THE
HUMANITIES

LIBRARY AND INFORMATION SCIENCE TEXT SERIES

The School Library Media Center. 5th ed. By Emanuel T. Prostano and Joyce S. Prostano

Library and Information Center Management. 5th ed. By Robert D. Stueart and Barbara B. Moran

The Academic Library: Its Context, Its Purpose, and Its Operation. By John M. Budd

The Social Sciences: A Cross-Disciplinary Guide to Selected Sources. 2d ed. Nancy L. Herron, General Editor

Introduction to United States Government Information Sources. 6th ed. By Joseph Morehead

The Economics of Information: A Guide to Economic and Cost-Benefit Analysis for Information Professionals. By Bruce R. Kingma

Reference and Information Services: An Introduction. 2d ed. Richard E. Bopp and Linda C. Smith, General Editors

Developing Library and Information Center Collections. 4th ed. By G. Edward Evans with the assistance of Margaret R. Zarnosky

The Collection Program in Schools: Concepts, Practices, and Information Sources. 2d ed. By Phyllis J. Van Orden

Information Sources in Science and Technology. 3d ed. By C. D. Hurt

Introduction to Technical Services. 6th ed. By G. Edward Evans and Sandra M. Heft

The School Library Media Manager. 2d ed. By Blanche Woolls

The Humanities: A Selective Guide to Information Sources. 5th ed. By Ron Blazek and Elizabeth Aversa

Wynar's Introduction to Cataloging and Classification. By Bohdan S. Wynar. 9th ed. By Arlene G. Taylor

Introduction to Library Public Services. 6th ed. By G. Edward Evans, Anthony J. Amodeo, and Thomas L. Carter

A Guide to the Library of Congress Classification. 5th ed. By Lois Mai Chan

The Organization of Information. By Arlene G. Taylor

Systems Analysis for Librarians and Information Professionals. 2d ed. By Larry N. Osborne and Margaret Nakamura

THE HUMANITIES
A SELECTIVE GUIDE TO INFORMATION SOURCES

FIFTH EDITION

Ron Blazek
Professor
Florida State University

and

Elizabeth Aversa
Professor
University of Tennessee, Knoxville

2000
Libraries Unlimited, Inc.
Englewood, Colorado

LIBRARIES UNLIMITED, INC.
P.O. Box 6633
Englewood, CO 80155-6633
1-800-237-6124
www.lu.com

Library of Congress Cataloging-in-Publication Data

Blazek, Ron.
    The humanities : a selective guide to information sources / Ron Blazek and Elizabeth
Aversa.--5th ed.
        p. cm.
    Includes bibliographical references and index.
    ISBN 1-56308-601-8 (cloth) -- ISBN 1-56308-602-6 (paper)
    1. Humanities--Bibliography of bibliographies. 2. Humanities--Bibliography. 3.
Humanities--Reference books--Bibliography. 4. Humanities--Information
services--Directories. I. Aversa, Elizabeth Smith. II. Title.

Z6265 .B53 2000 AZ221
016.0160013--dc21   99-089831

Contents

Preface to the Fifth Edition xiii

Acknowledgments xvii

List of Abbreviations and Symbols xix

1 INTRODUCTION TO THE HUMANITIES 1

Working Definitions of the Humanities 1

Nature of Scholarship in the Humanities 2

Information Seeking and Use in the Humanities 4

Computers in the Humanities 8

Digital Libraries 9

Helpful Resources for Students, Librarians, and General Readers 10

Notes 11

2 SOURCES OF GENERAL IMPORTANCE TO THE HUMANITIES 13

Bibliographic Guides and Directories 13

Reference Books and Research Guides 13

Periodical Guides 14

Computerized Databases/CD-ROM 16

Library Collections 17

Museums 18

Annuals and Current Awareness Sources 19

Indexes, Abstracts, and Serial Bibliographies 19

Dictionaries, Encyclopedias, and Handbooks 22

Biographical Sources 23

3 ACCESSING INFORMATION IN PHILOSOPHY 27

Working Definition of Philosophy 27

Major Divisions of the Field 28

Helpful Resources for Students, Librarians, and General Readers 30

Use and Users of Philosophy Information 31

Major Classification Schemes 32

Subject Headings in Philosophy 33

Computers in Philosophy 35

Major Societies, Information Centers, and Special Collections in Philosophy . . . 37

Notes 39

**4   PRINCIPAL INFORMATION SOURCES
     IN PHILOSOPHY** 41

Bibliographic Guides. 41
    General 41
    Periodicals 42
    Internet Resources 42
Bibliographies and Catalogs 42
    General 42
    Specialized by Topic, Region, or Period 44
Indexes, Abstracts, and Serial Bibliographies 47
Dictionaries, Encyclopedias, and Handbooks 50
    General 50
    Specialized by Topic, Region, or Period 55
Directories and Biographical Sources 58
Histories 62

5   ACCESSING INFORMATION IN RELIGION. 65

Working Definition of Religion 65
Major Divisions of the Field 66
Helpful Resources for Students, Librarians, and General Readers 67
Use and Users of Information in Religion 69
Computers in Religion 70
Major Religious Organizations, Information Centers, and Special Collections . . . 72
Notes 73

**6   PRINCIPAL INFORMATION SOURCES IN
     RELIGION, MYTHOLOGY, AND FOLKLORE** 75

Bibliographic Guides. 75
    General 75
    Periodicals 77
    Internet Resources 78
Bibliographies and Catalogs 79
    General 79
    Christian 79
    Non-Christian 82
    New Alternatives: New Age, Occult, Etc. 84
Indexes, Abstracts, and Serial Bibliographies 86
Dictionaries, Encyclopedias, and Handbooks 89
    General 89
    Christian 96
    Non-Christian 103
    New Alternatives: New Age, Occult, Etc. 107
Directories, Annuals, and Current Awareness Sources. 109
Biographical Sources 113
Histories and Atlases 117
The Bible 120
    Versions and Editions. 121
        Christian 121
        Non-Christian. 123

Multiple Versions. 123
Bibliographies, Indexes, and Abstracts 124
Concordances and Quotations 126
Dictionaries, Encyclopedias, and Handbooks 128
Commentaries. 134
Histories and Atlases 137
Mythology and Folklore 138
Bibliographies, Indexes, Abstracts, Etc. 138
Dictionaries, Encyclopedias, Handbooks, Etc. 140

7 ACCESSING INFORMATION IN THE VISUAL ARTS 147

Working Definition of the Visual Arts 147
Major Divisions of the Field 148
Helpful Resources for Students, Librarians, and General Readers 149
Use and Users of Art Information 152
Computers in the Visual Arts. 152
Major Art Organizations and Special Collections in Visual Arts 154
Notes 156

8 PRINCIPAL INFORMATION SOURCES IN THE VISUAL ARTS. 157

Arts in General 157
Bibliographic Guides 157
Reference Books and Research Guides 157
Periodicals 158
Internet Resources and Computerized Databases 159
Bibliographies and Catalogs 159
Indexes, Abstracts, and Serial Bibliographies 163
Art Work and Reproductions—Catalogs, Etc. 166
Art Sales and Exhibitions—Catalogs, Etc. 170
Dictionaries, Encyclopedias, and Handbooks 172
Directories. 178
Biographical Sources 181
Histories and Chronologies 188
Painting, Drawing, and Print 193
Bibliographic Guides and Bibliographies. 193
Art Work and Reproductions—Catalogs, Etc. 194
Sales and Exhibitions—Catalogs, Etc. 198
Dictionaries, Encyclopedias, and Handbooks 200
Biographical Sources 202
Histories. 204
Architecture, Interior Design, and Landscape Architecture 205
Bibliographic Guides and Periodical Directories 205
Bibliographies and Catalogs 207
Indexes, Abstracts, and Serial Bibliographies 208
Dictionaries, Encyclopedias, Handbooks, Etc. 209
Directories. 213
Biographical Sources 215
Histories. 216

8 PRINCIPAL INFORMATION SOURCES IN THE VISUAL ARTS *(continued)*

Sculpture 217
    Bibliographic Guides and Bibliographies. 217
    Art Work and Reproductions—Catalogs, Etc. 218
    Dictionaries, Encyclopedias, Handbooks 219
    Biographical Sources 220
    Histories. 221
Photography. 221
    Bibliographies and Catalogs 221
    Collections, Reproductions, and Sales—Catalogs, Etc. 223
    Dictionaries, Encyclopedias, Handbooks, Etc. 224
    Biographical Sources 226
Applied Design, Crafts, and Decorative Arts. 228
    General 228
        Bibliographic Guides, Bibliographies, and Indexes 228
        Dictionaries, Encyclopedias, Handbooks, Etc. 229
        Directories and Annuals 233
        Biographical Sources 234
    Furniture and Woodcraft 236
        Bibliographies, Indexes, and Abstracts. 236
        Dictionaries, Encyclopedias, Handbooks, Etc. 236
    Jewelry and Metalcraft 237
        Dictionaries, Encyclopedias, Handbooks, Etc. 237
    Ceramics, Pottery, and Glass 239
        Bibliographic Guides and Bibliographies 239
        Dictionaries, Encyclopedias, Handbooks, Etc. 240
    Textiles, Weaving, and Needlecraft. 242
        Bibliographic Guides and Bibliographies 242
        Dictionaries, Encyclopedias, Handbooks, Etc. 243
    Fashion and Costume 244
        Bibliographies and Indexes. 244
        Dictionaries, Encyclopedias, Handbooks, Etc. 245
        Biographical Sources 247

9 ACCESSING INFORMATION IN THE PERFORMING ARTS 249

Working Definition of the Performing Arts 249
Major Divisions of the Field 249
Helpful Resources for Students, Librarians, and General Readers 251
Use and Users of Performing Arts Information. 254
Computers in the Performing Arts 254
Major Organizations, Information Centers, and Special Collections. 256
Notes 258

10 PRINCIPAL INFORMATION SOURCES IN THE PERFORMING ARTS. 259

Performing Arts in General. 259
   Bibliographic Guides 259
   Bibliographies and Indexes. 260
   Directories and Biographical Sources 260
Music. 263
   Music in General 263
      Bibliographic Guides. 263
      Bibliographies and Catalogs 267
      Indexes, Abstracts, and Serial Bibliographies 270
      Printed Music Sources—Bibliographies, Indexes, and Catalogs. . . . 272
      Thematic Catalogs and Anthologies 280
      Dictionaries, Encyclopedias, and Handbooks 281
      Directories, Annuals, and Current Awareness Sources 286
      Biographical Sources. 288
      Histories and Chronologies. 290
      Recordings 293
   Serious Concert Music and Opera 295
      Bibliographies and Indexes. 295
      Dictionaries, Encyclopedias, Handbooks, Etc.. 295
      Directories, Annuals, and Current Awareness Sources 300
      Biographical Sources. 301
      Recordings 303
   Popular Music (Jazz, Folk, Rock, Country, Etc.). 304
      Bibliographic Guides. 304
      Bibliographies and Indexes. 305
      Printed Music Sources—Bibliographies, Indexes, and Catalogs. . . . 306
      Dictionaries, Encyclopedias, Handbooks, Etc.. 308
      Directories, Annuals, and Current Awareness Sources 312
      Biographical Sources. 312
      Recordings 316
   Musical Theater and Film. 319
      Bibliographies and Catalogs 319
      Dictionaries, Encyclopedias, Handbooks, Etc.. 320
      Recordings 323
   Musical Instruments and Technology. 323
Dance. 326
   Bibliographies, Catalogs, and Indexes 326
   Dictionaries, Encyclopedias, and Handbooks 328
      Dance in General. 328
      Ethnic and Regional Dance. 329
      Ballet 330
   Directories, Annuals, and Current Awareness Sources. 332
   Biographical Sources 334
   Histories. 335
Theater and Drama 336
   Bibliographic Guides 336
      Periodicals 337
   Bibliographies, Catalogs, and Indexes 337
   Play Sources—Bibliographies and Indexes. 339

**10 PRINCIPAL INFORMATION SOURCES IN
THE PERFORMING ARTS** (*continued*)

Theater and Drama (*continued*)
Dictionaries, Encyclopedias, and Handbooks 342
General 342
Specialized by Time Period or Geographic Region 344
Directories, Annuals, and Current Awareness Sources. 346
Biographical Sources 349
Histories and Chronologies. 352
General 352
Specialized by Time Period or Geographic Region 352
Reviews and Criticism 357
Play Production 359
Film, Radio, Television, and Video 361
Bibliographic Guides 361
Periodicals 362
Bibliographies and Catalogs 362
Film/Video Sources—Bibliographies, Indexes, and Catalogs 364
Indexes, Abstracts, and Serial Bibliographies 369
Dictionaries, Encyclopedias, and Handbooks 369
Directories, Annuals, and Current Awareness Services 378
Biographical Sources 381
Histories. 385
Reviews and Criticism 386

**11 ACCESSING INFORMATION IN LANGUAGE
AND LITERATURE** 391

Working Definitions of Language and Literature 391
Major Divisions of the Field 392
Use and Users of Information in Language and Literature. 393
Computers in Language and Literature. 394
Major Organizations, Information Centers, and Special Collections 395
Notes 396

**12 PRINCIPAL INFORMATION SOURCES IN
LANGUAGE AND LITERATURE**. 399

Language and Linguistics 399
Bibliographies and Guides 399
Internet Resources 401
Indexes, Abstracts, and Serial Bibliographies 401
Linguistics Dictionaries, Encyclopedias, and Handbooks 403
English-Language Dictionaries. 406
Unabridged and Scholarly 406
Desk and College. 409
Usage, Slang, Idioms, and New Words 410
Etymology, Synonyms, Pronunciation, Etc. 414
Foreign-Language and Bilingual Dictionaries 416
Histories and Directories 421

Literature 422
  General (Various Genres and Languages) 422
    Bibliographic Guides and Introductory Works. 422
    Bibliographies 424
    Indexes, Abstracts, and Serial Bibliographies 425
    Dictionaries, Encyclopedias, and Handbooks 426
    Biographical and Critical Sources 432
    Writers' Guides and Directories 440
    Quotations and Proverbs 442
  Fiction (Various Languages) 445
    Dictionaries, Encyclopedias, and Handbooks 445
    Biographical and Critical Sources 446
    Writers' Guides and Directories 449
  Poetry (Various Languages) 450
    Dictionaries, Encyclopedias, and Handbooks 450
    Biographical and Critical Sources 450
    Writers' Guides and Directories 451
    Quotations 451
  Literature in English 451
    General (Various Genres) 451
    Fiction 480
    Poetry. 497
  Literature from Languages Other Than English 505
    General (Various Languages) 505
    Classical Literature, Greek and Latin 508
    Romance Languages 509
    Germanic/Scandinavian Languages 519
    Slavonic Languages 521
    Arabic Languages 523
    Asian Languages 523
  Children's and Young Adult Literature. 525
    Bibliographies and Indexes. 525
    Dictionaries, Encyclopedias, and Handbooks 529
    Biographical and Critical Sources 532

    Author/Title Index 537

    Subject/Keyword Index 589

PREFACE TO THE FIFTH EDITION

Librarians, scholars, and teachers of literature and reference sources in the humanities had depended upon the efforts of A. Robert Rogers in producing *The Humanities: A Selective Guide to Information Sources* through its first two editions in 1974 and 1979. The untimely death of Dr. Rogers in 1985 left a wide gap that needed to be addressed. While working on the third edition, issued in 1988, the co-authors became aware of the magnitude of the task they had taken on in developing the new product. Six years later they were able to complete the updating and expansion, embracing new developments in the electronic environment and new emphases on the multi-cultural and female influence and accomplishments in producing the fourth edition. Now, in 2000, the objective of the fifth edition remains the same: to provide a work useful to teachers and students in schools of library and information science, reference librarians, collection development officers in libraries, humanities scholars, and others who have information needs in the broad discipline.

Permission to incorporate still useful segments of the text from the "Access" chapters of the second edition had been obtained earlier from Mrs. A. Robert Rogers through Libraries Unlimited, Inc., when developing the third edition. Basically, the format utilized originally by Rogers was retained, although there have been several revisions of varying magnitude with respect to the information environment and its impact on graduate schools of library and information science. This necessitated a more comprehensive as well as updated guide to humanities information resources. As was true of the fourth edition, the co-authors divided the task, with Professor Blazek assuming responsibility for revision and updating of the "Sources" chapters and Professor Aversa the "Access" chapters.

"ACCESS" CHAPTERS

The odd-numbered chapters (1, 3, 5, 7, 9, and 11) relate to accessing information. Each odd-numbered chapter consists of several sections: a "working definition" of the field, a section on "use and users," a section on major divisions of the field, and a "computers" section. Finally, each access chapter has a few pages on important collections, research centers, and organizations. We have continued to retain the "Computers in . . ." section for each chapter, because we believe that users vary with the subfields in the humanities and that the varied forms of electronic information have yet to be fully integrated into library collections and scholars' desks.

A new section was added to each chapter in the fourth edition of the *Guide*. This section, "Helpful Resources for Students, Librarians, and General Readers," serves to point the user to additional resources to read, acquire, or consider for purchase, and has been retained in this edition. These sections are designed to serve as aids to students with limited backgrounds in the fields described. A section on "use and user studies" was added to each "Access" chapter in the earlier edition, with the goal of directing the reader to relevant use and user studies for the specific disciplines of the humanities. Although there have been few additions to the "use and users" sections since the last edition, the sections have been retained and updated.

The greatest change in accessing information in humanities during the past five years has occurred because of the phenomenal increase in the number of electronic resources and the affordability of access to the resources. In this edition, online and CD-ROM databases appropriate to the humanities are noted in sections of the "Access" chapters, as are useful Internet resources.

The advent of the World Wide Web and its availability to end users everywhere has changed much of library and scholarly practice. Whether a search should be begun or concluded on the Web remains an interesting question, but whatever the answer, resources on the Web are now extremely important to the practice of librarianship and humanities scholarship. Thus, we have included Web resources and their URLs for the first time in this *Guide*. However, the coverage is limited to a very few resources out of the hundreds of thousands of Web pages that are presently available to the searcher. The librarian and teacher will do well to check on continuing availability of the sources noted before recommending particular Web pages to their patrons or students. This caution reflects the present and growing importance, as well as the rapidity of change, in the World Wide Web as a valuable, but dynamic, resource for all fields of the humanities.

In identifying World Wide Web resources, we tried to include those that offered clear organization, breadth of coverage, helpful links, reasonably up-to-date information, and some identifiable authority, either personal or institutional. We checked every URL during the last month of preparation of the *Guide*'s manuscript and noted the access date with each address. Of course, this provides no insurance of the continued presence of individual sources, but only indicates when the sources were last accessed by the authors. The sources were identified through the use of an array of search engines that included, but was not limited to, AltaVista, Excite, HotBot, Infoseek, Lycos, and Yahoo.

We believe that accessing information in the humanities is at once easier, and more difficult, than ever before. The resources are more available than ever, but evaluation of the resources is increasingly difficult for the casual user. Thus, we have tried not to be exhaustive, but to identify some representative resources that will serve the user directly, as well as some that may serve only as examples of what is possible. The latter should remind the user of new approaches to take, new types of material to access, and new tools to be used in searching for appropriate information to answer questions and fill requests in the humanities.

"SOURCES" CHAPTERS

The even-numbered chapters (2, 4, 6, 8, 10, and 12) describe the reference works, both print and electronic. Bibliographic advice was given by specialists in the field regarding inclusion and deletion of titles from the previous edition. These specialists are identified in the acknowledgments section. It was clear after examining all their reports that a great deal of selectivity was necessary in determining which sources should be included. Priority was given to the more recent sources with emphasis on those published in the past two decades. Even so, those of classic value were retained regardless of age.

As before, there was an attempt to provide in-depth annotations to serve the needs of students and educators as a textbook as well as librarians and scholars as a literature guide. Again, titles of periodicals were not considered as entries in this section unless they had reference value. In such cases they were placed in appropriate sections on current awareness or serial bibliography. There is a systematic attempt to identify guides and directories to serial publications in each "Sources" chapter. Computerized databases, both online remote and CD-ROM, are integrated with the books. When any of the print items are available online (including the World Wide Web) or in CD-ROM format, this is noted and described. Several of these resources appear only in computerized format rather than print; they are also treated within their appropriate reference category (index, bibliography, etc.). Online service, Internet, or CD-ROM availability is indicated by an asterisk in both the numbered entries and the indexes. Although this work is not intended as a directory of Web resources, URLs are included for such resources that provide links to other such resources and/or to bibliographies. Additionally, we hope that we have identified every print title on our list that is accessible on the Web.

All chapters identifying the principal information sources have been reviewed; all annotations from the fourth edition have been examined and, where necessary, updated, revised, and expanded. Every numbered entry is described in enough detail to provide adequate comprehension of the scope and coverage of the tool covered. In most cases, additional details concerning audience, arrangement, special features, authority, and even history of the work are furnished. Annotations range from 75 to 275 words in length, with an average of about 150 words each. Similar to the fourth edition is the inclusion of numerous cross-references linking the entries.

The job of writing annotations was completed in a seventeen-month period from July 1998 to January 2000. The job of selection, identification, and location of new materials, along with updating of existing entries, had begun two years earlier and was continued throughout the writing phase. Emphasis has been given to the need to identify new titles and new editions, and the project was conducted with the assistance of a cadre of interested and energetic young people, students in the humanities reference and advanced reference classes, DIS students, friends, and volunteers. The names composing this talented group are given in the acknowledgments section.

Titles were also added during the editing phase through January 2000, and forthcoming titles and editions have been identified. In regard to the recency of material, the extended writing period worked as an advantage in finding the latest entries. Criteria for inclusion remained the same as in the past, with each item receiving at least one of three support elements: recommendations from experts, favorable reviews, and/or familiarity of the co-author through his experience as instructor of humanities reference for the past twenty-nine years.

The final product is a literature guide of 1,374 major entries, as compared to a total of 1,250 in the fourth edition and 973 in the third edition. This represents a substantial increase of 124 titles, or 10 percent over the previous issue. These entries identify useful or important items, for which information is presented in depth and is up-to-date at time of writing. It does not include the hundreds of additional titles actually embraced within the annotations given to the major entries. These "co-equal entries," or "minor entries" as the case may be, were used cautiously in the third edition, liberally in the fourth edition, and generously in the current effort.

The numbers of entries in all areas have increased, with proportions of the total number of major entries within the "Sources" chapters remaining approximately the same as in the fourth edition. There are slight increases in three of the six major divisions, balanced by a slight decline in two, while the percentage of language and literature entries is the same.

REFERENCE SOURCES

	Fourth edition		Fifth edition	
	#	%	#	%
General	29	2.3	39	2.6
Philosophy	60	4.8	70	4.7
Religion	188	15.0	229	15.3
Visual Arts	266	21.3	313	20.9
Performing Arts	353	28.2	425	28.3
Language and Literature	354	28.3	424	28.3
Total	1250	100.0	1500	100.1

The bibliographic style of the entries is similar to the fourth edition, and arrangement of entries is alphabetical by title within the form categories and topical sub-categories. Names of authors, editors, and compilers are placed in the same field position following the edition statement, regardless of Library of Congress designation of their status. This should alleviate certain frustrations in determining whether the title or its editor belong in the main entry position. It resolves all difficulties in determining why certain individuals are accorded author status while others who do the same type of work are identified as editors or compilers. In any case, the indexes are to be employed to provide access when either a name or a title is known. Series are identified, and ISBN and ISSN designations are included for major entries (although not for co-entries or minor entries).

Acknowledgments

Obviously, a work of this kind cannot be completed without the help of others. The co-authors take this opportunity to express their deep appreciation to the bibliographic specialists and experts who took the time to respond to our request for evaluation of titles in the fourth edition and continued their assistance with the fifth edition. They are Dr. Hans E. Bynagle, Chief Librarian, Whitworth College, Spokane, Washington (Philosophy); Dr. Edward Teague, University Librarian, Architecture and Fine Arts Library, University of Florida (Visual Arts); and Mr. Blake Landor, Bibliographer in Religion and Philosophy, also at University of Florida (Religion). We are deeply appreciative also to Mr. Dan O. Clark, head of the music library at Florida State University, who for the first time joined us and provided excellent assistance.

Professor Blazek also wishes to thank his wife, Genevieve Blazek, for her continued input regarding the structure of the visual arts segment. Special mention must go to the graduate assistants who served so well over the entire period: Parichart "Trish" Webster, Julia Spencer, Rita Haydar, Amy Arnold, and Patric Kruger, all of whom proved to be quick learners in all phases of the search operation as chief bibliographic assistants and took on the added burdens of coordination of volunteers, word processing, and more during the critical writing period. Special thanks are given to Daniel Blazek, David Blazek, Dr. Theresa Griffin Maggio, and Dr. Anna E. Perrault, who continued to provide sound suggestions and advice. Thanks to Janet Capps and David Minor of the Computer Laboratory for their can-do attitudes regarding technology, and to Dr. Maria Chavez as head of interlibrary loan at Florida State University's Strozier Library.

Among the most deserving of recognition are students and former students of Florida State University's School of Library and Information Studies, who over the past three years participated in the identification of titles, searching of Web sites, and location of reviews: Max Anderson, Amy Arnold, Rachel Augello, Chris Barber, Alex Beguiristain, Gabe Burke, Marta Demopoulous, Guy Frost, Bob Goldman, Bob Guttman, Todd Gwinn, Melissa Hatch, Priscilla Henry, Ron Jarnagin, Becky Jones, Cara Keaton, Cindy Killingsworth, Scott Kinney, Kirsten Kinsley, Teresa Knapp, Patric Krueger, Abby Krystal, Greta Lowe, Lisa Lowell, Linda Most, John Nemmers, Mona Niffenegger, A. J. Price, Pat Reakes, Scott Routsong, Peter Thanos, Rebecca Walch, Tiffany Wiems, Jeff Wheelahan, Janet L. Williams, Gloria Woody, and Jennifer Zalenka. Thank you all wherever you may be.

The second author, Professor Aversa, acknowledges the support of her colleagues at the two institutions at which she "deaned and directed" during the preparation of this edition of the *Guide:* the School of Library and Information Science at The Catholic University of America and the School of Information Sciences at the University of Tennessee, Knoxville. Professor Aversa especially thanks her research assistant and recent graduate of UTK, Valerie Frey, for her many hours of checking and verification of material for the "Access" chapters of this *Guide;* her office manager, Gerri Littlejohn, for help with the manuscript and scheduling; her colleagues, for their patience; and her husband, Rocco Aversa, for his tolerance for late hours and frozen pizza.

LIST OF ABBREVIATIONS AND SYMBOLS

2/yr.	twice a year
Ann.	annual
Bienn.	biennial
Bimo.	bimonthly
Biwk.	biweekly
Corr.	corrected, corrections
Cum.	cumulative, cumulation
Enl.	enlarged
Exp.	expanded
Irreg.	irregular
Mo.	monthly
Pbk.	paperback
Q.	quarterly
Quin.	quinquennial
Repr.	reprinted
Rev.	revised
Semiann.	semi-annual
Trans.	translated
Trienn.	triennial
Wk.	weekly

SYMBOL

Asterisk (*) before entry number indicates electronic file availability (CD-ROM, online database, or World Wide Web) in both "Sources" chapters and author/title index.

CHAPTER 1

INTRODUCTION TO THE HUMANITIES

WORKING DEFINITIONS OF THE HUMANITIES

What disciplines constitute the humanities? The question of the classification of knowledge, or of scholarly endeavors, into *fields*, *disciplines*, *research areas*, or *subjects* is itself a humanistic problem. It is also a very practical problem for librarians and information specialists who need to categorize the literature into workable systems for storage, retrieval, preservation, and physical access to information sources and for educators who design curricula and establish the organizational components of schools, colleges, universities, and systems of higher education. Although the Commission on the Humanities suggested, in a 1980 report, that "fields alone do not define the humanities," and that "the essence of the humanities is a spirit or attitude toward humanity,"[1] scholars have, at various times, classified different areas of study as "humanistic disciplines," as opposed to those in the social and behavioral sciences or those in the physical and life sciences.

In classical and early Christian times, the scope of the humanities seemed very broad. Literature constituted the core, but virtually every discipline relating to the human mind was considered a part of the humanities. In the Renaissance period the term *humanities* was used in opposition to the term *divinity* and seemed to embrace all areas of study outside the field of religion. In the nineteenth century, *humanities* included those disciplines that could not be considered part of the natural sciences. By the twentieth century the fields of study that dealt with social, rather than natural, phenomena had emerged, along with "scientific" methods of investigation in the several social sciences. In the last years of the twentieth century, the humanities remained those fields of scholarship and study that are "dedicated to the disciplined development of verbal, perceptual, and imaginative skills needed to understand experience."[2] The fields of study that we include in this guide are philosophy, religion, the visual arts, the performing arts, and language and literature.

The reader may ask, "What about history?" and that is a worthwhile question. Although many consider history to be a central humanities field, research methods in history and indications of similarities between information use in that field and in the social sciences lead us to place history closer to the social sciences than to the humanities, at least for the purpose of constructing a guide to bibliographic sources. We believe that this source therefore reflects the migration during the second half of the twentieth century of history from a narrative enterprise to one using many approaches that are closely related to those of the social and behavioral sciences. This is not to suggest that the reader should overlook the many studies of

1

information-seeking behavior among historians; these works have contributed considerably to our understanding of how scholars work, and they are indeed must reading for the librarian.

The student wishing to explore the nature and scope of the humanities can access many useful resources. For an excellent general overview, the article entitled "The Humanities" in *Encyclopaedia Britannica (Encyclopædia Britannica Online,* http://members.eb.com/bol/topic?artcl=41479&seq_nbr=1&page=n&isctn=2 [accessed June 13, 1999]) should be consulted. The article also provides useful links to articles on the several disciplines identified as constituting the humanities. Kenneth McLeish's readable *Key Ideas in Human Thought* (Facts on File, 1993) offers brief, signed articles on the many disciplines and subfields that constitute the humanities, with a definite 1990s perspective. Volumes of the *Princeton Studies: Humanistic Scholarship in America* (Princeton, 1963–) provide a reflective look at the field.

The place of the humanities in higher education and the curriculum in general is addressed in Robert E. Proctor's *Education's Great Amnesia: Reconsidering the Humanities from Petrarch to Freud* (Indiana University Press, 1988) and also in Walter Kaufman's earlier work, *The Future of the Humanities* (Crowell, 1977). The former offers a curriculum that incorporates the humanities and suggests what students should be expected to know in the area; the latter suggests the logic behind teaching the humanities in the first place. Kaufman states that, among other reasons, the humanities should be taught to ensure the conservation and cultivation of humanity's greatest works and to teach broad truths and "vision."[3] Other popular works have addressed education as it relates to the humanities. Allan Bloom's *The Closing of the American Mind* (Simon & Schuster, 1987) continues to provoke discussion and debate more than a dozen years after its publication. In *What's Happened to the Humanities?* (Princeton University Press, 1997), Alvin Kernan brings together a variety of viewpoints on the current state of the humanities, including the important aspects of education and funding. Included in the volume are statistics on graduate degrees in the humanities and helpful bibliographic references to additional works.

The previously mentioned report, *The Humanities in American Life* (University of California Press, 1980) continues to be cited in many articles on the state of this large discipline. Most relevant to librarians will be the chapter "Cultural Institutions." Additional relevant readings on libraries at the close of the twentieth century and the implications of the changes for scholars are collected in *Daedalus* 125 (Fall 1996).

Finally, two additional works provide extensive retrospective views of the fields of the humanities and the role of the library in documenting and promoting this area of study. Lester Asheim's classic *The Humanities and the Library* (American Library Association, 1956) is still worthy of the reader's attention, while many of the sources and articles have been brought up to date in the more recently published revised second edition by Nena Couch and Nancy Allen, *The Humanities and the Library* (2d ed., American Library Association, 1993).

NATURE OF SCHOLARSHIP
IN THE HUMANITIES

The nature of scholarship in the humanities and the literature of librarianship and information services for the fields within the broad discipline are considered in the remainder of this chapter. At the outset, it should be remarked that humanistic research is differentiated most sharply from that in the natural sciences by the constant intrusion of questions of value. To the scientist qua scientist, such considerations are, indeed, intrusions. They interfere with and damage the quality of research concerned with objective, empirically verifiable data and with experimental results that can be replicated by other researchers. "Informed judgment" might play a part in determining which experiments to conduct, but "refined sensibility" would have no impact on the experimental outcome. Yet these are the "bread of life" for the humanistic scholar, whether dealing with a poem, a piece of music, a painting, a religious doctrine, or a philosophical theory. Thus, humanistic scholarship has traditionally been intimately intertwined with considerations of value.

One consequence of this connection between scholarship and value systems is the peculiarly personal and individualistic nature of humanistic research. Unlike colleagues in the natural sciences, or even, to a lesser degree, in the social and behavioral sciences, the humanist finds the research to be such an intimately personal matter that it is more difficult than in other disciplines to function effectively as a team. The results of team effort, it is felt, are more likely to be compromise and mediocrity than a productive division of labor. Collaborative efforts are possible, but they require special planning and are not considered nearly as "normal" as in the natural sciences.

On the other hand, it has also been suggested that it is not necessarily the content of the scholarship in the humanities that leads to independent and solitary work, but rather that it may be that there is something different about the training and education of humanistic scholars that leads to the lack of collaborative work. For a perspective on this aspect of humanities scholarship, see "Knowledge Collaboration in the Arts, the Sciences, and the Humanities—Part 3—The Humanities and Social Sciences," edited by Carla M. Borden, in *Knowledge: Creation, Diffusion, Innovation* 14 (September 1992): 110–32.

Regardless of the reason that humanists work alone, a further result of this is the general lack of ability on the part of the humanities scholar to delegate bibliographic searching to others. The interconnections within the researcher's mind appear to be so subtle or complex that it is necessary to examine personally the index entry or abstract to identify an item of potential relevance, and to see the book or article to determine its actual relevance. This problem continues to be compounded by the relative lack of standard or controlled vocabularies of the sort that are common in the pure and applied sciences. Yet the humanistic scholar needs help in the form of the availability of a wide variety of finding aids and access tools. Besides needing help in accessing print-on-paper resources, humanities scholars have now come to expect to find digitized texts through their libraries; this expectation is growing but is sometimes frustrated by the added costs that libraries must cover to provide electronic resources and the personnel to assist scholars in using them.

Part of the problem faced by the humanistic scholar also relates to the nature of knowledge in the humanities. Such knowledge is not likely to consist of hard, identifiable facts such as formulas in chemistry, population and income statistics from census data, or the content of genetic matter. Of course, there are plenty of facts in the humanities, but their sum total is considerably less than what the humanist is searching for. To know the number of times Shakespeare used the word "mince" in *Hamlet* will tell us very little about the importance of *Hamlet*. Yet the patient accumulation and analysis of this sort of factual data, now more possible than ever with electronic text and analytical tools, can lay the foundation for knowledge of the order sought by the humanistic scholar.

Closely related to the nature of knowledge is the question of progress. In the natural sciences, knowledge tends to be progressive or "cumulative." Each successive finding confirms, modifies, or overturns some piece of existing knowledge. This is true whether the problem is the identification of a new virus that has been detected through more sophisticated laboratory equipment or a far-ranging perception of relationships, such as the replacement of Newtonian physics with Einsteinian. In the humanities, no such "progress" is observable. Neither Sophocles's *Antigone*, Wagner's *Der Ring des Nibelungen*, nor Michelangelo's *Pieta* are superseded as was the "phlogiston" theory of chemistry. This is not to say that works based upon the same or similar themes do not appear and that patterns of influence are not clearly evident. What is not cumulative is our perception of beauty, our insight into the human condition, our understanding of how people act in terms of artistic creativity.

The reader should not overlook the fact that, despite the differences outlined above, the sciences and the arts and humanities actually have many connections. Increasingly, scholars and educators for professions in the sciences recognize that the humanities add value to the curricula in fields such as medicine and engineering. Earlier on, Michael Moravcsik, Eugene

Garfield, and others wrote of the relationships between the broad disciplines and the shared objectives of practitioners from both "cultures."[4] Indeed, a bibliography by D. R. Topper and J. H. Holloway, "Interrelationships Between the Visual Arts, Science, and Technology: A Bibliography," (*Leonardo* 13 [1980]: 29–33), provides a number of resources on the topic. An update of this bibliography, to include publications of the 1990s, would be a useful contribution to the field.

INFORMATION SEEKING AND
USE IN THE HUMANITIES

The factors noted in the previous paragraphs have their impact on patterns of use of information and library materials. They influence how humanities scholars seek information and the nature of the literature in their disciplines. For the humanist the library remains at the heart of the research enterprise, even as electronic access allows some research to be done at the desk. For the natural scientist, by contrast, the laboratory is at the center, with the library providing a supporting role. In this respect, the creative artist, as distinct from the researcher in the humanities, may be more nearly like the scientist—as anyone who has witnessed dialogue between a sculptor and an art historian can testify! Here the library provides support to the studio, just as the library is supportive of the lab activities of the scientist. Regardless of the type of work the humanist engages in, the library is often an important resource. Humanities scholarship and the library's role in supporting it are discussed in Ross Atkinson's "Humanities Scholarship and the Research Library," *Library Resources and Technical Services* 39 (January 1995): 79–84.

The centrality of the library for the humanistic researcher is still accompanied by the centrality of the monograph as distinct from the periodical article. Although there have been fewer user studies in the humanities than in other fields, the pattern of preference for books and pamphlets continues to emerge, in contrast to the ongoing preference of the natural and physical scientist for journal articles, reprints, and preprints. Book production in the humanities continued to grow at a healthy pace during the 1980s and 1990s.[5] Recently attention has been given also to book reviews. See, for example, Amanda Spink and others, "Use of Scholarly Book Reviews: Implications for Electronic Publishing and Scholarly Communications," *Journal of the American Society for Information Science* 49 (April 1998): 364–74, and Y. Lindholm-Romantschuk, "Scholarly Book Reviewing in the Social Sciences and Humanities," *College and Research Libraries News* 59 (May 1998): 375. The availability and popularity of reader reviews of books on commercial Web sites such as that of the bookseller Amazon.com (http://amazon.com/ [accessed May 2, 2000]) attest to the importance of the book in both scholarly and popular cultures. Even as humanities scholars, regardless of discipline, turn increasingly to electronic sources of information, the importance of the book cannot be ignored.

The advent of the World Wide Web has begun to change the way humanities scholars access and utilize information. Excellent Web sites provide links to related materials that would likely be overlooked in a search of printed indexes or a linear search in an online bibliographic database. Marlene Manoff predicted correctly that "It looks as if the World Wide Web is potentially a more promising technology for nontechnical fields than Gopher."[6] She also noted the value in having the ability to combine text and image, to consult either or both, and to view various versions of text and image simultaneously. For the first time in this guide, useful Internet sources and their URLs are noted in subsections of the "Access" chapters.

Another characteristic reported in the few user studies we have is the greater spread of individual titles used by researchers in the humanities. Whereas a relatively small number of journals contain a high proportion of frequently cited articles in fields such as chemistry and mathematics, the same high degree of concentration in journal or monographic titles has not been observed in the humanities. This is not to deny that critical studies tend to cluster around certain landmark works, but the spread of titles in which the criticisms appear is greater and the concentration much less intense.

A third use pattern that continues to distinguish humanistic from scientific researchers is a much wider time spread in the materials that are used. Whereas publications of the past five years seem more crucial to scientific research, with usage dropping off rapidly beyond that, the humanist is likely to be interested in works of twenty, forty, fifty, or a hundred or more years ago. Indeed, if one considers the classics in each field, the range of interest may extend to items 200 or 300 years old. This characteristic of humanities scholarship provides interesting challenges in the preservation of older materials; fortunately these challenges are being addressed by groups such as the Council on Library and Information Resources. The Council was formed in 1997 through the merger of the Council on Library Resources and the Commission on Preservation and Access. (See http://www.clir.org/about/about.html [accessed June 13, 1999] for specifics of the Council's missions, projects, and publications.) Newsletters of the former Commission on Preservation and Access are available in print under the title *Ensuring Access to the Accumulated Human Record As Far into the Future As Possible* (1997/1998).

A fourth distinguishing use pattern is that the humanist appears to have a greater need to browse than do scientists and social and behavioral scientists. Although little systematic evidence has been collected to support this use pattern, anecdotal accounts suggest this practice. Additional work is still needed to substantiate this claim and to determine if the need to browse is inherent in the humanistic researcher and his or her work or if the lack of systematic organization of the materials in the field makes browsing a necessity. Studies in use of the electronic networks will enable us to collect more data and to analyze such information with regard to the browsing issue.

Finally, we must mention citation practices and studies of publication and citation data in the arts and humanities. When the Institute for Scientific Information introduced its *Arts and Humanities Citation Index* in 1978, Eugene Garfield pointed out that inconsistent citation practices, citations to unpublished manuscripts and catalogs, and references to original sources embedded in texts without explicit citation were but three of the problems that were considered in developing the *Index*. The need to "enhance" titles for the Permuterm subject index has also been discussed in Garfield's works. See Eugene Garfield, "Will ISI's Arts and Humanities Citation Index Revolutionize Scholarship?" in *Essays of An Information Scientist Volume 3, 1977–1978* (ISI Press, 1980, pp. 204–8) and "Is Information Retrieval in the Arts and Humanities Inherently Different from that in Science?" *Library Quarterly* 50 (1980): 40–57. The nature of titles in humanities publications is explored in M. Yitzhaki's "Variation in Informativity of Titles in Research Papers in Selected Humanities Journals: A Comparative Study," *Scientometrics* 38 (February 1997): 219–29. An argument for increased journal coverage by the *Arts and Humanities Citation Index* and *Social Sciences Citation Index* is presented in Edward Funkhouser's "The Evaluative Use of Citation Analysis for Communication Journals," *Human Communication Research* 22 (June 1996): 563–74.

User studies that clarify the generalizations about humanists' scholarly practices and information seeking are not numerous, but their numbers have increased in recent years. The studies seem to fall into three broad categories: first, the broad, comprehensive studies that cut across disciplinary lines; second, the more limited studies that look at a single aspect of information seeking or at one or just a few users or disciplines; and finally, the studies that focus entirely on electronic information and how humanists respond to it. The third category has dominated work on humanities information seeking and use since the fourth edition of this guide was published.

Among the broad and general reviews, a good starting point remains Sue Stone's "Humanities Scholars: Information Needs and Uses," *Journal of Documentation* 38 (December 1982): 292–313. A good background is also provided by Paul Sturges in "Research on Humanities Information and Communication in Britain," *The Electronic Library* 10 (February 1992): 21–26. Judy Reynolds's more recent article, "A Brave New World: User

Studies in the Humanities Enter the Electronic Age," *Reference Librarian* 49–50 (1995): 61–81, provides over seventy-five references to works on humanities scholars' information needs and work habits in both print and electronic environments. A sweeping, though earlier, view of changes in scholarly communications is provided by a series of articles edited by Paula T. Kaufman and Tamara Miller in *Library Hi Tech* 10 (1992): 61–68. Of special interest is Deanna Marcum's contribution, "New Realities, Old Values" (pp. 62–67). William G. Jones's "The Disappearance of the Library: Issues in the Adoption of Information Technology by Humanists," *New Directions for Higher Education* 90 (Summer 1995): 33–41, suggests that libraries will continue to serve humanities scholars despite the advent of widely available electronic resources.

Two long works by Helen R. Tibbo deserve special mention because of the wealth of bibliographic information found in them. Tibbo's "Information Systems, Services, and Technology for the Humanities," *Annual Review of Information Science and Technology* 26 (edited by Martha E. Williams) (1991): 287–346, remains the most recent comprehensive review, with an extensive bibliography encompassing all aspects of communication and use of information by humanists and researchers in the subfields of the humanities. (The bibliography alone accounts for over twenty pages of the review.) The second of Tibbo's contributions is *Abstracting, Information Retrieval, and the Humanities* (American Library Association, 1993). Although this work is subtitled "Providing Access to Historical Literature," chapters on abstracting and the humanities and on technology and the humanities will prove useful to readers from other disciplines as well. As with the *ARIST* review cited above, the bibliography is exhaustive.

Other general studies should enhance the librarian's basic reading on user needs and behaviors. Results of a major study by the Research Libraries Group are presented in Constance Gould's "Information Needs in the Humanities: An Assessment," (RLG, 1988), referenced elsewhere in this guide. "Patterns of Information Seeking in the Humanities," by Stephen E. Wiberley, Jr., and William G. Jones (*College and Research Libraries* 50 [November 1989]: 638–45), reports on sources typically consulted by humanist researchers and suggests further questions for resolution in future studies of humanists' information-seeking behavior. Susan S. Guest's "The Use of Bibliographic Tools by Humanities Faculty at the State University of New York at Albany," *Reference Librarian* 18 (Summer 1987): 157–72, confirms the findings of some earlier studies but also suggests an increasing importance to both the journal literature and more recent publications than had been previously acknowledged.

Many specific studies of use and users in individual disciplines are covered in the remaining "Access" chapters of this guide. However, two that are not mentioned elsewhere, because they are essentially addressing the area of history, may be helpful to the reader interested in humanities librarianship. These are both by Donald O. Case: "The Collection and Use of Information by Some American Historians: A Study of Motives and Methods," *Library Quarterly* 61 (1991): 61–82, and "Conceptual Organization and Retrieval of Text by Historians: The Role of Memory and Metaphor," *Journal of the American Society for Information Science* 42 (October 1991): 657–68.

The number of works on use and information seeking in electronic information resources, the impact of electronic information on the humanities, and the future of humanities communication in light of electronic information continues to overwhelm the literature on humanities scholarship and librarianship. Only a few titles can be mentioned here. "The Lonely Scholar in a Global Information Environment," by Donald N. Langenberg, in *New Technologies and New Directions: Proceedings from the Symposium on Scholarly Communication*, edited by G. R. Boynton and Sheila D. Creth (Meckler, 1991, pp. 27–40) provides a good, though dated, introduction. More specific to librarians are Edward Shreeves, "Between the Visionaries and the Luddites: Collection Development and Electronic Resources in the Humanities," *Library Trends* 40 (Spring 1992): 579–95, and James H. Sweetland's "Humanists, Libraries, Electronic Publishing and the Future," in the same issue of *Library Trends* (pp. 781–803). Deborah Shaw and Charles H. Davis report on an investigation on the use of computer-based tools for MLA in "The Modern Language Association—Electronic and Paper Surveys of Computer-Based Tool Use," *Journal of the American Society for Information Science* 47 (December 1996): 932–40, and S. S. Lazinger and others report on "Internet Use by Faculty in Various Disciplines: A Comparative Case Study," *Journal of the American Society for Information Science* 48 (June 1997): 508–18.

Two important project reports give additional insights into the use of electronic materials by humanities scholars. "The Getty End-User Online Searching Project in the Humanities: Report No. 6: Overview and Conclusions," by Marcia J. Bates (*College and Research Libraries* 57 November 1996]: 514–23), concludes a series of reports by describing the challenges and opportunities of providing online information for humanities researchers. "The Use of Electronic Scholarly Journals: Models of Analysis and Data Drawn from the Project Muse Experience at Johns Hopkins University," by James G. Neal, was presented at the Conference on Scholarly Communicating and Technology (Atlanta, Georgia, April 23–24, 1997).

More technological changes affecting information services for the humanities are discussed in "The Changing Face of Research Libraries," by R. C. Alston, in *New Technologies for the Humanities*, edited by Mullings et al. (Bowker-Saur, 1996), as well as in Stephen E. Wiberley and William G. Jones's article, "Humanists Revisited: A Longitudinal Look at the Adoption of Information Technology," *College and Research Libraries* 55 (November 1994): 506ff. An older but still useful review for archivists is "Scholarly Communication and Information Technology: Exploring the Impact of Changes in the Research Process on Archives," by Avra Michelson and Jeff Rothenberg (*American Archivist* 55 [Spring 1992]: 236–315). Like the Tibbo review mentioned above, this one has an extensive bibliography and provides much general background as well as specific observations on information technology. Also, the American Council of Learned Societies' *Information Technology in Humanities Scholarship: Achievements, Prospects, and Challenges. The United States Focus* (Occasional Paper No. 37, 1997) by Pamela Pavliscak and others, provides additional observations from the disciplinary perspective.

The importance of new technological developments, including electronic publishing, is addressed by several organizations. The Coalition for Networked Information (CNI), Association of Research Libraries (ARL), and American Association of University Professors (AAUP) have followed the developments and implications of electronic publishing in several recent conferences on scholarly communications. Information about the conferences, lists of participants, and some conference papers are available on the World Wide Web. See, for example, http://www.arl.org/scomm/epub/papers/index.html (accessed June 10, 1999) for ARL's 1997 conference on monograph publishing, *The Specialized Scholarly Monograph in Crisis or How Can I Get Tenure if You Won't Publish My Book?* CNI's site at http://cni.org/archives/ (accessed February 28, 2000) provides coverage of a 1992 conference, *Technology, Scholarship and the Humanities*. The three organizations have ongoing interests in scholarly communications, libraries, and publishing, and their main Web pages should be consulted often for the most up-to-date information.

Publishing in the humanities, and especially the new "electronic publishing," has also been the topic of many articles in recent years. A "must-read" for those interested in scholarly publishing in the electronic age is *Scholarly Publishing The Electronic Frontier*, edited by Robin P. Peek and Gregory B. Newby (MIT Press, 1996). An additional important work on the topic is *Proceedings of the Second Conference on Scholarship and Technology in the Humanities* (Elvetham Hall, Hampshire, United Kingdom, April 13–16, 1994), edited by Stephanie Kenna and Seamus Ross and published by Bowker-Saur (1995). It contains papers on technical aspects (such as standards) as well as broader issues and implications of electronic publishing in the humanities.

Finally, the collection of articles entitled *Acquisitions and Collection Development in the Humanities*, edited by Irene Owens (Haworth Press, 1997) provides a section entitled "The Electronic Environment" that will point the reader to many additional articles and books covering important aspects of the digital environment. The work is also a very helpful guide to building collections in several specific areas within the humanities.

COMPUTERS IN THE HUMANITIES

The impact of computers in the humanities is illustrated by the number of computerized resources and tools now available to the humanist scholar, by the size of the literature describing those resources, and by the phenomenal increase in the number of electronic texts. From the few electronic texts that were available when this guide was last published, an entire area of humanities computing has emerged. Online databases for bibliographic access, CD-ROM resources for use at the scholar's workstation, tools for the analysis of texts, and the resources on the World Wide Web influence how the actual work of the humanist scholar is done. Word processing, database searching, electronic publishing, the use of analytical and statistical packages, graphical software, user friendly interfaces, and digital library collections have been discussed in the literature.

Because of the large number of publications in the humanities area, only a few can be mentioned here. Others, discipline specific, are mentioned in the "Access" chapters of this guide. Reviews and compilations are increasingly important because they help the reader to sort through the hundreds of sources that are available. The only pitfall is that things change so rapidly that even a hastily prepared review is soon obsolete. Nonetheless, a few resources will get the reader started.

The American Council of Learned Societies (ACLS) maintains an excellent guide to Web sites for computing in the humanities at http://www.acls.org/jshome.htm (accessed February 28, 2000). Click on "Online Scholarly Resources." The Society's Occasional Paper No. 41 has valuable appendices, including *Illustrative Websites for Computing and the Humanities* at http://www.acls.org/op41-ape.htm (accessed February 28, 2000).

The journal *Computers and the Humanities*, now in its third decade, is the journal of the Association for Computers and the Humanities. The journal is an invaluable source of articles on all aspects of computing in all areas of the humanities. It is available online and in print. An informative overview of humanities computing to the 1990s, written by the founding editor on the occasion of the twenty-fifth anniversary of the journal, is Joseph Raben's "Humanities Computing 25 Years Later," *Computers and the Humanities* 25 (1991): 341–50; a history of the journal can be found on the World Wide Web at http://kapis.www.wkap.nl/aims_scope.htm/0010-4817 (accessed February 28, 2000).

Other journals that the librarian should consult on matters of computers and information services in the humanities include *Library HiTech, Database, Online, CD-ROM Professional*, and *Journal of the American Society for Information Science*. Special issues of more general library journals will also offer some articles of interest for the humanities librarian; a good example is the spring 1994 (v. 42) issue of *Library Trends*. Edited by Thomas D. Walker, the issue is entitled "Libraries and the Internet: Education, Practice and Policy," and contains, among others, an article by Susan Hockey, "Evaluating Electronic Texts in Libraries" (pp. 76–93).

The topic of electronic texts has provided a large proportion of the recent literature on computers in the humanities. Along with Hockey's article noted above, the reader is directed to Natalia Smith and Helen R. Tibbo, "Libraries and the Creation of Electronic Texts for the Humanities," *College and Research Libraries* 57 (November 1996): 335–53. Brett Sutton edited *Literary Text in an Electronic Age: Scholarly Implications and Library Services* (Graduate School of Library and Information Science, University of Illinois, 1994). A very useful overview of the electronic text and its history can be found at the Web site of the Center for Electronic Texts in the Humanities (CETH) at http://scco1.rutgers.edu/ceth/ (accessed February 28, 2000). Also of interest is M. Gaunt's "CETH, Electronic Text Centers, and the Humanities Community," *Library Hi Tech* 16 (1998): 36–42. Another important resource on the topic is the University of Michigan's Humanities Text Initiative (HTI), an organization for the creation, maintenance, and promotion of electronic text. Information on HTI can be found at http://www.hti.umich.edu/ (accessed February 28, 2000). Many colleges and universities host electronic text projects, and their institutional Web sites should be consulted for links to project descriptions and access to texts. (For example, the University of Virginia and University of Pittsburgh collaborate on the *Japanese Text Initiative*, an effort to make classical Japanese text available to scholars. The URL is http://etext.virginia.edu/japanese/ [accessed February 28, 2000]. Other text projects are discussed in relevant chapters in this guide.)

Online searching is an area of computer use that has continued to receive attention in the literature. Whereas "how-to" articles dominated in the 1970s and 1980s, the more recent focus has been on search behavior, database identification and choice, and the overall impact of online information on the humanities scholar. For example, the vocabulary used in online searching in the humanities was studied, along with other aspects of searching, by Marcia J. Bates, Deborah N. Wilde, and Susan Siegfried, in the Getty Online Searching Project (*Library Quarterly* 63 [January 1993]). Also of interest are "Discovering Online Resources Across the Humanities: A Practical Implementation of the Dublin Core," by P. Miller and D. Greenstein, *Program* 33 (January 1999): 86–88, and the periodic reports in *Online and CD-ROM Review* by Martha E. Williams and others. A recent example is "New Database Products: Social Science, Humanities, News and General Use," *Online and CD-ROM Review* 22 (October 1998): 323–36.

Digital Libraries

No discussion of developments in library services in the humanities could be complete without mention of digital libraries. Projects abound, but they are too numerous to list in this guide. However, links to examples can be found by consulting the resource guides listed here. For an extensive bibliography, list of projects, journals, and conferences, consult the International Federation of Library Associations and Institutions (IFLA) *Digital Libraries: Resources and Projects* on the Web at http://www.ifla.org/II/diglib.htm (accessed June 16, 1999). For an up-to-date resource guide to digital libraries and issues surrounding their development and use, consult http://sunsite.berkeley.edu/Info/ (accessed February 28, 2000); this one provides links appropriate to readers just starting to learn about digital libraries as well as to those who have followed this literature from the beginning. An excellent example of the digital library collection concept, and the attendant literature about its development, is the *Library of Congress American Memory Project* at http://www.loc.gov/ (accessed February 28, 2000). A British project that collects, catalogs, and preserves digital information is the *Arts and Humanities Data Service* (AHDS), which is described on their Web pages at http://ahds.ac.uk/ (accessed February 28, 2000).

Besides exploring the many Internet resources on digital libraries, the reader may also benefit from reading the journal literature on the topic. See Steven Ellis, "Toward the Humanities Digital Library: Building the Local Organization," *College and Research Libraries* 57 (November 1996): 525–34; Gregory Crane, "The Perseus Project and Beyond: How Building a Digital Library Challenges the Humanities and Technology," *D-Lib Magazine* (January 1998): 1. (Available at http://www.dlib.org/dlib/january98/01crane.html [accessed February 28, 2000]); and Margaret Hedstrom, "Digital Preservation: A Time Bomb for Digital Libraries," *Computers and the Humanities* 31 (1997–1998): 189–202.

Directories of online, World Wide Web, and CD-ROM databases, as well as vendor literature, should be consulted for recent offerings from hundreds of database producers and publishers. Examples of useful print resources include *Directory of Electronic Journals, Newsletters and Academic Discussion Lists*, compiled by Lisabeth A. King and others (5th ed.,

Association of Research Libraries, Office of Scientific and Academic Publishing, 1995). Useful for leads is Louis Rosenfeld's *The Internet Compendium: Subject Guides to Humanities Resources* (Neal Schuman, 1995), but note that additional sources will need to be consulted for up-to-date results.

Often more current directories to resources will be found on the World Wide Web. Fruitful strategies include accessing organizational sites for lists of their print and electronic resources or accessing directories through topical searches.

HELPFUL RESOURCES FOR STUDENTS, LIBRARIANS, AND GENERAL READERS

Two additional topics must be mentioned. First, the nature of the materials in the humanities deserves attention, and second, funding of the humanities enterprise is always of interest. The working scholar in a humanistic discipline tends to perceive the materials with which to work as falling into four broad categories: original texts or artifacts, critical literature, literature designed for specific groups and purposes, and professional literature of the field. Each requires further elaboration.

The heart of humanistic study is the original work, whether a poem, painting, symphony, or discourse on ethics. The creative contribution is what is studied by the humanist scholar.

The second major category is the critical literature, which takes the form of analysis, interpretation, or commentary on the creative work. It may later be regarded as a creative work in and of itself.

The literature designed for special groups or purposes may be subdivided into popularizations, access tools, and professional literature. These are all of special interest to the librarian or information specialist. Popularizations allow for the dissemination of special interest material to wider audiences, thus enabling libraries to play a greater educational role. Access tools, of course, enable libraries to provide information services; here we think of bibliographies, indexes, abstracts, encyclopedias, dictionaries, handbooks, and the other finding aids needed to access information for scholarship and research.

Finally, the professional literature in each humanities field comprises publications by associations and professional societies, with journals, indexes and abstracts, conference proceedings, and current awareness services as typical outputs.

The excellent library collection will include all four categories of humanities-related material, and the librarian will need to be familiar with all types. This guide provides information on the materials required for the major subject areas in the field, but because no single collection can provide everything, the librarian should also have access to such tools as *Subject Collections*, edited by Lee Ash and William G. Miller (7th ed., Bowker, 1993), to lead the researcher to special collections of libraries and museums in the United States and Canada.

Additional resources that provide a starting point for accessing both popular and scholarly materials for learning and teaching can be accessed on the Internet. Consult, for example, *Top Humanities Websites*, at http://edsitement.neh.gov/websites-lit.htm (accessed February 28, 2000) and H-Net at http://www.h-net.msu.edu/ (accessed May 23, 1999). H-Net is a consortium of scholars and educators interested in using the Internet and information technology to further work in the humanities, arts, and social sciences and is described in "Conversational Scholarship in Cyberspace: The Evolution and Activities of H-Net, the Online Network for the Humanities," *Australian Universities' Review* 39 (1996): 12–15.

Funding for the humanities, especially as it affects libraries, continues to be discussed in a wide-ranging literature. The Web site of the National Endowment for the Humanities at http://www.neh.fed.us/ (accessed February 28, 2000) provides up-to-date information on grants and funding opportunities for the humanities. Two print reference tools that are also helpful are the *Directory of Grants in the Humanities, 1999–2000* (13th ed., Oryx Press, 1999) and the *Directory of Research Grants 1999*, also published by Oryx. Amounts of funding, types of projects, dates and restrictions on applications, and address information about sponsors are part of each entry, and subject, program type, and sponsor indexes allow for a variety of access methods. (The reader should consult http://www.oryxpress.com/ [accessed February 28, 2000] for information on the forthcoming Web-based directory, entitled *GrantSelect.*)

Potential sources of funding for humanities projects and programs can also be located on the World Wide Web. See, for example, the *Directory of State Humanities Councils* at http://www.neh.gov/state/states.html (accessed February 28, 2000). The main page of the National Endowment for the Humanities, at http://www.neh.fed.us/ (accessed February 28, 2000), provides links to other resources as well.

NOTES

[1]Commission on the Humanities, *The Humanities in American Life* (Berkeley, CA: University of California Press, 1980).

[2]Ibid.

[3]Walter Kaufman, *The Future of the Humanities* (Crowell, 1977).

[4]Michael J. Moravcsik, "Scientists and Artists: Motivations, Aspirations, Approaches, and Accomplishments," *Leonardo* 7 (1974): 255–57. Garfield, Eugene. "Art and Science. Part 1. The Art-Science Connection," in *Essays of an Information Scientist* v. 12 (ISI Press, 1989), pp. 54–61. This article contains a list of journals that cover the science-art connection.

[5]Dennis Dillon, "The Changing Role of Humanities Collection Development," in *Acquisitions and Collection Development in the Humanities*, edited by Irene Owens (Haworth Press, 1997), pp. 7–8.

[6]Marlene Manoff, "Revolutionary or Regressive? The Politics of Electronic Collection Development," in *Scholarly Publishing The Electronic Frontier*, edited by Robin P. Peek and Gregory B. Newby (MIT Press, 1996), p. 225.

CHAPTER *2*

SOURCES OF GENERAL IMPORTANCE TO THE HUMANITIES

BIBLIOGRAPHIC GUIDES AND DIRECTORIES

Reference Books and Research Guides

1. **American Popular Culture: A Guide to the Reference Literature.** Frank W. Hoffman. Englewood, CO: Libraries Unlimited, 1995. 286p. ISBN 1-56308-142-3.

Another in the line of popular culture reference books by Hoffman is this selective reference literature guide to all aspects of the study from comic books to motion pictures. Organization of the work is by type of information source, and coverage is given to 1,215 annotated entries placed under categories by type of tool: guides to the literature; general and subject encyclopedias; subject dictionaries; handbooks and manuals; biographical compilations; directories; indexes and abstracts; bibliographies; discographies; videographies; and supplemental sources such as periodicals, research centers, and associations. These segments are then subdivided by topic or subject: general, popular arts (music and fine arts), mass media (radio, computers), folkways/oral tradition, and social phenomena (fads, events, trends). Annotations are informative, providing description and in some cases evaluation of sources.

2. **American Reference Books Annual.** Bohdan S. Wynar et al., eds. Englewood, CO: Libraries Unlimited, 1970– . Ann. ISSN 0065-9959.

This is the most complete and detailed source of information on reference books published in this country in a single year; the 2000 volume contains 1,543 entries. Reviews are thorough and average about 200–225 words in length, although there are variations depending upon the individual reviewer or the tool being reviewed. The work is divided into four major segments, one of which is the humanities, accounting for some 34 percent of the total coverage in ten chapters ("Decorative Arts," "Fine Arts," "Literature," "Music," and so forth). Access is easily provided through a detailed table of contents and excellent indexes covering author/title, subject, and contributor. Quinquennial indexes are available for 1970–1974, 1975–1979, 1980–1984, 1985–1989, 1990–1994, and 1995–1999 to facilitate searching.

13

3. **Guide to Reference Books.** 11th ed. Robert Balay, ed. Chicago: American Library Association, 1996. 2020p. ISBN 0-8389-0669-9.

The eleventh edition of this massive source, prepared by a distinguished line of editors, contains annotations of over 14,000 reference books, the most recent issued in 1994. Similar to the previous editions, it is divided into five major sections: "General Reference," "Humanities," "Social Sciences," "History and Area Studies," and "Pure and Applied Sciences." The last area was considered underrepresented in the past, and this edition includes a 14 percent increase in titles in the sciences. Predictably, reference works in the humanities represent approximately one-third of the total number of entries. Although the coverage is international in scope, there is a known emphasis on both U.S. publications and the English language in general. This edition also contains a significantly larger number of titles on women in specific countries. Arrangement is by subject and type of tool, employing a unique alphanumeric system now familiar to its audience. Annotations tend to be brief and descriptive. This remains the most important reference literature guide for the majority of U.S. librarians because of its comprehensive nature. Its excellent detailed index, larger than in previous editions, expedites the search for titles as well as names of individuals responsible for them. Biennial supplements had updated previous editions, but the tenth edition (the last to be edited by Eugene P. Sheehy) was followed by Balay's 1992 supplement, *Guide to Reference Books: Covering Materials from 1985-1990. Supplement to the Tenth Edition*, treating 4,668 entries published over a six-year period.

4. **Walford's Guide to Reference Material.** 7th ed. A. J. Walford et al., eds. London: Library Association, 1996–1998. 3v. ISBN 1-85604-165-4 (v.1). 1-85604-223-5 (v.2). 1-85604-300-2 (v.3).

The British counterpart to Balay (entry 3), Walford is another standard source of information and remains a close second to its U.S. rival among academic reference librarians in the United States. Considered by some to be more balanced in perspective, with better annotations in some respects, there is, indeed, greater international coverage. Walford and Balay complement each other and generally are found side by side. Walford's seventh edition follows an established pattern of publication in three volumes issued at different times, *Science and Technology* being first (1996). Volume 2, *Social and Historical Sciences, Philosophy and Religion*, was issued in 1998, and volume 3, *Generalities, Language & Literature, the Arts* in 1999. Volumes 2 and 3 provide a sound basis for humanities reference work. Arrangement of entries in all volumes is under categories established by the Universal Decimal Classification. Access is provided by author/title and subject indexes in each volume. Volume 1 of the eighth edition was issued in November 1999.

Periodical Guides

5. **Magazines for Libraries.** 9th ed. Bill Katz and Linda Sternberg Katz, eds. New York: R. R. Bowker, 1997. 1402p. ISSN 0000-0914.

Like its previous issues, the ninth edition of *Magazines for Libraries* seeks to identify and describe the best and most useful magazines for the average primary or secondary school, public, academic, or special library. Numerous consultants in different subject areas selected and annotated over 7,300 titles from among over 165,000 possibilities. As in the previous editions, entries are organized by subject and coded according to the appropriate audience. New to this edition is the inclusion of Internet resources; after each section of print titles, where applicable, there is a subsection of electronic journals. This is an extensive revision with review, modification, or deletion of all entries as well as addition of new titles. About 85 percent of the titles have been revised and returned from the previous edition and 15 percent are new. Humanities areas are well served from the standpoint of reference and collection management through the inclusion of such subject headings as art, music, and dance. Titles of indexing and abstracting services are supplied following the full bibliographic description. The annotations show purpose, scope, and audience, with some evaluation provided. Each subject section begins with a short introduction and a recommended list of core periodicals essential for a basic collection.

*6. **1999 Gale Directory of Publications and Broadcast Media: An Annual Guide to Publications and Broadcasting Stations.** Julie Winklepleck et al., eds. Detroit: Gale Research, 1999. 4v. Ann. with interedition updates. ISSN 1048-7972.

Regarded as a standard and operating under a variety of titles since its initial edition in 1869, this directory has been known as *Ayer Directory of Publications* (1972 to 1982), *IMS/Ayer Directory of Publications* (1983 to 1985), and *IMS Directory of Publications* (1986). In 1987 it became *Gale Directory of Publications* and added "Broadcast Media" to the title in 1990, indicating an expanded scope. The complete subtitle following the word "Stations" reads "Including Newspapers, Magazines, Journals, Radio Stations, Television Stations, and Cable Systems." The 1999 issue is the 132d edition of this useful work that continues to provide full marketing information on newspapers, periodicals, radio, television, and cable stations and systems in the United States, Canada, and Puerto Rico. This edition contains hundreds of new entries, with emphasis on publications also available online. Directory information includes address, printing method, advertising rates, and circulation statistics for the print media, with similar identification given to the broadcasting units. Statistical summaries are furnished by state and by type; a master index provides quick access. The directory is also issued in CD-ROM format by SilverPlatter.

*7. **Ulrich's International Periodicals Directory, 2000: Including Irregular Serials and Annuals.** 38th ed. New York: R. R. Bowker, 1999. 5v. Ann. ISSN 0000-0175.

Having begun in 1932 and now in its thirty-seventh edition, this is the leading guide to world periodical publications, treating some 165,000 serials in nearly 900 subject categories. Irregular serials, annuals, and infrequent periodicals were incorporated within the text after the demise of Bowker's *Irregular Serials and Annuals: An International Directory* following its thirteenth edition (1987–1988). Entries are arranged alphabetically by subject and include title, frequency, publisher, country of publication, and Dewey Decimal Classification number. Additional information such as ISSN, year of inception, circulation, subscription price, URLs, etc., is included when known. The new edition adds 9,000 new titles and updates 120,000 entries from the previous issue. Electronic publications are included, with more than 3,000 serials on CD-ROM and some 9,000 titles issued online. Volume 5 identifies several thousand daily and weekly newspapers. Nearly 10,000 cessations are identified. *Ulrich's* has set the standard in the field.

Updating has taken place on a quarterly basis since 1992 through **Ulrich's Update*, formerly issued three times per year (1988–1991). Prior to that it was a quarterly known as *Bowker International Serials Database Update* (1985–1988). This had continued an earlier title, *Ulrich's Quarterly* (1977–1985), which in turn had superseded *Bowker Serials Bibliography Supplement* (1972–1976). The initial publication was *Ulrich's International Periodicals Directory. Supplement* (1966–1972). The Bowker listings are available online through DIALOG, OVID, and Lexis-Nexis, as well as the World Wide Web. The database (same name as entry) is updated monthly. Also available is **Ulrich's on Disc* (formerly *Ulrich's Plus Computer File*), providing CD-ROM quarterly coverage on cumulative compact disks. Scheduled for publication soon is *Ulrich's American Periodicals Directory 1998–1999*, which will focus similar coverage on U.S. publications only.

Computerized Databases/CD-ROM

*8. **CD-ROMs in Print 1998: An International Guide to CD-ROM, CD-I, 3DO, MMCD, CD32, Multimedia & Electronic Products.** 12th ed. Amy R. Suchowski, ed. Detroit: Gale Research, 1998. 1450p. Ann. ISSN 0891-8198.

Now published by Gale, this edition covers 15,000 titles (over 2,400 new listings reflecting business and social trends) in a variety of subject areas: "Business & Industry," "Science and the Professions," "Entertainment," "Games and Hobbies," and "Culture, History and Education." This is the first source to consult for CD-ROM availability. With steady growth of CD-ROM products, it has become a most important tool for librarians. Included are those titles that have been discontinued. Products listed are all commercially available, thus offering an excellent purchasing directory for prospective buyers. Entries supply the usual directory-type information, much of which is accessible through the various indexes (subject, audience level, CD-ROM company, electronic books/other platforms, etc.). It is available as a CD-ROM version similar to the coverage given in print.

*9. **Gale Directory of Databases.** Erin E. Braun, ed. Detroit: Gale Research, Jan/July 1993– . 2v. Semiann. ISSN 1066-8934.

This comprehensive directory was formed as a result of a merger of Gale's *Computer Readable Databases* (1979–1992) and Cuadra/Gale's *Directory of Online Databases* (1979–1992) and *Directory of Portable Databases* (1990–1992). The September 1999 issue profiles more than 6,000 online databases in volume 1 and 7,000 portable databases in volume 2. Each volume opens with a state-of-the-art essay describing market conditions for the appropriate product types. Volume 1 is divided into three major sections, the first of which lists alphabetically the online databases and describes them in terms of content, producer, contact, language, year, time span, updating, rates, and so forth. The second segment describes some 2,500 database producers in terms of products, contact persons, and branch offices. The third section provides contact information for online services through which the databases listed in the "Online Databases" section are accessible. Volume 2 treats CD-ROM, diskette, magnetic tape, handheld, and batch access database products, and enumerates system requirements as well as detail and description of products, producers, and vendors. Both volumes supply excellent indexing through subject and geographic location of producers and distributors. The work is available online through ORBIT/Questel, Data-Star, and DIALOG; on CD-ROM from SilverPlatter; and on diskette and magnetic tape through the publisher.

*10. **The Multimedia and CD-ROM Directory.** 17th ed. London/New York: TFPL Multimedia/Stockton Press, 1997. 2v. Semiann. ISBN 1-561592-20-X.

This British publication was formed by the union of *Multimedia Yearbook* and *CD-ROM Directory* and provides a selective listing of some 2,500 CD-ROM titles in a variety of fields. About 20–25 percent are representative of the humanities, with coverage given to the arts, language and linguistics, and more. Architecture is combined with construction in a separate class. The work is divided into several useful segments, beginning with one on copying information, followed by the main sections on CD-ROM titles, which are arranged alphabetically. Entries supply information on type, language, scope, time span, subject, updating, and system requirements of both regular and multimedia CD-ROMs. Subsequent sections treat hardware companies and software companies, as well as conferences and exhibitions useful for planning sales and marketing. Several indexes supply access. The directory is available on a semiannual basis in CD-ROM format from the publisher (18th ed., 1997).

CD-ROM Finder: The World of CD-ROM Products for Information Seekers, edited by James Shelton, is now in its sixth edition (Learned Information, 1995). Coverage is similar to the *Multimedia and CD-ROM Directory*, but it is more selective in its listing, with fewer titles. This number has been rising steadily from one annual edition to the next and indicates the growth of the CD market. Product profiles include a description and identification of scope, system requirements, and market data. Several indexes are supplied. It is available on CD-ROM from the publisher.

11. **World Databases in Humanities.** C. J. Armstrong and R. R. Fenton, eds. London: Bowker-Saur, 1996. 1060p. (World Databases Series). ISBN 1-857-39048-2.

A real boon to searchers is this recent entry to the publisher's series designed to provide essential data regarding databases in electronic format. Comprehensive in design, this work treats all computer-accessed products available in the humanities online, via the Internet, on CD-ROM, on magnetic tape, on diskettes, and even by fax. Entries are informative and evaluative in nature, comparing each database to others of similar purpose and scope. Entries are arranged alphabetically under subject category (religion, philosophy, fine arts, crafts, music, performing arts, language, and literature). Entries furnish identification of type of database, number of records and years covered in the file, details of search software, aids and manuals, along with a general profile. Several indexes provide excellent access.

Library Collections

*12. **Smithsonian on Disc: Catalog of the Smithsonian Institution Libraries on CD-ROM.** 4th ed. Boston: G. K. Hall, 1997. ISBN 0-78381-809-2. (CD-ROM).

Through the wonders of the electronic age, users are now given "instant access to a national treasure." G. K. Hall, the longtime publisher of catalogs in print format, has introduced this CD-ROM version in what has been a prototype for subsequent activity. The entire holdings of the Smithsonian Institution Libraries embrace 1.2 million volumes through nineteen major collections with several affiliates. Relevant to the humanities are the holdings of Cooper Hewitt/National Museum Design Branch, National Museum of African Art Branch, National Museum of American Art Library, National Portrait Gallery Library, and numerous others with collections in architecture, textiles and tapestries, decorative arts, and so forth. Important also is the ability or opportunity to combine searches on the art objects with information on the ethnic or historical significance obtained through materials from other collections (Anthropology Branch, National Museum of American History, Museum Reference Center Branch, etc.). Searching by keyword, name, or subject should be effective.

13. **Subject Collections: A Guide to Special Book Collections and Subject Emphasis As Reported by University, College, Public, and Special Libraries and Museums in the United States and Canada.** 7th ed. Lee Ash et al., eds. New York: R. R. Bowker, 1993. 2v. ISSN 0000-0140.

The seventh edition of *Subject Collections* provides access to thousands of collections from nearly 6,000 libraries and museums in the United States and Canada, down from 11,000 libraries in the sixth edition. (Many of the subject collections are no longer separate and have been incorporated into the main collection; a number of the libraries also have closed.) As was true of the previous edition, "virtually all libraries included in this book are listed in the *American Library Directory*" (Bowker, 1923–). Libraries are listed under an alphabetical subject arrangement based upon thousands of LC subject headings. There are 65,818 entries in all,

with good coverage given to museums as a result of continuing efforts to gain greater participation on their part. This is an important consideration because of the relative uniqueness of
such collections. This work has become a standard purchase for most libraries. One should
use the *Library of Congress Subject Headings* list to make full use of available entries. Reviewed
as an extremely laudable and much-needed work.

Museums

14. **The Cambridge Guide to the Museums of Europe.** Kenneth Hudson
and Ann Nicholls. New York: Cambridge University Press, 1991. 509p.
ISBN 0-521-37175-9.

This is a well-constructed directory of museums in twenty countries of Western
Europe, providing the traveler and information seeker with a good source of information.
Holdings are described briefly along with information on address, telephone number,
dates/hours of opening, admission charges, parking, refreshments, tours, and facilities. Provisions for disabled patrons are enumerated. Arrangement of entries follows the normal directory
prescription: first by country, then by city or town, then name of unit. All types of museums are
included, ranging from the major national and regional operations to the smaller and more
specialized facilities, including homes of notables and such varied topical phenomena as
oysters or firefighters. Emphasis has been placed on sites other than in capital cities, and an
attempt is made to include those museums furnishing exhibits of cultural or historical relevance within the country. A subject index aids access.

15. **Museums of the World.** 6th ed. Bettina Bartz et al., eds. Munchen:
K. G. Saur, 1997. 673p. ISBN 3-598-20605-4.

With publication of the first edition in 1973, this directory established a reputation
for comprehensive coverage of a variety of museums throughout the world. Included among
the various units devoted to the sciences, technology, history, and specialized studies are
those devoted to the arts and archaeology. Arrangement is by continent, then by country and
city. The museums are listed alphabetically. Names of the museums are in the native language although the descriptions are in English. The new edition covers some 24,000 museums
in more than 180 countries. Entries supply information on telephone and fax numbers along with
address, date of founding, current director, holdings, special collections, library, and additional
facilities. A new feature in this edition is the inclusion of e-mail and Web site addresses, where
available. Entries are arranged alphabetically under geographical headings. There is a museum
name index along with a personnel index and a comprehensive subject index.

The Directory of World Museums, by Kenneth Hudson and Ann Nicholls (2d ed.,
Facts on File, 1981) provides similar coverage and lists the museums under the English
form of their name.

16. **The Official Museum Directory.** 29th ed. New Providence, NJ:
R. R. Bowker, 1961– . 2v. Ann. ISSN 0090-6700.

Since it began over thirty years ago, this work has undergone changes both in title
and in frequency, but since 1980 it has appeared annually. Canadian museums were excluded
beginning in 1983. Regarded as the standard tool for the identification of museums in the
United States and now in its 29th edition (1999), it identifies over 7,000 institutions of various
types (museums, associations, zoos, gardens, etc.). Entries include name, address, founding
date, key personnel, governing authority, activities, publications, hours, special collections,
and admission. Art, history, science, and various other areas are represented among the subject areas. There are four major sections, beginning with an alphabetical listing by state, then
city, then name of institution. A second section lists the institutions alphabetically by name,

while the third section provides an alphabetical arrangement by names of directors and department heads. The final section lists institutions by type or category.

Annuals and Current Awareness Sources

17. **Artists and Writers Colonies: Retreats, Residencies, and Respites for the Creative Mind.** Gail H. Bowler. Hillsboro, OR: Blue Heron, 1995. 285p. ISBN 0-936085-34-7.

Of real interest to practitioners (both artists and writers) is this useful directory of existing art colonies, scholarships, fellowships, situations of patronage, and creative societies. The work is designed to identify various possible venues for "creative minds" to seek support and inspiration for continuing their efforts in contributing to an enlightened and enriched society. All areas of the country are tapped; descriptions are full and informative, providing awareness of conditions and types of facilities. Program deadlines are enumerated; conditions and eligibility for awards are explained. There is a separate section treating centers in foreign countries. A variety of indexes provide ready access to relevant data.

18. **Money for Graduate Students in the Humanities 1998-2000.** 2d ed. Gail A. Schlachter and R. David Weber, eds. San Carlos, CA: Reference Service Press, 1998. 296p. ISBN 0-918276-68-3.

Another welcome resource from the team that in the past has collaborated to provide awareness of resources for receiving financial support and assistance is this biennial directory focused on funding students in the humanities. All types of financial support are identified: scholarships, fellowships, traineeships, research grants, and loan funds. Works of this type must be clearly presented and well-organized to identify potentially viable awards; this title provides a good explanation of its use and value in revealing those funds that are applicable to the user's situation. The work is attractive and easy-to-read and presents information relevant to potential applicants. There is a useful annotated bibliography; indexes provide access to program titles, organizations, geographic restrictions, and so forth.

INDEXES, ABSTRACTS, AND SERIAL BIBLIOGRAPHIES

19. **The American Humanities Index.** Troy, NY: Whitston Publishing, 1975– . 2v. Ann. ISSN 0361-0144.

Designed for the scholar and serious student, this small-circulation work indexes some 400 creative, critical, and scholarly journals in the arts and humanities. All journals indexed are located at the College of William and Mary. From 1975 to 1987, the work was issued quarterly with annual cumulations and initially indexed some 100 titles not normally found in other indexing sources. Through the years the policy has changed and there is some duplication with *MLA International Bibliography* (entry 1060), *Arts & Humanities Citation Index* (entry 20), and *Humanities Index* (entry 24). Many of the titles indexed are little magazines devoted to the work of a single author or subject. Published short fiction is listed under "Stories" as well as under the authors' names, true also of poetry and poets. Although a number of the entries are currently found in indexes not considered uncommon, the work is useful in identifying those titles not otherwise covered. The 1997 edition was published in two volumes, as will be the 1999 edition to be published in the year 2000.

*20. **Arts & Humanities Citation Index.** Philadelphia: Institute for Scientific Information. 1978– . Semiann. ISSN 0162-8445.

Since it began as the third of the three major citation indexes from ISI, this work has established itself as a leading source for scholars and students. Initially issued in three parts—January/April, May/August, and finally an annual cumulation of six volumes—it changed to semiannual frequency in 1989. It offers unparalleled coverage of journals in the manner of its companion works in the sciences and social sciences. It currently indexes some 1,300 journals fully and another 5,100 titles partially, representing all fields of the humanities. Reviews of books and performances are found easily, but novices should read carefully the explanation of the various indexes (source, permuterm subject, citation, and corporate) to exploit the work to its fullest degree. When these are understood properly, the searcher can move in either direction, beginning with an author listing of indexed journal articles in the source index or finding the references in the bibliographies or footnotes of those articles in the citation index. Key words from the titles can be used to locate the articles in the subject index.

The work is available online as *Arts & Humanities Search through both FirstSearch and DIALOG, on CD-ROM as *Arts & Humanities Citation Index Compact Disc Edition*, and via restricted Web access. It represents an extensive file from the various fields of the humanities and social sciences dating from 1980 to the present and is updated weekly. The student should not hesitate to use the publisher's *Social Sciences Citation Index* as well, for there are many items of historical and cultural interest relevant to humanities study (philosophy, history, archaeology, etc.). *Social Scisearch also is available online through both FirstSearch and DIALOG, on CD-ROM as *Social Sciences Citation Index (Compact Disc Edition)*, and via restricted Web access.

*21. **Current Contents: Arts & Humanities.** Philadelphia: Institute for Scientific Information, 1979– . Wk. ISSN 0163-3155.

This weekly current awareness service provides tables of contents from over 1,150 leading journals in art and architecture, performing arts, literature, language and linguistics, history, philosophy, and religion on an international basis. Each issue of each journal is covered as often as it is published. A section on current book contents, in which a few recent multi-authored books are highlighted, appears infrequently. There is a title word index listing the keywords in the titles of every article and book indexed in each issue. There is also an author index that lists professional addresses, along with a directory of publishers. A new pattern has been established for the inclusion of a semiannual cumulative index.

It should be remembered that this is one of several different publications in the series, and others may be useful, especially *Current Contents: Social & Behavioral Sciences (ISI, 1974–). This covers about the same number of journals and includes titles in linguistics. Of importance to researchers is the availability of all articles indexed through a document delivery service from ISI. Both services are available online through OVID and DIALOG, for which there is weekly updating; the social/behavioral sciences package is also available on CD-ROM through the publisher.

*22. **Dissertation Abstracts International.** Ann Arbor, MI: University Microfilms International, 1938– . Mo. with ann. cum. ISSN 0419-4209(A); ISSN 0419-4217(B); ISSN 1042-7279(C).

The major source of information on doctoral dissertations worldwide, this service appears in two major segments: A, "The Humanities and Social Sciences," and B, "The Sciences and Engineering." Humanities is divided into five major sections covering communications and the arts; education; language, literature, and linguistics; philosophy, religion, and theology; and social sciences. Section C, "Worldwide," initially appeared in 1976 as "European Abstracts" and has gradually increased its scope and indexing and is published quarterly. Entries in all sections are arranged by broad subject categories, with the authors choosing the categories that best describe the general content. The abstracts are prepared by the authors and run from 300 to 350 words in length. In most cases, it is possible to order the dissertation from University Microfilms. Each issue contains both a keyword title index and an author index; there is an annual cumulative author index.

It is recommended that one consult *Comprehensive Dissertation Index* to expedite a thorough search over a period of several years. *Dissertation Abstracts Online, available through FirstSearch, DIALOG, and restricted Web access, provides quick access to dissertations from 1861 to date. Full abstracts are presented and updating occurs with the same frequency as the publisher's various offerings (monthly for *DAI*, quarterly for *Masters Abstracts*, etc.). *Dissertation Abstracts Ondisc* offers the file in CD-ROM format.

*23. **Essay and General Literature Index, 1900–1933: An Index to About 40,000 Essays and Articles in 2144 Volumes of Collections of Essays and Miscellaneous Works.** Minnie Earl Sears and Marian Shaw, eds. New York: H. W. Wilson, 1934. 1952p. v.2–7 1934–1969. 1934– . Semiann. with ann. and quin. cums. ISSN 0014-083X.

Although other areas of the humanities are covered in this standard work, literature receives the greatest emphasis. Originally, the work succeeded the *ALA Index . . . to General Literature* (2d ed., American Library Association, 1901–1914), that indexed books of essays, travel, sociological matters, and so forth up to 1900. A supplement covered the publications of the first decade of the twentieth century. *EGLI* indexes essays in books published since 1900, the initial volume covering the first thirty-three years. The work is kept up-to-date in print on a semiannual basis, with cumulations annually and quinquennially since 1955–1959. Prior to that it furnished seven-year cumulations. Two comprehensive editions have been issued covering the periods 1900–1989 (11v., 1989) and 1990–1994 (1994). There are annual updates on disk, tape, and online. Hundreds of collections and anthologies (about 300 added annually) serve as sources of the indexed essays on authors, forms, movements, genres, and individual titles of creative works. The work is available online through WILSONLINE and OVID, and on CD-ROM through WILSONDISC.

*24. **Humanities Index.** New York: H. W. Wilson, 1974– . Q. with ann. cum. ISSN 0095-5981.

The leading cumulative index to English-language periodicals in the humanities, this work has been published in its present form since 1974, when *Social Sciences and Humanities Index* (1965–1974) was separated into two publications. Since that time both *Humanities Index* and *Social Sciences Index* have gained an excellent reputation among the other Wilson indexes. *Humanities Index* indexes the contents of some 400 periodicals from all areas of the humanities and, in some cases, the social sciences. The same can be said of *Social Sciences Index*, treating humanist subjects such as anthropology. Both should be employed regularly in searching the literature and both are available online with or without abstracts (*Humanities Abstracts* 1994–) through WILSONLINE, FirstSearch, and on CD-ROM from SilverPlatter. A full-text version of ninety-six periodicals published since 1995 was issued in 1997. Updating is monthly.

25. **Index to Social Sciences & Humanities Proceedings.** Philadelphia: Institute for Scientific Information, 1979– . Q. with ann. cum. ISSN 0191-0574.

Developed in the same format as its earlier publication in the sciences, this ISI product is an international multidisciplinary access tool for papers presented at conferences, seminars, symposia, colloquia, conventions and workshops, and published as proceedings. Humanities coverage includes art, architecture, classics, dance, film, television, folklore, theater, and so forth. The entries provide current awareness for the specialist, particularly important because innovations often are introduced when experts convene. For each entry, full bibliographic information is given for the publication, including the publisher and ordering information. This is followed by a list of individual papers with names and addresses of authors. Indexes give access to each main entry by title, authors and editors, category, sponsor, meeting location, and the organizational affiliation of each cited author. Although currency is indicated in the preface, users should be aware that proceedings are often published long after the event. The proceedings publications selected for the work are considered by the publisher to be the most significant ones for which the majority of the material is printed for the first time.

DICTIONARIES, ENCYCLOPEDIAS, AND HANDBOOKS

26. **Great Events from History II: Arts and Culture Series.** Frank N. Magill, ed. Pasadena, CA: Salem Press, 1993. 5v. ISBN 0-89356-807-4.

Following the initial twelve-volume series treating historical events in America, Europe, and in ancient, medieval, and modern times, this is the third specialized series following science/technology and human rights. Coverage is given to nearly 500 chronologically arranged topics relevant to cultural and artistic life (art, literature, cinema, music, etc.) from 1899 to 1992, providing a useful study guide for undergraduates. Articles are arranged chronologically in usual Magill format beginning with ready reference identification of category of event, time, and locale. Then comes a brief summary of the event and its significance followed by a listing of important relevant personalities. Following that is a detailed essay describing the nature of the event and its impact or significance, along with a brief bibliography and cross-references to related articles. The work is accessed through indexes by broad category, subject/keyword, individual, and place.

The Cambridge Companion to Renaissance Humanism, edited by Jill Kraye (Cambridge University Press, 1996) is part of the series (entry 1082) in which selected essays by individual scholars provide thorough examination of various aspects of a topic, along with a carefully selected bibliography of additional reading. In this case, there are fourteen essays beginning with examination of the origins of humanism and progressing through studies of its representation in rhetoric, the Bible, philosophy, art, literature, and more.

27. **The Oxford Guide to Classical Mythology in the Arts, 1300–1990s.** Jane Davidson Reid and Chris Rohmann. New York: Oxford University Press, 1993. 2v. ISBN 0-19-504998-5.

This effort is of immense value to a variety of users seeking to identify modern cultural achievements of the Western world relating to figures in mythology. It represents a topically classified chronology of more than 30,000 artworks of various kinds (painting, literature, drama, sculpture, music, dance, and opera) produced from the fourteenth century to the present day. Arrangement is under names of some 300 mythological figures, with volume 1 covering Auchelous–Leander and volume 2 treating Leda–Zeus. All important beings are treated, from gods and goddesses to heroes, nymphs, and satyrs. Artworks are arranged chronologically within each entry and are identified by title of work, date, publication or first performance, and present location. Subjects are listed under the Greek name with cross-references to the Roman. The work concludes with a list of sources and index of artists.

BIOGRAPHICAL SOURCES

28. **American National Biography.** John A. Garraty and Mark C. Carnes, eds. New York: Oxford University Press/American Council of Learned Societies, 1999. 24v ISBN 0-19-520635-5.

This recent twenty-four-volume effort serves as a comprehensive source of information on the lives of 17,000 Americans who have made a significant contribution to some aspect or area of society. It has been in preparation for ten years and represents the collective scholarship of more than 6,000 contributors. Coverage is given to an excellent cross-section of personalities who have died as recently as 1995. There is a great variety of professions and achievements represented (from sports to rocket science, with many artists, philosophers, theologians, musicians, writers, etc.). Entries are full, authoritative, and complete with bibliographies in the style of *Dictionary of American Biography*, the twenty-volume set that recently issued its tenth supplement (Scribner's, 1995). Various indexes provide access.

American Cultural Leaders: From Colonial Times to the Present, by Justin Harmon and others (ABC-Clio, 1993) is a one-volume work that provides treatment of 360 individuals considered to be cultural leaders. All aspects of the humanities and creative expression are represented, with brief, informative 1,000-word biographical sketches given to both men and women who have made important contributions. Included are personalities prominent in the visual arts including architecture, theater, dance, film, literature, and music. *European Culture: A Contemporary Companion*, edited by Jonathan Law (Mansell/Cassell, 1993) provides brief biographical coverage of 1,000 important contributors to world culture since 1945. Coverage is given to movements, issues, and genres relevant to sophisticated cultural development in painting, sculpture, architecture, music, literature, theater, and film. Somewhat less emphasis is placed on philosophy, religion, and the sciences. Popular culture is treated only slightly, with emphasis on the creators rather than the performers.

29. **The Annual Obituary.** Chicago: St. James Press, 1981– . Ann. ISSN 0278-1573.

Initially offered by St. Martin's Press for its first three years, this annual service has been issued by St. James since 1984. It documents the passing of notables in all fields of human activity on an annual basis, providing a chronological overview of death dates from January to December of each year. Within each month entries are arranged alphabetically by surname. Each volume treats 300 or more persons from all over the world, providing a brief biographical sketch running from 500 to 2,000 words. These essays are well-developed and informative, documenting the subjects' accomplishments as well as influences on their lives. The essays may be a little premature when they attempt to assess the individuals' place in history. Essays are followed by a section of listings supplying biographical data and vital statistics such as birth name, parents, marital status, education, awards and honors, cause of death, and so forth. Included also are publications and sources for further reading. There are indexes by name and by subject.

*30. **Biography and Genealogy Master Index.** 2d ed. Barbara McNeil and Miranda C. Herbert. Detroit: Gale Research, 1981. 8v. Ann. supp. with quin. cum. 1981– . ISSN 0730-1316.

The first edition of this compilation in 1975 had the title *Biographical Dictionaries Master Index*. The second edition indexes the biographies in over 350 current and retrospective reference works. Prior to the publication of the first edition, it was necessary to consult these works individually. The *Master Index* contains over 3 million entries from 675 biographical dictionaries, subject encyclopedias, indexes, and works of literary criticism. The emphasis is on Americans, but a number of foreign biographical tools are also included. Names are listed in one alphabetical sequence. For each name, abbreviated citations to biographical listings found for that person are supplied. Variant forms of names have not been reconciled, so personalities may be listed under more than one form of their name. Entries include birth and death dates and indicate when a portrait is included with the biography. The 1998–1999 annual volume identifies more than 460,000 biographical sketches appearing in over 100 biographical dictionaries. Cumulations have been issued for 1981–1985, 1986–1990, and 1991–1995.

The work is available online through DIALOG as *Biography Master Index and as a CD-ROM product from the publisher, and can be searched by name, birth or death years, source publication, and year of publication.

*31. Biography Index. New York: H. W. Wilson, 1946– . Q. with ann. and bienn. cums; twice-wk. (online). ISSN 0006-3053.

Biographical articles from periodicals and essays (chapters) from collected biographical works as well as monographs dealing with the careers and lives of notables of all types are identified in this standard source from the Wilson Company. The title provides excellent general coverage of personalities from all over the world, both living and dead, although there is an emphasis on English-speaking individuals. More than 2,700 periodicals are examined and 2,000 books indexed annually. The index is arranged alphabetically by the names of the biographees. A list by occupation or profession is also included. Basic bibliographic information on monographs indexed is given in a list of those works included in each issue. The number of years this index has been published makes it useful for comprehensive research. It is available online through FirstSearch and on CD-ROM through SilverPlatter.

32. Blacks in the Humanities, 1750–1984: A Selected Annotated Bibliography. Donald F. Joyce, comp. New York: Greenwood, 1986. 209p. (Bibliographies and Indexes in Afro-American and African Studies, no. 13). ISBN 0-313-24643-2.

The compiler has been an active contributor to African-American history and has produced a unique source in terms of its scope, covering leading black personalities and their contributions over a wide range of the humanities and creative arts and spanning a period of over 200 years. The humanities are defined broadly and black involvement is considered under different chapter headings such as art, music, drama, literary criticism, linguistics, philosophy, science, history, and even library science. Coverage is provided for over 600 monographs, journal articles, and dissertations, offering both students and researchers well-selected and carefully developed listings. Annotations range from brief to very full; entries have been taken from numerous sources (bibliographies, indexes, union lists, encyclopedias, biographical dictionaries, catalogs, textbooks, etc.). Access is provided by both subject and author/title indexes of comprehensive nature.

*33. Current Biography. New York: H. W. Wilson. 1940– . Mo. ISSN 0011-3344. Ann. cum. ISSN 0084-9499.

With publication of its initial edition nearly sixty years ago, this title assumed an important position in libraries for its coverage of currently notable personalities representing various fields of endeavor. They range from the heroes of popular culture, including sports figures, to serious diplomats and politicians, as well as sophisticated achievers in science, social science, and humanities. Emphasis is on people from all over the world who are in the headlines at the time. Biographical sketches are detailed and well-developed and run from 2,500 to 3,000 words, with coverage given to nearly 20 personalities per month or about 200 per year. To date, more than 15,000 have been covered, with retrieval made simple on the recently issued CD-ROM version. Sketches are based on news articles about the person. A photograph is included with the majority of the essays. Although the purpose of the tools is to give current biographical information on living individuals, obituaries are also included.

The annual cumulation is titled *Current Biography Yearbook*, which integrates all sketches issued in the previous year into one alphabetical arrangement. In tribute to its golden anniversary, Jill Kadetsky edited a cumulative index in 1991 covering the years 1940–1990; in 1996, a new index treating the period 1990–1995 superseded all previous efforts.

In 1995, the publisher produced a shortened CD-ROM version containing the full text of all biographies appearing in the print volume since 1983; the 1997 edition of this work provides biographies in full text from 1983 through 1996, with indexing of the entire set from 1940.

34. **Lives and Works in the Arts from the Renaissance to the 20th Century.** Armonk, NY: Sharpe Reference, 1997. 9v. ISBN 1-56324-817-4.

This recent set represents a detailed and relatively thorough biographical description with analysis of 168 significant writers, artists, and musicians from the Renaissance to modern times. Beginning with the volume 1 treatment of Renaissance artists, each of the first eight volumes covers twenty-one personalities in a standardized six-page format, describing their lives, accomplishments, and contributions to the art. Along with illustrations, which include color and black-and-white photographs of the artists' works, there are additional features: boxed listings of key dates and relevant events. A picture of the individual is included in each entry. Information is suitable for high school/undergraduate levels and should provide the type of commentary and introduction to the figures that is needed. Volume 9 contains the full indexing, historical timeline, glossary, and bibliography of additional readings, although each volume presents such material relevant to its scope and coverage.

35. **St. James Guide to Biography.** Paul E. Schellinger, ed. Chicago: St. James Press, 1991. 870p. ISBN 1-55862-146-6.

This is the first edition of a widely acclaimed biographical reference work described by reviewers as a "solid, well-edited, and annotated bibliography whose strongest feature is its currency." International coverage embraces 700 personalities in entries contributed by 300 academic specialists. Personalities have been included on the basis of their fame, notoriety, or contribution to their particular field. Van Gogh, Dali, and David are listed along with Caesar, Bogart, and Hitler in a diverse array of important figures. Each entry furnishes a listing of biographical sources in the English language and an essay-review comparing the sources and evaluating their scholarship and accuracy. Sources include critical studies, general histories, journals and magazines, autobiographies, and diaries. The cutoff date for the sources used is 1990. Essays are well-written and interesting, promoting the point of view of their authors.

CHAPTER 3

ACCESSING INFORMATION IN PHILOSOPHY

WORKING DEFINITION OF PHILOSOPHY

Although the term *philosophy* is derived from the Greek words usually translated to mean "love of wisdom,"[1] there is reason to believe that the original usage was somewhat broader, connoting free play of the intellect over a wide range of human problems and even including such qualities as shrewdness, curiosity, and practicality. McLeish, in fact, suggests that the definition "love of knowledge acquired by the exercise of the intellect" is more appropriate to the original meaning.[2]

There has been a gradual narrowing of the meaning of the term *philosophy* beginning in antiquity and proceeding in stages up through the present time. Socrates differentiated his activity from that of the sophists by stressing the raising of questions for clarification in the course of discussion, as distinct from giving answers or teaching techniques for winning arguments. This emphasis on critical examination of issues remained central to philosophic method in the succeeding centuries. Stanley Chodorow, in "Transformations in the Humanities," states it more simply: "The one thing nearly all philosophers agree on is . . . that philosophical investigation rests on the making and analysis of arguments."[3]

The encyclopedic concepts of philosophy were shattered by the rise of modern science in the seventeenth century. First the natural sciences emerged as separate disciplines, then the social and behavioral sciences effected their separation from philosophy, and eventually the social sciences migrated into distinct scholarly and applied fields. The combination of philosophy and psychology that characterizes some reference tools produced at the beginning of the twentieth century is evidence of the relatively late departure of psychology and the other behavioral sciences from the broad field of philosophy.

Stripped of the natural and social sciences, what remains now of philosophy? First, there are questions about the nature of ultimate reality. Then there is the matter of knowledge as a whole as well as the interrelationships of the specialized branches of it. There are questions of methodology and presuppositions of the individual disciplines. (The phrase "philosophy of . . ." is often assigned to this type of endeavor: philosophy of science, philosophy of education, and the like.) Finally, there are those normative issues for which there are no scientifically verifiable answers.

It may be said, then, that philosophy is the discipline that is concerned with basic principles of reality; methods for investigation and study; and the logical structures, systems, and interrelationships among all fields of knowledge. For additional definitions of philosophy and discussions of some of the problems of defining the discipline, the reader should see Alan R. Lacy's *A Dictionary of Philosophy* (3d ed., Routledge Kegan Paul, 1996) and Anthony Flew and Jennifer Speake's *A Dictionary of Philosophy* (2d rev. ed., St. Martin's Press, 1984). A more recent brief description of the field is Kenneth McLeish's *Key Ideas in Human Thought* (Facts on File, 1993).

MAJOR DIVISIONS OF THE FIELD

Philosophy continues to be divided into five broad areas: metaphysics, epistemology, logic, ethics, and aesthetics. Each of these broad areas, in turn, can be further subdivided.

Metaphysics may be further subdivided into ontology and cosmology. Ontology is concerned with the nature of ultimate reality, sometimes referred to as "being." It includes consideration of whether reality has one, two, or many basic components (monism, dualism, or pluralism, respectively). Monistic philosophies consider whether reality is ultimately mental or spiritual (idealism) or physical (materialism). Dualistic philosophies commonly regard both matter and mind as irreducible ultimate components, while pluralistic philosophies allow for many possibilities. Pluralistic ideas are most often argued in the political realm.

Cosmology is concerned with questions of origins and processes. The nature of causality has been a frequent topic of debate. Although a few have argued for pure chance, more philosophers have emphasized antecedent causes (that is, preceding events that cause the event under consideration to happen) or final causes (ends or purposes that exert influence on the outcome of events). Many of the former persuasion are convinced that there is no room for either chance or freedom in the chain of causality. The determinists are called *mechanists* if they also believe that reality is ultimately physical. Those who emphasize final causes are known as *teleologists.* P. F. Strawson's *Individuals* (Methuen, 1959) is a recommended reading for cosmology.

Epistemology is concerned with the scope and limits of human knowledge. What can we know, and with what degree of certainty? Rationalists stress the role of human reason as the source of all knowledge, while empiricists believe that knowledge is derived from experience. It is generally agreed that there are two types of knowledge: *a priori*, which is knowable without reference to experience and which alone possesses theoretical certainty (for example, the principles of logic and mathematics); and *a posteriori*, which is derived from experience and possesses only approximate certainty (the findings of science, for example). T. E. Burke's chapter, "What Can Be Known?," in Davis and Park's *No Way: The Nature of the Impossible* (W. H. Freeman, 1987) is an example of an epistemological work.

Logic deals with the principles of correct reasoning or valid inference. It differs from psychology in that it does not describe how people actually think but rather prescribes certain canons to be followed if they would think correctly. Deductive logic (sometimes known as Aristotelian or traditional logic) is concerned with the process by which correct conclusions can be drawn from a set of axioms known or believed to be true. Its most familiar form is the syllogism, which consists of three parts: the major premise, the minor premise, and the conclusion.

Major premise: All men are mortal.

Minor premise: Socrates is a man.

Conclusion: Therefore, Socrates is mortal.

Inductive logic is a result of the development of modern scientific methods. It deals with the canons of valid inference, but is concerned with probabilities rather than certainties and often involves the use of statistics. In a sense the opposite of deductive logic, inductive logic attempts to reach valid generalizations from an enumeration of particulars.

Although logic arose in antiquity and was summarized in Aristotelian works, few advances were made until the last half of the nineteenth century, when symbolic and Boolean logic provided forms of notation useful in mathematical reasoning and later in computer science and information retrieval.

In ethics, the questions relate to human nature and to matters of conduct. Can certain actions be considered morally right or wrong? If so, on what basis? Should the interests of self have priority (egotism) or should the interests of others be the driving principle (altruism)? Or is there some greater good to which both self- and other-interest should be subordinate? Ethical theories may be classified by the manner in which criteria for right actions are established or by the nature of the highest good.

Andrew Jack suggests that ethics can be conveniently divided into three parts: "normative ethics, practical ethics, and meta-ethics."[4] The first deals with normative principles or moral rules such as "The Golden Rule." Meta-ethics considers the nature of metaphysical issues that can arise for any moral principle. Practical ethics considers specific applications of ethical thinking to particular problems.

Discussions in the popular literature have brought the consideration of practical ethics to newspaper readers and viewers of the television evening news. Such issues as euthanasia, assisted suicide, the death penalty, abortion, equality of the sexes or races, and the use of animals for biomedical research are but a few topics. Peter Singer's *Practical Ethics*, first published in 1979 and thoroughly revised in 1993 (Cambridge University Press), is a highly acclaimed work on the subject and includes chapters on equality and discrimination, treatment of animals, and environmental concerns, as well as an excellent discussion of the nature of ethics. Singer, now professor of bioethics at Princeton University, has recently been the focus of controversy in the popular press. See, for example, Paul Zielbauer, "Princeton Bioethics Professor Debates Views on Disability and Euthanasia," *New York Times* (October 13, 1999) p. 8. An ethics Web site that will be of interest to both scholarly and lay readers is Lawrence Hinman's *Ethics*, at http://ethics.acusd.edu/index.html (accessed February 28, 2000). The site includes pages on both theoretical and applied ethics.

The nature of beauty is the subject matter of aesthetics. The concerns of the philosopher may be differentiated from those of the psychologist and those of the critic. The psychologist concentrates on human reactions to aesthetic objects. The critic focuses on individual works of art or on the general principles of criticism, usually within the confines of a particular discipline. The philosopher is broadly concerned with beauty per se, whether in art or in nature. Does beauty adhere in the beautiful object? Are there objective criteria by which it may be determined? Or is beauty a subjective experience, with no universally valid norms? Classical theories stress objectivity, while romantic theories emphasize individualism and subjectivity. Further, aesthetics explores the nature of the arts and considers similarities and differences between the visual and performing arts and questions concerning what art represents and expresses.

Section 1 of Alexander Dey's *Philosophy in Cyberspace, A Guide to Philosophy-Related Resources on the Internet* [Online], available at http://www-personal.monash.edu.au/~dey/phil/section1.htm (accessed February 28, 2000), lists the divisions of philosophy and online resources on them. (The Philosophy Documentation Center, Bowling Green State University, publishes the guide in print form as well.) Definitions of many subfields of philosophy also can be found in the guides listed at Thomas Ryan Stone's comprehensive *Episteme-Links.Com*, at http://www.epistemelinks.com/index.asp (accessed February 28, 2000). This site is frequently updated, so it should be checked routinely for new material.

HELPFUL RESOURCES FOR
STUDENTS, LIBRARIANS, AND
GENERAL READERS

The reader needing a starting point in philosophy will find the *Encyclopaedia Britannica Online* article "History of Philosophy" to be most helpful. Available on the Web at http://www.members.eb.com/bol/topic?eu=115379&sctn=1 (accessed May 23, 1999), the entry provides an extensive outline that will lead the reader to related topics in the electronic encyclopedia. Several *Encyclopaedia Britannica Online* entries are also helpful, providing the reader or librarian with clear introductory reading and basic bibliographic leads. Access "philosophy" in the *Encyclopaedia Britannica Online* at http://members.eb.com/bol/topic?eu=61236&sctn=1#s_top (accessed June 16, 1999) and follow the guides to "Schools and Doctrines" and "Branches." Both offer insights into the divisions of the field, history of philosophical thought, and defining principles. The focus is on Western philosophy.

Still highly useful is John Passmore's "Philosophy," in the print *Encyclopedia of Philosophy* (reprint, Macmillan, 1996). Passmore's "Philosophy, Historiography of," in the same volume of the *Encyclopedia* provides historical perspectives. Another helpful work with brief signed articles on all manner of philosophical topics is Kenneth McLeish's *Key Ideas in Human Thought* (Facts on File, 1993). And a promising recent addition to the literature is the online *Stanford Encyclopedia of Philosophy*, edited by Edward N. Zalta and located at http://plato.stanford.edu/ (accessed May 23, 1999).

Several works are of particular importance to the librarian. *The Encyclopedia of Philosophy*, referenced above, contains three articles by William Gerber: "Philosophical Bibliographies," "Philosophical Dictionaries and Encyclopedias," and "Philosophical Journals," in volume 6 (reprint, 1996, pp. 166–216). The article on philosophy in Lester Asheims's *The Humanities and the Library* (American Library Association, 1956, pp. 61–99), despite its age, is still a valuable description, and Martin Bertman's *Research Guide in Philosophy* (General Learning, 1974) presents the literature of the field in a well-organized, practical manner. A more recent perspective is offered by Richard H. Lineback's chapter on philosophy in Nena Couch and Nancy Allen's *The Humanities and the Library* (2d ed., American Library Association, 1993, pp. 212–39). Finally, a recommended source for all librarians is Richard T. de George's *Philosopher's Guide to Sources, Research Tools, Professional Life, and Related Fields* (University of Kansas Press, 1980).

Many introductions and histories of philosophy are extremely technical and therefore forbidding to the layperson, but the librarian can guide readers to two classic popularizations: Bertrand Russell's *A History of Western Philosophy* (Simon & Schuster, 1945) and Will Durant's ever-popular *Story of Philosophy* (Simon & Schuster, 1926). Bertman's guide, mentioned earlier, contains an easy-to-read history. The reader needing only a synopsis of a particular work in philosophy will find useful *Masterpieces of World Philosophy*, edited by Frank N. Magill (HarperCollins, 1990) or the more exhaustive five-volume *World Philosophy: Essay Reviews of 225 Major Works* (Salem Press, 1982).

Neither the reference librarian nor the collection development librarian should overlook Hans E. Bynagle's *Philosophy: A Guide to the Reference Literature* (2d ed., Libraries Unlimited, 1997). Andrew D. Scrimgeour, "Philosophy and Religion," in *Selection of Library Materials in the Humanities, Social Sciences, and Sciences*, edited by Patricia A. McClung (American Library Association, 1985), also offers information useful to the selector.

To maintain currency, the selector of philosophical materials will need to consult articles such as "Forthcoming Philosophy and Religion Publications, 1998–1999," *Choice* 36 (December 1998): 645–55 as they appear in the professional journals.

For the reader who wishes to *read* philosophy, rather than read *about* philosophy, texts of the works of many important philosophers can now be accessed on the Internet. For example, *The Internet Encyclopedia of Philosophy*, edited by James Fieser, has links to many philosophical texts online. Access the "Philosophy Text Collection" at http://www.utm.edu. research.iep.philtext.htm (accessed February 28, 2000).

USE AND USERS OF PHILOSOPHY INFORMATION

A thorough search of the literature of use and user studies indicates that very little research has been done on literature use by philosophers. There is other evidence, however, that the literature of the field is widely used and that particular authors are well-cited both within the humanities and by writers in the sciences and social sciences.

A listing of the 100 most cited authors from the 1977–1978 *Arts and Humanities Citation Index* (ISI Press, 1978) includes Plato and Aristotle, with over 1,200 citations each, as well as contemporary writers like Karl Popper, Paul Ricoeur, and John Rawls. The most cited author was Karl Marx, whose works received over 1,600 citations in the year under study (1977–1978), and half of the citations were in philosophy journals, according to Eugene Garfield, whose article is the source of these data.[5]

Garfield has compiled a listing of the fifty twentieth-century books most cited in the *Arts and Humanities Citation Index* during the period 1976–1983. The field of philosophy is well represented on the list, as are criticism, linguistics, and fiction. In the philosophy area, the works of Wittgenstein, Popper, and Kuhn are among the most cited on the elite list.[6]

Garfield has also identified the arts and humanities journals that were most cited in the entire ISI family of citation indexes in 1981. The second and seventh most highly cited journals were *Journal of Philosophy* and *Philosophical Review*, with 640 and 435 citations, respectively.[7] Since citations in the sciences, the social sciences, and the humanities were combined for the purposes of ranking, the influence of philosophy across all fields of knowledge is apparent.

Although the citation rankings are, of course, dependent on the coverage of ISI's databases, they nonetheless indicate the relative impact of certain works as compared to all others referenced in the ISI-covered publications. Most important, citation does represent a quantitative measure of literature use.

Although carried out as a library collection evaluation, a study by Jean-Pierre V. M. Herubel at Purdue University ("Philosophy Dissertation Bibliographies and Citations in Serials Evaluation," *The Serials Librarian* 20, nos. 2/3 [1991]: 65–73) provides insight into the literature used by philosophy scholars in preparing dissertations in one university environment. Reflecting Garfield's earlier findings, *Journal of Philosophy* and *Philosophical Review* were among the most highly cited journals (first and fourth) with sixty-three and forty-four citations respectively. The dissertations, which are dated between 1970 and 1988, reflect the humanist's heavy reliance on monographs (71.3 percent of all references) and lesser use of the journal literature (28.7 percent).[8]

The importance of monographs is reaffirmed in the more recent study by Ylva Lindholm-Romantschuk and Julian Warren, "The Role of Monographs in Scholarly Communication: An Empirical Study of Philosophy, Sociology and Economics," *Journal of Documentation* 52 (December 1996): 389–404.

Studies of scholars' information seeking for the Research Libraries Group (Constance Gould, "Philosophy," *Information Needs in the Humanities: An Assessment* [Stanford, CA: RLG, 1988]) suggest that relatively few philosophers use traditional reference sources to stay current in their field, particularly when compared to researchers in other disciplines.

As for books, Henry J. Koren, in his still useful *Research in Philosophy—A Bibliographical Introduction to Philosophy and a Few Suggestions for Dissertations* (Duquesne University Press, 1966), divides philosophy books into "popularizing works, text books, and strictly scholarly works."

MAJOR CLASSIFICATION SCHEMES

Utilization of shelf arrangement as a tool for philosophic information retrieval must be considered secondary to other approaches, but some knowledge of the major library classification schemes will be advantageous. The two most frequently used schemes are the Dewey Decimal Classification (DDC) and the Library of Congress Classification (LC).

From the user's standpoint, there are three principal approaches to the arrangement of philosophic writings: by individual philosophers, by specialized branches (subdivisions) of philosophy, and by interrelationships and influence groupings. The first approach is particularly helpful if one wishes to study a specific philosopher's thought system or specific works of an individual. It is especially convenient if the library shelves secondary works, such as criticism and commentary, with the primary works.

The second approach to organizing philosophical materials, by subdivisions, would group together works on metaphysics, epistemology, logic, ethics, and aesthetics.

Finally, the interrelationships and influences approach would organize a collection of materials around the works attributed to a temporal period, language, school of thought, nationality grouping, and so forth.

Clearly, no truly useful classification system would follow a single approach to organizing. Hence, both DDC and LC attempt to balance the differing and sometimes conflicting approaches.

The DDC was first devised by Melvil Dewey in 1876, and although revised and expanded over the years, it still reflects a late nineteenth-century view of the world. Its handling of philosophy (100–199) has been frequently criticized for its separation of philosophical viewpoints from the period-specific sections, for placing aesthetics with the arts (in the 700s), and for its inclusion of psychology (150). In spite of these problems, however, the DDC is the most commonly used scheme, especially in public, school, and smaller academic libraries.

The major DDC subject divisions for philosophy and related disciplines are:

110   Metaphysics

120   Epistemology, Causation

130   Paranormal Phenomena and Arts

140   Specific Philosophical Viewpoints

150   Psychology

160   Logic

170   Ethics

180   Ancient, Medieval, Oriental Philosophy

190   Modern Western Philosophy

The Library of Congress (LC) schedule for philosophy was first published in 1910 and has also been revised. Although it, like the DDC, includes psychology, it is generally considered to be superior in its handling of philosophy. For example, LC includes aesthetics.

Subclass B is designed to keep the works of individual philosophers together and to place them in relation to periods, countries, and schools of thought. The general pattern for individual philosophers is 1) collected works, 2) separate works, 3) biography and criticism. LC also has sections for major divisions of the field. The principal divisions are:

B	Philosophy (General)
	Serials, Collections, etc.
	History and systems
BC	Logic
BD	Speculative Philosophy
	General works
	Metaphysics
	Epistemology
	Methodology
	Ontology
	Cosmology
BF	Psychology
	Parapsychology
	Occult sciences
BH	Aesthetics
BJ	Ethics
	Social usages, Etiquette

Although some special philosophy classifications have been developed, their use appears to have been confined to the arrangement of certain bibliographies and special collections.

SUBJECT HEADINGS IN PHILOSOPHY

Searching library catalogs (whether in card, book, or computer form) continues to play an important role in the retrieval of philosophical information. Although many subject indexes in recent years have been constructed on the basis of keywords from document titles, or from text, most library catalogs use a controlled or standardized vocabulary embodied in a list of subject headings. Such lists usually include guidance on choice of main headings, methods of subdividing major topics, and cross-references to lead the user to the headings chosen or to related topics.

The majority of large American libraries today follow the *Subject Headings Used in the Dictionary Catalogs of the Library of Congress*, available in print, on microfiche, and on magnetic tape. The subject headings enable the reader looking for a specific topic to go directly to that heading. The disadvantage of this approach for this discipline is that philosophic topics are scattered throughout an entire alphabetical sequence. This is true whether the library uses an integrated "dictionary" catalog or a divided catalog (in which the subject portion is separated from the author-title section). The subject headings are used in many online library catalogs, and thus some knowledge of them is helpful to the library user.

To use subject headings as a guide in the formulation of a search strategy, it is helpful to understand the basic forms subject headings may take:

1. *Simple noun headings*. This form is the most direct, immediate, and uncomplicated. If adequate to the text, it is the preferred method. The most obvious example, in this context is "Philosophy."

2. *Adjectival headings*. These may be in natural or inverted form. An example of the natural form is "Philosophical anthropology," while an example of the inverted form is "Philosophers, Ancient." The choice is determined by the need to emphasize those search words of greatest importance to the intended user. In the first example, the term "philosophical" is more significant to the

philosophy student than the word "anthropology." In the second example, the term "American" would be of significance to the person seeking information on American philosophy, but the natural order would bury the topic among dozens of other entries beginning with "American." Because the prime topic is philosophy, with American philosophy as one variety, the inverted form is chosen.

3. *Phrase headings.* These usually consist of nouns connected by a preposition. An example is "Philosophy in literature." Another type of phrase heading is the so-called compound heading, made up of two or more coordinate elements connected by "and." An example is "Philosophy and cognitive science."

It often happens that the approaches described above do not result in headings that are sufficiently specific. In such cases, further division of the topic will be required. The techniques most frequently used for division are as follows:

1. *By form.* The plan of division is not based on the content of a work but on its manner of arrangement or the purpose it is intended to serve. Examples include "Philosophy—Bibliography;" "Philosophy—Dictionaries;" "Philosophy—Study and teaching."

2. *By political or geographic area.* Generally, this is not a consideration in the field of philosophy because the need for geographic subdivision is accomplished by the use of the inverted form of adjectival headings, such as "Philosophy, French" or "Philosophy, Chinese."

3. *By period.* This technique for subdivision can cause some confusion for the uninitiated, especially in a field like philosophy. This represents a departure from the customary alphabetical approach in that headings for different historical periods are arranged chronologically. In philosophy, the technique is used to divide under separate countries, as in "Philosophy, French—17th century," which precedes "Philosophy, French—18th century." (Notice that alphabetical presentation would put eighteenth ahead of seventeenth.) The situation is further complicated by the use of subject headings for broad periods for philosophy (for example, "Philosophers, Ancient") that are arranged in the customary alphabetical way. The searcher will be wise to double check until thoroughly familiar with the subject matter and the approaches to its headings.

A subject heading system must make provisions for the user who may choose as the initial search term a word or phrase other than the one used in the system. The necessary connections have customarily been made by means of *see* references that direct readers from terms that are not used to those that are used. Similarly, the user has traditionally been provided access to other headings that might lead to relevant information by *see also* references. More recent subject headings use additional symbols for such cross references, for example:

USE

UF   (Used for)

BT   (Broader term)

NT   (Narrower term)

RT   (Related term)

SA   (See also)

This thesaurus-type approach eliminates the need for symbols indicating reverse patterns of *see also* references and other sometimes confusing notations.

Scope notes are sometimes, although not frequently, provided to remove doubt or confusion as to what may or may not be covered by certain subject headings. An example found under the heading "Philosophy, Ancient" in the LCSH is "Here are entered works dealing with ancient philosophy in general and with Greek and Roman philosophy in particular."

In practice, many more subject headings are used than are enumerated on any list of subject headings. However, the headings are most often formed in accordance with the principles followed in the LCSH.

It should also be remembered that no subject heading list should be static, even in a field as stable as philosophy. New terms are constantly coming into use and older terms are being revised or deleted. A comparison of the subject headings in various editions of the LCSH shows a dynamic, rather than a static list. *Library of Congress Subject Headings in Philosophy*, edited by Barbara Berman, is scheduled for publication by the Philosophy Documentation Center.

Searching in printed library catalogs and browsing machine readable catalogs are made considerably easier if the reader understands the filing system in use by the particular catalog. The dictionary catalog or subject portion of a divided catalog will most often follow an alphabetical arrangement, but a chronological arrangement may be used wherever a division by date seems more logical than a strictly alphabetical sequence.

Alphabetical filing arrangements usually follow one of two patterns. The first is the "letter-by-letter" method used by many reference tools, including several indexes and encyclopedias. With this method, all the words in the heading are treated as parts of one unit. Filing proceeds strictly on the basis of the order of the letters in the unit as a whole, regardless of whether they are in separate short words or in a single long word. Thus, "Newark" would precede "New York." Libraries have not favored this method because it tends to scatter closely related topics.

Most libraries have adopted the "word-by-word" or "nothing before something" approach, in which each word is treated as a separate unit for filing purposes. Using this method, "New York" would precede "Newark" in the catalog.

For the controlled indexing terms used in online and CD-ROM bibliographic databases, the user should consult the thesaurus for the database in question. The use of controlled subject terms will likely improve the search by complementing the use of keywords and enhancing precision. Many online thesauri have print counterparts that can be consulted in advance of the search in preparation for it. The area of online access is only one of the many areas in which computers influenced the way the work of the field was carried out in the late 1990s.

The advent of the Internet and World Wide Web brings new challenges to organizing materials. Methods of describing, indexing, and searching are rapidly changing to accommodate the enormous mass of information that is being made available electronically. Humanities librarians are involved in developing the systems by which philosophical materials can be organized for convenient access by users.

COMPUTERS IN PHILOSOPHY

Increasing use of computers by philosophy scholars is evidenced by the coverage in reviews of information systems in the humanities. The *Annual Review of Information Science and Technology* (*ARIST*) has included reviews of the situation in the humanities three times: in 1972 (J. Raben and R. L. Widmann, "Information Systems Applications in the Humanities," *ARIST* 7 [1972]: 439–69), in 1981 (J. Raben and S. K. Burton, "Information Systems and Services in the Arts and Humanities," *ARIST* 16 [1981]: 247–66), and in 1991 (Helen R. Tibbo, "Information Systems, Services, and Technology for the Humanities," *ARIST* 26 [1991]: 287–346). In 1972 and 1981, philosophy was neither singled out, nor even mentioned, as a field in which computer applications deserved discussion. Tibbo, however, noted several applications of computers to the work of philosophers: word processing, text analysis, theorem proving, logic studies and teaching.

Preston K. Covey, "Formal Logic and Philosophic Analysis," *Teaching Philosophy* 4 (July–October 1991): 277–301, and Larry Wos et al., *Automated Reasoning: Introduction and Applications* (Prentice-Hall, 1984), describe applications in logic. Donald Sievert and Maryellen Sievert, "Humanists and Technology: The Case of Philosophers," in *Information and Technology: Planning for the Second 50 Years: Proceedings of the American Society for Information Science 51st Annual Meeting* v. 25 (1988), pp. 94–99, consider philosophy scholars' earlier use of information technology.

Concordances and word indexes, among the primary applications of computers to literature, are also used for the analysis of philosophical works. The development of *The Index Thomisticus*, covering the work of St. Thomas Aquinas, is described in "The Annals of Humanities Computing: The Index Thomisticus," *Computers and the Humanities* 14 (October 1989): 83–90. Many new thesauri have been developed with the assistance of computers; lists of them appear in the *Web Thesaurus Compendium* at http://www-cui.darmstadt.gmd.de:80/~lutes/thesoecd.html#literature (accessed February 28, 2000), but the reader should begin in the "literature" category because philosophy, to date, is not included as a category. A list of online concordances can be accessed at William A. Williams's *Concordances of Great Books* at http://www.concordance.com/ (accessed February 28, 2000) or through the philosophy sites described elsewhere in this chapter.

Although there is no evidence that philosophers are heavy users of commercially available online and CD-ROM information resources, it has been reported that they are often aware of such resources as *Philosopher's Index* (Sievert and Sievert, "Humanists and Technology: The Case of Philosophers," in *Information and Technology: Planning for the Second 50 Years: Proceedings of the American Society for Information Science 51st Annual Meeting* v. 25 [1988], pp. 94–99).

The number of machine readable philosophy indexes and bibliographies is limited, but the availability of the Internet has resulted in tremendous growth in the number of resource lists and texts available electronically. A. Robert Rogers's "A Comparison of Manual and Online Searches in the Preparation of Philosophy Pathfinders," *Journal of Education for Library and Information Science* 26 (Summer 1985): 54–55, which suggested that manual searching has not been replaced by the use of online services, might have a different conclusion today.

Two major online bibliographic resources in the field are *Philosophers Index*, published by the Philosophy Documentation Center at Bowling Green State University, and the philosophy section of FRANCIS (Fichier de Recherches bibliographiques Automatisses sur Nouveautes, la Communication et l'Information Sciences sociales et humaines), which corresponds with the print *Bulletin Signaletique—Sciences Humaines Section 519 Philosophie.* Both databases include journals and other forms of publications, and coverage of both goes back to the 1940s. The latter has undergone several title changes, so the reader should consult Chapter 4 of this guide for the correct title to look for to do a particular search.

There are many Internet sites providing access to texts of philosophical works. A few example are listed here, but many more are available. James Fieser edits the *Internet Encyclopedia of Philosophy*, located at http://www.utm.edu.research.iep.philtext.htm (accessed February 28, 2000), and includes links to a modest number of texts; the *Noesis* Web site at http://noesis.evansville.edu/ (accessed May 23, 1999) leads the reader to hundreds of texts, indexed by philosopher and by collection; and Peter Suber's resource list at http://www.earlham.edu/~peters/philinks.htm#etexts (accessed February 28, 2000) provides even more links to electronic texts. The reader should also consult the larger text collections for philosophical texts.

Electronic journals in philosophy are listed on several Web sites: Access lists through Peter Suber's site at http://www.earlham.edu/~peters/philinks.htm#journals (accessed February 28, 2000) or through the Philosophy Documentation Center's *Poiesis (Philosophy Online Serials)* page at http://www.nlx.com/posp/ (accessed February 28, 2000). See also *Project Muse* at http://muse.jhu.edu/journals/index_text.html (accessed February 28, 2000) for additional journal titles. Print journals are also listed in online sources; the Philosophy Documentation Center's page at http://www.bgsu.edu/pdc (accessed February 28, 2000) lists those for which the Center handles subscriptions.

Because of its very nature, philosophy is a field where interactive forms of scholarship appear especially likely to develop as more students and teachers become knowledgeable about communicating on the Internet. An extensive guide to discussion groups in philosophy can be found at http://web.syr.edu/~dhoracek/lists.html (accessed February 28, 2000). This resource, maintained by David Horacek, offers addresses and subscriber information for discussion groups on individual philosophers. Another extensive listing of mailing lists and discussion forums in philosophy can be found at Alexander Dey's *Philosophy in Cyberspace* site, http://www-personal.monash.edu.au/~dey/phil/section4.htm (accessed February 28, 2000).

Finally, the reader should note that the computer still makes it possible for researchers to access remote library catalogs worldwide. Most Internet guides list library catalogs that are available, methods of access, and sources of additional information. If, indeed, the library is the laboratory of the humanities, the Internet expands that laboratory by orders of magnitude.

MAJOR SOCIETIES, INFORMATION CENTERS, AND SPECIAL COLLECTIONS IN PHILOSOPHY

It has become a truism to say that the competent librarian will employ information sources far beyond the collection of a single library. Indeed, since the last edition of this guide, emphasis has increasingly been on "access to" rather than "ownership of" information resources. The role of bibliographies, indexes, union catalogs, and remote library catalogs is familiar. Still, some discussion of supplementary information sources may be of help to the researcher. In philosophy, the supplementary resources may be grouped into three categories: philosophical societies, information centers, and print and electronic special collections. Following is a sampling of major sources of additional information; the list is by no means exhaustive, but is meant to jog the librarian or researcher's memory and to suggest where to turn when other resources do not provide what is needed.

The Philosophy Documentation Center at Bowling Green State University publishes *Directory of American Philosophers*, now in its nineteenth edition. International philosophical societies and groups outside North America are listed in the latest edition of the *International Directory of Philosophy and Philosophers* (Bowling Green, OH: Philosophy Documentation Center).

Over the years, UNESCO has provided support for many international philosophical activities. In 1946 it recognized the International Council of Scientific Unions (The Hague) as coordinating body. One of its branches is the International Union of the History and Philosophy of Science, which maintains affiliations with both national and international organizations. The International Council for Philosophy and Humanistic Studies, composed of many international non-governmental organizations, is also recognized by UNESCO, and has received funding for activities of its member organizations.

The most comprehensive philosophical society in the United States is the American Philosophical Association, founded in 1900 to promote the exchange of ideas among philosophers and to encourage scholarly and creative activity in the field. Membership is restricted to those qualified to teach philosophy at the college or university level, and national and regional groups elect officers and sponsor annual conferences and meetings. The Association publishes *APA Bulletin*, *Proceedings and Addresses of the American Philosophical Society*, and several newsletters. The reader may learn more by contacting the Association at the University of Delaware, Newark, DE 19716. The Web address is http://www.udel.edu/apa/index.html (accessed February 28, 2000).

Phi Sigma Tau was founded in 1931 to promote ties between philosophy students and departments of philosophy. It is the publisher of *Dialogue* and a newsletter. The contact address for the organization is Department of Philosophy, Marquette University, Milwaukee, WI 53233.

The American Catholic Philosophical Association, an example of a more specialized association in the field, was founded in 1926. It publishes *American Catholic Philosophical Quarterly* and its *Proceedings*, and has a membership of over 1,600. Write to the Association at American Catholic Philosophical Association at Fordham University, Bronx, NY 10458. The organization has a Web site at http://acpa-main.org/index.html (accessed February 28, 2000).

Two associations address the interests of people working in the field as journalists and teachers. The first of these is the Association of Philosophy Journal Editors (Journal of Philosophy, Columbia University, 709 Philosophy Hall, New York, NY 10027). It was founded in 1971 and meets annually in conjunction with the American Philosophical Association. The International Association of Teachers of Philosophy promotes teaching of philosophy at the secondary and college levels and sponsors professional training for philosophy teachers. An international association founded in 1975, it holds a biennial conference and publishes its proceedings. The address is Am Schirrof 11, 32427 Minden, Germany.

Some associations are organized around a particular subdivision of philosophy. An example is the International Association of Ethicists, which acts as a clearinghouse for information in ethical studies worldwide and promotes "ethical and moral" studies. The Association publishes in the area of applied ethics. The address is 117 W. Harrison Bldg., Ste. I-104, Chicago, IL 60605.

The C. S. Pierce Society (State University of New York, Philosophy Department, Baldy Hall, Buffalo, NY 14260) is but one example of the many societies organized around the work and influence of a single philosopher. The Pierce Society was founded in 1946 and publishes its *Transactions* quarterly. The Kant Society (Saarstrasse 21, 55122 Mainz, Germany) furthers the study of Immanuel Kant by conducting research and publishing studies of Kant and his work.

The Society for Women in Philosophy (SWIP) was begun in 1972 to promote women in philosophy and their activities. The Society has a Web page at http://www.uh.edu/~cfreelan/SWIP/ (accessed February 28, 2000) that includes statistics on women philosophers, publications, courses, and special areas of philosophy related to women. Links to feminist sites and to other associations are provided. The International Association of Women Philosophers can be reached by mail (Ulrike Ramming, Schriftfuehrerin der IAPh, Kaecheleweg 4, D-70619 Stuttgart, Germany). The international association holds conferences and publishes its proceedings, and can be reached via the Web at http://www.iaph.org/ (accessed June 17, 1999).

Lists and addresses of other philosophical societies may be found in the "Societies" section of the latest *Directory of American Philosophers* or on the Web at http://www.earlham.edu/~peters/philinks.htm (accessed February 28, 2000).

Information centers in the United States and abroad continue to work on publication, indexing, and retrieval of information in philosophy. The previously mentioned Philosophy Documentation Center (Bowling Green State University, Bowling Green, OH 43404) collects, stores, and disseminates bibliographic data in the field. The Center publishes *The Philosopher's Index*, which is available in print and online.

The Philosophy Information Center (University of Dusseldorf, Dusseldorf, Germany) cooperates with the publication of *The Philosopher's Index* and produces other bibliographic indexes as well.

Over twenty-five national centers participate in the work of L'Institut International de Philosophie (8, Rue Jean Calvin, F75005, Paris, France) which publishes the quarterly bulletin *Bibliographie de la Philosophie*. L'Institut Superieure de Philosophie de l'universite Catholique de Louvain, like l'Institut International de Philosophie, has received funding from UNESCO; it publishes *Repertoire bibliographique de la philosophie*.

Special collections in philosophy may attempt to cover the discipline as a whole, a period of history, a special topic, or the works of a single philosopher. Many examples are listed in *Subject Collections,* compiled by Lee Ash and William G. Miller (7th ed., R. R. Bowker, 1993). A few special collections of note include the following:

1. The House Library of Philosophy at the University of Southern California contains over 40,000 volumes and covers all time periods from medieval manuscripts to contemporary publications. A catalog of this collection was published by G. K. Hall.

2. The Renaissance period is the topic of the Professor Don C. Allen Collection at the University of California, San Diego.

3. The General Library of the University of Michigan has a large collection dealing with Arabic philosophy.

4. The Weston College Library attempts to be comprehensive in collecting works of Catholic philosophy, and the Dominican College Library specializes in Thomist works and attempts to collect all works by Dominican authors.

5. The Van Pelt Library at the University of Pennsylvania holds nearly 3,000 manuscripts of fifteenth- through nineteenth-century Hindu philosophy, religion, and grammar.

6. McMaster University Library in Hamilton, Ontario, holds the papers of Bertrand Russell, more than 250,000 items. Information is disseminated in *Russell: The Journal of the Bertrand Russell Archives.*

NOTES

[1]"Philosophy," in *Encyclopædia Britannica* [Online] Available: http://members.eb.com/bol/topic?eu=61236&sctn=1 (accessed June 6, 1999).

[2]Kenneth McLeish, ed. *Key Ideas in Human Thought* (New York: Facts on File, 1993), p. 556.

[3]Stanley Chodorow, "Transformations in the Humanities," in *Perspectives on the Humanities and School-Based Curriculum Development,* Occasional Paper No. 24 (American Council of Learned Societies, 1994), p. 27.

[4]Andrew Jack, "Ethics," in McLeish, *Key Ideas,* pp. 248–49.

[5]Eugene Garfield, "Is Information Retrieval in the Arts and Humanities Inherently Different from That in Science . . . ?" *Library Quarterly* 50 (1980):40–57.

[6]Eugene Garfield, "A Different Sort of Great-Books: The 50 Twentieth-Century Works Most Cited in *The Arts and Humanities Citation Index,* 1976–1983, in *Essays of an Information Scientist* v. 10 (ISI Press, 1989), p. 101.

[7]Eugene Garfield, "Journal Citation Studies. 38. Arts and Humanities Journals Differ from Natural and Social Sciences Journals—But Their Similarities Are Surprising," *Essays of an Information Scientist* v. 5 (ISI Press, 1983), p. 763.

[8]Jean-Pierre V. M. Herubel, "Philosophy Dissertation Bibliographies and Citations in Serials Evaluation," *The Serials Librarian* 20 (1991): 67.

CHAPTER 4

PRINCIPAL INFORMATION SOURCES IN PHILOSOPHY

BIBLIOGRAPHIC GUIDES

General

36. Library Research Guide to Philosophy. Charles J. List and Stephen H. Plum. Ann Arbor, MI: Pierian Press, 1990. 102p. ISBN 0-876-50264-8.

This brief guide designed for the needs of the undergraduate student provides well-constructed examination of the bibliographic process with emphasis on term paper development. Treatment is given to use of the library and utilization of library catalogs, specialized bibliographies, and indexes in surveying a topic and preparing for its elaboration. Advice is provided for term paper writing in the field, and basic reference sources are enumerated. Although it needs updating, the work represents a still-useful resource.

A recent work is *World Philosophy: A Contemporary Bibliography*, edited by John R. Burr and Charlotte A. Burr (Greenwood, 1993), that provides a listing of the most important books and monographs on philosophy published all over the world between 1976 and 1992. Nearly 4,000 entries are arranged into geographical regions such as Africa, Asia, the Americas, etc., then into countries. Many of the entries are annotated briefly with indication of special features as well as content. Author and subject indexes provide access. This is a useful complement to John R. Burr's *Handbook of World Philosophy: Contemporary Developments Since 1945* (entry 84).

37. Philosophy: A Guide to the Reference Literature. 2d ed. Hans E. Bynagle. Englewood, CO: Libraries Unlimited, 1997. 233p. ISBN 1-56308-376-0.

The second edition contains annotations to 572 leading reference works in the field of philosophy. Especially useful is the emphasis given to electronic sources. There are chapters on the various types of reference tools: general bibliographic and research guides, dictionaries, and handbooks, as well as chapters devoted to specialized branches of study. Lengthy annotations make it possible for the user to make an assessment of the content or utility of every item. Although the emphasis remains on English-language publications, there are a number of foreign-language efforts included. Bibliographic tools receive especially careful attention through coverage in five chapters (indexes, abstracts, serial bibliographies, etc.). There is a chapter on basic or core journals and one on professional associations, which should be helpful to the individual in locating additional information regarding topics or movements. Standard histories are not included. The guide continues as a leading source of information regarding reference material in the field.

Periodicals

38. **Philosophy Journals and Serials: An Analytical Guide.** Douglas H. Ruben, comp. Westport, CT: Greenwood, 1985. 147p. ISBN 0-313-23958-4.

Although somewhat dated, this work is a thorough and well-designed guide to 335 journals and serials in the English language, and should be of use to those who are seeking information regarding possible purchase or submission of manuscripts. Entries provide full annotations regarding publishers, prices, circulation, acceptance rates, target audiences, and coverage in abstracting and indexing services. There is commentary regarding the journal's point of view and some indication of strengths and weaknesses. Special features are also pointed out. An examination of the journals covered reveals a wide range of subject matter, from the traditional studies of metaphysics to such specialties as learning and behavior and even psychic phenomena. Arrangement is alphabetical by title and access is provided through subject and geographical indexes.

Internet Resources

39. **Philosophy in Cyberspace: A Guide to Philosophy-Related Resources on the Internet, Second Edition.** Dey Alexander, ed. Bowling Green, OH: Philosophy Documentation Center, 1998. 500p. ISBN 1-889680-00-1.

This is the most recent edition of the handy and useful guide to Internet resources on philosophy. At the time of its initial publication in print format (1996), it was intended to be an annual publication, but evidently has opted for biennial appearance. It is essentially a print rendition of an online directory of the same name compiled by the editor and maintained at Monash University in Australia (http://www.-personal.monash.edu.au/~dey/phil/ [accessed December 1999]). In the new edition there are more than 1,500 Web sites, along with over 300 mailing lists, and some 60 newsgroups. Arrangement is under five major sections with some 50 categories: "Branches" (aesthetics, metaphysics, etc.), "Text-Related" (bibliographies, electronic journals, etc.), "Organizations" (associations, societies, etc.), "Forums" (news-groups and mailing lists), and "Miscellaneous" (conferences, courses, job vacancies, etc.). For the user it represents a comprehensive source of information.

*Yale University Library Research Guide, compiled by Sarah Prown (1996), is not only a useful guide to library resources at Yale, but also furnishes links to databases on the World Wide Web, some of which can be searched without special passwords. It is a good example of a university Web site and can be located at http://www.library.yale.edu/pubstation/subjectlist.html#PHILOSOPHY (accessed December 1999).

BIBLIOGRAPHIES AND CATALOGS

General

40. **Bibliography of Philosophy, Psychology, and Cognate Subjects.** Benjamin Rand. New York: Macmillan, 1925. 2v. Repr., Part 1, Bristol, UK: Thoemmes, 1992. 542p. ISBN 1-85-506174-0.

One of the landmark bibliographies in the field, this work was published as volume 3 of James Mark Baldwin's *Dictionary of Philosophy and Psychology*, initially issued at the turn of the century. It attempts to provide comprehensive coverage of the major books and periodical articles up to about 1900. It was published in two parts, sometimes referred to as volumes, although this may confuse the fact that the work itself was considered a single volume of a larger publication. The first volume or part covers bibliography and the history of philosophy and includes individual philosophers listed alphabetically. The second part treats the topics of systematic philosophy, logic, aesthetics, ethics, and so forth, subdivided by both form and subject. Although criticized for omissions in coverage of philosophy of certain disciplines, the importance of this work is understood and it remains an important source of bibliographic information, especially for materials of the nineteenth century.

41. **Grundriss der Geschichte der Philosophie.** Friedrich Ueberweg. 11.–12. Aufl. Berlin: Mittler, 1916–1928; repr., Basel, Switzerland: Schwabe, 1951–1956, 1960–1961. 5v.

An important history of philosophy first appearing in the 1860s, this work has received even more attention through the years for its rich bibliographic coverage. For this reason, it is considered a necessary tool for philosophical study and has often appeared in the bibliographic sections of literature guides (as it does here). The eleventh and twelfth editions were especially important in this regard and several reprintings have taken place over the years. The coverage represents ancient to modern philosophy. Bibliographies include both primary and secondary sources, both periodical and monographic, up to about 1920. It should be noted that the English translation of this work was completed in the nineteenth century from the fourth edition, and lacks the bibliographies. In 1991, the ATLA Monograph Preservation Program produced a microfiche version of the English translation of volume 2 that includes bibliographical references. Currently, there is a new edition in progress.

42. **Handbuch der Geschichte der Philosophie.** Wilhelm Totok. Frankfurt, Germany: Klosterman, 1964–1990. 6v. ISBN 3-465-01665-3.

Developed as a supplementary history and bibliography to the Ueberweg work (entry 41), this title covers the literature of philosophy from 1920 to the time of the publication of each of the volumes. It is a work of great magnitude and judged to be thorough in its coverage of the history of philosophy, beginning with ancient philosophy in volume 1 and progressing through modern philosophy during the twentieth century in volume 6. The work is international in its coverage of books. Bynagle (entry 37) warns of its forbidding nature through extensive use of abbreviations and its presentation of bibliographic listings in paragraph form. Nevertheless, it must be regarded as an extraordinary vehicle for bibliographic control, especially for writings in the Western languages. Author and subject indexes conclude each volume. Work on the second edition has begun, with publication of the first volume in 1997.

43. **The History of Ideas: A Bibliographical Introduction.** Jeremy L. Tobey. Santa Barbara, CA: ABC-Clio, 1975–1977. 2v. ISBN 0-87436-143-5 (v.1).

These two volumes present a series of well-developed and thoughtful bibliographic essays of importance to both the student and the specialist. Volume 1 covers classical antiquity and volume 2 embraces medieval and early modern Europe. Considered to be a useful resource in its treatment of "important research and reference tools and scholarly works on the history of ideas and its related fields," much of the coverage in both volumes is devoted to philosophy and aesthetics. The philosopher will find much of value also in the treatment given science and religion. There appears to be an emphasis on English-language resources identified in the bibliographic essays, and Tobey's ideas are expressed clearly. These are welcome because they give evidence of his depth of understanding of the issues and serve to clarify certain alternatives for the reader. There is an index of periodicals and an author-title index.

44. **A History of the Bibliography of Philosophy.** Michael Jasenas. New York: George Olms, 1973. 188p. ISBN 3-487-04666-0.

Informative essays describe bibliographies of philosophy published in Western languages between 1592 and 1960. Concentrating on bibliographies that cover the whole of philosophy, the content is divided into five major chapter headings or phases of bibliographic growth ("Renaissance," "Modern," "German Aufklarung," "Post-Kantian," and "Twentieth Century"). The essays are useful not only in describing the bibliographies themselves but also in providing insight into the historical influences regarding their production and development. In describing these influences, attention is given to major figures. Appendix 1 arranges the bibliographies both chronologically and alphabetically, thus providing a handy bibliography of bibliographies. A second such listing covers bibliographies not described in the text. Appendix 2 is a short-title list of major philosophical works. Finally, there is a name index.

45. **Manuel de bibliographie philosophique.** Gilbert Varet. Paris: Presses Universitaires de France, 1956. 2v.

Another of the standard works in the field, this is a selective bibliography of approximately 20,000 books and articles published primarily from 1914 to 1934. This emphasis on World War I and the postwar era complements the coverage of de Brie's *Bibliographia philosophica* (see below), completed just two years earlier. Volume 1 treats the subject historically, beginning with Oriental philosophy and moving forward to the present. There are subdivisions by period and by individual. Works in all languages are included. For prolific authors, the most important editions are mentioned. Volume 2 is concerned with the development of systematic thinking. One section covers philosophy of art, religion, and history; another, philosophy of the sciences; and a third, political philosophy, educational psychology, and so forth. There are many brief annotations. A general index of names is given at the end of volume 1.

Bibliographia philosophica, 1934–1945, by G. A. de Brie (Editiones Spectrum, 1950–1954), is a two-volume standard in the field of philosophy bibliography dealing with a very brief, specific time period. The major purpose is to fill the gap in bibliographic control after the war because of the suspension of publication of one of the leading serial bibliographies, *Bibliographie de la philosophie* (entry 53). The first volume covers the history of philosophy and is arranged chronologically, while the second volume employs a classified arrangement in identifying 49,000 publications (books, reviews, and articles from journals and encyclopedias) in the major Western languages.

Specialized by Topic, Region, or Period

46. **A Bibliographic Guide to the Comparative Study of Ethics.** John Carman et al., eds. New York: Cambridge University Press, 1991. 811p. ISBN 0-521-34448-4.

Sponsored by the Berkeley-Harvard Program in Comparative Religion, this collaborative effort of scholars and specialists seeks to address questions of morality of a cross-cultural nature. These questions are examined and analyzed through bibliographic listings designed to furnish enlightenment about individual traditions and to address differences and similarities with others. This global approach to topical considerations such as friendship, spirituality, and various other ingredients of moral behavior represents a unique and valuable approach for scholars and serious students as well as practitioners in the areas of business or government. Listings emphasize primary documents from various traditions, both Eastern and Western, concerned with the topics.

Ethics: An Annotated Bibliography, by John K. Roth et al. (Salem Press, 1991) is an introductory guide to the topic furnishing a well-annotated bibliography of a selective nature for undergraduates. Listings include both primary source documents and books on current issues of concern. Most of the books were published in the 1980s.

47. **Business Ethics and Responsibility: An Information Sourcebook.** Patricia Ann Bick. Phoenix: Oryx Press, 1988. 204p. (Oryx Series in Business and Management, no. 11). ISBN 0-89774-296-6.

This is an interesting example of a specialized bibliography devoted to a field of growing interest. There are over 1,000 annotated entries arranged under thirteen subject divisions, which themselves are divided into more specific topics. These divisions or sections cover such areas as corporate social responsibility, employee rights, and international aspects. It is important to note the specialized section on South Africa in view of contemporary interest in socially responsible investments. Various types of literature are treated but represent primarily business publications and dissertations rather than periodicals of the legal profession or social services. Most helpful to librarians is the "Core Library Collection" identifying useful reference sources and the listings given to research centers, major journals, and relevant organizations. Omissions have been noted, such as AIDS in the workplace and ethical standards of major business schools. Author, title, and subject indexes aid access.

*48. **The Collaborative Bibliography of Women in Philosophy.** Noel Hutchings and William Ramsey, eds. Bowling Green, OH: Philosophy Documentation Center, 1997. 375p. ISBN 0-912632-65-8.

Defining itself as a collaborative effort, this work is a print version of an ongoing online project that had its beginnings in 1995. Collaboration in this case is facilitated using the Web site to enable users to contribute by providing bibliographic entries as well as corrections and enhancements to the extensive database, entitled NOEMA: The Collaborative Bibliography of Women in Philosophy (http://billyboy.ius.indiana.edu/WomeninPhilosophy/WomeninPhilo.html [accessed December 1999]). The print version contains over 11,000 citations by 3,500 female philosophers dating from ancient times to the present. Access is aided by good indexing, including a subject index and named person index. To indicate how quickly the database is growing, as of November 1998 there were 16,000 records representing the work of over 5,000 women as currently indicated on the Web site.

49. **Encyclopedia of Indian Philosophies. Bibliography.** 3d rev. ed. Karl H. Potter. Delhi: Motilal Banarsidass, 1995. v.1 in 2 parts. ISBN 8-120-80308-6 (v.1).

The first volume of this revised and expanded version of the 1983 revision of the *Encyclopedia* (entry 82) remains the standard bibliography in the field. The earlier revision had listed some 13,000 sources in an attempt to present the concepts of Indian philosophy and the content of Indian philosophical texts to a wider public. The bibliography helped to establish the scope and reputation of the entire work. The new revision has added several thousand items, incorporating the supplementary lists published in the *Journal of Indian Philosophy* (Dordrecht, Holland: D. Reidel, 1970–), as well as new material. Sanskrit texts, authorship, and dates are emphasized along with secondary literature in Western languages. Several indexes (name, title, subject) provide access. "Since 1999, an expanded and updated version has been made available on the World Wide Web by the University of Washington Center for Advanced Research Technology of the University of Washington (http://www.cartah.washington.edu/cartah/indic/). Work is continuous in identifying material found subsequent to the third edition."

Guide to Indian Philosophy by Karl H. Potter et al. (G. K. Hall, 1988) is part of the same series as *Guide to Chinese Philosophy* (entry 50), and furnishes an annotated bibliography of nearly 900 books and articles published during the twentieth century up to 1985, with emphasis on the decade prior to publication. Primarily intended for the undergraduate or interested layperson, all works are in English with the articles being at least ten pages in length. All areas of Indian philosophy are covered, from metaphysics to politics. Arrangement of entries is alphabetical by author; there are both name and subject indexes to aid access.

50. **Guide to Chinese Philosophy.** Charles Wei-Hsun Fu and Wing-tsit Chan. Boston: G. K. Hall, 1978. 262p. ISBN 0-8161-7901-8.

This is an annotated bibliography, mainly of English-language sources useful to the student or non-specialist, and of peripheral interest to the serious scholar, who would be more interested in Chinese-language texts. The guide is divided into sixteen sections, beginning with "History of Chinese Philosophy," which covers the various schools in sequence from pre-Confucian to Marxist. Topics such as ethics and human nature are treated in the next twelve chapters, while the final three chapters concern analytical sources, comparative philosophy, and significant texts. There is an author and title index. Prepared as part of the Asian Philosophies and Religions Project of the Council for Intercultural Studies and Programs, this work supersedes Chan's *An Outline and an Annotated Bibliography of Chinese Philosophy* (Yale University, 1969).

Guide to Buddhist Philosophy, by Kenneth K. Inada (G. K. Hall, 1985) is another of the publisher's resource guides in both Eastern religion and philosophy geared to the undergraduate level and serves as a companion volume to Frank E. Reynolds's *Guide to Buddhist Religion* (G. K. Hall, 1981) for purposes of providing a thorough study of Buddhism. There are over 1,000 books, articles, and dissertations listed, most of which are in English. Arrangement of entries is under categories similar to those employed in other works of this series such as history, metaphysics, and so forth. Annotations are brief but informative; there are detailed author-title and subject indexes.

51. **Marxist Philosophy: A Bibliographical Guide.** John Lachs. Chapel Hill: University of North Carolina Press, 1967. 166p.

A good example of a bibliography specialized to a philosophical school or movement, Lachs's work is still considered an excellent research tool, since it has not been superseded. This is a scholarly effort with comprehensive coverage of both books and periodical articles in thirty-eight chapters. Full bibliographic description is given but no annotations are provided. Many texts translated from the Russian are included in the total of over 1,500 publications, primarily in English, but with French and German items as well. Most chapters represent some aspect of Marxist-Leninist thought and all begin with a brief critical essay. There are chapters on journals of importance as well as reference works and bibliographies, and an author index.

Soviet books and articles in philosophy are found in *Bibliographie der sowjetischen Philosophie/Bibliography of Soviet Philosophy* (Dordrecht, Holland: Reidel, 1959–1968, 7v.). Writings on the subject of Soviet philosophy are represented in the bibliographies reported in *Studies in Soviet Thought* (Kluwer Academic Publishers, 1961–1992, 8/yr.). Beginning as an annual, it was issued as a quarterly from 1962 to 1990, when it changed to eight times per year. *Social Theory: A Bibliographic Series*, compiled by Joan Nordquist, has been issued since 1986 by Reference and Research Services and furnishes brief (60 pages) but informative and useful bibliographies of writings by and about a leftist thinker. To date about forty have been produced, treating such luminaries as Foucault, Marcuse, Heidegger, de Beauvoir, and Sartre.

52. **Resources in Ancient Philosophy: An Annotated Bibliography of Scholarship in English 1965–1989.** Albert A. Bell and James B. Allis. Metuchen, NJ: Scarecrow, 1991. 799p. ISBN 0-8108-2520-1.

This is an excellent resource bibliography to over 7,000 scholarly books and articles on the subject of ancient philosophy written over a twenty-five-year period. The philosophers are analyzed through introductory narratives that highlight accomplishments. Major contributions are noted. Annotations for entries tend to be brief but informative, furnishing a clear understanding of the topic. Arrangement of entries is under chapter headings, which treat the subject chronologically, for example, "Thales to Augustine." Schools of thought are then treated alphabetically by authors of the secondary source material listed. In establishing this order, the authors have enabled users to search a particular document such as Plato's *Republic* to find what specifically has been done by contemporary scholars. This book should prove useful to all levels of inquiries although the subject index is less than precise. There is no author index.

A more recent effort is *The Presocratic Philosophers: An Annotated Bibliography*, by Luis E. Navia (Garland, 1993), which identifies and describes 2,700 books and articles from the international scholarly literature. Various points of view are embraced, giving a well-rounded perspective to the individual philosopher and his or her accomplishments. Materials are cited from nearly 450 journals and represent diverse levels of inquiry and sophistication. Coverage is given to bibliographical works, source collections, and general studies, followed by single chapters for each of the eleven major philosophers treated. Entries are in the language of the original with English translations supplied.

INDEXES, ABSTRACTS, AND SERIAL BIBLIOGRAPHIES

53. **Bibliographie de la philosophie/Bibliography of Philosophy.** Paris: Vrin, 1954– . Q. ISSN 0006-1352.

A dual-language title accompanied the change in editorial policy of this work (see below). Published under the sponsorship of several international organizations, including the Institut Internationale de Philosophie and the International Federation of Philosophical Societies, it receives aid from UNESCO and the French National Centre for Scientific Research. Now published as an abstract journal for books only, the abstracts appear in the language of the original work if in English, French, German, Italian, or Spanish. Abstracts of books written in other languages are provided either in English or French. There is a classified arrangement under ten broad divisions of philosophy. Indexes appear only in the final issue of each volume, in which access is provided through authors, titles, and keywords. An "Index of Names" is also provided that gathers all publishers, translators, and individuals mentioned in titles and in abstracts. *Bibliographie de la philosophie*, issued as a serial bibliography from 1937 to 1953, was the original work published under the auspices of the Institut International de Philosophie. It furnished listings without annotations of philosophical books and articles and covered the field in a comprehensive manner, enumerating both well-known and obscure publications. During the postwar period, it reviewed over 700 journals for relevant articles. It was suspended during the war years (mid-1939–1945), creating the need for the subsequent publication of de Brie's *Bibliographia philosophica, 1934–1945* (entry 45n). Coverage of periodical articles was dropped in a change of editorial policy by its successor (see above).

A selective but worthy source is *Philosophical Books* (Oxford: Blackwell, 1960–), providing in-depth, high-quality reviews of a variety of philosophical books. Many of these have not been reviewed extensively and thus are more elusive. The tool is presently issued on a quarterly basis and furnishes about twenty reviews per issue. *Cumulative Index of Philosophical Books: Volumes 1–15 (1960–1974)*, compiled by Julius Ariail (Statesboro, GA: Sweet Bay, 1980) furnishes access to the first fifteen years of reviews. After 1974, the reviews are indexed in *Philosopher's Index* (entry 57).

*54. Bibliography of Bioethics. Detroit: Gale Research (publisher varies), 1975– . Ann. ISSN 0363-0161.

Presently sponsored by the Kennedy Institute of Ethics at Georgetown University, this annual bibliography has taken on added importance in the past few years owing to the increased publicity and volatility of ethical and public policy issues relating to medicine, health care, and related research. Abstracts have appeared since the ninth volume (1983). The coverage includes several forms of material, primarily journal articles, but also books, newspaper articles, and monographs, all in the English language. Entries are arranged by numerous subject headings such as abortion, contraception, and so forth; an annual thesaurus has been issued since 1984. Author, title, and subject indexes facilitate access. *Bioethics Thesaurus* has been issued as a section of this work since 1984, and is also published separately. It furnishes a controlled vocabulary to aid the searcher.

Corresponding to the printed work is the computerized database *BIOETHICSLINE (Kennedy Institute of Ethics), which provides cumulative coverage online of the entire file from the beginning to the present. Although not issued through any vendor service, access is possible through searching MEDLARS/MEDLINE and also through Questel. Direct searches are available to authorized individuals and organizations such as selected academic, medical, and special libraries.

*55. Francis bulletin signaletique. 519, Philosophie. Nancy, France: Institut de l'Information Scientifique et Technique (INIST), 1947– . Q. with ann. cum. ISSN 1157-3694.

Having undergone several name changes, this work continues as part of the large-scale Francis computerized operation to provide quarterly coverage of philosophy periodical literature from all over the world. It started out as *Bulletin analytique: Philosophie* (1947–1955), then became *Bulletin signaletique*, with a variety of subtitles. From 1970 until 1990 it was **Bulletin signaletique: 519* and was produced by the Centre National de la recherche scientifique (CNRS). After 1990, INIST took over the major responsibility from CNRS. The work employs a classified arrangement to embrace articles from over 4,000 periodicals. Brief abstracts are given in French regardless of the language of the original article. Book reviews are cited and abstracts given, although books are not listed routinely. Separate author and subject indexes appear in each issue as does an index of journals covered. All three indexes cumulate annually.

The database, **Philosophie (CNRS-INIST)*, is available online and in CD-ROM as part of the ongoing indexing and abstracting program (FRANCIS) of the French Centre National de la Recherche Scientifique now being conducted with INIST. Coverage of philosophy is available from 1972 to the present. **Philosophische Dokumentation* (University of Dusseldorf, 1968–) is a German-language abstracting and indexing service for 250 current philosophical and historical periodicals. Presently, it is published and distributed on a quarterly basis in print form by Kraus Thomson Organization. It is available online from the University of Dusseldorf and covers the period from 1970 to the present.

56. International Philosophical Bibliography/Repertoire bibliographique de la philosophie/Bibliografisch repertorium van de wijsbegeerte. Louvain, Belgium: Institut Superieur de Philosophie, 1949–1990. Q. ISSN 0034-4567. Continuation 1991– . Same ISSN.

This important serial bibliography, known for years by the French title, *Repertoire bibliographique de la philosophie*, has an interesting and varied past, beginning as an appendix to *Revue neo-scholastique de philosophie* from 1934 to 1948. After 1939 it also was issued under the title *Bibliografisch repertorium* as a supplement to the Dutch *Tijdschrift voor filosofie*. It continued in this manner even during World War II, when the *Revue neo-scholastique* was suspended. From 1949 to 1990, it operated as an independent supplement to *Revue philosophique de Louvain* and gained an excellent reputation for providing an exhaustive bibliography of books and articles in Catalan, Dutch, English, French, German, Italian, Latin, Portuguese, and Spanish. There was a single classified listing, aided by a name index that was issued in November of each year.

Its past associations helped shape the *Bibliography*'s present status; in 1991 it was merged with the still-active *Bibliografisch repertorium van de wijsbegeerte* to form a new quarterly continuation, the English/French language publication *International Philosophical Bibliography=Repertoire bibliographique de la philosophie=Bibliografisch repertorium van de wijsbegeerte*, published jointly by the Institut and by Universite catholique de Louvain.

*57. **The Philosopher's Index: An International Index to Philosophical Periodicals and Books.** Bowling Green, OH: Philosophy Documentation Center/Bowling Green State University, 1967– . Q. with ann. cum. ISSN 0031-7993.

Today considered the most important source for philosophers in the Anglo-American tradition, this work provides abstracts in English for articles from all major philosophy journals in English, French, German, Spanish, and Italian, with selective inclusion from journals in other languages. Originally limited to articles from British and U.S. periodicals, the scope expanded as it matured, and books were added in 1980. Book material is limited to that in the English language only but includes monographs, translations, bibliographies, biographies, textbooks, dissertations, dictionaries, and anthologies. There are both subject and author listings for all entries, with the abstracts appearing in the author section. There is a separate index for book reviews.

A corresponding database, *PHILOSOPHER'S INDEX, is available online and in CD-ROM. It is updated on a quarterly basis and includes abstracts from the retrospective publications (entry 58) as well. Book reviews are not included online. The service is available through DIALOG and EasyNet gateway system. There is an aid to the database written by Richard H. Lineback and Lynn Walkiewicz, entitled *The Philosopher's Index Thesaurus* (Philosophy Documentation Center, 1992), which furnishes a brief introduction and description of the database along with some practical advice for searching both CD-ROM and DIALOG versions.

*58. **The Philosopher's Index: A Retrospective Index to U.S. Publications from 1940.** Bowling Green, OH: Philosophy Documentation Center/ Bowling Green State University, 1978. 3v. ISBN 0-912632-12-7.

Developed to expand the coverage of the ongoing current index, which began in 1967, this retrospective effort covers the journal literature from 1940 to 1966, and books published from 1940 to 1976. (Books were not picked up in the current series until 1980, so a small gap still exists.) Total coverage is of some 15,000 articles and 6,000 books. Developed in the style of the current index (entry 57), the first two volumes include the subject index, while volume 3 contains the author listing with abstracts.

A complementary work edited by Richard H. Lineback, **The Philosopher's Index: A Retrospective Index to Non-U.S. English Language Publications from 1940* (Philosophy Documentation Center, 1980, 3v.) follows a similar format and arrangement. It includes approximately 12,000 articles from seventy periodicals published between 1940 and 1966, and some 5,000 books published between 1940 and 1978. Entries from both retrospective publications are available online.

DICTIONARIES, ENCYCLOPEDIAS, AND HANDBOOKS

General

59. **The Cambridge Dictionary of Philosophy.** Robert Audi, ed. New York: Cambridge University Press, 1995. 882p. ISBN 0-521-40224-7.

One of the top one-volume dictionaries in the field, this work contains some 4,000 entries by 381 eminent contributors providing excellent insight and expertise. Alphabetically arranged, the entries are well-constructed and informative and treat individuals, schools, terms, ideas, and so forth. The dictionary may be used by a specialist or student with good results. International in scope, the work provides insight into Eastern as well as Western thought systems. Entries run between 500 and 1,000 words on the average, although there are lengthier survey articles on philosophical areas or subfields (ethics, logic, etc.).

The Cambridge Companion to Early Greek Philosophy, edited by A. A. Long, was recently issued (1999) by the same publishing house and is similar to those in the Cambridge Companions to Literature series (entry 1082). It provides a selective grouping of essays by different scholars treating in depth various aspects of ancient philosophy; the "Cambridge Companions to Philosophy" should prove to be a meritorious series for library collections.

60. **A Dictionary of Philosophy.** 2d ed. Antony Flew, editorial consultant and Jennifer Speake, ed. New York: St. Martin's Press, 1984. 380p. ISBN 0-312-20924-X.

Considered by some to be a useful and compact dictionary in the field, this provides concise treatment of the subject. Good lucid definitions for the most part are easily understood by the layperson, although some articles tend to be more technical. It is not clear to what degree Flew, the well-known British philosopher, now retired from the University of Reading, participated in the revision. His name, however, establishes authority for the work, and Rogers found precious little change from the earlier edition in his *American Reference Books Annual 1985* review. The dictionary includes biographical articles on philosophers which, although brief, serve to identify the individuals cited. There is some coverage of Oriental philosophy, but the emphasis is definitely Anglo-American, with coverage of continental European subject matter secondary in importance.

A recent publication receiving favorable reviews is *Dictionary of Philosophy* by Mario A. Bunge (Prometheus Books, 1999). Using examples from the sciences, Bunge enumerates and explains important concepts and principles of modern philosophy.

61. **A Dictionary of Philosophy.** 3d ed. A. R. Lacey. London: Routledge Kegan Paul, 1996. 386p. ISBN 0-4151-3332-7.

The third edition continues to do an excellent job describing the problems and questions of the discipline through its brief but informative definitions. The emphasis is on Anglo-American philosophy, particularly that which concerns epistemological or logical topics. It covers all periods, branches, and schools of ancient, medieval, and modern philosophy in Western thought, but no coverage is given to Eastern philosophy. There are entries for important philosophers, and excellent bibliographies are provided for many of the entries that are useful for suggesting related works to students and interested laypersons. There are numerous cross-references as well.

Another recent publication is *A Dictionary of Philosophy*, edited by Thomas Mautner (Blackwell, 1996); it is designed to facilitate comprehension by students and "newcomers." Over 100 philosophers have contributed the narratives (not all signed) of personalities, theories, movements, schools, and terminology. Emphasis is on Western orientation, although there is brief treatment of Islamic tradition. Annotations are concise with some 2,300 entries linked by useful cross-references.

62. **Dictionary of Philosophy.** Dagobert D. Runes. New York: Philosophical Library, 1983. 360p. ISBN 0-802-22388-5.

This is a revised edition of an old standard first published in 1942 to furnish clear and concise definitions and descriptions and to do so in a comprehensive fashion. This it succeeded in doing and still continues to do. Entries are signed by the contributors, and the work is of value now for its historical character as well as its comprehensive and accurate nature in treating various thinkers, issues, and ideological systems of the past.

Less sophisticated is the effort by Peter A. Angeles, *The HarperCollins Dictionary of Philosophy* (2d ed., HarperCollins, 1992). It supplies some 3,000 definitions of major philosophical concepts suitable for the beginning student or layperson in his or her study of Western philosophy. Definitions are brief and uniform in style; there are no references to sources consulted. Biographical treatments are included.

63. **Dictionary of Philosophy.** Murad Saifulin and Richard R. Dixon, eds. New York: International Publishers, 1984. 464p. ISBN 0-7178-0604-9.

This is an English translation of a standard Soviet dictionary and represents philosophy from the perspective of Marxism-Leninism. Non-Western philosophy and ancient philosophy are treated objectively, but modern thought and its various exponents are described in relation to the development of communism. Thus the definitions and identifications are sprinkled with a variety of labels such as "bourgeois." Stalin is not mentioned here, which reflects the position of the Soviet state subsequent to Khrushchev. The work is valuable, historically, in light of recent developments and for its inclusion of many Russian philosophers who are unfamiliar to those with a Western orientation. It is interesting to consider what type of "de-communized" editions might be issued in the future in view of the breakup of the Soviet Union.

64. **Dictionary of the History of Ideas: Studies of Selected Pivotal Ideas.** Philip P. Wiener, ed.-in-chief. New York: Scribner's, 1973–1974. 4v. plus index. repr., 1980. 5v. ISBN 0-684-16418-3 (pbk.).

A significant contribution to the reference literature and scholarship of philosophy and related fields, this encyclopedic work contains over 300 lengthy monographic articles, all signed, on a wide array of subjects in intellectual history. Distinguished scholars from various disciplines have served as contributors to "establish some sense of unity of human thought and its cultural manifestation in a world of ever-increasing specialization and alienation." Not restricted to philosophical material in its interdisciplinary, multi-cultural coverage, the work offers a rich body of information for philosophical inquiry. Broadly, the areas of coverage embrace the sciences and the external order of nature; anthropology, psychology, religion, philosophy, and human nature; literature and the arts; attitudes toward the historical sciences; economic, legal, and political institutions and ideologies; religious and philosophical ideas; and mathematics and logic. Bibliographies are included and the articles are arranged alphabetically. A separate index volume provides access.

Hutchinson Dictionary of Ideas, edited by Anne-Lucie Norton (Helicon/ABC-Clio, 1994) is a more recent, concise, and popular effort targeted at the general reader. It contains some 4,000 brief entries providing descriptions and definitions of personalities, ideas, thought systems, and topics, with emphasis on Western culture. Treatment includes various disciplines (religion, psychology, mathematics, education, computer science, etc.). An interesting special feature is a group of diverse listings of miscellaneous information.

65. **Enciclopedia filosofica.** 2d ed. Florence: Sansoni, 1968–1969. 6v. Repr. and rev., Rome: Lucarini, 1982. 8v.

Now in its second edition, the initial offering of this Italian work in four volumes was considered to be the most comprehensive tool of its kind, prior to publication of *The Encyclopedia of Philosophy* (entry 66). It is a scholarly effort with signed articles and good bibliographies. Arrangement is dictionary style, with individuals, places, ideas, schools, movements, and other topical material in one alphabet. There is an emphasis on Continental European philosophy, the coverage of Italian thought and thinkers being especially strong, although the work is respected for its international coverage also. Eastern philosophy is treated, but as one might expect, much less fully than Western thought. The final volume has three major indexes (theoretical concepts, historical development, and terms and personal names for which entries do not appear but rather have received references in the text).

66. **The Encyclopedia of Philosophy.** Paul Edwards, ed.-in-chief. New York: Macmillan, 1967. 8v. Repr., 1996, 8v. in 4. Supp. 1996.

The compilers of this monumental set tried to cover the whole realm of philosophy (Eastern and Western) and its points of contact with other disciplines. The *Encyclopedia* contains nearly 1,500 articles, some monographic in length and most with copious bibliographies. There are excellent articles on philosophical movements, major ideas, the philosophy of various subject fields, the history of philosophy in different countries, and biographies of major philosophers. Coverage of ancient, medieval, and early modern philosophers is generally good. Coverage of contemporary philosophers is better for Western Europe, North America, and India than for what was the Soviet Bloc and the People's Republic of China. There are good articles on philosophical bibliographies, dictionaries, encyclopedias, and journals. The editor has tried to minimize editorial bias, but favors an Anglo-American tradition. The monographic approach has been preferred to a series of short articles, and smaller topics can be located by means of a detailed index in volume 8. More than 1,500 philosophers from all over the world contributed, while 150 scholars from the United States, Great Britain, and Europe served on the editorial board. The *Encyclopedia* was reprinted in 1996, and in that same year a single-volume supplement was issued. This has been the definitive English-language encyclopedia for many years, but will have to cede the position to the recently published *Routledge Encyclopedia of Philosophy* (entry 70).

The *Stanford Encyclopedia of Philosophy* is a dynamic work on the World Wide Web (http://plato.stanford.edu/info.html [accessed December 1999]), compiled by Edward N. Zalta and published by the Stanford University Center for the Study of Language and Information in 1997. It is an ongoing project, working toward completing the store of topics found in the table of contents. Entries are added and modified as needed; they are well-written and readable.

67. **Encyclopedie philosophique universelle.** Andre Jacob, ed. Paris: Presses Universitaires de France, 1989– . v.1– (in progress). ISBN 2-13041-440-0.

Progress has been slow but steady on this important new encyclopedia divided into four major segments or volumes. Volume 1 provides a series of essays by eminent scholars examining the philosophical universe; volume 2, with two tomes, provides a dictionary of terms and concepts classified by region of the world; volume 3, also in two tomes, furnishes summary and commentary on some 9,000 philosophical works, also classified by region of the world. Volume 4 has not yet been published but will provide an anthology of selections from important texts along with interpretations. There are over 1,000 contributors to this magnificent project.

68. **Historisches Worterbuch der Philosophie.** Joachim Ritter and Karlfried Grunder, eds. Basel, Switzerland: Schwabe, 1971– . v.1–10. ISBN 3-7965-0115-X.

Over 1,200 scholars have contributed to this revision of Rudolf Eisler's *Worterbuch der Philosophischen Begriffe* (Berlin: Mittler, 1910). Some subjects covered in the earlier work (e.g., psychology) have been dropped and new materials added. Other topics are revised and updated. The articles, ranging in length from a few sentences to several pages, treat the historical development of philosophical terms and concepts in a very scholarly manner. Documentation is abundant and up-to-date. An index and list of abbreviations is included in each volume. "It should be noted that articles on individual philosophers are not within the scope of this dictionary, although schools of thought based on the teachings of a single man are described." Work had slowed perceptibly since Ritter's death in 1974, but in the 1990s the quest was renewed to complete the project. Volume 7 was issued in 1990, volume 8 in 1992, volume 9 in 1995, and volume 10 in 1998, bringing the set through "T" in alphabetical sequence.

69. **The Oxford Companion to Philosophy.** Ted Honderich, ed. New York: Oxford University Press, 1995. 1009p. ISBN 0-19-866132-0.

Along with the *Cambridge Dictionary of Philosophy* (entry 59), this work stands out as the most useful and informative single-volume dictionary of philosophy to have come out in the past few years. The result of collaboration, with contributions from 248 primarily Anglo-American scholars, this engaging volume quite naturally provides a Western emphasis. It does not neglect Eastern thought, however, and with the nearly 2,000 entries of varying length, the entire realm of philosophy is examined, East and West, historical and current. As is true of similar works, *Oxford* treats personalities, topics, branches, schools, concepts, and terms, but does so in a comprehensible, informative, accurate, and interesting fashion. Included are maps, a chronological table, and a well-constructed index. Brief bibliographies accompany the narratives.

Oxford Dictionary of Philosophy, by Simon Blackburn (Oxford, 1994) is less than half the size of its newer partner but provides a handy and useful reference tool to accommodate the needs of less-sophisticated users. The work provides some 2,500 entries, briefly identifying personalities, terms, ideas, and issues of importance to philosophical inquiry from ancient times to the present. There is a real effort to include modern thinkers such as Chomsky and up-to-date topics such as euthanasia and abortion.

*70. **Routledge Encyclopedia of Philosophy.** Edward Craig, ed. New York: Routledge Kegan Paul, 1998. 10v. ISBN 0-415-07310-3.

This is a much-anticipated and now much-heralded English-language encyclopedia that has lived up to its promise of becoming the definitive and most thorough work in the field. As such it has replaced the *Encyclopedia of Philosophy* (entry 66) as the first choice for those needing in-depth, clearly presented information regarding philosophers, theories, concepts, issues, schools, and so forth, especially for recent developments. All of philosophy is covered in the 2,000 individual articles contributed by more than 1,300 scholars. Entries vary in size from relatively brief (500 words) to extensive survey articles of 19,000 words. Each entry is preceded by an overview providing the essentials of the topic and finishes with a bibliography. This is in addition to an outline provided for lengthier articles. Volume 10 is the index and contains more than 78,000 entries. It is available in CD-ROM format as well.

71. **Talking Philosophy: A Wordbook.** A. W. Sparkes. New York: Routledge Kegan Paul, 1991. 307p. ISBN 0-415-04222-4.

This extraordinary tool furnishes useful information to a variety of users, providing a thematic and conceptual awareness of the meanings of terms and their position with respect to other related words. Similar to *Roget's Thesaurus* in its structure, words are first located through the detailed alphabetical index, where references are made to the proper chapters, which cover such categories as "saying things" and "relations." Words defined in each section have parallels or similarities in context or previous use that are supported with references to sources listed in a bibliography of 800 entries at the end. These sources vary in nature and range from the philosophical to the literary. Entries contain numerous cross-references.

A Dictionary of Philosophical Quotations, edited by A. J. Ayer and Jane O'Grady (Blackwell, 1992; 1994 pbk.) identifies quotations from nearly 350 philosophers representing the Western European tradition. Emphasis is placed on modern philosophers of the late nineteenth or twentieth centuries, providing a useful perspective of contemporary thought. Quotations are thorough, providing analysis of a topical nature, and vary from a single line to a full page but average a paragraph in length. A glossary is included along with a subject index.

72. **Vocabulaire technique et critique de la philosophie.** 5th ed. André Lalande, ed. Paris: Presses Universitaires de France, 1999. 2v. ISBN 2-13-044512-8.

This is an old standard in the field, the first complete edition having been published in 1926. It has been consistent and predictable in its revisions and retains a position of importance as a reference tool. Prior to the first complete edition it appeared in twenty-one segments published in the *Bulletin de la Societe Francaise de Philosophie* between 1902 and 1923. Definitions are good; additional coverage is given to examples of use by philosophers, along with etymologies and bibliographic notes. German, English, and Italian equivalents are provided as well. The emphasis is on clarification of terms and ideas; therefore there are no biographical entries.

73. **World Philosophy: Essay-Reviews of 225 Major Works.** Frank N. Magill, ed. and Ian P. McGreal, assoc. ed. Englewood Cliffs, NJ: Salem Press, 1982. 5v. ISBN 0-89356-325-0.

This is an expansion of Magill's earlier *Masterpieces of World Philosophy in Summary Form* (Salem Press, 1961), in which 200 philosophical classics were summarized in a manner similar to other works by the noted editor. The new set retains the summaries or essay reviews of the earlier edition and adds twenty-five more, but with a new feature considered by the editors to be its major purpose. The inclusion of a section on pertinent literature supplies at least two critical commentaries for each essay-review. These critical studies are as detailed as the essay-reviews (600–1,000 words) and are significant additions. Following the critical commentaries are annotated lists of relevant English-language secondary sources for additional reading. The work is meant to appeal to a wide audience, with emphasis on the needs of laypersons, high school students, and undergraduates.

A more recent publication is Magill's *Masterpieces of World Philosophy* (Harper-Collins, 1990), which is simply an abridged edition of the five-volume work. About 100 documents ranging from those of Confucius to those from the twentieth century have been selected by John Roth from the earlier effort and arranged chronologically. Entries contain essay-reviews followed by brief listings of additional secondary sources to consult.

Specialized by Topic, Region, or Period

74. **Blackwell Companions to Philosophy** series. Cambridge, MA: Blackwell, 1991– . ISBN 0-631-16211-9 (v.1).

This recent series has already produced numerous volumes, most of which are devoted to either a topical area or an historical period: *A Companion to Ethics*, edited by Peter Singer (1991, repr. with corr., 1993); *The Blackwell Companion to the Enlightenment*, edited by John W. Yolton (1992); *A Companion to Aesthetics*, edited by David E. Cooper et al. (1992); *A Companion to Epistemology*, edited by Johnathan Dancy and Ernest Sosa (1992); *A Companion to Metaphysics*, edited by Jaegwon Kim and Ernest Sosa (1995); *A Companion to the Philosophy of Mind*, edited by Samuel D. Guttenplan (1995); *A Companion to Contemporary Political Philosophy*, edited by Robert E. Goodin and Philip Pettit (1995); *The Blackwell Companion to Philosophy*, edited by Nicholas Bunnin and E. P. Tsui-James (1996); *A Companion to the Philosophy of Law and Legal Theory*, edited by Dennis M. Patterson (1996); *A Companion to the Philosophy of Language*, edited by Bob Hale and Crispin Wright (1997); and *A Companion to World Philosophies*, edited by Eliot Deutsch and Ronald Bontekoe (1997). The series is generally of high quality and is carefully supervised by the eminent scholars and bibliographers who serve as editors of the individual volumes. Included in each are brief biographical and topical essays by an array of contributors. Selective bibliographies are furnished for each entry, which makes the volumes useful to a variety of potential users from scholars and serious students to interested laypersons. The series fulfills a need for treatment of specific areas of philosophy within a comprehensive planned program of publishing. The years 1998–1999 witnessed continuing publishing activity with coverage of such areas as language, bioethics, business ethics, cognitive science, law and legal theory, continental philosophy, feminist philosophy, religion, and world philosophies.

75. **The Concise Encyclopedia of Western Philosophy and Philosophers.** New ed. completely rev. James O. Urmson and Jonathan Ree, eds. Boston: Unwin Hyman, 1989; repr., London: Routledge Kegan Paul, 1991. 331p. ISBN 0-41-507883-0.

Long a staple reference tool, this continues to appeal to the intelligent layperson or non-specialist. Numerous distinguished contributors participated in the effort, and the work continues as a useful source of information on Western philosophers and their contributions. In addition to the biographies, there is coverage of trends and, of course, definition of terms. Articles are brief to moderate in length and favor the contributions and individuals associated with Anglo-American thought. Additional new articles furnish coverage of important developments subsequent to publication of the second edition in 1975, and needed corrections have been made. No bibliographies are provided, which limits the volume's use to identification purposes.

76. **Dictionary of Logic As Applied in the Study of Language: Concepts/ Methods/Theories.** Witold Marciszewski, ed. The Hague: Martinus Nijhoff, 1981. 436p. ISBN 90-247-2123-7.

This is a specialized work of international coverage. The phrase in the title "as applied to the study of language" is important for an understanding of its scope. Articles are lengthy, signed by the authors, and have both citations and bibliographies. There is a general bibliography at the end, as well as an index of symbols. Brief definitions of specific topics and references to the articles in which more extended discussion occurs are found in the "Subject Index and Glossary." The general bibliography is international in scope, with a strong emphasis on mathematical logic. Individual articles make heavy use of mathematical formulae.

A recent highly specialized source is *Encyclopedia of Phenomenology*, edited by Lester Embree (Kluwer Academic Publishing, 1997). This is volume 18 of the publisher's Contributions to Phenomenology and provides excellent description and identification of the topics, issues, and personalities associated with the study of phenomenology for both students and specialists. It is a work of collaborative scholarship, with academic scholars as the major contributors. Entries are clear, well-constructed, and informative.

77. **A Dictionary of Marxist Thought.** 2d ed. Tom Bottomore, ed. Cambridge, MA: Blackwell, 1991. 647p. ISBN 0-631-16481-2.

The initial edition (1983) established itself as a useful work although it was criticized for uneven quality in the array of topics and subjects presented. As a product of Anglo-American scholarship it examined the essence of contemporary Marxist thought in such areas as aesthetics, ethics, and theory of knowledge. The second edition updates its predecessor and goes beyond Marxist philosophy in its analysis of the concepts involved. New treatments include "analytical Marxism," "crisis in socialist society," and "market socialism." Continued excellent coverage is given to standard elements such as "alienation and dialectics." Philosophical schools and movements within Marxism are treated and individual philosophers are identified and described. In light of events leading to the dismantling of the U.S.S.R., this tool provides a needed Western perspective on Marxist thought. Because of the timeliness of the topic and the nature of the ongoing debates regarding Marxism, it remains an important source.

*78. **Encyclopedia of Bioethics.** Rev. ed. Warren T. Reich, ed.-in-chief. New York: Simon & Schuster/Macmillan, 1995. 5v. ISBN 0-02-897352-X.

This is an expansive revision of the comprehensive 1978 four-volume work on the important field of bioethics, updating the treatment of the ethical and social issues of life sciences, medicine, health care, and the health professions. Philosophical perspectives are provided, among others, since the work is interdisciplinary in nature. Elements are included that embrace the study of history, theology, science, law, and the social sciences. For the philosopher, there is value not only in the specialized area of bioethics but also in the excellent coverage given general ethical theory, which can still be used to supplement and update the coverage in *The Encyclopedia of Philosophy* (entry 66). Entries are arranged alphabetically and include the addition of the major issues of modern times (AIDS, sexuality and gender, animal welfare and rights, etc.). In many cases the perspectives of different authors are presented. There is an attempt to avoid technical language and to achieve a universal perspective, with contributions from over 400 scholars representing every continent. The work has a comprehensive index and cross-references are supplied. A CD-ROM version was issued in 1996.

79. **Encyclopedia of Cosmology: Historical, Philosophical, and Scientific Foundations of Modern Cosmology.** Norriss S. Hetherington, ed. New York: Garland, 1993. 686p. ISBN 0-8240-7213-8.

This one-volume compendium examines the whole realm of cosmology with all its ramifications from philosophical to scientific through a well-developed collection of scholarly articles. Such diverse aspects as Aristotle's cosmology, anthropic principle, creation, multiple universes, plurality of worlds, and philosophical elements within the origins of modern cosmology are treated along with aspects of particle physics, dark matter, deceleration of the universe, and galaxy formation. In addition to Aristotle's theories, the ancient theories of Ptolemy and Plato are analyzed together with such illustrious Renaissance personalities as Copernicus, Kepler, Descartes, and Newton. Modern figures such as Einstein and Hubble receive scrutiny as well. Numerous scholars have contributed to the volume, producing well-developed, cogent exposition. An important characteristic of this work is its inclusion of debates, contested issues, and alternative theories along with the accepted versions. All entries contain suggestions for additional readings; an index is furnished.

80. **The Encyclopedia of Eastern Philosophy and Religion**: Buddhism, Hinduism, Taoism, Zen. Ingrid Fischer-Schreiber et al., eds. Boston: Shambhala, 1989; 1994 pbk. 468p. ISBN 0-87773-433-X.

This is considered an indispensable recent source for information on Eastern traditions that previously had been treated only by highly specialized sources along with *Dictionary of Asian Philosophies*, by St. Elmo Nauman (Philosophical Library, 1978). It is an English translation of a German work, *Lexikon der ostlichen Weisheitslehren* (Bern: Barth, 1986), and furnishes some 4,000 definitions and biographical sketches. Arrangement is alphabetical and narratives vary in length according to importance of topic. Entries furnish cross-references that are helpful in linking associated subjects and issues. Some of the lengthy entries furnish expositions of doctrines and examine their cultural and historical impact. There are bibliographical references to relevant studies as well as a final detailed bibliography identifying both primary and secondary sources. No index is furnished, but the cross-references within entries are useful for access. A good feature is the lineage chart, which furnishes insight into the transmission of the Eastern traditions.

Companion Encyclopedia of Asian Philosophy, edited by Brian Carr and Indira Mahalingam (Routledge Kegan Paul, 1997) is the most recent one-volume reference work on the topic and provides the greatest depth of coverage in its more than 1,100-page format. Entries provide information regarding terminology, events, developments, ideas, and personalities.

81. **Encyclopedia of Ethics.** Lawrence C. Becker and Charlotte B. Becker, eds. New York: Garland, 1992. 2v. (Garland Reference Library of the Humanities, v. 925). ISBN 0-8153-0403-X.

Recognized by experts as one of the best of the specialized information sources in the field, this work furnishes over 400 signed articles dealing with ethics on a broad scale. Emphasis is given to perceptions of the English-speaking world, but also includes moral concepts as viewed by other cultures. From general to the level of serious inquiry as practiced by scholars and university students, the work is well-written. Essays vary from 500 to 9,000 words, with most articles ranging between 1,000 and 5,000 words depending upon the significance of the topic. Essays are thorough and informative, enumerating the various aspects of theories and alternatives regarding issues. Covered here are individual philosophers, ethics of specific fields such as business or government, theories, values and traits, and so forth. Useful bibliographies are furnished within each entry. There is an extensive subject index and an index to authors cited in the bibliographies.

82. **Encyclopedia of Indian Philosophies.** Ram Shankar Bhattacharya et al. Princeton, NJ: Princeton University, 1977– . v.1– .

Originally begun as a monumental project of an Indian publishing house in 1970, the work has been continuing under the auspices of Princeton University since 1977. Produced by teams of scholars, each volume furnishes another segment of what is considered to be a definitive encyclopedia of the various systems of classical Indian philosophy. Much of the work has been done by Karl H. Potter, whose initial bibliographic volume has been revised on two occasions. The first seven volumes have been issued, with volume 6 appearing in 1992 and volume 7 in 1996. At the same time volume 1 (*Bibliography*) was issued in its third revised edition in 1995 (entry 49).

A Concise Dictionary of Indian Philosophy: Sanskrit Terms Defined in English, by John A. Grimes, has been issued in a new and revised edition (State University of New York, 1996). It continues to provide a basic introduction to the terminology of the major schools of

Indian philosophy. Because Sanskrit is basic to the understanding of various concepts and themes, this dictionary of several thousand terms is useful to those at all levels of inquiry. Definitions vary in length from simple translations of a phrase to thorough descriptions and interpretations of usage and doctrine. Arrangement of entries is by roman alphabet; special features include charts showing relationships of works, categories, and source books for the various schools. There is an index of important terms.

83. **Handbook of Metaphysics and Ontology.** Hans Burkhardt and Barry Smith, eds. Philadelphia: Philosophia Verlag, 1991. 2v. ISBN 3-88405-080-X.

Considered to be an excellent source of information on the ancient study of metaphysics and ontology, this work furnishes excellent coverage of the issues and debates that have endured over thousands of years. Conversely, systematic treatment is given to more recent developments of the past four decades. All periods are treated along with various schools of thought, although the central framework resides within the Aristotelian traditions. There are nearly 500 articles furnished by specialists and vary from one page to over ten pages in length. Essays are highly technical; contributors have been straightforward and objective in their descriptions. In a highly selective work of this kind, questions inevitably follow regarding inclusions and exclusions, but generally speaking the work is well-conceived. Bibliographies to secondary sources accompany each entry. There is a detailed index, which has been criticized for certain difficulties in locating relevant articles.

84. **Handbook of World Philosophy: Contemporary Developments Since 1945.** John R. Burr, ed. Westport, CT: Greenwood, 1980. 641p. ISBN 0-313-22381-5.

A collection of twenty-eight essays grouped by six regions (Western Europe, Australia, and Israel; Eastern Europe; the Americas; Africa and the Republic of South Africa; Islamic Countries; and Asia), this work provides an international survey of philosophical directions, tendencies, and crosscurrents since 1945. The essays describe the thoughts, work, and activities up to about 1977. Within the regions, there are many subdivisions by country and each essay/article is accompanied by a substantial bibliography. The work has been criticized for a certain unevenness of coverage; for example, "France receives twice as much space as any other country." Nevertheless, this is a worthwhile tool because much of the coverage by country is not duplicated elsewhere, not even in the multi-volume encyclopedias. There are both subject and name indexes, as well as a directory of philosophical associations and a list of congresses and meetings in the appendices.

DIRECTORIES AND BIOGRAPHICAL SOURCES

85. **Biographical Dictionary of Twentieth-Century Philosophers.** Stuart Brown et al., eds. New York: Routledge Kegan Paul, 1996. 947p. ISBN 0-415-06043-5.

This is an important, informative, and lucid source, providing background information for college students and specialists on more than 1,000 philosophers from all over the world. Over 100 scholars have contributed the entries, with an emphasis on Anglo-American and European personalities; however representation is given to philosophers from China, Japan, Russia, the Mid-East, and so forth. Entries vary in length from 250 to 1,250 words and identify demographics, field of study, and accomplishments, and provide a bibliography along with an essay describing the individual's life and thought.

Essays on Early Modern Philosophers: From Descartes and Hobbes to Newton and Leibniz, edited by Vere Chappel (Garland, 1992), is in twelve volumes and furnishes some 300 essays by various scholars and specialists on early modern philosophers of the seventeenth century and their work. These articles were written over a period of sixty-three years from 1926 to 1989 and were published in fifty different sources. Volumes treat Descartes, Grotius to Gassendi, the Cartesians, Port-Royal to Bayle, Hobbes, British philosophers, Locke, Spinoza, Malebranche, and Leibniz. Each volume supplies from thirteen to thirty-seven articles dealing with some aspect of the subject's work and thought.

86. **Blackwell Philosopher Dictionaries** series. Cambridge, MA: Blackwell, 1992– . ISBN 0-631-17568-7 (Rousseau).

Another series from Blackwell (see entry 74) is this useful and informative compendium devoted to the life and work of individual philosophers. With the purpose of being scholarly as well as accessible, the content of each title provides a summary of the individual's life and impact, along with a dictionary of key terms and concepts integral to the philosopher's theories and thought systems. A well-conceived bibliography of important works by and about the philosopher and an index conclude the volume. Thus far there are seven titles: *A Rousseau Dictionary,* by N. J. H. Dent (1992); *A Hegel Dictionary,* by Michael J. Inwood (1992); *A Descartes Dictionary,* by John Cottingham (1993); *A Locke Dictionary,* by John Yolton (1993); *A Kant Dictionary,* by Howard Caygill (1995); *A Hobbes Dictionary,* by Aloysius P. Martinich (1995); and *A Wittgenstein Dictionary,* by Hans-Johann Glock (1996). Most recent is *A Heidegger Dictionary* by Michael J. Inwood (1999).

87. **Dictionnaire des philosophes antiques.** Richard Goulet, ed. Paris: Editions du Centre national de la recherche scientifique, 1989. v.1– . ISBN 2-222-04042-6 (v.1); 2-271-05195-9 (v.2).

Volume 1 of this multi-volume biographical encyclopedia was issued in 1989, followed by volume 2 in 1994. The two volumes have given an indication of what is to become a comprehensive biographical encyclopedia of early philosophers. Time span ranges from the beginning of philosophy to about the sixth century. Articles vary considerably in length depending upon the importance of the subject, with over 100 pages given to Aristotle while others receive a single paragraph. The biographical essays contain references to other sources dating from all time periods and furnish exposition of the subject's influence and thought systems. There is a listing of textual histories and standard editions for each philosopher. Volume 1 contains indexes of subjects, Greek words, and names.

Medieval Philosophers, edited by Jeremiah Hackett (Gale Research, 1992) is volume 115 of the publisher's Dictionary of Literary Biography series and is of use to both students and specialists. Using the same format and approach as other volumes in the series, the work provides in-depth treatment of forty-one philosophers, both Eastern and Western, who lived between the fourth and sixteenth centuries. A list of works is provided along with a biographical/cultural/historical essay. The contents of this work are indexed in *Gale's Literary Index CD-ROM* (entry 1090).

88. **Directory of American Philosophers, 1998–1999.** 19th ed. Archie J. Bahm et al., eds. Bowling Green, OH: Philosophy Documentation Center/ Bowling Green State University, 1998. 545p. ISBN 0-912632-74-7.

The recent edition of this biennial work basically continues the familiar format of the previous publications. The main body is composed of a directory of American college and university departments of philosophy arranged alphabetically by state, then by name. There is a listing of faculty members for each entry, along with the address and telephone number of the department. Canadian colleges and universities receive similar treatment in a separate listing and are arranged alphabetically by province, then name. Additional information is provided in separate sections on assistantships, societies, institutes, publishers, and journals in the field. Separate indexes provide ready access through names of philosophers (primarily the faculty members), institutions, publishers, journals, centers and institutes, and societies. The final section provides statistics on size of philosophy departments, number of philosophers, etc. A companion or complementary source is *International Directory of Philosophy and Philosophers* (entry 92).

89. **Fifty Major Philosophers: A Reference Guide.** Diane Collinson. New York: Routledge Kegan Paul, 1987. 170p. ISBN 0-4150-3135-4.

This modest effort was written primarily for non-specialists or students to enable them to understand the views of fifty of the most important philosophers from Thales to Sartre. It represents a highly-selective collective biography that provides a good read. As is true of any other work of similar nature, the major criticism relates to the judgment or decision rendered with respect to which philosophers are to be omitted. All subjects are deceased and are major thinkers who have had some influence on the Western tradition. Biographical sketches are clearly written and easily digested and are accompanied by a brief exposition of the philosopher's thought system and chief directions. Each entry contains a brief bibliography of suggested readings designed to aid further inquiry. Arrangement of entries is chronological; there is a glossary of some fifty terms.

90. **Great Thinkers of the Eastern World: The Major Thinkers and the Philosophical and Religious Classics of China, India, Japan, Korea, and the World of Islam.** Ian P. McGreal, ed. New York: HarperCollins, 1995. 505p. ISBN 0-062-70085-5.

In joining its counterpart, which treats Western thinkers (entry 91), this work's publisher has continued to produce an excellent biographical resource in a much needed area of inquiry. Numerous contributors have furnished the 109 entries examining the major ideas and theories of a variety of theologians and philosophers of the Eastern regions. Included are the major figures, both ancient and modern (Confucius, Buddha, Gandhi, Tagore, and Mao) along with those less heralded. Arrangement is chronological within geographic regions, and entries furnish biography, major ideas, major works, and bibliography.

Another useful resource for undergraduates (although highly selective) is *Thirty-Five Oriental Philosophers*, by Diane Collinson and Robert Wilkinson (Routledge Kegan Paul, 1994). Arranged in five geographical segments—China, Islam, India, Tibet, and Japan—the entries are readable and average three to five pages in length, providing a good description of the individual and his or her ideas. Period coverage ranges from ancient (Zoroaster) to modern (Mao).

91. **Great Thinkers of the Western World: The Major Ideas and Classic Works of More Than 100 Outstanding Western Philosophers....** Ian P. McGreal, ed. New York: HarperCollins, 1992. 572p. ISBN 0-06-270026-X.

Written at the undergraduate level, this work provides a useful perspective on the thoughts and thought systems of 116 thinkers from various fields of philosophy, the sciences, and the social sciences. Thinkers range from ancient Greek philosophers to twentieth-century scientists. All are major in terms of their importance and influence on Western culture. The work is similar to the Magill publication (entry 73) in its arrangement and narrative treatment. Entries are arranged chronologically by birth date of subjects and begin with a summary of the individual's principal ideas, followed by a biographical and descriptive commentary on writings and contributions. Entries conclude with a brief bibliography of secondary sources.

Thirty-five contributors, specialists in the field, have signed their essays and furnished a total package that successfully conveys the subject matter with clarity and lucidity.

A less comprehensive and more focused work is *Fifty Key Contemporary Thinkers: From Structuralism to Postmodernity*, by John Lechte (Routledge Kegan Paul, 1994), which emphasizes European, especially French, thinkers. Included here are linguists, writers, social theorists, and historians, as well as philosophers with such names as Joyce, Kafka, and Chomsky joining Freud, Peirce, and Nietzsche. The entries are in-depth and about five pages in length; bibliographies are included.

92. **International Directory of Philosophy and Philosophers, 1999–2000.** 11th ed. Ramona Cormier and Richard H. Lineback, eds. Bowling Green, OH: Philosophy Documentation Center, Bowling Green State University, 1999. 652p. ISBN 1-889680-03-6.

A companion and complementary work to *Directory of American Philosophers* (entry 88), this publication excludes the United States and Canada. Happily, a pattern has emerged in which the work is issued on a biennial basis, a real improvement over its earlier irregular frequency (1st ed., 1966; 2d ed., 1972). It continues to grow, with the current edition containing over 100 pages more than its predecessor. Like its companion work, the format is predictable. Part 1 covers international organizations of philosophy, while part 2 remains the major contribution, listing college and university philosophy departments alphabetically by country or region and providing listings of faculty members. Part 3 contains the indexes, which permit access by name of philosopher, university, center, society, journal, or publisher.

93. **Thinkers of the Twentieth Century.** 2d ed. Roland Turner, ed. Chicago: St. James Press, 1987. 977p. ISBN 0-912289-83-X.

An excellent biographical dictionary that first appeared in 1984 and then was considerably expanded through recommendations of librarians and reviewers for more mathematicians and scientists. With the addition of 50 individuals, there are now 480 persons covered. About 100 of these are philosophers in the strict sense (Sartre, Buber, Wittgenstein, etc.), but many others were known for their philosophical impact (Gandhi, Durkheim, C. S. Lewis, etc.). Most of the thinkers were writers whose contributions influenced our times. There is a biographical sketch for each individual, accompanied by a listing of his or her books. Also, a list of biographies and a list of critical studies are included. An excellent feature is the interpretive essay of approximately 2,000 words, written by an informed contributor, which analyzes the individual's life and influence. The lack of a subject index is the main drawback to an otherwise extraordinary research tool.

94. **Women Philosophers: A Bio-Critical Sourcebook.** Ethel M. Kersey and Calvin O. Schrag, eds. New York: Greenwood, 1989. 230p. ISBN 0-313-25720-5.

This work opens with an excellent informative essay furnishing a useful thematic perspective on the historical influence of women in philosophy. Included here are some 150 biographical sketches of women who have been identified as having written or taught in the field. All traditional areas of philosophy are represented, such as metaphysics and logic, and the work is of historical nature because most biographees were born before 1920. All or nearly all are contributors to the Western tradition, and their major ideas are examined in clear fashion. Both primary and secondary sources are listed in bibliographies for each entry. There is a useful table of quick reference in the appendix identifying dates, countries, and so forth for women in the field; there is a name index.

A bibliographic effort that seeks to help establish the work of women philosophers within the corpus of the field is Elsie M. Barth's *Women Philosophers: A Bibliography of Books Through 1990* (Philosophy Documentation Center, 1992). Listings include books both by and about women philosophers. Arrangement is by category and there are cross-references to related works. Most of the books are products of the twentieth century. The works are not evaluated critically. There is a name index.

HISTORIES

95. **A History of Greek Philosophy.** William K. C. Guthrie. Cambridge: Cambridge University Press, 1962–1981; repr., 1986. 6v. ISBN 0-521-05160-6 (v.2).

Since the appearance of the first volume in 1962, this work has been extolled by scholars for its erudition, technical accuracy, and insight, while at the same time remaining lucid and readable. Beginning with the pre-Socratics of early vintage in volume 1, it progresses to the later pre-Socratics in volume 2, and to the fifth century in volume 3. Plato is covered in his earlier period in volume 4 and in his later period in volume 5. The final volume is devoted to Aristotle. The six volumes make up a monumental contribution to the study of classical philosophy, even though Guthrie died before fulfilling his intention to provide a complete link to neo-Platonism. Each volume is thoroughly documented with references and provides a strong bibliography and an index.

Although technically not a series, Cambridge later began to publish single-volume histories, through the efforts of influential scholars, that provide excellent perspective for students and specialists. *The Cambridge History of Later Greek and Early Medieval Philosophy*, edited by Arthur H. Armstrong (1970), established the pattern for this sequential coverage through a collaborative effort of eight scholars. Historical exposition is excellent, treating the development of variations of Platonic-Aristotelian systems and their impact over a 1,400-year period from 300 B.C. to A.D. 1100. Cogent thinking, historical accuracy, and excellent documentation have been continued in subsequent publications. *The Cambridge History of Later Medieval Philosophy: From the Rediscovery of Aristotle to the Disintegration of Scholasticism, 1100–1600*, edited by Norman Kretzmann et al. (1982; 1988 pbk), continues the coverage another 500 years. *The Cambridge History of Renaissance Philosophy*, edited by Charles B. Schmitt et al. (1988), treats the historical development of the Renaissance from 1500 to 1600, while *The Cambridge History of Seventeenth-Century Philosophy*, edited by Daniel Garber and Michael Ayers (1997), covers the next 100 years. In all these volumes, bibliographies of primary and secondary sources are recognized for their value to students and specialists.

96. **A History of Philosophy.** Frederick Charles Copleston. New York: Image Books, 1985. 9v. in 3. ISBN 0-385-23031-1 (v.1); 0-385-23032-X (v.2); 0-385-23033-8 (v.3). Repr. in progress, 1993– . v.1– . ISBN 0-385-46845-8 (v.1).

Written from the standpoint of a scholastic philosopher (Copleston was a Jesuit priest and Professor of the History of Philosophy at Heythrop College, Oxford), this work first appeared in 1945. It has become a standard history of philosophy in the English language through frequent addition and reprinting. Beginning with ancient times (Greece and Rome), the coverage progresses through the various schools of Western philosophy—Neoplatonism, Scholasticism, Rationalism, Empiricism, Romanticism, and Utilitarianism—using representative philosophers as labels for each of the volumes. The ninth volume is the most recent and covers French philosophy through Existentialism and Sartre. Each volume was published with a good bibliography and index. This edition employs a compact format that combines three volumes in one for the entire set. The current reprint treats the single volumes individually; four volumes have been issued, bringing coverage up to Leibniz.

97. **The Oxford Illustrated History of Western Philosophy.** Anthony Kenny, ed. New York: Oxford University Press, 1997. 407p. ISBN 0-19-285335-X.

Initially published in 1994 (without *Illustrated* in the title), this remains an excellent one-volume product from Oxford. It furnishes a brief and readable yet informative survey describing idea systems, writings, and important developments from ancient times through the twentieth century. The work is organized chronologically into six major divisions, each by a different scholar, beginning with ancient philosophy and ending with political influences. Some 150 color illustrations are provided, along with maps and a chronological table.

The second edition of Bertrand Russell's *A History of Western Philosophy* (Simon & Schuster, 1961; repr., 1995) presents philosophy as an "integral part of social and political life," and is still regarded as one of the important popularizations. There is an emphasis on social, economic, and political conditions reflecting the author's progressive leanings. Coverage is given to all major philosophers and many minor ones. It remains one of the more interesting works in the field.

98. **Routledge History of Philosophy.** New York: Routledge Kegan Paul, 1993–1999. 10v. ISBN 0-415-06272-1 (v.1).

This excellent and comprehensive history of Western philosophy now begins its term as the leading multi-volume English-language work of its kind. Each volume is edited by an individual scholar who has worked with ten to twenty experts who have contributed chapters of approximately forty pages each to the topical coverage. Volume 1 (1997) treats the early beginnings of Western philosophy to Plato; volume 2 will cover Aristotle to Augustine; volume 3 (1998) examines medieval philosophy; volume 4 (1993), the Renaissance and rationalism; volume 5 (1996), British philosophy/Enlightenment; volume 6 (1993), German Idealism; and volume 7 (1994), the nineteenth century. The final three volumes deal with the twentieth century; volume 8 (1994), continental philosophy; volume 9 (1997), science, logic, and mathematics; and volume 10 (1999), meaning, knowledge, and value.

Recently initiated by the same publisher and utilizing similar style and format is *Routledge History of World Philosophies*, which examines the nature and development of the philosophies of the world in individually edited volumes with numerous contributors. Volume 1 (1996), in two tomes, covers Islamic philosophy; volume 2 (1997), treats Jewish philosophy.

CHAPTER 5

ACCESSING INFORMATION IN RELIGION

WORKING DEFINITION OF RELIGION

The word *religion* is thought to derive from the Latin *religare*, which means "to bind," thus offering two alternative explanations for the general use of the term: either as a set of beliefs to which the follower is devoted or bound, or as McLeish suggests, "that which binds things together . . . and which enables mankind to live in harmony with the animal world and with the gods."[1]

More broadly stated, the study of religion includes both the beliefs and the behaviors that, according to John F. Wilson and Thomas P. Slavens, "express as a system the basic shape or texture of the culture or subculture under observation."[2] Lester Asheim suggested a more familiar definition: religion is "the study of man's beliefs and practices in relation to God, gods, or the supernatural."[3] Either definition allows for the more traditional concept of religion as well as more recent New Age concepts of spirituality.

Religion influences other disciplines of the humanities and the social sciences in a way no other discipline, with the possible exception of language, does. Every student will be able to identify religious influences and themes in art, music, literature, drama, history, anthropology, law, sociology, and psychology. Walter Kaufmann's chapter on religion in *The Future of the Humanities* (Crowell, 1977, pp. 126–53) suggests that the only appropriate way to teach religion in higher education is to use an interdisciplinary approach. In recommending that mode, he states, "Religion is far too important to be left to theologians."[4]

There are many approaches to the study of religion; the most prevalent include the historical approach, the social science approach, and the study of the spiritual/phenomenological aspects. A broad perspective on religion and its literature is offered by Jaroslav Pelikan in the introductory chapter of a compendium entitled *The World Treasury of Modern Religious Thought* (Little, Brown, 1990). The articles on religion in the *Encyclopaedia Britannica Online* offer excellent background reading for the librarian. See "Religion, study of" at http://members.eb.com/bol/topic?eu=117377&sctn=2 (accessed February 28, 2000). J. Gordon Melton's *Encyclopedia of Occultism and Parapsychology* (Gale Research, 1996) identifies other aspects of spiritual issues, as does his earlier publication, *New Age Encyclopedia* (Gale Research, 1990).

MAJOR DIVISIONS
OF THE FIELD

Religions are commonly classified as being predominantly sacramental, prophetic, or mystical. Sacramental religions place great emphasis on the observation of ritual and on the sacredness of certain objects. Eastern Orthodoxy and Roman Catholicism are familiar examples. Prophetic religions emphasize the communication of the Divine Will in verbal form, often with strong moralistic emphasis. Islam and Protestantism reflect this approach. Mystical religions stress direct encounter with God and view words, rituals, and sacred objects as auxiliary at best, or hindrances at worst, to the full communion that is seen as the ultimate goal of all religious striving. Certain branches of Hinduism and Buddhism are examples of this type of religion.

The literature generated by the religions of the world may be conveniently analyzed under four predominant headings: 1) personal religion, 2) theology, 3) philosophy of religion, and 4) science of religion.

Personal religion is the primary and most direct source of religious writing. It is intimately related to the experiences of the individual and reflections about his or her significance. A major class of documents in this category would be the sacred scriptures of the world's great religions. Closely related to the sacred writings are those documents of explication and interpretations commonly known as commentaries. Finally, there is a much larger body of literature that does not have the same authoritative standing as the sacred scriptures and their commentaries. Works in this category may be devotional, autobiographical, or biographical. In this group would also be included a large number of popularizations.

Theology is an attempt to express in intellectually coherent form the principal doctrines of a religion. It is the product of reflection upon the primary sources of religion. It differs from philosophy in that the basic truth of the religious position is accepted and attention is given to its systematic and thoughtful exposition. The field has many subdivisions. Within the Christian tradition, systematic (or topic-oriented) theology and biblical theology have been especially important, but there is also a substantial body of literature on moral, ascetic, mystical, symbolic, pastoral, philosophical, liturgical, and natural theology as well.

The philosophy of religion is an attempt to relate the religious experience to other spheres of experience. It differs from theology in that it makes fewer assumptions about the truth of a religious position, at least in the beginning. It differs from philosophy in its selection of religion as the area for speculative investigation. Perhaps it is best described as a bridge between philosophy and theology. The article in the *Encyclopaedia Britannica Online* treats philosophy of religion in a direct and informative way; see "Religion, philosophy of" at http://members.eb.com/bol/topic?thes_id=327014 (accessed February 28, 2000).

The science of religion has also generated a substantial body of literature. Here, emphasis is placed on comparative and historical methods, with no presuppositions about (and possibly no interest in) the truth or falsity of the religions being examined. Whereas the locus of interest in the first three categories is usually one of the world's living religions, this is not always the case in the scientific study of religion, where a purely objective approach to the description and comparison of religious phenomena represents the ideal.

HELPFUL RESOURCES FOR STUDENTS, LIBRARIANS, AND GENERAL READERS

The student wishing to read more about religion and its subfields will find it helpful to consult *Religion: A Humanistic Field*, by Clyde A. Holbrook (Prentice-Hall, 1963), *Religion*, edited by Paul Ramsey (Prentice-Hall, 1965), and *Religion in America*, by Winthrop S. Hudson (4th ed., Scribner's, 1987). (Unfortunately, these titles, still excellent despite their age, are now out-of-print.)

More recent guiding material specifically for the librarian and serious researcher are Edward D. Starkey's *Judaism and Christianity: A Guide to the Reference Literature* (Libraries Unlimited, 1991) and *Religion and the American Experience, 1620–1900: A Bibliography of Doctoral Dissertations*, by Arthur P. Young and E. Jens Holley (Greenwood, 1992). The latter is one title in Greenwood's extensive series, Bibliographies and Indexes in Religious Studies, a series that should be consulted for other useful titles. In the same series, Michael A. Fahey's compilation *Ecumenism A Bibliographical Overview* (Greenwood, 1992) will lead the user to over 1,300 books and journal titles on ecumenism. A newer source for the scholar is reviewed in L. D. McIntosh, "Religion and Theology: A Guide to Current Reference Sources," *Australian Library Journal* 47 (February 1998): 120–21. Another title for the librarian and scholar of religion is the third edition of James P. McCabe's *A Critical Guide to Catholic Reference Books* (Libraries Unlimited, 1989), still useful despite its age.

E. T. Thompson's "Religious Records," in *Researcher's Guide to Archives and Regional History Sources* (Library Professional Publications, 1988, pp. 74–77) addresses the use of archival materials in religious studies. The student should not overlook entries in the literature indexes under headings such as "Religious Archives" for help in locating guides and finding tools for special collections. See, for example, *Researching Modern Evangelism; A Guide to the Holdings of the Billy Graham Center, with Information on Other Collections*, by R. D. Schuster and others (Greenwood, 1990).

A general perspective for the librarian is still well represented by Lester Asheim's chapter on religion in *The Humanities and the Library* (American Library Association, 1956). Gary Ebersole and Martha S. Alt's chapter "Religion," in the second edition of *The Humanities and the Library*, edited by Nena Couch and Nancy Allen (American Library Association, 1993), adds more recent profiles of religion librarianship and references to readings for specialists and generalists as well. The anthology of works mentioned above and edited by Jaraslov Pelikan, *The World Treasury of Modern Religious Thought* (Little, Brown, 1990) offers the broadest coverage of carefully selected representative authors, from Karl Marx to Mahatma Gandhi, Martin Luther King, and Paul Tillich. The anthology, along with Anne H. Lundin and Edward Lundin's equally thoughtfully prepared *Contemporary Religious Ideas Bibliographic Essays* (Libraries Unlimited, 1996), will prove of great help in working with all types of users: ministers and rabbis, religious educators, library selection committees, and students at all levels, from high school to seminarian.

Religious scholar John F. Wilson has contributed a great deal to the librarian's understanding of religious studies. With Paul Ramsey, he edited *The Study of Religion in Colleges and Universities* (Princeton University Press, 1970), a report that places the evolving area we call "religious studies" in the context of the seminary, the graduate school, and the full-service university. More recently, Wilson contributed the survey of religious literature portion to *Research Guide to Religious Studies*, co-authored with Thomas P. Slavens (American Library Association, 1982). As noted in Chapter 6, this source is now more useful for the scholarly articles than for the resource chapters, which are somewhat dated.

Bibliographic guides by Cyril J. Barber, including his *Introduction to Theological Research* (Moody Press, 1982), reflect the more conservative religious viewpoint. The book includes information on how to use the library, useful material for the intended audience of beginning Bible students.

Recent articles on user instruction, or bibliographic instruction, include "One-Shot Bibliographic Instruction," a brief report of a roundtable discussion at the 1998 ATLA conference, reported by Clayton H. Hulet in *Summary of Proceedings of the 52nd Annual Conference of the American Theological Library Association* (ATLA, 1998, pp. 297–300), and "Bibliographic Instruction in Religion: A Survey of the Field," a presentation to the College and University Interest Group at the 1996 ATLA Annual Conference and reported in the *Summary of Proceedings of the 50th Annual Conference of the American Theological Library Association* (ATLA, 1996, pp. 106–12). Section 5.2 of the Association of Theological Schools (ATS) Accreditation Standards requires that libraries provide bibliographic instruction as well as other services. (See the ATS Web site for the complete standards: http://www.ats.edu/sets/accfst.htm [accessed February 28, 2000].)

The librarian has a wide range of journal articles, brief publications, and chapters to consult on religious material, although a good many of the sources are older. A search of the index *Library Literature* (H. W. Wilson) for the period 1994 through 1998 reveals a considerable emphasis on acquisitions and materials now available on the World Wide Web.

Collection development and evaluation of resources are served well by L. Garrett's bibliographic essays and reviews in *Publishers Weekly*; *PW* regularly features listings (for example, "Keeping the Faith: Fall/Winter Religion Books," in the August 18, 1997 issue) as well as periodic coverage of religious bestsellers. Garrett and others edited "Religion Update" (*Publishers Weekly* 245 [May 25, 1998]: 3ff.). Reviews are also featured regularly in the journal *Catholic Library World*. With religion being a large and diverse area of publishing, religious books are well represented in the library and publishing literature.

Selection and acquisition of religious material for libraries are addressed in B. E. Deitrick's *A Basic Book List for Church Libraries* (Church and Synagogue Library Association, 1988). A special issue of *Library Acquisitions* (15, no. 2 [1991]: 145–227) is devoted to collection development of religious material. R. Singerman edits the issue that includes articles on such diverse materials as Liberation theology in Latin America and obtaining and preserving Buddhist materials. The issue also includes W. J. Hook's "Approval Plans for Religious and Theological Libraries" (pp. 215–27).

T. D. Lincoln's "A Contextual Approach to Collection Management in Religious Studies for North American Libraries," *Acquisitions Librarian* 17/18 (1997): 63–76, has been reprinted in *Acquisitions and Collection Development in the Humanities*, edited by Irene Owens (Haworth, 1997, pp. 63–76).

Collection development in specialized areas is addressed by David H. Partington in "Islamic Literature: Problems in Collection Development," *Library Acquisitions: Theory and Practice* 15 (1991): 147–54, and in the same journal issue by S. Peterson, "From Third World to One World: Problems and Opportunities in Documenting New Christianity" (pp. 177–84).

Other special areas are covered in articles such as C. Olson's "Essential Sources on Thai Theravada Buddhism," *Behavioral and Social Sciences Librarian* 16 (1997): 1–10, and "Choosing Resources on Social Ministry," by Bonnee Lauridsen Voss and Gary L. Harke in *Christian Social Action* 10 (February 1997): 37–38. See also, for example, "Multifaith Information Resources," *Bulletin of the British Theological and Philosophical Libraries* 5 (June 1998): 19–33. Statistics on holdings and services among theological libraries are published as appendices to the annual proceedings of the ATLA conferences.

The special area of children's books in religion is thoroughly covered in the periodical literature. Both *Publishers Weekly* and publications of the Church and Synagogue Library Association offer recommendations for teachers and librarians who work with children. Another article, based on presentations at the 1994 ALA conference, is J. P. Thomas, P. Scales, and P.

Klipsch, "Into the Lion's Den: Youth Access to Religious Materials: Building Strategies, Building Coalitions, Building Collections," *Journal of Youth Services in Libraries* 8 (Fall 1994): 37–52.

Organizing religious materials is another important area for the librarian. "The Classification of Philosophy, Religion, and the Occult," in D. W. Langridge's *Classification and Indexing in the Humanities* (Butterworths, 1976, pp. 59–77) remains useful, but the user will also want to see *Classifying Church or Synagogue Library Materials*, by D. B. Kersten (2d rev. ed., Church and Synagogue Library Association, 1989). J. L. Gresham, "The Place of Religion in the Universe of Knowledge According to Various Systems of Bibliographic Classification," *Journal of Religious and Theological Information* 2 (1994): 29–43, provides a view of several mainstream, as well as more obscure, classification schemes and their handling of religion. Specific issues related to the organization of religious materials are also discussed in the literature; for example, see A. R. Carr and N. S. Strachan, "Development of a System for Treatment of Bible Headings in an OPAC Catalog at Aberdeen University," *Catalogue and Index* no. 95 (Winter 1989): 5–6. The librarian involved with cataloging will need to keep up-to-date by consulting any ongoing revisions of both the Dewey Decimal and Library of Congress schemes. Annual conferences of the American Theological Library Association (ATLA) also provide opportunities for librarians interested in religious materials to network on technical issues, and their proceedings publications provide access to information for those who did not attend the conferences.

The subject of publishing in the area of religion is the subject of W. M. Linz's "A Religious Country Reflected in Its Publishing Industry," *Logos* 7 (1996): 6–11. Statistics reported in the article show overall stability in terms of book production in the United States. Henry J. Carrigan's "Reading Is Believing: Religious Publishing Toward the Millennium," *Library Journal* 120 (May 1, 1995): 36–40, also examines publishing trends.

Ruth E. Fenske and N. J. Mayer address the coverage of indexes in religion in "Title Coverage of Seven Indexes to Religious Periodicals," *Reference and User Services Quarterly* 37 (Winter1997): 171–75, 178–89. From a different perspective, Suzanne Smailes also examines coverage of periodical indexing in "Reliability of Coverage of Periodical Indexing of Lesbian Theological and Womanist Theological Articles in the ATLA Religious Database 1995" (master's research paper, Kent State University, 1996).

The librarian will also want to be aware that the Internet has enabled a number of organized religions, religious organizations, and individual houses of worship to communicate their aims, missions, goals, and services "on the Web." Web sites such as the International Bible Society's http://www.gospelcom.net/ibs/ (accessed February 28, 2000) offer, in addition to the usual links to other resources, e-mail services that deliver daily scriptures, prayers, and other materials usually associated with popularized or "personal religion" over the Internet.

USE AND USERS OF INFORMATION IN RELIGION

There continues to be a distinct lack of use and user studies in the area of religion. This may be the result of the very diverse nature of religious literature and the multiple viewpoints represented, along with the wide audience served by this literature. Users of historical materials, for example, are unlikely to be users of devotional and inspirational literature; indeed, few libraries will include devotional, informative, historical, and the wide range of doctrinal-interpretive works. The difficulty of investigating uses of literature through citation studies, a method useful in some other fields in the humanities, is compounded by the fact that many uses of the religious literature do not result in publication, that many references made to scriptural works are not formally cited, and that religious publications have a remarkably low rate of citation in general. Indeed, David P. Hamilton, in "Research Papers: Who's Uncited Now?" (*Science* 251 [January 4, 1991]: 25), notes that 98.2 percent of published papers in religion are uncited five years after publication. There is a continuing need for further investigation into the use of religious materials; Gleason and Deffenbaugh called for such studies in their *Collection Management* article (6 [Fall/Winter 1984]: 107–17), cited in the last edition of this guide.

Two religious periodicals were among the humanities journals sampled for the age of references cited in Derek J. de Solla Price's now classic "Price's Index" paper ("Citation Measures of Hard Science, Soft Science, Technology and Non-Science" in *Communication among Scientists and Engineers*, edited by C. E. Nelson and D. K. Pollock [Heath, 1970, pp. 3–22]). Both journals (*Anglican Theological Review* and *Journal of the American Academy of Religion*) cited more references, and more recent references, than any other humanities journals among the seventeen studied. The Price study suggests a methodology that could be fruitfully used to look more closely at citation, a measure of use, in the religious literature.

Bibliometric methods have been employed in several theses and dissertations in the field. John W. Heussman's "The Literature Cited in Theological Journals and Its Relation to Seminary Library Circulation" (Ph.D. dissertation, University of Illinois, 1970) provides a broad view of the use of theological journals in a specific setting. Moshe Itzchaky's Ph.D. thesis is a bibliometric study of the literature used in Biblical and Near-East Studies in 1923 and 1971; it is entitled "The Structure and Citation Patterns of the International Literature of Biblical and Ancient Near-East Studies" (Ph.D. thesis, Rutgers the State University of New Jersey, n.d.). Kevin L. Smith's, "A Study in Interdisciplinarity: Bibliometric Analysis of Periodical Publication in Religion and Literature" (Master's research paper, Kent State University, 1996) examines authorship and citations in the fields of religion and literature and suggests useful characteristics for comparison and contrast between the two fields. Finally, a much-needed look at the information seeking of clergy is provided in Donald Albert Wicks, "The Information-Seeking Behavior of Pastoral Clergy: A Study of Their Work Worlds and Work Roles" (Ph.D. dissertation, University of Western Ontario, 1997).

COMPUTERS IN RELIGION

Since the late 1980s there have been scores of articles on topics related to computers in religion; subjects addressed include the use of online databases, methods and tools for text analysis, Internet resources, new electronic archives for scholarly use, and concordance construction methods and programs. Concordancing and word index construction were the primary focuses for computing in the area of religion until very recently. D. M. Burton has written extensively on the subject in the journal *Computers and the Humanities*.

Since the mid-1990s, the emphasis on concordancing and indexing has been replaced by a heavy focus in the literature on Internet resources. K. Moroney's "Scholarly Religious Sites on the World Wide Web," *Collection Building* 17 (1998): 80–83, is an example. A good list of Internet resources is also included in "Selection and Access to Electronic Texts in the Theological Library," by Donald M. Vorp, in *Summary of Proceedings of the 52nd Annual Conference of the American Theological Library Association* (ATLA, 1998, pp. 53–67). An example of coverage of a specific resource is "God in the Information Age: Salt of the Earth Web Site," by Brett Grainger (*Sojourners* 27 [January/February 1998]: 60–61).

The most up-to-date resources can be accessed most directly from the Web: see, for example, the annotated directory of religious studies resources produced by the department of religion and culture at Wilfrid Laurier University at http://www.wlu.ca/~wwwrandc/internet_links.html (accessed February 28, 2000) or the very extensive *Links for Research on Religion* at http://religion.rutgers.edu/links/ (accessed February 28, 2000).

Online and CD-ROM databases serving the field of religion include Religion Index One and Two, produced by the American Theological Library Association and available through multiple vendors. See Barbara Pease, "Religious Indexes on CD-ROM," *Journal of Religious and Theological Information* 2 (1994): 137–49, and Tami Luedtke, "Present and

Future Forms of the ATLA Religion Database," in *Summary of Proceedings of the 52nd Annual Conference of the American Theological Library Association* (ATLA, 1998, pp. 243–47).

Electronic texts enable scholars to study grammar, syntax, and semantics, as well as to investigate authorship, influences, and relationships between various texts and authors. Text archives held at several American institutions support Biblical and religious studies: Duke University holds the Duke Data Bank of Documentary Papyri; the Center for Computer Analysis of Texts (University of Pennsylvania) has materials for Septuagint studies; and the Thesaurus Linguae Graecae (TLG) at the University of California at Irvine contains texts of Greek literature from 750 B.C. to about A.D. 600. Other electronic publication projects in the classics that are of interest to religious scholars include Chadwyck-Healey's Patrologia Latina Database and the Perseus Project, a hypertext and image database of classical Greece. The evaluation of the latter is the subject of Delia Neuman's "Evaluating Evolution: Naturalistic Inquiry and the Perseus Project," *Computers and the Humanities* 25 (August 1991): 239–45, and Gregory Crane's "The Perseus Project and Beyond: How Building a Digital Library Challenges the Humanities and Technology," *D-Lib Magazine* (January 1998): 1. (Available at http://www.dlib.org/dlib/january98/01crane.html [accessed February 28, 2000].)

L. Mealand, of the University of Edinburgh, argued persuasively for increased use of computers in the field of Biblical research in "On Finding Fresh Evidence in Old Texts: Reflections on Results in Computer-Assisted Biblical Research," *Bulletin of the John Rylands University Library of Manchester* 74 (Autumn 1992): 67–88. Mealand stated that the electronic availability of large texts gives the religious and literary scholar "something far, far more useful than index or concordance. We can discover all that such invaluable tools can tell us, and far more." The availability of many religious texts on the Internet has allowed scholars to do the work envisioned by Mealand.[5] For just a few examples of guides to available texts, see *Full Texts Recognized by Religious Scholars*, at http://www.religion-online.org (accessed February 28, 2000); *Academic Information: Religious Studies*, at http://www.academicinfo.net/ Religion.html (accessed February 28, 2000), and the text page of Wilfred Laurier University's extensive resource site at http://www.wlu.ca/~wwwrandc/internet_links.html#texts (accessed February 28, 2000).

The most prevalent electronic text in the area of religious studies is, of course, the Bible. Several dozen computer "versions" have been reported in the literature, and they are available online from commercial vendors, on diskettes and CD-ROMs, and from various Internet resources. For more on electronic Bibles and Biblical texts, see J. A. Wilderotter, *Electronic Bibles and Electronic Texts in Biblical Studies* (Georgetown University, Center for Text and Technology, 1991). Mark Stover's "Religious Studies and Electronic Information: A Librarian's Perspective," *Library Trends* 40 (Spring 1992): 687–703 describes some of the first electronic texts in the field, research projects involving machine readable texts, and software products that serve varied purposes in religious studies.

Newer are the numerous Bible versions and other related texts available on the Internet. For more information, see Harry Hayne's Web page *Selected Internet Resources on Computer-Assisted Biblical Research*. The pages at http://www-writing.berkeley.edu/chorus/ bible/links/index.html (accessed February 28, 2000) include bibliographic information, an extensive resource list, and listings of Internet discussion groups of interest to the biblical scholar. The best link from the site, since it has not been uniformly updated, is *Internet Resources for Computer-Assisted Biblical and Theological Research*, located at http://www.chass.utoronto.ca/ ~hahne/webclass.htm (accessed February 28, 2000).

"Electronic Resources in Theological Librarianship and Religious Publishing: Interest Group Presentations from ATLA 49th Annual Conference" can be found in the *American Theological Library Association Proceedings* 49 (1995): 111–45. Scholars in religion will also find searches of the following databases to be of importance: Dissertation Abstracts Online, Arts and Humanities Search, SocialSciSearch, Magazine Index, Books in Print, and Philosophers Index. General history and periodical indexes will also be helpful for some topical searches.

MAJOR RELIGIOUS ORGANIZATIONS, INFORMATION CENTERS, AND SPECIAL COLLECTIONS

Religious organizations are major sources of information. They may be denominational, ecumenical, or academic. The number of denominational organizations is immense. Certain useful generalizations can be made about the larger religious groups. Generally, they maintain national offices and have extensive publishing programs. Much of their publishing is designed to serve the needs of local congregations for devotional and educational materials. However, a number of the denominational groups do maintain research staffs at the national level, and nearly all of them gather such basic statistics as size of membership, number of congregations or suborganizations, and attendance at religious education programs. They issue directories as well as reports of proceedings of national, regional, or state conferences and other activities. A rapidly increasing number of organizations have a presence on the Internet by mounting and maintaining a World Wide Web site or by providing other Internet services for members or subscribers.

Many of the national church offices also maintain collections of historical materials pertaining to the denomination, and some actively promote church libraries among local congregations.

Ecumenical cooperation is exemplified by the work of the National Council of the Churches of Christ in the U.S.A. (475 Riverside Dr., Rm. 850, New York, NY 10115). The work of the Council includes the collection of data for and publication of *Yearbook of American and Canadian Churches*. The Church and Synagogue Library Association (Box 19357, Portland, OR 97280-0357), supportive of library activities regardless of denominational affiliation, publishes *Church & Synagogue Libraries* bi-monthly.

The oldest of the academic organizations is the Association for the Sociology of Religion (Room 108 Marist Hall, The Catholic University of America, Washington, DC 20064), which was founded prior to World War II and which publishes the quarterly journal *Sociological Analysis* as well as a newsletter and biennial directory. A larger academic group is the Society for the Scientific Study of Religion (875 SWKT, Department of Sociology, Brigham Young University, Provo, UT 84602). Its publication is *Journal for the Scientific Study of Religion*.

Very specialized organizations serving the religious community may also have useful information on very focused topics. Examples of these organizations include the nonprofit Religious Conference Management Association, the Religious Education Association (P.O. Box 15399, Atlanta, GA 30333-0399) and the Religious Public Relations Council (357 Righters Mill Rd., Box 315, Gladwyne, PA 19035). These organizations publish quarterly newsletters or journals and hold periodic meetings.

An organization that developed in response to the need for greater coordination of research and improved dissemination of religious information is ADRIS, the Association for the Development of Religious Information Systems. It publishes *ADRIS Newsletter* and, irregularly, a directory (ADRIS, c/o Department of Social and Cultural Sciences, Marquette University, 526 North 14th St., Milwaukee, WI 53233). In Europe, the source of coordination is the International Federation of Institutes for Social and Socio-Religious Research at Louvain, Belgium.

There are far too many educational organizations to mention them all. However, a good starting point in a search for information in this area is the Council of Societies for the Study of Religion (Valparaiso University, Valparaiso, IN 46383), publisher of the *Directory of Departments of Religion* (annual).

Only a few major information and research centers can be mentioned here. The Office of Research, Evaluation and Planning of the National Council of Churches is noteworthy for its extensive research efforts and the computerized inventory of more than 2,000 documents in the H. Paul Douglass Collection of research reports.

The American Theological Library Association (820 Church St., Ste. 300, Evanston, IL 60201) publishes *Religion Index One*, the index available online, in print, and now on CD-ROM; *Religion Index Two;* the newly combined Religious Indexes on CD-ROM; and many monographs, bibliographies, and a newsletter. The Association publishes summaries of the proceedings of its annual conferences annually; especially noteworthy is the *Summary of Proceedings: Golden Anniversary Annual Conference of the American Theological Library Association* (Denver, CO, 1996), edited by Melody S. Chartier. ATLA also participates in scholarship and research with other organizations as well; see, for example, Dennis Norlin, "Ecumenicity and Electronic Publishing: ATLA and CLA in Partnership," *Catholic Library World* 67 (June 1998): 24–28.

The Catholic Library Association (100 North St., Ste. 224, Pittsfield, MA 01201) probably has the widest range of activities of the denominational library associations, including a publishing program that includes *Catholic Library World* and *Catholic Periodical and Literature Index.* A national conference each year also draws many participants.

Ellen Bosman's Web page, *Selection Sources for Congregational Libraries: Congregational Library Associations*, at http://www.lib.iun.indiana.edu/churchlib.htm (accessed February 28, 2000), identifies almost a dozen additional religious library associations and their publications and services, including the Association of Christian Librarians, the Association for Jewish Libraries, the Church and Synagogue Library Association, and the Evangelical Church Library Association. Each association listed has a Web site and links are provided to them by Bosman.

A major Catholic research effort is conducted by the Center for Applied Research in the Apostolate (CARA, Georgetown University, Washington, DC 20057).

The subject of special collections in the field of religion would provide material sufficient for an entire book. The best starting point for a search is under "Religion" in *Subject Collections* (7th ed., R. R. Bowker, 1993) by Lee Ash and William G. Miller. For more specialized inquiries, look under names of denominations, individual religions, and personal names of religious leaders.

The literature will also guide the reader to articles on individual special collections, exhibits, and reviews. Two recent examples are R. Simon, "Saved: The Gambold Collection of Moravian Devotional Books," *North Carolina Libraries* 56 (Spring 1998): 4–10, and Guy Lamolinara, "Let There Be Light" *Library of Congress Information Bulletin* 56 (July 1997): 248–52.

G. K. Hall has published library catalogs of some outstanding collections, including the American Jewish Archives (Cincinnati), the Pontifical Institute of Medieval Studies (Toronto), Union Theological Seminary (New York), the Klau Library of Hebrew Union College (Cincinnati), Dr. Williams' Library (London), and Institut des Etudes Augustiniennes (Paris).

Thomas Slavens's *Theological Libraries at Oxford* (Saur, 1984) will also be of interest to students of special collections and religious libraries.

NOTES

[1] Kenneth McLeish, ed. *Key Ideas in Human Thought* (New York: Facts on File, 1993), p. 626.

[2] John F. Wilson and Thomas P. Slavens, *Research Guide to Religious Studies* (Chicago: American Library Association, 1982), p. 4.

[3] Lester Asheim, *The Humanities and the Library* (Chicago: American Library Association, 1956), p. 2.

[4]Walter Kaufmann, *The Future of the Humanities* (New York: Thomas Y. Crowell, 1977), p. 152.

[5]David L. Mealand, "On Finding Fresh Evidence in Old Texts: Reflections on Results in Computer-Assisted Biblical Research," *Bulletin of the John Rylands University Library Manchester* 74 (Autumn 1992): 68.

CHAPTER 6

PRINCIPAL INFORMATION SOURCES IN RELIGION, MYTHOLOGY, AND FOLKLORE

BIBLIOGRAPHIC GUIDES

General

99. Church and State in America: A Bibliographic Guide. The Colonial and Early National Periods. John F. Wilson, ed. New York: Greenwood, 1986–1987. 2v. ISBN 0-313-25236-X (v.1); ISBN 0-313-25914-3 (v.2).

This is a collection of bibliographical essays prepared by young scholars in the field. Following each essay is a bibliography of recent writings (the past twenty-five years), although some of the very important older studies are also included. Wilson explains the work in the introduction, in which he describes his preference for the listing of references that are broadly based rather than narrow in scope and are critical rather than prescriptive in tone. Volume 1 covers the colonial and early national periods and volume 2 covers the Civil War to the present. Each volume furnishes eleven bibliographic essays prepared by young scholars covering historical periods, geographical divisions, or topical elements. Each essay is accompanied by a listing of 250 publications. This work is a product of the Project on the Church-State Issue in American Culture at Princeton University, where Wilson holds an endowed chair. It represents an important attempt to enumerate those books and articles of comparative and historical natures that examine the early relationships between religious and political interests in our country. There is an author-subject index.

100. Church History: An Introduction to Research, Reference Works, and Methods. James E. Bradley and Richard A. Muller. Grand Rapids: Eerdmans, 1995. 236p. ISBN 0-8028-0826-3.

This is a brief but useful guide to the serious study and writing of church history, with excellent advice and recommendations of both resources to be utilized and strategies to be followed. Treated here are the difficulties of topic selection, the use of primary sources, and the manner of writing and documentation. There is a solid and well-constructed bibliography of resources, including reference tools and online databases. A chapter deals with perspective and meaning in history and examines the nature of objectivity in historical research.

The second edition of *A Reader's Guide to the Great Religions*, edited by Charles J. Adams (Free Press, 1977) is a more detailed but older volume that has been considered one of the leading authoritative guides in the field. It is a collection of thirteen bibliographical essays providing coverage of the history and traditions of the world's major religions. Each chapter is written by a specialist and includes a brief introduction followed by authoritative evaluation of many of the cited works. Topical coverage is given to primitive religion, the ancient world, Mexico, Central and South America, Hinduism, Buddhism, Sikhs, Jainas, China, Japan, Judaism, Christianity, and Islam. The appendix contains an essay entitled "The History of the History of Religions."

101. **Judaism and Christianity: A Guide to the Reference Literature.** Edward D. Starkey. Englewood, CO: Libraries Unlimited, 1991. 251p. (Reference Sources in the Humanities Series). ISBN 0-87287-533-4.

This is a handy guide to reference sources in religion, furnishing descriptive, and in some cases evaluative, annotations to more than 750 titles. The author is an experienced librarian with a master's degree in religious studies who has focused on what is called the Judeo-Christian tradition. Choice of entries is excellent, providing a fundamental listing of the most important English-language resources, with coverage given to numerous dictionaries as well as bibliographical sources. Annotations vary in length, with a number receiving in-depth commentary. Biblical sources are included and represent a substantial portion of the total. Arrangement of entries is by format or type of source within twenty-one chapters, such as bibliographies or encyclopedias. There is a useful and informative introduction furnishing some insight into the nature of research and acquisition of resources. An author/title index along with a subject index furnish access.

102. **Library Research Guide to Religion and Theology: Illustrated Search Strategy and Sources.** 2d ed. rev. James R. Kennedy, Jr. Ann Arbor, MI: Pierian Press, 1984. 59p. (Library Research Guides Series, no. 1). ISBN 0-87650-185-4.

Since the appearance of the first edition in 1974, this compact little volume has become recognized as an important aid to students in conducting their library research. As the reference librarian at Earlham College (noted for its heavy involvement in bibliographic instruction), Kennedy has produced useful and informative literature guides. In this most recent edition of the work on religion, he has continued his coverage of various aspects that have proved to be of interest, such as the choice and refinement of term paper topics. His "Library Knowledge Test" is still featured to help the user determine his or her ability. Most important, of course, is the information provided on the various tools and resources (bibliographic sources, commentaries, dictionaries, etc.) as well as databases that have come into the field. Sample questions are provided and a title index is included.

103. **Reference Works for Theological Research: An Annotated Selective Bibliographical Guide.** 3d ed. Robert J. Kepple and John R. Muether. Lanham, MD: University Press of America, 1992. 250p. ISBN 0-8191-8564-7.

Developed originally as a textbook for students of his course on theological research methods, the author's third edition represents an enlargement and expansion of the earlier offerings. It now provides annotated entries for some 800 titles arranged within thirty-nine chapters. Similar to the second edition in format, the first section is devoted to chapters containing general reference works and religious/theological works of a general nature (encyclopedias, handbooks, directories, bibliographies, etc.). There is a newly added chapter on computer-assisted research identifying online and CD-ROM databases as well as their guides. The second section furnishes a topical approach and covers reference literature for research on subjects such as practical theology, worship and liturgy, biblical studies, and various aspects of church history. The scope is limited for the most part to the Christian religions, with only brief coverage of Catholic materials because they are covered by McCabe's *Critical Guide to Catholic Reference Books* (entry 116). Nevertheless, it is extremely useful for the number of reference items listed. There is an index to authors, editors, titles, and variant titles.

104. **Religious Information Sources: A Worldwide Guide.** J. Gordon Melton and Michael Koszegi. New York: Garland, 1992. 569p. (Garland Reference Library of the Humanities, v. 1593; Religious Information Systems Series, v. 2). ISBN 0-8153-0859-0.

Melton, a prolific writer in the field of religion, has combined with Koszegi to produce a handy guide to reference books, bibliographies, databases, microform materials, and other publications. The work also serves as a directory of such resource units as oral history collections, professional associations, and research centers. There are over 2,500 entries arranged in various segments, beginning with the general concept of religion and proceeding to particular religions, organized geographically. Christianity is treated in a separate section, with chapters on the various denominations as well as church history. The scope is broad and sweeping (atheism and the occult are not overlooked). The breadth of the work may be faulted for resulting in superficial treatment of any particular element, denomination, or tradition, although certain areas are more thoroughly covered than others. The tool is convenient, however, and will find favor among reference librarians and their patrons.

World Religions Index (http://wri.leaderu.com/ [accessed December 1999]) is a useful Web site designed to provide Christians with an awareness of other world faiths and religious philosophies. It contains the text of informative articles on these religions as well as personal testimony; there are tables of data and links to relevant sites.

105. **Theological and Religious Reference Materials.** G. E. Gorman and Lyn Gorman. New York: Greenwood, 1984–1986. 3v. (In progress, projected 4v.). (Bibliographies and Indexes in Religious Studies). ISBN 0-313-20924-3 (v.1); ISBN 0-313-24779-X (v.2); ISBN 0-313-25397-8 (v.3).

The objective of this series of guides is to introduce students to the complete range of reference sources likely to be encountered in a program of religious studies. At present, three of the projected four volumes have been published, which when completed will approximate the generally accepted divisions of theology. Volume 1 represents general theology; volume 2 establishes coverage of doctrine and church history; and volume 3 embraces practical theology. The final volume, still in progress, will deal with comparative theology, and will also cover non-Christian religions. Each volume is meant to be used separately and provides several thousand annotated entries on the subject matter. There is useful introductory material regarding the nature of the topic in volume 1. Each volume is indexed separately by author, title, and broad subject.

Periodicals

106. **Religious Bibliographies in Serial Literature: A Guide.** Michael J. Walsh, comp. Association of British Theological and Philosophical Libraries. Westport, CT: Greenwood, 1981. 216p. ISBN 0-313-22987-2.

A useful and practical listing, this particular work targets the serial literature in terms of its ability to provide bibliographic coverage. There is a listing of 178 titles, most of which are indexes or journals with regular or major bibliographic sections or segments. The descriptions are detailed and provide awareness of content and analysis of completeness, availability, and general utility. Arrangement is also described. The scope is broad and includes most serials in the Western languages, as well as certain peripheral titles although they may not deal primarily with religion. There are subject and title indexes to provide ready access. Although the work exhibits a slight bias toward European serials, it represents an important contribution to the literature.

107. Religious Periodicals Directory. Graham Cornish, ed. Santa Barbara, CA: ABC-Clio, 1986. 330p. (Clio Periodicals Directories). ISBN 0-87436-365-9.

Religion is interpreted in a broad manner for purposes of inclusion in this directory, and it embraces periodical titles from a variety of related fields (history, anthropology, art, literature, etc.). The scope is international and includes periodicals from a range of denominations and sects. Periodicals are arranged alphabetically under one of six geographic regions: Canada and the United States, Latin America, Europe, Africa, the Middle East, and Asia and the Pacific Region. Countries are listed alphabetically within the regions, and entries include title, publisher, language, frequency and years of publication. Coverage by indexing and abstracting services is also indicated. There are both title and subject-geographic indexes. Over 1,700 periodicals are covered.

A more recent, but more restrictive, title is *Religion Journals and Serials: An Analytical Guide*, compiled by Eugene C. Fieg, Jr., as part of a series for Greenwood Press (1988). It serves as a very selective guide to some 330 English-language serials selected from a pool of 1,900 on the basis of importance. Entries are arranged alphabetically by title under various subject headings, such as history of religions, denominations, modern faiths, and so forth. Reviewers have criticized both the quality of annotations and selections for inclusion.

108. Religious Periodicals of the United States: Academic and Scholarly Journals. Charles H. Lippy, ed. Westport, CT: Greenwood, 1986. 607p. (Historical Guides to the World's Periodicals and Newspapers). ISBN 0-313-23420-5.

This is a highly selective but useful guide for those who seek to identify scholarly and academically oriented journals in the field of religion and religious studies. It is the only guide of its type to provide a complete focus on journals published in this country. It is likely to be the only one to treat the topic in such detail. Slightly more than 100 journals are covered. Each entry is described in terms of its subject matter, publishing history, and extraordinary features. Indexing services are identified. Information regarding title changes, volumes, publication, circulation, and editors are included. Appendices provide material of interest, such as a chronology of the periodicals covered and a listing of denominations. A comprehensive index by titles and authors concludes the work.

A more recent companion in the same series is *Popular Religious Magazines of the United States*, edited by Mark P. Fackler and Charles H. Lippy (Greenwood, 1995). It identifies about 100 popular religious periodicals that have been published in this country from colonial times to the present. The history and content of each magazine is described along with library locations and indexing sources.

Internet Resources

109. High Places in Cyberspace: A Guide to Biblical and Religious Studies on the Internet. 2d ed. Patrick Durusau. Atlanta: Scholars Press, 1998. 302p. (Scholars Press Handbook series). ISBN 0-788-50034-1.

The author has provided an increasingly comprehensive guide to the vast resources available to scholars, specialists, students, and interested laypersons in what appears to be a biennial effort. Access is made possible to a variety of religious studies, classics, and archaeological tools to aid not only religious and archaeological inquiry, but papyrology and history as well. In such a work it is difficult to remain current, and a periodic publication is warranted. The ongoing and dynamic nature of resource pursuits in this medium is described, and the varied aspects of Internet use are examined, some of which, like FTP (file transfer protocol), currently have less impact in view of the ascendancy of the World Wide Web. Treatment is accorded e-mail discussion lists, listservs, Web browsers, and telnet. There are suggestions for further reading, and a subject index provides access.

BIBLIOGRAPHIES AND CATALOGS

General

1 1 O. **Modern American Popular Religion: A Critical Assessment and Annotated Bibliography.** Charles H. Lippy. Westport, CT: Greenwood, 1996. 250p. (Bibliographies and Indexes in Religious Studies, no. 37). ISBN 0-313-27786-9.

Lippy has provided an important focus on modern religions in this country in an annotated bibliography of contemporary influences. Some 560 entries examine the nature, composition, customs, and practices of various nontraditional groups, both Christian and non-Christian. Coverage is divided into sections with listings on evangelicalism, fundamentalism, and the religious right; radio and television ministries; popular religions in the arts; self-help and recovery movements; traditional and unconventional approaches to personal spirituality; ethnic dimension; and biographical studies. Each section contains an overview of the topic. Several indexes provide good access.

*1 1 1. **World Council of Churches Catalogues.** Geneva, Switzerland: World Council of Churches Library, 1989– .

Available since 1989 as an online database, this work identifies the holdings of the library of the World Council of Churches, the international membership organization. Representing one of the well-developed collections of global perspective, the emphasis is on ecumenical history and theology. The work is divided into three major files: the Archives Catalogue, the Library Catalogue, and the Documentation Service Catalogue. Languages employed in the database are English, French, and German. Coverage begins with 1910 and continues to the present day. Updating occurs on a daily basis. The database is available from the World Council of Churches in Geneva, through payment of an annual subscription fee.

*World Council of Churches (http://wcc-coe.org/ [accessed December 1999]) is a Web site providing description of the organization's publications and projects as well as links to relevant text and sites of various religious groups.

Christian

1 1 2. **American Evangelicalism: An Annotated Bibliography.** Norris A. Magnuson and William G. Travis. West Cornwall, CT: Locust Hill, 1990. 495p. ISBN 0-933951-27-2.

Both this bibliography and *Twentieth Century Evangelicalism* appeared at the same time and cover much of the same ground. This one has twice the number of books and articles, however, and is the more extensive. Even so, there is a surprising lack of duplication in areas touched by both works, such as "The Bible." One is able to detect a greater emphasis on monographic literature as compared to periodical literature in this title. Also, there is a greater focus on the literature of evangelicalism rather than on literature about the topic of evangelicalism. Although this work is primarily focused on the twentieth century, the nineteenth century is surveyed as well. Annotations are brief, and there is an author index. This coverage is extended by the same authors in their recent continuation, *American Evangelicalism II: First Bibliographical Supplement, 1990–1996*, identifying the literature of the decade.

Twentieth Century Evangelicalism: A Guide to the Sources, by Edith L. Blumhofer and Joel A. Carpenter (Garland, 1990) is another offering of Garland Reference Library of Social Science (v. 521). More selective than *American Evangelism*, it serves as a useful complementary vehicle with a helpful introductory segment and a good subject index. Annotations are slightly longer than are those of Magnuson and Travis. Another useful tool is *Holy Ground: A Study of the American Camp Meeting*, by Kenneth O. Brown (Garland, 1992), which furnishes good bibliographical coverage of the literature as well as an informative history of the phenomenon that originated in the South during the late eighteenth and early nineteenth centuries.

113. **Bibliography of Published Articles on American Presbyterianism, 1901–1980.** Harold M. Parker, Jr. Westport, CT: Greenwood, 1985. 261p. (Bibliographies and Indexes in Religious Studies, no. 4). ISBN 0-313-24544-4.

Students and scholars of American Protestantism will find this recent work to be of great value in revealing the development of Presbyterianism in this country through a variety of published articles. This work includes but does not limit itself to national and regional secular reviews of a historical nature. Church reviews are also used, but house organs of churches are excluded. The author has compiled an excellent bibliography of nearly 3,000 articles, some of which would most assuredly be overlooked due to their nondescriptive or misleading titles or their surprising presence in certain journals. Entries are arranged by author and indexed by topic. Library locations are indicated because much of the material is difficult to obtain.

114. **Black Theology: A Critical Assessment and Annotated Bibliography.** James H. Evans, comp. Westport, CT: Greenwood, 1987. 205p. (Bibliography and Indexes in Religious Studies, no. 10). ISBN 0-313-24822-2.

Evans has provided a broadly developed, annotated bibliography of the black church in all its aspects. There are 461 books and periodical articles, primarily from religious journals. The work comprises three major divisions or sections, beginning with the origin and development of black theology, followed by liberation, feminism, and Marxism, and concluding with cultural and global discourse. Within the sections, the entries are arranged alphabetically by author under classifications by denomination and geographical region. A well-developed, cogent essay opens the work and furnishes insight into the nature of black theology. Annotations are informative, providing an awareness of the scope of the selected items. There is an index of names, along with a title index and subject index.

Black Holiness: A Guide to the Study of Black Participation in Wesleyan Perfectionist and Glossolalia Pentecostal Movements, by Charles E. Jones (Library Association/Scarecrow Press, 1987) furnishes a listing of 2,400 books and articles on the Holiness Movement. Existing on the periphery of mainstream religion, these charismatic movements influenced the lives of blacks even before their impact was felt on whites around the turn of the twentieth century. Jones has furnished historical and biographical commentary and notes that precede the various sections. This title represents a commendable effort to organize material that is elusive and difficult to locate, and is appreciated by scholars and students.

115. **Christian Communication: A Bibliographical Survey.** Paul A. Soukop. New York: Greenwood, 1989. 400p. (Bibliography and Indexes in Religious Studies, no. 14). ISBN 0-313-25673-X.

The author acted on a perceived need to provide a comprehensive bibliography treating all aspects of communication used by Christian churches or utilized in a style consistent with Christian ethics or practices. The work opens with a bibliographic essay identifying issues within a historical framework, while chapter 2 lists general resources, periodicals, directories, bibliographies, and catalogs. Chapters 3 to 9 furnish the topical approach, covering communication theory, history, rhetoric, interpersonal communication, intercultural communication, and mass communication. There are 1,311 entries; all are numbered sequentially. Annotations are thorough, reflecting the author's expertise in both theology and communications; books, articles, and dissertations are treated. The work is indexed by author, title, and subject.

A specialized tool is *Speaking in Tongues: A Guide to Research on Glossolalia*, edited by Watson E. Mills (Eerdmans, 1986), who supplies a collection of essays, commentaries, and research studies written between 1954 and 1980 along with a bibliography of relevant writings. The work opens with an introductory essay providing a historical overview of the topic. The essays are written by theologians, scholars, historians, and psychologists, and provide divergent opinions on the nature of this widespread phenomenon. There are indexes of names and of Bible references.

116. **Critical Guide to Catholic Reference Books.** 3d ed. James Patrick McCabe. Englewood, CO: Libraries Unlimited, 1989. 282p. (Research Studies in Library Science, no. 20). ISBN 0-87287-621-7.

Both of the earlier editions (1971 and 1980) were considered meritorious efforts in their thorough coverage of the subject, furnishing well-written descriptive and evaluative annotations of about 1,000 reference works expressing Catholic perspectives on both theological and secular issues. The new edition has been expanded somewhat in its inclusion of older titles excluded in previous editions as well as new titles. It retains its basic format of five major chapters dealing with general reference works, theology, the humanities, the social sciences, and history. The main emphasis continues to be on English-language titles, although foreign-language works are given ample coverage if available on this continent. Annotations are cogent, and access is provided through a comprehensive author, title, and subject index.

117. **Liberation Theologies: A Research Guide.** Ronald G. Musto. New York: Garland, 1991. 581p. (Garland Reference Library of Social Science, v. 507). ISBN 0-8240-3624-7.

With the increasing interest in freedom of individuals, there has been an impetus toward what is called "liberation theology," emphasizing the liberalizing influences and emancipation from oppression. Musto is an acknowledged advocate of these reforms generally opposed by conservative and fundamentalist theologians, and begins with an informative introductory essay describing the meaning and significance of liberation theology. Nearly 1,300 books are listed along with full and detailed annotations. Some contain vigorous emotional description; for example, Cardinal Ratzinger is labeled a "witch hunter." Entries are arranged in nine chapters by time period, geographical area, and topic. In perceiving that liberation theology originated almost as a grassroots Christian response to oppression (poverty, sexism, racism), Musto has represented the works of gay theology, black theology, and feminist theology in a fair manner, along with the writings of conservative opponents. There is an index of authors and one of titles.

118. **Women and Religion: A Bibliographic Guide to Christian Feminist Liberation Theology.** Shelley D. Finson, comp. Buffalo, NY: University of Toronto Press, 1991. 207p. ISBN 0-8020-5881-7.

As part of the increasing vigor with which the new liberation theology is being pursued comes this listing of books, articles, dissertations, reports, and other materials published over a thirteen-year period from 1975 to 1988. Feminist theology, along with gay and black theology, represents part of the reform movement forcing changes in mainstream religion and language usage within the Bible. The writings included here are recognized for their liberation perspective and critical interpretation of the female experience within the church traditions. Arrangement of entries is by subject, for example, Bible, history, ministry, and spirituality. This tool is of value to those students and teachers who wish to examine the various issues surrounding feminism and the church and serves as an excellent resource for women's studies. Of course, one must consult current indexes for the large amount of material that has appeared subsequent to its publication.

Non-Christian

119. **Bibliography of English-Language Works on the Babi and Baha'i Faiths, 1844–1985.** William P. Collins. Oxford: G. Ronald, 1990. 521p. ISBN 0-85398-315-1.

The author had served as the director of the International Baha'i Library at the Baha'i World Centre in Haifa, Israel from 1977 to 1990 and was well-prepared to take up this task. This is the most comprehensive bibliography of the subject in its attempt to identify all books, pamphlets, theses, and journal articles published in the English language on the Babi and Baha'i faiths. Approximately 7,400 entries are furnished within thirteen sections. The first six cover Baha'i writings of Baha'v'llah, the Babi 'Adbu'l-Baha, and others. The remaining sections treat the secondary sources. There is a well-developed introduction that outlines the Baha'i literature. Each section contains explanatory notes, with annotations for the most important entries. This has become the standard work in the field, and there are plans to continue the coverage with supplements for the period subsequent to 1985. There are detailed indexes by name, title, and subject.

120. **Guide to Buddhist Religion.** Frank E. Reynolds et al. Boston: G. K. Hall, 1981. 415p. (The Asian Philosophies and Religions Resource Guides). ISBN 0-8161-7900-X.

One of the initial publications in a projected seven-part series to provide basic resources for the study of Asian religions and philosophies, this guide provides an annotated listing of 4,000 items. Categories used in all volumes are general history, religious thought, sacred texts, popular practices, religious involvement in social life and politics, ritual and practice, and so forth. There is particular attention paid to the inclusion of appropriate articles from research journals. It has been noted that there is no annotated listing of journals used in this particular guide. There is an emphasis on English-language materials, and access is provided through author-title and subject indexes. (entries 121, 122)

The most recent addition to the series is David C. Yu's *Guide to Chinese Religion* (1985), which is complementary to the Reynolds guide because it excludes Buddhism. Instead, Yu identifies books and articles on Taoism, Confucianism, Lao Tzu, and even Maoism. Ancient superstitions are included within the same format as others in the series.

121. Guide to Hindu Religion. David J. Dell et al. Boston: G. K. Hall, 1981. 461p. (The Asian Philosophies and Religions Resource Guides). ISBN 0-8161-7903-4.

An annotated bibliography of 2,000 items, this work follows the procedure and pattern for the series (entries 120, 122). There is an excellent breadth in terms of coverage, with consideration given to art and anthropology. Annotations are well developed and descriptive of the topic under which the entry appears. Singled out for special praise by reviewers is this guide's section on bibliographies and research aids. An attractive special feature of this work is its annotated listing of journals. An unfortunate circumstance is the author's oversight in providing adequate access. There is neither a subject nor a title index but only an author approach. Happily, this inadequacy is not shared by other volumes in the series. Still, the work is extremely important for what it does.

122. Guide to Islam. David Ede et al. Boston: G. K. Hall, 1983. 261p. (The Asian Philosophies and Religions Resource Guides). ISBN 0-8161-7905-0.

Following the pattern of other volumes in the series (entries 120, 121), this guide is intended to provide the English-language reader with a sufficient choice of significant publications to learn about Islam as a religion and a civilization. Intended for the student at both graduate and undergraduate levels, the guide provides an annotated bibliography of nearly 3,000 items, mostly English-language books and articles. Most were published prior to 1977, a drawback for those expecting more recent coverage. As is true of all guides in the series, any of the publications listed may be obtained through the Institute for the Advanced Study of World Religions in xerography or microformat when not available elsewhere. It is reported that a supplement is being prepared to update the coverage. Like others in the series, this is a useful and welcome effort.

123. Judaica Americana: A Bibliography of Publications to 1900. Robert Singerman, comp. New York: Greenwood, 1990. 2v. (Bibliographies and Indexes in American History, no. 14). ISBN 0-313-25023-5.

Sponsored by the Center for the Study of the American Jewish Experience at Hebrew Union College, Singerman, a librarian of Judaica at the University of Florida, has produced an extensive bibliography on the topic. In so doing, he has incorporated all the entries from the standard resource, *American Jewish Bibliography . . .* , by A. S. W. Rosenbach (American Jewish Historical Society, 1926; repr., Canonymous Press, 1998), and its three supplements published in 1954, 1958, and 1971. Singerman has extended the coverage to 1900 (from 1850) and has added hundreds of titles. The present effort lists over 6,500 books, pamphlets, and serials written by both Jews and non-Jews examining the American Jewish experience. Entries are arranged chronologically, and library locations are supplied when known. This is a significant work with appeal to a wide audience ranging from scholars to interested laypersons. A detailed general index provides access by authors, titles, publishers, printers, and subjects.

A similar publication is *Judaica Americana: An Annotated Bibliography of Publications from 1960 to 1990,* by another librarian, Nathan M. Kaganoff (Carlson, 1995). The work is a two-volume cumulation of the bibliographies compiled by Kaganoff for the periodical *Judaica Americana.* Both adult and juvenile literature is included in book, periodical, and nonprint format; about 7,000 brief annotations are given.

Jewish Heritage in America: An Annotated Bibliography, by Sharad Karkhanis (Garland, 1988) is volume 467 of the Garland Reference Library of Social Science and presents a good array of nearly 325 books and 800 articles of both popular and scholarly literature. The author is the librarian of a community college in New York City and drew his entries from nearly ninety journals spanning a period of over sixty years from 1925 through 1987. Selection was based on the perceived significance of the topic and its treatment, with recognition of the need to furnish a balanced listing. Excluded are autobiographies, biographies, poetry, and fiction. Availability was a factor, with some emphasis on access through medium-sized libraries. Arrangement of entries is under seven broad categories, all of which are further divided by subcategories. Descriptive annotations are lengthy. Author, title, and subject indexes are furnished.

124. **Sikhs in North America: An Annotated Bibliography.** Darsan Singh Tatla. New York: Greenwood, 1991. 180p. (Bibliographies and Indexes in Sociology, v. 19). ISBN 0-313-27336-7.

As an authority on Sikh culture in the West, Tatla furnishes an excellent listing of books, articles, dissertations, reports, newspaper articles, and even audiovisual materials. Annotations tend to be brief, but vary considerably in size, with conferences and symposia treated in greater depth. Arrangement of entries is within topical chapters covering such aspects as employment, education, and family life. These follow an initial chapter on general sources, which includes useful listings of special libraries and archives, as well as newspapers and journals. There is an index of names but not subjects. The work follows the pattern set in Tatla's earlier effort, *Sikhs in Great Britain* (Coventry, UK: Centre for Research in Ethnic Relations, 1987) and continued in *Sikhs in Britain: An Annotated Bibliography* (1994).

Sikhism and the Sikhs, by Priya M. Rai (Greenwood, 1989) provides an annotated listing of English-language books and articles published since 1965. Entries are topically arranged and represent scholarly effort. There are author, title, and subject indexes.

125. **The Yogacara School of Buddhism: A Bibliography.** John Powers. Metuchen, NJ: Scarecrow Press, 1991. 257p. ISBN 0-8108-2502-3.

Sponsored by the American Theological Library Association, Powers has produced a unique specialized bibliography on the Yogacara school of Mahayana Buddhism. As an esoteric study, this work will appeal to a limited number of users primarily from the ranks of academe. The purpose is to list all writings on Yogacara in any languages of the world. The work is divided into two major segments, the first dealing with the primary sources of scripture written in Sanskrit, Tibetan, and Chinese. The second segment treats secondary sources or studies by modern authors and represents all languages both Oriental and Occidental. Five separate indexes furnish access to authors and titles of modern-, Indian-, Tibetan-, Chinese-, and Japanese-language publications.

A specialized bibliography of more popular nature is *Zen Buddhism: A Classified Bibliography of Western-Language Publications Through 1990*, by James L. Gardner (Wings of Fire Press, 1991). This is a comprehensive listing of more than 2,800 books, articles, dissertations, and essays written in various languages. Entries cover the concepts, functions, philosophy, people, and movements; and are classified by topic. The work opens with a brief introduction explaining the purpose and composition of the bibliography. There are well-constructed indexes to authors and subjects.

New Alternatives: New Age, Occult, Etc.

126. **Bibliography of New Religious Movements in Primal Societies.** Harold W. Turner. Boston: G. K. Hall, 1977–1992. 6v. ISBN 0-8161-7927-1 (v.1).

Planned as a series of four volumes initiated in 1977, only volume 1, *Black Africa*, and volume 2, *North America*, had appeared prior to 1990. Then, with a burst of productive energy following delays caused by relocation and the need to microfilm the documentation, Turner issued volume 3, *Oceania*, in 1990; volumes 4, *Europe and Asia*, and 5, *Latin America*, both in 1991; and volume 6, *Caribbean*, in 1992. This appears to have completed the project, for which the focus has been to represent those religious movements "which arise in the interaction of a primal society with another society where there is great disparity of power or sophistication." The volume on black Africa was designed to correct, supplement, and update *A Comprehensive Bibliography of Modern African Religious Movements*, by Turner and Robert Cameron Mitchell (Northwestern University Press, 1966; repr., University Microfilms, 1985). The second volume, on North America, emphasizes the United States, with subdivisions of Native American tribes, cults, and so forth, with smaller sections for Canada and northern Mexico. The additional volumes continue in the same tradition and now provide an important resource for study and scholarship. All volumes contain indexes of authors and sources.

Diane Choquette treats the emergence of new religious movements in North America in *New Religious Movements in the United States and Canada: A Critical Assessment and Annotated Bibliography* (Greenwood, 1985). She lists and describes nearly 740 books, articles, and papers housed mainly in the collection of the Graduate Theological Union Library at Berkeley. These movements began to emerge in the 1960s; they are accessed by author/title and subject indexes.

127. Channeling: A Bibliographic Exploration. Joel Bjorling. New York: Garland, 1992. 363p. (Garland Reference Library of Social Science, v. 589). ISBN 0-8240-5691-4.

A salient characteristic of New Age religious activity is trance channeling or the transmission of a message from the spirit world through a selected human being. This work is the most extensive bibliography of its kind, identifying more than 2,700 items dealing with this activity. They are listed in several chapters dealing with the history of channeling; channel revelations as found in books; UFO contactee channeling, including messages from extraterrestrials; and contemporary channeling, treating personalities and groups. An important feature is the introductory essay that precedes the chapters and furnishes exposition of various aspects such as the literature of channeling, mediums, history of different movements, and so forth. These essays furnish references that are linked to the entry numbers of listed works, affording a handy guide to especially relevant materials.

The Palmist's Companion: A History and Bibliography of Palmistry, by Andrew Fitzherbert (Scarecrow Press, 1992), is an up-to-date guide to the history and literature of palmistry. There are essays on various aspects of the art preceding an annotated bibliography of 560 entries. A title index provides access.

128. Magic, Witchcraft, and Paganism in America: A Bibliography. 2d ed. J. Gordon Melton and Isotta Poggi. New York: Garland, 1992. 408p. (Religious Information Systems, v. 3; Garland Reference Library of Social Science, v. 723). ISBN 0-8153-0499-4.

In this, the second edition of what has become a standard bibliography in the field, the authors have produced an updated and important volume. The magical community in this country increased greatly during the 1980s, and revision was needed since publication of the first edition took place in 1982. The work is divided into eight major segments, the first seven of which identify relevant topics such as ceremonial magic and traditional Earth religions. These sections supply 2,540 entries representing relevant books and articles. Secret works of various groups are excluded. The eighth section identifies current periodicals from all over the world. Appendices contain a listing of titles on witchcraft found in the New York Public Library in 1908 as well as the curriculum of the A.A. (Argenteum Astrum) employed by magical lodges. A name index of authors, editors, compilers, and translators provides access, format with special collections noted, and publications. Arrangement is alphabetical by state or city. There are additional listings of educational programs in universities, recording companies, and other helpful directories.

129. Parapsychology: New Sources of Information, 1973–1989. Rhea A. White. Metuchen, NJ: Scarecrow Press, 1990. 699p. ISBN 0-8108-2385-3.

With this work it would appear that White has established herself as the leading bibliographer on the topic of parapsychology, a field employing scientific methodology in examining unexplained phenomena. This useful bibliographic guide is a continuation and expansion of White's earlier effort issued in 1970, *Parapsychology: Sources of Information.* The present effort covers a period of more than sixteen years of published writings. Over 480 books are arranged under twenty-seven subject headings in the chapter on books. These subjects represent content, publication, format, or scope. Entries are numbered in sequence beginning with 343 (because the 1970 work ended with 342). In addition to the books, another 300 entries are furnished in chapters on periodicals, organizations, general sources, government reports, and theses. Entries are arranged alphabetically by author within each section. Annotations for books and organizations are detailed and in some cases are evaluative. There is a glossary along with various listings in the appendices. There are indexes by author, title, and subject.

INDEXES, ABSTRACTS, AND SERIAL BIBLIOGRAPHIES

*130. Catholic Periodical and Literature Index. Haverford, PA: Catholic Library Association, 1967/1968– . v. 14– . Bi-mo. with bienn. cum. ISSN 0008-8285.

The leading current index of the Catholic faith, this work was created from a combination of two earlier efforts. *Guide to Catholic Literature, 1888–1940* (Romig, 1940) provided an author-subject-title approach, identifying books and booklets pertinent to the Catholic faith or by Catholic authors. This was continued as an annual publication with four-year cumulations until 1967. *Catholic Periodical Index* (Catholic Library Association) indexed periodicals in the English language from 1939 to 1967 on a quarterly basis, with coverage back to 1930. The present work covers both books and articles. It provides annotations and an author-title-subject approach to several thousand adult books either by Catholics or on subjects of interest to Catholics, published during each calendar year. It regularly indexes some 150 periodicals, primarily in the English language. Articles are indexed by author and subject. In 1996, the publisher issued the work in CD-ROM format for the first time, covering the period from 1981 to 1994.

131. Critical Review of Books in Religion. Atlanta: Scholars Press, 1988– . Ann. ISSN 0894-8860.

This annual compilation of book reviews has been issued since 1988 as a cooperative venture of the American Academy of Religion and the Society of Biblical Literature. It is a full and detailed effort of some 450–500 pages that begins with several lengthy (as much as 100 pages) essays on important works such as the *Encyclopedia of Religion* (entry 151). These are followed by a number of shorter reviews of two to three pages classified in some twenty categories. Reviewers are specialists in their fields and sign their contributions. There is a list of new editions and translations in the appendix; indexes of authors and reviewers conclude the work.

*Index to Book Reviews in Religion is a bimonthly effort issued by the American Theological Library Association since 1986. It supersedes the book review index segment of **Religion Index One* (entry 135) and appears as an annual cumulation with the December issue. It indexes reviews published in nearly 500 journals. Online and CD-ROM availability is through **Religion Indexes* and begins with the year 1975. There is a three-volume cumulation, *Index*

to Book Reviews in Religion 1949–1974 (American Theological Library Association, 1990–1991), containing reviews that appeared in the initial effort, *Index to Religious Periodical Literature* (entry 135n).

*132. FRANCIS 527: Histoire et sciences des religions. Nancy, France: Institut de l'Information Scientifique et Technique (INIST); Paris: Centre National de la Recherche Scientifique (CNRS), 1970– . v. 24– . Q. ISSN 0180-9296.

This important abstracting service is part of the massive indexing effort undertaken by the Centre National, now taken over to a great degree by INIST. The Centre began indexing periodical literature of the sciences in 1940, then added humanities coverage in 1947. Many disciplines have been added as it progressed, including journals in the social sciences. All are covered by separate indexes bearing a number and subtitle. Thousands of international journals are covered on a quarterly basis in the humanities and social sciences and monthly in the sciences.

Coverage of religion has changed over time, with the print abstract journal undergoing various name changes. Initially, philosophy and religion were covered together in *Bulletin analytique: Philosophie* (v. 1–9); *Bulletin signaletique: Philosophie. Science humaines* (v. 10–14); *Sciences humaines: Philosophie* (v. 15–22); and *Philosophie, sciences religieuses* (v. 23). They were separated in 1970, with each discipline retaining the volume number in its new journal title. From 1970 to 1978, this title was known as *Bulletin signaletique 527: Sciences religieuses*. From 1979 to 1994 it was *Bulletin signaletique 527: Histoire et Sciences des religions*.

The current title ceased publishing in printed format as a quarterly abstracting journal in January 1995, and now operates as an online service with publication in CD-ROM. Bibliographic information is stored in a computerized database identified by the collective acronym *FRANCIS and is available online and in CD-ROM as part of *FRANCIS. The database for *Histoire et Sciences des Religions* contains over 200,000 citations, half of them with abstracts, dating from 1972 to the present. It adds about 10,000 records per year.

133. Index Islamicus. London: Mansell, 1958– . Q. with quinquenn. cum. ISSN 1360-0982.

This index provides a good coverage of books, articles, and essays on Islamic subjects. Hundreds of periodicals are examined, as are anthologies and Festschriften. There has been an increased coverage of social science issues in the past few years. This serial grew out of an earlier monographic publication, *Index Islamicus, 1906–1955*, by J. D. Pearson (London: University. School of Oriental Studies Library, 1958). This provided a catalog of some 26,000 articles in many languages on Islamic subjects. After issuing four supplements (1956–1960, 1961–1965, 1966–1970, and 1971–1975) in which 33,000 additional articles were identified, Pearson began his editorship of the *Quarterly Index Islamicus* in 1977. The fifth supplement (1976–1980) is in two volumes, with both monographs and articles receiving separate treatment. It cumulates the contents of the first five volumes or twenty issues of the *Quarterly*. Bowker-Saur began *Index Islamicus* in 1995.

*Islam is an annual index of books, journals, and newspapers available on CD-ROM. Coverage begins with the year 1991 and it is published and distributed by Hassan. The software is produced by Computerland.

134. **Index to Jewish Periodicals.** Cleveland Heights: The Index, 1963– . Ann. ISSN 0019-4050.

Beginning as a publication of the College of Jewish Studies in Shaker Heights, Ohio, this small index has held its own through the years. It generally indexes forty to forty-five periodicals relating to the Jewish faith or regarding Jewish life. It is considered an excellent source of information in identifying the thoughts and writings especially of American Jewry. All periodicals are in the English language, and book reviews are indexed. The material is indexed by author and subject and represents a wide range of interests and scholarship. Both popular and scholarly journals are included. The work is numbered as a quarterly, with each of the two issues receiving two numbers (1–2, July–December, and 3–4, January–June) per year; it is available through INIST.

*LC MARC: Hebrew is the quarterly computerized tape version from the Library of Congress, which furnishes its cataloging copy of all monographs in Hebrew and Yiddish. It is part of the MARC (machine readable cataloging) operation and is available through membership in Research Libraries Information Network (RLIN, p. xxi) or from the Library itself. Listing began in 1989.

*135. **Religion Index One: Periodicals.** Chicago; Evanston: American Theological Library Association, 1949/1953– . Semiann. with bienn. cum. ISSN 0149-8428.

Beginning in 1953 with indexing from 1949, the *Index to Religious Periodical Literature* established itself as the leading current index representing the Protestant viewpoint. With the title change in 1977, this tradition has continued and *RIO* has expanded its coverage to embrace over 1,400 titles in Western languages. Book reviews are listed separately, as always. While primarily concentrating on Protestantism, the index has traditionally demonstrated an ecumenical outlook and still selectively includes several Jewish and Catholic periodicals. It is indexed by subject and author, with a separate index for book reviews. *Religion Index Two: Multi-Author Works* (1976–) first appeared in 1978. *RIT* represents an annual index of composite works (compilations, anthologies, Festschriften, proceedings, etc.) published during the year covered.

The entire line of this very important family dating back to 1949 is available online through FirstSearch as *ATLA Religion Database. It is updated semiannually also and has about 1,000,000 records. CD-ROM versions are also available; *Religion Index One on CD-ROM has provided coverage of both *RIO* and *Index to Book Reviews in Religion* with coverage beginning in 1980. *Religion Indexes: RIO/RIT/IBRR 1975–on CD-ROM* (April 1993) furnishes coverage of *RIO*, *RIT*, and *IBRR* from 1975 to the present. Complete details of all publications and projects as well as the conference are found on the World Wide Web at the *ATLA Site Index (http://www.atla.com/s_index.html [accessed January 2000]).

*136. **Religious and Theological Abstracts.** Myerstown, PA: Religious and Theological Abstracts, 1958– . Q. ISSN 0034-4044.

Highly regarded as a nonsectarian abstracting service that covers 300 journals on an international basis. Abstracts are in English and average about 100 words in length. Journals represent a wide range of interests and beliefs and include representative titles of Christian (primarily Protestant), Jewish, and Muslim origins. There are five major categories or topical divisions: biblical, theological, historical, practical, and sociological. Each section is further subdivided, with numbers being given to each entry. Subject, author, and scripture indexes appear on an annual basis in the final issue of each volume. A list of abstractors accompanies each issue and abstracts are generally signed with initials. The work is available from the publisher on CD-ROM as *R&TA on CD-ROM;* it is updated on an annual basis.

137. **Science of Religion: Abstracts and Index of Recent Articles.** Amsterdam: Free University, and Leeds, England: University of Leeds, 1980– . v.5– . Q. ISSN 0165-8794.

This provides a continuation of an earlier bibliography that enjoyed an excellent reputation in the field. *International Bibliography of the History of Religions* (Leiden, Netherlands: Brill, 1952/1954–1973) was published under the auspices of the International Council for Philosophy and Humanistic Studies by the International Association for the History of Religions and received UNESCO support. An annual publication, it listed books, articles, and reviews for the year covered on the history of the various religions of the world. International in coverage, listings appeared in the language of the original document in a classified arrangement. An author index was provided. The present work retains the same sponsorship, with volumes 1–4 appearing under the title *Science of Religion Bulletin*. It covers nearly 300 journals representing all religions and time periods. Each issue is indexed by author and subject, both of which cumulate in the final issue of each volume.

DICTIONARIES, ENCYCLOPEDIAS, AND HANDBOOKS

General

138. **Angels A to Z.** James R. Lewis and Evelyn D. Oliver. New York: Gale Research, 1996. 485p. ISBN 0-7876-0489-5.

This is a handy compilation of information treating angels in various religious traditions and systems of belief, including the occult. Arranged alphabetically, the work furnishes some 300 entries on both individual angels by name and on topics relevant to their study and understanding of them. Such topics include their treatment in art, folklore, literature, music, film, and television. Entries furnish brief bibliographies that are supplemented by a concluding bibliography, filmography, and directory of organizations and firms. Included are black-and-white reproductions and a good index.

Another recent publication is *Encyclopedia of Sacred Places*, by Norbert C. Brockman (ABC-Clio, 1997), providing a good overview of important sites. Places of significance to various faiths and traditions are described briefly with a section on maps to identify specific locations. Appendices are quite useful in identifying sites by religious tradition and by country. A glossary is furnished along with a bibliography and index.

139. **Abingdon Dictionary of Living Religions.** Keith Crim et al. Nashville, TN: Abingdon, 1981; repr., **The Perennial Dictionary of World Religions.** San Francisco: Harper & Row, 1989. 830p. ISBN 0-06-061613-X.

Developed as a guide to the historical background as well as the belief systems and rites of religions that are still being practiced, this volume provides coverage of relevant issues and topics in an alphabetical arrangement. There are approximately 1,600 signed articles of varying length, with the religions receiving extensive coverage of anywhere from twelve to fifteen pages each. Many of the entries are biographical in nature and cover personalities associated with the religions. There is a fair amount of illustrative material: colored plates, maps (both in color and black-and-white), photographs, figures, and diagrams. Designed to be less technical than *A Dictionary of Comparative Religion* (entry 142), the work remains useful but certain parts such as canon law should have been updated with the reprinting. Cross-references and bibliographies are included.

140. **Contemporary Religions: A World Guide.** Ian Harris et al., eds. Harlow, Essex, UK: Longman; distr., Detroit: Gale Research, 1992. 511p. ISBN 0-582-08695-7.

This is a comprehensive information resource for all faiths and religious branches existing today throughout the world. Coverage is handled through three major segments beginning with a collection of seven essays on "Major Religious Traditions." These provide background information of the contextual framework of the various entries. Part 2, "Religious Groups and Movements," is the longest segment, incorporating over 800 articles on an array of faiths, cults, and denominations ranging from specific churches to movements and organizations. Included in this directory-segment are survey-length articles on such topics as Native-American religions. Entries vary in length from brief overviews of 100 words to lengthier expositions of 2,000 words. Coverage is distributed fairly, with approximately equal representation of denominations within and outside the Judeo-Christian tradition. Part 3 is a "Country by Country Summary" showing the distribution and influence of the different religions. There is a glossary but no bibliography, a serious deficiency for serious students.

Religions of the World, by Niels C. Nielsen et al., is now in its third edition (St. Martin's Press, 1993) and continues the excellent tradition of its predecessors, furnishing a first-rate aid for students at all levels. Each of the sections is compiled by an eminent scholar and represents a useful resource for both students and specialists. The initial section explores the basic questions and concepts that all religions share and also treats the important extinct religions of the past (Middle East, Greece, and Rome). The remaining segments describe the major living religions from both East and West: Hinduism, Buddhism, Judaism, Christianity, and so forth. There are many illustrations and there is balanced treatment of the various faiths.

141. **Crimes of Perception: An Encyclopedia of Heresies and Heretics.** Leonard George. New York: Paragon House, 1995. 358p. ISBN 1-557-78519-8.

Heresies or alternative perceptions of religious truths form the basis for this interesting and informative compendium of religious controversies in both Christian and Jewish traditions. The work provides coverage of personalities, cults, rituals, and practices in some 600 entries of varying length. Heretical influences in the West are featured, although Eastern Christian elements are included in some cases where there is influence on Western thought. Arrangement is alphabetical, and a good introduction places the topic in perspective. Concluding bibliographies provide additional reading, largely of historical matter.

142. **A Dictionary of Comparative Religion.** S. G. F. Brandon. New York: Scribner's, 1970; repr., Macmillan, 1988. 704p. ISBN 0-684-15561-3.

Considered a standard in the field, this work of British scholarship covers the beliefs, rituals, important personalities, schools, councils, and sacred books of the various religions of the world. Articles are brief, signed by the contributor, and generally have bibliographies. There is a certain degree of complexity associated with the comprehension of some of the articles, not true of *Abingdon Dictionary of Living Religions* (entry 139). Unlike *Abingdon*, however, this work includes religions not extant and provides a strong focus on intellectual history in its efforts "to treat the various religions proportionately to their significance in the history of human culture." Coverage of the Eastern religions is very strong and sectional editors describe Buddhism, Hinduism, Islam, China, and the Far East. There are no illustrations. The work has a synoptic index that groups all relevant entries under the name of the religion, as well as a general index of names and subjects. For optimal reference service, both Brandon and *Abingdon* should be used.

143. A Dictionary of Judaism and Christianity. Dan Cohn-Sherbok. Philadelphia: Trinity Press International, 1991. 181p. ISBN 0-281-04538-0.

The author is a rabbi and known advocate and promoter of Christian-Jewish relations who has succeeded in producing a useful comparative dictionary. Its format and style present a brief treatment of terms, concepts, topics, and issues spanning a wide segment of theology and religion. The design of the work is to represent these matters and furnish an explanation of how they are treated or accommodated by the two religious faiths. Such elements as anointing, education, original sin, and racism (which includes anti-Semitism) are juxtaposed in such a way that commonalities are readily seen and appreciated. The treatment of ecumenicism, for example, furnishes an excellent comparison of efforts within each faith and with each other. Few personalities are singled out for separate articles: Abraham, Adam, David, Elijah, and Jesus are among them. The tone of the work is fair, and it is written in a spirit friendly toward Christianity.

144. Eerdmans' Handbook to the World's Religions. Rev. ed. Pat Alexander, organizing ed. Grand Rapids, MI: Eerdmans, 1994. 464p. ISBN 0-8028-0853-0.

Another fine product from this reputable publishing house is this second edition of this comprehensive handbook that covers the world's religions. History, scriptures, worship, and customs are described in a lucid and comprehensible fashion. The new edition has been revised extensively and is generated through the work of some fifty specialists from a number of geographic regions. Generally brief in coverage, there is great breadth in the scope of this effort, which includes religions both living and dead. The work is divided into seven segments beginning with general history and proceeding to ancient, primal, then living religions. Development of religion is handled through descriptions of the nature of religious study, personalities and places of major importance, and origins and history. Unlike Brandon (entry 142), this volume treats Christianity separately. The "Rapid Fact-finder" is a glossary of terms and personalities. Subject access is provided through a general index.

145. The Eliade Guide to World Religions. Mircea Eliade et al. San Francisco: HarperSanFrancisco, 1991. 301p. ISBN 0-06-062145-1.

Begun shortly before his death in 1986, this work bears Eliade's name as his final publication. Like other products and projects with which he was connected, this guide is an excellent and authoritative handbook to the study of religions. Following a brief introductory essay, there are thirty-three chapters on different religious traditions both living and defunct. Emphasis has been given to the major traditions (Christianity, Buddhism, Judaism, and Islam). Described in concise but thorough fashion are the histories and doctrines, which are accompanied by useful bibliographies.

The Facts on File Dictionary of Religions, edited by John R. Hinnells (Facts on File, 1984), is a similar product from a noted scholar and authority, in which an attempt has been made to provide an exposition of all religions of the world in relatively compact format. It has succeeded as a reference tool of convenience and covers the various aspects associated with religious bodies. Good coverage is given to astrology, magic, and the occult. Technical terms, leading figures, and deities are covered in a lucid and learned manner. From the same publisher, *The Encyclopedia of World Religions*, by Robert S. Ellwood and Gregory D. Alles (Facts on File, 1998), is a resource designed for young readers from junior high to high school levels and seeks to provide more depth of coverage of personalities, topics, major religions, practices, and belief systems. Some 500 entries treat the subjects in a comprehensible and informative manner, although there is a danger of oversimplification in some respects.

146. Encyclopaedia of Religion and Ethics. A. J. Hastings et al., eds. New York: Scribner's, 1910–1927; repr., 1961, 1969, 1980. 13v. ISBN 0-567-06501-4(v.1).

Through the years, this work has been recognized as an outstanding example of scholarship and erudition. It remains the most comprehensive religious encyclopedia in the English language and has never been superseded or equaled in its treatment. Although old, it is not outdated, and provides long, scholarly articles on belief systems, customs, various religions, and national characters of religious movements in various countries of the world. Most impressive are the comprehensive articles on various social topics relating to ethical or religious matters, and the depth provided for exposition of various abstractions such as happiness. Anthropology, mythology, folklore, biology, psychology, and economics are among the elements considered in this expansive work. Articles range from brief (personalities get only a few lines of identification) to monographic in length. The final volume has an analytical index, an index to foreign words, an index to scripture passages, and an index to authors of articles. Although the work is of liberal, Protestant authorship, there is little sectarian bias.

147. Encyclopedia of African American Religions. Larry G. Murphy et al., eds. New York: Garland, 1993. 1006p. (Religious Information Systems, v. 9; Garland Reference Library of Social Science, v. 721). ISBN 0-8153-0500-1.

With the emphasis in the past few years on the black experience comes this comprehensive one-volume encyclopedia on the African-American religious traditions. There are some 1,200 entries, two-thirds of which are devoted to personalities. In addition to people, coverage is given to churches, organizations, topics, and issues dating from the eighteenth century to the present. All predominantly black denominations are included along with participation in mainstream traditions. The Nation of Islam is treated in depth with exposition of black Muslim developments of the twentieth century. Opening the work is a well-constructed introductory essay providing a detailed summary of black religion. This is followed by a chronology of major events. There are about thirty survey-length entries on major topics and issues such as the Civil Rights movement and abolitionism. An appendix lists organizations, and there is a comprehensive bibliography. Indexes of names, subjects, and organizations furnish access.

148. The Encyclopedia of American Religions. 5th ed. J. Gordon Melton. Detroit: Gale Research, 1996. 1150p. ISBN 0-8103-7714-4.

The initial edition of this important work was issued in 1978 by McGrath Publishing and later by Gale Research. The second edition appeared nine years later in 1987, followed by the third edition in 1989, and the fourth in 1993. It may have settled on a three-year frequency with publication of the present effort. The title has established itself as a solid source of information, and the new edition resembles its predecessors in scope and format. The present effort treats hundreds of religious bodies on the North American continent. Canadian groups continue to receive good coverage. There is a categorical arrangement that embraces the different religious families under various chapter headings. Both essays and listings furnish insight and perspective on traditional groups such as Lutheran and Reformed Presbyterian, along with more modern systems like the Communal, Metaphysical, Psychic, and New Age families. Information is provided on the various bodies (history, development, organizational aspects) as well as a bibliography and bibliographic notes.

A useful companion work is Melton's two-volume *Encyclopedia of American Religions: Religious Creeds* (Gale Research, 1993–1994), which enumerates more than 450 religious creeds, confessions, statements of faith, summaries of belief, and articles of religion associated with all types of religions practiced in the United States and Canada. There are indexes by creed/organization name and by keyword. Another useful source with a fine reputation is Frank S. Mead's *Handbook of Denominations in the United States*, revised by Samuel S. Hill for its tenth edition (Abingdon, 1995). Although not as detailed as the Melton effort, information in Mead is well-developed, furnishing history, doctrine, governance, and statistics for more than 200 religious groups. Useful listings are given in an appendix; glossary, bibliography, and index are provided.

149. Encyclopedia of American Religious History. Edward L. Queen et al. New York: Facts on File, 1996. 2v. ISBN 0-8160-2406-5.

Similar in scope to *Encyclopedia of the American Religious Experience* (entry 152) but with less depth, this serves as an excellent source of brief information, treating an array of religious topics, issues, denominations, personalities, movements, and so forth found in the United States. It examines both traditional and nontraditional influences with entries of varying length arranged alphabetically to expedite information retrieval. More than 500 entries are used, in which the diversity of the religious influences are examined within each of the major faiths represented.

Encyclopedia of Religious Controversies in the United States, edited by George Shriver and Bill J. Leonard (Greenwood, 1997) is more narrowly focused on the identification and descriptive treatment of personalities, themes, issues, terms, and topics associated with religious controversy in the United States. Included are controversies of both general nature such as homosexuality and those of consequential significance only to certain denominations. The emphasis is on Christianity, but other faiths are covered.

150. The Encyclopedia of Native American Religions. Arlene Hirschfelder and Paulette Moulin. Facts on File, 1992. 367p. ISBN 0-8160-2017-5.

This one-volume encyclopedia is the only reference tool devoted to Native American religions and will be a welcome resource for libraries serving a variety of students from junior high school to undergraduate levels. It furnishes easily comprehended descriptions of spiritual and religious traditions and personalities associated with Native American observance. Included here are ceremonies, rituals, terminology, and biographies of Native American healers, Christian missionaries, and others; relevant court cases; religious sites; and mythology. All entries are alphabetically arranged, vary in length from a few sentences to several pages, and furnish dates and tribal affiliations. Most entries run one or two paragraphs. To facilitate learning, there are photographs, line drawings, and maps. Hirschfelder is a prolific writer who has worked for the Association on American Indian Affairs for more than thirty years; Moulin is a member of the Ojibwa (Chippewa) tribe.

*151. The Encyclopedia of Religion. Mircea Eliade, ed.-in-chief. New York: Macmillan, 1987; repr., 1993, 1995. 16v. in 8. ISBN 0-02-897135-3.

Eliade's comprehensive encyclopedia represents an extraordinary project, furnishing over 2,700 entries by 1,400 eminent scholars. Entries generally consist of broad descriptive narratives on religious traditions, individuals, and themes. The book's coverage is worldwide, with especially good treatment of Eastern religions and cultures. Emphasis is on detailed examination of individual traditions and comparative study of religions. Articles provide an overview of the topic, details on particular aspects of the topic, and some bibliography (although this is not complete). Biographical and narrow topics occasionally receive briefer treatment. The work is aimed at the student or nonspecialist, but the great amount of information provided makes it valuable to the serious scholar as well. The final volume was issued a year after the encyclopedia was first published and provides a thorough topical index along with a synoptic outline of contents. In 1996, the publisher made the work available on CD-ROM.

An Encyclopedia of Religion, by Vergilius T. A. Ferm (Philosophical Library, 1945; repr., 1981), retains a place in the minds of reference librarians and on the shelves of reference collections. It represents a broad coverage of all religions even though it is written from a Protestant point of view. Entries are generally brief and cover a variety of topics—terms are identified; feast names are identified; persons, movements, and institutions are explained—and are particularly good in the coverage of Oriental religion. The *Encyclopedia* furnishes brief treatment of various denominations, theologies, and personalities associated with all faiths. Bibliographies are included.

152. **Encyclopedia of the American Religious Experience: Studies of Traditions and Movements.** Charles H. Lippy and Peter W. Williams, eds. New York: Scribner's, 1988. 3v. ISBN 0-684-18062-6.

This three-volume encyclopedia recalls an earlier period of encyclopedia production featuring monographic-type essays of substance and depth. There are 100 essays of about seventeen to eighteen pages each produced by young scholars writing in a clear and readable style. Each essay concludes with a summary paragraph and a bibliography of books and articles. The work is scholarly in terms of breadth and depth of coverage; both historical and contemporary conditions are covered. Entries are organized into nine major segments dealing with approaches to religion, principal religious groups, movements, the arts, politics, education, and other pertinent topics. It serves as a reference tool both for students and scholars and an agreeable reading experience for those interested.

153. **New Handbook of Living Religions.** John R. Hinnells, ed. Cambridge, MA: Blackwell, 1997. 902p. ISBN 0-63-118275-6.

This is a revised and expanded edition of the original work published by Viking in 1984 and retains its clarity and lucid treatment. The living religions of the world are described in much more depth than is true of *Abingdon Dictionary of Living Religions* (see entry 139). The detailed survey describes the religions of our time in regard to their practices, tenets, rites, customs, teachings, and traditions. Christianity and Judaism are covered, as are Hinduism, Islam, Zoroastrianism, Sikhism, Bahaism, and so forth. As in the past, there are many contributors. The general pattern for each religion includes several segments beginning with an introduction (primary sources) and progressing to historical development, critical assumptions, main teachings, practices, traditions, and twentieth-century development. There is a brief bibliography for each religion; a general index and a general bibliography conclude the work.

154. **The New Westminister Dictionary of Liturgy and Worship.** J. G. Davies, ed. Philadelphia: Westminster, 1986. 544p. ISBN 0-664-21270-0.

Published in both Great Britain and the United States, this excellent reference tool first appeared in 1972. The new edition represents a revision and slight expansion of the earlier publication, with about sixty new entries as well as modification of existing ones. It has been described by reviewers as having a greater spirit of ecumenicism that provides an attitude more receptive to ethnic pluralism and greater participation by the laity in church ritual. Treatment of women is timely, with articles on ordination of women, the feminist liturgical movement, and women and worship. Emphasis is on conceptual awareness rather than definitions of precise terms, and it is quite possible that a person unfamiliar with terminology may not come away with a precise understanding. Articles vary in length and cover both Christian and non-Christian religions. The tool provides a necessary ingredient to the religion collection.

A more recent but somewhat less authoritative and less exhaustive publication is *The ABCs of Worship: A Concise Dictionary*, by reform Presbyterian pastor Donald Stake Wilson (Westminster/John Knox Press, 1992). This handy work provides generally useful definitions of 176 terms both historical and contemporary. Definitions average close to a page in length, although some are much briefer.

*155. **On Common Ground: World Religions in America.** New York: Columbia University Press, 1997. (CD-ROM). ISBN 0-231-10898-2.

This is an impressive multi-cultural work originating at Harvard University, and is the result of several years of effort. It contains 3,000 pages of text, 2,000 photographs and maps, and 100 sound bites, treating fifteen religious traditions in terms of their history, belief systems, customs, and practices. The work is dynamic in that additional sites will be added and texts will be updated as the work progresses. It represents a potent source of information on the various religions both traditional and nontraditional, and serves as a prototype of the future of such sources in terms of design and search qualities.

In contrast to the modern quality of *On Common Ground* is the much-respected standard source, *Profiles in Belief: The Religious Bodies of the United States and Canada*, by Arthur C. Piepkorn (Harper & Row, 1977–1979). Piepkorn had prepared four volumes of what was to be a seven-volume work. These four volumes were published posthumously under his name. The first two volumes on Catholicism and Protestantism still are considered outstanding by scholars and students for their exposition of history, beliefs, statistics, liturgy, and practice. Volume 3 ("Holiness and Pentecostal") and Volume 4 ("Evangelical, Fundamentalist, and Other Christian Bodies") were issued in one binding, with volume 3 approaching the level of quality associated with the earlier volumes. Although volume 4 displays less familiarity with the subject matter, when taken as a set the work represents a still-useful tool for scholarly inquiry. It furnishes coverage of the historical background of the various religious bodies in the United States, with each volume examining history, beliefs, statistics, and practices.

156. **Die Religion in Geschichte und Gegenwart. Handworterbuch fur Theologie und Religionwissenschaft.** Tubingen, West Germany: Mohr, 1957–1965; repr., 1986. 7v. ISBN 3-16-145098-1.

One of the outstanding multi-volume sets, this work has earned a reputation for excellence in scholarship. Known and identified simply as *RGG*, it features signed articles and bibliographies of considerable length. Coverage is given to all religions, and it remains an important contribution by German Protestant scholarship. This authoritative tool includes biographical sketches of living as well as dead persons. Biographical notes on the more than 3,000 contributors are found in volume 7, the "Registerband." There is an extensive subject index.

157. **Religion: A Cross-Cultural Encyclopedia.** David Levinson. Santa Barbara, CA: ABC-Clio, 1996. 288p. (Encyclopedias of the Human Experience). ISBN 0-87436-865-0.

This is a concise but useful source of information on the doctrines, rituals, superstitions, and belief systems of an array of world religions in some fifty entries. Entries tend to be brief and treat either an individual religion (Christianity, Buddhism, Islam, Judaism, etc.) or common elements in the religions such as prayer, festivals, and the soul. Entries include statistical and comparative data and conclude with a bibliography. Special features include a chronology and maps; access is provided by a detailed index.

Religious Cultures of the World: A Statistical Reference, by Philip M. Parker (Greenwood, 1997), is volume 1 of *Cross-Cultural Statistical Encyclopedia of the World*, and provides a statistical demographic survey of the world's religions today. The author serves as an academic in business and marketing in France, and treats the statistical study of religion as a critical factor in economic development and demographic behavior. More than 26,000 statistics are furnished for more than seventy religious groups, with comparisons of religious cultures in economic resources.

158.   This Day in Religion. Ernie Gross. New York: Neal-Schuman, 1990. 294p. ISBN 1-55570-045-4.

Developed in the tradition of the "book of days," this religious chronology provides a needed, comprehensive, and easy-to-use reference tool. Each day of the year is given coverage through a tabular format, supplying one or two sentences identifying the religious events that occurred on that particular day. Emphasis has been placed on the Western Christian tradition, although important dates from the Jewish and Eastern faiths have been included. Coverage ranges from about A.D. 300 to the time of publication, providing an up-to-date source of information. The greatest limitation of the tool is its emphasis on mainstream religion, with little attention given to the smaller sects and religious bodies. In other respects, it is a solid effort and represents a good source of information for a variety of uses. Also included are a glossary and bibliography, along with an extensive general index.

Religious Holidays and Calendars: An Encyclopedic Handbook, by Aidan Kelly et al. (Omnigraphics, 1993), is a slender volume providing identification of some 300 religious holidays. The work is divided into two segments, the first of which supplies a relatively detailed introductory history of religious calendars, followed by the main text describing the various holidays and their dates of observance. There is a general bibliography and several indexes.

159.   Treasury of Religious Quotations. Gerald Tomlinson, comp. and ed. Englewood Cliffs, NJ: Prentice-Hall, 1991. 341p. ISBN 0-13-276429-6.

This is a unique tool in its focus on religious quotations, and draws from a wide array of talent and perspective. Philosophers from Martin Buber to Woody Allen are included, along with religious leaders from all faiths and denominations. Stature and status vary among the quoted personalities, and source material includes the Bible, Book of Mormon, Koran, ecclesiastical writings, and more. There are over 2,000 quotations, preceded by an introductory section explaining the purpose and method of selection. Arrangement of entries is alphabetical by subject, beginning with "achievement" and concluding with "zeal." A useful feature is the segment of brief biographies of the personalities quoted, which follows the main body. This is followed by an exposition of thirty religions and philosophies, then a bibliography of some 250 basic sources. A general index concludes the work.

Christian

160.   The Cambridge Companion to Christian Doctrine. Colin F. Gunton, ed. New York: Cambridge University Press, 1997. 307p. ISBN 0-521-47118-4.

This recent effort is divided into fourteen chapters, each by different scholars, examining the historical development, intellectual basis, and essential elements of Christian doctrine. There is emphasis on the recent inquiries of modernism and post-modernism, and critical exposition of such aspects as the Trinity, church and sacraments, Christ, the Holy Spirit, and the Creation is presented. There is a glossary along with a chronology of major thinkers and church councils and a useful bibliography.

The Westminster Dictionary of Christian Theology, edited by Alan Richardson and John Bowden (Westminster, 1983), is based on Richardson's earlier work in 1969 (a standard for Protestant theology), but this effort represents an important tool because of the contributions of 175 scholars representing Protestant, Anglican, Catholic, and Orthodox traditions. Theological thought is presented in a historical context in nearly 600 signed articles, most of which are accompanied by bibliographies treating biblical, patristic, medieval, reformation, and modern periods. There are no biographical sketches in this version.

161. **The Coptic Encyclopedia.** Aziz S. Ataya, ed.-in-chief. New York: Macmillan, 1991. 8v. ISBN 0-02-897025-X.

This is a monumental source of information on the Coptic people and their representation in culture, history, and religious tradition, and will be the standard for years to come. Some 2,800 articles in the first seven volumes provide comprehensive coverage of movements, doctrines, rites, canonical literature, art, history, geography, customs, and personalities of this Eastern branch of Christianity that developed in Egypt during the late classical and early medieval periods. Today the Coptic church represents a small but spiritually active segment for which reference tools were noticeably lacking. The present effort has filled the void with its authoritative treatment; articles have been signed by over 260 specialists and scholars. There are numerous photographs and line drawings to illustrate points and provide insight. Volume 8 furnishes maps, technical articles on Coptic linguistics, and an index to the set.

162. **Dictionary of Christian Lore and Legend.** J. C. J. Metford. New York: Thames and Hudson, 1983. 272p. ISBN 0-500-11020-4.

This work succeeds in its purpose to provide a guide to the major elements of the Christian tradition as represented in the arts, music, and literature. There are over 1,700 generally brief definitions, covering architectural features of church buildings as centers of worship, the liturgy, symbols and symbolism, biblical characters, saints, and tales of the Christian religion. "Lore" is interpreted to be knowledge relating to Christian culture, while "legend" represents narrative that should be read regardless of belief in its veracity. Developed as a resource for the nonspecialist, the work is written in a clear, readable style, and provides numerous illustrations in black-and-white. There are cross-references but no bibliographies.

Another title of popular interest is *The Dictionary of Bible and Religion*, by William H. Gentz (Abingdon, 1986), which provides clear exposition not only of the Bible, but also of the history and doctrine of Christianity. Various religions are explained in a lucid manner. The text is accompanied by photographs, illustrations, and colored maps. The work is the product of twenty-eight ecumenically Christian contributors whose viewpoints range from conservative to liberal.

163. **Dictionary of Christianity in America.** Daniel G. Reid et al., eds. Downers Grove, IL: Intervarsity Press, 1990. 1305p. ISBN 0-8308-1776-X.

This one-volume dictionary furnishes comprehensive coverage of Christianity in English-language countries of North America, providing 2,400 articles embracing some 4,000 topics contributed by 500 scholars. Reid and his team begin the work with an introductory essay on the history of Christianity in America and supply a guide to its use as a reference tool and source of information. The publisher is generally associated with evangelical materials, but has succeeded in producing an objective, descriptive work giving insight and enlightenment to American traditions. Included here is clear treatment of denominations, movements, events, institutions, and personalities; all are alphabetically arranged and easy to read. Emphasis has been placed on historical development rather than contemporary conditions, although popular living personalities (Billy Graham, Jerry Falwell, Jimmy Swaggart, and others) are included. Bibliographies accompany many of the entries. An abbreviated version, *Concise Dictionary of Christianity in America*, was edited by Reid and his associates in 1995. The work is a severe condensation, omitting the bibliographies and many of the longer essays and shortening all articles.

Dictionary of Heresy Trials in American Christianity, edited by George H. Shriver (Greenwood, 1997), is similar to the editor's *Encyclopedia of Religious Controversies in the United States* (entry 149n) but is limited to the Christian faith. This effort treats fifty heresy trials ranging from the colonial period to the present day. Entries are arranged alphabetically and seek to provide historical description and analysis of the organizations or personalities involved. One is able to detect a bias in favor of the heretics in the descriptions.

164. **Dictionary of Pentecostal and Charismatic Movements.** Stanley M. Burgess et al., eds. Grand Rapids: Zondervan, 1988; repr. with corr., Regency Reference Library, 1993. 914p. ISBN 0-310-44100-5.

The segment of evangelical Christianity treated here represents the fastest growing Christian movement in the world, a fact that justifies the specialized treatment of this one-volume effort. There are some 800 entries providing description and awareness of denominations, issues, topics, and personalities important to the understanding of the Pentecostal and Charismatic movements. They furnish bibliographies also. Personalities range from the famous to the obscure and represent a wide array of intellect and advocacy. Reviewers have pointed out a bias in favor of born-again individuals. Entries are supplied by over sixty contributor-specialists from seminaries, pastorates, and university religious departments. A good five-page introduction opens the work by providing a historical perspective; a general bibliography concludes the effort. There is no index, but access is aided through cross-references within the entries.

165. **Dictionary of the Ecumenical Movement.** Nicholas Lossky et al., eds. William B. Eerdmans, 1991. 1196p. ISBN 0-8028-2428-5.

Produced under the auspices of the World Council of Churches, this dictionary supplies over 600 entries relevant to the understanding of the ecumenical movement. This twentieth-century phenomenon has sought to provide a unity among the diverse Christian groups on matters of doctrine, worship, and organization. It has proven to be a controversial effort, inspiring heated debate and fierce criticism that has not been fully addressed within the entries. Entries furnish awareness of important ecumenical themes, events, activities, topics, and personalities. Different regions of the world and various denominations are considered in terms of their ecumenicism. Entries contain bibliographies, and in some cases are accompanied by illustrations. Articles vary in length, with detailed treatment of doctrinal topics and brief coverage of personalities. Various scholars have contributed. Access is aided by a detailed index and cross-references within the entries.

166. **Dictionary of Theology.** 2d ed. new rev. ed. Karl Rahner and Herbert Vorgrimler. New York: Crossroad, 1985. Repr., 1990. 541p. ISBN 0-8245-0691-X.

The original edition of this work was intended for the educated German layperson interested in Catholic dogmatic theology, and the English translation in 1965 was heralded as a success. The new edition has been thoroughly revised on the basis of subsequent revisions of the German edition. The dictionary represents an excellent effort by two Roman Catholic theologians to provide a handy and useful exposition of Catholic theology and represents a wide array of non-biblical subject matter. Considered a modern work for the modern Catholic, its related areas of coverage include philosophy, psychology, and sociology. The entries are relatively short but show variation depending on the term being defined. There are numerous cross-references, and no bibliographies. It remains a worthwhile effort for purposes of brief identification of all elements related to Catholic theology.

A useful and convenient work is Millard J. Erickson's *Concise Dictionary of Christian Theology* (Baker Book House, 1994). It continues to serve as a compact but informative dictionary describing terms, individuals, and issues, with some coverage of related areas of philosophy and church history.

167. **Dictionnaire d'archeologie chretienne et de liturgie.** Fernand Cabrol and Henri Leclercq. Paris: Letouzey, 1907–1953. 15v.

A standard in the French language, this excellent and profound treatment of Christian liturgy and archaeology is without peer. Originally published as the third multi-volume set in a series of sets collectively entitled *Encyclopedie des sciences ecclesiastiques* (Paris, Letouzey, 1907–), it remains the most important and unique work of the series. There are excellent articles, all signed, with good bibliographies on all aspects of liturgy and archaeology of the early Christian religion to the time of Charlemagne. Coverage includes monuments, iconography, epigraphy, designs, diagrams, rites and ceremonies, numismatics, and symbols. Latin terms are defined as well. No other compendium of antiquities rivals this work for depth of coverage.

168. **Encyclopedia of Biblical and Christian Ethics.** Rev. ed. R. K. Harrison, gen. ed. Nashville, TN: Thomas Nelson, 1992. 472p. ISBN 0-8407-3391-7.

This is a paperback offering a "modest revision" of the first edition published in 1987, with only slight changes. Two new entries have been added treating AIDS and homelessness, the irrepressible societal phenomena of the past decade. Only nine entries have been updated, some understandably but others provoking some curiosity as to their selection. Revised entries appear for abortion, addiction, civil rights, contraception, euthanasia, fetal rights, the Kinsey report, nuclear warfare, and population control, while such topics as apartheid remain unchanged. There are the expected corrections of inaccuracies or errors in the previous issue, and greater emphasis on cross-references within the entries. Even now, the work has been criticized for omission of needed cross-references. It remains a solid effort, although relatively unchanged from its 1987 version.

169. **Encyclopedia of Early Christianity.** 2d ed. Everett Ferguson et al., eds. New York: Garland, 1997. 2v. (Garland Reference Library of the Humanities, v. 1839). ISBN 0-8153-1663-1.

There are nearly 1,300 entries contributed by 167 specialists in this revised and expanded handbook, initially published in 1990. All articles have been reviewed and many rewritten in the coverage relating to the doctrines, practices, art, liturgy, heresies, schisms, places, and personalities of early Christianity. Now in two volumes, the organization remains essentially the same, with treatment given to the period of some 600 years beginning with the life of Jesus and proceeding through the formative centuries of Christian development. Entries vary in length but tend to be brief, running from a few sentences to a half-page. Many obscure figures are treated, which adds greatly to the value of the work for academic libraries. Although the scholarship is primarily U.S. and Canadian, there is good representation from abroad. Entries are arranged alphabetically and supply definitions, background, and historical development during the early period. There is a detailed subject index providing excellent access.

Supplementing the *Encyclopedia* from the same publisher is an eighteen-volume set of writings and research studies by members of the North American Patristic Society: *Studies in Early Christianity* is also edited by Ferguson et al. and was published in 1993. Personalities, literature, worship, art, various doctrines, missions, acts of piety, and more are covered in the eighteen individual volumes, standardized at 400 pages each.

*170. **Encyclopedia of Mormonism: The History, Scripture, Doctrine, and Procedure of the Church of Jesus Christ of the Latter Day Saints.** Daniel H. Ludlow, ed. New York: Macmillan, 1992. 4v. ISBN 0-02-879605-5.

This is a detailed and comprehensive compendium of the Mormon Church, edited by a well-known professor of religion. Entries are well-written and organized under five major topics: history of the Church, scriptures of the Church, doctrines of Mormonism, organization of the Church, and practices of Church members in society. Certain controversial topics such as feminism, abortion, and racism are treated in a frank and forthright but succinct and nonjudgmental manner. Doctrinal concepts may be difficult to grasp. The first four volumes furnish more than 1,100 signed articles with bibliographies and cross-references. The optional fifth volume contains the sacred scriptures of Mormonism, including the Book of Mormon. Numerous illustrations accompany the text. Contributors to the encyclopedia are religious scholars of various affiliations. The CD-ROM version is available through Infobases of Orem, Utah; it does not contain the sample Mormon hymns.

171. **Encyclopedia of the Early Church.** Institutum Patristicum Augustinianum; Angelo Di Berardino, ed. New York: Oxford University, 1992. 2v. ISBN 0-19-520892-7.

This is a well-developed, informative work covering the history of early Christianity up to the eighth century A.D.. It is a translation of an Italian effort that was issued in 1983 and represents the combined scholarship of 167 specialists from seventeen countries and diverse Christian traditions. Entries vary in length but tend to be brief and cover aspects of archaeology, philosophy, linguistics, theology, and geography, with attention given to the influence of various personalities. Especially noteworthy is the excellent coverage given to the inter-relationships and interactions of Christianity with the pagan beliefs of the time. Lengthy coverage is given to certain philosophical systems such as Aristotelianism and Platonism. The work is well-illustrated with black-and-white photographs along with color maps, and a synoptic table of various events correlated with cultural/doctrinal elements. Bibliographies are up-to-date; a detailed index provides access.

Jesus and His World: An Archaeological and Cultural Dictionary, by John J. Rousseau and Rami Arav (Fortress Press, 1995), provides an examination of Christian antiquities useful to both students and specialists. There are 108 entries furnishing up-to-date information about personalities, sites, customs, and practices important in the comprehension of the cultural setting in which Jesus lived and worked. The work is illustrated with black-and-white drawings and photographs. Bibliographies will lead to additional reading.

172. **Encyclopedia of the Reformed Faith.** Donald K. Mckim, ed. Louisville: Westminster/John Knox Press, 1992. 414p. ISBN 0-664-21882-2.

The Reformed faith is viewed as the Calvinist perception of Christian faith based in the Protestant reformation along with that of the Swiss Reformation. Due to the impact of the Reformed tradition on Christianity in the United States, this work fills a void and represents an important acquisition. Although not detailed, it supplies a comprehensive effort with contributions from 200 scholars, mostly from the United States but representing international scholarship as well. Most important, these contributors represent the full range of thinkers from liberal to conservative and provide a balanced perspective for the work as a whole. There are some 600 entries, ranging in length from several lines to several pages according to the significance of the subject. Coverage is given to personalities, institutions, events, movements, issues, concepts, and topics. A brief bibliography of both modern and historical writings accompanies most of the entries.

173. **Encyclopedia of Theology: The Concise Sacramentum Mundi.** Karl Rahner, ed. New York: Seabury, 1975; repr., New York: Crossroad, 1982, 1989. 1841p. ISBN 0-8245-0303-1.

The parent work of this publication is the six-volume *Sacramentum Mundi: An Encyclopedia of Theology*, also edited by Rahner and others, and issued in the period 1968–1970. With it, the Roman Catholic faith received an eminent work of scholarship that reflected the perspective subsequent to Vatican II. Extremely technical in parts, it was not meant for the layperson but rather the scholar, specialist, or serious student. Topical material embraced a wide range of subjects. Five years later appeared this abridged edition, which was meant to appeal to the interested layperson. The emphasis was on ideas and movements, as it was in the original, and many of the articles were taken from the larger work and others of its kind. Coverage includes theological topics and current issues of importance. The language is clear and nontechnical, and references to source materials are provided within the text.

174. New Catholic Encyclopedia. New York, McGraw-Hill, 1967–1979; repr., Palatine, IL: Publishers Guild, 1981. 17v. Palatine, IL: Jack Heraty, 1989–1996. v.18–19. ISBN 0-07-010235-X.

Prepared under the supervision of an editorial staff from the Catholic University of America, this represents a completely new work rather than a revision of *The Catholic Encyclopedia* (1907–1922, 17v.). The older work continues to be used because of its excellent in-depth coverage of topics in medieval literature, history, philosophy, and art, as well as matters of Catholic doctrine. *New Catholic Encyclopedia* represents a timely and clearly written exposition from the perspective of the Catholic faith in the twentieth century. There are approximately 17,000 articles, all signed, on the Catholic Church in the world today, with an emphasis on the United States and the English-speaking world. Biographies are limited to deceased people. Bibliographies are given for most articles. Volume 15 is an index; volume 16 is a supplement covering developments from 1967 to 1974; volume 17 includes supplementary coverage of change in the Church; volume 18 furnishes an update of developments during the 1978 to 1988 period; and volume 19 treats the period 1989–1995. All supplementary volumes reflect a certain freedom of thought in the articles on abortion, contraception, women as priests, and so forth, which are handled in an objective and impartial manner.

A work that serves to supplement the encyclopedia is *The Catholic Fact Book*, by John Deedy (Thomas More, 1992). It contains much information on Church history, basic tenets, personalities, events, and documents, as well as definitions of terminology. Smaller libraries may use it as an alternative to the more costly encyclopedia. *Dictionary of the Liturgy*, by Catholic priest Jovian Lang (Catholic Book, 1989), provides details of the history of the development of Catholic liturgy since Vatican II. A bibliography of additional readings is included.

175. The New Dictionary of Theology. Joseph A. Komonchak et al., eds. Wilmington, DE: Michael Glazier, 1987; repr., Collegeville, MN: Liturgical Press, 1991. 1112p. ISBN 0-81465-609-9.

This is the first of a trilogy of refined works designed to provide exposition of the Catholic faith in the modern world. Subsequent to Vatican II there has been a review of theological positions held by many thinkers. In this work one finds both the traditional and the more contemporary perspectives with regard to the significance of the Bible as well as the various elements that combine to produce a prevailing theology. Issues and topics such as sin, sexuality, justice, and mercy are examined within the perspectives held by the contributors. Traditional, liturgical, and biblical positions are reviewed and explored by a group of Catholic scholars from English-language-speaking countries. Summations of contemporary thought are supplied. Bibliographies accompany the signed articles.

The New Dictionary of Sacramental Worship is the second of the publisher's offerings in this series and is edited by Peter E. Fink, S.J. (1990). The work seeks to inform the reader of the nature of liturgical reform since Vatican II. Most of the 300 entries examine the Latin rite of the Roman Church, although Eastern rites are included. Entries are long and represent detailed essays of the current scholarly position on large topics rather than specific terms.

176. The Oxford Dictionary of the Christian Church. 3d ed. F. L. Cross and E. A. Livingstone, eds. New York: Oxford University Press, 1997. 1786p. ISBN 0-19-211655-X.

This is a welcome new edition of a fine standard work (2d ed., 1974) known for its comprehensive treatment of all aspects of the Christian church. There are over 6,000 entries from several hundred contributors. It remains especially useful for its biographies, definitions, theologies, and heresies. Doctrines, movements, church bodies, events, and holidays are included. Bibliographies are routinely provided for most articles. The work has been reviewed and revised where necessary and shows changes in the sociological and theological perspectives, with new coverage given to such areas as feminist and liberation theologies, homosexuality, Russian Christianity, and influences in various developing countries. Intended for the intelligent layperson, its audience is well served by the new effort.

177. **The Oxford Encyclopedia of the Reformation.** Hans J. Hillerbrand, ed. New York: Oxford University Press, 1996. 4v. ISBN 0-195-10363-7.

Another major work from Oxford is this thorough reference work on all aspects of sixteenth-century European religious life. Not limited to treatment of Luther, Calvin, and the Protestant condition, some 1,200 entries with bibliographies, contributed by 450 scholars, give insight into the social-cultural aspects of the time that gave impetus to the Reformation. Such issues as prostitution, literature, capitalism, the arts, travel, and women are treated in the mix of social forces and influences that represent the spirit of the time and its impact. Covered here are sites, regions, historical events, religious groups, ecclesiastical institutions, creeds, theology, social history, religions of the masses, and personalities as well as Reformation studies. Various maps are furnished in the appendix; a useful index provides access.

178. **Schaff-Herzog Encyclopedia. The New Schaff-Herzog Encyclopedia of Religious Knowledge.** New York: Funk & Wagnalls, 1908–1912; repr., Grand Rapids, MI: Baker, 1949–1950. 13v; 1977. 15v. ISBN 0-8010-7947-0.

Based on the third edition of the monumental German work by J. J. Herzog, *Realenzyklopadie für Protestantische Theologie und Kirche* (Leipzig, Germany: Hinricks, 1869–1913), this remains one of the most important works from a Protestant perspective in the English language. It provides excellent, in-depth coverage on a variety of topics (historical, biographical, theological, etc.) relevant to Christianity. Some treatment is given to non-Christian religions and religious leaders of various affiliations. Much of the material from the German work has been revised and abridged to make it a more readable but no less authoritative effort. Considered to be weak in its treatment of biblical aspects, it furnishes a useful source of information on doctrine, practical theology, sects, denominations, churches, organizations, missions, and religious controversies.

A new work, *New Twentieth Century Encyclopedia of Religious Knowledge*, edited by J. D. Douglas (2d ed., Baker, 1991), is a major revision of the 1955 supplement to the *Encyclopedia*. It furnishes a useful tool in its own right with biographical sketches, articles on topics of more recent interest, and revisions of outdated entries. There are over 2,000 entries by 250 contributors. An example of ongoing, in-depth German Protestant scholarship is *Theologische Realenzyklopaedie* (de Gruyter, 1976–), which is projected to fill thirty volumes. So far, eighteen volumes have been completed, with volume 18 issued in 1988. The work contains long signed articles of a profound nature, complete with bibliographies. The focus is on theological issues with detailed exposition by specialists. It is less regimented to the strictly Protestant point of view than the *Realenzyklopadie*.

179. **The Westminster Dictionary of Christian Ethics.** James F. Childress and John Macquarrie, eds. Philadelphia: Westminster, 1986. 678p. ISBN 0-664-20940-8.

In this extensive revision of Macquarrie's *Dictionary of Christian Ethics* (Westminster, 1967), only about 40 percent of the entries were retained, and these were updated if necessary. Contributors from different parts of the English-speaking world, representing the various elements within the Judeo-Christian tradition, have provided a modern approach in examining the relevant issues of contemporary society. Not limited to theologians, this work presents the perspectives of philosophers, lawyers, and physicians in analyzing developments in science, health care, medicine, and so forth. Such sensitive bio-ethical subjects as abortion, euthanasia, and human experimentation are considered. Traditional concepts are covered, as are biblical ethics. There are no entries for individual thinkers; rather a thematic approach is taken in which individuals' values are described. A name index provides access within this context. Like its predecessor, this work should become a standard source.

A more recent treatment of a major ethical issue is found in *The Religious Right: A Reference Handbook*, by Glen H. Utter and John W. Storey (ABC-Clio, 1995). With the increasing ardor and sometimes unrestrained activity of this group, it is important that such a reference book examine its attitudes, belief systems, and activities. The work provides an annotated chronology from the nineteenth century to the present day in which events are described and explained. There are informative biographical sketches of various personalities; included also are a bibliography, directory of organizations, and glossary of terms.

180. **World Christian Encyclopedia: A Comparative Study of Churches and Religions in the Modern World, AD 1900–2000.** David D. Barrett, ed. New York: Oxford University Press, 1982. 1010p. ISBN 0-19-572435-6.

Based on an extensive survey and twelve years in the making, this work represents a major accomplishment, providing a detailed exposition of the entire realm of Christianity. Covering nearly 21,000 different denominations representing the beliefs of nearly 9,000 different groupings of people speaking over 7,000 languages, it is far and away the most comprehensive statistical reference work on churches and missions. Many non-Christian religions are covered as well. The volume is divided into fourteen major segments, beginning with a status report on Christianity in the twentieth century, followed by a chronology, a methodology of the survey, a cultural classification of peoples, and so forth. Of major importance is the seventh part, which presents the survey (arranged country by country), providing demographic and cultural information as well as narratives of the non-Christian religions and analyses of Christian history and current status. The remaining sections include statistics, a dictionary, a bibliography, an atlas, directories of individuals and organizations, and a set of indexes.

Non-Christian

181. **The Blackwell Dictionary of Judaica.** Dan Cohn-Sherbok. Cambridge, MA: Blackwell, 1992. 597p. ISBN 0-631-16615-7.

Designed by the author to provide students with a single-volume, comprehensive coverage of basic information regarding the Jewish people and their religion, it is conceded that this book affords no substitute for the multi-volume encyclopedia. The scope is broad and encyclopedic, however, in its treatment of all aspects of Jewish civilization. There are about 7,000 entries arranged alphabetically, covering terms, personalities, organizations, events, issues, topics, and objects relevant to the Jewish faith. Cross-references are well-designed and useful in revealing related entries. There is a chronology of Jewish history along with two maps.

Encyclopedia of Jewish History, edited by Joseph Alpher (Facts on File, 1986), is a one-volume effort designed to appeal to the popular interest, providing a comprehensive history of world Jewry. Information is brief and clearly presented with respect to Jewish history and culture. Personalities are included. *The Encyclopedia of Jewish Symbols*, by Ellen Frankel and Betsy Plakin Teutsch (Jason Aronson, 1992), is more specialized in its focus on some 250 ceremonial objects, concepts, and motifs as well as personalities, places, and events symbolic of Jewish culture. Description is lucid and detailed indexing and cross-referencing facilitate access.

182. **Dictionary of Non-Christian Religions.** 2d ed. Geoffrey Parrinder. Amersham, Bucks, England: S. Thornes, 1981. 320p. ISBN 0-7175-0972-9.

A slight revision, but not an expansion, of the author's earlier edition of 1971, this remains an important and useful work for its rather unique general coverage of non-Christian faiths. The belief systems, practices, gods, heroes, cults, and observances of non-Christian religions are covered. There is an emphasis on the systems of Hinduism, Buddhism, and Islam because they represent the largest non-Christian faiths, but other parts of the world are not neglected. Post-biblical Judaism, the Americas, Australasia, and Africa are covered in ample fashion. Entries are generally brief but informative and include cross-references when necessary. There are numerous illustrations, both photographs and drawings. Entries lack bibliographies but a general reading list is supplied at the end. Also included are lists of dynasties from different regions.

*183. **Encyclopaedia Judaica.** New York: Macmillan, 1972. Geoffrey Wigoder, ed. 16v. Repr., Jerusalem: Keter, 1982. 17v. ISBN 0-685-36253-1.

A comprehensive and authoritative treatment of all aspects of Jewish life is provided in approximately 25,000 articles, most of which are signed by a panel of some 1,800 international contributors and 300 editors. Most entries conclude with bibliographies, which stress English-language materials. An interesting point worth noting is the placement of the index in volume 1 to ensure its use to exploit the resource to its fullest degree. Biographical sketches are included and represent universal coverage of both living and deceased people. A yearbook series was begun the year following publication of the encyclopedia, but its frequency varies. Wigoder edited the CD-ROM edition in 1997 for Grolier; it contains the entire text with some updating and new entries. In 1999, the Encyclopaedia was issued in paperback format.

The work never succeeded in replacing its equally massive twelve-volume predecessor, *The Jewish Encyclopedia* (Funk & Wagnalls, 1901–1906), which remains an excellent scholarly resource for historical interpretation of the customs, cultural traditions, and practices of Jewish life.

An important publication in 1982 was the *Encyclopedia Judaica Decennial Book, 1973–1982* (Jerusalem, Encyclopedia Judaica), which covers the ten-year period 1972–1981 and includes updates, revisions, and so forth, complete with cross-references to the major work.

184. **Encyclopaedia of Islam.** New ed. H. A. R. Gibb et al., eds. Leiden, Netherlands: Brill, 1954– . v.1– ; London, Luzac, 1960– . 5v. and supp. and fasc.

The original 1913 edition of this work served as a dictionary of the geography, ethnography, and biography of the Islamic peoples and was regarded as a scholarly and authoritative publication. Revision began in 1954 and has proceeded slowly since that time, with no publication since 1986. The pattern of publication has been in separate fascicles that later become parts of bound volumes. Five volumes have been completed, with several fascicles to volume 6, placing it in the "Ms" in terms of coverage. Supplements 1–6 accompany the volumes at present. The new work, if and when completed, will have succeeded in providing a more current exposition of the Islamic tradition, with greater attention given to history, geography, and culture. Arrangement is alphabetical but includes terms from the Arabic which in translation may not be as familiar as English expressions. Cross-references are provided in many cases. Articles vary in length from a paragraph to several pages depending upon the topic. An index produced in 1989 covers the first five volumes and supplements.

Shorter Encyclopaedia of Islam, edited by Gibb and J. H. Kramers (Brill, 1953; repr., 1991) is a one-volume abridgment of the earlier edition and contains only those articles dealing with law and religion. *The Concise Encyclopedia of Islam*, by Cyril Glasse (Harper, 1989), is the most recent compendium on Islamic culture and religion. It is an excellent one-volume reference work that provides brief but lucid definitions and well-developed expositions of religious forms, ideologies, observances, and important personalities. Appendices include maps showing the spread of Islam, genealogical tables, and a chronology. More recently, *Islamic Desk Reference* (Brill, 1994) was issued as a source of quick information regarding personalities, terms, and events based on what has been completed of the new edition.

185. Historical Dictionary of Buddhism. Charles S. Prebish. Metuchen, NJ: Scarecrow Press, 1993. 387p. (Historical Dictionaries of Religions, Philosophies, and Movements, no. 1). ISBN 0-8108-2698-4.

This is a well-designed and important reference tool initiating a new series of historical dictionaries for the publisher. The author is a well-known scholar in the field and has done an excellent job not only in selection of terms, issues, personalities, events, texts, doctrines, practices, institutions, and movements for inclusion but in their accurate representation and exposition. Slightly over 250 pages of the text are used for the dictionary proper, while nearly 100 pages are given to a fine classified bibliography of real value to students and specialists. The remainder of the work includes introductory material: preface, foreword, and pronunciation guide, as well as an overview of Buddhist scriptures, a map, and a chronology. Most important is the excellent introductory history describing the origin and spread of the religion. Although the entries contain cross-references, an index would have been a desirable feature.

A Glossary of Indian Religious Terms and Concepts, by Narenda Nath Bhattacharyya (South Asia Books, 1990), is a compact and handy volume providing definitions and explanations of Hindu, Jain, and Buddhist terms. Distinctions are noted and nuances and subtle differences are described. Definitions tend to be brief and are intended to aid the beginner, but users at all levels will profit from the comparative approach. The work begins with a useful introduction covering philosophical aspects of meanings and examines the history of Sanskrit lexicography developed within a Western perspective. A bibliography is included, along with an index of words for which definitions have been provided under variant terms.

186. Historical Dictionary of Hinduism. Bruce M. Sullivan. Lanham, MD: Scarecrow Press, 1997. 345p. (Historical Dictionaries of Religions, Philosophies, and Movements, no. 13). ISBN 0-8108-3327-1.

This is a useful, up-to-date effort that not only explains the terminology relevant to the Hindu faith but also provides historical description and doctrinal exposition in a useful introduction. The author, an academic at Northern Arizona University, has also provided an extensive bibliography in several parts, such as historical development, sacred places, and so forth. There are 570 entries of varying length treating all aspects of the faith in lucid fashion. This includes personalities, movements, rituals, doctrinal aspects, schools, and so forth. Similar to other titles in the series, the work examines religious texts, the social order, the arts, and literature, and provides a useful chronology of historical developments.

Encyclopaedia of the Sikh Religion and Culture, by R. C. Dogra and Gobind S. Mansukhani (Vikas, 1997), is a reprint of a 1995 publication that succeeded in providing concise but comprehensive coverage of Sikhism, an offshoot of the Hindu faith that includes only about 2 percent of Indian population. Customs, castes, festivals, practices, gods, demons, animals, geographical features, and so forth are identified and defined in entries of varying length. Historical development is presented in a fine introduction.

187. Islam in North America: A Sourcebook. Michael A. Koszegi and J. Gordon Melton. New York: Garland, 1992. 414p. ISBN 0-8153-0918-X.

Up to now there has been a dearth of information sources regarding the development of the Islamic religion in this cotinent and region of the world. The *Sourcebook* furnishes a carefully selected array of documents that otherwise might not be found by students and researchers. There is a good mix of articles, bibliographies, and directories based on the holdings of the specialized collections at the University of California. The articles are written by Arab Islamic scholars and will be useful for black studies as well (Nation of Islam, African-American Muslim community, and more). Certain articles have been written for this work, others are reprints of historical value (Muhammad A. R. Webb's 1893 address on the spirit of Islam). The work is divided chronologically into eighteen chapters; most furnish relevant articles along with bibliographies. The last two chapters supply a directory of Islamic organizations and centers in North America and a listing of nonprint sources.

Islam and Islamic Groups: A Worldwide Reference Guide, edited by Farzana Shaikh (Longman; distr., Gale Research, 1992) treats the political focus rather than the doctrine of Islam. Coverage is given to Islamic political presence in more than 100 countries, describing the origins and developments, demographic representations, relationships to the government, and modern political activities. Arrangement of the work is by country, with narrative text followed by listings of organizations and publications.

188. Jewish-American History and Culture: An Encyclopedia. Jack Fischel and Sanford Pinsker, eds. New York: Garland, 1992. 710p. (Garland Reference Library of the Social Sciences, v. 429). ISBN 0-8240-6622-7.

This is considered by reviewers to be a groundbreaking work, presenting a well-designed and clearly written one-volume source of information of comprehensive nature revealing the richness and depth of contribution of the Jewish experience in America. Entries are alphabetically arranged and describe all aspects of life such as arts, economics, history, humanities, military, sciences, social institutions, organizations, and popular culture. Personalities are covered in liberal fashion. Entries range in size from brief to detailed survey length and furnish not only description but in many cases critical evaluation as well. Useful bibliographies accompany most entries, allowing the reader to research the topic further. Contributors to the work are specialists in the field of Jewish studies who provide an enlightening and fair-minded exposition. Useful listings include Jewish Nobel Prize winners and libraries with extensive collections on the subject.

189. The New Standard Jewish Encyclopedia. 7th ed. Geoffrey Wigoder, ed. Facts on File, 1992. 1001p. ISBN 0-8160-2690-4.

Now in its seventh edition, this well-known and frequently used one-volume information source was edited initially by Cecil Roth. Wigoder, the editor-in-chief of *Encyclopaedia Judaica* (entry 183), has continued the tradition of an easy-to-use reference tool furnishing definitions of terms and exposition of institutions, organizations, and personalities. Arrangement of entries is alphabetical and articles have been updated to include such elements as German reunification and the dissolution of the U.S.S.R. Population figures are up-to-date as of 1991, as are death dates of personalities. The work continues to serve as a useful source of brief exposition and identification.

Also edited by Wigoder is *The Encyclopedia of Judaism* (Macmillan, 1989), which in similar fashion supplies definitions, identifications, and brief biographies, arranged alphabetically. Organizations, associations, and issues are treated in brief but effective articles numbering over 1,000. U.S. coverage is excellent, with treatment of both Conservative and Reform movements. The work is well-illustrated and is accessed through an index along with useful cross-references.

190. Oxford Encyclopedia of the Modern Islamic World. John L. Esposito, ed. New York: Oxford University Press, 1995. 4v. ISBN 0-19-506613-8.

This is a monumental work, with contributions from more than 450 scholars from various parts of the world. It contains some 750 entries of varying length, but all of sufficient depth in treating personalities, topics, issues, beliefs, rituals, practices, arts, economics, and customs relevant to Muslim existence during the past two centuries. Its emphasis on the modern world serves to complement rather than replace the coverage in *Encyclopaedia of Islam* (entry 184). The work is divided into five categories examining thought and practice, politics, communities, society, and Islamic studies. Fine coverage is given to geographical influence of Islam both in regions of the world and in specific countries.

The Muslim Almanac: A Reference Work on the History, Faith, Culture, and Peoples of Islam, edited by Azim A. Nanji (Gale Research, 1996) is similar in scope but provides a comprehensive one-volume overview of Islam from its origins in the seventh century to the present day. Beginning with a chronology, it is divided into thirty-nine chapters or essays contributed by various scholars, each treating an aspect of Islamic history, belief, or culture. Various perspectives are furnished and bibliographies are provided.

New Alternatives: New Age, Occult, Etc.

191. Dictionary of Cults, Sects, Religions and the Occult. George A. Mather and Larry A. Nichols. Grand Rapids, MI: Zondervan, 1993. 384p. ISBN 0-310-53100-4.

This work provides informative descriptions of cults, sects, and other forms of alternative religion judged to be the most popular, interesting, and influential in this country. The authors write from an admittedly evangelical Christian perspective, treating groups, movements, topics, issues, and personalities. Terms are defined and doctrines explained. For each group or personality there is fairly detailed exposition of history and teachings as well as concluding commentary. Arrangement of entries is alphabetical and cross-references are provided. Four appendices and a bibliography are classified by major group or movement.

The Illustrated Encyclopedia of Active New Religions, Sects, and Cults, by Benjamin Beit-Hallahmi (Rosen, 1993), provides comprehensive treatment, with over 2,200 entries relevant to the study and comprehension of elements of new religions. These are defined by their age of less than 200 years, an avowed new claim to divine truth, and belief in a supernatural setting with deities, dead souls, angels, or devils. Sects are generally thought to have developed out of a schism or separation from an earlier religious organization, while cults have arisen without previous connections. Included in this work are Mormons and Second Day Adventists, along with Krishna groups, "Moonies," and Scientologists. Entries are alphabetical and range from a single sentence to several hundred words in length.

192. The Encyclopedia of Ghosts and Spirits. Rosemary Ellen Guiley. New York: Facts on File, 1992. 374p. ISBN 0-8160-2140-6.

One of the increasing number of resources appearing on the supernatural or pseudo-scientific is this well-constructed, one-volume encyclopedia. It is a handy tool furnishing a great deal of information on the supernatural. Scientific explanations for certain phenomena are rendered along with legend and folklore. Topics vary from ouija boards to apparitions and famous hauntings. There are more than 400 entries accompanied by some seventy illustrations. They treat not only events and happenings but also personalities associated with spiritualistic endeavor or serious research. Brief bibliographies accompany each entry; a topical index provides access.

Another effort by Guiley is *The Encyclopedia of Witches and Witchcraft* (Facts on File, 1989), considered to be a solid and informative piece. All aspects of the subject are treated, again furnishing over 400 entries on animals, beliefs, myths, personalities, practices, and so forth. Entries are straightforward and vary in size. There is a good general bibliography and a thorough index.

193. **Encyclopedia of Occultism & Parapsychology: A Compendium of Information.** . . . 4th ed. J. Gordon Melton, ed. Detroit: Gale Research, 1996. 2v. ISBN 0-8103-5487-X.

This is an update and extension of a work issued first in 1978 and conceived as a combination of 1,000 modern entries, with entries from two old standards in the field, *Encyclopaedia of Psychic Science*, by Nandon Fodor (Arthurs Press Limited, 1933) and *Encyclopaedia of Occultism*, by Lewis Spence (Routledge, 1920). The second edition, issued in 1984 in three volumes, represented an updating and extension of the earlier effort developed within an improved format. The third edition retained that format and provided corrections of errors and updates as well as hundreds of new entries in response to interest in recent phenomena, concepts, cults, personalities, organizations, and publications. The fourth edition has received a thorough review and revision, with the addition of 300 new entries to cover new developments. The complete title continues to identify this work as "a compendium of information on the occult sciences, magic, demonology, superstitions, spiritism, mysticism, metaphysics, psychical science and parapsychology." It is considered to be most comprehensive and is a product of scholarly effort.

Another unique work from the same publisher is *The Astrology Encyclopedia*, edited by James R. Lewis (1994). It is the only reference work on astrology now in print, and contains some 780 entries alphabetically arranged from the asteroid "Abundantia" to the "Zodiac." There are numerous graphics, including line drawings. The entries are clear and concise and conclude with a brief bibliography. Appendices contain lists of organizations and of relevant periodicals. *Parapsychology: A Concise History* by John Beloff (St. Martins, 1997), is the first attempt to provide a one-volume historical overview of parapsychology from its beginnings in medieval Europe to the present.

194. **The Encyclopedic Handbook of Cults in America.** Rev. ed. J. Gordon Melton. Hamden, CT: Garland, 1992. 407p. ISBN 0-8153-0502-8.

With the continuing interest in the topic, this work replaces the edition published in 1986. It remains a timely and informative handbook of alternative religions and represents an extensive revision and expansion. Melton, long an authority on religion in American life and founder of the Institute for the Study of American Religion, presents an objective treatment of thirty-three different groups, ranging from the more established Rosicrucians to the more recent Unification Church and the Krishna affiliates. Especially useful are opening essays defining cults and their opposition in the United States. Each group is described in terms of leading figures, belief systems, organizational structure, and controversies. Bibliographies are provided. A name index and a detailed table of contents facilitate access.

195. **Harper's Encyclopedia of Mystic & Paranormal Experience.** Rosemary Ellen Guiley. San Francisco: Harper, 1991. 666p. ISBN 0-06-250365-0.

As part of the increased representation of the occult in libraries and bookstores, this effort is designed to provide the general audience with information and insight. Articles are brief and arranged alphabetically for easy access. They are clearly written and cover a variety of topics, including the New Age movement, psychical research, astrology, and so forth. Personalities are included, but in a selective manner because emphasis is placed on topical material.

Entries supply cross-references that link related items; there are references to more than 1,100 books and almost as many articles. The strength of this effort lies in its recency and coverage of contemporary issues.

Dictionary of Mysticism and the Occult, by Nevill Drury (Harper & Row, 1985), supplies nearly 3,000 entries describing elements of magic, spiritualism, parapsychology, mysticism of both the East and West, folklore, divination, tarot, and astrology. Rites, terms, personalities, and topics are treated in an informative fashion with relevant research findings. The author is a recognized authority in the field.

196. **New Age Encyclopedia: A Guide to the Beliefs, Concepts, Terms, People, and Organizations. . . .** J. Gordon Melton et al. Detroit: Gale Research, 1990. 586p. ISBN 0-8103-7159-6.

Melton, the well-known author and editor of religion reference tools, has embraced the New Age movement, defined as "the new global movement toward spiritual development, health and healing, higher consciousness." There are nearly 335 entries identifying beliefs, concepts, terms, personalities, and organizations related to the New Age, made popular by such personalities as Shirley MacLaine. This work provides thorough coverage and furnishes a useful introductory essay explaining the origin, development, and conceptual basis of the belief system. Seven contributors have joined with Melton to supply an objective and systematic explanation of important aspects; the work is not judgmental but rather descriptive in its approach. All major topics have been treated, although there are the usual number of controversial omissions and inclusions. Entries contain bibliographies; there is a chronology, a listing of educational institutions, and a general index.

Also from the same publisher, *Encyclopedia of Afterlife Beliefs and Phenomena,* by James R. Lewis (1994), examines the concept of life after death in some 250 entries of varying length containing cross-references. These are alphabetically arranged and cover personalities, religious traditions, movements, belief systems, phenomena, and so forth. In a one-volume work of this kind, there is danger of being overly simplistic and superficial in attempting to explain complex elements. There are black-and-white photographs and line drawings; an index furnishes access.

DIRECTORIES, ANNUALS, AND CURRENT AWARENESS SOURCES

197. **American Jewish Yearbook.** Philadelphia: Jewish Publication Society; New York: American Jewish Committee, 1899– . Ann. ISSN 0065-8987.

Designed by the Jewish Publication Society to review events of the year relating to Jewish affairs in the United States and other countries of the world, this tool has been published by the American Jewish Committee since 1950. Feature articles appear at the beginning of the work, followed by signed articles on a variety of subjects regarding developments in the American Jewish community. These are treated in some detail, followed by briefer treatment of conditions in other countries. Included also are directories of various organizations in the United States and Canada, biographies, necrologies, and bibliographies. Among these resource items are a useful listing of Jewish periodicals and a summary Jewish calendar. Volume 97 (1997) continues the fine tradition in which each volume is approached through a detailed name and subject index.

*198. **Catholic News Service.** Washington, DC: Catholic News Service. 1988– . (database)

Available online since 1988 is this database of news and miscellaneous information regarding the activities of the Catholic Church both in the United States and around the world. The Service's satellite newswire acts as the supplier for those who wish to be informed on a continual basis. Coverage begins with January 15, 1988, and continues to the present day, with daily updates. Regular features include "Washington Letter" and "Vatican Letter" columns, along with reviews of books, motion pictures, and television previews.

*Catholic Trends is another online product of the Catholic News Service; it targets the current news and furnishes analysis of Church activities as they relate to public policy, ecumenicism, court decisions, education, and the ministries. Coverage begins with April 2, 1988, and continues to date. The database is updated on a biweekly basis. Both the *Catholic News Service and *Catholic Trends databases are available through Newsnet, Inc.

199. **Directory of African-American Religious Bodies: A Compendium by the Howard University School of Divinity.** 2d ed. Wardell J. Payne, ed. Washington, DC: Howard University Press, 1995. 382p. ISBN 0-88258-174-0.

The second edition retains the excellent tradition established by the 1991 effort. It continues as a thorough and comprehensive reference tool devoted to the African-American religious experience, comprising a series of directories with historical essays and a full set of appendices. Several categories are treated: African-American religious bodies (by far the most extensive part); African-American religious councils, ecumenical organizations, and service agencies; African-American religious educational institutions; and white religious bodies and agencies with significant African-American membership. Personalities with scholarly interest in religion are identified. The work provides basic description of history, purpose, composition, and location of units and name, title, affiliation, education, and address of personalities. There are historical essays on various religious groups.

200. **Directory of Departments and Programs of Religious Studies in North America.** David G. Truemper, ed. Macon, GA: Mercer University Press, 1987– . Ann. ISBN 1-88313-506-0.(1996).

This annual directory was issued first in 1987 and furnishes a useful listing of schools, as well as departments and programs offering at least a bachelor's degree. Information on both graduate and undergraduate programs in religious studies at American and Canadian four-year colleges, universities, and specialized theological schools is furnished in a clear and easy-to-assimilate fashion. Entries include contact persons, and supply profiles of faculty, programs, facilities, degrees, and financial aid. Descriptive data are based on responses to a questionnaire. This coverage of hundreds of institutions represents a more comprehensive treatment than is true of other sources.

Another directory of this type is *Guide to Schools and Departments of Religion and Seminaries in the United States and Canada: Degree Programs in Religious Studies* (Modoc Press, 1987). This work furnishes more in-depth treatment of just over 700 regionally or nationally accredited schools. Arrangement is alphabetical by state or province, then by name of institution. Indexes furnish access.

201. **Directory of Religious Organizations in the United States.** 3d ed. J. Gordon Melton and Amy Lucas, eds. Detroit: Gale Research, 1993. 728p. ISBN 0-8103-9890-7.

A classified listing of nearly 2,500 religious and lay organizations in the field of religion, this is an update of a work published eleven years earlier. Its reception has been excellent, and the tool is well-developed, with information presented in a handy and useful manner. The new edition adds nearly 1,000 organizations to the total covered in the previous effort, not surprising considering the amount of time or degree of religious activity subsequent to the earlier work. All organizations listed are regarded as having a religious purpose. Representative organizations are departments of national churches, professional associations and societies, volunteer groups of various types, government agencies, businesses, and fraternal societies. Information given includes religious affiliation, address and location, fax and telephone numbers, officers, purpose, activities, founding date, publications, and membership. Information is supplied by the organization. Many of these organizations are not easily found elsewhere; therefore, the work represents a desirable addition to the collection. It is indexed by personal name, function, affiliation, and keyword.

202. **Fund Raiser's Guide to Religious Philanthropy.** 12th ed. Bernard Jankowski, ed. Detroit: Taft Group/Gale Research, 1998. 1149p. ISSN 1042-0053.

As one of several titles in the field of religious philanthropy, the twelfth edition of this well-received, useful source continues to grow and expand, furnishing profiles of hundreds of philanthropic sources. There are numerous helpful articles and descriptions designed to provides a source of information and reference for fund seekers and units needing support in the area of religion. Arrangement of entries is alphabetical by state, then by foundation name. Entries furnish name, address, telephone number, officers, description of purpose, activities, limitations of support, and application process. There are numerous indexes (donors, officers, places, subjects, types of support, etc.).

National Guide to Funding in Religion, edited by James E. Baumgartner (Foundation Center, 1999), is now in its fifth edition and is a similar publication intended to be a beginning point for grant seekers looking for financial support. More than 3,000 foundations and programs are listed; drawn from the Center's extensive listings in *National Directory of Corporate Giving* (Foundation Center, 1989–) and *The Foundation Directory* (Russell Sage Foundation, 1960–). Another effort is the fifth edition of *Foundation Guide for Religious Grant Seekers,* edited by Kerry A. Robinson (Scholars Press, 1995). This is a revised and enlarged issue of what is considered a useful source of information on Christian, Jewish, and interfaith foundations providing aid to those seeking charitable gifts and endowments.

*203. **Methodists Make News.** Nashville, TN: United Methodist News Service, 1983– . W. (database)

Another of the online databases available through Newsnet, Inc., is this file of news and features of interest to the United Methodist Church. Formerly known as United Methodist Information, the service provides the full text of the weekly print newsletter of the same name. Information is given concerning members, activities, projects, issues, and related matters. Coverage ranges from May 1983 to the present.

The *Lutheran News Service, published by the Evangelical Lutheran Church in America, is a database supplying the complete text of the *Lutheran News,* a print weekly. Articles cover social issues, theology, and miscellaneous news from the Evangelical Lutheran Church in America and the Lutheran World Federation. Similar to Methodists Make News, it covers the time period from January 10, 1986 to date, with the file updated on a weekly basis. It also is available through NewsNet, Inc.

204. **National Directory of Churches, Synagogues, and Other Houses of Worship.** J. Gordon Melton, ed. Detroit: Gale Research, 4v. 1993– . Trienn. ISSN 1070-3314.

Melton is a prolific writer and editor who has a knack for providing needed reference sources for the study of religion. This comprehensive directory, projected as a triennial publication, contains more than 350,000 churches, synagogues, mosques, and so forth representing thirty-five primary religious traditions in the United States. Entries are presented in four volumes, each treating a different region of the country (Northeastern States, Midwestern States, Southern States, and Western States). The intent is to provide identification of worshipping congregations, both urban and rural, throughout the country. Within each volume, listings are given by state, then city, then denomination, then by church and congregation name. Entries supply name, address, telephone number, date established, size of congregation, and name of church leader. There is a guide to denominational locations and an index to churches and congregations in each volume.

205. **The Official Catholic Directory for the Year of Our Lord 1999. . . .** New Providence, NJ: P. J. Kenedy/Reed Reference Publishing, 1886– . Ann. ISBN 0-87217-987-7.

Although there have been some variations in title through the years, this directory has been a predictable commodity and represents a standard reference tool. Developed with the purpose of providing up-to-date, accurate information on a yearly basis, it serves an important function in disseminating the reports of statistical and institutional information as provided by diocesan authorities. The 1999 issue represents the 182d edition of this reputable work. Coverage includes the organization, clergy, missions, schools, churches, and religious orders of the Catholic Church in the United States, its affiliates and territories, as well as Canada and Mexico. Arrangement is by hierarchical order of the Church under countries and subdivisions of countries. Dioceses are listed by states and detailed information is provided regarding names of individuals serving in various positions. Traditionally, the index has appeared at the beginning of the volume. Numerous classified advertisements help subsidize the costs of the publication.

206. **Religious Bodies in the United States: A Directory.** J. Gordon Melton. New York: Garland, 1992. 313p. (Religious Information Systems Series, v. 1; Garland Reference Library of Humanities, v. 1568). ISBN 0-8153-0806-X.

From the time of its initial publication under a slightly different title in 1977, this directory has earned the respect of librarians and their patrons for its excellent brief coverage of hundreds of religious bodies in this country. The present effort continues the excellent tradition with a needed update. Unlike the earlier effort there is no attempt to classify the denominations under families. Chapters are given to the various religions (Hindu, Jewish, Christian, Buddhist, Occult/Magical, etc.). Arrangement is alphabetical by name of the body in the directory sections and information is provided regarding origin, history, address, and telephone number. Publications are treated, as are interfaith organizations. There is a bibliography of materials relating to American religious groups at the end.

The Directory of Publishers in Religion, compiled by Mike Farry (Scholars Press, 1997), is a compact volume providing an alphabetical listing of U.S. publishers of religious literature. The work begins with a preface describing the nature of the business, and the customary directory information is furnished in the main text. Several indexes provide good access.

207. **Yearbook of American and Canadian Churches.** Nashville, TN: Abingdon, 1916– . Ann. ISSN 0195-9034.

Although its title, publisher, and frequency of appearance have varied in the past, this work has assumed an important position as a reporting tool for statistics and developments of major religious bodies in the United States and Canada. Originally limited to Protestant religious bodies, it has changed character through time and now covers the organizations and activities of all faiths. Consisting of several major sections plus an index, greatest coverage is in the "Directories," which is classified by categories. Separate listings are given for American and Canadian groups, but each entry provides a brief historical overview, a listing of officers, organizational information, and a list of periodicals. A calendar of future major religious dates is given for all faiths, and there is a section presenting statistics regarding financial conditions and membership. The index groups denominations under generic headings such as "Baptist Bodies." The 1998 edition is edited by Eileen W. Lindner and contains 372 pages.

BIOGRAPHICAL SOURCES

208. Biographical Dictionary of American Cult and Sect Leaders. J. Gordon Melton. New York: Garland, 1986. 354p. ISBN 0-8240-9037-3.

Melton has had a great deal of success in reading the desires of the marketplace, and this title was developed in response to a clear need for material on leaders of divergent, nonmainstream groups and their leading figures. Both scholars and students should profit from the focus on what has come to be called alternative religions. This is a comprehensive biographical dictionary of 213 founders and major leaders of American cults and sects. Coverage is limited to deceased personalities. A sect is considered to be a group in protest against a mainstream church, and a cult is defined as a more radical new spiritual option. Some of the groups have become mainstream, such as the Mormon church. The biographies are well written and informative, from 300 to 500 words in length, and include bibliographies by and about the personality. Appendices provide classification of the personalities by tradition, birthplace, and religious influences. A good general index is given.

209. The Book of Saints: A Dictionary of Servants of God. 6th ed., entirely rev. and reset, 1st American ed. Benedictine Monks of St. Augustine's Abbey, Ramsgate, comps. Witton, CT: Morehouse, 1989. 605p. ISBN 0-8192-1501-5.

This new edition of a standard biographical dictionary was issued twenty-three years after its predecessor and has updated and enlarged its coverage. There are nearly 10,000 entries, doubling the number treated in the fifth edition and at the same time extending the scope to embrace a greater proportion of non-English saints. Those entries for saints removed from the General Calendar in 1969 are noted as having questionable authenticity. Recently canonized saints are treated. Entries are brief but informative and furnish name, appellation, feast day, dates, liturgical group, and religious order, along with a biographical sketch. They are arranged alphabetically and in many cases are accompanied by illustrations of Christian art. The work supplies a brief bibliography along with an index of emblems, a list of patron saints representing the various professions and activities, and a list of the twelve sibyls or prophetesses of the pre-Christian world.

210. Butler's Lives of the Saints. Herbert Thurston and Donald Attwater, eds. New York: P. J. Kenedy, 1956; repr., Westminster, MD: Christian Classics, 1990. 4v. ISBN 0-87061-0457.

In Attwater's revision and abridgment of Thurston's earlier twelve-volume edition (1926–1938), which itself was a revision of the eighteenth-century effort by Butler, much of the original material has been included without change. Some brief treatments were deleted and some biographies of recently canonized saints have been added. The homilies have been omitted. The purpose of the work is to present information on the principal saints familiar to English-speaking Catholics. The saints are listed by months and days, which requires in many cases the use of the index to locate the entry. A good biography of the individual's life is followed by a listing of sources. Each volume is indexed, and a general name index for the set appears in volume 4. A one-volume concise edition, revised and updated, was issued by HarperSanFrancisco in 1991. In 1995 a new, full edition of twelve volumes was published by Burns & Oates.

211. **The Conversion Experience in America: A Sourcebook on Religion Conversion Autobiography.** James C. Holte. New York: Greenwood, 1992. 228p. ISBN 0-313-26680-8.

A specialized effort in which Holte furnishes in-depth treatment of religious conversions described by thirty Americans, some well-known (Amy Semple McPherson, Frederick Douglass), others obscure (Ann Eliza Young, Black Elk), over a period of 350 years. Most are Protestant but also represented are Roman Catholics, Black Muslims, Shakers, and others. Seven of the subjects are female and nine are from minority groups. The entries are full and well-developed, averaging five to ten pages in length. They are divided into four sections, beginning with "Biography," which supplies an introduction to the individual; this is followed by "The Autobiography," a detailed analysis of the subject's writing, then "Criticism," rendering a brief commentary on the significance of the writing. Finally, there is a "Bibliography" of related sources. The work is accessed through an index.

212. **Dictionary of American Catholic Biography.** John J. Delaney. Garden City, NY: Doubleday, 1984. 621p. ISBN 0-385-17878-6.

In this volume an attempt has been made to provide factual information regarding the lives and activities of Catholics who have been influential in this country. The work covers about 1,500 individuals, all of whom are deceased but whose dates range from the colonial period to the present. In addition to theologians, the entries include a distinguished listing of performers, artists, athletes, and politicians. Such people as Bing Crosby, Arturo Toscanini, Babe Ruth, and John F. Kennedy are included as well as those of more controversial nature such as Joseph McCarthy. Each entry covers birth information, education, activities, achievements, and date and place of death. This appears to be a useful source for its stated purpose.

A useful eight-chapter narrative history providing detailed bibliographical notes on periods and topics along with biographical sketches is Patrick W. Carey's *The Roman Catholics* (Greenwood, 1992; 1996 pbk.). Included here are brief biographies of 145 major personalities who influenced the Catholic faith in this country. Bibliographies accompany each of the sketches. For coverage on an international basis see the earlier work, *Dictionary of Catholic Biography*, by Delaney and James Edward Tobin (Doubleday, 1961), which covers nearly 15,000 individuals from earliest times to the time of publication.

213. **Dictionary of American Religious Biography.** 2d ed. rev. and enl. Henry Warner Bowden. Westport, CT: Greenwood, 1993. 572p. ISBN 0-313-27825-3.

A retrospective biographical dictionary that is limited to religious figures who died before July 1, 1992, expanding the first edition, which provided coverage up to July 1, 1976. Detailed treatment is given to religious leaders who represent a wide range of denominations and belief systems. Of the 425 treated in the first edition, all have been retained, with most having been updated and revised. About 125 names have been added, for a total of 550 persons. Included are such diverse figures as Increase Mather and Martin Luther King, Jr. Each entry begins with a brief career overview and personal and educational data. Following this is a detailed narrative sketch that includes both expository and evaluative commentary. A special attempt has been made to include women and minorities as well as dissidents from mainstream activity. Bibliographies providing references by and about the biographee are included with each entry. A selected general bibliography has been added at the end of the new edition. There is a name and subject index.

214. **Jewish Profiles: Great Jewish Personalities and Institutions of the Twentieth Century.** Murray Polner, ed. Northvale, NJ: Jason Aronson, 1991. 410p. ISBN 0-87668-793-1.

This is a selective biographical and informational tool furnishing forty articles taken from *Present Tense*, a now-defunct Jewish magazine of liberal persuasion. Most articles are reports of interviews held with subjects who figured prominently in the affairs of the day. Featured are artists, politicians, educators, and others wielding influence (Elie Wiesel, Teddy Kollek, Betty Friedan, etc.). Also covered are certain institutions such as Brandeis University and the *Jewish Daily Forward.* A detailed index provides access. The work was issued on audiotapes in 1994.

Reform Judaism in America: A Biographical Dictionary and Sourcebook, edited by Kerry M. Olitzky of Hebrew Union College and others (Greenwood, 1993), provides first-rate coverage of the American reform movement, treating the lives and achievements of the most influential leaders. Rabbis, cantors, scholars, and volunteers are profiled in biographical sketches along with bibliographies of primary and secondary sources. Several essays provide historical perspective on important organizations.

215. The Oxford Dictionary of Popes. J. N. D. Kelly. New York: Oxford University Press, 1986; repr., 1988. 347p. ISBN 0-19-213964-9.

This is the leading biographical dictionary, covering all 264 popes who followed Peter up to 1981, and remains a useful source of information, even though it is dated. Entries for each pope are arranged chronologically and cover family, social and educational background, life prior to becoming the head of the Church, and career activities while shouldering the responsibility of office. In general, the bibliographies are considered to be impartial and informative, although at times gossip and innuendo find their way into the descriptions. There is an appendix on "Pope Joan," which explores the myth of a female pope. Each entry provides a bibliography of source materials for both the individual's life and official acts. An excellent detailed index provides easy access.

A more recent effort is *The Pope Encyclopedia: An A to Z of the Holy See* by Matthew Bunson (Crown Trade Paperbacks, 1995), which provides some 2,000 entries on individual popes, the papacy, and related topics, issues, events, associations, and quotations. Written in the popular vein and suitable for the less sophisticated individual, the work has met with mixed reviews in terms of factual consistency and value to the user.

216. The Oxford Dictionary of Saints. 4th ed. David Hugh Farmer. New York: Oxford University Press, 1997. 512p. ISBN 0-19-280058-2.

The initial edition of this informative biographical dictionary treating the lives of the saints of Great Britain was published in 1978 and was updated with the second issue in 1987 with coverage of over 1,000 saints. The third edition, issued in 1992, provided updated, and in some cases revised, accounts of more than 1,100 saints. The fourth edition in paperback continues in the same vein. Like those in the previous efforts, some of the saints were native to England, others considered important by the British, and still others died in England. Entries are concise and supply useful facts for all the saints recorded in English place names, the calendar of the Book of Common Prayer, the Sarum Rite, and the Calendar of the Roman Catholic Church. The book also includes coverage of the leading saints of Ireland, Scotland, and Wales. Arrangement is alphabetical by Christian names for those who lived prior to the sixteenth century and by surname for those who followed. There are selective bibliographies, which provide references to official sources. An index of places associated with particular saints is also included.

217. The Presbyterians. Herbert Randall Balmer and John R. Fitzmier. Westport, CT: Greenwood, 1993; 1994 (pbk.) 274p. (Denominations in America, no. 5). ISBN 0-313-26084-2.

This is a comprehensive history and biographical dictionary of the Presbyterian church in this country, and it fills a void in the library collection. Part 1 provides a detailed historical account of the European origin of the Church and the influence of Zwingli, Calvin, and Knox in the creation of Reformed and Presbyterian theology. The Church's development and growth in the United States is described in a lucid manner and the immigration of the Scottish-Irish Presbyterians in the late eighteenth century is explained. The Church later was to split over the issue of slavery and the two factions were not reconciled until recent years as part of the ecumenical movement. Part 2 supplies a biographical dictionary of Presbyterian leaders to complement the historical survey. This must be considered an important tool for academic and religion libraries.

218. **Religious Leaders of America: A Biographical Guide to Founders and Leaders of Religious Bodies, Churches, and Spiritual Groups in North America.** J. Gordon Melton. Detroit: Gale Research, 1991. 604p. ISSN 1057-2961.

This most recent effort by this prolific author represents a biographical dictionary of nearly 1,050 personalities, all of whom made their contribution subsequent to the Civil War. Coverage extends over a wide range of figures representing both the traditional Judeo-Christian heritage and the alternative or fringe areas as well. Included are minority figures, females, blacks, and Native Americans, in a purposeful attempt to be inclusive. Although most of the entries are deceased, there is a good representation of living people. Thus we have Pat Robertson along with Jesse Jackson and Billy Graham; Mother Cabrini along with Madalyn Murray O'Hare. Entries furnish birth and death dates, birthplaces, and religious affiliations together with well-developed biographies. There is an appendix of religious affiliation classifying the subjects into various groups. A comprehensive index identifies individuals, organizations, publications, and so forth.

Twentieth Century Shapers of American Popular Religion, edited by Charles H. Lippy (Greenwood, 1989), is a most unusual and welcome tool for both scholars and students in its detailed biographical essays on the leading figures, both living and dead, who represent some form of popular religion. Religions of this type are considered to be outside the mainstream, and focused on a charismatic leader utilizing (or exploiting) the media. Television evangelists of today, along with the capable spokespersons of the past, are represented. Coverage is highly selective and is limited to just over sixty men and women who created a unique presence (Harvey Cox, Marcus Garvey, Amy Semple McPherson, Malcolm X, and Pat Robertson). Others have been included for their influence, such as Sinclair Lewis for his *Elmer Gantry*. Entries include an evaluation, critical summary, and bibliography. A detailed index is given.

219. **Who's Who in Religion, 1992–93.** 4th ed. Wilmette, IL: Marquis Who's Who, 1992. ISBN 0-8379-1604-6.

Although this effort began with what appeared to be a yearly or possibly biennial publication schedule, with the first two editions published between 1975 and 1977, there was a hiatus that happily ended with the publication of the third edition in 1985. The earlier editions covered individuals in a much more extensive fashion (16,000 in the first edition and 18,000 in the second edition) while the third issue limited itself to around 7,000 religious and lay leaders, church officials, clergy, and educators. The fourth edition continues the tradition of its predecessors, treating those who achieved a position of prominence in the United States, and selections for inclusion were aided by a special advisory board. Biographies provide information on occupation, family, creative works, activities, memberships, and so forth. The work covers all denominations and faiths and represents a valuable resource tool.

Who's Who in Christianity, by Lavinia Cohn-Sherbok (Routledge Kegan Paul, 1998), is a recent effort focused on those who have had a "continuing effect on the life of the Church." Some 1,200 prominent individuals representing not only the clergy but all areas of endeavor from different time periods are treated in brief fashion with paragraph-length entries. Also included is a chronology of Christian history along with a glossary and a short bibliography.

220. **Who's Who in the Old Testament: Together with the Apocrypha.** Joan Comay. New York: Oxford University Press, 1993; 1995 pbk. 398p. ISBN 0-19-521029-8.

Initially issued in 1971 by a different publisher, this is for the most part a reprint without the illustrations of the original issue. It provides well-developed and informative entries for every character who appears in the OT. These entries are arranged alphabetically and describe in detail the lives and activities of biblical personalities, with more extensive treatment given to the major figures. In this work, some 3,000 men and women are covered, beginning with Adam and Eve and including the great prophets such as Isaiah as well as influential rulers such as David and Solomon. Entries are developed within the context of modern biblical scholarship and recent research. A separate section treats the Apocrypha.

Who's Who in the New Testament, by Ronald Brownrigg (Oxford University Press, 1993), is a reprint of a companion piece also published initially in 1971 by a different publishing house. It offers a comprehensive coverage, treating every character who appears in the NT in a detailed and informative manner. Exposition of the various versions of the gospels is provided in light of recent biblical scholarship, with special attention given to sites of major events in Jesus's life.

221. **Who's Who of World Religions.** John R. Hinnells, ed. New York: Simon & Schuster, 1992; repr., Penguin Books, 1996. 560p. ISBN 0-14-051439-3.

This is one of the few biographical dictionaries to attempt a balanced coverage between the Christian and non-Christian religions of the world. All regions and all time periods are covered in this universal approach that embraces such diverse personalities as Sun Myung Moon, Pope John Paul II, and Ayatollah Khomeini. Both men and women are included and founders such as L. Ron Hubbard are positioned with creative artists and poets such as J. S. Bach or Giotto. The majority of figures are Christian as might be expected, but the 1,500 entries represent a good mix, with coverage given to twenty-six religious groups. Some sixty scholars have contributed to this effort. Bibliographies, maps, and indexes are included.

Religious Leaders, by Jacques Brosse (Chambers, 1988; repr., 1991), is a highly selective biographical dictionary of leaders (those concerned solely with guiding others to the truth). Selflessness, along with a lack of interest in worldly status, is the primary characteristic shared by the 163 personalities (Socrates, Joseph Smith, George Whitefield) and groups (Sikhs, Neoplatonists). Entries run from one to two pages in length and are accompanied by illustrations along with a glossary and index.

HISTORIES AND ATLASES

222. **The Cambridge History of Judaism.** W. D. Davies and Louis Finkelstein, eds. New York: Cambridge University, 1984– . v.1– . ISBN 0-521-21880-2 (v.1); 0-521-21929-9 (v.2).

Projected for completion in four volumes, this authoritative work presents a scholarly history of the Jews from the destruction of the Temple in 586 B.C. to the period of the closure of the Mishnah in A.D. 250. Two volumes have been completed, which examine not only the developments in Israel but in Babylonia and Egypt as well. Volume 1 presents an introduction, covering the geography of Palestine and the Levant; it is termed the "Persian Period."

This consists of a series of sixteen essays, erudite but readable, related to the development of Jewish culture in this period. Volume 2 (1989) continues the exposition with cogent coverage of the Hellenistic Age. New data are utilized in the inquiry, which represents a work of ecumenical proportions because the contributors are of various backgrounds and national origins. As is true of other Cambridge efforts, the bibliographies are full and of value to those who would research further. There are chronological tables and an index.

The Origins of Judaism: Religion, History, and Literature in Late Antiquity, edited by Jacob Neusner with William Scott Green (Garland, 1990), is a scholarly, thirteen-volume compilation of articles and essays providing detailed examination of all aspects of early Judaism. More than 300 writings of classic importance completed during the past fifty years are organized in thematic volumes covering such elements as "Normative Judaism," "The Pharisees and Other Sects," and "Controversies in the Study of Judaic Religion and Theology," along with historically sequenced volumes.

223. **The Cultural Atlas of Islam.** Ismail R. al Faruqi and Lois I. al Faruqi. New York: Macmillan, 1986. 512p. ISBN 0-02-910190-5.

Considered by the authors (who unfortunately met with violent deaths prior to publication date) to be a "first production" in the exposition of the Islamic culture, this is an important work combining informative narrative along with maps, charts, diagrams, tables, line drawings, and photographs. Sources utilized were chosen carefully on the basis of historical/cultural integration; the result was a collection of seventy-seven maps illustrating various aspects and phenomena of the Islamic tradition. The work is divided into four major parts—"Origin," "Essence," "Form," and "Manifestation"—without regard to national or regional boundaries. Within these segments one is able to read of the history, art, and cultural identity of Islam. As part of the new phenomenological approach employed in the development of contemporary cultural atlases, this represents an impressive and useful work for both researchers and students. There is an index to aid access.

224. **Eerdmans' Handbook to Christianity in America.** Mark Noll et al. Grand Rapids, MI: Eerdmans, 1983. 507p. ISBN 0-8028-3582-1.

The work is divided into four sections, chronologically sequenced: "God and the Colonies," "Christianity and Democracy," "The Era of Crisis," and "Christianity in the Secular Age." It provides an exposition of the entire Christian experience in America in an historical context, beginning with the early Puritans and bringing the reader to the modern evangelicals. There are numerous graphs, charts, and diagrams illustrating the points made in the text. The work is both interesting and useful in its interpretation of the Christian experience in this country. For purposes of enlightenment, quotations help the reader comprehend the thoughts of those being studied. There is a detailed table of contents, but no index.

225. **Handbook of Church History.** Hubert Jedin and John Dolan, eds. New York: Herder & Herder, 1965–1981. 10v. Repr., Crossroad, 1986–1989. ISBN 0-824-50314-7 (v.1).

Translated from Jedin's *Handbuch der Kirchengeschichte* (3d ed., New York: Herder, 1962–1979; 7v. in 10), this represents a major contribution to church history from a Roman Catholic viewpoint. The purpose is to examine both the Church's external career in the world and its inner life. Major events and personalities are described and explained with respect to their impact on or relationship to such elements as church doctrine, liturgy, dogma, organization, and literature. Beginning with volume 1, "From the Apostolic Community to Constantine," by Karl Baus, the sequence of events is presented in scholarly fashion. Each volume is a work of separate authorship, with three written by Roger Aubert. The final volume treats the Church in the modern age and provides an appropriate capstone to an erudite, well-conceived effort.

Compact but comprehensive in coverage is *Catholicism in Early Modern History; A Guide to Research*, by John W. O'Malley (Center for Information Research, 1988). It comprises sixteen different state-of-the-art reviews by various scholars, treating geographical areas such as Germany and France and topical aspects such as spirituality and preaching. The essays examine current scholarship in a lucid manner. There is an excellent bibliography.

226. **Historical Atlas of the Religions of the World.** Isma'il Ragi al Faruqui. New York: Macmillan, 1974. 346p. ISBN 0-02-336400-9.

Developed by the editor with an international team of scholars, this work provides not only excellent and authoritative historical maps but also scholarly narratives on the histories of religion. These are integrated with the graphic material, which in addition to maps includes, photographs, tables, and charts describing the links of religion to cultural and geographic locations. Past religions are covered first, contemporary ethnic and universal religions next, and finally, specific areas and religions. There is an appendix of chronologies of the various religions treated, with the current religions being subdivided by the particular denominations they comprise. There is a detailed table of contents, and subject and name indexes provide access.

227. **The Macmillan Atlas History of Christianity.** Franklin Hamlin Littell. New York: Macmillan, 1976. 176p. ISBN 0-02-573140-8.

Arranged by historical periods, this work illustrates the development of Christianity through graphic representation of its encounters and in some cases its disputes with other ideologies and belief systems. Developed with a Protestant perspective, it provides chronological coverage of the emergence and growth of Christianity, considering such topics as the Jewish matrix, the Carolingian Empire, and the age of colonialism. There are nearly 200 maps and over 100 separate illustrations linked to the textual description, providing a useful framework for comprehension of the material presented. There is some variation in size and detail among the maps, but in general they are quite adequate. Access is provided through a general index.

228. **The Oxford Illustrated History of Christianity.** John McManners, ed. New York: Oxford University Press, 1993. 770p. ISBN 0-19-285291-4.

McManners is an acknowledged authority and professor emeritus of ecclesiastical history at Oxford University who has supervised the production of an attractive, well-illustrated volume with both black-and-white and color plates suitable for both reference and browsing purposes. Numerous specialists and scholars have contributed to the development of this highly readable and informative history. The work is divided into three segments, the first (and lengthiest) of which covers the earliest period, "From the Origins to 1800." The articles in this section are arranged chronologically, beginning with an essay by Henry Chadwick on the early Christian community. The second segment, "Christianity Since 1800," supplies several chapters representing different regions of the world. The final section, with briefest coverage, "Christianity Today and Tomorrow," treats contemporary theological doctrine and also trends of the future. There is a chronology of events and an annotated bibliography. A detailed subject index furnishes access.

Varieties of Religious Conversion in the Middle Ages, edited by James Muldoon (University Press of Florida, 1997), is a collection of eleven essays from different scholars providing exposition of important conversions taking place from the fourth century (Augustine) to the fourteenth century (Jews and Asians to Christianity). Background is furnished, as is insight into the nature of the religious and societal conditions, spiritual motivations, and status of those converted.

229. **Sacred Games: A History of Christian Worship.** Bernhard Lang. New Haven, CT: Yale University Press, 1997. 527p. ISBN 0-300-06932-4.

The author, a German academic, identifies six "games" that are played out as ritualistic behavior emanating from ancient pre-Christian influences. They are praise, prayer, sermon, sacrifice, sacrament, and spiritual ecstasy. These important components of worship are examined historically in terms of their origins and development through time, and comparisons are drawn between their practice in the past and in the present. There is a bibliography and index.

230. **World Spirituality: An Encyclopedic History of the Religious Quest.** Ewert Cousins, gen. ed. New York: Crossroad, 1985– . v.4, 6–8, 13–15, 16–22. ISBN 0-8245-0681-2 (v.16). (In progress).

Spirituality is generally defined as "that inner dimension of the person called by certain traditions, the spirit." The general editor of the series is Ewert Cousins, and the issuance of these volumes, each a separate work edited by individual scholars, represents a total effort of great magnitude. Attempting to respond to an increased consciousness on the part of the world's citizenry and increasing intercourse between Eastern and Western religions, this multi-volume history should have no equal in this field of endeavor. The volumes comprise a series of essays, each of which can be used alone or in context with others. The contributors and the editorial board are distinguished scholars of ecumenical character who have generated an outstanding narrative on spirituality of religious traditions in a variety of contexts (iconography, art, literature, Monasticism, etc.). An index is provided at the end of each volume. Completed thus far are volume 4, *South and Meso-American Native Spirituality* (1993); volumes 6–7, *Hindu Spirituality* (1989–1997); volumes 8–9, *Buddhist Spirituality* (1997–1999); volumes 13–14, *Jewish Spirituality* (1986–1987); volume 15, *Classical Mediterranean Spirituality* (1986); volumes 16–18, *Christian Spirituality* (1985–1987); volumes 19–20, *Islamic Spirituality* (1987–1991); volume 21, *Modern Esoteric Spirituality* (1992); and volume 22, *Spirituality and the Secular Quest* (1996). The most recent volume, *Reclaiming Spirituality*, was completed in 1998.

THE BIBLE

The books of the Old Testament were written in Hebrew at various times between 1200 and 100 B.C. Final decisions about which ones should be included in the Jewish canon (list of divinely inspired books) appear to have been made around A.D. 100. A notable translation into Greek, known as the Septuagint, was made in the third and second centuries B.C. It included some books not officially accepted as part of the Jewish canon. The books of the New Testament were written in Greek, mainly in the last half of the first century A.D. By the end of the second century, the contents of today's New Testament were fairly clear. The first complete list of the twenty-seven books accepted today appeared in the *Easter Letter* of Asthasius in A.D. 367. A major translation of the Bible into Latin (known as the *Vulgate*) was completed by Jerome in A.D. 404.

In the recent past, great efforts have been made in both modernization of language and treatment as well as interpretation. While retaining the accuracy of intent of the earlier translations, the modern versions have successfully negotiated the difficult passage to clear and, now, nonsexist language and treatment. These modern Bibles are more precise in language and lack the "elaborate eloquence" of their predecessors when making the important points. Of course, they are well-suited to the temper and tempo of our times.

The most detailed general description of Bible origin and development is found in *The Cambridge History of the Bible* (entry 282). A more up-to-date resource is *The English Bible from KJV to NIV: A History and Evaluation*, by Jack P. Lewis, now in its second edition

(Baker, 1991). The segment dealing with Bibles and related texts in *The Reader's Adviser* (14th ed., R. R. Bowker, 1994) continues to provide informative description of various versions and editions.

Recently, much effort has gone into computerization of files and creation of various databases leading to the development of either online or CD-ROM products for biblical studies. The *King James Version*, especially, has received the attention of such publishers. In reality, the large-scale efforts identified and described as entries in the section on multiple versions have rendered most major Bible editions accessible in this manner.

Only the principal English-language versions are listed here, and they are listed in chronological order of initial publication.

Versions and Editions

CHRISTIAN

*231. King James or Authorized Version (1611).

Because of the majestic beauty of its language, this version is still a favorite among Protestants. Numerous editions are in print. It remains possibly the most frequently used of all Protestant Bibles. As stated in the introduction to this segment, *KJB* has been computerized, and is available online through DIALOG. A CD-ROM version, *CD-ROM Bible Database* (Nimbus Information Systems), has been discontinued.

A recent edition, *The New King James Version* (Thomas Nelson, 1990) has introduced modern language "where necessary." It has updated archaic terms and replaced seventeenth-century verb forms but retains its lyrical style. It appears to follow the original text more closely than the other contemporary Bibles, although its language is simpler than either the *Revised Standard* or the *New American Standard* versions. There is a brief personal study guide: *Holy Bible: New King James Version, with Notes, Maps, Charts* (Thomas Nelson, 1995).

232. Douay Bible (1582–1610, rev. by Challoner in 1749–1750).

Translated from the *Vulgate*, this version has been for Roman Catholics what the *King James* has been for Protestants. It differs from Protestant versions inasmuch as the Apocryphal books are accepted as canonical and integrated in the text.

233. American Standard Version or American Revised Version (1901).

Published shortly after the *English Revised Version* (1885), this has been widely used by American Protestants since its publication at the turn of the twentieth century. It has been favored by the American evangelical population, and the subsequent revision was a product of that community. A revision first appeared in 1971 as the *New American Standard Bible* from World Publishing Company. Other publishers followed suit with various issues, the most recent being from the American Bible Society in 1998. In comparison to the new versions of the past few years, it is somewhat more complex and difficult to negotiate. It is generally considered a successful attempt to furnish a more modern version of *ASV*.

234. Revised Standard Version. Nashville, TN: Thomas Nelson, 1952.

This revision into modern English by a group of American scholars from many denominations attempts to follow the style of the *King James Version*. There is both a Protestant edition and a Catholic edition with the Apocrypha, as well as an ecumenical edition issued in 1973.

The Reader's Digest Bible, edited by Bruce Metzger, which reduced the *RSV* by some 40 percent by tightening the rhetoric and shortening the genealogies and listings, was issued in 1982, with a more recent publication in 1995. The *New Revised Standard Version* (*NRSV*) (Zondervan, 1990) is a truly contemporary offering in nonsexist language, with references to humankind rather than man. It is precise in wording and easily understood, while remaining true in terms of the message being delivered. More recently, Metzger et al. produced *The New Oxford Annotated Bible Containing the Old and New Testaments* (Oxford University Press, 1994), an edition of *NRSV* that contains the Apocrypha.

235. **The Jerusalem Bible.** Garden City, NY: Doubleday, 1966.

Preceded by a French edition (1956) prepared by the Dominicans at L'Ecole Biblique in Jerusalem, this English version is a direct translation from the original languages, with references to the French edition. It won the Thomas More Association Medal for "the most distinguished contribution to Catholic literature in 1966." A new edition appeared in 1985, entitled *The New Jerusalem Bible*, with a pocket edition issued in 1990 and a study edition in 1994.

236. **The New English Bible.** New York: Oxford University Press, 1971.

The result of more than twenty years of work by a group of scholars to translate the Bible into clear, modern English, this one differs from the *Revised Standard Version* in that no effort was made to follow the style of the *King James Version*. Representatives from the various Protestant churches of the British Isles combined to provide a faithful rendering of the available texts in a fluid, idiomatic, but still elevated prose and poetry. A study edition with the Apocrypha was produced in 1976.

The Revised English Bible (Oxford University Press, 1989) is a substantial revision of the *NEB* that further reduces passages of exaggerated prose and also eliminates the use of sexist language. *REB* represents a fresh and clearly developed version that has eliminated many inconsistencies with respect to translation of original Greek words and phrases as well.

237. **The New American Bible.** New York: P. J. Kenedy, 1971.

Sponsored by the Bishops' Committee of the Confraternity of Christian Doctrine, this is a thoroughly modern translation for American Catholics, including the deuterocanonical books. It includes textual books on Old Testament readings and an encyclopedic dictionary of biblical and general Catholic information. A revised edition was issued by Eerdmans in 1988; notes and introductory passages have been expanded. In 1994, Fireside Bible Publishers issued a school and church edition in large print, while Oxford University Press published a personal study edition in 1995.

238. **New International Version (NIV).** Grand Rapids, MI: Zondervan, 1978. ISBN 0-310-90000-X.

Based on a thirteen-year effort, initially begun by the Committee on Bible Translation in 1965, the work was sponsored by the New York Bible Society International in 1968. Participating in the process were over 100 scholars from various evangelical denominations representing various countries. It represents a successful modern approach in its use of current English, and is much more easily read and understood than the *ASV*. A useful device is the inclusion of quotation marks around quotes. Initially, the Bible Society issued the NT version as *The Great News* in 1973. In 1996, Zondervan produced *Holy Bible: New International Reader's Version*.

NON-CHRISTIAN

239. **The Holy Scriptures.** Jewish Publication Society, 1908; latest repr., 1988. ISBN 0827602529.

Various editions of the Old Testament Bible have appeared in English since this work was published. The most recently completed revision is a three-volume edition of a new translation of the *Holy Scriptures According to the Masoretic Text*, done over a twenty-year period, 1962–1982. It includes volume 1, *The Torah;* volume 2, *The Prophets;*, and volume 3, *The Writings.* In 1985, a single volume was issued, *Tanakh: A New Translation of the Holy Scriptures According to the Original Hebrew Text.* The *Tanakh* was issued on CD-ROM in 1994.

There has been other activity in computerization with the issuance of *Computerized Torah Treasure* on CD-ROM from the publisher with the same name as the title. It contains rabbinical literature in Hebrew and covers Tanakh, Mishnah, and various Talmudic interpretations, along with commentaries. *Global Jewish Database furnishes the complete text of 252 volumes of rabbinical responses covering over 1,000 years and over thirty countries. It includes the Bible and various commentaries and collected works; it is available online from the Institute for Computers in Jewish Life in Israel.

240. **Koran. al-Quran: A Contemporary Translation.** 2d rev. ed. Ahmed Ali. Princeton: Princeton University Press, 1988. 572p. ISBN 0-691-07329-5.

The first edition of the English-Arabic translation of the Koran was issued in 1984 and was warmly received in libraries and college teaching departments as a needed resource. The Ali translation is considered to be first-rate in terms of style and accuracy and furnishes parallel columns of the Arabic and English text to allow for quick comparison. The corrected second edition furnishes explanatory notes with informative material by its eighty-year-old author and translator. The lack of a contemporary English translation prior to publication of the first edition was considered a serious deficiency for Islamic studies. The work is indexed by subject and also by names of prophets for which both the English and Arabic name forms are furnished. A Book-of-the-Month Club version of this work was offered in 1993.

MULTIPLE VERSIONS

*241. **The Bible Library.** Oklahoma City: Ellis Enterprises, 1992. ISBN 1-566-73000-7.(CD-ROM).

This is an enormous tool furnishing access to nine versions of the Bible as well as various concordances, word-studies, dictionaries, commentaries, sermon outlines, and illustrations (including hymn stories). It is an excellent example of a class of computer-accessed comprehensive religious sources enhancing the library collection in a modestly priced manner ($600 or so). Bible versions treated are *American Standard Version, Hebrew-Greek Transliteration, King James Version, Literal English Translation, Living Bible, New King James Version, New International Version, Revised Standard Version,* and *Simple English New Testament.* The CD-ROM is a reissue of the 1988 offering available for purchase through the Faxon Company. As reference librarians begin to explore their complete systems of Bible information, they will appreciate the "one-stop shopping" convenience in the host of informational tools available. Updates are issued when needed.

The *CDWord Interactive Biblical Library*, produced by CDWord Library in 1990 in cooperation with the faculty of the Dallas Theological Seminary, is another of these CD-ROM publications of comprehensive nature selling for about the same price as the *Bible Library.* It furnishes access to sixteen of the world's most-used Bible texts and reference sources. These have been carefully selected by scholars and specialists; updates are issued on an annual basis. Included here are two complete Greek versions, four English texts, two dictionaries, three Greek word books, three commentaries, and parsing for each Greek word.

*242. **FABS Reference Bible System.** Foundation for Advanced Biblical Studies (FABS International), 1988. (CD-ROM).

This is another of the computerized systems, comprehensive in nature, producing convenient access to information from a variety of sources for the librarian and the patron. It provides eight English translations of the Bible, the Greek New Testament, the Greek Septuagint, six volumes of aids to language study, concordances, Apocryphal translations, Josephus, and Apostolic Fathers. The company has been developing such software for several years and is regarded as a major supplier of computer-accessible software in the field. It sells for around $400.

Another source from the same company is *FABS Electronic Bible System*, priced at less than half of the *Reference Bible System*. This one furnishes the text of five English-language versions along with a concordance for each version. It represents an excellent reference source for the librarian for accessing information for frequently asked queries.

Bibliographies, Indexes, and Abstracts

243. **International Zeitschriftenschau für Bibelwissenschaft und Grenzgebiete/International Review of Biblical Studies.** Dusseldorf, Germany: Patmos, 1951/1952– . Ann.

The *IZBG* is an annual publication that provides abstracts of Bible studies that appear as periodical articles, monographic works, or essays in collections. Titles of the studies appear in the language of the original document, although most abstracts are in German. Entries are arranged by classification of the subject covered; access is facilitated by an index of authors.

Another international bibliography of foreign extraction is *Elenchus of Biblical Bibliography, 1985–* , which has appeared under this title since 1988, with coverage beginning in 1985. This Italian publication provides extensive listings of biblical scholarship, also on an annual basis, and has author and subject indexes. Prior to that time, it had a distinguished run, first as part of the journal *Biblica*, then as *Elenchus Bibliographicus Biblicus* (Rome: Biblical Institute, 1968–1984).

244. **Multi-Purpose Tools for Bible Study.** Rev. and exp. ed. Frederick W. Danker. Minneapolis, MN: Fortress Press, 1993. 330p. ISBN 0-800-62598-6.

Finally, after more than twenty years, this highly respected and detailed literature guide was revised and updated and again has become the first choice of scholars and serious researchers when searching for sources of information in the field. Its predecessor (1970) had shown signs of obsolescence, but the new edition has reclaimed its leading position. Like the initial offering, it provides excellent coverage of the various tools and reference sources available for the study of the Bible in its various versions and will appeal to students as well as more sophisticated inquirers.

Another useful tool is *The Bible Study Resource Guide*, in its revised second edition by Joseph D. Allison (Thomas Nelson, 1984). This work has gone through several changes in seeking to fulfill its intent to provide an easy-to-follow-and-understand guide for the layperson in making decisions regarding the choice of Bibles and their study aides. It represents a handy information piece that should be of use to both librarians and students, although exposition tends to be brief. Explanations are given of Bible versions and reference sources of all kinds. Background and development of these tools are explained.

245. **New Testament Abstracts: A Record of Current Periodical Literature.** Cambridge, MA: Weston School of Theology, 1956– . 3/yr. ISSN 0028-6877.

Now in its thirty-eighth year, this is the oldest continuing abstract service on Bible studies in the English language. The abstracts cover the literature on the Bible that has appeared in a variety of Western languages from periodicals of varied extraction. Catholic, Protestant, and Jewish periodicals all contribute the source material. Each volume contains indexes of scripture texts, authors, book reviews, and book notices, published in the third issue. All abstracts appear in English regardless of the language of the original publication. The work indexes over 500 periodicals and lists over 500 books per year. There is a broad classified arrangement, with Gospels, Acts, Epistles, Revelations, and so forth.

A bibliography considered to be an extraordinary achievement is *New Testament Christology: A Critical Assessment and Annotated Bibliography*, compiled by Arland J. Hultgren (Greenwood, 1988). More than 1,900 books, articles, and essays representing the twentieth-century theological scholarship of numerous countries and languages are identified, described, and frequently evaluated with clarity and precision. Arrangement of entries is under major categories that are then subdivided by orientation. There are indexes by name, book title, and subject.

*246. **Old Testament Abstracts.** Washington, DC: Catholic Biblical Association of America, 1978– . 3/yr. ISSN 0364-8591.

Developed on the model of *New Testament Abstracts* (entry 245) in terms of its thrice-yearly frequency and its style of coverage, this newer work has also made a significant contribution in an area not previously covered by an abstracting service. Each year more than 200 journals from various denominations and geographic regions provide the source material for nearly 1,000 abstracts in English. These articles cover all aspects of Old Testament study (Pentateuch, the historical books, the writings, etc.). Like the earlier service, this one provides a separate listing of book reviews, and indexes of authors and scripture texts in the third issue. In addition, there is an index of Semitic words. In 1995, the publisher made the work available on CD-ROM.

247. **Old Testament Commentary Survey.** 2d ed. Tremper Longman III. Grand Rapids, MI: Baker Book House, 1995. 184p. ISBN 0-8010-2024-7.

Commentaries are among the most frequently consulted reference tools in the area of religion, furnishing explanation of the meaning of Bible passages. This work furnishes a useful guide to their selection, treating those commentaries focused on the Old Testament. Longman represents an evangelical tradition but furnishes objective evaluation in terms of ratings based on a five-point system recognizing merit rather than brand of theology. Included here are introductions, theologies, histories, and atlases, along with the commentaries, making the tool especially valuable in developing a collection. The second edition represents an expansion with the addition of fifty-five new entries.

A more broadly developed source is *A Guide to Selecting and Using Bible Commentaries*, by Douglas Stuart (Word Books, 1990). Not limited to Old Testament sources, Stuart furnishes an excellent guide to more than 1,100 commentaries of various types produced in the English language. The work opens with an exposition of the nature of commentaries, with attention given to such requisites as size, detail, level of readership, and theological perspective in their classification. The last chapter provides personal recommendations.

248. **The Word of God: A Guide to English Versions of the Bible.**
Lloyd R. Bailey, ed. Atlanta, GA: John Knox, 1982. 228p. ISBN
0-8042-0079-3.

A well-conceived and informative literature guide to nine different English-language versions of the Bible, this work presents the essays of distinguished authors who were given the task of evaluating the Bible in terms of the criteria they deem important. They were asked to consider the original manuscripts, interpretations provided by translators, and English usage. The Bibles selected were the *Revised Standard Version* (entry 234), *New English Bible* (entry 236), *New Jewish Version*, *New American Standard Bible* (entries 231n, 233n), *Jerusalem Bible* (entry 235), *Today's English Version*, *Living Bible*, *New American Bible* (entry 237), and *New International Version* (entry 238). The appendices include a commentary about the *King James Version* (see entry 231) as well as a summary comparison by Bailey. There is an index to scripture references.

Concordances and Quotations

249. **Complete Concordance to the Bible (Douay Version).** Newton
Wayland Thompson and Raymond Stock. St. Louis, MO: Herder, 1942;
repr., 1945, 1953, 1964; Woodbridge, CT: Research Publications, 1992
(microfilm). 1914p.

The Douay version (entry 232) is the old edition (still revered by many) that has occupied a prominent place in the rites of Catholics through the years. A parallel can be drawn to the *King James Version* (entry 231) in its remarkable longevity and appeal in the light of many subsequent discoveries, revisions, and new translations. Therefore, this concordance retains an important position in libraries that serve the needs of Catholic patrons. First published in 1942, the concordance was revised and expanded only three years later with the addition of many words and references. Citations to passages with excerpts from them are found after each listed word. It provides a good coverage of words in the Bible, except for those of very common, nondistinctive character.

250. **Cruden's Complete Concordance to the Old and New Testaments.** Grand Rapids, MI: Zondervan, 1976; repr., McLean, VA: MacDonald,
1984. 783p. ISBN 0-917006-31-3.

The most famous of the concordances, *Cruden's* was first published in 1737 and has achieved a classic position among reference books of this type. It has been revised, reedited, and published under a variety of imprints since that time. A paperback edition was published in 1976. It presents about 250,000 English words from the *King James Version* (entry 231) in alphabetical order. Not nearly as complete as some of its successors in coverage of the canon, it remains useful for its treatment of the Apocrypha. The work is divided into three sections: Common Words, Proper Names, and Apocryphal Words. It provides definitions for proper names and for common words with obscure meanings. Some of the modern reprints omit the Apocrypha section, which greatly affects its value as a reference tool.

251. **The Eerdmans' Analytical Concordance to the Revised Standard
Version of the Bible.** Richard E. Whitaker. Grand Rapids, MI: Eerdmans,
1988. 1548p. ISBN 0-8028-2403-X.

Whitaker and his associates at the Institute for Antiquity and Christianity have pre-pared an important analytical concordance of the whole *Revised Standard Version* (entry 234); it identifies the words being translated from the original language within their context. The *Revised Standard Version* is considered to be a more authoritative translation than is

King James (entry 231), and the analysis of the English and original Greek wording makes it an important vehicle for both students and scholars. Personal pronouns and certain prepositions and conjunctions are omitted as being nonessential. In addition to the major text, there are listings of proper nouns and of numbers along with indexes in Hebrew, Aramaic, Greek, and Latin.

An Analytical Concordance to the Revised Standard Version of the New Testament, by Clinton Morrison (Westminster, 1979), is an attempt to treat the *RSV* as did Young the *KJV*. It has proven to be a successful effort, creating a needed reference source. The concordance is divided into two parts, the concordance itself and an index-lexicon. The concordance provides for each English word reference to scripture as well as definitions, Greek phraseology, and English transliterations. The index-lexicon identifies the transliterated Greek words with the English words used in the Bible, thus serving as an index to the concordance.

252. Nelson's Complete Concordance of the New American Bible.
Stephen J. Hartdegan, gen. ed. Nashville, TN: Thomas Nelson, 1977. 1274p. ISBN 0-8407-4900-7.

The Nelson Company has been an early player in developing new concordances with the aid of the computer. This work on the *New American Bible* (entry 237) presents 300,000 entries grouped under 18,000 key terms. These major terms are arranged alphabetically and are subdivided by entries that are listed in order of their occurrence in the Bible. Keywords are set off in boldface capitals to facilitate their use. Frequency of appearance is indicated for keywords as well. References are provided for exact locations in the Bible. A list of omitted words representing nonsignificant descriptors is given in the preface.

253. The NIV Exhaustive Concordance. Edward W. Goodrick and John R. Kohlenberger III. Grand Rapids MI: Zondervan, 1990. 1853p. ISBN 0-310-43690-7.

This is an expanded offering of a 1981 publication with a slightly different title. Due to the increasing influence and popularity of the *New International Version* (entry 238), this concordance has become an important purchase and common feature of reference departments. It is a computer-produced concordance of exhaustive proportions, covering all words in the Bible, and furnishes easy access to required passages and phrases for both the scholar and the layperson. There are numerous special features, such as frequency counts, related word lists, cross-indexing to Strong's classic work (entry 255), and a listing of variant terms for British and American usage. The present edition identifies original Hebrew, Aramaic, and Greek words in separate indexes; articles, conjunctions, prepositions, and pronouns are treated also, with their biblical citations.

254. The NRSV Concordance Unabridged: Including the Apocryphal/ Deuterocanonical Books. John R. Kohlenberger III. Grand Rapids MI: Zondervan, 1991. 1483p. ISBN 0-310-53910-2.

This concordance, published one year after the issue of the *New Revised Standard Version* (entry 234n), is a computer-produced effort divided into four sections. The main concordance lists every major word and about 630 phrases, with a frequency count, related words, and cross-references to the *King James Version* (entry 231). In addition there are an index of articles, conjunctions, pronouns and particles; an index to *NRSV* footnotes; as well as a topical index identifying such elements as animals, athletics, and musical instruments of the Bible. The work is thorough and well-constructed, with good contextual information for each word.

NRSV Exhaustive Concordance, published by Thomas Nelson in the same year, is a competitor and provides similar coverage to the *NRSV Concordance Unabridged*. In similar fashion, it furnishes a main concordance with a new identical listing of words, but only about thirty phrases. Other parts are similar to the Kohlenberger effort, although the topical index is much more detailed in this title. There are some additional special features such as listings of laws of the Bible, Jewish calendar, Jewish feasts, prayers of the Bible, and so forth.

255. **Strong's Exhaustive Concordance of the Bible with Key-word Comparison.** Rev. ed. James Strong. Nashville, TN: Abingdon, 1980; repr., 1986. var. paging. ISBN 0-687-40033-3.

This is a reprint of one of the classic concordances, originally published in 1894, embellished with keyword comparisons. Strong's work is regarded as the most complete in terms of its coverage of every word of the *King James Version* (entry 231), including articles, adjectives, and other nondistinctive types of words. These are listed alphabetically in two places, with the important words in the main text and the forty-seven common words in the appendix. In addition, there is a comparative treatment of selected words and phrases to those found in five leading contemporary translations. There are brief dictionaries of the original Hebrew and Greek terms, with references to the English words. The apocryphal books are not covered. The cover title identifies it as *Abingdon's Strong's Exhaustive Concordance of the Bible*.

The New Strong's Exhaustive Concordance of the Bible (Thomas Nelson, 1997) is one of the modern computer-generated concordances, first issued in 1984. It has a pleasing appearance that was the result of changes in sequence of information presented in the entries, simplified instructions, and the addition of some helpful new features. A complementary effort is *NKJV Exhaustive Concordance: New King James Version*, published by Thomas Nelson (1992), providing coverage similar to that of the recent *NRSV* efforts (entry 254). It treats every word in the new translation; articles, possessives, and prepositions are found in extensive listings at the back of the volume. Words are cross-referenced with the *King James Version* (entry 231). There are no charts or explanatory articles as in the *NRSV* works.

256. **Young's Analytical Concordance to the Bible.** Newly rev. and corr. Robert Young. Nashville, TN: Thomas Nelson, 1982. 1428p. ISBN 0-8407-4972-4.

The subtitle reads: "Containing about 311,000 references, subdivided under the Hebrew and Greek originals, with the literal meaning and pronunciation of each: based upon the King James Version, including index-lexicons to the Old and New Testaments." Names of people and places are included. The main text consists of the word listings (nouns, adjectives, verbs, and adverbs) in alphabetical order. These are identified with scriptural passages as well as definitions and indications of original forms in Greek, Hebrew, and Aramaic when necessary. The analytical coverage of words in the ancient languages has given this work a reputation for comprehensiveness and has established it as a landmark effort for study and reference with the *King James Version* (entry 231).

A simplified edition was issued in 1992 as *Analytical Concordance to the Bible on an Entirely New Plan . . .* from Hendrickson Publishers. It is designed for the "simplest reader of the English Bible."

Dictionaries, Encyclopedias, and Handbooks

*257. **The Anchor Bible Dictionary.** David N. Freedman et al., eds. New York: Doubleday, 1992. 6v. ISBN 0-385-19360-2 (v.1).

This is a monumental effort designed to provide a reference source for serious Bible study. It can be used specifically with the Anchor Bible or generally with all versions. There are nearly 1,000 contributors (scholars and specialists in the field), who have furnished 6,200 entries over the period of six years that it took to bring the title to fruition. Articles are full and detailed, with each of the contributors providing his or her own perspective. Unfortunately, in many cases they have not provided indication of alternative theories. It would appear that this work will replace *Interpreter's Dictionary of the Bible* (entry 266) in those areas in which the *IDB* is outdated, although certainly not in all respects. It was originally planned in five volumes, but as work progressed it became obvious that a larger set was necessary. Although there are cross-references, the work suffers somewhat for lack of an index. In 1997, the work was offered in CD-ROM format through Logos Research Systems.

258. Dictionary of Jesus and the Gospels. Joel B. Green and Scot McKnight, eds. Downers Grove, IL: Intervarsity Press, 1992. 933p. ISBN 0-8308-1777-8.

This effort serves to supplement the earlier classic title by Hastings, *Dictionary of Christ and the Gospels* (Scribner's 1906–1908; repr., Baker Book House, 1973). Such an update was necessary due to the vast amount of inquiry and investigation into the topic. Numerous scholars have contributed to this work, an evangelical effort from an evangelical publisher. They have written in a manner that is both informative and critical, focusing on the authority of scripture and the accuracy of the gospels in furnishing perspectives on Jesus Christ. The work is noted as being easy to use and relatively free of needless jargon, enabling it to be employed with a wide-ranging audience in terms of scholarship and seriousness of purpose. Articles furnish cross-references as well as current bibliographies of useful reading materials.

259. Dictionary of Proper Names and Places in the Bible. O. Odelaine and R. Seguineau. Garden City, NY: Doubleday, 1981. 479p. Repr., Robert Hale, 1991. 528p. ISBN 0-7090-4400-3.

Translated from the French and adapted by Matthew J. O'Connell, this has proved to be a useful dictionary of proper names identified in the *Jerusalem Bible* (entry 235). Although the majority of these words can be found in other Bible dictionaries, it is unique in its coverage of this modern version. Coverage is provided of words in both the Old and New Testaments and entries include the English form of the name, transliteration of the Hebrew or Greek form as originally used, frequency of occurrence in the Bible, definition and etymology, as well as an indication of its importance. There is an introductory essay explaining the purpose of the work and the importance of biblical names. There are name listings and chronological tables. A word of caution: Indexing may not be complete for each word, and it may appear more frequently than the number of references provided.

260. Dictionary of Qur'anic Terms and Concepts. Mustansir Mir. New York: Garland, 1987. 244p. (Garland Reference Library of the Humanities, v. 693). ISBN 0-8240-8546-9.

An excellent supplementary resource to *Encyclopaedia of Islam* (entry 184) and *Shorter Encyclopaedia of Islam* (entry 184n) is this dictionary of some 500 terms drawn from the *Qur'an* (see entry 240), the Bible of the Islamic faith. Entries are generally brief, ranging from a few sentences to about two pages depending upon the significance of the topic. Arrangement is alphabetical by English translation and coverage includes definition and explanation of the significance of the various terms, with references to passages in the *Qur'an*. The work appears to fulfill its purpose of providing concise and methodical treatment of both major and minor terms and concepts. It is especially useful to a beginning student or to a general reader. No bibliography or index is provided, but entries have cross-references. Concluding the work is a twenty-page listing of terms included.

261. **The Eerdmans Bible Dictionary.** Rev. ed. Allen C. Myers. Grand Rapids, MI: Eerdmans, 1987; 1993 (pbk). 1094p. ISBN 0-8208-2402-1.

This is an important revised and expanded English translation of the reputable Dutch dictionary, *Bijbelse Encyclopedie*, first published in 1950 under F. W. Grosheide and later revised in 1975. Representing the evangelical Protestant tradition but presenting a fair perspective and treatment, it has nearly 5,000 entries contributed by nearly fifty North American scholars of various denominations. The work has been updated with the addition of current topics and recent archaeological studies, and is based on the *Revised Standard Version* (entry 234), although other modern translations are incorporated. Articles are not signed but scholarship is evident in the treatment given to every person and place named in the Bible and the exposition of theological concepts and cultural aspects. Some entries contain bibliographies, and there are a number of photographs, line drawings, and color maps by Hammond. There is a list of abbreviations along with a transliteration scheme and a pronunciation guide.

262. **Encyclopedia of Biblical Theology: The Complete Sacramentum Verbi.** 3d ed. Johannes B. Bauer. New York: Crossroad, 1981. 1141p. ISBN 0-8245-0042-3.

This work was translated from the German language and represents the combined efforts of biblical experts from West Germany, Austria, France, and Switzerland. It is a high point of erudition and consistency for Roman Catholic scholarship and covers important words, their changes of meaning, and their significance. Articles are cogent, well-written, and provide an analysis of the reasoning behind Catholic theological beliefs. Although of scholarly quality, the tool can be used by the laity. Entries range from a few paragraphs to several pages in length, depending upon the importance or significance of the topic. Articles are signed and provide bibliographies of both English- and foreign-language sources. There are indexes of biblical passages and of Hebrew and Greek words, among others.

263. **The HarperCollins Bible Dictionary.** Rev. and upd. ed. Paul J. Achtemeier et al., eds. San Francisco: HarperSanFrancisco, 1996. 1256p. ISBN 0-06-060037-3.

Taking a cue from the nonsectarian production of the 1976 supplementary volume of the *Interpreter's Dictionary of the Bible* (entry 266), the initial 1985 edition (*Harper's Bible Dictionary*) employed the talents of 180 members of the Society of Biblical Literature. Contributors represented all elements of Western traditions—Catholic, Protestant, and Jewish—mostly from the United States but also from the United Kingdom and Israel. Although not noted in the bibliographic statement, this actually was the ninth edition of this Harper & Row publication, first issued in 1952 and revised up to 1973. The new HarperCollins revision continues in the same vein, having disengaged from conventional piety and representing the concepts and personalities in a matter-of-fact fashion characteristic of historical scholarship. Such elements as the Shroud of Turin are categorically dismissed. Current topics are treated along with all important personalities and places named in the Bible. There are numerous illustrations (maps, photographs, drawings), some in color. A general index furnishes access. The earlier edition, *Harper's Bible Dictionary* (1985), is available on CD-ROM as a file in *CDWord Interactive Biblical Library* (entry 241n). It is expected that the new edition will soon be covered in that manner.

The sister publication is *Harper's Bible Commentary* (entry 276). The publisher prepared a two-volume set combining the two efforts in 1991, entitled *Harper's Bible Dictionary and Harper's Bible Commentary.*

264. **New Bible Dictionary.** 3d ed. D. R. W. Wood, ed. Downers Grove, IL: Intervarsity Press, 1996. 1298p. ISBN 0-830-81439-6.

Another revision and expansion of the popular *New Bible Dictionary* (Tyndale, 1962; 2d ed., 1980), this work, like its predecessors, has been prepared by a distinguished group of editors. Contributions from numerous specialists from various English-speaking countries retain its character as a work of international scholarship. Articles cover the *Revised Standard Version* (entry 234) in terms of its books, people, major words, and doctrines; 100 of these have been revised and embrace the latest findings and studies. History, geography, customs, and culture of Israel and surrounding countries are described. There are hundreds of photographs, maps, charts, diagrams, and tables. Bibliographies are furnished. The work appeals to all ages and backgrounds.

Another recent effort is *Illustrated Dictionary of Bible Life and Times* (Readers Digest, 1997), treating words selected from the *New Revised Standard Version* (entry 234n) for a popular and less-sophisticated audience. There are some 1,500 entries in the main text that are unique because they are names of things, ideas (mercy, patience, etc.), relationships, and physical objects (kitchen, husband, etc.) rather than personalities, places, or events. The narrative is accompanied by color illustrations. In addition, there is a secondary glossary of nearly 400 additional words deemed not important enough to appear in the main text.

265. **The International Standard Bible Encyclopedia.** Rev. ed. Geoffrey W. Bromiley, gen. ed. Grand Rapids, MI: Eerdmans, 1979–1988. 4v. ISBN 0-8028-8160-2.

Since its original edition in 1915 and revision in 1930, the *ISBE* has been regarded as a standard for library purchase and a classic in the field. The new edition has now been completed, and all indications are that it will assume a similar position of importance. Volume 1 (A–D) was published in 1979, followed by volume 2 (E–J) in 1981. Volume 3 (K–P) was completed in 1986 and volume 4 (Q–Z) was issued in 1988. Designed for teachers, students, pastors, and interested laypersons, it covers all persons and places mentioned in the *Revised Standard Version* (entry 234) along with references to similar words in the *King James Version* (entry 231), the *American Standard Version* (entry 233), and the *New English Bible* (entry 236). Entries include pronunciation, etymology, and evolution of meaning through both the Old Testament and New Testament. There are numerous illustrations, some in color. Also covered are terms relating to theology. Cross-references are supplied.

266. **The Interpreter's Dictionary of the Bible**: **An Illustrated Encyclopedia.** Nashville, TN: Abingdon, 1962. 4v. **Supps.** 1976, 1982. ISBN 0-687-19270-6.

Considered the leading scholarly encyclopedic dictionary, this covers both the *King James Version* (entry 231) and the *Revised Standard Version* (entry 234). Its full subtitle indicates its purpose: "identifying and explaining all proper names and significant terms and subjects in the Holy Scriptures, including the Apocrypha, with attention to archaeological discoveries and research into the life and faith of ancient times." It is a work of modern scholarship that includes references to the Dead Sea Scrolls and other recently investigated ancient manuscripts. Developed for the use of preachers, scholars, students, teachers, and general readers, it has met the needs of this diverse grouping in an extraordinary manner. Each important article receives a bibliography, and the work provides maps and illustrations, some of which are in color. An indispensable source, it proves to be an excellent companion to *The Interpreter's Bible* (entry 277). The supplements represent a departure from the past by adding new articles of ecumenical nature as well as updating material needing revision.

267. **Mercer Dictionary of the Bible.** Watson E. Mills et al., eds. Macon, GA: Mercer University Press, 1991–1992. 993p. ISBN 0-86554-402-6.

This is the third corrected printing in two years for this work, designed to serve the needs of college students of religion and Bible classes. It represents an important effort, reflecting the more conservative orientation but with a balanced perspective. It is a product of the scholarship of 225 specialists, all members of the National Association of Baptist Professors of Religion. Entries furnish exposition of the full range of possible topics: books of the Bible, characters, places and geographical features, theological concepts, history, and culture. They are well-developed, utilize current scholarship, and reflect a broadly informed and somewhat worldly view. There are 1,450 signed articles, alphabetically arranged. For the most part they furnish bibliographies of both liberal and conservative writings, and they vary in length from a few sentences to several pages. There are sixty-four pages of color maps and photographs; black-and-white photographs appear throughout. The work was reissued as *The Lutterworth Dictionary of the Bible* in 1994.

268. **Nelson's Bible Encyclopedia for the Family: A Comprehensive Guide to the World of the Bible.** Nashville, TN: Thomas Nelson, 1982. 288p. ISBN 0-8407-5258-X.

One of the several publications that in the recent past has established the family, especially young people, as its target audience. The format is attractive and tends to appeal to a variety of age levels. Coverage is given to the complete world of the Bible in twenty chapters, beginning with "The Bible's Story" and then leading into its content, translation, archaeology, the home, family, clothes, geography, and so forth. Chapters are subdivided by nations or geographic regions. The articles are written in simple, easy-to-understand language in a clear manner, and are well-illustrated in colorful fashion. Charts and drawings (some of comic book variety) are provided. The work was developed through the efforts of the Scripture Union, an interdenominational organization of international status.

269. **The New International Dictionary of Biblical Archaeology.** Edward M. Blaiklock and R. K. Harrison, eds. Grand Rapids, MI: Zondervan, 1983. 485p. ISBN 0-310-21250-2.

Considered to be an outstanding, comprehensive, scholarly dictionary that covers all aspects of biblical archaeology. Entries are provided for personal names, place names, deities, texts, languages, animals, architecture, archaeological techniques, furniture, and so forth. There are more than 800 articles from twenty contributors from all over the world. Articles are signed and include bibliographies and cross-references. They vary in length from a few columns to a dozen pages or more. There are more than 200 photographs, including a sixteen-page section in full color. Maps are incorporated, although possibly not as frequently as needed. Emphasis is on providing facts of interest to a wide audience; theological interpretation is left to the reader.

270. **The New Unger's Bible Dictionary.** Rev. ed. Merrill F. Unger, R. K. Harrison et al., eds. Chicago: Moody Press, 1988. 1400p. ISBN 0-8024-9037-9.

The third edition of Unger's reputable work was published in 1966 and since then has provided a serious and scholarly source of information based on a conservative perspective of the *New American Standard Bible* (entry 233n). The present effort continues the excellent coverage, and includes certain passages of the *King James Version* (entry 231) and the *New International Version* (entry 238). Unger was a Semitic scholar and prolific contributor to religious studies. Similarly, the present work is guided by the well-known scholar, R. K. Harrison, who now serves as editor. Emphasis has been placed on several areas of inquiry: archaeological treatment based on important recent scholarship, historical and geographical scrutiny of biblical lands of the Near East, the influence and activities of various personalities associated with biblical events, and thorough exposition of common doctrines and beliefs. The work is profusely illustrated with photographs, drawings, and maps. An index provides access.

The New Unger's Bible Handbook, revised and updated by Unger (Moody, 1984), has held a respected position among reference tools. It has a conservative orientation based on the evangelical tradition. The new edition continues in the same vein and has appeal for the layperson. Attractive in format, the descriptions provided are brief and to the point, with little identification of scholarly source material. There are numerous illustrations, including photographs, drawings, maps, charts, diagrams, and colorful chronologies. The books of the Bible are explained in regard to their place in canonical literature, authorship, and themes. Brief background articles cover related aspects of Bible study, such as history and archaeology.

*271. **The Oxford Companion to the Bible.** Bruce M. Metzger and Michael D. Coogan, eds. New York: Oxford University Press, 1993. 874p. ISBN 0-19-504645-5.

Another of the excellent one-volume handbooks in the Oxford Companion series, this recent effort furnishes over 700 signed entries describing and interpreting all aspects of Bible development and use. Unlike other Bible dictionaries, it is designed to track the continuing significance of the work in cultural developments relating to the law, arts, politics, and literature. More than 250 international scholars are listed as contributors and have provided a variety of insights and important perspective. Entries vary in length from a few lines to extensive essays, and treat personalities, books of the Bible, events, and rites. Coverage is given to religious concepts such as the Holy Spirit and immortality as well as contemporary social issues such as homosexuality and anti-Semitism. There are a number of well-constructed full color maps to illustrate locations and sites, along with an index to aid access. The work became available on computer disks in 1996.

A recent and useful work that complements the *Companion* in furnishing more concise treatment of a greater number of specific topics is *A Dictionary of the Bible*, by W. R. F. Browning, a clergyman and academician (Oxford University Press, 1996; popular title *Oxford Dictionary of the Bible*). Some 2,000 entries serve to identify and define terms, places, persons, practices, and events in a clear and lucid manner, and contain references to the Bible. A brief bibliography concludes the effort.

272. **Papal Pronouncements: A Guide, 1740–1978.** Claudia Carlen. Ann Arbor, MI: Pierian Press, 1990. 2v. ISBN 0-87650-266-4.

This is a complementary work to an earlier title by Carlen, *The Papal Encyclicals 1740–1981*, described below. *Papal Pronouncements* lists and describes all types of pronouncements, both formal and informal, beginning with Benedict XIV, who revived the encyclical. In addition to encyclicals, coverage is given to letters, apostolic constitutions, homilies, addresses, allocutions, and so forth. Sixteen popes are covered; volume 1 treats Benedict XIV to Paul VI and volume 2, Paul VI to John Paul I. Not included are the decrees from the two Vatican Councils. Identification is made by form and content, with entries supplying dates, titles, audience, type of pronouncement, length, summary, and sources where they can be found. There is a directory of collections of such material, a general bibliography, and a general index.

The Papal Encyclicals 1740–1981, completed by Carlen for the same publisher in 1981 and reprinted in 1990 as a five-volume set, provides the complete text in English of 280 encyclicals issued over a span of 240 years. The encyclical is described in an introductory essay as an instrument of papal teaching. Arrangement is chronological under the name of the pontiff; the encyclicals are numbered consecutively. The reign of each pope is described historically; the encyclical follows, then a listing of sources. References appear in endnotes.

*273. **Theological Dictionary of the New Testament.** Gerhard Kittel and Gerhard Friedrich, eds. Grand Rapids, MI: Eerdmans, 1985. 1356p. ISBN 0-8028-2404-8.

This is an abridgment of the author's monumental ten-volume work of the same name (Eerdmans, 1964–1976), translated from the German by Geoffrey W. Bromiley, who also was responsible for this shorter version. The earlier, major work brought contributions from many specialists. It defined in great length the Christian meanings of 2,300 Greek terms, some articles reaching monographic proportions. Known as *Kittel* or as *TDNT*, the multi-volume work is regarded as an indispensable aid for scholarship. The recent one-volume *Kittel* retains the same number of entries as does the original, but shortens them in drastic fashion. Entries still cover history, variant meanings, and connotations, but the emphasis is on biblical usage with far less attention given to original context. Designed to appeal to a wide range of users, from beginning students to scholars and specialists in need of a convenient information source who do not mind the deletion of bibliographical references. It is available on CD-ROM as part of the package provided by **CDWord Interactive Biblical Library* (entry 241n).

Less detailed and thorough is *Exegetical Dictionary of the New Testament* (Eerdmans, 1990–1993), the three-volume translation of a German work edited by Horst Balz and Gerhard Schneider. It represents a useful tool in its exposition of the meaning of biblical text for its first audience. Coverage is given to all words in the Greek New Testament, enabling the user to comprehend the original intent. It is convenient and readable and offers a solid source of information to both student and specialist.

274. **Theological Dictionary of the Old Testament.** Johannes G. Botterweck and Helmer Ringgren. Grand Rapids, MI: Eerdmans, 1974– . 8v. (In progress). ISBN 0-8028-2332-7 (v.8).

Projected as a twelve-volume set, *TDOT* is a translation of a German work also in progress. The English translation is progressing at a rate that closely matches its initial production in German. Volume 8 was issued in 1997. Considered to be an extremely valuable resource for students and scholars, it provides lengthy, technical articles on important words, tracing the etymology in ancient languages. Definitions are given, as are expositions of semantic relations and the word's social, cultural, and historical context. There is a liberal provision of footnotes and bibliographies, and students will appreciate the discussions of the theological importance of the words. Articles are signed by contributors who are noted scholars. It should be considered as a companion to the full set of Kittel's *Theological Dictionary of the New Testament* (entry 273), and is sometimes referred to as *OT Kittel*.

Commentaries

275. **Encyclopedia of Biblical Interpretations: A Millennial Anthology.** Menahem M. Kasher. New York: American Biblical Encyclopedia Society, 1953– . 9v. (In progress).

This is a translation by Rabbi Harry Freedman of an extensive thirty-five-volume set, which is being shortened somewhat in the process of translation. About half of the original edition has been covered in the nine volumes produced thus far. Unfortunately, nothing has been added since 1979. The work presents a collection of Jewish interpretations of and commentaries on the Bible from the time of Moses to the Talmudic-Midrashic period. Each verse of the Bible is covered and the sources are identified. Included among the commentary are both exegetical works and parables, with careful documentation of the sources, both modern and ancient. Bibliographies and indexes are included in each volume.

People of the Book: Canon, Meaning, and Authority, by Moshe Halbertal (Harvard University Press, 1997), furnishes a concise but sophisticated analysis of Jewish text-centered cultures through examination of the past impact of the sacred texts in establishing Jewish identity. This influence over identity has diminished over the years through Zionism and contemporary problems and questions that cannot be answered in traditional or even deviant interpretations of the Torah and Talmud. The work is a well-constructed exegesis.

*276.   Harper's Bible Commentary. James L. Mays et al., eds. San Francisco: Harper & Row, 1988. ISBN 0-06-065541-0.

This is a Bible commentary appearing twenty-six years after its predecessor from the same publisher. Sponsored by the Society of Biblical Literature, its purpose is to make available the fruits of current scholarship to an audience of general readers. As such, it represents a companion volume to *Harper's Bible Dictionary* (entry 263n) and furnishes cross-references to relevant entries in that work. In its focus on mainstream scholarship, it has been considered by some to be the natural successor to *Peake's Commentary on the Bible* (entry 281). Worthy of mention are the well-constructed introductory essays both on the entire Bible and on each of its parts or books, including the Apocrypha. There are black-and-white illustrations along with color plates and maps. More than eighty contributors have joined the six editors in producing a useful and up-to-date work. In 1991, Harper prepared a two-volume set of its two works entitled *Harper's Bible Dictionary and Harper's Bible Commentary*. Both parts are available in CD-ROM format through **CDWord: The Interactive Biblical Library* (entry 241n).

277.   The Interpreter's Bible. New York: Abingdon-Cokesbury, 1951–1957; repr., 1988–1989. 12v.

An outstanding work in every way; the subtitle states "The Holy Scriptures in the *King James* [entry 231] and *Revised Standard* [entry 234] versions, with general articles and introduction, exegesis and exposition for each book of the Bible." A product of the combined energies of some of the best minds in the area of biblical scholarship, most of the large Protestant denominations were represented among the consulting editors. Some 125 contributors were involved, providing both exegesis and exposition. (The former provides awareness of the setting and the meanings of words in the phrases, while the latter provides the present-day meanings of the passages.) The work also provides introductory material, maps, and topical articles. Developed for the general reader as well as the specialist, this is an indispensable tool for Bible study.

The New Interpreter's Bible: General Articles, Introduction, Commentary, & Reflections . . . (Abingdon, 1994–) is a completely new work, now in progress, providing comparative treatment of the *New Revised Standard Version* (entry 234n) and the *New International Version* (entry 238). Full texts and critical notes are furnished for the two versions in parallel columns in the same manner as the earlier effort. Volumes 1–9 and 12 were completed between 1994 and 1999; volumes 10 and 11 are projected for 2000.

278.   Interpreter's Concise Commentary. Nashville, TN: Abingdon, 1983. 8v. ISBN 0-687-19232-3 (v.1).

This is a revision of *The Interpreter's One-Volume Commentary on the Bible*, edited by Charles Laymon (Abingdon, 1971), and similarly is based on the *Revised Standard Version* (entry 234). It has been divided into eight paperback volumes, each of which deals with a different aspect or issue: "The Pentateuch," "Old Testament History," "Wisdom Literature and Poetry," "The Major Prophets," "The Minor Prophets and the Apocrypha," "The Gospels," "Acts and Paul's Letters," and "Revelation and the General Epistles." The contributors represent a wide range of scholars from different parts of the world. Commentary is generally lucid, with information given regarding historical, literary, and linguistic study of the Bible. Each volume has an introduction, bibliographies, and maps. In general, the set represents a good purchase at a reasonable price.

A more recent and more restrictive one-volume work is *An Introduction to the New Testament*, by Raymond E. Brown, a retired academician (Doubleday, 1997) who prepared the work for students beginning their Bible study of the established twenty-seven-book canon. Emphasis is placed on the documents in their current canonical form rather than on their sources and subsequent developmental history. It is a useful title in providing practical comprehension of the messages and matters relating to their study.

279. **The New Jerome Biblical Commentary.** Raymond E. Brown et al. Englewood Cliffs, NJ: Prentice-Hall, 1990; repr., London: Chapman, 1995. 1484p. ISBN 0-13-614934-0.

About two-thirds of the material is new, making this extensive revision of the initial 1968 publication a noteworthy new tool, and it continues to be recognized as an important work. It provides a brief but informative commentary by some seventy Roman Catholic scholars from North American universities on each book of the longer canon identified and defined at Trent as the various parts of the Bible. Numerous articles provide exegesis and interpretation of high quality and sophistication, expressing the range of varying belief within the Church today. Bibliographies are also provided. The perspective in which the work was undertaken reflects the ecumenicism developed through the Second Vatican Council, and like the initial edition, it has been issued as a result of the emphasis on the part of the Roman Catholic Church on biblical scholarship. The same editors produced a more concise tool based on this work, entitled *The New Jerome Bible Handbook*, for Liturgical Press in 1992.

280. **The Oxford Study Bible: Revised English Bible, with the Apocrypha.** M. Jack Suggs et al., eds. New York: Oxford University Press, 1992. 1597p. ISBN 0-19-529001-1.

This aid to Bible study treats analytically the *REB* (entry 236n), the revision of the *New English Bible* that had been issued through the publisher three years earlier. The work is a truly ecumenical product and includes seven Catholic and six Jewish scholars among the various contributors. There are over twenty expository articles placing the Bible within a historical and cultural context. These essays are comprehensive in their coverage and topical approach. Notes and annotations to Bible passages are thorough and well-developed, aiding interpretation. As is the case with other study Bibles, this work combines the Bible version with study materials designed to help distinguish the nuances of meaning within the passages and to help provide a general perspective. There are twenty-eight pages of plates and fourteen color maps.

281. **Peake's Commentary on the Bible.** Rev. ed. Matthew Black and H. H. Rowley, eds. New York: Thomas Nelson, 1962; repr., 1975, 1985; repr., New York: Routledge Kegan Paul, 1990. 1126p. ISBN 0-415-05147-9.

Another standard work based on the *Revised Standard Version* (entry 234), the original edition appeared in 1919, with a supplement in 1936. The present edition was completely revised and updated by a team of illustrious British and American Bible scholars. They have signed their articles and list their credentials. The revision was undertaken due to the discovery of ancient manuscripts requiring the development of new versions of the Bible and new interpretations of a number of the passages. There are articles on a variety of general subjects and topical matters as well as the analyses of the Bible passages. The work concludes with a general index, set of maps, and geographical dictionary.

Histories and Atlases

282. **Cambridge History of the Bible.** Cambridge, UK: Cambridge University Press, 1963–1970; repr., 1975 (pbk). 3v. ISBN 0-521-29018-X.

An important standard in the field, this is an authoritative and scholarly record of the development of the Bible. The volumes appeared at different times, with number 1 being the last to appear. Volume 1 covers the period from the beginning to Jerome and provides exposition of both the Old Testament and the New Testament and the Bible in the early Church. Volume 2 covers the Western world to the time of the Reformation, providing descriptions of book production and Bible illustration in early times. Volume 3, the first published, treats the most recent period, from the Reformation to the present day. Each volume has a table of contents, a bibliography, an index of biblical references, and a detailed, general index. There is no comprehensive index to the entire set.

283. **The Harper Atlas of the Bible.** James B. Pritchard, ed. New York: Harper & Row, 1987. 254p. ISBN 0-06-181883-6.

This atlas presents a well-developed, understandable graphic/narrative description of the land, events, and personalities associated with biblical times. The historical periods from the time of the Old Testament through the period of the New Testament and Byzantine Palestine are treated through maps, charts, graphs, illustrations, and informative commentary. There is a detailed chronology from prehistoric times to A.D. 150, providing an overview of the contextual coverage of the work. Cogent narrative supplies insight into the customs, beliefs, practices, scriptural styles, crafts, and military equipment of the period. Some fifty specialists (linguists, historians, archaeologists, and theologians) representing different parts of the world contributed their expertise to produce this excellent work. Also included is a glossary providing biographical data and an extensive place-name index.

The Harper Concise Atlas of the Bible (1991) is a product of the same editor and international team of contributors. They have rewritten the narrative in more concise form and eliminated certain areas of study such as crafts and city planning, and special features such as the chronology and the biographical glossary. Documentation of biblical times remains excellent in terms of scope and treatment; it is a carefully constructed and successful abridgment.

284. **The Macmillan Bible Atlas.** Completely rev., 3d ed. Yohanan Aharoni and Michael Avi-Yonah. New York: Macmillan, 1993. 215p. ISBN 0-02-500605-3.

Always considered a work of sound scholarship and skillful cartography, this atlas continues in the tradition of the earlier editions and remains an outstanding Bible atlas. Since publication of the second edition in 1977, there have been great strides in biblical study of ancient documents that have been incorporated into what now is a timely and up-to-date source of information. In keeping with modern theory, there has been greater interest in the ecology of the lands, especially the Ancient Near East and Greco-Roman world. The book contains a large number of maps that are well developed and carefully presented. The atlas covers the period from 3000 B.C. to A.D. 200, just as it did previously, and continues to geographically depict social and political events pertaining to the influence of religious, political, economic, and military events during the periods of the Old and New Testaments. The commentary in the Old Testament section has been thoroughly revised, along with parts of the New Testament section. There are many useful charts and drawings. The scholarship and fruitful yield are acknowledged by all.

285. New Bible Atlas. J. J. Bimson et al., eds. Wheaton, IL: Tyndale, 1985. 128p. ISBN 0-8423-4675-9.

This atlas was developed out of the same research activity that created *The Illustrated Bible Dictionary* (1980). A product of British scholarship, it provides some eighty maps, which compares favorably with other biblical atlases except for *The Macmillan Bible Atlas* (entry 284). Most of the maps are in color and illustrate a variety of events in biblical history. Cartographically, it is as good as or better than other current atlases, and it is superior to *Macmillan* in clarity and visual interest. Topography, geological features, vegetation, climate, and trade routes are depicted. There are numerous photographs and ample expository narrative providing summaries of biblical history. In general it is a far more attractive publication than most of the older atlases and should be welcomed by both laypersons and serious students.

286. Oxford Bible Atlas. 3d ed. Herbert G. May, ed. New York: Oxford University Press, 1984. 144p. ISBN 0-19-143452-3.

As part of the new breed of Bible atlases, much attention has gone into the physical appearance of this volume. It is a well-illustrated, attractive effort that emphasizes recent findings in biblical scholarship and archaeological study. Beginning with an introduction that describes the climate and geographic features of the area around Palestine, the story of the Israelites is graphically presented through maps and illustrative material from the time of Saul in 1025 B.C. to the fall of Jerusalem in A.D. 70. Both topographical and historical maps are used to enlighten the reader about the context in which biblical history was made. There is not as much textual narrative as is found in other atlases.

287. Zondervan NIV Atlas of the Bible. Carl G. Rasmussen. Grand Rapids, MI: Regency Reference Library, 1989. 256p. ISBN 0-310-25160-5.

Based on the *New International Version* (entry 238), this clear and well-constructed atlas supplies excellent maps, charts, diagrams, and pictures along with lucid text. The work is divided into two major segments, the first of which is the geographical section, providing insight into the geography of Israel and Jordan. Longitudinal zones are enumerated and such elements as weather patterns, roads and routes, and geographical regions are examined. Subsections are given to coverage of Egypt, Syria, Lebanon, and Mesopotamia. The second segment is the historical section and presents a historical overview from the pre-patriarchal period to the fall of Jerusalem. There is a total of 121 maps along with 33 charts and 61 plates, furnishing useful insight into biblical times. The work concludes with a grouping of appendices supplying endnotes, bibliography, glossary, and historical timeline, and there are indexes of scripture references and personalities. Also included is a gazetteer with index.

MYTHOLOGY AND FOLKLORE

Bibliographies, Indexes, Abstracts, Etc.

288. Folklore and Folklife: A Guide to English-Language Reference Sources. Susan Steinfirst. Hamden, CT: Garland, 1992. 2v. (Garland Folklore Bibliographies, v. 16). ISBN 0-8153-0068-9.

This is a comprehensive guide to reference material in folklore written in the English language and represents a needed tool in the field. With the increasing interest and growth of the study in recent years, there has been much more interdisciplinary effort embracing a variety of fields such as sociology, psychology, folk art, architecture, and literature. Targeted to the needs of students and beginning folklorists, the entries are arranged by subject, such as folk literature or folk belief systems. Journals and societies are treated as well. Annotations describe the scope of each item; there are indexes of authors, titles, and subjects.

Folklife Sourcebook: A Directory of Folklife Resources in the United States and Canada, by Peter T. Bartis and Hillary Glatt, has been issued in its second edition (Library of Congress, 1994). This revised and expanded work represents another effort to control resources in the field of American folklore. It continues as a directory of library collections and organizations that house materials, offer programming, or publish resource material on folklife. These include federal agencies, state folk cultural programs, societies and other organizations, institutions, and foundations. Serial publications are listed. All receive treatment in separate sections of the work. Entries provide address, initial year, telephone number, regulations regarding access and services, research facilities, and collection size and format, with special collections noted along with publications.

289. **Index to Fairy Tales, 1949–1972: Including Folklore, Legends and Myths in Collections.** Norma Olin Ireland. Westwood, MA: F. W. Faxon, 1973. 741p. **Supp. Four 1973–1977.** 1979. 259p. **Supp. Five 1978–1986.** Metuchen, NJ: Scarecrow Press, 1989. 575p. **Supp. Six 1987–1992.** 1994. 587p. ISBN 0-8108-2750-6.

Compiled as a continuation of Mary Huse Eastman's *Index to Fairy Tales, Myths, and Legends* (F. W. Faxon, 1926; supps., 1937,1952), this work indexes over 400 anthologies under titles and subjects. Collections of fairy tales, folklore, legends, and myths from all over the world are included in the coverage. Authors are identified only if their names appear in the titles, but the subject index is detailed, facilitating access. Since this volume presents itself as the third supplement to Eastman, its own supplements, which cover the period 1973–1977 and 1978–1986, are considered the fourth and fifth supplements to Eastman. An additional 130 collections are indexed, most of which were published during this time period in *Supp. Four*, 261 anthologies in *Supp. Five*, and 310 anthologies in *Supp. Six*.

290. **Jewish Folklore: An Annotated Bibliography.** Eli Yassif. New York: Garland, 1986. 341p. (Garland Folklore Bibliographies, v. 10). ISBN 0-8240-9039-X.

This is an annotated bibliography of international proportions on 100 years of contributions to the study of Jewish folklore. Textbooks and anthologies of folklore are not included. Annotations are both descriptive and evaluative and provide detailed information of the important and representative studies. The period ranges from 1872 to 1980 and represents over 1,300 numbered entries. The bibliography is arranged alphabetically by author and is selective. Areas of study excluded are East European Jewish culture and Judeo-Spanish folklore. A general index is provided for access; it covers themes, motifs, names, and approaches. The compiler is a professor at Ben-Gurion University in Israel and is a recognized authority in the field of Hebrew literature.

291. **Recent Studies in Myths and Literature, 1970–1990: An Annotated Bibliography.** Bernard Accardi et al., comps. New York: Greenwood, 1991. 251p. (Bibliographies and Indexes in World Literature, no. 29). ISBN 0-313-27545-9.

This volume may serve as a supplementary vehicle within the reference collection on literary criticism and serves a specialized audience of students and scholars. Mythic criticism in the vein of Frazer's *Golden Bough* (entry 293n) is identified within a twenty-year span. Over 1,000 entries are furnished, representing modern mythical scholarship, and demonstrating that the genre is one of continuing interest to researchers. Entries are located within seven chapters, beginning with studies of mythic personalities such as Orpheus and Faust, continuing with classical literature, then dividing into periods of British and American literature, with subsections on certain authors. Shakespeare, Milton, Melville, Joyce, and others are treated. Annotations are well-developed and informative. Providing access to mythical figures, themes, and theories is a well-developed subject index, along with an index of authors.

Dictionaries, Encyclopedias, Handbooks, Etc.

*292. **Brewer's Dictionary of Phrase and Fable.** 15th ed. Adrian Room, ed. New York: HarperCollins, 1995. 1182p. ISBN 0-06-270133-9.

Since its initial appearance in 1870, Ebenezer Brewer's work has undergone frequent revision and has come to be regarded as a standard in the field. Arranged alphabetically are allusions, heroes of mythology and fiction, popular colloquial and proverbial phrases, titles, and linguistic oddities of various sorts. Because of its eclectic character and expansive scope, it is considered a work of value both for general reference and for purposes of entertainment relating to the interest or curiosity of the user. (Brewer himself referred to it as a "treasury of literary bric-a-brac.") The current edition has been reviewed and revised where necessary by Room, a well-known literary figure in this field. It continues as one of the leading reference sources for this area of inquiry. In 1996, Data Text Publishing produced the first hypertext version by making the 1894 edition available on the World Wide Web at http://www.bibliomania.com/ Reference/PhraseAndFable (accessed December 1999).

Brewer's Dictionary of 20th-Century Phrase and Fable, now in its third edition (Cassell, 1996), continues to provide a focus on interesting and evocative words and phrases introduced during this century. Inclusion of contemporary fable or myth results in the coverage of famous events of sometimes sensational nature such as murders, military disasters, political scandals, and even legendary stars of the cinema. Adhering to the style of the original work, the new offering is a useful reference to British slang and idiom.

*293. **Bulfinch's Mythology.** Thomas Bulfinch. Richard P. Martin, ed. New York: HarperCollins, 1991. 732p. ISBN 0-06-270025-1.

Bulfinch was a nineteenth-century accountant who spent much of his leisure in the pursuit of classical studies, which he had begun earlier in life as a student at Harvard. By convention, his three books on mythology and legend have become part of a one-volume trilogy. This edition retains the original text and Bulfinch's notes and introductory material to the three parts: "The Age of Faith," "The Age of Chivalry," and "Legends of Charlemagne." Martin is an academic and a distinguished classicist who provides commentary and exposition of the Bulfinch perspective with respect to current scholarship. References to additional source material are given. A paperback edition was issued by Modern Library in 1998. Of real importance is the Showgate Web version (http://www.showgate.com/bulfinch/welcome.html [accessed December 1999]), created by Bob Fisher in 1996, containing the complete text along with relevant links and a brief but informative biography of Bulfinch.

Another standard in the field, *The Golden Bough: A Study in Magic and Religion*, by Sir James George Frazer (3d ed., Macmillan, 1990, 9v. in 13), provides an interpretation of the growth and development of mystical belief systems and their relationship to customs and institutions. The original two-volume edition (1890) was later expanded to twelve and thirteen volumes and the work has appeared in the form of one-volume abridgments since 1922. (The most recent one-volume issue was from Simon & Schuster in 1996.) Frazer's work has always been considered an outstanding piece of classical scholarship, with copious notes and references to source material.

294. **A Dictionary of British Folk-Tales in the English Language.** Katherine M. Briggs. Bloomington, IN: Indiana University Press, 1970–1971. 4v. Repr., New York: Routledge Kegan Paul, 1991. 4v. in 2. ISBN 0-415-06694-8 (v.1); 0-415-06695-6 (v.2).

This extensive collection of the folk narratives and folk legends of Britain, either represented in the original form or summarized, is compiled from various printed and manuscript sources found in the F. J. Norton Collection in London. Recognized as one of the leading authorities on British folktales, Briggs has provided a distinction between folk narrative (folk-fiction for purpose of entertainment) and folk legend (once believed to be true). Part A is devoted to folk narratives (fables, fairy tales, jocular tales, novelle, and nursery tales) in keeping with the standard Aarne-Thompson classification scheme. Part B covers the folk legends such as fairies, ghosts, or giants. Within each category, the entries appear alphabetically by title (creating some difficulties regarding those that have elusive titles). There are approximately 850 entries in part A and over 1,200 in part B. Each part contains a bibliography, a classified index, and an index of titles.

*295. **Dictionary of Celtic Mythology.** James MacKillop. New York: Oxford University Press, 1998. 402p. ISBN 0-19-869157-2.

This dictionary is an expansion and revision of the previous effort by Peter B. Ellis (ABC-Clio, 1992) and continues to provide a handy introduction to Celtic mythology for a wide audience. Irish and Welsh influences and culture are examined in this alphabetical listing of entries describing places, events, gods, heroes, weapons, and fantastic creatures. Irish and Welsh origins are identified by symbols for each entry. Like other Oxford publications, this work contains informative narrative and excellent introductory material. All elements of Celtic influence (Bretons, Irish, Cornish, Manx, Scots, and Welsh) are included. Definitions and descriptions vary in length depending upon the importance of the topic. There is a useful bibliography to sources.

Peter B. Ellis's *A Dictionary of Irish Mythology* (ABC-Clio, 1991) is more narrowly focused on the Irish culture than is the *Dictionary of Celtic Mythology*. It presents concise and convenient treatment suitable for a general audience. Entries vary in length from one or two lines to two pages and treat terms, events, personalities, and topics. There is an introductory essay and a select bibliography. Of further interest is the Web site maintained by Interactive Technologies since 1997, **Gods, Goddesses, and Myths*, providing insight into the mythologies of Ireland, as well as Gaul, Wales, and so forth (http://eliki.com/ancient/myth/ [accessed December 1999]).

296. **A Dictionary of World Mythology.** Rev. and exp. ed. Arthur Cotterell. Oxford: Oxford University Press, 1986; repr., 1997. 314p. ISBN 0-19-217747-8.

A revision and expansion of the 1980 edition, this work continues to be an important and useful source of information for the reference librarian. Unlike many of the other efforts in this category, this one provides excellent coverage of the more exotic and difficult to locate geographic locales. Although Europe is also covered, the major contribution is the inclusion of Asia, the Americas, Africa, and Oceania because this material is more unique and less duplicated in other sources. Sections are divided along geographic lines and each section provides an introductory overview of the historical development of myth and religion in that area. Under each section, entries are arranged alphabetically and include deities, place names, and terms. An index and maps have been added to the new edition. Also included are a bibliography and illustrations.

Encyclopedia of Creation Myths, by David A. Leeming and Martha A. Leeming (ABC-Clio, 1994), is a well-illustrated compendium of information on myths of creation from all lands, peoples, and time periods designed for a popular audience. The work contains about 280 alphabetically arranged entries of varying length. In each case, the myths are described and source references are furnished to the bibliography. Reviewers have identified factual errors, but it remains unique in its coverage.

297. **An Encyclopedia of Fairies: Hobgoblins, Brownies, Bogies and Other Supernatural Creatures.** Katharine M. Briggs. New York: Pantheon, 1977. 481p. ISBN 0-394-40918-0.

A standard in the field, this work provides an alphabetical arrangement of entries dealing with the realm of the supernatural. These include individual creatures, descriptive articles regarding various phenomena, and identifications of related elements. Illustrations in the form of twenty-one black-and-white plates are included. These may well have been improved had they been in color. The coverage is of the world of the supernatural as represented in the tradition of Great Britain over the past 1,000 years. Descriptions are brief but informative for the most part, with citations to sources and cross-references. Pronunciations are included where needed. The bibliography at the end is followed by an index of types and motifs based on Stith Thompson's *Motif Index of Folk Literature* (Indiana University Press, 1955–1958, 6v.). The Thompson work provides a scheme of classification of the narrative elements in folktales, ballads, myths, fables, romances, and so forth. Volume 6 is an index.

298. **The Facts on File Encyclopedia of World Mythology and Legend.** Anthony S. Mercatante. New York: Facts on File, 1988. 807p. ISBN 0-8160-1049-8.

This work may serve both reference and browsing purposes because it is a well-constructed and clearly written information tool with some 3,000 entries. Entries furnish plot descriptions of titles, definitions of terms, and identification of characters both fictitious and real, from saints and rulers to fantastic creatures. Most entries run less than a page, but are informative regarding origins, significance, and background. Numerous cross-references are utilized to reveal related entries. The work is valuable for its comprehensive coverage of the various elements associated with mythology. There is a useful bibliography along with an extensive general index and a cultural and ethnic index.

Adrian Room's *NTC's Classical Dictionary: The Origins of the Names of Characters in Classical Mythology* (National Textbook, 1990) is a reprint of his *Classical Dictionary*, published in 1983. It furnishes more than 1,200 entries alphabetically arranged, providing information regarding the origin and meaning of names of mythological characters. There are several appendices that furnish name listings of various kinds. This is a good tool for serious students.

299. **The Folklore of American Holidays: A Compilation of More Than 500 Beliefs, Legends, . . .** 2d ed. Hennig Cohen and Tristram Potter Coffin, eds. Detroit: Gale Research, 1991. 509p. ISBN 0-8103-7602-4.

The complete title goes on to identify "superstitions, proverbs, riddles, poems, songs, dances, games, plays, pageants, fairs, foods, and processions associated with over 120 American calendar customs and festivals." The second edition continues in the tradition of its predecessor as an entertaining and interesting as well as informative tool. The present effort has added seventy-eight pages to the total but has retained the organization and format of the earlier issues. Beginning with New Year's Day, holidays are covered in sequence until the end of the year. Treatment for each holiday includes an historical overview through excerpts from books, newspapers, and periodicals describing practices and observances. The new edition has included additional material for previously listed days and has added new days representing multicultural influences such as Greek Independence Day, and boosterism such as Cheyenne Frontier Days. The work is well-indexed, furnishing access by subjects, ethnic groups, locations, song titles, first lines, motifs, and so forth.

300. **Funk & Wagnall's Standard Dictionary of Folklore, Mythology, and Legend.** Maria Leach, ed. and Jerome Fried, assoc. ed. New York: Funk & Wagnalls, 1972; repr., San Francisco: Harper & Row, 1984. 1236p. ISBN 0-06-250511-4.

Originally published as a two-volume work in 1949–1950, this has become the basic tool for reference in the field. The present effort is a reprint of that original edition. It has been repackaged into one volume, with the addition of a key to the 2,045 countries, regions, cultures, areas, peoples, tribes, and ethnic groups described in the text. Entries are arranged alphabetically. Coverage is comprehensive and includes lengthy, signed survey articles of an authoritative nature on individual regions and major topics, complete with bibliographies, as well as concise articles on beliefs, customs, gods, heroes, songs, tales, dances, motifs, proverbs, games, and so forth. The dictionary is known for the richness of its material.

301. **Guide to the Gods.** Marjorie Leach. Santa Barbara, CA: ABC-Clio, 1992. 980p. ISBN 0-87436-591-0.

This is a highly useful reference tool, comprehensive in its inclusion of mythological gods from all parts of the world and developed within the current orientation to multiculturalism. Gods from the legend and myth of the Greeks are treated with those from other parts of Europe, Asia, Africa, and Polynesia. Entries are arranged alphabetically within chapters, falling under eight major sections: cosmogonical, celestial, atmospheric, terrestrial, life-death cycle, economic associations, socio-cultural concepts, and religion. There are over 20,000 gods covered in double-column format. Identifications are brief and include country, place, or culture. Within each section the chapters present different attributes or functions. Commonalities of the various cultural deities are easily determined in this manner, a useful strategy to benefit students. Entries provide references to a lengthy bibliography at the end of the work. A detailed name index provides access.

302. **Illustrated Who's Who in Mythology.** Michael Senior. New York: Macmillan, 1985. 223p. ISBN 0-02-923770-X.

This is an attractive, well-written, easy-to-understand dictionary of mythological figures from all over the world. Represented are Greek, Egyptian, Hindu, Indian, Chinese, Mayan, Hebrew, Scandinavian, Japanese, Russian, and other cultures. Entries are arranged alphabetically, beginning with Abraham, and number over 1,200. The real utility of the work is in its breadth of coverage, since material on many of these cultures is not easily found in other works of ready reference. As its title implies, illustrations are a major feature, and black-and-white photographs appear on almost every page. There is also a sixteen-page section of fine color plates. Entries are generally brief in terms of description of the characters, with those from the more literate traditions receiving more space. Sources are given at the end of many entries. The seven-page introduction provides an excellent explanation of what constitutes mythology. The work concludes with a four-page index of themes.

303. **Man, Myth and Magic: The Illustrated Encyclopedia of Mythology, Religion, and the Unknown.** New ed. Richard Cavendish, ed.-in-chief and Yvonne Deutch, comp. and ed. New York: Marshall Cavendish, 1995. 21v. ISBN 1-85435-731-X.

Originally published in Great Britain in weekly installments, the first edition of this work appeared in 1970 in twenty-four volumes and was criticized for presenting certain material that was not needed or irrelevant. This edition has eliminated those segments and has been updated considerably. Coverage embraces a wide variety of topical matter, with indexes provided to main articles and to topics. There is a bibliography with classified subject guides. Cross-references are used throughout. Illustrations are plentiful and appear on almost every page; some are in color. Coverage is given to such topics as alchemy, sorcery, witchcraft, magic, psychology and the paranormal, and so forth, with long survey articles on the religions of the world. Among the many contributors who have provided signed articles are some of the very distinguished scholars of our time. This has proved to be a valuable source of information for its objective and impersonal examination of supernatural influences and occultism.

304. **Mythical and Fabulous Creatures: A Sourcebook and Research Guide.** Malcolm South, ed. Westport, CT: Greenwood, 1987. 793p. ISBN 0-313-24338-7.

This is an important work that provides detailed studies by South and seventeen colleagues on twenty different creatures. Part I of the work is divided into four segments, beginning with "Birds and Beasts" (unicorns, dragons, phoenixes, rocs, griffins, chimeras, and basilisks). The coverage continues with "Human Animal Composites" (manticores, mermaids, sirens, harpies, gorgon medusae, sphinxes, minotaurs, satyrs, and centaurs). "Creatures of the Darkness" covers vampires and werewolves, and the work concludes with "Giants and Fairies." The essays provide in-depth information on each creature and cover its origin as well as its treatment in literature, film, and art from ancient to modern times. A useful bibliography is furnished at the end of each essay. Part II contains a bibliography of general works on the subject as well as on individual creatures that do not fit into the four categories established in part I. This is considered a top-notch reference book for both students and interested laypersons.

Another good title is *Encyclopedia of Things That Never Were: Creatures, Places, and People*, by Michael Page and Robert Ingpen (Viking Penguin, 1987). This is a handy and practical work for identification of fictional and fantastic characters. Over 400 entries from over 100 different source titles of witchcraft, mythology, astrology, and classic adventure fiction are furnished. Entries are ample and range from 150 to 2,000 words in length. The work is well illustrated in color.

305. **Mythologies: A Restructured Translation of Dictionnaire des Mythologies et des Religions des Societes Traditionnelles du Monde Antique.** Chicago: University of Chicago Press, 1991. 2v. ISBN 0-226-06453-0.

This is a translation of a collection of essays originally published in French and representing original research and creative applications. It is unique in its capacity to provide understanding in depth and context of myths treated. There are excellent insights rendered in the 395 essays contributed by French scholars. Arrangement is by cultural societies and topical elements such as cosmos, creation, and sacrifice. This is not a dictionary or encyclopedia in the normal sense but rather a model of erudition and enlightened critical interpretation, its strength being its emphasis on scholarship. This makes it a unique tool for scholars and serious students. Mythologies from all over the world are covered, with emphasis placed on their folklore and literature, especially French theory. There are excellent black-and-white illustrations; a general index provides access.

306. **Who's Who in Classical Mythology.** Michael Grant and John Hazel. New York: Oxford University Press, 1993. 352p. ISBN 0-19-521030-1.

With information drawn from a number of ancient literary sources, this represents an important tool for identification of all Greek and Roman mythological figures. Included here are all the gods and all the mortal heroes, both familiar and relatively obscure. Entries furnish well-developed, cogent description and exposition of these personalities and treat events associated with them. These articles are written in an interesting and even entertaining fashion, appealing to all types of library users. Grant and Hazel are both well-known classical scholars who have combined their expertise to produce a readable and authoritative work.

A companion effort, *Who's Who in Non-Classical Mythology* (Oxford University Press, 1993), represents a revision by Alan Kendall of *Everyman's Dictionary of Non-Classical Mythology*, by Egerton Sykes (4th ed., Dutton, 1968). It is important in its focus on the personalities from the mythology of cultures other than Greek and Roman. Covered are the Celts, Teutons, Slavs, Basques, the Americas, Africa, Australia, China, Japan, and Indonesia, providing a fresh and much-needed perspective of world mythology. A recent publication by Adrian Room, also entitled *Who's Who in Classical Mythology* (National Textbook, 1997) treats the origins of the names of some 1,200 Greek and Roman mythological characters rather than their deeds or exploits. This is a revision of an earlier work by a different title.

307. **Women of Classical Mythology: A Biographical Dictionary.** Robert E. Bell. Santa Barbara, CA: ABC-Clio, 1991. 462p. ISBN 0-87436-581-3.

This is an interesting and useful reference tool for students and the general public, covering 2,600 female personalities from mythology. Treated here are all types of goddesses, heroines, and monstrous beings. Entries vary in length from a single sentence to about four pages, and are written in clear and lucid manner. They provide excellent insight developed within a perspective sensitive to the social position of women. Both famous and obscure figures are included. Arrangement of entries is alphabetical, providing simple access to the personalities. Both Greek and Roman mythology serve as the basis for this work. Entries furnish references to ancient sources where the characters have been treated, a useful feature for student users. Another special feature is a listing of male figures cited in the various entries, entitled, "The Men in Their Lives."

More breadth but less depth is found in *Goddesses in World Mythology*, by Martha Ann Imel and Dorothy M. Imel (ABC-Clio, 1993). Designed for a popular audience, it contains over 8,000 entries spanning a period of some 3,000 years. Most entries furnish brief identifications of the subject, with her attributes, region, terse description, and references to sources listed in the bibliography. Included here are goddesses, monsters, evil spirits, fairies, and witches arranged within twelve geographic regions.

CHAPTER 7

ACCESSING INFORMATION IN THE VISUAL ARTS

WORKING DEFINITION OF
THE VISUAL ARTS

The term *art* is derived from the Latin word *ars*, which means skill or ability. At the time of the Italian Renaissance, the craft guilds were known as "arti," and the word "arte" denoted craftsmanship, skill, mastery of form, or inventiveness. The phrase "visual arts" serves to differentiate a group of arts that are generally nonverbal in character and that communicate by means of symbols and the juxtaposition of formal elements. Michael Greenhalgh and Paul Duro suggest a definition of visual arts: "the practice of shaping material, such as wood or stone, or applying pigment to a flat or other surface, with the intention of representing an idea, experience, or emotion."[1]

The representation is communicated by the creation of emotional moods and through expansion of the range of the aesthetic experience. "Beauty," as such, is not an integral part of art, but more a matter of subjective judgment. The difficulty here is that aesthetics deals with individual taste—a subjective issue from the outset. Nevertheless, certain concepts of balance, harmony, and contrast have become a part of our way of thinking about art as a result of Greek speculation about the nature of beauty.

Style normally refers to the whole body of work produced at a given time in history; however, there may be regional and national styles as well as one basic style for a period. In modern times, attention has even been given to the "styles" of individual artists. Style, like taste, is a subjective phenomenon.

Iconography is the use of symbols by artists to express universal ideas; the Gothic style of architecture, for example, symbolized humanity's reaching out toward God. On a more recent note, designers of graphical software have used "icons" to denote certain functions and messages; an example is the use of a timepiece (clock, hourglass, or wristwatch) to communicate that the user should wait and that processing is taking place.

147

MAJOR DIVISIONS OF THE FIELD

The visual arts may be conveniently divided into four main groups: 1) pictorial arts, 2) plastic arts, 3) building arts, and 4) minor arts.

The pictorial arts employ flat, two-dimensional surfaces. The term is most often applied to painting, but it can also include drawing, graphic arts, photography (including moving pictures and video), and mosaics. Painting may be done with a variety of materials: oil, tempera, water color, or other media. Drawing is done most often with pencil, pen and ink, wash, crayon, pastel, or charcoal.

The graphic arts are produced by the printing process, with three basic methods employed. Intaglio, in which the design is hollowed out of a flat surface and the ink is gathered in the hollows for transmission to the paper, is exemplified by etching or engraving. Cameo, or relief, in which the design is on a raised surface (as in woodcut, mezzotint, aquatint, or drypoint) and only the raised surface is inked, is the second method. Last is the planographic method, in which a completely flat surface is used and the design is created by using substances that will either attract or repel ink. Lithography is the term often used for this method because the flat surface was frequently made of stone.

The pictorial arts employ one or more of three basic forms: murals, panels, or pages. Murals involve pictures directly applied to walls of buildings or painted on canvases and permanently attached to the walls. Panels are generally painted on wood or canvas; these are sometimes known as easel paintings. Pages may be illuminated manuscripts or, more often, produced as a result of the printing process. The basic problems of the pictorial artist, regardless of the form used, include surface, design, movement, space, and form. These are commonly solved by the use of line, color, values (light and dark), and perspective.

In the plastic arts, of which sculpture is the most obvious example, ideas are expressed by means of three-dimensional objects. This type of art is perhaps the oldest form, predating even cave painting. The materials used include stone, metal, wood, plaster, clay, or synthetics (such as plastic). Tools of the artist may include chisels, mallets, natural and chemical abrasives, and punches. The techniques used are determined primarily by the materials and tools available, and include carving, casting, modeling, or welding. The finished product may be free standing or bas-relief (part of a wall or planar surface). In sculpture, the human figure has traditionally provided the most common subject matter, although the twentieth century has seen increased use of abstractions.

In the building arts (architecture), spaces are enclosed in such a way as to meet certain practical needs (as in schools, homes, offices, or factories) and to make some kind of symbolic statement of basic values. These values may be utilitarian and the symbolic statement very pedestrian, or they may be related to the highest aspirations of the human spirit. Factories and gasoline stations are frequently examples of the former, while Gothic cathedrals are often cited as examples of the latter. Architects design buildings of three basic types: trabeated, in which a lintel is supported by two posts; arcuated, in which arches support rounded vaults and domes; and cantilevered, in which only one post is required to support a lintel or beam. The materials used in the construction will determine the type of design used. Wood is useful for trabeated construction, but brick and stone can be better adapted to the requirements of arcuated building. Structural steel and reinforced concrete make possible large scale cantilevered construction.

The minor arts are a special group, often classified on the basis of the materials used: ceramics, glass, metals, textiles, ivory, precious gems, wood, reeds, synthetics, and the like. Ordinarily, they follow the same styles as the major art forms. The end products may be useful everyday objects such as coins, clothing, baskets, utensils, and furniture, or they may be ornamental items such as jewelry, stained glass, and many items of interior decoration. The minor arts are often referred to as "crafts," "decorative arts," or "collectibles," or some combination of these terms.

The topic of technology must be addressed as part of any discussion of the visual arts. The application of science to problem solving in all four divisions of the arts is obvious. In the discussion of the major divisions of the field, we have addressed aspects of the more traditional technologies: materials and tools. Just as the areas of sculpture and architecture have changed as new tools and materials have evolved, so too do all the visual arts change. Two good examples of where technology and art are melded are photography and computer art. The former has been around for over 100 years, while the latter is a creation of recent decades. Nonetheless, both depend heavily on technology—so much so, in fact, that it is hard to distinguish between the technology and the art, except in the final product.

More information on the divisions of the visual arts can be found in the *Encyclopaedia Britannica Online* article "Art" at http://members.eb.com/bol/topic?eu=9772&sctn=1 (accessed June 24, 1999). This and the related articles are intended for the general reader, although they are more advanced treatments than one finds in many other encyclopedias. For briefer articles and shorter histories of various divisions of the arts, see McLeish's *Key Ideas in Human Thought* (Facts on File, 1993). Entries on "Art(s), Visual" (pp. 47–49) and on Christian art (pp. 119–20), computer art (p. 149), architecture (pp. 44–45), and aesthetics (pp. 13–14) provide both introductions to the topics and suggestions for further reading. *The Encyclopedia of World Art* (Publishers Guild, 1959–1988) contains signed articles by experts on the various topics, and it should be consulted by the student or librarian looking for more technical, detailed encyclopedic coverage of art, its subfields, and related subjects. Finally, for histories of the visual arts, a recommended source is the *Encyclopedia of Visual Art* (Encyclopaedia Britannica Educational Corporation, 1989). A ten-volume set, the *Encyclopedia* covers the area fully, includes illustrations as well as text, and points the user to other material. An overview of the field of art history is found in *Research Guide to the History of Western Art*, by W. Eugene Kleinbauer and Thomas P. Slavens (American Library Association, 1982). A highly regarded guide to research methods is the recently revised *Art Research Methods and Resources: A Guide to Finding Art Information*, by Lois S. Jones (3d ed., Kendall/Hunt, 1990). Besides providing background material on different aspects of visual arts, both guides are also intended to help the reader find published information on the arts. The reader should access these titles in libraries because unfortunately they are now out-of-print.

HELPFUL RESOURCES FOR STUDENTS, LIBRARIANS, AND GENERAL READERS

Unlike philosophy and religion, where conventional techniques of librarianship and library research will cover most situations, the visual arts pose several distinct problems. As a result, art, or visual arts, librarianship has emerged as a specialized branch of the field. The chapter "Fine Arts" in Lester Asheim's now-classic text, *The Humanities and the Library* (pp. 100–150), suggests some basic tenants that still hold. First, different types of art libraries serve differing purposes, although the subject matter contained in them may be similar. Museum, art school, and departmental public and university libraries serve diverse, though sometimes overlapping, clienteles, and hence the institutions will have varying policies and practices in terms of management, collection development, user education, public services, and organization. Not only librarians, but also users of the libraries will benefit from awareness of the differences and similarities.

An article on art libraries appeared in each annual *ALA Yearbook of Library and Information Services* (American Library Association, 1975–1995), and each one- or two-page entry summarized the year's developments in the field. An old, but still helpful encyclopedic treatment of art libraries and special collections is Wolfgang Freitag's article in *Encyclopedia of Library and Information Science* (v. 1, pp. 571–621). Philip Pacey's *A Reader in Art Librarianship* (Saur, 1985) is a standard source.

An important consideration is the different types of materials found in an art library collection. In "How to Research a Work of Art," in *Guide to Basic Information Sources in the Visual Arts* (ABC-Clio, 1978; repr. 1980), Gerd Muehsam outlined several distinctive types of art catalog publications. The catalogue raisonné is defined as

> a systematic, descriptive, and critical listing or catalog of all known, or documented, authentic works by a particular artist—or of all his known works in one medium. Each entry aims at providing all ascertainable data on the work in question: (1) title, date, and signature, if any, as well as size and medium; (2) present location or owner and provenance (previously recorded owners and history of the work); (3) description, comments, analysis, or literary documentation; (4) bibliographical references to books and periodicals; (5) listings of exhibitions and reproductions. Usually there is also an illustration. The entries are numbered consecutively. These catalog numbers are often referred to in scholarly literature about the artist and permanently identify a particular work.[2]

The oeuvre catalog is similar but may omit documentation and provenance. Museum catalogs are defined as catalogs of a museum's permanent collection; exhibition catalogs, on the other hand, include works from many museums or owner's private collections that are brought together for a particular exhibition. Corpus catalogs attempt to do for an entire category of art what the catalogue raisonné does for an individual artist. Because of their scope, these often depend on international collaboration.

Catalogs are first-rate sources of art information, but the researcher must understand the difficulties of bibliographic control prior to publication of the ongoing *Worldwide Art Catalogue Bulletin* (1963/1964–). The subject of catalog collecting is addressed in B. Houghton and G. Varley, "A Local Approach to National Collecting: A UK Feasibility Study for the Cooperative Collection of Exhibition Catalogues," *Art Libraries Journal* 14 (1989): 38–43. Jack Robertson's "The Exhibition Catalog As Source of Artists' Primary Documents," *Art Libraries Journal* 14 (1989): 32–36, also addresses this special research resource. The chapter by Susan Wyngaard, "Fine Arts," in the second edition of *Humanities and the Library*, edited by Nena Couch and Nancy Allen (American Library Association, 1993), covers exhibition and sales catalogs in considerable depth. Artists' books and ephemera are also discussed in the same chapter. Finally, another approach to the use of exhibition catalogs is presented in Olivia Fitzpatrick, "Art Exhibition Catalogues: A Resource for Art Documentation," *An Leabharlaan* 12 (1996): 117–20.

Another special type of document for the art library is the so-called art book. Elizabeth Esteve-Coll discusses the medium in her provocative keynote paper, presented at the European Conference of the IFLA Art Libraries Section and published as "The Art Book: The Idea and the Reality," *Art Libraries Journal* 17 (1992): 4–6. Nikos Stangos' article addresses the issues in art book publishing in the same issue ("Art Book Publishing: Minority Issue, Popular Entertainment, or Kudos?," pp. 31–33).

Planning and developing visual art collections are covered from a management orientation in Nancy Shelby Schuller's *Management for Visual Resources Collections* (2d ed., Libraries Unlimited, 1990).

For the librarian, there are many sources in the journal literature on selecting and acquiring materials. The journals *Art Documentation* and *Art Libraries Journal* are the most specific to art library collection development, but *Library Journal* also covers art books on a regular basis. *AB Bookman's Weekly* is also a good resource.

An excellent annual source is "Annual Bibliography of Art Librarianship," in *Art Libraries Journal*; it covers all aspects of practice, including collection development.

Special materials are discussed in the following articles. Sales at auction sources are covered in C. H. Backlund, "The Cutting Edge: New Auction Sources and Computer Projects," *Art Documentation* 9 (Winter 1990): 175–78; special problems with Eastern European materials are discussed in E. Kasinec and R. H. Davis, "Materials for the Study of Russian/Soviet Art and Architecture: Problems of Selection, Acquisition, and Collection Development for Research Libraries" *Art Documentation* 10 (Spring 1991): 19–22; Native American art is discussed in "Balance and Harmony: Books on American Indian Art," by D. Seaman (*Booklist* 90 [October 1, 1993]: 238–39); and other special items are covered in M. R. Hughston's "Preserving the Ephemeral: New Access to Artists Files, Vertical Files, and Scrapbooks" (*Art Documentation* 9 [Winter 1990]: 179–81. Archives are the subject of Serena Kelly's "Collecting Archives: Changes and Consequences," *Art Libraries Journal* 21 (1996): 30–34. Daniel Lombardo's "Focus on Art Instruction Books," *Library Journal* 116 (August 1991): 65–68, adds to the librarian's knowledge in the area of collection development. Carla Conrad Freeman and Barbara Stevenson, eds., provide *The Visual Resources Directory: Art Slide and Photograph Collections in the US and Canada* (Libraries Unlimited, 1995). The topic is also addressed in various Occasional Papers issued by ARLIS/NA; see, for example, "Current Issues in Fine Arts Collection Development: Occasional Paper #3." See also "Slide Collection Management in Libraries and Information Units," by Elizabeth O'Donnell and Maryly Snow (*Visual Resources* 13 [1997]: 199–203).

Other aspects of art libraries and librarianship that are especially important include the special security problems presented by art materials, the development of art librarians and information specialists, and art library facilities. The first of these areas is discussed in Elizabeth H. Smith and Lydia P. Olszak, "Treatment of Mutilated Art Books: A Survey of Academic ARL Institutions," *Library Resources and Technical Services* 41 (January 1997): 7–16. The "Profile of Fine Arts Librarianship," in the chapter by Wyngaard referenced above, provides advice regarding qualifications and training for the field. Other articles on the visual arts library profession include Carla Conrad Freeman, "Visualizing Art: An Overview of the Visual Resources Profession in the U.S.," *Art Documentation* 16 (Fall 1997): 31–34; Clive Phillpot, "The Social Role of the Art Library," *Art Documentation* (Fall 1997): 25–26; and "What Does It Mean to Be a 'Professional' Art Librarian," by Max Podstolski (*Art Libraries Journal* 21 [1996]: 4–8). Two additional works that address staffing of art libraries are "Staffing Standards for Art Libraries and Visual Resources Collections," *Art Documentation* 14 (Winter 1995): 27–32, and "Criteria for the Hiring and Retention of Visual Resources Professionals," in the same issue of *Art Documentation* (pp. 35–37).

Regarding facilities, Betty Jo Irvine edited *Facilities Standards for Art Libraries and Visual Resources Collections*, published by Libraries Unlimited (1991) for ARLIS, the Art Libraries Society of North America. The latter includes an excellent bibliography on the subject of art and architecture library facilities (pp. 105–8). "Space Planning for the Art Library" was also the topic of ARLIS/NA Occasional Paper no. 9, published by the Society in 1991.

In the technical areas of librarianship, two older titles dealing with the organization of materials deserve mention. The first is Carolyn Frost's *Media Access and Organization: A Cataloging and Reference Sources Guide for Nonbook Materials* (Libraries Unlimited, 1989). The second is *Nonprint Cataloging for Multimedia Collections*, by JoAnn V. Rogers and Jerry D. Saye (2d ed., Libraries Unlimited, 1987).

Cooperative cataloging is addressed in "The Research Libraries Group: New Initiatives to Improve Access to Art and Architecture Information," *INSPEL* 32 (1998): 8–22.

Linda McRae and Lynda S. White edited the *ArtMARC Sourcebook: Cataloging Art, Architecture and Their Visual Images* (ALA, 1998), and Janet Stanley also addresses the organization of art materials in "Reference Librarian As Cataloger: Analytical Indexing As Front-End Reference," *Art Documentation* 14 (Winter 1995): 7–9.

USE AND USERS OF ART INFORMATION

Users of visual arts information can be categorized as art professionals (art historians, artists, art educators, critics, curators, and architects); students of the visual arts who are enrolled in art schools, colleges and universities, and secondary schools; and the interested public (museum goers, collectors, and others for whom art is a hobby or avocation). The article "Art Libraries and Collections" in the *Encyclopedia of Library and Information Science*, cited above, covers the myriad needs of visual art information users.

Interest in use and users of art materials is not a new phenomenon: An early article on use of art materials was "The Use of Art Books," by Katherine Patten (*Bulletin of the American Library Association* 1 [July 1907]: 183). More recent works include Phillip Pacey's enduring contribution, "How Art Students Use Libraries—If They Do," *Art Libraries Journal* 7 (Spring 1982): 33–38, and Deidre Corcoran Stam's "How Art Historians Look for Information," *Art Documentation* 3 (Winter 1984): 117–19 (reprinted in 16 [Fall 1997]: 27–30). Stam's contributions in this area have continued with "Tracking Art Historians: Information Needs and Information Seeking Behavior," *Art Libraries Journal* 14 (Fall 1989): 13–16. The latter article describes three prevalent methods for generating data on information needs: bibliometric tracking, autobiographical methods or participant observation, and user studies. Stam more recently presented "Artists and Art Libraries," *Art Libraries Journal* 20 (1995): 21–24.

Several chapters in Kusnerz's *The Architecture Library of the Future* address user needs. See especially Kurt Brandle, "What Do Researchers Want from the Architecture Library?" (pp. 21–26) and Hemalata Dandekar, "What Do Planners Want? What Do Planners Need?" (pp. 27–34).

The Getty Art History Information Project investigated information-seeking practices of art historians and published several reports between 1988 and the mid-1990s. See Chapter 1 of this guide for citations to articles based on the reports.

J. Cullars has investigated citation practices in the arts and has published "Citation Characteristics of Monographs in the Fine Arts," *Library Quarterly* 62 (July 1992): 325–42. Cullars is referenced elsewhere in this volume for other citation studies in the humanities. A more recent study on users is Susie Cobbledick's "The Information-Seeking-Seeking Behavior of Artists: Exploratory Interviews," *The Library Quarterly* 66 (October 1996): 343–72.

Despite the increase in use and user studies over the past decade, more information is needed, especially about users other than art historians and users of other than traditional print materials. The next decade may see expansion of our present definition of use and user studies, and the use of electronic resources will likely be the focus of such studies.

COMPUTERS IN THE VISUAL ARTS

The literature of computer applications in the visual arts is large and continues to expand rapidly. The computer is used in a wide variety of ways, from computer assisted design in architecture to computer graphics and computerized information retrieval in museums and libraries. As with all disciplines in the humanities, the visual arts area has been changed by the advent of the World Wide Web. A perfect medium for visual arts information, especially graphical in nature, the Web opens the door to new and expanded research possibilities for the future visual arts scholar.

The historical development of computer applications in art can be traced by referring to several review sources. *The Annual Review of Information Science and Technology* is a good starting point. "Information Systems and Services in the Humanities," by Joseph Raben and Sarah K. Burton, covers arts information systems through 1980 (ASIS, 1981, v. 16, pp. 254–56), and the review entitled "Visual Arts Resources and Computers," by Karen Markey, (ASIS, 1984, v. 19, pp. 271–309) is specifically directed at the visual arts and brings the reader up to the middle of the 1980s. Jasia Reichardt's *The Computer in Art* (Van Nostrand, 1971) is of historical interest.

R. Skinner's "Networking from the Ground Up: Implementing Macintosh Networks in a Newly Constructed Arts Library," in *Library LANs*, describes a system at Southern Methodist University (Meckler, 1992, pp. 50–62).

Information technology and its applications in architecture libraries are discussed in Part 2, "Information Resources in the Architecture Library," in Kusnerz's *The Architecture Library of the Future*, referenced above.

"Bringing Art Museum Images to the Classroom and Desktop," in *RLG News* 46 (Spring 1998): 3–6, is just one article on accessing images in the arts.

The number of online and CD-ROM resources in the visual arts continues to grow but, as noted above, the literature in this area has recently focused on Internet resources and access rather than on the "how to search" articles that were typical some years ago.

Among the most important bibliographic databases is Art Literature International (*International Repertory of the Literature of Art*), which includes all entries in the print *RILA* database since 1975. Art Literature International covers all aspects of Western art from late antiquity to the present. RILA's contents were merged with that of *Repertoire d'Art et d'Archeologie* to form the newly titled *Bibliography of the History of Art* (J. Paul Getty Trust, 1991–). The *Repertoire d'Art et d'Archeologie* was produced from 1910 through 1990 in Paris by the Centre de Documentation Sciences Humaines.

ARTbibliographies Modern (entry 327), another online bibliographic file, covers nineteenth- and twentieth-century art and design, as well as nineteenth-century themes begun in the eighteenth century. Updated semiannually, the database covers the literature from 1974 on. It is produced by ABC-Clio.

Two online files in architecture are available on DIALOG Information Services: Architecture Database and the Avery Architecture Index. The former is provided by the British Architectural Library at the Royal Institute of British Architects and comprises records from the *Architectural Periodicals Index* (from 1978 on) and the *Architectural Book Catalogue* (1984 to the present). The Avery Architecture Index is produced at the Avery Architectural and Fine Arts Library of Columbia University. It is part of the Getty Art History Information Program, and utilizes terms from the Art and Architecture Thesaurus, also sponsored by the Getty. All areas of architecture, including technical aspects, are included in the database, which covers from 1979 to the present.

Sales catalogs are indexed in SCIPIO (Sales Catalog Index Project Input Online), a tool that leads the user to libraries holding particular sales catalogs. Like the Avery Index, this tool has been sponsored by the Getty Art Information Project.

H. W. Wilson's *Art Index* (available in print, online, and on CD-ROM) continues to be one of the most used databases in fine arts. Available in machine readable form from 1984, *Art Index* serves as a good starting point for searching art periodicals and museum publications. Although it does include foreign-language materials, its scope and coverage will seem limited to the most scholarly art historian because of the omission of valuable art history materials such as books, theses, and dissertations.

There are many articles that will lead the reader to additional online, CD-ROM, and Internet resources in the visual arts.

The growth in the field of visual arts is rapid even when compared to the explosive growth of the Internet as a whole. Not only do we have text and resource-finding tools available, but a variety of image files are now accessible through the Internet.

Print materials to help the reader access Internet resources abound in the literature, so only a few are cited here. The following should get the reader started:

1. Jeanne M. Brown, "Architecture Reference Sites on the Internet," *Reference Librarian* 57 (1997): 147–51.

2. Barbara Q. Prior, "Art and Architecture Databases on the Internet," *Reference Services Review* 24 (Fall 1996): 81–96.

3. Jennifer Trant, "Images on the Internet: Issues and Opportunities," *ACLS Newsletter* 4 (February 1997): 6–8.

4. J. Griffin, "Fine Art on Multimedia CD-ROM and the Web," *Computers in Libraries* 17 (April 1997): 63–67.

5. Martin Kalfatovic, "Internet Resources in the Visual Arts," *College and Research Libraries News* 57 (May 1996): 289–93.

6. Lois Swan Jones, *Art Information on the Internet: How to Find It, How to Use It* (Oryx Press, 1998).

Finally, for the art librarian, "Content Guidelines for Art Museum Library Web Pages," *Art Documentation* 16 (Fall 1997): 44–50, by Polly Trump, is an excellent feature with a bibliography.

The Web itself provides guides to sources available there. Access resource pages on visual arts—from painting to body art—by going to Yahoo's links at http://dir.yahoo.com/arts/visual-arts/ (accessed March 8, 2000). For art history links, try *The Parthenet* site at http://home.mtholyoke.edu/~klconner/parthenet.html/ (accessed March 8, 2000). Another excellent site for links is *Mother of All Art History Links Pages*, at http://www.umich.edu/~hartspc/histart/mother/ (accessed March 8, 2000). The Getty site at http://www.getty.edu/ (accessed March 8, 2000) provides links to the major arts databases supported by the Getty. The ARLIS-NA site should not be overlooked as a source of publications. The Grove Dictionary of Art Online (http://grovereference.com/TDA/) (accessed March 8, 2000) is another useful Web source.

Finally, before leaving "Computers in the Visual Arts," we must add that digitization of images remains an important topic in the field. Two articles to peruse are "The Future of the Slide: Digitization Possibilities," by Lynn Williams (*Audiovisual Librarian* 23 [August 1997]: 191–94), and "Art History, Scholarship, and Image Libraries: Realising the Potential of the Digital Age," by Jennifer Durran (*LASIE* 28 [June 1997]: 14–27).

MAJOR ART ORGANIZATIONS AND SPECIAL COLLECTIONS IN VISUAL ARTS

At the international level, much of the impetus for the collection and dissemination of art information has come from projects aided by UNESCO. For example, since 1949 UNESCO and its national commissions have worked with art publishers to establish a central archives service of art reproductions. In this undertaking, UNESCO had the assistance of the International Council of Museums. Other organizations that have been active on the international scene include the Artists International Association, International Association of Art Critics, and the International Union of Architects (51 rue Raynouard, Paris F-75016, France).

Another major influence in the area of art information is the Getty Trust, of which the Art History Information Program, the Getty Center for the History of Art and the Humanities, and of course, the J. Paul Getty Museum in Malibu, California, are part. The main address is The Getty Center, 1200 Getty Center Dr., Los Angeles, CA 90049. Projects as diverse as Art and Architecture Thesaurus, the Census of Antique Art and Architecture Known to the Renaissance, and others based at various locations in the United States and abroad, are all supported by the Getty organizations. The J. Paul Getty Trust public affairs office is located at 1875 Century Park East, Ste. 2300, Los Angeles, CA 90067. The research institute is properly cited as The Getty Research Institute for the History of Art and the Humanities, and its URL is http://www.getty.edu/gri/ (accessed March 8, 2000).

Within the United States, the variety of national, regional, and state organizations concerned with art information is too large for an exhaustive listing, but several national organizations should be mentioned. The American Federation of Arts (41 E. 65th St., New York, NY 10021) was founded in 1909 to broaden public art appreciation, especially in areas of the country not served by large museums. Its membership includes 500 art institutions and 3,000 individuals. The program of the organization includes circulating museum collections and preparing curricula on visual arts education. The Federation advises on the publication of the *American Art Directory, Sources of Films on Art,* and *Who's Who in American Art.*

The National Art Education Association (1916 Association Dr., Reston, VA 22091) was founded in 1947 to promote the study of the problems of teaching art as well as to encourage research and experimentation in the visual arts. Affiliated with the National Education Association, the National Art Education Association has 8,000 art teachers, supervisors, and students as members. It publishes *NAEA News* and the journal *Art Education.*

Other national organizations include the American Association of Museums (1225 Eye St. NW, Ste. 400, Washington, DC 20005), the College Art Association (275 7th Ave., New York, NY 10001-6708), and the American Arts Alliance (805 15th St. NW, Ste. 500, Washington, DC 20004). There is also the American Art Association. The first two associations publish, respectively, *Museum News* and *Advisory CAA Reviews, The Art Bulletin,* and *Art Journal.*

Of special interest to librarians and information specialists are The Art Libraries Society, with headquarters in Bromsgrove, United Kingdom, which publishes *Art Libraries Journal,* and its American counterpart, Art Libraries Society/North America (401 Lake Boone Trail, Ste. 201, Raleigh, NC 27607), publisher of *Art Documentation.* ARLIS/NA celebrated its twenty-fifth anniversary in 1997; its history is chronicled by notable author Wolfgang M. Freitag in "ARLIS/NA at Twenty-five—A Reminiscence," *Art Documentation* 16 (Fall 1997): 15–19.

The Museums, Arts, and Humanities division of Special Libraries Association (SLA) was established in 1929 (as the Museum Group) and is now the fifth-largest SLA division, with over 1,000 members. SLA is located at 1700 18th St., NW, Washington, DC 20009. The American Society for Information Science (ASIS) (8720 Georgia Ave., Ste. 501, Silver Spring, MD 20910) also has a special interest group (SIG) on Arts and Humanities. According to the 1994 directory of ASIS, members of the SIG are "interested in retrieval of text, images, sound and humanistic implications of information technology." There is also the Association of Architectural Librarians (1735 New York Ave. NW, Washington, DC 20006), which publishes a newsletter for the membership.

There are also many special associations that will have information for the interested librarian or information specialist. General directories will give the particulars on organizations like the Glass Art Society, the Handweavers Guild of America, the National Sculpture Society, the National Watercolor Society, the American Pewter Guild, and the Art Dealers Association of America, to name just a few. Most also now maintain Web pages.

Collections in the fine arts are numerous and can be found in public, academic, and special libraries. Examples of public library collections of note include the Art and Architecture Division of the New York Public Library and the Fine Arts Library of the Westminster City Libraries (United Kingdom). Among university libraries we have the Avery Architectural Library at Columbia University (New York), the Fine Arts Library of Harvard University (Cambridge, Massachusetts), and the Marquand Library of Princeton University (Princeton, New Jersey).

Other notable U.S. library collections include the Dumbarton Oaks Research Library in Washington, D.C., The Frick Art Reference Library in New York, the libraries of the Art Institute of Chicago, and the Archives of American Art in Washington, D.C. Of course, the Smithsonian Institutions in Washington, D.C., of which the Archive of American Art is a part, offer extensive resources on site and on the Web.

Art Information: Research Methods and Resources, by Lois Swan Jones (Kendall/Hunt, 1990) has a section on research centers that should be consulted for other library and research collections. *Subject Collections*, by Lee Ash (7th ed., R. R. Bowker, 1993), is also a valuable source of information on special resources.

NOTES

[1]Kenneth McLeish, ed., *Key Ideas in Human Thought* (New York: Facts on File, 1993) pp. 47–49.

[2]Gerd Muehsam, *Guide to Information Sources in the Visual Arts* (Santa Barbara, CA: ABC-Clio, 1978), p. 12.

CHAPTER 8

PRINCIPAL INFORMATION SOURCES IN THE VISUAL ARTS

ARTS IN GENERAL

Bibliographic Guides

REFERENCE BOOKS AND RESEARCH GUIDES

308. **Art Research Methods and Resources: A Guide to Finding Art Information.** 3d ed. Lois S. Jones. Dubuque, IA: Kendall/Hunt, 1990. 373p. ISBN 0-840-35713-3.

The third edition of this title continues a useful and informative literature guide on the various reference tools in the field. Adequate coverage is given to both broad, general reference materials and also those that are highly specialized for scholars and specialists. The work continues to provide cogent information to the methodology of art research as well as important sources. There seems to be good balance among the coverage given to the resources, the methodology, and searching out relevant material. All sections have been updated and slightly expanded. Most encouraging is the attention given to the novice and his or her preparation. The fourth section covers the procedures for obtaining materials and describes research library collections. Appendices include multi-language glossaries of art terms; indexes are provided.

Visual Arts Research: A Handbook, by Elizabeth B. Pollard (Greenwood, 1986), covers information sources for both the fine and applied arts, with chapters devoted to separate categories of information.

309. **Fine Arts: A Bibliographic Guide to Basic Reference Works, Histories, and Handbooks.** 3d ed. Donald L. Ehresmann. Englewood, CO: Libraries Unlimited, 1990. 373p. ISBN 0-87287-640-3.

This is a welcome edition because its predecessor (1979) had begun to show its age. The title remains a useful source of information regarding reference literature in the arts. Having incorporated all relevant titles from Mary W. Chamberlin's *Guide to Art Reference Books* (American Library Association, 1959) in past editions, it continues to furnish a blend of older standard works, both articles and books of reference value, along with recent titles.

There are 2,051 entries representing the major body of reference literature published in the Western languages between 1830 and September 1988. Only tools that treat two or more of the three major media (painting, sculpture, or architecture) are included. Part I contains seven chapters representing reference types such as bibliographies or directories, but also includes iconography. Part II adds six chapters of histories and handbooks classified by historical period (prehistoric and primitive art) or by geography (oriental art). Annotations are relatively brief and descriptive for the most part but evaluative comments are found in some entries. There are detailed author-title and subject indexes.

310. **Reference Tools for Fine Arts Visual Resources Collections.** Christine Bunting, ed. Tucson, AZ: ARLIS/NA, 1984. 55p. (Occasional Papers, no. 4). ISBN 0942740025.

Developed as part of the series of Occasional Papers produced by the Art Libraries Society of North America, this small literature guide represents a cooperative effort of a number of specialists and practitioners in the various fields and subfields of the arts and architecture. Recognizing the need to provide up-to-date coverage of the vast array of materials of value to the professional, this work identifies several hundred titles of art books. There are three major sections, covering professional literature, art reference, and sources of art history, subdivided by medium. The reference works include indexes, directories, handbooks, and so forth. There is an author-title index.

311. **Research Guide to the History of Western Art.** W. Eugene Kleinbauer and Thomas P. Slavens. Chicago: American Library Association, 1982. 229p. (Sources of Information in the Humanities, no. 2) ISBN 0-8389-0329-0.

Another in the series of literature guides edited by Slavens (a now-retired professor of library science at the University of Michigan) in which he collaborates with an authority in the field, this work is designed for library school students and librarians. The first segment is by Kleinbauer and consists of a series of bibliographic essays on the field of art history. This is the major segment, and it presents interpretations of topical material such as "psychological approaches" and "studying the art object." The second segment is by Slavens and covers reference works. There is an annotated list of major reference tools. Although the annotations are full and informative, the entries represent standards in the field rather than newer reference books.

PERIODICALS

312. **Fine Arts Periodicals: An International Directory of the Visual Arts.** Doris Robinson. Voorheesville, NY: Peri Press, 1991. 570p. ISBN 1-879796-03-1.

This large-type, handy dictionary was developed in response to a need to control the periodical literature of art in a comprehensive and manageable way. The work identifies nearly 2,800 art periodicals, newsletters, and newspapers, a number of which are not found in *Ulrich's International Periodicals Directory* (entry 7). All media and fields of art are represented through inclusion of both major and minor sources, providing an excellent overview of publishing in the field. Entries are arranged under broad topical headings, such as "Information Sources," "Visual Arts," "Decorative Arts and Crafts," "Buildings and Interiors," and "Photography." These are subdivided by more specific or specialized aspects. Entries furnish current information regarding address, publisher, editor, subscription, audience, summary of content, and pointers for authors and advertisers. The work is adequately indexed by titles, publishers, organizations, ISSNs, and subjects.

INTERNET RESOURCES AND COMPUTERIZED DATABASES

313. **Key Guide to Electronic Resources: Art and Art History.** Martin Raisch and Pat Ensor, eds. Medford, NJ: Information Today, 1996. 128p. ISBN 1-57387-022-6.

Because the world of electronic resources in the field of art is especially dynamic and expanding and Web addresses change constantly, this tool will be issued as an irregular serial. As a basic source in identifying a reasonable proportion of available resources in the field at time of publication, it is useful and not limited to service as a Web directory. Instead it is divided into three major categories of resources—optical, magnetic, and network—and there are miscellaneous inclusions. In the case of network resources, emphasis is correctly given to electronic (Web) directories of Web sites along with a sampling of important URLs, rather than to an extensive listing of home pages. Also included are discussion groups (along with contacts and procedural routines) and electronic journals. Floppy disk material is treated under magnetic resources, and CD-ROM databases are identified in the optical category. Entries supply title, producer, descriptive narrative, price, and equipment requirements, and in some cases, evaluation. Several indexes facilitate access.

A useful resource on the Web is *Worldwide Art Resources*, compiled by the Worldwide Arts Resources Association, a commercial publisher (http://www.war.com/ [accessed December 1999]), providing a directory of artists, museums, galleries, education programs, and more found on the Internet. Included are discussion forums, chat sessions, and advertisements.

Bibliographies and Catalogs

314. **Action Art: A Bibliography of Artists' Performance from Futurism to Fluxus and Beyond.** John Gray, comp. Westport, CT: Greenwood, 1993. 343p. (Art Reference Collection, no.16). ISBN 0-313-28916-6.

The compiler serves as the Director of the Black Arts Research Center and has been a published bibliographer of the performing arts. He brings expertise and understanding to the development of this work. The result is a comprehensive bibliography of international proportions and a successful first effort to document performance art as a modern art form. There are more than 3,600 entries identifying both print and media materials issued from 1914 to 1992. The history of performance art is well treated here, with coverage given to its origins in various early twentieth-century movements such as Futurism, Dadaism, Russian Constructivism, and Bauhaus. The peak decades from the 1950s to the 1970s are identified through references to such developments as Fluxus, Guerrilla Art Action, and Situationism. Individual artists and groups are included. Appendices supply useful listings of reference sources, archival collections, country, and group.

315. **Art and Architecture in Canada: A Bibliography and Guide to the Literature to 1981. Art et Architecture au Canada. . . .** Loren R. Lerner and Mary F. Williamson. Toronto: University of Toronto Press, 1991. 2v. ISBN 0-8020-5856-6.

A well-developed introductory essay establishes the purpose of this important and unique work documenting the art history literature of Canada. There are now more than 9,500 entries identifying the most important publications issued between 1825 and 1981 relating to Canadian art and architecture regardless of place of publication. Arrangement of entries is by topical subject and geographical categories subdivided chronologically. Abstracts are furnished for each entry and written in the language of publication, either French or English. The authors bring expertise to the task from their professional positions, serving as art librarians in academic libraries. Volume 1 treats the arts: Painting, graphic arts, photography, decorative arts, sculpture, and so forth are covered in the first section, and architecture in all its aspects in the second section. Volume 2 supplies detailed indexes to authors and subjects.

316. **Art Books: A Basic Bibliography of Monographs on Artists.** 2d ed. Wolfgang M. Freitag. New York: Garland, 1996. 351p. (Garland Reference Library of the Humanities, v. 574). ISBN 0-8240-3326-4.

This represents an expansion and revision of the first edition, now listing about 14,000 monographs on 2,100 individual artists representing all time periods and geographic locations. There is an emphasis on European and North American artists, and the work is based on the collection of the Harvard Fine Arts Library, where Freitag served as librarian. The original bibliography was produced with a grant for aiding the study of art history from the Getty Trust. The major segment of the text is an alphabetical listing by artist of monographs, including biographies, bibliographies, exhibition and auction catalogs, and catalogues raisonnés. Of course, the major artists receive more entries than do the lesser-known ones. There is an author index, and the bibliography includes titles in various languages; it is definitely intended for the scholarly rather than for a popular audience.

This effort draws on the previous work by Edna Louise Lucas, *Art Books: A Basic Bibliography on the Fine Arts* (New York Graphic Society, 1968), which contains 4,000 entries, including many on individual artists.

317. **Arts in America: A Bibliography.** Bernard Karpel, ed. Washington, DC: Smithsonian Institution, 1979. 4v. ISBN 0-87474-578-0

This well-received, comprehensive bibliography, primarily of books on the fine and decorative arts of the United States, includes sections on theater, dance, and music. The first three volumes consist of twenty-one separate bibliographic listings, which provide over 20,000 separate entries. Volume 1 covers art of the Native Americans, decorative arts, design, sculpture, and art of the West. Volume 2 covers painting and the graphic arts, while volume 3 provides access to the related performing arts as well as photography. This volume also covers dissertations, theses, and visual resources. Volume 4 is an index of authors and subjects. The work has been criticized for the variations in the listings due to the varying styles and forms of the contributors. Although it is nearly twenty years old, this represents a fine contribution to art research and reference and an important bibliographic tool for American art.

*318. **The Arts of Africa: An Annotated Bibliography. 1986–** . Janet L. Stanley, comp. Atlanta, GA: Crossroads Press/African Studies Association, 1989–1997. v. 1–6. ISSN 1044-8640.

Volume 1 furnishes coverage of the 1986–1987 period and was issued in 1989 to initiate this annual publication based on the monthly library acquisition lists from the National Museum of African Art branch of the Smithsonian Institution. The final print volume was issued in 1997 and covered the period 1991–1992. The compiler serves as head librarian of the facility and has succeeded in producing a useful guide to the literature of African art. Volumes identified books, articles, reviews, and exhibition catalogs. There were two major sections dealing with general studies, divided into more than twenty different geographical regions of the continent. Entries represent the various art forms along with treatment of African culture and black imagery in the Western world. Entries are full and informative and include OCLC numbers for the serials. Detailed author and subject indexes furnish access. The work has been incorporated into and is being continued as part of the digital catalog, Smithsonian Institution Research System (SIRIS) and is available on the Web at http://siris.si.edu (accessed December 1999).

*319. Card Catalog of the Manuscript Collections of the Archives of American Art. Wilmington, DE: Scholarly Resources, 1981. 10v. **Supp. 1981–1984**, 1985. 542p. ISBN 0-8420-2235-X.

Originally housed in the library of the Detroit Institute of the Arts and now part of the Smithsonian Institution in Washington, the Archives was started in 1954 to provide documentation of all areas and aspects of American art history. The reproduction of its master catalog provides an excellent source of information on manuscripts in the collection. There are nearly 6,000,000 items in 5,000 different collections. All items are available on microfilm, either through interlibrary loan or at the regional centers in Boston, Detroit, New York, Washington, and San Francisco; thus the work furnishes complete bibliographic control. Most items are biographical and much of the information is accessed through names of artists. There is no subject approach. The supplement furnishes listings for an additional 1,000 new collections acquired during the early 1980s, along with modifications for some of the earlier entries. One may search the Smithsonian's manuscripts catalog, research bibliographies catalog, library catalog, and chronology catalog through its SIRIS information system at (http//www.siris.si.edu [accessed December 1999]).

*320. Dictionary Catalog of the Art and Architecture Division, the Research Libraries of the New York Public Library. New York Public Library. Art and Architecture Division. Boston: G. K. Hall, 1975. 30v. ISBN 0-8161-0061-6. **Supp. 1974**, 1976. 556p. **Ann. Supp.**, 1976– .

This is another of the G. K. Hall publications providing photoreproduction of the catalog entries of a major research collection. This specialized tool lists the holdings of the Art and Architecture Division, regarded as one of the most significant resource collections in the visual arts. It consists of material cataloged through December 1971, representing painting, drawing, sculpture, the applied arts, and architecture. It is estimated to cover about 200,000 items treating all periods of art history on an international basis. Included also are those relevant volumes from other departments, such as the Cyrillic, Hebrew, and Oriental collections, as well as the Local History and Rare Books Divisions and even indexing of related articles from journals in all parts of the library. A 1974 supplement was published in 1976 and covered material added from January 1972 to September 1974. Since 1972 all additions to the collection have been listed in the major general catalog of the library, *Dictionary Catalog of the Research Libraries*. Annual supplements have been issued since 1976 as *Bibliographic Guide to Art and Architecture* (entry 328). The entire catalog can be accessed on the Web at http://www.nypl.org./catalogs/catalogs.html (accessed December 1999).

*321. Dictionary Catalog of the Library of the Freer Gallery of Art. Smithsonian Institution. 2d enl. ed. Boston: G. K. Hall, 1991. 252 microfiche. ISBN 0-8161-1791-8.

Another in the G. K. Hall line of catalog reproductions, this, like the others, has reproduced the cards of a notable library. The Freer Gallery has excellent depth in Oriental, Near Eastern, and nineteenth-century American art and its library resources are useful to people with a serious interest. Now on microfiche, this edition represents an expansion of the six-volume print edition issued in 1967. The work is divided into two parts or sections; one for books in Western languages and the other for books in Oriental languages. More than 40,000 publications are represented, including books, pamphlets, and periodicals. An important feature is the inclusion of analytics for relevant periodical articles. Each section (Eastern and Western languages) is accessed individually through its authors, subjects, and titles in a unified, alphabetical arrangement.

Freer Gallery of Art Library (http://www.sackler-freer-library.si.edu [accessed December 1999]) is the related Web site, started in 1998 and continuously revised. It contains several features, the most important being an online catalog to all holdings (with the exception of the slide library and the Archives) acquired after 1987. Currently about one-third of the pre-1987 holdings have been entered, the remainder being added as an ongoing activity.

322. **Feminist Art Criticism: An Annotated Bibliography.** Cassandra Langer. Boston: G. K. Hall, 1993. 250p. (A Reference Publication in Art History). ISBN 0-8161-8948-X.

Developed by a well-known specialist, art historian, and critic, this effort marks the first attempt to provide extensive documentation to the field of feminist art and its culture, theory, and criticism. More than 1,000 publications are identified, including books, pamphlets, articles, periodicals, exhibition catalogs, newspapers, and even unpublished manuscripts. These vary from scholarly monographs to brief expositions in both mainstream and alternative press publications. Publication dates embrace the past 100 years and the Western tradition, but emphasis is placed on British and American scholarship over the past twenty-five years. An entry supplies the title, author, and imprint along with Langer's appraisal of its significance. Bibliographic references are included for some. Most valuable overall is the variety of perspectives offered by the listed titles, revealing a lack of systematic theory in their disagreements and contradictions concerning the feminist position.

323. **From Museums, Galleries, and Studios: A Guide to Artists on Film and Tape.** Susan P. Bessemer and Christopher Crosman, comps. Westport, CT: Greenwood, 1984. 199p. (Art Reference Collection, no. 6). ISBN 0-313-23881-2.

A timely and useful source of information on over 600 films, videocassettes, and audiocassettes available for loan, rental, or purchase. Educators, students, historians, and interest groups or professional organizations can use this guide to identify filmed and taped interviews with artists. This has been a useful tool at a time when oral history has been playing an increasingly important role in the planning of research and resource collections. For the most part, the work is restricted to the visual arts and includes painters, sculptors, architects, photographers, film and video artists, craftsmen, folk artists, and graphic artists. Annotations vary in length but complete bibliographic identification is provided for all entries.

Not so much a guide, but a more recent source is *Art on Screen: A Directory of Films and Videos About the Visual Arts*, edited by Nadine Covert (G. K. Hall, 1992). Five essays provide the context for this selective annotated bibliography of some 900 films and videos on the arts. These productions were released between 1976 and 1990 and have been judged to be of high quality in either substantive treatment or visual imagery. Several indexes provide access through subject, distributor, title, and more.

*324. **Library Catalog of the Metropolitan Museum of Art.** 2d ed., rev. and enl. Metropolitan Museum of Art. Boston: G. K. Hall, 1980. 48v. **Supp. 1–5,** 1982–1994. ISBN 0-78382-060-7. (Supp. 5).

Since the appearance in 1960 of the initial edition of this major source, it has been recognized as one of the chief bibliographic tools in the field. The new edition incorporates all holdings from the first edition that are still part of the collection, along with material from the eight supplements that followed it. (The supplements are still being produced for those libraries that do not wish to invest in this new edition.) This dictionary catalog of author, subject, and title cards of the library holdings is in the style familiar to users of G. K. Hall products. Much re-cataloging was done to update terminology and spelling and to include new art developments. Sales catalogs are accessed by subject and by collector or auction house in the final three volumes. The new edition has supplements of its own that have appeared since its publication. The third supplement covers the period 1983 to 1986 in three volumes and the fourth supplement covers materials added from 1987 to 1989 in three volumes, while the fifth supplement treats additional materials from 1990 to 1992, also in three volumes. As of December 1999, seventy percent of the cataloging done prior to 1980 is available online at the library's Watsonline Web site http://www.metmuseum.org/htmlfile/watson/watson-1.html. All cataloging subsequent to 1980 is available.

Indexes, Abstracts, and Serial Bibliographies

*325. **Annual Bibliography of Modern Art.** The Museum of Modern Art Library, New York. Boston: G. K. Hall, 1987– . ISSN 0898-7300.

Compiled for the RLIN records of both recent and earlier publications acquired by the Museum Library, this work is available in print and on microfilm and has proven to be a useful source for identification and verification of published materials. It serves to document the materials cataloged by this library and it affords bibliographers and specialists the opportunity to identify a wide range of materials. The collection at MOMA is one of the most comprehensive of its kind and treats modern art in all aspects and phases. As one might expect, this collection is international in scope and embraces a number of languages, although emphasis is given to the United States, Europe, and Japan. Books, periodicals, exhibition catalogs, manuscripts, rare documents, and books created as art objects are treated. Entries are arranged alphabetically by author, title, and subject and furnish cross-references. Main entries provide full information. The contents are available online through the Web site at http://www.moma.org/docs/research/library/index.htm (accessed April 28, 2000).

*326. **Art Index.** New York: H. W. Wilson. 1929– . Q. with ann. cum. ISBN 0-685-22229-2 (v.1–8); 0-685-22230-6 (v.9–28); 0-685-22231-4 (v.29–). Mo. on CD-ROM.

This major indexing tool in the field covers approximately 300 periodicals, yearbooks, and museum bulletins in all fields related to the arts (archaeology, architecture, art history, city planning, crafts, graphic arts, industrial design, interior design, landscape architecture, museology, photography, and film, as well as the fine arts). Coverage is international, with periodicals in five languages; it represents the most comprehensive source of bibliographic information on periodical literature. Listings of articles appear under both author and subject, while book reviews are listed separately under the author of the book being reviewed. Exhibitions are listed under the artist or appropriate form heading, and the tool now indexes reproductions of art works. Illustrations without accompanying text are indexed under artist's name. It is available online through WILSONLINE and on CD-ROM through WILSONDISC from September 1984 to the present. The disks are updated monthly, while the database is updated twice a week. Each is cumulative and contains well over 400,000 records. *Art Abstracts* has added abstracts to the indexing since 1994, is updated monthly, and is available through FirstSearch.

Ethnoarts Index (Data Arts, 1987–) is a useful quarterly tool indexing the periodical literature related to art of Native Americans. Initially published as *Tribal Arts Review* from 1984 to 1987, it supplies a geographical arrangement and a quinquennial cumulation. Unfortunately, the publication appears to be on shaky ground because no issues have appeared since 1991.

327. *ARTbibliographies MODERN. Santa Barbara, CA: ABC-Clio, 1973– . v.4– . Semiann. ISSN 0300-466X.

This work indexes and abstracts books, periodical articles, theses, and exhibition catalogs related to art and design of the nineteenth and twentieth centuries. Entries are arranged alphabetically and include artists' names and subjects. There are both an author index and an index of museums and art galleries. Online coverage is available through DIALOG; the database of the same name covers from 1974 to date. It is updated twice a year (the same as the print volume); there are well over 100,000 records with about 12,000 added each year. Recently it has become available on CD-ROM as *ARTbibliographies MODERN on DISC*, also on a semiannual basis. With the demise of *LOMA: Literature of Modern Art* (Lund Humphries, 1969–1971), this title established itself as the heir apparent and assumed the *LOMA* numbering system. The 1969–1971 volumes of *LOMA* are considered to be volumes 1–3 of the present effort. This left the 1972 period without coverage.

A competing publication, now defunct, *Art, Design, Photo* (Idea Books, 1973–1977) also regarded itself as the successor to *LOMA* and had the same editor. It began its coverage in 1972, thus providing uninterrupted access. It was unable to survive beyond the coverage of the 1976–1977 season, however.

*328. **Bibliographic Guide to Art and Architecture.** Boston: G. K. Hall, 1976– . Ann. ISSN 0360-2699.

Although this work serves as an annual supplement to the *Dictionary Catalog of the Art and Architecture Division* of the New York Public Library (entry 320), it has gained recognition as a serial bibliography in its own right. Providing comprehensive coverage of the field, it reflects the broad collection development scheme of the library. It is not limited to the cataloging done for the division but also includes entries from the MARC tapes of the Library of Congress. Coverage includes materials from the fields of painting, drawing, sculpture, architecture, and the applied arts. Entries are listed under authors, titles, and subjects in a dictionary arrangement and represent a variety of formats (monographs, serials, and nonbook materials). Contents of these volumes can be accessed on the Web at http://www.nypl.org./catalogs/catalogs.html (accessed December 1999).

*329. **Bibliography of the History of Art: BHA=Bibliographie d'histoire de l'arte.** Santa Monica, CA: J. Paul Getty Trust, Getty Art History Information Program, 1991– . ISSN 1150-1588.

Beginning with the 1990 volume, *BHA* emerged as the successor of *RILA* (entry 333) and *RAA* (entry 331). Sponsored as a cooperative enterprise of the International Committee for the History of Art, Comite français d'histoire de l'arte, College Art Association of America, and Art Libraries of North America, it operates as part of the J. Paul Getty Trust and of the Centre national de la recherche scientifique/institut de l'information scientifique et technique in Nancy, France. It represents an important abstracting service of international dimensions, with coverage given to some 4,000 periodical titles along with books, exhibition catalogs, and dissertations relating to the history of art. The initial 1990 volume (published in 1991) includes the 1989 period to continue the coverage of *RILA* and *RAA*. Coverage is given to European art from late antiquity and American art from the period of European discoveries. Eastern art is included only when it has influenced the West. All media are included, and each issue furnishes author, subject, and journal indexes. A fifth issue supplies a cumulative annual index. The work is available online through DIALOG as a continuation of the *RILA* file and through QUESTEL as part of FRANCIS.

Art and Archaeology Technical Abstracts started initially in 1955 as an abstracting service sponsored by the International Institute for Conservation of Historic and Artistic Works and for the first ten years was produced in London. Beginning in 1966, it was published through the Institute of Fine Arts at New York University, and since 1986 has operated as a part of the Conservation Information Network as a joint project of the Getty Conservation Institute and the Department of Communication, Canada. Throughout its existence it has continued to provide abstracts of technical studies of conservation and restoration drawn from monographs, journals, and technical reports. It is available online through the Conservation Information Network. Information on the Getty Research Institute for the History of Art and Humanities and its research library may be found at its Web site (http://www.getty.edu/gri/ [accessed December 1999]).

330. **Francis bulletin signaletique 526: art et archeologie, Proche-Orient, Asie, Amerique.** Paris: Institut de l'Information Scientifique et Technique, 1971– . Q. ISSN 0007-5612.

This quarterly abstracting service is part of the large-scale program of the Centre national de la recherche scientifique, now joined by the Institut in taking over the publishing activities of the CNRS Centre des Sciences Humaines et Sociales. This work covers international books and articles on the art of Asia, the Near East, and pre-Columbian America. These areas initially had been picked up by the *Bulletin* from the print quarterly, *Repertoire d'art et d'archeologie* (entry 331n) after that publication narrowed its coverage. Online availability is through FRANCIS; the database is *Francis: Art et Archeologie 526. The complete file of about 35,000 citations dates from its beginning as a print resource in 1972 and adds about 2,800 records per year.

*331. **FRANCIS bulletin signaletique 530: Repertoire d'art et d'archeologie.** Paris: Institut de l'Information Scientifique et Technique, 1971–1990. Q. ISSN 0080-0953.

This was a complementary quarterly publication to **FRANCIS bulletin siqnaletique 526* (entry 330), which abstracted journal articles and other international publications dealing with the history of art and archaeology of the Western world from the third century A.D. to 1940. It provided electronic access to the material in the well-known and respected quarterly publication, **Repertoire d'art et d'archeologie (RAA)*, which since 1910 had given comprehensive coverage to such aspects as art theory, popular art, aesthetics, civilization, conservation, restoration, and more from antiquity to the present day. A classified, annotated bibliography of books, pamphlets, and periodical articles, it was recognized for its extensive coverage of materials on an international basis. Books were included beginning in 1920, and classifications tended to be broad, generally by period and country. It ended when it merged with *RILA* (entry 333) to form *Bibliography of the History of Art* (entry 329). After its inception in 1910 it went through several changes in sponsorship and in scope. Since 1965, the series has focused on early Christian art, eliminating the coverage of antiquity, Islamic art, and Eastern art, which were taken over by **Bulletin signaletique 526* as part of the massive FRANCIS project. The work is available online from 1973 to 1989 in a database by the same name and on CD-ROM through the FRANCIS system. There are more than 200,000 electronic records dating back to 1973.

332. **Original Index to Art Periodicals.** Frick Art Reference Library. Boston: G. K. Hall, 1983. 12v. ISBN 0-8161-0387-9.

Another of the photoreproductions of the catalog cards of an important library collection by G. K. Hall, this multi-volume work presents a file of information developed over a forty-five-year period from 1923 to 1969. It furnishes analytics developed for English, French, and Italian journals of the nineteenth and twentieth centuries, with detailed coverage of artists cited in the indexed articles as well as individual art objects, reproductions, exhibitions, provenance, and locations. Entries are provided for authors, artists, galleries, exhibitions, and portraits in a single, unified, alphabetical arrangement. Information on the collection and the library may be found at the Web site *Frick Art Collection and Frick Art Reference Library* (http://www.frick.org [accessed December 1999]).

An earlier work of similar character that is recognized for its value is *Index to Art Periodicals*, by the Ryerson Library of the Art Institute of Chicago (G. K. Hall, 1962). This eleven-volume effort provides photoreproduction of the library's card file through 1960. The analytics are extremely useful because they do not duplicate the coverage of *Art Index* (entry 326). A supplement in 1975 covered the period 1961 to 1974.

333. **RILA, Repertoire international de la litterature de l'art/ International Repertory of the Literature of Art.** Williamstown, MA: Clark Art Institute/Getty Art History Information Program, 1975–1989. Semiann. ISSN 0145-5982.

This work ended with its merger with *Repertoire d'art et d'archeologie* (entry 331n) to form *BHA* (entry 329). It began with an introductory or demonstration issue in 1973, providing initial exposure to what turned out to be an important and comprehensive international abstracting tool treating books, periodical articles, newspaper articles, Festschriften, congress reports, exhibition catalogs, museum publications, and dissertations relating to post-classical European and post-Columbian American art. Its scope complemented *Bulletin signaletique 526: art et archeologie* (entry 330). The abstracts were arranged alphabetically by author under topical headings representing forms such as reference works or subjects and periods such as medieval art. An exhibition list and an author-subject index were included. The file of *RILA* is available online through DIALOG as *Art Literature International.* Coverage is complete from 1975 to 1989. It contains over 133,000 records.

334. **Twentieth Century Artists on Art: An Index to Artists' Writings, Statements, and Interviews.** 2d enl. ed. Jack Robertson. Boston: G. K. Hall, 1996. 834p. ISBN 0-8161-9059-3.

A work of interest to art specialists, librarians, students, and researchers in related fields is the second edition, indexing the statements of nearly 15,000 artists from all over the world. Art is defined broadly and includes the fine arts, photography, video, architecture, performance, and earthworks. Sources are in Western languages, with 75 percent in English. There are more than 27,000 citations to documents that have appeared in more than 900 different publications, including anthologies of interviews and group exhibition catalogs. These sources are listed separately and are accompanied by OCLC numbers. Indexing of such materials is truly unique and the work represents a plus for its intended audience.

Art Work and Reproductions—Catalogs, Etc.

335. **The Black Artist in America: An Index to Reproductions.** Dennis Thomison, comp. Metuchen, NJ: Scarecrow Press, 1991. 396p. ISBN 0-8108-2503-1.

This is a useful and comprehensive index to the reproductions appearing in books, magazines, and exhibition catalogs of the work of nearly 1,000 African-American painters, sculptors, printmakers, illustrators, and others in the visual arts. The compiler is a university librarian who brings both expertise and familiarity with abundant resources to his treatment of artists dating from the mid-eighteenth century (Joshua Johnson) to the present (Richard Hunt and Faith Ringgold). The work is divided into three principal sections, beginning with a list of publications and institutions cited in part 2, the main body of the effort. Part 2 supplies entries alphabetically arranged by artist and gives personal information and references to biographical sources, reproductions, and additional readings. The final section contains several bibliographic listings, including audiovisual materials and doctoral dissertations. A subject index is provided.

*336.   Electronic Library of Art: A Survey of Western Art. Milpitas, CA: EBook, 1992. 4v. (CD-ROM).

The study of art is aided immeasurably by the appearance of recent technology. CD-ROM (along with the World Wide Web) may be used for identification, exposition, and interpretation of art works. This effort supplies a variety of images along with exposition of artists and time periods. Thousands of pictures in full color help the student appreciate the nature of the work. Exposition is well-developed. The work embraces the various art forms: painting, sculpture, architecture, and photography. Text is culled from theater dictionaries and other information tools. The work is indexed by artist, title, medium, school, and subject and represents a comprehensive survey of Western art. Each volume is issued on a separate disk, with all four volumes appearing in 1992.

The *International Art Catalog* is an extensive set of twenty-two disks produced by Artificial Intelligence Publishing; it sells for more than $20,000. It supplies full-color reproductions of paintings and sculptures from all parts of the world and various time periods. Indexing is thorough and access is possible by artist, period, title, pseudonym, subject, and school.

337.   The Fine Art Index. North American ed. Chicago: International Art Reference; distr., New York: Distributed Art Publishers, 1991. 660p. ISBN 0-962816-0-5.

Not really an index, but more a catalog of illustrations of some 1,000 examples of North America's finest art work, this tool furnishes reproductions by some 350 artists. Illustrations are excellent, in full color, and provide awareness of the work of both established and aspiring artists. The effort is divided into the broad general categories of paintings, drawings and prints, conceptual and installed art work, sculpture, and photographs; crafts are excluded entirely. Omissions and inclusions remain a problem for any title that attempts to treat "the finest." Entries are brief and range from one to three photographs, with no prices or accompanying text other than basic identification information. Directory listings include galleries, museums, and business services; exhibition schedules along with maps of gallery communities are given. Indexes furnish access by galleries, artists, appraisers, associations, auction houses, and conservators.

338.   Harvard University Art Museums: A Guide to the Collections. Kristin A. Mortimer, with William G. Klingelhofer. New York: Abbeville, 1985. 344p. ISBN 0-89659-600-1.

Harvard's is one of the most distinguished university art collections, and this catalog presents a sampling of the many objects held by the three museums now designated the Harvard University Art Museums. The tool was produced in celebration of the opening of the Arthur M. Sackler Museum, which joins the William Hayes Fogg and the Busch-Reisinger museums in providing an excellent and well-balanced study of the visual arts. The guide has nearly 400 reproductions of art objects, of which 80 are in color, and represents a diversified collection scheme. The Sackler Museum contains ancient, Islamic, and Oriental art; the Fogg has Western, European, and American; while the Busch-Reisinger is limited to European with an emphasis on German art. Objects are identified by title, artist, date, medium, source, and acquisition number. Arrangement is generally by time period, medium, or country, and most items are given brief description and historical coverage. Information on the museums, events, and exhibitions may be found at the Web site (http://www.artmuseums.harvard.edu/ [accessed December 1999]).

Since 1987, Chadwyck-Healey has issued *The Artists File* of the New York Public Library in over 11,000 microfiche. This is mainly the clipping file of some 1,500,000 items treating 76,000 painters, sculptors, architects, and craftspeople and represents the most comprehensive source of biographical information available in the art world. It is also the single largest collection of reproductions ever issued. Files include brochures, newsletters, book jackets, and more, constituting an important pictorial resource.

339. **Historical Art Index, A.D. 400–1650: People, Places, and Events Depicted.** Mercedes Rochelle. Jefferson, NC: McFarland, 1989. 217p. ISBN 0-89950-449-3.

This is a unique and valuable tool for those seeking art work representing events, personalities, and places in Western history. It serves first to locate art objects of various kinds (paintings, woodcuts, tapestries, manuscripts, engravings, miniatures, etc.) in museums and galleries and second to identify reproductions in books. Emphasis is on the topic rather than the artist, with entries arranged alphabetically by subject of the art work. Although topical coverage is restricted to a period of 1,250 years, there are no limitations on the date of the art, with some entries created as recently as the early twentieth century. Most coverage is given to European nobility and portraiture. Entries furnish brief description of subject, date, artist, and medium along with indications of location and reproduction. Works are listed chronologically under each heading. There is a directory of collections and a bibliography of books cited.

340. **Illustration Index.** 2d ed. Lucile E. Vance and Esther M. Tracey. Metuchen, NJ: Scarecrow Press, 1966. 527p. **Supps. III–VIII**, 1973–1998. ISBN 0-8108-3484-7. (Supp. VIII).

This has become a standard tool for identification of photographs, maps, and drawings in eight to ten popular periodicals, as well as a selective listing of books. This second edition replaces the initial effort in 1957 and its 1961 supplement by including their content together with additional material in an expanded volume supplying coverage to July 1963. Several supplements have followed to provide continuous coverage and have been labeled as editions. *Illustration Index III*, by Roger C. Greer (Scarecrow Press, 1973), covers the period July 1963 to December 1971, while *Illustration Index IV*, by Marsha C. Appel (Scarecrow Press, 1980) embraces a five-year period, 1972–1976. *Illustration Index V*, also by Appel (Scarecrow Press, 1984), treats the period 1977–1981. *Illustration Index VI* (Scarecrow Press, 1988) identifies some 35,000 illustrations in nine magazines between 1982 and 1986. A variety of subjects such as animals, architecture, plants, Native Americans, furniture, personalities, and more are covered. Thousands of entries provide references, with description of type and illustration. Arrangement is by subject. *Illustration Index VII* (Scarecrow Press, 1993) provides access to more than 28,000 illustrations appearing in the media between 1987 and 1991, while *Illustration Index VIII* (1998) continues the coverage from 1992 to 1996. Entries are indexed under some 19,000 subjects.

341. **Index to Two-Dimensional Art Works.** Yala H. Kerwin. Metuchen, NJ: Scarecrow Press, 1981. 2v. ISBN 0-8108-1381-5.

This is a well-developed tool to complement the efforts of the Monros (entry 432), Havlice (entry 436), and Smith and Moure (entry 433) for identifying reproductions in books. Unlike the others, it is not limited to reproductions of paintings but represents original color flat surface media (paintings, collages, mosaics, murals, tapestries, embroideries, drawings, stained glass, and book illumination). More than 250 books, mostly published between 1960 and 1977, are indexed; there is some duplication with the previously mentioned publications. The author is both a librarian and a creative artist and has provided a good selection of items reflecting the Western tradition. About 35,000 reproductions are identical. Volume 1 contains the artist index, which includes brief biographical identification along with title and date of work, current location symbols, and citation to reproduction. Volume 2 lists the location symbols and names of art works lost, stolen, or destroyed, and furnishes a detailed title-subject index.

342. **Mythological and Classical World Art Index: A Locator of Paintings, Sculptures, Frescoes, Manuscript Illuminations. . . .** Mercedes Rochelle. Jefferson, NC: McFarland, 1991. 279p. ISBN 0-89950-566-X.

The complete title of this effort goes on: "Sketches, Woodcuts and Engravings Executed 1200 B.C. to A.D. 1900, with a Directory of the Institutions Holding Them." It complements the coverage of Rochelle's earlier effort, *Historical Art Index, A.D. 400–1650* (entry 339). The Greek and Roman worlds as depicted in paintings, sculpture, mosaics, and drawings over a period of more than 3,000 years are the focus. Personalities, places, and events, including those relating to the gods and goddesses, are listed as topics or subject headings. Under these topics come the art works, ranging from a single listing to around 250 in the case of Venus. Included for each is a brief description of the art, medium, artist, and museum location, along with references to one or more books to locate reproductions. There is a directory of museums, bibliography of cited works, and an index of artists and art works. This is similar in concept to the author's *Post-Biblical Saints Art Index* (entry 344).

343. **Picture Sources 4.** 4th ed. Ernest H. Robl. New York: Special Libraries Association, 1983. 180p. ISBN 0-87111-274-4.

This is an interesting directory of picture collections that has earned a place in the hearts of those who have an interest in picture research. The new edition has listings for nearly 1,200 collections, of which 200 have been added since the third edition in 1975. Information is gathered through a survey of existing facilities that house pictures, maps, art reproductions, and news photographs. Although entries in earlier editions were arranged by subject, the present effort lists all collections in one alphabetical sequence. Helping to provide access is a detailed subject index. Entries supply the usual directory-type information, including collection size and scope. An important tool for general reference, with special value for the art librarian.

A similar effort is *Picture Researcher's Handbook: An International Guide to Picture Sources and How to Use Them*, now in its sixth edition (Routledge Kegan Paul, 1996) and compiled by Hilary Evans and Mary Evans. This continues as a well-conceived directory of more than 1,000 commercial sources of illustrations. Arranged alphabetically under broad categories (general, regional, national, and specialist), entries furnish address, telephone number, telex, historical period of coverage, special subject collections, information on use, and access. The British slant is complementary to the emphasis on North America in *Picture Sources 4*.

344. **Post-Biblical Saints Art Index: A Locator of Paintings, Sculptures, Mosaics, Icons, Frescoes. . . .** Mercedes Rochelle. Jefferson, NC: McFarland, 1994. 357p. ISBN 0-89950-942-8.

Similar in concept and structure to the author's *Mythological and Classical World Art Index* (entry 342), this work identifies and locates on an international basis some 5,000 art works for which saints are used as themes and subjects. More than 4,200 Christian saints, both prominent and obscure, are treated in this work, for which information is provided about the saint's title, order, patronage and method of martyrdom if applicable, date of death, and feast day. Locations of art works are given and include museums, cathedrals, libraries, and churches, and furnish title, medium, and artists' names. There are references to books that contain reproductions of the art. Special features include an index of attributes and events, bibliography, and directory of relevant art museums and libraries.

Art Sales and Exhibitions—Catalogs, Etc.

*345. **ADEC 99/Art Price Annual & Falk's Art Price Index.** Peter Falk, ed. St. Romain au Mt. d'or, France: Ehrmann, 1987– . Ann. ISBN 2-907-12915-5.

This annual publication is the most detailed and exhaustive serial on the international art market. Its twelfth issue continues to represent the combination of the *Art Price Annual* with *Falk's Art Index* for the most complete coverage of sales at auction houses in both the United States and Europe. The current volume adds another 190,000 sales from 4,500 auction houses for a cumulative total of nearly two million sales over the twelve-year period. Various forms of art are included: painting, watercolor, pastels, prints, sculpture, graphic arts, and photography. Information includes dates of artist and work, title, size, sale price, and more. In 1998, a cumulative CD-ROM was issued providing coverage from the first volume on.

ADEC (Annuaire des cotes moyennes) has produced an annual print guide adding to its stature as a leading international source for art auction price information. *Art Price Indicator 2000* (1999) is an inexpensive guide of 1,800 pages providing information of over 100,000 auction records of paintings, drawings, prints, sculpture, and photographs by some 50,000 artists world-wide. Entries supply selling price, title, size, place and date of sale, and medium. Users should become familiar with their Web sites for up-to-date information, http://www.artmarket.com and http://www.artprice.com (accessed December 1999). *Art Prices Current* (London: Art Trade, 1908–1973) provided an annual record of sales at European and American auction houses over a period of sixty-five years, except for a brief suspension of publication during World War I. Its focus was narrower and was limited to paintings, drawings, miniatures, engravings, and prints. *SCIPIO (Sales Catalog Index Project) is a database begun in 1980 and available online through RLIN (Research Libraries Information Network). Citations are given to thousands of international auction catalogs held by eight major art libraries, including the National Gallery of Art, the Art Institute of Chicago, and the Getty Center for the History of Art and the Humanities. There are over 100,000 entries dating from 1600 to the present day.

346. **Art at Auction in America.** Silver Spring, MD: Krexpress, 1989– . Ann. ISSN 1046-4999.

Unlike the Sotheby Parke Bernet effort (entry 350), this is primarily an annual price guide for the art trade in this country. A total of sixteen American auction houses are treated each season, furnishing information on over 5,000 artists and 20,000 art works. Coverage is limited to paintings, watercolors, and drawings, but embraces all periods and artists, reflecting the wide variety of purchases in American auction houses. Only works identified with a particular artist are presented; works of anonymous creators or from a certain school are excluded. Entries furnish artist name, medium, size, title, date of creation, auction house, date of sale, and price (beginning with $25). Intended for a wide audience, the work includes valuable advice and suggestions regarding value and pricing. Due to the low threshold price, it serves as an excellent survey of the entire market.

347. **Art Sales Index: Oil Paintings, Drawings, Water Colours, and Sculpture.** Poughkeepsie, NY: Apollo Book, 1968/1969– . Ann.

The title of this work has changed several times in line with a change in scope, in which two of the publisher's serials, one covering oils, the other watercolors, were merged. Later, sculpture was added to the field of coverage. The text is written in both English and

French, with the summaries given in English. The index provides listings of thousands of art items sold at auction throughout the world. Details of the sale, including prices given in pounds, dollars, and currency of the sale identified and a physical description of the art work, are given. Name, nationality, and dates of artists are provided. Dates of sales are revealed as are references to illustrations in auction catalogs.

348. **Frick Art Reference Library Sales Catalogue Index.** Boston: G. K. Hall, 1992. 230 microfiche. ISBN 0-8161-1794-2.

Since its beginning in 1920, the Frick Art Reference Library in New York has been one of the leading research centers for the history of art and has developed one of the largest collections of photographic reproductions of art works. In an effort to document the photographs there has been an emphasis on the acquisition of sales catalogs that continues to this day. The collection of 60,000 auction catalogs is recognized as the most valuable and comprehensive of its kind. Nearly 1,200 of that number were issued prior to the nineteenth century; more than 2,100 are unique to the United States or to the world. Emphasis is on Western Art: paintings, drawings, sculpture, and illuminated manuscripts sold in Europe and the United States from the seventeenth century to the present. The index is organized in three sections, providing access by date of sale, auction house or place of sale, and owner or collector. As of 1996, the auction sales catalogs are cataloged in *SCIPIO (entry 345n).

Another important collection of exhibition catalogs is held by the Arts Library of the University of California at Santa Barbara. Chadwyck-Healey has issued an excellent access tool on thirteen microfiche. *Subject Index to Art Exhibition Catalogues on Microfiche* was issued initially in 1982. It now cumulates all entries in one sequence up to 1984. The work is valuable because of the international scope of the collection.

349. **Leonard's Annual Price Index of Art Auctions.** West Newton, MA: Auction Index, 1981– . Ann. ISSN 0747-6566.

Due to the immense size of the art market, a number of serial indexes of sales have been issued. *Leonard's Index of Art Auctions* was established initially as a quarterly publication to provide a record of original works of art sold at the major auction houses in this country. Because the season runs from September to the end of August, this annual cumulation appears around October. Unlike some of the other guides, there are no illustrations here; instead, listings identify sales from more than thirty major American auction houses. Purchases are arranged by artist in alphabetical order, and listings are by price with the most expensive items first. Art works include oils, watercolors, pastels, gouache, mixed media, drawings, and sculpture. There is a good annual review of paintings sold at auction for the year, a description of trends, and a brief bibliography.

350. **Sotheby's Art at Auction: The Art Market Review.** London: Sotheby Publications, 1967– . Ann. ISSN 0084-6783.

Sotheby's has been going for over 260 years, having joined with Parke Bernet to become one of the major art auction houses in the world. Offices and facilities are located in both London and New York as well as other metropolitan areas. For a number of years, librarians and art devotees have anxiously awaited the appearance of its annual review of the preceding season, *Art at Auction: The Year at Sotheby's*, as it was formerly called. With its 1986–1987 issue, the publication changed its name but retained its essential character as a generally slick and beautiful catalog, handsomely illustrated with photographs of objects sold. The sections with color may be described as lavish in appearance. The work is arranged according to medium, country, or style, with chapters on various topics. The format has changed at different times, but generally some of the prime items sold are highlighted in expository essays, which sometimes embrace historical topics as well. All forms of art are sold at Sotheby; therefore, it provides an excellent record of notable sales.

Christie's Review of the Season (Oxford: Phaidon; distr., Salem, NH: Salem House) is also a yearly record of an international auction house that provides a slick, detailed catalog with some illustrations of art objects to illustrate the sale of notable items. Its coverage dates back to the 1920s.

351. **The Worldwide Bibliography of Art Exhibition Catalogues, 1963–1987.** Millwood, NY: Kraus International Publications, 1992. 3v. ISBN 0-527-98004-8.

After twenty-four years, *The Worldwide Art Catalogue Bulletin* (Worldwide Books, 1963–1987), the quarterly publication valued by art librarians and specialists, ended with its fourth issue in 1987. It served to inform the user of the availability of exhibition catalogs, an important but elusive resource, from the leading jobber in the field, Worldwide Art Catalogue Centre, created in 1962 and supported by the major national art bodies. This cumulation furnishes information on the 17,500 exhibition catalogs treated during that twenty-four-year period. These catalogs are of immense value for their detailed descriptions of art objects contained in these exhibitions held throughout the world. Each catalog is described in detail and was available through the Centre. The cumulation is divided into four major sections: geographic, media, topic, and monographic (listing the catalogs of a single artist). Entries include title, English translation, first exhibiting institution, stock numbers, and references to the issue of the *Bulletin* in which the particular catalog was described.

An important work from the Archives of American Art is the *Collection of Exhibition Catalogs* (G. K. Hall, 1979), which gives the catalog cards for about 15,000 exhibition catalogs identified through a survey of libraries in both the public and private sectors. Arrangement is by name of gallery or museum and under the artist's name. Material covers the nineteenth and twentieth centuries, with an emphasis on the latter.

Dictionaries, Encyclopedias, and Handbooks

352. **American Artists: Signatures and Monograms, 1800–1989.** John Castagno. Metuchen, NJ: Scarecrow Press, 1990. 826p. ISBN 0-8108-2249-0.

This is a useful identification tool prepared by a creative artist-art representor, who has identified some 5,100 artists with 10,000 signatures, monograms, and estate stamps. Entries are arranged alphabetically and furnish facsimile signatures of 4,500 Americans and 600 Canadians and Latin Americans. Many of the nineteenth-century and late twentieth-century artists have not been treated elsewhere. Also included in the entries are dates, nationality, and references to various sources of biographical, bibliographical, and pictorial information. Citations to relevant auction catalogs from over twenty major galleries are supplied. Castagno has also produced a companion effort, *European Artists: Signatures and Monograms, 1800–1990, Including Selected Artists from Other Parts of the World* (Scarecrow Press, 1990). Like the American version, it provides reference source material along with some 9,000 facsimile signatures of 4,800 European and 400 Australian, South African, and Japanese artists.

A similar effort is Peter H. Falk's *Dictionary of Signatures and Monograms of American Artists: From the Colonial Period to the Mid-Twentieth Century* (Sound Vien Press, 1988), developed as a companion volume to *Who Was Who in American Art* (entry 399). It also identifies some 10,000 signatures arranged in three major segments: "Signatures and Monograms," "Initials and Monograms," and "Shapes and Symbols."

353. Artist Monograms and Indiscernible Signatures: An International Directory, 1800–1991. John Castagno. Metuchen, NJ: Scarecrow Press, 1991. 538p. ISBN 0-8108-2415-9.

Signature and monogram sourcebooks for artists received a big boost with publication of the Castagno efforts the year prior to this work (entry 352). This is the first title devoted to identification of difficult or illegible signatures. It furnishes around 5,200 monogram and signature facsimiles for some 3,700 artists worldwide who were active within a period of nearly 200 years. As is true of the author's other efforts, signatures are drawn from reference books, catalogs, and magazines. Included here are painters, cartoonists, poster artists, and illustrators. There are chapters and initials, symbols and Oriental signatures, Cyrillic, Hebraic, and more. This is an important title for its emphasis on contemporary American artists, and places it along with the other Castagno efforts as supplementary to the massive Goldstein work described below.

Monogramm-Lexikon: Internationales Verzeichais der Monogramme bildender Kunstler seit 1850, by Franz Goldstein (de Grunter, 1964), is the standard source for identification of monograms of artists active since 1850. Entries give dates, media, and references to various information sources such as Thieme and Becker (entry 383) and Benezit (entry 391). Arrangement is alphabetical by letters of the monogram. This work complements the earlier five-volume title by George Kaspar Nagler, *Die Monogrammisten und diejenigen bekannten und unbekannten Kunstler aller Schulen . . .* (Franz, 1858–1879; repr., de Graaf, 1966), which is a comprehensive dictionary of monograms and marks on all types of art work by artists up to the 1850s. Arrangement is by dominant letter of the monogram.

354. The Artist's Handbook of Materials and Techniques. 5th ed. Ralph Mayer. Rev. and updated by Steven Sheehan. New York: Viking, 1991. 761p. ISBN 0-670-83701-6.

This is an established source in the field that has gained an excellent reputation for depth of coverage and accuracy beginning with its initial appearance over fifty years ago. Librarians have recognized this title as a vital work for both the practitioner and the librarian serving the practitioner's needs. Originally published in 1940, the fourth edition was issued in 1981. The purpose of this tool has been and continues to be to provide the artist with a fully integrated, up-to-date account of both materials and procedures. The new edition by Sheehan (the director of the Ralph Mayer Center at Yale University) continues in the style of its predecessors, providing in-depth coverage with new information on pigments, oil painting, tempera painting, watercolor, solvents, new materials, conservation practices, and so forth. Outdated material has been deleted. Included also are notes, bibliographies, and an index.

355. Artwords: A Glossary of Contemporary Art Theory. Thomas Patin and Jennifer McLerran. Chicago: Fitzroy Dearborn, 1997. 153p. ISBN 1-884-96491-5.

The authors are academics who have put together a volume of interest to students and serious inquirers, defining more than 400 terms and phrases relevant to current theory and criticism of visual art and culture. In so doing, the work adopts an interdisciplinary approach and utilizes the terminology of cultural studies, literary theory, psychoanalytic theory, and criticism. In some cases, the terms used are abstract and difficult to comprehend, and definitions may include terms defined elsewhere in the volume. Within the definitions, there are references to theorists and artists whose work is connected to the individual terms. The work serves as both a guide and a dictionary, providing thematic access as well as alphabetical access to terms, cross-references, and a useful bibliography.

356. **The Classified Directory of Artists' Signatures, Symbols & Monograms.** Enl. and rev. ed. H.H. Caplan. Detroit: Gale Research, 1982. 873p. ISBN 0-8103-0977-7.

Originally appearing in 1976, this tool gained a reputation as a solid piece of work in helping to identify artists by their signatures or monograms. Several thousand artists are covered, with the first section alphabetically arranged by name and providing facsimile signatures. The second section treats monograms arranged under the first letter, while section 3 provides a listing of illegible signatures arranged under the first recognizable letter. The final segment presents symbols arranged by general shape, such as circle or star.

This emphasis is continued by Caplan's supplementary effort, *The Classified Directory of Artists' Signatures, Symbols, & Monograms: American Artists with New U.K. Additions*, published in London by P. Grahame Publishing Company in 1987.

357. **The Color Compendium.** Augustine Hope and Margaret Walch. New York: Van Nostrand Reinhold, 1990. 360p. ISBN 0-442-31845-6.

This work has provoked mixed reactions from its reviewers; it was felt in some quarters that it did not live up to its expectations as a comprehensive illustrated encyclopedia entirely devoted to color. Others have praised its scholarly yet popular approach, which combines profound essay-length articles with brief descriptive pieces. In all, there are 1,100 entries, arranged alphabetically, that touch on every facet, some of peripheral nature, relating to the exposition of color. This breadth is admired by certain critics and lamented by others, but the work represents a panoramic view of the meaning, impact, and influence of color as it affects the world today. Computer technology, food preparation, advertising, fashion, architecture, and the arts are covered. There are good color plates to illustrate specific points, and useful appendices provide listings of international color organizations, color specific systems, and a well-developed bibliography.

358. **Contemporary Masterworks.** Colin Naylor, ed. Chicago: St. James Press, 1991. 933p. (Contemporary Art Series). ISBN 1-55862-083-4.

This title represents a change in direction from others in the series because it emphasizes the art works rather than the artists. Coverage is given to 450 pieces of art recognized as having made an important contribution to twentieth-century culture. They are arranged alphabetically by artist in four segments, beginning with "Art" (painting, sculpture, performance work, etc.) and progressing through "Architecture," "Photography," and "Design" (automobiles, posters, fashions, etc.). Entries furnish a critical essay, catalog data, a bibliography, and a full-page black-and-white illustration for each work. One hundred sixty specialists have contributed the signed articles. Selections were made by an advisory board of twenty distinguished experts. The effort is noteworthy for its inclusion of a variety of art works ranging from pop art to serious artistic productions. There is a brief general bibliography and an index to individuals, studios, and manufacturers.

359. **A Dictionary of Art Quotations.** Ian Crofton, comp. New York: Schirmer Books, 1989. 223p. ISBN 0-02-870621-8.

First published in the United Kingdom by Routledge in 1988, this is the first American edition of this compact little volume targeted to quotations concerning Western art. The bulk of the text is given to the fine arts of painting, drawing, and sculpture, although there are separate segments addressing architecture and photography. It has been criticized for being somewhat whimsical in its approach to the subject and its selection of quotations and for being uneven in its coverage. The value of the work lies in its unique focus on art quotations and the variety of perspectives offered. Entries are arranged under numerous topical sections, including artists' names (architects and photographers are excluded). Quotations are drawn from a variety of written sources in a rather arbitrary manner. Bibliographic references are brief, and the work is geared to the interests of the curious rather than the needs of the scholarly. A general index provides access.

360. **The Dictionary of Art.** Jane Turner, ed. New York: Grove, 1996. 34v. ISBN 1-884-44600-0.

This much-anticipated, monumental effort was issued in 1996 as had been promised. Consisting of thirty-four volumes, it joins the celebrated Grove publication in music as the definitive general reference resource in its field. It supplies some 41,000 articles of varying length (with bibliographies) written by 6,700 art historians and specialists from all over the world and is considered to be the largest international collaboration in the history of art publishing. It is designed to provide broad context coverage of an interdisciplinary nature employing the most recent scholarship. The work provides insight into such areas as anthropology, archaeology, and the performing arts. It contains 15,000 illustrations integrated with the text, providing treatment of the entire realm of the visual arts on an international basis. There is an excellent, detailed index to facilitate access.

361. **Dutch Art: An Encyclopedia.** Sheila D. Muller, ed. New York: Garland, 1997. 489p. (Garland Reference Library of the Humanities, v. 1021). ISBN 0-8153-0065-4.

This is the first reference survey of Dutch art and occupies an important position as a source of information in a much-needed area. It provides comprehensive coverage from the late fifteenth century to the present and furnishes essays treating artists' biographies, historical development, and stylistic and developmental concepts. This pattern of coverage provides insight and understanding into the social and cultural forces that helped to shape and influence the creative energy and mode of expression of the individual artists. Entries provide cross-references to other essays in the work that provide additional coverage on the topic. Color and black-and-white illustrations provide the necessary visual representation, and the bibliography provides up-to-date listings of an international character. The work is well-indexed.

362. **Encyclopedia of Women in Religious Art.** Diane Apostolos-Cappadona. New York: Continuum, 1996. 442p. ISBN 0-826-40195-6.

Representative of the influence of gender studies in recent years is this compendium of information on the treatment of women in religious art. The work contains over 2,000 entries on themes, subjects, motifs, and symbolism as well as personalities (artists, critics, historians) considered important in such study. Female entities represented as the subjects in art from various traditions (Christianity, Judaism, Islam, Buddhism, Hinduism, etc.) are supplied in a comprehensive coverage of ancient to modern periods. Of real interest is the coverage given to the less familiar cultures such as the Druids. The presentation is aided by black-and-white illustrations of female images, symbols, and mythology from the different cultures and their inherent variations.

363. **Encyclopedia of World Art.** New York: McGraw-Hill, 1959–1987. 17v. ISBN 0-07-019467-X.

In the past, this has been considered to be the cornerstone of every reference collection in art, and it still must be considered a magnificent work. It was published simultaneously in Italian and in English. Providing treatment of considerable length, the signed articles represent excellent scholarship on an international level. Bibliographies are extensive and are regarded as a real strength. Entries are alphabetically arranged, but the emphasis on monographic-length articles makes use of the index (volume 15) mandatory. Biographies of artists, although numerous, tend to be brief, with the major emphasis on the articles regarding various schools, movements, and national characteristics in which the personalities are mentioned. The scope is broad and covers the entire field of visual arts in all countries and periods. Each volume contains about 500 plates, some of which are in color. The index volume is detailed and provides access through some 20,000 entries. Volumes 16 and 17 serve as supplements, providing coverage of contemporary art and new perspectives.

A recent tool of interest to the sophisticated student is *The Art of Art History: A Critical Anthology*, edited by Donald Preziosi (Oxford University Press, 1998), which provides a comprehensive and provocative analysis of the realm of art history. Introductions to some thirty-five critical readings by serious art critics and scholars are organized into nine chapters treating aesthetics; style; iconography and semiology; feminism; gender studies; formalism; post-modernism; deconstruction; and museography, hybridity, and multiculturalism.

364. **Glossary of Art, Architecture, and Design Since 1945.** 3d ed., rev., enl. and ill. John A. Walker. London: Library Association Publishing; distr., Boston: G. K. Hall, 1992. 500p. ISBN 0-8161-0556-1.

This has been one of the standard tools in the field since its initial publication in 1973 and its subsequent revision in 1977. At that time, its subtitle read: "Terms and Labels Describing Movements, Styles and Groups Derived from the Vocabulary of Artists and Critics." The third edition represents an effort augmented by the inclusion of 173 illustrations, all in black-and-white. There are 700 entries, each providing a concise but up-to-date and informative definition. A bibliography is furnished for each one, adding to the value of the work both for the curious information seeker and the more serious inquirer. The Library Association of Great Britain has produced an attractive tool with a wide appeal. Access is assured through use of cross-references within entries and provision of a detailed general index.

365. **The HarperCollins Dictionary of Art Terms and Techniques.** 2d ed. Ralph Mayer. Rev. and ed. by Steven Sheehan. New York: Harper-Perennial, 1991. 474p. ISBN 0-06-271518-6.

One of the standard art dictionaries in the field, the earlier edition of this work had been reprinted several times since its initial appearance. Sheehan, the director of the Ralph Mayer Center at Yale University, updated this effort as well as *The Artist's Handbook of Materials and Techniques* (entry 354). Using the Mayer pattern, the work continues to provide coverage of the terminology and techniques representing a broad spectrum of art activity. It contains several thousand entries that provide cogent and well-developed definitions and identifications. The purpose remains the definition of those terms encountered by the student or specialist in the literature of the field. There are entries on schools, styles, and periods, with some illustrations provided. The emphasis is on the procedures and materials of the artist.

366. **An Index-Dictionary of Chinese Artists, Collectors, and Connoisseurs with Character Identification by Modified Stroke Count....** Nancy N. Seymour. Metuchen, NJ: Scarecrow Press, 1988. 987p. ISBN 0-8108-2091-9.

The full title goes on: ". . . Including over 5,000 Chinese Names and Biographies from the T'ang Dynasty through the Modern Period." This gives an idea of the broad coverage and scope of this important reference work. It addresses the need for a source of identification for artists and other personalities related to the world of Chinese art. They are listed alphabetically using the Wade-Giles romanization system, but entries also furnish alternative spelling through the Pinyin system of romanization. Included in the entries are brief biographical sketches, number of strokes in the character of the surname, full script characters for each name, and references to additional biographical sources listed. The second section of this work presents a useful instructional approach to identifying and explaining Chinese characters and signatures. It supplies a methodology for identifying characters by a stroke-counting system, as well as a chronology of Chinese dynasties. There is a character index of Chinese names.

367. **The Oxford Companion to Art.** Harold Osborne, ed. Oxford: Clarendon, 1970; repr., 1984, 1986, 1989. 1277p. ISBN 0-19-866107-X.

Another useful tool in the Oxford Companion series, this one has been reprinted several times. There are about 3,000 entries, arranged alphabetically. The major focus is on painting and sculpture, although other aspects of the visual arts such as architecture and ceramics are covered. Applied arts and handicrafts receive little attention. Articles vary in length from a brief paragraph to a number of pages on broad topical categories such as perspective. Although the articles are not signed, the authors' expertise is evident in the exposition given the various elements covered: national and regional schools of art, movements, concepts, styles, techniques, themes, iconographies, biographies, and museums. Articles are introductory in nature and include cross-references but no bibliographies. An extensive bibliography in the appendix provides additional references.

368. **The Oxford Companion to Christian Art and Architecture.** Peter Murray and Linda Murray. New York: Oxford University Press, 1996. 596p. ISBN 0-19-866165-7.

This husband and wife team has produced a successful Oxford Companion with this guide, providing over 1,700 articles on major contributors, periods, figures, forms, and beliefs, as represented within the Judeo-Christian art tradition. Entries are alphabetically arranged and provide excellent insight into and exposition of the art topics and their relation to dogma, rites, and liturgy. Included are articles on personalities, artistic and religious movements, and architecture. As is true of other works in this series, the writing is clear and lucid and provides useful information on a variety of related topics, ranging from the basic and fundamental to the relatively obscure. There are black-and-white illustrations, sixteen full-page color plates, and a classified bibliography. Of interest is the seven-page glossary of architectural terms.

369. **The Oxford Companion to Twentieth-Century Art.** Harold Osborne, ed. New York: Oxford University Press, 1981; repr. with corr., 1985–1990. 656p. ISBN 0-19-866119-3.

One of the strong features of the earlier work, *Oxford Companion to Art* (entry 367) is the coverage given to contemporary art movements and artists. This newer title provides more timely information on the nature of the modern art scene. There are numerous biographies of individual artists as well as informative treatments of styles, movements, and schools. Terms are defined in a lucid fashion, in the manner of the previous works in this series. The tool is intended to serve as a handbook or guide for students and interested laypersons seeking enlightenment on the subject of modern art. Such recent aspects as computer art and body art are treated, along with the more standard manifestations of Dada and art deco. Living artists are covered, with their achievements summarized to the mid-1970s. Illustrations are included and a selective bibliography is appended.

370. **The Oxford Dictionary of Art.** Ian Chilvers and Harold Osborne, eds. New York: Oxford University Press, 1997. 647p. ISBN 0-19-860084-4.

Another of the useful one-volume Oxford efforts, this new edition, like its predecessor (1988), is based on *The Oxford Companion to Art* (entry 367), *The Oxford Companion to Twentieth Century Art* (entry 369), and *The Oxford Companion to the Decorative Arts* (entry 543). Much of the material has been revised and updated, and about 300 new entries have been produced. The lengthy survey articles in the Oxford Companions treating art in the various countries, architecture, and Oriental art have been omitted, and no artists born after 1945 are included. In all, some 3,000 entries provide brief but informative descriptions of various aspects of Western art, including personalities, periods, schools, techniques, paintings, graphics, and sculpture. Architecture is excluded. Coverage begins with antiquity and continues to the present.

The Concise Oxford Dictionary of Art and Artists, edited by Chilvers (2d ed., Oxford University Press, 1996), supplies a condensed version of the principal *Dictionary*. It provides brief and cogent entries on painting, sculpture, and graphic arts. This title retains the essential character of the parent effort but with one-third fewer entries.

Directories

371. **American Art Directory.** New York: R. R. Bowker, 1898– . Bienn. ISSN 0065-6968.

With publication of the 57th edition (1999–2000), this directory remains the acknowledged standard in the field. Originally entitled *American Art Annual* (vols. 1–37, 1898–1945/1948), it is now published biennially. The frequency has varied in the past, but it now seems to have established its pattern both in terms of frequency and format. The most recent edition provides information on several thousand art museums, libraries, associations, schools, and studios within the U.S. and Canadian sphere of influence. Major emphasis is given to treatment of museums, libraries, and associations, with geographical arrangement by state and city. Entries include address, key personnel, sources of income, descriptions of collections, and publications. Coverage also includes art councils, periodicals, scholarships, exhibitions, and booking agencies as well as schools and academic departments. Access is provided by three indexes: organization, personnel, and subject.

Art in America Annual Guide to Galleries, Museums, Artists is compiled by the editors of the well-known monthly periodical, *Art in America*. The *Guide* is regarded as a solid piece of work, identifying individuals as well as institutions of importance and interest to artists in this country. It has been issued since 1982.

372. **American Art Galleries: The Illustrated Guide to Their Art and Artists.** Les Krantz, ed. New York: Facts on File, 1985. 304p. ISBN 0-81600-089-1.

This is a comprehensive directory of nearly 1,100 art galleries of importance to art patrons, collectors, and dealers. Galleries are defined in terms of their activities, including both selling and exhibiting, thus eliminating those museums and exhibition centers not providing opportunity for purchase. Arrangement is alphabetical by state, then by city, with the galleries then arranged alphabetically under the city. Galleries from all fifty states and the District of Columbia are represented. Each entry provides a history of the gallery, identification of its leading artists and their media, and enumeration of any specializations in art styles or group exhibits. Addresses, telephone numbers, key personnel, and business hours are included. There are excellent illustrations of selected art objects, some of which are in color. An important feature is an extensive artist index.

373. **American Artists' Materials Suppliers Directory.** Alexander W. Katlan. Park Ridge, NJ: Noyes Press, 1987–1992. 2v. ISBN 0-815550-64-2 (v.1); 0-932087-19-1 (v.2).

Katlan, a painting conservator, prepared the initial volume to facilitate the identification and dating of unsigned American paintings of the nineteenth century through listings of some 3,700 art supply firms in the Boston and New York areas during that time. Unique stencil marks and labeling on the canvases prepared by these firms serve as excellent clues to their origin. Entries supply addresses and dates of the supply houses. In addition, there are brief histories of eight major firms and black-and-white photographs of the marks and labels.

Volume 2 emphasizes the actual art materials, with entries furnishing exposition along with illustrations of stretchers, panels, artist boards, and canvas. Included are listings of stretcher patents from 1849 to 1949, segments of original trade catalogs, and a directory of art supply houses in Philadelphia and Baltimore. Case histories are given on the materials used by three artists.

374. **Archives of American Art: A Directory of Resources.** Garnett McCoy. New York: R. R. Bowker, 1972. 163p. ISBN 0-8352-0598-3.

Since its appearance fifteen years ago, this tool has achieved recognition as a valuable source of information regarding the papers held by the Archives. The Archives was established in 1954 in Detroit, Michigan, to preserve and make available personal papers. The Archives has since become a part of the Smithsonian Institution but operates with five regional centers in Detroit, New York, Boston, San Francisco, and Washington, D.C. This print directory identifies 555 groups or collections of papers that are available for use in microfilm at any of the centers. By using the Web site (http://www.si.edu/artarchives [accessed December 1999]), one is able to secure information regarding the vast resources in some 5,000 collections. Another contribution of value is *The Card Catalog of the Manuscript Collections of the Archives of American Art* (entry 319).

*375. **Art on Screen: A Directory of Films and Videos About the Visual Arts.** Program for Art on Film; Nadine Covert, ed. Boston: G. K. Hall, 1991. 283p. ISBN 0-8161-7294-3.

This is a useful directory or catalog of more than 900 films and videos related to the study, enjoyment, appreciation, or understanding of the fine arts, decorative arts, archaeology, crafts, and so forth. Its intent is to draw a selective listing from the 17,000 entries in the *Art on Film Database, compiled by the Program for Art on Film and sponsored by the Getty Trust and the Museum of Modern Art. It does not duplicate the listings in *Films on Art* (Canadian Center for Films on Art, 1977) but rather treats favorably reviewed items issued between 1976 and 1990. Entries are listed under one of two major categories, treating documentaries and shorts and also feature films. Entries supply series title, running time, format, year of release, agency, and so forth, along with a synopsis and evaluation. There are several informative introductory essays; five indexes furnish access.

376. **Artist's & Graphic Designer's Market, 2000: 2,500 Places to Sell Your Art & Design.** Mary Cox, ed. Cincinnati: Writer's Digest Books, 1999. 720p. ISBN 0-89879-913-9.

This work continues its annual appearance and retains its reputation as an excellent resource for artists, designers, and illustrators in marketing their products. The format and presentation follow those of previous years, with introductory chapters devoted to marketing, self-promoting, and organizing a business, along with an overview of the art industry. Additional chapters examine some 2,500 markets, including advertising and public relations firms, studios, publishers, distributors, galleries, and so forth. Entries furnish telephone and fax numbers, personnel, and descriptions of companies. Most important is the information regarding submissions, with tips on how to best present the products to particular markets. Included are interviews with practicing professionals, illustrations of marketed works, a glossary, and a bibliography. A detailed index provides access.

*377. **International Directory of Art Libraries.** Thomas E. Hill, ed. Poughkeepsie, NY: Vassar College Libraries, 1997– . http://iberia.vassar.edu/ifla-idal (accessed April 5, 2000).

Produced by International Federation of Libraries (IFLA) Section of Art Libraries in cooperation with other international art organizations, this Web site is administered on facilities provided by Vassar College Art Library. Data on nearly 3,000 art libraries—either with more than 2,500 volumes or, if of lesser size, with unique or important collection distinctions—and library departments with specialized holdings in art, architecture, and archaeology are provided on an international basis. Data have been collected through use of an electronic survey form; entries furnish name, address, e-mail addresses of librarians, Web links to home pages, telephone number, fax number, access hours, periods of closing, number of volumes, founding date, names of librarians, and date of last entry. A printed edition may be ordered from K. G. Saur.

378. **International Directory of Arts.** 1998–1999. 24th ed. New Providence, NJ: KG Saur/Reed Reference Publishing, 1998. 3v. ISBN 3-598230-78-8.

This is the most comprehensive international directory in the art field, identifying a host of representative organizations and personalities associated with the arts. The 24th edition of what has turned into a regular publication is in three volumes for the first time and contains more information than previous efforts, providing data on over 150,000 addresses and related facts, with hundreds of new listings and review and revision of the previous listings. Information is gathered through a survey of organizations and individuals throughout the world. There is expanded coverage of museums and institutional galleries and broader inclusion of universities, academies, and schools of art, along with associations. There is continued inclusion of dealers and their galleries, publishers, periodicals, book dealers, restorers, auctioneers, and collectors. Arrangement is generally alphabetical by country, then by city. Frequency of publication has varied in the past but appears to have settled on a biennial issuance. The tool is especially useful for museums, universities, research libraries, professional associations, and specialized collections. It has been criticized for its lack of indexing.

379. **Looking at Art: A Visitor's Guide to Museum Collections.** Adelheid M. Gealt. New York: R. R. Bowker, 1983. 609p. ISBN 0-8352-1730-2.

Different from most catalogs and guides to specific collections, this work provides background knowledge and insight into the nature of the types of art produced through time. It is a good information piece on the thoughts and influences that have shaped various styles and developments. The book is divided into two major sections, the first of which covers the history of collecting and the growth and practices of art museums. The second part contains a number of chapters devoted to the history of art in the Western world from ancient times to the present. There is also coverage of Asian, pre-Columbian, and tribal arts. There are lists of major museums and lists of artists, which identify their media as well as dates. The volume also provides a concluding bibliography and a detailed, comprehensive index.

A selective survey of collections is *Art Museums of the World*, edited by Virginia Jackson (Greenwood, 1987, 2v.). It covers some 200 museums, each provided with a lengthy historical essay. Directory-type information such as directors, departments, and telephone numbers is not given.

380. **Slide Buyers' Guide: An International Directory of Slide Sources for Art and Architecture.** 6th ed. Norine D. Cashman, ed. Englewood, CO: Libraries Unlimited, 1990. 190p. (Visual Arts Resources Series). ISBN 0-87287-797-3.

Since its initial edition in 1972, this directory has established a solid reputation for its comprehensive coverage of sources of slides on a worldwide basis. Originally a biennial with a different publisher, the work has settled into a less frequent but more viable pattern of four to five years between editions (5th ed., 1985; 4th ed., 1980; 3d ed., 1976). It remains an extremely important tool for those who work with this medium, for there is nothing else like it. Listings emphasize U.S. and Canadian sources in the first section, while the second section provides coverage of Asia, Australia, Great Britain, Europe, Ireland, and the Middle East. Commercial sources are grouped separately from museum sources for each country. The evaluative commentary is slight, but helpful. Appendices supply listings of vendors who did not reply to the questionnaire and of sources of textbook slide sets. Both name and detailed subject indexes provide access.

381. **The Visual Resources Directory: Art, Slide, and Photograph Collections in the United States and Canada.** Carla Conrad Freeman and Barbara Stevenson, eds. Englewood, CO: Libraries Unlimited, 1995. 174p. ISBN 1-56308-196-2.

This is an important resource tool for librarians and specialists, the first comprehensive directory of visual resources to be published in years. Coverage is given to over 500 individual collections housed in the United States and Canada. These represent the broad expanse of the visual arts through all media, including architecture and design. Entries are arranged under state or province, then city and institution, and identify contact persons, telephone and fax numbers, e-mail addresses, borrowing privileges, hours, size of collection and staff, and type of visual media in collection. Also of value to the user is the description of the manner of cataloging and classification utilized in the organization of modern collections and identification of imaging projects underway. Access is assured through indexing by subject, institution, and personnel.

382. **World Museum Publications: A Directory of Art and Cultural Museums, Their Publications and Audiovisual Materials, 1982.** New York: R. R. Bowker, 1982. 711p. ISBN 0-8352-1444-3.

The first issue of what purported to be a serial directory, this work provided the most comprehensive information up to that time on museum publications. Developed through a survey of nearly 10,000 museums in 111 countries, it presents listings of over 30,000 publications in various formats (books, catalogs, bulletins, journals, newsletters, pamphlets, posters, and picture books). Audiovisual titles, such as films, filmstrips, slides, recordings, and videotapes, are also included. Material is presented in five different indexes: geographic guide to museums; museum publications and audiovisual materials arranged alphabetically by museum; author index; publications by title; and audiovisual materials by title. A listing of publishers and distributors completes the volume. This has been a valuable resource for academic libraries and specialized art libraries through the years.

Biographical Sources

383. **Allgemeines Lexikon der bildenden Kunstler von der Antike bis zur Gegenwart.** Ulrich Thieme and Felix Becker. Leipzig, Germany: W. Engelmann, 1907. 37v. Repr., Munchen: Deutscher Taschenbuch Verlag; distr., Land O' Lakes, FL: Dealer's Choice Books, 1992. ISBN 3-423-05098-7.

This is considered the most complete and scholarly biographical reference work in the entire art field. It includes nearly 50,000 artists from all countries and all time periods. The emphasis is on painters and engravers, but architects and sculptors are also covered. Articles vary in length but generally provide good depth of coverage, with the longer ones signed by the contributors. Locations are provided for works of art, and this title is known for the bibliographies accompanying the majority of entries. These include references to books, catalogs, and periodical articles. Entries are arranged alphabetically by names of personalities.

The work is extended by a supplementary effort by Hans Vollmer, entitled *Allegemeines Lexikon der bildenden Kunstler des XX Jahrhunderts* (Seeman, 1953–1962, 6v.). Although there is some overlap with Thieme (which included a few living persons at time of publication), the concentration on twentieth-century artists is for the most part unique. It includes about 6,000 brief biographies with bibliographical references. *Internationale Kunstler Datenbank* (1990–) is an annual CD-ROM publication from K. G. Saur providing complete listings of popular artists and contact information.

384. **Artist Biographies Master Index: A Consolidated Index to More Than 275,000 Biographical Sketches of Artists Living and Dead.** Barbara McNeil, ed. Detroit: Gale Research, 1986. 700p. (Gale Biographical Index series, No. 9) ISBN 0-8103-2107-6.

As part of the Gale Biographical Index series, this is a spinoff from the *Biography and Genealogy Master Index* (entry 30). These specialized indexes are convenient and furnish some economy in terms of time needed for searching; therefore, most art collections will purchase this work even though the *BGMI* may be kept in another part of the library. The index identifies references in over seventy English-language biographical dictionaries, some of which are multi-volume publications covering a broad spectrum of the art world. Included are the usual painters and sculptors along with architects, photographers, cabinetmakers, fashion and graphic designers, illustrators, and ceramics and computer graphics artists. Thousands of individuals are covered, many with multiple references. Although it will not replace other biographical sources in the library because it is limited to English-language source material, this work represents a good addition to any art collection.

An older, more specialized tool is Theresa Dickason Cederholm's *Afro-American Artists: A Bio-bibliographical Directory*, published by the Boston Public Library in 1973. It is still regarded as an important source for identification of some 1,500 African-American artists of all types (painters, sculptors, illustrators, designers, craftspeople, etc., along with educators and historians). Brief biographical information is given for individuals both past and present.

385. **Artists of the American West: A Biographical Dictionary.** Doris Ostrander Dwady. Athens, OH: Swallow Press, 1974–1985. 3v. Repr. v.1, 1990. ISBN 0-8040-0607-5.

A comprehensive biographical source, this covers over 4,000 artists who worked and lived in the western part of this nation. Limited to artists born before 1900, there is excellent coverage given to twentieth-century art because many of the individuals achieved their greatest success during this period. Limited to painters, illustrators, and printmakers for the most part, entries are arranged alphabetically and include dates and places of birth and death, primary area of residence, location of works, and references to additional sources of information in books and periodical literature. Biographical information is brief. There is a classified bibliography of source materials relating to all three volumes and a general index to the set in volume 3.

386. **Biographical Dictionary of Japanese Art.** Yutaka Tazawa, ed. Tokyo: Kodansha International; distr., New York: Harper & Row, 1981. 825p. ISBN 0-87011-488-3.

Developed as the final volume of a three-volume dictionary on Japan, this should prove to be of value to the reference collection in its focus on the art and artists of the East. Coverage is broad, as it should be in a general purpose tool intended to represent the multi-faceted artistic production of the Japanese. Included are biographical sketches grouped by media and type of art (painting, printmaking, architecture, sculpture, calligraphy, graphic design, tea ceremony, gardens, ceramics, swords, metalwork, textiles, and lacquer). Heaviest emphasis is placed on figurative artists. Arrangement is alphabetical by names in English translitera-tion and entries are adequate (in some cases anecdotal). Appendices are varied and useful and include a glossary, maps, bibliography, and historical charts and tables.

387. **Contemporary Artists.** 4th ed. Joann Cerrito, ed. Detroit: St. James Press, 1996. 1340p. ISBN 1-55862-183-0.
The first edition of this work appeared in 1977 and covered over 1,300 artists world-wide. The second edition deleted 450 of those artists while adding 150 new names, for a total of 1,000. This weeding and reduction process continued with the third edition, which deleted 200 while adding 50 new ones, for a total of 850. The fourth edition contains about the same number, having deleted some older names in favor of more recent artists, including those in video and computer art. Generally, there are no artists included who died before 1965, as compared to 1960 in the third edition, which signals a continuously narrowing selection policy. Artists from various media in the fine and applied arts are covered if they have exhibited their work in important art galleries, have been included in museum shows, or are exhibited in the permanent collections of major museums. Entries include a brief biography, references to exhibitions and collections in which the artist has been represented, a bibliography by and about the artist, name of agent or dealer, and a signed critical essay. Photographs are included along with comments by the artists themselves. It is recommended that libraries retain the previous editions together with this revision, to provide fuller coverage.

388. **Dictionary of Contemporary American Artists.** 6th ed. Paul Cummings. New York: St. Martin's Press, 1994. 786p. ISBN 0-312-08440-4.
This biographical dictionary continues as a standard for identification of American artists, most of whom are still living. The present edition treats some 900 artists, having deleted 27 and added 41 to those covered in the fifth edition. The artists have attained a certain stature or status (museum representation, exhibitions, recognition in the field) for which brief information is provided regarding education, teachers, teaching career, scholarships or prizes, address, dealer, exhibitions, collections, special commissions, and notes on the artist's specialty. A bibliography of books by and about the subject is included. There are over 100 black-and-white illustrations scattered throughout the work. There is much more detail here than in *Who's Who in American Art* (entry 400), although Cummings is much more selective in terms of number of artists covered. Emphasis is on painters, but sculptors and printmakers are included as well. There is an index of artists, with a pronunciation guide for difficult names, and a key to museums and galleries in which the artists are represented.

389. **Dictionary of Women Artists.** Delia Gaze, ed. Chicago: Fitzroy Dearborn, 1997. 2v. ISBN 1-884-96421-4.
This large-scale work is an important product of an expert group of 330 advisors and contributors, who have combined to supply an important biographical reference work of some 600 women who have worked in various media at both the professional and amateur levels. It represents current historical thought in its emphasis on societal and cultural chal-lenges and obstacles faced by women artists rather than the commercial success they enjoyed. These challenges and societal implications are examined in twenty introductory essays, all signed, that precede the scholarly biographical articles. The subjects were chosen from lists prepared by the panel, and range from those who worked around A.D. 1000 to those born in 1945. Arrangement is alphabetical by professional name, with cross-references to alternate names. A chronology is furnished.

390. **Dictionary of Women Artists: An International Dictionary of Women Artists Born Before 1900.** Chris Petteys et al. Boston: G. K. Hall, 1985. 851p. ISBN 0-8161-8456-9.

More than 21,000 female artists are covered, making this the most comprehensive source of information to date. Painters, printmakers, illustrators, and sculptors are included, while photographers, architects, craftswomen, and designers are not. Although this is one of several publications recently dedicated to the identification of women artists, it is unequaled in terms of its utility in identifying elusive or obscure names. Entries provide full name, married name, pseudonyms, birth and death dates, medium, subject or thematic matter, residence, education, exhibitions and awards, and references to source material from which the biographies are derived. Bibliographic references to additional material are also included. This is of major value in art reference work.

391. **Dictionnaire critique et documentaire des peintres, sculpteurs, dessinateurs, et graveurs de tous les pays.** New ed. Emmanuel Benezit. Paris: Grund, 1976. 10v. ISBN 2700001494.

In the past, this multi-volume biographical dictionary has been rated by art librarians as a vital source. It has retained its reputation through the years since its initial appearance in three volumes (1911–1923). The present edition is a complete revision of the 1948–1955 effort of eight volumes, although the format is the same and similar information is given. Coverage includes artists from the fifth century B.C. to the mid-twentieth century, and represents both Eastern and Western cultures. Entries vary in length from a few lines to several columns, but generally provide a list of the artist's chief works and museums where they are displayed. Reproductions of symbols and signatures, including those of anonymous artists, are placed at the end of each key letter of the alphabet. There is a brief bibliography of sources in volume 10.

392. **Guide to Exhibited Artists.** Santa Barbara, CA: ABC-Clio, 1985. 5v. ISBN 0-90345-095-X.

Each volume of this important multi-volume set covers a different medium and each can be purchased separately. The most extensive volume is the one on European painters, but the most unique are the volumes on printmakers and on craftsmen. The remaining volumes cover sculptors and North American painters. The set as a whole provides listings of 16,000 contemporary artists, for which information is given on nationality, address, type of work, medium, date and place of birth, gallery representation, and recent exhibits. Information is relatively up-to-date and should be welcomed by librarians, students, and collectors, as well as critics and writers. Each volume is indexed separately.

393. **International Dictionary of Art and Artists.** James Vinson, ed. Chicago: St. James Press, 1990. 2v. ISBN 1-55862-001-X (Art); 1-55862-000-1 (Artists).

The volume on artists supplies a biographical dictionary of the most important European and American artists ranging from the thirteenth to the twentieth centuries. Entries treat 500 personalities chosen by a panel of specialists and provide a biographical sketch highlighting the careers and achievements of painters, sculptors, and engravers who have earned recognition as master artists. Following a detailed critical essay on the consequence of each artist's works is a listing of the most important collections of that person's works, along with bibliographic references. The volume on art treats 500 individual works of art in a chronological arrangement. Information regarding artist, location, size, and date are given along with a signed critical essay. Articles are written by specialists, primarily art historians; for the most part the same scholar contributes both the article on the artist and the one on the artist's work. There is an index of artists and of artwork locations.

394. **Mallett's Index of Artists, Including Painters, Sculptors, Illustrators, Engravers, and Etchers of the Past and Present.** Daniel Trowbridge Mallett. New York: R. R. Bowker, 1935. 493p. **Supp.**, 1940. 319p. Repr., Detroit: Gale Research, 1976; Editions Publishers, 1986. 2v. ISBN 0-317-57518-X.

Another of the standard biographical sources, along with Thieme (entry 383) and Benezit (entry 391), this work covers over 25,000 artists whose works are exhibited in leading galleries or who are subjects of inquiry of modern students. Artists represent many different phases and media of the art world and come from all countries and time periods. Since this is primarily an index, limited biographical information is provided in each entry (name, pseudonym, nationality, period of productivity, residence, and dates). There are references to twenty-two general reference works and over 1,000 specialized sources providing fuller biographical treatment. The supplement provides entries for artists of all countries and periods not covered in the main edition, with a necrology from 1935 to 1940. Although criticized for certain inaccuracies, it remains a likely first source for biographical information.

395. **Mantle Fielding's Dictionary of American Painters, Sculptors, and Engravers.** 2d ed., rev. and enl. Mantle Fielding; Glenn B. Opitz, ed. Poughkeepsie, NY: Apollo Book, 1986. 1081p. ISBN 0-938290-04-5.

There have been several reprints and revisions of this standard biographical tool since its appearance in 1926. The 1965 work was a reprint with addenda containing corrections and new material, while the 1983 effort is a complete revision that doubled the coverage from about 5,000 to over 10,000 names. The present edition provides information on nearly 13,000 American artists of all time periods. They are arranged alphabetically and the volume is by far the most attractive in terms of typeface. Material has been updated and corrections have been made. (Although Fielding had a good reputation for inclusiveness, the work has been criticized for inaccuracies in the past.) It provides a comprehensive source of information on both major and minor artists of the United States.

396. **Modern Arts Criticism: A Biographical and Critical Guide to Painters, Sculptors, Photographers, and Architects from the Beginning of the Modern Era to the Present.** Joann Prosyniuk et al., eds. Detroit: Gale Research, 1991– . ISSN 1052-1712.

Another of the biocritical tools from Gale, this title emulates the publisher's Literary Criticism series in providing thorough and well-developed treatment of visual artists from all media. A volume was issued annually in 1991 and in 1992; both the third and fourth volumes appeared in 1993, indicating that the series is alive and well even in these days of diminished purchasing budgets. Each volume treats around twenty-five painters, sculptors, architects, photographers, and so forth active from the latter part of the nineteenth century to the present. These are major figures such as Ansel Adams, Frank Lloyd Wright, Dali, and van Gogh. Entries furnish biographical sketches along with excerpts from critical appraisals drawn from books and periodical articles. Also included are reading lists and reproductions of works for each artist. The title is indexed by individual art works and by medium.

397. **St. James Guide to Native North American Artists.** Roger Matuz, ed. Detroit: St. James Press, 1998. 691p. ISBN 1-55862-221-7.

This recent addition to the publisher's biographical reference line provides a needed service, supplying comprehensive coverage of 400 twentieth-century native North American artists both living and dead. Various forms and media of art work are included: painting, fabrics, jewelry, drawing, photography, sculpture, bead work, carving, pottery, basketry, and so forth. Entries include tribal affiliation, medium, listing of exhibitions and galleries in which they were held, and publications. Most important are the well-written, informative, and extensive narratives regarding the artist's life and work. In addition, there are illustrations identifying the work of some of the biographees, and in some cases, pictures of them. The work is well-indexed, with cross-references to variant names, tribal listings, and geographical identifications.

398. **Spanish Artists from the Fourth to the Twentieth Century: A Critical Dictionary.** Frick Art Reference Library. New York: G. K. Hall, 1993–1997. 4v. ISBN 0-8161-0614-2 (v.1).

With the publication of the first volume of this set, it was apparent that the complete set would be a real asset to students and scholars alike. In citing biographical sources on this little-documented target group, this tool filled a real void. Volume 1 treats the artists alphabetically, A–F, and provides an introductory guide for use of the work in English, Spanish, German, and French. Volume 2 (1996) treats G–L, while volume 3 (1997) concludes the coverage with M–Z. There is a comprehensive index, chronological list, and complete bibliography in volume 4 (1997). Some 10,000 personalities who were born in Spain or worked there are treated. Artistic endeavors vary and include architecture, painting, sculpture, printmaking, drafting, and the applied arts. Entries supply dates, medium, and variant names as well as listings of biographical sources.

399. **Who Was Who in American Art.** Peter Hastings Falk, ed. Madison, CT: Sound View Press, 1985. 707p. ISBN 0-932087-00-0.

This work is compiled from the original thirty volumes of *American Art Annual* (entry 371n) between 1898 and 1933 that included biographies, and the four subsequent volumes of *Who's Who in American Art* (entry 400) between 1936 and 1947. It represents an excellent source of information on 25,000 deceased personalities associated in some way with American art. Included among the entries are painters, sculptors, printmakers, illustrators, photographers, cartoonists, critics, curators, educators, and craftspeople whose creative activity spanned a fifty-year period from the 1890s to the 1940s. Entries include name, profession, last known address, dates of birth and death, education, location of works, exhibitions, awards, memberships, and references to the volume of either of the two source works in which the artist was last covered.

400. **Who's Who in American Art 1999–2000.** New Providence, NJ: Marquis Who's Who 1936/1937– . Bienn. ISSN 0000-0191.

Originally published as part 2 of the *American Art Annual* (entry 371n) in volumes 1–4, 1936–1947, this work has appeared irregularly in the past, but seems to have settled into a biennial pattern since 1953. A standard in the field, the 23d edition (1999–2000) continues under the well-known and highly respected Marquis Who's Who Publishing which had taken over the responsibility from R. R. Bowker in 1998. This represents a comprehensive biographical dictionary of living personalities from various related disciplines from all spectra of the arts in the United States as well as Canada and Mexico. Media represented are painting, sculpture, graphic arts, illustration, design, and various crafts. In addition to artists, there are important educators, administrators, collectors, critics, historians, curators, and dealers. There are over 11,500 entries, alphabetically arranged, with each entry given about 200 words. Entries include birth date, education, publications, collections, commissions, professional affiliations, honors and awards, style and techniques, media, dealer, and mailing address. The work is indexed by geographic location and professional classification.

401. **Who's Who in Art: Biographies of Leading Men and Women in the World of Art Today.** Havant, Hants, UK: Art Trade Press, 1927– . Bienn. ISBN 0-900083-15-8 (1994).

The frequency of this comprehensive biographical directory of primarily British artists has varied widely in the past (including a hiatus of fourteen years between the third and fourth editions). It is one of the oldest continuing reference tools in the field, and has established itself as a predictable two-year offering during the past decade. The twenty-eighth edition (1998) continues to provide a comprehensive listing of living artists working in a variety of media in the United Kingdom, with a few other "representative" (outstanding) artists included. It has been decided to restrict the inclusion of foreign artists to those already listed and eventually produce an all-British listing. Presently, some 3,000 artists and craftspeople as well as related professionals (designers, teachers, critics, writers, etc.) are covered, of which fewer than 10 percent are not British. Entries vary somewhat but are generally one paragraph in length. They provide birth dates, education, memberships in professional societies and organizations, a list of exhibitions, and a list of collections in which the subjects are represented. Also included are present addresses and manner of signing their work.

402. **Women Artists in the United States: A Selective Bibliography and Resource Guide on the Fine and Decorative Arts, 1750–1986.** Paula L. Chiarmonte. Boston: G. K. Hall, 1990. 997p. ISBN 0-8161-8917-X.

This is a comprehensive work of substance in terms of breadth and depth. It serves as an excellent bibliography and resource guide to female American artists of all types, with the exception of needleworkers. (This is to receive its own volume in the future.) An important contribution is the set of introductory essays by sixteen specialists in the field explaining the criteria used in selection. The work is divided into two segments, with the first providing essays on feminist critics and organizations, directories of manuscript repositories, and special collections. The second cites the literature; books (including biographical tools), catalogs, and articles. This section supplies some 4,000 references covering more than 2,500 female artists, with special attention given to African-Americans, Native Americans, Asian-Americans, and Latinas. Author/title and artist indexes furnish access.

The two-volume effort by Eleanor Tufts, *American Women Artists, Past and Present: A Selected Bibliographic Guide* (Garland, 1984–1989), is another useful resource. Volume 1 identifies monographs and journal articles on 500 artists of all media but excludes the crafts. These range from the eighteenth century to contemporaries born before 1950. Volume 2 adds another 700 figures.

403. **World Artists 1950–1980.** Claude Marks. New York: H. W. Wilson, 1984. 912p. **Supp.**, 1980–1990. ISBN 0-8242-0827-7.

The Wilson Company offers a line of fine biographical dictionaries, and editor Marks provides a useful source of information for any library collection. Biographies of over 300 artists who achieved some prominence in the years following World War II are included. Painters, sculptors, and graphic artists from many countries and representing numerous styles and movements are listed. These are generally the important personalities who influenced the field in some fashion. Entries provide full names, dates of birth and death, and a detailed biographical-critical essay of two to five pages (identifying locations and dates of exhibitions and museums and galleries showing the subject's work). There is also a brief bibliography of books and articles about each artist. Pictures generally accompany the entries.

Marks has produced a supplementary volume, *World Artists 1980–1990* (H. W. Wilson, 1991), which continues the coverage. Some 120 new artists who have been influential during the 1980s are featured, with biographical coverage averaging four pages in length. Many countries are represented, and photographs are supplied.

404. **World Encyclopedia of Naive Art.** Oto Bihalji-Merin and Nebojsa Tomasevic. New York: Scala/Philio Wilson; distr., New York: Harper & Row, 1984. 735p. ISBN 0-93-574862-8.

Naive artists are defined by the authors as those who practice their art worldwide "but outside historical and stylistic categories." This type of classification and coverage given to those who practice in this manner generally without benefit of formal instruction makes this a unique and useful reference tool. Opening with an expository essay on 100 years of naive art, the purpose of the work is described through an explanation and summary of the subject. There are biographical sketches for over 800 artists from nearly fifty countries, although many more are listed. There is a bias toward artists in the authors' native land, with Yugoslavian artists receiving 86 entries while the United States receives 59 entries. Included are a number of historical surveys of naive art in various countries and a listing of relevant art exhibitions, museums, and galleries throughout the world.

Histories and Chronologies

405. **African Art: An Introduction.** Rev. ed. Frank Willett. New York: Thames & Hudson, 1993. 288p. ISBN 0-500-20267-2.

This represents a revision of an old favorite, first issued in 1971 and reprinted on several occasions. Coverage is the same, providing a comprehensible introduction to African art. The work represents a successful survey and excellent overview of the development of African art in its social and historical context. There are 261 illustrations, with 61 in color, that serve to highlight the various art forms and their distinctive character. Willett served as a professor of African art at Northwestern University and brings a high level of expertise and understanding to this work. He provides a useful and informative description of and commentary on the geography, culture, and social conditions in which African art developed. He is able to provide exposition of such elements as ancient sculpture, rock drawings and paintings, masks, and decoration. There is a useful seven-page bibliography; an index provides access.

Suzanne P. Blier has recently published *The Royal Arts of Africa: The Majesty of Form* (Abrams, 1998), which examines the African tradition as influenced by kings who utilized palace art and finery to demonstrate and support their power. An introduction to this phenomenon is provided, followed by five chapters on different regional monarchies and their artistic achievements. Over 200 photographs enhance the text.

406. **American Visions: The Epic History of Art in America.** Robert Hughes. New York: Alfred A. Knopf, 1997. 635p. ISBN 0-679-42627-2.

The author is a well-known critic and writer who has produced a history of 350 years of American art, as part of the PBS television series *American Visions*. Beginning with the period of the Puritans, such epochs as the Revolutionary Era, westward expansion, and the age of discovery are examined for their influences on artistic expression. We are given an opinionated but intriguing view of those events, personalities, and developments that have created the American art scene today. In examining the development of American art, the whole character of American society reveals itself to the interested observer. All parts of the country are treated—East, West, North, and South—and all are explained in terms of the societal influences, with the facts, observations, and most important, the perceived revelations, supplied by this most interesting writer.

407. **Art: A History of Painting, Sculpture, Architecture.** 4th ed. Frederick Hartt. Englewood Cliffs, NJ: Prentice-Hall, 1993. 1127p. ISBN 0-1305-2432-8.

This comprehensive history by a distinguished expert was first issued in 1976 and since then has earned the respect of both librarians and art students. The text is well-written and there are nearly 1,300 illustrations. The second edition appeared in 1985, but since then the frequency has been every four years. Currently, this now-standard work has been modernized, with more emphasis on women artists as well as a change in chapter sequence. The first part treats the period from prehistoric times to the late Gothic, while the second part embraces the period from the Renaissance to the present day. Considered by reviewers to be a valuable item combining erudition with lucidity, events and achievements are described and schools and movements are explained. Serving as the basis for the revision are the results of the latest research in the field. Similar to the initial effort, the present work has a glossary, bibliography, and detailed index.

408. **Art and Life in Renaissance Venice.** Patricia F. Brown. New York: Prentice Hall Press, 1997. 176p. ISBN 0-136-18455-3.

This is an interesting and informative survey of one of the most creative geographic areas in one of its most productive periods of artistic expression. Art and its creators blossomed and flowered during the fifteenth and sixteenth centuries in Venice because of the influence of those in power who were determined to have art serve as a demonstrable testimony of elegance, sophistication, and achievement for both institutions and individuals. Coverage is given to the status of artists, female and male portraiture, and the use of antiquity in helping to adorn and ornament building interiors. There are illustrations to augment the text, along with a timeline, useful maps, and a good bibliography.

Art of the Mediterranean World, A.D. 100 to 1400, by Hugo Buchthal (Decatur House, 1983), is a brief but effective tribute to the author, a renowned art historian and teacher. The work contains a selection of his insightful articles written over a thirty-five-year period from 1940 to 1975. There are four major segments: Islamic and Indian art, Sicilian manuscript illumination, Byzantine manuscript illumination, and iconography. Illustrations are carefully chosen and the format is attractive. The four editors (art historians and former students) have contributed commentaries or postscripts and provided additional bibliography.

409. **Art in China.** Craig Clunas. New York : Oxford University Press, 1997. 255p. (Oxford History of Art). ISBN 0-19-284244-7.

In this interesting and well-designed brief examination of Chinese art from ancient to modern times, the author has treated the topic in both thematic and chronological fashion. The work is organized into five major chapters: "Art in the Tomb," "Art at Court," "Art in the Temple," "Art in the Life of the Elite," and "Art in the Market-Place." All art forms are included in the broad sweep of Chinese culture, with clear and informative exposition provided of Chinese artifacts and art objects. The color illustrations are effective, enabling the reader to comprehend the nature and development of Chinese artistry. Special features include a chart of chronological developments as well an excellent bibliographic essay.

The third edition of *The Arts of China*, by Michael Sullivan (University of California, 1986), retains its broad coverage of the development of Chinese art from its beginnings to the present and is based on up-to-date research and study. It is a scholarly effort, well-illustrated, and furnishes background information in the introductory segments that will be useful to students at all levels of understanding. Art trends are described and examples of both typical and monumental nature are given. There is a bibliography as well as additional special features, with an index to facilitate access.

410. **5,000 Years of the Art of India.** Mario Bussagli and Calembus Sivaramamurti. New York: Abrams, 1971. 335p. ISBN 0-8109-0118-8.

Heavily illustrated with about 400 color reproductions, this is an attractive work on Asian art. It should be pointed out that the quality of color has been criticized by reviewers in the past, as has been the unevenness in style of writing. Although both authors have excellent credentials in art history, Bussagli's writing is much more stylistic and eloquent, whereas sections by Sivaramamurti are stiff and pedestrian. Coverage is given to Indian art through the Mughal period, but also embraces developments in Southeast Asia, Tibet, Ceylon, and Indonesia. Although the tool can be recommended for its content, there is no bibliography or index.

411. **The Formation of Islamic Art.** Rev. and enl. ed. Oleg Grabar. New Haven, CT: Yale University Press, 1987. 232p. ISBN 0-300-03969-7.

The first edition of this work in 1973 established Grabar as a leading interpreter of Islamic art. The revised and enlarged edition continues to furnish a lucid theory of the development of Islamic art and architecture in terms of its origin and subsequent development over a 400-year period from the sixth to the tenth centuries. Designed as a text for college students, it provides an excellent perspective on the nations under Muslim control during this period of Islamic expansion, examining the social forces that fashioned the style and contributions of artists. The work is scholarly in nature and places greatest emphasis on the design and ornamentation of architectural structures. There are 131 illustrations in black-and-white that provide further insight into the artistic elements. Each chapter has a bibliography and there is a chronology of important dates.

A recent effort is *Modern Islamic Art: Development and Continuity*, by Wijdan Ali (University of Florida, 1998), which provides a two-part examination. The first part treats the historical development of contemporary art in thirteen Islamic countries in chronological fashion, while part two examines the search for a suitable art form and the creation of the Contemporary Calligraphic School of Art, which produces abstract works. It includes brief biographies of artists and reproductions of their work.

412. **Gardner's Art Through the Ages.** 10th ed. Richard G. Tansey and Fred S. Kleiner. Fort Worth, TX: Harcourt Brace College Publishers, 1996. 1200p. ISBN 0-15-501141-3.

If a single work can be called a classic in the field, it must surely be this excellent encyclopedic history of art, originally produced in 1926 by Helen Gardner. Since then it has served the needs of both high school and college students as well as reference librarians in their search for information on schools, movements, art forms, and developments from ancient to modern times. Planned as a college text, it has undergone constant change and revision, ever increasing its scope of coverage. There are many illustrations, and bibliographies are provided at the ends of the chapters. Gardner was a professor of art history at the school of the Art Institute of Chicago and designed the original scheme in line with her teaching responsibilities. The present authorship continues Gardner's excellent treatment with expanded narrative and illustrations. Coverage is brought up-to-date.

Compiled by Chris Witcombe, Professor of Art History, for "Harcourt Brace College Publishers' Art History Resources on the Web," is a Web page, *Gateway to Art History* (http://www.harbrace.com/art/gardner [accessed December 1999]) intended to accompany the Gardner work. Divided into five chronological periods, from "The Ancient World" to "The Modern and Postmodern World," the twenty-eight links include recent essays and narratives on various geographic and stylistic influences. The second part provides a directory of research resources (images, prints/photography, museums and galleries).

413. History of Art: A Survey of the Major Visual Arts from the Dawn of History to the Present Day. 4th ed. Horst Woldemar Janson. Rev. and exp. by Anthony F. Janson. New York: Abrams, 1991. 856p. ISBN 0-8109-3401-9.

One of the standard histories in competition with *Gardner's Art Through the Ages* (entry 412), this work is now in its fourth edition. Since Horst Janson's death the work has been carried on by his son. Always regarded as a solid and comprehensive description of the development of Western art, the book emphasizes painting, sculpture, and architecture. Some attention is given to Oriental and pre-Columbian periods, with coverage brought to the present day. Although a separate chapter on sculpture since 1900 has been added, the contemporary segment has been judged to be the weakest element of an otherwise strong historical coverage. The fourth edition contains more color illustrations and more diagrams and architectural drawings than previous editions. It is one of the top choices as a textbook for art history classes. The bibliography is up-to-date, and a good index is included.

414. History of Italian Renaissance Art: Painting, Sculpture, Architecture. 4th ed. Frederick Hartt. Rev. by David C. Wilkins. Englewood Cliffs, NJ: Prentice-Hall, 1994. 696p. ISBN 0-13-393380-6.

The fourth edition retains the excellent readable qualities of previous efforts. Since its appearance in 1969, this title has been the first choice of American university professors selecting a textbook on the Italian Renaissance period for undergraduates. Much of its utility continues to lie in the integrated treatment given to painting, sculpture, and architecture in its exposition of the technical and stylistic qualities of that very creative era. There are numerous reproductions, and hundreds of individual works are described and analyzed in clear fashion. The illustrations enhance these analyses. Hartt, the original author, has conceded a bias toward Florentine art in the past that remains in the present effort, but there is a good survey of the period from about 1250 to 1575. A bibliography is provided, along with a glossary, chronology, and an index to works and subjects.

415. History of Modern Art: Painting, Sculpture, Architecture, Photography. 3d ed. H. H. Arnason. Rev. and updated by Daniel Wheeler. New York: Abrams, 1986. 744p. ISBN 0-8109-1097-7.

Another standard in the field that has been revised is this well-known survey of modern art covering developments in Europe and America from 1850 to the present day. The present edition represents the most timely history of what may be referred to as the current art scene, describing the origins and influences that have shaped the styles and fashions in painting, sculpture, and architecture. The work is arranged chronologically and designed to appeal to college students and interested laypersons. There are hundreds of attractive illustrations, so many, in fact, that earlier editions have been criticized for a somewhat limited text. Biographical sketches of major artists are included. A bibliography is provided.

The Museum of Modern Art Artists Files (Chadwyck-Healey, 1986) is an immense sourcebook of material on nearly 5,700 microfiche taken from the library holdings of the Museum. Some 200,000 items of diverse nature (announcements, magazine clippings, postcards, excerpts from anthologies, reviews, newspaper articles, etc.) are presented in full text with an index of names to provide access. *The Museum of Modern Art Artists Scrapbooks*, issued by Chadwyck Healey in four looseleaf volumes and in 642 microfiche, also in 1986, presents the scrapbooks of forty-four major artists of the twentieth century. Again, there is much diversity in the holdings that include newspaper and magazine articles, invitations, catalogs, and more.

416. **The Oxford History of English Art.** T. S. R. Boase, ed. Oxford: Clarendon, 1949–1978. 11v.

This large-scale project was designed as an eleven-volume comprehensive history of British art from its beginnings to 1940, and took nearly thirty years to complete. Each volume of this work was written by a different authority, who covers a time period in his or her area of expertise. Like the other Oxford multi-volume sets, it represents a grand attempt to provide in-depth coverage of a scholarly nature, complete with bibliographies. With Boase's death in 1974, future writing activity was uncertain, and completion of the set represents an important achievement for the publisher and the specialists involved. Coverage begins with volume 1 treating the period up to A.D. 871, and concludes with volume 11 (1870–1940). Outstanding scholars like Boase, Joan Evans, Peter Brieger, D. T. Rice, Eric Mercer, and Joseph Burke have authored the individual volumes.

417. **Pelican History of Art.** Nikolaus Pevsner et al., eds. New York: Penguin, 1953–1987. v.1–46. ISSN 0553-4755. (Yale University Press Pelican History of Art). 1993– .

Initially projected as a fifty-volume set by Penguin, the individual titles of this work cover time periods and/or nations of the world (largely Western Europe) with respect to the history of art and architecture. Volumes vary considerably in scope and cover a wide spectrum of topics and trends. Between 1953 and 1987 forty-six volumes appeared, some in their second or third revisions. Individual titles are by authorities and are highly regarded for both depth of coverage (e.g., the volume on Italian painting, 1500–1600) and useful surveys (e.g., the volume on Japanese art and architecture). Only two new titles were issued by Pelican in the 1980s, one covering the Indian subcontinent, the other Islam. In 1992, this useful series was purchased by Yale University, which agreed to issue the fifteen titles contracted by Penguin beginning in 1993. There are plans to redesign the series, placing more emphasis on regions other than Western Europe, and more than thirty titles have been issued by Yale up to the year 2000. Coverage has been given to Ancient Egypt, China, Ancient Orient, and Islam as well as Europe, ancient, medieval, and modern.

418. **The Visual Arts: A History.** 4th ed. Hugh Honour and John Fleming. New York: Abrams, 1995. 864p. ISBN 0-81-093928-2.

With its initial appearance in 1982, this work quickly developed a reputation for excellent coverage in certain areas considered weak in both Gardner (entry 412) and Janson (entry 413). Beginning with the earliest civilizations, this chronological survey of world art provides a descriptive narrative accompanied by more than 1,100 illustrations, some of which are in color. Each chapter is introduced with a chronology of events in art history along with other historical developments. This work is considered to be stronger than both Gardner and Janson in its treatment of modern art, with an excellent writing style that makes vivid the concepts and developments covered. The purpose is to be exploratory rather than critical in providing an idea of the visual arts in an historical and aesthetic context. Included are a glossary and bibliography as well as an index to provide access. The work has been issued in the United Kingdom as *A World History of Art* through Lawrence King Publishing.

419. **Visual Arts in the Twentieth Century.** Edward Lucie-Smith. New York: Harry N. Abrams, 1997. 400p. ISBN 0-810-93934-7.

Unlike the broader coverage of the title in entry 418, the author of this work, a noted art writer, has focused this recent effort on artistic development in the past 100 years. Even so, it represents an expansion of his earlier publication (1976), which examined artistic development since 1945. In the current work, chapters are organized in sequence by decades and each medium is described separately in terms of stylistic developments with an emphasis on the social influences of the period. Readers are given an informative view of political, intellectual, and cultural influences that worked upon the artists to shape their products. Coverage is given to painting, sculpture, graphic arts, photography, and architecture. Fine color illustrations support the text.

420. **Women Artists in the Modern Era: A Documentary History.** Susan Waller. Metuchen, NJ: Scarecrow Press, 1991. 392p. ISBN 0-8108-2405-1.

This documentary history supplies extracts and selections from sixty-one sources comprising artists' correspondence, journals, and memoirs as well as minutes and reports of professional associations and schools. These documents are selected to help explore the experience of women artists and their relationship with men. Also included are critical reviews of the artists' work as reported by the artists' contemporaries, both male and female. The time period ranges from the mid-eighteenth century to the mid-twentieth century and embraces a variety of media: painting, sculpture, ceramics, and textiles. The emphasis is on well-known artists, but amateurs are treated as well. Included here are such personalities as Harriet Hosmer, Angelica Kaufmann, and Berthe Morisot. The title serves as a useful, convenient tool for undergraduates beginning their research on these individuals; what is missing, of course, is the more complete picture contained in the whole documents rather than the snippets presented here.

PAINTING, DRAWING, AND PRINT

Bibliographic Guides and Bibliographies

421. **American Drawing: A Guide to Information Sources.** Lamia Doumato. Detroit: Gale Research, 1979. 246p. (Art and Architecture Information Guide Series, no. 11). ISBN 0-8103-1441-X.

The Gale series has been recognized as one of the best reference sources for bibliographic information, having achieved a high standard in coverage of the literature of the field. This work by Doumato, a former reference librarian at the Museum of Modern Art, maintains the high quality of the series. She provides an annotated bibliography of books, parts of books, exhibition catalogs, and periodical articles on American artists working from the 1890s to the present day. Several prominent illustrators are also included as subjects, although cartoonists are excluded. There is coverage of important library research collections as well. The initial effort in the series was Sidney Starr Keveaney's *American Painting* (Gale Research, 1974), in which he identified source materials published between 1946 and 1973.

422. **American Popular Illustration: A Reference Guide.** James J. Best. Westport, CT: Greenwood, 1984. 171p. (American Popular Culture). ISBN 0-313-23389-6.

This is of much value to the field because of its treatment of illustration, a more elusive field not generally the subject of bibliographic coverage. With the spread of popular culture in the past decades, this has proved to be a useful tool in both public and academic library settings. The author is an instructor in the field of American illustration and designed the bibliography to reflect his course coverage. There is a brief history of the topic from 1800 to the present day that should prove enlightening for those who need to research its origins. Then follows a critical analysis of the significant titles in a number of categories: histories, illustrated works, biographies, technique, social context, and so forth. Appendices list periodical titles, research collections, and illustrated books. The bibliography is well conceived and useful.

423. **Central Italian Painting, 1400–1465: An Annotated Bibliography.** Martha Levine Dunkelman. Boston: G. K. Hall, 1986. 351p. (A Reference Publication in Art History). ISBN 0-8161-8546-8.

The fifteenth century in Italy is an era rich in art history and is extremely important for study purposes. Accordingly, there is a large body of literature, making this annotated bibliography an appropriate addition to the reference collection of an academic library. As part of a series on the Italian Renaissance, coverage is given to the region composed of Tuscany, Umbria, the Marches, and Lazio, which has attracted more study and publication than any other period or place in Western art. There are over 2,000 references to books, documents, and articles culled from the major indexing and abstracting services. Coverage begins with early publications, but emphasis is placed on English-language writing of the past half-century. Additionally, there are references to Italian, French, and other European writings. The work is indexed by authors, editors, reviewers, and artists.

424. **Old Master Print References: A Selected Bibliography.** Lauris Mason et al. White Plains, NY: Kraus International, 1986. 279p. (Print Reference Series). ISBN 0-527-62196-X.

This is a selective bibliography on eminent printmakers, similar to the volume published earlier in the series (entry 425). It provides a listing of artists with birth and death dates, followed by a chronological listing of references. This particular volume covers printmakers from the fifteenth through the seventeenth centuries, with slight representation of eighteenth-century artisans. Bibliographic references range from seventeenth-century writings to 1984 publications. The book is international in coverage; foreign-language titles are translated into English. References include books, journal articles, exhibit catalogs, and book reviews. Mason has been a solid contributor to the bibliography of printmaking and has served as editor of *Print Collectors Quarterly* (KTO, 1977–), which publishes essays on eminent printmakers.

425. **Print Reference Sources: A Select Bibliography, 18th–20th Centuries.** 2d ed., rev. and enl. Lauris Mason and Joan Ludman. Millwood, NY: Kraus Publishing, 1979. 363p. ISBN 0-527-62190-0.

The first edition of this work appeared in 1975 and covered 1,300 printmakers listed alphabetically. Entries listed both primary and secondary sources about them. It is a useful tool because information on printmakers tends to be difficult to obtain. This edition was enlarged to cover an additional 500 printmakers, with a total of some 5,000 citations. The purpose remains the same: to provide a selective listing of source material on the printmakers of the eighteenth and nineteenth centuries. Sources identified represent a variety of types and forms, including catalogues raisonnés, oeuvre-catalogues, museum and dealer publications and checklists, and essays from both book and periodical literature. Both out-of-print and currently available items are identified, of importance to a varied audience ranging from librarians to print collectors and dealers.

A complementary work is *Old Master Print References* (entry 424), covering the period from the fifteenth through the seventeenth centuries.

Art Work and Reproductions—Catalogs, Etc.

426. **American Paintings in the Metropolitan Museum of Art.** Metropolitan Museum of Art. Kathleen Luhrs, ed. New York: The Museum, 1956–1980. 3v. Repr., 1994. ISBN 0-87099-244-9.

Volume 1 of a projected three-volume set was issued in 1956 as *American Paintings: A Catalogue of the Collection of the Metropolitan Museum of Art*, by Albert Ten Eyck

Gardner and Stuart P. Feld. This effort covers American painters born by 1815. Following its publication, there was a hiatus until Ms. Luhrs was authorized to serve as editor. Volume 2, by Natalie Spassky et al., treats the paintings by artists born between 1816 and 1845. Volume 3, by Doreen Bolger Burke, supplies the paintings by artists born between 1846 and 1864. Volumes 2–3 (1980) cover paintings accessioned by the Museum prior to January 1979. There are references to artists' biographies and sources of quotations. Works mentioned but not illustrated are identified by museum location or source of reproduction. This is an indication of the potential magnitude of the effort, and there is the possibility that it might continue to become a complete catalog of the paintings of American artists in the museum. Information on the Museum and its collections may be found at the Web site *The Metropolitan Museum of Art* (http://www.metmuseum.org/ [accessed December 1999]).

A similar coverage of paintings in British museums is *Subject Catalogue of Paintings in Public Collections*, published by Visual Arts Publishing. Volume 1, issued in 1989, treats the collections of London's National Gallery, The Wallace Collection, and The Wellington Museum, providing precise information on each work. Volume 2 (1990) continues the coverage of London collections, treating the old masters collection at the Tate Gallery. Entries supply names and dates of artist, school, title, year, size, and medium along with a detailed description of the painting. Several indexes are furnished that provide access through artist, subject, subjects of portraits, and location.

427. **American Prints in the Library of Congress: A Catalogue of the Collection.** Karen F. Beall, comp. Baltimore: Johns Hopkins University Press, 1970; repr., San Francisco: Alan Wofsy Fine Arts, 1991. 568p. ISBN 1-556-60088-7.

This is considered to be an outstanding reference book in the field of graphic arts. It identifies approximately 12,000 American prints from 1,250 different artists. These works span the complete history of our country from the colonial period to the year of publication. The Library of Congress has one of the truly outstanding collections in this area, and the catalog provides documentation difficult to find elsewhere. The arrangement is alphabetical by artist's name, under which are listed the prints in the Library's collection. Information includes date of execution, imprint, medium, and size. The analytical notes are useful. There are indexes for iconography, names, and print series. A seven-page bibliography is included. The work was copied and made available by University Microfilms in 1981.

Not so extensive, but more recent, is *Library of Congress Prints and Photographs: An Illustrated Guide* (Library of Congress, 1995), a selective, eighty-page overview with brief descriptive narratives on various collections categorized by different topics, such as pictorial journalism and architecture, design, and engineering. It is found on the Web (http://lcweb.loc.gov/rr/print/guide [accessed December 1999]).

*428. **Coates Art Review: Impressionism.** Minneapolis: Quanta Press, 1990, 1993. (CD-ROM).

With the increasing importance of computerized products, the study of art is benefited immensely by the ability to furnish graphic images in CD-ROM format. From Quanta Press comes this resource covering over 600 images of Impressionist art. Designed for both VGA and Super VGA viewing and compatible with both IBM and Macintosh equipment, this catalog and tutorial on Impressionism provides well-developed images. Brief identification information is included, making this title a useful educational device for both high school and undergraduate students as well as an information source for the general public. Entries supply the title of the work, artist, medium, date, size, and location. Biographies of artists are included along with a chronology of important events.

429. The Collections of The Nelson-Atkins Museum of Art, Italian Paintings, 1300–1800. Eliot W. Rowlands. Kansas City: Nelson-Atkins Museum of Art, 1996. 487p. ISBN 0-942-61425-9.

The author is the assistant curator of the Museum and has begun a project to catalog all the Museum holdings. This work identifies and describes fifty-seven paintings dating from the early Renaissance to the Baroque period of Italy. Each work is treated in-depth, with a biography of the painting, description of its aesthetic distinction and importance, technical description of its condition, provenance, exhibition history, and bibliography. Each painting is reproduced in full color along with black-and-white comparative study elements. Although the collection is relatively small in size, there are a number of important works such as those by Caravaggio, Titian, Tiepolo, and others. The book opens with introductory segments describing the history of the Museum's collecting activity and its study of Italian paintings and concludes with indexes of proper names and former collections.

430. Finder's Guide to Prints and Drawings in the Smithsonian Institution. Lynda Corey Claassen. Washington, DC: Smithsonian Institution, 1981. 210p. ISBN 0-8747-4317-6.

This was the first in a series of guides planned to enumerate the collections of the Smithsonian Institution to make these resources available or accessible to students and scholars. Individual prints and drawings in a total of forty-nine collections are indexed. Information provided includes artists, subjects, historical periods, and locations. Media and formats treated are watercolors, pastels, posters, scientific and engineering drawings, and books with original illustrations. General information regarding the collections includes availability of catalogs or directories, publications, photoduplication services, exhibition programs, loan policy, hours, and type of public access. A special feature of value is a location guide to graphic artists that identifies over 10,000 artists whose works are owned by the eight major Smithsonian art collections. The text has an index to facilitate access.

431. Fine Art Collections. Greenwich, CT: New York Graphic Society, 1986. ISBN 0821216449. **Supp.,** 1988– .

First published in 1946, this title, known initially as *Fine Art Reproductions, Old and Modern Masters*, has gone through numerous editions and has become a fixture in art reference departments, where its use varies widely from one library to another. This catalog of the reproductions available for purchase from the New York Graphic Society has itself become an attractive collection of reproductions. Arranged by groupings such as old masters, twentieth-century painting, and American painting, the catalog gives a historical overview, providing color illustrations for each work. Although they are small in size, they are extremely attractive and provide a good idea of how the reproductions will look. The society has high quality prints and is considered a useful source for libraries. Included are name and date of artists; nationality; title with date and location of the original; and catalog number, size, and price of reproduction. There are indexes of artists and subjects. A periodic looseleaf supplement was begun in 1988 that provides an updated master price list.

432. Index to Reproductions of American Paintings: A Guide to Pictures Occurring in More Than Eight Hundred Books. Isabel Stevenson Monro and Kate M. Monro. New York: H. W. Wilson, 1948; repr., 1972. 731p. **First Supp.,** 1964. 480p. ISBN 0-8242-0025-X.

An old standard in the field of art reference, this work will retain its value as long as its source materials (books that it indexed) remain in libraries. Especially useful for libraries through the years due to the great number of sources covered, the work indexes pictures of

American paintings in 520 books and over 300 exhibition catalogs. Alphabetically arranged by name of artist, title of the work, and in some cases by subject, entries include dates of artist, dates and locations of paintings, and references to books that provide reproductions. A supplement appeared in 1964 that indexed more than 400 books and catalogs published between 1948 and 1961. A more recent update is by Smith and Moure (entry 433).

A companion work is *Index to Reproductions of European Paintings: A Guide to Pictures in More Than Three Hundred Books* (H. W. Wilson, 1956; repr., 1967), by the same authors. It follows the same plan, except for its concentration on books with no listings from catalogs. A supplementary item is *World Painting Index*, by Patrice Havlice (entry 436).

433. Index to Reproductions of American Paintings Appearing in More Than 400 Books, Mostly Published Since 1960. Lyn Wall Smith and Nancy Dustin Wall Moure. Metuchen, NJ: Scarecrow Press, 1977. 931p. ISBN 0-8108-1084-0.

Commended for their thoughtful selection of source material, the authors have provided a useful continuation to the Monros' index and supplementary volume (entry 432). The arrangement is somewhat similar to the original, with artists listed alphabetically, followed by titles of paintings with references to reproductions in books. There are indications of ownership in permanent collections. Much of the source material is highly specialized in nature, making it more useful in libraries with more extensive art collections. The subject index makes access possible on a wide range of topics such as allegories, animals, architectural subjects, and Native Americans, as well as portraits of individuals. There is no index by title alone.

*434. The National Portrait Gallery, Smithsonian Institution: Permanent Collection of Notable Americans on CD-ROM. Washington, DC: Smithsonian Institution; Cambridge, MA: Abt Books, 1991. 3093 images. ISBN 0-8901-1618-0.

Since 1973, the National Portrait Gallery has been issuing a pictorial account of its collection. Its *Checklist of the Permanent Collection* has appeared at different intervals, ranging from two to seven years in 1973, 1975, 1982, and 1987. During that period it has grown from a slender, 72-page effort to a volume of 461 pages, documenting the continued growth of the collection. Illustrations in the *Checklist* during that time were in black-and-white. During the 1990–1991 period, the *Checklist* was converted to machine readable and made available on CD-ROM. The new catalog has begun to supply color images and convenient access to holdings such as the Hall of Presidents and the Meserve Collection (Matthew Brady). Searching is possible through title of portrait, occupation, artist, medium, and dates of birth and death. Information on the Gallery calendar and exhibitions is found at the Web site (http://www.npg.si.edu/ [accessed December 1999]).

435. Print Index: A Guide to Reproductions. Pamela Jeffcott Parry and Kathe Chipman, comps. Westport, CT: Greenwood, 1983. 310p. (Art Reference Collection, no. 4). ISBN 0-313-22063-8.

Useful in the art reference area is this index to the prints of more than 2,100 graphic artists. These prints appeared in over 100 English-language publications. With its focus on the graphic arts rather than the more customary painting and sculpture, the tool is somewhat unique. This uniqueness, of course, is its strength and serves to make it a good purchase for a reference department. Publication dates of the sources vary over a long span of time from the late nineteenth century to several published during the 1980s. Artists are identified with birth and death dates and nationality. There is an index of subjects and titles.

436. **World Painting Index.** Patrice Pate Havlice. Metuchen, NJ: Scarecrow Press, 1977. 2v. ISBN 0-8108-1016-6. **First Supp. 1973–1980**, 1982. 2v. ISBN 0-8108-1531-1. **Second Supp. 1980–1989**, 1995. 2v. ISBN 0-8108-3020-5.

This was intended to supplement and update both works by Monro and Monro (entry 432, 432n) because it covers both European and American paintings, among others. The basic edition covers reproductions in nearly 1,200 books and catalogs published from 1940 to 1975. Volume 1 is alphabetically arranged by names of artists and provides references to the books that contain the reproductions. Volume 2 is a title list that refers the user back to volume 1. Criticized for a noticeable bias in favor of Western art and lack of cross-references for variant names, it is still an important reference tool. The first supplement covers over 600 art books and catalogs published between 1973 and 1980. Arrangement and style are similar to the initial offering, including the feature of separate title listings of paintings by unknown artists. There is an increased emphasis on the work of lesser known Western painters as well as female and Third World artists. The second supplement supplies access to reproductions in an additional 697 books and catalogs. There is no subject approach in Havlice that approximates the one by the Monros.

437. **The World's Master Paintings from the Early Renaissance to the Present Day: A Comprehensive Listing of Works by 1,300 Painters and a Complete Guide to Their Locations Worldwide.** Christopher Wright. New York: Routledge Kegan Paul, 1992. 2v. ISBN 0-4150-2240-1.

This is an identification tool and locator of what has been termed the master paintings of the world. It is a comprehensive source of information, supplying coverage of some 120,000 paintings by 1,300 artists. More than 4,000 locations are identified. Described by a reviewer in *The Times Literary Supplement* as "awesome" in scope, the work represents a magnificent effort and an extremely valuable purchase for all types of users. Serious students and researchers will find it an excellent source of information on the products of certain artists who as yet have not been documented well in the literature. The general public will use it to identify the locations of those paintings that they would like to see or the holdings of a museum they plan to visit. Brief biographies are included for the artist. Indexing is by subject, artist, and title of painting.

Sales and Exhibitions—Catalogs, Etc.

438. **German Art from Beckmann to Richter: Images of a Divided Country.** Eckhart Gillen, ed. Cologne: DuMont; distr., Yale University, 1998. 550p. ISBN 0-300-07324-0.

This catalog of an exhibition held in Berlin features the work of eighty-eight artists who made their major contributions from the 1940s to the present and embraces the period of the two Germanies subsequent to World War II. This period of coverage is needed because it has received little attention from American scholars. The work focuses on a comparison of artistic development and expression between the two sectors and examines the links between these elements and the socio-political environments that shaped them. Artistic response to the horrors of Nazism and the Holocaust as well as other political developments are effectively presented. Several hundred illustrations, some in color, provide the vehicle for valid comparisons presented in seventy-six essays by scholars and critics. These essays examine individual works and issues and are organized into nineteen thematic chapters.

*439. **Gordon's Print Price Annual.** New York: Martin Gordon, 1978– . Ann. ISSN 0160-6298.

Still considered the leader's resource guide to fine print prices at auction, this tool provides a well-researched record of sales of prints, issued on an annual basis. Covering auction sales for the year, entries are listed alphabetically and include title, medium, size, date, references, measurements, notes, and remarks, as well as margins and conditions. Naturally, auction houses and prices are enumerated. Prints are of various combinations and represent not only individual pieces but also sets, pairs, groupings, and artists' portfolios. Coverage is provided of sales from about twenty-five leading auction houses worldwide. Useful information regarding exchange rates is given along with the addresses and telephone numbers in a listing of auction houses. The annual covers about 30,000 entries each year. The work is available online and on CD-ROM from the publisher.

440. **A Guide to Collecting Fine Prints.** J. H. U. Brown. Metuchen, NJ: Scarecrow Press, 1989. 152p. ISBN 0-8108-2228-8.

In the field of print collecting, as is true of any other collectible, it is important that one is apprised of the important considerations and factors in determining value. This tool is designed to provide such guidance to the fledgling collector by describing the various conditions relevant to the buying, selling, and collecting of prints. Consideration is given to the purchase of prints both at auction and from dealers and to the optimal ways to sell prints. There are sections on determining price and authenticity. Also treated are such concerns as conservation, framing, and tax factors when selling or donating prints. A brief, informative history of prints and printing opens the work. There are nearly fifty black-and-white illustrations. Appendices supply listings of art journals and print dealers as well as a glossary and bibliography. A detailed index provides access.

441. **Index of American Print Exhibitions, 1882–1940.** Raymond L. Wilson. Metuchen, NJ: Scarecrow Press, 1988. 906p. ISBN 0-8108-2139-7.

This is an important reference effort for identification and location of American prints. It provides a chronological listing of exhibition catalogs treating exhibits and exhibitions at the annual showings of the most important print societies in this country over a period of nearly sixty years. Included here are the New York Etching Club, Chicago Society of Etchers, California Society of Etchers, Printmakers Society of California, and Brooklyn Society of Etchers, as well as the New York World's Fair of 1939 and the Panama-Pacific International Exposition of 1915. Also included are the works treated in the major publications *Fine Prints of the Year* and *Fifty Prints of the Year*, altogether providing an excellent perspective of high quality print production. Artists are listed alphabetically under each catalog; title of print and medium are given. There is an index of artists but not of titles.

442. **Picasso—The Early Years, 1892–1906.** Marilyn McCully, ed. Washington, DC: National Gallery of Art/Yale University Press, 1997. 374p. ISBN 0-300-07166-3.

This is a catalog of a Picasso exhibition held at the National Gallery of Art in 1997, before it moved on to the Boston Museum of Fine Arts. This is an important undertaking, presenting a sampling of the great artist's productivity and mindset in his early years before reaching his great heights of recognition and reception. Many of the illustrations, both black-and-white and color plates, are relatively unfamiliar because the work begins with an examination of his works at the pre-teen stage until he was twenty-four. The work opens with a chronology providing key dates and achievements that is in effect an informative biographical study. This leads into a collection of essays examining his work and their influences. Picasso's art education, relations with friends and acquaintances, and environmental influences are explored, making for an interesting and useful resource tool.

443. **Print Price Index '94: 1992–1993.** Madison, CT: Sound View Press, 1991– . Ann. ISSN 1058-2339.

Another useful annual guide to the season's sales of prints from auction houses is this recently created price catalog. Included here are the records from some 450 auctions held in North America and Europe during the 1992–1993 season. This is only the third issue of this title and the present effort has been expanded considerably since the initial issue. Prints derived from etchings, engravings, and lithographs are featured but aquatints, wood engravings, woodblock prints, screenprints, and more are also included. Over 40,000 entries are listed alphabetically by artist and identify nationality, birth/death dates, auction price, title, medium, date of print, edition number, presence of signature, stamp or annotation, auction house and date, lot number, and so forth. There are listings for different categories of prints, such as books with original prints, natural history, Japanese and Oriental, and posters. A well-developed bibliography is provided along with a directory of print dealers, a glossary, and a listing of catalogues raissoneés by artist.

444. **The Printworld Directory: Contemporary Prints & Prices.** Bala-Cynwyd, PA: Printworld; distr., Poughkeepsie, NY: Apollo Book, 1982– . Ann./Irreg. ISSN 0734-2721.

Another useful entry in the field of art sales reporting is this directory to the world of printmaking. Over 1,200 contemporary artists are identified in the more than 1,000 pages of the fifth edition (1991–1992). Biographical information is provided, and gallery affiliations are enumerated. The directory is developed through surveys of the artists, who are listed alphabetically. They find it to their advantage to provide information regarding their works that have sold out as well as those currently available. Criteria for listing the prints are their price, signature (must be signed), and number (not more than 300). Emphasis is on today's artist, and most illustrations are of works from the past two or three years. There are indexes of the artists and of the print publishers and workshops. The work also contains a listing of galleries specializing in original graphics.

445. **World Collectors Annuary.** Voorburg, Netherlands: World Collectors Publishers, 1950– . Ann. ISSN 0084-1498.

Since its beginning in the years following World War II, this work has come to be recognized as an authoritative and well-developed selective listing of sales from nearly forty important auction houses in the art world. It has a reputation for reporting the most important and valued items sold during the year in Europe and the United States, with the range of prices somewhere between five and seven figures for each entry. Paintings, watercolors, pastels, gouaches, and drawings are represented; stylistic information is given along with description, provenance, place and date of sale, price, and bibliographic references. To facilitate access to individual items, a cumulative index to the first twenty-four volumes was compiled and published as *World Collectors Index 1946–1972* and later replaced with *World Collectors Index 1946–1982. World Collectors Index* (Voorburg, Netherlands: World Collectors, 1977–) began with coverage of the 1973–1974 season, the intent being to publish biennially thereafter.

Dictionaries, Encyclopedias, and Handbooks

446. **Artists As Illustrators: An International Directory with Signatures and Monograms, 1800–the Present.** John Castagno. Metuchen, NJ: Scarecrow Press, 1989. 625p. ISBN 0-8108-2168-0.

Another of Castagno's efforts to provide coverage of artists' signatures and monograms (entries 352, 353), this is a somewhat unique tool because it targets illustration as a medium. An interesting feature is that treatment includes many people from the fine arts who at some time have crossed the line to create illustrations for books, magazines, record labels, and posters. Thus we have not only professional illustrators but also painters and even sculptors, identified with their signatures as used on illustrations. There are more than 14,000 entries on nineteenth- and twentieth-century figures from all over the world. Unfortunately, of this number only about 4,000 facsimile signatures are furnished, with most entries containing the artist's name, nationality, dates, and references to biographical sources. Sources indexed include standard biographical tools and magazines, but only three museum publications, a real flaw for serious study. Supplements are planned for the future.

More recently, Castagno has continued his mission to document important artists' signatures with *Latin American Artists' Signatures and Monograms, Colonial Era to 1896* (Scarecrow Press, 1997). Eleven hundred artists are treated.

447. **Encyclopaedia of Oil Painting: Materials and Techniques.** Frederick Palmer. Cincinnati: North Light/Writer's Digest Books, 1984. 288p. ISBN 0-89134-078-5.

This handbook is considered to be a useful reference work that succeeds in its objective to explain in lucid fashion the purposes of the implements, equipment, and materials as well as the rationale and basic concepts of painting. Palmer is both an artist and a teacher and offers sound advice in his commentary. Such elements as easels, palettes, brushes, rags, and pigments are described in terms of their utility, and color is explained in thorough fashion. Techniques of glazing, collage, toning, encaustic, serigraphy, and painting from photographs are treated. Generally intended for the beginner rather than the advanced art student, the work is aided by the inclusion of over 250 illustrations, most of which are black-and-white. There is an index of painters as well as a general index.

448. **Encyclopedia of Themes and Subjects in Painting: Mythological, Biblical, Historical, Literary, Allegorical, and Topical.** Howard Daniel. New York: Abrams, 1971. 252p. ISBN 0-8109-0099-8.

This attractive handbook is quite distinctive and has been regarded as a useful reference source since the mid-1970s. Arranged alphabetically are the themes derived from the source elements identified in the title and used in European painting from the early Renaissance to the mid-nineteenth century. There are about 400 topics or themes, most of which are illustrated with reproductions of adequate size and quality. The largest proportion of the themes or subjects represents mythological or religious events; thus the work has value for students in the areas of religion and literature. There is a list of illustrations. The main weakness is the lack of an index.

449. **Looking at Prints, Drawings and Watercolors: A Guide to Technical Terms.** Paul Goldman. London: British Museum Publications; distr., Santa Monica, CA: J. Paul Getty Book Distribution Center, 1988. 64p. ISBN 0-89236-148-4.

This slender, authoritative, and readable wordbook, compiled by a staff member of the British Museum and co-sponsored by the J. Paul Getty Museum, is a useful information piece on certain elements of two-dimensional art work. Coverage is given to about 100 terms used by art critics, curators, and historians in describing prints, drawings, and watercolors. Techniques like metalpoint and squaring are defined, as are processes like etching, materials like gum arabic, and instruments like stylus and roulette. Terms represent traditional collections rather than modern or contemporary new techniques. British spelling is used ("watercolours") but certain Americanisms may be found buried within entries more common to English usage. Treatment tends to be detailed and provides exposition of such aspects as manufacture, qualities, components, and utilization by professionals. Approximately seventy illustrations accompany the entries.

450. **The Thames and Hudson Encyclopaedia of Impressionism.**
Bernard Denvir. New York: Thames & Hudson, 1990. 240p. ISBN
0-500-20239-7.

This slender little work has apparently succeeded in its purpose to furnish a brief
and up-to-date information tool relating to Impressionism in all its aspects and its practitioners.
Included are entries on models, dealers, and critics as well as artists, and on techniques as well
as locations and sites. Well-constructed articles treat general themes and furnish background
information on social, political, and cultural conditions. A number of the entries are illustrated in black-and-white, although there is some use of color. Bibliographies are included
that provide useful references for additional readings, and cross-references are given to related
entries. A unique feature is the subject index, which precedes the entries and groups them into
broad topical categories such as "The Art Market," "Patrons and Collectors," and "Dealers."
There is a general bibliography, along with a chronology of the Impressionist period, and a
directory of top collections of Impressionist art.

451. **What Great Paintings Say.** Rose-Marie Hagen and Rainer Hagen.
London: Taschen; distr., Random House, 1996–1998. 3v. ISBN
3-8228-8270-4 (v.3).

This set of writings has been compiled to both educate and inform the relatively
unsophisticated reader about the nuances and elements of art. It is similar in purpose to the art
series *History in Paintings* produced for television. Written in an interesting and popular
style, the work when viewed as a whole seems to have succeeded in presenting a useful
description of trends and lifestyles as depicted through the paintings and painters selected.
The volumes each contain about thirty essays examining works over several hundred years. Most
artists, although not all, are from Western Europe. Excellent color illustrations are employed
to clarify analyses, and commentary describes the impact of socio-political issues and religious
views on the art.

*Encyclopedia of Painting: Painters and Painting of the World from Prehistoric
Times to the Present Day*, edited by Bernard S. Myers (4th ed., Crown, 1979), remains a comprehensive, one-volume effort supplying numerous illustrations well integrated with the textual
description. Painters, movements, and styles are covered in one alphabetical dictionary-type
arrangement, the work having kept its format since the initial edition in 1955. Considered to
be strong in biographical coverage, much of the total information is provided through the
treatment of personalities; contemporary artists and influences were added to this edition.

Biographical Sources

452. **The Dictionary of British Artists, 1880–1940; An Antique
Collectors' Club Research Project Listing 41,000 Artists.** Jane Johnson
and A. Greutzner. Suffolk, UK: Antique Collectors Club, 1976; repr., 1986.
567p. ISBN 0-902028-36-7.

This dictionary provides an excellent source of information on British painters following the Victorian era, listing every artist who exhibited in any one of forty-seven selected
representative galleries during that time period. Entries are brief and provide dates of birth
and death, residence, memberships and honors, places and frequency of exhibitions, and
(sometimes) art schools attended. The introduction consists of a descriptive essay on the
groups, movements, societies, and galleries that developed during this time period. In each
entry there is an indication of when one of the artist's pictures brought more than 100 pounds
at an auction during 1970–1975.

453. **Innovators of American Illustration.** Steven Heller, ed. New York: Van Nostrand Reinhold, 1986. 224p. ISBN 0-442-23230-6.

An interesting introductory work is provided here by a distinguished authority in the field. The editor has served as art director for several periodicals, including *The New York Times Book Review*. He presents a collection of interviews conducted with twenty-one American illustrators between 1984 and 1985. Such individuals as Maurice Sendak, Milton Glaser, and Edward Sorel are questioned about their careers from the beginning to the present. They describe their working habits, motivations, and philosophical views on the role of illustration, as well as their education, training, and the personalities who were influential in their lives. Although not necessarily part of the reference collection, this book will have value for both teachers and students.

454. **Larousse Dictionary of Painters.** New York: Larousse, 1981; repr., New York: Mallard Press, 1989. 467p. ISBN 0-7924-5132-5.

Like other reference books bearing the Larousse name, this one is profusely illustrated with hundreds of reproductions, many of them in color. Unfortunately, they are somewhat cramped in the page layouts and not of the highest quality. The dictionary is a useful biographical tool providing coverage of the principal figures in painting in both Europe and North America. Information is given regarding the artist's life and contributions to the world of art, at a depth adequate to provide a reasonable awareness of his or her prominence. An important element is the inclusion of locations where the artist's works are displayed. Many nations are represented, including some that generally are not considered important for their artistic influences.

455. **Painting of the Golden Age: A Biographical Dictionary of Seventeenth Century European Painters.** Adelheid M. Gealt. Westport, CT: Greenwood, 1993. 770p. ISBN 0-313-24310-7.

About 300 major painters from all parts of Europe are treated in this well-constructed biographical dictionary. Essays are informative and provide an excellent overview of the career achievements and important contributions of each artist. In the past, the majority of titles covering artists of this time period (Brueghel, Caravaggio, Rubens, etc.) have been issued in French, German, or Italian, making this work of particular importance to English-speaking students and librarians. Entries vary in length from several pages to less than a page and are accompanied by listings of paintings not covered in the text along with a selective bibliography. Appendices supply listings of painters by geographical area, a detailed bibliography, and a thorough index.

Nineteenth Century Painters and Painting: A Dictionary, by Geraldine Norman (University of California, 1977), is an old favorite that opens with a brief but useful description of the major movements within the art world during the nineteenth century, such as Romanticism and Impressionism. Color reproductions illustrate the stylistic features. The major body of the text is given to biographies of about 700 artists of the period along with entries for schools, practices, and techniques. Many of these articles are illustrated in black-and-white. Entries vary in length, with some of the longer articles dedicated to less prominent individuals for whom in-depth information is generally not available. Considered a strength is the coverage given to Hungarians, Russians, and others who have escaped attention in the past.

Histories

456. **American Painting.** Jules David Prown and Barbara Rose. New York: Rizzoli, 1979–1987. 2v. ISBN 0-8478-0308-2.

Originally published in 1969, this history of American painting gained recognition as a detailed description of the events and happenings, with excellent exposition of the work of individual artists. Volume 1 is by Prown and covers the colonial period to the Armory Show. Fine treatment is provided of individuals like West, Copley, Stuart, Cassatt, Sargent, and Whistler. It ends with the emergence of the Ashcan School and the Armory Show, a landmark in modern art. Volume 2 is by Rose and continues the coverage to the present day, embracing the important as well as the faddish elements and movements that characterize contemporary art. Both volumes contain color reproductions and are handsome works. They were revised in 1979; Rose's volume was updated in 1986 and Prown's in 1987.

457. **Chinese Painting: Leading Masters and Principles.** Osvald Siren. London: Lund Humphries, 1956–1958; repr., New York: Hacker, 1974. 7v.

This multi-volume work has been considered a vital source of information since its first appearance forty-three years ago. It covers the history of Chinese painting, a complex and many-faceted subject, from the earliest times to the end of the Ch'ing dynasty in 1912. Siren's scholarship remains foremost in Chinese art and the coverage given to individuals and developments is authoritative and complete. Generally considered a necessary purchase for academic libraries, the reprint edition has been criticized for a lower quality of reproduction of the 900 black-and-white prints. The provision of the lists of works by Chinese painters is an asset to scholars and students; bibliographies are international in scope and include materials in the Chinese language.

458. **A Concise History of Modern Painting.** 3d ed., enl. and upd. Sir Herbert E. Read. New York: Praeger, 1974. 392p. ISBN 0-50020-141-2. Repr., Oxford University Press, 1985. ISBN 0-19-519940-5.

Considered in most quarters to be a fine one-volume history of the origins and development of modern art, this work made its initial appearance in 1959. Since then it has achieved popularity and wide distribution in libraries and is regarded as a staple in the reference department. Beginning with Cezanne, it clearly traces the elements, influences, and styles of modern painting. It includes quotes from the artists themselves and is well served in terms of number of illustrations, although at times they have been criticized for poor quality. Errors that appeared in the first edition have been corrected, and presently this is a useful tool for those needing a lucid and informative survey work.

459. **The Development of the Italian Schools of Painting.** Raimond van Marle. The Hague: Nijhoff, 1923–1938; repr., New York: Hacker, 1970. 19v. ISBN 0-87817-048-0.

An extensive and comprehensive treatment of Italian art, this survey of painting from the sixth century has no equal in the English language. Scholarly in nature, it provides many references and includes bibliographies for each chapter. Each volume has an index of artists, iconography, and places. The work has been criticized for certain instances of misleading information and obsolete commentary. Until Venturi's *Storia dell'arte italiana* (entry 459n) is translated, however, this is the best work available for those who must use the English language. An important feature is the total of more than 5,500 illustrations, which suffer somewhat in the reprint version. The final volume is a general index to the whole set.

460. Painting in the Twentieth Century. 2d ed., exp. Werner Haftmann. New York: Praeger, 1969. 2v. in 1.

A translation of a German work from the mid-1950s, this work provides a good survey of painting in the twentieth century. Volume 1 provides an analysis of the artists and their work, while volume 2 gives a pictorial survey that includes over 1,000 reproductions, some of which are in full color. Volume 1 is a profound examination of the psychological and philosophical elements associated with contemporary painting and the personalities who engaged in it. About 500 artists are covered, with short biographies, each of which is given a number of bibliographical references. Although it has been criticized for a bias toward German and Italian art, Haftmann's work provides enough information on other areas to be recommended as a general source. There are both name and subject indexes in volume 1.

ARCHITECTURE, INTERIOR DESIGN, AND LANDSCAPE ARCHITECTURE

Bibliographic Guides and Periodical Directories

461. Architecture: A Bibliographic Guide to Basic Reference Works, Histories, and Handbooks. Donald L. Ehresmann. Littleton, CO: Libraries Unlimited, 1984. 338p. ISBN 0-87287-394-3.

A companion piece to other guides by Ehresmann in the fine arts (entry 309) and in the decorative arts (entry 532), this is an essential tool for both collection development and reference. It provides an annotated bibliography of books that have proved to be useful and informative. Books listed are primarily in the English language but there is coverage of titles in Western European languages. Emphasis is on a practical bibliography and the titles listed are generally available in American libraries. There are 1,350 entries; arrangement is by form or type such as reference books, by chronological coverage (prehistoric), or by geographic coverage (Oriental). There are both author-title and subject indexes.

462. Architecture Sourcebook: A Guide to Resources on the Practice of Architecture. Kathryn M. Wayne, ed. Detroit: Omnigraphics, 1997. 417p. (Design Reference Series, v. 2). ISBN 0-7808-0024-9.

As volume 2 in the publisher's series, this work provides an excellent listing of publications in architectural design. It consists of eighteen chapters organized into two major parts. The first part contains fourteen chapters, each treating a building type (commercial office, cultural, government and public, educational, etc.) in which a variety of pertinent resources are assembled for easy access to the professional. The second part provides four chapters on additional reference sources (dictionaries and encyclopedias, indexes, handbooks and manuals, and periodicals). The editor is an architectural librarian, familiar with the field and its bibliography, and even more important with the manner in which such resources will be best utilized. The work is well-indexed.

Landscape Architecture Sourcebook: A Guide to Resources on the History and Practice of Landscape Architecture, edited by Diana Vogelsong (Omnigraphics, 1997), is volume 1 in the publisher's series and is somewhat similar in format. There are ten major chapters (reference works, general texts and histories, landscape architects and architectural firms, practical handbooks, plant materials, core works on places and projects, environmental concerns, periodicals, institutional resources, and computer and media resources). A glossary is supplied along with an index.

*463. **Cyburbia—Architecture Resource Directory.** Dan Tasman. Buffalo, NY: University of Buffalo, 1994– . http://www.ap.buffalo.edu/ pairc/architecture_resource_directory.html (World Wide Web) (accessed December 1999).

This Web site is the product of the University of Buffalo School of Architecture and Planning and contains over 8,000 links to architectural resources on the Web. Formerly called *The Planning and Architecture Internet Resource Center (PAIRC)*, the current site is maintained regularly and offers a classified directory of a wealth of material through a number of major divisions (architecture firms, architecture images and exhibits, buildings, education and career development, environment, history and preservation, landscape architecture, urban design, etc.). It also provides several interactive message boards.

*Landscape Architecture Virtual Library (http://www.clr.toronto.edu/VIRTUALLIB/ larch.html [accessed December 1999]), by Rodney Hoinkes (University of Toronto, 1994–), is a similar site maintained by an academic unit (University of Toronto Faculty of Architecture, Landscape, and Design) and provided through CLRnet. Numerous links relevant to the study and practice of landscape architecture are supplied.

464. **Directory of International Periodicals and Newsletters on the Built Environment.** 2d ed. Frances C. Gretes. New York: Van Nostrand Reinhold, 1992. 442p. ISBN 0-442-00792-2.

Considered to be an outstanding resource item for its audience of specialists when published initially in 1986, the second edition of this directory of serial literature is greatly augmented and updated. Over 1,500 publications are placed within fourteen sections similar to those used in the first edition. They deal with subjects relevant to the built environment (architecture, office practice, building types, historic preservation and architectural history, urban design, fine arts, planning, landscape design and gardening, building and construction, engineering, real estate development, etc.). Entries are arranged alphabetically within each topical division and include complete bibliographic information as well as description of the content. This is a welcome aid to the librarian who serves architects, engineers, designers, planners, and contractors, because the number of documents in these fields has increased dramatically over the past few years. Included are a listing of indexes and abstracts, a title index, and a geographical index of countries where the serials are published.

465. **Interior Design Sourcebook: A Guide to Resources on the History and Practice of Interior Design.** Susan A. Lewis. Detroit: Omnigraphics, 1998. 307p. (Design Reference Series, v. 3). ISBN 0-7808-0198-9.

Volume 3 of the publisher's series that includes *Architecture Sourcebook* (entry 462), this work focuses on the related field of interior design, furnishing resources in a comprehensive manner. It is organized into fifteen chapters (reference; design theory/philosophy; history; programming, planning, and pre-design; furniture, finishes, and textiles; building and interior systems; project types; visual communication methods; business and professional practice; competitions, awards, and scholarships; magazines; publishers and bookstores; professional and trade organizations and government agencies; research centers; and national product expositions and conferences). Each chapter has an introduction and is followed by a selective bibliography. Indexing is excellent.

Bibliographies and Catalogs

466. Catalog of the Avery Memorial Architectural Library of Columbia University. 2d ed., enl. Boston: G. K. Hall, 1968. 19v. **Supp.** 1–5, 1972–1982. ISBN 0-8161-0397-6 (Supp 5).

In addition to the extensive holdings of the Avery Library, one of the outstanding architectural collections in the country, this catalog contains all books on the subject of architecture and art held anywhere in the university in any of its libraries. Through the years, this has come to be recognized as one of the most comprehensive sources of bibliographic information in the field. A catalog first was issued in 1895 in printed form, and G. K. Hall produced the first catalog of this type in 1958, a six-volume work received warmly by librarians in the field. The supplements continue to update the coverage. The holdings of the various Columbia University libraries are listed at the Avery Web site through the CLIO information system (http://www.columbia.edu/cu/libraries/indiv/avery [accessed February 2000]).

For listings of films and videos, there is *Architecture on Screen: Films and Videos on Architecture . . .* (G. K. Hall, 1993), produced as part of the Program for Art on Film under the joint sponsorship of the Metropolitan Museum of Art and the J. Paul Getty Trust. Edited by Nadine Covert, it supplies detailed information, including synopses, references to reviews, and production and release information. Some 900 films and videos on architecture are treated in a manner similar to that used in *Art on Screen* (entry 375). Several indexes supply access.

467. Early Christian and Byzantine Architecture: An Annotated Bibliography and Historiography. W. Eugene Kleinbauer. Boston: G. K. Hall, 1992. 779p. (A Reference Publication in Art History). ISBN 0-8161-8316-3.

There is an extensive introductory section to this work that describes the origins and development of the study of early medieval architecture; useful narrative is given to the development of photography of Byzantine architecture in the appendix. Between these expository pieces there lies a well-constituted bibliography of more than 2,000 books, articles, and catalogs representing fifteen different languages. Arrangement of entries is by some 200 topical headings reflecting specific interests or needs of researchers such as basilicas, aqueducts, catacombs, sculptured decoration, and so forth. Christian architecture is treated from its beginning to the sixth century, while Byzantine work is examined from the third century until the fall of the Empire in 1453. Publication dates of sources listed run through 1990. There is a subject index containing geographic locales, along with an index to authors.

468. The Literature of British Domestic Architecture 1715–1842. John Archer. Cambridge, MA: MIT Press, 1985. 1078p. ISBN 0-262-01076-3.

A thorough and detailed bibliography of 360 titles printed in Great Britain and Ireland during the eighteenth and nineteenth centuries, this item will be of interest to bibliographers all over the world. Three major essays precede the bibliography and provide coverage of the relationship of architecture to the book trade, describe the elements of format and content, and discuss the development of architectural theory in Great Britain. The bibliography is detailed in its coverage of the early publications, and variant editions are noted, as are library locations. There are another 150 titles or so in the appendices, which join those in the main body of the work to provide excellent coverage of this elusive albeit important topic. Many of the works described are of landmark importance. The book is illustrated in black-and-white and contains an index as well as notes and references.

469. Romanesque Architecture: A Bibliography. Martin Davies. Boston: G. K. Hall, 1993. 340p. (A Reference Publication in Art History). ISBN 0-8161-1826-4.

This publication is the most comprehensive bibliography on the study of Romanesque architecture, providing an important tool for both students and specialists. All elements of Romanesque architecture are treated, the general decorative and ornamental aspects as well as the specific features incorporated within the style. There are more than 1,600 entries identifying lengthy studies and graphic documentation; no periodical articles are treated but rather coverage is given to monographs, theses and dissertations, guidebooks, series, maps, audiovisual materials, and atlases. These sources are in all languages. All related styles are embraced: Carolingian, pre-Romanesque, later Romanesque, and Transitional, as well as Romanesque. Entries are placed in geographically divided chapters treating Europe both in general and distinct regions; these are subdivided chronologically. Maps are provided along with indexes to ease access.

Indexes, Abstracts, and Serial Bibliographies

*470. Architectural Periodicals Index. London: Royal Institute of British Architects, 1972/1973–1994. Q. with ann. cum. ISSN 0266-4380.

This was a useful subject index to architectural periodicals found in the British Architectural Library of the Royal Institute of British Architecture (RIBA), and covered about 450 titles, the majority of which are British. Subjects were assigned through headings utilized in *Architectural Keywords*, a vocabulary control device developed by RIBA in 1982. Arrangement is classified by those subjects, with alphabetical arrangement of titles within the categories. Foreign titles are identified, with indication of language and presence of English abstracts or summaries. There is a name index as well as a topographical and building name index. The *Index* was available online through DIALOG during most of its life. It is continued by **Architectural Publications Index* (1995–) in CD-ROM format.

Comprehensive Index to Architectural Periodicals, 1956–1972 (London: World Microfilms, 1975) offers the card catalog file of the library on twenty-one reels of microfilm. This represents a retrospective index of some 200 periodicals in an arrangement similar to *Architectural Periodicals Index*. The majority of these listings first appeared in the quarterly issues of *RIBA Bulletin*.

*471. Avery Index to Architectural Periodicals. Columbia University. Avery Architectural Library. Boston: G. K. Hall, 1973. 15v. **Supp. 1–13**, 1975–1993. ISBN 0-8161-0615-0 (Supp 13).

One of the leading architectural collections in this country belongs to the Avery Library of Columbia University. G. K. Hall initiated this excellent service by reproducing the card file containing analytics of periodical articles in titles received at the library. The 1973 edition superseded the original 1963 work by absorbing all its entries and those of its supplements. Since then, supplements have appeared that continue to update the listings. Since 1984, the work has been supported by the Getty Art History Information program. The most recent supplement was issued in four volumes in 1993, and is now computer-generated. This set and its supplements include periodical titles not only in architecture but also in decorative arts, sculpture, city planning, and archaeology. There is good coverage of writings on individual architects. With about 800 periodicals indexed, this is the most comprehensive periodical source, although it is limited to periodicals in the Western languages. The index is available online through a database by the same name covering the period from 1979 to date; in 1996 it was issued in CD-ROM format providing retrospective coverage up to 1996.

472. Index to Historic Preservation Periodicals, National Trust for Historic Preservation Library of the University of Maryland, College Park. Boston: G. K. Hall, 1988. 354p. ISBN 0-8161-0474-3. **Supp. 1987–1990**, 1992. 548p. ISBN 0-8161-0524-3.

For those interested in the study of historic architecture and preservation, this is a useful index to nine years of serial publication from 1979 to 1987. More than 600 serials of all levels (international, national, regional, state, and local) were reviewed for pertinent writings, producing a comprehensive array of articles as entries. About 5,600 entries treat a full complement of topics, including design review, law, and fund-raising elements along with architecture, interiors, and preservation. Arrangement is alphabetical by topic or subject heading; there are some annotations. The major deficiency is lack of a subject index, since only one subject heading has been assigned to each entry. The supplement covers the 1987–1990 period and documents the growth of interest in the topic.

473. World Architecture Index: A Guide to Illustrations. Edward H. Teague, comp. New York: Greenwood, 1991. 447p. (Art Reference Collection, no. 12). ISBN 0-313-22552-4.

Some 7,000 illustrations of buildings and plans culled from 108 important books are indexed in this convenient source. Indexing is detailed and access is possible by site, architect, architectural type, and variant names of the structures depicted in the reproductions. All books are English-language sources and there is emphasis on Western architecture, although scope and coverage is global. The work is divided into four major segments, arranged alphabetically. Part 1 is the site index, with entries listed under the city. This is the major segment, with approximately half the text. Part 2 is an index of architects listing both individuals and firms responsible for the works portrayed. Brief biographical information is included in some of the entries. Part 3 is an index of building types (dwellings, waterworks, military structures, etc.) and part 4 lists the names and alternate names of the structures. This work is well-organized and handy to use.

A more specialized source compiled by Teague is *Index to Italian Architecture: A Guide to Key Monuments and Reproduction Sources* (Greenwood, 1992), which is number 13 in the same series. It identifies illustrations of some 1,800 Italian monuments and buildings in eighty books. Teague is an art and architecture librarian in academe; his expertise is evident in the excellent access provided by site, architect, chronology, type, and work.

Dictionaries, Encyclopedias, Handbooks, Etc.

474. Atlas of European Architecture. Brian Sachar. New York: Van Nostrand Reinhold, 1984. 369p. ISBN 0-442-28149-8.

An attractive and practical handbook for the study of European architecture is this country-by-country exposition of notable buildings. Each of the twelve chapters is devoted to a specific country (arranged alphabetically), in which towns and cities are also listed alphabetically. Entries for each of the 3,500 buildings covered are listed under cities in chronological order by date of construction. The book is sure to please individuals involved with architectural studies, such as architects, students, art historians, and preservationists, as well as laypersons with an active interest in architecture. Entries provide name, date, address, architect, photograph, and some notes of special features. Also listed when available is information regarding the tourist information office, architects' institute, and major museums with special collections. There is a bibliography, an index of architects and artists, and an index of cities and towns.

Another richly illustrated source, but more comprehensive in scope, is *World Atlas of Architecture* (G. K. Hall, 1984; repr., New York: Crescent Books, 1994), the English edition of a French title, itself derived from Mitchell Beazley's *Great Architecture of the World* (Random House, 1975). Fully 100 pages of this 408-page effort are devoted to non-Western architecture (China, Japan, Korea, Southeast Asia, India, Black Africa, etc.). The remainder is divided into historical periods beginning with the ancient world and ending with the modern era.

475. Concise Encyclopedia of Interior Design. 2d ed. A. Allen Dizik. New York: Van Nostrand Reinhold, 1988. 220p. ISBN 0-442-22109-6.

This slender volume represents an update of a 1976 publication and is intended to provide a source of information for homeowners, interior designers, students, and teachers. To appeal to such a diverse audience it employs a popular approach, furnishing articles ranging from one-sentence definitions and identifications to survey essays running two to four pages on such topics as color, lighting, and draperies. Coverage is broad and includes furniture, furniture periods, room arrangements, fabrics, and wall coverings along with the fine arts, architecture, antiques, and construction. Entries provide numerous cross-references (although some have been found to be defective). There are useful charts and tables that help to clarify the treatment given to such considerations as wallpaper coverage, tile coverage, types of carpet fibers, and so forth. Four pages of line drawings treat room arrangements.

Entourage: A Tracing File for Architecture and Interior Design Drawing, by Ernest Burden (3d ed., McGraw-Hill, 1996), provides a compilation of architectural and design renderings that may be traced to complete the various projects undertaken by specialists or students. All types of renderings are supplied (people, vehicles, plants, benches, flags, birds, etc.). These are shown in different perspectives and positions.

476. Dictionary of Architecture & Construction. 2d ed. Cyril M. Harris. New York: McGraw-Hill, 1993. 924p. ISBN 0-07-026888-6.

A well-known and important source, now in its second edition, this comprehensive effort has been expanded by some 2,300 entries to contain 22,500 terms and abbreviations in more than seventy-five working areas of architecture, construction, and the building trades. Both students and specialists will make this a first source of information for brief identifications of both contemporary and historical influences. Previous entries have been updated when necessary. Illustrations have been enhanced in size and detail; their number has been increased to about 2,000. Modern construction terminology embracing tools, techniques, equipment, and more are included along with the more traditional terms of architectural history.

Dictionary of Architectural and Building Technology, by Henry J. Cowan and Peter R. Smith (Elsevier Applied Science Publishers, 1986), is a useful but more compact, less comprehensive source providing treatment of the technical terminology of modern architecture and related areas. It contains about 5,000 terms, 1,500 of which have been added since publication of an earlier work by Cowan in 1973. The emphasis is on the science of architecture and building, with fine coverage of structures, materials, acoustics, lighting, thermal environment, building services, solar heating, and so forth. Definitions are brief but informative and are enhanced by over 120 illustrations, including diagrams and charts. This title is useful to those who are active in the construction of buildings or its study (teachers, students, architects, engineers, consultants, and contractors).

477. Dictionary of Islamic Architecture. Andrew Petersen. New York: Routledge Kegan Paul, 1996. 342p. ISBN 0-415-06084-2.

This is a useful tool providing information in a needed area of inquiry for less-sophisticated users. The work is clear and well-constructed; definitions begin with a one-sentence statement of explanation. Most, but not all, are then further developed to varying degrees depending upon the complexity or importance of the topic or concept. Reading lists are furnished for the lengthier descriptions. Most important is the comprehensive scope of the work, which includes a wide range of Islamic architectural production, including buildings in the United States, China, and the United Kingdom as well as the Arab world. Included among the entries are site descriptions, survey articles on historical origin and cultural influences, and biographical sketches as well as technical definitions. Numerous photographs, line drawings, diagrams, and maps help to explain the terms.

478. **A Dictionary of Landscape Architecture.** Baker H. Morrow. Albuquerque: University of New Mexico Press, 1987. 378p. ISBN 0-8263-0943-7.

This wordbook has received mixed reviews at best, having been criticized for its inclusions of such terms as "biology" and "sidewalk cafe" and for its frequent errors, such as the dates given to Charles Platt. On the other hand, it is commended for its attempt to clarify a body of knowledge about which little has been published. The purpose of the work is to identify the many aspects, details, and components of landscape architecture, while at the same time provide exposition of its essential wholeness. Entries vary in length from brief technical definitions of a few words or sentences to longer narratives such as a four-page description of English landscape architecture. There are cross-references that aid access to related articles, along with numerous black-and-white illustrations of drawings, plans, and some photographs. Unfortunately, these illustrations are of poor quality and do little to enhance the work.

479. **Encyclopedia of American Architecture.** 2d ed. Robert T. Packard and Balthazar Korab. New York: McGraw-Hill, 1995. 724p. ISBN 0-07-048010-9.

The second edition of this work continues as a practical and informative reference book for the layperson. It represents a compendium of miscellaneous facts and definitions. Written in nontechnical language, definitions and identifications are clear and adequate, and the work retains the basic character of the initial effort produced by William Dudley Hunt. This style favors the lengthier discursive article over the more modern and to-the-point, briefer entry. There are more than 200 articles on history, building types, systems and structures, materials, and preservation, with about 50 on prominent architects. There is a special attempt to include women and minorities in the various articles when appropriate. The work has been updated in terms of coverage and is considered to be a useful tool for the general reader, although not as technical as the advanced student might want or need. Comprehensive coverage is provided from the pre-Columbian period to the present. The encyclopedia contains excellent color illustrations, good cross-references, and brief bibliographies. An adequate index is included.

A good resource tool for the specialist in the field is the twelfth edition of *The Architect's Handbook of Professional Practice*, edited by David S. Haviland for the American Institute of Architects (1994). The segments identify architects, firms, tools, and projects as well as the documents concerned with building contracts and specifications in this country. *The Newsletter of the AIA Document Supplement Service* was issued in 1990 as a monthly looseleaf supplement to the *Handbook*.

480. **Encyclopedia of Architecture: Design, Engineering & Construction.** Joseph A. Wilkes and Robert T. Packard, eds. New York: John Wiley, 1989–1990. 5v. (A Wiley-Interscience Publication). ISBN 0-471-63351-8.

This five-volume encyclopedia was prepared over a period of six years and issued over a two-year period. It represents an up-to-date and comprehensive information tool. Included in the alphabetically arranged body of entries are architects; firms; types of buildings; materials; and various features, topics, and issues relevant to the comprehension of architecture and construction. Along with the processes and technical elements, there is excellent coverage of both the historical influences and the philosophical aspects such as aesthetics. This substantial tool has gained recognition as a standard in the field and the first source of information for those who need enlightenment in this area. Some 500 signed articles are contributed by specialists (architects, architectural histories, and academicians). There are 3,000 high-quality illustrations along with 500 tables. Volume 5 (T–Z) contains the index of subjects, personal names, and buildings, along with a 219-page supplement of additional topics.

481. **Encyclopedia of Interior Design.** Joanna Banham, ed. Chicago: Fitzroy Dearborn, 1997. 2v. ISBN 1-884964-19-2.

This work consists of a collection of signed essays bringing together a variety of elements integral to interior design. Treatment is given to the history and exposition of rooms such as parlors and bedrooms and of articles of furniture as well as the full range of topics, issues, and personalities important to the study of the field. Emphasis is given to the modern period in terms of depth of articles, but the coverage is comprehensive with respect to the history of style and accomplishments of all periods. Biographical data are presented for personalities, as well as their publications and a short bibliography for further reading. Black-and-white pictures are provided along with an index to facilitate access.

482. **Illustrated Dictionary of Historic Architecture.** Cyril M. Harris, ed. New York: McGraw-Hill, 1977; repr., New York: Dover, 1983. 581p. ISBN 0-486-24444-X.

Originally published under a different title, this work is still regarded as an excellent source of information on architectural history. There are about 5,000 terms, all of which are given clear definitions and explanations. There are no biographies among the entries; the emphasis is on styles, forms, and component elements of architecture. The illustrations are excellent: Some 2,100 line drawings and a few photographs help to define both the character and characteristics described in the entries. They are brought together from a variety of sources and are well-integrated, providing a cohesive coverage of topics. Entries vary from a single line to a half-page and cover about 5,000 years from ancient to modern architecture. Oriental terms are accompanied by their calligraphic symbols.

Providing more emphasis on contemporary accomplishments is the well-constructed source by John Fleming and Hugh Honour, *The Penguin Dictionary of Architecture* (4th ed., Penguin, 1991). The two collaborators are joined by an equally well-known expert, Nicholas Pevsner, in producing this useful and popular treatment of architects, their styles and accomplishments, and the terminology of the field. A standard source is *Encyclopedia of Modern Architecture*, edited by Wolfgang Pehnt (H. N. Abrams, 1964), providing strong focus on the twentieth century. The concise articles are arranged alphabetically and are contributed by more than thirty architectural writers from sixteen countries.

483. **The Illustrated Encyclopedia of Architects and Architecture.** Dennis Sharp, ed. New York: Whitney Library of Design/Watson-Guptill, 1991. 256p. ISBN 0-8230-2539-X.

Sharp serves as the editor of *World Architecture*, an international journal in the field, and has secured the services of a highly qualified group of contributors in producing this work. It is divided into two parts, the first being a biographical dictionary treating the lives and careers of 350 architects from both the historical past and contemporary times. The entries are brief and include a summary evaluation of the individual's work along with a bibliography for additional reading. In some cases, photographs of important achievements are supplied. The second section presents a historical overview of architecture through a series of brief essays illustrated with some 400 black-and-white and color photographs. In this way, one is able to comprehend the development of the styles and the nature of the movements and their influences in architectural history. There are cross-references to architects in part 1, along with a general index. A glossary also is furnished.

484. **Time-Saver Standards for Building Types.** 3d ed. Joseph De Chiara and John Hancock Callender, eds. New York: McGraw-Hill, 1990. 1413p. ISBN 0-07-016279-4.

First published in 1973 and revised in 1980, this work continues to provide a standard source of information on all major building types arranged under ten broad categories, including residential, educational, cultural, and health. A miscellaneous category treats farm buildings, nature centers, and others. The editors are practicing architects who have provided information on vital details within each section. Dimensions, facility needs, space criteria, layouts, schematics, and arrangements are supplied for all types of construction, thus providing a starting point in the design process. A detailed index is furnished.

Three other titles have been issued in this series. The second edition of *Time-Saver Standards for Housing and Residential Development*, also edited by De Chiara et al. (McGraw-Hill, 1995), treats the emerging trends in the largest segment of the construction industry. The same editor has collaborated with others to produce *Time-Saver Standards for Interior Design and Space Planning* (McGraw-Hill, 1991), providing further exposition of various types of buildings and construction details, as well as reference data. The most recent offering is the second edition of *Time Saver Standards for Landscape Architecture: Design and Construction Data* (McGraw-Hill, 1998), edited by Charles W. Harris and Nicholas T. Dines; it continues to provide a comprehensive exposition of important data along with illustrations organized in various sections such as historical landscapes and outdoor accessibility. A similar source is *Ramsey/Sleeper Architectural Graphic Standards* (9th ed., John Wiley, 1994). Sponsored by the American Institute of Architects and initiated by Charles George Ramsey and Harold Reeve Sleeper, both of whom died in the early 1960s, this continuing effort is now edited by John Ray Hoke, Jr. It represents a standard source of information regarding standards for building design and construction arranged in chapters according to principles established by the Construction Specifications Institute. Recently added chapters treat historic preservation and energy design. It is available in CD-ROM format.

Directories

485. **America Preserved: A Checklist of Historic Buildings, Structures, and Sites.** Washington, DC: Library of Congress, Cataloging Distribution Service, 1995. 1152p. ISBN 0-16-045255-4.

This is the second checklist of historic buildings, structures, and sites recorded by the Historic American Buildings Survey (HABS) and the Historic American Engineering Record (HAER). The first checklist was published as *Historic America* (Library of Congress, 1983) and succeeded in providing a systematic record of the country's built environment through identification of graphic and written records. The current effort adds 14,000 entries to the initial work, with fuller documentation and description. The *Checklist* identifies over 30,000 structures, 160,000 photographs, and 96,000 drawings, along with references to more than 15,000 documentary pages. Entries indicate full LC shelflist numbers to expedite ordering and in many cases are accompanied by black-and-white photographs.

*486. **National Register of Historic Places, 1966 to 1994: Cumulative List Through January 1, 1994.** Washington, DC: National Park Service, 1994. 923p. ISBN 0-891332-54-5.

This is the latest edition of this cumulative listing, replacing the 1991 issue that covered the period 1966–1991. There are more than 60,000 entries, representing an increase over its predecessor. Included here are all properties listed in the National Register over a period of twenty-five years. Arrangement of entries is directory-fashion, alphabetical by state, then county. Coverage is thorough for the United States and embraces the District of Columbia as well as American Samoa, Guam, Puerto Rico, the Virgin Islands, and Micronesia. This official listing is maintained by the National Park Service and published in cooperation with the American Association for State and Local History. It includes properties of local and state significance as well as those of national importance. The work is available online through the National Park Service and on CD-ROM from Chadwyck-Healey.

487. **Preservation Yellow Pages: The Complete Information Source for Homeowners, Communities, and Professionals.** Rev. ed. Julie Zagars, ed.; National Trust for Historic Preservation. Washington, DC: Preservation Press/John Wiley, 1997. 277p. ISBN 0-471-19183-3.

Originally published as *The Brown Book: A Directory of Preservation Information* (Preservation Press, 1983), this useful directory-handbook has been enlarged and revised over time. The work is designed to aid the National Trust for Historic Preservation to fulfill its responsibility to inform and advise states and local agencies in their desire to preserve old buildings of historical or architectural significance. Part 1 provides an overview of the nature and importance of preservation; part 2 gives practical information in topical chapters alphabetically arranged, covering architectural styles, lists of books, bookstores, libraries, periodicals, and so forth, along with a glossary and information on tax incentives; part 3 identifies regional, national, and international organizations and programs; and part 4 provides a state-by-state listing of preservation contracts. There is a general index of sites, names, and publications.

488. **ProFile: The Sourcebook of U.S. Architectural Design Firms.** American Institute of Architects. Atlanta: Construction Market Data, 1993– . Ann. ISSN 0190-8766.

This directory of architectural firms, published under the auspices of the AIA, actually began in 1978 and has appeared irregularly in the past. The 1996 issue (11th ed.) bears a slight change of subtitle along with continuing commitment to annual publication. Member firms are listed alphabetically by name within a geographical arrangement, in typical directory fashion. Each entry provides addresses of all offices of the firms and indication of types of practice, as well as the present name of the company. Also included are names of personnel, analyses of work distributions by gross income percentages, geographical work distributions, and awards. There are indexes of both companies and individuals.

The AIA also sponsored *American Architects Directory* (R. R. Bowker, 1955–1970), which furnished biographical information along with names and addresses of members and of other prominent architects. Included were a geographical index and lists of fellows and award winners.

Biographical Sources

489. **American Architects from the Civil War to the First World War: A Guide to Information Sources.** Lawrence Wodehouse. Detroit: Gale Research, 1976. 343p. (Art and Architecture Information Guide Series, v. 3). ISBN 0-8103-1269-7.

The author is a British architect who has rendered an important bibliographic guide to the study of architectural history that has stood the test of time. It represents a selective, annotated, biographical bibliography, treating the most important American architects from 1860 to the second decade of the twentieth century and continues the coverage initiated by Frank J. Roos, Jr.'s *Bibliography of Early American Architecture* (University of Illinois Press, 1968), which covered the field up to 1860. An annotated listing of 46 general reference books on American architects precedes the major section treating 175 important architects and partnerships. These entries are arranged alphabetically by surname and supply a brief biographical sketch along with a listing of the personality's publications, locations of his or her drawings, and a bibliography of books and articles offering biographical or critical commentary. There is a general subject index and a building location index.

Wodehouse continued his efforts with a similar work on major architects in his native land. *British Architects, 1840–1976: A Guide to Information Sources* is number 8 in the publisher's series and was issued in 1978. It treats 288 important architects from England, Wales, Ireland, and Scotland. Indexing as well as treatment are similar to *American Architects.*

490. **Contemporary Architects.** 3d ed. Muriel Emanuel, ed. Detroit: St. James Press, 1994. 1125p. (Contemporary Arts Series). ISBN 1-55862-182-2.

Another good source is this biographical dictionary, now in its third edition. This work furnishes biographical coverage of 585 of the greatest current architects, landscape architects, and structural engineers, along with coverage of some of the acknowledged masters from an earlier part of this century. Entries include a biographical sketch, list of major works, exhibitions, references to books by and about the architect, a photograph of a representative work, and an evaluative essay. In some cases there is commentary from the architect about his work. The fourth edition is about to be published in the year 2000. *Contemporary American Architects*, edited by Philip Jodidio (Taschen, 1997) is a recent but brief identification piece.

Avery Obituary Index of Architects (2d ed., G. K. Hall, 1980) provides some 17,000 references to obituaries contained in about 500 periodicals covered in the *Avery Index to Architectural Periodicals*, along with a selection of newspapers such as the *New York Times*. The work was initiated in 1934 and was last issued in 1963 as *Avery Obituary Index of Architects and Artists*. The indexing of artists ceased in 1960, however, accounting for the change in title. There is additional indexing of obituaries in four leading U.S. architectural periodicals from their beginnings, along with selective inclusion of English, French, and German periodicals.

491. **International Dictionary of Architects and Architecture.** Randall Van Vynckt, ed. Detroit: St. James Press, 1993. 2v. ISBN 1-55862-089-3.

This two-volume guide identifies and describes the lives and careers of 525 master architects and provides exposition of 464 major architectural works. Enhancing the work are numerous illustrations, 900 photographs, and 200 floor plans. Volume 1, "Architects," supplies an alphabetical arrangement of major architects dating from ancient Greece to the present. Entries begin with a biographical sketch and listing of the personality's architectural triumphs. An extensive bibliography of books and articles by and about the figure then precedes a detailed critical essay of up to 2,000 words in length, signed by one of the contributor-specialists. Volume 2, "Architecture," presents important architectural projects dating from the Middle Ages to the present. Included in each entry are the architect's name; location, size, and date of the structure; and a signed expository essay on historical, stylistic, and critical aspects. An index of locations is furnished.

492. Macmillan Encyclopedia of Architects. Adolf K. Placzek, ed. New York: Free Press/Macmillan, 1982. 4v. ISBN 0-02-925000-5.

This is a comprehensive biographical dictionary of 2,400 prominent architects from all countries and all time periods who either were born prior to 1931 or are deceased. The biographies were selected by an editorial board and approved by specialists of international stature. In addition to architects, there are engineers, bridge builders, landscape architects, and town planners as well as a few patrons and writers. Criteria imposed upon the biographees were their influence, the importance of their work, and their productivity. Articles generally are of essay length and may be 10,000 words long, although some personalities are covered in less than 100 words. There is also a glossary of terms, as well as indexes of names and of architectural works.

493. Who's Who in Interior Design. Laguna Beach, CA: Barons Who's Who, 1988– . Bienn. ISSN 0897-5914.

This title began with the 1988–1989 edition and has shown promise of becoming a useful source of information on current practitioners. The initial edition contained biographical sketches of 2,300 designers, mostly from the United States. The subsequent issue (1990–1991) on an international perspective, treated 3,300 designers active in sixty-one countries, republics, and principalities. Included were designers in architecture, contract health care, and industry, as well as residential and transportation design. Coverage was continued in this manner with the publication of the 1994–1995 editions in 1994. To accommodate the greater scope, the number of U.S. designers was reduced by some 500 personalities. Coverage was given to 550 Japanese designers, 200 French figures, and somewhat fewer British or Italian subjects. About 10 percent of the entries represented Africa, the Middle East, South America, and inner Asia. Entries are arranged alphabetically and supply the usual directory-type information. Also included is a directory of organizations; a geographical index aids access.

Histories

494. History of World Architecture series. New York: Rizzoli, 1985– .

This is the most recent of the several series to appear that treats the entire history of world architecture. More than fifteen volumes have been issued thus far. Now produced by Rizzoli, the series originated in the 1970s and was published in Italian by Electa of Milan, Italy. The present series has translated these works and, in addition, has incorporated the English-language series of the same name published by Harry N. Abrams, also produced during the 1970s. Rizzoli continues the tradition of its predecessors in selecting architecture of different regions and/or historical periods for individual treatment in the volumes. The Rizzoli efforts cover each major period, beginning with primitive and progressing to modern architecture. Each volume is written by a specialist in the field and presents a narrative history along with bibliography in slender volumes of some 200 pages. Indexes are provided.

495. Sir Banister Fletcher's A History of Architecture. 20th ed. Dan Cruickshank. Boston: Architectural Press, 1996. 1621p. ISBN 0-750-62267-9.

Upon his death in 1953, Fletcher left a trust fund to the Royal Institute of British Architects and the University of London for the revision and updating of his well-illustrated history. First published in 1896, the tool set a standard in the field for its excellent coverage of architectural styles and features of various historical periods. The present edition has continued the trend toward modern awareness of achievement in Eastern and other cultures (Asian, African, Australian, Oceanic, and American) as well as European development from the pre-colonial period to the present. It also has redefined itself by moving away from Fletcher's emphasis on the comparative method in favor of historical interpretation of international styles influenced by societal, cultural, and political factors. The organization is roughly chronological, with several major parts or segments, beginning with ancient Egypt and Greece and concluding with the twentieth century. This continues as an essential reference book for the amount of information it contains, this revision being the product of a distinguished group of contributors from various parts of the world.

SCULPTURE

Bibliographic Guides and Bibliographies

496. **American Sculpture: A Guide to Information Sources.** Janis Ekdahl. Detroit: Gale Research, 1977. 260p. (Art and Architecture Information Guide Series, v. 5). ISBN 0-8103-1271-9.

This is an especially useful resource in view of the lack of bibliographic coverage on the topic of American sculpture. Compiled by a college art librarian with a knowledge of the needs of both students and specialists, the work opens with a general section of research materials covering bibliographies, catalogs, indexes, biographical sources, encyclopedias, dictionaries, and directories. The second section treats the history and aesthetics of American culture in seven chapters, while the final section provides listings of sources for nearly 220 American sculptors. Books, parts of books, periodical articles, and exhibition catalogs are identified and described in terms of their principal features. There are author, title, and subject indexes, and a list of institutions with extensive collections of sculpture in the appendix.

497. **Fifteenth Century Central Italian Sculpture: An Annotated Bibliography.** Sarah Blake Wilk. Boston: G. K. Hall, 1986. 401p. (A Reference Publication in Art History). ISBN 0-8161-8550-6.

One of a series of twenty Renaissance bibliographies, from G. K. Hall, this work provides listings of 2,000 documents. Most entries are annotated and represent excellent bibliographic coverage of Florentine sculpture, with the inclusion of figures such as Donatello, Ghiberti, Brunelleschi, and Luca della Robbia. One section is given to modern scholarship, while others identify early sources and studies of technique and materials. There are surveys of a general nature as well as treatments of specific or specialized topics reported in monographs, and articles in several Western languages. Also included are theses and other unpublished works. Most coverage is given to works on individual sculptors. Unlike its subject matter, the tool is unattractive, with a typescript appearance, but it is a useful vehicle for both students and specialists.

498. **French Romanesque Sculpture: An Annotated Bibliography.** Thomas W. Lyman and Daniel Smartt. Boston: G. K. Hall, 1987. 450p. (Reference Publications in Art History). ISBN 0-8161-8330-9.

This is a comprehensive bibliography intended to capture all material published in books, periodicals, and catalogs on the topic of Romanesque sculpture in France and its earlier possessions, Corsica and Alsace. This artistic period embraces the late tenth century to the early fourteenth century and the work is divided into three major chronological periods of publication: 1700–1900, 1900–1944, and 1945 to the present. Of the 2,173 entries, more than 1,200 were issued in the most recent period, reflecting an increased interest among scholars since World War II. Each segment opens with an introductory essay providing historical perspective in terms of publication and research. There are separate listings for each of the three types of sources; entries are arranged chronologically within their form category. There is an extensive detailed index of authors, reviewers, subjects, places, and names in annotations.

Italian Romanesque Architecture: An Annotated Bibliography, by Dorothy F. Glass, is a 1983 publication in the same series. It contains 1,550 briefly annotated entries representing books and periodical articles based on the holdings of the Biblioteca Hertziana in Rome. Entries are arranged within topical sections identifying specific locales and art forms such as wood sculpture.

Art Work and Reproductions—Catalogs, Etc.

499. **Earth Scale Art: A Bibliography, Directory of Artists, and Index of Reproductions.** Patricia Pate Havlice. Jefferson, NC: McFarland, 1984. 138p. ISBN 0-89950-072-2.

Despite being of diminutive size, this is a most useful bibliography and index to reproductions in its unique coverage of earth-scale art. Sometimes termed earthworks, earth art, or land art, the medium uses the land itself within the context of the art form to produce the finished work. Some of its practitioners have achieved international acclaim or attention, such as Christo, who is one of thirty-two artists treated here. The work opens with a general bibliography of some 100 articles from magazines placing land art in perspective. Next is the major segment supplying entries for artists. These contain birth/death dates, training, awards, films about the artist, list of shows, relevant bibliography, and a listing of reproductions both in color and black-and-white. The final segments contain an author index and a title index to the earthworks.

500. **Renaissance Artists & Antique Sculpture: A Handbook of Sources.** Phyllis Pray Bober and Ruth Rubinstein. New York: Oxford University Press, 1986; repr., 1987, 1991. 522p. ISBN 0-19-921029-2.

This standard tool is now issued as a new impression with the assistance of the J. Paul Getty Trust. It treats over 200 pieces of monumental sculpture, primarily statues and reliefs, executed prior to the Sack of Rome in 1527. Selections are culled from the enormous catalog begun in 1949 under the sponsorship of the Warburg Institute and New York Institute of Fine Arts, *Census of Antique Works of Art Known to Renaissance Artists.* The purpose is to provide documentary evidence of the influence of ancient art works on the work of Renaissance artists. The work is organized into two segments: "Greek and Roman Gods and Myth" and "Roman History and Life." Entries furnish title, description, and history of the various subjects along with the identification of representations, especially drawings from sketchbooks of Renaissance artists. Appendices furnish an index of artists and sketchbooks and an index of Renaissance collectors.

501. **Romanesque Sculpture in American Collections.** Walter Cahn and Linda Seidel. v.1 New England Museums. New York: B. Franklin, 1979. 344p. ISBN 0-89102-131-0. v.2 New York, South Atlantic, Midwest, and West. Walter Cahn et al. Boston: G. K. Hall, 1994. 500p. ISBN 0-8153-0656-3.

When volume 1 was first published in 1979, it was to initiate a series of critical catalogs published under the sponsorship of the International Center of Medieval Art. Articles were based on studies published earlier in *Gesta*, the Center's journal, and revised and updated by specialists in the field. Stone and wood sculpture of monumental nature is treated; selections are excellent and description is well-developed. An illustration is furnished for each work treated. This is an important source for identification of Romanesque sculpture in the eastern United States. The second volume, also edited by Cahn with the assistance of others, did not appear until fifteen years later, in 1994. Like the earlier effort, it furnishes a critical inventory of Romanesque sculpture housed in public collections in the United States. Items are described and analyzed in terms of origin, meaning, and significance. Citations to the literature are supplied in both volumes, along with photographs.

French Sculptors of the 17th and 18th Centuries, the Reign of Louis XIV: Illustrated Catalogue, by Francois Souchal et al. (Oxford University, 1977–1987), was issued as a three-volume catalog in English translation. Entries are arranged alphabetically and treat the artist's life and career, along with a chronologically arranged listing of the individual's work with brief identification. Bibliographic sources are supplied. There is a general index of sites, names, and subjects. In 1993, a supplementary volume 4 was issued by Faber & Faber that served to augment and correct the earlier work.

502. **Sculpture Index.** Jane Clapp. Metuchen, NJ: Scarecrow Press, 1970–1971. 2v. in 3. ISBN 0-8108-0249-X.

This excellent index to pictures of sculpture in 950 publications, although aging, remains a staple in the reference departments of art libraries. Listings are dictionary style under names of artists, titles, and subjects, adding greatly to ease of use. Sources include art histories, collection and exhibition catalogs, and art reference books, and are generally available in public, school, college, and special libraries. Although the emphasis is on modern sculpture after 1900, all periods are represented. The sculpture of Europe and the contemporary Middle East is covered in volume 1, while volume 2 embraces the Americas, the Orient, Africa, the Pacific area, and the classical world. Locations of original sculpture are given, and there is an excellent list of both private and public collections by country and city. Entries include nationality and dates of sculptors, materials, size, museum identification numbers, and references to documents. All types of sculpture are included.

Dictionaries, Encyclopedias, Handbooks

503. **The Encyclopedia of Sculpture Techniques.** John Mills. New York: Watson Guptill, 1990. 239p. ISBN 0-8230-1609-9.

The author is a well-known English sculptor and academic who has utilized his expertise to produce a useful handbook and guide to sculptural techniques and processes. Arrangement of entries is alphabetized, with coverage given to an array of topics and considerations. The text is clear and concise; terms are defined, processes are explained, and instruments are described. Enhancing the articles are some 260 black-and-white illustrations, including photographs and line drawings presenting step-by-step sequences of activity and instructions as well as finished results. There is liberal use of formulas, charts, and diagrams. All aspects of sculpture are treated, with comprehensive coverage of the terminology that embraces both common and obscure terms. Techniques covered represent the traditional and the contemporary as well as experimental and innovative applications. A selective bibliography identifies titles of practical value.

504. **Looking at European Sculpture: A Guide to Technical Terms.**
Jane Bassett and Peggy Fogelman. Los Angeles: J. Paul Getty Museum;
distr., Oxford University Press, 1997. 103p. ISBN 0-89236-291-X.

Of both general interest to museum visitors and particular interest to those visiting
either the J. Paul Getty Museum outside of Los Angeles or the Victoria and Albert Museum in
London is this brief, small dictionary and guide to European architecture. As one would expect,
the definitions are concise and alphabetically arranged. They are selected for their frequency
of use in catalogs and museum labels and for their relevance to the holdings of the two museums,
but are appropriate to the art form as it exists anywhere. About 100 high-quality photographs
of European sculpture, two-thirds color, are documented with name of artist, dates of birth
and death, title, size, and location in either of the two museums. A useful bibliography concludes the effort.

505. **Sculpture in America.** New and rev. ed. Wayne Craven. Newark:
University of Delaware Press; distr., New York: Cornwall Books, 1984.
788p. ISBN 0-87413-225-8.

For many years, the author's name has been familiar to those who work with the
bibliography of art, and this particular effort has been regarded as a solid contribution to the
field since its initial publication in 1968. This edition supplies a new chapter on sculpture of
the 1960s and 1970s, with good treatment of the formalists and the representationalists. The
work provides a fine overview of the relationship between sculpture and the other arts in different art periods in this country. Individual sculptors are treated from colonial times to the
present. Most commendable in the view of critics is the excellent treatment given to the sculpture and sculptors of the nineteenth century because this period generally has been overlooked in the past. The work represents a good blend of scholarship, judgment, and
professional expertise, and has been regarded as a must purchase for libraries.

Biographical Sources

506. **Contemporary American Women Sculptors.** Virginia
Watson-Jones. Phoenix, AZ: Oryx Press, 1986. 664p. ISBN 0-89774-139-1.

A useful reference tool with an emphasis on the contribution of female artists, this
biographical dictionary covers over 300 American sculptors. A quick check reveals good
coverage of those who have earned recognition, such as Louise Nevelson, Nancy Grossman,
and Lee Bontecou. The inclusion of less-prominent personalities represents a real service in
helping to identify our contemporary artists. Much of the information appears for the first
time and was gathered through questionnaires mailed to art historians, museums, and art associations. Each entry provides brief biographical information, professional accomplishments,
and a statement from each artist. There is a black-and-white reproduction of one of each
artist's works.

507. **Dictionary of American Sculptors: 18th Century to the Present.**
Glenn B. Opitz, ed. Poughkeepsie, NY: Apollo Book, 1984. 656p.
0-938290-03-7.

This title covers over 5,000 American sculptors from the eighteenth century to the
present, although emphasis is on nineteenth- and twentieth-century figures. Those working in
this area are aware of the difficulty in finding any detailed commentary on individual sculptors
of this period; therefore, the work fills a real need for documentation of obscure and even
more prominent individuals. There are many living and now deceased personalities who had
submitted data directly. These entries join those for whom data were gathered from sources

such as *American Art Annual* (entry 371n). The work has been criticized for failure to include information subsequent to the 1970s, and a subsequent volume was planned but never carried out.

Histories

508. **A History of Western Sculpture.** John Pope-Hennessy. Greenwich, CT: New York Graphic Society, 1967–1969. 4v.

These four volumes are truly monographic works in their own right and are brought together under the collective title with the aid of a consultant editor. Volume 1, *Classical Sculpture*, is by George M. A. Hanfmann; volume 2, by Robert Salvini, is *Medieval Sculpture.* Herbert Keutner has contributed volume 3, *Sculpture: Renaissance to Rococo*, while volume 4, by Fred Licht, is entitled *Sculpture: 19th and 20th Centuries.* In all volumes, the connection between sculpture and social, political, and economic forces is described and carefully analyzed. Historical lines are traced and developed in a manner that provides insight into the reasons behind creative development in different eras. A good survey of sculpture is furnished through the four volumes, each of which has fine illustrations, a bibliography, and an index.

509. **An Introduction to Italian Sculpture.** 4th ed. John Pope-Hennessy. London: Phaidon Press, 1996. 3v. ISBN 0-714-835-803.

An important work in the field, first published in 1955, this is now in its fourth edition. Titles for the individual volumes have remained unchanged over the years, although succeeding editions have incorporated additional elements, modifications, and corrections when needed. Volume 1 covers Italian Gothic sculpture roughly from Pisano to Ghiberti, while volume 2 treats the Italian Renaissance from Donatello to Tullio Lombardo. Volume 3 describes the High Renaissance and Baroque. Typically, the volumes include introductory chapters on leading sculptors and trends, plates, notes on sculptors, an index of sculptors, and an index of places. Works are treated chronologically in each volume and biographies of artists are included.

Roman Sculpture, by Diane E. E. Kleiner (Yale University, 1993), is one of the few tools to focus exclusively on the sculpture of classical Rome, placing it in the context of cultural development and political and social events. The text is well-developed and informative and is enhanced by black-and-white illustrations of high quality. Organization of chapters is chronological in treating the historical influences. Chapters contain bibliographies; the index follows a glossary of Greek and Roman terms.

PHOTOGRAPHY

Bibliographies and Catalogs

510. **History of Photography: A Bibliography of Books.** Laurent Roosens and Luc Salu. New York: Munsell, 1989–1996. 3v. ISBN 0-7201-2008-X (v1).

This is an enormous project, over thirty years in the making, that provides comprehensive coverage of books issued between 1839 and 1914 and selective coverage of those published from 1915 to the mid-1990s. More than 21,000 books are listed under 3,000 alphabetically arranged subject headings and subheadings in the three volumes. Subject headings treat topics, personalities, and types of publications; citations are arranged chronologically under these subject headings. Photographers in volume 1 are those born prior to 1914, while volume 2 extends the coverage to those born before 1936. Volume 3 brings the coverage to

1950. A dozen languages of the Western world are represented; broad subjects are subdivided by language. Included here are monographs, dissertations, company literature, and exhibition catalogs; juvenile literature is excluded. Entries supply authors/editors/contributors, title and translation, imprint, pagination, number of illustrations in black-and-white and in color, and edition statements. Entries for photographers identify nationality and dates. There is a detailed, comprehensive index of photographers and authors.

511. **Library Catalog of the International Museum of Photography at George Eastman House.** International Museum of Photography. Boston: G. K. Hall, 1982. 4v. ISBN 0-8161-0294-5.

The International Museum of Photography at George Eastman House was created in 1949 as an independent, nonprofit institution under the joint sponsorship of the Eastman Kodak Company and the University of Rochester. It has amassed an enormous research collection of images, films, photographic equipment, and print publications. Included in this four-volume catalog are over 43,000 cards that identify 11,000 monographic titles treating the social, historic, cultural, and aesthetic qualities of photography and cinematography. Included are more than 2,700 rare and unique books. Neither periodical publications nor unpublished manuscripts are included. Volumes 1–2 treat authors and titles while volumes 3–4 identify subjects. All volumes are alphabetically arranged. The work is available from the publisher on sixty-six microfiche as well as four reels of microfilm.

512. **Nineteenth Century Photography: An Annotated Bibliography, 1839–1879.** William Johnson. Boston: G. K. Hall, 1990. 962p. ISBN 0-8161-7958-1.

This is a comprehensive annotated bibliography of an important forty-year period of development and innovation in photography. The author is a well-known researcher in the field who has spent over twenty years studying this topic. The result is a listing of more than 20,000 books and articles in the English language, the most thorough bibliography ever produced on this subject. Obscure photographers and much documentation are revealed for the first time in this effort. Entries are in two sections, the major one covering author or artist. Here, the entries are alphabetically arranged and include biographical information ranging from substantial description in some cases to indication of dates and nationality in others. The other segment treats broad special topics (bibliography, prehistory, history, country, apparatus or equipment, application or usage). Some of these broad topics are subdivided further. An author index completes the work.

513. **Photography and Literature: An International Bibliography of Monographs.** Eric Lambrechts and Luc Salu. New York: Mansell, 1992. 296p. ISBN 0-7201-2113-2.

This is a bibliography unique in its purpose: to study the relationship between photography and literature. Nearly 3,900 titles of books, exhibition catalogs, dissertations, and special issues of magazines in twenty different languages are identified. Books are of various types, from those providing monographic studies of the topic to those that treat photographic work produced by writers of literature, as well as those that furnish portraits of writers by credited photographers. Excluded from coverage are magazine articles, pictorial biographies, fiction, and biblical texts. Entries supply the bibliographic data and indicate language of publication. Arrangement of entries is alphabetical by author or photographer; numerous cross-references are included. Due to its unique approach and its theoretical slant, the work is best utilized by researchers, specialists, and serious students. A broad subject index completes the effort.

514. **Photography and Photographers to 1900: An Annotated Bibliography.** Robert S. Sennett. New York: Garland, 1985. 134p. (Garland Reference Library of the Humanities, no. 594). ISBN 0-8240-8728-3.

This is a useful, selective bibliography for the specialist and the student. Its purpose is to identify early books of merit in the field. The author is an academic librarian who utilizes his expertise in supplying annotated entries of 408 books of international origin. These were thought to be important for their impact, influence, literary quality, or innovative approaches. Arrangement is within four chapters treating technical treatises, theoretical treatises, monographic works on personalities, and photographic surveys. These chapters are further divided by specific subjects. Although the subject matter represents historical coverage, publication dates of entries run to the mid-1980s. Annotations are brief but informative in describing content; English-language editions are identified for foreign titles. There is a general index providing access by authors and subjects.

Collections, Reproductions, and Sales—Catalogs, Etc.

515. **Index to American Photographic Collections: Compiled at the International Museum of Photography at George Eastman House.** 3d enl. ed. Andrew H. Eskind and Greg Drake, eds. Boston: G. K. Hall, 1996. 1058p. ISBN 0-7838-2149-2.

The first edition of this directory and guide was published in 1982, compiled by James McQuaid, who had a longtime professional interest in the indexing of photographic collections and identification of photographers. The enlarged second edition, edited by Eskind and Drake, extended this coverage from 400 to 540 collections open to the public in museums, public and university libraries, art galleries, newspaper and magazine archives, historical societies, and other institutions. The number of photographers increased from about 19,000 to about 20,000 individuals. All previous listings were updated where necessary. The third enlarged edition continues in the same manner, with coverage increased to 582 collections with nearly 67,000 photographs. This large-scale, comprehensive coverage is thought to embrace all photographers who have inspired others to collect their works. Entries for collections include alphabetical listings of photographers as well as name of contact person. Name listings include cross-references, dates, and nationality.

A useful Web resource is *The American Museum of Photography* (wysiwyg://109/ http://www.photographymuseum.com/ [accessed December 1999]), which provides information and selective viewing of collections and exhibits.

516. **The Photographic Art Market: Auction Prices, 1997.** Robert S. Persky, ed. New York: Photographic Arts Center, 1998. 131p. ISBN 1-890488-14-3.

This is a small but informative continuing publication serving as a guide to the sales of important photographs in the large auction houses of Butterfield's, Christie's, Phillips, and Sotheby's. Published at various intervals since its inception in the early 1980s, it has become an annual catalog attesting to the increasing popularity of photography as a collecting medium. Arrangement is alphabetical by names of photographers, under which are listed the titles of photographs. Entries include price, auction house, lot number, physical description, and date of negative or print. Prices for individual prints are listed in a chronological sequence by date of auction. The work is plain in appearance, with listings provided without benefit of illustration. It represents a useful resource item for collectors and dealers.

Holography Market Place: HMP, the Reference Text and Directory of the Holography Industry, edited by Brian Kluepfel and Franz Ross (3d ed., Ross Books, 1991) provides specialized treatment of this recent technology. The work consists of thirteen mostly topical chapters covering the various aspects of holography. The final chapters supply listings of businesses and related elements (distributors, wholesalers, retailers, distributors, personalities, copyright holders, etc.). Businesses are organized by category, and individuals are covered. There is a bibliography and an index.

517. **Photography Books Index: A Subject Guide to Photo Anthologies.** Martha Moss. Metuchen, NJ: Scarecrow Press, 1980. 286p. ISBN 0-8108-1283-5. **Supp.**, 1985. 261p. ISBN 0-8108-1773-X.

This important work identifies and locates thousands of photographs by indexing twenty-two major titles of photography anthologies. The work is organized into three major sections, comprising a listing of photographers alphabetically arranged; a subject listing based on the Sears list of subject headings revealing topical matter contained in the photographs; and a listing of portraits of named individuals identifying children, men, and women alphabetically by name of model or sitter. These entries include dates, photographers, and source of pictures.

Photography Books Index II . . . published in 1985, serves as a supplement to the initial effort and continues the process of identification. The same format is followed in the indexing of an additional twenty-eight titles published between 1955 and 1982. Hundreds of personalities and classic photographs by masters of the camera are revealed along with photographic records of events and developments.

*518. **PhotoNet.** Coral Gables, FL: VMSI/PhotoNet. 1983– .

This online database has been available since 1983 and furnishes information useful to professional photographers, photo agencies, and purchasers. Requests for photographs are entered into the system by subscribers; buyers and sellers interact on the electronic bulletin board. Also included are travel itineraries of photographers, stocking information of photo agencies, a directory of photographers and agencies, professional services from Nikon, airline guides, and newswire services. The world of commercial photography is covered in all phases from equipment to services. General news of interest to the field is provided. Updating is continuous. Internet access is provided at the Web site (http://www.photonet.com/ [accessed April 5, 2000]).

*The Photoletter is a monthly newsletter available online through Newsnet since 1982. It is published by PhotoSources International of Osceola, Wisconsin, and identifies photo needs of magazines as received from editors of U.S. publications. Descriptions, prices, deadlines, and contacts are specified for photographers to market their wares. **Photomarket* (1984–) also comes from the same publisher and similarly identifies the types of photographs needed by middle-range magazine and book publishers. Both databases are updated biweekly.

Dictionaries, Encyclopedias, Handbooks, Etc.

519. **International Center of Photography/Encyclopedia of Photography.** William L. Broecker, ed. New York: Crown, 1984. 607p. ISBN 0-517-55271-X.

Designed for a more advanced and sophisticated audience, this encyclopedia contains 1,300 entries providing technical awareness, biographical coverage, and aesthetic understanding. Many cross-references appear in the entries and there are numerous illustrations to augment the exposition provided. Biographies cover prominent individuals over a 100-year period from 1840 to 1940 and are illustrated with examples of the biographees' work. Trends in the field are identified and described, and a bibliography is furnished.

520. International Guide to Nineteenth-Century Photographers and Their Works: Based on Catalogues of Auction Houses and Dealers. Gary Edwards. Boston: G. K. Hall, 1988. 591p. ISBN 0-8161-8938-2.

This is a unique and valuable information source for identifying photographers and their works from the historical past. Edwards' intent is to emphasize the finding of basic information on obscure photographers rather than obscure information on famous or well-known photographers. As a result the work is functional in two ways: it serves as both a catalog of auction sales and a directory of some 4,000 photographers, both obscure and well-known. It opens with a listing of the fifty auction catalogs that provide the source material, along with indication of auction dates. The main body of the work then places entries for all photographers in alphabetical order. Entries supply nationality, dates, principal subject matter, date of activity (earliest to latest known photographs), processes and formats (portraits, genre, etc.), geographical range for topographic and documentary photographers, and locations of photographs in sales catalogs.

521. Looking at Photographs: A Guide to Technical Terms. Gordon Baldwin. Malibu, CA: J. Paul Getty Museum with British Museum Press, 1991. 88p. ISBN 0-89236-192-1.

This slender volume, produced by the Getty Museum in cooperation with the British Museum Press, is designed to provide an up-to-date wordbook for specialists, scholars, students, and collectors. All technical terms of some magnitude are included in what amounts to a surprising amount of information, considering the diminutive size of the work. All important details concerning the words are treated, with coverage in most cases ranging from one to three paragraphs in length. Arrangement of entries is alphabetical; some of the technical terms are not included in other, more general photography information sources. Entries are enhanced in many cases with illustrations designed to clarify the topic being treated. Alternative terms are identified for the various processes, and cross-references are noted within the entries.

522. Photographers: A Sourcebook for Historical Research. Richard Rudisill et al.; Peter E. Palmquist, ed. Brownsville, CA: Carl Mautz Publishing, 1991. 103p. ISBN 0-96219-402-6.

Due to the increased interest in historical figures and their work in photography, Palmquist, a well-known scholar in the field, has created a manual for historical research. There are two major sections, with the first consisting of six essays on research and writing of regional history, each by a different specialist. The second segment presents a briefly annotated listing of directories of photographers developed by Rudisill, a curator of a photographic history collection in New Mexico. Arrangement is geographic by country, region, or state. Rudisill has contributed one essay of the six in the first section, describing his ruminations related to the compilation of his bibliography of directories. Another of the essays is written by Palmquist, a personal narrative researching California photographers and regionalism in practice. Methods and techniques are further explained by writers of the other essays. There is an index of authors.

523. The Photographer's Bible: An Encyclopedic Reference Manual. Bruce Pinkard. New York: Arco, 1983. 352p. ISBN 0-668-05851-5.

Since its publication, this encyclopedia authored by a British photographer has been used frequently by a wide range of users who appreciate its concise yet informative entries. Arrangement of articles is alphabetical, with coverage given to all aspects of photography, mechanics, techniques, hardware such as cameras and filters, aesthetics, and personalities. Entries vary in length from a single-line definition to a four-page exposition of the exact procedures in utilizing a process. Cross-references are included within entries as are suggested readings. The work is well-illustrated with 100 diagrams, 260 black-and-white photographs, and an eight-page color section. Charts and tables provide quick access to pertinent data. There is an extensive appendix supplying listings of personalities, organizations, sources of equipment and film, galleries, periodicals, and more. Both British and U.S. units are treated.

524. **Price Guide to Antique and Classic Cameras, 1997–1998.** 10th ed. James M. McKeown and Joan C. McKeown, eds. Grantsburg, WI: Centennial Photo Service, 1996. 608p. ISBN 0-931-83829-0.

The tenth edition of this guide to appear in the last twenty-six years remains an excellent source of information on the specialized interest of antique cameras. One of several guides in this field, it affords a useful and convenient source of information on a subject that has received increased attention on the part of collectors. Arranged alphabetically by manufacturer and chronologically within that category, both still and motion picture cameras are treated separately. Several thousand cameras from all over the world and all periods of time are listed, making it a useful source for identification. It is illustrated with more than 2,000 black-and-white photographs. Each entry provides valuation and brief description (including dates and history whenever possible) and is accessed through a detailed index. Photographic accessories and novelties are included as well.

Biographical Sources

525. **American Photographers: An Illustrated Who's Who Among Leading Contemporary Americans.** Les Krantz, ed. New York: Facts on File, 1989. 352p. ISBN 0-8160-1419-1.

This is a comprehensive and attractive biographical dictionary treating more than 1,000 living photographers representing all areas of the field. Information on the well-known personalities appears to have been culled from standard reference books; others have supplied much of their data through mail questionnaires. Treated in this volume are some of the most prominent names in fashion and advertising media as well as prize-winning photojournalists; the majority of entries, however, represent little-known commercial photographers who at times have contributed what might be called exaggerated descriptions of their competencies. Entries furnish brief mention of type of work, address, telephone number, situations, awards, and education. Personalities have at least five years' experience and are expected to have had their work reproduced in at least five media in 1988. Whether this standard is enforced or not is difficult to judge.

526. **Contemporary Photographers.** Martin M. Evans, ed. Detroit: St. James Press, 1995. 1145p. ISBN 1-55862-190-3.

The current edition of this useful biographical dictionary has added 140 new entries while deleting the names of photographers who died before 1975. Thorough treatment is given to around 750 prominent photographers, either living or recently deceased. This work provides a distinctive and useful source on what is generally elusive information. Planned as a quinquennial publication, the second was issued in 1988, six years after the initial effort (1982), while the third edition appeared seven years later. It covers photographers from all over the world, including a good representation of those from Eastern Europe and the former Soviet Union. Selection was determined by an advisory board composed of distinguished authorities. Entries provide the usual biographical information as well as listings of exhibitions, group expositions, galleries, and museums that display the subjects' work, and a bibliography of books and articles by and about them. A distinctive feature is the critical essay on the style and quality of the photographers' work as well as statements from the artists themselves.

*527. **Encyclopedie internationale des photographs de 1839 a nos jours = Photographers Encyclopedia International 1839 to the Present.** Michele Auer and Michael Auer. Hermance, Switzerland: Editions Camera Obscura, 1985. 2v. ISBN 2-903671-04-4.

This bilingual biographical dictionary represents a Herculean effort on the part of the authors to identify and describe the life and work of some 1,600 photographers over a period of 145 years. The great value of the work lies in its excellent coverage of contemporary photographers and the nature of their work because, in most cases, only the well-known early photographers are treated. Information was obtained through actual visits with 600 of the personalities as well as contact with agencies and use of published sources. All entries receive a full page of coverage, opening with a biographical sketch in both English and French accompanied by photographs of the artists and reproductions of their signatures along with listings of exhibitions, collections displaying their work, and a bibliography. There is also an illustration of each person's craft. There is a list of abbreviations and a chronology, along with indexes of photographers by country and by other names. A CD-ROM version was later issued, for which the Auers created a print index in 1992.

528. **Macmillan Biographical Encyclopedia of Photographic Artists and Innovators.** Turner Browne, ed. New York: Macmillan, 1983. 722p. ISBN 0-02-517500-9.

An extensive biographical dictionary of 2,000 photographers and photographic artists, this volume includes individuals both living and dead. The major photographers are covered, of course, but more important is the utility of the tool in identifying individuals who are less prominent and relatively difficult to find. About 25 percent of the personalities date from the nineteenth and early twentieth centuries, and selection for inclusion is generally based on contribution to the field. Coverage is international and those included have generally had works shown, have published, or have received awards. There are nearly 150 reproductions of representative works and separate listings of museums and galleries. This is a valuable resource because of the number of individuals covered.

529. **World Photographers Reference** series. Anne Hammond and Amy Rule, eds. Boston: G. K. Hall, 1992– . ISBN 0-8161-0577-4 (v.1).

This is an important new series of volumes, each of which treats an individual photographer in a standard format running about 200 pages. Volumes supply a brief chronology of the photographer's life and work and a biocritical essay. Also included are a listing of texts written by and about the artist, an annotated critical bibliography or bibliographic essay utilizing both primary and secondary sources, and a selection of twenty-five to thirty reproductions illustrating the nature of the subject's art. The volumes are beautifully illustrated and combine the appeal of "coffee table items" with good scholarship. The general editors are professionals in the field and have assisted the authors in producing useful works. Ms. Hammond authored the first volume in the series, on Frederick H. Evans; subsequent volumes have treated Imogen Cunningham, Henry Fox Talbot, Carleton Watkins, Bill Brandt, and James Craig Annan.

APPLIED DESIGN, CRAFTS, AND DECORATIVE ARTS

General

BIBLIOGRAPHIC GUIDES, BIBLIOGRAPHIES, AND INDEXES

530. **American Decorative Arts and Old World Influences: A Guide to Information Sources.** David M. Sokol. Detroit: Gale Research, 1980. 294p. (Art and Architecture Information Guide Series, v. 14; Gale Information Guide Library). ISBN 0-8103-1465-7.

Like others in this Gale series, this is a well-developed and carefully constructed, selective bibliography on the topic. That the subject is the decorative arts makes the work highly desirable for libraries because the area has not been well-documented in the past. More than 1,300 published works are organized within eleven topical and format chapters. The first two chapters treat bibliographies and general reference books, followed by three chapters surveying time periods and geographic regions. Six chapters deal directly with the decorative arts, beginning with a general overview and progressing through the specialized treatment of ceramics, furniture, glass, metalwork, and textiles. Entries represent books and articles, with good coverage of exhibition catalogs. Concluding the effort are three separate indexes providing access by author, title, and subject.

531. **American Graphic Design: A Guide to the Literature.** Ellen Mazur Thompson, comp. Westport, CT: Greenwood, 1992. 282p. (Art Reference Collection, no. 15). ISBN 0-313-28728-7.

This is a unique effort developed by a specialist-librarian in cooperation with the American Institute of Graphic Arts. It furnishes an annotated listing of 1,100 publications relevant to the field of graphic art and commercial design in this country. All types of publications are included: reference books, textbooks, manuals, sourcebooks, catalogs, periodical articles, films, and online databases. Materials are placed within eighteen sections, beginning with one on general reference sources. Following are topical sections dealing with subjects such as design education, computer technology, visual resources, advertising, color, comics, and photography. Excluded are the book arts, cartography, and commercial printing. Each section treats various types of materials (reference sources, online databases, etc.) useful to the topic, with cross-references to separate listings of some 200 annuals and serials in the appendix. Also included is a directory of associations and organizations.

532. **Applied and Decorative Arts: A Bibliographic Guide.** 2d ed. Donald L. Ehresmann. Englewood, CO: Libraries Unlimited, 1993. 629p. ISBN 0-87287-906-2.

A companion volume to the author's other publications on the fine arts (entry 309) and architecture (entry 461), this is a useful and needed literature guide in the broad field of the decorative arts. The new edition doubles the number of entries of the previous issue (1977) and triples the number of pages. Basically, it is a classified and annotated bibliography of 2,482 books in the Western languages published between 1875 and 1991. It embraces the various fields in twenty separate chapters, beginning with a general section on applied and decorative arts, followed by ornaments, folk art, arms and armor, ceramics, clocks and watches, costumes, enamels, furniture, glass, ivory, jewelry, lacquer, leather and bookbinding, medals and seals, metalwork, musical instruments, textiles, toys and dolls, and wallpaper.

Excluded are drawing, graphic arts, and mosaic, because they are considered adjuncts to the fine arts. There are author and subject indexes.

533. **Decorative Arts and Household Furnishings in America, 1650–1920: An Annotated Bibliography.** Kenneth L. Ames and Gerald W. R. Ward, eds. Winterthur, DE: Henny Francis du Pont Winterthur Museum; distr., Charlottesville: University Press of Virginia, 1989. 392p. ISBN 0-912724-19-6.

This useful bibliographic guide covers a period of 270 years of involvement with the decorative arts in this country and represents the efforts of twenty-two specialist-contributors. It opens with an excellent introductory essay linking the decorative arts to cultural history and discussing the nature of interdisciplinary research in the area. There are nine major sections, each beginning with an introductory essay, covering domestic architecture, furniture, metals, ceramics, glass, textiles, time pieces, household systems, and finally, artisans and culture. The Arts and Crafts Movement in this country is well covered. There are twenty-one individual bibliographies within these segments, each beginning with an introduction and furnishing well-constructed, descriptive annotations of useful and important books and articles published to the mid-1980s. Research needs are identified within the essays. The work is indexed by author and title.

*534. **Design & Applied Arts Index.** Burwash, UK: Design Documentation, 1988– . Semiann. with trienn. cum. ISSN 0953-0681.

Beginning with the 1987 publication year, this work indexes nearly 100 periodicals from the fields of design and the applied arts to fully cover related design elements and issues within the areas of art, engineering, and technology. Entries are arranged in a single alphabetical sequence incorporating both broad and specific topics along with names of personalities. Documentation is thorough and includes articles, news reports, conference reports, reviews of books and exhibitions, obituaries, and illustrations. Entries are selected for inclusion based on their treatment of current topics of interest and/or research value. Because of its interdisciplinary and thorough nature, as well as its international scope, this work shows great promise in achieving recognition as an important indexing source in the field. Computerized access was provided in 1994 with the availability of the entire file on CD-ROM; it is continued on a quarterly basis.

A good resource is available from the Frances Loeb Library at the Graduate School of Design at Harvard University (http://www.gsd.harvard.edu/library/ [accessed December 1999]), providing research guides to design-related subjects and useful links to Internet resources.

DICTIONARIES, ENCYCLOPEDIAS, HANDBOOKS, ETC.

535. **The Arco Encyclopedia of Crafts.** H. E. Laye Andrew. New York: Arco, 1982. 432p.

As one might expect, a variety of information is included in this work, and coverage ranges over a wide spectrum of craftwork from the very traditional to the very new. Emphasis is on techniques employed in the crafts rather than on specific projects. There are more than 120 crafts enumerated, with 850 illustrations to enhance the text. Historical information is given for a number of crafts described. There are many useful charts and diagrams included in the appendices that facilitate the successful completion of projects such as conversion charts and diagrams (metric) and color charts. There are lists of suppliers, craft associations, and museums organized by countries.

536. **Design on File.** The Diagram Group. New York: Facts on File, 1984. 320 leaves. ISBN 0-87196-270-5.

As part of the publisher's On File series, in this book about 275 designs are presented in looseleaf format and individually treated. The leaves are of heavy paper stock and suitable for reproduction by students at the high school or college level. Permission to reproduce the designs is granted to purchasers of the work involved in educational or nonprofit activity. Entries are organized under nine design categories: geometry, patterns, projections, diagrams, scales, maps, planning, lettering, and human forms. Like others in the series, this work provides excellent background source material for instructional purposes; it would be especially useful for studying the concept of design in the arts and applied arts as well as mathematics or science. Lost or worn-out leaves can be replaced at small cost, an important consideration for library purchase. A general index aids access.

537. **Dictionary of 20th-Century Design.** John Pile. New York: Facts on File, 1990. 312p. (A Roundtable Press Book). ISBN 0-8160-1811-1. Repr., Da Capo Press, 1994. ISBN 0-3068-0569-3.

This is a broad-based, comprehensive information source by an academic and specialist in the field who has defined design as that which determines the form of a functional object. Thus, information related to shape, size, color, texture, and pattern of a variety of objects is provided (furniture, tableware, glass, silver, graphics, etc.) as these features relate to interiors or industrial design on an international level. There are more than 1,000 entries, all alphabetically arranged for easy access. Styles, periods, movements, firms, individuals (critics, designers, writers, and instructors), journals, schools, museums, and dealers as well as technical terms all are presented. Entries vary in length but tend to be brief (60–100 words). Illustrations in black-and-white accompany a number of the articles. A bibliography of frequently used sources and a detailed index conclude the work.

A recent effort devoted to a single style of ornamentation is *Art Deco Style*, by Bevis Hillier and Stephen Escritt (Phaidon, 1998). It provides informed description of the energetic 1920s and 1930s and the emergence and development of this distinctive application in both the fine arts and mechanical arts. Excellent illustrations are mostly color and serve to point out the nuances and attributes of this enormously popular design. The work contains biographical descriptions of leading personalities and concludes with a good bibliography.

538. **The Dodge Collection of Eighteenth-Century French and English Art in the Detroit Institute of Arts.** Alan P. Darr. New York: Hudson Hills Press/Detroit Institute of Arts, 1996. 272p. ISBN 1-55595-135-X.

This may be thought of as a catalog of sixty-eight of the most important items in the decorative arts section of the at the Institute and contains examples of furniture, painting, ceramics, metalwork, and so forth. Each item is illustrated with an excellent color photograph and is described in appropriate essays. A biographical sketch is furnished for each artist. The Dodge Collection was created through the philanthropy of the Dodge family (Horace Dodge's widow, Anna Thomson Dodge), who had acquired a fortune in the automobile industry. Mrs. Dodge had collected French decorative arts over a fifty-year period when decorating her homes and had accumulated one of the leading collections of its kind in the country. The book includes brief descriptive entries, some illustrated, of other objects that have been added to the collection.

539. **The Encyclopedia of Crafts.** Laura Torbet, ed. New York: Scribner's, 1980. 3v. ISBN 0-684-16409-4.

This is a detailed and comprehensive encyclopedia that provides in-depth information on about fifty different crafts. There are approximately 12,000 entries for specific terms associated with these crafts. Designed as a basic tool for the craftsperson as well as the fledgling operative, coverage is given to such activities as basketry, mosaics, block printing, fabric printing, jewelry, ceramics, stained glass, metalworking, and batik. Articles vary in length from a short paragraph to several pages. Many cross-references are provided, with indication given in boldface type within an article to a routine that has its own entry. Considered an excellent source book, the arrangement is alphabetical, and 2,500 illustrations are furnished. There is no index.

540. **Encyclopedia of Design.** New York: Hart, 1983. 399p. ISBN 0-8055-1276-4.

Artists and craftsmen who need designs of various kinds benefit from this title, which provides over 4,000 illustrations from different cultures throughout the world. The illustrations appear in the twenty-nine chapters devoted to various cultures of the world such as Assyrian, Celtic, Chinese, and Coptic. Most important is the fact that the pictures belong in the public domain and are freely available for reproduction without seeking permission or paying fees. Chapters vary considerably in depth of coverage and range from two to ten pages in length. Numerous designs are furnished in different media, including pottery, masks, tapestry, furniture, and stained glass. There is a bibliography of source material with precise references given.

541. **Graphic Arts Encyclopedia.** 3d ed. George A. Stevenson; rev. by William A. Pakan. New York: Design Press, 1992. 582p. ISBN 0-8306-2530-5.

The third edition has been increased by about 100 pages and represents an augmented and updated effort of the previous issue published in 1979. It remains an excellent source of information, supplying comprehensive coverage of the graphic arts. Arrangement is alphabetical and entries vary in length from brief identifications to essays. Terminology, technical applications, equipment, and processes embrace a variety of activities such as copy preparation, art reproduction, copying, and printing. The coverage of equipment is brought up-to-date with treatment given to electronic and computer applications as well as traditional processes. Machinery covered includes word processors, keyboard equipment, video display terminals, typesetters, printing presses, microfilm equipment, process cameras, and color copiers. The writing is clear and free of technical jargon and the definitions are still accompanied by a number of black-and-white illustrations. There are numerous tables and charts, but no index.

542. **Graphics, Design, and Printing Terms: An International Dictionary.** Ken Garland. New York: Design Press, 1990. 248p. ISBN 0-8306-3448-7.

This is an up-to-date and handy wordbook, needed in the world of graphic arts with the recent emergence of new technology in the field. Covered here are the terms utilized in such important developments as desktop publishing, computer graphics, and photocomposition. Some 2,800 terms are covered relating to typography, advertising, printing, computers, publishing, photography, and film. Older terms have been updated where necessary and technical terms are defined in a lucid manner. Important is the inclusion of slang expressions, abbreviations, and acronyms recently employed. Also included in many of the entries are charts and diagrams (over 300 in number) to illustrate features and numerous cross-references to related terms. Both British and American usage are clearly indicated by Garland, an Englishman with work experience in the United Kingdom.

543. **The Oxford Companion to the Decorative Arts.** Harold Osborne, ed. New York: Oxford University Press, 1975; repr., 1985. 880p. ISBN 0-19-281863-5 (pbk.).

Basically a reprint of the earlier edition, which was well received by librarians as another useful source of information in the Oxford Companion series, this new edition provides a bibliography on the final page for the article on decorative papers. The decorative arts as a study embraces those fields and crafts not covered in the *Oxford Companion to Art* (entry 367) and may be defined as "creations that are valued primarily for their workmanship and beauty of appearance." These include leather working, ceramics, furniture, jewelry, costume, glass-making, landscape gardening, clock-making, enamels, lacquer, toys, lace, embroidery, and so forth. Entries vary in length from brief to survey-type, and articles are unsigned. The emphasis is on Western arts, with the countries of the East and Eastern Europe receiving less coverage.

544. **The Penguin Dictionary of Decorative Arts.** John Fleming and Hugh Honour. New York: Viking, 1989. 935p. ISBN 0-67-082047-4.

This is another edition of the well-known and popular resource tool, long recognized as a useful and comprehensive source of information. The authors are well known in the field of art history, have published extensively in the past, and furnish impeccable authority for a work of this kind. The emphasis is on furniture and accessories found in both European and American homes past and present. There are about 5,000 entries (including increased coverage of new movements and designers) that supply definitions, expositions, and descriptions of materials, techniques, manufacturers, and individual personalities associated with the decorative arts; cross-references are provided. Bibliographies are furnished for most entries that enable the user to pursue additional readings on the subject. The work is well-illustrated with the addition of sixty-seven color plates along with the hundreds of black-and-white pictures from the previous edition.

545. **The Poster: A Worldwide Survey and History.** Alain Weill. Boston: G. K. Hall, 1985. 422p. ISBN 0-8161-8746-0.

Bringing a great deal of expertise to the subject from his career as head of Collection at Louvre's Museum of Decorative Arts, and presently a consultant on the topic, Weill provides an informative and substantial history of posters from 1469 to the 1980s. Developments are explained and landmark events described in a clear and revealing style. Personalities are identified in a separate section and a bibliography is furnished. Coverage is chronological by country and is enhanced by over 650 illustrations, with 300 in color. With the increased interest in posters, as indicated by the number of sales and prices paid, this is a timely and useful tool for collectors, illustrators, and students.

546. **The Thames and Hudson Encyclopaedia of Graphic Design and Designers.** Alan Livingston and Isabella Livingston. New York: Thames & Hudson, 1992. 215p. (World of Art). Repr., 1998. ISBN 0-500-20259-1.

Another volume in the publisher's World of Art series, this, like the others, is for the most part clearly written and informative. The danger of presenting an encyclopedic work on such an extensive topic is apparent, however, and results in a product that functions in part as a catalog, in part as a directory, and also as a dictionary and fact book. Included here are biographies of important personalities; definitions of various technical processes; and descriptions and identifications of journals, magazines, and design organizations. Information tends to be brief, with broad coverage of historical developments treated within a European emphasis and perspective. The tool has been criticized as being too limited in its treatment of certain major elements, such as typology. Special features include a chronology covering the development of graphic design from 1840 to the present and a color section. The current issue is a reprint with revisions of the 1992 publication.

547. **Twentieth Century Design.** Jonathan M. Woodham. New York: Oxford University Press, 1997. 288p. ISBN (Oxford History of Art series). ISBN 0-19-284204-8.

This work is organized into ten chapters, each examining a design component (modernism, consumerism, reconstruction after World War II, nostalgia, etc.). It appears to be successful in its purpose to present an illustrated survey of modern design in both the Western and Eastern worlds. Some sixty-five color plates help to explain the attributes and design features of a varied array of objects, including the Coca-Cola bottle and the McDonald's logo, as representative of an industrialized culture in which taste and public consumption are intertwined.

The author's *Twentieth Century Ornament* (Rizzoli, 1990) is a chronological examination of the major trends in ornamentation from 1900 to the time of publication. The text is clear and points of comparison are developed in an interesting and sometimes provocative manner. All major trends that occurred in both North American and European styles are treated with over 400 illustrations, 200 in color, utilized in the description. A brief bibliography and adequate index complete the work.

DIRECTORIES AND ANNUALS

548. **Artist's Market: Where and How to Publish Your Graphic Arts.** Susan Conner, ed. Cincinnati: Writer's Digest Books, 1975– . Ann. ISSN 0161-0546.

Another of the Writer's Digest publications that has become standard fare for those seeking to market their wares is this annual guide, intended primarily for those in the graphic arts. Each issue supplies several thousand entries identifying relevant purchasers; these are arranged under one of fourteen types of markets, such as advertising, audiovisual and public relations firms, art/design studios, magazines, and book publishers. Prefatory notes are given for each section. Each year there are several hundred new listings and previous entries are updated, making these efforts timely and representative of the current market. Entries generally supply address, telephone number, contact person, brief description, and type of client along with an indication of needs, terms of contract, and contact person. "Tips" are sometimes included. Illustrations are sometimes furnished as examples of desired products. A glossary and general index are furnished.

549. **The Crafts Supply Sourcebook: The Comprehensive Shop-By-Mail Guide for Thousands of Craft Materials.** 5th ed. Margaret A. Boyd. Cincinnati: Betterway Books, 1999. 304p. ISBN 1-55870-506-6.

Using the same format as its predecessors in 1989, 1992, and 1996, the fifth edition continues to provide directory listings of more than 2,500 merchants and suppliers of materials and equipment. Because many of these craft dealers are small suppliers, there is less longevity than would be true of other segments of the manufacturing and trade industries; the new edition is needed to provide up-to-date listings. The work is divided into three major sections, the first of which covers the general arts, crafts, and hobbies (stained glass, jewelry making, photography, cake decorating, Native American crafts, etc.). The second section treats needlecrafts, including batik, costume, and weaving. All entries receive the usual directory treatment of address, telephone number, and so forth, along with description of supplies available. The final section covers resources and identifies aids, publications, and associations.

A useful source of purchasing information is *Graphic Design Materials and Equipment*, by Jonathan Stevenson (London: Studio Vista/Cassell, 1987). This slender volume of 192 pages provides a comprehensive listing of suppliers, distributors, manufacturers, and sellers of all types of equipment and supplies needed by graphic artists, photographers, and printers. A more recent publication is *Directory to Industrial Design in the United States . . .* , by Charles Burnette (Van Nostrand Reinhold, 1992). It provides listings for independent consulting firms, corporate design departments, schools with degree programs, institutions, organizations, and publications in the field.

550. The Guide to Arts & Crafts Workshops. Coral Gables, FL: Shaw Associates, 1990. 253p. ISBN 0-945834-05-5.

This is a well-designed guide and directory to instructional offerings for those interested in the creation and sale of fine and decorative arts. Coverage is comprehensive for short-term programs held throughout the world and treating all types of media. Arrangement is alphabetical using the title of the sponsoring agency, and entries list seminars, workshops, retreats, and residencies for artists, near artists, and aficionados. Media covered include painting, drawing, sculpture, and crafts of all kinds (fiber, metal, wood, glass, ceramics, and gems). Entries supply descriptive information on the program, faculty, costs, accommodations, and locations. Student-teacher ratios are enumerated in the style of college directories. Indexing is excellent, with access furnished by a detailed general index as well as specialty and geographical indexes. In addition, there is a listing of workshops for youngsters.

BIOGRAPHICAL SOURCES

551. Contemporary Designers. 3d ed. Sara Pendergast, ed. Detroit: St. James Press, 1997. 981p. ISBN 1-55862-184-9.

The first edition of this work was issued in 1984 and provided information on the lives and careers of 600 contemporary figures in the world of design. The second edition treated about the same number of individuals, having deleted some and added others. The third edition represents a major advance, with the inclusion of 685 designers, 85 of whom have just been added. Previous entries have been updated and in many cases expanded to reflect recent activities and accomplishments. Coverage is international and includes important personalities for the many and varied fields of design (architecture, interiors, display, textiles, fashion, film, stage, costume, industry, etc.). A panel of international specialists have recommended the personalities as major figures; numerous critics, historians, and designers have contributed articles. Entries furnish a detailed biography, listings of major design works, bibliography of publications by and about the personality, and a critical-evaluative essay. Comments from the designer are included. The work is well-illustrated in black-and-white, with examples of art work.

552. Contemporary Graphic Artists: A Biographical, Bibliographical, and Critical Guide to Current Illustrators, Animators, Cartoonists, Designers, and Other Graphic Artists. Maurice Horn, ed. Detroit: Gale Research, 1986–1988. 3v. ISSN 0885-8462.

Developed on a plan similar to that of *Contemporary Authors* (entry 1083), the important serial biography by the same publisher, this title was initially projected as a semi-annual publication but became a short-lived annual instead. Prior to its termination, three volumes had been issued. Each provides bio-critical coverage in the Gale Research manner for about 100 graphic designers, editorial and magazine cartoonists, book illustrators, animators, and comic strip artists. Arrangement is alphabetical by name. There appears to be an emphasis on cartoonists, which was justified because biographical information on cartoonists is, at best, difficult to find. The definition of "contemporary" is broad; several of the artists are nineteenth-century figures. Biographies are brief but informative and the bibliographical references are good. There is no index for the volumes.

553. **The Facts on File Dictionary of Design and Designers.** Simon Jervis. New York: Facts on File, 1984. 533p. ISBN 0-87196-891-6.

This dictionary has been recognized as a fine reference tool on design and has earned the respect of those who work in the field of art reference. It is useful in its treatment of personalities, providing biographies of designers, patrons, and historians from the mid-fifteenth century to the present, and is important for its coverage of obscure individuals as well as prominent ones. Biographies are brief and provide dates, place of birth, training, and influences upon the personalities as well as their achievements. The terminology of design and designing is also covered, with entries given to the various types, such as ceramics, furniture, glass, interior decoration, and metalwork. Generally the emphasis is on the styles and techniques of Europe and North America. Many cross-references are provided in the entries.

554. **Folk Artists Biographical Index: A Guide to Over 200 Published Sources of Information on Approximately 9,000 Folk Artists.** George H. Meyer et al., eds. Detroit: Gale Research, 1987. 496p. ISBN 0-8103-2145-9.

The editor is Director of the Museum of American Folk Art and brings his expertise to bear in creating this comprehensive index to information on over 9,000 folk artists found in over 200 biographical dictionaries and collective works. It is of substantial benefit to librarians, as biographies of folk artists tend to be elusive and difficult to locate. As one might expect, the variety of media represented in the folk arts is great and covers such activity as sculpture, furniture making, carving, weaving, pottery making, and quilting, and such products as samplers, coverlets, decoys, and canes. Individuals are listed alphabetically and entries include birth and death dates, type of work, period, and citations for source materials. The work provides excellent access through the indexes of museums in which the artists' works are displayed, ethnic origin, medium, and type of work.

555. **Museum of American Folk Art Encyclopedia of Twentieth-Century American Folk Art and Artists.** Chuck Rosenak and Jan Rosenak. New York: Abbeville Press, 1990. 416p. ISBN 1-55859-041-2.

The authors are serious collectors and enthusiasts who have traveled widely in this country to cultivate their collection and enrich their knowledge. Folk art as the expression of the feelings of common people, largely unschooled, embraces a wide range of media and applications, including painting and sculpture as well as pottery and other decorative arts. This work treats the lives and art work of 257 contemporary folk artists who have been identified by the Rosenaks. Most of the artists were interviewed and photographed by the authors, resulting in a rich and full treatment. Several well-known specialists have contributed segments. Entries treat biographical data, general background, artistic background, subjects and sources, media and processes, as well as recognition and popularity. Individuals vary from the famous to the lesser known. Appendices list major exhibitions from 1924 to 1990, and there are a bibliography and detailed general index.

Information regarding the Museum, its programs, exhibits, and schedules as well as numerous links can be found at *Museum of American Folk Art Online* (Note: This Web site was undergoing change at time of access [December 1999]).

Furniture and Woodcraft

BIBLIOGRAPHIES, INDEXES, AND ABSTRACTS

556. **American Furniture Craftsmen Working Prior to 1920: An Annotated Bibliography.** Charles J. Semowich, comp. Westport, CT: Greenwood, 1984. 381p. (Art Reference Collection, no. 7). ISBN 0-313-23275-X.

This is a comprehensive annotated bibliography of value to a variety of users from specialists and researchers to dealers and the general public. More than 2,000 entries are supplied representing secondary sources treating furniture craftsmen in the early years. Biographical coverage, critical interpretation, and exposition are presented. The work is divided into four major sections, with the first segment identifying titles dealing with the lives and work of individual craftsmen and the second section citing those that cover groups of furniture makers. The third part supplies reference works of general nature, while the fourth lists furniture trade catalogs. Annotations vary in length and quality, with some being too brief. The appendix contains a listing of trade publications from 1880 to 1930 and one of manuscript archives. Indexes furnish access by author-title, subject, and name of craftsman.

DICTIONARIES, ENCYCLOPEDIAS, HANDBOOKS, ETC.

557. **American Furniture, 1620 to the Present.** Elizabeth Bidwell Bates and Jonathan L. Fairbanks. New York: Richard Marek/Putnam, 1981. 561p. ISBN 0-399-90096-9.

An extraordinary reference work providing comprehensive coverage of the development of American furniture styles from the colonial period to the present day. Furniture is treated chapter-by-chapter in different periods, which are illustrated with reproductions of both paintings and photographs. About 1,400 reproductions (100 in color) show the pieces in their museum setting, and diagrams are provided of the structure of the furniture. Informative commentary helps the reader understand the place of the furniture within the social and historical context. Fairbanks is curator of American decorative arts at the Boston Museum of Fine Arts, and together with Bates brings expertise and authority to the topic. Included also are a glossary of cabinetry terms, a bibliography, and an index.

558. **The Antiques Directory of Furniture.** Rev. ed. Judith Miller and Martin Miller, eds. Boston: G. K. Hall, 1995. 639p. ISBN 0-5171-4118-3.

This standard in the field maintains the quality and informative content of its predecessor published ten years earlier. Furniture from all over the world is treated, with some 7,000 items dating from the sixteenth century on. Hundreds of photographs, many in full color, help to illustrate the differences in style and appearance. Intended as a guidebook for those who seek profit or collect in the field, the work accommodates the needs of its intended audience in a country-by-country arrangement, subdivided by form or type (tables, chairs, etc.). As with most guidebooks, the commentary at the beginning of each section is brief and serves only to introduce the reader to the furniture of a particular country. Pictures are described in terms of styles, dates, sizes of objects, and periods represented. The emphasis is on British furniture. There is a useful outline chronology of developments by country from 1450 to 1920. The work contains an index but no bibliography.

559. **A Complete Dictionary of Furniture.** Rev. ed. John Gloag. Rev. and exp. by Clive Edwards. Woodstock, NY: Overlook Press; distr., New York: Viking Penguin, 1991. 828p. ISBN 0-87951-414-0.

Gloag's work has been a standard in the field since its initial publication in 1952 and its revision in 1969 under a different title. The present effort by Edwards, a specialist with the furniture department of the Victoria and Albert Museum in London, is more a reprint, including the original 3,000 terms along with an additional fifteen pages in the appendix treating about 85 contemporary terms. The work is divided into six sections covering the development of furniture in England since A.D. 1100 and in North America since the mid-seventeenth century. These sections offer narratives of furniture and of its design, a dictionary of names and terms (the major segment), and listings of furniture makers, along with a bibliography of books and articles. A series of tables outlines furniture production from 1100 to 1950. It remains the most extensive work of its kind in terms of its vast scope.

560. **Dictionary of Furniture.** Charles Boyce, ed. New York, Facts on File, 1985; repr., New York: Henry Holt, 1988. 331p. ISBN 0- 8050-0752-0.

An up-to-date, comprehensive source of information on furniture and furniture making in all countries and time periods, this work was readily accepted by librarians in the field. Furnishing brief entries, alphabetically arranged, coverage is given to numerous topics, issues, styles, personalities, and terms. These are explained in an informative and lucid manner, in enough detail to satisfy most queries. Both Western and Eastern influences and individuals are treated. The tool is especially helpful in its treatment of modern furniture and designers, since biographical information on twentieth-century furniture makers is elusive.

An old favorite, first published in 1938, is *The Encyclopedia of Furniture*, by Joseph Aronson (Cronson, 1965). This older work can be used to supplement the coverage of the newer one, since each contains material not found in the other.

Jewelry and Metalcraft

DICTIONARIES, ENCYCLOPEDIAS, HANDBOOKS, ETC.

561. **American Silversmiths and Their Marks IV.** Rev. and enl. ed. Stephen Guernsey Cook Ensko; comp. by Dorothea Ensko Wyle. Boston: D. R. Godine, 1989. 477p. ISBN 0879237783.

Since this work was first issued in 1948 (and reprinted in 1984), it has been recognized as an important and unique source for identification of American silversmiths over a 200-year period, 1650–1850. This revised and expanded edition was compiled by Ensko's daughter. Little is known of individual artisans plying a craft in a unique style for those formative years. American silversmiths had chosen a more simple but elegant execution of American pieces in comparison to the flourishes and ornamentation of their European counterparts. Included in the new edition are thousands of gold- and silversmiths with identification of their marks. There are numerous illustrations along with a set of maps identifying location of silversmith shops. The bibliography is up-to-date; there is an index of silversmiths located in the maps.

562. **Answers to Questions About Old Jewelry: 1840 to 1950.** 4th ed. Jeanenne Bell. Florence, AL: Books Americana, 1996. 402p. ISBN 0-89689-115-1.

This work continues as a useful guide, with a detailed table of contents providing access to the wealth of information contained in this volume. As before, there is no index. A continuing growing interest in the collection of jewelry has made a guidebook of this type a necessity in most libraries. The current issue replaces the third edition, published in 1992 in much the same format. Section 1 provides the historical background and describes the different motifs and personalities associated with the creation of jewelry in different periods, such as Victorian, Art Deco, and modern. Section 2 treats the materials used in making jewelry, while section 3 identifies simple tests to determine the authenticity of the composition of these materials. Section 4 provides a catalog of marks and a biographical dictionary of prominent designers and craftsmen. Valuations are given along with small black-and-white pictures of the pieces.

563. **Collector's Dictionary of the Silver and Gold of Great Britain and North America.** 2d ed. Michael Clayton. Ithaca, NY: Antique Collectors Club, 1985. 481p. ISBN 0-907462-57-X.

Those individuals for whom silver and gold play an important role in their collecting habits will appreciate the comprehensive nature and breadth of coverage of this fine dictionary. First published in 1971, it has come to be recognized as a standard item in reference departments for its excellent treatment of gold and silver work from the Middle Ages to the nineteenth century. Entries are generally short, ranging from one to two paragraphs in length, but they cover a wide variety of topics and include cross-references. General topics such as "American silver" are explained and defined along with specific artifacts, objects, personalities, styles, and techniques. Formerly associated with Christie's Auction House, the author brings expertise and authority to the descriptions and interpretations he provides. There is a bibliography of books and catalogs on selected topics at the end.

564. **Encyclopedia of American Silver Manufacturers.** 3d ed. rev. Dorothy T. Rainwater. West Chester, PA: Schiffer, 1986. 266p. ISBN 0-88740-046-9.

This is another standard tool in the field; the first edition was published in 1966 and the second edition in 1975. The third edition has updated and embellished the previous issues with additional entries and revision where necessary. It continues to supply the names of some 1,500 silver manufacturers operating in this country. This comprehensive coverage is enhanced with illustrations of over 2,000 silver trademarks. Sources utilized were old company catalogs and records from the U.S. Patent Office, as well as current manufacturers and antique shop owners. Reproductions are clear and adequate in terms of detail. Entries are arranged alphabetically by manufacturer's name, supplying location, trademark, and narrative description of the firm's activity. A brief glossary defines terms. Unfortunately the bibliography has not been updated.

565. **An Illustrated Dictionary of Jewelry: 2,530 Entries Including Definitions of Jewels, Gemstones, Materials. . . .** Harold Newman. New York: Thames & Hudson, 1981; repr., 1994. 334p. ISBN 0-500-27452-5.

This is a paperback reprint of the earlier edition considered to be a unique and important work with its comprehensive coverage of jewelry. The complete title indicates its vast scope: "Processes, and Styles, and Entries on Principal Designers and Makers, from Antiquity to the Present Day." Indeed, there is an abundance of information within the more than 2,500 entries, all alphabetically arranged for easy access. Included here are definitions of terms, descriptions of processes and styles, and biographical narratives of designers and craftspersons from the beginning of such art work to modern day practice and practitioners. Important gems are identified and locations are indicated. There is a conscious effort to avoid technical terminology; bibliographies accompany certain entries. Articles are well-constructed and informative. Both color and black-and-white illustrations are utilized to enhance many of the entries.

566. **Professional Goldsmithing: A Contemporary Guide to Traditional Jewelry Techniques.** Alan Revere. New York: Van Nostrand Reinhold, 1991. 226p. ISBN 0-442-23898-3.

The author is a well-known figure and a master goldsmith who has issued an excellent manual to smithing technique. The work opens with several short chapters on the composition of metals, types of tools, and nature of the craft. Then follow step-by-step sequenced activities, all described in clear fashion and accompanied by color illustrations for purposes of clarification. Thirty projects involving a wide range of smithing techniques are described and illustrated. Intricate processes involve the creation of forged rings and bracelets, mesh chains, and necklace clasps. These techniques have been handed down for generations and represent the traditional approaches so highly prized today. This work may be used as a shop text or as a manual for self-learning. Appendices treat relevant information such as weights and measures. There is a general index.

567. **The Sotheby's Directory of Silver, 1600–1940.** Vanessa Brett. London: Sotheby's Publications; distr., New York: Harper & Row, 1986. 432p. ISBN 0-85667-193-2.

Although there is no shortage of reference works on silver, this survey of 2,000 elegant pieces sold at auction by Sotheby's spans a period of sixty years of auctioneering from the 1920s to the mid-1980s. It is regarded as an important tool not only for the record it provides of prices and costs over the years but also for identifying the work of high-quality silversmiths from both Europe and the United States. Each piece is illustrated, and information is given on category, manufacture, size, and weight as well as sales. Additional information is furnished regarding the silversmith. Unfortunately, makers' marks and monograms are not included, which may be regarded as a deficiency in an otherwise useful work. The arrangement is by country and then by maker, in a sequence that is roughly chronological. An index facilitates access.

568. **Traditional Jewelry of India.** Oppi Untracht. New York: H. N. Abrams, 1997. 431p. ISBN 0-8109-3886-3.

The author is an experienced collector and researcher who is able to convey the compelling importance of jewelry to the Indian people and to their way of life. Beginning with the body decorations of Bengal Bay Islanders and religious ornamentation of different regions some 5,000 years ago, the work proceeds to examine the tradition of entire-body decoration; the use of gold, silver, and precious stones; gradual development of artistry within the Mughal dynasty; and the cross-cultural elements of European and Indian jewelry design. The text is readable and informative and appeals to a popular audience. The pictures are well-chosen and serve to provide a cohesive resource tool to aid the comprehension of the subject matter.

Ceramics, Pottery, and Glass

BIBLIOGRAPHIC GUIDES AND BIBLIOGRAPHIES

569. **Pottery and Ceramics: A Guide to Information Sources.** James Edward Campbell. Detroit: Gale Research, 1978. 241p. (Art and Architecture Information Guide Series, v. 7). ISBN 0-8103-1274-3.

Designed for use by students, practitioners, and collectors, this is another useful tool from this Gale series. The author is a specialist in the field and has rendered a well-constructed, selective literature guide to the study of ceramics and pottery. All the clay arts are embraced for documentation in primarily English-language books, articles, pamphlets, and catalogs. Annotations are useful and informative, and range from purely descriptive to evaluative in nature. Opening chapters treat reference works of general nature, with subsequent chapters organized within a historical framework. Publications of more than 700 authors are treated, with possibly too little inclusion of government documents when considering the historical context. There are useful listings of periodicals, organizations, societies, and museum collections. Access is provided through author, title, and subject indexes.

570. Stained Glass: A Guide to Information Sources. Darlene A. Brady and William Serban. Detroit: Gale Research, 1980. 572p. (Art and Architecture Information Guide Series, v. 10; Gale Information Guide Library). ISBN 0-8103-1445-2.

This is a comprehensive guide and bibliography supplying over 1,700 annotated entries treating English-language books and articles relating to both American and European traditions in stained glass and its manufacture. It continues the coverage begun initially by George Sang Duncan's *A Bibliography of Glass: (From the Earliest Records to 1940)* (Dawsons of Pall Mall, 1960). The present effort extends the period to 1976, with the idea of providing a source useful to a variety of individuals from general readers and hobbyists to art historians and practitioner-specialists. Entries are arranged under format categories such as reference works, bibliographies, dissertations, and periodicals. In addition, three specialized periodicals are indexed for the first time. Specialized chapters supply information on conducting library research and furnish directory-listings of collections, museums, organizations, and supply houses. There is a general subject index as well as specialized indexes by author, title, name of artist, and location of art work.

DICTIONARIES, ENCYCLOPEDIAS, HANDBOOKS, ETC.

*571. The Collector's Encyclopedia of Heisey Glass 1925–1938. Neila Bredehoft. Paducah, KY: Collector Books; distr., Newark, OH: Heisey Collectors of America, 1989; repr. with upd., 1996. 463p. ISBN 0-89145-307-5.

This encyclopedia furnishes a detailed record of the Heisey lines and the thousands of desirable items that were produced by the factory. It begins with an historical overview of the fortunes of the Heisey Company. The major segment of the text is catalog material based on information contained in Heisey catalogs of the period covered. All photographs are taken from these sales catalogs and are mostly black-and-white. Each color in the line is illustrated, however, with representative pieces from that line. Entries contain pattern numbers, names, dates, decorations, and indication of marks. Included with the purchase of the encyclopedia but also selling as a separate item is a price guide that provides price ranges for all items and lines described in the encyclopedia. The present edition provides values updated to 1989. It has been available on CD-ROM through the publisher since 1991. The 1996 reprint contains values updated that year.

572. Encyclopedia of Pottery and Porcelain 1800–1960. Elisabeth Cameron. New York: Facts on File, 1986. 366p. ISBN 0-81601-225-3.

An important work is this compendium of the world of pottery and porcelain covering a period of 160 years. The approximately 9,500 alphabetically arranged entries include decorators, designers, factories, materials, styles, techniques, and basic terminology as well as individual potters. Marks are described within the context of the entries for individuals or firms although they generally are not illustrated. The emphasis is on European (especially English) and American pottery, although Japanese ceramics are not overlooked. There are

450 black-and-white reproductions, with 32 illustrations in color, providing a good indication of nature or character of the representative forms and styles. Considered to be the best single guide available for its coverage of major personalities and elements within this important time span, the encyclopedia provides bibliographic references as well.

A standard source for identification of potters' marks is William Chaffers's *Marks and Monograms on European and Oriental Pottery and Porcelain* (London: William Reeves, 1965). This two-volume tool was last issued in its fifteenth edition and treats the whole field of European and Oriental pottery in scholarly fashion; adequate illustration of objects is furnished. Volume 2 is geared specifically to British porcelain.

573. An Illustrated Dictionary of Ceramics. . . . Rev. ed. George Savage and Harold Newman. New York: Thames & Hudson; distr., Boston: Little, Brown, 1985. 319p. ISBN 0-500-27380-4.

This is a paperback reprint of a hardcover edition published in 1974, issued with a warning that the paperback edition should not be lent, resold, hired out, or otherwise circulated without the publisher's consent. The hardcover edition is still preferred by art departments because the paperback does not contain the color reproductions. Other than that, there is not much difference between them, and the black-and-white illustrations are of good quality. The definitions are brief but informative and will be useful for those seeking to define the terminology of the field. Many cross-references are furnished. The subtitle aptly describes the scope as "Defining 3,054 Terms Relating to Wares, Materials, Processes, Styles, Patterns, and Shapes from Antiquity to the Present Day." The emphasis is on English ceramics.

574. An Illustrated Dictionary of Glass. Harold Newman. London: Thames & Hudson, 1977; repr., 1987. 351p. ISBN 0-500-27451-7.-8.

The title page of this comprehensive dictionary, now a standard in the field, goes on: "2,442 entries, including definitions of waves, materials, processes, forms, and decorative styles, and entries on principal glass-makers, decorators, and designers, from antiquity to the present." Scope is universal in terms of international coverage, but emphasis is placed on American and European influences. The entries are arranged alphabetically in dictionary fashion and vary in length from a single sentence to a half-page. Bibliographic references are given in only a small proportion of the entries, an unfortunate decision because there is no bibliography of additional readings. An excellent introductory essay by Robert J. Charleston surveying the history of glass-making opens the work. Then follows the text with its brief entries for countries and regions as well as technical terms and related aspects.

575. The Illustrated Guide to Glass. Felice Mehlman. Englewood Cliffs, NJ: Prentice Hall, 1982; repr., London: Peerage, 1985. 256p. ISBN 1-85-052020-8.

This was originally published as *Phaidon Guide to Glass* and earned a reputation as a concise but solid information source. It opens with an excellent introduction describing the materials and processes utilized in the making of glass objects along with various stylistic and technical features. Popular decorative styles are explained in reviewing the history of glass as it has evolved in different parts of the world. Objects are categorized by type or function and include drinking glasses, jewelry, mirrors, and paperweights. Both color and black-and-white photographs accompany the narrative. Emphasis is placed on historical development throughout the text with treatment given to important events and developing influences. The exposition is handled well and enables both collector and student to gain a better understanding and appreciation of the craft. There is a brief bibliography and a general index.

576. **The Potter's Dictionary of Materials and Techniques.** 4th ed. Frank Hamer and Janet Hamer. Philadelphia: University of Pennsylvania Press, 1997. 406p. ISBN 0-8122-3404-9.

The third edition of this well-known, now standard work in the field was issued four years after its predecessor; the fourth edition followed five years later. It has updated the majority of the entries and has added a number of new suppliers. There are three major segments treating general arts, crafts, and hobbies; needlecraft, sewing, and fiber arts; and finally, resources such as associations, books, general craft business, and so forth. Within these sections are the listings of supply houses categorized alphabetically by type of service or product. Recently identified environmental and safety hazards are explained fully. The remainder of the work is essentially the same, with continued emphasis on information relevant to potters in the performance of their craft. Coverage is comprehensive, with entries describing technical terms, processes, techniques, and important concepts. Cross-references are supplied within the entries and tabular data are included in the appendices. The authors are Welsh potters who have the experience and insight to provide cogent and practical commentary. Spelling generally follows British conventions.

Textiles, Weaving, and Needlecraft

BIBLIOGRAPHIC GUIDES AND BIBLIOGRAPHIES

577. **Embroidery and Needlepoint: An Information Sourcebook.** Sandra K. Copeland. Phoenix, AZ: Oryx Press, 1989. 150p. ISBN 0-89774-442-X.

This slender bibliography supplies access to more than 1,700 books and more than 150 periodical titles treating the subject of needlework. Publications range from 1950 to the mid-1980s and represent English-language titles. Foreign-language publications are included when their illustrations are useful even without the text. Entries are placed within chapters by form, such as the initial chapter on general information sources and the second chapter devoted to periodical titles, or by topic, as in subsequent chapters treating specialized techniques: appliqué, blackwork embroidery, stumpwork, samplers, shisha mirror work, and so forth. The author is both a librarian and a needlework artist who has used her expertise to produce brief but informative annotations for a majority of the entries. She has also rendered a service, providing a useful segment of ninety-one works serving as the core library collection. Author, title, and subject indexes are furnished.

578. **Handweaving: An Annotated Bibliography.** Isabel Buschman. Metuchen, NJ: Scarecrow Press, 1991. 250p. ISBN 0-8108-2403-5.

This is a well-developed bibliography of more than 550 books and periodical titles published over a sixty-year period from 1928 to 1989. Coverage is given to basic texts for students as well as monographs on looms and equipment, patterns, fabrics, historical development, Native American influences, and so forth. Emphasis is placed on technical applications and projects. Publications are placed within five major chapters examining important broad topical and format areas. Covered first are the materials, tools, techniques, and products of hand-weaving, followed by chapters on history, reference works, and journals. In addition, a full chapter is given to Native American weaving methods. Entries are arranged alphabetically by author within the various chapters. Annotations vary in length but are lucid and informative. There are author, title, and subject indexes.

DICTIONARIES, ENCYCLOPEDIAS, HANDBOOKS, ETC.

579. **The Batsford Encyclopaedia of Embroidery Techniques.** Gay Swift. London: B. T. Batsford, 1984; repr., 1991. Distr., North Ponfret, VT: Trafalgar Square/David & Charles. 240p. ISBN 0-7134-6781-9.

This useful information source was initially published in 1984, and due to its success was reprinted in 1990. It represents a unique source in its description of technical terms, concepts, styles, and applications in a comprehensive manner. All aspects of the embroidery arts are included, with coverage given to appliqué, quilt making, buttons, lace, and so forth. Excellent illustrations accompany the text and enable the user to gain a sense of perspective with regard to the breadth and patterns of composition. Use of color is exceptional and places this work among others suitable for coffee table display. In addition there is a listing of the most important embroidery collections, with emphasis on those in the United Kingdom, in the bibliography section at the end. There is no index but access is aided by italicized cross-references within the entries.

580. **The Complete Stitch Encyclopedia.** Jan Eaton. Woodbury, NY: Barron's Educational Series, 1986; repr., 1989. 173p. ISBN 1-8628-2053-8.

This is a detailed and comprehensive manual to the various forms of stitchery that have been popular through the years. Identification is furnished for over 450 different stitches, arranged by type. Categories are organized according to degree of difficulty, with the simplest techniques listed first. There are numerous illustrations in full color for each stitch and detailed instructions given for successful application. The photographs are integrated with the narrative, and sequence photographs are provided for the more complicated techniques. Advice is given regarding such matters as choice of thread, along with brief historical information on some of the older techniques.

581. **Encyclopedia of Batik Designs.** Leo O. Donahue. Philadelphia: Art Alliance; distr., East Brunswick, NJ: Associated University Presses, 1981. 630p. ISBN 0-8453-4729-2.

Batik as a form of textile decoration employing wax resist methods emerged in the eighteenth century, having been introduced by the Dutch East India Company. It very quickly became high fashion and through the years has enjoyed a steady popularity marked by spurts of increased interest. In this volume, exposition is given not only to the creation of the batik but also to the block on tjap for printing on cloth. The processes are explained in detail and many photographs enhance the descriptions provided of the routines and the creation of various effects. There is a glossary of terms, along with a bibliography and an index.

582. **Encyclopedia of Textiles.** Judith Jerde. New York: Facts on File, 1992. 260p. ISBN 0-8160-2105-8.

This relatively compact volume furnishes a broad view of the topic with coverage of design, manufacture, care, and utilization of fabric. Fiber types, patterns, and weaves are explained and illustrated, as are dyes, printing techniques, and technical processes. Entries furnishing definitions, descriptions, and explanations vary in length, with the various fibers receiving the most detailed narrative. The title should be useful to a wide audience ranging from the novice to the skilled artisan. Personalities are also treated with brief biographical sketches.

An earlier work, *The A F Encyclopedia of Textiles* (Prentice-Hall, 1980), is now in its third edition and provides a fine exposition of various fibers, designs, and processes involved in the manufacture of textiles. Brief chapters cover the various topics and include numerous illustrations.

583. **The Illustrated Dictionary of Knitting.** Rae Compton. Loveland, CO: Interweave Press, 1988. 272p. ISBN 0-934026-41-6.

This well-constructed information source is more a handbook of knitting technique and process rather than simply a dictionary of terms. Of course, terms and relevant topics are described and historical information is included along with narrative of stylistic differences between ethnic and cultural groups. Such coverage is brief and of secondary importance, however, and this book should be considered a manual of practice. When entries deal with a technique or process, the activity is generally defined briefly at the outset, followed by a more detailed exposition of the manner in which it is performed along with possible variations of the application. Specific parts of clothing and apparel such as zippers, gloves, or socks are handled individually. The work is well-illustrated in color and black-and-white, enabling the user to examine the sequence of steps as well as the finished products.

584. **The Macmillan Atlas of Rugs and Carpets.** David Black, ed. New York: Macmillan, 1985. 255p. ISBN 0-02-511120-5.

A useful and detailed expository work on the history and development of the craft of carpet-making, this atlas furnishes information on the individual countries involved in the practice. Beautiful illustrations (200 in color and 150 in black-and-white) show the various designs and techniques. The work begins with a description of the methods of weaving and carpet design and provides general guidelines for analyzing carpets. The next chapter covers the history of carpets and examines and compares developments in countries considered most desirable for their products (Turkey, Persia, India, etc.). The largest portion of the work covers individual countries with maps, and detailed information is given for each style produced. Included are the braided, hooked, and embroidered rugs of the United States as well as Navaho blanket weaving.

Fashion and Costume

BIBLIOGRAPHIES AND INDEXES

585. **Fashion and Costume in American Popular Culture.** Valerie B. Oliver. Westport, CT: Greenwood, 1996. 279p. ISBN 0-313-29412-7.

Written by a librarian at the University of Connecticut, this guide provides an array of bibliographic essays furnishing exposition and description of the various types of resources, each chapter concluding with a full bibliography of the titles used in the description. Although the majority of the chapters are structured by type of resource such as encyclopedias, there is a chapter dealing with specific clothing and accessories as well as one on psychological and sociological aspects. Listings of research centers are supplied along with coverage of periodical titles but not articles, exhibition catalogs, theses, and more. Coverage of monographic literature and ERIC documents makes the work useful to both students and specialists.

Costume Index: A Subject Index to Plates and to Illustrated Text, by Isabel Stevenson Monro and Dorothy E. Cook (H. W. Wilson, 1937), and its 1957 supplement, remain as old standards in the field, indexing plates appearing in over 950 books of costume through 1956. Any full-page illustration has been defined as a plate. Coverage is broad and historical costumes from any period with the exception of biblical times are identified under geographic locations, classes of persons, or details of costume. A continuation of coverage is supplied by Jackson Kesler's *Theatrical Costume: A Guide to Information Sources* (Gale Research, 1979), a bibliography of materials dating from 1957 to the 1970s.

DICTIONARIES, ENCYCLOPEDIAS, HANDBOOKS, ETC.

586. **American Costume, 1915–1970: A Source Book for the Stage Costumes.** Shirley Miles O'Donnol. Bloomington: Indiana University Press, 1982; repr., 1989. 270p. ISBN 0-253-30589-6.

An essential work for any costumer is this exposition of American costume over a period of fifty-five years. Beginning with the era of World War I, it provides separate chapters in chronological sequence: "World War, 1916–1919"; "The Twenties (1920–1929)"; "Depression (1930–1939)"; "World War (1940–1946)"; "The 'New Look' (1947–1952)"; "Space Age (1953–1960)"; and the "Sixties (1960–1970)." The background of each period is described along with general information on dress, then specific coverage is accorded men's, women's and children's fashions. Also included are details on grooming, hair styles, and accessories as well as colors and motifs. There are suggestions for costumers and lists of plays for the different time periods. Illustrations are provided.

587. **The Chronicle of Western Fashion: From Ancient Times to the Present Day.** John Peacock. New York: H. N. Abrams, 1991. 224p. ISBN 0-8109-3953-3.

This is a useful chronology of fashion and dress ranging over a period of 4,000 years from antiquity (Egypt, 2000 B.C.) to the year 1980. Major historical periods (ancient civilizations, Middle Ages, and Renaissance) lead into sequential century-by-century coverage from the sixteenth through the twentieth. A work such as this depends on its illustrations, and there are over 1,000 detailed full-color drawings. Illustrations number about 10 per page and furnish examples of a variety of styles, with emphasis on the dress of the upper and middle classes. Also shown are the garb of royalty, military, sports, and various occupations from the lower working classes to the professions. Outfits from formalwear to sleepwear are depicted. Descriptions of each illustration appear at the end of each segment. Included is a glossary of fashion terms, along with a bibliography of sources.

588. **The Dictionary of Costume.** R. Turner Wilcox. London: B.T. Batsford, 1969; repr., 1992. 406p. ISBN 0-7134-7026-7.

This reprint of a standard tool in the field provides a convenient source of information on all aspects of costume on a broad-based international basis. More than 3,200 entries are arranged alphabetically for easy access and present the technical terminology, major personalities, articles of apparel, jewelry, cosmetics, hair and even beard styles, instruments and equipment, and fabrics and materials. The author is an acknowledged authority and writer. This effort is useful to a variety of audiences from fledgling students to accomplished specialists in its treatment of all periods of history. Entries vary from precise explanations of particular terms to lengthy survey articles on such topics as "eighteenth century." Numerous illustrations accompany the text and illustrate the apparel and accessories described. Cross-references are provided, a useful practice because there is no index. A brief bibliography concludes the effort.

A recent work, similar in scope, is Mary B. Picken's *A Dictionary of Costume and Fashion: Historic and Modern, with Over 950 Illustrations* (Dover, 1999). Entries vary in length but generally provide adequate exposition and description of topics and developments in the world of fashion over time.

589. **The Encyclopaedia of Fashion: From 1840 to the 1980s.** Georgina O'Hara. London: Thames & Hudson, 1986; repr., 1989. 272p. ISBN 0-500-27567-X.

This is well-developed source of information on terms, personalities, styles, articles of apparel, fabrics, movements, trends, furs, and even media that influenced the fashion world over a period of 140 years. A variety of individuals is treated: designers, jewelers, milliners, hairdressers, illustrators, artists, and so forth. There are over 1,000 entries, arranged alphabetically with numerous cross-references. The text is accompanied by more than 350 illustrations, some in color.

The Fashion Encyclopedia: An Essential Guide to Everything You Need to Know About Clothes, by Catherine Houck (St. Martin's Press, 1982), is an interesting, revealing, and highly readable survey of the field of fashion that provides much information from a variety of sources. Coverage is given to style, personalities, production, care, and purchasing of a variety of material, clothing, and accessories. Arrangement is alphabetical by topic and there are many black-and-white illustrations. Among other things, such topics as furs, jewelry, discount houses, mail order, and thrift shops are treated. An especially useful feature is the list of trademarks, copyright, and certification marks of the various products, firms, and processes. Although not scholarly, the tool will prove to be useful for the variety of information it provides.

590. **Essential Terms of Fashion: A Collection of Definitions.** Charlotte Mankey Calasibetta. New York: Fairchild Publications, 1986. 244p. ISBN 0-87005-519-4.

This dictionary is especially useful for its inclusion of contemporary terminology. It also provides good coverage of the traditional terms of the field and has been commended for its historical precision. Arrangement is by broad categories of articles of clothing, accessories, or style such as boots, robes, and pleats. These are subdivided by specific types. Definitions are brief for the most part, but adequate, and cross-references are furnished. Illustrations in the form of line drawings are useful and accompany many of the entries. The terms are those used in the fashions of men, women, and children, and the work has been received well by both librarians and designers.

The second edition of *Fairchild's Dictionary of Fashion*, by Charlotte Mankey Calasibetta (Fairchild, 1988) is a detailed and comprehensive source of information on the world of fashion from the time of antiquity to the present, and supplies over 15,000 entries. Arrangement is alphabetical and entries provide brief definitions, identifications, expositions, and biographical descriptions. Nearly 100 of these terms are given broad categorical representation, such as "cuffs," "shoulders," and "heels," under which are grouped numerous related terms, which themselves are listed alphabetically in the main text along with cross-references back to the categories. Included here are numerous black-and-white illustrations along with a section of color. No bibliography is given.

591. **Fashion in Costume 1200–1980.** Joan Nunn. Lanham, MD: New Amsterdam Books, 1999. 256p. ISBN 0-941-53379-4.

This brief but informative survey history of costume in the Western world provides several hundred line drawings to accompany the narrative. Clothing is described in terms of its design and production within a framework of social and historical development, and manufacturing techniques are examined in some detail. Fashion trends and stylistic changes are explained in a lucid manner. A brief bibliography is furnished to make the work a useful reference for students and others.

Costume and Fashion: A Concise History, by James Laver and Amy De La Haye (Thames & Hudson, 1995), is a well-illustrated narrative survey of developments in costume and fashion of the world. The text is easy-to-read and emphasizes styles and fabrics of England. Students will find the pictures especially beneficial to the understanding of design changes in clothing of the different periods.

592. The Illustrated Encyclopaedia of Costume and Fashion: From 1066 to the Present. Jack Cassin-Scott. London: Studio Vista; distr., New York: Sterling, 1994. 192p. ISBN 0-289-80093-5.

This is an expansion in scope of the 1986 publication that covered the years 1550 to 1920. As before, it supplies 180 color reproductions providing excellent images of more than 300 costumes. Detail is clearly shown and reveals the styles worn by lords and ladies, children, military figures, peasants, and musicians. Costumes are described briefly and dates are furnished. In most cases, type of fabric is given and country of origin established. The earlier work had been criticized for certain oversights among the illustrations provided, such as cropping of the lady's train in one plate and a portion of a skirt in another. The new edition is somewhat more polished as well as more extensive. Its comprehensive coverage adds to its value as a worthwhile addition to the reference department.

593. A Visual History of Costume: The Twentieth Century. Penelope Byrde. London: Batsford; New York: Drama Book Publishers, 1987; repr., 1992. 152p. ISBN 0-71346-830-0.

This is the final volume of a highly stylized five-volume series on costume; each volume is done in the exact same format with the same number of pages. An English publication from Batsford, it is sold in the United States by Drama Book Publishers. The series begins with *A Visual History of Costume: The Sixteenth Century*, by Jane Ashelford (1984), followed by *A Visual History of Costume: The Seventeenth Century* by Valerie Cumming (1987), *A Visual History of Costume: The Eighteenth Century*, by Aileen Ribeiro (1983), and *A Visual History of Costume: The Nineteenth Century*, by Vanda Foster (1984). The volumes are considered useful sources of information on the styles of costume, and are illustrated through a series of reproductions of the art work of the time. Illustrations are chronologically arranged, appear both in color and black-and-white, and depict men and women dressed in fashions of the day. These are mostly English, and captions describe the costume features. Each volume begins with an introduction surveying the world of fashion in that century and provides an index and a selective bibliography.

BIOGRAPHICAL SOURCES

594. Contemporary Fashion. Richard Martin, ed. Detroit: St. James Press, 1995. 575p. ISBN 1-55862-173-3.

Another from the St. James line of biographical sources is this collective work providing detailed coverage of nearly 400 established personalities and firms representing twenty-seven countries in the world of fashion. Designers, milliners, footwear specialists, and others serving an array of tastes and budgets from high fashion to department store lines are treated. Entries supply a brief biographical sketch followed by a brief bibliography, and when possible, a statement from the artist. Entries for companies provide a brief history. Entries, in some cases, are enhanced with a black-and-white photograph of the work.

Who's Who in Fashion, by Anne Stegemeyer (Fairchild, 1996), is the third edition of a useful work providing an alphabetical listing about 300 influential and established designers from all over the world. Illustrations (some in color) are furnished for designers and their work. Entries vary in length from a few paragraphs to three pages and treat background, career, education, and achievements of the personalities.

595. Costume Design on Broadway: Designers and Their Credits, **1915–1985.** Bobbi Owen. New York: Greenwood, 1987. 254p. (Bibliographies and Indexes in the Performing Arts, no. 5). ISBN 0-313-25524-5.

Only since 1936 have costume designers in theater been granted recognition by the union; thus there has been relatively little documentation or consideration of their achievements. The author is a scholar in the field who has produced a well-constructed and useful source of information for specialists and students. More than 1,000 designers who contributed at least one costume to a Broadway production within a seventy-year period from 1915 to 1985 are treated. Entries are alphabetically arranged and supply a biographical sketch along with a listing of Broadway credits. Following this is a segment of black-and-white sketches of selected costumes. Three appendices identify award-winning designers, with separate listings for Tony, Marharam, and Donaldson winners. Finally, there is an index of 7,000 plays checked, along with their designers if available.

CHAPTER 9

ACCESSING INFORMATION IN THE PERFORMING ARTS

WORKING DEFINITION OF THE PERFORMING ARTS

The term *performing arts* has not become standardized in its usage. It is used to differentiate the arts or skills which, by their nature, require public performance, as opposed to those whose beauty is appreciated through the sense of sight or some surrogate, as in the visual arts. McLeish states: "In the performing arts . . . the performer, the intermediary, is a crucial part of the process."[1] Generally, there are three elements necessary for consideration as a performing art: the piece or work being performed; the performer or performers; and an audience hearing, viewing, or experiencing the performance. Sometimes the three elements originate in the same individual, as is the case where a songwriter composes the work and performs it for himself or herself in the privacy of the practice room or studio. Most often, however, the entities are different individuals or groups, and we treat the performing arts in that sense in this guide.

MAJOR DIVISIONS OF THE FIELD

As used in this guide, the performing arts include music, dance, opera, the theater, film, radio, television, and video. An interesting, though slightly different approach, is taken in the second edition of *The Humanities and the Library*, edited by Nena Couch and Nancy Allen (American Library Association, 1993). In that update of Asheim's earlier work, the editors present music and performing arts as separate chapters. Both are useful for the librarian and student; the music chapter is by Elizabeth Rebman (pp. 132–69) and Couch and Allen provide the performing arts section (pp. 173–211). Here, however, we maintain the arrangement of previous editions and include music within the performing arts chapter.

Music is commonly defined as the art of organizing sound. Its principal elements are melody (single sounds in succession), harmony (sounds in combination), and rhythm (sounds in a temporal relationship). The two major divisions are vocal music and instrumental music. Vocal music includes songs, opera, oratorios, and so forth, while instrumental music includes solos, chamber music, and orchestral music. Musical instruments may be classified as stringed (violin, harp, guitar), woodwind (flute, bassoon, oboe, English horn), brass (trumpet, cornet, bugle, trombone), percussion (drums, bells, gongs, chimes), keyboard (piano, organ, electronic keyboard) and others (accordions, harmonica, bagpipes, concertina). The modern system of musical notation came to be used in about 1700.

The librarian responsible for a music collection will need to keep in mind three major elements: 1) the music itself, which follows to some degree the divisions outlined above; 2) the literature about music, which is divided more along the conventional lines for all disciplines, but with some special characteristics; and 3) the vast array of recordings on records, discs, tapes, cassettes, and video, which are a part of any modern music library and which pose problems in terms of organization, preservation, retrieval, and use.

The dance may be defined as movement of the body to a certain rhythm. There are three major divisions of the field: folk dancing, ballroom dancing, and theater dancing. Folk dancing, which originated in open-air activities, is characterized by great vigor and exuberance of movement. Ballroom dancing had its origin in the European courts of the Renaissance and is an indoor participant activity. Theater dancing is a spectator activity that may be traced to religious dances in the ancient world and to performances known as masques in the courts of Renaissance Europe. Its most characteristic form is the ballet. The dance is usually (though not always) accompanied by music. The subject of dance notation is of ongoing interest, and new material on dance notation can be accessed on the Internet. (A starting point is the *Dancewriting* site at http://www.dancewriting.org/ [accessed June 22, 1999]; an alternative is The Dance Notation Bureau's site at http://www.dancenotation.org/ [accessed June 22, 1999].)

Theater is the art of presenting a performance to a live audience. In modern usage the term is restricted to live performances of plays. A distinction is sometimes drawn between theater and drama; theater is restricted in meaning to those matters having to do with public performance, while drama includes the literary basis for the performance (that is, the text of plays). The texts are often classed with literature in libraries, leading to the seemingly illogical separation of the texts of plays from works about performance of those plays. Topics that are closely related to theatrical performance, and that help to differentiate it from drama, are acting, costume, makeup, directing, and theater architecture.

Film may be divided into two types: feature length (an hour or longer) and shorts. Many feature length films are fictional, often based on books of some popularity. Others, known as documentaries, are prepared for informational purposes. The fictional and documentary form may be combined to make colorful travelogues or the so-called docu-dramas, in which real situations are presented in fictional, or partly fictional, form. Two other forms of film are animated cartoons and puppet features. Recent technology has allowed for the melding of live action and animated cartoons, so that cartoon characters mix with live casts. Shorts are often filmed by independent producers and sold to distributors of feature length films or video to complete an "entertainment package" for viewing in theaters or homes.

Films are widely used in schools, universities, churches, and other institutions for informational, educational, and training purposes. Films of this type are likely to constitute the bulk of many library collections.

Video is a relative newcomer to the performing arts field, particularly as a form available to most of the public. Feature length films, educational films, "how-to" instructions in a variety of fields, and music performance are all widely distributed on tape for home consumption. The inclusion of the tapes in public library collections, while attracting some new users to libraries, may pose problems from the standpoint of preservation, censorship, and fees for services.

Radio, which depends entirely on sound for its effects, and television, relying on sound and pictures, can be presented either "live" or in prerecorded form. For libraries, it is the residual audio and videotapes that may be included in collections. These materials share with the other performing arts some of the problems of organization and preservation.

Coverage of music, dance, theater, and film is reasonably good in many general encyclopedias. The pivotal article on music in *Encyclopaedia Britannica Online*, "Music" (located at http://members.eb.com/bol/topic?tmap_id=141375000&tmap_typ=aa [accessed June 20, 1999]), can be followed up by reviewing such topics as musical forms and genres; similarly, the dance article ("Dance" at http://members.eb.com/bol/topic?tmap_id=53513000&tmap_typ=aa [accessed June 20, 1999]) can be followed by articles such as the one on "theatrical dance" or any of the many other subdivisions, such as "dance notation." Articles in the same encyclopedia on theater and motion pictures are also excellent, especially if an historical perspective is wanted.

The reader can obtain a psychiatrist's view of music, and the role of audience and listener, in Anthony Storr's *Music and the Mind* (Ballantine, 1992). Bibliographical references abound in Linda H. Hamilton's book on the psychology of performing artists, *The Person Behind the Mask: A Guide to Performing Arts Psychology* (Ablex, 1997).

For divisions of the field of music and related performing arts, the reader should not overlook the monumental *New Grove Dictionary of Music and Musicians*, edited by Stanley Sadie (6th ed., Groves, 1980). Articles are accompanied by highly authoritative bibliographies that will lead the reader to additional publications on all aspects of music and related fields.

HELPFUL RESOURCES FOR STUDENTS, LIBRARIANS, AND GENERAL READERS

There are many helpful resources for students, librarians, and general readers who wish to understand more about materials on the performing arts, how they are selected for libraries, and how they are organized for both preservation and retrieval. Although some of the readings date to the early 1990s, the basic information is still useful if the reader overlooks references to specific bibliographic sources that have been updated or revised. Of course, if an historical perspective is needed, the older sources will serve the reader well.

Many resources that were previously available only in print form are now accessible in electronic formats. A review of hundreds of World Wide Web sites related to the performing arts reveals the widest array of offerings encountered by this author in any subject area. The resources range from well-organized and maintained sites to poorly designed and outdated resources that do little but muddy the research waters. An outstanding example of a helpful resource is the comprehensive Indiana University *Worldwide Internet Music Resources* at http://www.music.indiana.edu/music_resources/ (accessed June 21, 1999).

Performing arts are addressed in Carolyn A. Sheehy, ed., *Managing Performing Arts Collections in Academic and Public Libraries* (Greenwood, 1994) and in a title in the Reference Sources in the Humanities Series, Linda Keir Simons's *The Performing Arts: A Guide to the Reference Literature* (Libraries Unlimited, 1994). A journal that covers all aspects of the performing arts is *Performing Arts Journal*, online since 1996 at http://muse.jhu.edu/journals/performing_arts_journal/indexold.html (accessed June 21, 1999). *PAJ* began as a print journal in 1976.

The writing of reviews of the performing arts is taken up in W. U. McCoy's *Performing and Visual Arts Writing and Reviewing* (University Press of America, 1992).

The music chapter in Lester Asheim's classic *The Humanities and the Library* (pp. 151–98) remains a good introduction to the basic organization and use of a music collection. It is supplemented and somewhat updated by "Music Libraries and Collections," by Guy A. Marco, in *Encyclopedia of Library and Information Science* (Dekker, 1976, v.18, pp. 328–493). A classic in the field is *Music Libraries*, by Jack Dove (Deutsch, 1967), which was a revision of the 1937 work of the same title by L. R. McColvin and H. Reeves.

More recent entries in the literature of music librarianship include E. T. Bryant and Guy Marco's *Music Librarianship: A Practical Guide* (2d ed., Scarecrow Press, 1985), and *American Music Librarianship: A Biographical and Historical Survey*, by Carol J. Bradley (Greenwood, 1990). The former title was written for general librarians and students and gives more than an introduction to such topics as administration, reference, cataloging and classification, and recordings. A long bibliography is also a useful feature. Michael Och's *Music Librarianship in America* (Harvard University Press, 1991) is a set of papers presented at a symposium in honor of the first music library chair in the United States, the Richard F. French Chair in Librarianship at Harvard. The papers were also published as the *Harvard Library Bulletin* 2 (Spring 1991).

Guides to the literature of music are numerous, but among the best is *Music Reference and Research Materials: An Annotated Bibliography*, by Vincent Duckles, Ida Reed, and Michael A. Keller (5th ed., Schirmer, 1997). The guide, referred to by librarians simply as "Duckles," consistently received high ratings because of the quality of the annotations. Duckles (1913–1985) contributed much more to music librarianship and music scholarship; a bibliography of his publications appeared in *Notes*, the journal of the Music Library Association, as a memorial tribute from his colleagues in the field. (See "Vincent Duckles: A Bibliography of His Publications," compiled by Patricia Elliott and Mark S. Roosa, *Notes* 44 [December 1987]: 252–58.)

Other guides that will be helpful to the librarian or student include Elizabeth A. Davis, ed., *Basic Music Library: Essential Scores and Sound Recordings* (American Library Association, 1997).

Many special topics in music librarianship and research have been addressed in special reports (Technical Reports Series) issued by the Music Library Association. These have focused largely on cataloging and processing issues in terms of contents, but some reports have addressed space use in music libraries: Report no. 20 (1992), by James Cassaro, and "Careers in Music Librarianship," Report no. 18 (1990), by Carol Tatian.

Besides the special issues published by the Association, the journal literature and recent books have covered the topic of technical services and the organization of the materials. Richard P. Smiraglia, who has written and spoken extensively on the topic, has published *Describing Music Materials: A Manual for Descriptive Cataloging of Printed and Recorded Music, Music Videos, and Archival Music Collections: For Use with AACR2 and APPM* (Soldier Creek Press, 1997). Specific issues related to organizing twentieth-century music and scores are discussed in "Nailing Jell-o to a Tree: Improving Access to 20th Century Music," by Michael D. Colby (*Cataloging and Classification Quarterly* 26 [1998]: 31–39). And Elwood McKee addresses the organization of private collections in "Developing and Selecting Cataloging Systems for Private Collections," *ARSC Journal* 27 (Spring 1996): 53–58. An additional work in the cataloging area is Sherry Vellucci's *Bibliographic Relationships in Music Catalogs* (Scarecrow Press, 1997).

Articles addressing other technical aspects of handling and organizing music materials include Michelle Koth and Laura Gayle Green, "Workflow Considerations in Retrospective Conversion Projects for Scores," *Cataloging and Classification Quarterly* 14 (1992): 75–102; "ARIS Music Thesaurus: Another View of LCSH," *Library Resources and Technical Services* 36 (October 1992): 487–503; and "Cataloging Musical Moving Image Material: A Guide to the Bibliographic Control of Videorecordings and Films of Musical Performances and Other Music-related Moving Image Material." MLA Technical Report No. 25 (1996), was published by the Music Library Association Working Group on Bibliographic Control of Music Video Material.

"Preservation Policies and Priorities for Recorded Sound Collections," by Brenda Nelson-Strauss (*Notes* 48 [December 1991]: 425–36), is one of many works addressing the physical preservation issue. *Knowing the Score: Preserving Collections of Music*, compiled by Mark Roosa and Jane Gottlieb (MLA, 1994) is another. A specific preservation program is described in Sion M. Honea, "Preservation at the Sibley Music Library of the Eastman School of Music," *Notes* 53 (December 1996): 381–402.

On the technical front, D. Jessop's "DVD Basics for Libraries and Information Centers," *Computers in Libraries* 18 (April 1998): 62–66, will be of interest to the librarian.

Finally, rounding out the large selection of materials focused on technical aspects of music librarianship are articles on instruction for library users. Recent articles include "Bibliographic and User Instruction within Music Libraries: An Overview of Teaching Methodologies," by Judith L. Marley, in *Music Reference Services Quarterly* 6 (1998): 33–34; Mark Germer's

"Whither Bibliographic Instruction for Musicians?" *Notes* 52 (March 1996): 754–60; and Amanda Maple et al., "Information Literacy for Undergraduate Music Students: A Conceptual Framework," *Notes* 52 (March 1996): 744–53.

A recent work on collection development in music libraries is *Collection Assessment in Music Libraries*, edited by Jane Gottlieb (MLA, 1994). This is number 22 of the MLA Technical Report Series, a series that offers many other useful and practical reports.

There are many sources that will help to identify reference materials and other items that might be included in collections. Besides the guides and bibliographies discussed in Chapter 10, a good bibliography of the basics is found in Anne Gray's *The Popular Guide to Classical Music* (Birch Lane Press, 1993, pp. 337–40). A bibliography focusing on recorded sound is found in *The Iconography of Recorded Sound 1886–1986*, by Michael G. Corenthal (Yesterday's Memories, 1986). For scores and sound recordings, the Davis work, published by ALA and cited above, is also an important resource.

The journal literature is rich with shorter articles describing the current offerings or recommended titles on specific topics. A sampling of articles on diverse topics includes R. A. Leaver's "Hymnals, Hymnal Companions, and Collection Development," *Notes* 47 (December 1990): 331–54; H. J. Diamond's "The Literature of Musical Analysis: An Approach for Collection Development," *Choice* 27 (March 1990): 1097–99; C. A. Pressler's "Rock and Roll: Dimensions of a Cultural Revolution," *Choice* 29 (April 1992): 1192–1201; and P. Garon's "A Survey of Literature on the Blues," *AB Bookman's Weekly* 89 (February 17, 1992): 619–21. Two more recent entries are R. M. Cleary's "Rap Music and Its Political Connections: An Annotated Bibliography," *Reference Services Review* 21 (1993): 77–90, and Leta Hicks's "A Review of Rap Sound Recordings in Academic and Public Libraries," *Popular Music and Society* 21 (Summer 1997): 91–114. All of the articles listed here provide bibliographic citations for materials on the focal topics. The journal *Collection Management*, volume 12 (1990) carried two views of library collection building: W. E. Studwell presented the music researcher's viewpoint (pp. 92–94) and H. S. Wright the music librarian's perspective (pp. 95–99).

The journals *Notes* (published by the Music Library Association) and *Fontis Artis Musicae* (International Association of Music Libraries) should not be overlooked. The former carries substantive articles and regularly reviews new publications as well as reference materials and recorded music. The latter, which is multilingual and international in scope, covers activities of the association, proceedings of its conferences, and other topics of broad interest to performing arts librarians. A third source to consult for collection building is *BBC Music Magazine*, which carries a regular reviewing feature entitled "Building a Library."

An important special source of leads for materials in the performing arts is the Internet. Articles describing some good sources are J. Stinson's "Medieval Music on the Web: Music Resources for the 21st Century," *Australian Academic and Research Libraries* 28 (March 1997): 65–74; Kellie Shoemaker's "Net Notes: Music on the World Wide Web," *Voice of Youth Advocates* 21 (February 1999): 425ff.; and "Music Library Online," by K. Sloss and C. Duffy (*Brio* 35 [Spring/Summer 1998]: 9–12).

Although the field of music contributes the bulk of material in performing arts librarianship, there are important readings for librarians in the other subfields. For example, the reader may find the following titles helpful on matters related to collection development. Henry Wessells, "Publishing Roundup: Recent Books on Music, Film, and Television," *AB Bookman's Weekly* 102 (December 7, 1998): 1088ff. "Webwatch (Resources on Theater)," by Joan R. Stahl (*Library Journal* 123 [December 1998]: 27ff.), will help locate online resources. "Video Reviews," *Notes* 54 (June 1998): 973–77, discusses the video medium, as does R. E. Provine, "Issues in Video Collections and New Technologies," *College and University Media Review* 3 (Spring 1997): 47–57. In "Let's Go to the Videotape," Diane Ney (*American Theatre* 16 [April 1999]: 47–48) discusses the importance of videotape to performing arts scholarship. The Society for the Preservation of Film Music has published H. Stephen Wright and Stephen M. Fry, eds., *Film Music Collections in the United States: A Guide* (1996).

"Archival Guidelines for the Music Publishing Industry," by Kent D. Underwood et al. (*Notes* 52 [June 1996]: 1112–18), outlines a framework for the music industry's contribution to research needs of the field.

Also helpful across the performing arts fields is the Greenwood Press series Bio-Bibliographies in the Performing Arts. Its titles have excellent bibliographies, discographies, and filmographies on important individuals in the performing arts.

Library Journal, Library Quarterly, and other general journals in librarianship include the performing arts, publishing articles on collection development, technical processes, reference services, nonbook materials, and other topics of special interest. These titles should not be overlooked as sources of information for the librarian, student, or general reader.

USE AND USERS OF PERFORMING ARTS INFORMATION

Of the performing arts, music has been the most studied in terms of use and users of information. Malcolm Jones's *Music Librarianship* (Saur, 1979) introduces, very generally, types of music libraries and their users in "Music Libraries and Those They Serve" (pp. 13–23). The chapter on music by Elizabeth Rebman in *The Humanities and the Library* (2d ed., American Library Association, 1993) offers a brief user perspective in the section entitled "The Work of Composers, Performers, and Music Scholars" (pp. 136–37).

More specific studies of the use of the literature of music can be found largely in the older journal literature. The reader will want to see, for example, R. Griscom, "Periodical Use in a University Music Library: A Citation Study of Theses and Dissertations Submitted to the Indiana University School of Music from 1975–1980," *Serials Librarian* 7 (Spring 1983): 35–52; R. Green, "Use of Music and Its Literature Over Time," *Notes* 35 (September 1978): 42–56; and David Baker, "Characteristics of the Literature Used by English Musicologists," *Journal of Librarianship* 10 (July 1978): 182–200. Miranda Lee Pao investigated the behavior of authors and publications in computational musicology in "Bibliometrics and Computational Musicology," *Collection Management* 3 (Spring 1979): 97–109. A more recent study is S. M. Clegg's "User Surveys and Statistics for Music Librarians," *Fontis Artis Musicae* 32 (January 1985): 69–75. One of the very few *recent* citation studies in the performing arts is Lois Kuyper-Rushing's "Identifying Uniform Core Journal Titles for Music Libraries: A Citation Study," *College and Research Libraries* 60 (March 1999): 153–63.

Mary Kay Duggan stressed the music scholar's need for information in diverse formats in "Electronic Information and Applications in Musicology and Music Theory," *Library Trends* 40 (Spring 1992): 756–80. The number of electronic resources now available to musicologists and other scholars of the performing arts would suggest that they are adopting the new information technologies. The next few years will undoubtedly yield new studies of users in the electronic environment.

COMPUTERS IN THE PERFORMING ARTS

Computers are being used in a variety of ways in the performing arts. As with other aspects of performing arts information, music is the field for which we have the most literature on computer use. In the field, we see computers used in musicological research and analysis, by the creative composer for writing music, and by music educators for the teaching of music. In libraries, information centers, and music archives, computers are used to search and retrieve material via online vendors, the Internet, or CD-ROM databases. And in the 1990s we saw musicians, scholars, music librarians, and music historians using the Internet as a resource for commerce, discussion groups, and electronic mail. Music librarians use computers for the same purposes as other librarians and information specialists.

An older, though comprehensive, article on electronic information in music is Mary Kay Duggan's "Electronic Information and Applications in Musicology and Music Theory," *Library Trends* 40 (Spring 1992): 756–80. The article covers all aspects of computers in music and music librarianship, and an extensive bibliography accompanies the article. It is a good place to begin reading about electronic resources in music.

The primary online database for music and related areas is *RILM Abstracts*. The counterpart to this database in print form is *RILM Abstracts of Music Literature (Repertoire Internationale de Litterature Musicale)*. The database covers all areas of music and some other aspects of performing arts that relate to music; the coverage begins at 1969. A thesaurus is available also. *RILM Abstracts* is available online through FirstSearch, and the files are available on CD-ROM for the decade between 1981 and 1992.

An invaluable source for periodical literature is Chadwyck-Healey's *International Index to Music Periodicals Full Text*. On the Web at http://iimpft.chadwyck.com/ (accessed June 21, 1999), this database covers over 300 periodicals useful to the music librarian or scholar.

Other databases of interest to the performing arts scholar are Magazine Index, Books in Print, Dissertation Abstracts Online, and ISI's Arts and Humanities Search. All have print counterparts. H. W. Wilson's *Readers' Guide to Periodical Literature* covers the general periodical literature.

Database searches in the performing arts fields of dance, theater, television and radio, and film are usually carried out in what we might term "general" or "multidisciplinary" databases. *Magill's Survey of Cinema* is the exception.

The Internet and CD-ROM offer great potential for performing arts materials, and a number of CD-ROM products include sound and textual material together in true multimedia PC products. A good source of information about music, dance, and theater Internet sites is the *Library of Congress Performing Arts Reading Room* page at http://lcweb.loc.gov/rr/perform (accessed March 8, 2000).

Electronic music applications are well covered in the journal *Computer Music Journal* at http://mitpress.mit.edu/e-journals/journal=home.tcl?issn=01489267 (accessed March 8, 2000). The site also offers copious links to organizations, publications, projects, manufacturers, and others important for research into computing in music.

Even the earliest music forms are accessible through online databases. See, for instance, the *Gregorian Chant* site at http://www.music.cua.edu/cantus/ (accessed March 8, 2000). Another unique site in music is *Music in the Public Domain*, which can be accessed at http://www.pdinfo.com/ (accessed March 8, 2000). As well as providing lists of music that is in the public domain, there are useful pages on copyright and other issues surrounding the use of music for performance.

The Computer Music Association (P.O. Box 1634, San Francisco, CA 94101-1634) publishes proceedings of its conferences on the subject of computing in music. Journals to consult on the topic include *Music Theory Online, Computing in Musicology*, and *Computers and the Humanities*. Other that are available online are listed on the MIT pages referenced above.

The Internet is such a rich source of performing arts material that we can only direct the reader to those sources that will lead elsewhere. The more limited Internet resources are especially numerous in the performing arts, and they range from sites on specific artists or particular genres to lists of companies offering hard-to-find sheet music. These resources can be found through the hundreds of music Web sites managed by the associations in the performing arts world or those maintained by garage bands and fans of particular performers. To access these, begin a search in any of the meta-indexes on performing arts and follow the links to the category of information needed.

MAJOR ORGANIZATIONS, INFORMATION CENTERS, AND SPECIAL COLLECTIONS

The number of national and international organizations in the performing arts is so great that attention can only be given here to those that are most significant to the librarian. Guides to the specific fields in the performing arts will offer additional information in much greater detail, as will the many directories now in print.

The International Association of Music Libraries has branches in most developed countries. It currently sponsors the *International Inventory of Music Sources/Repertoire International des Sources Musicales* (RISM), *Repertoire International de Litterature Musicale* (RILM), and *Repertoire International d'iconographie Musicale* (RIDIM). Since 1954, it has published *Fontis Artis Musicae*, the journal cited frequently in this chapter. The U.S. address for the IAML is c/o Lenore Coral, President, Cornell University Music Library, Lincoln Hall, Ithaca, NY 14853-4101. The International Music Council (UNESCO House, 1 rue Miollis, Paris F75732, France), one of the first nongovernmental agencies established by UNESCO, studies the development of music and produces many publications. The International Musicological Society (Case Postale 56, CH-4001, Basel, Switzerland) was founded in 1927 to promote research and has published the journal *Acta Musicologica* since 1928.

The Music Library Association (P.O. Box 487, Canton, MA 02021) supports a wide range of activities, including the publication of *Music Cataloging Bulletin* and, since 1943, *Notes*. Music Library Association activities may be followed on the Web at http://www.musiclibraryassoc.org/ (accessed April 5, 2000).

The Association for Recorded Sound Collections (P.O. Box 75082, Washington, DC 20013) was founded in 1966 and includes in its membership people in the recording and broadcasting industries as well as librarians in the performing arts. It publishes *ARSC Journal* and *ARSC Bulletin*. The Music Educators National Conference (1902 Association Dr., Reston, VA 22091) was founded in 1902 and has over 65,000 members. It publishes *Music Educators' Journal* and the quarterly *Journal of Research in Music Education*. The American Musicological Society (201 S. 34th St., Philadelphia, PA 19104) publishes *Journal of the American Musicological Society* and periodic lists of theses and dissertations in the field. An index to the dissertations is available on the Web at http://www.music.indiana.edu/ddm/ (accessed March 8, 2000). The American Symphony Orchestra League (777 14th St. NW, Ste. 500, Washington, DC 20005) was founded in 1942 and has a library pertaining to all aspects of the symphony orchestra. The American Guild of Organists (475 Riverside Dr., #1260, New York, NY 10115) is one of many specialized groups. Like many others, it publishes a monthly journal, *Music/AGORCCO*, as well as a journal, *The American Organist*.

Music industry statistics are published annually by the American Music Conference (5790 Armada Dr., Carlsbad, CA 92008). The Conference has a Web site at http://www.amc-music.com/ (accessed March 8, 2000) that provides links to pages on topics such as musical equipment, hardware and software for music applications, publications, and the like.

By contrast, the number of organizations devoted to dance is small; those that do exist seem to be largely concentrated in the areas of ballet and the teaching of dance. The Ballet Theatre Foundation (890 Broadway, New York, NY 10003) appeals to a broad audience for support and publishes *Ballet Theatre Newsletter*. The Imperial Society of Teachers of Dancing (Imperial House, 22-26 Paul St., London, UK EC2A 4QE) has a branch in the United States (4338 Battery Lane, Bethesda, MD 20814). The Society publishes a bimonthly, *Imperial Dance Letter*. The Dance Educators of America and Dance Masters of America both consist of dance teachers and have regional groups that supplement the activities of the national groups. The Dance Educators can be reached at P.O. Box 607, Pelham, NY 10803, and the Dance Masters at 12 Lucille Dr., Shelton, CT 06484.

The International Federation for Theatre Research (Department of French, University of Lancaster, Lancaster, UK) disseminates scholarly information through *Theatre Research International*. The American Society for Theatre Research http://www.theatre.uiuc.edu/theatre/ astr/ (accessed June 22, 1999) issues a newsletter and the semiannual publication *Theatre Survey*. The International Theatre Institute, established in 1948, has a branch in the United States (47 Great Jones St., New York, NY 10012) and publishes *Theatre Notes* and *International Theatre Information*.

The American Theatre Association (1010 Wisconsin Ave., NW, Washington, DC 20007) is concerned with all areas of educational theater. Its publications include *Theatre News*, *Placement Service Bulletin*, and an annual convention program and directory.

The Theatre Library Association (TLA) includes not only librarians but also actors, booksellers, writers, and researchers in its membership. Located in New York (Shubert Archive, 149 W. 45th St., New York, NY 10036), the Association publishes *Broadside*, a newsletter focusing on performing arts collections, and an annual, *Performing Arts Resources*. TLA also has undertaken other publishing projects, especially notable ones in the preservation and historical areas.

The University Film and Video Association (Chapman University, School of Film and Television, 333 N. Glassell St., Orange, CA 92866), publisher of a journal and digest, was formerly the University Film Association. *Film Society Bulletin* and *Film Critic* are published by the American Federation of Film Societies (3 Washington Square Village, New York, NY 10012). The American Film Institute (John F. Kennedy Center for the Performing Arts, Washington, DC 20566) supports a wide range of archival, research, and production activities. Publications have included *American Film* and *Guide to College Courses in Film and Television*. The Federation of Motion Picture Councils publishes *Motion Picture Rating Preview Reports*. The American Film and Video Association (920 Barnsdale Rd., #152, LaGrange, IL 60525) evaluates books and films and publishes *AFVA Evaluations*, *Sightlines*, and *AFVA Bulletin*.

Because music publishing often occurs outside the usual trade channels, two associations offer information about publishers of music. The National Music Publishers' Association, founded in 1917, was originally established as the Music Publishers Protective Association. Its focus is the publishing of popular music. The address is 711 Third Ave., New York, NY 10017. The Music Publishers' Association of the United States, also located in New York, is concerned with serious and educational music publishing. Its communications vehicle is *MPA Press*. The Association maintains a Web page that has many helpful links, including copyright information resources, important for performing artists, composers, and others in the creative fields, at http://www.mpa.org/ (accessed March 8, 2000).

The American Composers' Alliance (170 W. 74th St., New York, NY 10023) was founded in 1937. It publishes its *Catalogues* of new music and works for the protection of the rights of its members.

The Committee on Research in Dance (New York University, Dept. of Dance Education, 35 W. 4th St., New York, NY 10003) serves as a clearinghouse for research information in the field.

The Wisconsin Center for Theater Research (University of Wisconsin, Madison, WI 53706) concentrates on the performing arts in America. The Institute of Outdoor Drama (1700 Airport Rd., University of North Carolina, Chapel Hill, NC 27599) provides advisory and consultation services as well as bibliographic information on the specialty and a newsletter.

The most outstanding music collection in the United States is at the Library of Congress, which benefits from copyright deposit. The Music Division, established in 1897, has issued numerous catalogs, several of which are listed elsewhere in this book. Another notable collection is found in the Music Division of the Research Library of the Performing Arts in Lincoln Center (part of the New York Public Library). Music from the twelfth to the eighteenth centuries is a specialty of the Isham Memorial Library of Harvard University, while primary sources in early opera scores and librettos are a strength of the University of California Music Library in Berkeley. The Center for Research Libraries has several microform collections of research materials. In Europe, the Austrian National Library (Vienna), the Royal Library of Belgium (Brussels), the Biblioteque Nationale (Paris), the Deutsche Staatsbibliothek (Berlin), the British Museum (London), the Biblioteca Nazionale Centrale (Florence), and the Vatican Library (Rome) all have outstanding collections.

The Dance Collection in the Research Library of the Performing Arts (New York Public Library) includes photographs, scores, programs, prints, posters, and playbills, as well as instruction manuals and other literature on the dance. The Archives of Dance, Music and Theatre (University of Florida Libraries) contains about 20,000 similar memorabilia related to the performing arts in the twentieth century.

The Theater Arts Library (University of California at Los Angeles) has screenplays and pictures in addition to the general collection of English- and foreign-language books on film. The Harvard Theatre Collection (Houghton Library) has rare letters, account books, diaries, drawings, promptbooks, and playbills from the United State, Great Britain, and continental Europe. Similar materials relating to British and American theater from 1875 to 1935 (especially the Chicago Little Theatre Movement, 1912–1917) are found in the Department of Rare Books and Special Collections, University of Michigan. The Theatre Collection in the Research Library of the Performing Arts (New York Public Library) is one of the most notable anywhere. Bibliographic access is provided through its published catalog. The Free Library of Philadelphia has over 1.2 million items relating to the theater, early circuses, and minstrel and vaudeville shows.

The Library of Congress has several notable film collections, including those received on copyright deposit. The Dell Publishing Company has a collection of over 3.5 million pictures dealing with movie and television personalities.

This is only a small sampling of the performing arts collections in the United States and Europe that contain specialized information in a rich diversity of formats. Ash's directory and specialized guides to the different areas of performing arts will lead the reader to ample numbers of other libraries, information centers, and archives.

The World Wide Web offers a wealth of information on the performing arts. This should not be overlooked by the researcher beginning a search on associations, special collections, or arts societies. The sources listed below provide links to other resources and are worth the reader's perusal. (All were accessed on March 8, 2000.) For musicology societies and organizations, and music related links, see http://www.bishops.ntc.nf.ca/music/links.htm/. For community theater links, see the American Association of Community Theater site at http://www.aact.org/acctlink.html. For Motion Picture Association resources, check http://www.mpaa.org/. The Association has information about copyright, rating, and other issues important to the industry.

NOTES

[1] Kenneth McLeish, "Performing Arts," in *Key Ideas in Human Thought* (New York: Facts on File, 1993), pp. 548–49.

CHAPTER 10

PRINCIPAL INFORMATION SOURCES IN THE PERFORMING ARTS

PERFORMING ARTS IN GENERAL

Bibliographic Guides

596. The Literary Adviser: Selected Reference Sources in Literature, Speech, Language, Theater, and Film. Thomas P. Slavens. Phoenix, AZ: Oryx, 1985. 196p. ISBN 0-89774-236-2.

Still one of the most comprehensive specialized guides of this type, this compact work provides an annotated listing of nearly 650 reference sources. Arrangement is by geographical division and genre headings representing the types or forms of reference tools, such as dictionaries and encyclopedias or biographies. Annotations describe purpose and coverage of the individual titles, which are primarily American and British although others are included. This should prove to be a useful source of information for those interested in the major tools of the wide group of fields categorized as the performing arts. There is a table of contents, and a set of indexes provides access through author, title, and subject.

597. The Performing Arts: A Guide to the Reference Literature. Linda Keir Simons. Englewood, CO: Libraries Unlimited, 1994. 230p. (Reference Sources in the Humanities Series). ISBN 0-87287-982-8.

Another useful literature guide from Libraries Unlimited is this treatment of reference and information sources relevant to theater, dance, and such related arts as puppetry, mime, and magic. Excluded from coverage are music, film, and television, which are covered by other works in the series, as well as those tools dealing primarily with drama as literature rather than performance. The emphasis is on recent English-language works but old standards and foreign titles are included. Arrangement of entries is by type of material, with chapter coverage given to the most important directories, encyclopedias, handbooks, bibliographies, catalogs, chronologies, and so forth. These chapters are then subdivided by subject (theater, dance, etc.), providing easy access for the librarian or student user. Secondary sources such as core journals, electronic discussion lists, associations and societies, and libraries and archives are identified and described in additional chapters.

259

A useful Web site is **Performing Arts Library Guide* (http://www.lib.umd.edu/UMCP/MUSIC/LINKS.HTM [accessed December 1999]) at the University of Maryland, which provides databases, online journals, links, and guides to performing arts resources.

598. **Popular Entertainment Research: How to Do It and How to Use It.** Barbara J. Pruett. Metuchen, NJ: Scarecrow Press, 1992. 581p. ISBN 0-8108-2501-5.

Beginning with a fine introduction to the methods of conducting research, including the searching of databases and employment of interviews, Pruett has produced a useful guide to the reference literature of the various elements of popular culture. Coverage is given to film, theater, popular music, and broadcast media. Chapters furnish annotated listings of archive collections, research centers, databases, journals, and compilations of resources, and so forth. Annotations describe the resources and furnish hints on gaining access and making contacts. Listings of reference materials published before 1990 are given in each chapter.

*American Variety Stage, Vaudeville and Popular Entertainment 1870–1920 (http://lcweb2.loc.gov/ammem/vshtml/vshome.html [accessed December 1999]) is a useful Web-site maintained by the Library of Congress through its *American Memory* program. It supplies listings and images of theater playbills, sound recordings, motion pictures, Houdini memorabilia, English and Yiddish plays and scripts in the Library collections related to popular entertainments.

Bibliographies and Indexes

599. **Index to Characters in the Performing Arts.** Harold S. Sharp and Marjorie Z. Sharp, comps. Metuchen, NJ: Scarecrow Press, 1966–1973. 4v. in 6. ISSN 0072-873X.

Since its publication, this four-volume set has been regarded as an excellent source of information for the identification of characters in the various genre of the performing arts. Volume 1 covers non-musical plays (two volumes), volume 2 treats operas and musical productions (two volumes), volume 3 lists characters in ballets, while volume 4 covers radio and television. The established pattern was for a two-part coverage, beginning with an alphabetical listing of characters for which cross-references were provided to productions and followed by a list of citation symbols identifying title, type of production, number of acts, author or composer, name of theater, and place and date of first performance. Thousands of characters, both fictitious and real, major and minor, are treated.

Directories and Biographical Sources

600. **Bibliotheques et musees des arts du spectacle dans le monde/ Performing Arts Libraries and Museums of the World.** 4th ed. Andre Veinstein and Alfred S. Goulding. Paris: Centre Nationale de la Recherche Scientifique, 1992. 740p. ISBN 2-222-04604-1.

The first edition of this work appeared in 1960, the next edition seven years later. After seventeen years, the third edition was issued in 1984. Eight years later, the fourth edition was published; the work continues as an outstanding source of information on the collections of performing arts held in museums and libraries all over the world. Traditionally the text is written in both French and English. Entries provide information regarding size and composition of collections, regulations governing their use, and business hours of the various public and private institutions covered. Information is gathered through questionnaires, and arrangement of entries is alphabetical by country, then by city, with place names given in French. There is an index of names and of collections.

601. Contemporary Theatre, Film, and Television: A Biographical Guide Featuring Performers, Directors, Writers, Producers, Designers. ... Detroit: Gale Research, 1984– . Bienn. v.1– . ISSN 0749-064X.

The first volume of this work expanded and superseded two of the standard long-running serials, *Who's Who in the Theatre* (Gale, 1981) and *Who Was Who in the Theatre* (Gale, 1978). Since then, it has continued to provide good biographical sketches of hundreds of currently employed personalities as well as prominent retirees from the United States and Great Britain. The subtitle continues: "Managers, Choreographers, Technicians, Composers, Executives, Dancers, and Critics in the United States and Great Britain." There is an emphasis on U.S. nationals. Entries provide personal data, education, debut dates, credits, awards, and so forth, and vary somewhat in length because of the amount of material furnished by the biographee or found in secondary sources. Subsequent volumes each cover some 450 additional personalities, in a manner similar to that of *Contemporary Authors* (entry 1083), and update entries for those covered in *Who's Who in the Theatre*, including recently deceased individuals. The publication of volume 11 in 1993 brings the total to around 6,500 persons covered. Included is a cumulative index to the entire series as well as *Who's Who in the Theatre* and *Who Was Who in the Theatre*.

602. Directory of Blacks in the Performing Arts. 2d ed. Edward Mapp. Boston: G. K. Hall, 1990. 594p. ISBN 0-8108-2222-9.

The initial edition of this directory was issued in 1978, and this replacement effort is welcome. It expands previous coverage by some 150 pages and 300 entries and provides needed updates and revision of previous entries. It is now more comprehensive in its inclusion of musical groups as well as individual performers. All areas of the performing arts are treated and brief biographical information is provided for actors, playwrights, singers, composers, producers, broadcasters, choreographers, agents, and others associated with film, recording, television, and theater. There are some 1,100 entries alphabetically arranged and supplying listings of credits along with identifications. Coverage appears to be up-to-date in terms of the reporting of deaths and the work is especially helpful in identifying figures who have recently been discovered. There is an index classified by field of activity.

603. Money for Performing Artists. Suzanne Niemeyer, ed. New York: ACA Books/American Council for the Arts, 1991. 268p. ISBN 0-915400-96-0.

One of several directories of sources of support for artists published under the auspices of the American Council for the Arts, this tool is extremely useful in view of the diminished resources available during the past few years. Listed here are nearly 225 organizations, alphabetically arranged for easy access. Those organizations provide financial support to practitioners of all kinds rather than students, even though there are some awards for fledgling artists. All areas of the performing arts are included, with grants, awards, fellowships, residencies, competitions, and technical assistance identified. Entries supply description of types of support and requirements, details of the application process, and types of programs and services. Names of contact persons are given along with their addresses. There are indexes by organization, discipline, geographic area, and type of support offered.

604. Performing Arts Biography Master Index: A Consolidated Index to over 270,000 Biographical Sketches of Persons Living and Dead. 2d ed. Barbara McNeil and Miranda C. Herbert, eds. Detroit: Gale Research, 1982. 701p. (Gale Biographical Index Series, no. 5). ISBN 0-810310-97-X.

This is a convenience tool derived from the massive coverage of *Biography and Genealogy Master Index* (entry 30). Beginning as *Theatre, Film, and Television Biographies Master Index* (Gale Research, 1979), this new title expanded and increased coverage by more than double the number of citations to sketches in biographical dictionaries. The number of biographical dictionaries indexed was increased in similar fashion from about 40 to over 100 sources. It continues as a biennial publication, providing coverage of personalities representing a wide spectrum of the performing arts (theater, film, television, classical and popular music, dance, puppetry, magic, etc.). Entries provide dates of birth and death and references to the biographical dictionaries (including page numbers). The biographical sources are considered to be readily available in library reference collections, making this a practical reference tool.

605. **Performing Arts Resources.** New York: Drama Book Specialists, 1974– . Ann. ISSN 0360-3814.

This is an annual publication sponsored by the Theatre Library Association; in each issue there are articles describing the location, identity, and content of various collections of the performing arts. Earlier volumes covered such diverse units as the research collections in New York City, the motion pictures of the Library of Congress, and the Federal Theatre Project holdings at George Mason University. The work is intended for the use of serious students, scholars, and archivists to facilitate the search for materials on theater, film, broadcasting, and popular entertainment. More recent volumes have tended to emphasize collections on very specific topics as well as performance aspects. The Association's Web site, **Performing Arts Links*, provides access to the sites of a number of international organizations.

Handel's National Directory for the Performing Arts (5th ed., 1992) is an annual publication that began in 1988 and is issued by Bowker/Reed. It replaces both the *National Directory for the Performing Arts and Civic Centers* and the *National Directory for the Performing Arts/Educational* through its two-part coverage. Volume 1 lists institutions and organizations relevant to dance, instrumental and vocal music, theater, and performing arts in general by state and city subdivided by specialty. Volume 2 lists educational institutions and their programs in the performing arts. Several indexes provide access.

606. **Sourcebook for the Performing Arts: A Directory of Collections, Resources, Scholars, and Critics in Theatre, Film, and Television.** Anthony Slide et al., comps. New York: Greenwood, 1988. 227p. ISBN 0-313-24872-9.

This is a comprehensive directory of the performing arts in terms of scope, but selective in terms of its listings. It comprises three major segments, the first a listing of institutions (colleges, universities, libraries, etc.) and historical societies with major research collections. The second lists 200 major personalities involved in scholarly inquiry and/or criticism, while the third enumerates bookstores, production companies, journals, studios, and more. Information is brief (considered skimpy by some) and covers little more than the basics of addresses and telephone numbers of relatively few persons and units.

The Lively Arts Information Directory: A Guide to the Fields of Music, Dance, Theater, Film, Radio, and Television in the United States and Canada . . . , edited by Stephen R. Wasserman and Jacqueline Wasserman O'Brien (2d ed., Gale Research, 1985), provides more detailed and thorough coverage. Its magnitude is expressed in the complete subtitle, which goes on to state that it covers national, international, state, and regional organizations; government grant sources; foundations; consultants; special libraries; research and information centers; educational programs; journals and periodicals; and festivals and awards. The first edition appeared in 1982; and it was hoped that it had adopted a triennial frequency. Unfortunately, there have been no subsequent editions. Indexing varies with each component: the national and international organizations are accessed through a KWIC index while foundations are approached through subject and geographical indexes. There are over 9,000 listings, over a third more than in the initial edition, and the work is derived in part from the publisher's database of listings from the *Encyclopedia of Associations* (Gale Research, 1984; available in CD-ROM since 1997) but with enough additional material from a variety of publications to make it a worthwhile purchase.

607. **Variety Obituaries: Including a Comprehensive Index.** Chuck Bartelt and Barbara Bergeron, proj. eds. New York: Garland, 1988– . v.1– . ISBN 0-8240-0835-9 (v.1).

From Garland Press comes this multi-volume compilation of obituaries and related articles on entertainment figures as they appeared in *Variety* over a time span of more than eighty years; the work is of real value to researchers and serious students. Arrangement and format are similar to *Variety Film Reviews*, and entries appear in chronological sequence, beginning with volume 1, which contains obituaries published between 1905 and 1928. Much of the material originated as news stories and editorials as well as obituary listings. All aspects of entertainment are represented through listed personalities, who range from performers to business employees in fields from circus to television. No photographs are included. Volume 11 is an index to the first ten volumes and completes the initial set covering the years 1905–1986. The work continues with separately indexed volumes on a biennial basis. Volume 12 was issued in 1990 and covers the period 1987–1988, and volume 13 (1992) treats the years 1989–1990.

Jeb H. Perry has authored *Variety Obits: An Index to Obituaries in Variety, 1905–1978* (Scarecrow Press, 1980) for those who have *Variety* on microfilm and need only an index to the material.

608. **Variety Who's Who in Show Business.** Rev. ed. Mike Kaplan, ed. New York: R. R. Bowker, 1989. 412p. ISBN 0-8352-2665-4.

This revised issue represents what amounts to the third edition of this well-established biographical dictionary of show business personalities and updates earlier volumes published in 1983 and 1985. Included here are biographical data for some 6,500 contemporary major figures, including executives as well as performers in the areas of film, television, music, and theater. Also treated are writers and technicians along with directors and producers. Personalities are selected for achievement and for influence, with inclusions monitored by *Variety* (entry 959). Only living persons and individuals deceased subsequent to November 30, 1988, are considered. International figures are included for the first time. Information is concise for all entries, with listings of credits accompanying simple identifications.

MUSIC

Music in General

BIBLIOGRAPHIC GUIDES

609. **Baroque Music: A Research and Information Guide.** John H. Baron. New York: Garland, 1993. 587p. (Music Research and Information Guides, v. 16; Garland Reference Library of the Humanities, v. 871). ISBN 0-8240-4436-3.

To address the needs of specialists, students, performers, and others interested in the Baroque period of Western European music, this bibliographic guide cites some 1,400 books, dissertations, anthologies of essays, and to a lesser degree, periodical articles on the topic. Defining the Baroque period broadly, scope of coverage ranges from 1580 to 1730, with most entries published between 1960 and 1991. They represent various languages of Western Europe, with emphasis on English and German efforts. All aspects of Baroque music are treated, including publications on the stylistic elements, museums, institutions, and instruments, as well as theoretical and philosophical issues. Annotations vary in length from brief identifications of a few sentences to full-page descriptions. Entries provide cross-references and are indexed separately by subject, name, and author.

610. **Bibliographical Handbook of American Music.** D. W. Krummel. Champaign: University of Illinois Press, 1987. 269p. ISBN 0-252-01450-2.

The guide serves as an annotated bibliography of some 700 bibliographies, described in-depth, that help to define the literature of American music. There are four major sections, each of which is divided into chapters. The major sections are "Chronological Perspectives," covering major national bibliographies; "Contextual Perspectives," treating bibliographies of regions, ethnic elements, and persons; "Musical Mediums and Genres," with bibliographies of concert, popular, and sacred music; and "Bibliographical Forms," identifying and describing bibliographies of collections and writings about music as well as discographies. Books, articles, dissertations, and databases are covered in this work.

Another useful source by the same author is *Resources of American Music History: A Directory of Source Materials from Colonial Times to World War II* (Urbana: University of Illinois, 1980). This work identifies collections of importance to the study of music history. Under development and expanding since 1996 is *American Music Resource* (http://www.uncg.edu/~flmccart/amrhome.html [accessed December 1999]), providing information on and links to primary bibliographical sources for American music.

611. **Early American Music: A Research and Information Guide.** James R. Heintze. New York: Garland, 1990. 511p. (Music Research and Information Guides, v. 13; Garland Reference Library of the Humanities, v. 1007.) ISBN 0-8240-4119-4.

As part of the publisher's series, this annotated guide adds another important dimension to the organization and control of literature treating early American music prior to 1820. Books, articles, and dissertations are included, with coverage given to both primary and secondary source material. Included are such diverse items as published sermons, church records, and travelers' accounts, along with secondary descriptive matter. Publication dates run through 1987 and entries are placed within two major sections covering reference works (encyclopedias, dictionaries, bibliographic sources, etc.) and historical studies (general histories, topical writings, biographical sources, etc.). Nearly 2,000 entries are furnished, with annotations varying in length and substance. For the most part, coverage of folk, African-American, and Native American music is limited due to its treatment in other works. Author-title and subject indexes are supplied.

A complementary work by Heintze is *American Music Studies: A Classified Bibliography of Master's Theses*, published in 1989 by Information Coordinators. This effort supplies nearly 2,400 entries organized in a topical arrangement. This material is purposely omitted in *Early American Music*.

612. **Information on Music: A Handbook of Reference Sources in European Languages.** Guy A. Marco and Sharon Paugh Ferris. Littleton, CO: Libraries Unlimited, 1975–1984. 3v. ISBN 0-87287-096-0.

Originally planned as an eight-volume work to supplement the coverage of reference and research materials provided by Duckles (see entry 614) and others, this important series was apparently concluded with the publication of volume 3, *Europe*, in 1984. The set begins with volume 1, *Basic and Universal Sources* (1975), which furnishes annotated entries for over 500 tools in the field of music and related areas. Volume 2 (1977) covers the Americas and annotates over 800 reference sources relating to music in the Western hemisphere. The final volume on Europe appeared seven years after volume 2, and continued the same tradition of providing citations to numerous sources, including individual encyclopedia articles from M.G.G. (entry 668) and *The New Grove* (see entry 670). Annotations are for the most part brief but informative, and there are references to additional reviews. Each volume is separately indexed, although volume 2 contains a comprehensive index for volumes 1 and 2. An appendix in volume 3 updates materials in the preceding volumes.

613. **Music: A Guide to the Reference Literature.** William S. Brockman. Englewood, CO: Libraries Unlimited, 1987. 254p. (Reference Sources in the Humanities Series). ISBN 0-87287-526-1.

Designed to supplement the coverage found in Marco's *Information on Music* (entry 612) and the third edition of Duckles's *Music Reference and Research Materials* (entry 614), Brockman's guide is useful in its identification of important English-language sources issued since 1972. There are 841 entries describing both current and retrospective sources and providing a valuable perspective on the major reference and bibliographical sources, bibliographies of music literature, as well as music and discographies. There are sections treating current periodicals, associations, research centers, and other organizations in detailed fashion. Annotations are well-constructed and informative and vary in length. Generally, they provide ample description and in some cases, evaluation and comparison. The work has been commended for its excellent selection of items. Access is aided by author/title and subject indexes. A needed new edition is expected in early 1999.

Research Guide to Musicology, by James W. Pruett and Thomas P. Slavens (American Library Association, 1985), is the fourth in a series of literature guides edited and co-authored by Slavens, a professor of library science at the University of Michigan. The first part of the two-part format is by Pruett, a musicologist, who provides a series of survey essays on various subjects relating to music scholarship, elements of musicology, and periods of music history. The surveys close with selective bibliographies listing the important sources of information on the topics described. The final section, by Slavens, is an annotated bibliography of reference tools classified by form or type. Although somewhat narrow in conception, the work is still found to be useful. A more recent effort by academics is *Sourcebook for Research in Music*, by Phillip D. Crabtree and Donald H. Foster (Indiana University Press, 1993). It furnishes identification of information sources on the practice, history, and criticism of music, as well as listings of important bibliographies.

614. **Music Reference and Research Materials: An Annotated Bibliography.** 5th ed. Vincent H. Duckles and Ida Reed, eds. New York: Schirmer Books, 1997. 812p. ISBN 0-02-870821-0.

The single most important and popular guide for music students, teachers, and librarians, the fifth edition, as did its predecessors, represents a substantial revision and has an improved index. The basic format remains unchanged, with arrangement by category of tool such as dictionaries, encyclopedias, and so forth, but the chapter on electronic information resources should prove useful to those using the Internet. The work provides bibliographic information and annotations for more than 3,500 different reference books, an increase over the previous issue. About 1,300 are new to the work after having deleted a number of outdated items. With Duckles's death in 1985, Michael A. Keller, who succeeded him as head of the music library at the University of California at Berkeley, edited the fourth edition and served as an advisor to the current effort. The work has maintained the standards that made the title an indispensable work for students and specialists. There are indexes of persons, subjects, and titles.

Periodicals

615. **International Music Journals.** Linda M. Fidler and Richard S. James, eds. New York: Greenwood, 1990. 544p. (Historical Guides to the World's Periodicals and Newspapers). ISBN 0-313-25004-9.

This well-constructed directory supplies useful listings of some 200 mainstream and specialized periodicals. Selections are based on the popularity and importance of the journals in terms of either historical or contemporary impact. Entries are alphabetically arranged by title, and coverage is given to the history and significance of the journal along with its physical properties, overview of its content, and critical appraisal. Also provided are bibliographic references and locations of buildings. Some fifty contributors, specialists in the field, have supplied the well-developed and informative narratives as well as the bibliographies. The work opens with a concise account of the origins and development of music journals in the Western world. The appendix contains listings of recent journals and indexing/abstracting journals. Chronological, geographical, and subject lists of journals are furnished along with a name and title index.

616. **Music and Dance Periodicals: An International Directory & Guidebook.** Doris Robinson. Voorheesville, NY: Peri Press, 1989. 382p. ISBN 0-9617844-4-X.

This is a useful and comprehensive (although not exhaustive) directory of music and dance periodicals and annuals currently available. There are 1,867 entries arranged under nineteen broad subject categories and supplying detailed information. Given in each entry in addition to bibliographic identification are indication of date of inception, frequency, price, format, types of music covered, number and types of reviews, indexing, advertising, and circulation. Annotations describe such considerations as scope, purpose, and reference features. Various types of serials are included, ranging from fanzines to scholarly journals, but membership directories are omitted. Entries represent publications from more than fifty countries, largely from the Western world, making the directory valuable to a wide variety of users. The work is indexed in thorough fashion, supplying access through five approaches: title, publisher/organization, subject, country, and ISSN.

Internet Resources

*617. **The Virtual Musician: A Complete Guide to Online Resources and Services.** Brad Hill. New York: Schirmer Books, 1996. 257p. ISBN 0-028-64583-9.

From this music publishing house comes this guide or "musician's map" to an extensive array of resources now available on the Internet. The author is a well-known writer and expositor of the electronic elements surrounding the music industry, who began his career writing inspirational essays. He has examined the World Wide Web as a research tool and is wedded to various message boards and Usenet sites. Included here is a useful mix of fan forums, music publications, and Web sites treating music education, record labels, and MIDI addresses where music can be heard. These sites range from the well-known commercial pages to the obscure fan pages, and are organized into ten chapters examining the superhighway along with various providers with their sites. The final chapter covers CD-ROM. The work comes complete with a CD-ROM copy.

BIBLIOGRAPHIES AND CATALOGS

618. **African Music: A Pan-African Annotated Bibliography.** Carol Lems-Dworkin. Munich/Providence: Hans Zell/K. G. Saur, 1991. 382p. ISBN 0-905450-91-4.

This is a useful bibliography, comprehensive in scope because it treats the entire continent of Africa, identifying more than 1,700 books and articles in a variety of languages (European, African, and Middle-Eastern). Annotations are cogent and provide both descriptive narrative and exposition of the documents. Entries are arranged alphabetically by author and are indexed by subject. Inclusion of entries is highly selective when contrasted to a complementary tool produced by John Gray, *African Music: A Bibliographical Guide to the Traditional Popular Art and Liturgical Musics of Sub-Saharan Africa* (Greenwood, 1991), which supplies over 5,800 entries in treating a much smaller segment of the Continent. All types of writing, including newspaper articles and unpublished papers, are identified in this exhaustive work.

Indian Music Literature, by Mohammed Haroon (Indian Bibliographic Bureau, 1991), supplies 4,000 entries representing scholarly efforts and emphasizes the Hindustani and Carnatic systems. Entries are arranged into types of studies (general, biographical, musicological, etc.). The work is useful for its emphasis on Indian literature as opposed to proportional representation of North American or European publications. The work is not annotated, and there is no subject index.

619. **Bibliography of Black Music.** Dominique-Rene De Lerma. Westport, CT: Greenwood, 1981–1984. 4v. (Greenwood Encyclopedia of Black Music). ISBN 0-313-21340-2 (v.1).

There has been a recent emphasis on bibliographic coverage of black music, and this work has earned praise from reviewers for its comprehensive nature and ambitious scope. Volume 1 provides a bibliography of reference works (catalogs, bibliographies, encyclopedias, discographies, iconographies, directories, dissertations, etc.). Especially useful is a listing of nearly 200 periodicals related to the topic. Volume 2 represents the Afro-American idiom and covers general histories and works on spirituals, ragtime, musical theater, concert music, blues, gospel, popular, and jazz. Volume 3 covers geographical studies, including books, articles, dissertations, essays, and so forth, on the music of various geographic regions; it furnishes a section on ethnomusicology. Volume 4 covers theory and education and enumerates sources on instrumentation, performance, notation, and so forth. The arrangement of material over the entire set follows the organization established by *RILM* (entry 633). Volumes 3 and 4 have indexes.

620. **Dictionary Catalog of the Music Collection.** New York Public Library. Boston: G. K. Hall, 1982– . 45v. ISBN 0-8161-1387-4.

One of the leading collections of both music literature and printed music is presented in this set. The first edition appeared in 1964 and was supplemented in 1973 and 1976. Like its predecessor and similar publications from G. K. Hall, this is a photographic reproduction of the catalog, which offers detailed information on books, pamphlets, essays, periodical articles, and micro-materials as well as scores and librettos. The present edition includes imprints through 1971 and represents more than 3,500,000 individual documents. Special strengths of this collection are acknowledged to be in the areas of folk songs, Americana, music periodicals, programs, and various elements of printed music such as operas, historical editions, and vocal music. There is also an annual supplement, entitled *Bibliographic Guide to Music* (entry 629).

Music in the Royal Society of London 1660–1806, by Leta Miller and Albert Cohen (Information Coordinators, 1987), is a catalog of journal reports and manuscripts of this eminent scientific society on the subject of music. Acoustics, the ear and hearing, and various instruments and inventions are among the topics covered.

*621. Doctoral Dissertations in Musicology. 7th North American ed., 2d International ed. Cecil Adkins and Alis Dickinson, eds. Philadelphia: American Musicological Society, International Musicological Society, 1984. 545p. **Ann. Supp.**, 1985– . **Second Series**, 1990– . ISSN 1088-4281; 1088-6238.

This represents the seventh cumulative edition of combined listings of American and Canadian doctoral dissertations and the second cumulative listing of international doctoral dissertations. It is a comprehensive bibliography of 6,500 dissertations from all over the world, which superseded its predecessors due to its cumulative nature. Most dissertations are North American (nearly 35 percent), while the remainder are products of thirty countries (listed since 1972). Arrangement is by period covered and classified by topical subdivisions. There are references to abstracts in **Dissertation Abstracts* (entry 22) and the *RILM* work (entry 633). Works-in-progress are identified with asterisks and there are separate indexes for both subject and author. In 1990, the authors issued the first cumulative edition of what is termed the second series of this work. It is a compact volume of 171 pages providing a cumulation of annual supplements published since 1985. In 1996, the second cumulative edition was issued covering the period from 1984 to 1995.

The Office of Doctoral Dissertations then moved to Indiana University, where the work was continued in online format as **Doctoral Dissertations in Musicology Online* (or DDM) (http://www.music.indiana.edu/ddm [accessed December 1999]). It is in the process of converting all earlier records to digital format.

622. Electronic and Computer Music: An Annotated Bibliography. Robert L. Wick. Westport, CT: Greenwood, 1997. 198p. (Music Reference Collection, no. 56). ISBN 0-313-30076-3.

Developed within a classified format but employing historical application is this well-constructed and unique annotated bibliography of material treating electronic and computer music. The work is organized into chapters (each of which contain entries) following a general introduction describing the history and development of electronic music. Chapters treat histories and general works, synthesizers, instruments and devices, composition, MIDI, and teaching. Subsequent chapters examine bibliographies, dictionaries, and electronic music conferences. Some 250 books are identified and described in thorough and distinctive fashion. In the appendices are listings of online sources from the Internet, theses and dissertations, system manuals, and relevant periodicals. The work concludes with both a name and subject index.

623. Ethnomusicology Research: A Select Annotated Bibliography. Ann Briegleb Schuursma. New York: Garland, 1992. 173p. (Garland Library of Music Ethnology, v. 1; Garland Reference Library of the Humanities, v. 1136). ISBN 0-8240-5735-X.

This effort is designed to complement the coverage given to materials on ethnomusicology in earlier bibliographic sources: *Ethnomusicology*, by Jaap Kunst (M. Nijhof, 1959), and Bruno Nettl's *Reference Materials in Ethnomusicology* (Information Coordinators, 1973). Schuursma has produced a useful annotated listing of nearly 470 English-language items published since 1960, organized into five sections on history of the field, ethnomusicological theory and method, fieldwork method and technique, musical analysis, and influential related fields (anthropology, linguistics, folklore, sociology, and psychology). Entries are arranged alphabetically within each section, with cross-references utilized when items belong under more than a single category. Annotations are brief and are descriptive rather than evaluative. Both dance and popular music are excluded from coverage because each area will be covered in separate volumes. Name and subject indexes supply access.

624. **Literature of American Music III, 1983–1992.** Guy A. Marco. Lanham, MD: Scarecrow Press, 1996. 451p. ISBN 0-8108-3132-5.

This is the third volume of a set of bibliographies initiated by David Horn, a British music librarian, with *The Literature of American Music in Books and Folk Music Collections: A Fully Annotated Bibliography* (Scarecrow Press, 1977), providing comprehensive coverage of books and monographs in classified arrangement. That volume was followed by *The Literature of American Music in Books and Folk Music Collections. Supplement I* (Scarecrow Press, 1988) by Horn and Richard Jackson, an American, which continued the style and organization of the earlier effort. The current work by Marco supplements the coverage for succeeding years and provides critical commentary and background information. Organization is by LC classification. Marco's *Checklist of Writings on American Music, 1640–1992* (Scarecrow Press, 1996) is an index to the three volumes, citing author, title, publisher, and date.

625. **Medieval Music: The Sixth Liberal Art.** Rev. ed. Andrew Hughes. Toronto: University of Toronto, 1980. 360p. (Toronto Medieval Bibliographies, no. 4). ISBN 0-80202-2358-4.

This edition adds over 250 citations to the 2,000 or so items covered at the time of initial publication in 1974. These documents are listed separately and receive separate indexing. Classification numbers for these materials are interpolated into the main body of the text by use of cross-references. Indexing is thorough and there is exposition in the text to facilitate the search for subject classifications, which are based on twenty-nine main categories with numerous subcategories (geographical, chronological, individuals, genres, etc.). Essentially a bibliography of books and periodical articles on all aspects of medieval music, this work appeals to the relatively unsophisticated user who needs to find out about the topic. Annotations are brief and there are separate indexes of authors and subjects.

626. **Music Analyses: An Annotated Guide to the Literature.** Harold S. Diamond. New York: Schirmer Books/Macmillan, 1991. 716p. ISBN 0-02-870110-0.

This is a selective listing of some 4,650 citations to analyses issued in books, periodicals, doctoral dissertations, and master's theses. Emphasis is on those items that provide critical evaluation or exposition of the structural elements that justify and validate the artistic quality of the musical selections treated. The work seeks to update Diamond's initial effort, published eleven years earlier under a slightly different title. The present volume is annotated briefly, with indication of level of complexity of analysis presented. The work is intended for a wide audience from advanced students to laypersons, but is limited to analyses in the English language. Arrangement of entries is alphabetical by title under composer's name, with references to general criticism followed by those for individual works. There is an index of distinctive titles.

627. **Music Theory from Zarlino to Schenker: A Bibliography and Guide.** David Damschroder and David Russell Williams. Stuyvesant, NY: Pendragon Press, 1990. 522p. (Harmonologia Series, no. 4). ISBN 0-918728-99-1.

This is an important work serving both as a bibliography of Western music theory and a guide to important theorists. More than 200 works are covered, with entries treating theorists individually. Entries supply brief but informative essays on their writings, providing exposition of the distinctive and unique elements in their scholarship as well as their fit within groupings of musical theory. The essays are followed by a listing of citations to primary source material that includes translations, then by a listing of related works. The scope of the work actually is greater than the title implies, beginning with Glarean's "Isagogue in Musicen" in the early sixteenth century and ending with an analysis by Schoenberg published posthumously in 1967. Access is provided by cross-references along with a set of four indexes, assuring location of desired information.

*628. **Repertoire international des sources musicales/International Inventory of Musical Sources.** Munich: Henle, 1960– . ISBN 3-7618-0512-8, (ser. A, v.1, pt.5).

This is a joint effort on the part of the International Musicological Society and the International Association of Music Libraries and is commonly referred to as *RISM*. It is a catalog of all bibliographies of music, writings about music, and textbooks on music published up to 1800, identifying locations where they can be found. Over 1,000 libraries worldwide are cooperating in this venture. The two major series are A, alphabetical, and B, systematic or classified. Series A (followed by volume number in Roman numeral) includes individual editions in circulation from 1500 to 1800, which are arranged alphabetically by composer or editor. Series B (followed by volume number in Roman numeral) arranges the materials chronologically by category or genre, such as "manuscripts of polyphonic music." Bibliographical descriptions are generally given in greater detail in the B section. This large-scale effort has earned the respect of music bibliographers everywhere. Since 1997, segments have been made available on the World Wide Web as *RISM Online* (http://hplus.harvard.edu/alpha/rismonline.html [accessed December 1999]) through the HOLLIS project at Harvard University.

Series C has begun as a continuation of a series of directories of international libraries (entry 678). Progress is constant and volumes continue to appear in steady fashion on a wide variety of themes and topics, from Hebrew notated manuscript sources to ancient Greek music theory.

INDEXES, ABSTRACTS, AND SERIAL BIBLIOGRAPHIES

629. **Bibliographic Guide to Music.** Boston: G. K. Hall, 1975– . Ann.. ISSN 0360-2753.

A serial bibliography in its own right, this work serves as an annual supplement to the *Dictionary Catalog of the Music Collection* for the New York Public Library (entry 620). Beginning with coverage of the year 1975, it enumerates all types of music materials (including printed music) cataloged by the library during the period under scrutiny (September through August). Additional cataloging is included through use of MARC tapes from the Library of Congress in the areas of music literature (bibliography, history, criticism, and philosophy of music) and music instruction. The age of materials cataloged in any single year varies considerably, with both recently acquired items and older documents cataloged for the first time. Produced by computer, it serves many purposes including those of reference, acquisition, and cataloging.

630. **Music, Books on Music, and Sound Recordings.** Washington, DC: National Union Catalog, 1973–1989. Semiann. with ann. cum., quin. cum. ISSN 0041-7793.

As part of the National Union Catalog series, with its quinquennial cumulation, this work represented a reproduction of the catalog cards supplied by the Library of Congress and seven other leading music libraries. It covered music in breadth and identified printed music and recordings as well as books about music and musicians. The recordings are not limited to musical works, but represent a vast range of materials (educational, literary, political, etc.). It superseded *Library of Congress Catalog: Music and Phono-records* (Library of Congress, 1953–1972), which appeared semiannually but was limited to entries from LC printed cards. The effort ceased with the 1989 volume, and presently is continued as a microfiche publication, *Music Catalog (Washington, D.C.)*. It remains an important serial publication for reference, cataloging, and acquisition purposes.

*631. The Music Index. Warren, MI: Harmonie Park Press, 1949– . Mo. with ann. cum. ISSN 0027-4348.

This is the major indexing service for music literature and covers approximately 350 periodicals worldwide, some of which are indexed selectively. Indexing is by author and subject and the work surveys the world of music in comprehensive manner from musicology to the music industry. Obituaries, reviews of recordings, and book reviews are included. Music reviews are listed under name of performer. The major problem with the print version has always been its tardiness of appearance, with annual cumulations several years behind and monthlies delayed about six months. Recently, however, the problem has been alleviated; the 1997 cumulation has nearly 1,100 pages.

*Music Index on CD-ROM has been available since 1991 through Chadwyck-Healey and Harmonie Park Press. It is updated on an annual basis, combining the print editions from 1981 on into a single database easily searched by its users.

632. Music Library Association. Notes. Canton, MA: Music Library Association, 1934– . Q. ISSN 0027-4380.

The leading periodical for music librarians is the official publication of the Association. From 1934 to 1942, frequency was somewhat irregular and the publication was suspended during 1939. Since 1942, it has appeared on a quarterly basis and continues to provide excellent, comprehensive listings of recently published books and a section of excellent book reviews. Music scores are also identified and reviewed. There is a listing of current music publishers' catalogs and frequent reviews of new music periodicals.

*633. RILM Abstracts of Music Literature. New York: International RILM Center, 1967– . Ann. ISSN 0889-6607.

From 1967 to 1983 this title was issued on a quarterly basis. *RILM* is an acronym for the original parent organization's name in French (Repertoire International de Litterature Musicale). Now an annual, it is still regarded as a major contribution to the field of music bibliography. It provides abstracts of articles from some 3,500 periodicals, books, reviews, dissertations, iconographies, catalogs, and so forth in the field of music. Over 300 journals in 200 languages are treated. Abstracts are signed and include identification of keywords for purposes of indexing. There are various major divisions, including reference materials, collected writings, ethnomusicology, and instruments. An English language thesaurus was begun in 1992 in looseleaf format.

It is available online through FirstSearch and has a file size of 250,000 items, covering the period 1969 to the present with monthly updating. The CD-ROM version has been known as **MUSE (MUsic SEarch)* and provides complete coverage from 1969. It is available from National Information Services Corporation and now receives quarterly updating.

PRINTED MUSIC SOURCES—BIBLIOGRAPHIES, INDEXES, AND CATALOGS

634. **American Music Before 1865 in Print and on Records: A Biblio-Discography.** Rev. ed. James R. Heintze. New York: Institute for Studies in American Music, Brooklyn College, 1990. 248p. (Institute for Studies in American Music Monographs, no.30). ISBN 0-914678-33-7.

This is a revision and expansion of the useful classified and annotated bibliography of American music issued for the Bicentennial. It lists music originally printed prior to 1865, some of which is still available for purchase through normal channels. Additionally, there is a discography of LPs issued up to 1987. The useful features have been retained and include a segment on music in performing editions that lists works containing the music as it was conceived by its composers. Another segment on facsimile reprints includes references to music unavailable in other editions. Purchasing information is furnished along with series identification and content of anthologies. This is a reliable and well-constructed, work now made more valuable because it presently has over 1,300 entries, almost doubling its previous coverage. Access is aided by an excellent index; the work remains an important choice for reference departments.

635. **Anthologies of Music: An Annotated Index.** 2d ed. Sterling E. Murray. Warren, MI: Harmonie Park Press, 1992. 215p. (Detroit Studies in Music Bibliography, no. 68). ISBN 0-89990-061-5.

The initial edition began as a project for Murray's class and represented a useful pedagogical tool because it indexed the contents of about forty historical anthologies of musical examples. The second edition indexes some 4,670 pieces (as compared to the previous 3,560) in sixty-six anthologies. Coverage is given to more than sixty composers (forty in the first edition). These anthologies are organized chronologically and supply either complete movements or total compositions for music students. They are generally available through college libraries. Selections are arranged alphabetically by title under the composer's name. Entries vary in length and furnish general location information along with additional information about text translations, available recordings, partial signatures, and more. In general, selection of anthologies cannot be faulted and the practical value of the *Index* is evident. A useful feature is the genre index at the end of the work that classifies the entries into correct genres.

Harmonium Bibliography-Anthologies of Music (http://shift.merriweb.com.au/harmonium/books/anthologies.html [accessed December 1999]) is an excellent listing as part of a broad music bibliography.

636. **A Basic Music Library: Essential Scores and Sound Recordings.** 3d ed. Elizabeth Davis et al., eds. Chicago: American Library Association, 1997. 665p. ISBN 0-8389-3461-7.

Originally published in 1978, and again in 1983, this work initially emphasized scores and book material. The new subtitle indicates the shift in scope to provide a strong focus on sound recordings (rather than books). Nevertheless, it continues to provide awareness of books (reference books, biographies, etc.) although on a reduced basis, with some 240 titles listed as "Bibliographic Resources." Otherwise the work has been expanded and lives up to the standard that has earned it an enviable reputation among music librarians for its excellent coverage of materials useful to a music collection. Coverage includes identification of scores of all types, including anthologies of scores, study scores, performing editions, vocal scores, instrumental methods, and so forth. This edition is an extensive revision and expansion of the earlier efforts; it continues to supply a listing of music dealers. The index is well constructed and provides easy access to material within.

637. **The Book of World-Famous Music, Classical, Popular and Folk.**
4th ed., rev. and enl. James J. Fuld. New York: Dover, 1995. 718p. ISBN
0-486-228445-X.

First published in 1966, this work has been a favorite of reference librarians since it
first became available. Now in its fourth edition, it traces the development of hundreds of
popular melodies back to their original sources. Included are the various types of music mentioned in the title, along with identification of original singers and interesting commentary.
The new edition is essentially a reprint of previous works but with a supplementary section
that contains new information and corrections to entries in the main text. Entries provide
symbols as cross-references to the supplement for revisions. The work thus has the same
scope and remains a listing of musical compositions both vocal and instrumental written over
a period of 500 years. Arrangement of entries is by title; incipits or opening bars are provided
as are opening words for the vocal compositions. Entries include identification of the earliest
publication and information regarding its use and performance. Much of this information is only
chatty and much is important, such as biographical notes on composers, but all is interesting.

Music and War: A Research and Information Guide, by Ben Arnold (Garland,
1993), is a specialized bibliography identifying relevant art music concerning war developed
within the Western tradition. The work is divided into eight chapters, four of which treat music
(wars) of the twentieth century. Chapters supply a detailed essay along with annotated listings
of selected works and unannotated supplementary listings. Footnotes are useful in tracing primary
sources and related materials. Inclusion is appropriate and both familiar and lesser known
music are treated.

638. **The Catalogue of Printed Music in the British Library to
1980.** Laureen Baillie and Robert Malchin, eds. New York: K. G. Saur,
1981–1986. 62v. ISBN 0-851-57900-0; UK: Bowker-Saur, 1987. ISBN
0-86291-300-4.

Although this set represents a costly investment, it is a vast resource that provides
access to about 1,000,000 entries previously found in an array of bibliographic tools utilized
by the *British Catalogue of Music (BCM)* (slip catalog, accession lists, Royal Music Library
catalog, and a catalog of music published between 1503 and 1800). Much of the inconsistency and diversity of cataloging styles has been ameliorated through the computerization
process. Of interest to those primarily interested in printed music is the fact that this tool has a
much higher proportion of this material when compared to the New York Public Library's
Dictionary Catalog of the Music Collection (entry 620). Entries are found under composer's
names or under form headings such as "Songs," in which individual titles are identified.

Two computerized products have served to update the coverage. *Catalogue of
Printed Music in the British Library* was published in its second edition on CD-ROM by
Bowker-Saur in 1997 and provides access to such materials published between 1503 and
1996. It provides many search options, such as composer, title, key word, arranger, and pub-
lisher. *British Library Catalogue: Music Library* continues the coverage of the print set by
providing both online and CD-ROM access to the *British Catalogue of Music*, a monthly publication that lists both popular and classical music scores published in the United Kingdom.
Another work is *The Catalogue of Music in the Bath Reference Library to 1985*, by Jon A
Gillaspie (K. G. Saur, 1986, 4v.), which furnishes a listing of manuscripts and related items.
Because Bath served as a center for the performance of music during the eighteenth and nineteenth centuries, the work provides a panorama of musical history.

639. **Chamber Music: An International Guide to Works and Their
Instrumentation.** Victor Rangel-Ribeiro and Robert Markel. New York:
Facts on File, 1993. 271p. ISBN 0-8160-2296-8.

Considered to be a practical and up-to-date guide to the repertory of chamber music, this useful tool supplies 8,000 citations to musical works for a variety of instrumental combinations ranging from three to twenty performers. The work is divided into three major segments, the first of which treats composers up to the time of Haydn and Mozart. The second segment covers composers from Beethoven to the present day, while the third part supplies an index to combinations of instruments required in the pieces identified. Both vocal and instrumental pieces are included. Entries are well-constructed and provide exposition and description of year of composition, duration, and publication elements. Utilizing a grid format, information on alternate scoring is supplied, making it a well-rounded and useful source.

640. **Collected Editions Historical Series & Sets & Monuments of Music: A Bibliography.** George R. Hill and Norris L. Stephens. Berkeley, CA: Fallen Leaf Press, 1997. 1349p. (Fallen Leaf Reference Books in Music, no. 14). ISBN 0-914913-22-0.

This is the successor to Anna H. Heyer's classic effort (discussed below). This is a superb effort to identify historically important collected editions and sets. The current work is much more extensive in its coverage than Heyer's and enumerates over 8,000 numbered sets, collected editions of composers, as well as important anthologies and publishers' series. Access for each musical work is provided by name of composer and reference to the sets in which the work appears. Entries furnish composer, uniform title, instrumentation, thematic catalog number, original source where available, and so forth. There is a listing of catalogs and sets. The work was supported by a grant from the NEH. It appears that future editions will appear in CD-ROM format.

The third and final edition of *Historical Sets, Collected Editions, and Monuments of Music: A Guide to Their Contents*, by Anna H. Heyer, was published in two volumes (American Library Association, 1980). First published in 1957, it has been a standard work, identifying over 1,300 sets and collections of music published in the Western world up to 1980. At Duke University there is an important collection of nineteenth- and twentieth-century century American sheet music for which access is provided at the Web site, *Historic American Sheet Music* (http://scriptorium.lib.duke.edu/sheetmusic/ [accessed December 1999]). There is an attempt to provide comprehensive coverage of nineteenth- and twentieth-century sets, thus making this an excellent tool for scholars in locating scores.

*641. **The Music Cataloging Collection.** Dublin, OH: OCLC, 1991– . Q. (CD-ROM).

For the past few years the bibliographic records for musical scores and sound recordings in the OCLC Online Union Catalog have been available in CD-ROM format on a quarterly basis. This is of great value to music librarians in their endeavor to stay abreast of collection development in an elusive area of concern. The *LC Authorities Collection* is included automatically with the purchase. The CD-ROM format has become increasingly popular for both new editions of standard information tools and serial offerings of bibliographic sources. With the enormous cataloging database at OCLC, this resource is proving to be a wise selection. It is issued on two disks each quarter and provides full cataloging data for bibliographic identification.

642. **Music in Harvard Libraries: A Catalogue of Early Printed Music and Books on Music in the Houghton Library and the Eda Kuhn Loeb Music Library.** David A. Wood. Cambridge, MA: Houghton Library; distr., Harvard University Press, 1980; repr., Woodbridge, CT: Research Publications, 1985. 306p. ISBN 0-674-59125-9.

This important bibliography contains both music literature and music in print. The material here, regarded as early music, was printed before 1801 and had been cataloged at Harvard by January 1967. Thus, it serves as a resource tool for library use but is even more important as an identification or verification tool for the serious student and scholar of music. Songsters and sheet music for songs are excluded, as are liturgical books, hymnals, psalters, libretti, and musical manuscripts. Coverage embraces monographs, treatises, pamphlets, music periodicals, as well as a large collection of scores, part-books, and so forth. Arrangement is alphabetical by author, composer, publisher, or title. Full bibliographic descriptions are provided. *Eda Kuhn Loeb Music Library* (http://www.rism.harvard.edu/MusicLibrary/Welcome.html [accessed April 5, 2000]) contains links to various components and instructions for finding materials through the online catalog.

Music and CRC Catalogs, issued by the University of West Ontario through APAR Systems, Ltd., has provided a CD-ROM version of its library catalog since 1991. It contains bibliographic description of some 70,000 titles of its music collection, along with 10,600 related items from the catalog of the University's Curriculum Resource Center.

643. Music Library Association Catalog of Cards for Printed Music, 1953–1972: A Supplement to the Library of Congress Catalogs. Elizabeth H. Olmstead, ed. Totowa, NJ: Rowman & Littlefield, 1974. 2v. ISBN 0-87471-474-5.

The title provides an indication of the content of this work, which was four years in the making under the sponsorship of the Music Library Association, aided by numerous volunteers. What Olmstead (the music librarian at Oberlin) and her fellow workers have done is to identify 30,000 entries of music cataloging that had been submitted to the Library of Congress by cooperating libraries but for some reason had not been entered into the *National Union Catalog*. The volunteers did a good job of editing to provide at least some conformity to acceptable standards of the Library of Congress, although there is some unevenness among the entries. Most deficient is the poor quality of reproduction: Some entries are virtually unreadable. Although it serves partially as a supplement to the *Library of Congress Catalog: Music and Phono-records* (entry 630n), this does not identify the libraries responsible for the cataloging, except for New York Public and Harvard University.

*LC MARC: Music is an online database available from the Library of Congress that furnishes bibliographic coverage of monographs of printed and manuscript music as well as non-music sound recordings cataloged by the Library from 1984 to the present. It is also available on CD-ROM as part of the Current Cataloging Database project. Updates are provided every month.

644. Music-in-Print Series. Philadelphia: Musicdata, 1974– . Irreg. Supp., 1979– . Ann; also irreg. specialized supps. ISSN 0146-7883.

Corresponding somewhat to *Books in Print* are these much-needed listings of available music in print. Individual volumes cover different types of music, both vocal and instrumental, and are compiled from publishers' catalogs to provide a continuous record of music available to the performer, instructor, and student. There are seven volumes to date; each is supplemented every few years. Volume 1 covers sacred choral music (2d ed., 1985; supps., 1988, 1992); volume 2, secular choral music (2d ed., 1987; supps., 1991, 1993); volume 3, organ music (2d ed., 1984; supp., 1990); volume 4, classical vocal music (1976; supp., 1985), volume 5, orchestral music (1979; supp., 1983), volume 6, string music (2d ed., 1980; supp., 1984), and volume 7, classical guitar music (1989). An arranger index was begun in 1987; as were a master composer index in 1989, a master title index in 1990, and a master index to both types of choral music in 1991. The continuous record is maintained through these new editions and specialized supplements; as well as a general annual supplement to the whole set.

Thousands of pieces have been identified from nearly 1,000 different publishers worldwide. Entries provide title, composer, arranger, instrumentation, and publisher.

The most comprehensive listing of printed music currently available, both popular and serious, can be found at the Web site of the J.W. Pepper Company, "the world's largest sheet music retailer". *Pepper Music Network* (http://www.jwpepper.com/ [accessed April 5, 2000]) furnishes a small image of the score and a sound byte as well.

Vocal Music

(Library patrons should note that additional works of this kind can be found by searching under the catalog subject heading "Vocal Music—Bibliography.")

645. **American Choral Music Since 1920: An Annotated Guide.** David P. Devenney. Berkeley, CA: Fallen Leaf Press, 1994. 278p. (Fallen Leaf Reference Books in Music, no. 27). ISBN 0-914-91328-X.

This work completes the author's line of titles surveying American choral music, and catalogs original choral music written by American composers from 1920 to the time of publication. Some 3,000 compositions by seventy-six composers have been identified and described. Arrangement is alphabetical by composer then by title with entries supplying opus number, date of composition, instrumentation or other performing forces needed, author of text, publisher, location of composer's manuscript, reviews, and references to items in the extensive annotated bibliography. Items in the bibliography were included for their treatment of the history and performance practice. The music is indexed by author and source of text, title, performing force, and duration.

Devenney's *Nineteenth-Century American Choral Music: An Annotated Guide* (Fallen Leaf, 1987) is similar in format, covering the nineteenth century, while his *Early American Choral Music: An Annotated Guide* (Fallen Leaf, 1988) catalogs the music of the eighteenth and early nineteenth centuries.

646. **American Oratorios and Cantatas: A Catalog of Works Written in the United States from Colonial Times to 1985.** Thurston J. Dox, comp. Metuchen, NJ: Scarecrow Press, 1986. 2v. ISBN 0-8108-1861-2

This is a work of major proportions and one that was needed by reference librarians because it identifies 3,450 choral pieces spanning the history of our country from its beginnings to the present day. Dox is a professor of music at Hartwick College and used his expertise to construct a tool that received plaudits for both its organization and detail. There are four sections, beginning with oratorios, followed by choral cantatas, ensemble cantatas, and choral theater. Entries provide publication information, locations for both published and unpublished items, performance requirements, text (source), length, and number of movements. Some annotations are given as well as commentary from composers and critics.

647. **Choral Music Reviews Index, 1983–1985.** Avery T. Sharp. New York: Garland, 1986. 260p. (Garland Reference Library of the Humanities, v. 674). ISBN 0-8240-8553-1.

This is a useful source of reviews of over 2,000 pieces of choral music in sixteen English-language journals for a three-year period. Most of the works are Christian sacred hymns, making this especially valuable for religion collections, choir directors, and choir members. The secular music listed is generally intended for schools, and therefore is of interest to school libraries and music instructors. Arrangement of entries falls under three main categories—octavos (single compositions), collections, and extended choral works (liturgy, oratories, etc.)—and is alphabetical by title. Entries include titles, composers, arrangers or editors, performers, publishers, vocal ranges, and languages, as well as commentary on accompaniment and use. Separate indexes are furnished for composer, arranger, editor, use, level of group, instrumentation, and voicing.

Sharp has continued his work with *Choral Music Reviews Index II 1986–1988* (Garland, 1990), which follows the same format and indexes fourteen journals. Although there are two fewer journals, the total number of entries has increased substantially.

648. **Musical Settings of American Poetry: A Bibliography.** Michael Hovland. Westport, CT: Greenwood, 1986. 531p. (Music Reference Collection, no. 8). ISBN 0-313-22938-4.

Of interest to students of both music and literature is this important source of information that serves as a guide to musical settings of American poetry. Included here are some 5,800 musical settings of 2,400 poems by nearly 100 American writers. The art songs and choral literature represent the efforts of some 2,000 composers. Only published music is listed (both commercial and private), along with recorded music and music in facsimile form. Arrangement is by poet, subdivided by title of poem. Included in the entries are indications of publication information, voice specifications, accompaniment, and collection that contains the song. Information is given on the poet in terms of dates, and for some entries, library holdings are given along with notes of discographies. Access is provided by both a composer index that supplies dates and names of the poets and an index of literary titles.

649. **A Singer's Guide to the American Art Song 1870–1980.** Victoria E. Villamil. Metuchen, NJ: Scarecrow Press, 1993. 452p. ISBN 0-8108-2774-3.

This is a useful resource for a variety of specialists and interested parties, treating the musical composition of nearly 150 composers. Songs were selected for their history of performance or perceived quality and are limited to those composed only for solo voice either with or without accompaniment. In this regard, the work serves as a good complement to the others in this section that focus on choral music. Entries for composers include a biographical sketch and a catalog of works. Songs are described and identified in a manner to facilitate their use by performers. A bibliography and discography are furnished, and there are indexes to titles and poets/lyricists.

Repertoire for the Solo Voice, by Noni Espina (Scarecrow Press, 1977), is an older two-volume guide from the same publisher with extensive listings of solo vocal literature identifying 9,726 songs and arias. The music covers a time period of 600 years and entries furnish title, voices for performance, authorship, range, descriptive commentary on the general character, specific features of the work, level of difficulty for accompanist, and bibliographical source. Indexes identify sources, with names of poets and librettists as well as composers.

650. **Vocal Chamber Music: A Performer's Guide.** Kay Dunlap and Barbara Winchester. New York: Garland, 1985. 140p. (Garland Reference Library of the Humanities, v. 465). ISBN 0-8240-9003-9.

This work has proved to be of value in music libraries. It defines vocal chamber music as composition for one voice and one instrument (other than keyboard or guitar) up to a dozen solo voices and twelve solo instruments. Compositions for solo voices and chorus also are given when no instrumentation is needed. Works included cover more than 300 years, dating from 1650 to 1980, and generally are available for purchase, making this a practical listing for the music instructor. Entries provide composer, title, publisher, and scoring. There are indexes to publishers or collections and to voice type. Unfortunately, there is no index to instruments identified.

Instrumental Music

(Library patrons should note that additional material can be found under the catalog subject heading "Instrumental Music—Bibliography." Material for specific instruments may be found under the name of the instrument, for example, "Piano—Music—Bibliography.")

651. **Guide to the Pianist's Repertoire.** 2d ed., rev. and enl. Maurice Hinson. Bloomington: Indiana University Press, 1987. 856p. Repr., 1994. ISBN 0-253-20885-8 (pbk.).

The author has compiled a number of books on music for the piano. Fourteen years after its initial appearance, the second edition of this useful and important title was issued in an enlarged form. Known for its extensive coverage of composers and their works in the past, the new edition assures continued recognition in this regard. Hundreds of composers from countries all over the world are listed and their compositions enumerated. Works have been graded for each composer, and related bibliographic entries of books and periodical articles have been integrated into the main body of the work. The general bibliography includes books, articles, and dissertations, and the appendices include a useful directory of publishers. Several indexes to composers and others conclude the work.

652. **Guitar and Lute Music in Periodicals: An Index.** Dorman H. Smith and Laurie Eagleson. Berkeley, CA: Fallen Leaf Press, 1990. 104p. (Fallen Leaf Reference Books in Music, no. 13). ISBN 0-914913-16-6.

Generally, specialized music periodicals issue supplements that carry original compositions, which then become somewhat fugitive and difficult to retrieve even if the periodicals are covered in *The Music Index* (entry 631). This tool indexes the musical compositions appearing in six periodicals devoted to the lute or guitar, three of which have not been treated in *The Music Index*. They vary considerably in longevity, from the short-lived *Chelys* (1976–1977), *Electric Chelys* (1977–1978), and *Guitar and Lute* (1974–1983), to the still-current *Lute Society of America Journal* (1968–), *Lute Society of America Newsletter* (1966–), and *Guitar Review* (1946–). The cutoff date is December 1988 for the continuing publications, resulting in a listing of 780 musical pieces. Arrangement is under four categories: composer, title, medium, and source/arranger. Entries under composer are full and supply information regarding notation, format, and presentation.

653. **A History of Keyboard Literature: Music for the Piano and Its Forerunners.** Stewart Gordon. New York: Schirmer Books/Macmillan, 1996. 528p. ISBN 0-02-870965-9.

This is a comprehensive work presenting the history of literature for all stringed keyboard instruments. It presents a clear description and catalog through its examination of basic structure, key features, schools of composition, trends, and influential forces. The work opens with a chapter on the history and development of keyboard instruments and then treats European contribution with a number of separate chapters devoted to individual composers. The final chapter covers North American developments in the twentieth century thus completing the survey of Western achievement in keyboard music.

Instrumental Music Printed Before 1600: A Bibliography by Howard M. Brown (Harvard University Press, 1965) is a scholarly work that attempts to include all known publications in the field prior to 1600, beginning with the period of the 1480s, shortly after the development of the printing press. Arrangement is chronological, and under each year publications are listed alphabetically by author or publisher. The contents are described and references are provided to modern editions that contain the entries. Much of the music included has been lost or was never published, making the work of great value to music historians. Vocal music is included only if it contained instrumental parts or segments. Although the work has been criticized for omissions (the inevitable challenge to an all-encompassing bibliography), Brown has succeeded in providing a work that has been admired by those it was designed to serve.

654. Music for Oboe, 1650–1800: A Bibliography. 2d ed., rev. and exp. Bruce Haynes. Berkeley, CA: Fallen Leaf Press, 1992. 432p. (Fallen Leaf Reference Books in Music, no. 16). ISBN 0-914913-15-8.

This specialized bibliography of Baroque oboe music was developed by a scholar/ performer with the purpose of treating every solo and chamber piece that was intended to be played by that instrument. The oboe has been broadly interpreted to include the English horn and certain variant forms. Within the 3,000 entries are included some 10,000 musical pieces. Entries are arranged alphabetically by name of composer and coded for instrumentation. Enhancing its utility for scholarship is coverage given to national origin and information furnished with respect to manuscripts, original publications, library locations, and contemporary editions. The first edition of this work was issued in 1985, and the second edition represents a more expansive approach in terms of supplying greater detail and refined treatment of the entries.

655. Organ Literature: A Comprehensive Survey. 3d ed. Corliss Richard Arnold. Metuchen, NJ: Scarecrow Press, 1995. 2v. ISBN 0-8108-2964-9 (v.1); 0-8108-2965-7 (v.2).

The initial edition was issued as a single volume in 1973. It was organized into two major parts, treating the historical survey and the biographical catalog. The second edition (1984) simply reprinted the first part, with slight modification of tables but no updating of chapter bibliographies or text, as volume 1. Volume 2, however, was a revised and expanded dictionary of composers and their works (originally part 2). Volume 1 offers a chronological overview of the various periods of musical history and development of the organ and its music. Chapters cover different periods and developments and conclude with bibliographies. The biographical catalog (now volume 2) doubled in size and presents a detailed but not exhaustive listing of individual works and anthologies under the composer's name. The third edition updates its predecessor with greater coverage of modern composers and composition through 1993. The source remains an excellent survey of the primary literature, although certain entries may be faulted for omissions.

Harpsichord and Clavichord Music of the Twentieth Century, by Frances Bedford (Fallen Leaf, 1993), supplies listings of about 5,600 compositions by 2,700 composers. Like others in the Fallen Leaf line, there is hope that such a compilation will inspire renewed interest in study and performance of the instruments. The first section treats harpsichord music while the second covers the literature of the clavichord. Appendices supply directories of composers and of publishers, music centers, and libraries. Various indexes assure access.

656. The Piano in Chamber Ensemble: An Annotated Guide. Maurice Hinson. Bloomington: Indiana University Press, 1978; repr., 1996 570p. ISBN 0-253-21055-0 (pbk.).

Even with Hinson's comprehensive *Guide to the Pianist's Repertoire* (entry 651), there is still a call for this more specialized volume. Limited to those works in which the piano shares the performance with other instruments, its arrangement of entries makes it a useful source for any performer or instructor. First covered are works for the piano and a solo instrument in which a number of unusual instruments are identified; second are compositions for the piano and two other instruments, progressing up to the piano and seven other instruments. Entries generally provide a brief musical analysis that is valuable in furnishing insight into the nature and character of the piece. There is a list of American publishers and agents and their publications.

657. **Subject Guide to Classical Instrumental Music.** Jennifer Goodenberger. Metuchen, NJ: Scarecrow Press, 1989. 171p. ISBN 0-8108-2209-1.

This guide provides educators and radio, television, and film production people with a handy and convenient index to classical instrumental music classified by topic or subject, such as "wind," "occupations," and "Shakespeare." Subject headings are conceived by the author and lack the uniformity of a standard thesaurus, but appear to be functional. Entries provide composer's name and dates, title and nickname of composition, opus number, translation, and type. Goodenberger's experience as a radio programmer enables her to select a core body of instrumental music primarily from the nineteenth century. Operas are included when it is felt that they have a central theme. Selection criteria are unclear; there are many omissions of appropriate musical pieces under the 200 non-musical subject headings chosen. Availability is a major factor; entries are thought to be accessible as recordings in libraries and stores. The work suffers somewhat from the lack of a composer index.

THEMATIC CATALOGS AND ANTHOLOGIES

Thematic catalogs are those highly specialized reference tools used by musicologists and trained music librarians to identify compositions. They provide a listing of incipits (beginnings or opening bars up to twelve notes) and serve as exact identifiers of particular pieces. Various editions may differ in their inclusiveness, possibly due to the inability of the authors to gain copyright permission. An important contribution to music reference since their initial appearance in the eighteenth century, thematic catalogs are developed on a variety of subjects (single composer, form, style, historical period, or school). Only a few are given here, along with a few anthologies of musical compositions, for which the numbers are legion.

658. **Dictionary of Musical Themes.** Rev. ed. Harold A. Barlow and Sam Morgenstern. New York: Crown, 1975; repr., London: Faber, 1983. 642p. ISBN 0-571-11998-0.

Called by Sheehy and others the "Bartlett" for musical themes, this has been a vital work; it has evolved from Barlow's earlier efforts in the 1940s and subsequent years. The first few notes from 10,000 themes of instrumental music are listed (rather than the notation from the initial lines most typical of thematic catalogs). Arrangement is by composer, followed by titles. The notation index is what makes this work a useful identification source, since it arranges the themes alphabetically by notation after having transposed them to the key of C. The tune or melody of the theme can be played on a keyboard or vocalized for ready identification. An index of titles provides easy access if a title is known and one wishes to check its theme. There is a companion volume, *Dictionary of Opera and Song Themes . . .* (entry 659).

659. **Dictionary of Opera and Song Themes, Including Cantatas, Oratorios, Lieder, and Art Songs.** Rev. ed. Harold A. Barlow and Sam Morganstern. New York: Crown, 1976. 547p. ISBN 0-517-52503-8.

Originally published in 1950 under a different title, this is a companion work or complementary volume to *Dictionary of Musical Themes* (entry 658). Over time it has changed only slightly except for the title. It lists notations from themes of vocal composition of all types (operas, oratorios, cantatas, art songs, and miscellaneous vocal works). Its basic approach and format are similar to *Dictionary of Musical Themes*, and the initial notes of some 8,000 themes are enumerated alphabetically by composer, then by title of work. Opera themes are identified by act and scene and words are included with the musical bars. The notation index is similar to that of the companion volume, with transposition to key of C and alphabetical arrangement of notes. There are also indexes of first lines and of songs.

660. **National Anthems of the World.** 9th ed. W. L. Reed and M. S. Bristow, eds. New York: Blandford Press; distr., Sterling, 1997. 608p. ISBN 0-3043-4925-9.

This is a new edition of this anthology or collection of both music and words of the national anthems of various nations. A new edition generally appears about every five years; although necessity dictates change, as in the case of the seventh edition, which was issued only two years after the sixth. During that period of time there were changes in lyrics, vocal scores, and even language for twenty-five countries. In the past this work not only has documented such changes but also has introduced the anthems of newly created countries. Generally, both words and music are included, with the text in the original language. English translations are furnished, and both authors of texts and composers are identified. In addition, there are brief historical descriptions that include the dates that the works were officially designated as national anthems. More than 180 nations are represented in alphabetical order.

A nice feature of *E-Conflict Encyclopedia* is the section on "National Anthems of the World" (http://www.emulateme.com/anthems [accessed December 1999]), providing a recording in MIDI of national anthems of many countries.

661. **Thematic Catalogues in Music: An Annotated Bibliography.** 2d ed. Barry S. Brook. Stuyvesant, NY: Pendragon Press, 1997. 602p. ISBN 0-918728-86-X.

Barry Brook of New York University has been one of the most respected names in music bibliography and also one of the influential figures in the creation of *RILM Abstracts . . .* (entry 633). The first edition of this work (1972) established itself as a standard for scholarship and utility, receiving excellent reviews and warm reception from music librarians. Now it has been updated and provides coverage of thematic catalogs from 1645 to 1996. Essentially, it is a bibliography of thematic catalogs, which have been the most useful and at the same time the least controlled category of reference tool until Brook's initial effort. Arrangement is by composer or compiler if more than one composer is treated. Annotations vary from several words to detailed listing of contents. This is without a doubt the most comprehensive source of its kind, and supersedes earlier, less detailed efforts. It is of inestimable importance to the music librarian, with its full bibliographic descriptions and references to related works. There are a good exposition on thematic catalogs, useful appendices, and a detailed index of subjects and authors.

DICTIONARIES, ENCYCLOPEDIAS, AND HANDBOOKS

662. **Encyclopedia of Music in Canada.** 2d ed. Helmut Kallman et al., eds. Buffalo, NY: University of Toronto Press, 1992. 1524p. ISBN 0-8020-2881-0.

This is a timely expansion of what had already been the largest, most comprehensive, and most detailed reference source on Canadian music. The initial edition was published in 1981 and was warmly received by both reviewers and librarians. The new issue continues to fulfill its purpose to describe music in Canada and to help define the country's musical relations with the rest of the world. There are several thousand entries, with numerous extensive survey-type articles on such topics as ethnomusicology. Biographies are provided; they include living persons as well as those deceased. Music of all types is treated although the emphasis is on art music. Performing groups, institutions, organizations, manufacturers, and musical compositions are covered as well. There are many cross-references and bibliographies as well as discographies. An interesting feature is the index of persons, places, and things that did not receive a separate entry.

663. **Encyclopedia of Recorded Sound in the United States.** Guy A. Marco and Frank Andrews, eds. New York: Garland, 1993. (Garland Reference Library of the Humanities, v. 936). ISBN 0-8240-4782-6.

In what represents a unique effort, the editors have created a compendium of information on the recording industry in this country from its beginnings with the Edison cylinders to the CD era today. All related aspects and topics are treated, with entries on companies, organizations, personalities, societies and associations, sound archives and libraries, laws, technologies, issues, and so forth. As its title indicates, the primary focus is recorded sound in the United States, but some coverage is given to Canada, Europe, Australia and New Zealand. The major emphasis is on the two early periods relevant to the 78 rpm era (1877–1948) and the LP era (1949–1982). Entries are written by the editors and contributor-specialists; a board of experts has reviewed and approved them. Illustrations accompany the entries. A bibliography is provided, and a subject/person index is provided.

664. **The Garland Encyclopedia of World Music.** James Porter and Timothy Rice, eds. New York: Garland, 1998– . 7v. (In progress). ISBN 0-8240-6035-0 (v.1).

Garland Publishing has moved quickly on this planned ten-volume musical encyclopedia with emphasis on ethnomusicological treatment. It was planned by Timothy Rice and James Porter and supplies individual volumes on the major areas of the globe. Each volume is edited by scholars and provides an overview of music in the region along with treatment of musical issues and music of the cultures or nations. These volumes are accompanied by a sound disc. Volume 1 treats Africa and is edited by Ruth M. Stone and James Porter (1997); volume 2, South America, Mexico, Central America, and the Caribbean, edited by Dale Olson and Daniel Sheehy (1998); volume 4, Southeast Asia, edited by Terry E. Miller and Sean Williams (1998); volume 5, South Asia and the Indian Subcontinent, edited by Alison Arnold (1999); volume 6, The Middle East, edited by Sakata (1999); volume 8, Europe, edited by Porter (1999); volume 9, Australia and the Pacific Islands, edited by Jacob W. Love and Adrienne L. Kaeppler (1998). Yet to come are volumes 3, 7, and 10 to be published in the year 2000 covering the United States and Canada, providing insight into global perspectives, and a cumulative index.

665. **The Guinness Book of Music.** 4th ed. Robert Dearling and Celia Dearling. London: Guinness Books, 1990. 256p. ISBN 0-85112-363-5.

This is a revised and somewhat expanded edition of the author's earlier volume (1986). Like other works from Guinness, this is a highly readable and interesting survey designed both to appeal and to enlighten. There is a topical arrangement, beginning with instruments of the orchestra and followed by non-European instruments. The typical Guinness touch is seen in the listings and approaches provided for the various topics, such as groupings of composers who lived to be ninety, those who had the same last name, and those who committed suicide. Various chronologies are included, such as one on vocal music and another on instrumental music. There is even a chapter on keys that lists popular works by their respective keys. There are name and instrument indexes.

666. **The International Cyclopedia of Music and Musicians.** 11th ed. Oscar Thompson, ed. New York: Dodd, Mead, 1985. 2609p. ISBN 0-396-08412-5.

This is regarded as one of the most comprehensive one-volume reference books in the field and has maintained this reputation since its initial appearance in 1939. It is a useful source of information, providing brief articles but also some lengthier survey-type essays. It gives accurate and reliable data on a variety of topics, issues, individuals, and developments. Included are entries on music history, criticism, folk music, opera, compositions, and so forth. Extensive articles are signed by contributors, many of whom are known scholars of the subject. Biographical coverage of composers is excellent and the narratives are accompanied by calendars of their lives and a listing of their works. The new edition contains an addendum of nearly 100 pages recording the developments in music from 1975 to the present. It adds significant bits of information to entries from the main text as well as entirely new entries on individuals, topics, and organizations.

667. **The Musical Woman: An International Perspective.** Judith Lang Zaimont et al., eds. Westport, CT: Greenwood, 1984– . v.1–3. ISSN 0737-0032.

This is designed as a continuing series targeting women's achievements in music. Volume 1 covers the year 1983, while volume 2 treats events and happenings in 1984 and 1985. The most recent volume, issued in 1991, is the most comprehensive and had suggested future continuation on a quinquennial basis with its coverage of 1986–1990. No additional volumes have been issued, however. Volumes are divided into two principal segments. The first identifies performances, awards, festivals, commissions, recordings, films, books and so forth for the period of time covered. The second consists of a series of essays by different authors on a variety of subjects. The 1986–1990 volume contains nineteen articles under such topical headings as "The Music Profession" and "Music Education." There is value in the mixture of information offered both within the unique listings of part 1 and in the variety of topics treated in part 2. A general index is furnished.

A good Web site, **IAWM*, is maintained by the International Association of Women in Music (http://music.acu.edu/WWW/iawm/home.html [accessed December 1999]). It provides bibliographic listings, directory data, and general information.

668. **Die Musik in Geschichte und Gegenwart.** Kassel, Germany: Barenreiter-Verlag, 1949–1986; repr., 1989. 17v. ISBN 3-423-05913-3.

Known by all who are involved in any way with music reference, the *MGG*, edited by Friedrich Blume, is considered the most scholarly and comprehensive work of its kind. Not until publication of the *New Grove Dictionary* . . . (entry 671) was there anything even approaching it in the English language. The work is international in scope and the product of a team of experts who contributed signed articles covering individuals and compositions. Serious music is covered in-depth and popular elements are treated more concisely. There are extensive bibliographical notes and numerous illustrations. A product of nineteen years of labor, the alphabetical arrangement is covered in volumes 1–14. More recently, the supplements have been issued in volumes 15–16, also covering the entire alphabet. The valuable index has recently been published as volume 17; it provides access to over 330,000 names and terms. The same publisher began on the second edition, edited by Ludwig Finscher, in 1994, and to date eight volumes have been completed.

669. **The New American Dictionary of Music.** Philip D. Morehead and Anne MacNeil. New York: E. P. Dutton, 1991. 608p. ISBN 0-525-93345-X. Repr., Meridian, 1992. ISBN 0-452-01100-0 (pbk.).

Recognized for its great scope of coverage, this handy dictionary supplies information on personalities, events, terms, concepts, instruments, and so forth. All periods and forms of music are covered, from early to contemporary and from popular to classical. Entries are generally quite brief, although there is lengthier coverage of especially important topics. Translations are given for foreign terms; there is a glossary of terms in English, French, German, and Italian. There are some illustrations of musical instruments and musical examples. It is a useful source for quick identification. The reprint version has been renamed *The New International Dictionary of Music.*

The New College Encyclopedia of Music, edited by J. A. Westrup and F. L. Harrison (Norton, 1981), basically is a reprint in paperback of the 1976 edition, which had been revised by Conrad Wilson. A British work, it was first published in this country in 1960. It has earned an excellent reputation as a useful reference source emphasizing the coverage of major contemporary figures and their work. It contains about 6,000 entries on a variety of topics, including composers, musical instruments, genres, operas, and performers. Terms are defined in a clear and concise manner, and there are illustrations to accompany a good proportion of the entries. Short bibliographies are furnished with some of the descriptions given. Although there are notable omissions of some popular American figures, the work is successful in providing a useful resource for non-scholarly interests.

670. **The New Grove Dictionary of American Music.** H. Wiley Hitchcock and Stanley Sadie. New York: Grove's Dictionaries of Music, 1987; repr., 1992. 4v. ISBN 0-943818-36-2.

This is the most recent effort to be published in the Grove's series, and like the major twenty-volume publication (entry 671), it has earned the respect of those who must minister to information needs of both scholars and nonspecialists. With four volumes, it is by far the most comprehensive and detailed work on the subject and provides good expositions, descriptions, and identifications of both personalities and subjects in the realm of American music. Known to music librarians as "Amerigrove," it describes the whole range of American musical culture from acid rock to serious concert music and, naturally, embraces grand opera as well as country and western contributions. There are 2,500 entries, two-thirds of which are biographical. Articles vary in length from 200 to 10,000 words depending upon the importance of the subject.

671. **The New Grove Dictionary of Music and Musicians.** Stanley Sadie, ed. London: Macmillan; Washington, DC: Grove's Dictionaries of Music, 1980; repr. with corrections, 1994. 20v. ISBN 0-33-323111-2.

Possibly the single most valuable title in the reference department, this multivolume tool has had a distinguished history in terms of its recognized quality. A British work first published at the turn of the century, it has continued to grow in stature with each succeeding edition. The most recent issue is basically a reprint with minor corrections of the monumental 1980 publication that made it the closest competitor to the *MGG* (entry 668) in depth and comprehensiveness. Its coverage is timely and authoritative, with about 23,000 articles, 8,000 cross-references, 3,000 illustrations, and 17,000 biographies of all types of personalities associated with music. This is a masterful publication that is useful to both specialists and nonspecialists and has succeeded in providing an international perspective through purposeful elimination of its former British bias. Arrangement is alphabetical and articles are signed by their distinguished authors, with more Americans than Britons serving as contributors. Definitely an outstanding item and a must for the music library collection. At this time the publisher is working on an online version. The second edition of this massive work is planned for November 2000.

The Norton/Grove Concise Encyclopedia of Music, edited by Sadie and Alison Latham and initially published by Norton in 1988, was revised and enlarged in 1994. It is a spinoff of the multi-volume *Grove Dictionary* and is intended to provide quick and easy access to important information for all levels of users. There are more than 10,000 brief entries derived from material in the larger work covering a variety of topics: performers, composers, instruments, terms, musical works, and so forth. Major topics are given lengthier treatment, up to a page or more. The work provides a useful one-volume reference source that compares favorably with others.

672. **The New Harvard Dictionary of Music.** Don Michael Randel, ed. Cambridge, MA: Belknap/Harvard University Press, 1986. 942p. ISBN 0-674-61525-5.

This tool earned an excellent reputation under its original editor, Willi Apel, with its initial publication in 1944 and the revision that followed twenty-five years later. This new edition with a new editor should retain its status as an indispensable reference tool. There are nearly 6,000 entries contributed by seventy distinguished scholars, all specifically commissioned to update, rewrite, or add material. The result is a complete overhaul that makes a notable work all the more useful. Continuing the established pattern, there are no biographies, but instead excellent definitions and descriptions of a wide range of topics embracing all aspects of music, including individual compositions. It is recommended that the earlier edition be retained because much material was deleted or revised to include more modern concepts. As in the earlier work, there are a number of good illustrations.

The New Everyman Dictionary of Music, edited by David Cummings (6th ed., Fitzhenry & Whiteside, 1988), is based on the 1971 edition, edited by Eric Blom. Cummings has refurbished, renewed, and updated this old favorite into a timely and useful new source by introducing some 1,500 new entries and revising some 1,000 more. Alphabetical arrangement is given to composers, performers, orchestras, and musical terms. Listings of major works are given for composers; there has been a special concern to include singers (who were not well covered in previous editions). Cross-references provide access to related entries; there is a table of abbreviations and a listing of operatic roles.

673. **The New Oxford Companion to Music.** Denis Arnold, ed. New York: Oxford University Press, 1983; repr. with corr., 1994. 2v. ISBN 0-19-311316-3.

The 1983 edition was a thorough revision of *The Oxford Companion to Music*, by Percy Scholes (10th ed., 1970), and was essentially an entirely new work. The Scholes volumes, which began in 1938, were known for their anecdotal style and inherent charm, but the new publication is far more comprehensive in coverage, and provides greater breadth and precision. Treatment in the first effort was somewhat uneven, and this issue, therefore, is a far better reference tool. Coverage is international, with an acknowledged emphasis on Western culture. Entries cover composers and their works, opera plots, terms, and institutions as well as theory, form, notation, and so forth. Bibliographies are included. Contemporary music receives much better coverage than in the past. There are many illustrations to enhance the text, and the work should appeal to a varied audience. It is primarily aimed at the interested layperson.

Michael Kennedy's *The Oxford Dictionary of Music*, now in its second edition with corrections (Oxford University Press, 1997), covers personalities, compositions, instruments, and terms in brief fashion, and serves as a condensed version of the *New Oxford Companion*.

674. **Selected Musical Terms of Non-Western Cultures: A Notebook-Glossary.** Walter Kaufmann. Warren, MI: Harmonic Park Press, 1990. 806p. (Detroit Studies in Music Bibliography, no. 65). ISBN 0-89990-039-9.

The author, who died in 1984, was a former academic who spent a lifetime researching, studying, and in effect, collecting terms relevant to music in Eastern cultures, with emphasis on the terminology of India. This source represents a wordbook of personal rather than comprehensive nature, but is useful to students and researchers in the field for the uniqueness of its subject. Coverage is especially noteworthy for India but there is ample treatment of other parts of Asia and Africa. There are about 12,000 terms defined in entries that are generally concise but vary in length from one or two sentences to a half-page. Terms were selected at random through the author's vast experiences, and origins are indicated in the entries along with references to additional sources listed in the bibliography of over 300 items at the end.

675. **Webster's New World Dictionary of Music.** Nicolas Slonimsky and Richard Kassel, ed. New York: Macmillan General Reference, 1998. 613p. ISBN 0-02-862747-4.

This is an abridged version of *Baker's Dictionary of Music* (Schirmer Books, 1997) and like its sire, combines definitions of terms with brief biographies of musicians as well as listings of their most important works. There are over 12,000 entries explaining musical concepts, describing instruments and features, and contributions of leading composers and performers. Although libraries will not use it as a replacement source for *Baker's Dictionary of Music*, which serves as a rather complete one volume source for musical terms, personalities, locations, performances, pieces, genres, instruments and more for the world of serious music reference, it represents a useful convenience tool for those with less sophisticated information needs.

An important effort by Horace Leuchtmann is *Dictionary of Terms in Music: English-German, German-English* (4th ed., K. G. Saur, 1992). It continues the style and format of the third edition (1981), and remains a useful tool for those seeking a bridge to link English and German terminology. The English segment is treated first, followed by the section on German terminology. A special feature is the listing of musical works in both languages at the end; these contain references to the form in the other language.

DIRECTORIES, ANNUALS, AND CURRENT AWARENESS SOURCES

676. **Directory of Record and CD Retailers.** 1990–1991 ed. Keith Whelan. Wharton, NJ: Power Communication Group, 1990. 368p. ISSN 1057-7181.

This is a useful listing of significant record and CD stores located in this country. It is limited to those stores that carry specialty recordings or deal with rare items, making it an important tool for serious collectors, specialists, and librarians. The popular chains (Musicland, Goody, etc.) therefore are not listed. The work is divided into several sections, the first of which identifies locations, hours, formats carried, music categories, and services provided. This is followed by a listing of stores by recording format (CD, LP, etc.); and finally, there is a segment containing county maps for each state, which aid in establishing location.

*The Music Yellow Pages (http://www.musicyellowpages.com [accessed December 1999]) is at this time likely to be the most comprehensive industry trade directory for music and all its providers, producers, retailers, wholesalers, equipment producers, distributors, agents, instrument makers, and so forth. It furnishes classified advertisements, news, and current awareness of trade shows.

677. **Directory of Music Faculties in Colleges and Universities, U.S. and Canada.** Binghamton, NY: College Society, 1967– . Ann. ISSN 0098-664X.

Both the title and frequency of this important computer-produced tool have varied in the past. The first three editions (1967–1970) were entitled *Directory of Music Faculties in American Colleges and Universities*, and appeared on an annual basis. The fourth edition (1970–1972) initiated the change in title, which signaled an expansion of the scope to include Canadians, and in frequency, to a biennial publication. Currently, it is back to annual status. The most recent edition is the twenty-first (1999–2000), published in 1999. The tool furnishes a listing of music faculty members in colleges and universities and provides several approaches. There are several listings: alphabetical by state of colleges and universities accompanied by a listing of faculty members with area of interest; faculty members alphabetically arranged; and schools by type of degrees offered.

678. **Directory of Music Research Libraries.** Kassel, Germany: distr., New York: Barenreiter, 1967– . Irreg. (Repertoire international des sources musicales, Series C). 5v. 2d rev. ed. 1979– . ISBN 3761806841 (v.1).

This outstanding directory began publication with the first edition in 1967, furnishing the student and scholar with an international guide to the holdings and practices of music research libraries all over the world. It was developed as series C of *RISM* (entry 628). Volume 1 (1967) covered libraries in the United States and Canada that had been inventoried in series A and B (pre-1800 material). Volume 2 (1970) covered thirteen European countries (Austria, Belgium, Switzerland, East and West Germany, Denmark, Ireland, Great Britain, Luxembourg, Norway, the Netherlands, Sweden, and Finland). It included sources for the nineteenth century and some libraries not inventoried in *RISM*. Volume 3 (1972) treated Spain, France, Italy, and Portugal and provided increased depth in descriptions of the collections. These early volumes were published by the University of Iowa. The German publisher, Barenreiter, took it over from the University of Iowa and issued a set of the previously published parts as volumes 1–3 in 1975. Volume 4 appeared in 1979 as part of the second revised edition and covers Australia, Israel, Japan, and New Zealand. This was the first volume to be issued directly under the auspices of *RISM* as part of its recently created series C. A change of editorial policy established the directory as dealing with the total problem of gaining access to the collections described, and information is given regarding not only library collections but also such important aspects as public holidays, names of *RISM* contacts, copyright information, and library systems. Most recently, volume 5, covering Czechoslovakia, Hungary, Poland, and Yugoslavia, appeared in 1985. A second edition of volume 1 was issued in 1983.

RISM Online Resources (http://rism.harvard.edu/rism/online.html [accessed December 1999]), provides directory information for more than 5,500 libraries holding music material relevant to the series, as well as access to certain RISM databases.

679. **Music Festivals from Bach to Blues: A Traveler's Guide.** Tom Clynes. Detroit: Visible Ink Press, 1996. 632p. ISBN 0-787-60823-8.

Selected as an outstanding reference source for 1996 by the Reference and Adult Services Division of the American Library Association, this is a comprehensive guide and listing of music festivals of all types of music in the United States and Canada. Some 200 are selected as the biggest and best and receive full description, embracing artistic direction, performers, and expectations. In all, 1,001 festivals are identified with dates, times, costs, location/travel details, lodging, map, and more. A useful and increasingly popular Web site is *Festival Finder* (http://www.festivalfinder.com/ [accessed February 2000]), which provides listings of more than 1,500 music festivals in North America. Identification is possible by date, location, performers, or festival name.

The fourth edition of *Music Festivals in America: Classical, Opera, Jazz, Pops, Country, Old-Time Fiddlers, Folk, Bluegrass, Cajun*, by Carol Price Rabin (Berkshire Traveler Press, 1990), is a similar effort for the music lover who is willing to travel. It covers all types of musical styles and is organized into six musical categories (classical; opera; jazz, ragtime, and Dixieland; pops and light classical; folk and traditional; and bluegrass, old-time fiddlers, country, and Cajun). These sections are then divided by state, followed by other locations (Bermuda, Puerto Rico, and Canada). A complementary work is *The Music Lover's Guide to Europe: A Compendium of Festivals, Concerts, and Opera*, edited by Roberta Gottesnan and Catherine Sentman (John Wiley, 1992). Cogent paragraph-long descriptions of specific festivals are furnished along with listings of recent performers. Coverage of Eastern Europe is scanty.

680. **Musical America: International Directory of the Performing Arts.** New York: ABC Leisure Magazines, 1969– . Ann. ISSN 0735-7788.

Originally appearing as a special directory issue of *High Fidelity* magazine and bearing separate pagination, this work is now an independent and essential reference tool. During its formative period, it was published under the auspices of *Billboard* magazine (entry 750), but it now appears under the masthead of ABC Leisure, which continued to publish *High Fidelity* until 1989, when it ceased. The directory furnishes names and addresses by state, then city, of solo performers, orchestras, performing art series, dance companies, opera companies, choral groups, festivals, music schools, contests, foundations and awards, music publishers, service and professional music organizations, artist managers, music periodicals, and music critics. Coverage is international, with the inclusion of a foreign listing of companies and organizations. The tool also serves as a yearbook, with a section of articles covering the events in music and dance for the previous year. The 1998 edition contains 912 pages.

681. **The Schirmer Guide to Schools of Music and Conservatories Throughout the World.** Nancy Uscher. New York: Schirmer Books/ Macmillan, 1988. 635p. ISBN 0-02-873030-5.

This is a useful tool for students planning to choose an educational institution for either graduate or undergraduate programs. Some 750 schools from all over the world are given detailed treatment regarding their history, enrollment, number of faculty, entrance requirements, admission procedures, degrees, and areas of study. Coverage extends to types of facilities, specialized programs, and financial aid, with commentary given to especially noteworthy or important considerations. To be included, a U.S. or Canadian department, school, or conservatory must have either a minimum of ten full-time faculty members above the instructor rank or offer a master's degree. European institutions must prepare students to become professional musicians rather than theorists or researchers. Guidelines vary somewhat for non-European institutions outside the United States or Canada. Three indexes are supplied, providing access by institution, program area, and instrument.

BIOGRAPHICAL SOURCES

Two of the most important series of individual biographies should be mentioned at the outset; they are the Composer Resource Manuals from Garland Publishing, for which the most recent issue is volume 48, *Giacomo Puccini: A Guide to Research*, by Linda B. Fairtile (1999); and Bio-bibliographies in Music from Greenwood Press (Number 69 is *Malcolm Arnold*, by Stewart R. Craggs, 1998.). Each series has a distinctive format but both include a biography, list of works with some performances, and a bibliography, discography, and so forth on each personality.

682. **Baker's Biographical Dictionary of Musicians.** 8th ed. Nicholas Slonimsky. New York: Schirmer Books/Macmillan, 1992. 2115p. ISBN 0-02-872415-1.

Now in its eighth edition, this standard work has been an indispensable item in reference departments since its initial appearance in 1900. It has established a reputation for comprehensiveness, which the new edition maintains, covering more than 14,000 personalities, both living and dead, from all geographic areas and periods of time. It has been criticized in the past for relative weakness in coverage of living performers, and the new edition furnishes an additional 1,100 biographical sketches, while revising 1,300 of the existing entries. Many represent contemporary popular crooners, rock singers, and so forth, and there is greater emphasis on ethnomusicologists and female composers. Along with performers and composers, there are conductors, scholars, educators, and librarians. Biographies vary in length from a few lines to several pages and include bibliographies, which have been updated, and lists of composers' works.

An abridged version of the eighth edition was issued by Slonimsky as *The Concise Baker's Biographical Dictionary of Musicians* (Schirmer/Macmillan, 1994). Some 5,000 major figures from all time periods have been taken from the complete edition and represented in a 1,155-page volume selling at less than half the price. In 1995, a children's version was issued in 291 pages as *The Portable Baker's Biographical Dictionary of Musicians*, edited by Richard Kostelanetz. With Slonimsky's death in 1995 at the age of 101, Laura Kuhn has begun to edit a series of more specialized Baker spinoffs covering musicians representing a certain period or style. The first is *Baker's Biographical Dictionary of Twentieth-Century Classical Musicians* (Schirmer Books, 1997). It is done in the style of the earlier work and contains more personalities from this period than did its parent.

683. **Black Music Biography: An Annotated Bibliography.** Samuel A. Floyd, Jr., and Marsha J. Reisser. White Plains, NY: Kraus International, 1987. 302p. ISBN 0-527-30158-2.

From the same writers who created *Black Music in the United States: An Annotated Bibliography* for the same publisher in 1983, this is a major work for documentation of black musicians of all types and styles of performance. Coverage is given to a relatively small but important segment of eighty-seven composers and performers over a hundred-year period beginning with the 1850s. Nearly 150 monographic works have been identified and described in detail. Performers range from Michael Jackson to Leontyne Price, and there is an excellent detailed introduction providing a summary of the literature.

684. **The Harvard Biographical Dictionary of Music.** Don M. Randel, ed. Cambridge: Belknap/ Harvard University Press, 1996. 1013p. (Harvard University Press Reference Library series). ISBN 0-67-437299-9.

Edited by an academic, this comprehensive new biographical reference work is considered to be a natural companion to the editor's *New Harvard Dictionary of Music* (entry 672). It treats nearly 5,500 personalities both important and relatively obscure, primarily but not limited to representatives of Western concert music. Included here are composers, musicians, theorists, and instrument makers from the classical period to the music of today, with especially good coverage of modern popular and genre music. Entries furnish dates and places of birth and death, with simple identification of each person's career; this is followed by a descriptive passage of varying length, generally briefer than those found in *Baker's* (entry 682) but adequate to inform the reader. In some cases, listings of works are given and bibliographies are furnished. Sources are identified.

685. **International Encyclopedia of Women Composers.** 2d ed., rev. and enl. Aaron I. Cohen. New York: Books & Music, 1987. 2v. ISBN 0-9617485-2-4.

With the recent emphasis on documentation of the contributions of minority groups to both culture and progress in society, the decades of the 1970s and the 1980s brought a new interest in the work of both blacks and women. This is a highly useful encyclopedia that provides descriptions of the lives and accomplishments of female composers of all ages and from all parts of the world. The present edition has over 6,200 entries providing biographical sketches, listings of contributions, and publications by and about the composer. Separate sections furnish photographs of a number of the individuals. Appendices include a listing of sources from which the biographies were derived, a bibliography of additional reading, lists of operas by women, pseudonyms, and discography. Indexes give access by country and century, profession, instrument, musical form, and so forth.

An earlier work that documents the contributions of female musicians is Women in Music: A Biobibliography, by Don L. Hixon and Don Hennessee (Scarecrow Press, 1975). It presents an alphabetical list of women musicians who are identified briefly; coded references refer to any of the appropriate forty-eight sources from which the entries were derived.

686. Who's Who in American Music: Classical. Jaques Cattell Press, ed. New York: R. R Bowker, 1983–1985. Bienn. ISSN 0737-9137.

This was published only twice and was then discontinued. It was a typical Cattell effort, giving great attention to details and covering more than 9,000 individuals associated primarily with classical and semi-classical music in America. Musicians, critics, publishers, and editors are among the various groups represented in the listing. The arrangement of entries is alphabetical, and they furnish addresses, personal data, and information on major accomplishments and writings. *American Classical Music Hall of Fame and Museum* (http://www.classicalhall.org [accessed December 1999]) is an interesting Web site celebrating the many aspects of classical music in this country. It contains an event calendar and news as well as links to other sites.

First issued in 1935 is a similar British publication, *International Who's Who in Music and Musicians' Directory in the Classical and Light Classical Fields*, edited by David M. Cummings and Dennis K. McIntire (14th ed., International Biographical Centre, 1994). This provides biographical sketches of several thousand musicians from the Western world. Entries are concise, furnishing background information on lives and accomplishments of musicians and related personnel such as teachers and librarians. Various indexes are provided.

HISTORIES AND CHRONOLOGIES

687. A Chronicle of American Music, 1700–1995. Charles J. Hall. New York: Schirmer Books, 1996. 825p. ISBN 0-028-60296-X.

This is a detailed chronology supplying year-by-year coverage of important events in music: births, deaths, debuts, founding dates of organizations, publications, and so forth. Both serious art/concert music and popular music are treated in a comprehensive manner within a broad-based context including memorable societal developments. Historical, world cultural, as well as American art and literature categories embrace political, literary, and artistic occasions. This work embraces and expands three earlier chronologies by the author, a radio personality and university professor.

Hall's *An Eighteenth Century Musical Chronicle: Events 1750–1799* (Greenwood, 1990), *A Nineteenth Century Musical Chronicle: Events 1800–1999* (Greenwood, 1989), and *A Twentieth-Century Musical Chronicle: Events 1900–1988* (Greenwood, 1989) form a three-volume set within the publisher's Music Reference Collection series. As in the *Chronicle of American Music*, musical events are treated along with biographical highlights, musical compositions, and musical literature identified in the context of various societal happenings.

688. A History of Western Music. 5th ed. Donald Jay Grout and Claude V. Palisca. New York: W. W. Norton, 1996. 862p. ISBN 0-393-96904-5.

Now in its fifth edition, this highly acclaimed historical survey of Western music was originally published in 1960. It has been considered an outstanding textbook for music history classes and represents one of the fine contributions of the W. W. Norton Company. The current effort, like the previous edition, bears the stamp of Palisca, the editor who took over the fourth edition after Grout's death. He has continued to delete, rewrite, or modify many of the earlier articles, as well as add entries in line with current thinking and recent research. Current thinking on early musical periods is evident. The work continues as a standard survey history of Western music employing musical examples. There is a glossary and bibliography, along with a chronology of musical development. A number of illustrations help to define and explain the musical character and development of the various periods. Title, subject, and name indexes are furnished.

Concise History of Western Music, by Barbara R. Hanning, was issued by Norton in 1998. It is a 585-page volume based on the Grout and Palisca work. A 1941 work from Norton, reprinted in 1997, is Paul Henry Lang's *Music in Western Civilization*, which treats musical development within a social, political, and cultural context. Another similar effort is *Ideas and Styles in the Western Musical Tradition*, by Douglass Seaton (Mayfield, 1991).

689. Music History from the Late Roman Through the Gothic Periods, 313–1425: A Documented Chronology. Blanche Gangwere. Westport, CT: Greenwood, 1986. 247p. ISBN 0-313-24764-1.

This is an outline or chronology of musical history covering early musical developments over a period of over 1,100 years. Greenwood has planned a series of these, which eventually will cover the entire history of music in Western civilization. This work identifies important elements with respect to contributions and theoretical influences, and covers terms, notations, and musical instruments. References to sources provide exposition and interpretation and furnish examples of the technique, form, or style under scrutiny. Many of these references are to encyclopedia articles as well as separate monographs. Information is given regarding geographical regions; maps are included. This should become one of the most frequently used tools for answering historical inquiries.

Continuing the coverage is Gangwere's *Music History During the Renaissance Period, 1425–1520: A Documented Chronology* (Greenwood, 1991). This chronological sourcebook identifies personalities, events, documents, and so forth relating to this brief but important musical period. Arrangement is broadly under three chronological segments: 1425–1450, 1451–1479, and 1480–1520. Source references are given for listed events and individuals along with brief exposition. The index furnishes adequate access for scholars and serious students.

690. Music Since 1900. 5th ed. Nicholas Slonimsky. New York: Schirmer Books, 1994. 1260p. ISBN 0-02-872418-6.

First published in 1938, this has been one of the standard historical chronologies, providing a day-by-day treatment of musical developments in the twentieth century. The author, a 100-year-old Russian-born musicologist, has been the editor of *Baker's Biographical Dictionary* (entry 682) through the past four editions and is considered one of the experts in the field. The current effort is primarily a listing and exposition of stylistic developments from 1900 to 1991, thus updating the 1971 fourth edition and its 1986 supplement. It includes letters and other primary source material as well as the dictionary of terms, while supplementing the previous coverage with an additional 500 new entries on events of six years (1986–1992). Treatment is cogent and well-developed and presents trends, styles, and tastes in both serious and popular music. Included are dates of performances, debuts, and so forth. Indexes are clear and effective.

An Outline History of Western Music, edited by Milo Wold (WCB McGraw-Hill, 1997), is the ninth edition of a standard work of value to less sophisticated readers in providing an introduction to the history of Western music. Performers and compositions are treated; there are discographies of relevant recordings in the appendices.

691. New Oxford History of Music. London: Oxford University Press, 1954–1990. 10v. ISBN 0-19-316329-2. Repr., 1994. ISBN 0-19-816447-5 (pbk).

Carrying the name of Oxford University, this multi-volume history of music has earned an excellent reputation for detailed coverage and scholarly bearing. Its overall effectiveness has been limited in the past by its lack of timeliness; it took about thirty years to complete the set (with several reprints and reissues of various volumes along the way). Individual volumes, all by scholars of distinction, have proved to be valuable tools in their own right, but finally the entire set represents a powerful reference history. In its entirety it represents a comprehensive and detailed survey of music from the earliest times to the present. The set consists of ten volumes, each by distinguished scholars: volume 1, *Ancient and Oriental Music*, by Egon Wellesz (1957); volume 2, *Early Medieval Music up to 1300*, by Dom Anselm Hughes and Gerald Abraham (1954), and in its second edition by Richard Crocker and David Hiley (1990); volume 3, *Ars Nova and the Renaissance, c. 1300–1540*, by Dom Anselm Hughes and Gerald Abraham (1960, 1977); volume 4, *The Age of Humanism, 1540–1630*, by Gerald Abraham (1968, 1988); volume 5, *Opera and Church Music, 1630–1750*, by Nigel Fortune and Anthony Lewis (1975, 1986); volume 6, *Concert Music, 1630–1750*, by Gerald Abraham (1986); volume 7, *The Age of Enlightenment, 1745–1790*, by Egon Wellesz and Frederick W. Sternfield (1973, 1981); volume 8, *The Age of Beethoven, 1790–1830*, by Gerald Abraham (1982, 1985); volume 9, *Romanticism, 1830–1890*, by Gerald Abraham (1990); and volume 10, *Modern Age, 1890–1960*, by Martin Cooper (1974).

Not officially a series, but serving to provide comprehensive coverage, are the works of Norton Publishing produced over a span of twenty-five years. The emphasis in these works is on the style, characteristics, and development of musical thought rather than an account of happenings or descriptions of a biographical nature. The titles, listed chronologically by period of coverage, are *The Rise of Music in the Ancient World: East and West*, by Curt Sachs (1943); *Music in the Middle Ages*, by Gustav Reese (1940); *Music in the Renaissance* (1959), also by Reese; *Music in the Baroque Era: From Monteverdi to Bach*, by Manfred F. Bukofzer (1947); *Music in the Romantic Era*, by Alfred Einstein (1947, 1975); *Music in Our Time: Trends in Music Since the Romantic Era*, by Adolfo Salazar (1946); and William W. Austin's *Music in the Twentieth Century: From Debussy to Stravinsky* (1966).

692. **The Prentice Hall History of Music Series.** Englewood Cliffs, NJ: Prentice-Hall, 1965– . v.1– .

Similar in concept to the earlier standardized series from Norton (entry 691n), is this more popular and less expensive series of slender volumes, each completed by an American scholar. Coverage is less detailed than that of Norton, but personalities and their careers are given more emphasis. Separate volumes treat historical periods of Western music, along with individual volumes on certain non-Western nations or cultures. Thus far the following titles have been issued: volume 1, *Folk and Traditional Music of the Western Continents*, by Bruno Nettl (3d ed., 1990); volume 2, *Music Cultures of the Pacific, the Near East, and Asia*, by William P. Malm (3d ed., 1996); volume 3, *Music in the Medieval World*, by Albert Seay (2d ed., 1975); volume 4, *Baroque Music*, by Claude V. Palisca (3d ed. 1991); volume 5, *Music in the Classic Period*, by Reinhard G. Pauly (3d ed., 1989); volume 6, *Nineteenth-Century Romanticism in Music* by Rey M. Longyear (3d ed., 1989); volume 7, *Twentieth-Century Music: An Introduction*, by Eric Salzman (3d ed., 1988); volume 8, *Music in the United States: A Historical Introduction*, by H. Wiley Hitchcock (3d ed., 1988); volume 9, *Music in the Renaissance*, by Howard Brown (1976); volume 10, *Music in India: The Classical Traditions*, by Bonnie C. Wade (1978); and volume 11, *Music in Latin America, an Introduction*, by Gerard Behague (1979).

693. **Source Readings in Music History.** Rev. ed. W. Oliver Strunk and Leo Treitler, eds. New York: W. W. Norton, 1998. 1558p. ISBN 0-39303752-5.

The earlier multi-volume set was considered a landmark publication at the time it first appeared in 1950 as an anthology of nearly 100 writings on the subject of music. The revised edition has been issued in one volume but is being revised in all its individual volumes as well. The documents represented convey the thoughts of various cultures and geographic regions in all periods of time from the ancients to the Romantics. The individual volumes expand the single-volume edition, treating the periods in separate volumes. Volume 1 covers Greek views of music (1997); volume 2, the Renaissance (1966), volume 3, the Baroque (1966); volume 4, the Classic era (older ed.), and volume 5, the Romantic period (1966). Volume 6, treating the nineteenth century, is in a new edition (1998). Writings of both composers and theorists as well as philosophers and scientists and numerous others are represented and provide a rich array of opinions and pronouncements. All foreign documents have been translated into English.

RECORDINGS

Discographies or lists of recordings are of prime importance to both specialists and aficionados and compose a prolific segment of the reference literature. They are done on a variety of topics representing musical forms, schools, types, and individual composers and performers. Generally, they are arranged by name of performer or by title of composition, possibly in chronological sequence.

694. **Bibliography of Discographies.** New York: R. R. Bowker, 1977– . v.1– . ISBN 0-8352-1023-5(v.1).

This valuable list of discographies has been planned in five volumes, each of which is dedicated to a different category or type of music. Volume 1, *Classical Music, 1925–1975*, by Michael H. Gray and Gerald D. Gibson, was issued in 1977 and again in 1983, and listed over 3,000 discographies of serious concert music under the name of the composers or performers or subject of the efforts. Entries provide name of compiler and imprint of book or periodical title, whichever is the source, but do not indicate the quality or comprehensiveness of the discography. Coverage embraces works in all European languages. The volume has been supplemented by Gray with *Classical Music Discography, 1976–1988: A Bibliography* (Greenwood, 1989). The supplement gives an excellent listing of discographies culled from books, articles, dissertations, and program notes. Volume 2, *Jazz*, by Daniel Allen, appeared in 1981 and identified more than 3,500 discographies of jazz, blues, ragtime, gospel, and rhythm and blues published between 1935 and 1980. Although there are a few variations, the general format and arrangement parallels those of the first volume. Volume 3, *Popular Music*, by Gray, was published in 1983 and covers rock music; motion picture and stage show music; country, old time, and bluegrass music; and finally, the pop music of balladeers and orchestral themes up to 1982. Unfortunately, the other volumes have yet to appear. Volume 4 is to deal with ethnic and folk music, and volume 5 with general discographies. *The Journal of the Association for Recorded Sound Collections* has been supplementing the volumes through its column "Bibliography of Discographies."

695. **CD Review Digest.** Voorheesville, NY: Peri Press, 1987– . Q. with ann. cum. ISSN 0890-0213.

This quarterly digest of reviews of both popular and serious concert music recordings established itself as an extraordinary indexing tool of international proportions. It served the needs of a wide-ranging audience, from interested listeners to serious specialists and collectors. In 1989, it split into two separate parts. *CD Review Digest: Jazz, Popular, Etc.* is a quarterly digest of reviews of popular music, both audio and visual: jazz, country, rock and roll, folk, and show tunes are all treated with extracts of reviews published in some fifty magazines. Entries are arranged alphabetically by performer; recordings are listed with information regarding locations and dates of recordings, along with extracts of reviews. Awards for excellence are identified. *CD Review Digest: Classical* is structured in the same way, with the focus on recordings of serious concert music. Both tools supply separate indexes to recording labels, reviewers, titles, and performers. Their annual cumulations follow the same pattern and organization, each covering some 6,000 audio and visual recordings per year. These annual cumulations are especially valuable for purposes of reference due to their comprehensive listings.

There are two spinoff publications. *Best Rated CDs: Jazz, Popular, Etc.* (Peri Press, 1992) is designed as an annual guide. This is a selective listing of reviews of the top 10 percent of CDs of popular music contained in the first five volumes of *CD Review Digest*, covering the period 1983–1991. It contains excerpts for nearly 2,100 recordings, each of which has been reviewed at least twice and has received an award for excellence from at least one of the reviewers. Ratings are assigned on a five-point scale. Indexing follows the pattern set in the host publication. The other is the sister effort, *Best Rated CDs: Classical* (Peri Press, 1992), structured in the same manner and providing its record ratings and critical assessments under eight categories.

696. **Ethnic Music on Records: A Discography of Ethnic Recordings Produced in the United States, 1893–1942.** Richard K. Spottswood. Champaign: University of Illinois Press, 1990. 7v. (Music in American Life). ISBN 0-252-01719-6.

This comprehensive and important discography identifies all foreign-language recordings made in the United States over a period of fifty years and represents an outstanding effort. The work was sponsored in part by the Library of Congress, for which Spottswood had previously edited the series of fifteen records, "Folk Music in America." Volume 1 treats Western Europe; volume 2, Slavic; volume 3, Eastern Europe; volume 4, Spanish, Portuguese, Philippine and Basque; and volume 5, Middle East, Far East, Scandinavian, English language, American Indian, and international. Volume 6 provides artist and title indexes, while volume 7 supplies record and matrix number indexes. Omitted are certain forms of music such as operatic and classical and Hawaiian music. Neither language instruction nor U.S. reissues of foreign releases are included. More than 130 record labels are treated, with entries arranged by performer under thirteen national or language groups.

697. **Opus: America's Guide to Classical Music.** Chatsworth, CA: Schwann Publications, 1990– . Q. ISSN 1047-2371.

The *Schwann* catalogs have been popular guides to available recordings since the initial appearance of the basic guide in 1949, *Schwann Long Playing Record Catalog*. Since that time, the work has undergone several name changes and changes of scope, but it has always been highly regarded as the best single source of purchasing information on thousands of sound recordings, both disc and tape, available from hundreds of record distributors and publishers. Classical, popular, rock, jazz, country, opera, ballet, and electronic music recordings were covered in various separate publications at different times. Beginning in 1990, *Opus* was issued as a quarterly guide to all classical recordings in all formats, including CD-videos, and is organized like its predecessor, *The Schwann Quarterly*. Also treated are recordings of electronic music, musicals, New Age, and film/television soundtracks.

The companion publication is *Spectrum*, begun at the same time, which covers all other music: rock, pop, jazz, blues, gospel, religious, and Christmas music, as well as children's and spoken recordings. It also duplicates the *Opus* treatment of soundtracks, musicals, and New Age. Both titles are indispensable to the music library. A similar effort of long standing is *Phonolog Reporter*, which has been issued since 1948 by Trade Service Publications and provides comprehensive weekly looseleaf updates of currently available phonograph recordings. The work is divided into classical and popular segments and is accessed by titles of albums and songs, composers, and performers. *Laserlog Reporter*, from the same publisher, treats current compact discs.

Serious Concert Music and Opera

BIBLIOGRAPHIES AND INDEXES

698. **Index to Opera, Operetta and Musical Comedy Synopses in Collections and Periodicals.** Jeanette M. Drone. Metuchen, NJ: Scarecrow Press, 1978. 171p. ISBN 0-8108-1100-6.

This work has retained its value in the music library for its extensive coverage of seventy-four collections as well as of four periodical series. The tool is divided into four sections covering operas, operettas, and musical comedies from 1926 to the time of publication. Part 1 is a listing of collections and periodicals used, followed by an index of titles of specific musical works, with references to their source documents in the second part. The third segment lists the composers and their works, while the final section provides a bibliography of additional sources of synopses. Although subsequent editions were planned to index the periodical literature more extensively, this is the only volume published to date.

DICTIONARIES, ENCYCLOPEDIAS, HANDBOOKS, ETC.

699. **Annals of Opera, 1597–1940.** 3d ed., rev. and corr. Alfred Lowenberg, comp. Totowa, NJ: Rowman & Littlefield, 1978. 1756col. ISBN 0-87471-851-1.

This is one of the standards in the field of music reference and has been regarded as an indispensable source of information on the identification of operas since its initial publication in 1943. The second edition (1955) separated the indexes into a second volume and was somewhat less convenient. The new work joins the basic text to the indexes in a single unit. Several thousand operas are listed in chronological order according to date of first performance. Entries provide name of composer, title of opera, author of text, place of first performance, name of theater when known, number of acts, and history of later performances. References are furnished to translations of text and revivals as well. There are four indexes to provide access: operas; composers (with dates of birth and death and titles of operas); librettists; and a general index listing other individuals, subjects, and places. This work was edited by Harold Rosenthal, who has prepared a supplementary volume, *Annals of Opera, 1940–1981* (Barnes & Noble, 1983).

700. **The Definitive Kobbe's Opera Book.** Gustav Kobbe; Earl of Harewood, ed. New York: G. P. Putnam's Sons, 1987. 1404p. ISBN 0-399-13180-9.

The 1979 edition was an extensive revision of an old standard in the field, which had been expanded to include 319 opera plots. First published around 1920, the work has undergone frequent revision and substantial change under the Earl of Harewood, who has edited it since 1954. This edition has added twenty-nine operas while dropping twenty, and is considered the most complete source of opera synopses because the storylines are given in great detail. Arrangement is by century, subdivided by country. Brief notes are given on composers, and musical motifs are described. Older operas are included if they are still being performed, and there is good coverage of modern operas as well. Dates of first performance and important revivals are enumerated with names of important singers. The work is especially generous in its coverage of Wagner, Verdi, and Britten.

Opera Glass is a participatory Web site (http://rick.stanford.edu/opera/main.html [accessed December 1999]) that provides varied information. Included here are performance histories, synopses, reviews, libretti, discographies, images, and links to other relevant Web sites.

701. **Enciclopedia della musica.** Milan, Italy: Rizzoli, 1972–1974. 6v. Considered by most music librarians to be an outstanding source of information on all aspects of music development, this important tool provides over 15,000 signed articles on a variety of topics. Coverage includes biographies, histories, definitions, and expositions on the music and musicians of all countries and time periods. There are over 300 black-and-white illustrations and 48 color plates. To be sure, there is an emphasis on Western tradition, especially European development and contribution. Major figures are given detailed treatment with a complete catalog of their works. Those needing to identify particular pieces by Bach, Beethoven, Brahms, Chopin, Debussy, Donizetti, Handel, Haydn, Liszt, Mozart, Palestrina, Schubert, and Vivaldi need go no farther than the appendices.

702. **Great Opera Classics.** Rev. ed. Arthur Jacobs and Stanley Sadie. New York: Gramercy, 1984; repr., 1987. 563p. ISBN 0-517-64108-9. This is a revision of a work originally issued in 1964, and itself is a reissue of *The Limelight Book of Opera* (Limelight Editions, 1985). It describes in considerable depth the features of eighty-seven major operas by forty-one composers. The operas cover a time span of 400 years, and therefore this tool would be an excellent reference guide in any library serving the needs of both specialists and nonspecialists. The operas are described through a three-part approach: a general introduction placing the opera and its composer in historical perspective, followed by a plot synopsis, and finally, a musical commentary. Although the commentaries are brief, they have been commended for their clarity and use of musical excerpts. Arrangement of operas is by composer within chronological time period groupings, beginning with Purcell in the seventeenth century and ending with contemporaries Britten and Menotti. There is an additional chapter on twentieth-century composers not previously described, as well as a general bibliography.

703. **International Dictionary of Opera.** C. Steven LaRue, ed. Detroit: St. James Press, 1993. 2v. ISBN 1-55862-081-8. This useful new source furnishes a comprehensive examination of important operas and related personalities. There are over 1,050 entries treating 400 operas, 200 composers, over 300 performers, and a number of designers, producers, conductors, and librettists. There are over 450 illustrations. Entries are alphabetically arranged with volume 1 covering A–K and volume 2 concluding the alphabet and supplying the indexes. Operas vary in popularity and renown, from the most famous of classic stature to contemporary works still somewhat obscure. The entries on personalities supply a brief biography, followed by a signed essay on the importance or significance of the individual's career and body of work. They conclude with a bibliography of additional sources. Entries on the operas provide composition and production information along with a signed critical evaluative essay and bibliography. Indexes in volume 2 give access by nationality and by title.

Soon to appear is the first edition of *Baker's Dictionary of Opera*, edited by Laura Kuhn. Published by Schirmer and bearing the "Baker's" designation, it promises to be a valuable source of varied information on the topic.

704. **Metropolitan Opera Encyclopedia: A Comprehensive Guide to the World of Opera.** David Hamilton, ed. New York: Simon & Schuster, 1987. 415p. ISBN 0-671-67132-X. The editor is a well-known figure who has served as music critic and contributor to various journals. He has produced the most extensive treatment of opera offered by a single-volume reference tool while also providing a distinctive focus on performers of the Metropolitan Opera Guild through the 1986–1987 season. There are 2,500 entries featuring 550 opera synopses, including every opera ever performed at the Met. There are biographies of 800 singers; nearly 300 composers and librettists; and some 300 conductors, producers, designers, and executives. More than 200 relevant musical terms are defined. The work is well-illustrated in black-and-white. Entries are alphabetically arranged and supply place, dates, and cast of world premieres and U.S. premieres, as well as Metropolitan productions. There are twenty-four guest essays by such luminaries as Pavarotti, Domingo, and Sutherland. There is an opera chronology and brief bibliography.

705. **The Metropolitan Opera Stories of the Great Operas.** John W. Freeman. New York: W. W. Norton, 1984–1997. 2v. ISBN 0-393-01888-1 (v.1); 0-393-04051-8 (v.2).

This is an excellent choice for the reference collection because each volume presents the description of plots of 150 operas by seventy-five composers presented at the Metropolitan Opera House. These not only represent the major works, which are more readily found, such as those by Mozart, Verdi, Wagner, and Puccini, but more important, lesser known selections on the periphery of the Met's repertoire. For each opera, the source and language of the libretto are furnished along with information about initial performances at the Met and elsewhere and a listing of characters. Story lines are furnished by scenes and acts along with titles of the important arias. There is a picture along with a biography for each composer. There are no cast listings.

An important complementary tool is *Annals of the Metropolitan Opera Guild: The Complete Chronicle of Performances and Artists, Chronology 1883–1985*, edited by Gerald Fitzgerald (Metropolitan Opera Guild, 1989). This title provides a chronological record of the casts of the operas performed from the first season in 1883 to the mid-1980s. It replaces an earlier work begun in 1947 and continuously supplemented since then. Volume 1 provides the chronology of nearly 22,000 performances, while volume 2 furnishes an array of indexes (performances, cocomposers, librettists, directors, etc.). The New York City Opera Company maintains a Web site, *The New City Opera* (http://nycopera.com/ [accessed February 2000]) that provides a link to synopses of some forty major operas and to biographies of fifteen major composers.

706. **The New Grove Dictionary of Opera.** Stanley Sadie, ed. New York: Grove's Dictionaries of Music, 1992; repr. with corr., 1994. 4v. ISBN 0-935859-92-6.

This is slated to be the final small-volume set derived from Sadie's comprehensive multi-volume effort (entry 671). It contains some 10,000 entries alphabetically arranged from "Aachen," the headquarters of an important German opera company, to "Zylis-Gara," the Polish-born soprano. The signed articles cover all aspects of opera in the Western tradition and treat not only performers but also composers and directors, as well as companies, theaters, locations, terms, and stagecraft. Plot summaries are provided along with performance history for individual operas. Secondary bibliographies are supplied for most of the entries. Included are black-and-white illustrations. Some 1,300 specialists have contributed to the work, and in most cases they have provided lively and opinionated exposition. Much of the material is newly written since publication of the 1980 large-scale set. Volume 4 contains appendices of role names and first lines.

707. **Opera in History: From Monteverdi to Cage.** Herbert S. Lindenberger. Stanford: Stanford University Press, 1998. 364p. ISBN 0-804-73104-7.

This is a sophisticated work for those familiar with opera, by a university professor who provides an excellent description and exposition of the origin and development of opera within the context of the time. Social and artistic influences are identified and examined to shed light on the manner and reasons behind musical development within the genre. Opera in general is described, as well as specific works as reflections of the influences and attitudes of their time. The time period ranges from the early seventeenth century to the present day, and the work is organized into eight chapters, beginning with Monteverdi and his peers in the arts and literature; subsequent treatment is given to Handel. Rossini, Wagner, and more, concluding with Cage and opera aesthetics. A bibliography is supplied along with an index.

708. Opera Plot Index: A Guide to Locating Plots and Descriptions. . . . William E. Studwell and David A. Hamilton. New York: Garland, 1990. 466p. (Garland Reference Library of the Humanities, v. 1099). ISBN 0-8240-4621-8.

This comprehensive information source indexes nearly 3,000 operas and musical productions listed in nearly 170 books written in ten languages. It is an excellent tool for all types of users, from the general public to the serious student and specialist, whose purpose is to identify composers, dates, and themes or to determine plots, nature of criticism, and additional sources of information. Entries supply the title of the work, composer, and date of first performance, with references to sources of information and type of information contained in them. In addition to plots, musical illustrations are identified and historical background is provided. An index of composers aids access.

The Opera Handbook, by John Lazarus (G. K. Hall, 1987; repr., 1990), as part of the publisher's Performing Arts Series, complements *Opera Plot Index* as a less comprehensive but more detailed source. Treated here are the 200 operas most frequently performed by major companies during the decade of the 1980s. Arrangement is by country or national origin in different sections, opening with an introductory chapter. Entries describe plot, characterization, musical idiom, and influences of other works. Special features include a glossary, as well as several directories and bibliographies.

709. Operas in German: A Dictionary. Margaret Ross Griffel. Westport, CT: Greenwood, 1990. 735p. ISBN 0-313-25244-0.

This is a unique and valuable resource for a wide range of users, from scholars and professionals to devotees and collectors. The principal segment is composed of alphabetically arranged entries treating 380 major operas composed to German text. Entries supply information on premieres and first performers in Germany, the United States, and Great Britain; plot summaries; cast listings; major roles; and some historical/analytical commentary. Scores, librettos, recordings, and bibliographic references are treated. Appendices include additional coverage of some 1,250 operas not treated in the first section due to space limitations or lack of information. Appendices then list composers, librettists, and authors whose works inspired operas, as well as sources used by librettists. There is a chronology of German operas from the seventeenth century to the present. The work concludes with a bibliography along with indexes of characters and premiere participants.

710. The Oxford Dictionary of Opera. John Warrack and Ewan West. New York: Oxford University Press, 1992; repr., 1994. 782p. ISBN 0-19-869164-5.

This is an expansion of the previous effort by Warrack and Harold Rosenthal, the current edition of which is described below. In the Oxford manner, it serves as an excellent one-volume handbook to the subject, and in this case contains 4,500 entries. Coverage is given to 750 composers and 900 performers. There is selective inclusion of current performers; a number of obscure performers of the past have been deleted from the *Concise Dictionary*. About 600 operas are described in thorough fashion regarding plot and performance aspects; included are listings of casts and treatment of premieres. There are numerous entries for countries and cities providing background information on the nature of their involvement with opera. Coverage is given to characters, institutions, companies, and festivals. The work is international in scope, with a British perspective, and describes the major themes and contributions of individuals rather than providing an extensive listing of their credits.

The Concise Oxford Dictionary of Opera, by Rosenthal and Warrack (3d ed., Oxford University Press, 1996), has been a quick and convenient source of information since the initial effort in 1964, followed by the second edition in 1985. Based on the second edition of the *Oxford Dictionary of Music* (entry 673n), it continues as a comprehensive reference title on the opera. It serves as an excellent first source for brief treatment of operas, performers, composers, and terminology. Obscure singers of the past are included, as well as a sampling of important contemporary groups.

711. **The Paris Opera: An Encyclopedia of Operas, Ballets, Composers, and Performers.** Spire Pitou. Westport, CT: Greenwood, 1983– . v.1– . ISBN 0-313-26218-7.

The Paris Opera and Opera Comique are documented thoroughly, with every extant work produced and all relevant personalities. Volume 1, issued in 1983, treats the period 1671–1715, and sets the pattern for the encyclopedia. Volume 2 was published in 1985, covering the period from 1715 to 1815. Pitou died before volume 3 was issued in two volumes (1990), treating the pivotal period from 1815 to 1914, when the Paris Opera achieved international recognition and acclaim. Volume 4 will complete the set, with coverage from 1915 to 1982; publication is assured because Pitou's widow has organized his manuscripts. Entries describe the operas or ballets with a detailed plot summary, performance history of the work including its Paris premiere, indication of critical recognition, and bibliography. Biographical entries of singers, dancers, choreographers, librettists, scenarists, and executives are ample. Each volume has its own index.

712. **Recent American Opera: A Production Guide.** Rebecca Hodell Kornick. New York: Columbia University Press, 1991. 352p. ISBN 0-231-06920-0.

The author is an academic who researched this material while preparing her doctoral dissertation; it is published with the intent of updating standard works in the field, *Opera Production I* and *Opera Production II*, by Quaintance Eaton (Da Capo, 1974). Eaton covers American opera production through 1972, and most works treated in the present effort premiered after that year. Information is given on 213 productions in American opera and musical theater of serious nature, with no duplication of Eaton's coverage. Entries are arranged by composer and supply brief appraisals, plot summary, production requirements, and references to reviews. Information on genre, acts, scenes, length, and style of music is provided. The book's value lies in the array of composers and their works, from the well-known to the obscure and from the highly sophisticated to the more popular (Sondheim, Berlin, etc.).

A good Web site linked to a commercial CD sales merchant is *Opera of America* (http://www.best.com/~chapka/opera/us [accessed December 1999]), maintained by Christopher Hapka. It furnishes a chronology, list of American composers, synopses of some forty operas, and a selection of scores and musical segments in MIDI.

713. **A Short History of Opera.** 3d ed. Donald Jay Grout and Hermine W. Williams. New York: Columbia University Press, 1988. 913p. ISBN 0-231-06192-7.

At long last, after twenty-three years, the third edition of this work was issued. Originally published in 1947, the second edition appeared in 1965 with the purpose of updating the material by bringing the historical coverage to 1960. Biographies were updated, and additional illustrative material was included. For the third edition, Grout's failing health placed a large responsibility on co-author Williams, and the pair have produced another excellent textual history up to 1986. The opera is treated in a comprehensive manner, as it was before, beginning with the lyric theater of the Greeks. Arrangement is chronological, with attention given to musical styles. Descriptions are scholarly and the intended audience (specialists and students) continues to derive much value from both the articles and the excellent bibliography. Coverage of twentieth-century opera in the last few chapters is somewhat less successful because much of the change in style and many of the prevailing influences defy neat chronological categorization by decade.

DIRECTORIES, ANNUALS, AND CURRENT AWARENESS SOURCES

714. **Opera America. Season Schedule of Performances.** Washington, DC: Opera America, 1999– . Ann. (no ISSN).

A recently initiated chronicle of the opera season (former title: *Opera America. Repertoire Survey*), this useful source lists mainstage repertoire performance dates. Included here are the production teams, performance halls, and seating capacities for all professional company and international company members of Opera America. It is joined by *Opera America. Annual Field Report* (1999–) providing statistics on attendance, operating budgets, and income; and by *Opera America. Directory of Production Materials for Rent* (1999–), a biennial with 1,400 listings of sets, costumes, and other essentials.

715. **Opera Companies of the World: Selected Profiles.** Robert H. Cowden, ed. Westport, CT: Greenwood, 1992. 336p. ISBN 0-313-26220-9.

This is a directory of about 140 professional opera companies from different parts of the world generally performing on a regular seasonal basis, although there is selective inclusion of some of the major opera festivals. Arrangement of entries is alphabetical by country and city; entries supply description of the history and current operations along with a bibliography of secondary sources, as well as principal administrator, address, and telephone and fax numbers. Smaller companies are treated briefly in the appendix.

Another title providing worldwide coverage is *The International Opera Guide*, by F. M. Stockdale and M. R. Dreyer (Trafalgar Square/David & Charles, 1990). This tool supplies a directory of opera houses and festivals from all over the globe. Individual opera houses are treated in some detail, providing history and exposition along with maps and seating charts. Facilities are described and transportation is explained. Arrangement is alphabetical by city. The second part is a biographical dictionary of composers with synopses of their most important works and listings of characters and major arias.

716. **Symphony Orchestras of the United States.** Robert R. Craven, ed. Westport, CT: Greenwood, 1986. 521p. ISBN 0-313-24072-8.

This useful directory contains a great deal of information on American orchestras not readily available elsewhere. Descriptions are brief, generally running about three pages, but are well written and describe adequately the significant characteristics of each unit. Selection of orchestras was based on membership in the American Symphony Orchestra League (ASOL), where they were designated as either major and regional orchestral units or metropolitan orchestras with the highest budgets. In addition, an orchestra was included from each state that was not represented in the previous categories, for a total of 126 orchestras. Coverage includes descriptions of the history, organization, budget, and activities as well as discography, chronology of music directors, bibliography, and an address and contact person for each orchestra. Included are a general bibliography, a chronology of orchestra founding dates, and a detailed index to the contents.

BIOGRAPHICAL SOURCES

717. **Concert and Opera Conductors: A Bibliography of Biographical Materials.** Robert H. Cowden, comp. New York: Greenwood, 1987. 285p. (Music Reference Collection, no. 14). ISBN 0-313-26075-3.

In this companion to his works on concert and opera singers (entry 724n) and instrumental virtuosi (entry 723), Cowden employs a similar pattern in this biographical bibliography of conductors. Nearly 1,250 conductors are treated alphabetically with entries supplying dates and places of birth and death. There are citations to listings in seven major reference books, articles in ten music periodicals, biographies and autobiographies, and any additional books that contain pertinent information. Criteria for selection of the composers were treatment in at least two publications and appointment to a permanent post as conductor. This eliminates guest conductors such as Domingo or others who have had such experience on different occasions. Other sections provide a listing of collective works and related books. Appendices furnish additional reference sources as well as an index to over 1,600 conductors treated in the seventh edition of *Baker's* (entry 682). There is an author index.

718. **Contemporary American Composers: A Biographical Dictionary.** 2d ed. Ruth E. Anderson. Boston: G. K. Hall, 1982. 528p. ISBN 0-8161-8223-X.

First published in 1976, this work has been revised to omit certain categories of individuals, such as those who have written only one or two compositions and those who did not respond to the questionnaires. Still, the number of entries has increased and presently the tool identifies over 4,000 composers of concert music. These people were born after 1869 and are American citizens or have resided in this country for an extensive period of time. Entries furnish dates of birth and death, education and training, professional and academic appointments, awards and commissions, and mailing address. Due to the reliance on the questionnaire, some caution should be exercised in reporting the information as accurate, but all things considered, the tool is valuable for its breadth of coverage.

A more recent work is *A Dictionary of American Composers*, by Neil Butterworth (Garland, 1984), which provides greater depth but sacrifices breadth. It supplies well-developed treatment of 558 composers of serious music from the eighteenth century to the present in detailed fashion.

719. **Contemporary Composers on Contemporary Music.** Exp. ed. Elliott Schwartz et al., eds. New York: Da Capo, 1998. 512p. ISBN 0-306-80819-6.

This has been a standard in reference departments since its initial appearance in 1967, and provides personal commentary from the composers on music in general and their music in particular. The entries are based on interviews and/or personal writings; much insight is given into perspectives held by both the great and the obscure. One might quibble with the term "contemporary" here because the work includes Debussy and Busoni, but the book has great value in explaining the character of the music of those who contributed to musical development (both traditional and non-traditional) in the twentieth century.

Contemporary Composers, edited by Brian Morton and Pamela Collins (St. James Press, 1992) covers some 500 composers living at the time that the project was initiated in 1989. Coverage is international in scope and includes composers from Japan and Korea, although there is emphasis on U.S. and European nationals. More than 100 specialists contributed the entries. Entries provide a brief biographical sketch and detailed listing of works arranged chronologically and categorized by type. Dates are given for completion and first performance, and citations refer to works by and about the composer. Concluding each entry is a critical-evaluative commentary establishing the position or status of the composer within the broader musical fabric.

720. **A Dictionary of Pianists.** Wilson Lyle. New York: Schirmer Books/Macmillan, 1984; repr., London: Hale, 1985. 343p. ISBN 0-7090-1749-9.

One of the rare biographical sources devoted to the artists of the piano, this tool provides information on 4,000 classical pianists from the eighteenth century to the present day. Listings are arranged alphabetically and the entries are straightforward except for the inclusion of occasional editorial comments, which may seem anomalous within the context of the work. Coverage excludes those individuals whose performance can be categorized as jazz, ragtime, blues, and pops (but interestingly enough embraces an entry on Liberace). There appears to be a slight bias toward including figures of British or European extraction but, in general, the tool should prove of value to music librarians and their patrons.

Another biographical dictionary on instrumentalists of a special type is *Great Masters of the Violin: From Corelli and Vivaldi to Stern, Zuckerman, and Perlman*, by Boris Schwarz (Simon & Schuster, 1983; repr., 1987). This is a highly useful survey of the lives and times of violinists from the sixteenth century to the present day. It is written in an anecdotal and informal style and draws upon a wealth of information derived from a variety of sources, including the author's personal knowledge.

721. **Greene's Biographical Encyclopedia.** David Mason Greene. Garden City, NY: Doubleday, 1985; repr., London: Collins, 1986. 1348p. ISBN 0-004-34363-8.

A recent biographical tool, this work covers over 2,400 prominent composers representing all nations and time periods. Greene is known for his irreverence in the columns he has done as a contributing editor to *Musical Heritage Review* (Paganiniana Publications, 1977–), and these biographical sketches are presented in an interesting, informal, and entertaining manner sure to appeal to the intended audience of nonspecialists. Entries are rich in detail and include information on personal traits and habits as well as the more convenient standard material. They give personal data, analysis of the major works, and a listing of their availability as recordings. Arrangement is chronological to facilitate comparisons within schools or periods.

A narrower time span is covered by Jerome Roche and Elizabeth Roche in *A Dictionary of Early Music from the Troubadours to Monteverdi* (Oxford University Press, 1981). This work provides brief but well-written sketches of 700 early composers whose works appear on recordings, in published editions, or in textbooks, or who are the subject of current scholarship. An informative commercial offering is *Classical Music Website* (http://www.hnh.com/qc_f3.htm [accessed December 1999]). By clicking on this URL you are led to listings of brief biographical coverage of major composers.

722. **Index to Biographies of Contemporary Composers.** Storm Bull. Metuchen, NJ: Scarecrow Press, 1964–1987. 3v. ISBN 0-8108-1930-9 (v.3).

The first volume of this work appeared in 1964 and identifies biographical material on nearly 6,000 composers active between 1900 and 1950 from sixty-nine sources. The second volume, published ten years later, indexes another 108 sources and updates material on 4,000 of the previously covered personalities while adding another 2,000 individuals to their ranks. The massive third volume has listed 13,500 composers with almost 6,000 new entries culled from ninety-eight biographical sources. Arrangement is alphabetical in all volumes, with brief identification given along with references to listed sources. These individuals are contemporary in that they were born during the twentieth century, were still living at time of publication, or died after 1949. This work is recognized as a useful source for quick identification of modern personalities.

723. Instrumental Virtuosi: A Bibliography of Biographical Materials.
Robert H. Cowden, comp. New York: Greenwood, 1989. 349p. (Music
Reference Collection, no. 18). ISBN 0-313-26075-3.

Completing his trilogy of efforts for Greenwood Press, Cowden has produced this
biographical bibliography on instrumental virtuosi to accompany earlier works on singers
(entry 724n) and conductors (entry 717). The pattern is the same as that of the earlier efforts,
opening with a section listing thirty-seven collective works that treat virtuosi. Following that
is another segment identifying nearly 140 related publications. Then follows the major segment, listing 1,215 virtuosi alphabetically. Entries supply birth and death dates, with references to treatment in books previously identified. Virtuosi represent twenty-six different
instruments (woodwinds, brass, strings, organ, percussion, piano, etc.). Most frequent listings
are for artists of the cello, organ, violin, and piano. Serious concert musicians as well as jazz
and pop instrumentalists are included. Appendices supply several indexes to entries as well as
indexing to instrumentalists treated in *Baker's* (entry 682) and in *New Grove* (entry 671).

724. Opera and Concert Singers: An Annotated International Bibliography of Books and Pamphlets. Andrew Farkas. New York: Garland,
1985. 363p. (Garland Reference Library of the Humanities, v. 466). ISBN
0-8240-9001-2.

This is a comprehensive bibliography of 1,500 biographies and autobiographies in
twenty-nine different languages. Also included are 300 monographs covering more than one
subject, which are listed in a separate section. Annotations are excellent, providing useful information and written in a sprightly style. There is a warning from the author that most libraries
do not possess more than half the books listed; therefore, this should serve as a purchasing
guide to strengthen the collection. A list of unpublished manuscripts is given at the end. All in
all, this is an impressive and complete contribution.

Another bibliography published in the same year is *Concert and Opera Singers: A
Bibliography of Biographical Materials*, compiled by Robert H. Cowden (Greenwood,
1985). Although personalities are duplicated to a great extent in the two works, the latter
includes entries from reference books and periodicals. It has only a small number of annotations. It is the first of three such efforts completed by Cowden for the publisher (see entries
717 and 723).

RECORDINGS

725. International Discography of Women Composers. Aaron I.
Cohen, comp. Westport, CT: Greenwood, 1984. 254p. ISBN
0-313-24272-0.

The increased interest in the contributions of females to society and culture has led
to the production of several reference sources in the field of music, and Cohen has been a contributor in this regard (entry 685). This discography furnishes listings of the recorded music
of 468 women composers of concert music. It is hoped that with efforts like this, there will be
an increased awareness, not only of the quantity but also of the quality of much of this work,
so that it is more frequently performed. The entries are arranged alphabetically by name of
composer, under which the recordings are listed along with performers, instruments, record
label and number, and dates and nationality of composer. Included are a directory of record
companies and a list of composers by country of origin and by instrument and form. Treatment of composers is comprehensive, dating from the twelfth century to the present day. An
index of titles provides access.

Popular Music (*Jazz, Folk, Rock, Country, Etc.*)

BIBLIOGRAPHIC GUIDES

726. **Folk Music in America: A Reference Guide.** Terry E. Miller. New York: Garland, 1986. 424p. (Garland Reference Library of the Humanities, v. 496). ISBN 0-8240-8935-9.

This is a selective listing of scholarly articles, books, dissertations, and even encyclopedia articles on the topic of folk music. Annotations, although brief, are informative, and emphasis is given to relatively recent writings from the past three decades. The introduction provides an understanding of what may or may not be considered folk music. Treatment is subsequently given to such elements as the music of Native Americans and Eskimos; Anglo-American folk songs and ballads; and the more contemporary bluegrass, country and western, and protest music. There are sections on instruments and instrumental music such as banjo and dulcimer as well as black and ethnic folk music. This should prove to be a basic reference tool in the music collection.

727. **Popular Music: A Reference Guide.** Roman Iwaschkin. New York: Garland, 1986–1993. 2v. (Garland Reference Library of the Humanities, v. 642). ISBN 0-8240-8680-5 (v.1). (Music Research and Information Guides, v. 15). ISBN 0-8240-4449-5 (v.2).

Another of the Garland bibliographies, this two-volume bibliography represents a real contribution to the literature of popular music in all phases. Volume 1 provides coverage of more than 5,000 items, some of which receive annotations. There is comprehensive coverage of the vast field of popular music, with such categories as folk, country, Cajun, black, jazz, and stage and screen, as well as rap music, African pop, Grand Ole Opry, and jazz in Germany. The book includes a section on biographies, another on education and instruments, and another on the music business. Songs and recordings receive separate treatment, as do literary works, including novels and poetry. The listing of periodicals is a useful resource feature. Volume 2 is an update to the coverage of volume 1 treating the literature from 1984 to 1990. It contains an improved author and title index.

A timely effort is Judy McCoy's *Rap Music in the 1980s: A Reference Guide* (Scarecrow Press, 1992), important for its documentation of a sociological phenomenon and grassroots style of performance. Coverage is given to 1,000 books and articles published from 1980 to 1991 on the various aspects of rap music. Entries are annotated and serve to provide awareness of the content; as a plus, there is an annotated discography of seventy-six recordings. The work is indexed by artist, album title, and subject.

728. **Rockabilly: A Bibliographic Resource Guide.** B. Lee Cooper and Wayne S. Hamey. Metuchen, NJ: Scarecrow Press, 1990. 372p. ISBN 0-8108-2386-1.

For enthusiasts at various levels of sophistication, this is a unique resource tool providing documentation of books and articles treating this particular form of popular music of the 1950s. Rockabilly represents a merger of musical elements (country music, rock and roll, and the blues) into what is today regarded as an innovative and distinctive genre. This work contains nearly 1,950 entries largely citing the popular media (*Rolling Stone* and *Crawdaddy*) as well as historical studies and reviews. Arrangement of entries is alphabetical by name of performers, with such well-known practitioners as Carl Perkins along with those of more questionable linkage to the rockabilly movement. There is a separate discography of more than 200 albums that should be useful to both collectors and students, along with a separate bibliography of general books. An author index is furnished.

BIBLIOGRAPHIES AND INDEXES

729. **Fire Music: A Bibliography of the New Jazz, 1959–1990.** John Gray, comp. New York: Greenwood, 1991. 515p. (Music Reference Collection, no. 31). ISBN 0-313-27892-X.

Avant garde or free form jazz performed in unorthodox and unconventional fashion by a large number of musicians between the 1960s and 1970s abandoned some of the more traditional "roles" of harmony, rhythm, melody, and so forth to produce this short-lived variation. Documentation is heavy and this work lists more than 7,100 entries representing all types of literature: books, newspaper and periodical articles, dissertations, videos, films, and tapes. Various Western languages are represented, with emphasis on English and French publications over a thirty-year period. The work is divided into six sections, providing a general chronology with reference to relevant material, along with segments on African-American cultural history, county and regional studies, jazz collectives, jazz lofts, and biographical-critical studies. Appendices provide listings of reference works, research centers, and performers by country and by instrument. There are author, subject, and artist indexes.

730. **The Literature of Jazz: A Critical Guide.** 2d ed., rev. Donald Kennington. Chicago, American Library Association, 1980. 236p. ISBN 0-8389-0313-4.

Originally published in Great Britain by the Library Association, this bibliography has earned a respected position among the useful reference works in the field of music. Essentially, it is a listing of the important books on jazz and it attempts to enumerate all the significant material in the English language published through 1979. Chapters cover various aspects of the literature beginning with general background and following with such categories as histories, biographies, analysis, theory and criticism, reference sources, periodical literature, and organizations. There are full bibliographies at the end of each chapter. Chapters on the blues and jazz education are new to this edition. Emphasis is still on English-language materials. There are name and title indexes.

An excellent Web site is provided by the University of Chicago Library Information System: *Jazz Research* (http://www.lib.uchicago.edu/LibInfo/Libraries/CJA/research.html [accessed April 5, 2000]). It serves as a guide for high school and undergraduate students researching the topic. Included are listings of research tools, bibliographies, indexes, recordings, and so forth. There are a number of links to relevant Web sites.

731. **The Literature of Rock, III, 1984–1990: With Additional Material for the Period 1954–1983.** Frank Hoffman and B. Lee Cooper. Metuchen, NJ: Scarecrow Press, 1981–1995. 3v. in 4. ISBN 0-8108-2762-X.

This work is a continuation of two earlier works by the authors from the same publisher. Hoffman authored *The Literature of Rock, 1954–1978* in 1981, covering a twenty-five year period of writings on rock music. Then Hoffman and Cooper added *The Literature of Rock II, 1979–1983*, supplementing the initial effort with additional material omitted in the earlier issue and at the same time extending the coverage a few more years. The present effort continues the pattern. All works furnish a selective annotated bibliography of books and periodical articles arranged in subject categories reflecting a chronological sequence. Such periods as doo-wop, rhythm and blues, and soul are included. Most entries are for individuals, although some subjects are given. Source materials include fanzines, trade magazines, books, and undergrounds. Each volume has a detailed index and a useful discography.

PRINTED MUSIC SOURCES—BIBLIOGRAPHIES, INDEXES, AND CATALOGS

732. **The Great Song Thesaurus.** 2d ed., upd. and exp. Roger Lax and Frederick Smith. New York: Oxford University Press, 1989. 774p. ISBN 0-19-50548-3.

The first edition of this important index to popular songs was issued in 1984 and was hailed as an "invaluable source." Coverage now has been extended by an additional 1,000 songs popular between 1980 and 1987, for a total of 11,000 popular songs in the English language from the Elizabethan period through 1986. The value of the work lies in the many approaches offered in the ten sections. Included here are year-by-year inventory of significant songs (1558–1986); listing by performance medium; thesaurus of songs by subject, key word, and category; song-title catalog, identifying composers and lyricists, year, and recording artists; award winners in chronological sequence for both film and television; themes, trademarks, and signatures; elegant plagiarisms; and more. With the inclusion of an index of lyric keylines, one is able to identify titles when only the important lines are remembered.

733. **Musi*key: "The Reference Guide of Note."** Fort Collins, CO: Musi*Key, 1987– . Bimo. ISSN 0895-1543.

This serial publication is purchased by yearly subscription and supplies six bimonthly issues, each of which represents an updated, complete listing of currently available song sheets and collections of popular music. This is important to those who need to keep abreast of materials in this elusive area. Included here are listings for the songs of Broadway, as well as folk music, gospel, jazz, pop, rock, and so forth. Purposely omitted are classical music, choral arrangement, band charts, and method works. Each issue treats some 155,000 songs in addition to 10,000 pieces of sheet music and more than 8,000 anthologies. The work is divided into four sections listing the entries under song title, book title, sheet title, and composer/recording artist. Each of these sections contains complete ordering information along with types of musical arrangement.

A complementary service is provided by the *Music Library Association Sheet Music Collections* site on the World Wide Web (http://www.lib.duke.edu/music/sheetmusic/collections.html [accessed December 1999]). It provides listings of such collections as are available through public access either on the Web or an online service.

734. **Popular Music, 1920–1979: An Annotated Index of over 18,000 American Popular Songs.** 2d ed. Nat Shapiro and Bruce Pollock, eds. Detroit: Gale Research, 1985. 3v. **Supp. 1 1980–1984,** 1986. **Supp. 2– ,** 1986– . Ann. ISSN 0886-442X.

This is a major cumulation of what was an eight-volume set that indexed the popular music of this country in five- or ten-year intervals. This comprehensive work organizes the entries alphabetically by title and describes alternate titles, country of origin for songs from other countries, lyricists, composers, dates, history, performers, and record labels. There are indexes of composers and lyricists, important performances, and awards. There is also a list of publishers. The original eight volumes are still available for those libraries that have collected them and do not wish to invest in the new work, but the new edition facilitates access and provides up-to-date publisher lists. The series continues with subsequent publications that serve as supplements; volume 9 is a cumulation for 1980–1984 (Gale Research, 1986) followed by annual supplements beginning with 1985 (volume 10– , 1986–).

A retrospective cumulation for the early years, *Popular Music, 1900–1919: An Annotated Guide to American Popular Songs . . .* , was edited by Barbara N. Cohen-Stratyner (Gale Research, 1988), providing extraordinary access to music of the twentieth century and facilitating the search for information.

735. Popular Song Index. Patricia P. Havlice. Metuchen, NJ: Scarecrow Press, 1975. 933p. **First Supp.**, 1978. **Second Supp.**, 1984. **Third Supp.**, 1989. ISBN 0-8108-2202-4.

This is an extensive index of 301 songbooks, mainly U.S. but also including several British, Canadian, and French works. The emphasis is on folk songs, as it is in Leigh's *Index to Song Books* (entry 736n), although coverage is from 1940 to 1972. This book is complementary to the work by de Charms and Breed (entry 737), beginning its coverage with 1940 imprints and emphasizing popular music rather than classical. Main entries are under titles, with cross-references from actual first lines and first lines of choruses. There is also an index of composers and lyricists. The supplements continue the coverage, with the first supplement adding seventy-two anthologies published between 1970 and 1975. The second supplement covers another 145 songbooks published between 1974 and 1981, while the third supplement identifies songs in another 181 anthologies published between 1979 and 1987.

736. Song Index. . . . Minnie Sears. New York: H. W. Wilson, 1926. 650p. **Supp.**, 1934; repr., Hamden, CT: Shoe String Press, 1966, 1990. 2v. in 1. ISBN 0-7812-9019-8.

The complete title of the basic edition indicates that it is "an index to more than 12,000 songs in 177 song collections comprising 262 volumes." This was the original work that other song indexes were designed to supplement. Despite its age, it remains a useful index and is still used in all kinds of libraries. Sears established an excellent pattern of coverage with titles, first lines, and names of lyricists and composers all in one listing for ease of access. The supplement adds another 7,000 songs from 104 song collections published up to 1932. More recent song indexes by Leigh (see below), de Charms and Breed (entry 737), Havlice (entry 735), and Shapiro and Pollock (entry 734) supplement this work but do not supersede it.

Robert Leigh's *Index to Song Books: A Title Index to over 11,000 Copies of 6,800 in 111 Books Published Between 1933 and 1962* (repr., Da Capo, 1973) picked up where Sears left off, much like de Charms and Breed. Coverage differs substantially between the two, however, because Leigh places greater emphasis on folk, community, and popular songbooks published in this country, although there is international representation. Songs include popular hits, children's songs, carols, hymns, and operatic arias. Only songbooks that provide both words and music are included.

737. Songs in Collections: An Index. Desiree de Charms and Paul F. Breed. Detroit: Information Service, 1966. 588p.

Designed to supplement to a degree the coverage of Sears's *Song Index* (entry 736), this represents a good companion to the original edition of *Popular Song Index* (entry 735) because they both begin their coverage with 1940 imprints. Anthologies in de Charms range from 1940 to 1957. De Charms concentrates primarily on anthologies of art songs and operatic arias, with less emphasis on traditional folk song collections. (There are just a few popular songbooks, which are, of course, the primary focus of *Popular Song Index.*) Songs in 400 collections are indexed, with separate sections given to composed songs, anonymous and folk songs, carols, and sea chanteys. There is an index to first lines and one to authors, with the collections listed at the beginning of the volume.

738. **Where's That Tune? An Index to Songs in Fakebooks.** William D. Goodfellow. Metuchen, NJ: Scarecrow Press, 1990. 449p. ISBN 0-8108-2391-8.

This index identifies 13,500 songs in sixty-four fakebooks. Fakebooks are collections of popular songs for which the words, melody lines, and chord notations are provided; they are utilized by musicians to support and enhance their repertoire. Fakebooks indexed in this source were published generally within the past decade and are available in libraries. There are three major parts or segments to the index, with part 1 listing the sixty-four fakebooks treated. Citations include OCLC number along with brief descriptive annotations supplying the number of songs or amount of musical notation. Popular songs of all kinds are included: jazz, pop/rock, children's songs, country, show tunes, Christian music, and so forth. The second part is a title index to all the songs, with coded references to the fakebooks; part 3 supplies an index of composers that lists the song titles but not the fakebooks.

DICTIONARIES, ENCYCLOPEDIAS, HANDBOOKS, ETC.

739. **Encyclopedia of the Blues.** 2d ed. Gerard Herzhaft. Fayetteville: University of Arkansas Press, 1997. 300p. ISBN 1-55728-452-0.

Since blues music represents a crossover form and shares the musicians and certain elements of rock, gospel, soul, and so forth, this is a useful tool for focusing on the genre. Initially a French work, the translation reads well, providing coverage of personalities, instruments, and places, with entries arranged alphabetically. Treatment of instruments is interesting and geographical locations are described in terms of their influences, styles, and connection with the development of blues music. The second edition contains seventy-five black-and-white photographs, and the work concludes with a bibliography and discography of selective nature. Access is aided by a general index along with an index by instrument.

A good World Wide Web source is *The Delta Blues Museum* (http://www.deltabluesmuseum.org/bluesnews.html [accessed December 1999]) in Clarksdale, Mississippi. Information regarding the topic and the Museum is furnished along with links to news and issues.

Hit Parade: An Encyclopedia of the Top Songs of the Jazz, Depression, Swing and Sing Eras, by Don Tyler (Quill/William Morrow, 1985), is an interesting and useful chronology of a variety of popular songs that appeal to a wide audience, and is a desirable addition to a general reference collection. Entries are alphabetically arranged by title in chapters, which are classified in chronological order. Each entry furnishes name of composer and lyricist, followed by a fairly detailed description of the song. This normally covers circumstances of its introduction, performers, rivals, and so forth. Introductory material preceding each chapter describes in a highly informal manner the nature of the period. Some errors have been pointed out but, in general, this is a good purchase for a general audience. There are indexes of song titles and of proper names.

740. **Country Music: The Encyclopedia.** Irwin Stambler and Grelun Landon. New York: St. Martin's Press, 1997. 672p. ISBN 0-312-15121-7.

This is a useful source of information on personalities and musical developments from the early days to Shania Twain. It is the most recent work by the well-known writer combination and serves as an update to their well received *The Encyclopedia of Folk, Country, & Western Music* (St. Martin's, 1984). All varieties of country music are represented; there are numerous photographs accompanying entries and interviews with top stars. Biographical sketches are well written, providing detail regarding the performer's career and a list of notable recordings. Appendices provide lists of award winners, and the work is well-indexed by artist, album, and song title.

A History and Encyclopedia of Country, Western, and Gospel Music, by Linnell Gentry (McQuiddy, 1961; repr., St. Clair Shores, MI: Scholarly Press, 1979), is an older work but still useful for the diversity of information it contains. Part of its vitality lies in the choice of thirty-seven reprint articles taken from a variety of journals covering numerous topics in an informative manner. Other sections provide biographical coverage of over 300 prominent figures, a listing of country music radio shows since 1924, and a comprehensive listing of 3,800 names.

741. **Facts Behind the Songs: A Handbook of American Popular Music from the Nineties to the '90s.** Marvin E. Paymer, ed. New York: Garland, 1993. 560p. ISBN 0-8240-5240-4.

This is a handy source of information on popular music in this country, organized into two major sections. The first part supplies about 325 articles on popular songs, describing their origins, such as classic or film musical; foreign influences if any; domestic roots or influences such as Motown or Bluegrass; means of popularization, such as "Your Hit Parade"; genre, such as doo-wop or protest song; subject or topic, such as humor or money; and style, such as harmony or scat. Entries on the "Depression Years" and "Roaring Twenties" treat the musical development of those historical periods. The second section lists the songs and identifies year, lyricist, composer, type, source, production, and so forth, with cross-references to articles in the first segment. There are fifteen specialized tables identifying various award winners and source listings. Bibliographies accompany some of the entries.

Eyeneer Music Archives (http://www.eyeneer.com/index.html [accessed December 1999]) is progressing as a useful commercial Web site of educational nature seeking to provide comprehensive information about music, musicians, and recordings. The section on "American Music Archives" covers blues, folk/bluegrass, r&b/soul, and gospel. Images accompany the entries.

742. **The Guinness Encyclopedia of Popular Music.** 2d ed. Colin Larkin, comp. and ed. Chester, CT: New England Publishing Associates, 1995. 6v. ISBN 1-56159-76-9.

This continues as the most comprehensive reference work on the topic of popular music and provides alphabetically arranged listings of "every important artist, band, genre, group, event, instrument, publisher, promoter, and musical style." Thousands of entries are treated within the six-volume work (expanded from four volumes in the 1992 edition); these vary in length depending upon the importance of the topic, from about 150 to 3,000 words (as in the case of Duke Ellington). Numerous specialists have contributed their efforts. Popular music of the twentieth century is covered thoroughly, with some emphasis on the more recent era of rock. Artists of all nations are covered, including those of the East such as Ryuichi Sakamoto of Japan. Biographical entries give basic factual data along with interpretation of influences, motivation, and success. Events treated include festivals, and there is coverage of organizations. A massive bibliography and a detailed index are provided. A one-volume concise edition with the same title was issued in 1993.

743. **Lissauer's Encyclopedia of Popular Music in America: 1888 to the Present.** Robert Lissauer. New York: Facts on File, 1996. 3v. ISBN 0-8160-3238-6.

This is a revision and update of a 1991 publication from another publishing house. It is another useful source of information for identification of popular music in this country, written by an expert in the field. Nearly 20,000 songs spanning a period from 1888 to roughly 1994 are listed alphabetically in the first section of the work. Entries may supply lyricist, composer, dates, brief history, musical productions, performers, and recordings in narratives varying in length from about ten to sixty-five words. Academy award winners are noted.

Volumes 1 and 2 treat all types of songs, country, rock, jazz, blues, show tunes, and other forms popular in their eras, with cross-references to alternative titles along with a chronology listing titles by year of recording or height of popularity. Volume 3 lists the writers alphabetically. Special features include a glossary of terms and a selective bibliography.

744.   The New Grove Dictionary of Jazz. Barry Kernfield, ed. London: Macmillan; New York: Grove's Dictionary of Music, 1988. 2v. Repr. in one volume, St. Martin's Press, 1994. ISBN 0-312113-57-9.

This is a comprehensive and well-constructed encyclopedia from a fine publishing house on topics and various personalities related to jazz. All periods and styles are described, with coverage on an international basis. There are some 4,500 entries covering soloists and groups, bands, styles, topics, instruments, record labels, organizations, and terminology. Most of the biographical entries treat performers, although coverage is given to composers, writers, producers, arrangers, editors, discographers, and others. There are some 200 entries on jazz theory, with lengthy discourse given to survey articles on such topics as "arrangement" and "beat." Specific musical terms receive briefer treatment, several paragraphs in length; most entries supply detailed bibliographies. Coverage given to instruments emphasizes their use in jazz and contrasts that use with other genres. Some 350 recording studios are treated historically, with indication of achievements. There is an extensive bibliography of bibliographies in the appendix.

745.   Night Beat: Collected Writings on Rock & Roll Culture and Other Disruptions. Mikal Gilmore. New York: Doubleday, 1998. 352p. ISBN 0-385-48435-6.

This is an entertaining and informative collection of articles penned by the author during his long career as a critic and journalist for *Rolling Stone*. Included here is the text of critical articles, reviews, philosophical pieces, and interviews, providing a fine overview of the music, its entertainers, and its essential nature. Gilmore refers to the sampling as "an outline, a shadow, of rock & roll history" in which important personalities and their contributions are examined and described. Impact of these people on music is assessed, and excellent commentary is provided on musicians from Elvis to Tupac Shakur. Both icons and peripheral contributors are analyzed.

The New Rolling Stone Encyclopedia of Rock & Roll (Fireside, 1995), edited by Patricia Romanowski et al., is both a biographical dictionary and a treatment of issues and events, providing some 2,000 entries of varying size from a couple of paragraphs to three pages. Selective discographies are given with each of the artists, who date from the earliest days and precursors of rock to the current crop of performers, both top-drawer and those of lesser impact.

746.   The Oxford Companion to Popular Music. Peter Gammond. New York: Oxford University Press, 1991; repr. with corr., 1993. 739p. ISBN 0-19-280004-3 (pbk.).

Defining popular music as "not serious or classical," this inexpensive reprint is another of the specialized one-volume handbooks in the Companion series. Like others, it provides descriptions of one or two paragraphs along with articles of several pages on major topics or important personalities. Popular music of the Western world is treated (jazz, blues, ragtime, country, operetta and music hall pieces, folk, military, rhythm and blues, etc.). The emphasis is on music in the English language; coverage runs from 1850 to 1985. There is greater coverage of the first half of the twentieth century; relatively brief coverage is given to the major rock and rollers of the recent past. Entries provide biographical sketches of all types of personalities, from performers to executives; plot descriptions of shows and films; and individual songs. The work is indexed by personalities, shows and films, and albums.

747. Resource Guide to Themes in Contemporary American Song Lyrics, 1950–1985. B. Lee Cooper. Westport, CT: Greenwood, 1986. 458p. ISBN 0-313-24516-9.

A tool that has proved valuable for research on song themes is this handbook covering American song production over a thirty-five-year period. Categories are defined in terms of socio-economic elements of importance today, such as death, education, marriage and divorce, occupations, race relations, urban life, and youth culture. These categories are then subdivided into more specific themes. A most interesting sociological study is possible through the linking of these topics with music of our time, and comparisons are surely in order with other decades. Several tables show relationships of songs to various events. Both the bibliography and the discography are lengthy and useful.

748. Variety Music Cavalcade, 1620–1969: A Chronology of Vocal and Instrumental Music Popular in the U.S. 3d ed. Julius Mattfeld. New York: Prentice Hall Press, 1971. 766p. ISBN 0-13-940718-9.

One of the important works in the field is this highly respected chronology of popular music. It spans a period of 350 years beginning with the Pilgrims, and provides brief descriptions of various events along with the listings of songs. The events are social, political, and literary and help to provide some idea of the context of the period in which the songs were developed. Songs are of a varied type and include hymns, all types of popular secular music, sacred songs, choral compositions, and instrumental and orchestral works. Only musical elements (not social events) are indexed, along with dates that lead the user to the proper year. Songs are listed alphabetically under the year of publication and are accompanied by information on composer, lyricist, publisher, and copyright date.

749. Year by Year in the Rock Era: Events and Conditions Shaping the Rock Generations That Reshaped America. Herb Hendler. Westport, CT: Greenwood, 1983; repr., New York: Praeger, 1987. 350p. ISBN 0-313-23456-6.

This is a detailed chronology of the twenty-eight-year period from 1954 through 1981, in which rock music is placed within the context of social events in much the same manner as *Variety Music Cavalcade* (entry 748) treats popular music. The author is a former record company executive and has provided a wealth of information, covering each year individually and listing major performers, dancers, and news of the rock music industry along with social, cultural, and political information gleaned from the news. Statistics, fashions, slang, and so forth are included. In addition, there is an interesting section analyzing the rock era by category such as cost of living, *Time* "Man of the Year" winners, and top television shows. The work concludes with a detailed bibliography.

Another chronology of the same period is *Rolling Stone Rock Almanac: The Chronicle of Rock and Roll*, by the editors of the rock journal (Collier Books/Macmillan, 1983; repr., 1984). The introduction describes the history and development of rock and roll and its relationship to rhythm and blues, country and western, and more. The years 1954–1982 are described individually, first with a brief introductory essay, then by a calendar of events. *Shake, Rattle & Roll: The Golden Age of American Rock n' Roll, Volume 1 1952–1955*, by Lee Cotten, is a recent entry in the field (Popular Culture Ink, 1990). Projected to be a four-volume history beginning with coverage of the early formative years in this volume, it has been followed by *Reelin' and Rockin'* . . . *1956–1959* (1995) and *Twist and Shout* . . . *1960–1963* (to be published in 2000). The set furnishes detailed chronologies of daily occurrences, events, and happenings such as openings and closings of concert runs, stage appearances, and details of performance. Several indexes furnish access.

DIRECTORIES, ANNUALS, AND CURRENT AWARENESS SOURCES

*750. Billboard. New York: Billboard Publications, 1984– . Wk. ISSN 0006-2510.

Considered to be the equivalent to music of what *Variety* (entry 959) is to theater and film, this well-known publication appears in a newspaper/magazine format. With a weekly circulation of nearly 50,000, it represents one of the most popular offerings and provides excellent current awareness of news in the music field. The focus is on publishing, recording, and selling music, and articles cover personalities, recent contracts, shows recently given or soon to be seen, as well as new albums and tapes. The writing style is snappy and informal, and the publication does an excellent job of keeping readers abreast of developments in rock, pop, country, and folk music. Although there is a rather costly index, all materials including reviews are indexed in *Music Index* (entry 631). The publication is available online through NEXIS as *Billboard Online, and is on the Web (http://www.billboard-online.com/ [accessed December 1999]).

*Rock Net is another daily service available online through Compuserve. It furnishes reports on the rock music industry (news, concert schedules, reviews, etc.). The system includes online conferences and interviews with rock stars.

751. Songwriter's Market: Where and How to Market Your Songs. Cincinnati: Writer's Digest Books, 1979– . Ann. ISSN 0161-5971.

The 1997 edition of this popular guide to the marketplace, edited by Cindy Laufenberg, continues in the same manner as its previous issues and of other titles in the Writer's Digest series. There is an introductory narrative on the profession of songwriting, followed by extensive listings of commercial firms involved in the sale and purchasing of songs. Content of articles varies with the importance of issues in the music industry. The work contains some 2,500 listings. General information is given regarding address, description, contacts, and so forth for the various firms and individuals. Emphasis is on the American music industry, although there are listings for international firms based in other countries of the world. Music publishers, record companies, record producers, audiovisual firms, managers, classical groups, and theater companies are all included. Appendices provide information on a host of topics such as contracts and management of records. A glossary and detailed index are furnished.

BIOGRAPHICAL SOURCES

752. American Musicians: Fifty-Six Portraits in Jazz. Whitney Balliett. New York: Oxford University Press, 1986; repr., 1990. 415p. ISBN 0-19-506088-1 (pbk.).

Described by the author as a "highly personal encyclopedia," this collective biography represents a compilation of Balliett's numerous contributions to *The New Yorker* over a twenty-five-year period beginning with the early 1960s. The book begins with biographies of two writers: jazz historian Hughes Panassie and discographer Charles Delaunay. It then treats jazz musicians in chronological sequence. The names are well known to most people who have even a passing acquaintance with jazz: "King" Oliver, Sidney Bechet, Duke Ellington, Coleman Hawkins, and so forth. The author has used his personal interviews with the subjects or their associates as well as standard biographies and various accounts to produce cogent and well-developed narratives as well as biographical highlights. Numerous quotations provide real insight into each subject's nature.

Gene Lees, an excellent authority, and editor of the privately published monthly newsletter, *Gene Lees Jazzletter* (1981–), has created a number of informative works, both of collective and individual biography/criticism, drawn from his newsletter essays. Two of the most popular are *Waiting for Dizzy* (Oxford University Press, 1991) and *Cats of Any Color: Jazz Black and White* (Oxford University Press, 1994). His most recent (and most extensive) effort is *Leader of the Band: The Life of Woody Herman* (Oxford University Press, 1995). Lee writes in a clear and interesting style, both informative and passionate.

753. **American Women Songwriters: A Biographical Dictionary.** Virginia L. Grattan. Westport, CT: Greenwood, 1993. 279p. ISBN 0-313-28510-1.

This work fills a basic need, providing coverage of women songwriters overlooked by such dictionaries of music as David Ewen's *American Songwriters* (H. W. Wilson, 1986). This is the first work of this type to target this group, resulting in a biographical dictionary of more than 180 women who have written songs for the theater, film, concert hall, and recording label. Included here are all types of popular music: country, blues, jazz, folk, gospel, and rock. Madonna, Janet Jackson, and Mariah Carey are treated, along with now-obscure writers of the nineteenth and twentieth centuries. Issue will be taken with omissions rather than inclusions, and treatment is cursory in nature. Entries supply mostly one-page coverage that includes a biographical sketch with career highlights, listing of most important or famous songs, and a few additional sources of information.

754. **Blues Who's Who: A Biographical Dictionary of Blues Singers.** Sheldon Harris. New Rochelle, NY: Arlington House, 1979; repr., Da Capo, 1994. 775p. ISBN 0-306-80155-8.

Considered to be the most substantial and complete source of biographical information on blues singers, this work lists the personalities by their real names. As a result, there are many cross-references from variations and stage names to the proper entries. Hundreds of personalities are covered (although Mahalia Jackson and Billie Holliday have been omitted) and coverage is excellent among those local singers, both urban and rural, who achieved some measure of national or international recognition. Howlin' Wolf, Muddy Waters, and B. B. King are listed, of course, among many others. Entries include a biographical sketch, birth date and place, marriages, children, instruments, songs composed, influences, and critical comments concerning their work. A detailed list of professional concert appearances, television and radio shows, films, and so forth is provided.

A useful Web site is *Blues Online*, created by Joel Snow, who holds the copyright (http://mathrisc1.lunet.edu/blues/blues.html [accessed December 1999]). It provides directories of styles (based on regions) and resources as well as artists and bands. Access to sound bytes is included.

755. **Composers and Conductors of Popular Orchestral Music: A Biographical and Discographical Sourcebook.** Reuben Musiker and Naomi Musiker. New York: Greenwood, 1998. 360p. ISBN 0-313-30260-X.

This recent effort identifies and treats members of a relatively overlooked group in its focus on conductors as well as composers of popular orchestral music. Some 500 personalities who have worked in such genre as film, theater, show, and mood music are identified and described. Coverage is international, with emphasis on the United States and the United Kingdom and limited for the most part to the latter half of the twentieth century, focusing on the period from the 1940s to the 1960s. The entries are of varying length and are arranged alphabetically. Major composers such as Kern, Berlin, Rodgers, and Coward and major conductors such as Kostelanetz and Faith are treated along with less famous or popular personalities. Entries furnish a biographical sketch with some evaluative commentary, selected works, and discographies; in some cases bibliographies are furnished. The work concludes with a general bibliography and name index.

756. Contemporary Musicians. Detroit: Gale Research, 1989– . Semiann. ISSN 1044-2197.

The first issue of this serial publication appeared in 1989, the intent being to continue it as a semiannual production. Each issue covers from 80 to 100 well-known performers and writers of the popular music scene. Included here are personalities and groups from jazz, rock, blues, folk, country, and rhythm and blues as well as rap, New Age, and reggae. As one might imagine, coverage has been diverse: Anita Baker, the Kingston Trio, Reba McIntyre, and Metallica all have been featured. Entries are signed by their contributors, specialists in the field, and furnish bio-critical essays of about 2,000 words. There are a section of biographical data, a selective discography, and a bibliography as well. Like others in the Gale lineup, this work is regarded as an in-depth biographical resource. There are indexes of musicians and of subjects.

Artists of American Folk Music: The Legends of Traditional Folk Music . . . , edited by Phil Hood (William Morrow, 1986), is a highly selective and more restrictive biographical encyclopedia, covering only thirty-one different groups or solo performers. Treatment is detailed, with articles running from three to six pages in length. The selection includes such individuals as the Kingston Trio, Peter, Paul, and Mary, Bob Dylan, Woody Guthrie, Pete Seeger, and Leadbelly, who are considered leaders in the troubadour tradition.

757. The Harmony Illustrated Encyclopedia of Rock. 7th ed. Mike Clifford and Pete Frame. New York: Harmony Books/Crown, 1992. 208p. ISBN 0-517-59078-6.

This work of British authorship has appeared frequently in the past (6th ed., 1988) and is an important biographical source on rock music. It has been a consistent favorite among devotees of the genre for nearly twenty years, and covers approximately 1,000 performers thought to be significant. There is some emphasis on British stars, thus overlooking some reasonably important American contributors. As is true of any work of this type, there are some errors and oversights, but the quality of writing is excellent and the content is well presented in an entertaining fashion with many illustrations. Coverage tends to be mainstream.

758. The Heritage Encyclopedia of Band Music: Composers and Their Music. William H. Rehrig; Paul E. Bierley, ed. Westerville, OH: Integrity Press, 1991. 2v. ISBN 0-918048-08-7.

Regarded by its makers as a seminal volume on band music and its composition, this important tool attempts to document all editions of all music ever published for concert and military bands. The result is an extensive bio-bibliography treating some 9,000 composers of band music and their works. Entries are arranged alphabetically and supply listings of compositions along with references to source materials. Omitted are brass band music, treated well by other tools, and the continents of South America and Africa due to the scantiness of information on them. The utility of this work lies in its coverage of personalities and compositions not included in standard works of the field. Other specialized sources have not been as comprehensive; therefore this is becoming the standard reference tool for band music. Numerous appendices provide additional information; a title index provides access.

Treatment of personalities and bands is included in an earlier multi-volume history by David Whitwell, a noted author on the subject. *History and Literature of the Wind Band and Wind Ensemble* (Winds, 1982–1984, 9v.) provides description, commentary, and criticism from the period before 1500 to the end of the nineteenth century.

759. **The Harmony Illustrated Encyclopedia of Country Music.** 3d ed. Alan Cackett. New York: Crown, 1994. 208p. ISBN 0-51788139-X.

This remains a useful source of information, as was the first edition in 1987. It has been completely revised and updated, and has been expanded to include more than 700 entries from the previous 500 treated in the second edition. Concise but informative biographical sketches are furnished, providing revealing insight into the musical influences and background of performers from the early days to the present. The work is informal in tone, well-illustrated, and enjoyable; it provides some 500 photographs, most in color, to accompany the articles.

Kingsbury's Who's Who in Country & Western Music, by Kenn Kingsbury (Black Stallion Country Press, 1981), is an older but still useful biographical dictionary of country music personalities furnishing brief but informative biographical portraits of 716 individuals (performers, publishers, executives, disc jockeys, composers, agents, etc.). Biographies are adequate in identifying and describing the various personalities. Pictures are included as well. There are listings of 2,000 radio stations, record companies, publishers, talent agencies, and award winners.

760. **The Rock Who's Who.** 2d ed. Brock Helander. New York: Schirmer Books, 1996. 849p. ISBN 0-028-71031-2.

Now in its second edition, the work continues to supply the rock fan with a useful biographical source on the lives of 400 individuals, including disc jockeys, music industry people, songwriters, and performers. Inclusion is selective and implies a significant contribution to the development of contemporary popular music. This selectivity allows for thorough biographical and critical treatment for selected personalities; of real importance are the detailed discographies following each biographical sketch. The trade-off, of course, is less comprehensive coverage and fewer individuals included.

The third edition of *The Rolling Stone Illustrated History of Rock & Roll*, edited by Anthony DeCurtis and others (Random House, 1992) is a comprehensive and authoritative history providing excellent critical biographical coverage and interpretation of major artists and performers such as Chuck Berry, the Beatles, the Rolling Stones, and more.

761. **Soul Music A–Z.** Hugh Gregory. Rev. ed. New York: Da Capo, 1995. 344p. ISBN 0-306-80643-6.

Gregory, a British writer, had chosen to examine a musical element developed by black Americans but later expanded to include white performers who have operated within that synthesis of rhythm and blues and gospel. The revised edition contains sketches of some 1,000 (up from 600 in the previous effort) performers, songwriters, and producers, varying in length from a single paragraph to several columns. The range is extensive, from early practitioners like Little Willie John to today's Mariah Carey, rapper LL Cool J, and Gladys Knight. Entries are arranged alphabetically; in addition to biographies, they furnish highlights of careers, listings of hits, chartings of both the British and U.S. markets, and discographies (for some of the performers). All the big-name performers and groups seem to be treated, but the book's real value lies in the documentation of the lives and efforts of the obscure individuals covered. Numerous cross-references are given; a brief bibliography is included.

762. **Who's Who of Jazz: Storyville to Swing Street.** 5th ed. John Chilton. London: Papermac, 1989. 375p. ISBN 0333483758 (pbk.).

This is a well-developed biographical dictionary of more than 1,000 jazz personalities born before 1920 and raised in the United States. Biographies vary in length with the prominence of the individual and range from a brief paragraph to two full pages. Emphasis is placed on the person's career and musical development rather than on his or her personal life. A section with photographs and a list of jazz periodicals arranged by country of publication are included.

Leonard Feather has provided an excellent series of biographical dictionaries keyed to different decades. *The Encyclopedia of Jazz* (Horizon, 1960; repr., Da Capo, 1984) is a revised edition of an earlier work and furnishes biographies and illustrations of more than 2,000 performers of that time, with a guide to their recordings. *The Encyclopedia of Jazz in the Sixties* (Horizon, 1966; repr., Da Capo, 1986) updates its predecessor; and Feather and Ira Gitler collaborated on *The Encyclopedia of Jazz in the Seventies* (Horizon, 1976; repr., Da Capo, 1987). This volume extends the coverage of the series to 1975, and adds lists of jazz films and recordings.

RECORDINGS

763. **All Music Guide to Country: The Experts' Guide to the Best Recordings in Country Music.** Michael Erlewine et al., eds. San Francisco: Miller Freeman, 1997. 611p. (AMG All Music Guide series). ISBN 0-879-30475-8.

This work contains identifications and reviews of some 4,000 recordings, along with biographies of performers, and twenty essays on country music. It is one of several guides to recordings from the same publisher that have captured the interest and enthusiasm of music librarians because of their comprehensiveness, thorough treatment, and frequency of updating.

The first offering in this AMG line was a comprehensive guide to more than 23,000 recordings in twenty-two categories, *All Music Guide, The Best CDs, Albums & Tapes: The Experts' Guide to the Best Releases from Thousands of Artists in All Types of Music*, edited by Erlewine and Scott Hultman in 1992. Since then the guides have been specific to a certain genre or format. *All Music Guide to Jazz: The Best CD's, Albums & Tapes* (3d ed., 1998), edited by Ron Wynn and Erlewine, contains 18,000 reviews and 1,700 biographies; *All Music Guide to Rock: The Best CDs, Albums & Tapes, Rock, Pop, Soul, R&B, and Rap* (2d ed., 1997), edited by Erlewine et al., treats 15,000 recordings and 2,500 performers. The second edition of *All Music Guide to the Blues* . . . (1999), edited by Erlewine et al., covers 3,000 recordings and 500 personalities. The initial appearance of *All Music Guide to Electronic Music: The Experts' Guide to the Best Electronic Recordings*, edited by Erlewine et al. is to follow in 2000. One should visit the Web site *AMG All-Media Guide* (http://www.allmusic.com [accessed December 1999]) for an array of listings as well as essays on all aspects and styles of music.

764. **Billboard Top 1000 Singles, 1955–1992.** Joel Whitburn, comp. Milwaukee, WI: Hal Leonard Publishing, 1993. 143p. ISBN 0-7935-2072-X.

Based on data culled from *Billboard* magazine (entry 750), this slender but useful revision of earlier publications covers the period beginning in 1955. It supplies a listing of the top 1,000 hits over a span of thirty-seven years along with a year-by-year ranking of the top 40. Rankings are based on the highest position attained, and longevity as number 1, in the top 10, and in the top 40. These listings and rankings are taken from *Billboard* and are of interest to those who find the need to examine the field of popular music.

Billboard's Hottest Hot 100 Hits, by Fred Bronson is available in a revised and enlarged edition (Billboard Books, 1995). It identifies forty years of hits, beginning with "Rock Around the Clock" in 1955 and extending through 1994. This work is quite thorough, listing the performers and their top 100 hits, with sections listing top songs by artists, writers, producers, labels, chart appearance, type of performer, year, and subject. Descriptive sketches are furnished for each. There is a history of most important chart singles for different record companies. There is also a listing for the top 5,000 hits of the rock era in ranked order. *The Billboard Book of Top 40 Albums*, by Joel Whitburn, also in its revised and enlarged edition (Billboard Books/Watson-Guptil, 1995) has been updated to 1994, with focus on the most successful artists and their albums.

765. **The New Blackwell Guide to Recorded Blues.** John Cowley and Paul Oliver, eds. Cambridge, MA: Blackwell, 1996. 372p. ISBN 0-631-19639-0.

Oliver has earned a well-deserved reputation as a competent jazz and blues critic and historian, and now with Cowley has joined to produce a revised and updated edition. This historical discography and guide for collectors of blues music initially appeared in 1989, and was updated in 1991 with the addition of "CD Supplement" to the title. The work is divided into several chapters, each written by noted specialists; the first chapter is authored by Oliver, who describes the origin of blues as a Southern variant of earlier folk music and religious music. Chapters are arranged historically, with each one treating a particular style or time period. In addition to the narratives, the work identifies thousands of recordings as well as a listing of an essential collection of 140 CDs and a basic library of 560. The historical discography works well for both collectors and serious students in addressing their information needs. Included are a bibliography and several maps along with a general index.

A complementary guide is *The Down Home Guide to the Blues*, by Frank Scott and the staff of Down Home Music (A Cappella Book; distr., Independent Publishers Group, 1991). This is a more comprehensive tool, supplying over 3,500 reviews of blues recordings culled from twelve years of a newsletter produced by Down Home Music, a mail order supplier of blues records. Both individual and group recordings are treated. Arrangement is alphabetical by name of performer; a second section treats prewar and postwar anthologies. Reviews address the quality and style of recordings. There is a listing of 100 essential recordings. Unfortunately, there are no indexes.

766. **The Cash Box/Black Contemporary Singles Chart, 1960–1984.** George Albert and Frank Hoffman. Metuchen, NJ: Scarecrow Press, 1986. 704p. ISBN 0-8108-1853-1.

Formerly called rhythm and blues, black contemporary music appeals to an ever-growing audience of white Americans. *Cash Box* magazine has treated the music in a variety of ways over the past twenty-five years. Its listings were fragmented and scattered in different sections and under different categories. This work follows a format established by these authors in previous publications on pop and country music and makes the weekly chart information of twenty-five years of listings easy to find and convenient to use. Arrangement is alphabetical by performers, with a list of recorded songs alphabetically organized under their names. Entries provide name of song, date of entry onto the chart, record label and number, weekly position, and total weeks on the chart. Another alphabetical listing of song titles includes cross-references to the performers. Additional interesting information is given in the appendices.

The same authors have produced a companion publication, *The Cash Box Black Contemporary Album Charts, 1975–1987* (1989), also based on weekly charts from the magazine. There is an extensive artist index that furnishes dates of chart entry, album, label, and weeks on the chart. An album-title index is also included. An interesting and unique work is *Doo-Wop: The Forgotten Third of Rock n' Roll*, by Anthony J. Gribin and Matthew M. Schiff (Krause, 1992), which provides treatment of that distinctive vocal style of the 1950s marked by group harmony and a range of voices that may include falsetto. The work opens with several useful introductory essays describing the characteristics of the music, followed by a listing of artists and their recordings, for which year and label are given.

767. **The Decca Hillbilly Discography: 1927–1945.** Cary Ginell, comp. New York: Greenwood, 1989. 402p. ISBN 0-313-26053-2.

An important tool from the standpoint of historical documentation is this listing of more than 1,500 discs issued by Decca, the leading record label for country and rural music in those early years. Included here are the recordings in the important and prolific 5000 series, 17000 or Cajun series, 45000 or Champion series, and all Decca productions issued on the

Montgomery Ward label. Unreleased recordings are included in the comprehensive coverage given to the 5000 and 17000 series. The compiler, an academic who used his personal collection to begin the study, has provided an opening introductory essay giving historical perspective. Listings are by catalog number and identify artists, titles, and instruments. Adequate indexing is furnished by artist, location, composer, and title.

The Billboard Book of Number One Country Hits, by Tom Roland (Billboard Books/Watson Guptill, 1991), covers the period 1968–1989 and identifies all songs ranked number 1 by *Billboard*. Some 825 songs are treated, with entries providing description of their stories and their eras. Recordings are identified fully and dates are included. About 150 photographs are furnished. The work is indexed by performer and title.

768. **The Jazz Discography.** Tom Lord. West Vancouver, BC: Lord Reference; Redwood, NY: Cadence Jazz Books, 1992– . 22v. (In progress). ISBN 1-881993-17-5 (v.19).

Projected as a multi-volume work, this comprehensive effort by Tom Lord was scheduled for publication over a period of several years. It was anticipated to cover approximately 100,000 entries treating every known jazz recording in unprecedented, comprehensive fashion from 1898 to date of publication. Jazz in all its forms (early, contemporary, Dixieland, swing, etc.) is included. As of 1999, twenty-two volumes had been issued, with coverage organized in encyclopedia fashion using alphabetical arrangement by name of band leader. Information is given for each recording session (band leader, album title, name of group, performers and their instruments, location and date, names of songs and selections, and album numbers).

A recent selective effort is the second edition of *The Blackwell Guide to Recorded Jazz* edited by Barry Kernfeld (Blackwell Reference, 1995). As part of a series of discographies for the publisher, this work identifies and describes various aspect of jazz from hot jazz to freebop in separate sections. Description is provided for 230 CD recordings in various stylistic categories. Contributors are specialists in the field who provide a well-developed overview and commentary, some of which is highly subjective.

769. **Jazz Records 1897–1942: Fifth Revised and Enlarged Edition.** Brian Rust. Chigwell, UK: Storyville Publications, 1982. 2v. ISBN 0902391046.

Considered the standard source for both music librarians and devotees, the fifth edition of this title is an update, correction, and extension of earlier versions. It lists over 30,000 jazz recordings by American and British artists in standard format, arranged by name of performer. Entries include personnel, instruments, and listing of recording sessions. Information is given about the matrix number, label, and catalog issue number (78s only), with indication of vocals. A song index covers over 16,000 titles and an artist index includes over 10,000 band leaders, musicians, singers, and arrangers. There are numerous cross-references to clarify obscure pseudonyms. Since publication of *The Complete Entertainment Discography from the Mid-1890's to 1942*, by Rust and Allen G. Debus in 1973, and its second edition by Rust, entitled *The Complete Entertainment Discography, from 1897 to 1942* (Da Capo, 1989), as well as Rust's *The American Dance Band Discography, 1917–1942* (Arlington House, 1975), the jazz discography now more closely restricts the entries to jazz and blues recordings.

A useful foreign contribution that complements this work is *Jazz Records, 1942–1980: A Discography*, by Erik Raben (Copenhagen: Stainless/Wintermoon; Jazz Media Aps, 1987–). This is a new edition of a multi-volume effort initially published over a seven-year period from 1963 to 1970 and covering the era from 1942 to 1969. Volume 1 of the new edition (A–Barnes) continues in the same tradition, providing a detailed compilation of jazz records and earning respect for its comprehensiveness.

770. **1900–1965 American Premium Record Guide: 78's, 45's, and LP's Identification and Values.** 4th ed. L. R. Docks. Florence, AL: Books Americana, 1992. 447p. ISBN 0896890880.

This is an especially useful discography and guide to the recordings of popular music over a sixty-five-year period. It gives an additional fifteen years of coverage, dating from 1900 rather than from 1915, as in the third edition. It treats a variety of record types, as enumerated in the title, but is limited to the disc format. Format is similar to the previous effort, with recordings divided into four major styles: jazz/big band, blues, country and western, and rhythm and blues. The jazz/big band section receives the most coverage, followed by rhythm and blues, which includes rock and roll. Entries are listed by name of performer and provide evaluative commentary as well as identification, making this a useful source for record collectors. The guide provides a glossary of terms and valuable hints for collecting and for understanding the market.

A popular source is *The Rolling Stone Album Guide*, edited by Anthony DeCurtis et al. (3d ed., Random House, 1993). First issued in 1979, it provides coverage of thousands of albums, claiming to have included every essential album and essential artist available in the area of rock, pop, soul, country, soul, blues, jazz, and gospel. The comprehensiveness is impressive, although the coverage of rock and soul is more exhaustive than is true of some of the other areas. Another staple is *The Trouser Press Guide to '90s Rock*, edited by Ira A. Robbins (4th ed., 1991; 5th ed., Simon & Schuster, 1997). This revised edition remains the most comprehensive source, treating some 2,300 important artists and 8,500 CDs and cassettes available for purchase.

Musical Theater and Film

BIBLIOGRAPHIES AND CATALOGS

771. **A Comprehensive Bibliography of Music for Film and Television.** Steven D. Wescott, comp. Detroit: Information Coordinators, 1985. 432p. ISBN 0-89990-027-5.

To complement the earlier efforts by Limbacher (entry 772), this more comprehensive compilation identifies nearly 6,350 books, periodicals, and other materials on the popular topic. Treated in these works is the dramatic aspect of music in film and television as well as its presence in documentaries, advertising, experimental and innovative applications, and its socio-cultural context. Radio music is also included in this broad-based bibliography that contains the works of more than 3,700 authors from twenty-eight countries representing eighteen different languages. The work is divided into three major areas: "history," with nearly 3,000 entries identifying surveys and critiques; "composer" (nearly 1,350 entries), treating personalities; and "themes" (over 2,000 entries), providing sections on aesthetics, special topics, and research. Entries supply full bibliographic descriptions, with publication dates through January 1984. A detailed general index supplies access.

If seeking appropriate recordings for theater and film presentations, it is recommended that one search the Web for "sound effects libraries."

772. **Film Music: From Violins to Video.** James L. Limbacher, ed. and comp. Metuchen, NJ: Scarecrow Press, 1974. 835p. ISBN 0-8108-0651-7.

Because the area of film music has been relatively overlooked, this book has filled a need in reference work. Although it has been criticized for certain omissions and lack of clarity regarding its selection criteria, it has been used by both serious students and interested laypersons in pursuit of information on the nature of film music up to 1972. Part 1 consists of excellent notes and commentary on film music by composers such as Dimitri Tiompkin and Sir William

Walton, while part 2 provides various listings. These include an alphabetical list of titles with dates, chronological list of films with composers, composers and their films, and musical scores by film title.

A supplementary work by the same author is *Keeping Score: Film Music 1972–1979* (Scarecrow Press, 1981), which continues the listings in three major sections arranged by film titles, composers, and recorded musical scores. Both of the above works are updated and expanded through Limbacher's most recent effort, *Keeping Score: Film and Television Music 1980–1988 (with Additional Coverage of 1921–1979)* (Scarecrow Press, 1991), which furnishes a chronological listing of films and television programs from 1921 to 1988, followed by a listing by composer and date of production. A discography follows.

A comprehensive effort is *Movie Song Catalog: Performers and Supporting Crew for the Songs Sung in 1460 Musical and Nonmusical Films, 1928–1988* (McFarland, 1993), by Ruth Benjamin and Arthur Rosenblatt. The title is self-explanatory in its intent to identify song titles from sixty years of motion picture making. Entries supply year, country, running time, music directors, writers, and vocalists. The work is accessed through indexes by title, performer, and songwriter.

773. A Guide to Critical Reviews: Part II The Musical, 1909–1989. 3d ed. James M. Salem. Metuchen, NJ: Scarecrow Press, 1991. 820p. ISBN 0-8108-2387-X.

This is part 2 of a five-volume set that covers American drama (entry 893n) as well as foreign drama and the screenplay (entry 978n). The third edition furnishes listings of critical reviews for nearly 2,700 Broadway and off-Broadway shows performed between 1909 and 1989. These reviews appeared in popular magazines or in the *New York Times* and provide both the researcher and the theater buff with useful information. Arrangement of entries is alphabetical by title of play; entries furnish openings and closings and number of performances, as well as names of writers, lyricists, choreographers, and others concerned with the production. Cast listings are not given.

DICTIONARIES, ENCYCLOPEDIAS, HANDBOOKS, ETC.

774. American Musical Theatre: A Chronicle. 2d ed. Gerald Bordman. New York: Oxford University Press, 1992. 821p. ISBN 0-19-507242-1.

This is an update and revision of Bordman's 1978 and 1986 editions, which covered the musical theater from 1866 to the 1970s and 1980s, respectively. Beginning with a prologue that summarizes the development of musical theater in this country from its beginnings to 1866, the new work covers each year in detail through the 1989–1990 season. Developments of the season are described, "hits" are identified, and musicals are arranged by date of opening. Included are plot synopses, names of performers, important songs, and a brief analysis of the impact of the show or its relative position in the context of musical theater. Critical comments from reviewers are included. Biographies are given for various personalities (composers, playwrights, actors, etc.). An index for shows and sources identifies original sources from which the musicals were derived. Also included are a song index and an index of personal names.

More comprehensive listings are found in the second edition of Ken Bloom's *American Song: The Complete Musical Theatre Companion* (Schirmer Books/Simon & Schuster, 1996). This is a two-volume collection of information on nearly 4,800 musical productions from 1877 to 1995. Included are musical plays from Broadway, off-Broadway, regional theater, touring groups, burlesque, vaudeville, and even foreign productions by major American composers. There are no plot summaries or critical analysis. Indexing is vast, with more than 42,000 songs and 58,000 personalities. Now in its fourth edition is *Broadway Musicals: Show by Show*, by Stanley Green, revised and updated by Kay Green (Hal Leonard Publishing,

1994). Less comprehensive than either Bloom or Bordman, coverage is given to 325 hit Broadway musicals from 1866 to the present. Green's widow continues the wealth of informative coverage with synopses, lists of credits, and miscellaneous interesting facts regarding plot, reception, and so forth, along with photographs. Several indexes provide access.

775. **The Broadway Song Companion: An Annotated Guide to Musical Theatre Literature by Voice Type and Song Style.** David P. Devenney. Lanham, MD: Scarecrow Press, 1998. 210p. ISBN 0-8108-3373-5.

This is a recent effort by a noted music writer to provide a selective handbook along with bibliographic listings. As an instructor, the author was keenly aware of the difficulty in identifying and selecting useful and appropriate pieces for his students to use in their recitals. This led to preparation of this volume listing more than 2,000 songs from Broadway shows. Each entry supplies information regarding voice, vocal range, and song style. The work is organized alphabetically by name of show, with entries for songs listed in order of performance within the show. Access is furnished through indexes by voice part, composer, and lyricist.

Songs of the Theater: A Definitive Index to the Songs of the Musical Stage, by Richard Lewine and Alfred Simon (H. W. Wilson, 1984), is an earlier publication that expands two previous works by the same authors. It is comprehensive and identifies 17,000 songs from 1,200 American musicals on stage, film, or television. Songs are both published and unpublished and span a time period from 1891 through 1983. Songs are identified from every theater production seen on Broadway since the 1920s. The book also includes songs of off-Broadway productions if they run at least fifteen days. Listings of shows and of songs are supplied; they include composers and lyricists. There is a separate index of films and television productions.

776. **Encyclopaedia of the Musical Film.** Rev. ed. Stanley Green. New York: Oxford University Press, 1988. 344p. ISBN 0-19-505421-0.

With the popularity of the musical film in American entertainment, it is important that libraries provide some resource tools in keeping with the interests of their patrons. Generally intended for the interested layperson as well as the film specialist, this work provides useful information on those films developed in this country and in Great Britain. Arrangement of entries is alphabetical and general information is given on a variety of personalities (actors, producers, directors, composers, etc.), along with identification of their best-known works. In addition to personalities, the films, and even major songs, receive separate entries. There is an index of title changes, as well as a general bibliography and a discography.

Clive Hirschhorn's *The Hollywood Musical* (2d ed., Pyramid, 1991) is a good pictorial chronology of American musicals, from the "Jazz Singer" in 1927 to the year 1990. Included are synopses, cast lists, song listings, and miscellaneous information, accessible through several good indexes. One is able to trace the musical in terms of its popularity during different time periods. For detailed information on the topic, it is recommended that one use **Musical and Dance Films*, by Tim Dirks, located on the Web at http://www.filmsite.org/musicalfilms.html (accessed December 1999). It provides good exposition with links to relevant sites.

777. **Encyclopedia of the Musical Theatre.** Kurt Ganzl. New York: Schirmer/Macmillan, 1995. 2v. ISBN 0-02-871445-8.

This is a comprehensive encyclopedia by a recognized expert on musical theater, including some 2,700 entries alphabetically arranged. It treats all aspects of the musical theater from the mid-nineteenth century to the present day. Plot summaries are furnished for more than 1,000 musicals and represent a well-chosen array of productions from Broadway, London, and the European continent. More than half the entries are given to coverage of personalities; performers, writers, composers, producers, designers, costumers, arrangers, and so forth. More than 300 photographs are included. The work is well-indexed.

Ganzl's Book of the Musical Theatre, is an earlier, more selective effort by Ganzl and Andrew Lamb (Schirmer/Macmillan, 1989), designed to complement the Kobbe work on the opera (entry 700) and provide similar coverage for musical theater. More than 300 musicals, operettas, and comic operas are treated in entries ranging from three to four pages in length that provide synopses and listings of productions, cast of characters, and references to songs. Arrangement of entries is in five major geographical segments, treating sixty-nine musicals of Great Britain (1782–1987); fifty-three of France (to 1980); ninety-five from the United States (1890–1983); seventy-four from Austria, Germany, or Hungary (1865–1964); and seven from Spain (to 1932). Selection is based on popularity and frequency of performance, historical significance, and the authors' personal preferences. Sections are preceded by introductory essays on the history of musical theater in respective locales. Included are a discography, an index of names and titles, and an index of songs.

778. **The Gilbert and Sullivan Companion.** Leslie Ayre. London: Allen, 1972; repr., Papermac, 1987. 485p. ISBN 0333443705.

This work was warmly received at the time of publication and has demonstrated its value as a useful tool for librarians in their dealings with both specialists and laypersons. There is a good description of the famous partnership at the beginning, which most readers will find interesting as well as informative. The major segment of the text is an alphabetical arrangement of entries related to the Gilbert and Sullivan productions. These include major performers, plot summaries, songs, and explanations of obscure references dating from 1871 to the time of publication. Entries for the operettas themselves, in addition to providing synopses of plots, provide full song texts, although not complete libretti. This work will remain an important source as long as Gilbert and Sullivan productions are prominent stage offerings.

779. **The Great Hollywood Musical Pictures.** James Robert Parish and Michael R. Pitts. Metuchen, NJ: Scarecrow Press, 1992. 806p. ISBN 0-8108-2529-5.

This work identifies about 340 musicals considered to be great by the authors and provides detailed descriptions of plot, history, and criticism, sometimes citing previous reviewers. Also included are the usual identification data along with listings of credits for all personalities associated with the production (authors, designers, choreographers, editors, music arrangers, music directors, composers, lyricists, sound and camera people, and of course, cast members). The work is well-illustrated with over 100 black-and-white photographs. Entries are alphabetically arranged beginning with "Annie" and concluding with "Ziegfeld." Coverage is broad and includes those of classic reputation to the more contemporary efforts; animated musicals as well as live-action vehicles are treated. The work concludes with a chronology of motion pictures covered, from *The Jazz Singer* (1927) to *School Daze* (1988). There is no index.

780. **Opening Night on Broadway: A Critical Quotebook of the Golden Era of the Musical Theatre,** *Oklahoma* **(1943) to** *Fiddler on the Roof* **(1964).** Steven Suskin. New York: Schirmer Books/Macmillan, 1990; repr., 1993. 810p. ISBN 0-02-872628-6.

Suskin, an obvious aficionado, provides treatment of 300 Broadway musicals that played during a twenty-year period identified as the "golden era." Entries are arranged alphabetically by title and supply personal credits, date of opening, name of theater, and selections or extracts from opening night reviews with identification of critic and newspaper. Most interesting is the Broadway scorecard, which tallies the types of reviews in terms of their favorability. Profit or loss of the show is similarly indicated. Suskin's evaluative commentary is cogent and useful to the reader. There are numerous illustrations of art work used in window cards and advertisements. The work opens with an introductory essay on the musical theater from 1943 to its decline at present. Appendices supply a chronology of shows and directories of notable careers. A name and subject index provides access.

781. **Stage It with Music: An Encyclopedic Guide to the American Musical Theatre.** Thomas S. Hischak. Westport, CT: Greenwood, 1993. 341p. ISBN 0-313-28708-2.

This is a convenient source of varied information by a professor of theater history on the American musical theater from its beginnings in the nineteenth century to the present. Some 300 entries are packed into a one-volume format treating various issues, genres, shows, personalities, musical series, production companies, and institutions. All types of individuals are included: performers, producers, choreographers, orchestrators, composers, lyricists, directors, designers, and so forth. A useful special feature is a chronology of musical shows; a bibliography is furnished. The work is well indexed to ease access.

Nineteenth-Century American Musical Theater (Garland, 1994) is a series edited by Deane L. Root that identifies and supplies original sources (scores) for important musical productions of that period. Each of the sixteen volumes reproduces manuscript sources for one or two productions of historical interest and supplies expository material. Volumes treat such topics as early and later melodrama; British and Italian opera; Irish-American, African-American, and Yiddish theater; operetta; burlesque; and grand opera. Volume 5 is language material for "Uncle Tom's Cabin"; the rest of the volumes comprise musical scores. These play scripts with songs and musical scores are of real value to scholars, performers, and teachers as well as students. Each volume opens with an introductory essay summarizing careers of the creative personalities, describing plots, and evaluating the historical value of the pieces.

RECORDINGS

782. **Film and Television Composers: An International Discography, 1920–1989.** Steve Harris. Jefferson, NC: McFarland, 1992. 302p. ISBN 0-89950-553-8.

Derived in part from an earlier work by Harris described below, the new effort provides updated and more comprehensive coverage of film and television music than did its predecessor. Here are nearly 8,000 entries on phonograph records arranged alphabetically by composer. Entries supply production title, country, record format, label, and catalog number. This effort contains an additional three years' production of films along with inclusions from earlier dates omitted in the previous effort. Composers from fourteen countries are represented, with special emphasis on the United States, Great Britain, France, and Italy. Treated here is original music as well as compositions adapted for television or film.

Harris's earlier work, *Film, Television, and Stage Music on Phonograph Records: A Discography* (McFarland, 1988), supplies about the same number of entries (8,000). About 1,200 deal with stage music, however, which is omitted in the sequel. Coverage runs through 1986; date of release is included here but not in the more recent title described above. Entries are labeled by title; emphasis is on U.S. and British recordings.

Musical Instruments and Technology

General technical handbooks are emphasized here. Check the specialized bibliographic guides, especially Duckles (entry 614) for material on particular instruments.

783. **Compendium of Modern Instrumental Techniques.** Gardner Read. New York: Greenwood, 1993. 276p. ISBN 0-313-28512-8.

The author is a recognized composer and erudite professor emeritus who has developed an important handbook for music instruction. It codifies and synthesizes those modern techniques utilizing conventional instruments in unconventional ways to produce novel effects. Such applications form the essential character of contemporary art music and represent an important creative element of recent composition and performance. The work is divided into two segments, with the first part treating techniques applicable to all instruments. The second section covers particular instruments, with representation of all categories of the orchestral setting.

784. A Dictionary of Electronic and Computer Music Technology: Instruments, Terms, Techniques. Richard Dobson. New York: Oxford University Press, 1992. 224p. ISBN 0-19-311344-9.

One of the reference tools dealing with music automation and electronic configuration is this well-constructed dictionary. Entries tend to be lengthy, establishing this tool as a combination dictionary and handbook on the new technologies. There are numerous cross-references from specific terms to more general categories such as "acoustics," which receive full treatment of their various aspects and components. Exposition and narratives are clear and cogent, with technical aspects well defined and explained. The work is indexed by names and also by product/manufacture, covering more than 350 products.

A complementary effort is *Illustrated Compendium of Musical Technology*, by Tristram Cary (Faber & Faber, 1992), which supplies more entries but briefer treatment. This is considered a practical glossary of the basic concepts, with much greater emphasis on audio technology. Cary's *Dictionary of Musical Technology* (Greenwood, 1992) also provides excellent coverage of audio topics along with computer music and electronic elements among the 800 entries included. Line drawings and flow charts are included. An earlier work is Bo Tomlyn's *Electronic Music Dictionary: A Glossary of the Specialized Terms Relating to Music and Sound Technology of Today* (H. Leonard Books, 1988). It contains some 400 terms with cross-references to related words and to general categories or subjects.

785. Encyclopedia of Keyboard Instruments. Robert Palmieri, ed. New York: Garland, 1994–2000. 3v. (Garland Reference Library of the Humanities, v. 1131). ISBN 0-8240-5685-X.

This is the first encyclopedia devoted to keyboard instruments and was planned as a three-volume effort. Volume I, "The Piano," edited by Robert Palmieri and Margaret W. Palmieri, was issued in Spring 1993, and followed by volume II, "The Organ," edited by Douglas E. Bush in 1994. Volume III, "The Clavichord and Harpsichord," edited by Igor Kipnis is to be published in the year 2000. Each volume supplies some 600 articles alphabetically arranged and dealing with personalities of various types along with events, topics, companies, instrument technology, culture, discoveries, trends, and so forth. Articles vary in length from a few sentences to over 7,000 words. There are illustrations and charts to augment the narratives. Entries contain selective bibliographies for further reading.

A similar effort from Garland is the one-volume *Encyclopedia of Percussion*, edited by John H. Beck (1995). Articles are alphabetically arranged and provide details of each instrument such as manufacturer, designer or inventor, country of origin, musical examples, and publisher. All types of percussion instruments are covered (drums, bells, chimes, cymbals, whistles, shakers, etc.). There is a segment of twenty-five survey articles signed by experts exploring various topics in detail. Both a chronology and bibliography are included. A comprehensive index provides access along with cross-references within the entries.

786. Musical Instruments: A Comprehensive Dictionary. Corr. ed. Sybil Marcuse. New York: W. W. Norton, 1975. 608p. ISBN 0-393-00758-8.

This work was first published in 1964, and this edition is essentially a reprint with some corrections. It has become a staple in music libraries for its coverage of musical instruments from all periods from the earliest times to the present day. Although the information provided here may be found in other more general sources, this specialized dictionary is highly convenient for music patrons. Entries are furnished for hundreds of different instruments and the identifications are clear and accurate. Instruments are listed in English, with equivalent foreign terms identified. There are some illustrations, which are excellent in quality but few in number. A more recent work by the same author is *A Survey of Musical Instruments* (Harper & Row, 1975), which places the instruments in technical groupings or families such as idiophone and chordophone.

787. **Musical Instruments of the World: An Illustrated Encyclopedia.** The Diagram Group. New York: Paddington/Two Continents, 1976; repr., Oxford: Facts on File, 1985. 320p. ISBN 0-84-670134-0.

The strength of this work lies in its illustrations of the musical instruments: There are over 4,000 drawings that identify every conceivable piece of music-making equipment. The arrangement of this impressive work is by type, with sections on vibrating air instruments, self-vibrating instruments, vibrating membrane instruments, vibrating string instruments, and mechanical electronic instruments. Divisions by geographical areas, time periods, and instrumental ensembles are also given when appropriate. The Diagram Group is an organization of artists, writers, and editors that promotes understanding of essential features of construction and technique through the publication of highly illustrated works of this type. There is a small section with twenty-five to thirty biographies of important instrument makers, virtuosos, and writers as well as a bibliography and a directory of museums. A name-subject index provides access.

Musical Instruments of the World (1997) is a useful Web site maintained by the International Music Archives (http://www.eyeneer.com/World/Instruments/index.html [accessed April 5, 2000]). It provides photographs, sound samples, and explanatory text for instruments from varied regions of the world.

788. **The New Grove Dictionary of Musical Instruments.** Stanley Sadie, ed. New York: Grove's Dictionaries of Music, 1984; repr. with corr., 1995. 3v. ISBN 0-94318-05-2.

More than just a spin-off of the *New Grove Dictionary of Music and Musicians* (entry 671), this specialized survey of musical instruments from all periods and geographical regions expands the coverage given the topic in the magnificent general encyclopedia. Sadie edited both works, and for this specialized set has revised, modified, updated, and in some cases replaced the articles as they appeared in the major work. The attempt here was to achieve complete coverage of the world of musical instruments, whereas the original set, although comprehensive, was still subject to certain limitations in this regard. Especially well covered are non-Western and folk instruments. There has been some criticism of the quality of illustrations, but there is no argument with the depth and quality of the identification, and description of the history, structure, creation, and use of the various instruments. Several reprints with minor corrections have been issued since 1984.

DANCE

Bibliographies, Catalogs, and Indexes

789. **Ballet Plot Index: A Guide to Locating Plots and Descriptions of Ballets and Associated Material.** William E. Studwell and David A. Hamilton. New York: Garland, 1987. 249p. (Garland Reference Library of the Humanities, v. 756). ISBN 0-8240-8385-7.

This collective index to fifty-four reference sources in English, French, German, Danish, Russian, and Polish supplies entries to 1,600 ballets ranging from the well-known to the obscure. Entries provide not only plot synopses but, more important, descriptive narrative concerning the creation and performance of the ballet. The *Index* is remarkable for its coded notation, which serves to identify not only the presence of bibliography and illustrations but also treatment and historical background, criticism and analysis, and musical themes. Arrangement of entries is alphabetical by title of ballet, and identification includes name of composer and year of first performance. The work is geared to the needs of a varied audience, ranging from dance researchers and students to patrons of the performing arts. Access is aided by a well-constructed composer index listing the works by each composer.

790. **A Bibliography of the Dance Collection of Doris Nyles and Serge Leslie.** Serge Leslie and Doris Nyles; Cyril Beaumont, ed. London: C. W. Beaumont, 1966–1981; repr., Dance Books, 1981. 4v. ISBN 0-903102-56-0.

From the time of its original appearance in the 1960s, this small-scale publication of the holdings of a private collection has been regarded as a valuable bibliography. It covers 2,000 items related to the dance. The most recent reprint of this work continues in the earlier tradition of restrictive printing, since it also is a limited edition of only 525 copies. Regardless of the relatively few copies available through the years, the work has been considered a real asset in identifying useful source materials. The emphasis is on the ballet, but folk dancing and social dancing are included as well. The arrangement is alphabetical by author; volume 1 treats A–K and volume 2, L–Z. Each volume has an index that provides subject access. Volumes 3–4 were published by Dance Books and cover mainly twentieth-century publications.

791. **Dance on Camera: A Guide to Dance Films and Videos.** Louise Spain, ed. Lanham, MD: Scarecrow Press, 1998. 238p. ISBN 0-8108-3303-4.

This is the revised and updated version of *The Dance Film and Video Guide*, compiled by Deirdre Towers (Dance Film Association/Princeton Book, 1991). It remains one of the few film and video guides to focus exclusively on dance and retains its value as an important purchase for dance collections in all types of libraries. The earlier work has been reviewed for needed change, and corrections to errors have been incorporated. It continues to identify well over 2,000 dance performances available commercially. All forms of dance are treated (ballet, folk, ballroom, jazz, and even instructional). Several useful introductory essays precede the body of the index. Entries furnish information on length, format, distributor, production, company, dancers, and so forth. Brief scope notes describe content. All types of videos and films that include dance scenes are treated. The work is indexed thoroughly by title, series title, dance style, purpose of video or film, and geographical region as well as dancer, choreographer, composer, dance company, and director. A directory of distributors is provided.

792. **Dictionary Catalog of the Dance Collection.** New York Public Library. Boston, G. K. Hall: 1974. 10v. **Ann. Supp.**, 1976– .ISSN 0360-2737.

The complete title of this work goes on: "a List of Authors, Titles, and Subjects of Multi-media Materials in the Dance Collection of the Performing Arts Research Center of the New York Public Library." As it has done for other important specialized collections, G. K. Hall has produced a listing of catalog cards based on the cataloging done prior to October 1973. The catalog includes some 300,000 entries for nearly 10,000 items, as well as relevant materials in other parts and divisions of NYPL. Included are books, periodicals, playbills, letters, pamphlets, manuscripts, films, scrapbooks, tapes, and dance scores. Some of the entries have detailed descriptions of contents. This collection is considered to be the most comprehensive of its kind.

The Bibliographic Guide to Dance has continued the coverage as an annual supplement since 1976, listing material cataloged during the preceding year. As is true of the main set, there are numerous cross-references along with scope and history notes. The twenty-third supplement (G. K. Hall, 1998) was issued in three volumes and covers the period from September 1996 through August 1997. *Dance on Disc: The Complete Catalog of the Dance Collection of the New York Public Library on CD-ROM* was first issued early in 1992 and published by G. K. Hall. It is a cumulation of the library's entire catalog of dance materials on CD-ROM. It is updated annually, and contains both the catalog and the authority file of the Dance Collection.

793. **Index to Dance Periodicals.** Dance Collection, New York Public Library. Boston: G. K. Hall, 1990– . Ann. ISSN 1058-6350.

Another contribution by the New York Public Library (see entry 792) is this recently initiated index to dance periodicals. It represents an extensive project, identifying information on all aspects of the field (biography, performance, news, features, videos, book reviews, television programs, motion pictures, etc.). The work begins with an introductory section explaining the criteria for inclusion and organization along with a listing of periodicals examined. It is an important tool for students, specialists, librarians, and dance enthusiasts.

Guide to Dance Periodicals (University of Florida, 1931–1962) represents one of the few specialized indexes in the field of dance and was a respected publication for over thirty years. The specialized index varied in frequency, beginning with a series of four quinquennial editions, 1931/1935–1946/1950. Subsequently, its appearance was biennial from 1951/1952 through the final issue in 1961/1962. Although criticized for lack of timeliness, it was a useful index of nineteen periodicals by subject and author, compiled originally by S. Yancey Belknap and later by Louis Rachow. It was then incorporated into the annual, *Guide to the Performing Arts* (Scarecrow Press, 1960–1972) as one of the important additions to that more comprehensive publication.

794. **Resources in Sacred Dance: An Annotated Bibliography from Christian and Jewish Traditions....** Rev. ed. Kay Troxell, ed. Lancaster, PA: Sacred Dance Guide, 1991. 55p. ISBN 0-9623137-1-8.

Three hundred resources are supplied in this slender volume, representing a specialized tool that would be a good purchase for both religion and dance collections. It has expanded by some 135 new entries and an additional 15 pages over the previous edition of 1986. As before, the target audience is those who are interested in dance as a spiritual expression. Most materials are English-language, relatively recent publications covering Judeo-Christian dance traditions. Annotations describe usefulness to the practitioner and means of acquiring the items. Following the pattern set in the earlier edition, entries are organized by format, with sections on books; booklets and pamphlets; articles; and nonprint media, embracing film, audiotapes, and videotapes. Reference sources are treated in a final section that includes bibliographies as well as lists of libraries with important collections and professional associations.

Dictionaries, Encyclopedias, and Handbooks

DANCE IN GENERAL

795. **The Dance Encyclopedia.** Rev. and enl. ed. Anatole Chujoy and Phyllis Winifred Manchester, comps. New York: Simon & Schuster, 1967. 992p. ISBN 0-67-122586-3.

Originally published in 1949 and now out-of-print, this work is still respected as a fine source of information even with the recent publication of *International Encyclopedia of Dance* (entry 799). The 1967 revised edition almost doubles the original size, and it furnishes about 5,000 entries covering all phases of the dance, with emphasis on ballet. Personalities are covered but dance forms are given the most extensive treatment; individual ballets are covered with synopses and performance data. This work is considered especially strong in coverage of American ballet.

The Encyclopedia of Dance and Ballet, edited by Mary Clarke and David Vaughan (G. P. Putnam's Sons, 1977) places emphasis on contemporary dance styles as well as classical ballet. Because it is ten years younger than *The Dance Encyclopedia*, it provides somewhat more recent information. The focus of the work is on dance, which has been raised to a theatrical level in many of the media of the twentieth century. Entries cover a variety of topics, including individual dancers, companies, choreographers, individual ballets, and different dance types. Over 2,000 entries have been prepared by specialists from various countries, and illustrations are included. A glossary of technical terms and a general bibliography are supplied.

796. **The Dance Handbook.** Allen Robertson and Donald Hutera. Boston: G. K. Hall, 1988; repr., 1990. 278p. (Performing Arts Handbooks). ISBN 0-8161-9095-X.

This is a selective information source treating Western ballet and modern dance in eight chronological sections, ranging from ballet's romantic era to innovative experimental techniques of today. Within these sections exposition is provided regarding the nature and development of dance styles in these eras. Following these introductory essays are entries treating choreographers, dancers, and dance companies. In all, there are 200 main entries providing factual information; critical evaluation and commentary; and bibliographies of books, films, and videos containing additional information. An interesting aspect of each entry is the lineage feature, supplying links to related dances or dancers. The work is selective, of course, but treats a broad range of topics; ethnic and social dance are purposely excluded. Special features include a glossary, additional readings, and a directory of international information sources (periodicals, companies, and festivals). There is a detailed general index.

797. **Dance Words.** Valerie Preston-Dunlop. Newark, NJ: Harwood Academic/Gordon & Breach, 1995. 718p. (Choreography & Dance Studies, v. 8). ISBN 3-7186-5605-1.

This is a unique artistic wordbook in that it bears a classified arrangement organized under seven categories relevant to choreographic studies: dance domain, performers, movement, choreographic concepts, sound and space, events, and research. Each concept is handled with up to four chapters, in which the terms are not arranged alphabetically but rather clustered by similarity of concept element or area of interest. The purpose of the work is to provide common understanding of choreographic perspective for all who work in the field: choreographers, performers, critics, and so forth. The entry words are up-to-date and include quotations drawn from classes, workshops, books, journals, and media events. The indexes are essential to full utilization and embrace every term along with personal names. A full bibliography is supplied.

798. **Dictionary of the Dance.** W. G. Raffe, comp. New York: A. S. Barnes; distr., London: T. Yoseloff, 1964; repr., 1975. 583p. ISBN 0-498-01643-9.

Always considered a comprehensive source of information on dance and dancing, this continues to be one of the important reference tools. All countries and time periods are included, and coverage is excellent for specific dances and dance types. There are over 5,000 entries, alphabetically arranged. Information covers development and origin as well as form and technique. It is especially strong on folk and ethnic dances; coverage is aided by a geographical index that arranges the dances by country. No biographies are included, but the work is heavily illustrated with a variety of pictures. There is a comprehensive bibliography of items from the fifteenth century to the present, and a subject index facilitates access.

799. **International Encyclopedia of Dance: A Project of Dance Perspectives Foundation, Inc.** Selma J. Cohen, et al., eds. New York: Oxford University Press, 1998. 6v. ISBN 0-19-509462-X.

This recent and welcome effort serves as a comprehensive source of information on all aspects and forms of dance from serious to popular. More than 600 contributors from fifty countries have provided a tool to satisfy the needs of a host of users and to serve as a starting point for more serious inquiry. Within the multi-volume set, there are thousands of entries treating personalities, styles and schools, topics, and issues such as composition and criticism. Individual dance forms from all time periods and geographic regions are defined and described in terms of their origins and historical development. There are survey articles on dance in more than 100 individual countries that supply information on research and education in those environments, along with numerous photographs and illustrations. An extensive index is furnished, along with an outline of the complete set.

800. **The Tap Dance Dictionary.** Mark Knowles. Jefferson, NC: McFarland, 1998. 254p. ISBN 0-786-40352-7.

Written by a specialist who has performed, taught, and choreographed, this work serves as a manual for technical improvement and enlightenment of the practitioner. No biographical sketches are included but comprehensive coverage is given to techniques. These are described in detailed and lucid fashion; insightful historical accounts are given regarding the origins and development of the techniques. Carefully researched through examination of old books and articles, the end result is a resource that is distinctive and at the same time appealing. Many anecdotes are furnished in establishing the sequential history of steps, forms, and styles and it has been possible to provide cross-references to those that are known by more than one name. Treatment is given to several ballroom dances as well as some social dances.

ETHNIC AND REGIONAL DANCE

801. **The Square Dance and Contra Dance Handbook: Calls, Dance Movements, Music, Glossary. . . .** Margot Gunzenhauser. Jefferson, NC: McFarland, 1996. 304p. ISBN 0-89950-855-3.

The complete subtitle of this work goes on to include "Bibliography, Discography, and Directories" and gives an idea of the comprehensive nature of this moderately sized offering. Although not identified as a second edition, it is an updated version of a 1981 effort published in the Danish language. With such a broad focus survey coverage is brief, although the work is accurate in what it represents. It supplies an overview or summary of both square and contra dancing, with sections on the basics including "how to call" and various types of dances. Lists of dances are furnished along with a glossary of dance terminology, as mentioned in the title. The directory is of organizations supplying relevant materials, the discography identifies over 150 recordings, and the bibliography contains just over 100 items.

802. **Theatre in the East: A Survey of Asian Dance and Drama.** Faubion Bowers. New York: Nelson, 1956; repr., New York: Books For Libraries, 1980. 374p. ISBN 0836992784.

This is an extensive survey of the dances of fourteen different countries or regions, each of which is treated in an individual chapter. Illustrations are abundant and some are taken from the work of *Life* magazine photographers. Hailed as a great asset to both specialists and laypersons who wish to study or to travel to the Orient, the work provides historical overviews and excellent descriptions of folk, traditional, and modern dances in India, Ceylon (Sri Lanka), Burma, Thailand, Cambodia, Laos, Malaysia, Indonesia, Philippines, China, Vietnam, Hong Kong, Okinawa, and Japan. The author and his wife visited these areas, and have produced an impressive and attractive guide.

A good source on the Web is *USF Asian Theatre Site—General* (http://www.usfca.edu/fac-staff/davisr/thtrasia.html [accessed April 5, 2000]), maintained by the University of San Francisco and providing links to articles, resources, and organizations by region or country.

BALLET

803. **Ballet Guide: Background Listings, Credits and Descriptions of More Than Five Hundred of the World's Major Ballets.** Walter Terry. New York: Dodd, Mead, 1976; repr., 1982. 388p. ISBN 0-396-08098-7.

Based somewhat on an earlier work by the author, this handbook provides brief synopses and identifications of 500 important ballets. In addition to synopses, the tool furnishes historical information, dates of first performance, choreographers, composers, scenery and costume designers, ballet company, principal dancers in first performances, and major recreations of roles. The synopses themselves are well done and informative, and the additional background information is highly useful. The arrangement of entries is alphabetical by the title of the ballet, and the work is well illustrated. It covers ballet on an international level. A glossary of terms and a good index are included.

804. **Classical Ballet Technique.** Gretchen Ward Warren. Tampa: University of South Florida Press; distr., Gainesville: University Presses of Florida, 1989. 395p. ISBN 0-8130-0895-6.

This is a well-constructed and useful manual of ballet technique and process, the idea being to clarify and define ballet theory and tradition as well as movements. Ballet steps and positions are presented in narrative form along with excellent illustrations of professional dancers from major ballet companies who serve as models. There are more than 2,500 black-and-white photographs helping to clarify step-by-step instruction and sequenced movements. Information is presented with the intention of providing instruction with respect to the pattern and artistry of ballet. Steps and positions are arranged by category and are given technical treatment. The theoretical commentary enhances the practical exposition. All major schools of classical ballet are defined. Special features include a pronunciation guide, glossary, and selective bibliography.

805. Complete Stories of the Great Ballets. Rev and enl. ed. George Balanchine. New York: Doubleday, 1977. 838p. ISBN 0-385-11381-1.

This is a leading handbook of ballet synopses because of its detailed and comprehensive coverage. Originally published in 1954 with a revision in 1968, none of its three editions has had the same title. The latest edition covers over 400 ballets, either of classic stature and of lasting importance or significant and written in the past twenty-five years. The main part consists of stories and reviews by Balanchine, followed by sections on history, chronology, and careers; an essay on how to enjoy the ballet; and notes on dancers, dancing, and choreography. There are an illustrated glossary, an annotated section on ballet records, and a general bibliography. A detailed analytical index facilitates access.

Balanchine and Francis Mason have issued a new edition of a less-comprehensive work, *101 Stories of the Great Ballets* (Anchor/Doubleday, 1989). Ballets are arranged alphabetically and represent both the old favorites or historically important ballets and those identified as the most important to appear between 1968 and 1975. Another source is *The Ballet Goer's Guide*, by Mary Clarke and Clement Crisp (Random House, 1981). It applies a British perspective to the coverage of nearly 150 of today's most frequently performed ballets. Included is information on choreography, plot, and historical background, and it contains numerous illustrations, some of which are in color. Descriptions are lively and cogent, and the work is important to ballet enthusiasts.

806. The Concise Oxford Dictionary of Ballet. 2d ed., upd. Horst Koegler. New York: Oxford University Press, 1987. 458p. ISBN 0-19-311330-9.

Since its first appearance in English in 1977, this tool (based on an earlier German work) has come to be regarded as a first-rate reference book providing brief and informative descriptions, identifications, and definitions. This is a reprint with corrections of the second edition, published in 1982. The second edition did not supersede the first issue inasmuch as many entries from the original effort were deleted to create a more compact and more convenient volume. New subjects and topics of interest were added, making this the most up-to-date ballet dictionary. Many of the entries furnish biographical references to further reading on the topic, and various personalities are covered. Possibly more coverage could have been given to the younger and recently successful individuals, because the emphasis on established stars duplicates much of what is available elsewhere. Coverage is comprehensive and the whole spectrum of ballet is considered, with treatment given to modern and ethnic dance.

807. A Dictionary of Ballet Terms. 3d rev. ed. Leo Kersley and Janet Sinclair. London: A & C Black, 1977; repr., New York: Da Capo, 1981. 112p. ISBN 0-306-80094-2.

This work has taken a turn toward the more technical side since its initial publication in 1952. At that time, it was meant for popular consumption, but more recently the definitions have appealed to a more sophisticated audience. It remains a compact little volume with several hundred entries; some of the definitions are lengthy and detailed. It brings together related terms, sometimes in its liberal use of cross-references, at others in treating several terms under a single subject heading. There are many line drawings, which serve to illustrate a number of the techniques defined.

Another useful tool is Gail Grant's *Technical Manual and Dictionary of Classical Ballet*, now in its third edition (Dover, 1982). Unlike the Kersley and Sinclair work, this one provides pronunciations as well as definitions of dance terms. It also furnishes line drawings of main positions.

808. **The Guinness Guide to Ballet.** Oleg Kerensky. Enfield, UK: Guinness Superlatives; distr., New York: Sterling, 1981. 224p. ISBN 0-8511-2226-4.

Kerensky is a noted authority and writer on the subject of ballet and has succeeded in developing an interesting and comprehensive guide. The emphasis is on British and American ballet, although coverage is of international proportions. Brief treatment is given to a broad spectrum of aspects and considerations, such as history, language, training of dancers, careers, stars, music, costume and decoration, and choreographers. There are good, colorful illustrations, and a well-developed index provides access.

An older work that has been a familiar reference tool in past years is *The International Book of Ballet*, by Peter Brinson and Clement Crisp (Stein & Day, 1971). The emphasis is on the ballets of thirty-eight major choreographers, under whose names are listed 115 different ballets grouped by period and type. It covers a time period from the seventeenth century to the time of publication. Works in the general repertoire at time of publication have been included. There is a bias toward British choreographers among the contemporary contributors.

809. **International Dictionary of Ballet.** Martha Bremser, ed. Detroit: St. James Press, 1993. 2v. ISBN 1-55862-084-2.

An important effort, this two-volume compendium provides comprehensive coverage of the topic on a worldwide scale. Entries treat individual ballets beginning with the period of the Renaissance in the late sixteenth century to contemporary productions. There are more than 800 entries that provide detailed exposition averaging two pages in length. These are arranged alphabetically for ease of access and include ballets, ballet companies, and personalities (dancers, choreographers, designers, composers, and instructors). The entries are prepared by contributing specialists and supply bibliographies. Accompanying the entries are some 550 illustrations.

A Dictionary of Ballet, by George Buckley Wilson, last issued in its third edition (London: A & C Black, 1974) is still considered a useful tool, furnishing about 2,500 entries on a variety of topics and issues pertinent to the study of ballet. Originally published as a Penguin imprint in 1957, it was revised in 1961. All aspects are treated: history, choreography, individual ballets, stage design, ballet companies, and various personalities. Although coverage includes modern dance as well as Spanish and Indian dances, the emphasis is on classical ballet, and definitions and identifications relate primarily to ballet in Great Britain, France, West Germany, and the United States.

Directories, Annuals, and Current Awareness Sources

810. **Dance Directory.** Beverly J. Allen, ed. Reston, VA: National Dance Association, 1990– . ISSN 0070-2676.

The National Dance Association is an association of the American Alliance for Health, Physical Education, Recreation and Dance, and sponsors this guide to programs in professional dance at schools, colleges, and universities in the United States. Institutions are arranged geographically, with entries supplying faculty listings, degrees awarded, performance groups within the schools, and course listings. Coverage of the college credit courses is unique and detailed enough to include credit hours for each offering. Schools are neither compared nor rated. There is a separate listing for high schools in the performing arts that gives their address and telephone number.

National Square Dance Directory 1999, edited by Gordon Goss (National Square Dance Directory, 1999) has varied in frequency from annual to biennial since its inception in 1979. This effort was the last to be published. It provides directory-type information on thousands of dance and folk clubs with interests in square dance, round dance, contra, clogging, and so forth. Each state in the United States is treated, followed by listings for Canada, Australia, Europe, the Far East, the Middle East, the Pacific, and South America.

811. **Dance Resources in Canadian Libraries.** Clifford Collier and Pierre Guilmette. Ottawa: National Library of Canada, 1982. var. paging. (Research Collections in Canadian Libraries: Special Studies, no. 8). ISBN 0660510227.

This is an extensive survey of research and educational materials and centers available in Canada for the study of dance. It is bilingual (French/English), and provides a good state-of-the-art assessment, while serving as a tool for collection development for new and existing collections. There are several sections or parts, the first one dealing with the methodology used in the collection of data, followed by a historical overview in part 2. Part 3 furnishes a statistical summary identifying size of monograph and serial collections and presence of non-book collections in Canadian libraries arranged by province, while the final section considers observations and suggestions for the future. Appendices identify serials available in Canada, reference works related to dance, and a directory of colleges and other post-secondary institutions that offer diplomas or degrees. There is a list of collections by province with numerical information on holdings, as well as an index.

812. **Dancemagazine.** New York: Dance Magazine, 1927– . Mo. ISSN 0011-6009.

This is the most popular and widely known dance periodical in the country, enjoying a wide circulation and continued interest. It began life as the *American Dancer* in 1927 and was absorbed into *Dancemagazine* in 1942. Today it is an excellent current awareness tool providing coverage of dance activities throughout the world. An important monthly calendar is impressive in its comprehensiveness and attention to detail. Another important feature for reference work is the directory of dance schools. Articles cover all aspects of the subject, including information on performers, tours, costumes, and dance companies. Excellent photographs contribute to the informational qualities of this periodical. In 1986, the magazine issued *Performing Arts Directory* for the city of New York, now replaced by Ruth Leon's *Applause: New York's Guide to the Performing Arts* (Applause Trade Book Publishing).

A useful Web site is *Dance Links* (1996) (http://www.dancer.com/dance-links/ [accessed December 1999]), created by Amy Reusch, a dance videographer. It provides access to links in several categories such as ballet companies, performance listings, dance resources, and funding resources.

813. **World Ballet and Dance 1993–1994: An International Yearbook.** Bent Schonberg et al., eds. New York: Oxford University Press, 1994. ISBN 0-19816-427-0.

This annual publication has gained a wide following for its comprehensive coverage and its value as both a critical-evaluative tool and descriptive or expository volume. It serves as a review of the previous year and covers the major performances all over the world. Critical commentary is provided on policies and trends and various parts of the world are analyzed in terms of their developments. The current edition contains the usual listings of personalities and companies along with nearly forty black-and-white photographs. Special coverage is given to conditions in Cuba and in South Africa, along with obituaries of Nureyev and MacMillan.

Dance World, edited by John Willis (Crown, 1966–1979), had provided an annual survey of the New York dance season before it ceased publication. The fourteen volumes are still regarded as a vital collective resource in reference work. Similar to *Theatre World* (entry 857) in the use of illustration, arrangement, and format, each volume provides an excellent pictorial overview, including much useful information on the season just completed (June 1 to May 31). Although the focus is on the New York stage, there is some coverage of other companies and productions, with a section on regional U.S. companies. There are lists of personnel of various companies, repertoires, opening and closing dates, cast lists for dance events, festivals, and biographies of choreographers and key performers. Both dance scenes and individuals are highlighted in the high-quality photographs.

Biographical Sources

814. **Biographical Dictionary of Dance.** Barbara Naomi Cohen-Stratyner. New York: Schirmer Books/Macmillan, 1982. 970p. (A Dance Horizons Book). ISBN 0-02-870260-3.

Nearly 3,000 figures are described in this most comprehensive of biographical dictionaries. Included are individuals representing all aspects of dance and performance, such as performers, choreographers, composers, impresarios, designers, theorists, and teachers. They span a period of over 400 years in both Europe and America. Entries are alphabetical and furnish personal and career information, including education, training, development, and accomplishments, with special attention given to roles and choreographical productions. All forms of dance are covered in various theatrical styles (opera, ballet, striptease, Broadway musical, etc.) and even include television variety performances. Obviously, the greatest value of a comprehensive work of this type is that it sheds light on some of the obscure and little-known personalities for whom information is difficult to locate.

815. **Dancers and Choreographers: A Selected Bibliography.** Leslie Getz. Wakefield, RI: Asphodel Press, 1995. 305p. ISBN 1-55921-108-3.

The author is the editor of the dance newsletter, *Attitudes and Arabesques,* and is familiar with the need for improved bibliographic access to materials on personalities associated with the field of ballet and modern dance. Arrangement of the work is alphabetical by name of artist, followed by a list of biographical writings and documented interviews. Included here are books, dissertations, and monographic publications treating a single individual, along with references to relevant sections of a select grouping of seventy-nine major books and seventeen scholarly periodicals. References are also made to chapters and parts of other books and to articles from more general periodicals. The work concludes with an extensive listing of general reference tools, critical writings, and histories.

816. **Film Choreographers and Dance Directors: An Illustrated Biographical Encyclopedia, with a History and Filmographies, 1893 Through 1995.** Larry Billman. Jefferson, NC: McFarland, 1997. 652p. ISBN 0-899-50868-5.

The work begins with an excellent bibliography containing books and articles relevant to historical treatment of dance on film, including references to interviews with various choreographers. This is followed by a well-written and informative history, beginning with a section on the origins from 1893 to 1930. It is then segmented into succeeding decades from the 1930s to the 1990s. These sections include filmographies identifying important films of the period. The collective biography then follows, treating nearly 1,000 choreographers and dance directors, for whom information is given regarding dates and places of birth and death; description of type of choreography; awards received; and credit listings for work on film, television, stage, video, night club, and concert. The work is illustrated with black-and-white photographs.

817. **International Dictionary of Modern Dance.** Taryn Benbow-Pfalzgraf and Glynis Benbow-Niemier. Detroit: St. James Press, 1998. 891p. ISBN 1-558623-59-0.

Another useful biographical dictionary from St. James is this collection of 425 biographical sketches on dancers, choreographers, teachers, designers, writers, and other specialists associated with the world of dance during the twentieth century, as well as dance forms and companies. The focus on modern dance, with its roots in theatrical performance of "popular" nature, justifies the exclusion of ballet and social dance, with their earlier origins. Entries are informative and contain career and background highlights, awards, writings, and a critical essay. Numerous black-and-white photographs are provided. The work opens with a chronology and concludes with a bibliography and index.

The Complete Guide to Modern Dance, by Don McDonagh (Doubleday, 1976), although older, retains its utility with its emphasis on choreographers, for whom it provides detailed coverage of some 100 personalities. Material is arranged in a chronological sequence of five periods, beginning with the forerunners of modern dance and culminating with contemporary contributions. Choreographers are arranged alphabetically within the time frames. Entries furnish a biographical sketch, accompanied by descriptions of one or more of the major works along with a chronology of all the person's works.

Histories

818. **Ballet & Modern Dance: A Concise History.** 2d ed. Jack Anderson. Princeton, NJ: Princeton Book, 1992. 287p. (A Dance Horizons Book). ISBN 0916622428.

This is the second edition, somewhat expanded, of Anderson's informative and easily comprehended history of dance from classical times to the present. The first edition was issued in 1986 and was well received by its audience of general users and music students. Anderson is a long-time dance critic and writer, whose narrative is informal and appealing. He begins with a segment on the pleasures of dance history and then takes the reader through an interesting survey of ballet history from its place in the royal courts through its professionalization and its rise in the United States. Contemporary dance is examined on the international level. Selected readings from various historical periods are included along with numerous biographical sketches. A lengthy bibliography is provided.

This work updates Anderson's earlier effort, *Dance* (Newsweek Books, 1979), a slender trade paperback edition based on the 1974 hardbound issue. It was prepared as part of a series covering areas of the arts and humanities (music, theater, painting, architecture, etc.), and traces the development of dance from the ritualistic stages to today's intricate choreography of modern and classical styles. Coverage runs from the latter part of the sixteenth century to the mid-1970s, with a good selection of both artists and techniques. A useful chronology identifies dance events along with historical phenomena.

819. **Dance History: An Introduction.** 2d ed., rev. and upd. Janet Adshead-Lansdale and June Layson. New York: Routledge Kegan Paul, 1994. 289p. ISBN 0-415-09029-6.

This is included here primarily because it is one of the more recently published general histories of dance. It provides an informative survey of the development of dance on an international basis. Especially useful as a textbook for students, the text is comprehensible and well-constructed. Bibliographical references to useful sources are supplied, along with a good index to facilitate access.

Another recent and useful teaching tool is Selma Jeanne Cohen's *Dance As a Theatre Art: Source Readings in Dance History from 1581 to the Present* (Princeton Book, 1992) which provides a selection of important writings on dance. First published in 1974, the work has been received well by users of all levels. Introductions have been prepared for each of the documents, the selection of which represents exemplary planning.

820. **The Dance in America.** Rev. ed. Walter Terry. New York: Harper & Row, 1971; repr., Da Capo, 1981. 272p. ISBN 0-306-76059-2.

This work has been judged to be of exceptional importance. The complete history of the American contribution is chronicled, along with illustrations and excellent descriptions of the work of people like Isadora Duncan, Ted Shawn, and Martha Graham. A recognized expert in the field who served as the dance critic of the *New York Herald Tribune*, the author has published widely. Beginning with the earliest developments in this country, he furnishes excellent descriptions of European and Oriental influences and surveys all periods to the present day. There are biographies of leading performers, and coverage is given to ethnic dancers, black dance, and the regional ballet movement. It continues to be a much-used and highly popular work.

821. **World History of the Dance.** Curt Sachs. New York: W. W. Norton, 1937; repr., 1965. 469p. ISBN 0-393-00209-8.

An older work in contrast to the two preceding entries is this important contribution from the Norton Company. It has been considered a standard in the field ever since it was translated in 1937 from a German work completed in 1933. It provides more depth than the more recent works and successfully categorizes and describes the development of dance through an interpretation of its forms, themes, and steps from antiquity to the present day. Emphasis is on sociological conditions attached to dance origins and the significance of religion, war, fertility, or social dance within the time frames presented.

THEATER AND DRAMA

Bibliographic Guides

822. **American Theater and Drama Research: An Annotated Guide to Information Sources, 1945–1990.** Irene Shaland. Jefferson, NC: McFarland, 1991. 157p. ISBN 0-89950-626-7.

This slender volume contains 536 entries with annotations of varying length ranging from a single sentence to a paragraph. These annotations provide factual description along with critical and comparative commentary. Entries are organized within several major sections and subsections such as general reference sources, major sources after 1945, theater arts sources, alternate theater sources (treating black, Jewish, Hispanic, and musical theater), and other sources (periodicals, databases, organizations, etc.). The title is somewhat misleading because the scope or period covered is 1945–1990, with publications dating from 1965 to 1990. The work is intended to cite the most relevant and important sources dealing with the history of American theater and drama and excludes works treating technique, theory, and performance aspects. It is most useful for its currency and timeliness. An author index is supplied; unfortunately there is no subject or title access.

823. **A Guide to Reference and Bibliography for Theatre Research.** 2d ed., rev. and exp. Claudia Jean Bailey. Columbus: Publications Committee, Ohio State University, 1983. 149p. ISBN 0-88215-049-9.

An annotated guide to a broad range of materials available to students and researchers in the field, this tool is divided into two major sections. The first part represents general reference, standard tools, national bibliography, library catalogs, indexes of periodicals and newspapers, and lists of dissertations. The second section covers theater and drama and furnishes more specialized materials. Emphasis is on British and American theater. Arrangement in both sections is classified, with entries by author, geographical location, or chronological sequence. Over 650 titles are included, with publication dates up to mid-1979. There is an author-title index.

PERIODICALS

824. **American Theatrical Periodicals, 1798–1967: A Bibliographical Guide.** Carl Joseph Stratman. Durham, NC: Duke University Press, 1970. 133p. ISBN 0-8223-0228-4.

This guide lists nearly 700 titles of serials of all kinds, from dailies to annuals, and includes directories published over a period of more than 175 years. These represent the publications of 122 cities in thirty-one states. Locations are given in nearly 140 libraries in the United States and Canada, and include even the British Library. Arranged chronologically by year of initial issue, then alphabetically by title, the entries list original title, editor, place of publication, publisher with address, frequency, notes on missing issues, dates of first and last issue, changes in title, and so forth. Included is an index of titles and names. This is a companion work to *A Bibliography of British Dramatic Periodicals, 1720–1960* (entry 825). A photocopy reprint was made available through UMI Books on Demand in 1997.

825. **A Bibliography of British Dramatic Periodicals, 1720–1960.** 2d ed., rev. Carl Joseph Stratman. New York: New York Public Library, 1962. 58p. ISBN 0-87104-034-4.

The author was a distinguished bibliographer in the field of theater and drama. His untimely death in 1972 ended a period of extensive productivity in providing researchers, specialists, and students with useful listings in both English and American theater studies. This work serves as a companion to the more recent *American Theatrical Periodicals, 1789–1967* (entry 824). It furnishes 674 titles of British periodicals over a span of 240 years. It is a compact volume, with entries arranged chronologically, giving locations of complete files in both American and British libraries. A variety of periodicals is treated, and for those libraries that have the bibliography, it remains a useful resource item.

Bibliographies, Catalogs, and Indexes

826. **American Theatre History: An Annotated Bibliography.** Thomas J. Taylor. Pasadena, CA: Salem Press, 1992. 162p. (Magill Bibliographies). ISBN 0-89356-672-1.

As part of the Magill Bibliography series, this slender volume supplies entries to about 500 books, dissertations, and society or university press publications covering the history of American theater from its beginnings to the present day. Especially good coverage is extended to autobiography of recent personalities of all types. The work is divided into five sections, the first three of which are chronological: "Beginnings to 1914"; "1914 to 1948," which includes coverage of Federal Theater, musical theater, and playhouses; and "New York: 1945 to the Present." The two concluding sections treat various topical elements such as regional, experimental, ethnic, and community theater, along with periodicals. Entries supply paragraph-long descriptive annotations identifying the content, style, range, and critical capacity of the works. Additional sources are cited. A general index is provided.

827. **Bibliography of Medieval Drama.** 2d ed., rev. and enl. Carl Joseph Stratman. New York, Ungar, 1972. 2v. ISBN 0-8044-3272-4. **Supps. 1969–1972**, 1986; **1973–1976**, 1986; **1977–1980**, 1988.

This is one of Stratman's most important works, updating the initial edition published in 1954. It is arranged in several sections (primarily geographical), which cover general studies, Festschriften, liturgical, Latin drama, English drama, Byzantine drama, French drama, German drama, Italian drama, Low Countries drama, and Spanish drama. Many plays are identified in manuscripts, published texts, and various editions. Works about them from a variety of sources—books, articles, and dissertations—are also listed. Devised primarily to aid the student of English drama, this work should be considered only supplementary to any specialized bibliographies on any of the countries covered. There are over 9,000 entries, with library locations given for manuscripts and book material. Entries provide author, title, imprint, pagination, and so forth, with asterisks marking the most important works. A general index provides access.

Subsequent to Stratman's death in 1972, the work was continued with subsequent publications from the School of Graduate and Professional Studies at Emporia State University. *Bibliography of Medieval Drama, 1969–1972* edited by Maria S. Murphy and James Hoy was issued in 1986, as was *Bibliography of Medieval Drama, 1973–1976*. Hoy and Carole Ferguson produced *Bibliography of Medieval Drama, 1977–1980* in 1988.

828. **Catalog of the Theatre and Drama Collections.** New York Public Library. The Research Libraries. Boston: G. K. Hall, 1967–1976. 51v. ISBN 0-685-02808-3 (Part 1 no.1); 0-8161-0106-X (Part 1 no.2); 0-8161-0107-8 (Part 2). **Supp.** to Part I *Drama Collection*, 1973. 548p. **Supp.** to Part II *Theatre Collection*, 1973. 2v. **Ann. Supp.**, 1976– . ISSN 0360-2788.

Another of the important contributions to reference and research by G. K. Hall is this massive reproduction of the card catalog of this outstanding collection of theater and drama materials established in 1931. Publication of this catalog has been in several parts, related to different components of the collection. Parts I and II were published in 1967. Part I, *Drama Collection: Author Listing* (6v.) and *Listing by Cultural Origin* (6v.), consists of 120,000 entries for plays published separately or in anthologies and even periodicals. Part II, *Theatre Collection: Books on the Theatre*, has over 120,000 entries from over 23,500 volumes relating to all aspects of the theater (history, biography, acting, etc.). A 548-page supplement to part I and a two-volume supplement to part II were published in 1973. Part III, *Non-Book Collection*, was published in thirty volumes in 1975 and represents over 740,000 cards on such items as programs, photographs, portraits, and press clippings.

Coverage for parts I and II has been continued by an annual supplement, *Bibliographic Guide to Theatre Arts*, appearing since 1976. This lists materials newly cataloged by the New York Public Library, with additional entries furnished from the Library of Congress MARC tapes.

829. **International Bibliography of Theatre.** New York: Theatre Research Data Center, Brooklyn College, City University of New York; distr., New York: Publishing Center for Cultural Resources, 1985– . Ann. ISBN 0-945419-03-1.

This is a recently conceived, comprehensive annual bibliography of theater on an international basis. The year 1982 was covered initially in the 1985 publication, with 1983 coverage being issued in 1986. The delay continues: The 1995–1996 issue (volume 11) was published in 1998, and the 1997 issue in 1999. Nevertheless, this is a valuable source of information for students and specialists in locating information about all essential components and personalities related to theater. Aided by the computer, this work identifies periodical coverage in various languages (Catalan, English, French, German, Italian, Polish, Russian, the

Scandinavian languages, and Spanish). Books published in Austria, Canada, England, France, East and West Germany, Italy, Poland, the U.S.S.R., Spain, and the United States are treated. Some 6,000 entries are classified by subject, with some 18,000 references to books, articles, dissertations, and other theater documents.

Play Sources—Bibliographies and Indexes

830. **American Women Playwrights, 1900–1930: A Checklist.** Francis D. Bzowski. Westport, CT: Greenwood, 1992. (Bibliographies and Indexes in Women's Studies, no. 15). ISBN 0-313-24238-0.

This work targets the early years of the twentieth century as a time when women were given opportunity to express themselves alongside a growing little-theater movement that afforded them production outlets in this country. The onset of the Great Depression in 1930 marked the decline of women's social freedom and creative opportunities. Some 12,000 plays by American women were written during this time, and this checklist is an attempt to document those efforts in a comprehensive fashion. Entries are arranged alphabetically by name of writer (not all of whom are known to be American or even women). Writings of various types are cited, with operettas and exercises included along with plays. Biographical data are spare; library locations are identified in the entries. Unfortunately, there is no subject or title index.

831. **Gay and Lesbian American Plays: An Annotated Bibliography.** Ken Furtado and Nancy Hellner. Metuchen, NJ: Scarecrow Press, 1993. 231p. ISBN 0-8108-2689-5.

A product of its time is this unique bibliography of more than 700 plays in which either a primary character is gay or lesbian or the primary theme involves homosexuality. The effort signals and is representative of a burgeoning body of work in contemporary theater examining the gay lifestyle and its ramifications on people's lives. Entries supply plot descriptions along with names of playwrights and titles; information is given regarding acts, characters, settings, and music. Such material is most useful for play groups, producers, directors, and actors as well as researchers and students. Appendices furnish much useful information, such as listings of theaters that produce such plays, names and addresses of playwrights and agents, and related bibliographic references, as well as a chart or matrix identifying plays by certain criteria.

832. **Index to Full Length Plays, 1895 to 1925.** Ruth Gibbons Thomson. Boston: F. W. Faxon, 1956. 307p. **Supp. 1926 to 1944**, 1946. ISBN 0-87305-085-1.

This is another of the landmark indexes necessary to identify authors and titles in the field. An earlier effort by Thomson spanned the period 1926–1944 (F. W. Faxon, 1946). Ten years later, she produced this more extensive volume, which preceded it in coverage, establishing the first publication as a supplement. Both titles overlap to some extent the coverage given by Firkins (see entry 834). Thomson's focus in both volumes is on full-length plays, and the work provides a title index that includes author, translator, number of acts, number of characters, subject, and scene. There are author and subject indexes with cross-references to the title index for full information. A bibliography identifies publishers and dates at the end.

Norma Olin Ireland's *Index to Full Length Plays, 1944 to 1964* (F. W. Faxon, 1964) continues the coverage with another twenty years of indexing. There is a dictionary index of authors, subjects, and titles. Both anthologies and separate play texts are included.

833. **An Index to One-Act Plays.** Hannah Logasa and Winifred Ver Nooy. Boston: F. W. Faxon, 1924. 327p. (Useful Resource Series, no. 3). **Supp. 1–5**, 1933–1964. 5v. ISBN 0-81081-208-8.

Logasa was one of the pioneers of this century in indexing. Her early effort concentrated on one-act plays. Children's plays and adult plays are both included, as are both anthologies and separate publications. The basic volume covers plays published from 1900 to 1924. These are limited to English-language dramas but do include translations from foreign works. Each supplement continues the coverage, adding another eight to nine years of indexing up to 1964. The third supplement (1941–1948) adds radio plays, while the fourth and fifth supplements (1948–1964) include television plays as well. Access is provided by title, author, and subject indexes in each volume.

834. **Index to Plays 1800–1926.** Ina Ten Eyck Firkins. New York: H. W. Wilson, 1927. 307p. **Supp. 1927–1934**, 1935. 140p. ISBN 0-404-02386-X.

An early commitment of the Wilson Company was the indexing of plays, and Firkins was one of the pioneers in this area. Her basic work is a comprehensive index of nearly 8,000 English-language plays by over 2,200 authors over a period of 126 years. The plays are identified with the name of anthology or other source provided. The first part is the author index, in which complete bibliographic information is provided for each entry and additional description is given of the number of acts and type (comedy or tragedy, etc.). The second part is a title and subject index, with references to the author list. Firkins produced a supplement eight years later that identifies over 3,000 plays by over 1,300 authors.

A more recent index is Gordon Samples's *The Drama Scholars' Index to Plays and Filmscripts: A Guide to Plays and Filmscripts in Selected Anthologies, Series, and Periodicals* (Scarecrow Press, 1974–1986). With the publication of volume 3 in 1986, coverage of the index is through 1983. This work provides a balanced selection of plays from all periods and various parts of the world. Due to its remarkable comprehensive coverage, it is an extremely important tool in identifying sources of plays that have not been indexed elsewhere.

835. **Index to Plays in Periodicals.** Rev. and exp. ed. Dean H. Keller. Metuchen, NJ: Scarecrow Press, 1979. 824p. ISBN 0-8108-1208-8. **Supp. 1977–1987**, 1990. 391p. ISBN 0-8108-2288-1.

This has been an important reference tool since it first appeared in 1971. The expanded edition is cumulative, including the nearly 7,500 entries from the first edition and its 1973 supplement along with 2,145 new citations. Thus, nearly 10,000 plays from all over the world appearing in nearly 270 periodicals through 1976 are enumerated. There are two major sections. The first is an author listing that identifies the author's name and dates, title, brief description, number of acts, and volume and date of periodical. The second is a listing by title that provides references to the author entries. All types of plays in various languages are covered, and cross-references are given for joint authors, translators, and so forth. The work continues to serve as a valuable identification tool along with other indexes in the collection. Keller's ten-year supplement treats another 4,000 plays.

836. **Ottemiller's Index to Plays in Collections: An Author and Title Index to Plays Appearing in Collections Published Between 1900 and 1985.** 7th ed., rev. and enl. by Billie M. Connor and Helene G. Mochedlover. John Henry Ottemiller. Metuchen, NJ: Scarecrow Press, 1988. 523p. ISBN 0-8108-0919-2.

An old favorite among reference librarians is this index to plays appearing in anthologies. Since its initial appearance in 1943, the work has gained a position of prominence for those who must identify dramatic titles or authors. The present edition furnishes thousands of citations to several thousand plays and authors. Hundreds of anthologies or collections have been identified, with increased coverage of feminist, ethnic, and gay perspectives. English-language materials from various parts of the world are represented, and foreign translations are identified. Plays are universal in nature, ranging from ancient to modern; excluded from coverage are collections of children's plays, amateur plays, one-act plays, holiday and anniversary plays, and radio and television plays. If plays of this type appear in an anthology that is indexed, then they are included in the listing. Main entries are listed by author; there is a title index, as well as a list of collections analyzed.

837. **Play Index.** New York: H. W. Wilson, 1949/1952– . Quin. ISSN 0554-3037.

This continuing publication from the Wilson Company is the chief reason why some of the other indexes have ceased publication (see entries 832 and 833). Coverage at this point is from 1949 to 1992, and has been handled in eight volumes that have varied in frequency from five to ten years. Basically, it appears as a quinquennial publication, with the last volume issued in 1993 and covering the period 1988–1992. Editorship has changed hands over time, with such names as Dorothy H. West and Estelle A. Fidell giving way to the current editor, Juliette Yaakov. The work itself is comprehensive and includes all types of plays from all types of sources—one-act plays, full-length plays, children's plays—either separately published or parts of collections. All are English-language items, but translations are included, as are publishers from all over the world. Generally about 4,000 plays are covered in each volume (4,397 in 1988–1992), and more than 30,000 plays have been treated overall. The main listing is a dictionary index of authors, titles, and subjects followed by a list of collections indexed. A cast analysis is provided that lists plays under gender of cast and number of characters. Finally, there is a directory of publishers.

A more recent work is Herbert H. Hoffman's *Recorded Plays: Indexes to Dramatists, Plays and Actors* (American Library Association, 1985). This source may be of use to scholars and theater buffs in identifying various types of recorded plays (LPs primarily, but also cassettes, video, film, and other discs).

838. **Plays for Children and Young Adults: An Evaluative Index and Guide.** Rashelle S. Karp and June H. Schlessinger. New York: Garland, 1991. 580p. ISBN 0-8240-6112-8. **Supp. 1,** 1989–1994, 1996. 369p. ISBN 0-8153-1493-0.

Designed for all types of individuals or organizations that select material for youngsters, this tool is a comprehensive index to more than 3,500 plays appropriate for children and young adults ages five to eighteen. The plays identified in this volume are primarily American efforts published between 1975 and 1989. Various types of productions are treated, such as choral readings, scenes, musical reviews, readers' theater, and skits, as well as full length and one-act plays. Entries are arranged alphabetically by title and provide grade level, cast analysis, playing time, and number of acts as well as plot summary, source of story, subject headings, and evaluation by symbol. Numerous contributors have supplied the plot descriptions, which run several lines, as well as the concluding statements of recommendation. The work is well-indexed, giving access by author/original title, cast gender, grade level, subject/type, and playing time.

The same authors have produced the first supplement, continuing the coverage from 1989 to 1994; it lists 2,158 plays both from anthologies and separately published in the same style as the original work.

Dictionaries, Encyclopedias, and Handbooks

GENERAL

839. **The Cambridge Guide to World Theatre.** Rev. and upd. ed. Martin Banham, ed. New York: Cambridge University Press, 1992. 1104p. ISBN 0-521-42903-X.

This is a comprehensive, one-volume handbook of the history and practice of theater around the world. It treats personalities, techniques, issues, and topics of varied nature, some of which are overlooked by other tools of this kind. Much of the topical material is covered by the *Oxford Companion to the Theatre* (entry 845), but the *Cambridge* offers a more inclusive coverage in dealing with popular culture and the theater presence in the Third World. All aspects of theater are covered, from production to theory to legal considerations of copyright. There are more than 100 contributors, all of whom have signed their articles. Bibliographies are furnished for the topical entries; there are several hundred black-and-white illustrations.

840. **The Facts on File Dictionary of the Theatre.** William Packard et al., eds. New York: Facts on File, 1988. 556p. ISBN 0-81601-841-3.

This is a well-constructed dictionary providing more than 5,000 definitions, expositions, and biographical sketches. Coverage is given to both performers and playwrights as well as all other aspects of the theater. Styles, genres, forms, techniques, design technology, and companies are treated; schools, organizations, and major plays are included. Entries tend to be brief, and greater length would have been desirable in some cases.

The Encyclopedia of World Theater: With 420 Illustrations and an Index of Play Titles, by noted theater critic Martin Esslin (Scribner's, 1977), is an old standard created as an amplified and expanded version of a German reference work published in 1969. The volume presents an excellent overview and furnishes brief entries for various personalities (actors, actresses, playwrights, directors, designers) and various facets of the theater. Although somewhat dated, the 2,000 articles and 400 illustrations furnish useful perspective on scenes, theaters, and individuals. As one might expect, coverage is better for continental Europe than is true of most works of this type.

841. **International Dictionary of Theatre.** Mark Hawkins-Dady, ed. Chicago: St. James Press, 1992–1995. 3v. ISBN 1-55862-094-X.

Similar to coverage afforded in the publisher's *International Dictionary of Films and Filmmakers* (entry 967), this is an important, three-volume compendium treating plays, playwrights, and performers. Volume 1, "Plays," issued in 1992, covers 620 of the world's most significant or notable plays. Selection of foreign plays is based upon their recognition and performance within the English-speaking world; entries are prepared by a large group of specialist-contributors. Information is supplied regarding first date of publication as well as production, and references are given to critical material. There is a critical summary and evaluation of the play's significance. Occasional photographs are provided. Volume 2, "Playwrights," published in 1993, treats 500 playwrights and supplies biographical sketches, chronologies, and bibliographies of critical studies. It includes a title index. Volume 3, "Actors, Directors, and Designers," published in 1995, provides biographical and critical treatment of some 300 personalities.

842. **An International Dictionary of Theatre Language.** Joel Trapido et al. Westport, CT: Greenwood, 1985. 1032p. ISBN 0-313-22980-5.

Considered by reviewers to be an excellent choice because of its scope and depth of coverage, this is the most recent dictionary of theater terminology. Coverage is broad, with approximately 15,000 terms described, two-thirds of which come from the English language. The remainder represent terms derived from sixty foreign languages. Selection of foreign terms was limited to those that have been used in English-language theater publications in a romanized form. The terminology spans theater history from ancient times to the present day. Entries identify language, literal meaning, and definition. Some entries include additional description, with references to supporting documents. Cross-references are numerous, and an extensive bibliography concludes the effort.

843. **Masterplots II: Drama Series.** Frank N. Magill, ed. Pasadena, CA: Salem Press, 1990. 4v. ISBN 0-89356-491-5.

This is the sixth effort in the series of sets supplementing the 1976 edition of *Masterplots* (entry 1094). It treats 327 twentieth-century plays by 148 playwrights. Plays have all been issued in the English language, although some are translations from their native tongue. Detailed entries are written by over 230 contributors and run five pages in length, opening with an overview of production and publication history along with a listing of major characters. Coverage continues with a plot summary followed by narrative describing themes, dramatic devices, and critical context. Entries conclude with a brief bibliography of additional sources. The work is useful for students at both high school and undergraduate levels with respect to its detail and treatment of a wide variety of themes and subjects. It is highly selective, however, and includes only works of major importance. There is an author index.

844. **McGraw-Hill Encyclopedia of World Drama: An International Reference Work.** 2d ed. Stanley Hochman, ed.-in-chief. New York: McGraw-Hill, 1984. 5v. ISBN 0-07-079169-4.

This is a most welcome revision and expansion of the 1972 edition, which was received in a lukewarm manner. The revised edition provides more complete coverage of national and ethnic theater traditions and of theater in specific countries, while retaining the pleasant and useful illustrated format. As in the earlier edition, the emphasis is on dramatists, with individuals receiving the majority of the entries. Entries for major personalities include biographies, critiques of their work, synopses of selected plays, and a bibliography of editions that includes references to plays in anthologies or collections. Biographical and critical references are given as well. Bibliographies for most entries are useful and up-to-date. Articles on theater companies and title entries for anonymous plays are provided. Articles are signed for the most part. Volume 5 furnishes a general index to facilitate access.

845. **The Oxford Companion to the Theatre.** 4th ed., repr. with corr. Phylliss Hartnoll, ed. New York: Oxford University Press, 1993. 934p. ISBN 0-19-211546-4.

An old standard in the reference department since the initial edition in 1951, the fourth edition (1983) was forced to cut back its coverage to maintain a suitable price level. The final product is a most worthwhile tool although it does not supersede the third edition entirely. All peripheral entries (ballet, opera, vaudeville) have been deleted and the survey articles on theater in individual countries have been shortened considerably. The cuts have been most drastic (50–80 percent) in stage management and production articles (lighting, scenery, makeup, etc.). The product does an excellent job in its focus on the "legitimate theater." Scholarship is up-to-date and there is frequent reprinting with corrections. Coverage is given to a variety of new topics, such as "Chicano Theatre." Improved treatment of U.S and British regional theater is evident, with larger numbers of contemporary personalities and developments included. It remains an indispensable tool.

A more abbreviated tool is *Concise Oxford Companion to the Theatre*, edited by Hartnoll and Peter Found (Oxford University Press, 1992). It is considered the second edition, and represents a condensed version of the fourth edition. Some of the less important entries have been deleted to cover new personalities and topics.

SPECIALIZED BY TIME PERIOD OR GEOGRAPHIC REGION

846. **Cambridge Guide to American Theatre.** Don B. Wilmeth and Tice L. Miller, eds. New York: Cambridge University Press, 1996. 463p. ISBN 0-521-56444-1.

This work rivals *The Oxford Companion to American Theatre* (entry 850) as a single-volume information source on the topic. It is an updated, corrected, and expanded paperback version of the 1993 edition and continues in the vein of other Cambridge guides. Coverage is comprehensive, providing a well-developed survey of the American theater from its origins to the present day. There are more than 23,000 entries for personalities, representing all aspects of performance and production, plays, musicals, theaters, organizations, and terminology. A number of the entries are based on earlier coverage in the *Cambridge Guide to World Theatre* (entry 839), but are revised and updated where necessary. The entries are signed and are arranged alphabetically to provide informed description and identification. Excellent indexing is provided along with an extensive bibliography.

847. **A Companion to the Medieval Theatre.** Ronald W. Vince, ed. New York: Greenwood, 1989. 420p. ISBN 0-313-24647-5.

Designed to appeal to the general reader or student of the theater rather than the medieval scholar, this is a useful tool, providing some 250 entries on all aspects of medieval theater, alphabetically arranged. Emphasis has been placed on performance considerations rather than literary analysis in treating theater over a 650-year period, A.D. 900–1550. Entries supply factual description and exposition of place-names, personalities, technical terms, theater forms, genres, and so forth. They vary in length from several sentences to survey articles of several pages on such topics as dance, music, art, and secular drama, and on geographic regions such as Iberia, the Low Countries, and the British Isles. Cross-references are furnished along with bibliographies for many of the entries. A useful and detailed chronology precedes the main text. Four indexes provide access by person, place, play, and subject.

The Cambridge Companion to Medieval English Theatre, edited by Richard Beadle (Cambridge University Press, 1994), is part of a series that features a selected group of essays by scholars treating various aspects of the topic. In this case, twelve experts provide chapters on English drama of the time, mystery cycles, morality plays, and so forth. From the same publisher is a similar tool, focused on a different period of English productivity: *The Cambridge Companion to English Renaissance Drama*, edited by A. R. Braunmuller and Michael Hattaway (1990) provides insightful commentaries treating the early modern and Elizabethan period through the seventeenth century.

848. **Cambridge Companion to Greek Tragedy.** P. E. Easterling, ed. Cambridge, UK: Cambridge University Press, 1997. 392p. (Cambridge Companions to Literature series). ISBN 0-521-41245-5.

Following the pattern of the series (entry 1082), this work provides a selected group of essays by different scholars examining a variety of aspects of the topic. In this case, the work is divided into three major parts, beginning with "Tragedy As an Institution: The Historical

Context," which embraces four chapters examining the theater as a process of Greek life, its audience, and its art. Part II, "The Plays," contains four chapters treating their sociology, language, structure, and form. Part III "Reception," supplies the final four chapters, examining the plays' acceptance, their adaptation into film and opera as well as stage performance, and modern critical approaches. A chronology, a glossary, and a bibliography of additional readings are provided.

Crowell's Handbook of Classical Drama, edited by Richmond Y. Hathorn (Thomas Y. Crowell, 1967; repr., 1971), is an old standard used by both students and specialists for its convenient coverage of Greek and Roman drama. Unlike the *Cambridge Companion*, it features hundreds of alphabetically arranged entries that supply biographies of dramatists, summaries of myths and legends, identification of gods and heroes, and definitions of historical and dramatic terms. Placenames and even major characters from the plays are included. Plays are identified with date of composition or first performance; entries include brief synopses and some evaluative commentary.

849. **Dictionary of the Black Theatre: Broadway, Off-Broadway, and Selected Harlem Theatre.** Allen Woll. Westport, CT: Greenwood, 1983. 359p. ISBN 0-313-22561-3.

There are two major sections in this useful work describing theatrical contributions related to the black experience. Part 1 enumerates the shows themselves and describes some 300 plays, revues, and musicals "by, about, with, for and related to blacks" from "A Trip to Coontown" in 1898 to "Dreamgirls" in 1981. Entries furnish information on playhouse, opening date, number of performances, writing and production credits, casts, songs, content, and analysis of critical reception. This analysis is enhanced through the inclusion of excerpts taken from the reviews and press coverage of the time. The second section lists and describes the relevant personalities and organizations. Coverage is given to career developments and achievements as well as stage credits of both individuals and groups. To facilitate access, cross-references are supplied between the two sections.

850. **The Oxford Companion to American Theatre.** 2d ed. Gerald Bordman. New York: Oxford University Press, 1992. 735p. ISBN 0-19-507246-4.

This is the second edition of this specialized version of the Oxford Companion series, and it provides a comprehensive source of information on the American theater. Especially strong is the biographical coverage of performers, playwrights, composers, librettists, choreographers, producers, managers, directors, and designers, as well as orchestrators, photographers, publicists, critics, scholars, and even architects. Represented in addition to the legitimate stage are various forms of live theater, such as minstrel shows and vaudeville. Excellent coverage is given also to individual plays, musicals, and revues, a feature not included in *Oxford Companion to the Theatre* (entry 845). Entries include production date, plot summary, and commentary. Organizations, companies, unions, clubs, societies, periodicals, and newspapers are included, making this an extremely welcome resource for the specialist and the layperson alike.

Bordman also developed *The Concise Oxford Companion to American Theatre* (Oxford University Press, 1987; repr., 1990), which is a pared-down version of the first edition published in 1984. About 40 percent, or nearly 300 pages, was deleted, thus eliminating coverage of all minor and obscure personalities and topics. Exposition has been reduced, and the composition of the work has been altered somewhat due to the cuts.

851. **The Oxford Companion to Canadian Theatre.** Eugene Benson and L. W. Conolly, eds. New York: Oxford University Press, 1989. 662p. ISBN 0-19-540672-9.

Another of the Oxford Companions, this one supplies 703 articles, signed by their contributors and covering all aspects of Canadian theater. Articles vary in length from brief identifications to detailed and extensive narratives. Coverage is given to genres, early ritual ceremonies, personalities (actors, directors, designers, dramatists), theaters, theater companies, movements, regional theater, and so forth. Like others in the Companion series, entries are arranged alphabetically and furnish description, exposition, and biography. Plot descriptions are given for some fifty major plays. Both English and French Canadian theater are treated. A unique feature of this particular work is its inclusion of more than 180 illustrations to accompany the text. Many articles contain bibliographies of additional readings and cross-references to related entries. There is a detailed topical index to aid access.

852. **Theatre Backstage from A to Z.** 4th ed. Warren C. Lounsbury and Norman Boulanger. Seattle: University of Washington Press, 1999. 262p. ISBN 0-295-97717-5.

This dictionary was first published in 1967, revised in 1972, and again in 1989. Lounsbury stepped out of retirement to co-author what was perceived as a needed revision in view of innovations and new technology. It represents an important tool for both novices and theater students in bringing together up-to-date terms and treatments important to the understanding of lighting, sound, scene design, set construction, properties, and so forth in the United States. There is an abundance of new material concerning computers and electronic equipment of varied nature. Most useful is a lengthy and detailed introductory essay providing an overview of historical development of scenery and lighting practices in this country from the seventeenth century to the present. The work is profusely illustrated with line drawings and black-and-white photographs. Also included are an up-to-date bibliography and a directory of manufacturers and distributors.

853. **Variety Presents: The Complete Book of Major U.S. Show Business Awards.** Mike Kaplan, ed. New York: Garland, 1985. 564p. (Garland Reference Library of the Humanities, v. 572). ISBN 0-8240-8919-7.

The focus of this handbook is on awards, and treatment is given to Oscars, Emmys, Grammys, Tonys, and Pulitzer Prizes for plays. All winners and runners-up are listed for each prize from the beginning, with coverage given to the end of the year 1983. The work is well illustrated with pictures of award winners and presenters and furnishes titles and casts. No evaluative commentary is given, but the tool furnishes many facts on movies, plays, and television, which are accessed by a detailed index. *Variety International Showbusiness Reference* (Garland, 1983) is a more comprehensive (and expensive) Kaplan effort that compiles a great deal of information on show business. It furnishes biographies of over 6,000 personalities; award listings; film, television, and stage credits; festivals; long-running plays; necrology; and so forth.

Directories, Annuals, and Current Awareness Sources

See the section "Reviews and Criticism" for more detailed evaluative commentary on either a genre in general or on individual titles. For current awareness tools on play productions, there are computerized databases linked to specific cities, providing information on entertainment events.

854. **Dinner Theatre: A Survey and Directory.** William M. Lynk. Westport, CT: Greenwood, 1993. 128p. ISBN 0-313-28442-3.

The author is especially well-qualified to examine the topic as executive director of the American Dinner Theater Institute, columnist on dinner theater for *Back Stage*, and publicist for the largest dinner theater in the country in Akron, Ohio. His work serves as a handbook or manual of practice, source of historical information, and directory. In an introductory essay, he treats the nature of dinner theater and provides historical perspective on its development. Then follows practical advice on operations regarding food service, play production, and business considerations. Various insights are presented, citing the wisdom of practitioners, performers, and others; profiles of successful operations are supplied. A geographical directory then follows that identifies individual units. Illustrations of theaters and productions accompany the text; a selection of menus is included. A bibliography of information sources concludes the effort.

855. **Directory of Historic American Theatres.** John W. Frick and Carlton Ward, eds. New York: Greenwood, 1987. 347p. ISBN 0-313-24868-0.

The editors are academicians who have prepared this comprehensive directory of nearly 900 theaters built between 1800 and 1915 for the League of Historic American Theatres. It represents an important tool for the theater historian for its identification and factual description of particular theaters. Entries are arranged by state, then city, and supply, when available, name, address, opening date, opening show, architects, style of architecture, type of building, facade, type of theater, restoration activity, closing date, current status, stage and auditorium dimensions, seating capacity, and so forth. Sources of information used to compile the work are found in the Gene Chesley Collection at Princeton University, although these sources are not listed. The work expands the efforts of Chesley, the first president of the League, who published two such directories in the 1970s. There is a bibliography along with indexes of theaters and subjects.

856. **Directory of Theatre Training Programs: Profiles of College and Conservatory Programs Throughout the United States.** . . . 7th ed. Jill Charles et al., eds. Dorset, VT: Theatre Directories, 1999. 244p. ISBN 0-933919-45-X.

This biennial directory has expanded in size and coverage since its first edition in 1987. It represents an important source of information for its treatment of theater schools and their programs. The seventh edition (1999–2001) covers more than 400 college and conservatory performing arts programs in this country and provides up-to-date information concerning their composition and practices. Entries are based on written and oral responses to questionnaires and telephone interviews. Arrangement is alphabetical by state; entries supply information on contacts and admission, lists of degrees and classes, faculty, facilities, production, number of graduates, curriculum, professional associations, guest artists, and a statement describing the department's philosophy of training. As in most works of this type, entries vary in terms of completeness. Varied appendices and indexes supply information on theater training and the performing arts as a career.

857. **John Willis' Theatre World.** New York: Theatre World, 1944/1945– . Ann. ISSN 0082-3856.

This important survey of the year in theater has undergone several name changes, but began life with its present title. From 1950 to 1965 it was called *Daniel Blum's Theatre World* in honor of its editor, and for a time it was called *John Willis' Theatre World* in tribute to the subsequent editor. After being called *Theatre World* for many years, it has reclaimed its second title with its coverage of the 1996–1997 season (1998). Regardless of the appellation, it has remained an excellent pictorial and factual record of theater productions in the United States. Its emphasis is on Broadway, but coverage is given to off-Broadway, regional theater, and touring companies. It provides opening and closing dates, cast lists, producers, directors, authors, composers, song titles, theaters, designers, agents, technicians, and so forth. Biographies of cast members are given in a brief, stylized format, and many pictures are included of scenes and personalities involved. There is an extensive index that expedites access to the information in legitimate plays, solo performances, and musicals. Some of this information (without illustrations) may be found in *Best Plays* (entry 876).

858. **New York Theatrical Sourcebook.** Association of Theatrical Artists and Craftsmen. New York: Broadway Press, 1984– . Ann. ISBN 0-964267-93-4(1998).

This remains a highly useful directory of sources and services in the New York City area for those involved with the entertainment industry. The largest segment is "Products and Services," which furnishes a classified listing of some 3,000 different businesses organized under such categories as "Books, Fake." Props, stage designs, costumes, special effects, puppets, and other paraphernalia are acquired through the listings, which furnish address, telephone number, hours of operation, and sometimes, descriptive notes. Cross-references are given between entries. There is an alphabetical listing of these companies with references to the "Products" section. The appendices are useful and provide additional listings, including design collections, unions, and concert halls. Especially noteworthy is a listing of services available during odd hours.

859. **Regional Theatre Directory: A National Guide to Employment in Regional & Dinner Theatres. . . .** Jill Charles et al., eds. Cambridge, MA: Blackwell, 1985– . Ann. ISBN 5-559-66031-0 (1998–99).

The complete subtitle goes on: "for performers (Equity and non-Equity), designers, technicians & management: with internship opportunities for students." This paperback guide to the employment opportunities in regional theater contains union addresses and Equity contracts, organizations, audition lists, references to useful publications, theater listings with information regarding contracts and hiring practices, as well as estimated salaries. Applications, apprenticeships, internships, and so forth are given by geographical region. Each issue contains thematic articles treating evaluations of various services such as computerized casting services in New York City and narratives on job hunting. The 1998–1999 edition was issued in 1998.

Also available is *Summer Theatre Directory*, which began as an annual in 1984. It is organized along the same lines. Edited by Jill Charles and published by Theatre Directories, it is designed as a summer placement aid for actors, technicians, designers, and so forth seeking employment. The new edition (1998) lists 385 summer theaters and seventh-five summer training programs around the country. Indexing is excellent in both titles.

860. **Theatre Companies of the World.** Colby H. Kullman and William C. Young, eds. Westport, CT: Greenwood, 1986. 2v. ISBN 0-313-25667-5 (v.1), 0-313-25668-3 (v.2).

This is a comprehensive directory of theater companies around the world. The definition proposed in the text for theater companies suggests permanent acting groups under contract for a specific period each year who perform a season of plays that includes nonmusical productions. There is some hedging on the criteria, however, to accommodate the practices in various regions, which may be disposed to handle repertory theater in their own way. Thus, part-time companies without contracts are included, as well as those who engage in mime, puppetry, dance, and so forth. Entries provide name, address, significance, history, names of playwrights associated with a company, philosophy of production, facilities, and future plans. Plans are to produce a separate listing for the United States; therefore, representation from this country is limited.

Biographical Sources

861. A Biographical Dictionary of Actors, Actresses, Musicians, Dancers, Managers, and Other Stage Personnel in London, 1660–1800. Philip H. Highfill et al. Carbondale: Southern Illinois University Press, 1973–1993. 16v. ISBN 0-8093-1803-2 (v.16).

This important biographical dictionary was designed to serve somewhat as a companion piece to *The London Stage, 1660–1800* (entry 882) and was completed after twenty years of effort. Biographical sketches vary in length from a few lines to monographic essays for all persons who were members of theatrical companies, occasional performers, patentees or servants of the patent theaters, opera houses, amphitheaters, pleasure gardens, theatrical taverns, music rooms, fair booths, and other places of public entertainment. Some 8,500 persons are treated in this remarkable and extremely valuable tool. Its coverage of the unheralded as well as the famous represents a treasure house of information. The information is derived from a variety of sources, and there are many fine portraits and illustrations.

862. British Dramatists Since World War II. Stanley Weintraub, ed. Detroit: Gale Research, 1982. 2v. (Dictionary of Literary Biography, v. 13). ISBN 0-8103-0936-X.

This is a detailed description and analysis of sixty-nine of the most significant or potentially most significant playwrights in modern British play production. Such individuals as Tom Stoppard, Samuel Beckett, Harold Pinter, and Christopher Fry are treated in-depth in articles that include production lists, books published, biographical sketches, critical commentary, production photographs, programs, playscript drafts, and bibliographic references. Appendices provide a collection of essays on a variety of topics, such as Britain's postwar theater, theater companies, and stage censorship. There is a general bibliography for further reading. This tool is an extremely useful resource for both students and specialists seeking further information about important dramatists.

863. Contemporary American Dramatists. K. A. Berney and N. G. Templeton, eds. Detroit: St. James Press, 1994. 771p. (Contemporary Literature series). ISBN 1-55862-214-4.

From the now-familiar St. James series comes this well-developed, in-depth biographical dictionary treating the best and most prominent currently active playwrights, along with some who have died since 1950. The work is selective and treats 200 individuals in detailed manner, furnishing biographical sketch, complete listing of published or produced plays, and listing of separately published books. Also provided is a list of bibliographies and critical studies on the dramatist along with a critical essay of his or her work. This critique is signed by the scholar/author. Playwrights vary in terms of style and thematic focus, with such personalities as Ossie Davis, Tennessee Williams, and Edward Albee represented. There is a good general index that includes listings of plays, radio plays, television plays, and screenplays.

864. Contemporary British Dramatists. K. A. Berney and N. G. Templeton, eds. Detroit: St. James Press, 1994. 886p. (Contemporary Literature series). ISBN 1-55862-213-6.

Another of the St. James works designed to focus on a national grouping, as opposed to the more established *Contemporary Dramatists* (entry 865), which has a broader scope in its treatment of those who write in English. This work in selective fashion presents coverage of 200 British and Irish playwrights who have contributed to the stage art of the United Kingdom. As in other titles from this series, the subjects have been active within the past forty-five years and are either alive today or died after 1950. Among those treated are Samuel Beckett, John Osborne, Terence Ratigan, and David Hare. Entries furnish a biography, a bibliography, and a 1,000-word critical essay signed by a scholar, examining the writer's body of work. Also provided are a full listing of works by the playwright for stage, screen, radio, and television; play publication and production dates; and his or her own statements when available. Librettos and musicals are included. The work is well-indexed to provide easy access.

865. **Contemporary Dramatists.** 6th ed. Detroit: St. James Press, 1998. 850p. (Contemporary Writers of the English Language). ISBN 1-55862-371-X.

Continuing in the tradition and style of the earlier editions, which received considerable praise from critics, is this sixth edition which, like the others, covers in excellent detail the lives and works of some 450 living playwrights who write in the English language, an increase of nearly 100 personalities from the previous issue (1993). They have been selected by a panel of critics and scholars. Earlier material has been revised or rewritten with information updating the contributions and activities of the dramatists. More than just a biographical dictionary, this tool continues to provide excellent evaluative commentary as well as a full bibliography of each dramatist's published works. There are references to critical studies; manuscript collections are identified. An appendix provides an additional listing of playwrights who have died since the 1950s. A title index is included.

866. **Contemporary Women Dramatists.** K. A. Berney and N. G. Templeton, eds. Detroit: St. James Press, 1994. 335p. (Contemporary Literature series). ISBN 1-55862-212-8.

This title with a gender-based focus from the St. James series treats both American and European playwrights who write in the English language. As in other titles in the series (see entries 863, 864) the writers are generally currently active, although some have died since 1950. The work covers eighty-five women dramatists in the same manner as the other titles in the series. Included among those treated are Alice Childress, Wendy Wasserstein, and Ntozake Shange. Each entry contains a detailed biography, a bibliography of books and critical studies, and a 1,000-word critical essay examining the dramatist's body of work, along with her observations when available. It also supplies lists with dates of play production credits and of publication of play texts. An index facilitates ready access.

867. **Early Black American Playwrights and Dramatic Writers: A Biographical Directory and Catalog of Plays, Films, and Broadcasting Scripts.** Bernard L. Peterson, Jr. New York: Greenwood, 1990. 298p. ISBN 0-313-26621-2.

Developed as a companion volume to an earlier work on contemporary black playwrights, *Contemporary Black American Playwrights and Their Plays*, this work continues Peterson's tradition of careful and systematic effort in creating an important tool revealing information not easily found elsewhere. Nearly 220 playwrights, screenwriters, and dramatists are profiled in a thorough manner. Entries are alphabetically arranged and provide detailed biographical sketches of individuals dating from the 1820s to the 1940s. Included are the well-known, such as poet and writer Langston Hughes and the film writer Oscar Devereaux Micheaux, along with the now obscure, such as Mister Brown of the Africa Company of the early nineteenth century. Included in each entry are listings of commentary about individual works, a bibliography of other writings, and additional sources. Appendices supply pre-1950 titles, chronology of plays and radio/screen scripts, and musical librettists. There is a general index.

Peterson's earlier work, *Contemporary Black American Playwrights and Their Plays: A Biographical Directory and Dramatic Index* (Greenwood, 1988), treats the more recent writers of stage, television, radio, and film subsequent to 1950. Current addresses are supplied, with brief biographical sketches and plot descriptions and identifications. A highly selective work is Doris E. Abramson's *Negro Playwrights in the American Theatre, 1925–1959* (Columbia University Press, 1969; repr., 1991), although more in-depth analysis is given to the twenty plays (and playwrights) selected. Biographical coverage and critical appraisals are included.

868. **The Great Stage Stars: Distinguished Theatrical Careers of the Past and Present.** Sheridan Morley. New York: Facts on File, 1986. 425p. ISBN 0-8160-1401-9.

One of the more attractive biographical dictionaries, this work covers a period of 400 years, with an emphasis on those who performed in London rather than New York. Of those personalities who are living (definitely in the minority), few could be said to be young, and many are vintage. The author is the son of Robert Morley and has been a critic and an author of biographies of theatrical personalities. His descriptions are excellent and his use of comments taken from reviews blends in well with the quotes from the performers themselves. Approximately 200 personalities are covered and there are about fifty photographs, which help the reader have an informative and enjoyable experience.

869. **Stage Deaths: A Biographical Guide to International Theatrical Obituaries, 1850 to 1990.** George B. Bryan, comp. New York: Greenwood, 1991. 2v. ISBN 0-313-27593-9.

Of most use to a library supporting an extensive theater collection, this is a comprehensive index to obituaries of stage personalities found in any of nine Anglo-American newspapers (*New York Times, Los Angeles Times, Boston Transcript, London Times,* etc.) or in English-language biographies or autobiographies. All types of stage people are represented (actors, playwrights, motion picture actors, directors, composers, etc.). Entries supply brief biographical identification; alternate names, family information, dates, and theatrical work along with references to obituaries and death notices. There are numerous cross-references to related personalities. The contribution of this title is greatest in the study of regional theater and the identification of obscure personalities about whom little is known. Although the work is valuable for its inclusiveness, biographies of well-known individuals are more easily accessed directly through other tools.

870. **Theatrical Designers: An International Biographical Dictionary.** Thomas J. Mikotowicz, ed. New York: Greenwood, 1992. 365p. ISBN 0-313-26270-5.

This is a unique and valuable source for its emphasis on theatrical designers for whom biographical information is difficult to locate. This work treats 270 designers from various historical periods, beginning with the fifteenth century up to the present day. Both practitioners and theorists of the field are included as long as they have made an important or significant contribution. Most of the designers are of the modern era, with about 65 percent of them having been born since 1900. The editor is an academic who has been joined by ten contributors in producing this work. Entries are arranged alphabetically and vary in length from a few sentences to a page or two; a list of productions is included. Appendices list designers chronologically and by country of birth; a selective bibliography is furnished. There is an index of names and play titles.

Histories and Chronologies

GENERAL

*871. **History of the Theatre.** 8th ed. Oscar G. Brockett. Boston: Allyn & Bacon, 1998. 720p. ISBN 0-205-28171-0.

From the time of its initial publication in 1968, this work has been regarded as one of the best one-volume general histories of the theater. The new edition continues this tradition and provides an excellent overview of the theater from the primitives to the contemporary stage in the mid-1990s. Scholarship and attention to detail are apparent in this carefully researched and well-documented survey of theatrical practices all over the world. The emphasis has been on European theater, with American theater as an outgrowth of those influences, but there now is increased coverage of Africa, Asia, and non-Western theater. Excellent coverage is given to the Greek, Roman, and Renaissance theaters. Such elements as performance practices, architecture, and theatrical conditions are covered. There is a selective bibliography, and an index provides access. It is frequently updated (7th ed., 1995).

To help keep the resource current, a Web site was developed by Franklin J. Hildy prior to publication of the eighth edition (http://www.abacon.com/brockett/page1.html [accessed December 1999]) as *Digital Supplement to Oscar Brockett's History of the Theatre.* The purpose is to assess ways in which the new technology can be utilized to enhance educational value. Included here are updates and corrections to the printed volume.

872. **The History of World Theatre.** Margot Berthold and Felicia H. Londre. New York: Continuum, 1972–1991. 2v. ISBN 0-8264-0480-4 (v.1).

Volume 1 was first issued in 1972 and was a highly successful and scholarly effort by a German professor (Berthold). It provided a European perspective useful to American scholars and students. This volume treats the period up to the Baroque, while volume 2, by Londre, covers the frequently neglected modern period of the English Restoration to the present. Important here is the worldly view provided in a history of the theater from the time of ancient ceremonies and ritualistic practices to the trends and developments of the twentieth century. The authors are academics and furnish insight into the topic derived from awareness of historical, anthropological, and aesthetic influences. The work remains a useful tool for laypersons as well as those with professional interest.

SPECIALIZED BY TIME PERIOD OR GEOGRAPHIC REGION

873. **The American Theatre: A Chronicle of Comedy and Drama, 1865–1914.** Gerald Bordman. New York: Oxford University Press, 1994. 832p. ISBN 0-19-503764-2.

Similar in format and design to Bordman's *American Musical Theatre: A Chronicle* (entry 774), this work provides chronological coverage by opening date of every Broadway comedy and drama over a period of fifty years of early production. Sequence is season by season, and individual shows are described in terms of their plots, major cast members, and production statistics. Additional commentary treats scenery and costuming, along with quotes from contemporary critics giving indication of literary value. Useful to scholars and theater students are the excerpts taken from the plays, some of which are quite extensive. These provide perspective on and insight into the period dialogue and dramatic style characteristics of the past. In addition to plot description, this work supplies brief biographical sketches of the major personalities such as Booth, Barrymore, and Belasco. An index provides access.

874. American Theatre Companies 1749–1887. Weldon B. Durham. Westport, CT: Greenwood, 1986. 598p. ISBN 0-313-20886-7.

The first of a three-volume set on resident acting companies in this country, this work covers a most interesting and creative period, 1749–1887. Included are P.T. Barnum's American Museum Stock Company and the Thalia Theatre Company, a prominent and successful German-language theater in New York City. Coverage begins with the first important English-speaking company in the colonies and continues through the beginning of the last company organized and managed in the style of the English playhouse. Eighty-one theater groups are treated. Entries provide dates and locations of operations, manager, description of artistic and business practices, performers, designers, technicians, and so forth. An analytical description of the group's repertory and a bibliography of published and archival resources for further study are included. The excellent factual analysis makes this an important tool.

American Theatre Companies, 1888–1930, also edited by Durham (1987), is the second volume of the series and continues the first-rate coverage with treatment of 105 more companies ranging over a span of forty-plus years. *American Theatre Companies, 1931–1986* (1989) completes Durham's effort on behalf of Greenwood Press, with coverage given to an additional fifty-five years.

875. Annals of the New York Stage. George Clinton Densmore Odell. New York: Columbia University Press, 1927–1949. 15v. ISBN 0-404-07830-3.

This massive set chronicles the period from 1699 to 1894 and remains the legacy of a single individual, who persevered in the effort for over twenty years. Unfortunately, Odell was to fall short of his goal of reaching the year 1900, but his scholarship, care, and attention to detail have enabled thousands of scholars, researchers, students, and critics to draw upon a wealth of well-organized information. Each volume proceeds in chronological sequence, covering a period of years (volume 1, to 1798; volume 2, 1798 to 1821, etc.). Included in the record are the actors, plays, theaters, critical commentary, and historical background of the period. Plays are identified along with cast listings and comments from contemporary critics and reviewers. Many portraits of now obscure performers are included, for which access has been facilitated through the publication of *Index to the Portraits in Odell's Annals of the New York Stage* (American Society for Theatre Research, 1963).

876. Best Plays of 1894/1899–1989 and Yearbook of the Drama in America. New York: Dodd, Mead, 1920–1989. Ann. ISSN 0197-6435.

This annual review of play production has been an excellent vehicle for keeping abreast of developments in the world of theater. Although the title has varied in the past, as did the frequency in the early years, it is now simply referred to as the Best Plays series, or "Burns Mantle" after its initial editor. Mantle provided retrospective coverage of the early years with two volumes: *1899/1909* (1944) and *1909/1919* (1933). These volumes identify plays and furnish lists of plays produced with date, theater, and cast. The annual began in 1920 under Mantle; after his death in 1948, others later completed the final retrospective volume, *1899–1909*, in 1955. The annuals provided digests and evaluations of selected plays as well as title lists of plays produced in New York, including author, number of performances, theater, and cast. Various listings of actors, productions, awards, and statistics were supplied. There are indexes of authors, plays, casts, producers, and so forth.

After 1990 the work was renamed *The Burns Mantle Theater Yearbook* (Applause Theater Book Publishers), edited by Otis L. Guernsey and Jeffrey Sweet, then subsequently *The Otis Guernsey-Burns Mantle Theater Yearbook*. Guernsey's *Directory of the American Theater, 1894–1971* (Dodd, Mead, 1971) is a convenient index to the series by authors, titles, and composers for a period spanning seventy-seven years.

877. **Calendar of English Renaissance Drama, 1558–1642.** Yoshiko Kawachi. New York: Garland, 1986. 351p. (Garland Reference Library of the Humanities, v. 661). ISBN 0-8240-9338-0.

This is an important new work for those interested in the study of English drama. It furnishes a detailed chronology on a day-to-day basis of the Elizabethan period and carries it to the time of Cromwell, when the theaters were closed. Compiled form a variety of primary and secondary source material, the calendar identifies all types of staged entertainments, including masques, regardless of whether they were performed by professionals or amateurs. Included in the entry are dates, name of company, place, title of play, type (tragedy or comedy), author, and source of play text. There are indexes to plays, playwrights, and dramatic companies to facilitate access to the contents of this useful tool.

878. **The Cambridge History of American Theatre. V.1. Beginnings to 1870.** Don B. Wilmeth and Christopher Bigsby, eds. New York: Cambridge University Press, 1998. 525p. ISBN 0-521-47204-0.

This volume marks the beginning of a projected three-part history of the American theater from a respected and authoritative publisher. Beginning with a timeline of the period under investigation, the work is divided into six major chapters by ten prominent authorities, examining the theater in context, structure and management, plays and playwrights, actors, scenography, and so forth. Development of performance and theater art and its evolving role are described within a framework of social, political, and economic history. A bibliography and index are furnished.

The Encyclopedia of the American Theatre 1900–1975, by Edwin Bronner (A. S. Barnes, 1980), is an older work providing a useful chronology of information on non-musical plays by American or Anglo-American authors which were performed either on or off-Broadway during the first three quarters of this century. Arrangement is alphabetical by title and entries provide date of opening, theater, number of performances, and brief synopses or "capsule reviews." Authors are sometimes listed within the body of comments, with quotations from contemporary reviews as well as critical comments from Bronner. Cast members, producers, directors, and revivals are also noted, as are some set and costume designers. A specialized tool is *A History of Hispanic Theatre in the United States: Origins to 1940* by Nicolas Kanellos (University of Texas Press, 1990). The work describes the development of playhouses and theatrical groups in the United States, Spain, Mexico, and Puerto Rico from the nineteenth century through the first decades of the twentieth century.

879. **The Encyclopedia of the New York Stage, 1920–1930.** Samuel L. Leiter and Holly Hill, eds. Westport, CT: Greenwood, 1985. 2v. ISBN 0-313-23615-1 (v.1); 0-313-25037-5 (v.2).

This is the first issue of a series covering all plays, musical and non-musical, revues, and revivals staged either on or off-Broadway and reviewed by the press in the decade between 16 June 1920 and 15 June 1930. Included are the productions of ethnic and foreign-language groups as well as important "amateur" companies like the Princetown Players. Entries provide information on author, director, producer, opening, length of run, plot reviews, and in some cases, interesting anecdotes about staging, performance, or writing. There are a number of useful appendices, including a chronology, a subject listing, locales, foreign-language productions, ethnic groups, awards, sources of plays (novels), institutional theaters, foreign companies and stars, critics cited, seasonal statistics, and theaters. Indexes by proper name and title and a bibliography are furnished.

Continuing the coverage are subsequent publications, *The Encyclopedia of the New York Stage, 1930–1940* (1989) and *The Encyclopedia of the New York Stage, 1940–1950* (1992), both by Leiter.

880. The Federal Theatre Project: A Catalog Calendar of Productions.
George Mason University. Fenwick Library. Westport, CT: Greenwood,
1986. 349p. (Bibliographies and Indexes in the Performing Arts, no. 3).
ISBN 0-313-22314-9.

Much has been written in recent years about the Federal Theatre Project, a product
of the New Deal through the WPA. It was the only federally funded theater in this country and
operated between 1935 and 1939, employing many professionals and helping young people
to shape their careers. Unfortunately, hopes for a permanent national theater were shattered
by mounting criticism regarding its moral and political character. The materials from FTP
were housed in the archives of George Mason University's Fenwick Library on indefinite
loan from the Library of Congress and remained there for ten years between 1974 and 1984.
This catalog calendar identifies nearly 2,800 individual productions, arranged alphabetically by
title and includes date and location of performance, theater, name of director or choreographer,
and so forth. Materials in the collection are identified and indexed and include costume and
set designs, playscripts, music, photographs, and programs.

The New Deal Stage Selections from the Federal Theatre Project 1935–1939 is a
1998 Web site from the Library of Congress (http://lcweb2.loc.gov/ammem/fedtp/fthome.html
[accessed December 1999]). It contains information about the Project and 3,000 images of
items selected from the Collection: photographs, stage and costume designs, posters, and
even several notable playscripts. In keeping with the national library's goal to facilitate broad
public access, additional documents will be added.

881. **Historical Guide to Children's Theatre in America.** Nellie
McCaslin. Westport, CT: Greenwood, 1987. 348p. ISBN 0-313-24466-9.

McCaslin is an academic specializing in educational theater and has authored an
important reference tool for the field. The work opens with an historical essay describing the
beginnings of children's theater in 1903 and continuing through various stages, including the
enriching element of gradual participation by colleges and universities. The history is followed by an interesting selection of black-and-white photographs of important personalities
and productions. The major segment of the work is part 2, which supplies alphabetically arranged
entries treating over 400 production companies and theater associations relevant to children's
theater. Articles vary in size but generally are brief accounts of the origin, development, purpose,
goals, and physical quarters as well as touring activities. Useful appendices include a chronology
of important events from 1903 to 1986, listing and brief identification of 60 personalities, and
directory of theaters. A general index provides access.

882. **The London Stage, 1660–1800: A Calendar of Plays, Entertainments and Afterpieces. . . .** Carbondale: Southern Illinois University
Press, 1960–1968. 5 pts. in 11v. ISBN 0-8093-0437-6.

Proceeding in chronological sequence in the manner of Odell's *Annals of the New
York Stage* (entry 875) is this record of play production in London covering a period of 140
years. The work furnishes a treasury of information to the scholar and serious inquirer, as
expressed in its complete subtitle, which continues: "Together with Casts, Box-receipts and
Contemporary Comment, Compiled from the Playbills, Newspapers, and Theatrical Diaries
of the Time." Much detail is gleaned from the materials presented and one is able to determine not only the types of plays appealing to Londoners during this time period but the reception given them by the critics. Each volume is preceded by an introduction that provides
monographic treatment of the conditions of the theater and its activity.

Ben Ross Schneider's *Index to the London Stage, 1660–1800* (Southern Illinois
University, 1979) is a computer-produced index to all names and titles appearing in the set.

883. **The London Stage, 1890–1899: A Calendar of Plays and Players.** J. P. Wearing. Metuchen, NJ: Scarecrow Press, 1976. 2v. ISBN 0-8108-0910-9.

Clearly following *The London Stage, 1660–1800* (entry 882), Wearing has furnished a listing of the plays and players on the London stage during the last decade of the nineteenth century. Derived from a variety of sources, the format is established for the entries as a series of playbills. Arrangement is chronological by date of opening and by theater when there was more than one play opening on the same night. Entries furnish title, author, genre, theater, length of run and number of performances, cast, production staff, and references to reviews of opening night performances. A detailed general index facilitates access.

Wearing's subsequent efforts continue the coverage: *The London Stage, 1900–1909* is a two-volume effort published in 1981; *The London Stage, 1910–1919* was published in two volumes in 1982; *The London Stage, 1920–1929* was issued in three volumes in 1984; *The London Stage, 1930–1939* appeared in three volumes in 1990; *The London Stage, 1940–1949* was published in 1991 as a two-volume effort; and *The London Stage 1950–1959* was issued in two volumes in 1993.

884. **The Medieval Stage.** Edmund Kerchever Chambers. London: Oxford University Press, 1903; repr., Dover, 1996. 2v. ISBN 0-486-29229-0.

An old standard in the field, this work is still considered the most comprehensive and authoritative history of the period. The medieval stage is considered from the fall of the Roman Empire to the Tudor period. The work is divided into four major sections. Part 1, "Minstrelsy," and part 2, "Folk Drama," are covered in volume 1. Part 3, "Religious Drama," and Part 4, "Interludes (Tudor)," are covered in volume 2. Bibliographies are provided, and appendices contain original documents. A subject index facilitates access.

Another major effort by Chambers is *The Elizabethan Stage* (London: Clarendon Press, 1923; repr. with corr., 1974). This is a four-volume work that is also a standard in the field, although parts of it, such as the section on the Elizabethan playhouse, have been updated in other histories. The variety of topics includes the Court and control of the stage, companies and playhouses, staging at Court and in the theaters, and various plays and authors. Appendices contain original documents, and a general index is provided.

885. **Theatre in the United States: A Documentary History.** Barry B. Witham, ed. New York: Cambridge University Press, 1996– . (In progress). ISBN 0-521-30858-5.

This is the first of a projected two-volume set providing insight into the origin and development of theater through presentation and exposition of various documents. This volume covers the period from 1750 up to the early days of World War I in 1915, and is organized into three distinct chronological sections:1750–1810, 1810–1865, and 1865–1915. Each section is handled by a different scholar and contains an introductory essay, array of documents (business transactions, letters, newspaper reports, reviews, memoirs, etc.), and interpretation/commentary.

Famous American Playhouses is a two-volume set, also a documentary history, by William C. Young (American Library Association, 1973) and is part of a documentary series. Young describes famous playhouses, with volume 1 covering the period 1716–1899 and volume 2 treating the years 1900–1971. A variety of materials has been collected, including excerpts from newspapers, periodicals, letters, diaries, journals, autobiographies, reviews, magazines, playbills, publicity materials, and architectural descriptions. Some 200 buildings of historical, architectural, or cultural prominence are examined.

886. **20th Century Theatre.** Glenn Meredith Loney. New York: Facts on File, 1983. 2v. ISBN 0-87196-463-5.

An attractive and easy-to-use chronological record of theatrical developments in the United States and Great Britain, this work has proved to be a popular choice for librarians and their patrons. The arrangement is year-by-year from 1900 to 1979, classified by topics such as American premieres, British premieres, revivals and repertoires, births/deaths/debuts. and theaters/productions. Within each topic, the activities are listed chronologically from 1 January to 31 December. Many production photographs are used. A chronology of this type will work as a date finder, personality identifier, and event locator when the indexes are sufficient to provide access. It appears that this is true in this case, with a general index of names, production tables, and miscellaneous subjects (awards, companies, schools, etc.).

Reviews and Criticism

Additional evaluative and descriptive commentary on both individual titles and theater in general may be found in the section "Dictionaries, Encyclopedias, and Handbooks."

887. **American Drama Criticism: Interpretations, 1890–1977.** 2d ed. Floyd Eugene Eddleman, comp. Hamden, CT: Shoe String Press, 1979. 488p. **Supp. I.,** 1984. 255p. **Supp. II.,** 1989. 269p. **Supp. III.,** 1992. ISBN 0-208-01713-5. **Supp. IV.,** 1996. 239p. ISBN 0-208-02393-3.

This work supersedes the first edition by Palmer and Dyson (1967) and its two supplements (1970, 1976). It provides a listing of interpretations of American plays published over a period of nearly ninety years. These interpretations (critiques, reviews, etc.) appeared in 200 books and monographs and in over 400 periodicals. The arrangement of entries is by playwright and then by title. Only the works of dramatists who are or were citizens of the United States are included, except for a few Canadians and Caribbean writers whose works are performed here. The date of first production is noted and musical plays are included. There are indexes of critics and of adapted authors and works. The supplements, also by Eddleman except for Supp. IV (edited by Lanelle Daniel), furnish listings of hundreds of additional interpretations published from 1978 through 1993.

888. **Chinese Drama: An Annotated Bibliography of Commentary, Criticism, and Plays in English Translation.** Manuel D. Lopez. Metuchen, NJ: Scarecrow Press, 1991. 525p. ISBN 0-8108-2347-0.

This is a comprehensive bibliography of both primary and secondary source material concerning Chinese drama. Books, articles, and dissertations are identified in either of two sections, providing a total of some 3,300 citations. The first part provides historical treatment with references to literature covering Chinese drama from its origins to the mid-1980s. Arrangement is topical, such as "background and development" or "comparison with other national theatres," which in turn is subdivided by format (books, articles, dissertations, parts of books). Part 2 identifies the plays themselves, all of which have appeared in English translation. These are listed alphabetically by title, with citations arranged by type of coverage (summaries, commentaries, etc.). Only about 25 percent of the citations are annotated, and then very briefly, producing some unfavorable comments from reviewers. Nevertheless, it is a useful tool for students or specialists in theater or Asian studies.

889. **Critical Survey of Drama: English Language Series.** Rev. ed. Frank N. Magill, ed. Pasadena, CA: Salem Press, 1994. 7v. ISBN 0-89356-851-1.

Begun in the early 1980s, with coverage of short fiction (entry 1119), poetry (entries 1284, 1294), and long fiction (entries 1251, 1293), the Critical Survey series treats the different genres in standardized manner, with individual writers arranged alphabetically. The initial edition of this work was published in 1985 as a six-volume set, followed by a single-volume supplement in 1987. The current effort provides an update and revision following the same pattern. Coverage begins with a listing of the author's major works within the genre and progresses with brief description of the writer's success with other literary forms, an assessment of his or her major achievements, a biography, an analysis of major works in this genre, and a list of publications in other forms, ending with a bibliography of secondary sources. It treats over 200 dramatists representing all historical periods and includes British, Irish, Canadian, Australian, African, and West Indian as well as U.S. nationals. Arrangement is alphabetical by dramatist. In the final volume, there is a collection of essays on the drama in all its phases through different historical periods and in various nations.

Critical Survey of Drama: Foreign Language Series (Salem Press, 1986) is another Magill product in six volumes and completes the critical survey series. The first five volumes cover 199 dramatists from antiquity to the present. There is a European bias, with 44 percent having written in French or German, 23 percent in Spanish or Italian, 15 percent in languages of central or southeastern Europe (including Russian), and 7 percent in Scandinavian. Asian languages represent 3 percent and Latin American 1 percent. There is no African inclusion. Updating both of the works is *Critical Survey of Drama: Supplement* (1987). It supplies forty-nine additional entries not included in the two major editions. Most of the new entries are from the twentieth century; there is African representation along with the others.

890. Drama Criticism: Criticism of the Most Significant and Widely Studied Dramatic Works from All the World's Literature. Lawrence J. Trudeau. Detroit: Gale Research, 1991– . 8v. (In progress). ISSN 1056-4349.

This new entry in the Gale line of bio-critical series in the area of literature provides a focus on the evaluation and literary merit of plays and playwrights of international consequence and representing various countries of origin. In volume 1 (1991), coverage is given to fourteen dramatists thought to have contributed to a considerable degree to the development of such literature. Among the principals treated are Arthur Miller, Lillian Hellman, Yukio Mishima, and Karel Capek. Since that time eight more volumes have been issued, with volume 9 published in 1999. Entries furnish biographical sketches and critical commentary, both from critics and the playwrights themselves, providing much insight for the student and scholar.

An older but still useful title in two volumes is *Drama Criticism*, by Arthur Coleman and Gary R. Tyler (Alan Swallow, 1966–1971). This is one of the several checklists from this publisher of interpretations generally found in reference collections. The work cites interpretations in English that appeared in books or periodicals, but the plays are from different countries of origin. Volume 1 lists critiques or interpretations of American or English plays published between 1940 and 1964. Volume 2 (published five years later) covers classical and continental plays for which the interpretations were published between 1950 and 1968. Arrangement of entries is alphabetical by dramatist, then by title of play.

891. Major Modern Dramatists. Rita Stein et al., comps. and eds. New York: Ungar, 1984–1986. 2v. (Library of Literary Criticism). ISBN 0-8044-3267-8 (v.1), 0-8044-3268-6 (v.2).

This set is part of the well-known Library of Literary Criticism series, which seeks to provide a collection of excerpts of literary criticism on various literary efforts. This is the first effort to capture the literary tradition of a genre rather than those of a time period. Volume 1, issued in 1984, covers American, British, Irish, German, Austrian, and Swiss dramatists, while volume 2 (1986) extends European coverage to French, Belgian, Russian, Polish,

Spanish, Italian, Norwegian, Swedish, Czech, and Hungarian playwrights. The format and purpose of the set are similar to those of previous efforts, providing an overview of the critical reception given to a dramatist from the beginning of his or her career up to the present time through excerpts from reviews, articles, and books. Treatment is given only to major dramatists, beginning with Isben and late nineteenth-century realism up to the present.

892. **The New York Times Theatre Reviews, 1870–1992.** Hamden, CT: Garland, 1992. 27v. ISBN 0-8153-0351-3. **Bienn. Supp.**, 1971– . ISSN 0160-0583.

The first segment to be published of this chronological collection of reviews, published by the New York Times and covering the years 1920–1970, appeared in ten volumes in 1971, with the final volume given to indexes and appendices. The segment covering the early years, 1870–1919, was published in five volumes in 1976. Garland has continued the coverage of the biennial supplements that began in 1971/1972, and now offers a twenty-seven-volume set through 1992. Thus we are able to consult a review as it appeared in the *New York Times* for a period of 122 years. Reviews are arranged chronologically and there are excellent appendices of awards and prizes and of productions and runs by season. The work is indexed by titles, production companies, names of performers, and names of others associated with the staging of the play; separate indexes are available for the initial two segments. Biennial supplements are separately indexed. Reviews are detailed and have earned a reputation for quality and perceptiveness. If a party subscribes to the online version of the *New York Times* (http://www.nytimes.com), he or she is able to access a file of recent reviews in full text.

New York Theatre Critics Reviews (New York Theatre Critics Reviews, 1940–) is a useful weekly publication that furnishes copies of reviews as they appeared in a variety of New York newspapers as well as periodicals and even on network television. It is a useful tool for comparing reviews from different critics.

893. Selected Theatre Criticism. Anthony Slide, ed. Metuchen, NJ: Scarecrow Press, 1985–1986. 3v. ISBN 0-8108-1811-6 (v.1), 0-8108-1844-2 (v.2), 0-8108-1846-9 (v.3).

The complete set of three volumes covers the first half of the twentieth century, providing a collection of original reviews to productions of the New York stage. Reviews are reproduced in their entirety from an array of periodicals including *Century Magazine*, *The Critic*, and *The Forum*. Volume 1 covers the period 1900–1919, volume 2, 1920–1930, and volume 3, 1931–1950. All types of shows are included: dramas, revues, comedies, and musicals, over 500 in all. Arrangement in each volume is alphabetical by title, and production information is given along with the reviews.

James M. Salem's *Guide to Critical Reviews* (Scarecrow Press, 1984–) appears in several parts, each dealing with a different entertainment form. Citations to critical reviews are furnished rather than the reviews themselves. Part 1 covers the American drama 1909–1982 and was last issued in 1984. It is a continuing publication. (See entry 978 for more information.)

Play Production

894. Movement: From Person to Actor to Character. Theresa Mitchell. Lanham, MD: Scarecrow Press, 1998. 117p. ISBN 0-8108-3328-X.

This is a concise but highly useful manual for novice actors, dancers, and others to use in gaining control of their body movement while on stage. The writing is clear and forthright, with enumeration of exercises to follow in developing awareness of what the body is doing in terms of appropriate behavior in keeping with the nature of the staged action. In addition to exercises and anatomical exposition, the work addresses the importance of relaxation with mental routines and helpful suggestions. As an academic, the author is familiar with the needs of young actors and emphasizes the importance of personal responsibility in the learning process through self-analysis by keeping a journal or log. An index helps to provide access.

895. Producing Theatre: A Comprehensive Legal and Business Guide. 2d ed. Donald C. Farber. New York: Limelight Editions, 1997. 472p. ISBN 0-8791-0103-2.

Farber, an attorney, had combined and updated the contents of two earlier works published in the 1960s to provide the first edition of this guide in 1981. The second Limelight edition maintains the tool's reputation as a comprehensive and comprehensible guide to the legal documents and procedures involved in play production. It is geared to the business of producing plays anywhere, be it on Broadway, resident theater, or stock, and covers all possible and probable aspects. Information on contractual agreements is presented in precise and understandable fashion, furnishing samples of actual contracts. Revised and expanded by some ninety pages over the earlier work, it represents the most authoritative and up-to-date legal and business guide in the realm of theater, with fourteen chapters given to coverage of all aspects of commercial production. It begins with acquisition of a property, then examines options, contract, and license possibilities, and ends with considerations regarding pre-opening, during run, and after-opening periods. A general index provides access.

896. The Small Theatre Handbook: A Guide to Management and Production. Joann Green. Harvard, MA: Harvard Common; distr., Port Washington, NY: Independent Publishers Group, 1981. 163p. ISBN 0-916782-20-4.

The small theater is defined as having an annual budget of under $100,000; this work is a manual of management practice for these theaters. The author has served as the artistic director for the Cambridge Ensemble Theatre and therefore is well equipped to handle the discussion of problems and to provide practical directions. The work is considered most useful in regard to organization and administration, furnishing many examples, such as budgeting and fund raising. Information on production, such as choosing the play, directors, actors, and so forth, is somewhat sketchy. In general, the tool should be helpful to people associated with the business end of play production in colleges, neighborhood theaters, repertoires, and so forth.

Another work in this vein is *The Complete Play Production Handbook*, by Carl Allensworth et al. (Harper & Row, 1991). This is more focused on the production end in its goal of assisting schools, colleges, and little theaters in mounting a creditable production. *Play Directing in the School: A Drama Director's Survival Guide* (Meriwether, 1998), by David Grote, is a complete manual for those involved in school productions. Treatment is given to all the pitfalls and hurdles regarding budgeting, scheduling, and school politics, as well as motivation and discipline of young actors.

897. Stage Makeup. 8th ed. Richard Corson. Englewood Cliffs, NJ: Prentice-Hall, 1990. 411p. ISBN 0-13-840539-5.

This specialized handbook is a standard in the field and has been revised frequently (6th ed., 1981; 7th ed., 1986). Although a new edition has not appeared in a decade, it continues as a major resource for instructors, makeup artists, and actors responsible for their own makeup. The handbook is detailed in its exposition and well-illustrated to facilitate the user's comprehension of the techniques and applications. Factors include skin tone, facial anatomy, and lighting. Application of greasepaint, beards, wigs, artificial limbs, hair styles, fashions and more is described in-depth.

Stage Makeup Step-By-Step: The Complete Guide to Basic Makeup, Planning and Design Makeup, Adding and Reducing Age, Ethnic Makeup, Special Effects, by Rosemarie Swinfield (Betterway Books, 1994), is another fine manual. Although quite brief, it provides excellent color illustrations along with needed explanatory text regarding selection, application, and cleanup of the process. Swinfield's *Period Make-up for the Stage: Step By Step* (Betterway Books, 1997) targets different makeup preparations for both men and women by historical period from ancient Egypt to the 1980s. The most recent addition is *Stage Makeup: The Actor's Complete Step-By-Step Guide to Today's Techniques and Materials* (Backstage Books, 1999), edited by Laura Thudium. Her work is designed to benefit the teacher and student rather than the advanced professional.

898. **Stagecraft: The Complete Guide to Theatrical Practice.** Trevor R. Griffiths, ed. Oxford, UK: Phaidon, 1982; distr., New York: Drama Book, 1984; repr., 1990. 192p. ISBN 0-7148-2644-8.

This British work is a practical handbook to all basic aspects of nonprofessional play production. Its ten chapters cover such considerations as directing, stage management, acting, set design, light design, costumes, makeup, and even the conduct of a workshop. Chapters are contributed by authorities in these topical areas, and the work is heavily illustrated both in color and black-and-white. Although the British terminology may seem awkward at first, the material furnished is useful and in keeping with the overall purpose, which is to achieve the best possible production with the fewest pitfalls. A glossary is provided, and a general index aids access.

A more specialized effort is Francis Reid's *The Stage Lighting Handbook*, now in its fifth edition (A & C Black, 1996). Geared to the needs of amateurs, this tool describes the purposes, equipment, rigging, and so forth and enumerates the basic steps in lighting design for a variety of stage presentations. *The ABC of Stage Lighting*, also by Reid (Drama Book, 1992), provides definitions for terminology employed in lighting. Reid is an expert in the field and provides practical and up-to-date technical terms, with both illustrations and cross-references.

FILM, RADIO, TELEVISION, AND VIDEO

Bibliographic Guides

899. **On the Screen: A Film, Television, and Video Research Guide.** Kim N. Fisher. Littleton, CO: Libraries Unlimited, 1986. 209p. ISBN 0-87287-448-6.

Coverage is given to primarily U.S. writings from the 1960s to the 1980s, furnishing information on film, television, and video in all aspects of production. Arrangement of entries is alphabetical within broad-based topical categories, each receiving an entry number and accompanying description. Information includes author, title, imprint, pagination, and ISBN or other identifying number. The value of the work lies mainly in its well-developed annotations, combining both descriptive and evaluative commentary, and on its scope in treating three different media within a single work. Databases are identified, as are research centers, archives, societies, and associations. There are both author-title and subject indexes.

PERIODICALS

900. **Film, Television, and Video Periodicals: A Comprehensive Annotated List.** Katharine Loughney. New York: Garland, 1991. 431p. (Garland Reference Library of the Humanities, v. 1032). ISBN 0-8240-0647-X.

This is a useful and comprehensive listing of about 900 of the most widely used and accessible periodicals in the fields of film, television, and/or video. Emphasis is placed on the inclusion of titles in the English language, although some foreign periodicals are treated as well. The titles represent a wide diversity of interests and audiences, from the scholarly (*Film Criticism*) to the technical (*Broadcast Engineering*), and even the popular (*TV Guide*). Arrangement of entries is alphabetical by title, supplying publisher, address, telephone number, frequency, ISSN, LC and Dewey call number, and OCLC number. Annotations vary in size but are generally brief, running thirty to fifty words. Most impressive is the comprehensiveness of the coverage given video periodicals, with nearly 275 titles. Cross-references are supplied to related entries; there are several indexes providing access by country, genre, level, and title.

901. **Union List of Film Periodicals: Holdings of Selected American Collections.** Anna Brady. Westport, CT: Greenwood, 1984. 316p. ISBN 0-313-23702-6.

To facilitate research in the field, this finding list covers the periodical holdings of thirty-five American libraries with important film collections. Periodical titles are from nearly sixty countries and include a broad range of emphases in the field, such as film and art, industry and entertainment, and sociological and psychological perspectives. Over 1,600 titles are listed, and country of publication, language, ISSN, publication dates, and title changes are given. Numbers of volumes the various libraries hold are enumerated. There is an index of title changes that includes those titles having undergone at least three changes, and a geographical index lists the titles under country of publication.

Bibliographies and Catalogs

902. **The Film Index: A Bibliography.** Writers Program of the Work Projects Administration of the City of New York. Volume 1. New York: H. W. Wilson, 1941; repr., Kraus, 1988. Volume 2. New York: Kraus International, 1985. Volume 3. New York: Kraus International, 1985. ISBN 0-527-29326-1 for the set.

This three-part annotated bibliography has had a long and interesting history since the first volume appeared in 1941. It was not to be completed until forty-four years later, because of cutbacks in the budget of the WPA in 1939. The Wilson Company published the first volume, *The Film As Art*, with the Museum of Modern Art. This is an extensive, annotated bibliography of books and articles on the history, technique, and types of motion pictures, based primarily on the collections of the Museum of Modern Art and the New York Public Library. The remaining cards for the other two volumes had been held in the Archives of the Museum; Kraus finally arranged for their publication in the 1980s. Volume 2, *The Film As Industry*, covers English-language materials, excluding newspapers, based on the holdings of the New York Public Library, with additional listings derived from periodical indexes. Entries are classified under major subject headings in alphabetical order. Volume 3, *The Film in Society*, identifies books and articles under such topics as education, censorship, and moral and religious aspects. All annotations are original from their period of preparation and the complete set is an important contribution to film research.

903. **Film Study: An Analytical Bibliography.** Frank Manchel. Rutherford, NJ: Fairleigh Dickinson University Press; distr., Cranbury, NJ: Associated University Presses, 1990. 4v. ISBN 0-8386-3186-X(v.1).

The author is a knowledgeable academic and writer who has updated and expanded his 1974 effort, *Film Study: A Resource Guide.* The new edition supplies introductory essays and bibliographies to each of six approaches to the teaching of cinema. Individual chapters are given to genres, stereotypes, themes, comparative media, periods, and film history. These chapters are subdivided by various topics, with listings of relevant monographs and films. There are over 2,000 books covered along with annotations of varying length in the first three volumes; volume 4 supplies various appendices, including directories, along with indexes to authors, titles, and film personalities.

904. **The Macmillan Film Bibliography: A Critical Guide to the Literature of the Motion Picture.** George Rehrauer. New York: Macmillan, 1982. 2v. ISBN 0-02-696400-7.

A long-time contributor to the reference literature of film study, the author has served as professor at Rutgers University and used his expertise to produce his most extensive work. This two-volume set covers, in a profound and analytical manner, the contributions of nearly 6,800 books on the topic. Although there are a few items that are not annotated, most of the entries provide excellent descriptions of the content and an assessment of value. Some of these annotations are quite lengthy and have been praised for their wit and sometimes caustic commentary. Arrangement is alphabetical by title in volume 1, while volume 2 provides indexes by subjects, authors, and scripts.

905. **Radio and Television: A Selected, Annotated Bibliography.** William E. McCavitt, comp. Metuchen, NJ: Scarecrow Press, 1978. 229p. ISBN 0-8108-1113-8. **Supp. One: 1977–1981**, 1982. 155p. ISBN 0-8108-1556-7. **Supp. Two: 1982–1986**, 1989. ISBN 0-8108-2108-3.

The basic edition furnishes 1,100 annotated entries representing selections from the literature of broadcasting over a period of fifty years from 1926 to 1976. There is a classified arrangement of twenty-one broad subject headings, including such topical matter as history, regulation, organization, broadcasting, and audience. These categories are generally subdivided further. The work has been criticized in the past for lack of sufficient access because of the fragmentation and scattering of entries on similar subjects, and the general categories are awkward as subject headings for some of the entries. There is an author index that provides access by name when known. The first supplement added six new subject headings (news, advertising, corporate video, home video, etc.) but still contained no detailed subject index. The second supplement, by P. K. Pringle, continues the coverage with another 1,000 entries. The work is recommended for those with a serious interest.

906. **Radio Broadcasting from 1920 to 1990: An Annotated Bibliography.** Diane Foxhill Carothers. New York: Garland, 1991. 564p. (Garland Reference Library of the Humanities, v. 967). ISBN 0-8240-1209-7.

The importance of this title lies both in its inclusiveness and its currency. Designed to appeal to a wide audience, from scholar to hobbyist, this bibliography by a communication librarian in academe provides comprehensive coverage of writings over a period of seventy years. Emphasis is on books, although there are government documents and some serials among the 1,704 titles treating radio broadcasting. Theses and dissertations are omitted. Coverage is provided in eleven chapters representing full coverage of the field: history, biography, production concerns, programming, regulations, international and educational aspects, technology, careers, amateur radio, women and minorities, and reference sources. Annotations supply brief but informative description. Unfortunately, there are no cross-references between entries and no subject indexing, which may hinder access to particular entries. Author and title indexes are supplied.

907. Television & Ethics: A Bibliography. Thomas W. Cooper et al. Boston: G. K. Hall, 1988. 203p. ISBN 0-8161-8966-8.

This unique work is represented by its authors as a seminal work in a field where it is sorely needed. The authors are academics at Emerson College, where study of television ethics has been emphasized within the communications curriculum. The authors have utilized the talents of a number of scholars to serve as advisors on the development of this work, designed to reveal the influence of television and its ethical implications. Coverage is thorough and embraces 1,171 entries spanning antiquity to the present day, organized under various categories. Criteria for inclusion and strategies of searching out the items are described for the user, affirming its scholarly nature and its emphasis on relevance and substance of the documents. Annotations are supplied for nearly half the entries; these are brief and mainly descriptive of content. Author and subject indexes are given.

Film/Video Sources—Bibliographies, Indexes, and Catalogs

Film listings and catalogs are extremely valuable for both reference and research in film work. Catalogs of important collections are available, as are numerous filmographies based on genres (horror, western, science-fiction, detective, etc.) or an individual's work. Additional items to identify films or persons associated with them can be found in the sections "Dictionaries, Encyclopedias, and Handbooks" and "Reviews and Criticism."

908. African American Films Through 1959: A Comprehensive, Illustrated Filmography. Jefferson, NC: McFarland, 1998. 312p. ISBN 0-7864-0307-1.

This is an important information tool, providing identification and in some cases detailed exposition of 1,324 feature films, short subjects, and musical soundies featuring African-American casts or providing topical treatment of African-Americans. The Negro film industry was flourishing in the 1920s, with studios in several of the major cities in this country. Their products were shown in theaters catering to this audience before the time of integration and lasting until the 1950s. Their record of accomplishment represents an important element in the history of American film making. Each film entry supplies production date, producer, director, company, distributor, cast, type, genre, and so forth along with synopsis of plot and references to reviews. Appendices provide film credits for 1,850 actors and listing of film companies and their films.

909. The American Film Institute Catalog of Motion Pictures Produced in the United States. New York: R. R. Bowker, 1971–1988. Repr. and continued, University of California, 1988– .

This multi-volume work is the most extensive listing of films ever compiled. Based in the Library of Congress and funded by grants from both public and private sources, it was developed in several series or parts. Part A treats films 1893 to 1910, parts F1 through F6 describe feature films from 1911 through 1970, parts S1 through S6 will identify short films from 1911 through 1970; and parts N1 through N6 will identify newsreels from 1908 through 1970. Regarding feature length films (F1–F6), the most recent issues represent a reprint series begun in 1988 and published by the University of California. Available now are the volumes treating the period 1893–1910 (1995), 1911–1920 (1988), 1921–1930 (1996), 1931–1940 (1993), and 1961–1970 (1996). The 1941–1950 coverage will be available in 1999. In addition, an comprehensive volume treating the period 1950–1994 was published in 1996. The first volume of each unit lists films alphabetically by title and furnishes complete information on physical description, production credits, cast credits, and content (genre, source, summary). There are indexes of credits and of subjects.

The Film Catalog: A List of Holdings in the Museum of Modern Art, by Jon Gartenberg et al. (G. K. Hall, 1985), was published in honor of the fiftieth anniversary of MOMA's film department. The catalog describes some 5,500 titles acquired between 1935 and 1980, ranging form fiction and documentary to television commercials.

910. **American Film Cycles: The Silent Era.** Larry Langman. Westport, CT: Greenwood, 1998. 400p.(Bibliographies and Indexes in the Performing Arts, no. 22). ISBN 0-313-30657-5.

Another reference source from this prolific and respected teacher and freelance writer provides a listing of more than 1,000 silent films organized into forty categories or themes relevant to societal forces operating at the time of their release. These themes, not to be confused with genres, range from the biographical and detective dramas to such categories as the "Black Hand." The work is divided into two major periods; 1900–1919 was dominated by the one- and two-reelers, while 1920–1929 (Golden Age) saw the ascendancy of the feature length film. Essays on the thematic categories are detailed and full, providing insight into the political and social context; synopses of film titles treat their success or failure to represent a social perspective.

911. **Bowker's Complete Video Directory.** New Providence, NJ: R. R. Bowker, 1990– . Irreg. ISSN 1051-290X.

This monumental and comprehensive guide to available videos of all kinds was first issued in 1990, then 1992, and again in 1993 and 1994. It appears to have settled on an annual frequency, with coverage in three volumes beginning in 1993. Within the three-volume effort are entries treating more than 100,000 programs from more than 1,500 manufacturers and distributors. There are over 40,000 entertainment and performance videos and over 60,000 educational and special interest videos. Entries generally supply brief annotations, along with full purchasing information and identification of formats. Presently it is highly competitive with the well-established *The Video Source Book* (entry 919) as the major tool in the field.

Prior to this, from 1988 to 1989, Bowker had issued *Variety's Complete Home Video Directory* as an annual with quarterly supplements targeting the entertainment, cultural, and general interests of the home video market. *Variety's Video Directory Plus* was made available on CD-ROM, providing not only brief annotations of all available home videocassettes and videodiscs but also several thousand full-length reviews from *Variety* (entry 959). It has been updated quarterly.

912. **The British Film Catalogue, 1895–1985: A Reference Guide.** Denis Gifford. New York: Facts on File, 1986. 1000p. ISBN 0-8160-1554-6.

This important source replaces an earlier effort published in 1973, which covered the period 1895–1970, and is divided into two sections. The first embraces the material in the earlier issue and treats every film made in Great Britain or Ireland, whether released or not, from 1895 to 1970. The second section presents the new material, covering the period from 1971 to 1985. Arrangement of entries is chronological in both sections. Nearly 15,300 films are identified, with entries supplying information regarding production company, plot summary, indication of subject, length, producer, director, source of story, cast list, and awards. Many abbreviations are utilized. The second section, 1971–1985, contains a separate introduction and key to abbreviations. There is an alphabetical index to titles, but not to other elements.

913. **Enser's Filmed Books and Plays: A List of Books and Plays from Which Films Have Been Made, 1928–1991.** Upd. ed. Ellen Baskin and Mandy Hicken, comps. Brookfield, VT: Ashgate Publishing, 1993. 970p. ISBN 1-85742-026-8.

Enser's standard work has been revised by other compilers for the first time and now cumulates the content of the previous issues (first published in 1968) while adding another five years of coverage to the last issue published in 1988. Basically, it is a list of some 6,000 English-language films derived from books and plays. It provides a unique approach to both film buffs and serious students for identifying such works over a sixty-three-year period beginning with the onset of talking pictures. Never claiming to be a completely exhaustive listing, the bibliography is accessed through excellent indexes. Entries in the title index give the name of the distributing company and year of registration, as well as author, publisher, and book title. The author index list works by the author that have been made into films and includes publisher, as well as film distributor. There is a "change of original title" index that lists original book titles when they differ from their motion pictures.

An effort that complements this coverage is *Books and Plays in Films, 1896–1915: Literary, Theatrical, and Artistic Sources of the First Twenty Years of Motion Pictures*, by Denis Gifford (McFarland, 1991). Gifford lists some 3,000 film presentations derived from artistic or literary works (ballet songs, operas, and comic strips, as well as novels and short stories). Most of these early silent films were relatively short and thus have not received much attention from writers of guides such as this. Arrangement is alphabetical by name of author or creator, after which are listed the films in chronological order. Companies are given and genre is identified.

914. **The Films of Mack Sennett: Credit Documentation from the Mack Sennett Collection at the Margaret Herrick Library.** Warren M. Sherk. Lanham, MD: Scarecrow Press, 1998. 321p. ISBN 0-8108-3443-X.

This is a fine filmography of the work of a real pioneer in the industry and one of the most prolific film producers of all time. Sennett died in 1960 at the age of eighty. He was famous for his comedy series, especially the Keystone Kops. The work is based primarily on the film collection of the Academy of Motion Picture Arts and Sciences in Beverly Hills, but has also utilized other sources for as complete a list as possible. There are 855 entries, each supplying production company, distribution company, release date, cast list, director, cinematographer, and length. Arrangement is alphabetical by title, and the text follows an introduction and guide to using the filmography. Appendices include a chronological index of film titles and a listing of production numbers. A name index provides access.

915. **From Headline Hunter to Superman: A Journalism Filmography.** Richard R. Ness. Lanham, MD: Scarecrow Press, 1997. 789p. ISBN 0-8108-3291-7.

Based on the author's doctoral dissertation, this filmography seeks to examine the changing role and perception accorded journalists of various media and journalistic endeavor as portrayed in feature films from the silent era to 1996. Most films are American, although some foreign productions are included. This is a comprehensive and detailed effort, providing entries to 2,165 motion pictures of varying quality organized alphabetically within chrono-logically arranged chapters by decade. Chapters begin with an introductory essay examining the important social developments of that period and relating them to changing film images and portrayals. Individual entries supply studio, running time, production credits, and cast members, with brief narrative of varying length providing plot summary and critical analysis.

The Media in the Movies: A Catalog of American Journalism Films, 1900–1996, by Larry Langman (McFarland, 1998), is a similar effort about half the size of the *Headline Hunter*. An introductory essay opens the work. It is a filmography identifying more than 1,000 feature films and serials whose central characters or plots were focused on journalism. Most of the titles treat newspaper reporters and reporting, but radio, television, and photojournalism also are represented in the mix. Entries are arranged alphabetically and furnish production credits, casts, and brief plot descriptions, and sometimes analysis.

*916. **The International Film Index, 1895–1990.** Alan Goble, ed. New Providence, NJ: K. G. Saur, 1991. 2v. ISBN 0-86291-623-2.

This work was developed as a comprehensive reference tool by a single individual, who has devoted twenty years to its production. The end-product is a massive, two-volume listing of more than 177,000 films from 25,000 directors listed under 232,000 titles. Listings were culled from over 400 reference books listed in the bibliography in volume 2. About 90 percent of all mainstream motion pictures for the United States and Europe have been listed, although accuracy is dependent upon the veracity of the reference books used as sources. Also included are listings for 120 countries outside of Europe. Feature length films, animated films, art films, documentaries, serials, and shorts are all treated. Volume 2 provides a filmography for directors, identifying their country, dates, and films in chronological order. The work represents a synthesis of the content of numerous reference books; its omissions, gaps, and inaccuracies are representative of past oversights. In 1995 **International Film Index on CD-ROM* was issued by Bowker-Saur and contained 245,000 titles covering films released in over 165 countries between 1895 and 1996.

Directors and Their Films: A Comprehensive Reference, 1895–1990, by Brooks Bushnell (McFarland, 1993), provides excellent coverage of more than 108,000 films of various types, not limited to those of feature length, along with their directors. The first part supplies alphabetical listings of directors, under which are listed their motion pictures in chronological sequence. Part 2 lists the films alphabetically and supplies name of director and year of release. Variant titles are all included, both in English and foreign languages. The work does not include those films made for television.

917. **Leonard Maltin's Movie & Video Guide, 2000.** 19th ed. Leonard Maltin. New York: Plume, 1999. 1641p. ISBN 0-452-28123-7.

This is one of the well-known, cumulative annual guides providing comprehensive and somewhat controversial (overly critical??) coverage of motion pictures. Unlike a number of others, it is not limited to films that appear in video. The author is one of the leading critics, and in this work he treats more than 20,000 titles, having added several hundred new ones up to the summer of 1999. Reviews are very brief but informative and employ a rating scale ranging from four stars to "bomb." Maltin's brief reviews are lively, employing a sense of humor in the capsule commentaries. Included are release dates, running time, director, major cast, and video availability. Entries are arranged alphabetically and are accessed through indexes by performers and directors.

Video Movie Guide 2000, by Mick Martin et al. (14th ed., Ballantine, 1999), is another well-known, comprehensive guide to more than 17,000 films, serials, and television programs found on video. Newly added entries (about 500) are identified with a symbol, and are part of the alphabetically-arranged text. Capsule reviews are furnished, along with a rating system from five stars to "turkey." Included also are release dates, directors, and principal cast. As in the Maltin guide, there are indexes by director and cast members.

*918. National Union Catalog. Audiovisual Materials. Washington, DC: Library of Congress, 1983– . Q. ISSN 0734-7669.

This catalog, also available in microfiche, is the latest entry in a line of resource tools to the cataloging of the national library, which began with the *Library of Congress Catalog: Motion Pictures and Filmstrips*. This was issued quarterly and in quinquennial editions between 1953 and 1973. Its identity was established at that time as part of the *National Union Catalog* as well, and it attempted to cover all educational motion pictures and filmstrips released in this country. From 1972 to 1978, it was known by the title *Films and Other Materials for Projection*, and added sets of slides and other transparencies to its field of coverage. From 1979 to 1982, it was the *Library of Congress. Audiovisual Materials* and included video recordings and kits. Presently bearing the masthead of NUC, its purpose and organization remain much the same, and it contains 124,000 films, videos, filmstrips, and so forth. Succeeding issues in a volume cumulate those before it, furnishing indexes by name, subject, title, and series. The work is available online and on magnetic tape as *LC MARC; Visual Materials beginning with the year 1972, as part of the Current Cataloging Database from the Library of Congress.

919. The Video Source Book. Detroit: Gale Research, 1979– . Ann. ISSN 0277-3317.

Begun by the National Video Clearinghouse in 1979 as an annual publication, this comprehensive tool is now issued by Gale Research. It identifies and describes prerecorded video program titles of all types available on videotape and videodisc. Arrangement is by title, and several indexes, including one by subject category, are furnished to provide access to materials of interest to home, business, or educational institutions. As an early entrant in the field of video documentation, it is now in its twenty-third edition (1999) and issued in two volumes. It acts as a guide for some 150,000 programs currently available from several thousand sources.

920. VideoHound's Golden Movie Retriever 2000. Martin Connors and Jim Craddock, eds. Detroit: Visible Ink Press, 2000. 1700p. ISBN 1-578-59042-6.

Since its first issue in 1991, this annual work has joined Leonard Maltin's work (entry 917) as one of the most popular comprehensive guides to motion pictures on video. It has more titles (over 22,000) and, like the other guides, provides capsule reviews along with a rating (ranging from four bones to "woof," the equivalent of a bomb). The reviews are informative and provide interesting facts. Also included in each alphabetically arranged entry are release dates, running time, video availability, and major credits (principal cast members and directors, but also individuals responsible for writing, camera work, and music). About 1,000 new movies are added to each edition. There are credit listings for these people as well.

VideoHound's World Cinema: The Adventurer's Guide to Movie Watching, by Elliott Wilhelm (1999), is one of the new resource tools from the same publisher. Wilhelm is a film curator and provides brief description and analysis of more than 800 foreign films. These reviews are done from the perspective of a viewer and provide lively fare, offering suggestions to make the viewing experience as beneficial as possible. Brief profiles are given for certain leading personalities as well. About 100 photographs accompany the text. Several indexes provide excellent access.

Indexes, Abstracts, and Serial Bibliographies

*921. Film Literature Index: A Quarterly Author-Subject Periodical Index to the International Literature of Film. Albany, NY: State University of New York at Albany Film and Television Documentation Center, 1973– . Q. with ann. cum. ISSN 0093-6758.

This work complements the coverage of *The Critical Index: A Bibliography of Articles on Film in English 1946–1973* (Teachers College Press, 1973), which limits itself to U.S., British, and Canadian journals. *Film Literature Index* covers material from some 300 periodicals, which are scanned for pertinent articles. Recently, it has included television periodicals as well. Since it was first issued in 1973, it has developed an excellent reputation not only for its coverage of some 160 journals from thirty countries but also for its organization and ease of use. Developed originally as a pilot offering at SUNY-Albany with a grant from the New York State Council on the Arts, the work has continued without interruption and occupies a prominent position among such tools. The work is available online from the publisher.

922. International Index to Film Periodicals. New York: R. R. Bowker, 1972– . Irreg. ISSN 0000-0388.

An excellent example of a cooperative indexing project of international proportions is this effort sponsored by the International Federation of Film Archives (FIAF). It was begun by Bowker and now is published through FIAF. It provides a convenient package of index entries cumulated over the year at various archives in Europe and North America and contributed by them to this effort. These entries originally appeared on catalog cards, which were distributed to subscribers of the service from FIAF. About sixty to eighty film periodicals are selected from the index based on their representation of their country's thinking and articles of lasting quality. There are separate sections of reviews, biographies, and studies of individual films. It has been made available on CD-ROM. The sixth edition was published in 1996.

The counterpart to this work in the field of television is *International Index to Television Periodicals: An Annotated Guide* (London: International Federation of Film Archives, Bienn., 1979/1980–), which provides cumulations of entries indexed on cards by a service. It covers important articles from nearly 100 periodicals worldwide. There are separate indexes for general subjects, individual programs, and biography, as well as an author index.

Dictionaries, Encyclopedias, and Handbooks

For additional listings of film and video as well as evaluative and descriptive material on individual titles, see "Film/Video Catalogs and Listings" and "Reviews and Criticism" in this chapter.

923. The American Film Industry: A Historical Dictionary. Anthony Slide et al., eds. Westport, CT: Greenwood, 1986: repr. Limelight ed., 1990. 431p. ISBN 0-313-24693-9.

Slide and his team of eight research associates have put together a rather unique and detailed dictionary of the historical development of the film industry in this country. Coverage is given to about 600 entries, alphabetically arranged; the writing is smooth and the descriptions well-developed, and cross-references are furnished. The work treats many facets of the industry, with special attention given to business organizations, industrial techniques, and technology. Also covered are producing and releasing companies, film series, genres, organizations, and specific terms peculiar to the field. Entries vary in length from only a few lines to several pages depending upon the importance of the subject, and may include addresses, bibliographies, and archival resources. The work concludes with a general bibliography for additional reading on film history and a name index of persons, subjects, and organizations.

924. **Blacks in Black and White: A Source Book on Black Films.** 2d ed. Henry T. Sampson. Metuchen, NJ: Scarecrow Press, 1995. 735p. ISBN 0-8108-2605-4.

Initially published in 1977, this history of a unique era in motion pictures has been expanded considerably. It remains the only detailed source of information on the origin and development of the genre of motion pictures featuring all-black casts, producers, and directors intended to be shown to primarily black audiences. These theaters were mostly in black neighborhoods in cities and towns, and many were owned and managed by black businessmen. Coverage begins around 1910 with the introduction of the genre and its preparation and ends in 1950 with its demise. Treated here are the achievements of performers and filmmakers, most of whom are now obscure. The second edition enhances the previous coverage given to black producers, describes more films, and provides expanded listings of film titles and cast members. There is a new chapter on whites in blackface. Photographs accompany the text; a detailed general index is provided.

925. **Chambers Film Quotes.** Tony Crawley, comp. and ed. New York: Chambers, Kingfisher Graham, 1991. 296p. ISBN 0-550-21024-5.

Of interest to a wide variety of users is this quotation handbook identifying more than 2,000 celebrity quotations. It is unique in its focus on Hollywood and those associated with film and filmmaking. Sources of quotations are actors, directors, producers, and so forth, whose remarks or comments have been arranged by topic or category. Quotations vary widely in terms of their wit, humor, and profundity; in many cases the abrasiveness, vanity, ego, and jealousy of this part of the entertainment industry is revealed clearly. There are more than 260 topics or categories, ranging from the "casting couch" to the "method." Each quote in its own way provides insight into the life and character of its creator, thereby addressing the interests of moviegoers and film buffs. Printed sources of quotations are identified. There is an index of speakers to aid access.

926. **The Complete Actors' Television Credits, 1948–1988.** 2d ed. James Robert Parrish and Vincent Terrace. Metuchen, NJ: Scarecrow Press, 1989–1990. 2v. ISBN 0-8108-2204-0 (v.1); 0-8108-2258-X (v.2).

This unique two-volume set separates male and female television performers, with volume 1 treating 1,587 actors and volume 2 covering 1,739 actresses. It serves as an enlargement and expansion of an earlier work by Parrish that, together with its three supplements, covered the years 1950–1985. The term "complete" in the title represents the tool's inclusiveness in covering all entertainment programs broadcast on network and cable television as well as those made in syndication. Experimental television from 1931 to 1946 is treated, as are variety series, specials, and dramatic series. Coverage of performers is selective; some but not all cast members are identified. Entries in both volumes are arranged alphabetically by performer, for whom the television credits are listed chronologically. Name of show is given along with episode, date, and network.

927. **The Complete Directory to Prime Time Network TV Shows, 1946–Present.** 6th ed. Tim Brooks and Earle Marsh. New York: Ballantine Books, 1995. 1385p. ISBN 0-345-39736-3.

Defining prime time in broad terms as the time period from 6:00 P.M. to sign-off, this now-familiar work furnishes the librarian and patron with a comprehensive listing of all regularly scheduled programs ever aired on network television during the choice hours. First published in 1979, it has been updated three times and has followed a pattern of about three years between issues. In addition to network series, it includes the top shows in syndication. Offerings of the Fox network are furnished in this edition for the first time. Entries are arranged by title of the program and include dates of showing, broadcast history, cast, story line, and memorable episodes. The present work covers series through the early 1990s and is indexed by names. There are several interesting and useful appendices.

A work that overlaps in coverage is Vincent Terrace's *The Complete Encyclopedia of Television Programs, 1947–1979* (A. S. Barnes, 1979). Much of the same information is provided for series television, but the two titles can be used together to assure that coverage is as complete as possible.

928. **The Complete Film Dictionary.** 2d ed. Ira Konigsberg. New York: Penguin, 1997. 469p. ISBN 0-670-10009-9.

The second edition continues as a comprehensive tool that provides definitions along with history, theory, technical awareness, and business practice of the motion picture industry, It remains an excellent resource for all types of inquirers. Definitions are thorough and vary in length with the topic; the work provides clear and well-developed text. Terms are not only of American coinage but include a European perspective in the vocabulary covered. Around 4,000 entries treat terms, studios, organizations, and so forth. There are numerous line drawings and photographs, making it an especially useful aid in understanding both technical aspects of instrumentation and the nature of film genres.

Filmmaker's Dictionary, by Ralph S. Singleton (Lone Eagle, 1986; repr., 1990), is a concise and compact volume filled with the terminology of filmmaking practice. It is written in simple language but provides a useful service, helping the user to become familiar with both technical terms and slang expressions employed by professionals in the field. More than 1,500 terms, representing every aspect of the art, are defined. There are abundant cross-references from the entries to other related definitions, making this a convenient and practical dictionary. Most interesting are the almost anecdotal bits of background information attached to many of the definitions.

929. **Dictionary of Television and Audiovisual Terminology.** Moshe Moshkovitz. Jefferson, NC: McFarland, 1998. 175p. ISBN 0-7864-0440-X).

This is an up-to-date and practical dictionary providing coverage of both common technical and slang terminology relevant to the world of television broadcasting and audiovisual production. There is some representation of the vocabulary of electronics and computer science. The author is an academic, who began by compiling a glossary for his students. The dictionary contains over 1,500 words and phrases representing the common speech of professionals in the field and of those writing for publication. Arrangement is alphabetical; acronyms are placed as if words and numbers as having been spelled out. Definitions are clear and well-constructed, with many providing examples illustrating the meanings. They vary in length from a few lines to more than a page, depending upon the topic.

930. **The Encyclopedia of Novels into Film.** John C. Tibbets and James M. Welsh. New York: Facts on File, 1998. 448p. ISBN 0-816-03317-X.

This work will find a welcoming audience in those interested in novels that serve as sources for subsequent motion pictures. Coverage is given to more than 300 novels and their screen adaptations, including a wide range in terms of seriousness of purpose, from *Schindler's List* to *Valley of the Dolls*. Drama, comedy, film noir, science fiction, westerns, suspense, and action all are represented in two-part entries. The first part describes the original novel, while the second provides comparative examination and assessment of the film(s).

An earlier effort is the two-volume *A Title Guide to the Talkies: A Comprehensive Listing of 16,000 Feature-Length Films from October, 1927, Until December, 1963*, by Richard B. Dimmitt (Scarecrow Press, 1965), which provides more extensive coverage with the purpose of identifying the sources of films, whether novels, stories, plays, or even poems. Motion pictures are listed alphabetically and indication is given of the original work and authorship. This work has been updated by Andrew Aros's *A Title Guide to the Talkies, 1964 Through 1974* (Scarecrow Press, 1977) and by his *Title Guide to the Talkies, 1975 Through 1984* (Scarecrow Press, 1986), continuing the pattern of coverage for a few thousand more titles.

931. The Facts on File Dictionary of Film and Broadcast Terms.
Edmund F. Penney. New York: Facts on File, 1991. 251p. ISBN 0-8160-1923-1.

Another of the publisher's dictionaries specialized to various fields is this reference tool containing 2,500 definitions of trade words. Definitions are brief and emphasis is given to utilitarian needs in explaining technology, equipment, broadcast formats, audiovisual considerations, production staff/activities, networks, unions, and so forth. Some coverage is given to film theories and to production companies, but personalities are not included. Definitions are pithy and cogent albeit brief, and are expressed in a personal manner and casual style. There is no attempt to indicate historical background of the words. There are twelve appendices providing script forms, budget forms, releases, and other examples of practical documentation.

Chambers Concise Encyclopedia of Film and Television, edited by Allan Hunter (Chambers, Kingfisher Graham, 1991), provides more depth in its treatment of some 700 technical terms, personalities, major films, and television programs. Hunter has also provided his own perspective based on his experience and expertise in the field, beginning with the preface describing film and television as "symbiotic companions."

932. The Film Encyclopedia. 3d ed. Ephraim Katz et al. New York: HarperPerennial Library, 1998. 1504p. ISBN 0-062-73492-X.

This is the most respected single-volume reference source in the field today even though there are no entries for individual film titles. The two previous editions were largely the work of a single individual; although Katz died prior to completion of the current effort, it bears his stamp in terms of charm, style, vigor, detail, and depth of knowledge. The work continues its excellent, in-depth coverage of personalities associated with most areas of performance and production (actors, directors, choreographers, cinematographers, writers, editors, critics, etc.). For each one a filmography is supplied. In addition, there are numerous facts and trivia, detailed survey articles on motion picture history and development in every country that contains this industry, and definitions of technical terms.

933. Film-Video Terms and Concepts. Steven E. Browne. Boston: Focal Press, 1992. 181p. ISBN 0-240-80111-3.

Designed for those who have had some experience in film or video in its use of at-times technical language to define technical words, this slim dictionary provides an excellent blend of film and video terminology. Similarities and differences between the two media are examined through definitions bearing symbols for their status. Such symbols indicate whether a term is applicable only to film, only to video, to both media, to both media with different meanings, or to both media with equivalent or highly similar definitions. Terms are basic to the fields and represent both production and post-production activity, equipment, and process. Entries are alphabetically arranged and supply definitions that are clear and comprehensible to the intended audience. Cross-references are supplied, and illustrations enhance the text along with charts and diagrams.

934. **Guide to African Cinema.** Sharon A. Russell. Westport, CT: Greenwood, 1998. 183p. (Reference Guides to the World's Cinema series). ISBN 0-313-29621-9.

This is an interesting and up-to-date handbook, combining biographical coverage of directors with film exposition in a selective single volume. The author is an academic, whose selection of entries in part was based on their availability and, more important, their qualities in representing an African perspective. She limits her choices to only sixteen directors and forty motion pictures. No actors are treated because in African filmmaking their position, influence, and impact are of less consequence than is true in the West. Entries are arranged alphabetically, with biographical description and critical commentary given to directors along with a filmography and bibliography. Films are given thorough treatment, with excellent, informative essays containing lengthy plot summary, critical examination, and bibliography. An index provides access.

935. **A Guide to World Cinema: Covering 7,200 Films of 1950–84. . . .** Elkan Allan, ed. London: Whittet Books; distr., Detroit: Gale Research, 1985. 682p. ISBN 0-9054-8333-2.

Rather than being a guide, which implies a certain selectivity or evaluative nature, this is a listing of the thousands of motion pictures shown at the British Film Institute over a thirty-four-year period. With such a huge quantity, naturally a wide variety of films are listed, ranging from the classic to the absurd. This is in part what gives this work strength as a valuable identification tool for all libraries supporting film research and inquiry. The work provides for each film what are referred to in the subtitle as "capsule reviews": brief but informative commentaries taken from the original program notes. Most entries also include a very small production still. The comprehensive coverage and relative depth of information provided make this a notable purchase for the collection, even though it has been criticized for its small print size.

Screen World (Crown, 1949–) has been appearing annually since it was started by Daniel Blum. Since 1966, it has been edited by John Willis and has continued as a highly regarded resource for its survey of film releases in the previous year. Screen World 1998 (1999) is volume 49 in the series and, like the others, it identifies major films with the cast lists and production credits. The volume is profusely illustrated with film scenes. There are no plot summaries, but it does have a useful biographical section. Recently, the publisher has reprinted the first twenty volumes of this notable serial.

936. **Halliwell's Filmgoer's Companion.** 12th ed. Leslie Halliwell and John Walker, eds. New York: HarperPerennial/HarperCollins, 1997. 514p. ISBN 0-06-273478-4.

The name Halliwell is a familiar one to librarians and patrons of the entertainment arts because of the useful and convenient guides he has produced over the years. The twelfth edition of this work (two to three years between issues) has added much new material covering the period up to the time of publication. The current effort contains some 10,000 entries. Since Halliwell's death in 1989, Walker has edited the subsequent editions and continues the tried-and-true format. Arrangement of entries is alphabetical and coverage is given to films, personalities (actors, directors, writers, etc.), and other related elements. It remains a storehouse of information on the cinema.

Halliwell's Film and Video Guide 2000, also by Halliwell and Walker (HarperPerennial/ HarperCollins, 1999), the successor to *Halliwell's Film Guide* (1980–1995), continues to expand and grow, and remains a favorite for identification and description of films. It is issued annually and the current edition contains more than 23,000 entries providing brief reviews and cast listings. Coverage of early films from the 1930s is excellent, and critical commentary is provided from the time of the film release. Films are listed alphabetically.

937. Handbook of Old-Time Radio: A Comprehensive Guide to Golden Age Radio Listening and Collecting. Jon D. Swartz and Robert C. Reinehr. Metuchen, NJ: Scarecrow Press, 1993. 825p. ISBN 0-8108-2590-2.

This well-developed guide to old-time radio is designed for the nostalgia buff as well as the serious student and researcher. More than 2,000 programs are treated in descriptive narrative highlighting the casts, announcers, network affiliations, length of program, duration or longevity, and availability. Story lines are included for certain programs when appropriate. Programs are categorized by type, with chapter coverage given to each type of program. Guidelines are supplied regarding the comprehension and research of the various categories. Also treated are the most well-known premiums offered by the various programs to their listening audience. In addition, the work describes the history of the major networks, providing useful background information, and there is a listing of resources available for acquisition of old-time programs. Indexing treats more than 8,000 performers and programs.

938. Historical Dictionary of American Radio. Donald G. Godfrey and Frederic A. Leigh, eds. Westport, CT: Greenwood, 1998. 485p. ISBN 0-313-29636-7.

This is a comprehensive and valuable resource, providing coverage not only of terminology but also of a variety of elements, issues, and events in the history and development of radio. It opens with an introduction by the editors, both academics, that provides an historical framework for the coverage; a chronology highlights developments from 1837 to 1997. Nearly 100 scholars have served as contributors. Entries vary in length with importance of the topic, from several lines to three pages, and are arranged alphabetically. They furnish excellent insight and exposition of more than 600 topics (radio personalities, radio coverage of historical events, stations, networks, characters, programs, etc.); these are cross-referenced and signed by the authors. In addition, there are bibliographic references for further reading and study.

939. Hollywood's Indian: The Portrayal of the Native American in Film. Peter C. Rollins and John E. O'Connor, eds. Lexington: University of Kentucky, 1998. 226p. ISBN 0-8131-2044-6.

This is a collection of twelve essays examining the treatment given to Native Americans in cinema from the silent film era to the present day. Both general history of film development in this regard and specific titles are treated in an effort to provide insight into the nature of changing perspective within American society. Twelve motion pictures are examined in depth, beginning with *The Vanishing American* (1926) and ending with *Indian in the Cupboard* and Disney's *Pocahontas* (both 1995). Essays examine the manner in which the films may represent the attitudes and perceptions held by the movie-going public. Review and exposition of such cultural attributes enables one to understand the issues, conflicts, and forces that shape the final products.

940. The International Film Industry: A Historical Dictionary. Anthony Slide. New York: Greenwood, 1989. 423p. ISBN 0-313-25635-7.

Serving as a companion volume to Slide's effort on the American film industry (entry 923), the present effort has utilized the same basic pattern, providing treatment on an international level. It supplies 650 entries pertinent to both historical and contemporary aspects of filmmaking, with coverage given to directors, films, studios, production companies, theaters, awards, techniques, and organizations. Useful information is given on genres, movements, publications, processes, distributors, and series. Entries have been prepared by numerous contributors although articles are not signed. They vary in length from a single sentence to several pages; many contain bibliographies. Although all nations are covered, there is emphasis on the British film industry. Listings are included for archives and film festivals.

International Film Prizes: An Encyclopedia, by Tad Bentley Hammer (Garland, 1991), supplies information on awards given in forty-two nations, with emphasis on those presented to feature-length motion pictures entered in domestic competitions. Arrangement is by country and entries provide historical overview of the award and chronology of winners. There is a bibliography; the work is indexed by title and by personality.

941. Motion Picture Series and Sequels: A Reference Guide. Bernard A. Drew. New York: Garland, 1990. 412p. (Garland Reference Library of the Humanities, v. 1186). ISBN 0-8240-4248-4.

With series and sequels so much a part of filmmaking and the business, reference tools on the phenomenon are used by all types of audiences. This is a comprehensive effort, with 800 entries identifying 936 English-language motion pictures dating from 1899 to the present, including those made for television. These films had one or more major sequels or remakes, and embrace all genres (mystery, comedy, etc.); animated films, documentaries, and short comedies are excluded. Entries supply plot descriptions, studio, year, directors, major performers, and alternate titles. The work is illustrated in black-and-white and indexed by title.

Cinema Sequels and Remakes, 1903–1987, by Robert A. Nowlan and Gwendolyn Nowlan (McFarland, 1989), treats all films (silent or sound) having at least one English-language sound remake or sequel. Although not as inclusive as Drew's work in number of films, coverage is more detailed. Entries supply studio, country, release date, cast, credits, and source of story, along with a summary of the story line. The work is indexed in extensive fashion. *Haven't I Seen You Somewhere Before? Remakes, Sequels, and Series in Motion Pictures, Videos, and Television, 1896–1990*, by James L. Limbacher (Pierian Press, 1991), is an expansion of an earlier edition published in 1979. The work is divided into three sections, the first of which is on remakes. This is followed by sequels (one or two films that follow in the events of the original). Finally, the series section lists those efforts with three or more films using the same characters, ideas, or actors.

942. The New Video Encyclopedia. Larry Langman and Joseph A. Molinari. New York: Garland, 1990. 312p. ISBN 0-8240-8244-3.

This is a revised and updated version of an earlier work issued in the mid-1980s; it treats the burgeoning world of video with an expanded offering. It now supplies more than 1,500 entries defining every conceivable term pertinent to the field in various aspects of production, equipment, business, and marketing. Additionally, there is coverage given to magazines as well as notable personalities like Sarnoff and Zworykin. Entries tend to be brief, at around 50 words, although some survey topics provide descriptions as long as 200 words. They are alphabetically arranged and many are accompanied by line drawings or black-and-white photographs. Cross-references are indicated through use of capitalization. The audience for this tool is specialized, but ranges from the technician to the student and interested layperson.

A more specialized handbook is *Cheap Shots: Video Production for Nonprofits*, by Pat Kardas (Scarecrow Press, 1993), which focuses on reasons and reasoning behind video production. In providing its unique emphasis on nonprofit agencies as a target group, the work examines potential audience, basic equipment needs, sources of funding and free talent, scriptwriting, editing, and polishing the product.

943. The New York Times Encyclopedia of Film. Gene Brown and Harry M. Geduld, eds. Hamden, CT: Garland, 1984. 13v. ISBN 0-8129-1059-1.

Similar to the *New York Times Film Reviews* (entry 982) in format, this monumental collection of articles from the *New York Times* is arranged chronologically from 1896 to 1979. Included are all types of writings pertaining to motion pictures: news items, features, interviews, reports, and promotional pieces. As one might expect, reviews are studiously avoided, allowing the *New York Times Film Reviews* to retain its uniqueness in that area. Many illustrations are included, although the work has been criticized for the poor quality of the reproductions. Many subjects are covered, with a good proportion of the articles on personalities (producers, commentators, critics, and news correspondents, as well as performers). There is an index volume, which is alphabetically arranged, providing access to the desired subject. Initially published by the New York Times, Garland is marketing the work at a bargain price because it is going out of print.

944. On the Air: The Encyclopedia of Old-Time Radio. John Dunning. New York: Oxford University Press, 1998. 822p. ISBN 0-19-507678-8.

This is an updated and revised effort of the author's 1976 publication and offers a veritable treasury of information related to old-time radio programming from the 1920s to the early 1960s. Some 1,500 entries are alphabetically arranged and provide essential details about radio shows: dates of the run from beginning to end, day and time of broadcast, network, sponsorship, cast members, announcers, musicians, producers, directors, sound technicians, and so forth. A narrative then provides extensive description of program details. Especially lengthy description, the product of extensive research, is given to the history and development of major series such as *Gunsmoke*; there are also detailed survey articles on types of programming, such as "news broadcasts." A bibliography is provided; an index supplies access.

945. Radio Programs, 1924–1984: A Catalog of over 1800 Shows. Vincent Terrace. Jefferson, NC: McFarland, 1999. 399p. ISBN 0-786-40351-9.

This is an update and expansion of the author's work treating radio's golden years (1930–1960), published in 1981 and treating 1,500 programs. It retains the solid character and informative approach of the earlier effort in its identification of network and syndicated programs over a period of sixty years. Arrangement is alphabetical by title of the program; entries include story line, cast lists, announcer and music credits, sponsors, program openings, network and syndication information, length, and dates. All types of programming are included, representative of the range of entertainment afforded the public (adventure, comedy, crime, drama, game shows, musicals, mystery, science fiction, and westerns). A name index provides access.

Primetime Radio Classics is a database available online through CompuServe. It provides information on episodes of classic radio programs from the 1930s to the 1950s in a variety of categories. Cassettes may be ordered.

946. Radio Soundtracks: A Reference Guide. 2d ed. Michael R. Pitts. Metuchen, NJ: Scarecrow Press, 1986. 337p. ISBN 0-8108-1875-2.

The purpose of this revised edition of an earlier work is to identify programs from the golden age of radio (1920s to 1960s) that are available on tapes and records. It is divided into five parts, the largest of which lists over 1,000 programs available on tape. Entries are arranged by name of program and include network, length, stars, and brief commentary. Part 2 covers radio specials on tape, while part 3 identifies those available on long-playing records. Part 4 is "Performers' Radio Appearances on Long Playing Records" and part 5 describes compilation record albums composed of radio material. Over 2,700 entries are furnished in all, and the work should be extremely useful both for identification of the historical factual material and for information regarding the recording.

947. Television Character and Story Facts: Over 110,000 Details from 1,008 Shows, 1945–1992. Vincent Terrace and Steven Lance. Jefferson, NC: McFarland, 1993. 539p. ISBN 0-899-50891-X.

Great trivia and interesting facts are supplied for more than 1,000 television shows from this country. Entries are arranged alphabetically and identify the cast, network, broadcast dates, and theme song credits. Of real interest is the host of facts, much of it trivial, but nevertheless welcome, presented about the characters, plots, and settings, as well as the identification of performers who appeared briefly or as guests. Also given in some cases is information regarding pilots for the show or unseen episodes. Over 100 photographs serve to enhance the text.

Also for the trivia buff is Terrace's *1350 Toughest TV Trivia Questions of All Time* (Citadel, 1999), an expansion of his 1997 offering of 1,201 "toughest TV questions." These are drawn from several hundred television shows of varied quality but of popular interest; a library patron can spend some carefree hours enjoying the recollection of some character trait or setting element from entertainment choices of the past.

948. **The Television Industry: A Historical Dictionary.** Anthony Slide. New York: Greenwood, 1991. 374p. ISBN 0-313-25634-9.

This effort completes what has been referred to as Slide's "trilogy" of historical dictionaries, joining his two works on the film industry (entries 923, 940). There are more than 1,000 entries on various aspects of television, such as production companies, distributors, organizations, various genres, and themes, as well as technical terms and popular language. The programs themselves are excluded because there are many available tools dealing with programming. Emphasis is on the United States, then on Great Britain, although the coverage is international in scope. Entries vary in length from brief identifications of a few sentences to two-page articles treating the major networks. An interesting feature is the inclusion of biographical essays on the three magnates of network television: Sarnoff, Paley, and Golderson.

Another useful tool is *Les Brown's Encyclopedia of Television* (3d ed., Gale Research, 1992). Brown has furnished 800 entries treating performers, programs, and events in alphabetical order. Coverage is international in scope and a bibliography is given. There are numerous listings in the appendices. There is a subject index.

949. **Variety International Film Guide.** Peter Cowie, ed. Hollywood, CA: Samuel French. 1990– . Ann. ISBN 1-879-50547-9 (1999).

This familiar effort, once known as *International Film Guide* (1964–1989), continues in the 1999 edition its comprehensive treatment and detailed reporting of the state-of-the-art of filmmaking in nearly seventy countries. Peter Cowie has remained steadfast as the editor of this annual throughout its existence and is recognized for his efforts. Countries are arranged alphabetically and the essay-reports are produced by scholars or critics, who summarize the condition of film production and attendance. New films are described and biographical sketches of important personalities are included within those entries. Top box office attractions are listed as well. In addition to the reports, there are various listings such as international film festivals, film archives, journals, and book stores. Unfortunately, there is no title index to the films described.

Roger Ebert's Book of Film (W. W. Norton, 1996) is Ebert's tribute to or celebration of the first century of the movies. He has selected and compiled an anthology of 100 pieces of outstanding film writing from the work of newspaper columnists, novelists, essayists, screenwriters, technicians, and others who have provided outstanding assessments or descriptions of a wide range of motion picture artistry and individual performers.

Directories, Annuals, and Current Awareness Services

*950. **Baseline**. New York: Baseline II Inc. (Database)

This is a comprehensive computerized system that contains biographies of creative, technical, and administrative personnel for various segments of the entertainment industry (film, television, theater); listings of over 40,000 films released in the United States for both theaters and television, theater productions, and television series since 1970; current production information on over 1,400 films and television series; citations to articles in major entertainment trade journals, including *Variety* (entry 959); demographics on audiences attending opening nights; daily information on the Hollywood entertainment community; and synopses and evaluations of literary properties available for purchase, calendar, stocks, and travel. E-mail and bulletin board services are furnished. It is updated daily.

A daily print publication also available online is **HOLLYWOOD HOTLINE*, edited by Eliot Stein. Online access is through CompuServe, NewsNet, and GEnie, among others. It provides news about the entertainment industry, including films, music, and home entertainment. It covers programming, contracts, movie summaries, soap operas, weekly ratings, record albums, and so forth from 1983 to the present. It is updated daily.

*951. **Entertainment Weekly**. New York: Entertainment Weekly, 1990– . Wk. ISSN 1049-0434.

This relatively new entertainment journal is linked to its companion television show. The print version is designed to cover the trends and developments in the entertainment industry in this country, and furnishes feature stories, reviews of books, motion pictures, musical recordings and television programs of all kinds. This concept is shared by the television program, which highlights developments and happenings in the careers of performers and production people. Like *Variety* (entry 959) and *Billboard* (entry 750), it stands four-square in the realm of popular culture. The publication is also available online through VU/TEXT Information Services, under the auspices of Time, Inc. The service provides full-text of the complete file from the inception of the weekly in February 1990 to the present day.

952. **The Film Festival Guide: For Filmmakers, Film Buffs, and Industry Professionals.** Adam Langer. Chicago: Chicago Review Press Club, 1998. 269p. ISBN 1-556-52285-1.

This is an important tool for libraries serving the needs of professional and prospective professional film people; it provides needed information regarding film festivals held around the world. It fills a need for a convenient source for such data in its classified coverage, beginning with a chapter on the author's selection for "Best of the Fests" and followed by regional chapter divisions: North America, Europe, Asia, Africa and Middle East, Australia, and South America. Entries supply place, time, description, award winners, number of films, celebrity attendance in the past, prices, and admission and contact information.

The Ultimate Film Festival Survival Guide: The Essential Companion for Filmmakers and Festival-Goers, by Chris Gore (Low Eagle, 1999) is more of a handbook than a directory in its emphasis on the marketing and selling of films at some 500 festivals held around the world. The author is a knowledgeable film writer and editor who has written and directed films as well as served as judge at different festivals. He offers a manual of steps to follow in submitting a film, marketing the film, and closing the deal.

953. **International Directory of Film and TV Documentation Collections.** Rene Beauclair, ed. London: Federation Internationale des Archivs du Film, 1994. ISBN 0-906973-26-0.

This slender volume began in 1976 under the auspices of FIAF; the International Federation of Film Archives, with fewer than half the entries found in the present edition. The directory now lists dozens of collections from countries all over the world. Information is given for each unit regarding available documentation services, nature and availability of holdings, and publications issued. These centers are varied in nature and include film schools, state institutions, and specialized agencies. Collections also vary and include scripts, clippings, stills, posters, programs, scrapbooks, diaries, recordings, and slides along with books and periodicals. Most are archival in nature and are available for research purposes. Listings of FIAF members are given; there is an index to special collections.

*Footage 91: North American Film and Video Sources, edited by Richard Prelinger et al., was issued as a supplement to *Footage 89* and identifies services and policies of some 1,600 television stations, film archives, and university collections containing films and videotapes available for use. Entries describe collections and supply contact information. It was made available on CD-ROM in 1992.

954. International Motion Picture Almanac. New York: Quigley, 1929– . Ann. ISSN 0074-7084.

This has been a leading directory of services and products and an important purchase for film libraries throughout its long history and its issuance under varying titles. It is a treasure-house of miscellaneous information and statistical data. Included is a who's who providing brief biographical sketches of numerous film personalities. There are also sections on pictures, corporations, theater circuits, buying and booking, equipment and suppliers, services, talent and literary agencies, organizations, advertising, world market, press, non-theatrical motion pictures, censorship, and so forth.

International Television & Video Almanac (Quigley, 1956–) is also published on an annual basis. Statistical reporting and information on people and developments make it a useful tool for the study of television. It identifies television stations, shows, networks, personnel, festivals, awards, producers, feature releases, and so forth, and provides information on the television and video industries.

955. Money for Film & Video Artists. 2d ed. Douglas Oxenhorn, ed. New York: American Council for the Arts, 1993. 309p. ISBN 1-9879903-09-1.

The American Council for the Arts sponsors this directory in response to a need not addressed by such established tools as *Foundation Directory* (entry 202n). It is a comprehensive guide to resources for film and video artists and identifies more than 200 organizations that offer assistance or support. Most of these units are found in the United States, but some Canadian agencies are also treated. These vary in size and prominence as do their grants and awards, and range from the well-known national operations to obscure local and state organizations. Included in these pages is information regarding grants, awards, fellowships, artists' residencies, access to equipment, loan programs, and technical assistance. Entries treat each of the organizations separately and supply pertinent data regarding funding, eligibility, types of award and assistance, application process, and requirements. Several indexes provide access.

956. The Nostalgia Entertainment Sourcebook: The Complete Resource Guide to Classic Movies, Vintage Music, Old-Time Radio and Theatre. Randy Skretvedt and Jordan R. Young. Beverly Hills, CA: Moonstone Press, 1991. 158p. ISBN 0-940410-25-7.

This unique directory targets the pre-television era and provides sources and source listings on a variety of elements within the popular culture. Included here are record shops, film and video dealers, jazz festivals, radio shows, and revival cinemas, representing the interests of bygone eras. More than 1,100 sources are cited in all; also treated are fan clubs, research centers, conventions, and radio stations. Separate sections are given to movies, music, radio, and theater, each with its own sequence of entries. Coverage of nostalgia extends from the 1920s to the 1940s; sports are not included. Entries supply the normal directory-type information along with brief annotations. Collectors and nostalgia buffs will utilize the listings of museums as well as the sources of available memorabilia. Appendices contain bibliographies; an index is provided.

957. Television & Cable Fact Book. Washington, DC: Warren Publishing, 1982– . Ann. ISSN 0732-8648.

This has proved to be a most useful reference tool for those needing up-to-date information on the television and cable industries. It appears in two separate publications. The "Stations" volume covers technical facilities, ownership, personnel, rate, and audience data for all television stations in the United States. Entries are arranged by state, then alphabetically by city, with separate treatment for Canadian and international stations. The "Cable and Services" volumes provide similar coverage of those aspects related to cable industries. Since 1991, there has been a weekly supplement entitled *Television & Cable Action Update*, which reports actions affecting television stations and cable networks.

From the same publisher comes the weekly current awareness tool *Television Digest*, which covers political, social, industrial, and educational issues and developments pertaining to television, cable, and allied fields. It is available online through NewsNet, and coverage is furnished from March 15, 1982, to the present. Also from Warren Publishing is *Public Broadcasting Report*, which is a biweekly report also available online through NewsNet, dealing with the financial, regulatory, and programming developments concerning public radio and television. Coverage dates from May 7, 1982, to the present. *The Home Video & Cable Report* (Knowledge Industry Publications, 1982–) is another up-to-date tool, providing a weekly service. It is the most current print tool for information on the home video and cable industries. *Bacon's Radio/TV Directory* (Bacon's Information, 1986–) is a well-developed and informative annual directory providing complete programming and format information for all radio and television stations in this country. The seventh edition (1992) treats some 10,000 stations and lists some 70,000 key personnel along with address, network, type of programming, target audience, power, and so forth.

958. Television Writers Guide. 4th ed. Lynn Naylor, comp. and ed. Los Angeles: Lone Eagle, 1995. 442p. ISSN 0894-8658.

Initially projected as an annual publication, this serial effort was first issued in 1989 and incorporated writers' credits dating from the 1978–1979 season through the 1988–1989 season. The fourth edition retains the format of the earlier issues, updating the coverage through the 1993–1994 television season. The work provides lists of Emmy awards and nominations along with the listing of writers. Writers are arranged alphabetically, with television credits furnished for the time period covered. Membership in the Writers Guild of America is identified, along with names of co-writers or contact telephone numbers. Also treated are comedy series, daytime, drama, variety shows, and so forth, listed with their networks and production companies. There is excellent access through indexes by show, agent or manager, and advertiser.

959. Variety. New York: Variety, 1905– . Wk. ISSN 0042-2738.

This is the leading current awareness journal and official newspaper of show business, analogous to *Billboard* (entry 750) in the music field. There are sections on movies, radio and television, music, records, and vaudeville, providing information of a varied nature on recent developments, trends, personalities, and so forth. Theater is covered in detail, with reviews of various shows, information on casting, gate receipts, and so forth. It is well-known for its reviews of top records of the week. Excellent coverage is given to the business aspects of this wide range of performing arts.

Art Murphy's Boxoffice Register (Art Murphy's Boxoffice Register, 1982–) has established itself as an annual publication. It provides financial reporting from *Variety* for film distributors for the box office year. Films are identified and income given; arrangement is alphabetical by title.

Biographical Sources

960. Art Directors in Cinema: A Worldwide Biographical Dictionary.
Michael L. Stephens. Jefferson, NC: McFarland, 1998. 350p. ISBN 0-7864-0312-8.

This is a useful biographical dictionary that treats a segment of endeavor that has received little attention. The work describes the lives and achievements of 300 important personalities representing the world of production design. Individuals from all aspects of art direction and design creativity in film are covered on an international basis. Although this activity emanated from the legacy of those who labored for the stage, the demands of motion pictures were monumental in comparison. Entries are well written and readable and are arranged alphabetically. They vary in length from a single paragraph to several pages; each biographical sketch is followed by a filmography of credits. The work concludes with a general bibliography; a good general index provides access to names, film titles, issues, and studios.

961. A Biographical Dictionary of Film. 3d ed. David Thomson.
New York: Alfred A. Knopf, 1994. 834p. ISBN 0-394-58165-2.

The first edition of this work was published in 1976 and was praised by reviewers for its literate and witty, albeit opinionated, coverage of actors and directors. The second edition, published in 1981, updated and expanded the initial effort. Published thirteen years later, the current product continues the excellent and perceptive treatment, covering 1,000 actors, directors, and producers on an international scale. It remains a vital source, entertaining in style but at the same time cogent and effective as a critical tool. Thomson is a Briton whose "obsessive work provides a sharp expression of personal taste, jokes, and digressions, insults, and eulogies." The work retains its charm and continues to be a top-rated biographical dictionary for its clarity, depth, and provocative nature.

962. A Biographical Dictionary of Scenographers, 500 B.C. to 1900
A.D. Robin Thurlow Lacey. New York: Greenwood, 1990. 762p. ISBN 0-313-27429-0.

Although criticized for his personal and unpolished style of writing in developing his entries, Lacey has provided a needed service with this biographical dictionary of all known scenographers working in the Western tradition from antiquity to the beginning of the twentieth century. As a group, set designers and scenery painters have received little attention in the past, and efforts to document their achievements are considered useful to both scholars and students. Keying the entries to the bibliography of 435 published sources and archival collections, Lacey has produced a biographical dictionary of 3,000 scenographers. Entries vary in length from a single credit to more extended narratives bearing numerous credits of the artist's work. Of interest are the major artists not generally known to have been scenographers. There is a geographical-chronological list in the appendix.

963. **The Film Handbook.** Geoff Andrew. Boston: G. K. Hall, 1990. 362p. ISBN 0-8161-9093-3.

Andrews is a British film critic who has compiled a useful biographical dictionary of 200 leading directors dating from the silent era to the present day. Entries are detailed and run about 800 words, providing factual information and biographical narrative examining the individual's life and career along with evaluative commentary of his or her work. Also, short, critical bibliographies are supplied, along with filmographies of the major works. In providing treatment of directors whose films are easily available, the focus is primarily on mainstream cinema, which is covered well. It should be noted, however, that Andrew is more prone to favor the mavericks and social critics among this mainstream. A glossary is supplied along with a bibliography of film books, as well as a listing of information sources divided by country. A general index provides access.

964. **From Silents to Sound: A Biographical Encyclopedia of Performers Who Made the Transition to Talking Pictures.** Roy Liebman. Jefferson, NC: McFarland, 1998. 309p. ISBN 0-7864-0382-9.

This is a most interesting and specialized biographical resource, focusing on actors and actresses who bridged the gap and made the transition from silent film to talking pictures. Coverage is limited to 500 screen personalities who had made at least three silent movies as either a star or major supporting figure and then had appeared in at least one talking picture. A further limitation omits those who had silent film careers in countries other than the United States. The roster of individuals included varies considerably in terms of their current fame and popularity, although they were prominent in their day. Entries vary in length and furnish birth place, dates, nicknames and pseudonyms along with real names, citations to sources for filmographies, and career description along with excerpts from film reviews. Appendices supply additional listings and the work concludes with a general bibliography followed by an index.

965. **Hollywood Baby Boomers.** James Robert Parish and Don Stanke. New York: Garland, 1992. 670p. (Garland Reference Library of the Humanities, v. 1295). ISBN 0-8240-6104-7.

This work is specialized to the needs of those who are seeking biographical or career information on that particular generation of Hollywood achievers born between 1946 and 1960. It is this group that is dominant in terms of box office and popularity today, with such names as Dan Akroyd, Arsenio Hall, Meryl Streep, Oprah Winfrey, Sean Penn, and Robin Williams. Detailed coverage is given to eighty actors, singers, and comedians. Entries open with a quote from the biographee followed by essays of some six to eleven pages in length describing the person's life and furnishing a chronology of the star's work along with a summary of his or her present and future status. Film, theater, television, and recording credits are enumerated. A black-and-white photograph is given for each entry. There is a detailed general index providing access.

966. **The Illustrated Who's Who of the Cinema.** Upd. ed. Ann Lloyd and Graham Fuller, eds. New York: Portland House, 1988. 480p. ISBN 0-51-764419-3.

More than 2,500 biographies covering people from all areas of the cinematic world are furnished, along with some 1,500 photographs of varied size. Actors, actresses, producers, directors, scene designers, costumers, art directors, composers, screenwriters, cinematographers, and so forth are represented along with critics and censors. Generally conceded to be a record of the personalities of what may be called "mainstream cinema," there is excellent coverage of people from the 1920s to the 1940s. Less elaboration is given to personalities of the 1950s and 1960s. Biographies are brief and include a short filmography that identifies the person's first and last motion picture and some others in between. This volume updates the previous 1983 edition published by Macmillan.

A quite different work is *The Illustrated Encyclopedia of Movie Character Actors*, by David Quinlan (Harmony Books/Crown, 1985), which supplies more detailed narrative. The work furnishes interesting and informed descriptions of 850 British and American character actors. The glib and witty characterizations make this work a pleasure to read.

967. **The International Dictionary of Films and Filmmakers.** 3d ed. Nicolet V. Elert et al., eds. Detroit: St. James Press, 1997. 4v. ISBN 1-55862-042-7.

The new edition of this work is a revision of the earlier issue (1990–1993). Thorough coverage is still given to a variety of personalities associated with filmmaking. There are numerous illustrations, which enhance the appeal of the new edition. Volume 1 provides information on hundreds of the world's most frequently studied films, along with a name index. Volume 2 examines the genius of numerous directors and filmmakers of international renown. The arrangement is alphabetical by name and entries provide brief biographies; filmographies; credits; production information; selective bibliographies of books and articles, both by and about the personality; and an informative critical evaluation of the individual's work. Volume 3 treats actors and actresses of international stature and provides coverage similar to that accorded the directors in volume 2. Volume 4 covers the contributions of writers and production artists. The previous edition contained an index volume; in this edition volumes 2–4 contain individual title indexes instead. As one might expect, there is some variation in the quality of the critical essays, as well as in the fullness of the biographical entries, but in general the tool is useful for its depth and detail.

968. **Michael Singer's Film Directors: A Complete Guide.** Michael Singer, comp. and ed. Beverly Hills, CA: Lone Eagle, 1984– . Ann. ISSN 0740-2872.

This annual biographical directory has continued to serve as a useful resource and covers more than 1,800 living directors from all over the world. Arrangement of entries is alphabetical by name and each entry furnishes basic information of interest to those who wish to identify or further examine the work of an individual filmmaker. Included are birthdate, birth place, agent's name, address, and telephone number, as well as a chronological listing of films (including television works) with year of release, country of origin, and distributor. The value of this work lies in the comprehensive coverage of contemporary figures that one might not find elsewhere. Directors of the past are given coverage in separate segments. The tenth edition (1993) continues the tradition and contains 584 pages.

A Biographical Dictionary of Film (entry 961) or George Sadoul's *Dictionary of Film Makers* (University of California Press, 1972) should be used for greater biographical detail. The latter is a translation of a French work and is a selective biographical dictionary of 10,000 producers, directors, scenarists, photographers, and others associated with filmmaking, excluding actors and actresses. Entries are brief but informative and commentary is subjective. More limited in scope but also important is Larry Landman's *A Guide to American Film Directors: The Sound Era, 1929–1979* (Scarecrow Press, 1981, 2v.).

969. **Who Was Who on Screen.** 3d ed. Evelyn Mack Truitt. New York: R. R. Bowker, 1983. 571p. ISBN 0-8352-1578-4.

Since its initial appearance in 1974, this retrospective biographical dictionary has been a popular purchase for reference collections serving the needs of both film buffs and specialists. With each edition its has enlarged its coverage, and the present work covers no fewer than 13,000 individuals who died between 1905 and 1981. Where needed, entries from the previous editions have been revised. The arrangement of entries is alphabetical. They furnish brief biographical identification along with a complete listing of film credits with dates. The latter contribution especially establishes this tool as a basic reference work. Both shorts and features are identified. Inclusion is not limited to actors alone but extends to prominent personalities who have had cameo appearances, such as Picasso, Hitchcock, and Maugham. A condensed version of this work was published in 1984 as the illustrated third edition. It covers 3,100 personalities and provides sixteen pages of pictures.

970. **Who's Who in Hollywood: The Largest Cast of International Film Personalities Ever Assembled.** David Ragan. New York: Facts on File, 1992. 2v. ISBN 0-8160-2011-6.

This is a comprehensive listing of some 35,000 entries identifying anybody who appeared in motion pictures from 1893 to 1991. The range is great, embracing the very famous, near famous, and never famous, from international celebrities to bit players. Living actors are described, with date and place of birth, current address, and sampling of motion picture credits. Deceased performers are supplied year of death and age along with sampling of credits. In some cases brief biographical sketches are included as well as career insights. Entries are alphabetically arranged and range in size from a single sentence to a page. Actors are listed by stage names; a brief general bibliography completes the effort.

Who's Who in the Motion Picture Industry: Directors, Producers, Writers, . . . (Packard Publishing, 1981–) began as an annual, then changed to biennial, and later triennial, frequency. It is not limited to performers; the subtitle goes on: "cinematographers, executives, major studios, production companies, and distribution companies." Arrangement of entries is alphabetical; there is a name index. *Who's Who in American Film Now*, by James Monaco (2d ed., Zoetrope, 1987), is an update of the initial publication that emphasized the 1970–1980 period. The second edition lists some 11,000 individuals and their credits in thirteen categories of film production, beginning with writers and ending with editors. These personalities were associated with 6,000 films between 1975 and 1986. Data are taken from the *Baseline database (entry 950). Entries are alphabetically arranged within each category and supply film credits in chronological order. Unfortunately, no comprehensive name index is given, a real detriment for locating individuals that appear in several categories.

971. **World Film Directors.** John Wakeman, ed. New York: H. W. Wilson, 1987–1988. 2v. ISBN 0-8242-0757-2.

Designed primarily for students and hobbyists, this biographical dictionary provides detailed biographical sketches ranging from 1,500 to 8,000 words on 400 major directors whose films are available in English-speaking countries. Volume 1 treats those individuals born prior to 1920, while volume 2 covers directors who gained prominence during the latter half of the twentieth century, some of whom were still active at the time of publication. The work contains the contributions of some fifty specialists, who together have produced a useful reference tool. Essays treat highlights of directors' lives and careers and supply production details of their major motion pictures along with a digest of critical response and popular reception. Quotations from the directors are included, providing insight into their personalities. A photograph, filmography, listing of published screenplays, and brief bibliography accompany each entry.

Histories

972. **Early American Cinema.** Anthony Slide. Rev ed. Metuchen, New Jersey: Scarecrow Press, 1994. 263p. ISBN 0-8108-2711-5.

This revision appeared some twenty years after the initial effort, and represents an update and expansion. It remains a brief history of the motion picture industry up to 1920. Coverage is given to pre-cinema, independent filmmakers, the star system, and D. W. Griffith, as well as technologies and genres. New material has been incorporated into the development of the topics, and the work provides an excellent overview of the developments of the silent era and early beginnings of the modern talkie. Benjamin Hampton's *A History of the Movies* (Friede, 1931; repr., Arno, 1970) is a valuable history of the American film industry and is a classic work regarded as a major contribution even today.

American History, American Television: Interpreting the Video Past, edited by John E. O'Connor (Ungar, 1983; repr., 1985), is a collection of fourteen essays of a historical and critical nature regarding the role of television in the American culture. The essays cover a variety of subjects, ranging from Milton Berle to the 1980 political campaign, with treatment given to programming and production issues and industry and public response. News documentaries and entertainment programming are also covered in this fashion.

973. **A History of Narrative Film.** 3d ed. David A. Cook. New York: W. W. Norton, 1996. 1087p. ISBN 0-393-96819-7.

This continues as the most complete and comprehensive history of cinema on an international basis, focused on the development of narrative film. The first edition (1981) and the second edition (1990) established it as an important information source; it proved to be of use to a variety of patrons from serious students to laypersons. The new edition has expanded its coverage, adding 106 pages; it is presented in scholarly fashion, well documented throughout, and provides 1,500 illustrations of major scenes from many of the films described. Detailed information is found on individual filmmakers, and their movies are examined in a critical manner. National cinemas and many films are covered. Film elements are analyzed, and in some cases public reaction and influence on the field are gauged. The layperson will be especially interested in the quantity of production stills taken from a variety of motion pictures over the years. The current edition has a section on Hollywood from 1965 to the present. There are both a good bibliography and a good glossary. Both public libraries and academic libraries are well served by this tool.

974. **History of the American Cinema.** Charles Harpole, ed. New York: Charles Scribner's Sons/University of California Press, 1991– . 6v. (In progress). ISBN 0-684-80539-1.

When the projected ten volumes are completed, this will be the definitive history of the motion picture in this country, examining all aspects of the business, technology, and art of the industry. It will cover the beginnings in the nineteenth century and take the user through the end of the twentieth century. Each volume is by a different expert, resulting in a masterful effort combining scholarship and readability under the general editorship of an academic from the University of Central Florida. There are excellent photographs and valuable charts. Volume 1 (1991) treats the emergence of cinema up to 1907; volume 2 (1991) examines the transformation of cinema, 1907–1915, in which the film industry was shaped; volume 3 (1991) describes the age of the silent feature from 1915–1928; volume 4 (1997) treats the emergence of the talkies and the impact of the new technology, 1926–1931; volume 5 (1995) chronicles the Depression years and the grand design of the industry in representing political and social issues (1930–1939); and volume 6 (1997) supplies an informative look at the 1940s, with changes in the studio system and movement toward independent production.

Reviews and Criticism

Additional evaluative sources are found in "Film/Video Catalogs and Listings" and "Dictionaries, Encyclopedias, and Handbooks," previously treated in this chapter. This segment is targeted to sources of more lengthy reviews.

975. **Film Review Index.** Patricia King Hanson and Stephen L. Hanson, eds. Phoenix, AZ: Oryx Press, 1986–1987. 2v. ISBN 0-89774-153-6.

Treating nearly 8,000 films, this is the most comprehensive index of reviews in its coverage of over 100 years of filmmaking. Volume 1 examines the period from 1882 to 1949; volume 2 completes the effort with coverage from 1950 to 1985. Although comprehensive in terms of time covered, the title includes only those films established as being of most interest to researchers and students and those lesser efforts that have the potential to attract researchers due to their popularity or their relationship to sociological trends. Arrangement of entries is alphabetical by title of American release, with cross-references from foreign or subsequent titles, and supply country, director, and date along with citations to reviews in magazines, journals, books, and trade publications. Indexes of director, country, and year are found in volume 2.

976. **Film Theory and Criticism: Introductory Readings.** 4th ed. Gerald Mast and Marshall Cohen, comps. New York: Oxford University Press, 1992. 797p. ISBN 0-19-506398-8.

The essential character of this work has remained the same through the years, and it has earned an excellent reputation for the selection of articles and essays by theorists of various traditions and backgrounds. Much of the material is repeated from the third edition (1985). Despite being fifty-five pages shorter than the previous edition, there is similar broad representation of critical theory and well-developed coverage of the new breed of critic who has been schooled in the nature of the film art rather than literary criticism. The categories or sections of the work examine important issues and topics identified as basic to the study of film theory, with groupings of an expository nature relating to film and reality, the medium, audience, and so forth. The essays generally run from twenty to thirty pages, but vary in length.

977. **Great Italian Films.** Jerry Vermilye. Secaucus, NJ: Carol Publishing, 1994. 254p. ISBN 0-806-51480-9.

The author is a prolific writer and critic of film, and with this work has provided a needed service, examining the nature and composition of some of Italy's great films as well as some of the more obscure but similarly well-conceived efforts. Coverage is given to such works as *The Bicycle Thief, La Strada*, and *The Garden of the Finzi-Continis*. The work of such directors as De Sica, Rossellini, Monicelli, Fellini, and Antonioni is described and analyzed in an insightful manner. Numerous photographs and stills enhance the coverage and help explain the impact of the works, their makers, and their performers (Mangano, Mastroianni, Magnani, etc.).

Five Hundred Best British and Foreign Films to Buy, Rent or Videotape is an earlier effort by Vermilye (William Morrow, 1988), developed as a companion volume to a 1985 offering of the 500 best American films. It includes the most significant British and foreign titles as identified by the National Board of Review of Motion Pictures and editors of the Board's journal, *Films in Review*. Entries are alphabetically arranged and supply nationality, cast list, director, release date, running time, indication of color or black-and-white, and a page of critical-descriptive commentary. Unfortunately, there are no illustrations and no index.

978. Guide to Critical Reviews, Part IV: The Screenplay, Supplement One: 1963–1980. James M. Salem. Metuchen, NJ: Scarecrow Press, 1982. 698p. ISBN 0-8108-1553-2.

Since the initial volume of this four-part listing of critical reviews of stage and screen came out more than twenty-five years ago, the parts or basic four volumes have appeared at different times and in different editions, with various supplements. Part I of the main volume is now in its third edition (1984) and covers American drama from 1909 to 1982. Part II (3d ed., 1991) covers the Broadway musical from 1909 to 1989. Part III (2d ed., 1979) treats foreign drama from 1909 to 1974. This supplement is to part IV, which has not been revised since the first edition in two volumes in 1971. Part IV is entitled *The Screenplay from The Jazz Singer to Dr. Strangelove*, and covers the period from 1927 to 1962, documenting the critical commentary accorded the first thirty-five years of the talkies. This supplement continues the coverage of that work by adding another seventeen years of reviews. The reviews are generally from well-known periodicals such as *Film Quarterly*, *Life*, *Newsweek*, *Rolling Stone*, and *The New Yorker*, and the reviews should not be difficult to find. All volumes, including this one on the screenplay, continue to be a popular, useful purchase for the reference department.

979. Magill's Cinema Annual. Detroit: Gale Research 1982– . Ann. ISSN 0739-2141.

Gale has taken over production of this handy and extremely useful guide to a select number of films of the previous year from Salem Press. Beginning with coverage of the year 1981, it has served as a supplement to the extensive multi-volume *Magill's Survey of Cinema* (entry 980). The reviews are lengthy and well-constructed and cover an average of eighty films released in the United States. Entries include production credits, direction, screenplay, cinematography, editing, editing, art direction, music, MPAA rating, running time, and principal characters. Foreign films are included if they were released in this country during the time period. There is also a section of additional films that treats briefly the same number of films that appear in the "Selected Films" category. In addition, there are an obituary section and a listing of popular awards. A number of indexes provide excellent access, including subject, title, performer, and screenwriter. The 1999 *Annual*, edited by Michelle Banks, is the eighteenth edition and examines the films of 1998.

980. Magill's Survey of Cinema: Foreign Language Films. Frank N. Magill, ed. Englewood Cliffs, NJ: Salem Press, 1985. 8v. ISBN 0-89356-243-2.

This is another of the extensive multi-volume sets that are parts of a series bearing the Magill name. This set covers more than 750 foreign films arranged alphabetically by the title used in the United States. The reviews themselves are new and the result of a fresh viewing of the films by about 180 contributors. The reviews are preceded by identifications that include origin, release date, U.S. release date, producers, directors, screenplay, photographer, editor, art, costume, sound and music direction, and running time. Cast lists are also given.

The original set in the series appeared in 1980 as *Magill's Survey of Cinema: English Language Films, First Series*. This was a four-volume set treating over 500 important English-language films, followed in the next year by a six-volume set, the *Second Series*, covering another 750 films. The third issue was *Magill's Survey of Cinema: Silent Films*, a three-volume set published in 1982. It covered some 300 silent motion pictures from 1902 to 1936. In all cases, the essays are well-written and range from 1,000 to 2,500 words in length, including plot summaries and critical commentaries. *Magill's Cinema Annual* (see entry 979) serves as an update each year. A useful convenience tool is *Magill's Survey of Cinema-Title Index, All Series* (Salem Press, 1987), which furnishes a cumulative index for all series published between 1980 and 1986.

981. **The Motion Picture Guide, 1927–1984.** Jay Robert Nash and Stanley Ralph Ross. Chicago: CineBooks, 1985–1987. 12v. **Ann. Supp.**, 1986– . ISBN 0-933997-00-0.

This ten-volume set and two index volumes (vols. xi, xii) form one of the most comprehensive and detailed of all reference tools for the identification and description of films. There are 25,000 entries on English-language motion pictures as well as notable foreign films, with a separate volume devoted to silent films. Volumes are arranged sequentially in alphabetical order, and entries are arranged by title. Ratings are provided from zero to five stars and included are year of release, running time, production/releasing company, and color status. Cast lists are given, and most important, good analytical reviews are provided. The reviews are interesting, with their sometimes incisive and sometimes anecdotal commentary. Interesting background information regarding the performers or the making of the films is also included. The two-volume index, published in 1987, provides access to alternate titles, series, and awards. *The Motion Picture Guide: Annual* supplements the *Guide*, and covers all films from the previous year that have been released to movie theaters in the United States, as well as some that have gone straight to video. The 1999 annual (covering the films of 1998), edited by Edmond Grant, is published by Cinebooks. It is the thirteenth annual supplement and provides well-constructed, detailed reviews of some 500 feature films.

The Movie Guide, edited by James Pallot (3d ed., Perigee, 1998), continues to provide excellent in-depth reviews and descriptions, along with detailed cast and credit listings, ratings, and an array of useful appendices. Several thousand motion pictures are treated.

982. **The New York Times Film Reviews, 1913–1992.** Hamden, CT: Garland, 1993. 18v. **Bienn. Supp.**, 1969/1970– . ISSN 0362-3688.

This monumental work is one of the best sources of available reviews for motion pictures. The original six-volume set was issued by the *New York Times* and covered a period of fifty-five years from 1913 to 1968. Garland is now continuing the coverage through biennial supplements as well as offering a complete eighteen-volume set through 1992. For the early years of silent pictures through all the great periods of Hollywood genre films, the reviews are chronologically arranged by date of appearance in the newspaper and are reproduced. Thousands of films are covered in excellent fashion; the newspaper's critics have had a reputation for being thorough and perceptive. Volume 6 is an index volume to the first five volumes and contains appendices of overlooked reviews, New York Critic's Circle Awards, Academy Awards, and many illustrations. This index is detailed and is divided into separate sections for titles, people, and corporations. The series is kept up-to-date with biennial cumulations beginning with the period 1969–1970, generally published a year or two following the period of coverage, such as volume 20, the 1995–1996 supplement, published in 1998. These supplementary volumes are indexed individually.

The New York Times Directory of the Film (Arno, 1971; abridged ed., 1974) is a reprinting of the personal name and corporate index sections from the index volume of the main set. It is useful for its references to the date and page of the newspaper.

983. **Roger Ebert's Movie Yearbook 2000.** Kansas City: Andrews & McMeel, 1999. Ann. ISBN 0-7407-0027-8 (2000 ed.).

Ebert and his late colleague, Gene Siskel of the *Chicago Tribune*, have provided insightful commentary and have been enjoyed on national television by millions of motion picture fans. This is a new work providing every full-length review written by Ebert for his newspaper, the *Chicago Sun-Times*, and every interview he conducted in the last two and a half years. It represents an important source in its inclusion of a wide variety of motion pictures from blockbuster to small art film, both foreign and domestic, that have come under the scrutiny of this perceptive analyst. Some 500 new reviews are furnished, but equally important is the indexing provided to every review that has appeared in *Roger Ebert's Video Companion* annual series since its beginning as *Roger Ebert's Movie Home Companion* in 1983. The 1998 issue (published as the 12th ed. in 1997) is a cumulation of 1,500 reviews written and interviews conducted over the years. About 150 new reviews are added to each new annual. Coverage has been limited to those films available on video. Ebert's writing simulates his television commentary and provides insightful commentary in a lively manner. A four-star rating system is employed, and entries enumerate running time, year, cast, and credits, along with the review.

984. **Variety Film Reviews, 1907–1980.** New York: Garland, 1983–1985. 16v. **Bienn. Supp.** v.17– . 1981/1982– . R. R. Bowker. ISSN 0897-4373.

Using the idea developed for the production of the *New York Times Film Reviews* (entry 982), this is another multi-volume collection of reviews from a single source. In this case, the film reviews are taken from *Variety* (entry 959) and cover a period of seventy-three years in fifteen volumes. Volume 16 serves as an index of titles. The reviews are furnished in chronological sequence in order of their appearance in the magazine. Since feature-length films and shorts were not distinguished from each other until 1927, both types are included up to that time. After June 1927 only feature-length films are included. The R. R. Bowker Company continued the work with biennial supplements beginning with volume 17, covering the 1980–1981 period and ending with Volume 21 (1989–1990), issued in 1991. *Variety Movie Guide*, edited by Derek Elley and published by Berkeley Publishing Group, now provides reviews of over 8,500 selected films on a periodic basis. The most recent issue was in 1999, and the next edition is to be issued in March 2000.

Similar to the *New York Times Directory of the Film* (entry 982n) is Max Joseph Alvarez's *Index to Motion Pictures Reviewed by Variety, 1907–1980* (Scarecrow Press, 1982). It furnishes a separately published title index to the reviews and includes short subjects and re-releases.

985. **Variety Television Reviews 1923–1992.** Howard H. Prouty, ed. Hamden, CT: Garland, 1993. 17v. **Bienn. Supp.,** 1989/1990– . ISBN 0-8153-0363-7.

Developed in the same style and pattern as the *Variety Film Reviews* (entry 984), this is a large-scale attempt to capture the history of television through more than 40,000 reviews published over a seventy-year period. These date from the experimental years through the emergence of color and cable. Arrangement of entries is chronological; facsimile reviews are furnished as they appeared in *Variety* (entry 959). All types of programming are included, making the set a treasure-house of information on otherwise elusive local programs from all regions of the country, foreign broadcasts, and daytime fare as well as prime-time and syndicated offerings. Volume 15 is an excellent index that identifies even titles of episodes of documentary broadcasts; cross-references are provided. Like other works of its type, the biennial supplements are separately indexed; the 1993–1994 supplement (volume 18), edited by Prouty, was published in 1996 as *Variety and Daily Variety Television Reviews*.

CHAPTER 11

ACCESSING INFORMATION IN LANGUAGE AND LITERATURE

WORKING DEFINITIONS OF LANGUAGE AND LITERATURE

Language and literature are treated together in this guide because they are interdependent and because one of the primary ways of organizing literature is by the language of the literary work under consideration.

The common definitions of *language* and *literature* suggest that language has to do with spoken and written words and the systems for their use, while literature comprises the writings that capture ideas. Although literature, it can be said, is dependent on language for its very essence, it is probably wise to look at the definitions of the two fields separately, at least at the outset. Because language is a requirement of literature, it is considered first.

Language, according to one commonly used reference tool, is "systematic communication by vocal symbols";[1] another dictionary states that language is the "form or style of verbal expression";[2] while a third suggests that it is "communication by voice in the distinctively human manner."[3] All of these definitions, spanning nearly thirty years, seem to suggest that language must be spoken, when in fact some languages (notably sign languages and artificial languages) are not vocal yet constitute a means of communication within a community nonetheless. Some might argue that sign language is a substitute for spoken language, while other researchers suggest that it is indeed a language in its own right and not a surrogate at all. The same may be said for computer programming languages that sometimes substitute for foreign-language requirements for admission to academic programs.

Languages are subdivided into families and stocks, based upon the relationships among and derivations of each. Often, but not always, the distribution of languages is of geographic origin: Sino-Tibetan languages, for example, are most often used in a particular Asian region.

Closely involved with the study of language are the fields of linguistics (the scientific study of language) and anthropology (the study of social and cultural constructs and how humans live within them). Language is sometimes claimed as a subdiscipline of both.

To clarify the definitions of language, the reader should consult Edward Sapir's *Language: An Introduction to the Study of Speech* (Harcourt, 1921; repr., 1955), a classic cited in later textbooks. Literature is easier to define. Helen Haines, in the now-classic *Living with Books* (2d ed., Columbia University Press, 1950), offers: "Literature, in familiar library classification and definition, embraces the whole domain of imaginative and creative writing as well as the history, philosophy, and art of literary expression and various distinctive forms in which literary art finds manifestation."[4] Although Haines later differentiates literature from science, we can assume from her definition that the "distinctive forms" might include writings in the sciences and social sciences, thus constituting the literature of science, social sciences literature, and indeed, the literature of library and information science. These "literatures of . . ." refer to writings in a special discipline or field of study. Sometimes definitions of literature suggest a value judgment: that the literature has "lasting value" or is of "permanent interest."

The importance of the literature of various academic disciplines is made apparent in the curricular offerings of graduate schools of library science, information science, and information studies. Courses such as "Social Sciences Literature," "Resources in the Humanities," and "Sources and Services: Science and Technology" are just a few examples.[5] The role of the literatures, as vehicles for scholarly communication, is stressed in courses entitled "Scientific and Technical Communications" and the like. Few courses in contemporary programs put the whole emphasis on titles; most now include coverage of structures of the literature, the roles of various types of publications, and the unique forms of communications that one finds in the fields under study.

Some are inclined to define literature by the genres, or forms, that are usually included: fiction, poetry, drama, essays, and criticism. Asheim included oratory, excluded essays, and suggested that "imaginative writings" in those forms should define the area of literature.[6] The same parameters are observed in this guide.

The issue of value in literature is an important one. While this issue is of interest in all fields of the humanities, the fact that criticism of one work may ultimately become a part of the body of literature itself is nowhere more evident than in the area of literary scholarship. The critical literature, then, is subject to subsequent criticism as well.

MAJOR DIVISIONS OF THE FIELD

Both of the basic approaches to the division of literature, by language and by form, are usually taken into account in the customary divisions of the field. *The Reader's Adviser: A Layman's Guide to the Literature* (R. R. Bowker, 1988, v. 2) divides literature by language group and form, covering drama and then other literature.

Division of literature on the basis of the language in which it is written may require some refinements and modifications. For example, the volume of literature written in English is so large that further subdivision is desirable. In this case the term "English literature" is restricted to the literary output of the United Kingdom that appears in English, or even to the literature of England alone. Separate provision is customarily made for American literature, Australian literature, and so forth. At the other extreme, some of the world's smallest literatures may be grouped together under a single parent language.

As suggested above, the basic forms of literature are poetry and prose. Prose is normally divided into novels, short stories, and essays. Poetry is normally treated as a single unit, but it can be subdivided by type (lyric poems, epic poems, etc.). The drama, as a literary record of what is to be performed on the stage, has an independent life of its own and may also be considered as a major literary form. Modern drama is ordinarily prose, but it may also be verse, or it may consist of both prose and verse.

Another approach to the organization of literature is by historical periods or literary movements. These are often combined with the forms outlined above. J. B. Priestly's classic *Literature and Western Man* (Harper, 1960) divides the field by form (poetry, drama, and fiction) and by chronological period. Another detailed approach to the divisions of language and literature is offered by The Modern Humanities Research Association in *ABELL: The Annual Bibliography of English Language and Literature* (MHRA, 1920–1997, v1–72). Many of the divisions and subdivisions can be applied to other than English materials; see the Web pages at http://www.lib.cam.ac.uk/MHRA/ABELL/ (accessed March 8, 2000).

In addition to the extensive coverage of literature and of individual language literatures in general encyclopedias (*Encyclopedia Americana* and *Encyclopaedia Britannica* both have excellent articles), Haines's *Living with Books* should be consulted for the classic librarian's view of the fields of literature, drama, poetry, and fiction. A more recent discussion, also directed to the librarian, is James K. Bracken's "Literature," in *The Humanities and the Library*, edited by Nena Couch and Nancy Allen (American Library Association, 1993, pp. 86–131). The sources in the historical section of Chapter 12 of this guide provide additional background reading on literature.

A recommended source for more current Internet resources is Pam Day's "Internet Reference Resources in Language and Literature" *The Reference Librarian* 57 (1997): 153–59.

USE AND USERS OF INFORMATION IN LANGUAGE AND LITERATURE

Of all the disciplines covered in this guide, literature is the one in which scholars have been subjected to greatest scrutiny in terms of their information needs and information-seeking behaviors. Surveys, observational studies, and unobtrusive citation analyses provide an interesting and varied picture of the literature scholar's work habits and literature use. Because of the number of studies in this area, only those reported after 1980 are listed here; for earlier work, see earlier editions of this guide.

R. Heinzkill looked at English literary works in "Characteristics of References in Selected Scholarly English Literary Journals," *Library Quarterly* 50 (July 1980): 352–65. M. Stern's "Characteristics of the Literature of Literary Scholarship," *College and Research Libraries* 44 (July 1983): 199–209, is another frequently cited article. In 1985–1986, three significant studies were published: John Cullars's "Characteristics of the Monographic Literature of British and American Literary Studies," *College and Research Libraries* 46 (November 1985): 511–22; John Budd's "Characteristics of Written Scholarship in American Literature: A Citation Study," *Library and Information Science Research* 8 (April 1986): 189–211; and John Budd's "A Citation Study of American Literature: Implications for Collection Management" *Collection Management* 8 (Summer 1986): 49–62.

John Cullars has investigated the characteristics of other special literatures in "Citation Characteristics of French and German Literary Monographs," *Library Quarterly* 59 (October 1989): 305–25; "Characteristics of the Monographic Scholarship of Foreign Literary Studies by Native Speakers of English," *College and Research Libraries* 49 (March 1988): 157–70; and, more recently, "Citation Characteristics of Italian and Spanish Literary Monographs," *Library Quarterly* 60 (October 1990): 337–56.

Richard Hopkins's doctoral dissertation, "The Information Seeking Behaviour of Literary Scholars in Canadian Universities" (University of Toronto, 1988), confirmed and refined findings of some earlier works, and suggests that constraints of time and cost affect information seeking among scholars. The findings are summarized in Hopkins's "The Information Seeking Behaviour of Literary Scholars," *Canadian Library Journal* (April 1989): 113–15.

Broader studies of humanists' information seeking and use have included faculty members and literary scholars. Two still useful reports are Stephen E. Wiberley, Jr., and William G. Jones, "Patterns of Information Seeking in the Humanities," *College and Research Libraries* 50 (November 1989): 638–45; and "The Humanistic Scholars Project: A Study of Attitudes and Behavior Concerning Collection Storage and Technology," *College and Research Libraries* 51 (May 1990): 231–40.

As we predicted in this guide's fourth edition, the recent years have yielded many studies of the use of electronic materials; scholars' attitudes toward electronic sources and texts; and studies of new work methods made possible by networks, document delivery services, and other information technologies. See, for example, "Bibliographic Database Searching by Graduate Students in Language and Literature: Search Strategies, System Interfaces, and Relevance Judgments," by Debora Shaw (*Library and Information Science Research* 17 (Fall 1995): 327–45).

COMPUTERS IN LANGUAGE AND LITERATURE

The area of computing in language and literature continued to grow in the 1990s. In the fields of language and literature, computational linguistics, language teaching, writing and editing, text analysis, and automated translation are some of the areas for which we have an extensive literature. But perhaps the most prevalent growth has been in the area of Internet and Web resources. Bibliographies such as the *Annual Bibliography of English Language and Literature* are now available on the Web as well as on CD-ROM. Records in the bibliography from 1920 through 1996 are available at http://www.lib.cam.ac.uk/MHRA/ABELL/online.html (accessed December 14, 1999). *MLA International Bibliography, Linguistics and Language Behavior Abstracts* (LLBA) and other important resources are available in a variety of machine-readable formats.

Another important Web resource is *Voice of the Shuttle* at http://humanitas.ucsb.edu/ (accessed December 14, 1999). This site includes numerous resources in all areas of the humanities and is particularly strong in the areas of literature and linguistics. A page on "technology of writing" is included. See http://vos.ucsb.edu/shuttle/english.html (accessed December 14, 1999) for the English-language pages on the VOS site.

An extensive list of sources and an excellent review of literary texts is still Helen R. Tibbo's "Information Systems, Services, and Technology for the Humanities," *Annual Review of Information Science and Technology (ARIST)* 26 (1991): 287–346. This provides a good starting point and can be updated by many articles, including Perry Willett, "Building Support for a Humanities Electronic Text Center: The Experience at Indiana University," *Library Hi-Tech* 16 (1998):51–56; and Marianne Gaunt, "CETH, Electronic Text Centers, and the Humanities Community," *Library Hi-Tech* 16 (1998): 36–42. An earlier article that will provide background on the topic is Anita Lowry "Electronic Texts in English and American Literature," *Library Trends* (Spring 1992): 704–23. Here the reader can find information about Shakespeare and other English-language text files and also about basic considerations such as descriptive markup language and encoding. Avra Michelson and Jeff Rothenberg discuss all aspects of electronic text in "Scholarly Communication and Information Technology: Exploring the Impact of Changes in the Research Process on Archives," *American Archivist* 55 (Spring 1992): 236–315. The article describes projects such as the Thesaurus Linguae Graecae (TLG) and American and French Research on the Treasury of the French Language (ARTFL).

Electronic text projects, such as Michael Hart's Project Gutenberg and the Online Book Initiative, have made the full text of many great literary works available. Dartmouth's Dante Project provides the full text of *The Divine Comedy*, along with six centuries of commentary on the work, in searchable form. Other sources of information on the availability of electronic text include *The Georgetown University Catalogue of Projects in Electronic Text*, *The Humanities Computing Yearbook* (latest edition), Oxford University Press, and Chadwyck-Healey. The impact of electronic text is covered in *Literary Texts in an Electronic Age: Scholarly Implications and Library Services*, edited by B. Sutton (Urbana-Champaign: ASLIS, University of Illinois, 1994).

Database searching is also important in the fields of literature and languages. MLA Bibliography (file 71 on Dialog, also available on CD-ROM) covers 1963 to the present and provides access to books and journals on language, literature, and linguistics. LLBA (Linguistics and Language Behavior Abstracts), produced by Sociological Abstracts, Inc., covers the period 1973 to the present. Included are articles from over 1,000 journals. It is file 36 on Dialog. Other popular databases that literary scholars use include Arts and Humanities Search (produced by the Institute for Scientific Information and available in a variety of formats, including the new Web of Science), and Dissertation Abstracts Online.

The Internet resources related to literature and linguistics are vast and include list-servs and electronic journals on many literary genres, writers, and special topics. Search the Web for the particular genres or authors, and access to a wealth of resources will result. A good starting point for links to resources and reviews of them is the Argus Clearinghouse at http://www.clearinghouse.net/arthum.html (accessed March 8, 2000).

Finally, scholarly publishing is the subject of John Unsworth's "Electronic Scholarship or Scholarly Publishing and the Public," *Journal of Scholarly Publishing* 28 (October 1996): 3–12.

MAJOR ORGANIZATIONS, INFORMATION CENTERS, AND SPECIAL COLLECTIONS

The oldest, largest, and best known of the organizations that promote the study and teaching of languages in this country is the Modern Language Association of America (10 Astor Pl., New York, NY 10003). Founded in 1883, it has more than 30,000 members, primarily university or college teachers, and it conducts an immense range of programs and activities. Publications include *PMLA* (quarterly). *Job Information Lists—English and Foreign Language* versions are available on the Web. An important contribution of the Association is its style manual, available in high school and scholar's versions, and also on the Web. The *MLA International Bibliography*, covered in detail in Chapter 12, is among the world's most important bibliographic resources covering drama, English, folklore, foreign languages, humanities, language, linguistics, and literature. The Web site for MLA is at http://www.mla.org (accessed December 15, 1999).

The American Council on the Teaching of Foreign Languages (6 Executive Plaza, Yonkers, NY 10701) was founded by MLA in 1967, but now exists as a separate entity. Its publications include *Foreign Language Annals* (6/yr.) and *Series on Foreign Language Education* (annual).

The National Federation of Modern Language Teachers Associations (659 57th Ave., Omaha, NE 68132) is a federation of national, regional, and state associations in the United States that publishes *The Modern Language Journal*, a quarterly.

The American Association of Language Specialists (1000 Connecticut Ave., NW, Ste. 9, Washington, DC 20036) is a group of interpreters, editors, and translators who provide language services worldwide. The members' directory is available on the Web. The Web address is http://www.taals.net (accessed June 1, 1999).

U.S. English (1747 Pennsylvania Ave. NW, Ste.1100, Washington, DC 20006) is an organization active in promoting English as the official governmental language of this country. It maintains a Web site at http://www.us-english.org/ (accessed March 8, 2000) that keeps members and the press up-to-date on legislative matters related to their goals.

There are a wide variety of organizations concerned with specific languages, and some maintain a Web presence. An example of the latter is Esperanto Language Society of Chicago (http://members.aol.com/chiesper/esc/ [accessed March 8, 2000]). Other organizations concerned with specific languages include the International Association for the Study of the Italian Language and Literature and the League for Yiddish, Inc. (200 West 72d St., New York, NY 10023).

The American Comparative Literature Association (University of Alabama, Box 870262, Tuscaloosa, AL 35487-0262) promotes the study and teaching of comparative literature in American universities, cosponsors *Yearbook of Comparative and General Literature*, and maintains a list of links to Web sites concerned with comparative literature. Its Web address is http://www.acla.org (accessed March 8, 2000).

The Council of Literary Magazines and Presses (666 Broadway, 11th Fl., New York, NY 10012) assists "little magazines" in a variety of ways. The Council maintains a Web presence with links to many small presses at http://www.litline.org/ (accessed March 8, 2000).

Regional interests are served by such groups as the Society for the Study of Southern Literature and the Western Literature Association (Department of English, Utah State University, Logan, UT 84322-3200).

Various library, literary, and children's literary associations serve a host of special clienteles with interests in all aspects of books, literature, and publishing. General association directories will lead the reader to the many organizations that are too specialized to be listed here.

Special collections in language and literature are numerous—they include those in information centers, libraries, associations, and scholarly societies—and there are far too many of them to list here. Good sources to use as supplements to this section are *Subject Collections*, compiled by Lee Ash and William G. Miller (7th ed., R. R. Bowker, 1993) and the Web sites identified above. Besides this guide to subject collections by Ash and Miller, publications of the American Library Association, Special Libraries Association, and the Center for Research Libraries will guide the reader to other collections of note.

Some special collections remain noteworthy. They include the Folger Shakespeare Library (201 E. Capitol St. SE, Washington, DC 20003-1094) which has an active research and publication program in British civilization of the Tudor and Stuart periods and theatrical history as they relate to Shakespeare. See http://www.folger.edu (accessed March 8, 2000).

The Center for Hellenic Studies (3100 Whitehaven St., Washington, DC 20008) is an international center associated with Harvard University. It conducts research in such areas as classical Greek literature, philosophy, and history.

Other giant collections are held by the Library of Congress (http://www.loc.gov [accessed March 8, 2000]), the British Library (http://portico.bl.uk/ [accessed March 8, 2000]), the Bibliotheque Nationale (http://www.bnf.fr/ [accessed March 8, 2000]), the New York Public Library (http://www.nypl.org/ [accessed March 8, 2000]), and Harvard University (http://www.harvard.edu [accessed March 8, 2000]). Information about the institutions and their holdings is readily accessible now via the Internet; many services can be provided electronically.

NOTES

[1]*The Concise Columbia Encyclopedia* (New York: Avon, 1983), pp. 465–66.

[2]*The Merriam-Webster Dictionary* (New York: Pocket Books, 1974), p. 397.

[3]*The American College Dictionary* (New York: Random House, 1961), p. 685.

[4]Helen E. Haines, *Living with Books*, 2d ed. (New York: Columbia University Press, 1950). p. 418.

[5]Course descriptions for courses offered by ALA-accredited programs were scanned for titles. For a list of accredited programs and linked access to their Web sites, see http://www.alise.org (accessed March 1, 2000) and click on "Schools."

[6]Lester Asheim, *The Humanities and the Library* (Chicago: American Library Association, 1956).

CHAPTER *12*

PRINCIPAL INFORMATION SOURCES IN LANGUAGE AND LITERATURE

LANGUAGE AND LINGUISTICS

Bibliographies and Guides

986. **Bibliography and Index of Mainland Southeast Asian Languages and Linguistics.** Franklin E. Huffman. New Haven, CT: Yale University Press, 1986. 640p. ISBN 0-300-03679-5.

A comprehensive listing that has proved useful to the field, this bibliography divides languages into five major categories: Austroasiatic, TibetoBurman, Tai-Kadgi, Miao-Yao, and Mainland Austronesian. About 10,000 titles on Southeast Asian languages, published up to 1985, are identified; they represent all forms of published materials as well as informal papers including conference presentations. Arrangement of entries is alphabetical by author, with cross-references furnished from multiple authors and variant names. Materials written in various languages of the world are identified and English translations are provided for entries in other than the common European language systems. An informative introduction describes the language classifications employed, and a detailed index provides ready access.

987. **Bibliography of Semiotics, 1975–1985.** Achim Eschbach et al., comps. Philadelphia: John Benjamins, 1986. 2 pts. (Library & Information Sources in Linguistics, v. 16; Amsterdam Studies in the Theory and History of Linguistics Science, Series V). ISBN 90-272-3739-5.

This is the most recent contribution to this important series under the direction of E. F. Koerner, which has included bibliographies on various aspects of linguistics. Semiotics embraces the study of signs and signaling systems and is interpreted by some to include such areas as pragmatics, semantics, and syntactics. Nearly 11,000 entries are furnished for the ten-year period covered. Books, monographs, dissertations, articles, conference proceedings, Festschriften, and reviews are all included. The coverage is international and several countries and languages are represented. Part 1 consists of an alphabetical list of nearly 700 periodicals that publish in this field, followed by the first half of the bibliographical entries; part 2 provides the second half of the bibliographical listings as well as indexes of reviews, subjects, and names.

Another useful product is *Semantics: A Bibliography, 1986–1991*, by W. Terrence Gordon (Scarecrow Press, 1992). This is the third issue of a continuing series in which the first book covered 1965–1978 (Scarecrow Press, 1980), while the second volume treated the years 1979–1985 (Scarecrow Press, 1987). The new work opens with an overview of the divisions and fields of semantics and a glossary of terms. The main text consists of an annotated bibliography of books, articles, and papers organized under topics such as ambiguity, synonymy, and idioms. There is an author index and an index of words treated.

988. **Dictionaries, Encyclopedias and Other Word-Related Books.** 4th ed. Annie M. Brewer, ed. Detroit: Gale Research, 1988. 2v. ISBN 0-8103-0440-6.

This is a large-scale, enumerative work treating some 35,000 dictionaries, encyclopedias, thesauri, and other wordbooks. The utility of this work lies in its arrangement of entries under Library of Congress subject classification, permitting the librarian to identify sources of word information relevant to different topics. All types of dictionaries are included: monolingual, bilingual, and polyglot dealing with all types of specialties and specializations. There is no indication of selection criteria, and various editions appear while others are omitted. There is a detailed subject/title index to aid access.

A recent specialized effort is David E. Vancil's compilation, *Catalog of Dictionaries, Word Books, and Philological Texts, 1440–1900* (Indiana State University, 1993). This is a useful tool for scholars and students, providing a catalog of the holdings of the Cordell Collection at the University. The Cordell Collection of Dictionaries is the largest in the world and contains more than 5,100 dictionaries issued before 1901 along with thousands of more recent origin. Foreign and English-language entries are interfiled in this catalog of the early works. Emphasis on the early titles is especially useful to historical research. Access is aided through indexes by date, language, and subject.

989. **Kister's Best Dictionaries for Adults & Young People: A Comparative Guide.** Phoenix, AZ: Oryx Press, 1992. 438p. ISBN 0-89774-191-9.

This excellent guide opens with an informative sixty-one-page introductory essay describing the different uses, history, compilation, and various types of dictionaries as well as the debates between prescriptive and descriptive orientation and inclusion of four-letter words. It serves as an update of Kister's earlier work on dictionaries, issued in the late 1970s, but in this case omits related tools like thesauri and secretarial handbooks. The present effort is divided into two major sections treating 132 adult dictionaries (unabridged, college desk, family and office, etc.) and 168 young people's dictionaries (high school, junior high, upper elementary, etc.). Entries provide description and evaluation and range from one to ten pages in length. Five appendices provide useful listings of associations and publications; there is an author-title-subject index.

From the British perspective is Brendan Loughridge's *Which Dictionary? A Consumer's Guide to Selected English-Language Dictionaries, Thesauri, and Language Guides* (American Library Association, 1990). Preceded by an introductory description of the seven criteria or checkpoints used in evaluating dictionaries, coverage is given almost exclusively to British publications. Some 300 titles are treated, most of which are of the small and specialized nature. An appendix supplies a list of 50 recommended titles. A title index is furnished.

990. **Linguistics: A Guide to the Reference Literature.** 2d ed. Anna L. DeMiller. Englewood, CO: Libraries Unlimited, 2000. 396p. (Reference Sources in the Humanities Series). ISBN 1-56308-619-0.

Designed to serve the needs of a wide range of users, from undergraduates to specialists and researchers, this useful tool describes over 1,000 reference sources published between 1957 and 1999. The work is divided into three major sections, the first of which treats general linguistics and includes morphology, syntax, semantics, and other aspects of theoretical linguistics. Part 2 treats allied areas such as socio-linguistics, psycho-linguistics, semiotics, and so forth, while part 3 provides good descriptions of major reference works which include: bibliographies, encyclopedias, indexes, abstracts, biographies, as well as online, CD-ROM databases, periodicals, and associations. Fifty useful Web sites are identified as well. Annotations are detailed and informative. Three well-developed indexes provide access by author, title, and subject.

INTERNET RESOURCES

*991. **Summer Institute of Linguistics.** Dallas: International Linguistics Center, updated 1999. http://www.sil.org (accessed December 1999).

The Institute (SIL) is a leader in linguistics study and from its home page it furnishes an excellent directory of World Wide Web resources along with information about its history and development. The page is categorized by topic or area of interest; currently links are provided to such academic domains as linguistics, anthropology, translation, literacy, language learning, computing, and humanities. Under "linguistics" one may search "SIL Linguistics Resources," "Conferences, Workshops, Meetings, Symposia," "Universities and Other Academic Sites," "Electronic Texts, Dictionaries, and Data," "Computing Resources," "Journals and Newsletters," and "Resources Listed Topically" (speech, phonetics, grammar, semantics, etc.). There is a useful listing of "Other Indexes to Linguistics on the Internet" leading to a variety of sources from different organizations and individuals.

Indexes, Abstracts, and Serial Bibliographies

992. **Bibliographie linguistique des annees.** Comite International Permanent de Linguististes. Utrecht: Spectrum, 1939/1947. 1949– . Ann.

With its initial publication covering an eight-year period in two volumes, this service in both French and English (*Linguistic Bibliography for the Year...*) has achieved worldwide recognition as a massive work of documentation. It provides coverage of linguistics on an international level and identifies books, reviews, and articles from such diverse countries as South Africa, Belgium (Flemish publications), Czechoslovakia, Finland, France, Italy, the Netherlands, Norway, Poland, Spain, and Switzerland in volume 1. Coverage in volume 2 furnishes listings from Austria, Belgium (French publications), Denmark, England, Greece, India, Ireland, Portugal, the Soviet Union, Sweden, Turkey, and the United States. There is an author index to both volumes. The title continues as an annual publication and is highly regarded for its comprehensive coverage of periodical articles. There is no subject index, but the detailed table of contents facilitates access. Since 1994 it has been issued through Kluwer Academic Publishers of Boston.

*993. **Francis bulletin signaletique 524: Sciences du langage.** Nancy, France: Institut de l'information scientifique et technique, 1947– . Q. ISSN 1157-3740.

Part of the massive international documentation service undertaken initially by the Centre National de la Recherche Scientifique in Paris, this work has been taken over by the Institut since 1991. It is issued on a quarterly basis and provides listings of periodical articles in the field. It began as an abstract journal, with linguistics covered in *Bulletin signaletique: Philosophie, sciences humaines* from 1947 to 1960; from 1961 to 1966, linguistics was treated in *Bulletin signaletique, Sec. 21: Sociologie, sciences du langage*, and from 1967 to 1968 in *Bulletin signaletique 24: Sciences du langage*. It became the *Bulletin signaletique 524: Sciences du langage* after 1968, at which time it ceased providing abstracts and became a bibliography only. At present, it covers the biology and pathology of language, psycholinguistics, sociolinguistics, ethnolinguistics, historical linguistics, descriptive studies, semiotics, and communications. There is a classified arrangement with author and subject indexes. It is available online from the Institut as *FRANCIS: SCIENCES DU LANGAGE, providing coverage from 1972 to date. It contains nearly 85,000 citations, adding about 800 records per quarter.

*994. **Linguistics and Language Behavior Abstracts: LLBA.** La Jolla, CA: Sociological Abstracts, 1967– . Q. ISSN 0023-8925.

Formerly *LLBA: Language and Language Behavior Abstracts*, edited at the University of Michigan Center for Research, this abstract journal changed its title in 1985. It continues to cover an array of disciplines related to language and linguistics and treats a variety of journals, books, and monographs from communications and education as well as linguistics. Included are titles in acoustics, anthropology, comparative literature, ethnology, information science, medicine, psychiatry, psychology, and philosophy. Abstracts are grouped in broad divisions such as linguistics and philosophy and are subdivided by more specific topics. Over 1,000 journals are surveyed for articles of potential relevance and represent a number of languages and countries. There is an author index. The work is available online through DIALOG, with a file size of some 200,000 records from 1973 to date, and on CD-ROM on a semiannual basis from SilverPlatter.

995. **Modern Language Review.** Belfast: Modern Humanities Research Association, 1905– . Q. ISSN 0026-7937.

This is one of the most respected review journals in the humanities and provides reviews of studies of medieval and modern languages and literatures. Known for its lengthy, detailed, and thoughtful book reviews, it is a top priority in those libraries emphasizing or supporting communication and language studies. As in many review journals in the humanities, there is a certain amount of delay following publication of the items prior to their review in the journal. It is being made available in microform by the Association.

Modern Language Quarterly is an American contribution published through the University of Washington since 1940. Several studies of literary works and literary forms appear in each issue and represent Western European and American scholarship. The publication features comparative reviews on topics and issues in the field. The journal has issued the *Annual Bibliography of English Language and Literature* since its inception.

996. **Year's Work in Modern Language Studies.** London: Modern Humanities Research Association, 1929/1930– . Ann. ISSN 0084-4152.

The war years witnessed an extended suspension of publication for this useful reviewing source; therefore, volume 11 covers the period 1940 to 1949, in which year it resumed its annual frequency. Language and literature are treated in a variety of settings and time periods: medieval Latin, Romance languages, Germanic languages, and Slavonic languages. The focus is on developments from the medieval period to the present day. During the past two decades, general linguistics has been treated and today is regarded as an important component.

Studies in Philology, from the University of North Carolina, is a quarterly journal that began in 1906. It furnishes textual and historical research in classical and modern languages and literature. It is of use primarily to the scholar and specialist and is available on microfilm through Maxwell House, Microforms International.

Linguistics Dictionaries, Encyclopedias, and Handbooks

997. **The Cambridge Encyclopedia of Language.** 2d ed. David Crystal. Cambridge, UK: Cambridge University Press, 1997. 480p. ISBN 0-521-55050-5.

Developed by a British professor of linguistics, this second edition continues to utilize a thematic arrangement in achieving its intent to promote an informed awareness and understanding of the importance and complexity of human language. Aided by an excellent team of editorial advisers, the work retains its stature as a scholarly but readable tool, well-illustrated with maps, diagrams, and photographs. There are several major sections or parts, treating such topics as popular ideas about language; language and identity; structure of language; medium of language; child language acquisition; and language, brain, and handicap. Especially useful is the segment on languages of the world. These parts are divided into numerous subsections treating the different components of the category. There are many cross-references to related sections along with extensive bibliographic references. Several appendices furnish a glossary and a table of the world's languages along with indexing by language, authors and personalities cited, and topic.

998. **Compendium of the World's Languages.** George L. Campbell. New York: Routledge Kegan Paul, 1991. 2v. ISBN 0-415-02937-6.

This is a scholarly tool treating more than 300 languages in a comparative manner. Both individual languages and families are described in terms of their historical development and structure, providing the reader with treatment of the script, phonology, morphology, syntax, and word order. Entries identify the number and location of language speakers as well as language composition. There is general diversity in the languages selected, from Chinese, spoken by over a billion people, to various African dialects spoken by several thousand at the most. In some cases languages are grouped, with a heading for North American Indian languages along with headings for certain individual tribes. Sources used by the author are listed as a general bibliography at the end of volume 2, along with a chart providing exposition of some forty scripts. There is no general index.

999. **A Dictionary of Linguistics and Phonetics.** 4th ed. David Crystal. Oxford: Blackwell, 1997. 426p. ISBN 0-631-20096-7.

The author, a prominent British linguist and editor of the quarterly journal *Linguistics Abstracts* (Blackwell, 1985–), has provided an updated edition of his well-received work issued in 1980, 1985, and 1987. These earlier efforts had achieved a prominent position among those dictionaries designed for both students and researchers in the field. The new work has added new words that make it more useful to current students. Terms are treated as main entry items and include many that came to prominence during the 1980s and 1990s. They serve to indicate the directions taken by the field of study with respect to both current and traditional linguistic theory models. Government-binding theory has received excellent coverage. Many of the definitions have been reworked or expanded. Entries may include descriptions, examples, diagrams, and references to additional reading. The new edition continues the tradition of high quality established by the earlier efforts.

Crystal's *Encyclopedic Dictionary of Language and Languages* (Penguin, 1994) is a paperback reprint of a 1992 publication intended for the popular market. It is a non-technical glossary of some 2,750 terms culled from various areas of language and linguistics study and is geared toward everyday use. Cross-references are supplied and definitions are clear and comprehensible.

1000. An Encyclopaedia of Language. N. E. Collinge, ed. New York: Routledge Kegan Paul, 1990. 1011p. ISBN 0-415-02064-6.

This is a comprehensive collection of essays by various scholar-contributors representing their specialties within the study of language. There is a total of twenty-six essays by twenty-eight contributors, arranged under three general topics or categories, accompanied by numerous diagrams and illustrations. The first category, "The Inner Nature of Language," contains nine essays treating such topics as phonetics, phonology, grammar, semantics, and pragmatics. The second category, "The Larger Province of Language," also has nine essays. Coverage includes psycho-linguistics, neurolinguistics, language therapy, anthropological linguistics, sociolinguistics, and so forth. The final segment "Special Aspects of Language," supplies eight essays treating such topics as lexicography, history of linguistics, language engineering, and Collinge's contribution on the evolution of language. Each essay furnishes a list of references along with suggestions for further reading. There is an index of topics and an index of names to aid access.

1001. The Encyclopedia of Language and Linguistics. R. E. Asher and J. M. Y. Simpson, eds. New York: Pergamon Press, 1994. 10v. ISBN 0-08-0359434.

With the rapid development of language studies and linguistics during this century, there has been a profusion of theories, practices, and professional jargon. The development of a comprehensive work of this kind was seen as necessary to treat the diverse elements and personalities contained in over 3,000 years of history and hundreds of different languages from all over the world. This large-scale effort provides international scope and perspective, with an honorary editorial advisory board of fourteen members representing the United Kingdom, United States, Japan, France, Australia, Russia, India, and China. The executive editorial board of thirty-five members shows more British orientation, along with members from the United States, New Zealand, Italy, the Netherlands, and Australia. More than 1,000 contributors from fifty countries (primarily the United Kingdom and United States, but also from Asia and Africa) have produced detailed and informative articles on 2,000 subjects. There is a glossary of over 3,000 definitions along with indexes by subject, contributor, and name. The tool should become the standard for the field.

1002. Encyclopedic Dictionary of Semiotics. 2d rev. and upd. ed. Thomas A. Sebeok, ed. New York: de Gruyter, 1994. 3v. ISBN 0-31104-229-5.

Sebeok, a professor of linguistics at Indiana University, has performed an excellent service in coordinating the efforts of numerous individuals who served on the editorial board and the panel of contributors to produce this significant work. The first edition was issued in 1986 and utilized the talents of more than 200 specialists from all over the world, who contributed signed articles. This updated effort employs a similar pattern, supplying over 400 articles providing well-executed coverage. Exposition includes historical background and present usage of terms, with some recommendations to standardize current conventions; biographies of prominent personalities in semiotics; and appraisal of the impact of semiotics on inquiry in other fields. Articles vary in length from those of a monographic nature (over twenty pages on semantics) to explanations of one paragraph. The title remains a solid work and represents an important aid to specialists and advanced students.

1003. International Encyclopedia of Linguistics. William Bright, ed. New York: Oxford University Press, 1992. 4v. ISBN 0-19-505196-3.

This comprehensive and detailed work is intended primarily for the scholar and advanced student in its coverage of all known and extinct languages and language families. There are 750 articles, signed by specialist-contributors from twenty-five countries. Articles covering the languages generally supply historical perspective along with treatment of script, pronunciation, grammar, syntax, and relationship to neighboring languages. Articles on language families enumerate specific examples and identify the number of speakers. In addition, technical terms are defined and biographical sketches of important personalities are given. There are numerous cross-references along with a detailed index of more than 100 pages. A glossary is furnished along with synoptic outlines of entries placing them in perspective.

The Linguistics Encyclopedia, edited by Kirsten Malmkjaer (Routledge Kegan Paul, 1991; repr., 1995), is designed for a wider audience, ranging from educated laypersons to scholars. All relevant topics of linguistics are treated in enough detail and with enough clarity to achieve good results. Articles are supplied by a group of scholars from all over the world. There are numerous cross-references and illustrations; both a bibliography and an index are furnished.

1004. **Longman Dictionary of Language Teaching and Applied Linguistics.** Rev. ed. Jack Richards et al. New York: Longman, 1992. 423p. ISBN 0-582-07244-1.

The authors have established a reputation as experts in the field of applied linguistics with their work in the area of language teaching and other aspects. This is an update and expansion of a previous edition, issued in 1985. At that time it was the first dictionary to specialize in applied linguistics and furnished over 1,500 entries of terms used in the practice. The new edition has expanded the title to embrace the pedagogical element of language, which most certainly was an important component of its content in the past. New terms dealing with teaching and linguistics have been added. Definitions continue to be lucid and contain related terms within the body of a single entry. British and American pronunciations are given in most cases, and there are many cross-references between entries. Because it is focused primarily on the applied linguistics of language teaching, rather than language planning or lexicology, or translation, the work provides a good pedagogical overview of the field and includes many of the terms from theoretical linguistics as well. Useful for both the college student and the language teacher.

1005. **A Manual of European Languages for Librarians.** C. G. Allen. New York: R. R. Bowker, 1975; repr. with minor corr., 1981. 803p. ISBN 0-85935-028-2.

Especially useful for librarians and scholars is this handbook designed to facilitate the use and understanding of books published in some thirty-eight European languages, compiled by the former Superintendent of Reader Services at the British Library of Political and Economic Science. Arrangement is in seven language groups: Germanic, Latin/Romance, Celtic/Greek/Albanian, Slavonic, Baltic, Finno-Ugrian, and Other (Maltese, Turkish, Basque, Esperanto). Coverage of each language group follows a stylized pattern, beginning with general characteristics such as history and word order, followed by "bibliolinguistics," which examines the bibliographic elements of books and periodicals. Treatment is given to idiosyncrasies of authors' names, editions, titles, volumes, and so forth. Grammar and parts of speech then follow, concluding with a glossary of bibliographic terms and a grammatical index. The work is accurate and thorough in its coverage of the distinctive problems associated with the various languages.

1006. **The Oxford Companion to the English Language.** Tom McArthur and Feri McArthur, eds. New York: Oxford University Press, 1992. 1184p. ISBN 0-19-214183-X.

Another in the line of handy one-volume compendia from the publisher, this particular "Companion" supplies more than 3,500 signed entries by 100 scholars, treating all aspects of the English language. Diverse treatment includes historical considerations, dialects, grammar, style, rhetoric, pronunciation, usage, education, literature, culture, linguistics, politics, technology, and so forth. Articles tend to be well-constructed and concise but are thorough in their coverage and accurate in their treatment. Biographical sketches of important personalities such as Shakespeare, Noah Webster, James Joyce, and Mary Wollstonecraft are furnished. Scope ranges from the language of ancient times to contemporary considerations such as sexist language, jargon, political correctness, and black English. Placenames are included from all over the world, affirming the global representation of the language within the work. Arrangement of entries, as in other Oxford Companions, is alphabetical for easy access. In 1996, the editors issued an abridged edition of 1,053 pages, *The Concise Oxford Companion to the English Language* which concentrates on grammar, usage, dialect, pronunciation, and history of the language.

1007. A Pocket Guide to Literature and Language Terms. Benjamin W. Griffith. Woodbury, NY: Barron's Educational Series, 1986. 154p. ISBN 0-8120-2512-1.

Although one may wonder at the purchase of a paperback pocket-sized work for the reference department, it is felt that the inexpensive price of this item warrants its consideration. Designed for the college student who must operate in both linguistics and literature courses, this compact little volume does an admirable job and could be used in any library serving the needs of college and high school students. The first part of this convenient and easily handled work deals with literature terminology, while the second part is focused on grammar and composition. This latter segment also provides assistance in developing bibliographic entries. There is an index to both parts, and in general, although it is compact, the work is a worthwhile purchase.

1008. The World's Major Languages. Bernard Comrie, ed. New York: Oxford University Press, 1987; repr. with corr., 1990. 1025p. ISBN 0-41-506511-5.

This continues as an important and reliable handbook providing extensive information on particular languages and families of languages. The editor is a respected contributor and noted specialist in the area of Slavic languages and has written the introduction as well as two of the fifty chapters, each of which is devoted to a particular language or family. It is apparent that each chapter receives careful and thorough treatment by one of the forty scholars responsible for the work's development. Historical, sociological, and linguistic elements are covered, and detailed treatment is given to such aspects as graphic systems, morphology, word formation, and syntactic patterns. For inflected languages, charts indicate declension and conjugation classes. Most chapters have bibliographical notes and references. A general index provides access. The 1990 issue, in addition to correcting minor errors, updates the bibliography. In that same year Routledge issued reprints of sections of the work as *The Major Languages of Eastern Europe* and *The Major Languages of South Asia, the Middle East, and Africa.*

English-Language Dictionaries

UNABRIDGED AND SCHOLARLY

*1009. The American Heritage Dictionary of the English Language. 3d ed. Boston: Houghton Mifflin, 1992. 2140p. ISBN 0-395-44895-6.

Somewhat between the size of a desk dictionary and an unabridged edition is this important resource, now in its third edition. This useful tool was developed through the efforts of 175 contributors over a period of four years. It furnishes over 350,000 definitions for 200,000 main entry words. Also included are 4,000 illustrations. An important feature of this work is the usage panel of about 170 specialists, who make decisions on questions of current usage. Notes and commentary are provided in many cases. Word histories are furnished for some 400 selected words deemed to be especially interesting. Coverage is comprehensive, from the language of Shakespeare to that of present day idiomatic expression. The dictionary had quite an impact in the past in its attempt to provide guidance to proper usage, not only through labeling of words but also with usage notes regarding controversial terms. Etymologies are not so extensive. There are separate biographical and geographical segments, although certain proper nouns appear in the main text. The dictionary attempts to retain propriety but is not reluctant to portray the language as it is. It is available on CD-ROM as part of *Microsoft Bookshelf '95*.

1010. **Funk & Wagnalls New Standard Dictionary of the English Language: Complete in One Volume.** Isaac K. Funk et al. New York: Funk & Wagnalls, 1965. 2816p.

The 1964 edition is the latest in a long line of reprints, remediations, and added-on supplementary issues. In character and personality, it is still a 1913 work, which at the time represented a complete revision of the first edition, published in 1893. The style is, of course, that of a prescriptive dictionary in the manner of the traditional attempt to prescribe the nature of the language in terms of propriety or correctness. Usage labels are employed to show the status of a given term, and examples of usage are taken from the "great" writers of the past, even drawing from classical literature. Known for its excellent coverage in geography and biography, names and places are included alphabetically within the main text, rather than placed into separate glossaries.

1011. **Middle-English Dictionary.** Hans Kurath et al., eds. Ann Arbor: University of Michigan Press, 1952– . v.1– .

This monumental and definitive effort began in the 1930s at Oxford University, which joined with the University of Michigan to begin production in earnest in 1952. Since that time progress has been slow but steady and volumes have been issued in parts or fascicles. Volume 14 emerged in 1993, bringing coverage to "T" in the alphabetical sequence. Most recently, the first fascicle for "W" was issued in 1999. Editorship changed hands from Kurath to Sherman M. Kuhn (volumes G–P) and now resides with Robert E. Lewis (volumes Q–T). An interesting description of this lexicographic "trip" involving millions of data slips and six decades of work appeared in the *Washington Post* (May 27, 1992). Over 100 lexicographers and scholars have been involved in this systematic recording of the language from the Norman Conquest through the fifteenth century (A.D. 1100–1500). Entries supply definitions, variants, grammatical forms, citations, and quotations from numerous sources.

***1012.** **The Oxford English Dictionary.** 2d ed. J. A. Simpson and E. S. C. Weiner. New York: Oxford University Press, 1989; repr. with corr., 1991. 20v. ISBN 0-19-861186-2.

The original descriptive dictionary that portrayed the language as it was rather than prescribing what it should be, *OED* is unexcelled as a scholarly and comprehensive historical dictionary. The second edition was issued fifty-six years after the first effort, which itself was published forty-nine years after the work had begun. The enormous task of updating the earlier version and producing the second edition was conducted through the creation of machine-readable text allowing for computer access. It has been available on CD-ROM as *OED2 on CD-ROM* from the publisher since 1991. The title now furnishes convenient access to some 2,412,000 quotations, which continue to illustrate changes in meaning over time for some 500,000 words (290,000 main entries, or about a 15 percent increase) from their beginnings in the recorded literature. There are 5,000 new words in addition to the contents of the five supplements to the first edition, along with revisions and additions to entries. For the first edition, James A. H. Murray had served as initial editor from the beginning until his death in 1915, when William A. Craigie assumed his responsibilities.

A ten-volume set was issued in 1928, entitled the *New English Dictionary on Historical Principles (NED)* (Oxford: Clarendon Press), followed by a supplementary volume in 1933. Then the set was reissued in thirteen volumes as the *Oxford*, with some corrections of typographical errors. It remains an indispensable tool, the best of its kind in the English language. The second edition has deleted proper names, Anglo-Saxon terms that were not used beyond A.D. 1150, certain dialect words emerging since A.D. 1500, and some slang terms. The second compact edition of *OED* is now available as *The Compact Oxford English Dictionary: Complete Text Reproduced Micrographically*. Published in 1991, the work has been issued in greatly reduced form through a reduction process of nine pages to one. The twenty volumes now appear as one 2,416 page effort issued in slipcase with a microprint reader (batteries not included). To help the user find his or her way through this magnificent source, Donna Lee Berg has authored *A Guide to the Oxford English Dictionary* (Oxford University Press, 1993), providing systematic instructions. With examples taken from the *Dictionary*, Berg explains the various nuances and elements to more fully utilize its potential. The first volume of an "additions series" was published in 1997.

*1013. **The Random House Webster's Unabridged Dictionary.** 2d ed., rev. and upd. Stuart B. Flexner, ed.-in-chief. New York: Random House, 1997. 2230p. ISBN 0-679-45854-9.

Originally published in 1966, this is the most recent of the unabridged dictionaries (although it has been described as lying somewhere between an unabridged and a desk dictionary in size). The work contains about 310,000 terms, which represents an increase of some 50,000 terms over the first edition. There are about 75,000 new definitions, along with increased emphasis on illustrations of usage. There is greater inclusion of synonyms, antonyms, and illustrations, as well as a conscious effort to remove gender bias in the definitions. Although not as revolutionary in some respects as *Webster's Third* (entry 1015), it is more daring in its decision to appeal to a popular rather than a scholarly audience. (Editors compose usage examples rather than cite the literature.) It is of the descriptive type, but employs usage labels more frequently, and is therefore more prescriptive than *Webster's Third*. It is considered up-to-date in its definitions (AIDS, new wave, etc.) and no longer avoids obscenities. It furnishes personal and placenames within the body of the listings of foreign words (German, French, Spanish, and Italian) as well as an atlas and gazetteer segment. This effort is a revised and updated edition of the second edition published in 1987, and is also available in CD-ROM format.

1014. **Webster's New International Dictionary of the English Language.** 2d ed. William Allan Neilson, ed.-in-chief. Springfield, MA: Merriam-Webster, 1961 (1934). 3194p.

Descended from a line of distinguished dictionaries from the Merriam Company beginning in 1828, this edition was an important contribution to the prestige and respect accruing to the Webster name. The first edition of the *New International* appeared in 1909, and this work represented a complete revision in 1934. Subsequent printings and reissues showed slight modifications such as a new words section added to the front in 1939. This work remained available for several years following the publication of the third edition in 1961 (entry 1015). Basically, it remains an excellent dictionary based on the rationale of providing a prescriptive tool for maintaining the integrity of the language. Many usage labels are furnished and examples of usage are quoted from the fine literature of the past. Approximately 600,000 words are included, many of which are obsolete or archaic. Word meanings are in historical sequence, earliest to most recent (a Merriam characteristic), and there are a separate gazetteer and a biographical dictionary. The main volume is retained in libraries along with the newer edition.

1015. Webster's Third New International Dictionary of the English Language. Philip Babcock Gove, ed.-in-chief. Springfield, MA: Merriam-Webster, 1961; repr., 1996. 2662p. ISBN 0-87779-201-1.

It is difficult to imagine the controversy caused by the publication of this work, which placed the prestige and authority of the Merriam Company on the side of the new linguists as opposed to the traditional grammarians. No longer was this a prescriptive tool, but rather one that described the language as it was, using only a few usage labels. Many words regarded as vulgar, colloquial, or incorrect were not qualified as such. About 100,000 new terms were added, including the raw and racy language of the streets. About 250,000 of the older terms were deleted, furnishing a total of 450,000 words. Quotations include those from the popular literature and are taken from modern authors rather than classic writers. The biographical dictionary and gazetteer sections have been dropped, and about all that remains the same from the second edition (see entry 1014) is the historical sequence of definitions given. This is the preferred dictionary of the American people and is found in every library.

12,000 Words: A Supplement to Webster's Third New International Dictionary (Merriam-Webster, 1986) is an attempt to keep up to date with the changes in language and language use. This is not a self-contained dictionary but must be used in conjunction with the basic work. Of interest is the introductory essay describing the recent growth of English vocabulary.

DESK AND COLLEGE

Desk dictionaries are generally understood to be those that stand on the desk and can be found in the possession of secretaries, college students, professors, businesspersons, and others engaged in normal social routines. They are the most frequently purchased dictionaries for adults.

1016. The American Heritage College Dictionary. 3d ed. Boston: Houghton Mifflin, 1993. 1630p. ISBN 0-395-66917-0.

The third edition continues the good work of the earlier issues and is based on the 1992 edition of the oversize work (entry 1009). The present effort is nearly as comprehensive, providing coverage of 185,000 words and 200,000 definitions. It adds over 15,000 new words and supplies 2,500 illustrations, both photographs and drawings. It contains some 500 fewer pages than its parent by making use of a smaller typeface. Also, the usage examples have been shortened, abbreviations have been employed in the etymologies, and word histories have been eliminated. Biographical and geographical entries are treated within the main sequence, unlike the Merriam-Webster effort (entry 1014). There are an essay as well as a chart on Indo-European languages at the end.

The Concise American Heritage Dictionary (Houghton-Mifflin, 1987) is a revision of an earlier effort and furnishes some 60,000 definitions and 400 illustrations. *The American Heritage Illustrated Encyclopedic Dictionary*, also issued in 1987, is a merger of a dictionary and encyclopedia, offering lengthier descriptions of some 300 topics of interest to high school students. Numerous small maps and illustrations are included.

*1017. The Concise Oxford Dictionary. 10th ed. Judy Pearsall, ed. New York: Oxford University Press, 1999. 1666p. ISBN 0-19-860259-6.

Regarded in the past as a small desk dictionary; the eighth edition, entitled *Concise Oxford Dictionary of Current English* (1990), had tripled the coverage of the seventh edition (1982) from 40,000 to 120,000 entry words. The ninth edition treated 150,000 entries with 230,000 definitions. Prior to the eighth edition, the work had been based in large part on the supplements to the first edition of the *OED*; both the eighth and the ninth editions were derived from the second edition of the *OED* (entry 1012). The current edition continues in that tradition. The emphasis is on contemporary English, specialist, and technical vocabulary in current usage.

Like its predecessors it departs from the historical treatment in its arrangement of definitions in order of familiarity rather than chronological sequence. It contains more than 220,000 entries. Like the *OED*, it continues to be a descriptive rather than a prescriptive dictionary, and it records the language as it exists among English-speaking peoples. Alternative forms of the entry words appear in parentheses. The work has been made available on CD-ROM by the publisher as **Concise Oxford Dictionary*.

A recent effort is *The New Shorter Oxford English Dictionary*, edited by Lesley Brown (1993), a two-volume work that treats every word or phrase in use in the English language since 1700. Entries are well-developed, furnishing definitions, origins, pronunciation, and other elements. Unlike the *Concise Oxford*, it adheres to a historical approach, sequencing the 83,000 quotations as illustrations of changes of meaning. It should prove to be of value to both students and scholars. A more comprehensive work is *The Chambers Dictionary*, completely revised and updated in its eighth edition, and edited by Catherine Schwarz and others (Chambers, 1994). Included among the 300,000 definitions are 25,000 new terms. It achieves comprehensive coverage through its system of "etymological nesting," which treats derivatives from the same root word under the heading for the root word. Definitions for main entries and sub-entries are generally given in order of commonality. There are numerous appendices.

1018. **Merriam-Webster's Collegiate Dictionary.** 11th ed. Springfield, MA: Merriam-Webster, 1998. 1600p. ISBN 0-87779-709-9.

Comparable in size to the ninth edition, but using smaller typeface, the tenth edition (1993) of what is judged to be the best of the desk dictionaries maintains the excellence of its predecessors while adding "Merriam" to the title for the first time, firmly establishing its publishing identity. Some 10,000 new words (CD-ROM, E-Mail, glasnost, etc.) were added and others have been dropped. The current effort is a slight expansion of the 1993 tenth edition with more than 160,000 entry terms, 215,000 definitions, 35,000 verbal illustrations and illustrative quotations, 35,000 etymologies, 4,400 usage paragraphs, and 700 black-and-white illustrations. Treatment of slang and obscene terms has improved and become more courageous. This series has long been regarded as the top choice among college students and academicians. Like the others it is based on the entries in *Webster's Third* (entry 1015). There is a separate section for biographical and geographical names in the appendices, along with abbreviations and foreign terms. It is an excellent example of an abridged dictionary. This edition has been made available in CD-ROM since 1995 as **Merriam Webster's Collegiate Dictionary* (Deluxe Electronic Edition) which also contains the full text of *Merriam Webster's Collegiate Thesaurus* (1984).

Because the name "Webster's" is not copyrighted, Random House issued a collegiate dictionary entitled *Random House Webster's College Dictionary* in 1992, largely based on its unabridged edition (entry 1013). This succeeds the previous college dictionary issued in 1975, and furnishes 180,000 entries. There is good coverage of current informal speech, including slang and dialect. Also, *Webster's New World Dictionary of American English*, edited by Victoria Neufeldt (Webster's New World/Prentice-Hall, 1988), is another popular choice as a desk dictionary. It contains 170,000 entries and emphasizes words of American origin. It is strong in treatment of usage and of etymologies.

USAGE, SLANG, IDIOMS, AND NEW WORDS

1019. **A Dictionary of American Idioms: Based on the Earlier Edition.** 3d ed. Adam Makkai. New York: Barron's Educational Series, 1995. ISBN 0-8120-1248-8.

The first edition of this work was edited by M. T. Boatner and Makkai and appeared in 1975 from Rowman & Littlefield. It had earned its reputation as being the most significant dictionary of idioms and had been used by a wide-ranging audience. The second edition by

Makkai, a professor of linguistics, carried on the tradition and treated more than 5,000 idioms. The third edition continues the good work, with coverage of more than 8,000 idioms, idiomatic words and expressions, regionalisms, and so forth. These words and expressions have been incorporated into the language through varied elements of our society. Expressions from CB radio, computer technology, and drug or hippie cultures are supplied. Main entries include definitions, parts of speech, and usage. Many are accompanied by minor entries derived from the main entry. In addition, there are cross-references aiding access to variant forms of the idioms.

Another source of new coinage is *Acronyms, Initialisms and Abbreviations Dictionary*, edited by Mary Rose Bonk and issued in three parts as volume 1 (Gale Research, 1997). This is no less than the twenty-second edition of this important and popular work and identifies some 500,000 acronyms, contractions, and other shortened forms. About 20,000 new terms continue to be added from the literature of aviation, business, computer science, science, and the military. Entries supply meaning, source, language and country of origin, and subject category.

1020. **Dictionary of American Regional English.** Frederic G. Cassidy, ed. Cambridge, MA: Harvard University Press, 1985– . v.1– . ISBN 0-674-20511-1 (v.1); 0-674-20512-X (v.2).

Volume I, A–C, is the initial effort of an important project in providing what is to become a comprehensive five-volume dictionary of folk expressions, unused meanings of common terms, regional colloquialisms, and words belonging to ethnic or social groups in the United States. Entries include parts of speech, variant spellings, geographical roots, usage labels, cross-references, and definitions. Etymologies are sometimes covered. A series of computer-generated maps shows geographical distribution of the word and gives some idea of the density of the population affected. The initial volume contains an important essay on language changes in American folk speech, a guide to pronunciation, and an explanation of the maps. Volume II, D–H, was issued in 1991 and adds another 11,000 entries, continuing the detailed coverage. Both volumes contain cross-references to the content of subsequent volumes; initially it was hoped that the set would be completed in ten years (1995). *An Index by Region, Usage, and Etymology to the Dictionary of American Regional English, Volumes I and II* was issued by the University of Alabama Press in 1993.

1021. **The Dictionary of Cliches.** James Rogers. New York: Facts on File, 1985; repr., Wing Book, 1994. 305p. ISBN 0-51706-020-5.

An interesting and useful work identifying over 2,000 commonalties of language usage, this volume embraces idioms, proverbs, and quotations. Not surprisingly, Shakespeare and the Bible are two of the leading sources for the clichés, a language species much despised and denigrated by linguists. Nevertheless, they are important features of language study, and this dictionary provides useful treatment of meanings and definitions, as well as etymologies. Entries are covered in-depth, with enough information to provide insight and enlightenment (even though some of the etymologies are speculative). Entries are arranged alphabetically and there is a detailed index of cross-references at the end of the book. The work is thorough and should be of use to a variety of library patrons.

Catch Phrases, Clichés, and Idioms: A Dictionary of Familiar Expressions (McFarland, 1990) is a useful listing of trite phrases and banal expressions for which the compiler, Doris Craig, feels there is a ready market among advertising agency executives, among others. It furnishes a detailed index of keywords that should provide ready access.

1022. **A Dictionary of Slang and Unconventional English: Colloquialisms and Catchphrases. . . .** 8th ed. Eric Partridge. New York: Macmillan, 1984. 1400p. ISBN 0-02-594980-2.

The standard in the field, the Partridge work has been the original slang dictionary from the time of its initial appearance in 1937. Previous editions have reprinted the original and added supplements (addenda) at the back. Now, at last, there is an integrated work that brings together in one alphabetical arrangement the original and subsequent supplements as well as additional new words and corrections. (Cockney is no longer included as a label and such words have been deleted because it is now accepted as mainstream English.) Partridge had collected most of this material (5,000 of the 6,000 entries) prior to his death in 1979. The new editor, Paul Beale, initialed those entries that he contributed to the volume. The new work maintains the tradition of the old and will continue as the major work of its kind.

Dictionary of American Slang, by Robert L. Chapman, now in its third edition (Harper & Row, 1998) is a leader among dictionaries focused on American slang. It contains more than 19,000 terms ranging from the 1880s to the computer generation. Hundreds of new terms from the past twenty years are included. *Contemporary American Slang* by Richard A. Spears (National Textbook, 1991) is an interesting work in that it is intended for those using English as a second or non-native language. Examples of usage are given for each entry along with alternative forms to clarify shades of meaning. Pronunciations are given in International Phonetic Alphabet. *The Macmillan Dictionary of Contemporary Slang* by Jonathon Green (Macmillan, 1995) places emphasis on current usage, embracing thousands of entries from most parts of the English-speaking world. It identifies the place of origin for terms other than those that are obviously British.

1023. **Harper Dictionary of Contemporary Usage.** 2d ed. William Morris and Mary Morris. New York: Harper & Row, 1985; repr., 1992. 641p. ISBN 0-062-72021-X.

The second edition of this dictionary follows the original by ten years, in which time the title has gained recognition as the most comprehensive and up-to-date dictionary of American word usage. A prescriptive work by virtue of its nature and purpose, it features a lively style and an interesting commentary on some of the difficult elements of American usage. Experts on the panel were asked to vote and comment. An important consideration is the easy-to-read large print format. Such terms as "hot pants" and "house husband" are described, as are more traditional words from the past. This is definitely a needed reference work for most American libraries.

1024. **International English Usage.** Loreto Todd and Ian Hancock. New York: New York University Press; distr., Columbia University Press, 1987. 520p. ISBN 0-8147-8176-4.

This is a highly useful dictionary-style handbook that covers English usage in all parts of the world where English is either the first language or an important second language. Interesting and informative comparisons are made about various practices and pronunciations of different nations and regions. There is an attempt to establish coverage that is balanced between descriptive and prescriptive approaches, with distinctions made between logical regional characteristics and actual errors. Generally the style of writing is lucid, although some passages can be understood only by a specialist. This is a scholarly work, but it can be used successfully by the interested layperson. Access is facilitated by a good index and numerous cross-references.

1025. **Merriam-Webster's Dictionary of English Usage.** Springfield, MA: Merriam-Webster, 1993. ISBN 0-87779-132-5.

This work continues in the tradition of the 1989 issue, providing historical treatment of the common problems associated with disputed usage of words in the English language. Like its predecessor, it is constructed within a descriptive rather than a judgmental philosophy and supplies liberal use of quotations in illustrating points of consideration. Those who are opposed to this style will find little value in such a manual, one reviewer likening the first edition to the Humanist Association's publishing of a catechism. Others see it as a fair-minded presentation of summary comment from various authorities and an enlightened treatment of the debates and concerns over the use of language. From this standpoint, the avoidance of value judgments is seen as a positive rather than a negative characteristic.

1026. **Oxford Dictionary of Current Idiomatic English.** A. P. Cowie et al., comps. New York: Oxford University Press, 1975–1983; repr., 1985. 2v. ISBN 0-19-431146-5 (v.1); 0-19-431151-1 (v.2).

Volume 1 of this work, covering verbs with prepositions and particles, was published in 1975; volume 2, dealing with phrases, clauses, and sentence idioms, appeared eight years later in 1983. The intention of the set is to furnish a coverage sufficiently broad to answer various practical questions and inquiries regarding the use of idioms. Both volumes taken together cover some 40,000 idioms. Idiomatic statements are defined clearly, and examples of usage from contemporary literature and speech are furnished. Foreigners learning English will be aided by some of the warnings given to avoid wrong usage or construction. As is sometimes true of Oxford University Press titles, there is a British emphasis or slant.

1027. **The Oxford Dictionary of New Words.** 2d ed. Elizabeth Knowles and Julia Eliot, eds. New York: Oxford University Press, 1999. 368p. ISBN 0-19-860235-9.

Another of the increasingly popular dictionaries of new words, the second edition identifies over 2,500 new words and phrases that have entered the language since the late 1980s. Descriptions are well-written, informative, and interesting to a wide array of users. Entries treat pronunciation, and supply definitions, sample sentences of usage, origins, and histories for terms. Origins lie in all walks of life, culture, and subculture representing politics, the drug scene, and science/technology along with Wall Street and the computer industry. U.S. and British terms are covered in comprehensive fashion, but there is representation from Canada, Australia, and other parts of the English-speaking world. Origins lie in all walks of life, culture, and subculture, representing politics, the drug scene, and science/technology along with Wall Street and the computer industry.

Jonathan Green's *Tuttle Dictionary of New Words: Since 1960* (Charles E. Tuttle, 1992) is more inclusive but less detailed in its coverage of 2,700 new words and phrases that have entered the language since the 1960s. Emphasis is on British expressions and entries are arranged alphabetically in columns providing identification of part of speech, date, definition, and quotation. Computer terms are represented but there has been an effort to avoid esoteric scientific language. The *Facts on File Dictionary of New Words*, by Harold LeMay et al. (Facts on File, 1988), is a reprint of a 1985 paperback treating 500 new words and phrases and gives brief definitions, pronunciations, and quotations. Words are culled from the language of the streets and ethnic cultures as well as sports talk, business, politics, and so forth.

1028. **Third Barnhart Dictionary of New English.** Robert K. Barnhart et al., eds. New York: H. W. Wilson, 1990. 565p. ISBN 0-8242-0796-3.

This is a revision and expansion of the second edition published in 1980 and is intended to replace the previous issues rather than serve as a supplement (as did the second edition to the first). It treats 12,000 new words, abbreviations, and acronyms that have entered the language within the previous thirty years. As might be expected, much of the additional word coinage comes from the advances of science and technology, along with language patterns of cultural groups and recently incorporated slang. The previous edition covered only 5,000 words in its role as a continuation of the first issue. This specialized source represents a supplementary volume to the general purpose dictionaries and responds to the needs of those for whom current and contemporary language is paramount in importance. Entries supply well-developed definitions and numerous quotations and identify the year in which the terms became current.

ETYMOLOGY, SYNONYMS, PRONUNCIATION, ETC.

1029. **The Concise Oxford Dictionary of English Etymology.** T. F. Hoad, ed. New York: Clarendon/Oxford University Press, 1986; repr., 1991. 552p. ISBN 0-19-861182-X.

Another of the Oxford dictionaries, this, like the others, is a work of high quality. Its parent work, C. T. Onions's *The Oxford Dictionary of English Etymology* (Clarendon, 1966), was the first comprehensive etymological dictionary of the English language since 1910 and established an excellent reputation for scholarship and breadth of coverage. The concise edition was begun by an assistant editor to Onions, G. W. S. Friedrichsen, and finally completed by Hoad. In truth, it shows little change from the style or content of the original, although abridgment is noticeable within the entries. Many abbreviations are employed that require referral to a list. Entries furnish dates and origins of various senses of meaning, all arranged in chronological order for each term. Brief definitions are given, but the dictionary should not be used for that purpose. Not appearing here, unfortunately, is the interesting and helpful introduction summarizing the history of the English language, which was an important element in the original edition.

A supplementary work is Adrian Room's *NTC's Dictionary of Word Origins* (National Textbook, 1994), which in truth is simply a reprint of Room's 1986 effort under another title and different publisher. It identifies origins for about 1,200 words about whose beginnings popular misconceptions exist, and should be considered only as a second source for the library.

1030. **The Barnhart Dictionary of Etymology.** Robert K. Barnhart and Sol Steinmetz, eds. New York: H. W. Wilson, 1988. 1284p. ISBN 0-8242-0745-9.

This work is useful to both high school and college students who wish to trace the origins of some 30,000 words and related terms, with emphasis on their development within the vocabulary of American English. All types of words are included, traditional and contemporary, formal and slang. The tool opens with a rather sophisticated introduction treating Proto-Germanic and Indo-European elements, but the ensuing text and definitions are clear, detailed, and easily comprehensible. Included in the entries are pronunciation for unusual words, part of speech, definition, date, and language of origin, as well as alternative and foreign forms of the term, word history, and cross-references to related entries. Additionally, there are glossaries of linguistic terminology and a bibliography. In 1995, HarperCollins issued *The Barnhart Concise Dictionary of Etymology*, a revised and shortened version.

Initially published in 1987 by Facts on File and using that publisher's name in the original title is Robert Hendrickson's *The Henry Holt Encyclopedia of Word and Phrase Origins* (Henry Holt, 1990). With fewer than 600 pages, it is less than half the size of the Barnhart effort and is designed to entertain as well as inform. Origins of some 7,500 words are described; many of the origins are of doubtful veracity but are supplied for their interest and legendary status. All types of words are used, drawing from the Bible, technology, literature, placenames, foreign expressions, euphemisms, slang, and obscenities. Purists will need to verify or confirm the information in other sources.

1031. **Dictionary of Collective Nouns and Group Terms.** . . . 2d ed. Ivan G. Sparkes, ed. Detroit: Gale Research, 1985. 283p. ISBN 0-810321-88-2.

The second edition of a title originally published in 1975, this is a historical dictionary on collective nouns, group terms, and phrases. Over 1,800 of these terms are listed, with examples of their use and changes of meaning. The work is divided into two parts, the first of which provides a definition with examples of use within the meaning or sense given. The second part supplies an index that lists items about which a collective term has been furnished. There is a great curiosity value to a work of this kind and the dictionary will not only inform but also entertain. Most of the words tend to be obsolete, rare, or obscure (e.g., a kindle of cats).

1032. **Dictionary of Word Origins.** John Ayto. New York: Arcade/Little, Brown, 1991. 583p. ISBN 1-55970-133-1.

Designed to establish the historical connection between English words is this well-constructed etymological dictionary by a British lexicographer. Emphasis here is not on definition, nor is coverage given to part of speech or pronunciation. Instead, there is a fascinating linkage through use of cross-references to a wide variety of related terms and expressions, most of which seem far afield from the original reference. For example, the term "doctor" leads to eleven other entries, including "dainty" and "paradox"; there are similar connections provided between "bacterium" and "imbecile," "map" and "apron," and "bishop" and "spy." In all some 8,000 words are covered, with emphasis on their status in forming the "central core of English vocabulary." Also included are new words with interesting origins. Arrangement is alphabetical in double columns; either century of origin is indicated or there is designation of "OE" for Old English.

1033. **NBC Handbook of Pronunciation.** 4th ed. rev. Eugene Ehrlich and Raymond Hand, Jr. New York: HarperPerennial, 1991. 539p. ISBN 0-06-096574-6.

Initially published in the early 1950s, this unique work has become a standard in the field, providing pronunciation according to a "General American" speech pattern. Originally devised by NBC for use by its broadcasters around the country, a careful survey determined that the speech pattern chosen as amenable to most Americans and identified as "General American" was a cross between Midwestern and Western dialects. The present effort treats more than 21,000 entries used frequently by broadcasters and commonly mispronounced. Emphasis is on proper nouns, including such personalities as Boris Yeltsin and Mikhail Gorbachev and placenames like Riyadh. The major change from the third edition is the substitution of simple respelling for purposes of pronunciation instead of the previously used International Phonetic Alphabet (IPA). An interesting introduction by Edwin R. Newman provides perspective on the importance of pronunciation in terms of effectiveness of communication.

Another useful effort is *Pronouncing Dictionary of Proper Names: Pronunciations for More Than 23,000 Proper Names . . .* , edited by John Bollard et al. (Omnigraphics, 1993). Emphasis is placed on the selection of terms that are difficult to handle and include both current and historical personalities, places, things, and events. Similar to the *NBC Handbook*, this title employs a simplified phonetic respelling to indicate pronunciation, although in this case it does include the IPA transcription. Variants are given along with cross-references.

1034. **The Oxford Dictionary and Thesaurus.** American ed. New York: Oxford University Press, 1996. 1828p. ISBN 0-19-509949-4.

This work combines material from the *Oxford Thesaurus* (1992) and the eighth edition of *The Concise Oxford Dictionary of Current English* (entry 1017), providing a combination of definitions with synonyms. The work contains about 100,000 entries treated fully with pronunciation, part of speech, plurals and tenses, etymologies, and definitions in order of importance. Keywords are accompanied by synonym entries (about 300,000) corresponding to the definitions provided. *The Oxford Thesaurus*, edited by Lawrence Urdang, is organized into two principal parts, with an alphabetical listing of headwords and synonyms, along with a detailed index that includes words not listed in the first segment. Following the headword, the synonyms are grouped together by similarity of meaning. Variant meanings are illustrated with a sample sentence. Prescriptive labels are used to identify words as colloquial, slang, taboo, archaic, and so forth. Index entries are followed by headwords from the dictionary section with the particular connotation identified. This work was also published as *The Reader's Digest Oxford Complete Wordfinder* (Reader's Digest Association, 1996).

    The Random House Webster's College Thesaurus, by Jess Stein and Stuart Berg Flexner (Random House, 1997), is the latest publication of what was previously issued as the college edition of *The Random House Thesaurus* in 1984, and later as *The Random House College Thesaurus* (repr. 1992). It was based on *The Reader's Digest Family Word Finder* (1975). Random House had increased the number of entries by 10 percent to cover 11,000 terms along with a similar increase in the number of synonyms and antonyms furnished for the entry words. No coverage is given to word origins, pronunciation, or spelling, unlike the earlier *Reader's Digest* publication; usage labels such as slang are provided, however. The current effort is a revised and updated edition. Entries are alphabetically arranged for easy access; coverage is given to synonyms grouped according to meaning. Examples of usage are supplied by sentences prepared by the editors to illustrate the various contexts. Listings of antonyms conclude the entries for many of the terms. There is no index.

1035.   Roget's International Thesaurus. 5th ed. Robert L. Chapman, ed. New York: HarperCollins, 1992. 1141p. ISBN 0-06-270014-6. Repr. Econo-Clad Books, 1999.

    A true standard in the field, this thesaurus was originally produced by Peter Mark Roget in 1852. Since that time, it has established itself as the major tool of its kind, its contribution being the classification scheme developed originally by Roget and expanded by others who served as editors. Knowledge is divided into approximately 1,000 subclasses under several main headings, such as abstract relations, space, matter, and intellect. This edition treats some 350,000 words and phrases under 1,073 subclasses (31 newly added) that fall under 15 major classes. In this way, word relationships are shown within an idea framework, with terms placed under the topics that they represent or express. Other synonym dictionaries simply arrange words alphabetically and provide one-word definitions or alternatives. This edition is especially strong in contemporary language and expressions.

    An innovative effort is *Roget's II: The New Thesaurus* (Houghton Mifflin, 1995). Developed by the editors of the *American Heritage Dictionary*, this work, now in its third edition, offers a handy and convenient approach to the language, furnishing "rapid access to synonyms which are grouped by precise meanings." All synonyms are listed alphabetically, allowing one-step information recall under each category. In addition to main entries, there are secondary entries that act as cross-references to main entries. Brief definitions are furnished along with the synonyms and antonyms for all main entries. The work is based on the third edition of *The American Heritage Dictionary of the English Language* (entry 1009) and thus is up-to-date.

Foreign-Language and Bilingual Dictionaries

1036.   The American Heritage Spanish Dictionary: Spanish/English, English/Spanish. Boston: Houghton Mifflin, 1992. 512p. ISBN 0-395-32429-7.

    Continuing in the tradition of high-quality lexicography associated with the American Heritage name is this recent bilingual dictionary, a unique work providing excellent coverage of Latin American Spanish as well as European usage. For this reason it is especially useful to those in both the Southeastern and Southwestern regions of the United States. The work compares favorably in scope and depth to other dictionaries of its type, with good coverage given to idioms and to scientific and technical terms. Among the special features is a verb table at the beginning of the volume, to which are keyed the entries for all the irregular verbs. This is a real asset for students trying to conjugate verbs. A concise version was issued the same year by the publisher. This work was originally published as *American Heritage Larousse Spanish Dictionary* in 1986.

1037. **The Cambridge Italian Dictionary.** Barbara Reynolds, gen. ed. New York: Cambridge University Press, 1962–1981. 2v. ISBN 0-521-06059-1.

A span of nineteen years passed from the appearance of the first volume to publication of volume 2. With its completion, the librarian and the patron have been given an excellent translation tool. Volume 1 is Italian-English, and volume 2, English-Italian, the rationale behind the dictionary being the development of a wordbook useful to English-speaking individuals. With this idea in mind, it is understandable that the work provides no explanations of English grammar and includes no guides to English pronunciation. Unfortunately, Italian coverage is also lacking in that treatment, and remains the primary deficiency of an otherwise rich and useful source of words from all time periods and types. The work was translated into Italian and published by Signorelli for an Italian readership in 1985.

Harper Collins Italian Dictionary: Italian-English; English-Italian (Harper & Row, 1990) provides a useful tool supplementary to the *Cambridge Dictionary* in its inclusion of terms relevant to business and office automation. Treated here are 70,000 entries and 100,000 translations. Also covered is a selection of abbreviations as well as placenames.

1038. **Deutsches Worterbuch.** Jakob Ludwig Karl Grimm and Wilhelm Grimm. Leipzig: Hirzel, 1854–1960; 16v. ISBN 3740100001. Repr., 1984. 16v. in 33.

This is the great German dictionary, which was finally completed more than 100 years after it was started. It was the first dictionary to promote the idea of a compilation based on historical principles, and was the creation of Jakob Grimm, the great German philologist, who with his brother, Wilhelm, began the arduous process. The brothers Grimm today are probably better remembered by most Americans for their collection of fairy tales, produced early in their careers, but it is the dictionary that has served as their greatest legacy. It influenced the development of the *OED* (entry 1012) and others of its type. It was the purpose of this work to give an exhaustive account of the words of new High German, the literary language, from the end of the fifteenth century onwards. Etymologies and senses are illustrated by literary quotations. Since 1965, there has been an ongoing effort to develop a revised and expanded edition incorporating the results of new research.

A more practical purchase for most American libraries is *Cassell's German and English Dictionary*, compiled by H. C. Sasse et al. (Collier Books/Macmillan, 1966; repr., 1986). A small, inexpensive paperback, it provides a concise but useful dictionary for the traveler or student in the initial stages of learning the language. *Dictionary English-German, German-English* (CD-ROM Verlag Gmbh) furnishes access to some 200,000 words and word combinations on CD-ROM. There is a separate file of 3,000 idioms and concepts.

1039. **Harrap's Standard French and English Dictionary.** Rev. ed. J. E. Mansion and D. M. Ledbesert, eds. London: Harrap; New York: Prentice Hall Press, 1990. 4v. ISBN 0-1338-3068-3 (v.1).

This has long been one of the leading dictionaries of its kind, and this four-volume edition is the most recent issue of a work that had its beginning in the 1930s. Since then, it has undergone several name changes and modifications. The present edition is a thorough revision designed to provide a work that is reasonable in terms of size and of wide scope. Emphasis has been placed on modern, technical, scientific, and industrial elements as well as the modern language, complete with colloquialisms and idioms. These are labeled for propriety and indicate slang, vulgarism, and so forth. The work has been criticized for the inclusion of dated material from past editions but at the same time has been praised for the inclusion of modern technical terminology.

Harrap's Shorter Dictionary: English-French/French-English, edited by Timothy Gutteridge in 1996, continues a new edition of the condensed version in one volume of the four-volume effort. It is a high-quality title that retains the basic coverage needed by students and others learning the language. Treatment is less full, but adequate for most needs in presenting the common elements of the language. An unusual recent effort is *The Oxford Guide to the French Language*, by William Rowlinson and Michael Janes (Oxford University Press, 1992), which provides both a grammar and a dictionary for its users. Numerous examples are given from newspapers and magazines along with rules of grammatical construction in the first segment. Also treated are pronunciation peculiarities and translation problems. The second section contains a useful bilingual dictionary of 45,000 words. The work appeals to a diverse audience from traveler to beginning student.

*1040. Languages of the World. Lincolnwood, IL: National Textbook Company, 1990. (CD-ROM).

This unique kit supplies access to eighteen dictionaries in twelve languages including English, Danish, Finnish, German, Italian, Spanish, Chinese, and Japanese. Produced in Japan, it consists of one CD-ROM disk, three floppies for search systems with different CD-ROM devices, and a user's manual of forty pages. Only one of the dictionaries is American, NTC's own *American Idioms Dictionary*. No publication dates are given, which must be considered a negative factor. There is emphasis on the inclusion of Harrap's dictionaries, for whom NTC serves as U.S. distributor (*Harrap's Science*, *Harrap's Shorter*, *Harrap's Data Processing*, *Harrap's Business*, and *Harrap's Concise*). The advantage of such comprehensive coverage is evident in the opportunity to find definitions, synonyms, and antonyms in twelve languages. The disadvantage would appear to be in the age of the various editions used because many of the newer terms, such as "CD-ROM" do not "compute" into all language terminologies.

1041. A New English-Chinese Dictionary. Rev. and enl. ed. The Editing Group, comp. Seattle: University of Washington Press, 1988. 1769p. ISBN 0-295-96609-2.

This important effort originally was developed during the Cultural Revolution and published in 1975 by the Joint Publishing Company of Hong Kong with the participation of seventy scholars located in the Shanghai area. These scholars were faculty members at Fudan University, Shanghai Teachers' University, Shanghai Institute of Foreign Languages, and so forth. The University of Washington acquired the rights in 1988 after its publication in Hong Kong in 1987. The original 80,000 entries are furnished with 600 modifications and/or deletions of political references to Mao and the Cultural Revolution. Additionally, there is the inclusion of a 4,000-word supplement to the original edition. This contains new words and those that have changed in meaning or morphology since 1975. There are nine appendices supplying lists of English verbs, weights and measures, common marks and symbols, conversion tables, and so forth.

Vietnamese-English, English-Vietnamese Dictionary, by Le-Ba-Khanh and Le-Ba-Kong (Hippocrene Books, 1991), fills a need for a work of this type in view of the exodus and relocation of Vietnamese people in the United States following the war. It enables them to better understand the written and spoken English language, providing over 12,000 entries, a list of modern Vietnamese terms, and an appendix of synonyms and antonyms. For the English user, it is useful for its definitions and may be used for translation of the written word. Pronunciation is not given for Vietnamese terms, however.

1042. New Revised Velazquez Spanish and English Dictionary. Mariano Velazquez de la Cadena et al. Rev. by Ida Navarro Hinojosa et al. Piscataway, NJ: New Century Publishers, 1985. 788p. ISBN 0832902659.

Considered one of the best dictionaries of its kind, this edition replaces the one published in 1974. The tool is comprehensive, with over 150,000 entries for which information is given on pronunciation as well as translation. About 700 new entries have been added, providing up-to-date coverage that includes regional variations for Latin America and Spain. Always considered strong in technical terminology, obsolete terms, and esoteric language, the dictionary has a comprehensive nature that exceeds most works of this type. Revisions for terms requiring changes from the previous edition as well as new entries are included in the middle of the volume between the two sections of the work. In the appendices are brief grammars of Castilian and English, geographical terms, proper names, abbreviations, and other valuable listings.

Collins Spanish-English/English-Spanish Dictionary. Unabridged (HarperCollins, 1998), now in its fourth edition and edited by Colin Smith et al., has added over 40,000 references and some 50,000 translations since its initial appearance in 1971. It treats more than 250,000 entries and presents a new emphasis on Hispanic-American languages. Word treatment is up-to-date, with regional usage and slang identified and labeled. The fifth edition is to be published very soon. *The Random House Portuguese Dictionary: Portuguese-English, English-Portuguese* (Random House, 1991), edited by Bobby J. Chamberlain, furnishes 38,000 entries, the emphasis being Brazilian Portuguese. It identifies gender and serves as a practical manual through its numerous tables of basic measures, weights, days of the week, and so forth.

1043. NTC's New College Greek and English Dictionary. Paul Nathanail, comp. Lincolnwood, IL: National Textbook, 1992. 560p. ISBN 0-8442-8473-4.

Regarded as a useful and adequate dictionary since its publication in 1985, this reprint of a relatively inexpensive paperback edition packs a great deal of information into a small package. Related items are brought together while maintaining an alphabetical order. The vocabulary is considered to be well chosen and balanced, although there is a tendency to favor the contemporary demotic form. Although it is designed for English-speaking users (British-based), there is no guide to English pronunciation. Some hints in this direction for the Greek language would have been helpful even though Greek orthography is rather regular. There are more than 50,000 entries.

A comprehensive work is the two-volume treatment provided by D. N. Stavropoulos, which was initiated with publication of *Oxford English-Greek Learner's Dictionary* (Oxford University Press, 1977) and completed more than a decade later with *Oxford Greek-English Learner's Dictionary* (Oxford University Press, 1988). *The Oxford Turkish-English Dictionary*, by A. D. Alderson and Fahir Iz (3d ed., Clarendon/Oxford University Press, 1984), is considered the best existing tool for translation of contemporary Turkish texts. Many technical terms are included, and the complicated Turkish morphology and idiom are handled well.

1044. NTC's New Japanese-English Character Dictionary. Jack Halpern, ed. Lincolnwood, IL: National Textbook, 1993. 1992p. ISBN 0-8442-8434-3.

A solid publication is this effort providing comprehensive coverage of 60,000 definitions for 42,000 words. A central meaning considered to be the most important is supplied along with excellent treatment of kanji or Chinese characters by patterns. Entries are treated under four patterns (left-right, up-down, enclosure, and solid) and identify number of strokes, order of strokes, grade, frequency, compounds, synonyms, and so forth. Various appendices provide insight regarding rules and considerations.

A pocket-sized version is Noah S. Brannen's *The Practical English-Japanese Dictionary* (Weatherhill, 1991), a favorite of travelers and tourists. It supplies romanization of Japanese characters along with excellent examples of usage. Also included is an introduction to Japanese grammar identifying parts of speech, pronunciation, and conjugation tables. There are several CD-ROM dictionaries, not surprising with the emergence of Japan as an industrial and technical power. *English-Japanese, Japanese-English Dictionary* (Tokyo: Sanseido) aids the translation of Japanese to English, and English to Japanese. The software producer is Dai Nippon Printing Company, which has prepared this work based on the *Century's English-Japanese Dictionary and Crown's Japanese-English Dictionary*. Another CD-ROM issue is *Kojien: A Comprehensive Dictionary of the Japanese Language*, from Iwani-Jhaten Publishers, available since 1987, which treats a wide range of dialects as well as slang and technical expressions. Etymology and grammar are identified and quotations from Japanese literature are used. A similar revision is available from Fujitsu using a slightly different spelling in the title, *Kohjien (Japanese Dictionary) CD-ROM*. A comprehensive effort is *Kojien Dictionary*, published by Ayumi Software and Qualitas Trading Company. It supplies 200,000 entry words along with 2,000 graphics and sound. The CD-ROM product is compatible with Macintosh systems.

1045. **The Oxford Latin Dictionary.** P. G. W. Glare, ed. New York: Clarendon/Oxford University Press, 1982; repr., 1990. 2126p. ISBN 0-19-864224-5.

Another scholarly work in the Oxford lineup of dictionary and word source books developed through scholarly pursuits and careful attention to detail, this dictionary appeared in eight fascicles over a period of fourteen years from 1967 to 1981. A milestone was reached with the publication of the complete edition in one volume. The work has replaced an older and outdated standard in the field from Harper & Row as well as a more recent work that falls short in comprehensiveness and detail. There is a rich selection of entry words from the Latin literature; quotations illustrate in historical fashion the various senses or meanings the words have assumed through time. A thorough, precise, and valuable item for reference work.

1046. **The Oxford Russian Dictionary.** Rev. and upd. Colin Howlett. New York: Oxford University Press, 1995. 1340p. ISBN 0-19-864189-3.

This new work represents an expansion and update of the publisher's two volumes issued in 1984, *The Oxford English-Russian Dictionary* and *The Oxford Russian-English Dictionary*. The effort furnishes coverage of more than 180,000 words and phrases as compared to 160,000 in the earlier volumes, and treats 290,000 translations. It provides a complete approach to the study of the Russian language, identifying the terms derived from various dictionaries judged to be useful and of value. The work includes colloquialisms, idioms, and technical terms as well as general standard terminology. Explanations are given, as are translations, and useful appendices of official abbreviations and geographical names are furnished. Correctness of translation is emphasized in the English-Russian segment; the Russian-English section uses quotations from literature and newspapers. Like its predecessors, this work should be purchased by all libraries needing to provide services to specialists as well as students. In 1996, the publisher issued *The Concise Oxford Russian Dictionary*, derived from this work, in 1,007 pages.

Stephen Marder's *A Supplementary Russian-English Dictionary* (Slavica, 1994), a corrected reprint of the 1992 effort, furnishes 29,000 entries not found in the *Oxford* work. Included are recently coined terms along with those for which the meanings have changed substantially, as well as slang, technical terms, obscenities, and abbreviations.

1047. Webster's New World Hebrew Dictionary: Hebrew/English, English/Hebrew. Hayim Baltsan. New York: Prentice Hall General Reference, 1992. 827p. ISBN 0-13-944547-1.

This is an interesting and useful addition to the small body of work on Hebrew-English dictionaries and is unique in its use of romanized Hebrew words rather than Hebrew characters for the main headings in the Hebrew-English segment. This is in keeping with the work's intent to serve the needs of those with no prior knowledge of the Hebrew language. Transliteration does not follow standard practices as identified in the scheme developed by ALA and the Library of Congress but adopts a new system that appears to be accurate. In the Hebrew-English section, following the romanized entry the term is expressed in non-vowelized Hebrew characters, then defined. This non-vowelized Hebrew form is also used in the English-Hebrew section. Some 60,000 entries are treated in the two sections of the work. Practical in nature, the vocabulary includes socio-political terms and names of political parties.

Histories and Directories

1048. The American Language: An Inquiry into the Development of English in the United States. 4th ed., corr., enl., and rewritten. Henry L. Mencken. New York: Alfred A. Knopf, 1963; repr., 1984. 769p.

This monumental work is the most well-known and respected history of the American language. It was first completed over fifty years ago by H. L. Mencken, the famous journalist for the *Baltimore Sun*, and has gone through subsequent editions, supplements, and reprints. There is nothing to rival it either in breadth or depth of treatment of the English language in America. The work provides historical treatment of the development of the English language in the United States in eleven chapters covering a variety of topics. Included are such topical divisions as the two streams of English, the beginning and growth of the American language, pronunciation and spelling, common speech, proper names, slang, and so forth. The work contains an appendix that includes a segment on non-English dialects and a general index to provide access. A one-volume abridged edition was issued by Knopf in 1963, and again in 1977.

1049. A History of the English Language. 4th ed. Albert Croll Baugh and Thomas Cable. Englewood Cliffs, NJ: Prentice-Hall, 1993. 444p. ISBN 0-13-395708-X.

The initial edition of this work was published in 1935, and since that time it has become the leading reference history as well as a textbook for courses covering the historical development of the English language from its beginnings to the present. It includes a segment on the development of the language in this country, but for greater detail on that topic one should consult Mencken's *The American Language* (entry 1048). Treatment is given to the evolution of the language within the context of the political, social, and intellectual history of England. This is considered the best one-volume survey history on the topic. Bibliographies are up-to-date to time of publication and are linked to the recent scholarship in the field.

1050. World Guide to Terminological Activities, Organizations, Commissions, Terminology Banks. 2d completely rev. and enl. ed. Magdalena Krommer-Benz. Munich: Verlag Dokumentation; distr., New York: K. G. Saur, 1985. 158p. ISBN 3-598-21368-9.

For those interested in the development or maintenance of standards within the various disciplines and fields of study, this work will be of assistance in identifying organizations and activities on an international scale. It is felt that the lack of uniform terminology and inconsistency in language use in some fields or disciplines of study hamper the effectiveness of research and ultimate progress within the field. This is especially true of the newer areas of inquiry. Listed here are over 200 agencies and institutions and their committees concerned with terminology. All disciplines of study and all major languages are included, with an emphasis on Western European units. The arrangement is by UDC according to subject interest. There are indexes of names, subject, matter, and acronyms.

LITERATURE

General (Various Genres and Languages)

Sources in this segment treat literature from more than one language and include English.

BIBLIOGRAPHIC GUIDES AND INTRODUCTORY WORKS

1051. **The Art of Literary Research.** 4th ed. Richard D. Altick. Rev. by John J. Fenstermaker. New York: W. W. Norton, 1993. 353p. ISBN 0-393-96240-7.

Since its initial appearance in 1964, this standard source has been regarded as one of the more useful, well-constructed, and interesting introductory guides in the field of literature. The fourth edition carries on the good work of the earlier editions and provides excellent narrative and provocative exposition of the principles and practices involved in literary research. Fenstermaker's revision retains the original character of Altick's contribution, but furnishes a needed modification with respect to modern practice and theory. Bibliographies and exercises have been updated and there is more coverage of computerization in the field. Advice is still relevant regarding the consideration of bibliographic procedures, note taking, library practices, and writing as an art practice requiring high standards and commitment. The title continues as a top choice for reference departments.

1052. **The Comparative Reader: A Handlist of Basic Reading in Comparative Literature.** John T. Kirby. New Haven, CT: Chancery Press, 1998. 211p. (Comparative Studies, no. 1). ISBN 1-890657-00-X.

This is the first in a planned series from the publisher that will feature guides and bibliographic listings for the study of comparative literature at the college level. This concise but useful work begins with a general introductory essay establishing the criteria for selection of the items within the various listings and supplies the bibliographies developed by the Program in Comparative Literature at Purdue University. The various contributors to the volume are identified and described. There is a general listing of fundamental texts applying to various national groups and cultures; this is followed by individual listings for study of a varied array of national literatures. Included here are bibliographies for Australian, Breton, Cornish, Inuit, Aboriginal, Hungarian, Italian-American, and so forth. The listings vary in depth and focus with the individual contributors and may include historical and cultural expositions as well as literary efforts. Topical treatment may address such areas as feminist literature and gay studies.

*1053. **A Guide to Serial Bibliographies for Modern Literatures.** 2d ed. William A. Wortman. New York: Modern Language Association of America, 1995. 333p. ISBN 0-87352-965-0.

This is an expanded version of the initial 1982 effort, which was a compact but important annotated listing of serial bibliographies in the area of modern literature. The new edition has added 273 serial bibliographies in the areas of general humanities, national literatures, genres, themes, and so forth. The work is divided into several chapters covering scope; general bibliographies; British, American and foreign literatures; and alternative press serial bibliographies. These are primarily English-language works, but also include foreign-language products. Sources include standard reference works and electronic databases. Various types of bibliographies are enumerated (comprehensive, classified, author, and subject) as well as indexing and abstracting services. Entries furnish information regarding general coverage, bibliographic description, and publishing characteristics.

Serial Bibliographies (http://www.lib.muohio.edu/serial-bibliographies [accessed January 2000]) is a Web site maintained by William A. Wortman at Miami University of Ohio, designed to provide twice-yearly (January and June) updates and corrections to the MLA-sponsored *Guide*. The updates are cumulative and supply listings and descriptions of new or additional serial bibliographies, both electronic and print. Corrections and deletions are also furnished.

1054. **Problems in Literary Research: A Guide to Selected Reference Works.** 4th ed. Dorothea Kehler. Lanham, MD: Scarecrow Press, 1997. 230p. ISBN 0-8108-3216-X.

Continuing with the pattern established in previous editions, this effort treats a group of important basic literary reference works fundamental to literary research. The work is equally at home in the reference collection of a high school or undergraduate library or as a textbook for relevant coursework. Coverage is primarily of English and American literature sources but other literatures are not excluded. The work employs five chapters designed to promote understanding on the part of its readers. The pattern of coverage for each reference work begins with a brief description, then follows up with review questions and research problems requiring hands-on experience to resolve. Chapter 6 supplies a listing of supplementary sources. An index aids access.

Periodicals

1055. **The International Directory of Little Magazines and Small Presses.** Paradise, CA: Dustbooks, 1973/1974– . v.9– . Ann. ISBN 0-916685-70-5 (1999).

This annual guide and directory replaces the *Directory of Little Magazines* (1965–1972) and continues its volume numbering. Therefore, its initial volume under this title is volume 9. It continues to provide information of a directory nature for low-subscription literary and art magazines (address, telephone number, scope, editor, subscription price, average length, circulation figures), payment rates, and copyright arrangements, but also includes comments by the editors on the policies and types of material published. Lists of recent contributors are furnished as well. Small presses are covered in much the same fashion, with editor, address, scope, average price for books, production methods, and size of press runs. Editors' comments on the nature of the press are also given. Access is aided through subject and geographic indexes useful to those seeking publishing outlets. The 34th edition (1998–1999) furnishes information on more than 5,000 presses and journals.

Less comprehensive is *Directory of Little Magazines 1993–1994*, by R. I. Wakefield and Moyer Bell (Council of Literary Magazines and Presses, 1992). Similar information to that given by the *International Directory* is supplied for about 500 literary magazines from all over the world.

1056. **MLA Directory of Periodicals: A Guide to Journals and Series in Languages and Literatures.** New York: Modern Language Association of America, 1979– . Bienn. ISSN 0197-0380.

A companion volume to the important *MLA International Bibliography* (entry 1060), the ninth edition (1999) provides information on several thousand journals and series published in the United States and Canada that have been indexed in that work. This serial is without a rival in terms of providing up-to-date information on currently available titles of serial nature in the field. Arrangement is alphabetical by title of journal or series, with each entry furnished a sequence number referred to in the indexes. Various indexes provide excellent access: editorial personnel; language other than English, French, German, Italian, and Spanish; sponsoring organizations; subject; journal title abbreviations; and so forth.

Beginning in 1984, a useful biennial publication based on the *Directory* was published as a more narrowly based work. *MLA Directory of Periodicals: A Guide to Journals and Series in Language and Literature: Periodicals Published in the United States and Canada* draws from the complete version in furnishing coverage of about 1,200 titles published in the United States and its northern neighbor. It follows the same pattern of organization as does the parent work. There is also Margaret C. Patterson's *Author Newsletters and Journals . . .* (Gale Research, 1979), which identifies and annotates over 1,100 titles devoted to the collection and distribution of criticism, bibliographies, biographical information, and so forth on the lives and works of single authors.

Internet Resources

*1057. **A Celebration of Women Writers.** Mary Mark. 1994– . http://digital.library.upenn.edu/women/ (accessed April 5, 2000).

This is an interesting and informative Web site and is copyrighted by Mark. It is of expanding nature because it encourages contributions from its audience and participants. It represents a directory of Internet resources with links to biographical and bibliographical information on women writers throughout history. All types of writing are identified (novels, poems, letters, biographies, travel, religious commentary, history, science, etc.). Although emphasis is given to English-language resources, writers from many countries are included in an effort to make the public aware of the variety and quality of published material available from female writers. One may search the listings by century, country, or name of author. In addition, a major effort is being made to extend the resources by making older, out of copyright works available online; a listing of such resources is provided along with a standing request to add such sites that have not been identified.

BIBLIOGRAPHIES

1058. **Psychocriticism: An Annotated Bibliography.** Joseph Natoli and Frederick L. Rusch. Westport, CT: Greenwood, 1984. 267p. ISBN 0-313-23641-0.

This is a collection of annotated references to essays by writers who have applied psychological principles in their interpretation of literature. There are over 1,400 entries, representing essays published subsequent to 1969. These are organized by literary period, beginning with ancient and classical literature and ending with the twentieth century. There is an opening chapter that identifies essays of a general nature on psychology and literature. Following that are separate chapters given to the different periods. They begin with references to the period as a whole, then give citations to works on individual writers. Each entry is annotated with a brief description of the essay's content. Both an author index and a subject index are provided to facilitate access to the appropriate entry.

A work similar in perspective is *Psychoanalysis, Psychology, and Literature, a Bibliography*, edited by Norman Kiell (2d ed., Scarecrow Press, 1982). Approximately 20,000 psychologically oriented books, articles, and monographs about literature are classified by type, such as autobiography, criticism, drama, fiction, and myths. Writings date from 1790 to 1980 and are accessed through author and title indexes. *Psychoanalysis . . . Supplement to the Second Edition* (1990) continues the coverage with an additional 7,754 works written between 1980 and 1987.

INDEXES, ABSTRACTS, AND SERIAL BIBLIOGRAPHIES

*1059. **Francis bulletin signaletique 523: Histoire et sciences de la litterature.** Nancy, France: Institut de l'Information Scientifique et Technique (INIST), 1991– . Q.

Similar to other indexes and abstracts previously sponsored by the France Centre National de la Recherche Scientifique (CNRS), this abstract journal has been the responsibility of INIST since 1991. A quarterly publication, it has been issued since the early 1970s and continues to provide references and abstracts of journal articles, monographs, proceedings, and dissertations relevant to the history and science of all types of literature. As part of the enormous database known as FRANCIS, it is available online, with its file dating from 1972 and numbering around 122,000 records. The database is updated on a quarterly basis at the time the print copy is issued; it averages an increase of 4,000 items per year. Coverage includes French literature; African literature; Anglo-Saxon and German literature; and the literature of the Slavs, Italians, Latin Americans, and Caribbeans.

*1060. **MLA International Bibliography.** New York: Modern Language Association of America, 1921– . Ann. ISSN 0024-8215.

This is the monumental bibliography known and respected by language and literature students both in this country and abroad. A standard work in the field, it has changed title and scope since its inception in 1921, when it was limited to writings by Americans on the literature of various countries, and known as *American Bibliography*. Since 1956, it has been a more expansive source of bibliographic information and was named *Annual Bibliography* from 1956 to 1962. Since 1963, it has had its present title and includes writers from a variety of other languages, although still primarily American and European. Books, articles, monographs, and Festschriften representing critical analyses and interpretations on folklore, language, linguistics, and literature are all included. Presently, it appears in five volumes, with volume 1 given to the English-speaking nations; volume 2 to European, Asian, African, and South American literatures; volume 3 to linguistics; volume 4 to general literature; and volume 5 to folklore. The volumes may be purchased separately or in several combinations with author and subject index. The file is available online from MLA, FirstSearch, or WILSONLINE, and on CD-ROM through H. W. Wilson. There are more than 1,300,000 records online, covering the period from 1963 to the present, and about half that number on CD-ROM, with coverage beginning in 1981. More retrospective coverage is slated for the future. There is monthly updating of electronic versions.

Available through Research Libraries Group (RLIN) is *RLG Research-in-Progress Database, which furnishes some 2,500 references to articles accepted for future publication by fifty scholarly journals selected by the Modern Language Association, along with NEH-funded research in progress and feminist studies and conference papers from the National Council for Research on Women.

1061. **The Romantic Movement: A Selective and Critical Bibliography.** David V. Erdman, ed. West Cornwall, CT: Locust Hill Press, 1979– . Ann. ISBN 0-9339-5182-5 (1997).

This scholarly annual bibliography, formerly from Garland Press, is a continuation of a bibliography by the same title that appeared in *ELH*, a quarterly journal of English literary history, from 1936 to 1948; then in *Philological Quarterly*, 1949–1963; and finally in *English Language Notes*, from 1964 to 1978. The present work continues the plan and follows the rationale of the earlier publication in its desire to cover a movement rather than a time period. Time periods of Romanticism vary with different languages (the English section being stabilized between 1789 and 1837). Other languages covered are French, German, and Spanish, as well as Italian, which has recently been added.

The Romantic Movement Bibliography, 1936–1970 . . . (Pierian Press, 1973) is a compilation, in seven volumes with indexes, to the contents of the first thirty-four years of the bibliographic listings. It was edited by A. C. Elkins, Jr., and L. J. Forstner.

1062. Twentieth-Century Literary Movements Index: A Guide to 500 Literary Movements, Groups, Schools, Tendencies, and Trends.... Laurie Lantzen Harris and Helene Henderson, eds. Detroit: Omnigraphics, 1991. 419p. ISBN 1-55888-306-1.

This is the initial offering of a set or series of volumes designed for use at the high school and undergraduate level to aid comprehension of world literary movements and related elements. The title goes on: "covering more than 3,000 novelists, poets, dramatists, essayists, artists, and other seminal thinkers from 80 countries as found in standard reference works." Three volumes are planned for the twentieth century, with the second continuing essays on the literary movements and important personalities within them. The series is designed to cover one era at a time. The present volume indexes twenty-eight standard literary reference sources that contain entries on the movements. Part 1 provides an index to the movements; part 2 supplies a name index to the writers, critics, and theorists associated with them. Brief identification information is given along with citations to coverage in indexed sources.

DICTIONARIES, ENCYCLOPEDIAS, AND HANDBOOKS

1063. Benet's Reader's Encyclopedia. 4th ed. Bruce Murphy, ed. New York: HarperCollins, 1996. 1144p. ISBN 0-06-181088-6.

First published in 1948, with the second edition issued in 1965 and the third in 1987, this convenient and valuable handbook has been a standard in the field ever since it first appeared. The work furnishes brief articles on a variety of topics and personalities (scientists, artists, philosophers, as well as creative writers). The current edition represents a substantial revision, with more attention given to African, African-American, women, and multi-cultural influences. The emphasis on world literature continues, with treatment of the Orient, Russia, Latin America, and the Near East. All periods of time continue to be represented, with a large proportion of the entries either new or revised. The work remains an impressive attempt at comprehensiveness for a one-volume effort. Literature-related entries cover authors, titles, characters from fiction, literary terms, allusions, and movements. Important historical figures and topics are identified, as are terms from the sciences, fine arts, philosophy, and so forth. Entries for titles furnish plot summaries, and those for literary characters give full identification. Musical compositions and art works are also included.

1064. Calendar of Literary Facts: A Daily and Yearly Guide to Noteworthy Events in World Literature from 1450 to the Present. Samuel J. Rogal, ed. Detroit: Gale Research, 1991. 877p. ISBN 0-8103-2943-3.

The editor is well-known for his work in producing several reference works, including chronologies on British and American literature (see entry 1211). With this publication he has broadened the scope to embrace world literature over a period of 440 years, from 1450 to 1989. The chronology is divided into two sections: The first represents a generic day-by-day treatment of births and deaths of writers and includes their nationality and genre. The second part provides year-by-year coverage beginning in 1450 with the invention of printing from movable type. Categorical divisions for each year include births, deaths, major publications, and significant events relevant to literary interests. Brief annotations of each entry vary from a single sentence to a paragraph in length. Indexing is thorough for both sections.

1065. Characters in 19th-Century Literature. Kelly King Howes. Detroit: Gale Research, 1993. 597p. ISBN 0-8103-8398-5.

A more recent effort patterned after the earlier publication on the twentieth century described below, this is designed to aid high school students and undergraduates in their understanding of literary characters. It supplies plot summaries and character analysis for 275 major plays, novels, and short stories written by more than 150 nineteenth-century writers currently being studied in classrooms in this country. Minorities are purposely included. About 2,000 characters are identified and examined critically in terms of their status within the development of the theme and plot. A bibliography is furnished. Entries supply author, name, dates, nationality, and principal genres. Arrangement is alphabetical by author's name. There is an index of characters and titles.

Characters in 20th-Century Literature, edited by Laurie Lantzen Harris (Gale Research, 1990), and its *Book II* (1995), established the precedent for the above title, analyzing the characters and describing the plots of hundreds of works from hundreds of major novelists, dramatists, and short story writers who are either still alive or who have died since 1899. Special emphasis is given to the post-1960 period. Arrangement and format are similar to the more recent effort discussed above.

1066. Columbia Dictionary of Modern European Literature. 2d ed., fully rev. and enl. Jean Albert Bede and William B. Edgerton, gen. eds. New York: Columbia University Press, 1980. 895p. ISBN 0-231-03717-1.

Published initially in 1947, this was recognized as one of the best one-volume works on the subject of comparative literature of the modern period. The new edition maintains the high standard of scholarship, with excellent biographical sketches, critical evaluations, and survey articles on the various national literatures. "Modern" is defined as beginning with the period "toward the end of the nineteenth century when Europe was swept by a wave of new revolutionary movements, largely inspired by the French symbolists and known by different names . . . symbolism, decadence, and modernism." More than 1,850 biographical sketches are given for individual authors, each of which is furnished with bibliographical references. There are excellent survey articles on the various national literatures, and all articles are signed. Over 500 scholars have contributed to this comprehensive study. Many of the articles from the earlier edition have been revised and some have been deleted.

*1067. Cyclopedia of Literary Characters II. Frank N. Magill, ed. Pasadena, CA: Salem Press, 1990. 4v. ISBN 0-89356-517-2.

Designed as a companion to *Masterplots II* (entry 1094n) in the same manner in which that title complemented the original *Masterplots*, this work provides treatment of the characters portrayed in all literary works embraced by the *Masterplots II* series since its beginning in 1986. (*American Fiction*, *British and Commonwealth Fiction*, *World Fiction*, and *Drama*). Also included are a few selected titles from the *Short Story* series for a total of 1,437 works with over 12,000 characters. Format is similar to that of the initial effort, with articles arranged alphabetically by title of work. Articles provide in-depth coverage, treating characters individually, and pronunciation is given for difficult names. Articles are signed and provide description of the characters' role in plot development and relationship to other characters. Access is available on CD-ROM through *Masterplots II CD-ROM* (entry 1094n). The work is indexed by title, author, and character.

Magill's Cyclopedia of Literary Characters (Salem Press, 1963, repr., 1972) was issued in two volumes and treats over 16,000 characters from the 1,300 novels, dramas, and epics of world literature in the original *Masterplots*. Arrangement is alphabetical by the title of the work and information is given on author, time of action, and date of first publication or presentation. Characters are described in order of significance. An index by characters and authors facilitates access.

1068. **Dictionary of Concepts in Literary Criticism and Theory.** Wendell V. Harris. New York: Greenwood, 1992. 444p. (Reference Sources for the Social Sciences and Humanities, no. 12). ISBN 0-313-25932-1.

The author is a well-respected academic and writer who has developed a unique work primarily for scholars and serious students. It complements other work in the field, such as *A Handbook to Literature* (entry 1075) in its selectivity, choosing only seventy concepts, and also in its depth of analysis in providing exposition of them. Such major concepts in literary criticism as "allusion," "deconstruction," "semiotics," and "imagination" are treated in essays ranging from five to seven pages in length. These include current definition, etymology supported by numerous quotations, annotated references, and a bibliographical essay identifying related sources. The index is detailed and compensates somewhat for the generic organization of the work.

From the same publisher is Leonard Orr's 1991 effort, *A Dictionary of Critical Theory*, providing definitions specific to critical terminology. Terms from all over the world are treated including those derived from Asian as well as European languages. They represent various schools and thought systems and embrace both general concepts and specific elements of theory. The most likely audiences for the work are scholars and serious students, although the author suggests its utility for undergraduates as well.

1069. **A Dictionary of Literary Terms and Literary Theory.** 3d ed. J. A. Cuddon. Cambridge, MA: Blackwell Reference, 1991. 1051p. ISBN 0-631-17214-9.

First published in 1977 and revised two years later, this detailed dictionary has established itself as a useful source of information for serious students of world literature. The third edition has been expanded to provide over 2,000 terms from various literary genres and various parts of the world, with over a dozen foreign languages represented. In this respect, it is more comprehensive than other dictionaries of its type. Especially strong is the coverage of theater and rhetoric. Contemporary theory and critical movements are described. Entries vary in length from a single line to more than ten pages in the case of some survey articles. Literary forms and genres receive detailed exposition treating origin and history, examples from the literature, and important writers. Numerous cross-references link related entries. No bibliographies are furnished.

1070. **A Dictionary of Modern Critical Terms.** 2d ed. Roger Fowler, ed. New York: Routledge Kegan Paul, 1987; repr., 1995. 262p. ISBN 0-4150-5884-8.

This is an important and unique work due to the depth of coverage it gives to terms associated with modern literary criticism. Fowler has produced a handbook that is sharply focused on literary criticism and treats in essay-length articles the history and significance of such terms as well as their relationship to modern criticism. Such topics as poststructuralism, feminist criticism, and Marxist criticism are examined in-depth. Originally published in 1973, this edition supplies new essays and has updated the old ones. For more comprehensive coverage (with brief definitions) of literary terms, genres, and authors, it is recommended that the user consult other works listed in this section.

1071. **Encyclopedia of Literature and Criticism.** Martin Coyle et al., eds. Detroit: Gale Research, 1991. 1299p. ISBN 0-8103-8331-4.

This is an important work for scholars and serious students, providing ninety-one well-constructed and erudite essays treating the various concepts and elements of literary criticism. The essays are challenging and provocative and are arranged under ten categories, beginning with introductory essays treating the major issues and nature of literature and of criticism. Following are sections on "Literature and History," describing the development of Anglo-American literature; "Poetry," "Drama," and "The Novel," treating literary movements and periods with respect to the various genres; "Criticism," providing exposition of the various schools; "Production and Reception," identifying the socio-cultural conditions affecting literature, such as censorship, publishing, and libraries; "Contexts," examining literature in relation to the arts; "Perspectives," describing other English literatures (Australian, Canadian, etc.); and, finally, a provocative afterword. An index provides access.

1072. **Encyclopedia of World Literature in the 20th Century.** 3d ed. Steven Serafin, gen. ed. Detroit: St. James Press, 1999. 4v. ISBN 1-55862-373-6.

Based originally on a German work published in 1960–1961, the first English-language edition of this title appeared in three volumes between 1967 and 1971, the second in five volumes between 1981 and 1993. The current publisher acquired the work from Continuum Publishing and has published the complete third edition. It represents a good revision of the earlier work; approximately 50 entries have been added, providing up-to-date insight on a variety of topics, genres, movements, and trends. It continues its even-handed coverage and furnishes in-depth surveys of some 50 national literatures from around the world, along with 2,300 signed bio-critical articles (with bibliographies) on authors. Third World countries are not overlooked in the mix, and critical excerpts, along with photographs, are supplied for many of the writers covered. The title maintains the tradition and reputation established by the earlier issues.

1073. **A Glossary of Contemporary Literary Theory.** 3d ed. Jeremy Hawthorn. New York: E. Arnold, 1998. 393p. ISBN 0-340-69221-9.

The appearance of the first edition of this scholarly work in 1992, along with that of Harris (entry 1062), bears witness to the increased interest in the field regarding literary theory. Its revision and update only two years later was impressive. The third edition is a substantial revision in terms of expansion and updating, adding more than 100 pages to provide exposition of contemporary theory or terminology utilized by critics since 1920. It continues to blend well with the more intensive treatment of major concepts given by Harris, because Hawthorn has provided broad and comprehensive coverage of the modern era. Many of the terms are not found in other literary dictionaries and therefore add to the value of the work. Entries vary in size from a few sentences to several pages on survey topics such as "modernism." They generally define the terms with quotes from the originators and provide reference to sources included in the twenty-five-page bibliography at the end. There is no index but there are numerous cross-references.

Hawthorn's *A Concise Glossary of Contemporary Literary Theory* (Routledge Kegan Paul, 1994) is the second edition of a slimmed-down version (241 pages), providing similar coverage in abridged fashion. Intended for a wider audience beginning at the undergraduate level, the most useful information has remained unaltered; nonessential generic terminology has been deleted.

1074. A Glossary of Literary Terms. 6th ed. M. H. Abrams. Fort Worth: Holt, Rinehart & Winston, 1993. 301p. ISBN 0-03-054982-5.

The current issue of this established handbook, recognized as an outstanding tool since its initial publication in 1957, represents a good revision, updating, and slight expansion of material in the fifth edition (1988). It continues the useful added feature of a separate section containing several articles examining important critical movements since the 1920s. There are good illustrations, and a number of references to literary and critical material have been furnished. Rather than a list of entries with definitions, the work is more of a handbook, providing a series of essays bringing together related terms in the body of a textual narrative. There is an alphabetical index at the end to facilitate access to the desired term and related passages. The work is clearly written, comprehensive in coverage, and well-developed stylistically and substantively, and is a valuable addition to the reference collection.

1075. A Handbook to Literature. 7th ed. William Harmon and Hugh C. Holman. Upper Saddle River, NJ: Prentice-Hall, 1996. 669p. ISBN 0-13-234782-2.

For over fifty years students and teachers have relied on this title, originally referred to by the name of its initial author, W. F. Thrall. The new edition follows the established pattern, providing definitions of some 1,800 literary terms and phrases important to the study of English and American literature, an increase of 300 from the sixth edition (1992). The updated treatment provides more coverage of women and minorities and includes film studies. Entries are arranged alphabetically and vary in length from the briefest of identifications (one line or so) to several pages for the survey articles on movements. Cross-references are furnished between entries. There are a number of new terms and many others show evidence of revision or modification. The well-known and useful feature, the chronological "Outline to Literary History," is still present. Included also are the listings of Nobel and Pulitzer prize winners. A new feature is the inclusion of references for many of the entries, indicating from what source the definition or exposition was drawn. This work continues to be a top choice among librarians and their patrons.

The Harper Handbook to Literature, edited by Northrop Frye et al. (2d ed., Longman, 1997), is regarded as an important tool for defining literary terms in comprehensible fashion. Designed as a supplementary resource for college students, it is valuable to the general public and frequently used at the high school level. A useful feature is the detailed chronology identifying literature and world events from 3500 B.C. to the present.

1076. Literature and Its Times: Profiles of 300 Notable Literary Works and the Historical Events that Influenced Them. Joyce Moss and George Wilson, eds. Detroit: Gale Research, 1997. 5v. ISBN 0-7876-0606-5.

The title adequately describes the coverage of this expansive, broad-based effort to highlight and explain the origin, development, and subsequent publication of 300 important literary contributions over a span of 5,000 years. Included here are the historical "stories" of a selection of novels, short stories, biographies, speeches, poems, and plays selected by a panel of librarians, secondary teachers, and university professors in relation to their use in high school curricula. Entries supply information regarding the historical events of both the setting of each work and the period in which it was written and published. This enables students to begin their research for term papers and reports. Periods of coverage are treated chronologically, beginning with volume 1, "Ancient Times to the American and French Revolution," and proceeding to volume 2, "Civil Wars to Frontier Societies"; volume 3, "Growth of Empires to the Great Depression"; volume 4, "World War II to the Affluent Fifties"; and volume 5, "Civil Rights Movement to Future Times." Each volume contains a general index to the whole set.

1077. **The New Guide to Modern World Literature.** Martin Seymour-Smith. New York: Peter Bedrick; distr., HarperCollins, 1985. 1396p. ISBN 0-87-226000-3.

An expansion and updating of the author's earlier effort, *Funk & Wagnalls Guide to Modern World Literature* (1973), this work has been modified to provide much additional coverage on a variety of topics. For some reviewers, this title represents a storehouse of "provocative argument, wit, passion, humor, personal asides, philosophical speculation, and even wisdom," while others resent its "breathtakingly opinionated" manner. Of Jean Paul Sartre it states: "He is a sort of philosopher (but in the French, not the British sense: professional British philosophers shudder at his name and think of bedrooms, spit and semen)." Auden is considered to be "flash," while Windham Lewis is a "giant of letters." The work is divided into thirty-three chapters devoted to the literature of a nation or an ethnic group, in which twentieth-century themes are described and the various literary forms analyzed. This guide should be made available to library patrons, who might be forewarned of its extraordinary nature.

1078. **The Originals: An A–Z of Fiction's Real Life Characters.** William Amos. Boston: Little, Brown, 1985. 614p. ISBN 0-316-03741-9.

An innovative theme or focus of this work is the identification of real-life personalities who served as models for fictional characters. Almost 3,000 individuals are identified in this fashion and represent characters from novels, plays, essays, and poetry. A span of 400 years is covered, from the time of Shakespeare to date, with many nationalities included. The arrangement is alphabetical by fictional character, and entries furnish title, publication date, author, and the name of the real person who served as the model or partial model for the character. The length of entries varies considerably, and longer articles may describe the life and times of either the real or fictional characters or both. Photographs of some of the real people are given as well.

1079. **Plot Summary Index.** 2d ed., rev. and enl. Carol Koehmstedt Kolar. Metuchen, NJ: Scarecrow Press, 1981. 526p. ISBN 0-8108-1392-0.

A popular tool to identify location of plot summaries is this index of the contents of 111 reference sources. Literary works of all types are treated and entries are found for summaries of fiction, nonfiction, poetry, and even musical comedy. Emphasis is on American, then English literature, but coverage is international as long as the synopses are in English. The work is divided into two major sections treating titles and authors. Author entries identify the titles for which plot summaries have been indexed. Title entries supply references to any of the 111 digests, handbooks, and guides containing the summaries. Selection of those tools is somewhat extraordinary; excluded are several important and familiar works such as the Oxford Companion series, in favor of many less common and lesser known titles. The tool appeals to a wide-ranging audience, from serious students to laypersons.

A supplementary effort by Irving Weiss and Anne de la Vergne Weiss is *Thesaurus of Book Digests, 1950–1980* (Crown, 1981). About 1,700 fiction and nonfiction books published over a thirty-year period are included, as well as some earlier works of this century not covered by Haydn and Fuller. Plots, themes, or summaries are furnished. For lengthier treatments, one should consult other handbooks and critical works.

BIOGRAPHICAL AND CRITICAL SOURCES

1080. Author Biographies Master Index: A Consolidated Index to More Than 1,140,000 Biographical Sketches. 5th ed. Geri Speace, ed. Detroit: Gale Research, 1997. 2v. ISSN 0741-8655.

This biographical index updates the fourth edition, published in 1994, and contains 110,000 more citations to biographical sketches than did the previous issue. It represents a massive job, indexing some 300 separate English-language directories and biographical dictionaries in 700 volumes and editions from cover to cover. All time periods and most areas of the world are included, producing a universal index covering all genres as well as children's authors and illustrators. Typical coverage includes name, birth and death dates, and coded references, and is strongest on British and American authors of modern times. The work updates listings from the earlier editions with references to new editions of biographical works. Cross-references are lacking; therefore, a single author may appear in more than one place because of variant forms.

Barbara McNeil's *Twentieth Century Author Biographies Master Index: A Consolidated Index to More Than 170,000 Biographical Sketches* (Gale Research, 1984) is a convenience tool derived from the early editions of the above work. It is limited to living authors and those who have died during the twentieth century. It appears in paperback and is reasonably priced. Another useful index is Patricia Pate Havlice's *Index to Literary Biography* (Scarecrow Press, 1975), which provides references to biographical sketches of nearly 70,000 authors located in fifty collective biographies and literary dictionaries. The first supplement appeared in 1983, identifying 53,000 authors covered in fifty-seven literary dictionaries and biographical sources. Nationality and principal genre are given along with dates and coded references.

1081. Black Literature Criticism: Excerpts from Criticism of the Most Significant Works of Black Authors over the Past 200 Years. James P. Draper, ed. Detroit: Gale Research, 1992. 3v. ISBN 0-8103-8574-0.

Designed in the format of Gale's Literary Criticism series, this biocritical tool treats the lives and careers of 125 writers. Eighty-eight of the writers were born in North America, 25 in Africa, 9 in the Caribbean, 2 in Martinique, and 1 in Brazil. There is some question about the selectivity and the selection process in the attempt to treat important writers both established and new; there are many omissions pointed out by reviewers. Entries are arranged alphabetically and supply normal Gale coverage, beginning with a biographical sketch, followed by listings of principal works and then a selection of excerpts from critical essays by recognized authorities. These are carefully selected to reveal a broad range of the author's work. There is a photograph along with commentary taken from an interview with the writer. Access is aided by indexes of author, nationality, and title. The contents of this work are indexed in **Gale's Literary Index CD-ROM* (entry 1090).

1082. Cambridge Companions to Literature series. Cambridge, UK: Cambridge University Press, 1991– . ISBN 0-521-43117-4 (Ezra Pound).

Since its inception, this series has issued approximately forty different titles examining various literary topics. Most frequent and prominent are the volumes given to individual writers of note, but treatment has been extended to literary movements, national literatures, and periods. These begin with the title "Cambridge Companion to. . . ." The standard format is unlike the Oxford Companion series and represents a predictable pattern. providing a selected grouping of about fourteen to fifteen critical essays on various aspects of the topic written by individual scholars. A chronology and reading list are furnished in most cases. We have treated a number of these titles in this work as major entries, co-equal entries, and minor entries, all of which can be located through the title index. The most recent title (1999) treats Ezra Pound;

other examples are Arthur Miller, Beckett, Brecht, Conrad, Wharton, O'Neill, and Shaw among the individual personalities, and American realism and Greek tragedy among those themes receiving topical coverage.

1083. **Contemporary Authors: A Bio-Bibliographical Guide to Current Writers in Fiction, General Non-Fiction, Poetry, Journalism, Drama, Motion Pictures, Television, and Other Fields.** Detroit: Gale Research, 1962– . v.1– . ISSN 0010-7468.

The initial series in Gale's massive attempt to keep abreast of biographical coverage of authors in various fields, this work furnishes good biographical sketches of authors from many countries. Personal information, career highlights, previous works as well as those in progress, and sometimes bibliographical references are included in the entries. It generally favors American writers and excludes scientific and technical writers. The work continues, and access has been enhanced with the publication of a cumulative index. *Contemporary Authors, Cumulative Index, Volumes 1–160: Contemporary Authors New Revision Series, Volumes 1–62* (1998) indexes entries in *Contemporary Authors, Contemporary Authors New Revision Series, Permanent Bibliographical Series, Autobiography Series, Something About the Author, Dictionary of Literary Biography*, and so forth.

The *Contemporary Authors New Revision Series* includes entries from the original series that need revision; only those entries requiring significant changes are modified. Having begun in 1981, the *New Revision Series* reached its 62d volume in 1998, and is the favored method of updating the series at present. It replaces the *First Revision Series*, an ill-fated attempt to update whole volumes of the original series begun in 1975 and discontinued after four years and forty-four volumes. Also defunct is the *Contemporary Authors Permanent Series*, established in 1975 to furnish biographies of deceased personalities and retired individuals removed from the current series. This was discontinued after two volumes. These complicated, expensive, and time-consuming attempts to provide continuous biographical coverage mark Gale as a true leader in biographical publishing. Another contribution is the *Contemporary Authors Autobiographical Series*, begun in 1984 and furnishing about twenty autobiographical essays of important creative writers per volume. Volume 33 was issued recently; the plan is to include nonfiction writers in subsequent volumes. An annual index to the various series is now issued by the publisher. A recent spinoff is *Major 20th-Century Writers: A Selection of Sketches from Contemporary Authors*, edited by Bryan Ryan (Gale Research, 1991), which provides a selection of biocritical essays culled from the parent work. More than 1,000 well-established and known writers of fiction, poetry, drama, and essay are treated in slightly different format but with the same information provided by *CA*. The work is indexed by nationality and by genre/subject. Indexing of the contents of many of these titles is available in **Gale's Literary Index CD-ROM* (entry 1090).

1084. **Contemporary Literary Criticism: Excerpts from Criticism of the Works of Today's Novelists, Poets, Playwrights, Short Story Writers, Scriptwriters, and Other Creative Writers.** Detroit: Gale Research, 1973– . v.1– . ISSN 0091-3421.

Volume 121 was issued in October 1999 in this series begun in 1973. Presently, it provides selected excerpts from criticism of the work of about twenty-five authors per volume and is limited to those who are still living or who died after December 31, 1959. There is a heavy emphasis on English-language writers, although others are included if their work is fairly well-known in the United States. Almost any authors who have been critiqued are eligible for inclusion; therefore, there is a good mix of individuals represented. Each author receives about five excerpts taken from books, articles, and reviews. Citations to the source documents are furnished. Each volume contains a cumulative author index covering all *CLC* volumes as well as twenty-two other Gale series and sets. A nationality index is cumulative to the *CLC* series and a title index is limited to the volume itself.

    Contemporary Literary Criticism: Annual Cumulative Title Index is a separately bound publication that can be purchased if desired; the 1998 publication indexes volumes 1–107. The contents of this work also are indexed in *Gale's Literary Index CD-ROM* (entry 1090).

1085. Contemporary Literary Criticism: Yearbook 1984– . Sharon K. Hall, ed. Detroit: Gale Research, 1985– . Ann. ISBN 0-8103-4439-4 (1991).

    A recent addition to the *CLC* line, the subtitle of this work reads: "The Year in Fiction, Poetry, Drama, and World Literature and the Year's New Authors." The *Yearbook* began in 1985 with coverage of 1984, and was identified as volume 34 of the *Contemporary Literary Criticism* series (entry 1084). *Yearbook 1998*, published in 1999, is volume 101 in the series. Like other issues in the series, the yearbooks furnish the cumulative index to all author entries in the series. Sections of the yearbook include the year in review, new authors, prize winners, obituaries, literary biography, and literary criticism. There are several essays on the various genres covered during the year and highlights of important activities and developments of notable authors. Critical essays of new writers represent an important contribution to reference work.

1086. Cyclopedia of World Authors II. Frank M. Magill, ed. Englewood Cliffs, NJ: Salem Press, 1989. 4v. ISBN 0-89356-512-1.

    This is a continuation of the earlier issue described below and provides biographical and critical commentary on 700 authors. With its emphasis on modern writers, there is little overlap with the previous edition and only 20 percent of the previous entries are duplicated and updated. These authors are identified as having continued to publish or having inspired a substantial body of new criticism. Essays run about 1,000 words and are accompanied by a bibliographic narrative describing important secondary sources. In addition, there is a bibliography of the writer's major works divided by genre. The work is considered a companion to *Masterplots II* (entry 1094n) because it treats over 80 percent of the authors included in that series, and is available on the CD-ROM version of *Masterplots II*.

    Magill's *Cyclopedia of World Authors* was initially published in 1958 and was revised as a three-volume publication in 1974. It covers the lives and writings of some 1,000 authors, providing birthplace, dates, biographical sketches from 200 words to 1,000 words, list of works, and references to additional biographical sources.

*1087. Dictionary of Literary Biography. Matthew J. Bruccoli et al., eds. Detroit: Gale Research, 1978– . v.1– . ISBN 0-8103-0913-0 (v.1).

    A series of consequence, this work was started in 1978 with the purpose of providing information reflecting the changes and scholarship since publication of the *Dictionary of American Biography* (Charles Scribner's Sons, 1928–1937; repr., 1943, 21v.). *DLB* volumes continue to appear with great frequency. Initially, the intent was to cover writers, movements, and periods significant to the literature of the United States, Canada, and England, but in 1987 the focus was extended to include modern European literature (entry 1332n). More recently, the series has issued volumes on modern Spanish poets, modern Italian poets, German writers, Latin-American novelists, Chicano writers, and a first and second offering on modern Caribbean and Black African writers. The present mission is to cover all writers of significance to world literary history. All titles in the series treat a different subject, have different editors, and focus on either a specific period of literary history or a literary movement, beginning with volume 1, *American Renaissance in New England*, by Joel Myerson (1978). Presently, there are some 140 volumes, all of which follow a standard format, with major biocritical essays on the important figures that furnish career chronology, publications list, and a bibliography of works by and about the subject. Lesser figures are described in terms of life, work, and reputation. The contents are indexed in *Gale's Literary Index CD-ROM* (entry 1090), and since 1994 *DLB* has contributed to the content of the CD-ROM *DISCovering Authors* (entry 1088). Recently it has been made available on the World Wide Web through Galenet.

The Dictionary of Literary Biography Yearbook (1980–) updates and supplements entries that appeared in any of the volumes and surveys the year's literary issues and events. There is a section on tributes and obituaries, and a cumulative index to all volumes in the series is included. *The Dictionary of Literary Biography Documentary Series: An Illustrated Chronicle* (1982–) appears less frequently but is designed to provide a useful selection of documents, including galley pages, manuscript pages, proofs, and photographs of major literary figures linked to a particular literary movement, period, or genre in each volume. There is a listing of the author's books, as well as relevant biographies, bibliographies, and archival locations. Volume 19 was issued in 1998 and covered James Dickey.

*1088. **DISCovering Authors: Biographies & Criticism on 300 Most Studied Writers.** Detroit: Gale Research, 1992– . Ann. ISSN 1066-7792. (CD-ROM).

A total of 305 authors is treated in Gale's first CD-ROM product containing much bibliographical, biographical, and critical information drawn from its various print series. Selections were made on the basis of popularity and familiarity and include the most studied authors from ancient times to the present. Some thirty-five nationalities are represented, from the time of Aristotle to the present. Entries supply introductory information, biographical sketch, personal and career information, bibliographies of primary and secondary sources, identification of media adaptations, and several excerpts of criticism, with references to sources. Approximately 30 percent of the entries are original to this work. The remainder have been revised and updated prior to their inclusion. There are a variety of search options permitting access by author, title, subject-term/character, and personal data (birth date, death date, nationality, etc.).

The above work has provided a foundation for "*The Gale Discovering Authors Program" (1996–) which high school teachers, undergraduate instructors, and others have found to be useful. *Exploring Short Stories* (1998) is one of six teaching/learning kits produced to date and consists of a CD-ROM, user's manual, and teaching guide examining 100 short stories by British, American, and international authors of the nineteenth and twentieth centuries. Entries contain author biographies, introductory essays, plot summaries, character descriptions, critical articles, graphics, and so forth. Other titles relevant to the humanities are *Exploring Novels* (entry 1255), *Exploring Poetry* (entry 1285), and *Exploring Shakespeare* (entry 1189).

1089. **European Writers.** George Stade, ed.-in-chief. New York: Charles Scribner's Sons, 1983–1991. 14v. ISBN 0-684-19267-5.

With publication of the last seven volumes bringing the coverage into the twentieth century, this series was completed. The effort provides lengthy articles on the lives and achievements of European writers, as well as plot descriptions of their works. The essays run about 15,000 words and are written by qualified young scholars, professors emeriti, as well as critics, poets, and novelists. The first two volumes cover the Middle Ages and the Renaissance, while volumes 3 and 4 cover the Age of Reason and the Enlightenment. Volumes 5–7 deal with the Romantic century. Volumes 8–13 examine the twentieth century, beginning with Freud and ending with Czech novelist and poet Milan Kundera, born in 1929. Volumes average between twelve and twenty essay-articles each. They are arranged chronologically and are clearly written. There is a good overview of the periods covered in volume 1, written by the late editor, William T. H. Jackson of Columbia University. Volume 14 is an index to the set, and furnishes access by name, birth date, and language. It contains a general bibliography arranged by time period and nationality.

*1090. Gale's Literary Index CD-ROM. Detroit: Gale Research, 1993– . Ann. ISSN 1066-7709. (CD-ROM)

Beginning in February 1993, Gale Research issued a master index to every one of its literary series on a single CD-ROM disk. At the time this comprised 675 volumes and 32 titles. It is a serial publication, providing updates on a semiannual basis. Such important works as the *Dictionary of Literary Biography* (entry 1087), *Contemporary Authors* (entry 1083), *Black Literature Criticism* (entry 1081), *Literature Criticism 1400–1800* (entry 1093), *Nineteenth Century Literature Criticism* (entry 1097), *Twentieth Century Literary Criticism* (entry 1100), *Contemporary Literary Criticism* (entry 1084), *World Literature Criticism 1500 to the Present* (entry 1102), and *Poetry Criticism* (entry 1131) are now easily accessed and searched using the well-designed and user-friendly searching system. This permits one to search by author or title, then print or download the search results. Advanced techniques permit searching by nationality and dates of birth and death. The database contains more than 110,000 authors and over 150,000 titles dating from antiquity to the present day. Libraries are able to tag holdings, providing the user with instant awareness of availability of volumes.

1091. International Authors and Writers Who's Who. 16th ed. David Cummings, ed. Cambridge, UK: International Biographical Centre, 1999. 760p. ISSN 0143-8263.

The sixteenth edition follows the pattern established in the earlier editions and represents a useful and predictable source of information. At its high point, the eighth edition carried 14,000 writers, while the ninth edition provided 9,600 entries. The current effort, like its predecessor, treats about 8,000 writers, including journalists and magazine editors. There is heavy emphasis on English and American writers. Entries generally provide place and date of birth, profession, education, major publications, and address, although there is some variation in completeness of information supplied. Appendices supply listings of literary agents, organizations, awards and prizes.

1092. Literary Lifelines. Danbury, CT: Grolier Educational Corporation, 1998. 10v. ISBN 0-7172-9211-8.

This is an expansive effort examining the lives and works of a wide range of authors over a vast period of time. Included here are writers of classical Greece and Rome, the Middle Ages, the Renaissance, and so forth, down through the period of contemporary publication. It is an attempt to supply chronological exposition of the writer and his or her times, with a focus on providing an understanding of the social context in which such production took place. Included here are novelists, poets, playwrights, and short story writers from all over the world, providing suitable coverage for multi-cultural studies. Geared toward the needs of both high school and undergraduate students, the information is conveniently packaged and accessible for beginning the research process for term papers and reports. Entries are brief and coverage is limited to two pages that provide a brief biographical sketch, illustrations of both the writer and a book cover, a list of related writers, and a chronology of world events during the writer's life. Each volume contains a glossary; there is a comprehensive index to the entire set and a general bibliography in one volume.

1093. Literature Criticism from 1400 to 1800: Excerpts from Criticism of the Works of Fifteenth, Sixteenth, Seventeenth and Eighteenth Century Novelists, Poets, Playwrights. . . . Dennis Poupard, ed. Mark W. Scott, assoc. ed. Detroit: Gale Research, 1984– . ISSN 0740-2880.

Another series from Gale, this one serves as a complement to the others covering the nineteenth and twentieth centuries (entries 1097, 1100). Each volume of this series covers between seven and nine individuals from all over the world, along with one topical entry on a major theme or issue. Volume 1 appeared in 1984; volume 46 was issued in 1999. Such writers as Henry Fielding, Confucius, James Boswell, and St. Augustine are treated in terms of the critical response given to their work. Entries are arranged alphabetically within each volume and critical comments are furnished, beginning with the views of their contemporary critics and proceeding to modern-day reviews. It is useful to see the trend in critical acceptance or rejection and the relationship to time periods. Citations are given to the sources and there is a bibliography of additional references for each author. A cumulative index includes all entries from any of the titles in this series. The contents of this work are indexed in *Gale's Literary Index CD-ROM* (entry 1090).

*1094. **Masterplots Complete CD-ROM.** Frank N. Magill, ed. Englewood Cliffs, NJ: Salem Press, 1997. ISBN 0-89356-263-7. (CD-ROM).

Begun in the late 1940s and early 1950s, this work unfolded in four series over a period of nearly twenty years, covering various forms of literature (fiction, poetry, and essays), at which time it was known as *Masterpieces of World Literature in Digest Form.* Since that time, there have been many spinoffs and variations from Salem Press capitalizing on the popularity and prestige of this work, which was the most highly acclaimed source of plot summaries in the field. *Masterplots: 2,010 Plot Stories and Essay Reviews from the World's Fine Literature* (1976) brought together in one multi-volume set some of the detailed and well-constructed plot summaries culled from those first four series, which characteristically provided identification of form, author, period, type of plot, locale, date of first publication, principal characters, themes, and a brief critique. *Masterplots Definitive Revised Edition* (1978) brought together some 1,300 of the entries, but included in this set were approximately 700 new essay-reviews (in-depth, evaluative analyses) that had been added to the original coverage. These essay-reviews now characterize the products of Salem Press. In 1995, EBSCO issued *Masterplots Definitive Revised Edition: Nonfiction, Poetry, & Drama CD-ROM.* In 1996, Salem Press published *Masterplots: 1801 Plot Stories and Critical Evaluations of the World's Finest Literature*, an update and expansion of the *Definitive* edition, still retaining the purpose of its predecessor, to provide fundamental reference data and plot synopses, along with detailed critical evaluations of a large selection of world literature available in English. Now as a crowning achievement comes the current effort in CD-ROM, containing the entire contents of all twenty-one sets, 12,000 entries in eighty print volumes.

Masterplots Annual Volume appeared from 1954 to 1976, also edited by Magill. It furnished about 100 essay-reviews of outstanding books published in this country. It was succeeded by *Magill's Literary Annual* beginning in 1977, which to date supplies essay-reviews of some 200 new books each year from those appearing in the United States. Another important cumulation from the publisher is *Survey of Contemporary Literature* (rev. ed., 1977) in twelve volumes, furnishing updated reprints of 2,300 essay-reviews from the complete run of *Masterplots Annuals* between 1954 and 1976. It also includes material from the *Survey of Contemporary Literature* supplement. *Masterplots II: Short Story Series*, also by Magill (Salem Press, 1986), is a six-volume set describing over 700 short stories from all over the world. Titles are arranged alphabetically and coverage is given to story, theme, and style as well as setting, major characters, dates, authorship, and so forth. It is available on a separate CD-ROM through *Masterplots II CD-ROM* (1992), which supplies coverage of thirty-eight volumes from the *Masterplots II* series, which also includes American fiction (entry 1238), British and Commonwealth fiction (entry 1238n), world fiction (Salem, 1987), nonfiction (entry 1095), drama (entry 843), juvenile and young adult fiction (entry 1362), poetry (entry 1288), and *Cyclopedia of World Authors II* (entry 1086) and *Cyclopedia of Literary Characters II* (entry 1067). In 1995, there appeared the first issue of *Masterplots II: Women's Literature Series* (6v.).

1095. **Masterplots II: Non-Fiction Series.** Frank M. Magill. Englewood Cliffs, NJ: Salem Press, 1989. 4v. ISBN 0-89356-478-8.

This is the fifth set offered in the *Masterplots II* series that is designed to complement the original *Masterplots* issue. Nonfiction embraces a variety of works, such as autobiography and memoirs of important literary figures, essays, and monographs. Various subjects are treated as well, such as philosophy, literary theory, linguistics, sociology, and culture. Most of the works were published in the English language, or if foreign, have been issued in English translation. A total of 318 works are covered, with contributions from a diverse group including McLuhan, Chesterton, and William Buckley. Entries are arranged alphabetically by title and supply author, title, and date along with a three-page summary or overview treating origin, structure and content, analysis of major themes, ideas and motifs, and historical/critical context. A short bibliography of secondary sources completes the entry. The tool is indexed by author, title, and type of work.

1096. **Modern Black Writers.** Steven R. Serafin. New York: Continuum, 1995. 813p. (A Library of Literary Criticism). ISBN 0-826-40688-2.

This is another of the Continuum publications that has been acquired by St. James Press, which is developing a second edition about to be issued. The 1995 work is modeled after Moulton's *Library of Literary Criticism* (entry 1197) and serves as the second volume to the earlier effort by the same title, published in 1978. It supplies a collection of excerpts of critical interpretations of the creative work in various genres of 125 authors from thirty-two countries during the twentieth century. Among the novelists, poets, and dramatists who receive coverage are Maya Angelou, Toni Morrison, Wole Soyinka, and Alice Childress. There is an emphasis on those who have written in English or in French, but some treatment is given to works written in African dialects. Since a number of the writers also serve as critics, some of their critical work is included in the text as well.

The second edition will treat 170 of the most important writers, a sizable increase in terms of numbers. The critical analyses for those appearing in the earlier editions will be updated with the inclusion of more recent interpretations. The work will open with a good introduction examining the importance of black writers in the twentieth century and, like its predecessors, should contain adequate indexing.

1097. **Nineteenth Century Literature Criticism: Excerpts from Criticism of the Works of Novelists, Poets, Playwrights, Short Story Writers. . . .** Detroit: Gale Research, 1981– . ISSN 0732-1864.

Following the same plan as Gale's other series, which complement the coverage given here (entries 1093, 1100, 1102), this work treats those authors who died during the nineteenth century. All types of creative writers are included from Europe, Great Britain, and the United States. Each volume covers the works of from eight to fourteen different writers, with every fourth volume devoted to topics rather than individual authors. In 1996, the series reached volume 53. Entries furnish a brief biographical introduction, bibliography of works published, excerpts from the critics, and a suggested reading list for further inquiry. The brief excerpts of critical studies are well chosen and expressive of the critic's thoughts, and adequately convey the sense of the critique. Excerpts are arranged chronologically, beginning with contemporary criticism and proceeding to modern thinking. The first volume each year contains a cumulative title index to the entire series, while the last volume of the year has annual topic, nationality, and author indexes. The contents of this work are indexed in **Gale's Literary Index CD-ROM* (entry 1090).

1098. **Selected Black American, African, and Caribbean Authors: A Bio-Bibliography.** James A. Page and Jae Min Roh, comps. Littleton, CO: Libraries Unlimited, 1985. 388p. ISBN 0-87287-430-3.

This convenient and useful volume identifies the work of nearly 650 writers of African descent, the primary focus being on the Afro-American literature of the United States. Included also are some representative figures of the mother continent and also some from the Caribbean. To be included an author must have had at least one book published and must have been covered in collective works or handbooks. Poets must have had more than one book of poems published; playwrights at least one play published or performed; and essayists must have produced a body of works in the arts, biography, criticism, history, and so forth. The arrangement of entries is alphabetical by author and each entry furnishes dates, places of birth and death, family, education, address, career information, list of works, comments on career, and a list of sources.

1099. **Twentieth-Century Caribbean and Black African Writers. First Series.** Bernth Lindfors and Reinhard Sander, eds. Detroit: Gale Research, 1992. 406p. (Dictionary of Literary Biography, v. 117). ISBN 0-8103-7594-X. **Second Series**, 1993. 443p. ISBN 0-8103-5384-9 (v.125). **Third Series**, 1996. 461p. ISBN 0-8103-9352-2 (v.157).

These three volumes cover nearly 100 writers of Africa and the Caribbean as part of the *DLB* series (entry 1087). Similar to other bio-bibliographies in the series, there are separate chapters on about thirty-four modern writers, all individually authored. These are arranged alphabetically and treat the lives and careers of African and Caribbean authors. Included here are such well-known and important writers as Jean Rhys, Derek Walcott, and Wole Soyinka, along with the less-familiar Richard Rive and Nuruddin Farah. Chapters begin with a bibliography of the writer's works and follow with an essay ranging in length from four to twenty-three pages describing the writer's career. A photograph is included along with illustrations of dust jackets and manuscript pages, as are a bibliography of published interviews and critical writings about his or her work. A cumulative index is supplied to this and other works in the *DLB* series, and also in **Gale's Literary Index CD-ROM* (entry 1090).

1100. **Twentieth-Century Literary Criticism: Excerpts from Criticism of the Works of Novelists, Poets, Playwrights, Short-story Writers. . . .** Dennis Poupard, ed. Detroit: Gale Research, 1978– . 86v. ISSN 0276-8178.

This is another of the important sources from Gale that enable readers at various stages of scholarship to become familiar with the nature of critical interpretation and exposition. In this series, one is given excerpts of criticism of the major literary figures as well as nonfiction writers who wrote between 1900 and 1960. This complements the coverage of *Contemporary Authors* (entry 1083), in which the major focus is on living authors, and fits nicely with the other Gale series dealing with the nineteenth century (entry 1097). Each author entry provides a portrait, an in-depth bibliography, a bibliography of principal work, and most important, a selection of excerpts of literary criticism arranged chronologically from the time of publication of the work to the most recent efforts. Generally from eight to twelve authors are covered in each volume of this continuing publication, with every fourth volume devoted to topics rather than authors. Coverage of entries varies in length from ten to over thirty pages. Volume 86 was issued in 1999. The contents of this work are indexed in **Gale's Literary Index CD-ROM* (entry 1090).

*1101. World Authors, 1900–1950. Martin Seymour-Smith and Andrew C. Kimmens, eds. New York: H. W. Wilson, 1996. 4v. ISBN 0-8242-0899-4.

This is a revision and expansion of the original old favorite, *Twentieth Century Authors: A Biographical Dictionary of Modern Literature . . .* (1942), edited by Stanley J. Kunitz and Howard Haycraft, and its 1955 supplement, edited by Kunitz and Vineta Colby. These books were the original first choices for biographical information on modern authors. H. W. Wilson had commissioned Kunitz to develop a line of biographical dictionaries. They were all highly stylized, bearing a portrait and providing bibliographies of the author's work, along with a brief biography highlighting the career. This tool treated writers of all nations whose books were familiar to English-language readers. The new edition retains just about all authors in the initial effort and has revised and rewritten in extensive fashion. Also, it has added certain authors who were omitted in the first effort. It now takes its place as the lead publication of the World Authors series identified below. At this time Wilson is offering a new database, **Wilson Biographies Plus* that provides the content of several publications including *World Authors* (*Current Biography, World Artists* and *American Reformers*).

Kunitz and Colby had collaborated to produce *European Authors 1000–1900* (H. W. Wilson, 1967). This was done in the same general manner. Subsequently the publisher produced *World Authors, 1950–1970* (1975), edited by John Wakeman and providing biographical sketches of nearly 1,000 additional authors of literary importance or unusual popularity. Continuing in this vein are subsequent publications: *World Authors, 1970–1975*, edited by Wakeman (1980); *World Authors, 1975–1980* (1985); *World Authors, 1980–1985* (1991); and *World Authors, 1985–1990* (1995), the last three edited by Vineta Colby. Each of the five-year volumes furnishes sketches of several hundred authors. A useful tool is *Index to the Wilson Authors Series* (rev. ed., H. W. Wilson, 1997), which furnishes quick access to 11,000 entries in all of the Wilson authors series including those identified here.

1102. World Literature Criticism 1500 to the Present: A Selection of Major Authors from Gale's Literary Criticism Series. James P. Draper, ed. Detroit: Gale Research, 1992. 6v. ISBN 0-8103-8361-6.

From the publisher of the classic *Literary Criticism* series comes this set providing somewhat abbreviated coverage of 231 major dramatists, poets, novelists, and essayists from all over the world. These were selected by a panel of high school teachers and public and high school librarians as those most frequently studied in high school or college curricula. Such luminaries as Hans Christian Andersen, Jane Austen, Gertrude Stein, and Edgar Allen Poe are treated in entries arranged alphabetically by author. Special emphasis has been given to modern writers of European and U.S. origins, although Mexico, Africa, Argentina, New Zealand, and Colombia are represented. Entries supply portraits, biocritical sketches, a list of major works with indication of films, adaptations, representative excerpts of critical studies, and a bibliography of additional reading. Author, title, and nationality indexes provide access. The contents of this work are indexed in **Gale's Literary Index CD-ROM* (entry 1090).

WRITERS' GUIDES AND DIRECTORIES

1103. Grants and Awards Available to American Writers. 20th ed. John Morrone, ed. New York: PEN American Center, 1998. 274p. Bienn. ISBN 0-934638-15-2.

This biennial publication provides awareness of hundreds of grants and support funds for writers to help them continue their writing and to develop their careers. The twentieth edition treats the period 1998–1999 and covers various categories such as fiction, poetry, drama, journalism, general nonfiction, and children's literature, not only in the United States but in Canada and other countries as well. In most cases, the awards provide cash stipends of $500 or more or result in publication of a manuscript or production of a play. Residencies providing room and board are also included. Entries supply information regarding purpose of grant, nature of the award, eligibility, application procedure, deadlines, and contact person. Arrangement is alphabetical by key words derived from the names of the granting organizations. Appendices supply listings of arts councils; the work is indexed by award and by organization.

1104. **LMP 2000, Literary Market Place: The Directory of the American Book Publishing Industry with Industry Yellow Pages.** New Providence, NJ: R. R. Bowker, 1940– . 2v. Ann. ISSN 0075-9899.

LMP is the most well-known and frequently used directory of its type on the market. It provides up-to-date listings of organizations, periodicals, and some 3,000 publishing houses with officers and key personnel, all of whom are involved in the placing, promotion, and marketing of literary property. A variety of topical headings is used, including book publishing, book clubs, associations, book trade events, conferences and contests, and agents. *LMP 2000* (1999) retains the familiar eight major sections ("Book Publishers," "Electronic Publishing," "Editorial Services and Agents," etc.) embracing all relevant categories of publication. A useful alphabetical listing of names is accompanied by address and telephone number, as well as references to pages in the directory.

*Writer's Electronic Bulletin Board, issued by WEBB of Branson, Missouri, furnishes online access to certain marketing information provided by *LMP*, along with *Publishers Weekly*, *Writer's Monthly*, and others. Listings of literary agents, editors, and publishers are supplied along with writing tips, literary announcements, services, and clubs.

1105. **1999 Guide to Literary Agents : 500 Agents Who Sell What You Write.** Donya Dickerson, ed. Cincinnati: Writer's Digest Books, 1999. 300p. Ann. ISSN 1055-6087.

First published in 1991 and bearing the 1992 date in the title, this serial publication provides listings of agents and representatives in the United States and Canada. Agents listed here represent authors to publishers and purchasers. The format is similar to other *Writer's Digest* publications and opens with several introductory essays about literary agents relative to their activity, selection, and responsibilities to their clients. Articles have generally appeared in previous issues of *Writer's Digest Magazine*. The work is divided into sections treating fee and non-fee literary agents, script agents, and over 100 conferences of interest to writers. Over 500 agents and representatives are treated, with coverage given to date of inception of agency, member agents, areas of interest, conferences attended, and so forth. There are both a glossary and several indexes.

*Writer's Guide to Book Editors, Publishers, and Literary Agents, 1999–2000, edited by Jeff Herman, provides an alphabetical listing of more than 500 publishers and their contact editors, as well as 200 literary agents in the United States and Canada, with expository notes on the cover stating "Who they are! What they want! And how to win them over." The author is a literary agent who has provided a useful, honest, and straightforward manual of getting published as well as an excellent directory. Access is enhanced with an accompanying CD-ROM, making it an especially useful resource.

1106. **The Writer's Handbook 2000.** Sylvia K. Burack, ed. Boston: The Writer, 1936– . Ann. ISBN 0-87116-184-2 (1998).

The 2000 issue (published 1999) of this standard work, like earlier volumes, provides a number of essays and articles covering the art, craft, technique, and business of writing for publication, with contributions from significant (popular) authors. Both the writing scene in general as well as more specialized phases or areas are treated in more than 100 chapters authored by literary agents and writers. Covered are various forms of writing: fiction, nonfiction, poetry, drama and television, and juvenile and young adult. Business practices are also described. Possibly the most important feature is the market guide, which covers in up-to-date fashion some 3,200 markets or potential outlets for publication, including magazines with various subject emphases; fiction outlets; poetry; college, literary, and little magazines; humor; and juvenile. Prizes, organizations, and agents are also treated.

A similar tool is the third edition of *Writer's Encyclopedia* (Writer's Digest Books, 1996). It furnishes definitions and exposition of business practices, organizations, and general advice for writers. The emphasis is on print publishing but radio and television are also covered, as are advertising, songwriting, and so forth. Most useful is the appendix segment, with numerous entries furnishing samples of writing projects and identifying pay rates. Beginning with this edition, the work is available on CD-ROM and becomes an annual publication. *The Writer's Handbook 2000 International Edition* edited by Barry Turner (Trans-Atlantic Publications, 1999) is now in its thirteenth issue and provides some 5,000 entries embracing writing opportunities in the United Kingdom and Ireland as well as the United States.

*1107. **Writer's Market, 2000: 8000 Editors Who Buy What You Write.** Kirsten C. Holm, ed. Cincinnati: Writer's Digest Books, 1922– . 1112p. Ann. ISSN 0084-2729.

This is a no-nonsense, no frills, let's-get-to -the business-of-selling-your-work type of tool. In contrast to *Writer's Handbook* (entry 1106), which provides some 100 essays on the craft, art, inherent worth, and personal experiences of writing, *Writer's Market* treats issues of authors' rights, negotiation with publishers and editors, and dealing with agents. The coverage of the markets is detailed as compared to the brief one to two lines offered for each entry in the *Handbook*. The audience, as one might expect, is a more veteran group of writers who no longer need the type of inspirational push provided by the *Handbook*. Access is furnished through several indexes. Since 1996, it has been available on CD-ROM. The current edition identifies more than 1,100 book publishers, 1,500 consumer magazines, 450 trade magazines as well as script buyers, syndicates, and more.

Another useful directory is *The Writer's Resource: The Watson-Guptill Guide to Workshops, Conferences, Artists' Colonies, Academic Programs*, edited by David Emblidge and Barbara Zheutlin (Watson-Guptill, 1997), which provides awareness of various opportunities for professional development. It also serves as a manual to help writers select the most appropriate offering in view of their needs and tastes, with informative and interesting description of instruction, food, costs, and social interaction. Written in an entertaining style, it seems to have covered any questions that may occur prior to sending for brochures and applications. There are a number of illustrations that aid in making selections, and in addition, there are several useful essays examining the business of writing and the various genres.

QUOTATIONS AND PROVERBS

1108. **A Dictionary of American Proverbs.** Wolfgang Mieder et al., eds. New York: Oxford University Press, 1992; repr., 1996. 710p. ISBN 0-19-505399-0.

Fieldwork for this tool began in the 1940s with a committee of the American Dialect Society and input from numerous scholars and folklorists, who began systematic collection of proverbs and expressions. By the 1980s, some 150,000 examples had been collected and Mieder was appointed editor to do the selection. The total was narrowed down to some 15,000 proverbs by rigorously defining the proverb as a "concise statement of an apparent truth which has currency among people." The application of "apparent truth" rather than valid argument is meaningful in that many of the racial or gender-based proverbs are offensive and illogical. Entries have had common usage in the United States and Canada, and may include variant proverbs, historical or interpretative commentary, locations, citations to published sources, and cross-references. A bibliography is provided. Arrangement is alphabetical by key word from the proverb.

*1109. **Familiar Quotations: A Collection of Passages, Phrases, and Proverbs Traced Back to Their Sources in Ancient and Modern Literature.** 16th ed., rev. and enl. John Bartlett. Justin Kaplan ed. Boston: Little, Brown, 1992. 1405p. ISBN 0-316-08277-5.

This is the standard work of its kind; most searches for quotations or imperfectly remembered lines of poetry begin with Bartlett. The first edition of this landmark title appeared in 1855, and it has been a fixture in libraries ever since. New editions are issued on the average every seven to ten years, and each one generally adds contemporary authors to the coverage. The sixteenth edition retains the chronological arrangement of authors quoted, "a wonderfully eccentric way to organize a book," according to its new editor, an award-winning biographer of both Clemens and Whitman. Of the new entries quoted, forty-five are women and eighteen are black, demonstrating Kaplan's attempt to provide a better cross-section for purposes of representation. Among the new entries are Norman Mailer, Bernard Malamud, and Philip Roth, along with a Burma Shave jingle and the quote on genetic copying from the Watson and Crick paper on DNA. As always, the Bible and Shakespeare remain the leading sources of quotations. There is an author index, but most important for this tool (and others like it) is the detailed concordance index by key words. The ninth edition (1901) has been available free on the World Wide Web since 1995 at http://www.columbia.edu/acis/bartleby/bartlett (accessed January 2000).

1110. **The Home Book of Quotations, Classical and Modern.** 10th ed. rev. Burton Egbert Stevenson. New York: Dodd, Mead, 1967; repr., Greenwich House; distr., Crown, 1984. 2816p. ISBN 1-517-43130-0.

Another of the well-known standards in the field of quotation handbooks is the work of Stevenson, who published a series of "Home Books," all of which were warmly received by reference librarians. This particular tool was the mainstay of the Stevenson line and was first issued in 1934. It was frequently revised, each new issue adding new entries, until 1967. The tenth edition contains more than 50,000 quotations, all of which are arranged alphabetically by subject and then subdivided by smaller and more specific headings. Access is aided through an author index, which includes full name, identifying phrase, dates of birth and death, and references to all quotations listed. Most important, of course, is the key word index, which provides access to the quotations.

1111. **The New Penguin Dictionary of Quotations.** J. M. Cohen and M. J. Cohen. Rev. and exp. ed. London: Viking, 1992; repr., Penguin, 1996. 726p. ISBN 0-140-51244-6.

Initially developed in 1960 by a father/son team, the new edition still bears the name of the father, J. M. Cohen, although he died in 1989 shortly prior to its completion. The elder Cohen was a well-known editor, anthologist, and translator of quotations, and with his expertise in Spanish was able to translate quotations from the Spanish language. This expanded edition has increased the coverage of modern authors and there is judicious selection of the quotations having the potential to survive. For the great body of known or traditional quotations dating from the biblical and classical periods, authors have relied on previously published works in the field, especially *The Oxford Dictionary of Quotations* (entry 1114). Arrangement is similar to that of the *Oxford*, placing the quotations under the name of the authors, who are alphabetically sequenced. A subject index provides access.

1112. The New Quotable Woman. Rev. and upd. ed. Elaine Partnow, comp. and ed. New York: Facts on File, 1992. 714p. ISBN 0-8160-2134-1.

This work has been revised, altered, and expanded on several occasions since the initial publication of two volumes in 1977–1980. Quotations attributed to women between 1800 and 1899 were identified in volume 1; quotations from 1900–1975 are in volume 2. In 1982, two volumes were again issued, the first treating the period "From Eve to 1799" and the second "1800–1981." This revised and updated effort combines and updates the contents of those two volumes into one and adds 105 new personalities. There is a greater emphasis on cultural diversity and the words of contemporary world leaders are given more exposure. Some 300 quotations have been added, to reach a total of 15,000 chronologically sequenced quotations from about 2,500 women representing all times and locales. There is excellent access, with two new indexes by occupation and by nationality/ethnicity joining the subject and biographical index.

1113. The Oxford Dictionary of English Proverbs. 3d ed. rev. by F. P. Wilson. Oxford: Clarendon, 1970; repr., 1982. 930p. ISBN 0-19-866131-2.

It is difficult to imagine many libraries that provide services in language and literature not having this important title. It is generally a first choice when searching for proverbs in the English language, the emphasis, of course, being on the language as employed by Britons. The first edition appeared in 1935 and contained about 10,000 proverbs; since then the coverage has increased somewhat and there have been slight changes in arrangement. The present edition contains more proverbs than supplied by the second edition, but also includes material from the first edition that had been deleted from the second. Each proverb is dated, with references to its use in the literature from its beginning and subsequent changes of meaning identified. A concise version of 256 pages, edited by J. A. Simpson, was published in 1982.

Many proverbs are treated in Morris P. Tilley's *Dictionary of the Proverbs in England in the Sixteenth and Seventeenth Centuries* (University of Michigan Press, 1950; repr., AMS Press, 1982). The subtitle goes on: "A Collection of the Proverbs found in English Literature and the Dictionaries of the Period."

*1114. The Oxford Dictionary of Quotations. 4th ed. rev. Angela Partington, ed. New York: Oxford University Press, 1996. 1075p. ISBN 0-19-860058-5.

First published in 1941, this has been an important reference tool over the years. Proverbs and nursery rhymes are excluded because they are covered in other Oxford publications (entries 1113, 1365). This version was revamped and published four years after publication of the fourth edition in 1992. It continues to provide a comprehensive listing of more than 17,500 quotations, all of which are arranged alphabetically. Sources of the quotations are more than 2,500 authors of every description (poets, novelists, playwrights, public figures, etc., both English-language and foreign), as well as the Bible and Prayer Book. Also included are quotes from anonymous authors. Indexing is excellent, with approximately 70,000 entries indicating the author's name along with a page reference. Retained from earlier editions is a separate Greek index. The new revision contains the sections "Sayings of the 90s" and "Popular Misquotations." The work has been available through DIALOG, and in 1993, a disk version was issued that provides electronic access to the initial issue of the fourth edition and its companion volume, discussed below. The third edition of the concise version was issued in 1996.

The Oxford Dictionary of Twentieth Century Quotations edited by Elizabeth Knowles (Oxford University Press, 1999) furnishes some 5,000 quotations from a variety of media and disciplines, including songs, motion pictures, television, poetry, political movements, advertising, science, and more. It serves as an update of a 1991 publication with a different title, *Oxford Dictionary of Modern Quotations*, edited by Tony Augarde. Format and arrangement are similar to the work above with sources listed alphabetically. Quotations from writers are documented with references to printed sources. Inclusion begins with the Titanic period and continues to the present.

1115. **Writers on Writing.** Jon Winokur. Philadelphia: Running Press, 1990. 372p. ISBN 0-89471-877-0.

From a compact little volume of 160 pages in its 1986 edition, this collection of quotations of writers on the art and practice of writing has more than doubled its size. Its primary audience is still teachers and students of literature from high school to college levels. More than 2,000 quotations are classified under broad topics such as plagiarism. The claim is that the work results from twenty years of compulsive collecting in this area. It is a most pleasurable and interesting work, providing insight into writers' experience with frustration and their development of stylistic techniques.

Another of the books in this vein, now in its fourth edition, revised and expanded, is *The Writer's Quotation Book*, edited by James Charlton (Faber & Faber, 1997). First appearing in 1980, the present edition represents an expansion to several hundred quotations. These treat all aspects of literary production; writing, publishing, editing, and so forth. Reference use has been enhanced over the last two editions with the inclusion of an index.

Fiction (Various Languages)

Sources in this section treat fiction from more than one language and include English.

DICTIONARIES, ENCYCLOPEDIAS, AND HANDBOOKS

1116. **Reginald's Science Fiction and Fantasy Awards: A Comprehensive Guide to the Awards and Their Winners.** 3d ed., rev. and exp. Daryl F. Mallett and Robert Reginald. San Bernardino, CA: Borgo Press, 1993. 248p. ISBN 0-80950-200-3.

The present work has increased threefold in size over the initial edition published in 1981, and represents a comprehensive treatment identifying awards and award winners from all over the world. There are two major segments, English and foreign, with the first part covering the United States, Ireland, England, and Canada. The second part identifies foreign-language awards, including those for Japan and Russia as well as European countries. Awards in both segments are listed alphabetically and all winners are listed from the beginning of the award to the time of publication. The awards are described and explained briefly. A third section lists non-genre awards such as the Newberry, American Book, Emmys, and Oscars. Four appendices provide listings of association officers and conventions and indexes of authors and of awards. Also, there are statistical tables identifying outstanding winners.

1117. **Science-Fiction, the Early Years: A Full Description of More Than 3,000 Science-Fiction Stories. . . .** Everett F. Bleiler and Richard J. Bleiler. Kent, OH: Kent State University Press, 1990. 998p. ISBN 0-87338-416-4.

Considered by one reviewer to be a "gold mine of detail for researchers," this biocritical work provides excellent and comprehensive coverage along with adequate detail. Some 3,000 science fiction stories "from earliest times to the appearance of the genre magazines in 1930, with author, title, and motif indexes" are proclaimed in the complete title. Treatment is given to short stories, novellas, and novels written in English or in English translation, beginning with ideas represented in Plato's writings; most entries were issued from the seventeenth century on. A fine introductory segment categorizing science fiction motifs and providing historical perspective precedes the text. The stories are arranged alphabetically by author and supply biographical and publication data, extensive plot description, and critical commentary. Numerous indexes provide excellent access by motif, date, publication, title, and author.

BIOGRAPHICAL AND CRITICAL SOURCES

1118. **Caribbean Women Novelists: An Annotated Critical Bibliography.** Lizabeth Paravisini-Gebert and Olga Torres-Seda. Westport, CT: Greenwood, 1993. 427p. (Bibliographies and Indexes in World Literature, no. 36). ISBN 0-313-28342-7.

Due to its history of colonial control, the Caribbean region (islands of the Caribbean, Belize, Guyana, and Surinam) reveals linguistic traditions embracing English, French, Dutch, and Spanish, all of which are found among the listings provided for the 150 female authors covered. These writers either were born and raised in the Caribbean or have identified themselves as Caribbean and have written at least one novel since 1950. Entries are alphabetically arranged by name of writer and provide a biographical sketch and a comprehensive listing of works of all kinds (novels, short stories, poetry, essays, etc.). Novels are annotated. Entries conclude with an annotated listing of critical commentary and reviews. The work opens with a bibliography of general works and closes with a listing of authors by country; there are indexes by title of novel, critic, and themes/key words.

1119. **Critical Survey of Short Fiction.** Rev. ed. Frank N. Magill. Pasadena, CA: Salem Press, 1993. 7v. ISBN 0-89356-843-0.

This is a revision and expansion of the initial edition, published in 1981, and its supplement, published in 1987. Although British and American writers are emphasized heavily in this work, non-English-language authors are also covered. The work furnishes nearly 350 articles on major writers (with 65 new entries) and covers the influence, characteristics, and analysis of each individual's work along with biographical information and citations to additional works. All previous entries have been reviewed and revised. These essay-reviews combine both analysis and plot summaries of the short stories, and are characteristic of Magill's more recent efforts, unlike *Masterplots* (entry 1094), which was primarily concerned with the plot. Volume 7 contains twelve detailed essays on the nature and history of short fiction.

1120. **Detective and Mystery Fiction: An International Bibliography of Secondary Sources.** 2d ed., rev. and exp. Walter Albert. San Bernardino, CA: Brownstone Books, 1997. 672p. ISBN 0-941028-15-1.

Albert is an academic, who in 1973 began to produce the annual bibliographies of secondary literature for the leading periodical in the field, *The Armchair Detective*. This comprehensive bibliography expands those listings into a four-part coverage identifying more than 7,700 entries through 1990. They are numbered consecutively throughout the work. Part 1 provides an annotated listing of major sources (bibliographies, dictionaries, encyclopedias, and checklists). Part 2 contains annotated listings of books and articles providing general coverage and treatment. Part 3 lists criticism of dime novels, juvenile mystery series, and pulp magazines. The major segment, part 4, provides annotated listings of studies of individual writers, with references to treatment in sources listed in part 1. Collaborators from all over the world contributed to this effort, which accounts for the numerous foreign-language citations. There is an index of authors and one of series characters.

1121. **Popular World Fiction, 1900–Present.** Walton Beacham and Suzanna Niemeyer. Washington, DC: Beacham, 1987. 4v. ISBN 0-933833-08-3.

Designed as a companion work to Beacham's *Popular Fiction in America* (entry 1255n), this biocritical tool treats nearly 180 authors not included in the previous effort. Emphasis is on American and British writers who have achieved fame during the twentieth century, although other parts of Europe are represented as well. The criterion again is a test of "popularity" or best selling status, which will invite criticism for its omission of Danielle Steele, Georgette Heyer, and Kurt Vonnegut. Entries supply a brief publishing history along with an overview of the author's critical reception. Analytical commentary is given regarding themes, techniques, and adaptations of the works chosen along with a list of related titles by the author. Arrangement is alphabetical by name of author. Appendices list titles by social issues and themes; there are indexes by genre and by author/title.

1122. **Postmodern Fiction: A Bio-Bibliographical Guide.** Larry McCaffery, ed. Westport, CT: Greenwood, 1986. 604p. ISBN 0-313-24170-8.

Postmodernism, according to the author, is generally meant to embrace those writers who have established their careers since the 1960s. This places the guide in a unique position in terms of its focus on relatively recent individuals and their works. Most checklists and bibliographies have a much greater time span and pay little attention to the "post-moderns." A variety of writers is treated, ranging from genre specialists such as Gunter Grass, and Latin American contributors like Gabriel Garcia Marquez, to a number of critics and contributors to popular magazines. Part 1 provides 15 general articles analyzing the modes of postmodern fiction and criticism, while part 2 furnishes over 100 biocritical descriptions of individual writers. Also included is a bibliography of additional readings on postmodern criticism.

1123. **Reference Guide to Short Fiction.** 2d ed. Thomas Riggs, ed. Detroit: St. James Press, 1998. 1197p. ISBN 1-55862-334-5.

This recent entry to the St. James line (first edition, 1993) is a large-sized volume providing detailed treatment of 400 stories by 325 notable authors from all time periods and an array of geographic locales. It is especially useful to high school students and undergraduates in its focus on frequently studied writers selected for inclusion by a panel of experts. Personalities include Saul Bellow, Nikolai Gogol, Ernest Hemingway, James Joyce, Eudora Welty, and others of that level of accomplishment and popularity. The work is divided into two parts, the first providing biographical descriptions and evaluations of the body of work of each author in essays signed by the contributors. The second section provides critical essays of 400 important works such as "Kew Gardens" by Virginia Woolf and "A Hunger Artist" by Franz Kafka.

Short Story Writers and their Work: A Guide to the Best, by Brad Hooper, is also in its second edition (American Library Association, 1992), but unlike the above work is diminutive in size, with only seventy pages of text. Very brief coverage is given to more than 100 short story writers, both American and foreign, chosen by the author for their importance. It succeeds in furnishing critical assessment of the body of a writer's effort. Analysis is cogent and examines style, thematic influences, and settings, and assessment is made of the writer's impact or influence on the literary world. The first part treats the early masters of the nineteenth century; the second examines living writers with an additional brief segment on genre writers.

1124. Science Fiction and Fantasy Reference Index, 1878–1985: An International Author and Subject Index to History and Criticism. H. W. Hall, ed. Detroit: Gale Research, 1987. 2v. ISBN 0-8103-2129-7. **Supp. 1985–1991.** Englewood, CO: Libraries Unlimited, 1993. 677p. ISBN 1-56308-113-X. **Supp. 1992–1995.** Libraries Unlimited, 1997. 503p. ISBN 1-56308-527-5.

This is a comprehensive index to expository, descriptive, and evaluative writings on science fiction, as well as fantasy, horror, supernatural, and weird. About 19,000 books, articles, essays, audiovisual items, and news items are identified, dating from an early work treating Jules Verne in 1878 to works of the mid-1980s. Most of the writings were published between 1945 and 1985, with the great majority being in the English language. Treatment of European writings is more selective or representative than it is comprehensive. There is a total of 43,000 author and subject references provided to the 19,000 works. The recent supplementary volumes, also edited by Hall, contain some 16,250 and 10,600 new citations respectively, representing publications for an additional ten years.

Initially the work was derived from the coverage provided in the editor's *Science Fiction and Fantasy Research Index* annuals between 1980 and 1984 and his *Science Fiction Index*, published in 1980. Volume 1 supplies introductory material, a list of sources, and an author index. Volume 2 (entry 1230) provides a subject index along with a thesaurus.

1125. The Science Fiction Source Book. David Wingrove, ed. New York: Van Nostrand Reinhold, 1984. 320p. ISBN 0-442-29255-4.

This is a useful handbook to science fiction and will serve best the needs of those unfamiliar with the genre. The work opens with a brief history of the genre by Brian Aldiss and an exposition of some fifteen subgenres of the field by Brian Stableford. Also, there are lively discussions of its writing by twelve authors, including Ray Bradbury. The major text is a "consumer's guide" to the novels and short stories of 880 writers. Entries are arranged alphabetically by name of writer, for whom brief biographical sketches and publication data are furnished. Up to three representative titles of novels or short stories are given, with ratings of excellence based on a five-star system. These ratings utilize the criteria of readability, characterization, idea content, and literary merit in rendering judgment.

1126. Survey of Modern Fantasy Literature. Frank N. Magill, ed. Englewood Cliffs, NJ: Salem Press, 1983. 5v. ISBN 0-89356-450-8.

Responding to the obvious need for a work of this type for the genre of fantasy fiction, Salem Press has marshaled its considerable expertise and resources to provide an important and popular product. Fantasy literature includes both high and low fantasy, fairy tales, folklore, and horror dating from Victorian times to the present. Included here are 500 representative works of European and American authors, for which are furnished essay-reviews of approximately 1,000 to 3,000 words, depending upon the work's significance. Entries include brief author information, date of book publication, type of work, time period, locale, brief description of essay-review, plot, and bibliography.

An earlier product of the publisher is Magill's *Survey of Science Fiction Literature* (1979), also in five volumes. It follows the same pattern and format, furnishing in-depth analyses of 515 world-famous science fiction novels. Annotated bibliographies are supplied for nearly 300 titles. A supplementary volume was issued in 1982.

1127. The Vampire Gallery: A Who's Who of the Undead. J. Gordon Melton. Detroit: Visible Ink Press, 1998. 500p. ISBN 1-578-59053-1.

Melton, the well-known author of religious reference sources, published an initial encyclopedic work on vampires in 1994 and met with instant success in the market, indicating a real public interest in matters supernatural. This is a complementary vehicle, providing biographical coverage of some 350 vampires drawn from literature, motion pictures, and television. In so doing it provides insight into and critical awareness of the contributions of genre writers, actors, and directors over the past 100 years, and serves to document the emergence and development of the vampire myth. An introductory essay examines the Dracula myth and character as it evolved from Bram Stoker's original portrayal of a terrifying and evil figure to the more romanticized and even attractive antihero in motion pictures. All known vampires are treated in depth, some with illustrations and bibliographies in alphabetical arrangement. Included are Lestat, Vampirella, and of course, Barnabus Collins.

A recent publication is the second edition of Melton's *The Vampire Book: The Encyclopedia of the Undead*, from the same publisher (1999). Like its 1994 predecessor, it is a large, comprehensive volume (919 pages) and treats the whole world of vampires and their lore. It is well-researched although there are factual errors in some of the entries. There is a lengthy exposition on the cultural history of the vampire, listings of various types, a filmography, and a chronology supplementing the informative treatment of terms, events, personalities, issues, and topics arranged alphabetically for easy access.

WRITERS' GUIDES AND DIRECTORIES

1128. Fiction Writers Guidelines: Over 260 Periodical Editors' Instructions Reproduced and Indexed. 2d ed. Judy Mandell, comp. and ed. Jefferson, NC: McFarland, 1992. 337p. ISBN 0-89950-673-9.

Designed to expedite the process of writing for publication, this guide has established an excellent reputation since its first edition in 1988. The second edition retains the format of the original in its treatment of some 250 periodicals of all types. Included here are general purpose magazines, literary magazines, and children's periodicals of all sizes and degrees of popularity and importance, as well as a selection of pornographic titles. Entries are arranged alphabetically and supply reprinted guidelines for publication in each magazine. Instructions regarding format, type of manuscript, rate of payment, and availability of sample copies are presented in easy-to-read fashion. Reader characteristics are included in some cases. One might wish for more description of content that would be useful to teachers and students as well as writers. A comprehensive index provides access in detailed fashion.

Writer's Yearbook: Your Guide to Getting Published This Year, begun in 1930 by Writer's Digest Books, is an annual, enlarged version of *Writer's Digest Magazine*, with a number of feature articles and lists of publishing events for the preceding year. Features generally emphasize important aspects of selling one's writing to publishers and editors. *Writer's Digest*, the monthly magazine, started in 1920 and provides information, advice, tips, and techniques for both writing and selling.

1129. Novel and Short Story Writer's Market, 2000: 2,000 Places to Publish Your Fiction. Barbara Kuroff, ed. Cincinnati: Writer's Digest Books, 1989– . 675p. Ann. ISSN 0897-9812.

Replacing the publisher's previous annual guide, *Fiction Writer's Market*, begun in 1981, this work has been recognized as one of the most comprehensive and thorough in terms of its full treatment of the market for its audience. Several thousand markets have been identified, with excellent descriptive entries providing information on interests, needs, methods of payment, terms of agreement, and preferred formats when applicable. The 2000 edition continues the updating of the previous editions and adds new markets along with revisions of previously reported information. The current edition has new listings for conferences and workshops; retreats and colonies; and so forth to go along with the various indexes that continue to provide easy access.

Mystery Writer's Marketplace and Sourcebook, edited by Donna Collingwood and Robin Gee, was initiated in 1993 by the same publisher. It represents a specialized source of information for writers of a particular genre. Included are sections on trends, literary agents, organizations, conventions, contests, awards, a glossary, and so forth. Marketing information is up-to-date. Indexing is thorough and provides access by twenty categories of mysteries.

Poetry (Various Languages)

Sources in this section treat poetry from more than one language and include English.

DICTIONARIES, ENCYCLOPEDIAS, AND HANDBOOKS

1130. **The New Princeton Encyclopedia of Poetry and Poetics.** Alex Preminger and T. V. F. Brogan, eds. Princeton, NJ: Princeton University Press, 1993. 1383p. ISBN 0-691-02123-6.

This work is a major revision and expansion of the *Princeton Encyclopedia of Poetry and Poetics* (Princeton University Press, 1975), which itself was a reissue, with an added supplementary section, of the author's highly regarded *Encyclopedia of Poetry and Poetics*, published in 1965. The current effort has revised all previous entries that have been retained and added much new material. More emphasis has been placed on non-Western and Third World poetry, with inclusion of recent scholarship. Individual entries vary in length from descriptions, identifications, or definitions of only a few lines to monographic surveys on the poetry of regions and ethnic groups. The work is the product of some 375 contributors, who have produced a tool to suit a variety of needs ranging from those of the serious student to those of the interested layperson. History, theory, technique, and criticism of poetry are treated from the earliest times to the present. A successful blend of scholarship and lucidity has earned this publication a reputation as a standard work. Its updated focus on such topics as feminist poetics along with its excellent treatment of poetic traditions assure its continued status.

A Poetry Handbook by Mary Oliver (Harcourt, Brace, 1995) is a compact guide to the comprehension of the technical elements involved in writing poetry. Informational lessons are accompanied by examples in such areas as sound, form, tone, imagery, and more. The author is a poet who supplies inspiration along with expertise to those who aspire to pursue the quest for creative writing in the genre.

BIOGRAPHICAL AND CRITICAL SOURCES

1131. **Poetry Criticism: Excerpts from Criticism of the Works of the Most Significant and Widely Studied Poets of World Literature.** Robyn V. Young. Detroit: Gale Research, 1991– . v.1– . ISSN 1052-4851.

With publication of volume 1, the publisher begins another series of literary criticism treating world writers both ancient and modern. Volume 26 was issued in 1999. The series targets English-language poets; although foreign-language poets who have been widely studied and translated into English are also included. Each volume treats some twelve to fifteen major poets. Entries supply an introductory biographical sketch and description of important works. Also included are listings of critical analysis, with excerpts of commentary concerning major poems. Entries conclude with a brief bibliography of secondary sources for further reading. Volume 1 contains coverage of thirteen poets, among them Auden, Dickinson, Donne, Ferlinghetti, Frost, Plath, and Poe; volume 26 continues in the same vein. Cumulative indexes provide access by poet, title, and nationality. Contents of this work are indexed in *Gale Literary Directory CD-ROM* (entry 1090).

WRITERS' GUIDES AND DIRECTORIES

1132. **Poet's Market, 1998: 1,800 Places to Publish Your Poetry.** Chantelle Bentley, ed. Cincinnati: Writer's Digest Books, 1986– . Ann. ISSN 0883-5470.

One of the few guides focusing on the needs of the poet, the intention of this work is to help serious poets find the right outlets and derive appropriate rewards for their labor. The 1998 edition of this work covers more than 1,800 listings of various media of interest to the poet in publishing his or her work. Included here are small-circulation literary journals, mass circulation magazines, and book publishers, both small press and trade. The editors supply a code to identify what might be the most receptive houses, and identify specialties. Additionally, there are listings of greeting card companies, writing colonies, and poets' organizations. The contents are accessed through indexes of various types, including geographic region and subject.

QUOTATIONS

*1133. **The Columbia Granger's World of Poetry.** New York: Columbia University Press, 1995. (CD-ROM).

This is a major reference work, incorporating the content of both *Columbia Granger's Index to Poetry* (entry 1267) and *Columbia Granger's Dictionary of Poetry Quotations*. As a quotation book it provides 7,500 quotations from the most anthologized in-copyright poems (including those by anonymous poets) to be treated in the *Index*, selected by a panel of English professors. In addition, it contains the full text of 10,000 of the most anthologized non-copyrighted poems, as well as indexing to more than 135,000 poems by more than 20,000 poets in more than 700 anthologies and 70 collected and selected works. One is able to search by author title, subject, first line, last line, key word, or category. The end result is an incomparable source of information for revealing identity and location of poetry. Emphasis is on English-language poems from all time periods; various countries are represented.

Victoria Kline's *Last Lines: An Index to the Last Lines of Poetry* (Facts on File, 1991) further complements the identification of poetry with a two-volume treatment of the last lines found in poetry taken from 497 anthologies published between 1900 and 1987. Most are English or American in origin, although foreign poetry in English translation is included. The work is indexed by author and key word.

Literature in English

GENERAL (Various Genres)

Bibliographic Guides

1134. **American Prose and Criticism, 1820–1900: A Guide to Information Sources.** Elinore Hughes Partridge, comp. Detroit: Gale Research, 1983. 575p. ISBN 0-810-31213-1.

This is a useful bibliography and research guide designed to identify sources of information in books on nineteenth-century American nonfiction. It complements an earlier work completed in 1981 by Peter A. Brier, *American Prose and Criticism, 1900–1950*, from the same publisher, which covers the first half of the twentieth century. Both works are developed on the same lines and together are designed to help students and specialists identify significant primary and secondary titles treating their respective periods. Representative writings of various types are included, such as history, travel, narrative, diaries, science, and politics, as well as works by individual authors known primarily for belles lettre. The first section covers general secondary works (bibliographies, periodicals, historical and literary studies), the second section is arranged by genre and lists both primary and secondary sources, while the third section treats individual authors. There is an author/title index.

PAL: Perspectives in American Literature, a Research and Reference Guide, is an ongoing Web site (http://www.csustan.edu/english/reuben/pal/table.html [accessed January 2000]) developed and maintained by Professor Paul P. Reuben of the Department of English at California State University. The current effort (July 1998) is the eleventh edition and is free. It provides bibliographic coverage, overview and outline, and brief narrative in ten chapters beginning with literature up to 1700 and ending with the period from 1945 to the present.

1135. **A Reference Guide for English Studies.** Michael J. Marcuse. Berkeley: University of California Press, 1990. 790p. ISBN 0-520-05161-0.

One of the two important research tools covering both print and computerized sources in American and English literature is this guide to more than 2,700 entries arranged under twenty-four subject sections. These sections treat all periods and genres and supply well-developed descriptive and evaluative annotations of the important reference sources in the field. Designed to meet the needs of advanced students, the work explains use, content, and special features, and identifies complementary tools and related sources. Also furnished are unannotated listings of scholarly journals and of background titles. The work is accessed through detailed indexes of authors, titles, and subjects.

The other important tool is James L. Harner's *Literary Research Guide: A Guide to Reference Sources for the Study of Literatures in English and Related Topics* (2d ed., Modern Language Association of America, 1993). The first edition was issued in 1990 as a replacement for the second edition of Margaret Patterson's effort, published in 1984. This work, like Marcuse's, is designed for researchers and serious students. It has fewer entries but provides annotations. Harner's focus is on sources useful to the study of English and American literature, although there is a brief coverage of literatures in other languages. Annotations vary in length from a few sentences to a few pages and are arranged under twenty-one sections. The second edition contains about 1,200 entries that cite about that number within the body of the annotations. There are indexes to names, subjects, and titles.

1136. **Reference Works in British and American Literature.** 2d ed. James K. Bracken. Englewood, CO: Libraries Unlimited, 1998. 726p. (Reference Sources in the Humanities Series). ISBN 1-56308-518-6.

With publication of the first edition in two volumes in 1990–1991, literary researchers at the college level were provided with an annotated bibliography of reference and information sources serving a variety of needs. The current effort updates and expands the initial publication, extending its comprehensive coverage of useful reference sources (dictionaries, encyclopedias, handbooks, periodicals, etc.) treating English and American literature and writers. More than 1,500 resources on individual writers are described in detail, providing useful evaluations, critical interpretations, and description of content. Writers are organized by form, genre, or literary period. Valuable features and deficiencies are identified in relatively thorough and objective fashion. There are separate sections on core journals and principal research centers. Access is facilitated by numerous cross-references, as well as useful indexes.

R. H. Miller's *Handbook of Literary Research* (Scarecrow, 1995) now in its second edition treats sources considered by Miller to be essential for research. Employing a chapter arrangement, Miller enumerates the important reference sources as well as the procedures and strategies of locating works by and about U.S. and British authors. An additional section covers rhetoric and composition. Manuscripts, collections, and dissertations are treated with brief critical annotations to the resources.

Literature Online, offered by Chadwyck-Healey, is an excellent Web site (http://lion.chadwyck.com/html/homenosub.htm [accessed January 2000]) providing an online library of over 250,000 works of English and American literature in full text (poetry, drama, and fiction) along with an array of reference sources to study them. Access is furnished to libraries and others who pay to subscribe.

1137. **A Research Guide for Undergraduate Students: English and American Literature.** 4th ed. Nancy L. Baker and Nancy Huling. New York: Modern Language Association of America, 1995. 88p. ISBN 0-87352-566-3.

This compact little volume has gained popularity among undergraduate students as a useful bibliographic guide since its initial publication in 1982. Its design has been to acquaint students with all aspects of library use, including computer technology. The previous edition (1989) introduced the student to the potential of online search services in solving bibliographic problems with a chapter on the library catalog in which the user was introduced to online catalogs. The current effort continues this introduction with informative detailed coverage of the use of nearly forty print and electronic reference sources important to the completion of term papers. Separate chapters are given to bibliographies, the library catalog, *MLA International Bibliography*, locating periodical literature, finding book reviews, and other reference tools.

The third edition of *A Guide to English and American Literature*, by Frederick W. Bateson and Harrison T. Meserole (Longman, 1970; repr., 1976) continues the production of an excellent line of guides. Originally entitled *A Guide to English Literature*, the two previous editions from the same publisher (1965–1967) were recognized as important aids to both the graduate and undergraduate student in developing an awareness of existing sources of study. Although dated, it is still used to identify major editions and important commentaries by those pursuing literary topics in a serious manner. It opens with a general introductory section, followed by chapters on literary periods. Included are such studies as Medieval, Renaissance, Augustan, Romantic, and Modern English literature. American literature is given separate treatment, and there is a chapter on literary scholarship. A general index provides access.

Bibliographies and Catalogs

1138. **American Indian Literatures: An Introduction, Bibliographic Review, and Selected Bibliography.** A. LaVonne Brown Ruoff. New York: Modern Language Association of America, 1990. 200p. ISBN 0-87352-191-9.

Following by several years the earlier MLA publication by Paula Gunn, *American Indian Literature* (1983), Ruoff has provided a real service to students and teachers through identification of materials relating to the literature produced by Native Americans. Sources treating both oral and written traditions are included. The work is divided into three sections; the first serves as an introduction to the subject. Excellent and detailed exposition is given to the oral tradition, narrative, oration, drama, and song as well as the written literature. The second section provides a bibliographic review of the major works on the subject. These include bibliographies, research guides, and anthologies, along with study and criticism. Part 3 provides a more expanded treatment of the second section and includes Native American authors and their works, films, videos, journals, and small press publications. There is a chronology of Native American history, and an index is furnished.

Native American Authors is a Web site (http://www.ipl.org/ref/native/ [accessed January 2000]) offered through the Internet Public Library that represents an ongoing project. It supplies bibliographic coverage of Native American authors with links to a variety of Web resources. Emphasis is on contemporary authors, although writers of historical interest are included.

1139. **American Women Writers: Bibliographical Essays.** Maurice Duke et al., eds. Westport, CT: Greenwood, 1983. 434p. ISBN 0-313-22116-2.

This work is considered an important contribution to the body of reference literature developed on female authors in recent years. Much systematic effort is still needed, and publications like this help to develop the continuing body of critical inquiry. The essays cover twenty-four female writers, following the pattern established by James Woodress twelve years earlier in *Eight American Authors: A Review of Research and Criticism* (W. W. Norton, 1971), which itself was a revised edition of a work published fifteen years before that. In all these efforts, the essays describe and analyze a wide range of secondary works on the authors. Bibliographies, editions, manuscripts and letters, biography, and critical studies are covered. Both works treat authors ranging from the colonial period to the present.

1140. **The Annotated Bibliography of Canada's Major Authors.** Robert Lecker and Jack David, eds. Toronto: ECW Press; distr., Boston: G. K. Hall, 1979–1994. 8v. ISBN 0-920802-08-7.

This set moved steadily to completion with the publication of volume 6 in 1985, volume 7 in 1987, and volume 8 in 1994. The effort is divided evenly, with four volumes given to prose writers and four volumes to poets. Both primary and secondary sources are identified for about six writers in each volume. (Volume 7 treats four authors: Marian Engel, Anne Hebert, Robert Kroetsch, and Thomas H. Raddall.) No biographical information is given. Two sections contain works by the author and are divided between complete publications and contributions to publications. References are given to manuscript collections and audiovisual materials and reprints and individual titles within a work are identified. The other two sections contain works about the authors (articles, books, theses, interviews, audiovisuals, honors, book reviews, etc.). This is a highly useful work bringing together a body of material on significant Canadian writers.

1141. **Articles on Women Writers: A Bibliography.** Narda Lacey Schwartz. Santa Barbara, CA: ABC-Clio, 1977–1986. 2v. ISBN 0-87436-252-0 (v.1); 0-87436-438-8 (v.2).

Nine years after this bibliography of articles and dissertations on women writers was published, it was joined by a complementary volume, *Articles on Women Writers, Volume 2, 1976–1984.* In both works, coverage is limited to women writing in the English language, but from a number of countries of the Commonwealth, United States, and other areas. Volume 1 treats 600 personalities who were subjects of at least one scholarly or popular article published between 1960 and 1975. Volume 2 encompasses more writers, over 1,000 in a period of only eight years. This reflects both an increased interest and also a broadened search strategy on the part of the author. Schwartz has included feminist abstracting services as well as traditional indexes, providing another dimension and added perspective on women's writing. Sources are varied and range from literary journals to the common and popular periodicals. A most useful reference tool for literature study.

1142. **Bibliography of American Literature.** Jacob Blanck. New Haven, CT: Yale University Press, 1955–1991. 9v. ISBN 0-300-03839-9.

Originally projected for eight volumes, this monumental but highly selective series has finally concluded its slow journey to completion with publication of the ninth volume some thirty-six years following volume 1. Publication of volume 7 in 1983, ten years after the appearance of volume 6, and volume 8 seven years later in 1990, typifies the slow and painful labor that has required grants from both private and public agencies to sustain the effort. Volume 9, however, was issued in uncharacteristically quick fashion in 1991. The title complements the work of the early American bibliographers Charles Evans and Joseph Sabin. Some 300 American writers, dating from the Federal period to moderns who died before 1930, have been covered in thorough fashion. Arrangement is alphabetical, beginning with volume 1, "Henry Adams to Donn Byrne." Volume 9, "Edward Noyes Westcott to Elinor Wylie," includes such luminaries as Whistler, Whitman, and Whittier. About thirty writers are covered in each volume in systematic fashion, including first editions; reprints containing textual or other changes; and a selected listing of biographical, bibliographical, and critical works. Only authors of literary interest (popular in their time but not necessarily recognized today as major writers) are included. Bibliographic listings are organized chronologically under their classifications. Excluded from coverage are periodical and newspaper publications, later editions, translations, and volumes with isolated correspondence.

1143. **Black Authors: A Selected Annotated Bibliography.** James Edward Newby. New York: Garland, 1991. 720p. (Garland Reference Library of the Humanities, v. 1260). ISBN 0-8240-3329-9.

Newby is an academic at Harvard University who has compiled a useful bibliography of some 3,000 books, monographs, and essays written by African-Americans along with a few Africans and Caribbeans who are living and writing in the United States. In some cases, the items are unannotated. When there is doubt about the author being black, an asterisk is used; two asterisks are given to writers who are not black. The author identifies it as a selective bibliography, therefore there are many notable omissions (Richard Allen, Hallie Q. Brown, etc.) in the coverage given to writings over the period of 207 years from 1783 to 1990. There are nine chapters, representing subjects or genres such as history, education, juvenile literature, and biographies. Annotations vary in size but generally are brief. They may include brief comments on public reception to a work as well as description of content. Title and author indexes are furnished.

Black Literature, 1827–1940 (Chadwyck-Healey, 1990–1996) is a catalog of nearly 3,000 microfiche of source material. It identifies fiction, poetry, book reviews, literary notices, and obituaries from 900 newspapers and magazines published by black Americans from 1827 to 1940. This is part of the Black Periodical Literature Project, directed by Henry Louis Gates, and enumerates over 50,000 items; it is available on CD-ROM.

1144. **Index to British Literary Bibliography.** Trevor Howard Hill. New York: Oxford University Press, 1969– . v.1–2, 4–9. ISBN 0-19-818184-1 (v.1, 2d ed.)

This is an important and highly specialized bibliography, initially projected in six volumes, although volume 7 was issued in 1992. Volume 3 still remains unfinished. The set targets bibliographical works, books or articles, concerning British textual and bibliographic history. Volume 1, *Bibliography of British Literary Bibliographies*, is now in its second edition and covers books, parts of books, and periodical articles written in English and published in the English-speaking world after 1890. The subject of these works is the bibliographical and textual examination of British titles (manuscripts, books, printing, etc., of works published in England or written by British subjects abroad). The second edition of this volume, revised and enlarged, was published in 1987. Volume 2 provides identification and analysis of bibliographies of the work of Shakespeare. Volume 3 will deal with the period prior to 1890. Volumes 4–5 consider British literary and textual criticism and list writings and authors from 1890 to 1969. They describe bibliographical aspects of works printed in Britain from 1475 to the present day. Volume 6 is a combined index to volumes 1–2 and volumes

4–5. Volume 7 (1992) continues the coverage from 1970 to 1979, while supplementing the earlier volumes with works published from 1890 to 1969 that had been overlooked. Volumes 8–9 (two volumes in one), published in 1999, examine the period from 1980 to 1989 in a similar manner. Upon completion of volume 3, a new cumulative index will be issued.

1145. The New Cambridge Bibliography of English Literature. Cambridge, UK: Cambridge University Press, 1974–1977. 5v. ISBN 0-521-20004-0 (v.1).

The earlier edition of this work, *Cambridge Bibliography of English Literature* (1940, 4v.; Supp., 1957) was edited by F. W. Bateson. It established a standard for excellent and authoritative coverage of a larger number of sources relating to the periods and authors of Great Britain, beginning with Old English and Latin literature of the British Isles. The volumes are arranged chronologically for the years 600–1900, with volume 4 being an index volume. The more recent edition continues in the same tradition and is recognized as an indispensable reference and research tool in English literature. The pattern of coverage is similar to the original publication, treating hundreds of major and minor figures with listings of both primary and secondary sources. Each period is covered in terms of important sources of all types. This edition provides coverage to the mid-twentieth century, with volume 4 embracing the period 1900–1950 and volume 5 providing the index. Period studies are not limited to creative literary efforts, but include sections on travel, sports, education, and so forth. In most cases, this work has superseded the earlier edition, although the latter may be retained for certain background chapters not included in the present issue.

Intended for smaller libraries and for home and office use, *The Shorter New Cambridge Bibliography of English Literature*, edited by George Watson (Cambridge University Press, 1981) is an excellent abridgment of the main work. Following the plan of the original, as is usually the case with the "shorter" editions, it provides coverage from 600 to 1950, but eliminates the background material and a number of minor authors that have made the lengthier tool an important work for scholars. The primary section or the major corpus of an author's works have been retained, but the secondary section consisting of books and articles on the author has been reduced considerably. The coverage of periods retains the bibliographies, literary histories, anthologies, and critical surveys.

1146. The Pen Is Ours: A Listing of Writings by and About African-American Women Before 1910 with Secondary Bibliography to the Present. Jean Fagin Yellin and Cynthia D. Bond, comps. New York: Oxford University Press, 1991. 349p. (Schoenberg Library of Nineteenth-Century Black Women Writers). ISBN 0-19-506203-5.

Oxford University Press has been active in producing a series of bibliographies identifying the literature authored by black American women. This volume is one of ten published in 1991 providing a focus on the period prior to 1910. These volumes continue Oxford's activity, marked by publication of thirty volumes in 1988. This particular work supplies bibliographic coverage beginning in 1773, when Phyllis Wheatley's poetry was first published. There is a foreword by the director of the Schoenberg Center, after which the work is divided into five sections. These identify publications by and about writers of separately published works; by and about female slaves; publications appearing in periodicals and collections; publications on the subject of African-American women writers; and finally, a listing of contemporary writings about African-American women. A name index provides access to the first four sections.

1147. A Short-Title Catalogue of Books Printed in England, Scotland, and Ireland, and of English Books Printed Abroad, 1475–1640. Alfred William Pollard and G. R. Redgrave. London: Bibliographical Society, 1926; 2d ed., rev. and enl. W. A. Jackson, F. S. Ferguson, and Katharine F. Pantzer. 1976–1991. 3v. ISBN 0-19-721789-3 (v.1); 0-19-721790-7 (v.2); 0-19-71791-5 (v.3).

One of the most important and certainly most well known reference sources in English bibliography is this standard work, known as *STC*. Its coverage is comprehensive and the initial effort identifies over 26,500 editions covering a period of time rich in English history and creative thought. The arrangement is alphabetical by author and other main entries. The entries provide author's name, brief title, size, printer, date, reference to Stationers' registers entry for the item, and symbols for libraries possessing copies of the work. A serious attempt was made to locate all known copies of rare materials, and there is a representative listing of libraries for more common materials. Included among the 148 libraries are 15 in this country. The second edition was begun by Jackson and Ferguson and completed by Pantzer some ten years after their deaths. Volume 1 covers A–H; volume 2, I–Z; and volume 3 furnishes indexes, addenda, and appendices. The work has been continued by succeeding titles (entry 1148).

A complementary effort is William Warner Bishop's *A Checklist of American Copies of Short-Title Catalogue Books* (2d ed., University of Michigan Press, 1950; repr., Greenwood, 1968). This work identifies *STC* items held in over 110 libraries in this country.

1148. Short-Title Catalogue of Books Printed in England, Scotland, Ireland, Wales, and British America and of English Books Printed in Other Countries, 1641–1700. Donald Goddard Wing. New York: Columbia University Press, 1945–1951. 3v. 2d ed., rev. and enl. Index Committee of the Modern Language Association, 1972–1988. 3v. ISBN 0-87352-044-0 (v.1).

Developed as a complementary work to *STC* (entry 1147), this effort, known as Wing, continues the coverage for another sixty years. Over 200 libraries are identified in the initial effort through their holdings of English works published during this period. Common books are limited to five locations in the United Kingdom and five in the United States, with an attempt made to disperse the listings geographically to facilitate access for scholars and specialists. Wing devised his own location symbols identifying the various libraries involved. The second edition revised and enlarged the original coverage by identifying the holdings of another 100 libraries; bibliographic information has been enhanced in some cases. The revised edition began with the publication of volume 1, A1–E2926, in 1972. Ten years later, volume 2 appeared, covering E2927–01000. Volume 3, P1–Z28, completes the set. Both *STC* and Wing have served as models for a similar project of British holdings in the libraries of Australia as well as one that covers books printed in France.

Coverage continues with *The Eighteenth Century Short Title Catalogue*, a large-scale online catalog of the holdings of the British Library and some 1,000 other libraries throughout the world. *ESTC* contains some 315,000 records of books and other materials published in Great Britain and its colonial possessions between 1701 and 1800. Arrangement is by main entry (generally author) and material includes membership lists of societies, advertisements, and transportation time tables. The work is accessed through both RLIN and BLAISE-LINE, and is also available in CD-ROM version from Research Publications. There is a microfiche edition available through the British Library that furnishes some 300,000 records in the file at time of publication in 1990. *The Nineteenth Century Short Title Catalog*, has been issued in sixty-one volumes. Coverage is given to British publications dating from 1801 to 1918, and includes books, newspapers, journals, school texts, official documents, and others representing all subjects. Sources are the major libraries of England and Ireland as well as the

Library of Congress and Harvard University. An ongoing project begun in 1996 is making the work available on CD-ROM through Avero.

1149. **Small Press: An Annotated Guide.** Loss Pequeno Glazier. Westport, CT: Greenwood, 1992. 123p. ISBN 0-313-28310-9.

Small press publishing continues to represent an important element in the issuance of original literary effort and is not generally well understood. This slender little bibliography provides a needed resource for students and specialists in the literary arts, with its well-chosen sources treating the small press. In straightforward fashion it identifies nearly 175 sources on the small press and small press publishing since 1960. The work is divided into three major segments representing current information sources (directories, indexes, guides, and trade journals), core sources (writings on major social, historical, and commercial issues), and supplementary sources (catalogs, listings, and bibliographies). Annotations are well-developed and informative. Glazier is an academic librarian and subject specialist in the area of American literature who has provided an important tool for research on small presses in the United States.

A useful Web site is *Independent Publishers Group* (http://www.ipgbook.com [accessed January 2000]); IPG serves as a distributor for a number of independent publishers and small press operations. There is a directory of publishers with links to home pages; publishers catalogs may be browsed.

Indexes, Abstracts, and Serial Bibliographies

1150. **Abstracts of English Studies.** Calgary: University of Calgary, 1958– . Q. ISSN 0001-3560.

This is an important journal that provides abstracts of articles appearing in journals from various countries on the subject of literature in the English language. American, Commonwealth, and English literatures are covered. English philology is also within its scope. More recently, world literature and related languages have received attention. The journal has had an interesting and varied existence, beginning life as the monthly official publication of the National Council of Teachers of English. From 1962 to 1980, it was a monthly except for July and August (10/yr.). Beginning in June 1980, it was taken over by the University of Calgary, and in April 1981 it became a quarterly. Abstracts are taken from hundreds of different journals and represent an excellent selection of contemporary thought.

1151. **Annual Bibliography of English Language and Literature.** Modern Humanities Research Association. Cambridge, UK: Modern Humanities Research Association, 1920– . Ann. ISSN 0066-3786.

Located in Cambridge since its initial issue, this title represents one of the important annual bibliographies in the field, and is the most significant one targeted to English language and literature. It furnishes a variety of publications on English and American literature and identifies books, pamphlets, and periodical articles. Also included are reviews of books that have been listed. The work is divided into two major sections, language and literature. Arrangement of entries in the language section is by subject, while the entries in the literature segment are organized in chronological sequence, an arrangement that has been criticized by reviewers in the past. The work provides indexes of both authors and subjects to facilitate access.

1152. **Annual Bibliography of Victorian Studies.** Edmonton, Alberta: LITIR Database, 1977– . Ann. ISSN 0227-1400.

The Victorian period is defined as the time period from about 1830 to the beginning of World War I in 1914. This annual bibliography contains English-language materials of various kinds, including books, periodical articles, and reviews relating to that interesting period. It is not limited to literary subjects but attempts to treat the period in its entirety. The work is composed of seven major segments or categories, beginning with general and reference works, including fine arts, philosophy and religion, history, social sciences, and science and technology. Most important is the section on language and literature, which includes subsections on individual authors. Reviews are cited after the work itself. Indexing is provided by subject, author, title, and reviewer. There is a cumulative index issued every five years.

Victorian Studies (Indiana University Press, 1957–), a quarterly journal, has published an annual bibliography of books and periodical articles since its first year. "Victorian Bibliography" serves as a continuation of the list originally published in *Modern Philology* and was a project of a Committee on Victorian Literature of the Modern Language Association of America. Periodic cumulations of these bibliographies have been published by the University of Illinois Press as *Bibliographies of Studies in Victorian Literature: 1932–1944* (1945); *1945–1954* (1956); *1955–1964* (1967). AMS published the most recent volumes covering the periods *1965–1974* (1981), and *1975–1984* (1991).

1153. **Interviews and Conversations with 20th-Century Authors Writing in English: An Index. Series I–III.** Stan A. Vrana. Metuchen, NJ: Scarecrow Press, 1982–1990. 3v. ISBN 0-8108-2352-7 (III).

Series II of this work appeared in 1986 and augments the coverage of the earlier volume by adding more personalities. In Series I and II, the interviews were published between 1900 and 1980. Series III continues the coverage, indexing interviews published between 1981 and 1985. In all the volumes, arrangement is alphabetical by name of the author. Interviews are then listed chronologically. These interviews are taken from a variety of sources (newspapers and periodicals, both general and literary, from the United States and foreign countries). Also included, much to Vrana's credit, are African and Asian titles. Monographic sources are also covered, but are listed separately. About 3,600 interviews are identified in the first series, 4,500 in the second series, and 5,600 in the third series, providing an extraordinary and convenient access tool for this important material.

1154. **Shakespeare Survey: An Annual Survey of Shakespearean Study and Production.** Cambridge, UK: Cambridge University Press, 1948– . Ann. ISSN 0080-9152.

This is a highly useful and highly successful annual review of studies in a specialized but foremost area of literary research. In the past, it has been under the combined sponsorship of several scholarly and cultural organizations: the University of Birmingham, University of Manchester, Royal Shakespeare Theatre, and the Shakespearean Birthplace Trust. Volumes are given to specific themes that provide a focus for the articles of that year directed toward a particular element or feature of Shakespearean study. The scope is international and articles are furnished by scholars from a number of countries and regions. Most important in terms of bibliography is the regular feature "The Year's Contribution to Shakespearean Study," which is a critical survey of research and publication in the field.

1155. **The Wellesley Index to Victorian Periodicals, 1824–1900.** Walter E. Houghton, ed. Toronto: University of Toronto Press, 1966–1989. 5v. ISBN 0-4150-3054-4 (v.1).

After more than twenty years of work, this set was completed, furnishing both students and specialists with an extremely useful resource tool. Providing subject, book review, and author indexing, it is especially valuable for citations to contemporary criticism of Victorian writers. It is the most detailed index of Victorian periodicals in existence and includes certain journals not picked up by other sources. A total of forty-three periodicals is indexed in the set, with volume 1 covering eight major journals. Volume 2 treats twelve titles; and volume 3 another fifteen, including *Westminster Review*, while volume 4 concludes the text in its coverage of eight more. The volumes are divided into two major sections, with part A furnishing tables of contents for each issue of the titles and part B providing bibliographies of the contributors arranged by author. Volume 5, edited by Jean H. Slingerland, provides a comprehensive author index and tabular overview, with excellent detail, of the listings in all four volumes.

1156. **The Year's Work in English Studies.** Atlantic Highlands, NJ: Humanities Press, 1919/1920– . Ann. ISSN 0084-4144.

This is one of the leading review journals in the field and was originally published by the English Association through H. Milford and John Murray of London. It covers a wide range of studies of English literature. Similar to the *Annual Bibliography* (entry 1151) in scope, it has the additional feature of evaluating the importance or nature of the items indexed. The studies are drawn from both books and periodical articles published in Great Britain, the United States, and various countries of Continental Europe. Language is also treated as a subject and, since 1954, American literature studies have been included also. The arrangement of entries is chronological by period covered, and the work is indexed by author and subject.

Dictionaries, Encyclopedias, and Handbooks

For additional related information, see "Biographical and Critical Sources" in this section.

1157. **British English for American Readers: A Dictionary of the Language, Customs, and Places of British Life and Literature.** David Grote. Westport, CT: Greenwood, 1992. 709p. ISBN 0-313-27851-2.

This work serves as both a dictionary and "companion" or guide to the understanding of British literature and popular culture. Terms and expressions peculiar to British are defined, making it possible for the novice to comprehend the references and quotations expressed in both literary and broadcast media. Such references include places and commonplace objects used on a routine basis. Slang and idiomatic expressions are treated along with political, legal, and bureaucratic terminology. Social customs and routine existence are not overlooked. Grote is a prolific writer, playwright, and magazine editor who has succeeded in producing an unusual, comprehensive work of practical value to a wide-ranging audience. Six appendices provide well-developed perspective on the British scene as well as an extensive bibliography.

1158. **The Cambridge Guide to English Literature.** Michael Stapleton. Cambridge, UK: Cambridge University Press, 1983. 992p. ISBN 0-600-33173-3.

This work is similar to the *Oxford Companion to English Literature* (entry 1168) in structure, although it has greater scope, covering English writing in a number of countries including the United States. This handbook treats the various elements associated with English literature over the past 1,000 years or more. The focus is entirely on literature (somewhat unlike the *Oxford*). It appears that only 2 of the 3,100 alphabetically arranged articles were not written by Stapleton, a respected editor and writer. These two are lengthy survey articles, "The English Language," by M. H. Strang, and "The Bible in English," by C. H. Sisson. Entries include authors, titles, characters, and literary terms, and are arranged alphabetically. There are many cross-references between entries. Historical or mythological descriptions are excluded for the most part.

A more recent and more specialized tool is *The Cambridge Companion to English Literature*, edited by Steven N. Zwicker (Cambridge University Press, 1998). As part of the *Cambridge Companions to Literature* series (entry 1082), it furnishes fourteen well-constructed and insightful essays by different scholars examining various elements of British literary culture of that time period. Perspectives are up-to-date and the various literary forms are analyzed. Chronologies and bibliographies are supplied. *The Cambridge Companion to British Romanticism* (1993), edited by Stuart Curran, furnishes eleven original and quite contemporary essays focused on the period of British Romanticism of the eighteenth and nineteenth centuries. Exposition treats historical origin, development, and intellectual framework of the period, while chronology and bibliography provide enhanced learning. In the same manner, *The Cambridge Companion to Old English Literature* (1991), edited by Malcolm Godden and Michael Lapidge, furnishes selected essays on the early contributions to English literature dating from the Anglo-Saxon period.

1159. **The Cambridge Handbook of American Literature.** Jack Salzman, ed. New York: Cambridge University Press, 1986. 286p. ISBN 0-521-30703-1.

A rather slender and inexpensive work compared to most Cambridge efforts of this kind, the handbook can best be likened to *The Concise Oxford Companion to American Literature* (Oxford University Press, 1987). Coverage of this work includes literary movements, periodicals, plot summaries, biographical sketches of writers, and important bibliographical details. Entries are brief but informative and are arranged alphabetically. Personal opinions are avoided in the critical commentary in favor of the presentation of historical attitudes toward individual authors. Chronologies of American history and of American literature are placed side-by-side. Also included is a selective bibliography of important critical works published in the previous fifty years.

1160. **Companion to Scottish Literature.** Trevor Royle. Detroit: Gale Research, 1983. 322p. ISBN 0-8103-0519-4.

A specialized handbook to the whole realm of Scottish literature, this has been said to take up the study where *The Oxford Companion to English Literature* (entry 1168) leaves off. Entries are alphabetically arranged and include biographical sketches of various personalities (poets, novelists, dramatists, and critics) who have written either in English or Gaelic and have made solid contributions to the literary tradition. There are more than 1,200 entries of varying length depending upon the importance of the topic or the breadth of the issue. Historical events are included in the lengthy articles. Most important is the coverage of minor figures who may be difficult to find in the standard sources.

1161. **Encyclopedia of Southern Literature.** Mary E. Snodgrass. Santa Barbara, CA: ABC-Clio, 1997. 550p. (Literary Companions). ISBN 0-87436-952-5.

With the great influence of the southern United States in producing a large and varied array of literary effort, this encyclopedia represents a useful source of information regarding literary motifs, themes, titles, genres and authors both past and current. It is very selective, including only sixty-eight alphabetically arranged major entries (thirty-seven personalities, sixteen titles, fifteen literary periods, eras, movements, themes, etc.), but covers additional figures and elements within the narrative provided to these major entries. They vary in size from not quite two pages to about twenty pages; entries on particular titles furnish a thorough plot description along with background information and bibliographic citations to further reading. The writers chosen for such treatment (although few in number) receive good biographical coverage along with references, while the genres, historical periods, categories, and so forth. generally receive the lengthiest coverage in survey-length articles. Certain entries supply black-and-white photographs; there is a listing of major authors and chronologies of Southern writings and of subsequent films. A general bibliography contains books, articles, audiovisual materials, and Web sites and a general index furnishes adequate access.

1162. **Identities and Issues in Literature.** David R. Peck and Eric Howard, eds. Pasadena, CA: Salem Press, 1997. 3v. ISBN 0-89356-920-8.

This is an expansive and ambitious work responding to the need to review the "identities" of our dynamic society and the accompanying changes in the literary horizon during the past few decades. More than 300 contributors have supplied over 800 alphabetically arranged entries treating authors, titles, and subjects. These entries treat nearly 265 authors and 425 titles in about 500 words, but vary considerably in length of coverage given to a wide range of subjects that run from 500–4,000 words each. Each essay begins with the identity categories based on an extensive listing of such categories provided in the work and concludes with a brief bibliography. These identities vary in scope and breadth from such broad-based topics as "religion" and "women" to more focused thematic material such as "coming of age." Entries are well-written and useful to both high school and undergraduate students, and the work concludes with a general mediagraphy as well as an additional bibliography, both arranged by identity category. A general index supplies access.

1163. **Masterpieces of African-American Literature.** Frank N. Magill, ed. New York: HarperCollins, 1992. 593p. ISBN 0-06-270066-9.

This is another of the famous Magill critical/descriptive efforts in the style of *Masterplots* (entry 1094) developed for a different publisher. In response to growing demand for material on the black experience in America, Magill and his contributors have produced this compilation of summary reviews of 149 literary efforts by 96 African-American writers. Entries run about 2,500 words in length, and identify principal characters, describe plot, and provide analysis and critical commentary. Selected works represent the various genres: novels, short stories, plays, poetry, biographies, and essays by writers dating from the nineteenth century to the present. Most of the authors are major in terms of importance and impact (Baldwin, Haley, Hansberry, Morrison, etc.) although a few are lesser known. Several children's authors are included; there is a good selection of female writers. Author and title indexes provide access.

1164. **The New Arthurian Encyclopedia.** Upd. ed. Norris J. Lacy et al., eds. New York: Garland, 1996. 615p. ISBN 0-8153-2303-4.

The initial edition, published in 1986, was considered to be an important and comprehensive reference work focused on the world of King Arthur. It was not limited to literary coverage but included the treatment of Arthur in the arts, history, music, chronicles, archaeology, film, and folklore. The 1991 edition represented an impressive revision and expansion of the earlier effort, producing a significant contribution in its treatment of 1,200 entries classified by topics or categories, with a list of entries provided at the beginning of each category. The current effort is an updated paperback version. Because the time period for Arthurian themes is of course limitless, works represent all countries and eras. The tool remains handy and easy to use, covering both specific subjects and general categories in alphabetical order. Major characters and themes as well as individual works and authors are treated. Articles are signed by more than 100 contributors and there are many illustrations. A chronology is included along with a double-page map. A detailed subject index gives excellent access. In the current edition, there is a section compiling the various addenda that have appeared in *The Arthurian Yearbook* since 1991.

Ronan Coghlan's *Illustrated Encyclopaedia of Arthurian Legends* (Element, 1994) is smaller work from a minor publisher that opens with a good summary of literary treatment given the Arthurian legend. The bulk of the text is a listing with definitions or identifications of Arthurian names and places, some objects, and phenomena, along with illustrations. Entries vary from a single sentence to three or four columns in length.

1165. **The Oxford Companion to African American Literature.** William L. Andrews et al., eds. New York: Oxford University Press, 1997. 866p. ISBN 0-19-506510-7.

Publication of this title, edited by academics as part of the Oxford Companion line, marks a milestone in the general acceptance of this particular body of work among the mainstream genres. It represents the first comprehensive, one-volume source to embrace the rich tradition embodied in more than 250 years of effort, and is the product of more than 300 distinguished contributors. Brief biographical treatment is given to 400 authors dating from the colonial period to the contemporary scene, examining writers from Phyllis Wheatley to Gwendolyn Brooks. There are plot descriptions for 150 books, and coverage is given to individual characters from both fiction and drama. Other personalities, such as Marian Anderson, are included if they have had an impact on black culture. There is broad topical coverage of issues, genres, and thematic elements, for which lengthier articles are furnished.

1166. **The Oxford Companion to American Literature.** 6th ed. James D. Hart. New York: Oxford University Press, 1995. 779p. ISBN 0-19-506548-4.

This well-known standard in the field has been highly regarded since its first edition in 1941. The fifth edition (1983) was a long time coming, since the fourth was issued in 1965. After twelve years, the sixth edition arrived, although Hart, the original author, was unable to complete the effort prior to his death. The work has been revised in great measure, although only about 180 new entries have been added. Most of the new entries relate to contemporary authors, for whom the information is up-to-date. Many of the entries have been shortened, and many have been deleted, especially those on peripheral topics. As always, the work includes biographies of American authors with lists of their major writings and brief analyses of style and subject matter, descriptions of significant individual works in various genres, definitions, identifications of awards, societies, and other features, along with descriptions of various issues and topics relevant to society, politics, science, and so forth. It continues to be a leading source of information.

1167. **Oxford Companion to Canadian Literature.** 2d ed. Eugene Benson and William Toye, eds. New York: Oxford University Press, 1998. 1168p. ISBN 0-19-541167-6.

Another useful work in the Oxford Companion series, the initial edition (1983) succeeded Norah Story's *The Oxford Companion to Canadian History and Literature* (1967) and its supplement (1973). It had updated and expanded the coverage, with about 750 entries ranging from short biographical sketches to survey articles on such topics as children's literature or mystery and crime. The second edition, some fifteen years later, updates and expands the previous effort by providing much more emphasis on contemporary modern writers. Titles of individual works and various genres continue to be treated in an attempt to provide an encyclopedic overview of Canadian literary and cultural developments. French Canadian literature is included. Some entries provide references to additional reading, while many have cross-references to related passages.

*1168. **The Oxford Companion to English Literature.** 5th ed.; 2d rev. ed. Margaret Drabble, ed. New York: Oxford University Press, 1998. 1154p. ISBN 0-19-866233-5.

This is the oldest title and has served as a model for the now-extensive Oxford Companion series, having appeared initially in 1932. Drabble is a novelist who had conducted an extensive and thorough revision of the fourth edition, edited by Paul Harvey in 1967, to produce the fifth edition (1986) as well as an initial revision of that work in 1995. The changes in both revised editions have been modest, and the work remains a true standard in the field, with a reputation for brevity, accuracy, and comprehensiveness. It continues to furnish biographical sketches of several thousand authors among the 9,000 total entries; coverage of twentieth-century writers is excellent, following the pattern of the previous revision. Allusions were deleted in the fifth edition, but movements and individual works are covered in detail. There are also useful appendices. Biographies of earlier authors are well developed in the amount of detail provided. This work remains a staple for reference departments and is now available in disk versions for both the PC and Mac.

Drabble and Jenny Stringer produced an abridgment of the first revision in 1996, as they did for the fifth edition in 1987; the current edition of *The Concise Oxford Companion to English Literature* remains a useful tool. Their purpose was still to prune rather than delete the content of the earlier work to provide a reasonably priced resource for less-sophisticated needs. The work has been pared down to 5,000 entries, the emphasis being on basic information rather than critical appraisal.

1169. **The Oxford Companion to Irish Literature.** Robert Welch and Bruce Stewart, eds. New York: Clarendon Press, 1996. 614p. ISBN 0-19-866158-4.

As a recent entry to the Oxford Companion series, this work treats some 1,600 years of the great Irish literary tradition. More than 2,000 entries supply a comprehensive examination of poetry, drama, and fiction. Coverage follows the pattern of others in the series, and includes authors, specific titles, motifs, issues, periodicals, and associations, as well as events both historical and contemporary that influenced the literary endeavor. Political, religious, and social issues are examined and described in entries that vary in length from a single paragraph to several pages for major figures and monumental works.

The Oxford Companion to the Literature of Wales, compiled and edited by Meic Stephens (Oxford University Press, 1986; repr. with corr. 1990) is another that continues the Oxford tradition. Covering a period from the sixth century to the present, nearly 3,000 entries emphasize the writers in the Welsh language. Those who write or have written in English or Latin as well as foreign writers who have published works set in Wales also are included. Content coverage is similar to others in the series, treating historical figures, events, movements, critics, genres, motifs, characters, and titles of major works and periodicals.

1170. **The Oxford Illustrated Literary Guide to Great Britain and Ireland.** 2d ed. Dorothy Eagle and Meic Stephens, eds. New York: Oxford University Press, 1992. 322p. ISBN 0-19-212988-0.

In this, the second edition of an interesting and informative literary travel book, the editors have identified nearly 1,350 placenames worthy of consideration when planning a trip. There are more than 1,000 literary figures treated in terms of geographic locations of some significance to their lives or art. Cities, towns, villages, and dwellings are identified and described. Arrangement is alphabetical by placename and easily located. Entries for each vary from a few lines given to some small hamlets to a fifty-page spread on London. There are thirteen maps to help pinpoint grid position supplied by entries, and numerous illustrations, some in color.

The Oxford Illustrated Literary Guide to the United States, by Eugene Ehrlich and Gorton Carruth, from the same publisher, was published in 1982. Similar in format to its companion work, it appeals to the same audience of travelers with special interests in literary sites and locales. This work provides links or associations between authors and their towns and cities. The arrangement of entries is by state, then by city or town, then alphabetically by author as subject. Brief commentary is included on the sites and the literary figures associated with it. There are many illustrations and quotations, and a detailed author-as-subject index provides access.

1171. **Prentice Hall Guide to English Literature: The New Authority on English Literature.** Marion Wynne Davies. New York: Prentice-Hall, 1990. 1066p. ISBN 0-13-083619-2.

This was issued by the publisher as the *Bloomsbury Guide to English Literature*, and has been reprinted in paperback under that title (1992). As the product of a distinguished scholar, it lays valid claim to its position as an authoritative source, but is easily utilized by the layperson and serious student alike. It provides a comprehensive survey of English literature from Beowulf to the present. Most impressive is the opening segment, consisting of twelve monograph-length essays on topics important to the study of English literature such as political history, medieval literature, Shakespeare, and Victorian poetry. Following that is an encyclopedic treatment of some 6,000 entries supplying brief but informative descriptions of terminology, personalities, and issues. The text is accompanied by some 200 illustrations. A useful feature is a twenty-four-page chronology of important events in the history of English literature.

1172. **Pronouncing Shakespeare's Words: A Basic Guide from A to Zounds.** Dale F. Coye. Westport, CT: Greenwood, 1998. 744p. ISBN 0-313-30655-9.

This is the most recent of dictionaries on Shakespeare, providing assistance in pronunciation to more than 3,400 words that actors or students might find difficult to pronounce. Beginning with an introduction identifying problems with English pronunciation at this time and general description of variations, the work treats each play in alphabetical order, from "All's Well That Ends Well" to "The Winter's Tale." Pronunciations for each play's characters are listed, followed by words in sequence as they appear in the play from scene to scene. In some cases, definitions are provided. The text continues with coverage given to the poems, including the sonnets. Then follow several appendices relevant to correct pronunciation and the variation that exists and a general bibliography. The index of words is essential and the subject index furnishes useful access. The basic text from which the words were drawn is the well-known and respected 1974 publication, *The Riverside Shakespeare*. (The new two-volume edition was edited by J. J. M. Tobin for Houghton-Mifflin in 1997; like its predecessor it contains all the Bard's plays, poems, and sonnets.)

Biographical and Critical Sources

For additional relevant listings, see "Dictionaries, Encyclopedias, and Handbooks" in this section.

1173. **American Magazine Journalists, 1741–1850.** Sam G. Riley, ed. Detroit: Gale Research, 1988. 430p. (Dictionary of Literary Biography, v. 73). ISBN 0-8103-4551-X.

This is the first volume of a selective three-part coverage of journalists who were productive over a 220-year period from 1741 to 1960. This first volume covers the period from 1741 to 1850 and furnishes biographical essays about forty-eight individuals, most of whom have been treated in other volumes of this series and also in *Dictionary of American*

Biography (Scribner's, 1928–1937; repr. 1943. 21v.). The focus in the present work is on their magazine contributions; the biographical sketches are newly written by scholars and specialists. The essays are of considerable length and extensive bibliographies are furnished.

American Magazine Journalists, 1850–1900, also edited by Riley (Gale Research, 1989; DLB v. 79), is the second issue of this set and furnishes fifty biographical sketches of writers during this fifty-year period. Entries follow the same format as the previous effort and give lengthy coverage along with bibliographies. There is an informative expository essay on publishing trends relative to political, social, and economic developments of this time period. Photographs are included. *American Magazine Journalists, 1900–1960, First Series* (Gale Research, 1990; DLB v. 91) and *Second Series* (Gale research, 1994; DLB v. 137) represent a two-volume effort on this time period. Again, Riley serves as editor. Biographies and photographs of some thirty-seven editors and publishers of the twentieth century are treated in each volume in the manner of previous issues.

1174. **American Women Writers: A Critical Reference Guide from Colonial Times to the Present.** Lina Mainiero and Langdon Lynne Faust, eds. New York: Ungar, 1979–1982. 4v. ISBN 0-8044-3150-7. **Supp. v. 5**, 1994. 522p. ISBN 0-8264-0603-3.

This important work describes the lives and contributions of American women who made literature their career as well as those who wrote seriously about their work in a variety of professions (history, psychology, theology, etc.). The intention was to include all writers of established literary reputation, a representative segment of popular writers, and bibliographic references. The biography is critical and furnishes an assessment of the writer's contribution. A recognized deficiency is in coverage of black and lesbian writers, which the editors see as being alleviated with much of the biocritical material being published today. A two-volume abridged edition of this work, edited by Faust, was issued by the publisher in 1983, and reprinted in a single volume in 1988. The *Supplement*, edited by Carol H. Green and Mary G. Mason, provides additional entries for 145 women writers and updates entries on 90 more who remained active subsequent to their coverage in the initial volumes.

1175. **American Writers: A Collection of Literary Biographies.** Leonard Unger, ed.-in-chief. New York: Charles Scribner's Sons, 1974. 4v. ISBN 0-684-19196-2. **Supp. I–IV**, 1979–1996. 8v. **Retrospective Supp. I**, 1998.

This entire collection, including supplements, provides a series of critical studies designed to cover in depth the life and work of 219 notable poets, novelists, short story writers, playwrights, critics, historians, and philosophers from the seventeenth century to the present day. The emphasis is on the style, genre, and literary contribution of the individuals and their place within the literary tradition. The original four-volume set contains the material in a series of pamphlets published by the University of Minnesota; the essays on ninety-seven individuals have been updated bibliographically, re-edited, and newly indexed. The essays are excellent in terms of depth and documentation. The supplementary volumes continue the original plan and add 122 personalities designed to fill in gaps and to continue the coverage of major figures into the twentieth century. Included are such figures as Allen Ginsburg, E. B. White, and Sylvia Plath, along with Henry Adams, T. S. Eliot, and Ralph Waldo Emerson from the original set. The recent supplements have given more attention to African-American women, with the last supplement treating both Maya Angelou and Lorraine Hansberry as well as Neil Simon and Ayn Rand. The most recent issue is a retrospective supplement to the main set containing entirely new essays on nineteen classic American writers.

In 1991, two complementary publications were issued by the publisher to compensate for the limited coverage given to minorities in the past. *African American Writers*, edited by Lea Baechler and A. Walton Litz, treats thirty-four personalities, ranging from Olaudah Equiano, an eighteenth-century figure, to still-active Alice Walker. Eight of these writers had been covered in the previous set and/or its supplements. *Modern American Women Writers*, by the same editors, provides coverage of forty-one female writer, from Frances Ellen Watkins Harper (died 1911) to Walker. Of that number, twenty-two had been covered previously.

DiscLit: AMERICAN AUTHORS is a CD-ROM database issued for the first time in 1990 by G. K. Hall and consisting of 143 volumes of *Twayne's United States Authors Series*. There are over 127,000 citations drawn from OCLC Subject Bibliographies for the American Authors series, listing the works of American authors dating from the colonial period to the present. Twayne, a Canadian publishing house, started the series of biocritical volumes by various scholars, each generally dealing with a single author, in the 1960s. The series has thrived, and there are well over 600 volumes at this time. There are annual updates to *DiscLit.*

1176. **American Writers Before 1800: A Biographical and Critical Dictionary.** James A. Levernier and Douglas R. Wilmes, eds. Westport, CT: Greenwood, 1983. 3v. ISBN 0-313-22229-0.

Nearly 800 entries furnish biocritical sketches by 250 scholars who have contributed their talents to developing a useful source of information. Names of prominent individuals were selected by the editors from anthologies, histories, and bibliographies. Unlike many works of this kind, the length of the entries is not correlated with the importance of the individuals, and minor figures are treated as fully as are major ones. This is an important consideration for librarians who are asked to search out information on authors who are difficult to locate. Each entry provides a biographical sketch including comments on factors that influenced the writer's development, a critical appraisal of writings, and a list of selected reading about the writer. The tool is a worthwhile purchase and is used frequently.

1177. **A Bibliographical Guide to African-American Women Writers.** Casper LeRoy Jordan, comp. Westport, CT: Greenwood, 1993. 387p. (Bibliographies and Indexes in Afro-American and African Studies, no. 31). ISBN 0-313-27633-1.

Jordan is a retired librarian and library educator; she has compiled the most comprehensive bibliography to date on writings by and about black female authors. Some 900 writers are treated in alphabetical order and receive two-part coverage of primary and secondary sources. Writers represent all genres, including poetry, long and short fiction, memoirs, biographies, and diaries. Works date from the poetry of Lucy Terry to the popular writings of the 1990s by Terry McMillan and Alice Walker. All of the important and recognized writers are covered and many obscure individuals are identified. The comprehensive coverage of personalities is the great strength of the work because the listings of sources are limited rather than complete.

Complementing the above work is Ronda Glikin's *Black American Women in Literature* (McFarland, 1989), which provides more complete bibliographic coverage of a selective group of 300 women writers.

*1178. **Black Writers: A Selection of Sketches from Contemporary Authors.** 2d ed. Linda Metzger et al., eds. Detroit: Gale Research, 1993. 721p. ISBN 0-8103-7788-8.

Coverage is given to several hundred black writers, representing the most familiar and most studied authors of the Harlem Renaissance as well as socio-political activism and cultural expression from abroad. Of course, all the top-drawer individuals are included, such as Baldwin, Hughes, and Martin Luther King, Jr. Utilizing the style and coverage found in *Contemporary Authors* (entry 1083), the work is a tool of convenience and is in frequent use by students at both high school and undergraduate levels, who find it an asset in locating needed biographical information. Entries are thorough and contain excellent biographical sketches, addresses, awards, and memberships. Critical responses to the authors' works are included, providing insight into their influence and literary reputation. The work is available online through LEXIS-NEXIS.

1179. **The Bohemian Register: An Annotated Bibliography of the Beat Literary Movement.** Morgan Hickey. Metuchen, NJ: Scarecrow Press, 1990. 252p. ISBN 0-8108-2397-7.

This bibliography focuses on that anti-establishment literary period spanning the 1950s and early 1960s. It includes such proponents as Kerouac, Burroughs, and Ginsberg. Coverage is given to writings by and about some 200 authors and poets. There are about 700 titles, written from the late 1940s to 1989 and embracing little magazine publications, interviews, letters, essays, biographies, bibliographies, and book reviews. Entries supply biographical notes along with citations. The work is divided into three major segments, the first one listing fifty-six general works and critical studies. Part 2 identifies forty-two collections and anthologies; while the bulk of the work is contained in part 3 and cites titles by and about the beat writers. Annotations are informative, generally accurate, and at times irreverent. A chronology is given along with indexes by name, subject, and title.

1180. **British Writers.** Ian Scott Kilvert, ed. New York: Charles Scribner's Sons, 1979–1984. 8v. **Supps. I–V,** 1987–1999. ISBN 0-684-19714-6 (Supp. III).

Modeled after *American Writers* (entry 1175), for which it was designed as a companion set, this in-depth collection also originated as a series of separate pamphlets first published by the British Council in 1950. It is a collection of essays, all of which are signed by distinguished contributors, providing a detailed exposition of the life and work of significant authors. Articles range from 10,000 to 15,000 words and are placed into volumes that are arranged in chronological sequence (volume 1, "William Langland to the English Bible," to volume 7, "Sean O'Casey to Poets of World War II"). Volume 8 is the index. As in the case of *American Writers*, the essays describe the writer's life and period and provide a critical assessment of his or her works. The essays have been updated bibliographically and the content re-edited. The first two supplements are intended to add significant contemporary writers such as Tom Stoppard and Graham Greene not treated in the initial effort; the third supplement emphasizes earlier writers who have been neglected recently, such as Mary Shelley, Bram Stoker, and Beatrix Potter. The fourth and fifth supplements provide additional treatment of twentieth century writers. The work is useful to a variety of patrons as well as librarians themselves.

1181. **Canadian Writers and Their Works.** Robert Lecker et al., eds. Toronto: ECW; distr., University of Toronto Press, 1989. 20v. ISBN 0-9208-0243-5. 1995–1996. 2v (Fiction series).

This large undertaking is devoted to Canadian fiction and poetry of the nineteenth and twentieth centuries. The work is divided equally, with ten volumes on poetry and ten on fiction. Each volume furnishes an introduction and then covers in detail the work of five authors. The format for these essays, written by various experts in the field, provides for a brief biography, discussion of the tradition in which the author has worked, an analysis of major works, and a selective bibliography of primary and secondary sources. This is a worthwhile effort and merits inclusion in any library that values its coverage of literature north of the border. It is a most helpful vehicle for teachers, undergraduates, graduate students, and interested laypersons. In 1993, separate cumulative indexes were issued to both the poetry and the fiction series, and in 1995 and 1996, volumes 11 and 12 of the fiction series were issued.

French-Canadian Authors: A Bibliography of their Works and of English Language Criticism, by Mary Kandiuk (Scarecrow Press, 1990), is a well-constructed bibliography of critical reviews and interpretations of thirty-six major writers. Included here are novelists, poets, and playwrights such as Blais, Hebert, Roy, Hemon, and Brossard. Monographs, parts of books, dissertations, articles, and book reviews are enumerated. An index of critics is supplied along with a listing of Canadian publishers.

1182. **Concise Dictionary of American Literary Biography.** Detroit: Gale Research, 1987–1989. 6v. ISBN 0-8103-1818-0. **Supp. 1900–1998.** 1998. ISBN 0-7876-1695-8.

Designed to meet the needs of smaller libraries, this six-volume tool employs a streamlined style, utilizing entries taken from the *Dictionary of Literary Biography* (entry 1087). Each volume treats a literary period, beginning with coverage from 1640 to 1865 in volume 1 to the period 1968–1988, treated in volume 6. Each volume provides detailed biocritical essays of some thirty to forty important writers from that period. About 200 writers are treated in the six volumes and represent the authors and poets most frequently studied in high school and college curricula. Entries supply charts on "contextual diagrams," providing quick overview of places, themes, movements, influences, and so forth. relevant to the subject's work. A new edition should be out in 1999. A supplementary volume was issued in 1998 entitled *Modern Writers, 1900–1998*.

Structured in the same manner is *Concise Dictionary of British Literary Biography* (1992), with each of eight volumes treating some twenty to thirty writers. Volume 1 covers writers prior to 1660, while volume 8 treats contemporary writers from 1960 to the present. Materials in both these collections have been updated and presented in full when culled from the larger work. The final volume of each set provides cumulative indexes of people, places, and titles.

1183. **Contemporary Literary Critics.** 2d ed. Elmer Borklund. Detroit: Gale Research, 1982. 600p. ISBN 0-8103-0443-0.

Approximately 125 British and American critics of modern times are covered in this work, 9 of whom have been added since the earlier edition in 1977. Entries for those previously covered have been updated and revised. Entries furnish brief biographical summaries, bibliographies of major writings by and about the individual, and essays about the critical stance of each one. They run from two to six pages long and include quotations, some rather lengthy, of the subject's writings. The work represents an attempt to determine the objectives of each critic, the assumptions he or she makes, and his or her accomplishments. As is true of a number of Gale Research publications, the critical interpretations include personal judgment on the part of the author, who is willing to point out shortcomings in style or thought.

1184. **Contemporary Poets, Dramatists, Essayists, and Novelists of the South: A Bio-Bibliographical Sourcebook.** Robert Bain and Joseph M. Flora, eds. Westport, CT: Greenwood, 1994. 642p. ISBN 0-313-28765-1.

This work provides excellent coverage of a limited number of modern writers from various genres who have helped to make the southern literary contribution a major factor in our time. The forty-nine authors date from the early years of the twentieth century to the present and have qualified for inclusion by producing at least four books or plays that have inspired critical attention to a significant degree. Their work, regardless of form or genre, provides accurate and insightful representation of the human condition and the changing social values of the South. Essays provide in-depth biographical coverage along with critical examination of their efforts, and the entries are arranged alphabetically, beginning with Maya Angelou and ending with Charles Wright. They are prepared by individual scholars and experts, who have joined to produce a readable and informative resource appropriate for both high school and college level inquiry. A listing of their names is the last feature of the work, following the index that facilitates access.

1185. **Contemporary Popular Writers.** Dave Mote, ed. Detroit: St. James Press, 1997. 528p. ISBN 1-55862-216-0.

Another of the St. James volumes dealing with contemporary creative influences is this interesting and useful biographical dictionary treating 300 British and American authors of the twentieth century. Geared especially to the needs of high school and undergraduate students, the writers have been selected for their popularity both in school curricula and with the general public. Included here are Agatha Christie, Jackie Collins, Dave Barry, Michael Crichton, Stephen King, and Alex Haley, among others who give a well-rounded and varied representation of both creative and nonfiction influences. Entries are alphabetically arranged and supply brief but informative biographical treatment describing life, education, career highlights, and so forth. This is followed by a critical examination of the subject's body of work and selected individual titles. Access is facilitated through well-developed indexes of author, nationality, genre, and title.

1186. **Contemporary Southern Writers.** Roger Matuz, ed. Detroit: St. James Press, 1999. 442p. ISBN 1-55862-370-1.

The most recent entry to the St. James Contemporary line, this work responds to the growing interest in the Southern region as a fertile area for literary production. It is comprehensive in its coverage of 250 authors of varied genres; novelists, short story writers, poets, dramatists, editors, journalists, and nonfiction writers of the twentieth century, who are included in an alphabetical arrangement of entries. The entries are signed by individual contributors and vary in size from one to three pages. Each one contains a quick glance at the author's essential demographics, a bibliography of his or her works, a listing of critical reviews, and a good biocritical sketch. The work begins with a good introductory essay examining the rich literary tradition of the South and its impact on American literary development, enabling one to gain perspective regarding the contributions of the personalities treated (Harry Crews, Maya Angelou, Anne Rice, etc.). There is a time line that highlights important developments and significant events from the colonial period to the present day and a listing of additional important writers who were not covered. The work is well-indexed to assure access.

1187. **The Critical Temper: A Survey of Modern Criticism on English and American Literature from the Beginnings to the Twentieth Century.** Martin Tucker, gen. ed. New York: Ungar, 1969–1989. 5v. ISBN 0-8044-3303-8 (v.1–3); 0-8044-3307-0 (v.4); 0-8264-0435-9 (v.5).

This work serves as a supplement to Moulton's *Library of Literary Criticism* (entry 1197) in its provision of extracts from twentieth-century criticism of authors who wrote prior to that time. The set is arranged in chronological order from the Old English period to the beginning of the twentieth century. The first three volumes were published in 1969 and carry excerpts from modern literary critics from about 1900 to the 1960s. Volume 1 treats literature from Old English to Shakespeare; volume 2 covers Milton to Romantic literature; and volume 3 targets Victorian and American literature. Volume 4 was issued ten years later in 1979 as a supplement to the entire set, furnishing excerpts written in the previous ten years and bringing the critical coverage to the 1970s. Volume 5 (1989) is another ten-year supplement. In all volumes, critical studies from both books and periodicals are used.

1188. **The Essential Shakespeare: An Annotated Bibliography of Major Modern Studies.** 2d ed. Larry S. Champion. New York: G. K. Hall, 1993. 463p. (A Reference Publication in Literature). ISBN 0-8161-7332-X.

An especially useful tool for a student in identifying relevant and important critical studies is this annotated bibliography of more than 1,500 entries, now in its second edition. The coverage is limited to modern criticism, providing references to those studies published only in the twentieth century. Major sections or categories represented are general works, poems and sonnets, English history plays, comedies, and tragedies. Included in the general works section are bibliographies, editions, studies of sources, and film studies. Each of the specialized sections also contains an opening subsection on general studies. Annotations are detailed and furnish scope notes and dominant themes from each work. Although some oversights have been noted in the past edition, the work remains a useful source of information.

*1189. **Exploring Shakespeare.** Detroit: Gale Research, 1997. (The Gale DISCovering Program). ISBN 0-7876-0913-7. (CD-ROM).

Another in the publisher's program (entries 1255, 1285) presenting a resource kit for teaching/learning consisting of a CD-ROM along with a guide and manual, this is a comprehensive multimedia tool for high school and college students that examines four of the most frequently studied tragedies. Treated here are "Macbeth," "Julius Caesar," "Hamlet," and "Romeo and Juliet"; full text is provided, along with detailed plot summaries with synopses of each act, critical essays, thematic interpretations, and descriptions of historical context. There are listings of characters, related documents, and so forth. A good biography of Shakespeare is provided, as are a time line, notes, and a glossary. Hypertext links bring up relevant full-text documents as well as graphics, audio, and video clips.

Shakespeare (Creative Multimedia Corporation, 1989) is a CD-ROM publication offering the complete text of all plays, poems, and sonnets in both Queen's English and American English versions. A similar effort is *Complete Works of Shakespeare* (Andromeda Interactive, 1994), which provides full text of plays and sonnets along with numerous images.

1190. **The Feminist Companion to Literature in English: Women Writers from the Middle Ages to the Present.** Virginia Blain et al. New Haven, CT: Yale University Press, 1990. 1231p. ISBN 0-300-04854-8.

This is the most comprehensive biographical dictionary of its type, covering some 2,700 female writers from the Middle Ages to the mid-1980s who have written in the English language. The work has traded depth for its great breadth, and entries are limited to no more than 500 words. Arrangement is alphabetical by name of writer, with entries providing a biographical sketch, description of important writings, and a brief list of secondary source material for additional reference. Emphasis has been given to inclusion of British writers, although there is representation from the United States, Africa, Asia, the Caribbean, the South Pacific, Australia, and Canada. Novelists, poets, and playwrights are treated along with writers of diaries, letters, biographies, nonfiction, and children's' literature. Along with the biographical entries, there are about sixty on topics such as black feminist criticism and science fiction.

1191. **Feminist Writers.** Pamela Kester-Shelton, ed. Detroit: St. James Press, 1996. 641p. ISBN 1-55862-217-9.

This is a comprehensive bio-bibliography of nearly 300 writers who have directed their efforts to examining feminist themes through expression in varied genres and forms. Included here are novelists, poets, dramatists, journalists, short story writers, and writers of nonfiction. This represents a collection of international thought systems, primarily American and British, but inclusive of other cultures and nationalities. There is no limitation on time period and entries run from Sappho, the early Greek poet, to contemporary figures such as Gloria Steinem and Beth Hanley. Between them are such luminaries as Edna St. Vincent Millay, John Stuart Mill, Frederick Douglass, and Mary Wollenstonecraft. Entries are written by professors for the most part and are arranged alphabetically. They begin with identification of highlights of the person's life and career, followed by bibliographies by and about the subject. A critical essay examines the body of work related to feminism. The work is well-indexed by author, title, nationality, genre, and subject.

1192. **Gay & Lesbian Literature.** Sharon Malinowski, ed. Detroit: St. James Press, 1994. 488p. ISBN 1-55862-174-1; Volume 2, Tom Pendergast and Sara Pendergast, eds. 1997. 451p. ISBN 1-55862-350-7.

Endorsed by the Gay and Lesbian Task Force of the American Library Association's Social Responsibility Round Table, volume 1 provides comprehensive coverage of authors who have produced writings with gay themes. Included are two excellent introductory essays, one providing an introduction to gay male literature by noted writer Wayne R. Dynes and an introduction to lesbian literature by Barbara G. Grier. Some 200 authors of both fiction and nonfiction who have come to prominence in gay and lesbian culture since 1900 are covered. Entries are arranged alphabetically by name of writer and include such luminaries as James Baldwin, Oscar Wilde, and Gertrude Stein. Treatment is given to life and career, along with bibliographical coverage. Separate appendices identify authors not included as entries as well as writing awards, anthologies, and critical studies. There are a detailed table of contents along with genre and subject indexes. Volume 2 adds coverage of 200 writers born after 1900, such as Alice Walker and Camille Paglia.

1193. **Great Writers of the English Language.** New York: Marshall Cavendish, 1989; repr., 1991. 14v. ISBN 1-85435-000-5.

Biocritical treatment is accorded in this work to those writers considered to be enjoyable. Of course, such a subjective criterion leads to the usual questions regarding inclusion and omission of various important personalities. Only fifty-six authors are treated in the thirteen volumes of text and the index volume. Most volumes treat four authors each within a chronological arrangement for the set, beginning with volume 1 and what the editors have arbitrarily labeled as "The Early English Writers" (Shakespeare, Bunyan, Pepys, and Fielding). One volume treats eleven great poets, and another treats only Dickens and Hardy. Each entry is divided into four segments: biographical treatment; summary of one of the major works, including characterization and analysis of thematic influences; examination of literary devices; and finally, analysis of contemporary events that shaped the writing. The work is highly illustrated and should be popular with high school students for completing their assignments.

An authoritative recent work is *Reader's Guide to Literature in English*, edited by Mark Hawkins-Dady (Fitzroy Dearborn, 1998). It supplies nearly 575 entries treating a wide range of individual writers from all time periods and of varying popularity and renown, as well as topical elements (genres, periods, critical theories, schools, ethnic groups, and literature of various English-speaking countries). The work is the product of nearly 250 scholars and experts who have served as contributors. Narratives are full, at least a page in length, and open with a brief bibliography for which the items are described and evaluated. This is especially appropriate for college level students who are seeking to review an author or a literary topic. Several indexes facilitate access.

1194. **Index to Black American Writers in Collective Biographies.** Dorothy W. Campbell. Littleton, CO: Libraries Unlimited, 1983. 162p. ISBN 0-87287-349-8.

This is an alphabetical listing of 1,900 black writers whose biographical sketches have appeared in nearly 270 biographical dictionaries and other reference tools, including audiovisual collections and some children's works. These biographical sources were published over a span of nearly 150 years, from 1837 to 1982. Each writer has at least one listing or reference, and each source has at least two individuals from the list. Entries are alphabetically arranged and include dates, field of interest, and variant names as well as reference to a biographical source.

Black American Writers: Bibliographical Essays, edited by Thomas Inge et al. (St. Martin's Press, 1978), is a two-volume source of information of important biographical and critical writings on significant black American authors. It also identifies manuscript and special collections for further study. The essays cover individuals, groups, and specific genres.

1195. **Magill's Survey of American Literature.** Frank N. Magill, ed. New York: Marshall Cavendish, 1991. 6v. ISBN 1-85435-437-X. **Supp.** 2v. 1994. ISBN 1-85435-734-4.

Designed to meet the needs of both high school and undergraduate students in search of information about significant authors, Magill has produced a six-volume treatment of 190 writers from the seventeenth to the later twentieth centuries. In keeping with the time, attention has been given to gender, ethnicity, and racial considerations in the selection of writers. They are diverse in nature and represent the various genres (fiction and short story, poetry, drama, and nonfiction). Writers of young adult literature are not overlooked. Entries are arranged alphabetically and identify biographical highlights and literary achievements in boxed formats. There are essays ranging from seven to nineteen pages in length and supplying a sequential overview of the author's life, analysis of style, and treatment of specific titles. A listing of the author's works is given along with a bibliography of additional sources. There are a glossary and an index. The two-volume supplement extends the coverage by treating another seventy-six- influential writers, with emphasis on current authors (Tom Clancy) or past writers who have been neglected (Gertrude Stein).

1196. **Modern American Literature.** 5th ed. Detroit: St. James Press, 1999. 3v. ISBN 1-55862-379-5.

Established as a complementary work to Moulton's *Library of Literary Criticism* (entry 1197) by Continuum Publishing, this tool appeared for the first time in 1960. The fourth edition was issued in 1969 as a three-volume set, which updated and enlarged the previous edition (1964). Since then, three supplements have been issued, the last in 1998. The new edition has been taken over by St. James Press and furnishes cumulative coverage of 489 writers of the twentieth century, with approximately seventy having been added from the last supplement. Like Moulton, it provides a compilation of excerpts of critical essays on these prominent authors. The essays were originally published in both scholarly and popular books and journals. Citations are given to their locations. Arrangement is alphabetical, and volume 3 includes an index of critics. The new edition gives greater emphasis to the inclusion of African-American, Hispanic, Native American, and female writers, although each of the supplements to the fourth edition had done more in that regard.

In 1999, St. James issued a second edition of *Modern British Literature*, also previously produced by another publisher, Ungar (1966, and Supplements 1975, 1985). The new edition covers more than 400 writers, including 50 new to the work. All 350 entries from the earlier publication and supplements were reviewed and updated.

1197. **The New Moulton's Library of Literary Criticism of English and American Authors.** Harold Bloom, gen. ed. New York: Chelsea House, 1985–1990. 11v. ISBN 0-87754-779-3 (v.1).

This is a thorough revision of the classic *Library of Literary Criticism*, by Charles Wells Moulton (Moulton, 1901–1905). Like the original, which has been a library standard since its publication date, it serves as both an anthology of critical comment and an index to critical studies. It set the pattern for a number of works to follow in subsequent years by furnishing a compilation of extracts of quoted materials representing critical commentary. An additional 250 authors (British and American) who died before 1904 have been added to the new edition. Each author is given brief biographical coverage, followed by selected quotations of criticisms. These are classified and grouped as personal or individual works. Extracts can be quite lengthy, and adequately convey the sense of the critique. The period of criticism covered in the Chelsea House work remains the same (680–1904), beginning with volume 1, "Medieval-Early Renaissance," and ending with coverage of "Late Victorian-Edwardian" in volume 10. Volume 11 furnishes a bibliographical supplement and index.

Another supplementary effort is Martin Tucker's *Library of Literary Criticism of English and American Authors Through the Beginning of the Twentieth Century* (Ungar, 1966; rev. with additions, Continuum, 1989). This is a four-volume update as well as an abridgment of the Moulton work. New material has been added with new authors, and other authors were dropped.

1198. **The Oscar Wilde Encyclopedia.** Karl E. Beckson. New York: AMS Press, 1998. 456p. (AMS Studies in the Nineteenth Century, no. 18). ISBN 0-404-61498-1.

A good example of a reference source targeted to a specific author who has been gaining recognition in recent years, this treats both the artist and the man, describing important events, social developments, personalities, issues, and, most of all, his specific works and contributions. Entries are arranged alphabetically and supply informative essays, descriptive and analytical, on his poems, plays, fictional works, essays, and reviews, with dates of publication, subsequent revision, and inclusion in an anthology. Summaries of recent reviews of these titles are included also. The effort opens with an introduction by Wilde's grandson and contains a chronology; the index provides ready access.

The Cambridge Companion to Oscar Wilde, edited by Peter Raby (Cambridge University Press, 1997), treats the Wilde influence in different fashion, supplying fifteen essays by various scholars on the writer's contributions and significance. The first three essays frame his efforts within historical and cultural contexts, the next seven provide critical interpretation and analysis of the most important works, while the final five examine the thematic elements and societal forces that shaped his identity as a writer and as a person. There is a chronology and a bibliography for further reading; an index supplies access.

1199. **Reference Guide to American Literature.** 3d ed. D. L. Kirkpatrick, ed. Detroit: St. James Press, 1994. 1202p. ISBN 1-55862-31-8.

The second edition (1987) provided a combined and revised issue of the *St. James Reference Guide to American Literature*, a three-volume 1983 reprint of three 1980 publications from St. Martin's Press, in which volume 1 treats the history of American literature, volume 2 covers American writers to 1900, and volume 3 describes American writers since 1900. The format remains the same, with the current effort treating 555 major American novelists, poets, dramatists, and essayists. The entries for 410 authors covered in the second edition have been revised and another 145 have been added. Most of these indicate greater attention to contributions of African-Americans and other ethnic minorities as well as women and gay writers. Part 1 covers the writers and provides biographical and critical sketches, as well as listings of critical studies. Part 2 supplies 131 essays on individual, important works of American literature from their origins to the present. There are a chronology of important contributions to literary history in this country, a bibliography, and an index of titles.

1200. **Reference Guide to English Literature.** 2d ed. D. L. Kirkpatrick. Chicago: St. James Press, 1991. 3v. ISBN 1-55862-078-8.

This revision of the eight-volume *St. James Reference Guide to English Literature* (1986) has changed in coverage and format. All U.S. authors have now been excluded in favor of the publisher's *Reference Guide to American Literature* (entry 1199). Volume 1 opens with twelve essays by scholars on distinct periods; coverage is then given to some 900 of the most important writers of English-language literature from Great Britain, Ireland, Canada, Australia, New Zealand, Africa, Asia, and the Caribbean. Arrangement is simplified to an alphabetical listing rather than the previous organization under twelve literary periods and genres. Entries supply a brief biographical sketch, listings of the author's works in chronological order, a bibliography of additional readings, and critical essays from 300 to 1,500 words in length on the writer's work. Volume 3 supplies individual essays on 600 of the most important poems, novels, plays, and essay collections. A title index provides ready access.

1201. **Research Guide to Biography and Criticism.** Walton Beacham, ed. Washington, DC: Research Publishing, 1985–1991. 6v. ISBN 0-933833-00-8.

Designed for high school and undergraduate students, this series provides biocritical coverage of British and American poets, novelists, and nonfiction writers dating from the Middle Ages to the present. Dramatists from all periods are enumerated as well. Volumes 1–2 were issued in 1985 and provide signed articles from three to five pages long on 300 poets, novelists, and prose writers. Included in each article is a brief chronology, selected bibliography, evaluation of biographical and critical works, and references to biographical sources. Volume 3 was published in 1986 and embraces dramatists, while volume 4 (1990) provides an update, with revision of many entries covered in volumes 1–3. Volumes 5 and 6 were issued in 1991 and supply entries for nearly 130 writers who had not been treated previously. Most are contemporary Americans but there is some inclusion of notables from the past. There is a cumulative index in volume 6.

1202. **Who's Who in Writers, Editors & Poets: United States and Canada.** Highland Park, IL: December Press, 1987– . Bienn. ISSN 1049-8621.

The fifth edition of this biographical directory was issued in 1995, and like its predecessor it contains several hundred pages treating about 10,000 individual writers, editors, and poets. Canadians had been added to the third edition. Entries are brief and supply information regarding education, date and place of birth, family, awards, indication of publications, and current address. Information is gathered through questionnaire and inclusion is based on response; therefore omissions are evident. An interesting observation is the lack of representation among university press editors. The strength or value of the work lies in the great proportion of relatively unknown writers treated; it would appear that at least half the entries are for personalities not covered in biographical works by Gale Research or St. James Press. An index is provided.

1203. **The Writers Directory.** Detroit: St. James Press, 1971/1973–. Ann. ISSN 0084-2699.

Beginning as a biennial publication, this work continues to list thousands of living writers who have had at least one book published in the English language. Providing brief biographical sketches of the Who's Who variety, the entries give pseudonyms, citizenship, birth years, writing summaries, appointments, bibliographies, and addresses. Writers represent varied genres and include fiction, nonfiction, poetry, and drama. Coverage is geographically comprehensive, with all areas in which English is spoken or written represented (United States, England, Australia, Canada, South Africa, Ireland, etc.). A most useful feature is the "yellow pages," in which writers are classified and listed under different writing categories. The fourteenth edition (1999), published in 1998, seems to mark a change to annual rather than biennial frequency.

Who's Who in Canadian Literature, compiled by Gordon Ripley and Anne Mercer (Toronto: Reference Press, 1983/1984–), is a more specialized biennial directory and furnishes about 900 sketches of living Canadian poets, novelists, playwrights, critics, editors, and short story writers. The fourth edition for 1992/1993 was issued in 1992.

1204. **Writers of the Indian Diaspora: A Bio-Bibliographical Critical Sourcebook.** Emmanuel S. Nelson, ed. Westport, CT: Greenwood, 1993. 468p. ISBN 0-313-27904-7.

The author is an academic specialist in the area of Indic literature and has produced an important volume for high school and college students at all levels. A total of fifty-eight authors of noteworthy status who have written in the English language are covered in an attempt to be as comprehensive as possible. These writers represent a variety of geographical areas embraced within the Indian diaspora, from the South Pacific to the Americas, and including parts of Europe and Oceania. Entries are arranged alphabetically and supply well-constructed biographical sketches, a summary of major works, perspectives regarding critical reception, and listings of primary and secondary sources.

Nelson's earlier work, *Reworlding: The Literature of the Indian Diaspora* (Greenwood, 1992), is a slender volume providing exposition of literary development and achievement within separate chapters given to the different geographic regions. Writers are identified and elements of the literature are examined.

Histories and Chronologies

1205. **American Literary Magazines: The Eighteenth and Nineteenth Centuries.** Edward E. Chielens, ed. Westport, CT: Greenwood, 1986; repr., London: Greenwood/Eurospan. 503p. (Historical Guides to the World's Periodicals and Newspapers). ISBN 0-313-23985-1.

Designed as the first volume of a two-volume set covering the history of little (low-circulation literary) magazines in this country, this covers the period 1774 to 1900 and describes ninety-three of the most important titles of the time. Included for each entry is an extensive history of its publishing and editorial policy. The work is scholarly in nature, providing documentation through notes. Also furnished is a bibliography of additional sources for further reading. Reprint editions are identified, as are existing runs of the periodicals and availability of indexes. Title changes are recorded, and volume and issue data are given along with frequency and names of key figures. Also provided is an opening essay on periodical publishing during this period. The appendices contain listings of literary magazines and a chronology.

American Literary Magazines: The Twentieth Century, also edited by Chielens (1992), continues the coverage into the modern era and completes the two-volume set. The most familiar little magazines, seventy-six in number, are featured and described in the same manner as in the initial volume. A chronology is furnished, as is a descriptive analysis of nearly thirty repositories of little magazines in the United States. An appendix furnishes brief descriptions of an additional 100 magazines.

1206. **Annals of American Literature 1602–1983.** Richard M. Ludwig and Clifford A. Nault, Jr., eds. New York: Oxford University Press, 1986; repr., 1989. 342p. ISBN 0-19-505919-0.

Modeled after *Annals of English Literature* (entry 1207), this is a chronology of facts and dates focused on literary productivity. Listings are generally of books published in this country, but include some European titles considered important to an understanding of the pre-colonial and colonial periods and published during that time. Listings are year-by-year, with four genres identified (fiction, nonfiction, drama, and poetry). Authors are listed alphabetically each year in entries that include their birth dates, titles of their works, and genres. Parallel columns identify certain historical and literary events. Identified are the founding of newspapers, births and deaths of authors, and foreign literary works. Although there are a number of omissions in this selective work, it should prove to be of value for quick identifications.

1207. **Annals of English Literature, 1475–1950: The Principal Publications of Each Year Together with an Alphabetical Index of Authors and Their Works.** 2d ed. Oxford: Clarendon, 1961; repr., 1976. 380p. ISBN 0-19-866129-0.

Originally published in 1935 and covering the period up to 1925, this work has been a fixture in reference departments interested in providing services in the area of English literature. Recognized as an important chronology, it has served as a model for other works in its organization and format (entry 1206). Arrangement is year-by-year, with listings of authors given under each year. Important titles of their works are furnished. Complete listings are given major authors, and principal works of minor authors are given. Side columns give dates of birth and death of literary figures, founding of newspapers and important periodicals, as well as foreign events having a bearing on English literary contributions.

Another useful chronology is Samuel J. Rogal's *A Chronological Outline of British Literature* (Greenwood, 1980), which furnishes comprehensive coverage of literary events in England, Scotland, Ireland, and Wales. It is similar in style and format to Rogal's *A Chronological Outline of American Literature* (entry 1211).

1208. **British Literary Magazines.** Alvin Sullivan, ed. Westport, CT: Greenwood, 1983–1986. 4v. (Historical Guides to the World's Periodicals and Newspapers). ISBN 0-313-22871-X.

An impressive tool covering several hundred important British periodicals by historical period is this four-volume guide. Volume 1 covers the period of Johnson and the Augustan age, from 1698 to 1788; volume 2 covers the Romantic period, from 1789 to 1836; volume 3 surveys the Victorian and Edwardian years, from 1837 to 1913; and volume 4 provides coverage from 1914 to 1984. Entries are arranged alphabetically and each periodical is described in terms of its editorial history and general content. Significant contributors and regular features are listed. A useful bibliography of additional sources is given, and American and British library locations are enumerated. Each volume has an index of topics, titles, and names. Although not a history itself, this directory should prove to be an invaluable resource for the literary historian.

1209. **Cambridge History of American Literature.** 2d ed. Sacvan Bercovitch, ed. New York: Cambridge University Press, 1994–1999. 8v. ISBN 0-52-149733-7 (v.8).

This replaces the well-respected earlier edition in four volumes from Putnam, edited by William P. Trent, and continues its outstanding coverage of literary development in this country. The new edition divides the volumes between poetry and prose in the following manner: volume 1 (1994) provides comprehensive coverage of the earliest years, 1590–1820; volume 2 (1995), prose writing 1820–1865; volume 3 (2000), poetry and criticism for that same period; volumes 4, 5, and 6 are due in early 2000, and cover the middle years (1865–1940) in the same manner; volume 7 (1999) treats prose writing from 1940–1990; and volume 8 (1999), poetry and criticism, 1940–1995. The early years have been covered in detail through exposition of literary forms and important writers, and like its predecessor this work describes a host of less common considerations. Included are accounts of early travelers, explorers, colonial newspapers, literary annuals, and gift books. Coverage of children's literature, the English language in America, and non-English writings all serve to continue the tradition. Chapters are written by specialists, and the full bibliographies will appeal to both students and specialists.

1210. **Cambridge History of English Literature.** A. W. Ward and A. R. Waller, eds. Cambridge, UK: Cambridge University Press, 1907–1923; repr., 1976. 15v.

Considered for many years the most important general history of English literature, this massive work remains a model of scholarship and distinguished narrative. Individual scholars and specialists have prepared each of the chapters. The work begins with the earliest times and proceeds in chronological fashion, volume-by-volume, to the end of the nineteenth century. This century is given detailed coverage in three volumes, 12–14. The final volume provides an index to the whole set. Bibliographies are given in each volume and are generally extensive; although old, they are still useful. Designed originally for graduate students, the work has been reprinted several times, sometimes without the bibliographies. These cheaper reprints limit the reference value considerably in a literature department.

In 1998, David Wallace edited *The Cambridge History of Medieval English Literature*, the first in-depth historical examination of the topic in years. The work examines various literary texts and historical perspective are provided by more than thirty contributing scholars. There are a chronology and detailed bibliography.

1211. **A Chronological Outline of American Literature.** Samuel J. Rogal. Westport, CT: Greenwood, 1987. 446p. ISBN 0-313-25471-0.

Similar in format and style to a previous work by the author, *A Chronological Outline of British Literature* (entry 1207n), this chronology begins with the year 1507 and covers important events in American literature through 1986. The usual types of literary events are highlighted, such as births and deaths of literary figures; notable occurrences; and publications of various types, including poetry, fiction, drama, and essays. Both important and not-so-important American writers are treated, with the criteria for inclusion being their significance or representativeness. Although there are many omissions, the comprehensiveness of this chronology is commendable. A work of this type is useful to scholars, specialists, educators, and the general public as well. There are an introductory essay, a bibliography, and an index of authors and events. The lack of a title index might be considered an oversight.

1212. A Concise Chronology of English Literature. P. J. Smallwood, comp. Totowa, NJ: Barnes & Noble, 1985. 220p. ISBN 0-389-20597-4.

Another useful chronology that attempts to place literary contributions within the context of historical events is this recent work. Coverage begins with the period of Chaucer in 1375 and ends with the year 1975. This makes it a useful tool for those libraries that have been operating with the *Annals of English Literature* (see entry 1207) and its more limited time span (1475–1950). Two schemes are provided, one a listing of important events in English literature and the other giving important historical events that occurred at the same time. Certain European writers such as Boccaccio, Erasmus, and Machiavelli are included because of their significance in the development of English literature. The usual criticism about omissions or questionable inclusions applies. An index of authors' names provides access.

1213. A Literary History of England. 2d ed. Albert Croll Baugh. New York: Appleton-Century-Crofts, 1980. 4v.

This is the second issue of a highly regarded and important reference history in four volumes covering the same time period as the much more detailed *Cambridge History of English Literature* (entry 1210). Like the initial edition in 1967, the style of writing in the present effort is well developed and consistent from volume to volume, each of which is written by an American specialist on the topic. Volume 1 covers the Middle Ages in two parts: the Old English period to 1100 and the Middle English period 1100–1500. Volume 2 treats the Renaissance (1500–1660), and volume 3, the Restoration and eighteenth century (1660–1789). Volume 4 carries the coverage through modern times. The work is especially useful for its excellent documentation, with numerous bibliographical footnotes in the text. At the end of the new edition is a bibliographical supplement giving additional references to books and periodical articles.

1214. Oxford History of English Literature. Frank Percy Wilson and Bonamy Dobree. Oxford: Clarendon, 1945–1991. v.1–15.

Similar to the *New Oxford History of Music* (entry 691) in being a long-range project is this multi-volume history of English literature. Recognized as an important source for its detailed and authoritative coverage, it is hoped that the work will eventually reach fruition as a useful alternative to the much older *Cambridge History of English Literature* (entry 1210). Each volume or part of a volume is written by a specialist in the field, and each furnishes extensive bibliographies. Still in process are volume 1, part 1, ranging from before the Norman Conquest to Middle English literature, and a possible second part of volume 4 (part 1, "English Drama, 1485–1585"). Volume 15 brings the coverage to the early writers of the twentieth century. Most libraries follow the lead of the Library of Congress in cataloging the volumes separately and linking them together with a series added entry in the catalog.

A revised edition of *The Short Oxford History of English Literature*, edited by Andrew Sanders, was issued as an inexpensive paperback in 1996. It is in one volume and emulates the coverage of the larger work, beginning with a chapter on Old English literature and ending with a chapter on post-war and post-modern literature.

1215. The Oxford History of New Zealand Literature in English. 2d ed. Terry Sturm, ed. New York: Oxford University Press, 1998. 890p. ISBN 0-19-558385-X.

This continues as a well-executed survey of the literature of New Zealand, with chapters arranged by literary genre and produced by various scholar-contributors. New Zealand had been largely ignored in terms of its literary productivity until the recent past, with publication of Patrick Evans's *Penguin History of New Zealand Literature* (Penguin, 1990), a less-comprehensive work than the present effort. In addition to traditional elements, the *Oxford* provides chapters on popular fiction, children's literature, and nonfiction. The chapter on Maori literature in Maori is an especially useful source, revealing information difficult to find elsewhere. The concluding bibliographic essay identifies works to time of publication. An index is provided.

FICTION

Bibliographic Guides

1216. **Afro-American Fiction, 1853–1976: A Guide to Information Sources.** Edward Margolies and David Bakish. Detroit: Gale Research, 1979. 161p. (American Literature, English Literature, and World Literatures in English Information Guide Series, v. 25). ISBN 0-8103-1207-7.

Although this work is not without deficiencies in terms of omissions and inaccuracies, it still is important because of its comprehensive nature, incorporating several features not otherwise found in a single tool. First is a checklist of novels, a comprehensive listing of nearly 730 works dating from William Wells Brown's *Clotel* (1853) through publications in the year 1976. Second is a listing of anthologies of short stories, followed by an annotated list of bibliographies and general studies on black fiction and authors. All fictional works are listed chronologically in the appendix. Although there is little material that is not duplicated in other tools, it is convenient to have these features included in one work. There are indexes by author, title, and subject to provide access.

The contents of this title are indexed in **Gale's Literary Index CD-ROM* (entry 1090).

1217. **Dickinson's American Historical Fiction.** 5th ed. Virginia Brokaw Gerhardstein. Metuchen, NJ: Scarecrow Press, 1986. 352p. ISBN 0-8108-1867-1.

First published in 1958, this standard work has now been updated to include work published to 1984. It is a useful tool for reading guidance, providing a classified listing of over 3,000 novels published primarily between 1917 and 1984. For historical novels, time, place, and social/historical phenomena are identified. The arrangement of entries is by chronological period, beginning with colonial times and ending with the mid-1970s (the turbulent years). Annotations are furnished but are not evaluative, and describe briefly the setting and plot to give historical perspective. Included is a subject index as well as an author/title index.

Another useful source, although not as current, is Leonard Bertram Irwin's *A Guide to Historical Fiction for the Use of Schools, Libraries, and the General Reader* (10th ed., McKinley, 1971). This first appeared in 1930, written by Hanna Logasa, and still represents a standard source of favorably reviewed historical novels classified by geography and time period.

1218. **Science Fiction, Fantasy, and Weird Fiction Magazines.** Marshall B. Tymn and Mike Ashley, eds. Westport, CT: Greenwood, 1985. 970p. (Historical Guides to the World's Periodicals and Newspapers). ISBN 0-313-21221-X.

Regarded as an excellent source of information on magazines of this type, this work provides comprehensive coverage of English-language periodicals dating from 1882 to the present. It is divided into several sections, the first of which furnishes listings of magazines published in the United States, Great Britain, Canada, and Australia, which are devoted wholly or in part to genre literature. Entries provide a brief history of origin and development, bibliography and sources of indexing, sources of reprinting, and publication data, and include numerous cross-references. Other sections give English-language anthologies, information on significant fanzines and academic journals, and annotations of an additional 178 titles from twenty-three foreign countries. Appendices furnish an index to cover artists and a chronology of magazine origins.

Another important tool, *Anatomy of Wonder 4: A Critical Guide to Science Fiction* (R. R. Bowker, 1995), edited by Neil A. Barron, is now in its fourth edition and represents a major revision with the addition of about 500 titles from the previous 1987 effort. It now identifies some 2,100 novels and short story collections, as well as 800 nonfiction titles published up to 1994. It has eliminated all foreign-language contributions, film and television, and illustration as well as the major coverage of the primary literature, magazines, and others. Entries have been modified to include recent sequels and other interesting elements.

Bibliographies and Indexes

1219. **The Afro-American Short Story: A Comprehensive Annotated Index with Selected Commentaries.** Preston M. Yancy, comp. Westport, CT: Greenwood, 1986. 171p. (Bibliographies and Indexes in Afro-American and African Studies, no. 10). ISBN 0-313-24355-7.

This is a timely and important contribution, identifying over 800 short stories written in a thirty-two-year period between 1950 and 1982. These years are especially significant to the black experience in terms of its manifestation in the literature following the 1954 U.S. Supreme Court desegregation decision. Over 300 authors are represented in this tool, which is divided into several parts. The first part is a year-by-year chronological listing, with titles arranged alphabetically under each year. This is followed by a list of anthologies and collections, then by a section of commentaries on selected stories classified by type. There is an author index, which also provides references to biographical sketches in five biographical encyclopedias.

Helen Ruth Houston's *The Afro-American Novel, 1965–1975: A Descriptive Bibliography of Primary and Secondary Material* (Whitston, 1977) still holds a prominent position in reference departments with its listing of the works of fifty-six African-Americans published since 1964. Critical studies and reviews are identified.

1220. **American Fiction, 1774–1850: A Contribution Toward a Bibliography.** Additions and corr. appended. Lyle Henry Wright. San Marino, CA: Huntington Library, 1978. 438p. ISBN 0-87328-041-5.

This has become a standard reference tool since publication of the first edition in 1939. Since that time, it has been revised on several occasions, with over 700 titles added to the second revised edition in 1969. This issue contains additions and corrections. A total of 3,500 entries includes novels, romances, short stories, fictitious biographies and travel, allegories, and so forth. Copies of these works are located in twenty-two libraries. All works are by American authors, and entries are alphabetical by author. Entries furnish title imprints, pagination, and occasional notes. Juvenile fiction is excluded.

The work has been continued by Wright's *American Fiction, 1851–1875* (Huntington Library, 1965; repr., 1978) and *American Fiction, 1876–1900* (Huntington Library, 1966; repr., 1978). The former enumerates over 2,800 titles in nineteen locations, while the latter identifies copies of the first U.S. editions of 6,175 items in fifteen libraries. Most recent is *American Fiction, 1901–1925*, by Geoffrey D. Smith (Cambridge University Press, 1997), adding to the historical record in its identification of first printings of American fiction titles during the first quarter of the twentieth century.

1221. Crime Fiction II: A Comprehensive Bibliography, 1749–1990. Allen J. Hubin. New York: Garland, 1994. 300p. (Garland Reference Library of the Humanities, v. 1353). ISBN 0-8240-6891-2.

Based on earlier works by the same author, this edition adds another ten years of coverage and identifies some 70,000 titles. Newly added features are a listing of more than 4,000 films based on literary efforts, complete with release information, and a listing of individual short stories from 4,000 anthologies. All types of crime stories are included: mystery, detective, suspense, thriller, gothic, police, and spy. The major segment of the work is an author index, followed by titles arranged alphabetically, with cross-references to variant titles and pseudonyms. Access is facilitated through indexes by title, setting (geographical), series, and series character.

Another useful title is Albert J. Menendez's *The Subject Is Murder*, in two volumes (1968–1990) from the same publisher. Volume 1 identifies over 3,800 titles published between the 1930s and 1985 by subject or major thematic element such as medicine or politics, covered in separate chapters. Volume 2 supplies references to another 2,100 mystery titles under twenty-nine broad categories. Most of the titles were published between 1985 and 1989. *Murder . . . by Category: A Subject Guide to Mystery Fiction*, by Tasha Mackler (Scarecrow Press, 1991), is an annotated bibliography of mystery fiction published between 1985 and 1990. The author, a proprietor of a mystery bookstore, has supplied a classified arrangement with such subjects as "Getting Away with Murder" and "At Sea."

1222. Encyclopedia of Science Fiction and Fantasy Through 1968: A Bibliographic Survey. . . . Donald H. Tuck, comp. Chicago: Advent, 1974–1982. 3v. ISBN 0-911682-27-9 (set).

More of a bibliography than an encyclopedic source, this work was completed in three volumes over an eight-year period. Volume 1, "Who's Who and Works, A–L," consists of an alphabetical listing of authors, anthologists, editors, artists, and so forth, with biographical sketches where available. Listings of their works in the science fiction and fantasy area are furnished through 1968 and include all known editions and foreign translations. Tables of contents are given for anthologies and collections. Volume 2 covers the same territory for M–Z and also provides an alphabetical listing by title. Volume 3 covers a variety of topics: magazines in the field, paperbacks, pseudonyms (cross-references by pseudonym and real name), series, and general areas of interest such as publishers or films. Initially, the plan was to issue supplements on a quinquennial basis, but thus far this has not been done.

1223. Facts on File Bibliography of American Fiction, 1919–1988. Matthew J. Bruccoli and Judith S. Baughman, eds. New York: Facts on File, 1991. 2v. (Facts on File Bibliography Series). ISBN 0-8160-2674-2.

This bibliography is useful to libraries unable to afford the *Dictionary of Literary Biography* (entry 1087) who wish to provide a handy reference source for high school and undergraduate clientele. Nearly 225 fiction writers are treated, all of whom were born before 1941 and published their most important work between 1919 and 1988. All types of fiction are represented, with the inclusion of all genres and children's/young adult literature. Author entries are arranged alphabetically and supply listings of primary works identified by genre and secondary sources identified by type (bibliography, biography, books, articles, and special journal issues). Reviews and dissertations are listed also. These are signed by specialist-contributors. Special features include a chronology of authors and their works, an annotated bibliography of 110 titles considered essential to literature study, and a general bibliography. There is an index to authors of secondary works.

1224. Fiction Catalog. 13th ed. Juliette Yaakov and John Greenfieldt, eds. New York: H. W. Wilson, 1996. 973p. (Standard Catalog Series). ISBN 0-8242-0894-3.

As part of the well-known and highly respected standard catalog series, this work has had a long tradition; its first edition appeared in 1908. Presently, new editions are issued quinquennially, with annual updates. Considered a companion work to the *Public Library Catalog* (nonfiction), this tool furnishes a selective annotated listing of more than 5,461 English-language titles of prose fiction along with hundreds of analytic entries for novelettes and composite publications. Plot summaries are given in adequate detail, and arrangement and format are highly stylized. Both current authors and early authors are covered. The largest proportion of the volume consists of individual entries for specific titles. Arrangement is by author, then title; excerpts from reviews are included. There is a title-subject index providing ready access by topical matter, the subject approach being one of the strong features of this work.

1225. Fiction, 1876–1983: A Bibliography of United States Editions. New York: R. R. Bowker, 1983. 2v. ISBN 0-8352-1726-4.

Another of the Bowker spinoffs from *Books in Print* and *American Book Publishing Record* is this comprehensive listing of fictional works published in the United States over a period of more than 100 years. Included are novels, novellas, short stories, anthologies, and collections. There are over 170,000 entries, generally found to be reliable (although not error-free), as is true of other works in the Bowker line. Entries emulate those in *Books in Print* and may give author, editor, title, date, price, publisher, LC number, and ISBN. Volume 1 contains a classified author index listing authors by country and period as well as a main author index. Volume 2 furnishes a title index. Full publication information is found in entries in both indexes.

1226. Index to Crime and Mystery Anthologies. William G. Contento and Martin H. Greenberg. Boston: G. K. Hall, 1991. 736p. ISBN 0-8161-8629-4.

This is the first comprehensive index to anthologies of crime, mystery, detective, espionage, and suspense stories and appeals to a wide variety of users. The authors are both experienced writers and indexers of the genre and bring expertise to their treatment of 1,031 anthologies published between 1875 and 1990. More than 12,500 short stories, 3,700 novelettes, 500 novellas, 70 novels, and 300 articles represent the literary output of more than 3,600 authors. There are five major sections in the work: author listings of books, author listings of stories, title listings of books, title listings of stories, and a contents listing of anthologies. Entries for author listings supply information on authorship and publication, while title listings treat type of story and the source of its initial appearance. Anthology listings enumerate each story in the entry. The work is to be updated with subsequent volumes.

1227. A Mirror for the Nation: An Annotated Bibliography of American Social Fiction, 1901–1950. Archibald Hanna. New York: Garland, 1985. 472p. (Garland Reference Library of the Humanities, v. 595). ISBN 0-8240-8727-5.

This is a useful work, identifying some 4,000 titles of American fiction written during the first half of the twentieth century and showing their connection to social history. The emphasis is on novels, but also included are short story collections, plays, and narrative poems. Entries are arranged alphabetically by author, followed by indexes of subject, title, and illustrator. Subjects such as labor and capital or marriage and family life are used, but placenames predominate. Principal subject matter is described in brief annotations, and geographical setting is indicated. Excluded for the most part are the genres of Western and detective stories as well as juvenile literature.

1228. Nineteenth Century Fiction: A Bibliographical Catalogue Based on the Collection Formed by Robert Lee Wolff. Robert Lee Wolff, comp. New York: Garland, 1981–1986. 5v. (Garland Reference Library of the Humanities). ISBN 0-824-09474-3.

This set stands as the most complete bibliography of nineteenth-century English fiction available. Based on the important collection of Victorian fiction belonging to the late Robert Lee Wolff, the work identifies nearly 8,000 titles. They represent the intention of the collector to acquire any English novel published during the reign of Queen Victoria as well as any other novel published by those authors even though it might fall outside the range of 1827–1901. Volumes 1–4 consist of entries for the major segment of the collection, novels by known authors. Volume 5 lists anonymous works by title and pseudonymous works by pseudonyms; it also contains the title index to the entire set, as well as an index to all illustrators mentioned in the notes. *Nineteenth-Century Fiction* (Chadwyck-Healey, 1999) is a CD-ROM anthology of prose fiction of the Romantic and Victorian periods. It contains the full text of 250 works by 109 authors from 1781–1901.

1229. Science Fiction and Fantasy Series and Sequels: A Bibliography, Volume 1: Books. Tim Cottrill et al. New York: Garland, 1986. 398p. (Garland Reference Library of the Humanities, v. 611). ISBN 0-8240-8671-6.

Another of the Garland bibliographies that emphasize series publications of a genre (entry 1233) is this listing of 6,300 book titles in some 1,200 series. Since this work is identified as volume 1 and restricted to books, it might have been reasonable to assume that forthcoming volumes would cover series carried in periodicals. Unfortunately, there has been no further activity in this regard. Like the Western, science fiction and fantasy are well accommodated in the series format and much important work has appeared in this manner. Arrangement is by author, with entries furnishing series title, publisher, and publication date. Although some omissions are evident, the work is useful to those with an interest in the topic. There are good title and sequence indexes.

1230. Science Fiction Book Review Index, 1923–1973. H. W. Hall. Detroit: Gale Research, 1975. 438p. ISBN 0-8103-1054-6.

This is the lead volume and most comprehensive publication for an annual series cumulated on a quinquennial basis. The initial volume covers a fifty-year period and identifies reviews appearing in selected science fiction magazines. Arrangement is alphabetical by authors of the works. A directory of magazines indexed is furnished, and a title index provides access.

The work has continued annually and has cumulated as Hall's *Science Fiction Book Review Index, 1974–1979* (Gale Research, 1981), and most recently as *Science Fiction and Fantasy Book Review Index, 1980–1984 . . .* by Hall and Geraldine L. Hutchins (Gale Research, 1986). The recent title identifies more than 13,800 reviews published in over seventy magazines. An important addition is "Science Fiction and Fantasy Research Index," providing author and subject access points to books, articles, and essays of history or criticism. The effort has been issued annually under the new title since 1984 by SFFBRI. A similar work is *Science Fiction & Fantasy Book Review Annual* (Meckler, 1988–), a magazine of opinionated commentary and well-developed, cogent reviews. It supplies more than 500 reviews of books in the genre published during the previous year. The work has undergone several title changes since its initial appearance in 1978: *Fantasy Review, Science Fiction and Fantasy Review,* and *Fantasy.* (See entry 1124 for additional detail.)

1231. Short Story Index: An Index to 60,000 Stories in 4,320 Collections. Dorothy Elizabeth Cook and Isabel Stevenson Monro. New York: H. W. Wilson, 1953. 1553p. **Supps. 1950–1954, 1955–1958, 1959–1963, 1964–1968, 1949–1973, 1974–1978, 1979–1983, 1984–1988, 1989–1993.** ISSN 0360-9774.

A valuable and highly regarded standard tool, this work appeared originally in 1953. As its title indicates, the initial volume indexes 60,000 English-language stories published up to 1949 in several thousand collections. Indexing is by author, title, and subject, in typical Wilson dictionary arrangement. Since that time, the work has continued through periodic supplements, which are now issued annually and cumulated on a quinquennial basis. They identify several thousand stories in recently published anthologies and periodicals. Such subject headings as "AIDS," "Homeless," and "Lesbianism" are newly added. Inclusion of periodicals began with the 1974–1978 supplement. A list of collections indexed and a directory of periodicals appear in the back. In 1911, Ayer and Son Publishing began a reprint series of all anthologies indexed in *Short Story Index*. It produced many volumes through the years.

Roth Publishing has begun its *CoreFiche. Books Listed in the Short Story Index*, providing microfiche copy of the stories covered in the *Index*. An index of these stories is also issued, the most recent one being in 1998.

1232. War and Peace Through Women's Eyes: A Selective Bibliography of Twentieth-Century American Women's Fiction. Susanne Carter. Westport, CT: Greenwood, 1992. 293p. ISBN 0-313-27771-0.

This is a unique and important bibliography due to its treatment of novels and short stories with war themes written by female authors. It is highly selective in its coverage of 374 works from over 200 authors and excludes fiction of more popular than literary nature. This focus on quality makes it an especially useful tool for serious students as well as general readers. It opens with an introductory essay of scholarly nature placing war literature in perspective. The text is divided into five thematic chapters: "World War I," "World War II," "Vietnam," "Nuclear War," and "War and Peace." These chapters contain an introduction and separate sections on novels and short fiction and a bibliography of literary criticism and sources. Annotated entries supply an evaluative plot summary for each work. Author, title, and subject indexes are furnished.

1233. Western Series and Sequels: A Reference Guide. 2d ed. Bernard A. Drew et al. New York: Garland, 1993. 304p. (Garland Bibliographies on Series and Sequels; Garland Reference Library of the Humanities, v. 1399). ISBN 0-8240-9648-7.

As part of the extensive Garland line of bibliographies, this was introduced in 1986 as useful tool for identifying those westerns that appeared in series. This particular form of the genre has been common for decades, and the second edition adds 350 additional series to the 375 entries in the first edition. Series titles imply use of the same lead character in different books, each of which has an episode that is complete in itself. The coverage embraces those works set in Canada, the French and Indian Wars, and the Civil War, as well as the American West. Foreign series dealing with the theme are included; both juvenile and adult series are treated. There is a brief introductory history of the genre; a general index and author index provide access.

Dictionaries, Encyclopedias, and Handbooks

1234. **Critical Terms for Science Fiction and Fantasy: A Glossary and Guide to Scholarship.** Gary K. Wolfe. Westport, CT: Greenwood, 1986. 162p. ISBN 0-313-22981-3.

As the first literary glossary devoted to the area of fantastic literature, this tool has found a receptive audience among librarians and their patrons. Beginning with a twenty-six-page introductory essay on fantastic literature and literary discourse, it provides a list of nearly 500 terms, alphabetically arranged, complete with definitions and, in some cases, expositions and commentaries. Some terms are given multiple definitions—those of the author and those of other experts in the field. Certain broad concepts are defined with short essays. There are references given to authors and critics, whose efforts are listed in a section on works consulted. Both specialists and laypersons will find this tool to be helpful and rewarding. There is an index of primary authors.

1235. **Edwardian Fiction: An Oxford Companion.** Sandra Kemp, ed. New York: Oxford University Press, 1997. 464p. ISBN 0-19-811760-4.

A recent entry to the Oxford Companion series, this work is highly specialized in its coverage of fiction published primarily in Great Britain and Ireland in a brief period prior to World War I, from 1900 to 1914. Some 800 writers are treated with brief biographical passages; entries also provide descriptions of various works and topical considerations. There is some overlap with coverage in *The Oxford Companion to English Literature* (entry 1168), but such material is revised, updated, and in most cases expanded in this work. As in others from this series, entries are arranged alphabetically and are of varying length depending upon the topic. Coverage is much more inclusive for Edwardian writers of secondary or lesser status than in any other single-volume publication.

Another recent effort is *Cambridge Guide to Fiction in English* (Cambridge University Press, 1998), which, although more comprehensive in scope, has fewer pages than *Edwardian Fiction*. There are some 2,100 entries on novelists, novels, geographic regions, themes, trends, and genres, providing an excellent overview and a quick study guide. Certain of the entries dealing with themes and topical aspects are of greater length. A well-conceived introduction opens the work; there are a selective bibliography and a listing of prizes in the appendix.

1236. **Genreflecting: A Guide to Reading Interests in Genre Fiction.** 5th ed. Diana T. Herald. Englewood, CO: Libraries Unlimited, 2000. 553p. ISBN 1-56308-638-7.

Although the primary purpose of this item has been to serve as a text for library school classes in book selection and collection management, it also furnishes readers with interesting and useful information and awareness of currently available works by authors in the different genres. Using the rationale that no child or adult need apologize for his or her choice of reading matter, the authors survey the popular genres (crime, western, adventure, romance, science fiction, fantasy, and horror). There is an introductory chapter on genre literature, with succeeding descriptions of publishers, readers, and the place of such literature in libraries. Included in the coverage of each genre are listings of significant and popular authors, as well as anthologies, bibliographies, biographies, history, criticism, periodicals, and awards. This is a revision of the 1995 edition by Betty Rosenberg and Herald, to which more authors and titles have been added and older titles and authors deleted. A new sub-genre, "Legal Thriller," was added in 1995 while a new chapter covering historical fiction is in the current effort.

A Handbook of Contemporary Fiction for Public Libraries and School Libraries, by Mary K. Biagini with the assistance of Judith Hartzler (Scarecrow Press, 1989), is a practical, well-constructed listing of fiction titles organized by genre. Emphasis is on authors who have been prominent since World War II, although the classic writers have been included as well. The first part of the book provides the listings under nine different genres (mystery and detective stories, science fiction and fantasy, etc.). The second part categorizes the authors by national origin.

1237. Masterplots: Revised Category Edition, American Fiction Series. Frank N. Magill, ed. Englewood Cliffs, NJ: Salem Press, 1985. 3v. ISBN 0-89356-500-8.

Nearly 350 novels and collections of short stories have been taken from the original *Masterplots* (entry 1094) and reprinted here in a work limited to coverage of authors from the United States, Canada, and Central and South America. Thus, we have another spinoff of the monumental work originally begun in 1949. The "Revised Category Edition" has proved to be a useful convenience tool. Coverage is uniform, as we have become accustomed to in the *Masterplots* design: type of work, author and dates, type of plot, time setting, date of publication, principal characters, a brief critical essay, and an excellent summary of the plot. There has been slight modification and updating but basically this is a remake of the older work in a handy package.

Following the same pattern and rationale and published at the same time is Magill's *Masterplots: Revised Category Edition, British Fiction Series* (Salem Press, 1985). Nearly 400 works by authors from the British Commonwealth, with the exception of Canada, are reprinted in this three-volume set.

1238. Masterplots II: American Fiction Series. Frank N. Magill, ed. Englewood Cliffs, NJ: Salem Press, 1986. 4v. ISBN 0-89356-456-7. **Supp.**, 1994. 2v. ISBN 0-89356-719-1.

Another publication in the line-up from Salem Press is this four-volume edition focused on American fiction not previously treated in the *Masterplots* series (entry 1094). More than 350 modern works from the twentieth century are examined. Coverage is not limited to North America, but includes Latin America as well. Of the 198 authors whose works are treated, thirty-four, or 17 percent, are Latin American. Thus, Gabriel Garcia Marquez and Carlos Fuentes appear, as do Algren, Bellow, Faulkner, and Vonnegut. This makes it a more valuable resource because exposition of Latin American literature is not easily found. Entries differ somewhat from the traditional *Masterplots:* along with the plot summary, there is far more coverage given to the evaluation of narrative devices, characterization, and thematic elements. An interpretive summary is included. The two-volume *Supplement* provides coverage of 180 additional titles by contemporary or generally neglected authors. Arrangement follows that of the initial effort, and cumulative author and title indexes are provided to all volumes in the set.

*Masterplots II: British and Commonwealth Fiction Series (1987) is in the same mold and covers works of more than 150 authors of modern fiction from England, Ireland, Canada, India, Nigeria, and Australia. There are more than 350 evaluative essays of titles never covered in the previous series. Both the American and British series are accessible on CD-ROM along with other volumes in the *Masterplots II* line on **Masterplots II CD-ROM*.

1239. The Ultimate Guide to Science Fiction: An A–Z of Science Fiction Books by Title. 2d ed. David Pringle. Brookfield, VT: Ashgate Publishing, 1995. 481p. ISBN 1-85928-071-4.

While probably not the "ultimate guide," this is a comprehensive listing that has added about 500 titles since the previous 1990 edition. This effort covers about 3,500 novels, short stories, and collections written in the English language and enjoying continued popularity. Works published prior to 1970 and not reprinted since are excluded, along with foreign-language publications, lesser works of lesser writers, novelizations of motion pictures, spinoffs, fantasy, and scientific romance. The work opens with an introductory segment providing a "Bibliography and Acknowledgments" section listing important sources. Entries for individual titles are arranged alphabetically and provide information in keeping with the following pattern: title, date, star rating using four stars, classification, author's name and nationality, and a two-or-three sentence summary and evaluation providing names of sequels and film versions. There are cross-references to variant titles and parent novels of series and an author index.

Biographical and Critical Sources

1240. **The African Novel in English: An Introduction.** Keith M. Booker. Portsmouth, NH: Heinemann/J. Curry, 1998. 227p. ISBN 0-325-00030-1.

This work provides critical commentary in a chapter by chapter approach examining eight of the most important African novels written in English. Analysis of thematic representation, structure, and style are given for *Things Fall Apart*, by Chinua Achebe; *Nervous Conditions*, by Tsitsi Dangarembga; *The Joys of Motherhood*, by Buchi Emecheta; *The Beautyful Ones Are Not Yet Born*, by Ayi Kweh Armah; *Our Sister Killjoy*, by Ama Atta Aidoo; *Burger's Daughter*, by Nadine Gordimer; *In the Fog of the Season's End*, by Alex La Guma; and *The Devil on the Cross*, by Ngugi wa Thiongo. Bibliographies are supplied for each chapter and a general listing concludes the effort.

African Horizons: The Landscapes of African Fiction, by Christine Loflin (Greenwood, 1998), is an interesting and specialized commentary on the geographical landscapes of the continent as they are described and treated by African writers, which generally differ from those presented in work by non-Africans. Using the work of several African writers (some of whom are treated in the title above), Loflin examines the variety of ways in which description of the African landscape meshes with the thematic structure and meaning of the finished work in terms of ethnic identity and national pride. A good bibliography is provided.

1241. **American Short-Fiction Criticism and Scholarship, 1959–1977: A Checklist.** Joe Weixlmann. Chicago: Swallow, 1982. 625p. ISBN 0-8040-0381-5.

This work was initially developed as an update for the American portion of Jarvis A. Thurston's *Short-Fiction Criticism: A Checklist of Interpretation Since 1925 of Stories and Novelettes (American, British, Continental) 1800–1958* (Swallow, 1960; repr., 1963). It has exceeded the original work in comprehensiveness because it not only provides references to critical and scholarly works on short fiction but also includes citations to bibliographic publications, biographical studies, and interviews. There are around 10,000 entries to essays in 5,000 books and 325 serials. Individual authors are entered alphabetically by name, under which specific titles are listed. About 500 authors are treated.

The American Novel: A Checklist of Twentieth Century Criticism, by Donna Lorine Gerstenberger and George Hendrick (Swallow, 1961–1970), is the standard checklist in the field relating to novels or long fiction, with volume 1 identifying criticism published up to 1959. Volume 2 cites critical studies from 1960 to 1968. The arrangement is alphabetical by novelist. Citations to critical studies appear under individual novels. A second section gives general studies by century. Another important title is *The Contemporary Novel: A Checklist of Critical Literature on the English Language Novel Since 1945*, by Irving Adelman and

Rita Dworkin (2d ed., Scarecrow Press, 1996). This is a major revision of the 1972 effort, which was limited to British and American novels. The current work provides a comprehensive listing of critical commentary and evaluations of the fiction of some 600 modern authors of stature who have written in English, regardless of where they reside. Citations are furnished to critiques appearing in books and periodicals. Although there are the usual omissions and questioned inclusions, the work is an important contribution to literature study.

1242. **American Short Story Writers 1910–1945. Second Series.** Bobby Ellen Kimbel, ed. Detroit: Gale Research, 1991. 472p. (Dictionary of Literary Biography, v. 74). ISBN 0-8103-4582-X.

Designed primarily for undergraduate students, this work continues the coverage of the *Dictionary of Literary Biography* (entry 1087) series by Kimbel on American short story writers. It is a follow-up to the *First Series* effort published in 1989, in which coverage was given to twenty-five American short story writers active between 1910 and World War II. Pattern of coverage remains consistent as with other *DLB* offerings; the second series treats thirty-seven writers identified as having been contributors to the development of the short story in this country. Author profiles are written by individual contributors and supply name; dates of birth and death; cross-references to other *DLB* volumes; a bibliography of primary source material; and most important, a seven- to ten-page summary review and evaluation.

Earlier efforts by Kimbel cover the historical past, with *American Short Story Writers Before 1880* (1988) supplying a useful essay on the development of the American short story along with treatment of thirty-six notable writers. *American Short Story Writers, 1880–1910* (1989) is edited by Kimbel and William E. Grant and provides treatment of thirty-one authors. The contents of the *DLB* are indexed in *Gale's Literary Index CD-ROM* (entry 1090). Most recent is *American Short Story Writing Since World War II* (1993) edited by Patrick Meanor and *American Short Story Writers Since World War II. Second Series* (1999) edited by Meanor and Gwen Crane.

1243. **Contemporary African-American Novelists: A Bio-Bibliographical Critical Sourcebook.** Emmanuel S. Nelson, ed. Westport, CT: Greenwood, 1999. ISBN 0-313-30501-3.

Just off the press is this entry into the Greenwood line, providing focus on the lives and works of seventy-nine modern African-American novelists. Users at various levels of sophistication will acknowledge the value of this work in covering a wide range of personalities. Major writers such as Toni Morrison, Alice Walker, James Baldwin, Ralph Ellison, and Terri McMillan are treated along with important figures like Ntsoake Shang, Ann Allen Shockley, and Philip Lewis. The cross-section is revealing, including as it does forty-one female and twelve gay or lesbian writers. Like other products of Greenwood, each entry is by a contributing expert and supplies informative and clearly developed essays, beginning with a biographical sketch and followed by a critical analysis of the major works. Included also are a selection of thoughts and assessments from various critics and scholars, a bibliography of the author's works, and material written about him or her. Each entry is arranged alphabetically.

1244. **Contemporary Authors Bibliographical Series. Volume 1: American Novelists.** James J. Martine, ed. Detroit: Gale Research, 1986–1989. 3v. ISBN 0-8103-2225-0.

This series from Gale was designed to furnish a selective guide to the best critical studies done on major writers. Each volume covered ten personalities representing a particular genre. These were to complement the biographical sketches given in *Contemporary Authors* (entry 1083), primarily on English and American authors. Indexes to critics and writers were cumulative within each succeeding volume. Volume 1 treats such well-known personalities as James Baldwin, John Barth, Saul Bellow, John Cheever, Joseph Heller, Norman Mailer, Bernard Malamud, Carson McCullers, John Updike, and Eudora Welty. Entries furnish a listing of works by the author and a listing of works about the author that includes bibliographies, biographies, interviews, and critical studies. There is also a detailed bibliographical essay comparing and evaluating the critical studies. Volume 2 covers American poets (entry 1281). Unfortunately, the series expired after publication of volume 3, *American Dramatists*, in 1989. The contents of this title are indexed in **Gale's Literary Index CD-ROM* (entry 1090).

1245. **Contemporary Fiction Writers of the South: A Bio-Bibliographical Sourcebook.** Joseph M. Flora and Robert Bain, eds. Westport, CT: Greenwood, 1993. 571p. ISBN 0-313-28764-3.

This work retains the original format used by the editors in their two previous works, described below. The present effort focuses on forty-nine current authors (all but three of whom are still alive) who have received critical recognition and wide review transcending regional status. Pat Conroy, Alice Walker, and Alex Haley are included; Anne Tyler is the only repeat from the earlier volumes. All authors are known novelists; short stories are perceived as additional pursuits. Entries provide detailed biocritical essays ranging from nine to sixteen pages in length and following pattern coverage of life, themes, and critical assessment. A detailed index provides access. A second volume is planned to cover poets, playwrights, and essayists.

Covering the earlier period is the editors' *Fifty Southern Writers Before 1900* (Greenwood, 1987), treating fifty writers of varied renown (Mark Twain and William Alexander Carruthers) whose careers ended before 1900. *Fifty Southern Writers After 1900*, also published in 1987, treats the Southern renascence writers who published between 1917 and the 1950s. Such luminaries as Thomas Wolfe, Richard Wright, and Eudora Welty are included.

1246. **Contemporary Gay American Novelists: A Bio-Bibliographical Critical Sourcebook.** Emmanuel S. Nelson, ed. Westport, CT: Greenwood, 1993. 421p. ISBN 0-313-28019-3.

This work provides biocritical analysis and bibliographical coverage of fifty-seven male novelists, from the widely read James Baldwin, William S. Burroughs, and Christopher Isherwood to those of less prominence, such as John Fox and Peter Weltner. There is a conscious attempt to limit inclusion to serious writers (although several have been omitted by their own request). Entries supply biocritical coverage ranging from four to nineteen pages in length depending upon the influence of the subject; most have been prepared by gay scholars who are sensitive to the issues and in a few cases, overly exhortatory. Critical reception of the subject's work is treated and is most useful in furnishing insight into the literary existence or plight of a gay novelist. Bibliographies by and about the writers conclude the entries. The work fills a need in the growing interest in the study of the work of gay writers.

1247. **Contemporary Jewish-American Novelists: A Bio-Critical Sourcebook.** Joel Shatzky and Michael Taub, eds. Westport, CT: Greenwood, 1997. 506p. 0-313-29462-3.

Another in the Greenwood line of collective biographical/critical works is this treatment of more than seventy-five Jewish-American novelists whose major contributions were made subsequent to World War II. Their works either focused on Jewish themes or examined important concerns and considerations shared by those of the Jewish faith. The volume opens with a good introduction providing an overview of Jewish-American literary productivity during this time period. Like others in this line, the entries are written by expert scholars and writers and for each novelist provide a well-developed biographical sketch, a critical and interpretive essay on major works, a selection of commentary and reviews from critics and scholars, and a bibliography of the novelist's works as well as writings about him or her. There is a wide range of authors represented, from the renowned and heralded (Saul Bellow, Phillip Roth, Norman Mailer, Bernard Malamud, Leon Uris, etc.) to the socially conscious Paul Goodman, less familiar Walter Abish, and important newcomer Steve Stern. A good general bibliography provides additional reading references.

1248. Contemporary Novelists. 6th ed. Susan W. Brown, ed. New York: St. James Press, 1996. 1173p. ISBN 1-55862-189-X.

First published in 1972, this work is considered an important resource on the lives and contributions of the best-loved and most frequently studied current English-language novelists. Authors are carefully selected, with a good percentage of the several hundred entries in this edition being new to the series. A number of entries from the previous edition have been dropped because popularity and critical reception change with time. A panel of advisers makes recommendations for inclusion and deletion. The arrangement is alphabetical by author, and entries provide a brief biographical sketch, a bibliography of published works arranged chronologically by type (novels, plays, verse, and others), and a signed critical essay on the author's work, with references to additional reading. Information is given on other published bibliographies and locations of archival collections. Responses from the novelists are encouraged. There is a title index furnishing authors and dates of all novels and short stories. The work continues to maintain a high standard.

1249. Contemporary Southern Men Fiction Writers: An Annotated Bibliography. Rosemary M. Canfield Reisman and Suzanne Booker-Canfield. Lanham, MD: Scarecrow Press/Salem Press, 1998. 427p. ISBN 0-8108-3195-3.

This is a complementary effort to the earlier coverage given women by the publisher (see below) and generally follows the same pattern of delivery. As is true of the earlier model, it represents a useful regional treatment of a number of authors, most of whom have earned at least some degree of recognition for their work. There is a wide range, of course, in terms of popularity, style, setting, and critical acclaim achieved by the thirty-nine writers selected for inclusion, with such notables as John Grisham, Pat Conroy, James Dickey, Harry Crews, Larry McMurtry, and William Styron included along with those of lesser stature. Listings for each author include significant reviews and commentary addressing the style, theme, and characterization of both the body of work and individual titles. These reviews generally have been published in secondary works, but also include those from newspapers and periodicals. The brief annotations provide focus and evaluative summary.

Contemporary Southern Women Fiction Writers: An Annotated Bibliography, by Rosemary M. Canfield Reisman and Christopher J. Canfield (Scarecrow Press, 1994) is the earlier and more concise effort that serves as a model for the work above. It treats twenty-eight female writers, furnishing annotated references to published criticism and reviews. Over ninety critical works in the field of women's studies are identified and described. Another title focusing on women writers in the region and representing a multicultural context is *A Southern Weave of Women: Fiction of the Contemporary South*, by Linda Tate (University of Georgia Press, 1996). It examines such writers as Jill McCorkle, Alice Walker, Shay Youngblood, Ellen Douglas, and others representing both class and ethnic diversity characteristic of Southern literary productivity since World War II.

1250. **Critical Companions to Popular Contemporary Writers** series. Westport, CT: Greenwood, 1995– . ISBN 0-313-30249-9 (Anne Tyler).

This has been a prolific and frequent series of publications since its origin in late 1995 with coverage given to Mary Higgins Clark; since then, more than thirty writers have been treated in individual publications. These guides or "critical companions" are written by individual scholars and generally begin with chapters treating the author's life and literary background and influences, followed by separate chapters providing critical commentary and exposition of each of his or her major works and important series. A general bibliography and appropriate index conclude each effort. Titles of each volume begin with the author's name together with the standard series subtitle, such as Paul Bail's *Anne Tyler: A Critical Companion* (1998). Other authors covered in 1998 were Ernest J. Gaines, Leon Uris, Amy Tan, John Irving, Maya Angelou, and Toni Morrison; in 1997 treatment was given to Arthur C. Clarke, Erich Segal, Howard Fast, James Herriot, John Grisham, John Jakes, Robert Ludlum, Tom Robbins, and Gore Vidal. In the first full year, 1996, there had been a flurry of titles, with examination of Anne McCaffery, Michael Crichton, Robin Cook, Tom Clancy, V. C. Andrews, Anne Rice, Colleen McCullough, Dean Koontz, James A. Michener, James Clavell, John Saul, Ken Follett, Pat Conroy, Stephen King, and Tony Hillerman.

See also "Cambridge Companions to Literature" series (entry 1082), which provides volumes of commissioned essays, many of which are focused on an individual writer or group of writers and their writings in various genres. English-language novelists include Jane Austen (entry 1256n), Joseph Conrad (1996), William Faulkner (1995), Ernest Hemingway (1996), Henry James (1998), Herman Melville (1998), Mark Twain (1995), Edith Wharton (1995), and Oscar Wilde (entry 1198n).

1251. **Critical Survey of Long Fiction: English Language Series. Revised Edition.** Rev. ed. Frank N. Magill, ed. Pasadena, CA: Salem Press, 1991. 8v. ISBN 0-89356-825-2.

Another of the Magill offerings from Salem Press, this work furnishes nearly 350 critical essays on important writers. The volumes contain long biographical sketches of a wide range of writers, from Samuel Richardson to John Irving. The *Revised Edition* contains an additional 25 writers over the earlier 1983 issue. Such luminaries as Ray Bradbury, Joseph Wambaugh, and Salman Rushdie are now included. Over 150 articles have been revised and many have been completely updated. Critical assessments of each writer's contributions and an exposition of themes are rendered. Bibliographies are updated and annotated. Volume 8 completes the text (Wel–Z) and furnishes the index and fifteen background essays on various aspects of the novel.

1252. **English Fiction, 1900–1950: A Guide to Information Sources.** Thomas Jackson Rice. Detroit: Gale Research, 1979–1983. 2v. (American Literature, English Literature, and World Literatures in English, v. 21). ISBN 0-810312-17-4 (v.1); 0-810315-05-X (v.2).

Some forty influential British writers are treated in-depth in this two-volume work. Volume 1, published in 1979, provides a general bibliography and covers individual authors alphabetically from Aldington to Huxley. Volume 2 treats individual authors from Joyce to Woolf. Each entry furnishes an annotated list of all fictional works by the author and includes a representative selection of other writings. There is also a bibliography of secondary sources identifying journals, biographies, critical studies in books and articles, bibliographies, and studies of individual works. The cutoff date for volume 2 is 1980.

Part of the same series from Gale is S. K. Heninger's *English Prose, Prose Fiction and Criticism to 1660* (1975), which lists about 800 primary and secondary works by type, including fiction. Jerry C. Beasley's *English Fiction, 1660–1800: A Guide to Information Sources* (1978) continues the sequence of coverage.

1253. The English Novel, 1578–1956: A Checklist of Twentieth Century Criticisms. Inglis Freeman Bell and Donald Baird. Denver: Alan Swallow, 1959; repr., Hamden, CT: Shoe String Press, 1974. 169p. ISBN 0-208-02231-7 (Supp IV).

The English novel has been covered well in a series of publications providing citations to critical studies published in the twentieth century. This is the first of these checklists, giving a selective listing of critical studies that appeared in books and periodicals between 1900 and 1957 treating long fiction written over a period of 400 years. The arrangement of entries is alphabetical by name of author, followed by specific titles of his or her works.

This tool is supplemented by *English Novel Explication: Criticisms to 1972*, by Helen H. Palmer and Anne Jane Dyson (Shoe String Press, 1973), which lists criticism published between 1958 and 1972. This supplementary work is followed by its own *Supplement I*, by Peter L. Abernethy et al. (Shoe String Press, 1976), which covered the years 1972 to 1974. *Supplement II*, compiled by Christian J. W. Kloessel and Jeffrey R. Smitten (1981), extended coverage to 1979, and *Supplement III*, also by Kloessel (1986), covered the period from 1980 to 1985. *Supplement IV* (1990), treats the period from 1986 to mid-1989, and *Supplement V* (1998) brings the coverage to mid-1997. Another useful checklist, *The English Novel: Twentieth Century Criticism* (Swallow, 1976–1982), appeared in two volumes. Volume 1 identifies critical writings on the works of about forty-five novelists from Defoe to Hardy, while volume 2 covers eighty writers of the twentieth century.

1254. English Renaissance Prose Fiction, 1500–1660: An Annotated Bibliography of Criticism. James L. Harner. Boston: G. K. Hall, 1978. 556p. ISBN 0-8161-7996-4. **Supp. 1976–1983**, 1985. 228p. ISBN 0-8161-8709-6. **Supp. 1984–1990**, 1992. 185p. ISBN 0-8161-9088-7.

The initial volume was issued in the late 1970s and provided a bibliography of 3,000 critical items relevant to the study of fiction produced during the Renaissance period in England over a period of 160 years. The criticism, published between 1800 and 1976, is well-chosen and this tool and its supplements have gained a solid reputation among students and scholars. The basic volume identifies editions and studies (both original works and translations) written in England between 1500 and 1660. Included here are the various forms eventually leading to the development of the English novel, such as novelles, romances, histories, anatomies, and jest books. Listings are supplied of bibliographers, anthologies of Renaissance texts, and general studies. The major segment lists authors, translations, and titles. Entries supply informative annotations for the majority of critical books, parts of books, journal articles, and dissertations. The supplements continue to provide similar treatment of hundreds of additional critical works issued during the period of coverage. Indexes are supplied.

The subsequent literary period is treated in *The Eighteenth-Century British Novel and Its Background: An Annotated Bibliography and Guide to Topics*, by H. George Hahn and Carl Behm III (Scarecrow Press, 1985). This complements the previous source and supplies listings of nearly 3,200 books, chapters, and articles in English furnishing criticism, exposition, or bibliographical coverage of five major and thirty-nine minor novelists, as well as Johnson and Swift. Focused on the same period but with different content is *The Cambridge Companion to the Eighteenth Century Novel*, edited by John Richetti (Cambridge University Press, 1996). Furnished in this series (entry 1082) are selected essays providing exposition of the topic. In this work, there are twelve essays by different scholars who examine the origins and development of the novel in a modern and provocative manner. Coverage is given to the Gothic novel and women's fiction along with critical interpretation of the work of Defoe, Swift, Richardson, Fielding, Sterne, and Smollett.

*1255. **Exploring Novels.** Detroit: Gale Research, 1998. (The Gale DISCovering Program). ISBN 0-7876-1698-2. (CD-ROM).

One of the recent entries in the publisher's program for teaching and learning (entries 1189 and 1285) is this useful kit bearing a CD-ROM along with a manual and teaching guide. It examines sixty novels by British and American authors of the nineteenth and twentieth centuries in complete fashion. Entries furnish author biographies, introductory essays, plot descriptions, interpretation of historical context, character descriptions, critical articles, graphics, timelines, audio and video clips, and so forth. The eleventh edition of *Merriam-Webster's Collegiate Dictionary* (entry 1018) is included along with *Encyclopedia of Literary Terms.*

Beacham's Popular Fiction in America, edited by Walton Beacham and Suzanne Niemeyer (Beacham Publishing, 1986), is a four-volume set similar in design and purpose to the Magill efforts. The criteria for inclusion of an author as "popular" are that he or she be of the "best-selling" variety and that his or her works reflect social concerns. About 200 living or recently deceased novelists, primarily American, although there are some British, are included. The entries, written mostly by college professors, follow a set pattern covering publishing history as well as critical reception of each writer. Individual titles are analyzed in terms of social concerns, themes, techniques, literary precedents, and so forth.

1256. **A Jane Austen Encyclopedia.** Paul Poplawski. Westport, CT: Greenwood, 1998. 411p. ISBN 0-313-30017-8.

Another example of extensive treatment given to the life and work of a single author is this recent encyclopedia in which the biographical coverage is enhanced by three chronologies highlighting Austen's life and literary contributions; concurrent societal and historical development; and the literary tradition from which she emerged, furnishing identification of her reading and formative influences. All of Austen's writings are included, with entries arranged alphabetically and providing excellent exposition of her works in terms of characters, plots, themes, and reception given by critics. The essays vary in length and successfully blend biographical description with literary and critical context. Of importance is the general bibliography listing all of Austen's works, with publication history, books of criticism and commentary, and selected essays.

The Cambridge Companion to Jane Austen, edited by Edward Copeland and Juliet McMaster (Cambridge University Press, 1997), furnishes a comprehensive examination of Austen's works in both the perspective on her contemporary time period and in terms of current thinking. Exposition is given to her novels and letters along with essays on various social issues and factors such as religion, politics, and class consciousness. A useful chronology is furnished to enhance biographical description and critical assessment.

1257. **Jewish-American Fiction Writers: An Annotated Bibliography.** Gloria L. Cronin et al. New York: Garland, 1991. 1233p. (Garland Reference Library of the Humanities, v. 972). ISBN 0-8240-1619-X.

This annotated bibliography fills a void in the coverage of nineteenth- and twentieth-century Jewish-American writers of lesser literary status who have attained popularity among the reading public. The acknowledged greats such as Bellow, Mailer, Malamud, and Roth are purposely excluded, but coverage is given to such familiar personalities as Asch, Calisher, Ferber, Fiedler, Hecht, Jong, Ozick, Potok, Sontag, Uris, Wouk, and others. In all, sixty-two writers are given detailed bibliographic treatment. Entries are arranged alphabetically and supply listings of primary sources representing their own works (novels, short stories in anthologies and periodicals, and collected works) and of secondary sources written about them (books, book chapters, articles, biographies, bibliographies, and dissertations). The latter segment is annotated in a brief but informative manner. For the most part, these writers, although prominent, are not well-covered in the biocritical reference literature.

1258. **The Modern American Novel: An Annotated Bibliography.**
Steven G. Kellman. Pasadena, CA: Salem Press, 1991. 162p. ISBN
0-89356-664-0.

This bibliography of criticism and commentary is designed for the use of high
school and undergraduate students and provides treatment of sixteen important American
novelists of the early twentieth century who produced their major works between 1900 and
1940. Included among these luminaries are Cather, Dreiser, Fitzgerald, Hemingway,
Hurston, Lewis, Steinbeck, Wilder, and eight others of equal rank. They are recognized for
their contribution to the development or creation of a distinctive American expression among
the literatures of the world, and represent a sample of regional, ethnic, and expatriate writers.
The tool begins with an introductory section treating general works on the American novel.
This is followed by an alphabetical arrangement of authors. Each author entry supplies a bibliography of general studies followed by a listing of sources about individual works. Annotations are brief but informative. An index to authors of critical works is provided.

The Cambridge Companion to American Realism and Naturalism (Cambridge University Press, 1995) is part of a series (entry 1082) furnishing selected essays by various
scholars examining the background and development of the topic. This work examines ten
major works of fiction written in the late nineteenth century, from *The Rise of Silas Lapham*,
by William Dean Howells, to *Call of the Wild*, by Jack London.

1259. **St. James Guide to Crime and Mystery Writers.** 4th ed. Jay
P. Pederson, ed. Detroit: St. James Press, 1996. 1264p. (St. James Guide to
Writers series). ISBN 1-55862-178-4.

During the past few years St. James Press has been active in producing updated versions
and new editions of useful biocritical tools. Several of these resources treat the realm of modern
genre fiction. The fourth edition, with a changed title (formerly, *Twentieth Century Crime and
Mystery Writers*), examines the authorship of crime and mystery fiction, providing coverage
of 650 of the most important English-language writers, with emphasis on the modern era. Entries
supply brief biographical treatment of each author, followed by a complete listing of his or
her works, a listing of critical studies, and location of manuscripts. There are commentary
from the author about his or her work and a critical essay signed by its contributor. This informative work is accessed through a good title index.

The fourth edition of *St. James Guide to Science Fiction Writers* (1996), also edited
by Jay Pederson (formerly *Twentieth-Century Science Fiction Writers*), provides coverage of
more than 600 influential writers of this genre. More than 50 new entries have been added and
such people as Isaac Asimov and Roger Zelazny are treated. This was followed by the first
edition of *St. James Guide to Fantasy Writers*, edited by David Pringle (1996). More than 400
authors of fantasy, sorcery, fables, and fairy tales are treated, from the Brothers Grimm to the
modern scene. Tolkien, C. S. Lewis, Hans Christian Andersen, and Lewis Carroll are among
those covered. The most recent entry in the series (inevitable in treatment of genre writing) is
St. James Guide to Horror, Ghost and Gothic Writers (1998), edited again by David Pringle.
This work identifies and describes the life and work of more than 425 authors, most of whom
have written in English. Format and scope are similar to the other works described above and
examine writings with supernatural plots from ghost stories to the occult. *Twentieth-Century
Romance and Historical Writers*, edited by Aruna Vasudevan (3d ed., St. James, 1994),
examines more than 500 English-language writers of romance and historical fiction (the two
genres deemed epistemologically inseparable by the editors). Entries furnish biography, list
of works; signed critical essay; and identification of collections, critiques, and film adaptations for each writer. *Twentieth-Century Western Writers* (2d ed., St. James, 1991), edited by
Geoff Sadler, examines nearly 500 writers whose works are set in or relate to the American
frontier.

1260. **Short Story Criticism: Excerpts from Criticism of the Works of Short Fiction Writers.** Laurie Lanzen Harris and Sheila Fitzgerald, eds. Detroit: Gale Research, 1988– . v.1– . ISSN 0895-9439.

This series was initiated in 1988 to survey critical response to major writers. The initial volume treats fourteen important authors of short fiction issued in English or in English translation. Included in the inaugural edition are de Maupassant, Poe, John Cheever, and James Thurber. Entries are arranged alphabetically and some have been culled from the Gale Literary Criticism series. They supply biographical and critical description along with a listing of the authors' major works. Critical sources are listed chronologically to provide a historical perspective. Subsequent volumes have appeared in irregular fashion, with volume 28 published in 1998. This volume devotes about fifty pages to each of ten authors, who include Anton Chekhov, James T. Farrell, and Frank Norris. Background on the author's careers and critical commentary has maintained high quality, and the format remains unchanged. Entries are prepared by scholar-critics, who are described in explanatory notes. The contents of this work are indexed in *Gale's Literary Index CD-ROM* (entry 1090).

1261. **Supernatural Fiction Writers: Fantasy and Horror.** E. F. Bleiler, ed. New York: Charles Scribner's Sons, 1985. 2v. ISBN 0-684-17808-7.

Nearly 150 authors have been selected as major entries in this biographical dictionary of important contributors to the genre. Among those high-ranking individuals are Poe, Bradbury, Tolkien, Roger Zelazny, and Henry James. Because selection is so limited at this level, one might expect many omissions, and the tool has been criticized for slighting women writers in particular. Entries furnish well-developed, informative biographical essays that analyze notable works, make comparisons with other authors, and evaluate the influence and status of the writers. Bibliographies are included as well. The arrangement of entries is classified by time period and geographical region, but a detailed index provides ready access.

There is some overlap with Bleiler's *Science Fiction Writers: Critical Studies of the Major Authors from the Early Nineteenth Century to the Present Day* (Charles Scribner's Sons, 1982). This work covers seventy-five writers classified by period and is accessed by an index of names and titles. Essays are substantial and furnish scholarly exposition and thematic analysis of major writers such as Huxley, Poe, Bradbury, and Mary Shelley. The average length is about eight pages.

1262. **Twentieth-Century Short Story Explication: Interpretations 1900–1975 of Short Fiction Since 1800.** 3d ed. Warren S. Walker. Hamden, CT: Shoe String Press, 1977. 880p. ISBN 0-208-01570-1. **Supp. I–V,** 1980–1991. ISBN 0-208-01813-1 (Supp.1).

Originally published in 1961, the Walker effort is recognized as a standard in the field. The third edition cites interpretations since the turn of the century in books, monographs, and periodicals of short fiction published since 1800. For this series, a short story is a work not exceeding 150 average-sized pages. (Explications describe or explain the meaning of the story and include observations on theme, symbols, or structure.) The arrangement is by author, then story title. About 850 authors are covered by interpretations published through 1975. The supplements, numbered I–V, issued in 1980, 1984, 1987, 1989, and 1991, have added hundreds of authors.

Twentieth-Century Short Story Explication: An Index to the Third Edition and its Five Supplements 1961–1991, by Walker and Barbara K. Walker (Shoe String Press, 1991), furnishes an index to all citations to explications identified in the entire series. Nearly 16,750 stories by 2,300 authors are treated. Authors are listed alphabetically; their stories are listed alphabetically with references to the appropriate volume and page number in the series where

Literature 497

explications are cited. *Twentieth Century Short Story Explication: New Series, with Checklists of Books and Journals Used* is Walker's most recent offering (1993). It furnishes more than 5,700 entries providing interpretations for short stories by 815 authors published between 1989 and 1990.

1263. **Women's Fiction Between the Wars: Mothers, Daughters and Writing.** Heather Ingman. Edinburgh: Edinburgh University Press, 1998. 180p. ISBN 0-312-21514-2.

This is a concise but informative historical analysis to add to the body of feminist criticism, unique in its focus on the phenomenon of mother-daughter relationships in both the lives and works of certain British writers. It opens with an introductory essay exploring the historical context regarding the effect of a male-dominated society on the lives of women; this is followed by an examination of psychoanalytic theories of motherhood as portrayed in the works of several writers such as Lettice Cooper and May Sinclair. Various mother-daughter relationships are then examined, with individual chapters given to Rose Macaulay (flight from mother), Elizabeth Bowen (the mother betrayed), Ivy Compton-Burnett (tyrants and victims), Jean Rhys (the empty mirror), Virginia Woolf (retrieving the mother), and Dorothy Richardson (the artist's quest). The works are not judged for their value but emphasis is placed on the influences of the writers' family lives on their literary expression. There is a concluding essay along with a useful bibliography for additional reading.

POETRY

Bibliographic Guides

1264. **English Poetry, 1660–1800: A Guide to Information Sources.** Donald C. Mell. Detroit: Gale Research, 1982. 501p. ISBN 0-810312-30-1.

Recently the Gale Company has developed a series of guides in the area of English poetry; individual titles cover different chronological periods. This work covers poetry of the period 1660–1800 and furnishes annotated entries of critical research of the twentieth century through 1979. It is divided into two parts, the first of which furnishes a bibliography of general reference sources such as histories and guidebooks as well as collections of poetry and criticism. Also included are bibliographies, checklists, and background studies in related areas. The second part treats thirty-one poets, with listings of standard editions, collected works, bibliographies, and critical studies.

English Romantic Poetry, 1800–1835: A Guide to Information Sources, by Donald H. Reiman (Gale Research, 1979), identifies important studies relating to the work of five major poets (Wordsworth, Byron, Keats, Shelley, and Coleridge) and twelve secondary poets. Emily Ann Anderson's *English Poetry, 1900–1950: A Guide to Information Sources* (Gale Research, 1982) covers the modern period, with detailed coverage of sources of information on the work of twenty-one influential poets.

1265. **Middle Scots Poets: A Reference Guide to James I of Scotland, Robert Henryson, William Dunbar, and Gavin Douglas.** Walter Scheps and J. Anna Looney. Boston: G. K. Hall, 1986. 292p. (A Reference Guide to Literature). ISBN 0-8161-8356-2.

King James I, along with Henryson, Dunbar, and Douglas, constitute what has been termed a group of "Scottish Chaucerians" who until the twentieth century had been dismissed as minor figures. More recently, however, their stature has grown and their "Scottishness" has been treated more seriously rather than as a curiosity. This work identifies a variety of materials on each individual who is given separate treatment in the guide. All items are annotated.

There is a fifth section that lists general works treating the four poets collectively or providing background material. Each of the five sections has a separate index. The criticism covers a span of 457 years from 1521 through 1978, making this a useful tool for the serious inquirer.

Bibliographies and Indexes

1266. **The Bibliography of Contemporary American Poetry, 1945–1985: An Annotated Checklist.** William McPheron. Westport, CT: Meckler, 1986. 72p. ISBN 0-88736-054-8.

This slender little volume provides a wealth of information on published collections of poetry that include the work of American poets of our time. Coverage actually goes back to the early 1940s. The first section of this annotated bibliography lists multi-author sources arranged alphabetically by compiler, editor, or title. Only those anthologies that furnish a significant coverage of individual poets and of small presses that have published much of their work are included. The second section furnishes a list of 122 single-author studies of leading contemporary poets, arranged alphabetically by name of poet. There is a useful introduction describing key anthologies and problems in bibliographic control.

Contemporary American Poetry: A Checklist, by Lloyd Davis and Robert Irwin (Scarecrow Press, 1975), identifies 3,300 single-author collections of poetry published between 1950 and 1973. This work is continued by Davis's *Contemporary American Poetry: A Checklist, Second Series, 1973–1983* (1985), which lists 5,000 collections published during that ten-year period. Arrangement is by name of poet, and again coverage is limited to single-author works. An interesting Web site, *The Academy of American Poets*, is maintained by that organization (http://www.poets.org/ [accessed January 2000]) and provides calendar, news, awards, excerpts from recorded poetry, and details of programs.

1267. **The Columbia Granger's Index to Poetry.** 11th ed. Nicholas Frankovich and Edith Granger, eds. New York: Columbia University Press, 1997. 2299p. ISBN 0-231-10130-9.

Since 1904, *Granger's* has been the preeminent work in the field, indexing poems in anthologies by title, first line, author, and subject. The pattern of coverage and scope changed with the seventh edition (1982), no longer providing a cumulative coverage of preceding issues. Instead, the seventh edition indexed nearly 250 anthologies published between 1970 and 1981, thereupon supplementing the coverage of the sixth edition published in 1973. The eighth edition returned to the cumulative format, indexing anthologies published throughout the twentieth century and indexing over 400 titles. Of these, eighty-two were either new or indexed for the first time in this work. The ninth edition, the first to bear the imprint of Columbia University, added more than 150 new anthologies. Of these, fifty have been translated from other languages. The tenth edition was indicative of increased frequency under Columbia and followed the ninth by only three years. It supplied coverage of anthologies published through June 3, 1993. The eleventh edition followed in 1997 and treats some 75,000 poems found in anthologies published through January 31, 1997. The expected detailed indexing provides access by author, subject, title, first line, and last line.

1268. **Index to Poetry in Popular Periodicals.** Jefferson D. Caskey, comp. Westport, CT: Greenwood, 1984–1988. 2v. ISBN 0-313-22227-4 (v.1); 0-313-24810-9 (v.2).

The initial volume of this tool was issued in 1984 and treated poetry published in American general periodicals indexed in the *Reader's Guide to Periodical Literature* between 1955 and 1959. It was recognized as a well-constructed and useful index providing access to poems published in forty-five mass circulation magazines by author, title, first line, and subject.

Volume 2 provides an additional five years of coverage from 1960 to 1964. The work does not duplicate the *Reader's Guide* because *RGPL* did not index poetry during this period; therefore, most of the poems would be inaccessible otherwise. As one might expect, there are a wide range and diverse group of poets represented, from such stalwarts as e. e. cummings, Robert Frost, Ogden Nash, and Sylvia Plath to the less familiar James Merchant and Helen Singer. The strength of the tool lies in its inclusion of light verse not found in more scholarly indexes.

Index of American Periodical Verse, issued by Scarecrow Press, is an annual index to poems published in participating periodicals from the United States, Canada, and Puerto Rico. It began in 1973 with indexing of the year 1971. Coverage has increased each year, and the twentieth annual volume, issued in 1992 and treating the year 1990, analyzes 289 participating periodicals. There are more than 7,000 entries for individual poets and over 20,000 poems are indexed by title and first line.

1269. **Poetry by Women to 1900: A Bibliography of American and British Writers.** Gwenn Davis and Beverly A. Joyce, comps. Toronto: University of Toronto Press, 1991. 340p. ISBN 0-8020-5966-X.

This is the second volume of a series designed to provide bibliographic identification of the wealth of poetry by American and British women over a period of 425 years from 1475 to 1900. Poetry published only in the periodical literature is excluded because this work targets poems appearing in printed books. More than 6,000 books are treated; the poets are arranged alphabetically with a supplementary appendix providing a chronological listing. There is a valuable introduction by the compilers providing exposition and analysis of the literary situation, refuting certain misconceptions about the historical paucity of female poets, and offering a rationale for the relative oblivion of the great majority. The subject index is especially useful for its topical treatment of poetic themes; it provides the framework for potential comparative study.

Poetry by American Women, 1900–1975: A Bibliography, by Joan Reardon (Scarecrow Press, 1979), provides coverage of nearly 9,500 single-authored volumes of poetry written by 5,500 women over a span of seventy-five years. The work is comprehensive, the idea being to provide as complete a listing of those elusive publications as possible. Arrangement of entries is chronological, with access aided by a title index. Entries supply complete bibliographical identification. *Poetry by American Women, 1975–1989: A Bibliography*, also by Reardon (Scarecrow Press, 1990), continues the coverage through identification of nearly 2,900 volumes by 1,565 women published over a fifteen-year period. Format and treatment are the same as in the base volume.

1270. **Poetry Index Annual: An Author, Title, First Line and Keyword Subject Index to Poetry in Anthologies.** Great Neck, NY: Roth Publishing, 1982– . Ann. ISSN 0736-3966.

Rounding out the coverage given to poetry initially by the Granger Book Company (now Roth) is this annual index to English-language poetry appearing in anthologies. The purpose of this work is to index all anthologies published in a single year (including new editions of older works). This supplements the less frequent publication of *Granger's*, now published by Columbia University (entry 1267), and complements the coverage of single-author collections and periodical literature in *Roth's American Poetry Annual* (entry 1271). Indexing is by author, title, and subject, with all entries in a single alphabetical arrangement. From thirty to fifty anthologies are indexed per issue, providing access to several thousand poems. This is a useful resource for librarians and their patrons.

Poem Finder is Roth's computerized index, available on CD-ROM since 1992 and more recently on the Internet as a subscription service (http://www.poemfinder.com [accessed January 2000]). It supplies author, title, and subject access identification of more than 600,000 poems along with full text of over 50,000 poems.

1271. Roth's American Poetry Annual: A Reference and Guide to Poetry Published in the United States. Great Neck, NY: Roth Publishing, 1987– . Ann. ISSN 1040-5461.

When Roth Publishing took over the products of the Granger Book Company in 1989, one of their first acts was to combine *The Annual Survey of American Poetry*, begun in 1982; *American Poetry Index*, begun in 1983; and *Annual Index to Poetry in Periodicals*, which started up in 1982. The result was this important serial that furnishes a "unified index" identifying poems in books of poetry by a single poet and in periodicals issued during each year. Coverage of several thousand poems published in several hundred collections and standard magazines easily available to libraries make this a useful location tool for reference service. Arrangement of entries is alphabetical by poet and title in one alphabetical sequence. The work opens with the annual survey segment, furnishing a state-of-the-art essay; anthology of selected poetry; and several directories of grants, awards, schools, organizations, and publishers. It serves to complement the coverage of *Poetry Index Annual* (entry 1270), which indexes poetry in published anthologies. There is a list of periodicals indexed that shows a wide range of works, both well-known and relatively obscure.

The Granger Company had begun retrospective indexing in this area. *Index to Poetry in Periodicals: American Poetic Renaissance, 1915–1919* . . . (1981), *Index to Poetry in Periodicals, 1920–1924* . . . (1983), and *Index to Poetry in Periodicals, 1925–1929* . . . (1984) cite poems appearing in magazines and newspapers offering a wide range in terms of quality and popularity. Included are the products of top-notch poets as well as unknown versifiers who have written for both children and adults. Over 300 periodicals are indexed in each volume by name of poet, furnishing about 9,000 poems by over 2,000 poets per issue.

Anthologies and Collections

1272. The Columbia Granger's Guide to Poetry Anthologies. 2d ed. William Katz and Linda Sternberg Katz. New York: Columbia University Press, 1994. 231p. ISBN 0-231-07244-9.

Developed as a companion to the *Columbia Granger's Index to Poetry* (entry 1267), this work is useful to students and librarians. The work identifies, describes, and evaluates all the anthologies used by the *Index* from its seventh through its tenth editions. It succeeds its earlier issue (1991) due to the recent publication of the Granger tenth edition. The Katz publications are well-known in the literature of library science and the authors now demonstrate an excellent knowledge of poetry, especially that of American or British origin. Entries are classified by subject and supply detailed exposition of the anthology's comprehensiveness; ease of use; authority; and auxiliary features such as introduction, indexes, and notes. Critical commentary is reasoned and well-constructed and is effective in revealing excellence, oversight, omission, bias, or doubtful veracity of poetic text. As is true of other Katz works, the text is lucid and lively. The work is indexed by author and title.

*1273. English Poetry Full-Text Database. Cambridge, UK: Chadwyck-Healey, 1996. (CD-ROM).

This CD-ROM tool represents a sourcebook of poetry by 1,350 poets listed in the *New Cambridge Bibliography of English Literature* (entry 1145). The work treats a broad survey of English poetry dating from the Anglo-Saxon period to the end of the nineteenth century. The work is divided into three chronological segments, all of which can be purchased separately. They represent the periods 600–1660, 1661–1800, and 1801–1900. CD-ROM is an especially useful format for retrieval of material in full-text, and this work has been coded in a variety of ways. Included in addition to the poetry are epigraphs, dedications, notes, and bibliographical details pertinent to the edition used in the database. Boolean operators "or, not, and" may be employed to locate imagery, language, dates, and names.

The Columbia Granger's World of Poetry (entry 1133) contains complete text of 8,500 classic poems, quotations from 3,000 additional poems, and anthology citations to some 60,000 poems. These have been culled from three major sources from the publisher.

1274. **Moving Borders: Three Decades of Innovative Writing by Women.** Mary M. Sloan, ed. Jersey City, NJ: Talisman House, 1998. 720p. ISBN 1-883689-48-1.

This is an interesting anthology of innovative poetry drawn from the efforts of fifty American and Canadian women of the twentieth century. Certain poems push the envelope in poetic license in their use of a mix of genres (including fiction) and sequencing of words. Arrangement of poets and their work is chronological by publication date, providing a historical overview of poetic development. The first poem in this anthology was a previously unpublished and recently discovered effort, "Progression," by Lorraine Niedecker, who died in 1970, and coverage continues through the work of Melanie Neilsen, a poet of the 1990s. Also included is good representation of the poetry of Mary Rae Armantrout, Mei-mei Berssenbrugge, Nicole Brossard, Norma Cole, Tina Darragh, Jean Day, Patricia Dienstfrey, Rachel Blau Du Plessis, Kathleen Fraser, Barbara Guest, Lyn Hejinian, Fanny Howe, Susan Howe, Ann Lauterbach, and Karen Mac Cormack.

1275. **The New Oxford Book of American Verse.** Richard Ellmann, ed. New York: Oxford University Press, 1976. 1076p.

This is the standard anthology in the field and has been recognized as such since its first appearance in 1927. Both the 1927 and 1950 editions were compiled by Bliss Carman and F. O. Matthiessen and earned the respect of teachers and librarians for their excellent representation of both classic and modern poets. This edition continues in that tradition, listing the poets chronologically, beginning with seventeenth-century poet Anne Bradstreet and ending with Imamu Amiri Baraka (Leroi Jones), born in 1934. Inclusion is highly selective, and about seventy-five poets are treated. The intention is to include poems of intrinsic merit while at the same time representing the principal directions of modern poetry. The poems, like the poets who created them, appear in chronological sequence. There is an index of authors, titles, and first lines.

1276. **The New Oxford Book of Australian Verse.** 3d ed. Les A. Murray. New York: Oxford University Press, 1996. 438p. ISBN 0-19-553994-X.

One of the recent anthologies in the Oxford line, which made its initial appearance in 1986, is this collection of poems chosen by Les A. Murray, an important contemporary poet. His anthology has been carefully developed and represents the various elements within Australian poetry over a span of time beginning with the colonial period and running to the present day. The second edition (1991) was a reprint with additional poems, resulting in twenty-one additional pages. The third edition provides additional source material and another eighteen pages of text. Criteria for inclusion continue to reflect Murray's judgment of the amount of "poetry" found in a poem as well as its liveliness and readability. Standard poems are not always included and have given way to "untypical" works of high quality and expressive nature. Included are titles of aboriginal origin, which have not been included in standard anthologies. This remains a useful source for its unorthodox means of selection, which results in the inclusion of much obscure poetry.

1277. **The New Oxford Book of English Verse, 1250–1950.** Helen Louise Gardner. New York: Oxford University Press, 1972; repr. with corr., 1986. 974p. ISBN 0-19-812136-9.

The Oxford Book of English Verse is the oldest anthology in the Oxford line, first appearing in 1900 under the guidance of Sir Arthur Quiller-Couch. He was also responsible for the second edition in 1939. The first edition covered poetry up to 1900, the second edition to 1918. The present work is not a revision but a new anthology, and furnishes comprehensive coverage up to 1950. It contains nearly 900 poems. Whereas earlier editions had emphasized lyric verse, the new work represents the total range of English nondramatic poetry. American poets Ezra Pound and T. S. Eliot are also included. There are brief notes and references located at the back of the book, and access is furnished by indexes of authors and first lines. There are a number of Oxford anthologies of a specialized nature devoted to a particular period or century of English poetry that complement this general tool.

1278. **The New Oxford Book of Irish Verse.** Thomas Kinsella, ed. New York: Oxford University Press, 1986; repr., 1989. 464p. ISBN 0-19-812115-6 (pbk.).

This recent Oxford anthology of Irish poetry takes on a new challenge, covering the period from the beginnings to the fourteenth century. It thus represents a complementary work to the earlier edition, which covered the seventeenth to the twentieth centuries. Kinsella is a master poet in his own right and has not only selected the works, but has translated them faithfully, always keeping in mind the musical quality of the ancient verse. The anthology furnishes a well-balanced collection of Irish art, with representation of various elements of high quality as well as popular culture. The works of Swift, Goldsmith, Sheridan, Yeats, and Synge blend with the numerous folk poems, songs, prayers, and other contributions from lesser known but equally expressive poets.

Biographical and Critical Sources

1279. **American and British Poetry: A Guide to the Criticism, 1925–1978.** Harriet Semmes Alexander. Athens, OH: Swallow, 1984. 486p. ISBN 0-8040-0848-5.

Another of the Swallow checklists of literary criticism, this one provides references to critical studies appearing in books and periodicals between 1925 and 1978. A wide range of poets and poetry is treated, beginning with Spenser and ending with Dickey. References are to critical studies of the entire poem rather than certain parts of the poem, unless the poem is not covered more completely by any studies or the criticism is noteworthy in some way. The arrangement is alphabetical by poet, then by title of poem. This work is similar to *Poetry Explication* (entry 1287n) but includes poems up to 1,000 lines in length, whereas Kuntz limits his coverage to poems not exceeding 500 lines. Although there is overlap between the two, this work indexes titles not included in Kuntz and also treats a greater number of obscure poets.

1280. **American Poets 1880–1945. Third Series.** Peter Quartermain, ed. Detroit: Gale Research, 1987. 2v. (Dictionary of Literary Biography, v. 54). ISBN 0-8103-1732-X.

This is the third segment of a series that itself is part of the extensive *Dictionary of Literary Biography* (entry 1087). The first series appeared in 1986; the second series followed later that same year; and this, the third series, was first issued in two volumes in 1987. All volumes are in the same format, in keeping with the pattern of the parent series. In each volume, about forty-five American poets are listed alphabetically by name followed by dates of birth and death, then by name of the author of the entry. There is a bibliography of the poet's publications followed by a detailed biocritical essay of the poet's life and work. Concluding the entry is a bibliography of writings on the poet and library locations where manuscripts and letters may be found. One of the attractive features is the inclusion of photographs, copies of title pages, and manuscripts.

Continuing the coverage is *American Poets Since World War II. Fifth Series*, edited by Joseph Conte (1996). Treatment is given to additional contemporary poets (both acclaimed and lesser-known) who have contributed to the literary canon of North America in this series, which began in 1975. As parts of the *DLB* series, the contents of these titles are indexed in **Gale's Literary Index CD-ROM* (entry 1090).

1281. **Contemporary Authors Bibliographical Series. Volume 2: American Poets.** Ronald Baughman, ed. Detroit: Gale Research, 1986. 387p. ISSN 0887-3070.

This was designed as a companion series to the monumental Gale effort *Contemporary Authors* (entry 1083). The first volume covered American novelists (entry 1083) and set the pattern for the series, covering about ten major writers in a particular genre and nationality. In this work, eleven important poets of the post-World War II era are treated, including James Dickey, Randall Jarrell, Robert Lowell, and Anne Sexton. They are covered in separate chapters, each of which is written by a specialist, in a pattern providing bibliographic coverage of major works, followed by a listing of works about the authors and their work. Finally, there is a bibliographic essay analyzing the contribution of the critical studies. There are two indexes that are cumulative to volumes 1 and 2, an index of authors and an index of critics. The series ceased with volume 3, *American Dramatists*, in 1989. The contents of this series are indexed in **Gale's Literary Index CD-ROM* (entry 1090).

1282. **Contemporary Poets.** 6th ed. Thomas Riggs, ed. New York: St. James Press, 1996. 1336p. (Contemporary Writers Series). ISBN 1-55862-191-1.

Information on 779 living poets is furnished in this new edition of a standard reference tool. Individuals are carefully selected for inclusion by a panel of internationally known specialists. There are 120 newly added poets in this fully revised edition, retaining the pattern of coverage that has become familiar to users. There is a brief biographical chronology, followed by a full bibliography of the poet's writings arranged chronologically by type, including poetry, criticism, and biography; a personal statement on his or her work from the poet when available; and finally, a fine signed critical essay on the poet's work. There are listings of other published bibliographies and archival locations. A title index provides access to poems described in the main body of the work; there is also an index by nationality.

Less comprehensive and more narrowly focused is *The Cambridge Companion to English Poetry, Donne to Marvell*, edited by Thomas N. Corns (Cambridge University Press, 1993). Like others in the series (entry 1082), this work furnishes a limited number of thorough and informative essays on the topic. In this case, there are fourteen in-depth articles by various scholars on the work of major early modern poets of the sixteenth and seventeenth centuries. Donne, Jonson, Herrick, Herbert, Carew, Suckling, Lovelace, Milton, Crashaw, Vaughan, and Marvell are studied, as is the political-social-religious context in which they wrote.

1283. **Contemporary Women Poets.** Pamela L. Shelton, ed. Detroit: St. James Press, 1998. 400p. (Contemporary Writers Series). ISBN 1-55862-356-6.

About 100 of the 250 entries in this work are new poets who have begun to receive critical acclaim and are included for the first time in the St. James series. Others have been treated in *Contemporary Poets* (entry 1282) or other publications from the publisher. Included here are Gwendolyn Brooks, Nikki Giovanni, and Ntzoake Shange. This work opens with two general essays providing exposition of mostly (but not entirely) American and English women poets, their influence, and their use of various themes. Like other works in the series, individual entries furnish biographical treatment and critical commentary of those selected for inclusion; each entry begins with a biographical sketch examining the poet's background, career, education, honors, and impact. Following this is a bibliography of published anthologies and critical studies of the poet. Most important is the signed critical essay by a scholar, poet, or critic in the field, furnishing a readable analysis of the poet's contribution. In some cases, there are descriptive statements from the poets themselves. Indexing is by title and by nationality, providing good access.

1284. **Critical Survey of Poetry: English Language Series.** Rev. ed. Frank N. Magill, ed. Pasadena, CA: Salem Press, 1992. 8v. ISBN 0-89356-834-1.

Initially published in 1982 as an eight volume set, and supplemented in 1987 with a volume designed to give more detailed coverage to contemporary poets, the new edition serves as an excellent update and revision serving the needs of high school and undergraduate students. A total of 390 entries are provided with biocritical essays on 368 outstanding poets along with 22 comprehensive essays on periods and critical approaches to the genre. A number of minor poets have been dropped in favor of 27 completely new entries (Rita Dove, Carolyn Forche, Raymond Carver, etc.). There are 44 entries completely rewritten; all entries have updated bibliographies. Entries average five to ten pages in length, with treatment of poets providing sections on principal works, achievements, biography, and analysis. Entries are prepared by specialists and supply mainstream perspective. A detailed subject index provides access.

*1285. **Exploring Poetry.** Detroit: Gale Research, 1997. (The Gale DISCovering Program). 0-7876-0920-X. (CD-ROM kit).

Another of the teaching/learning sets from the publisher (entries 1189 and 1255), this work furnishes the full text of 275 of the most frequently studied poems by about 125 familiar poets, accompanied by detailed line-by-line explication of the content. In addition, each poem is given historical treatment and described in terms of its poetic structure and composition, and a time line is included. Also, there is general exposition of the critical background of the poem, along with a well-written biographical sketch of the poet. The entry is enhanced by a digital photograph. Along with the CD-ROM, there is a manual and teacher's guide that suggests questions for study and further resolution. Clips of audio and video readings as well as interviews add to the value and help to establish this effort as "a gold mine for high school and college students," in the words of one reviewer.

1286. **The Great American Poetry Bake-Off, Fourth Series.** Robert Peters. Metuchen, NJ: Scarecrow Press, 1991. 296p. ISBN 0-8108-2410-8.

The author is a witty and insightful poet and critic who initiated this series of critical handbooks in 1979. The second series was issued in 1982 and the third in 1987. With these previous efforts the series established an enviable reputation for its no-nonsense approach in examining strengths and weaknesses and providing fresh perspectives with regard to poetry and the work of poets such as Ginsburg, Cohen, and Creely. The fourth series continues in that tradition and Peters continues his controversial, iconoclastic commentary on the genre. Treatment is given to various poetry anthologies in a thorough and frank manner, and a number of poets writing outside the genre mainstream, such as Sharon Doubiago and James Broughton, are assessed. An important contribution to the critical literature for its penetrating and sometimes definitive exposition, its access is aided by a general index.

1287. Guide to American Poetry Explication. Boston: G. K. Hall, 1989. 2v. (Reference Publication in Literature). ISBN 0-8161-8919-6 (v.1); 0-8161-8918-8 (v.2).

This is the first of a two-part, multi-volume expansion of *Poetry Explication: A Checklist of Interpretation Since 1925 of British and American Poems Past and Present*, a standard in the field by Joseph M. Kuntz and Nancy C. Martinez, citing North American poetry explication from 1925 to 1987. This work was limited to those poems of 500 lines or less. Volume 1 of the current expansion is compiled by James Ruppert and treats "Colonial and Nineteenth Century" poems. Volume 2 is compiled by John K. Lee and covers "Modern and Contemporary" poems. The expansion is more comprehensive than was Kuntz in its inclusion of explications drawn from critical works on individual authors and of poems of more than 500 lines. All appropriate entries from the 1980 edition are incorporated in both volumes. There is a purposeful inclusion of diverse elements (gay and lesbian, African-American, and Native American poems) in volume 2.

Guide to British Poetry Explication completes the update and expansion of Kuntz in the same manner and format. Authored by Martinez and Joseph G. R. Martinez, the first two volumes of this four-volume effort were issued in 1991. Volume 1 treats "Old English-Medieval"; volume 2 examines the Renaissance; and volume 3, published in 1993, treats "Restoration-Romantic." The final volume, issued in 1995, examines "Victorian-Contemporary" poetry, with coverage from 1925 to the early 1990s. All appropriate entries from the Kuntz 1980 edition have been incorporated into the expanded offering. Similar to Kuntz in scope and purpose is Alexander's *American and British Poetry* (entry 1279), which treats poetry up to 1,000 lines in length.

1288. Masterplots II. Poetry Series. Frank N. Magill, ed. Pasadena, CA: Salem Press, 1992. 6v. ISBN 0-89356-584-9. **Supp.** 3v. 1998. ISBN 0-89356-625-X.

This is the eighth series developed as part of the *Masterplots II* set (entry 1095) and follows the pattern established in previous efforts. Emphasis is placed on English and American poetry, although there are a number of works in English translation included among the 760 poems by 275 poets. Poems are well-chosen and represent the most popular and most frequently studied works. Arrangement is alphabetical by title across the six volumes, and entries supply header information with poet's name, dates, type of poem, and initial year of publication, followed by a section on "the poem" treating structure, plot, and setting. "Forms and devices" covers form and technique, while "themes and meanings" provides a useful summary. Entries are signed by the 200 scholar-contributors and coverage is even-handed and suitable for the high school/undergraduate level. Bibliographies and indexes are furnished in volume 6. A supplement was published in 1998.

Literature from Languages Other Than English

GENERAL (Various Languages)

1289. Contemporary World Writers. 2d ed. Tracy Chevalier, ed. Detroit: St. James Press, 1993. 686p. ISBN 1-55862-200-4.

Initially entitled *Contemporary Foreign Language Writers* (St. James Press, 1984), this new edition continues its focus on important living writers of various genres (fiction, drama, poetry) who write in languages other than English and who have been translated into English. Treated are 358 writers, selected by a panel of twenty academic literary specialists. The entries represent a diverse group, ranging from writers who are recognized and established to those who are relative newcomers. Of the total, just over 100 are Western European, along with representation of Central and Eastern European, Latin American, and Oriental. The work follows the format previously established in the other titles in the publisher's series and supplies for each author a biographical sketch, bibliography citing English translations of his or her other works, listing of critical studies, and a critical essay of 800–1,000 words evaluating the writer's work.

1290. **An Encyclopedia of Continental Women Writers.** Katharina M. Wilson, ed. New York: Garland, 1991. 2v. (Garland Reference Library of the Humanities, v. 698). ISBN 0-8240-8547-7.

Designed as a companion piece to the publisher's *Encyclopedia of British Women Writers* (Garland, 1988), this work follows a similar format in providing biocritical treatment of more than 1,800 European (but not British) writers from ancient times to the current scene. All types of writers are included and there is a good sample of novelists, dramatists, poets, and essayists from all parts of Europe, representing various languages such as Yiddish and Arabic. Entries supply quick identification of dates and places of birth and of death, genre, and language. Biocritical essays are brief but informative and run from a half-page to a page in length, treating major works, literary impact, and themes of the various authors. A two-part bibliography concludes each entry and provides a listing of the writer's major works along with a selective list of secondary sources. The lack of indexing is unfortunate.

1291. **Women Writers in Translation: An Annotated Bibliography, 1945–1982.** Margery Resnick and Isabelle de Courtivron. New York: Garland, 1984. 272p. (Garland Reference Library of the Humanities, v. 288). ISBN 0-8240-9332-1.

The idea for this tool grew out of a meeting of the Modern Language Association, where foreign-language teachers had discussed the difficulty of locating good translations of works by women writers. The compilers coordinated this project while professors at MIT; it required the expertise of more than fifty contributors and specialists in Portuguese, French, German, Italian, Japanese, Russian, and Spanish. The relatively slender product reflects a disappointing situation of international proportions, which permits work of women writers to go out-of-print in a relatively short time. The annotations vary in quality, as is true of most compilations, but on the whole they are informative regarding theme, genre, and literary significance. This is a valuable tool for both teachers and librarians.

Fiction

1292. **The Continental Novel: A Checklist of Criticism in English, 1900–1966.** Elizabeth J. Kearney and Louise S. Fitzgerald. Metuchen, NJ: Scarecrow Press, 1968. 460p. **Supp. 1967–1980**, 1983. 496p. ISBN 0-8108-1598-2.

With its publication in 1968, this checklist provided a well-chosen sample of English-language criticism written between 1900 and 1966 about continental novels and novelle. There are six groupings representing country of origin: French, Spanish and Portuguese, Italian, German, Scandinavian, and Russian/East European. Entries are listed under authors, then titles of work in an alphabetical arrangement. The tool is useful to both students and scholars in its convenient treatment of novels and novelists representing both the old standards such as Balzac and Cervantes as well as those of modern times. The supplementary volume, produced by the same authors, was issued fifteen years later and continues the coverage with references to an additional fourteen years of critical writings appearing in books and some 250 journals. Again, both classic and current writers are included; some are relatively obscure.

1293. **Critical Survey of Long Fiction: Foreign Language Series.** Frank N. Magill, ed. Englewood Cliffs, NJ: Salem Press, 1984. 5v. ISBN 0-89356-369-2. **Supp.**, 1987. 408p. ISBN 0-89356-368-4.

Another of the Magill *Critical Surveys* from Salem Press (entries 889, 1119, 1251, 1284, 1294), this work follows the pattern set by the others. Volumes 1–4 cover 182 writers judged to be important contributors to the development of long fiction (novels or novel-like prose) in languages other than English. Entries for each writer furnish a list of principal long fiction, description of the writer's contribution to other literary forms, principal long fiction, description of the writer's contribution to other literary forms, assessment of his or her major achievements, a short biographical sketch, analysis of his or her major works of long fiction, a selective list of writings other than in the long fiction genre, and a brief bibliography of biographical and critical sources about the writer. There is a useful set of essays on the history of the novel in various areas of the world in volume 5. An author-title index provides access. The 1987 supplement adds another fifty novelists to the critical coverage.

Poetry

1294. **Critical Survey of Poetry: Foreign Language Series.** Frank N. Magill. Englewood Cliffs, NJ: Salem Press, 1984. 5v. ISBN 0-89356-350-1.

Similar in format and style to other Magill works in this series (entries 889, 1119, 1251, 1284, 1293), this work covers all major poetry of the world not in English. Nearly 200 poets are covered in the first four volumes. Each one is treated in signed articles divided into several sections: principal poems and collections, other literary forms, achievements, biography, analysis, major publications other than poetry, and a brief bibliography. Over 100 contributors are involved with the project, and the coverage is somewhat uneven in quality. The idea is to provide introductory information; most of the articles run less than ten pages in length. Volume 5 provides twenty essays on various aspects of the genre, including the oral tradition and linguistics.

Magill's *Critical Survey of Poetry: Supplement* (Salem Press, 1987) adds to the treatment of both the work above and its counterpart, *Critical Survey of Poetry, English Language Series* (entry 1284) by supplying more detailed coverage of contemporary poets from all over the world. Nearly fifty eminent individuals, including ten women, are arranged alphabetically and critiqued in a uniform manner in terms of principal poems and collections, achievements, biography, and so forth. Additionally, there is a section updating information on poets in earlier volumes.

1295. **Hoffman's Index to Poetry: European and Latin American Poetry in Anthologies.** Herbert H. Hoffman. Metuchen, NJ: Scarecrow Press, 1985. 672p. ISBN 0-8108-1831-0.

A recent work useful to students and teachers is this index, which excludes poetic output in the English language. It treats about 14,000 important poems in about 100 anthologies published since the mid-1930s. Nearly 1,800 poets are represented, with poems written in a number of languages: French, German, Spanish, Italian, Portuguese, Polish, Russian, and Ukrainian. Selection of anthologies is in part based on their availability in the English-speaking world, and adds considerably to the practical value. The main section is arranged by name of poet, alphabetically, with poems listed alphabetically by title. First lines are also given. A title listing and a first line listing are both grouped by languages.

CLASSICAL LITERATURE, GREEK AND LATIN

1296. **Ancient Writers: Greece and Rome.** T. James Luce, ed.-in-chief. New York: Charles Scribner's Sons, 1982. 2v. ISBN 0-684-16595-3.

This is a highly useful biocritical tool due to its depth of coverage of the writers. It consists of forty-seven essays by specialists from the United States, the United Kingdom, Canada, and Israel. The articles range in length from ten to more than fifty pages and are devoted primarily to individual authors, and in some cases to groups such as Greek lyric poets. The pattern of coverage renders a brief biographical sketch, followed by an extensive critical interpretation of the writer's works. There is a bibliography of currently available editions in the original language as well as major contemporary translations, along with a list of selected critical studies, primarily in English. It is an important purchase for academic and secondary school libraries.

The Cambridge Companion to Virgil, edited by Charles Martindale (Cambridge University Press, 1997), is another in the series that features excellent in-depth essays by individual scholars. This work contains fourteen essays examining the work of the great Roman poet, both within the framework of Roman society and in terms of its impact on subsequent literary development. Analysis of the poetry is insightful, and perspectives on Virgil's influence are up-to-date. Emphasis is placed on the critical reception given to the poetry through the ages.

1297. **Classical and Medieval Literature Criticism: Excerpts from Criticism of the Works of World Authors.** . . . Jelena O. Krstovic, ed. Detroit: Gale Research, 1988– . v.1– . ISSN 0896-0011.

This represents an important and comprehensive survey of classical/medieval literature and its criticism. Coverage ranges from the prebiblical epics of the ancient world to the end of the fourteenth century. The volumes are well-executed and follow an established pattern, providing extensive coverage of five or eight authors or major works per volume. Initiated in 1988, the series will issue its twenty-ninth volume in 1999. Such luminaries as Homer, Plato, Cicero, St. Augustine, and Seneca are treated along with such important works as the Koran, the Bible, *Beowulf*, and the Talmud. Entries open with vital statistics along with a picture and biographical treatment of the subject. There is a listing of English translations of the work, followed by what is most important, the extracts of criticism through time. An annotated bibliography concludes each entry. There is emphasis on criticism of the past 100 years. The contents of this work are indexed in **Gale's Literary Index CD-ROM* (entry 1090).

Greek and Roman Writers: A Checklist of Criticism, by Thomas Gwinup and Fidelia Dickinson (2d ed., Scarecrow Press, 1982), is a useful checklist of English-language criticism of the work of seventy classical authors. Critical studies are identified in both books and periodicals. It employs the normal checklist arrangement, with authors listed alphabetically, and with listings of general criticism followed by criticism of individual works. **The Online Medieval & Classical Library* (http://sunsite.berkeley.edu/OMACL [accessed January 2000]), maintained by Douglas B. Killings, supplies a collection of important literary works from different genres in full-English text. Most are in the public domain and can be downloaded. Several Roman and Greek epics are included.

1298. **The Classical Epic: An Annotated Bibliography.** Thomas J. Sienkewicz. Pasadena, CA: Salem Press, 1991. 265p. (Magill Bibliographies). ISBN 0-89356-663-2.

As is true of others in this Magill series, this retrospective bibliography of critical and expository materials on three classical epics is useful to high school and undergraduate students. Treatment is given to writings on the *Aeneid* by Virgil and the *Iliad* and the *Odyssey* by Homer. Listings are provided of books, book chapters, and essays within books; periodical literature is excluded. This is a retrospective bibliography and covers materials written from the turn of the twentieth century to the mid-1980s. Treatment is well-developed and most of the important English-language book material is included. Information is given on historical background of societies producing these epics along with excellent representation of pertinent sources providing biographies, plot summaries, character studies, and studies of particular episodes or passages. A detailed table of contents and author index provide access.

An important annual bibliography of publications in Western languages is *L'annee philogique critique et analytique de l'antiquite greco-latine* . . . which lists publications in a classified arrangement. It has been published since the 1920s by the International Society of Classical Bibliography and provides summaries in English, French, and German. English-language studies are reported by a branch established at Chapel Hill, North Carolina.

1299. **The Oxford Companion to Classical Literature.** 2d ed. M. C. Howatson, ed. New York: Oxford University Press, 1989; repr. with corr., 1990. 615p. ISBN 0-19-866121-5.

This is the latest edition of a true classic, begun in 1937 and edited by Sir Paul Harvey. It is regarded as one of the important tools in the field for use by students and general readers, and is a treasure-house of information on a variety of topics and subjects relevant not only to literature but to the study of classical antiquity as well. The work has been heavily revised and expanded due to the advances in scholarship made possible by the breakthroughs in deciphering the Linear B script. Entries are furnished not only for classical writers, literary forms and subjects, and individual works, but also for historical events and figures, institutions, and religious observations. The rationale is that knowledge of these elements is necessary to understand the plots and themes of classical literature. There are cross-references in place of an index and maps but no bibliography.

The Concise Oxford Companion to Classical Literature, edited by Howatson and Ian Chilvers (Oxford University Press, 1993), is a somewhat revised as well as shortened version. It omits background articles on general cultural topics and provides abbreviated treatment of historical, geographical, and political conditions, along with appendices. Little new material has been added, although there is some reorganization of content. *The Oxford Classical Dictionary*, edited by Simon Hornblower and Anthony Spawforth (3d ed., Oxford University Press, 1996), has been updated twenty-six years after the publication of the second edition. It has added more than 800 new entries, for a total of approximately 6,000 and remains a useful resource, although not focused on literature per se. It remains a scholarly dictionary but one that is readable and interesting, covering biography, mythology, religion, science, geography, and so forth as well as literature.

ROMANCE LANGUAGES

French

1300. **A Critical Bibliography of French Literature.** Syracuse, NY: Syracuse University Press, 1947– 1994. 6v.

Considered a work of major importance, this bibliography was originally edited by D. C. Cabeen and in most cases is still referred to as "Cabeen." There are six volumes along with various supplements, revisions, and parts. Each of the volumes is written by specialists in the field and treats a different time period. Volume 1, on the medieval period, was published originally in 1947 and enlarged in 1952. Volume 2 covers the sixteenth century, with the first edition appearing in 1956 and the revised edition in 1985. Volume 3 (1961) treats the seventeenth century; and 3A, a supplement, was issued in 1983. Volume 4 (1951) covers the eighteenth century, with a supplement in 1968. Volume 5, covering the nineteenth century in two parts, was the last to appear, in 1994. Volume 6 (1980) covers the twentieth century in different parts devoted to various genres. The series represents a selective, evaluative, and annotated bibliography of books, dissertations, and periodical articles with references to reviews. Each volume is separately indexed.

1301. **The Cambridge Companion to the French Novel: From 1800 to the Present.** Timothy Unwin, ed. New York: Cambridge University Press, 1997. 281p. (Cambridge Companions to Literature series). ISBN 0-521-49563-6.

Like others in the series (entry 1082), this work provide a selective group of commissioned essays by scholars on the topic. Much insight is furnished through the modern perspectives involving reassessments of personalities and their work, presented in the fifteen chapters beginning with the editor's view of the novel and the writing of literary history. Succeeding chapters treat the origin of the French novel, reality and its representation, women and fiction, popular fiction, the Proustian Revolution, and so forth, concluding with exposition of Postmodern French Fiction. As is true of the pattern set for the series, there is a useful chronology highlighting important developments, along with a bibliography for further reading.

Dictionary of Modern French Literature: From the Age of Reason Through Realism, by Sandra W. Dolbow (Greenwood, 1986), is a detailed and thorough dictionary of French literature of the eighteenth and nineteenth centuries from 1715 to 1880. All major writers and many minor figures of the period (philosophers, historians, novelists, dramatists, and poets) are included. Literary movements and individual works are identified and described. Biographical entries are adequate in size for identification and understanding. Similarly, good synopses and descriptions are rendered for individual works. Bibliographies are included for most entries.

1302. **French Women Writers: A Bio-Bibliographical Source Book.** Eva Martin Sartori and Dorothy Wayne Zimmerman, eds. Westport, CT: Greenwood, 1991. 632p. ISBN 0-313-26548-8.

Designed for a wide-ranging audience from general reader to scholar, this biographical dictionary provides coverage in depth of fifty-one writers identified with a substantial body of work in the French language. Certain omissions may be questioned, but in general the coverage of female writers in a variety of genres—novels, letters, memoirs, plays, and poetry—is comprehensive. One additional entry is generic, treating women troubadours of the twelfth and thirteenth centuries. Entries are approximately ten pages in length and provide treatment in a standard format that includes a biography, discussion of major themes, survey of criticism, and bibliography of primary works along with a list of English translations and a selection of critical studies. Arrangement of entries is alphabetical by name of writer. Special features include a chronology of women writers in French history and a listing of writers by birth date. There are detailed title and subject indexes.

1303. **Guide to French Literature: 1789 to the Present.** Anthony Levi. Detroit: St. James Press, 1992–1993; repr., 1994. 2v. ISBN 1-55862-159-8.

This two-volume effort provides a well-constructed comprehensive survey of French literature. Initially, volume 1 was the first volume to have been published, but it is actually the concluding volume, covering the period from 1789 to the present. Volume 2, the later issue, examined the beginnings to 1789. The reprint edition adjusted the sequence. Levi is an eminent scholar and specialist in French literature and has produced a useful tool for a variety of users ranging from serious students to the general public. Entries supply informative, detailed, and sometimes lengthy treatment of personalities and literary works and movements. Entries on writers provide a full biography, critical analysis and evaluation of all major works, plot summaries, listing of publications, and selective listing of secondary sources. Entries on a movement describe fully its aims, achievements, and major contributors. There is a detailed index providing excellent access.

Catharine Savage Brown has edited *Nineteenth Century French Fiction Writers: Romanticism and Realism, 1800–1860* (1992) as volume 119 of the *DLB* series from Gale Research (entry 1087), providing biographical coverage of nineteen major French writers whose work was issued during that sixty-year period. As is true of other numbers in the series, the essays provide detailed coverage of the writers' careers and literary styles and influences, and is especially useful for undergraduate users. The contents of this work are indexed in **Gale's Literary Index CD-ROM* (entry 1090).

1304. **Guide to French Poetry Explication.** Kathleen Coleman. New York: G. K. Hall, 1993. 594p. ISBN 0-8161-9075-5.

Explications or interpretations are important to students and scholars in providing a basis for their teaching/learning and research activity, and reference works of this kind are common to the study of poetry in the English language. This is the first G. K. Hall venture of this type with poetry in a foreign language, and it represents a milestone in that regard. Like other checklists and guides, the current effort is designed to locate and reveal these critical interpretations on the work of major poets. Emphasis is given to those poets generally included in French studies and those explications found in standard indexes and bibliographies available in this country. The poetry dates from the Middle Ages to the present, and explications were written between 1960 and 1990. Arrangement of entries is alphabetical by name of poet; titles of poems and their explications then follow in alphabetical sequence. An index of critics and several bibliographies complete the work.

1305. **The New Oxford Companion to Literature in French.** Peter France, ed. New York: Oxford University Press, 1995. 865p. ISBN 0-19-866125-8.

Continuing as a useful source is this most recent edition of a classic work, initially published in 1959 and abridged in 1976. It has become a broader-based and more comprehensive tool, covering various literatures in the French language rather than limited to the literature of France. The work contains some 3,000 entries treating a variety of topics pertinent to literary development. There are broad survey articles on the literature of each geographic area, such as "Haiti" and "Quebec," and on literary and intellectual movements. There is a greater emphasis on the work of women and much more inclusion of popular writing and writers. Of importance is the generous treatment given to contemporary literature and its components, such as feminism. The survey articles contain excellent bibliographies. Due to the broader structure, many minor writers were dropped from coverage, which should be reason enough to retain the earlier editions.

The Concise Oxford Dictionary of French Literature, edited by Joyce M. H. Reid (Oxford University Press, 1976; repr., 1985), is a successful condensation of the 1959 *The Oxford Companion to French Literature*, by Paul Harvey. Abridgment was achieved through compression in terms of style, format, and type size rather than elimination of articles. Several new articles were added where needed and older ones were updated and in some cases expanded. Articles of French-Canadian literature were deleted because of their treatment in *The Oxford Companion to Canadian Literature* (entry 1167). Like others in the Companion series, this volume is highly informative and contains entries for obscure writers as well as major figures.

1306. **Research and Reference Guide to French Studies.** 2d ed. Charles B. Osburn. Metuchen, NJ: Scarecrow Press, 1981. 532p. ISBN 0-8108-1440-4.

The first edition of this work received much acclaim when it was published in 1968, and it was followed by a useful supplement in 1972. The second edition represents a complete revision of the earlier one, with 6,000 entries of value to the study of French language and literature. The earlier edition was more comprehensive and was intended to cover the whole range of French studies. A variety of reference books is covered in the present work: concordances, dictionaries, iconographies, filmographies, encyclopedias, and so forth, primarily in English, French, and German. The coverage of bibliographies is excellent, and critical surveys are identified. This effort was intended as a link between the earlier edition and the machine-readable database of the *MLA International Bibliography* (entry 1060).

A good Web site is *French Studies Web* (http://www.nyu.edu/pages/wessfrench/ [accessed January 2000]), maintained by Jennifer Vinopal for the Western European Specialists Section /Association of College and Research Libraries of the American Library Association; the organization also has a Web site for German studies (entry 1329). This site is located at New York University and serves as a comprehensive directory of well-developed Web sites useful to French studies. *A Bibliographical Guide to the Romance Languages and Literatures*, by Thomas Rossman Palfrey et al. (8th ed., Chandler, 1971), is a comprehensive and well-respected guide to the Romance literatures such as French, Italian, Portuguese, and Spanish. First published in 1939, it has been the first choice of students and specialists for identifying important studies and literary contributions.

1307. **Six Contemporary French Women Poets: Theory, Practice, and Pleasures.** Serge Gavronsky and Leslie Kaplan, eds. Carbondale: Southern Illinois University, 1997. 144p. ISBN 0-809-32115-7.

This work provides in-depth examination of six French women poets of the twentieth century. Although the effort is concise, its limited scope permits an insightful view and provides the opportunity to develop an accurate perspective on the poetry of the subjects. Included for study is a body of work from Michelle Grangaud, Anne Portugal, Josee Lapeyr, Lillian Giraudon, Jacqueline Risset, and Leslie Kaplan, who has served as co-editor of the publication. There is an introductory chapter providing a brief overview; following that are six sections of poetry translated into English. A good bibliography is included.

Contemporary French Women Poets, by Michael Bishop (Rodopi, 1995), is a two-volume study of a broad array of women poets and their work since the mid-twentieth century. Volume 1 is subtitled "From Chedid and Dohollau to Tellermann and Bancquart," and provides critical examination of the work of eight women poets such as Andree Chedid and Heather Dohollau, as well as Jacqueline Risset (treated in entry 1306). These individual commentaries follow a broad introduction. The volume ends with a provisional concluding essay and bibliography. Volume 2 follows the same pattern, examining the work of eight more poets, including Jeanne Hyvard and Jeannine Baude, and ending with a final conclusion and bibliography.

*1308. **Textes and contextes.** CEDROM. (CD-ROM).

Available both abroad and in the United States, this CD-ROM tool supplies a comprehensive database of extracts from the masterpieces of French literature. Coverage is extensive, with about 6,000 extracts from the work of 1,500 authors. CD-ROM format provides excellent retrieval capabilities for students and teachers in locating literary passages in the original French language through employment of hypertext searching schemes. This work should not be confused with a two-volume print publication of the same title that treats French language and grammar.

*CD-Litterature is another CD-ROM tool covering French literature in the original language and was developed and published by Nathan Logiciels/Act Informatique in 1989. Coverage of French literature dates from 888 to 1899, and the tool provides 800 abstracts and 1,200 extracts of the work of 380 authors. Special features include a useful chronology of events for those years. Indexing is excellent through provision of a thematic index, form and technique index, author index, title index, and index of philosophic and literary terms.

Italian

1309. **Dictionary of Italian Literature.** Rev. and exp. ed. Peter Bondanella et al., eds. Westport, CT: Greenwood, 1996. 716p. ISBN 0-313-27745-1.

The new edition of the 1979 effort continues as a useful dictionary and guide to Italian literature; it now contains over 425 entries, alphabetically arranged, covering authors, genres, periods, movements, and related general topics. Most entries are on authors and provide informative sketches of their lives and achievements. Both major and minor writers are covered from the twelfth century through 1995. Many of the articles are signed by the contributors. Bibliographies are furnished for each entry and include English translations of important primary texts and critical studies in books and articles in various languages. There is a useful chronology in the appendix enumerating events in Italian literature, world literature, and philosophy. Access is provided by a good index.

Spanish (Includes Latin American, Hispanic)

1310. **Chicano Literature: A Reference Guide.** Julio A. Martinez and Francisco A. Lomeli, eds. Westport, CT: Greenwood, 1985. 492p. ISBN 0-313-23691-7.

At time of publication this filled a void through its coverage of Mexican-American authors and their works written since 1848. It is used frequently by librarians, scholars, students, and laypersons seeking to understand the careers and literary quality of nearly thirty important authors. Also included are ten thematic articles treating important subjects. Entries are arranged alphabetically, with author entries running from 2,500 to 5,000 words in length in proportion to the subject's importance. These entries supply biographical data relating to date and place of birth, background, and family, followed by a scholarly signed essay describing career highlights and achievements and assessment of contribution. A bibliography of works by and about the writer concludes each entry. There are four appendices that supply a chronology and glossary as well as bibliography. An index is furnished.

1311. **Contemporary Spanish American Poets: A Bibliography of Primary and Secondary Sources.** Jacobo Sefami, comp. New York: Greenwood, 1992. 245p. (Bibliographies and Indexes in World Literature, no .33). ISBN 0-313-27880-6.

This is a useful bibliography, treating eighty-six poets born between 1910 and 1952. Selection is based on coverage in national bibliographies and in the *MLA International Bibliography* (entry 1060), and treatment is divided between works by and about the poets. Included among the primary sources are poetic works, compilations and anthologies, and even other genres such as fiction and essay. Translations, for the most part, are not identified. Included among the secondary sources are bibliographies and critical studies of the subject's poetry. Although there is quarrel with certain omissions due to bias toward those countries with national bibliographies, there was no intention to be comprehensive; the work plays well as a selective survey of contemporary Spanish-American poets. A well-constructed and useful bibliography of general sources concludes the effort. An index is furnished.

1312. **Dictionary of Mexican Literature.** Eladio Cortes, ed. Westport, CT: Greenwood, 1992. 768p. ISBN 0-313-26271-3.

As the first of its kind, this dictionary of the literature of Mexico provides coverage needed by students and others to comprehend this body of work. There are some 550 entries following a nineteen-page introductory essay that provides an overview of Mexican letters and literature. Entries treat authors primarily; a few cover literary schools and cultural movements spanning Mexican literary history from the sixteenth century to the present day. Emphasis is given to the current scene and more than 80 percent of the writers chosen are either alive or have died during the twentieth century. Entries run from one to sixteen pages in length and provide a biography and analysis, listing of works, and bibliography of secondary sources. Cross-references are given within the entries. A bibliography of general sources and an index conclude the tool.

1313. **Dictionary of the Literature of the Iberian Peninsula.** German Bleiberg et al., eds. New York: Greenwood, 1992–1993. 2v. ISBN 0-313-21302-X.

This is an update and expansion of the editor's 1972 publication, bearing a Spanish-language title, that earned a reputation as an excellent work for students and specialists. The present effort continues its tradition under Bleiberg (a noted academic Hispanist), his co-editors, and his pool of 140 experts, who contributed the well-constructed, informative articles. Entries treat all elements of the major literatures of the Iberian peninsula (Spanish, Catalan, Galician, Portuguese) in a balanced manner. Included here are descriptions of literary figures, movements, genres, themes, styles, and forms along with definitions of terms. Entries generally conclude with listings of primary and secondary sources and English translations. Personalities are all Iberian-born and Spanish-American writers are excluded. Coverage spans a period of about 1,000 years from the tenth century to the mid-1980s. Cross-references are provided along with an index.

1314. **Handbook of Latin American Literature.** 2d ed. David William Foster, ed. New York: Garland, 1992. 799p. (Garland Reference Library of the Humanities, v. 1459). ISBN 0-8153-0343-2.

The initial edition of this useful work was issued in 1987 and attempted to bring an ideological approach to the description and analysis of the national literatures of twenty-one Latin American countries, including Puerto Rico. Information was presented through in-depth descriptive and analytical essays on each of the countries and covered a period dating from the colonial times to the time of publication. The second edition continues in the same tradition and supplies essays that have been thoroughly revised, expanded, and updated. Thematic aspects, major literary figures, and literary traditions are treated. Newly added chapters examine the literature of principal Hispanic groups in the United States, film, and para-literature. Annotated bibliographies conclude each entry. A name index provides access.

Literatura Hispanoamericana: Una Anotolgia, also edited by Foster (Garland, 1994), is designed as a companion volume to the *Handbook* and serves as a sourcebook or anthology of selections of the work of forty-five Spanish-American authors. Although the selections date from the colonial period, emphasis is placed on important twentieth-century authors. Two complete novels and two complete dramas are included, along with a complete slave narrative.

1315. **Hispanic Writers: A Selection of Sketches from Contemporary Authors.** Bryan Ryan, ed. Detroit: Gale Research, 1991. 514p. ISBN 0-81083-7688-1.

About 40 percent of the 400 entries for twentieth-century authors in this biographical dictionary have been drawn from *Contemporary Authors* (entry 1083) and updated; the rest have been prepared specifically for this tool. "Hispanic" in this case refers to writers from Mexico, the Spanish-speaking countries of Central America and South America, the Caribbean, and the United States. There is broad interpretation of "writers," with inclusion of major literary figures such as F. Garcia Lorca and Octavio Paz as well as socio-political personalities such as Che Guevara, and also scholars, historians, journalists, and media personalities. Entries supply personal information, address, career data, memberships, awards, writings, works in progress, a biographical sketch, critical reception and personal commentary, and a bibliography of secondary sources. All Spanish-speaking countries are represented; there is strong coverage of U.S. authors. An index by nationality of authors is provided.

1316. **Latin American Literary Authors: An Annotated Guide to Bibliographies.** David Zubatsky. Metuchen, NJ: Scarecrow Press, 1986. 332p. ISBN 0-8108-1900-7.

This is considered to be the most thorough and complete bibliography of bibliographies on Latin American authors of all types of literature. Novelists, dramatists, poets, essayists, literary critics, and others from all regions of Spanish-speaking America are included. A variety of sources is represented, including books, magazines, journals, dissertations, and Festschriften. All major writers seem to be represented, as well as scores of lesser known figures. Although there are some omissions, the work is commendable both for its inclusiveness and for its attention to detail. Entries are annotated and appear in two major parts, the first of which provides an alphabetical listing by author. Part 2 gives additional bio-bibliographical sources, arranged by country or region.

Zubatsky's *Spanish, Catalan, and Galician Literary Authors of the Twentieth Century: An Annotated Guide to Bibliographies* (Scarecrow Press, 1992) is developed within the same context and supplies a bibliography of both primary and secondary published bibliographies of the work or criticism of the work of several hundred novelists, playwrights, poets, short-story writers, linguists, literary critics, and historians who have published in Spanish, Catalan, or Galician during the twentieth century. In 1995, Zubatsky produced a companion work along the same lines, *Spanish, Catalan, and Galician Literary Authors of the Eighteenth and Nineteenth Centuries: An Annotated Guide to Bibliographies.* Another excellent resource, this one a Web site, is **Latin American Literary Review Press* (http://www.lalrp.org/ [accessed January 2000]), from Pittsburgh, Pennsylvania. The Press was established in 1980, expanding the work of the semiannual journal, *Latin American Literary Review*, by identifying and describing English translations of works by Latin American novelists and poets.

1317. **Latin American Literature in the 20th Century: A Guide.** New York: Ungar, 1986; repr., Harpenden: Oldcastle Books, 1988. 278p. ISBN 0-948353-15-5.

Based on the four-volume *Encyclopedia of World Literature in the 20th Century* (entry 1072), this one-volume work provides a compact but useful survey of literature written in Spanish and Portuguese from twenty countries of South and North America. Each country is treated separately and there is an introductory essay on literary trends and developments. This is followed by biographical sketches of a number of writers, discussion of their works, and a bibliography. There is a summary of each writer's accomplishments. The coverage in all cases has been praised for its high quality and clarity, especially important for examining some of the more complex and difficult works. This is a reliable source and one of the mainstays on the topic in most libraries providing reference services to students and interested laypersons.

1318. **The Latin American Short Story: An Annotated Guide to Anthologies and Criticism.** Daniel Balderston, comp. New York: Greenwood, 1992. 522p. (Bibliographies and Indexes in World Literature, no. 34). ISBN 0-313-27360-X.

This work opens with a well-developed introductory essay on the nature and role of anthologies. Latin-America is here defined as Spanish America and includes the Spanish-speaking countries of the Caribbean and Brazil. This well-constructed tool provides both a bibliography of anthologies of Latin-American short stories and listing of criticism and interpretations. The anthologies section is organized into separate segments treating general anthologies, regional anthologies, and anthologies from particular countries. Over 1,300 anthologies are cited in Spanish, Portuguese, or English translation and are briefly described. The second section contains an annotated bibliography of criticism, divided into segments on theory, general criticism, literary history, bibliography, regions, and particular countries. Annotations are brief but informative. There are more than 375 entries in this segment. The work is indexed by authors, critics, and titles of anthologies.

1319. **Latin American Writers.** Carlos A. Sole and Maria Isabel Abreu, eds. New York: Charles Scribner's Sons, 1989. 3v. ISBN 0-684-18463-X.

This important biocritical tool begins with a useful essay providing exposition of Spanish-American and Brazilian literature that places in perspective the information that follows on particular authors. A total of nineteen countries are represented by 176 writers of all genres (poetry, fiction, drama, journalism, biography, etc.). Writers are treated in chronological sequence by date of birth, beginning with the late fifteenth century and ending with the contemporary scene. Essays are detailed and range from 2,500 to 10,000 words depending upon the importance of the subject. Selective bibliographies of primary and secondary sources are given. Sixteen of the writers are women and contribute to the panoramic view of the literary history of Mexico, Central and South Americas, and the Spanish-speaking countries of the Caribbean. The articles are written by 135 specialist-contributors (academics, writers, critics, and diplomats). Most entries include quotations from the writer's work. A special feature is a chronology of literary and other events. A detailed index provides access.

1320. **Literatura Chicana: Creative and Critical Writings Through 1984.** Roberto G. Trujillo and Andres Rodriguez, comps. Oakland, CA: Floricanto Press/Hispanex, 1985. 95p. ISBN 0-915745-04-6.

This slender volume was completed in response to a need to help document the writings of an important American minority group which up to now has not received much attention in the area of bibliographic control. Limited to material found in books, the work is divided into various forms and genres, with headings such as poetry, novels, short fiction, theater, literary criticism, "literatura chicanesca," oral tradition, anthologies, literary periodicals, unpublished dissertations, bibliographies, autobiographical works, and video and sound recordings. The compilers are librarians at Stanford University and have used their bibliographic skills well in identifying nearly 800 items. Each entry furnishes the author's name, the title of the work, imprint, and pagination. There is a useful introductory essay by Luis Leal on bibliographies in the field. Indexes are by author and title.

1321. **The Oxford Companion to Spanish Literature.** Philip Ward, ed. Oxford: Clarendon, 1978. 629p. ISBN 0-19-866114-2.

Another useful resource in the Oxford lineup, this one follows the pattern of the Companions to other literatures, providing an alphabetical approach to articles on a variety of individuals, works, and topics. Of the personalities covered, most are authors, but also included are critics, historians, philosophers, and so forth. Plot summaries are given for important books, and good identifications are furnished for journals, libraries, publishers' series, literary movements, groups, and forms. All elements of Spanish literature are included—Basque, Catalan, and Galician as well as Castillian—but Portuguese is excluded. The literature of many countries is covered, representing most nations of Central and South America as well as

Mexico. Although no general bibliography is given, there are references to additional reading materials in many of the entries.

1322. A Sourcebook for Hispanic Literature and Language: A Selected Annotated Guide to Spanish, Spanish-American, and Chicano Bibliography. . . . 3d ed. Donald W. Bleznick. Metuchen, NJ: Scarecrow Press, 1995. 310p. ISBN 0-8108-2981-9.

First published in 1974, then revised in 1983, the third issue of this guide for both students and scholars furnishes over 1,400 entries in a classified arrangement. An introductory chapter describes the aims and methods of literary research, followed by individual chapters that cover style guides; general bibliographic guides; Hispanic literature bibliographies; literary bio-bibliographies, dictionaries, and encyclopedias; histories of Hispanic literatures; Hispanic literature in the United States (Chicano and Cuban); books on metrics; literature in translation bibliographies; Hispanic linguistics; scholarly periodicals; dissertation guides; other useful references; and selected book dealers. Author and title indexes are furnished to aid access.

Another title, also in its second edition, is *Argentine Literature: A Research Guide* (Garland, 1982), compiled by David William Foster. It has two major sections: general references with thirty chapters and the authors' segment, with nearly seventy-five writers. Each of the writers is given extensive bibliographic coverage (in some cases over 1,000 citations to studies in books, articles, and theses). Foster has also written *Mexican Literature: A Bibliography of Secondary Sources* (2d ed., Scarecrow Press, 1992). This is a useful bibliography of articles, monographs, dissertations, criticism, and review articles, the emphasis being on eight-three writers of the nineteenth and twentieth centuries. With access to many catalogs and bibliographic tools, Foster has maintained the excellence of the first edition and produced a valuable verification and identification tool.

1323. Twentieth-Century Spanish Poets. First Series. Michael L. Perna, ed. Detroit: Gale Research, 1991. 400p. (Dictionary of Literary Biography, v. 108). ISBN 0-8103-4588-9.

This volume is part of the *DLB* series (entry 1087) and follows the format and pattern of coverage established in the series, well-known for its excellent biocritical and bibliographical coverage. In this volume, twenty-nine of the most important twentieth-century Spanish poets are treated in essays ranging in length from seven to almost thirty pages. This is the first volume in the series to treat Spanish-language writers, and such luminaries as Federico Garcia Lorca and Miguel de Unamuno are included. Certain omissions are notable from this work, especially that of Nobel prize winner Juan Ramon Jimenez. Only three of the poets are female. As is true of other works in the series, the information is accurate and describes the ideology, contribution, and poetic technique of the subject. Included along with the essays are illustrations and listings of both primary and secondary sources for further study.

In 1994, Jerry P. Winfield edited *Twentieth-Century Spanish Poets. Second Series*, also published by Gale Research, as volume 134 in the *DLB* series. It treats sixty additional poets both of major stature (including the previously omitted J. R. Jimenez) and those less known. Similar coverage is provided, with each entry several pages in length. The contents of these titles are indexed in **Gale's Literary Index CD ROM* (entry 1090).

1324. U.S. Latino Literature: An Essay and Annotated Bibliography. Marc Zimmerman. Chicago: MARCH/Abrazo Press, 1992. 156p. ISBN 1-877636-01-0.

This is the second edition of a work initially commissioned and published by the Chicago Public Library in 1990, evidence of the growing interest in Latin-American clienteles. The new publisher is a cultural arts organization. This work was designed to provide needed enlightenment and initial orientation to readers and researchers regarding the complexity of Latino cultural identity and its expression in literature. The work opens with an introductory essay on this topic and examines the theories and strategies behind current critical approaches. Entries are annotated in a thorough manner and are placed within several categories or sections: "Chicano Literature," "U.S. Puerto Rican Literature," "U.S. Cuban Literature," "Latino-tending U.S. Latin American Writing," "Latino Children and Young Adult Books," "Chicanesque Literature," and "Secondary Materials." Emphasis has been placed on English-language publication or translation.

1325. **Women Writers of Spain: An Annotated Bio-Bibliographical Guide.** Carolyn L Galerstein, ed. Westport, CT: Greenwood, 1986. 389p. (Bibliographies and Indexes in Women's Studies, no. 2). ISBN 0-313-24965-2.

A combined effort of eighty contributors is this bio-bibliographical dictionary documenting the contributions of female writers in Spanish, Basque, Galician, and Catalan. In attempting to develop a useful tool for research, it was decided not to include those writers for whom no material could be found other than what has already been identified in a comprehensive standard bibliography by Manuel Serrano y Sanz, *Apuntes para una biblioteca de escritoras espanolas desde al ano 1401 al 1833* (Madrid: Establecimiento . . . , 1903; repr., Madrid: Atlas, 1975). Each author is given a biographical sketch with an annotated listing of her belles lettres contributions in book format. Several listings appear in the appendices: author by birth date, authors in Catalan, authors in Galician, and translated titles. A title index supplies access.

Women Writers of Spanish America: An Annotated Bio-Bibliographical Guide, edited by Diane E. Marting (Greenwood, 1987) is no. 5 in the same series. The pattern of coverage is similar, treating the Spanish-language contributions of Spanish-American women writers from twenty-one countries including the United States. Some seventy contributors have joined to provide a useful listing of entries, some fully annotated, furnishing the country of origin, dates, biographical information, and selective bibliography. *Women Authors of Modern Hispanic South America: A Bibliography of Literary Criticism and Interpretation*, by Sandra M. Cypess et al. (Scarecrow Press, 1989), is a useful resource tool for students and scholars in the areas of Hispanic literature and women's studies. It provides an unannotated listing of studies and critical interpretations of the work of 169 female writers from nine countries. Arrangement is first by country, then name and literary genre. References are included for books, articles, dissertations, and other materials.

1326. **Writers of the Caribbean and Central America: A Bibliography.** M. J. Fenwick. New York: Garland, 1992. 2v. (Garland Reference Library of the Humanities, v. 1244). ISBN 0-8240-4010-4.

This tool is especially valuable for its inclusiveness in examining the literary production of forty-three geographical areas bordering on the Caribbean. Coverage is given to nearly 6,500 personalities writing in the Spanish language, nearly 1,350 English-language writers, and some 700 in French, 100 in Dutch, and so forth Arrangement is by country, with entries duplicated under various countries where the authors have lived and worked. Entries supply a listing of the writer's works in chronological sequence, along with a listing of magazines and anthologies in which the works appear. Information is generally provided regarding vital years, genres, and major works, although entries vary considerably in treatment, with some providing only skeletal identification. With such comprehensive coverage, omissions are expected and pointed out by reviewers. Nevertheless, the work is unique for its breadth. An index is furnished.

GERMANIC/SCANDINAVIAN LANGUAGES

1327. **A Companion to Twentieth-Century German Literature.** 2d ed. Raymond Furness and Malcolm Humble. New York: Routledge Kegan Paul, 1997. 316p. ISBN 0-415-15056-6.

This is an updated and revised edition of the initial 1991 effort; the authors are academics and specialists in the field of German culture who have compiled a useful bio-bibliography for students at various levels. Additional entries have been included and many of the entries have been updated. More than 400 twentieth-century writers of imaginative texts are treated, with little consideration for the work of editors, publishers, producers, or critics. Instead, the focus is on poets, dramatists, and writers of fiction from the turn of the twentieth century to the present. Included here are all the well-known and most frequently studied German, Austrian, and Swiss writers, with excellent representation of females, those of Jewish faith, and those from the former German Democratic Republic. Entries take the form of bibliographic essays and run from a few sentences to a page in length. They provide biographical identification along with analysis of historical and literary context and critical judgment. Unfortunately, there is no index.

1328. **Dictionary of Scandinavian Literature.** Virpi Zuck et al., eds. New York: Greenwood, 1990. 792p. ISBN 0-313-21450-6.

Specialists from several countries contributed to this tool, providing coverage of five Nordic countries—Denmark, Norway, Sweden, Iceland, and Finland—and producing an important work for students and scholars interested in further study. Articles are arranged alphabetically employing English convention and supply biocritical essays ranging from 200 to 1,600 words long on 380 writers. Their works are described within the essays or are listed at the end along with secondary publications. In addition, there are numerous topical entries on such subjects as Old Norse poetry, library resources, literary journals, and children's literature. Especially useful are articles on the literature of the Faroese, Inuit (Greenland), and Sani (Lappland). Special features include a chronology comparing literary history in Scandinavia with other countries and an appendix of bibliographical sources. An index is supplied.

*1329. **German Literature on the Internet: Text Collections and Author Index.** James Campbell. Association of College and Research Libraries/Western European Specialists Section, last updated 1998. http://www.lib.Virginia.edu/wess/germtext.html (accessed January 2000).

As part of the American Library Association, the ACRL Western European Specialists Section has put together a useful hypertext resource providing links to general text collections, anthologies of poetry and prose, and oral history. Also included are sections on literary magazines and contemporary authors and individual Web pages treating German authors. The site functions as part of the *German Studies Web* and is restricted to literary texts written in German that generally have appeared in print. Translations are identified only when they accompany an original text or are part of a database that furnishes German language texts as well. There are links to ten sites for general texts, including such resources as *Projekt Gutenberg, Bibliotheca Germanica* and *University of Virginia Library Electronic Center.* There are thirteen anthology sites, including *German Corner*, *Projekt Alfred*, and *Buecher Online*.

1330. **Grundriss zur Geschichte der deutschen Dichtung aus der Quellen.** 2 ganz neubearb. Aufl. Karl Goedeke. Dresden, Germany: L. Ehlermann, 1884– . v.1– .

This is acknowledged to be the most complete bibliography of German literature, a necessary purchase for large reference libraries and those operating in a university environment. Bibliographical and critical comments are included regarding authors and their works, as well as extensive listings of various editions, treatises, histories, biographical and critical works, and sources. Each volume is separately indexed, and an alphabetical index of authors covered in the first fifteen volumes was published in 1975. There is a third edition of volume 4, dealing primarily with the work of Goethe, published in five parts over a period of more than fifty years (1906–1960). Since Goedeke's death in 1887, the work has continued under various editors. Volumes 14–17, edited by Jacob von Herbert, have added "aus der quellen" to the original title. Volume 17 was issued in 1989.

A convenient and informative guide is Michael S. Batts's *The Bibliography of German Literature: An Historical and Critical Survey* (Bern, Switzerland: P. Lang, 1978). This work provides a brief overview of bibliographical tools available, with a critical review of current sources.

1331. **Introduction to Library Research in German Studies: Language, Literature, and Civilization.** Larry L. Richardson. Boulder, CO: Westview Press, 1984. 227p. (Westview Guides to Library Research). ISBN 0-86531-195-1.

A useful resource tool for students because of its detailed coverage of the use of libraries and bibliographic searching techniques, this has become a popular guide to the field. It embraces not only the literature but related studies of history, art, philosophy, politics, religion, and film. About 250 reference sources are identified and described in a helpful manner. Designed for the student who is studying German literature, it provides many helpful definitions of the types of tools listed, such as usage dictionaries. Works of literary criticism are included, as are major periodicals in the field. Supplementary reference works, guides to research papers, and computerized databases are also covered. There is a glossary, and a comprehensive index covers authors, titles, and subjects.

German Literature: An Annotated Reference Guide, by Uwe K. Faulhaber and Penrith B. Goff (Garland, 1979), is an older but more extensive annotated bibliography of over 2,000 reference tools, works of literary criticism, and periodicals important to the study of German literature. There is a checklist of pertinent works in related fields such as art or music that is not annotated.

1332. **The Oxford Companion to German Literature.** 3d ed. Henry Garland and Mary Garland, eds. New York: Oxford University Press, 1997. 951p. ISBN 0-19-815896-3.

This edition, like its predecessor, is a considerable update of the initial effort, published in 1975, which covered the field through the early 1970s; the second edition (1986) treated the period up to the 1980s and included writers from both East and West Germany. The third edition continues the comprehensive coverage, spanning the entire history of German literature from its beginnings to the mid-1990s and encompassing German reunification. Treatment continues to be well-balanced, describing events, writers, plot summaries, genres, literary movements, characters, historical figures, artists, philosophers, and periodicals. Employing the general format of the previous editions (and, indeed, the pattern used in the entire Oxford Companion series), entries are alphabetically arranged and treat a variety of relevant topics. The current edition has added some eighty new entries and revised hundreds of others. Furnished here is information needed for background understanding and interpretation of German literature, with articles such as the one on anti-Semitism.

A new twist for the *Dictionary of Literary Biography* (entry 1087) began with the fifty-sixth volume of the series, *German Fiction Writers, 1914–1945*, edited by James Hardin (Gale Research, 1987). Formerly restricted to coverage of British and American authors, with this volume the series embraced modern European writers. Included are German and Swiss authors whose first important work appeared during the time period specified. Coverage is given to thirty-three individuals, from the obscure to the renowned. As usual, biographical essays provide basic bibliographies for each author. Work continues in this direction with the publication of *German Fiction Writers, 1885–1913*, also edited by Hardin, as volume 66 (in two parts) of the same series (1988). Treatment is accorded to thirty-eight fiction writers of the late nineteenth and early twentieth centuries. Length of coverage varies, from nearly fifty pages given to Thomas Mann to around five pages for lesser figures. The contents of these titles are indexed in *Gale's Literary Index CD-ROM* (entry 1090).

1333. The Twentieth-Century German Novel: A Bibliography of English Language Criticism, 1945–1986. Michael T. O'Pecko and Eleanore O. Hoffstetter. Metuchen, NJ: Scarecrow Press, 1989. 810p. ISBN 0-8108-2262-8.

This is an important tool of convenience for scholars and students, providing references to critical coverage published in books and periodicals after World War II on twentieth-century German novels. Coverage is comprehensive, with nearly 6,500 entries on these English-language studies. The work opens with a general section identifying histories and surveys of the German novel prior to World War II and general works on West German, East German, Austrian, and Swiss novels. The bulk of the text is given to individual authors and their novels, with arrangement alphabetical by name of author. Entries supply birth and death dates and references to bibliographies, general criticism, criticism of individual works, and book reviews. Coverage given to individual novels includes publication data, translations in English, and listings of criticism alphabetically by critic. Unfortunately, there is no index.

SLAVONIC LANGUAGES

1334. The Cambridge Companion to the Classic Russian Novel. Malcolm V. Jones and Robin F. Miller, eds. New York: Cambridge University Press, 1998. 312p. (Cambridge Companions to Literature). ISBN 0-521-47346-2.

A recent entry to the Cambridge series (entry 1082), this work furnishes fourteen insightful essays by scholars who provide contemporary perspective on the Russian novel. Beginning with an introductory essay by the editors, the treatment embraces thematic elements that structured the writing: the city, the countryside, the culture, politics, satire, religion, psychology, philosophy, romantic tradition, realist tradition, modernist tradition, writing technique, gender, and theory. Within these elements the major writers and their work are analyzed: Pushkin, Dostoevskii, Tolstoi, Turgenev, Nabakov, Bulgakov, Pasternak, Solzhenitsyn, and so forth. A chronology is provided along with listings for additional reading.

Handbook of Russian Literature, edited by Victor Terras (Yale University Press, 1985), has received much praise in the past for its impressive amount of information, precision of language, comprehensiveness of coverage, and interesting, enjoyable style. Over 100 scholars have contributed more than 1,000 entries, predominantly articles on individual writers. Coverage is given to literary terms and movements, historical events and figures, periodicals, societies, genres, and other relevant topics. There is an emphasis on pre-revolutionary subjects, a period that has been slighted by recent sources. Bibliographies accompany most articles and contain English-language publications.

1335. Nineteenth-Century Russian Literature in English: A Bibliography of Criticism and Translations. Carl R. Proffer and Ronald Meyer, comps. Ann Arbor, MI: Ardis, 1990. 188p. ISBN 0-88233-943-5.

In treating that important era of Russian literature marked by the contributions of Turgenev, Pushkin, Tolstoy, Chekhov, and Dostoevsky, this tool provides a real service to students at all levels. It serves as an excellent beginning source in its concentration on English-language translations and English-language study and criticism of sixty-nine important writers of that remarkable period. The work opens with a segment of general works on the topic and then proceeds with treatment of individual authors. Arrangement is alphabetical by name of author and entries supply references to bibliographies as well as translations and critical interpretations in books, articles, and doctoral dissertations. Both collective works and monographs are included, and thirty-four different journals are examined among the critical publications issued between 1890 and 1986. No annotations are given; nor is an index provided.

*1336. **REESWeb: Russian and East European Studies.** Karen Rondestvedt. Center for Russian and East European Studies, University of Pittsburgh, updated Nov. 1998, by Mark J. Weixel. http://www.ucis.pitt.edu/reesweb (accessed January 2000).

This is a university-maintained hypertext Web site identifying Internet material germane to the study of that relatively unfamiliar part of the world embraced by what was once known as the U.S.S.R. and its satellites. It represents a comprehensive and useful index of electronic resources treating such areas as the Balkans, the Baltic States, the Caucasus, Central Asia, Central Europe, the CIS, Eastern Europe, the NIS, and the Russian Federation. The Center for Russian and East European Studies of the University of Pittsburgh is recognized as a national resource center in this area. The majority of the resources are stored at other sites and are linked up to this site, for which there are three major categories of links. "REESWeb Shortcuts" provides access to such data as national home pages, resources by type, and World Wide Web servers in the former Soviet Union. "Directory of Internet Resources by Discipline" supplies sites on government and politics, media and journalism, history, geography, and sociology, and more, while "Directory of Internet Resources by Type" identifies sites for document depositories, interactive databases, listserv discussion groups, commercial vendors, and so forth.

1337. **Reference Guide to Russian Literature.** Neil Cornwell and Nicole Christian, eds. Chicago: Fitzroy Dearborn, 1998. 972p. ISBN 1-884964-10-9.

This is an important publication that begins with a set of thirteen introductory essays examining in survey fashion the various periods, topics, and genres of Russian literature. Following these contributions are insightful and thorough entries dealing with individual writers and individual works. Some 250 authors of creative works who have written in Russian are covered in this way, each entry with a brief biographical overview, bibliography of works arranged by date of publication, identification of critical studies, and essays about the writers and their individual works. Some 300 works are examined through critical essays which, like the essays about authors, are about 1,000 words in length. All entries are signed by the scholars and experts responsible for them.

Library Exorcisms of Stalinism: Russian Writers and the Soviet Past, by Margaret Ziolkowski (Camden House, 1998), is an interesting and useful exposition of the themes and motifs generally associated with Stalinism in novels written since 1953. It begins with a general introduction and is organized into seven major chapters, the first three of which examine the victimizers or despots such as Stalin and Pontius Pilate. The social-scientific establishment is treated in the next two chapters, while the final two chapters examine the conceptual basis of the victims, with emphasis on the Decembrists.

1338. **Women and Writing in Russia and the USSR: A Bibliography of English-Language Sources.** Diane M. Nemec Ignashev and Sarah Krive. New York: Garland, 1992. 328p. (Garland Reference Library of the Humanities, v. 1280). ISBN 0-8240-3647-6.

This work is useful to both researchers and students at all levels as a starting point for acquiring information on Russian women and their literary efforts. English-language works by and about women writers and about Russian and Soviet women in general are cited in four different sections. The first covers primary sources and lists the works by female Russian and Soviet writers; the second segment furnishes listings of biographical and critical sources; supplementary sources are treated in the third section; and the fourth part provides listings of bibliographies. The writings by the women writers are generally belletristic in nature, while the writings about women are issue-oriented and represent societal concerns such as education, health, religion, and ethnicity. Citations are up-to-date and run through 1990. Unfortunately, there is no index.

ARABIC LANGUAGES

1339. **Modern Arabic Literature.** M. M. Badawi, ed. New York: Cambridge University Press, 1992. 571p. ISBN 0-5213-3197-8.

This is a revised and expanded version of a 1987 publication issued through another publisher. It continues to furnish excellent coverage of the authors chosen for their importance and influence on post neo-classical Arabic literature. The emphasis is on twentieth-century writers, with representation from different parts of the Arabic world. There is a highly informative introductory essay furnishing a lucid summary of the highlights and important developments in Arabic literature, after which the material is organized into thirteen chapters. Some bias was reported by one reviewer regarding a possibly Eurocentric attitude toward Arabic literary creativity. There is a selection of critical analyses from a group of sources both Arabic and English in origin. (Arabic works are in English translation.) Specific works are analyzed, including collections and anthologies of poems and stories.

ASIAN LANGUAGES

1340. **Asian Literature in English: A Guide to Information Sources.** George Lincoln Anderson. Detroit: Gale Research, 1981. 336p. (American Literature, English Literature, and World Literatures in English, v. 31). ISBN 0-8103-1362-6.

This is a useful guide to translations into English and to critical studies and histories of the literature written in English. There are nearly 2,225 entries in the annotated bibliography, representing translations from a number of Asian countries (China, Japan, Korea, Burma, Cambodia, Indonesia, Laos, Malaysia, Singapore, Thailand, Vietnam, Mongolia, Tibet, and the Turkic regions of central Asia). Each literature section includes general bibliographies, anthologies, reference works, literary histories, literary forms, individual authors, and critical studies. Indian literature is excluded because it is treated in another volume in this series, *Indian Literature in English, 1827–1979: A Guide to Information Sources*, by Amritjit Singh (Gale Research, 1981). This is a bibliography of creative writing in English and includes works that have been translated from Indian languages by their authors.

1341. **Guide to Japanese Prose.** 2d ed. Alfred H. Marks and Barry D. Bort. Boston: G. K. Hall, 1984. 186p. ISBN 0-8161-8630-8.

Another of the G. K. Hall bibliographies, this work was published initially in 1975 and was acknowledged as a useful source of information focusing on a subject that has not received a great deal of attention from Western writers. The second edition, similar to the earlier issue, identifies literary prose that is available in English translation. A good essay opens the work, examining the historical and literary context. There are two major sections of the work: pre-Meiji literature, which covers the beginnings to 1867, and Meiji literature (1868 to the present).

Also issued by G. K. Hall is Richard J. Lynn's *Guide to Chinese Poetry and Drama* (rev. ed., 1984). First published in 1973, this has proven to be a valuable critical guide to works in English translation for students and interested laypersons.

1342. **The Princeton Companion to Classical Japanese Literature.** Earl Miner et al. Princeton, NJ: Princeton University Press, 1985. 570p. ISBN 0-691-06599-3.

The classical era designated in the title represents the time prior to the Meiji Restoration of 1867–1968, a lengthy and productive term. Within this time span are a number of distinctive literary periods, which are introduced with a brief history at the beginning. Many charts, maps, pictures, and figures help to supplement the narrative. Several chronologies are given, as are descriptions of social groups. There are segments on arts, clothing, housing, and other aspects. A section of major importance to reference work covers important authors and their work, with some biographies achieving essay length. Literary allusions are covered well in the glossary of literary terms.

The Indiana Companion to Traditional Chinese Literature, edited by William H. Nienhauser, Jr. et al. (Indiana University Press, 1986), is divided into two major sections. The first provides a series of ten essays on Buddhist and Taoist literatures and various genres. Part 2 contains over 500 entries on writers, individual works, genres, styles, and so forth. Each entry is accompanied by a bibliography.

1343. **Writers from the South Pacific: A Bio-Bibliographic Critical Encyclopedia.** Norman Sims. Washington, DC: Three Continents Press, 1991. 184p. ISBN 0-89410-594-9.

This is a useful work, treating some 2,000 writers from a geographic region only covered infrequently by sources of this kind. Coverage includes Malaysia and Singapore but excludes the Philippines and Indonesia. As one might expect, there is a diverse collection of ethnic groupings in this region and there is representation from the aboriginals in Australia, the Maori of New Zealand, the Vanatu of the New Hebrides, and native influences of the Wallis and Fortuna Islands. Emphasis is placed on Singapore and Malaysia, which together comprise about a third of the entries, although the entries in many of these cases are spare in terms of the information provided. Coverage runs from a single sentence to more than two pages in length, with the longer entries providing useful insight into the relationship of the writers to their society. An index is provided.

Children's and Young Adult Literature

BIBLIOGRAPHIES AND INDEXES

1344. **Best Books for Junior High Readers.** John T. Gillespie. New Providence, NJ: R. R. Bowker, 1991. 567p. ISBN 0-8352-3020-1.

This is one of three literature guides produced by Gillespie during this time period and provides brief annotated entries to about 5,675 books deemed to be worthy for students in grades seven through nine. Since the work was designed as a practical guide for purposes of selection, availability is an important consideration and all items were in print in 1990. Entries are arranged under broad categories corresponding to discipline or subject area, such as history and music. They are then arranged alphabetically by author under subheadings. Listings are taken from four retrospective bibliographies, including the *Junior High School Library Catalog* (H. W. Wilson, 1990), and are appropriate and well-chosen.

Best Books for Senior High Readers, also by Gillespie (R. R. Bowker, 1991), complements the above effort, identifying over 10,800 titles under sixty-seven major subject categories. These are culled from review journals and standard sources such as *Senior High School Library Catalog* (15th ed., 1997). *Best Books for Children* is the earliest of Gillespie's trilogy and is now in its fifth edition (R. R. Bowker, 1994). It identifies 15,647 titles recommended for grade school youngsters by at least two sources, such as *Children's Catalog* (17th ed., H. W. Wilson, 1996), *School Library Journal*, and *Booklist*.

1345. **The Best in Children's Books: The University of Chicago Guide to Children's Literature, 1985–1990.** Zena Sutherland et al. Chicago: University of Chicago Press, 1991. 492p. ISBN 0-226-78064-3.

Sutherland is a professor emeritus of the university and former editor of its *Bulletin of the Center for Children's Books*. This is the fourth volume in the series, in which earlier issues covered the periods 1966–1972, 1973–1978, and 1979–1984, maintaining the tradition begun by the initial work, *Good Books for Children 1950–1965* (1966). The present volume provides 1,150 reviews selected from those published in the *Bulletin* between 1985 and 1990. Reviews run from 75 to 225 words in length, providing summary and criticism of the fiction and nonfiction selections that are generally suitable for youngsters from preschool to junior high school levels. There is a fine introductory essay by Sutherland describing the importance of book selection for children and identifying the criteria used. Six indexes provide access.

1346. **The Best of Bookfinder: A Guide to Children's Literature About Interests and Concerns of Youth Aged 2–18.** Sharon Spredemann Dreyer. Circle Pines, MN: American Guidance Service, 1992. 451p. ISBN 0-88671-440-0.

Preceded by three earlier volumes, this work has been recognized for its excellent treatment of books suitable to youngsters at different levels of emotional and mental growth. The present effort identifies and describes over 675 books classified under 450 psychological, behavioral, and developmental topics. Many of these works have been culled from the earlier volumes, providing a well-constructed source of available materials. A few items of real value are labeled as out-of-print. It is the intent to provide books that are timely, representative of a universal theme, or are possibly the only work on a subject. Entries supply bibliographic description, primary themes, synopsis, reading level, availability in film, cassette, and so forth. Indexing is by author, title, and subject.

Sensitive Issues: An Annotated Guide to Children's Literature K–6, by Timothy V. Rasinski and Cindy S. Gillespie (Oryx, 1992), is designed especially for use by schools and their personnel involved in whole language programs. It cites juvenile titles treating such social issues as child abuse, cultural differences, death, and disability. Entries identify grade levels and provide annotations along with suggested activities.

1347. **Books by African-American Authors and Illustrators for Children and Young Adults.** Helen E. Williams. Chicago: American Library Association, 1991. 270p. ISBN 0-8389-0570-6.

The author is a librarian and professor of children's literature who has supplied a representative selection of books for young people written and illustrated by black writers and artists. A total of 1,200 titles published between 1900 and 1989 are identified within four chapters. The first three chapters treat books for very young children (picture books, concept books, folk and fairy tales, biographies, etc.); books for intermediate readers (folk literature, mystery, adventure, poetry, fiction and nonfiction for grades five to eight); and books for young adult readers, with more sophisticated works aimed at the senior high school level and above. Entries supply brief annotations describing content and identifying review sources. The fourth chapter treats illustrators and their works; entries describe style and technique of the illustrators and listings of their efforts. A bibliography, an appendix of awards, a glossary, and an index are furnished.

1348. **Children's Book Review Index, Master Cumulation, 1965–1984.** . . . Gary C. Tarbert and Barbara Beach, eds. Detroit: Gale Research, 1985. 5v. ISBN 0-8103-2046-0. 1975– . Ann. ISSN 0147-5681.

This is a twenty-year cumulation of what, in 1975, became an annual publication. It is a convenience tool, listing those materials in **Book Review Index* that are identified as children's books. The subtitle of the cumulation goes on: "a Cumulated Index to More Than 200,000 Reviews of Approximately 55,000 Titles." The work represents a treasure-house of information for those doing retrospective selection for purposes of collection development. It is also of importance to those in reference who are seeking to identify, verify, and locate critical reviews of children's materials for their patrons. The reviews cited have appeared in over 370 periodicals, for which references are provided. Listings are by author, then title. The 1997 annual cumulation furnishes more than 25,000 citations to reviews of thousands of children's books from the previous ten years.

1349. **Fiction, Folklore, Fantasy & Poetry for Children, 1876–1985.** New York: R. R. Bowker, 1986. 2v. ISBN 0-8352-1831-7.

Another of the comprehensive bibliographies produced from the Bowker database, this massive work identifies works of fanciful children's literature by author, title, and illustrator over a period of 110 years. Introductory sections on children's books and a history of the R. R. Bowker company are furnished in volume 1. Author and illustrator indexes follow. Volume 2 contains the title index as well as a section on book awards. Entries furnish author/illustrator dates and pseudonyms as well as title and imprint. The awards section seems to be less successful and has been criticized by reviewers. Newbery and Caldecott award winners are listed with date of publication rather than date of award. The first award winners in each of these categories have been omitted, and there are some misspellings. Despite these faults, the work must be considered a useful convenience tool.

1350. Index to Children's Poetry: A Title, Subject, Author, and First Line Index to Poetry in Collections for Children and Youth. John Edmond Brewton and Sara Westbrook Brewton. New York: H. W. Wilson, 1942. 965p. **Supps.**, 1954, 1965, 1972, 1974, 1984, 1989, 1994, 1998.

The original volume of what became a continuous series, this work indexed 130 collections of poetry for young people published up to the late 1930s. Title, subject, author, and first lines are indexed in a manner similar to that of *Granger's Index* (entry 1267). Over 15,000 poems by 2,500 poets are classified under a variety of subjects. The first supplement to this work appeared in 1954 and indexed over sixty-five collections published between 1938 and 1951. The second supplement was published eleven years later and covered eighty-five collections published between 1949 and 1963.

Index to Poetry for Children and Young People, 1964–1969, by Brewton and G. Meredith Blackburn (H. W. Wilson, 1972), began the series of supplements that placed increased emphasis on books at the seventh- to twelfth-grade levels. This was followed by *Index to Poetry for Children and Young People, 1970–1975*, by Brewton and Blackburn (H. W. Wilson, 1978). The same title and authorship continued with the supplement covering the period 1976–1981 (H. W. Wilson, 1984). Subsequent volumes have been compiled by Blackburn covering the periods 1982–1987 (H. W. Wilson, 1989), 1988–1992 (H. W. Wilson, 1994), and 1993–1997 (H. W. Wilson, 1998). Each of the supplements generally indexes over 100 collections with several thousand poems.

1351. Our Family, Our Friends, Our World: An Annotated Guide to Significant Multicultural Books for Children and Teenagers. Lyn Miller-Lachman. New Providence, NJ: R. R. Bowker, 1992. 710p. ISBN 0-8352-3025-2.

This is an important tool, identifying some 1,000 books published between 1970 and 1990 and useful in providing understanding of multi-cultural elements and diverse ethnic groups all over the world. It is the product of twenty-one contributor-specialists, who bring expertise to the development of the eighteen geographic/ethnic segments into which the work is divided. Included here are the four leading minority groups in the United States—African-Americans, Asian-Americans, Hispanic-Americans, and Native Americans—along with the peoples of Great Britain and Ireland, Sub-Saharan Africa, Eastern Europe and the Soviet Union, and so forth. Introductory essays provide a clear overview to the work itself and to each of the segments. Maps and statistical data are included. Entries follow the introductory passages and are annotated briefly. There is an appendix of professional sources, series titles, and publishers. A detailed general index is supplied.

A useful directory of Web sites is *Multicultural Resources for Children* (http://falcon.jmu.edu/%7Eramseyil/multipub.htm [accessed January 2000]), by the Internet School Library Media Center, which provides links to resources on the World Wide Web. Both general resources and bibliographies are furnished.

1352. Peoples of the American West: Historical Perspectives Through Children's Literature. Mary Hurlbut Cordier and Maria A. Perez-Stable. Metuchen, NJ: Scarecrow Press, 1989. 230p. ISBN 0-8108-2240-7.

This is a highly selective guide to reading for youngsters of all ages, providing historical perspective on the United States west of the Mississippi River from the sixteenth century to the early 1900s. Included here are both imaginative and factual works among the 100 items chosen for inclusion in this annotated bibliography, treating a variety of regional and social settings. Several of the works of Laura Ingalls Wilder and Patricia Beatty are included. Fiction entries are divided into thematic sections on homesteading and settling, overland journeys and major train trips, immigration, Native Americans, American Southwest, and

West Coast. Additionally, there is a nonfiction segment embracing the factual items. Both sections are then subdivided by grade levels K–3 and 4–9. Entries supply geographic location, dates, characterization, half-page synopses, and summaries of strengths and points for class discussion. Readability levels as determined by four formulas are included.

1353. **Portraying Persons with Disabilities: An Annotated Bibliography of Fiction for Children and Teenagers.** 3d ed. Debra E. J. Robertson. New Providence, NJ: R. R. Bowker, 1992. 482p. (Serving Special Needs Series). ISBN 0-8352-3023-6.

This useful guide continues to identify books for youngsters from kindergarten through senior high school chosen to help sensitize them to the problems of people with physical and mental disabilities. Earlier editions were entitled *Notes for a Different Drummer* (1977) and *More Notes for a Different Drummer* (1982). More than 450 books portraying characters with disabilities in realistic fashion are identified in the third edition, including of picture books, suspense novels, adventure novels, historical fiction, and so forth; folklore is excluded. All types of disabilities are embraced (physical, sensory, cognitive, behavioral, etc.). Entries are arranged under category of disability and supply bibliographic data and reading level along with an extensive annotation of plot summary and critical analysis. Additionally, there are well-constructed essays on stereotyping and publication trends in fiction.

A companion effort is *Portraying Persons with Disabilities: An Annotated Bibliography of Nonfiction for Children and Teenagers*, by Joan Brest Friedberg et al. (2d ed., R. R. Bowker, 1992). This tool identifies 300 biographies, case histories, and other sources published between 1980 and 1991.

1354. **The Young Adult Reader's Adviser.** Myra Immell, ed. New Providence, NJ: R. R. Bowker, 1992. 2v. ISBN 0-8352-3068-6.

Based on *The Reader's Adviser* (14th ed. R. R. Bowker, 1994. 6v.), this new tool for reading guidance is designed to help students, teachers, and librarians in their quest for good reading material on subjects and authors. Materials are suitable for youngsters from the middle grades through the high school years and are organized into four topical areas of the curriculum: literature and language arts, mathematics and computer science, social science and history, and science and health. Each segment contains entries on personalities that supply a biographical sketch as well as listings of primary and secondary source material. Along with the personalities, entries also treat major topics and issues, such as adolescence and aging, for which annotated bibliographies are furnished. Serving as both a critical bibliographic guide and a biographical encyclopedia, this work has earned a reputation as an important tool. It is indexed by author, title, and publisher.

An annual listing of value is *Young Adult Annual Booklist*, published by the Los Angeles Public Library since 1983. It identifies some 250 books and supplies reviews from library staff members. Arrangement of entries is under subject categories such as science and literature. Overall evaluations are indicated by symbols.

1355. **Young People's Books in Series: Fiction and Non-Fiction, 1975–1991.** Judith K. Rosenberg and C. Allen Nichols. Englewood, CO: Libraries Unlimited, 1992. 424p. ISBN 0-87287-882-1.

This is an update and expansion of Rosenberg's earlier efforts in the 1970s and supplies listings of series books for children in grades three to twelve. The segment on fiction is arranged alphabetically by author and provides numbers for titles within each series. Treatment in this section is comprehensive, and all series published during the sixteen-year period are included. Listings within each series appear to be complete in cases where the series has been included for the first time. Annotations tend to be brief, providing plot summaries and little more in many instances; age-level recommendations are indicated. The nonfiction segment is organized alphabetically by series title, and entries also supply brief evaluations and age-level recommendations. An index is furnished.

Vicki Anderson's *Fiction Sequels for Readers 10 to 16: An Annotated Bibliography of Books in Succession* (2d ed., McFarland, 1998) identifies some 2,500 titles that are part of a series. This represents an increase of 1,000 titles over the initial edition in 1990. Authors are listed in sequence to identify sequels. Most works were published after 1960; series such as Nancy Drew and the Hardy Boys have been excluded because sequels are distinguished from series by their greater emphasis on character development. Annotations are based on material provided on book jackets, catalog cards, reviews, and the books themselves.

DICTIONARIES, ENCYCLOPEDIAS, AND HANDBOOKS

1356. **Award-Winning Books for Children and Young Adults, 1990–1991.** Betty L. Criscoe and Philip J. Lanasa III. Metuchen, NJ: Scarecrow Press, 1993. ISBN 0-8108-2597-X.

Criscoe authored the initial edition of this guide in 1990, which covered award-winning books for 1989. It was to continue as an annual publication, but policy changes ensued and this second number was issued three years later, covering a two-year period. It would appear that either a biennial or a triennial pattern of frequency is to follow. The title has been received enthusiastically by reviewers, who consider it "a wonderful book for collection development, reading guidance, and research" and "invaluable in selecting the best from a year's publications." Its value is obvious to teachers and school librarians and those public librarians dealing with the needs of children and young adults, providing a valuable selection tool and purchasing guide. Awards are listed, with entries supplying background history of each award along with method and criteria of selecting winners. Winning books are identified and described; a reproduction of the book cover is given. For awards given to personalities, a biographical sketch and listing of credits is provided. Useful appendices include listings of publishers, authors and titles, and genres. Several indexes supply excellent access.

1357. **The Best Children's Books in the World: A Treasury of Illustrated Stories.** Byron Preiss and Kathy Huck, eds. New York: H. N. Abrams, 1996. 319p. ISBN 0-810-91246-5.

This is a well-devised collection that provides a selection of illustrated stories that have been received favorably by children from a variety of cultures from all over the world. All fifteen books included in the anthology were published separately and represent the artistic creativity of interesting and diverse regions: Belgium, Brazil, China, England, Germany, Ghana, Iran, Israel, New Zealand, Norway, Russia, the Slovak Republic, Spain, Sri Lanka, and Switzerland. The work begins with an excellent introductory essay by Jeffrey Garrett, providing insight into and interpretation of "international books." Each story is preceded by an informative introduction describing the author and illustrator; the stories with illustrations have been reproduced, and in most cases are accompanied by original text with English translations in the margins. Most of the stories have not been accessible to American audiences prior to this time.

1358. **The Black American in Books for Children: Readings in Racism.** 2d ed. Donnarae MacCann and Gloria Woodard, eds. Metuchen, NJ: Scarecrow Press, 1985. 298p. ISBN 0-8108-1826-4.

This is a valuable collection of essays for librarians and teachers who work with young people, written by specialists in children's literature, sociology, education, and history. Intellectual freedom is described in many of the essays, all targeted to the presentation of the black experience in literature for children. Titles such as *Sounder* and *Dr. Doolittle* are described and analyzed and trends are explained. Both illustrations and picture books are treated as well. Originally published in 1972, the second edition provides information helpful for establishing an informed perspective on the portrayal of the black experience. This work is extremely useful as a resource tool for courses in book selection and acquisitions.

1359. Characters in Young Adult Literature. John T. Gillespie and Corinne J. Naden. Detroit: Gale Research, 1997. 535p. ISBN 0-7876-0401-1.

This is a comprehensive guide to young adult literature, treating over 2,000 characters drawn from 232 works by 148 authors. Much information is given—birth and death dates of authors, genre, publication date, and listing of critiques—and sequels and series are identified. Plot summaries are provided for each title along with good characterization, providing a strong resource for study and analysis. An excellent and diverse array of authors embraces all styles and various genres and includes Verne, Conan Doyle, and Alcott along with Asimov and Tolkien. Contemporary favorites such as Ann Rice, Amy Tan, and Toni Morrison are also examined. There are numerous illustrations; an index of characters and titles provides access.

Characters from Young Adult Literature, by Mary E. Snodgrass (Libraries Unlimited, 1991) is a more compact publication but still treats hundreds of characters, both major and minor, from seventy-one works of fiction, drama, biography, and nonfiction dating from the sixteenth to the twentieth centuries. The works are listed alphabetically by title and all are English-language writings that have been popular with this age group and may have been included within school curricula. Entries furnish date of work, author's name and dates, genre, setting, and a brief plot synopsis. Characters are then described in terms of their gender, age, social circumstances, and nature. More extensive treatment is given to the major characters, but the reader is apprised of the role and situation of even the minor players. The introductory material regarding the characters is a welcome touch. An index is provided.

1360. Children's Literature Awards and Winners: A Directory of Prizes, Authors, and Illustrators. 3d ed. Dolores Blythe Jones. Detroit: Neal-Schuman/Gale Research, 1994. 678p. ISBN 0-8103-6900-1.

This is a revision and update of the 1988 edition, which was an expansion of the initial effort in 1983. About 7,000 prize-winning authors and illustrators are identified along with 5,000 books. Arrangement is in three parts, with part 1 being an alphabetical list of awards presented to works of children's literature by organizations in the United States and abroad. Entries include name of award, address, founder, history, criteria, purpose, time of presentation, and full citations to all award winners and runners-up, in chronological sequence. The second part furnishes an alphabetical arrangement of authors and illustrators, with indication of their books and the awards they won. Finally, there is a bibliography of source materials on children's literary awards.

Another useful tool is *Children's Books: Awards & Prizes, Includes Prizes and Awards for Young Adult Books* (10th ed., Children's Book Council, 1996). This guide groups the entries (awards) into four categories: U.S. awards selected by adults; U.S. awards selected by children; Australian, Canadian, New Zealand, and U.K. awards; and international and multinational awards. Entries describe the awards briefly and furnish listings of winners in chronological order. There is an award classification section that provides "subject" access, as well as a title index and a person index.

1361. Dictionary of American Children's Fiction, 1859–1959: Books of Recognized Merit. Alethea K. Helbig and Agnes Regan Perkins. Westport, CT: Greenwood, 1985. 666p. ISBN 0-313-22590-7. **Supp. 1960–1984**, 1986. 914p. **Supp. 1985–1989**, 1993. 368p. **Supp. 1990–1994**, 1996. 473p.

This is an interesting and useful tool that provides historical information on award-winning books of children's fiction covering a period of 100 years. Entries are listed alphabetically by title, with related entries for authors and for significant characters. Settings are also included in the index when important. Title entries furnish basic bibliographic data as well as an informative synopsis of the work and references to specific awards received. Cross-references are also provided. Most valuable is a detailed subject approach in the index, which identifies numerous specific subjects or topics relevant to the listed works. The index also provides access by age of protagonist, time period, and ethnic customs.

The work is continued by the two authors with publication of *Dictionary of American Children's Fiction, 1960–1984: Recent Books of Recognized Merit* (Greenwood, 1986). It identifies an additional 489 meritorious books written during that time period. The format remains the same with publication of *Dictionary of American Children's Fiction, 1985–1989: Books of Recognized Merit* (Greenwood, 1993), the first of what is projected to be a series of five-year supplements. It reveals 134 award-winning and significant books. *Dictionary of American Children's Fiction, 1990–1994: Books of Recognized Merit* by Alethea K. Helbig (Greenwood, 1996) continues the tradition in the same manner, treating 189 books by 136 authors.

1362. **Masterplots II. Juvenile and Young Adult Fiction Series.** Pasadena, CA: Salem Press, 1991. 4v. ISBN 0-89356-579-2. **Supp., 1997.** 3v. ISBN 0-89356-919-4 (v.3).

As part of Magill's *Masterplots II* series (entry 1095) this set provides a focus on fiction of interest to youngsters from the middle grades through high school. Picture books are excluded in its treatment of nearly 550 titles, all alphabetically arranged for easy access. Variety of selection is apparent, with inclusion of such general classics with appeal to youngsters as *Animal Farm* and *The Count of Monte Cristo* as well as popular children's works like *The Chocolate War*. Nearly 450 of the selections are new to the series and about 100 titles have been included in other sets. The entries have been completely rewritten and updated. Entries generally supply brief header information identifying dates, settings, principal themes, and recommended ages, along with plot synopsis and exposition of the story, themes and meanings, and context. Author, title and subject indexes are in volume 4. A three-volume supplement was published in 1997 as *Masterplots II: Juvenile and Young Adult Literature Series*, which continues both the fiction series as well as *Masterplots II. Juvenile and Young Adult Biography Series*. It includes poetry, drama, and short story collections as well as art, history, sociology, and science.

1363. **Newbery and Caldecott Medalists and Honor Book Winners: Bibliographies and Resource Material Through 1991.** 2d ed. Muriel Brown et al., comps. New York: Neal-Schuman, 1992. 511p. ISBN 1-55570-118-3.

Somewhat of a cross between a bibliography and a handbook is this interesting compilation of material on the Newbery and Caldecott medalists and Honor Book winners. A good introduction describes the medals. This is followed by the main listing of award winners—authors and illustrators—alphabetically arranged with dates provided. Listed for each illustrator and author are their award-winning books and other works. Also included are indications of media formats developed from their works, library collections, exhibitions, and additional readings. The time span covered is from the beginning of their careers to 1992.

A companion title is *Newbery and Caldecott Medal and Honor Books in Other Media*, compiled by Paulette B. Sharkey and Jim Roginski (Neal-Schuman, 1992). Listings of media publications based upon the award-winning books include audio, film, filmstrip, software, television, video, and so forth. There is a useful directory of producers and distributors and a good bibliography of resources. Another useful work is *The Newbery and Caldecott Awards: A Guide to the Medal and Honor Books*, issued annually by the American Library Association.

The 1999 volume contains annotations along with excellent essays on the history and terms of the awards. There is a listing of the media used in each of the award-winners and honor books. There are author/illustrator and title indexes. Worth noting are the Web sites maintained by the Association for Library Service to Children (ALSC) of the American Library Association on both the Newbery Medal (http://www.ala.org/alsc/newbery.html [accessed January 2000]) and the Caldecott Medal (http://www.ala.org/alsc/caldecott.html [accessed January 2000]), in which one can find descriptions of the current winners and honor books, lists of past winners, and history.

1364. **The Oxford Companion to Children's Literature.** Humphrey Carpenter and Mari Prichard. New York: Oxford University Press, 1999; 587p. ISBN 0-19860-226-6.

The authors are a husband and wife team working in much the same manner as Iona Opie and Peter Opie did in developing their *Oxford Dictionary of Nursery Rhymes* (entry 1365). This work covers children's literature on a broad scale and in a comprehensive manner, covering literature in all languages and countries where information could be found. There are approximately 2,000 entries in all, of which 900 are biographical sketches. Summaries are given for hundreds of children's titles and various topics, most of which are timely and of importance, such as "television and children." Articles vary in length in proportion to the importance of the topic, with lengthy descriptions given to Lewis Carroll and *Alice in Wonderland*. The work is used frequently by those writers whose interests parallel the topical coverage. This work represents an updated version of the 1984 edition.

1365. **The Oxford Dictionary of Nursery Rhymes.** New ed. Iona Opie and Peter Opie, eds. New York: Oxford University Press, 1997. 559p. ISBN 0-19-860088-7.

Working together, this husband and wife team had produced the most comprehensive and authoritative work ever developed on the English nursery rhyme in 1951. Since then it had been reprinted with corrections on several occasions. Now the Opies have given us a brand new edition, representing their fifty years of research and effort in the field. Some 550 nursery rhymes, songs, jingles, and lullabies are identified and described. All of them are in current use or have been used in the recent past. Annotations are excellent and provide information regarding earliest publication, origin, and changes in wording over the years. The arrangement is alphabetical by the most significant word; when nonsense language is employed, the entry is listed under the opening phrase. The work is well illustrated with reproductions from many of the early published works. Two indexes are given, the first of notable individuals associated with the nursery rhyme. There is also an index of first lines of both standard and original versions.

BIOGRAPHICAL AND CRITICAL SOURCES

1366. **American Writers for Children Since 1960: Fiction.** Glenn E. Estes, ed. Detroit: Gale Research, 1986. 488p. (Dictionary of Literary Biography, v. 52). ISBN 0-8103-1730-3.

This is one of the publications in the *Dictionary of Literary Biography* series (entry 1087). Like other volumes in the series, this one covers individuals determined to be influential in their genre. Nearly forty-five authors of children's fiction who have been productive since 1960 are included, thus providing useful information on some of the contemporary realistic writers. The coverage is of high quality, with well-developed entries providing good biocritical essays and furnishing career chronologies, publications lists, and bibliographies of works by and about the subject. Individuals represent the entire realm of children's fiction popular during this time in realism, historical fiction, fantasy, and so forth. Included are Judy Blume, Robert Cormier, Paul Zindel, and Katherine Paterson.

A more recent and more specialized effort is *Science Fiction for Young Readers*, edited by C. W. Sullivan (Greenwood, 1993), providing a collection of well-developed essays on a full range of topics relevant to science fiction for youthful readers. Leading writers such as Asimov and Heinlein are examined in terms of their contributions and particular titles and series are analyzed.

1367. **Biographical Index to Children's and Young Adult Authors and Illustrators.** David V. Loertscher. Castle Rock, CO: Hi Willow Research & Publishing, 1993. 320p. ISBN 0-931510-47-3.

This easy-to-use, comprehensive tool now indexes over 13,000 writers, illustrators, poets, filmmakers, and cartoonists covered in both collective and single biographies. This represents an increase of 6,000 personalities over the number treated in the 1992 edition. Individuals are from all over the world and are linked to biographical sketches appearing in more than 1,500 biographical works, both print and audiovisual. The initial edition (1992) grew out of an earlier publication designed as a state-by-state guide and limited to U.S. authors. Entries supply name, dates, country or state, and citations. The strength of this work lies in its extensive listing not only of children's and young adults' authors, but also of authors for adults whose works have appealed to high school students.

1368. **Black Authors & Illustrators of Children's Books: A Biographical Dictionary.** 2d ed. Barbara Rollock. New York: Garland, 1992. (Garland Reference Library of the Humanities, v. 1316). ISBN 0-8240-7078-X.

Rollock is retired head of children's services at New York Public Library. In 1988 she published the initial edition of this work, treating the lives and careers of 115 writers and illustrators. Since that time the contributions of black authors and illustrators have continued in a fashion commensurate with the nation's increased sensitivity to its multi-cultural composition. The new edition has added thirty-five new authors and has updated and revised the original entries, providing biographical treatment of 150 writers and illustrators of children's books that have been published in the United States between 1930 and 1990. Biographees are from the United States, Africa, the Caribbean, Britain, and France and provide an array of life-view perspectives important to the intellectual development of youngsters. There is a good introductory essay along with appendices containing award winners and listings of series.

Bookpeople: A Multicultural Album, by Sharron L. McElmeel (Libraries Unlimited, 1992), provides a selective treatment of fifteen authors and illustrators who either are members of a minority culture or have produced books about them. Entries supply biographical sketches, photographs, and description of their works. There are suggestions to teachers and media specialists that include discussion questions along with identification of related books by other authors.

1369. **Children's Literature Review. Excerpts from Reviews, Criticism, and Commentary on Books for Children and Young People.** Detroit: Gale Research, 1976– . Irreg. ISSN 0362-4145.

Another of the Gale efforts, this work has built a following, although the frequency of publication has been sporadic. Volumes 9–11 were issued during 1985–1986, which marked a period of increased activity. Since then publication has been steady, with volume 54 produced in 1999. Each volume contains excerpts from criticism and reviews published in books and periodicals on the writings of a dozen or so children's authors from all over the world, both past and present. Each author is treated in a separate section of the work, the entry beginning with a description of the writer's literary background and style along with a photograph. In some cases, there is an author's commentary permitting the writer to reflect on his or her own work. A general commentary by a reviewer is followed by the extracts of reviews of individual titles. There is a cumulative title index for the various volumes, along with those of authors and of nationality.

1370. **Homosexual Characters in YA Novels: A Literary Analysis, 1969–1982.** Allan A. Cuseo. Metuchen, NJ: Scarecrow Press, 1992. 516p. ISBN 0-8108-2537-6.

Cuseo initially began his literary investigation of the depiction of homosexuality in novels for young adults while working on his doctorate at Columbia University. This tool provides an analysis of sixty-nine realistic novels published between 1969 and 1982. In assessing their literary quality, the treatment given to their homosexual characters is examined in terms of the degree of realism and possible negativity or stereotyping present. This represents an earnest effort to determine whether such realistic literature in effect promotes myths about the gay/lesbian experience. Various elements are examined, such as the language, setting, image, violence, cultural diversity, relationships, and roles, with interpretation based on quotes from the literature. For this period, it was found that authors did indeed buy into a socially prejudiced view of homosexuality through their representation of stereotypes in these "realistic" novels.

1371. **The Junior Book of Authors.** 2d ed. rev. Stanley Jasspon Kunitz and Howard Haycraft. New York: H. W. Wilson, 1951; repr., 1991. 310p. ISBN 0-8242-0021-7; 0-8242-0777-7 (Sixth).

The second edition of this work by Kunitz and Haycraft furnishes biographical sketches of nearly 270 writers and illustrators, 160 of them repeated with revisions from the first edition in 1934. Of the 108 names deleted, most are of classic stature and are covered in other Wilson publications (entry 1101). This work marked the beginning of another series, since it was supplemented by Muriel Fuller's *More Junior Authors* (H. W. Wilson, 1963), which provided 268 biographical sketches of authors and illustrators. *Third Book of Junior Authors & Illustrators*, edited by Doris De Montreville and Donna Hill (H. W. Wilson, 1972), continues the coverage with over 200 biographical sketches, as does the *Fourth Book of Junior Authors and Illustrators*, edited by De Montreville and Elizabeth D. Crawford (H. W. Wilson, 1978). The most recent issues have been Sally Holtze's *Fifth Book of Junior Authors & Illustrators* (H. W. Wilson, 1983), treating nearly 240 individuals who "have come to prominence since 1978"; her *Sixth Book of Junior Authors & Illustrators* (H. W. Wilson, 1989), examining the contributions of another 250 personalities; and her *Seventh Book of Junior Authors & Illustrators* (H. W. Wilson, 1996), adding another 235. There is a cumulative index to all volumes in the back of each one.

Geared to the interests and needs of the middle school is *Junior DISCovering Authors*, a CD-ROM product first issued in 1994, and again in 1997, similar to the *DISCovering Authors* version treating writers for adults (entry 1088). Coverage is given to over 450 of the most popular and widely read English-language authors of books for children and young adults. Both past and present authors are included, with in-depth information along the same lines as the work above.

1372. **St. James Guide to Children's Writers.** 5th ed. Sara Pendergast and Tom Pendergast, eds. Detroit: St. James Press, 1999. 1406p. ISBN 1-55862-369-8.

First published in 1978, then revised in 1983, 1989, and again in 1995 as *Twentieth Century Guide to Children's Writers*, this work remains a useful source of information on modern children's writers of fiction, drama, and poetry. This edition, like its immediate predecessor, focuses on authors of books for children age ten and under, in contrast to the initial inclusion of authors suitable to young adults. The limited coverage embraces more than 700 writers as compared to more than 800 in the third edition, and the work now serves to complement the more recently conceived *St. James Guide to Young Adult Writers* (entry 1373). Of that total, seventy-five appear for the first time. Authors are selected carefully for inclusion. Entries are arranged alphabetically and treated with a short biography, a bibliography of published writings, and an informative critical essay by an expert of about one page in length. The essay treats their works and their significance. Locations of manuscripts are provided and references to critical studies are given. Emphasis is still on twentieth-century writers. A listing is provided of foreign-language writers of prominence. There is a title index that includes the author's name and year of publication.

1373. St. James Guide to Young Adult Writers. 2d ed. Sara Pendergast and Tom Pendergast, eds. Detroit: St. James Press, 1999. 1041p. ISBN 1-55862-368-X.

First published in 1994 as *Twentieth Century Young Adult Writers*, edited by Laura S. Berger, it continues to serve as the companion work to what is now the *St. James Guide to Children's Writers* (entry 1372), treating authors of books for older youngsters, ages eleven to nineteen. Format, coverage, and treatment are similar to the original effort in its presentation of 406 entries that include novelists, poets, and dramatists. A good range of popularity and acclaim is represented with such important writers as Robert Cormier, S. E. Hinton, William Golding, and Sylvia Plath, as well as Chris Crutcher and Anne Frank. Like others in the St. James series, it provides for each author a biographical sketch, bibliography of published works, and critical essay by an expert in the field. The writer's statement is furnished when available.

An interesting and useful Web site for librarians, teachers, and writers is *The Society of Children's Book Writers* (http://www.scbwi.org/ [accessed January 2000]), by an organization that serves the needs of people who write, illustrate, or promote children's literature. The site offers information about publishing for children, including grants, awards, and publications as well as upcoming events and activities.

1374. Something About the Author: Facts and Pictures About Authors and Illustrators of Books for Young People. Anne Commire, ed. Detroit: Gale Research, 1971– . ISSN 0276-816X.

Since 1971, this has been a prolific series, with ninety-two volumes published through 1997. Each of the volumes provides illustrated biographies of between 100 and 125 juvenile and young adult illustrators and authors. Both well-known and less-popular individuals are treated, with several writers selected for lengthy treatment and the rest receiving brief entries. Emphasis is on contemporary writing, with some 9,000 authors treated thus far. Primarily written for the youngster to read, the articles are lucid and well-developed stylistically, and contain complete name and pseudonyms, date of birth, career information including awards, titles of works, publication dates, and indication of genre. Numerous illustrations are reproduced from the works. Descriptions are noncritical, similar to the series from the Wilson Company (entry 1101). There is a two-part cumulative index in each volume, along with an illustrations index identifying volumes where art work is furnished, and the author index. Obituaries are included. The series is now edited by Donna Olendorf and Diane Telgen.

Something About the Author Autobiography Series, edited by Joyce Nakamura, began in 1986 and furnishes biographical sketches and commentary from the authors themselves. Treatment may include important events in their lives, sources of inspiration, and exposition of their style and method of writing. Each writer has been covered in *Something About the Author* prior to being selected for inclusion here. Volume 26 is to be issued in 1998, with coverage of about twenty authors per volume. *Major Authors and Illustrators for Children and Young*

Adults, edited by Nakamura and Laurie Collier (Gale Research, 1993), is a six-volume selection of updated entries initially appearing in *Something About the Author*. Intended for the small library, it supplies biographical sketches and bibliographies of the most popular and widely read authors. Emphasis is on the contemporary writers, but there is a good selection of those of classical importance. A supplementary volume was edited by Nakamura and Alan Hedblad (Gale Research, 1998). *Children's Authors and Illustrators: An Index to Biographical Dictionaries*, also edited by Nakamura, is now in its fifth edition (Gale Research, 1995). It is a comprehensive source identifying some 200,000 biographies of 30,000 individuals appearing in 650 biographical dictionaries.

AUTHOR/TITLE INDEX

Each item (book, serial, or database) that has been given a separate entry has also been given an item number. These numbers run consecutively from the beginning of the first sources chapter (chapter 2) through the final sources chapter (chapter 12). This index generally refers to item entry numbers, not to page numbers. Additional sources mentioned in the annotations to the main entries are considered to be either co-entries or minor entries and are indexed with the letter "n" following the entry number. Authors and titles identified or described in the access chapters are indexed by page numbers (preceded by "p" and in parentheses).

The following guidelines were used in alphabetizing index entries. Articles that occur at the beginning of titles have been omitted in the index. Lengthy titles have been shortened in cases where this could be done without ambiguity. Entries have been arranged in accordance with the word-by-word or "nothing before something" method of filing. Names beginning with "Mc" or "Mac" are treated as spelled; those with prefixes such as de or De are generally treated as a single word. Acronyms and initialisms such as UNESCO or LLBA are treated as single words. Numbers (including dates), when part of the title, are arranged as though written in word form except when they are part of a sequence or series. In such cases, the titles in the sequence are listed in numerical order from lowest to highest. Finally, all sources available online or in CD-ROM format are marked with an asterisk (*).

AB Bookman's Weekly, (p. 150, 253)
ABC of Stage Lighting, 898n
ABCs of Worship, 154n
ABELL: Annual Bibliography of English Language and Literature, (p. 393–394)
Abernethy, Peter L., 1253n
Abingdon Dictionary of Living Religions, 139, 142n, 153n
Abingdon's Strong's Exhaustive Concordance, 255n
Abraham, Gerald, 691n
Abrams, Meyer H., 1074
Abramson, Doris E., 867n
Abreu, Maria I., 1319
Abstracting, Information Retrieval and the Humanities, (p. 6)
Abstracts of English Studies, 1150
*Academy of American Poets, 1266n
Accardi, Bernard, 291
Achebe, Chinua, 1240n
ACLS Newsletter, (p. 154)
Achtemeier, Paul J., 263
Acquistions and Collection Development in the Humanities, (p. 11, 68)
Acquisitions Librarian, (p. 68)
Acronyms, Initialisms, and Abbreviations Dictionary, 1019n

Action Art: A Bibliography, 314
Adams, Charles J., 100n
*ADEC 99/Art Price Annual & Falk's Art Price Index, 345
Adelman, Irving, 1241n
Adkins, Cecil D., 621
ADRIS Newsletter, (p. 72)
Adshead-Lansdale, Janet, 819
Advisory CAA Reviews, (p. 155)
A F Encyclopedia of Textiles, 582n
Africa, 664n
African American...
    Films through 1959, 908
    Writers, 1175n
African Art, 405
African Horizons, 1240n
African Music...
    A Bibliographical Guide, 618n
    A Pan-African Annotated Bibliography, 618
African Novel in English, 1240
Afro-American Artists, 384n
Afro-American Fiction, 1853–1976, 1216
Afro-American Novel, 1965–1975, 1219n
Afro-American Short Story, 1219
AFVA Bulletin, (p. 257)
AFVA Evaluations, (p. 257)
Age of Beethoven, 1790–1830, 691n

Age of Enlightenment, 1745–1790, 691n
Age of Humanism, 1540–1630, 691n
Aharoni, Yohanan, 284
Aidoo, Ama Atta, 1240n
ALA Index ... to General Literature, 23n
ALA Yearbook of Library and Information
    Services, (p. 149)
Albert, George, 766
Albert, Walter, 1120
Alderson, Anthony D., 1043n
Alexander, Dey, 39
Alexander, Harriet S., 1279
Alexander, Pat, 144
al Faruqi, Isma'il R., 223, 226
al Faruqi, Lois I., 223
Ali, Ahmed, 240
Ali, Wijdan, 411n
*All Media Guide (AMG), 763n
All Music Guide (AMG), 761n
All Music Guide to...
    Country, 763
    Electronic music, 763n
    Jazz, 763n
    Rock, 763n
    the Blues, 763n
Allan, Elkan, 935
Allegemeines Lexikon der bildenden kunstler...,
    383
    des XX Jahrhunderts, 383n
Allen, Beverly J., 810
Allen, Charles G., 1005
Allen, Daniel, 694n
Allen, Nancy, (p. 4, 30, 150, 249, 393)
Allen, R. E., 1034n
Allensworth, Carl, 896n
Alles, Gregory D., 145n
Allis, James B., 52
Allison, Joseph D., 244n
Alpher, Joseph, 81n
Alston, R. C., (p. 7)
Alt, Marth S., (p. 67)
Altick, Richard D., 1051
Alvarez, Max J., 984n
America Preserved, 485
American and British Poetry, 1279
American Architects...
    Directory, 484n
    from the Civil War to the First World War, 489
American Archivist, (p. 7, 394)
American Art...
    Annual, 371n, 399n–400n, 507
    Directory, 371, (p. 155)
    Galleries, 372
American Artists
    Materials Suppliers Directory, 373
    Signatures and Monograms, 352
American Bibliography, 1060n
*American Book Publishing Record, 1225n
American Catholic Philosophical Quarterly, (p. 38)

American Choral Music Since 1920, 645
*American Classical Music Hall of Fame, 696n
American Costume, 1915–1970, 586
American Council of Learned Societies, (p. 7–8)
American Cultural Leaders, 29n
American Dance Band Discography, 769n
American Dancer, 812n
American Decorative Arts and Old World Influ-
    ences, 530
American Drama Criticism, 887
American Drawing, 421
American Evangelicalism..., 112
    II, 112n
American Fiction...
    1774–1850, 1220
    1851–1875, 1220n
    1876–1900, 1220n
    1900–1950, 1220n
    1901–1925, 1220n
American Film..., (p. 257)
    Cycles, 910
American Film Industry, 923
American Film Institute Catalog of Motion
    Pictures, 909
American Furniture Craftsmen Working Prior to
    1920, 556
American Furniture, 1620 to the Present, 557
American Graphic Design, 531
American Heritage...
    College Dictionary, 1016
    Dictionary, 1035n
    *Dictionary of the English Language, 1009,
        1035n
    Illustrated Encyclopedic Dictionary, 1016n
    Larousse Spanish Dictionary, 1036n
    Spanish Dictionary, 1036
American History, American Television, 972n
American Humanities Index, 19
American Indian Literatures, 1138
American Institute of Architects, 488
American Jewish Bibliography, 123n
American Jewish Yearbook, 197
American Language, 1048–1049n
American Library Directory, 13n
American Literary Magazines...
    The Eighteenth and Nineteenth Centuries, 1205
    The Twentieth Century, 1205n
American Magazine Journalists...
    1741–1850, 1173
    1850–1900, 1173n
    1900–1960, First Series, 1173n
    1900–1960, Second Series, 1173n
*American Museum of Photography, 515n
American Music...
    Before 1865 in Print and on Records, 634
    Librarianship, (p. 251)
    *Resource (AMR), 610n
    Studies, 611n
American Musical Theatre, 774, 833n

American Musicians: Fifty-Six Portraits in Jazz, 752
American National Biography, 28
American Novel, 1241n
American Oratorios and Cantatas, 646
American Painting, 421n, 456n
American Paintings: A Catalogue, 426
American Paintings in the Metropolitan Museum of Art, 426
American Photographers, 525
American Poetry Index, 1271n
American Poets...
    1880–1945, 1280
    Since World War II, 1280n
American Popular...
    Culture, 1
    Illustration, 422
American Premium Record Guide, 770
American Prints in the Library of Congress, 427
American Prose & Criticism...
    1820–1900, 1134
    1900–1950, 1134n
American Reference Books Annual (ARBA), 2, 60n
American Reformers, 1101n
American Renaissance in New England, 1087n
American Revised Version, 233
American Sculpture, 496
American Short-Fiction Criticism and Scholarship, 1241
American Short-Story Writers...
    Before 1880, 1242n
    1880–1910, 1242n
    1910–1945: First Series, 1242n
    1910–1945: Second Series, 1242
    Since World War II, 1242n
American Silversmiths and Their Marks, 561
American Song, 774n
American Songwriters, 753n
American Standard Version, 233, 241n, 265n
American Theater and Drama Research, 822
American Theatre...
    A Chronicle, 873
    Companies...
        1749–1887, 874
        1888–1930, 874n
        1931–1986, 874n
    History, 826
American Theatrical Periodicals, 1789–1967, 824–825n
American Theological Library Association Proceedings, (p. 71)
*American Variety Stage, 598n
American Visions, 406
American Women...
    Artists, Past and Present, 402n
    Playwrights, 1900–1930, 830
    Songwriters, 753

Writers...
    A Critical Reference Guide, 1174
    Bibliographical Essays, 1139
American Writers...
    A Collection of Literary Biographies, 1175–1176n
    Before 1800, 1176
    for Children Since 1960, 1366
Ames, Kenneth L., 1078
*AMG All Media Guide, 763n
Amos, William, 1078
An Leabharlaan, (p. 150)
Analytical Concordance to the...
    Bible, 256
    Revised Standard Version, 251n
Anatomy of Wonder, 1218n
*Anchor Bible Dictionary, 257
Ancient and Oriental Music, 691n
Ancient Writers, 1296
Anderson, Emily A., 1264n
Anderson, George L., 1340
Anderson, Jack, 818
Anderson, Ruth E., 718
Anderson, Vicki, 1355
Andrew, Geoff, 963
Andrew, H. E. Laye, 535
Andrews, Frank, 663
Andrews, William L., 1165
Angeles, Peter A., 62n
Angels A to Z, 138
Ann, Martha, 307n
Annals of...
    American Literature 1602–1983, 1206
    English Literature 1475–1950, 1206n–1207, 1212n
    Opera...
        1597–1940, 699
        1940–1981, 699n
    the Metropolitan Opera Guild, 705n
    the New York Stage, 875, 882n
Annotated Bibliography of Canada's Major Authors, 1140
Annual Bibliography...
    of English Language and Literature, 995n, 1151, 1156n
    *of Modern Art, 325
    of Victorian Studies, 1152
Annual Index to Poetry in Periodicals, 1271n
Annual Obituary, 29
Annual Survey of American Poetry, 1271n
Answers to Questions About Old Jewelry, 562
Anthologies of Music, 635
Antiques Directory of Furniture, 558
APA Bulletin, (p. 37)
Apel, Willi, 672n
Apostolos-Cappadona, Diane, 362
Appel, Marsha C., 340n
Applause, New York's Guide to the Performing Arts, 812n

Applied and Decorative Arts, 532
Apuntes para una biblioteca de escritoras, espanolas, 1325n
Arav, Rami, 171n
Archer, John, 468
Architect's Handbook of Professional Practice, 479n
Architectural Keywords, 470n
*Architectural Periodicals Index, 470, (p. 153)
*Architectural Publications Index, 470n
Architecture: A Bibliographic Guide, 461
Architecture Book Catalog, (p. 153)
Architecture Library of the Future, (p. 152–153)
Architecture on Screen, 466n
*Architecture Resource Directory, 463n
Architecture Sourcebook, 462, 465n
*Archives of American Art, 319n, 351n, 374
Arco Encyclopedia of Crafts, 535
Argentine Literature, 1322
Ariail, Julius, 53n
ARIST, (p. 6, 35, 152, 394)
ARL, (p. 7)
ARLIS/NA Occasional Papers, (p. 151)
Armah, Ayi Kweh, 1240n
Armstrong, Arthur H., 95n
Armstrong, C. J., 11
Arnold, Ben, 637n
Arnold, C. Richard, 655
Arnold, Denis, 673
Arnason, H. H., 415
Aronson, Joseph, 560
Aros, Andrew, 930n
Ars Nova and the Renaissance, 1300–1540, 691n
ARSC Bulletin, (p. 256)
ARSC Journal, (p. 256)
Art: A History of Painting, Sculpture, Architecture, 407
*Art Abstracts, 326n
Art and...
    *Archaeology Technical Abstracts, 329n
    Architecture in Canada, 315
    Life in Renaissance Venice, 408
Art at Auction...
    in America, 346
    the Year at Sotheby's, 346n, 350n
Art Books, 316
Art Bulletin, (p. 155)
Art Deco Style, 537n
Art, Design, Photo, 327n
Art Directors in Cinema, 960
Art Documentation, (p. 150–152, 154–155)
Art Education, (p. 155)
Art in...
    America Annual, 371n
    China, 409
*Art Index, 326, 332n, (p. 153)
Art Information...
    On the Internet, (p. 154)
    Research Methods and Resources, (p. 156)

Art Journal, (p. 155)
Art Libraries Journal, (p. 150–152, 155)
Art Murphy's Box Office Register, 959n
Art Museums of the World, 379n
Art of...
    *Africa, 318
    Art History, 363n
    Literary Research, 1051
    the Mediterranean World, 408n
Art on...
    *Film Database, 375n
    Screen, 323n, 375
Art Price...
    Annual, 345n
    Indicator, 345n
Art Prices Current, 345n
Art Research Methods and Resources, 308, (p. 149)
*Art Sales Index, 347
*ARTbibliographies MODERN..., 327
    *on DISC, 327n
ArtMARC Sourcebook, (p. 151)
Arthurian Yearbook, 1164n
Articles on Women Writers, 1141
    Volume 2 1976–1984, 1141n
Artist Biographies Master Index, 384
Artist Monograms and Indiscernible Signatures, 353
Artist's & Graphic Designer's Market 2000, 376
Artists' and Writers Colonies, 17
Artists as Illustrators, 446
Artists File (New York Public Library), 338n
Artist's Handbook of Materials and Techniques, 354
Artist's Market, 548n
Artists' Monograms and Indiscernible Signatures, 353
Artists of...
    American Folk Music, 756n
    the American West, 385
Arts & Humanities...
    *Citation Index, 19n–20, (p. 31)
    *on CD-ROM, 20n
    *Search, 20n
Arts in America, 317
Arts of...
    Africa, 318
    China, 409n
Artwords, 355
Ash, Lee, 13, (p. 10, 27–28, 39, 73, 156
Asheim, Lester, (p. 2, 30, 65, 67, 73, 149, 249, 251)
Ashelford, Jane, 593n
Asher, R. E., 1001
Ashley, Mike, 1218
Asian Literature in English, 1340
Astrology Encyclopedia, 193n
Ataya, Aziz S., 161
Atkinson, Rose, (p. 4)
*ATLA Religion Database, 135n

*ATLA Site Index, 135n
Atlas of European Architecture, 474
Attitudes and Arabesques, 815n
Attwater, Donald, 210
Aubert, Roger, 225n
Audi, Robert, 59
Audiovisual Librarian, (p. 154)
Auer, Michael, 527
Auer, Michele, 527
Augarde, Tony, 1114n
Austin, William W., 691n
Australian Academic and Research Libraries, (p. 253)
Australian Library Journal, (p. 67)
Australian Universities Review, (p. 10)
Author Biographies Master Index, 1080
Author Newsletters and Journals, 1056n
Authorized Version. *See* King James Version
Autobiography Series, 1083n
Automated Reasoning, (p. 36)
*Avery Index to Architectural Periodicals, 471, 490n
Avery Obituary Index of Architects and Artists, 490n
Avi-Yonah, Michael, 284
Award-Winning Books for Children and Young Adults, 1356
Ayer, A. J., 71n
Ayer Directory of Publications, 6n
Ayers, Michael, 95n
Ayre, Leslie, 778
Ayto, John, 1032

Back Stage, 854n
Backlund, David, (p. 151)
Bacon's Radio/TV Directory, 957n
Badawi, Muhammad M., 1339
Baechler, Lea, 1175n
Bahm, Archie J., 88
Bailey, Claudia J., 823
Bailey, Lloyd R., 248
Baillie, Laureen, 638
Bain, Robert, 1184, 1245
Baird, Donald, 1253
Baker, David, (p. 254)
Baker, Nancy L., 1137
Baker's Biographical Dictionary of...
    Musicians, 682, 684n, 690n, 717n, 723n
    Twentieth Century Classical Musicians, 682n
Baker's Dictionary of...
    Music, 675n
    Opera, 703n
Bakish, David, 1216
Balanchine, George, 805
Balay, Robert, 3
Balderston, Daniel, 1318
Baldwin, Gordon, 521
Baldwin, James M., 40n

Ballet and Modern Dance, 818
Ballet Goers Guide, 805n
Ballet Guide, 803
Ballet Plot Index, 789
Ballet Theare Newsletter, (p. 256)
Balliett, Whitney, 752
Balmer, Herbert R., 217
Baltimore Sun, 1048n
Baltsan, Hayim, 1047
Balz, Horst, 273n
Banham, Joanna, 481
Banham, Martin, 839
Banks, Michelle, 979n
Barber, Cyril J., (p. 67)
Barlow, Harold A., 658–659
Barnhart Concise Dictionary of Etymology, 1030n
Barnhart Dictionary of Etymology, 1030
Barnhart, Robert K., 1028, 1030
Baron, John H., 609
Baroque Music..., 692n
    A Research and Information Guide, 609
Barrett, David D., 180
Barron, Neil, 1218n
Bartelt, Chuck, 607
Barth, Elsie M., 94n
Bartis, Peter T., 288n
Bartlett, John, 1109
Bartz, Bettina, 15
*BASELINE, 950
Basic and Universal Sources (music), 612n
Basic List for Church Libraries, (p. 68)
Basic Music Library, 636, (p. 252)
Baskin, Ellen, 913
Bassett, Jane, 504
Bates, Elizabeth B., 1330n
Bates, Marcia J., (p. 7, 9)
Bateson, Frederick W., 1137n, 1145n
Batsford Encyclopaedia of Embroidery Techniques, 579
Batts, Michael S., 1330n
Bauer, Johannes B., 262
Baugh, Albert C., 1049, 1213
Baughman, Judith S., 1223
Baughman, Ronald, 1281
Baumgartner, James E., 202n
Baus, Karl, 225n
BBC Music Magazine, (p. 253)
Beach, Barbara, 1348
Beacham, Walton, 1121, 1201, 1255n
Beacham's Popular Fiction in America, 1121n, 1255n
Beadle, Richard, 847n
Beale, Paul, 1022
Beall, Karen F., 427
Beasley, Jerry C., 1252n
Beauclair, Rene, 953
Beautyful Ones Are Not Yet Born, 1240n
Beazley, Mitchell, 474n
Beck, John H., 785n

Becker, Charlotte B., 81
Becker, Felix, 353n, 383n
Becker, Lawrence C., 81
Beckson, Karl E., 1198
Bede, Jean A., 1066
Bedford, Frances, 655n
Behague, Gerard, 692n
Behavioral and Social Sciences Librarian, (p. 68)
Behind the Mask: A Guide to Performing Arts
        Psychology, (p. 251)
Behm, Carl, 1254n
Beit-Hallahmi, Benjamin, 191n
Belknap, S. Yancey, 793n
Bell, Albert A., 52
Bell, Inglis F., 1253
Bell, Jeanenne, 562
Bell, Moyer, 1055n
Bell, Robert E., 307
Beloff, John, 193n
Benbow-Niemier, Glynis, 817
Benbow-Pfalzgraf, Taryn, 817
Benedictine Monks of St. Augustine's Abbey, 209
Benet, Willam R., 1063n
Benet's Reader's Encyclopedia, 1063
Benezit, Emmanuel, 353n, 391
Benjamin, Ruth, 772n
Benson, Eugene, 851, 1167
Bentley, Chantelle, 1132
Bercovitch, Sacvan, 1209
Berg, Donna L., 1012n
Berger, Laura S., 1373n
Bergeron, Barbara, 607
Berman, Barbara, (p. 35)
Berney, K. A., 863–864
Berthold, Margot, 872
Bertman, Martin, (p. 30)
Bessemer, Susan P., 323
Best Books for...
        Children, 1344n
        Junior High Readers, 1344
        Senior High Readers, 1344n
Best Children's Books in the World, 1357
Best in Children's Books, 1345
Best, James J., 422
Best of Bookfinder: A Guide to Children's
        Literature, 1346
Best Plays (series), 857n, 866
Best Rated CD's...
        Classical, 695n
        Jazz, Popular, etc., 695n
Bhattacharya, Narenda N., 185n
Bhattacharya, Ram Shankar, 82
BHA, 329
Biagini, Mary K., 1236n
Bible. *See* individual versions as listed below
        American Standard Version
        Douay Version
        King James Version
        Jerusalem Bible

        Jewish Version (Holy Scriptures)
        New English Bible
        New King James Version
        New International Version
        New Jerusalem Bible
        New Revised Standard Version
        Revised Standard Version
*Bible Library, 241
Bible Study Resource Guide..., 244n
Biblica (Biblicus), 243n
Bibliografisch repertorium van de wijsbegeerte,
        56n
Bibliographia philosophica, 45n, 53n
Bibliographic Guide to...
        *Art and Architecture, 320n
        Dance, 792n
        Music, 620n, 629
        the Comparative Study of Ethics, 46
        Theatre Arts, 828
Bibliographic Relationships in Music Catalogs,
        (p. 252)
Bibliographical Guide to...
        African-American Women Writers, 1177
        the Romance Languages and Literatures, 1306n
Bibliographical Handbook of American Music, 610
Bibliographie de la philosophie/Bibliography of
        Philosophy, 45n, 53, (p. 38)
Bibliographie der sowjetischen philosophie, 51n
Bibliographie linguistique des annees, 992
Bibliographies of Studies in Victorian Litera-
        ture, 1152n
Bibliography and Index of Mainland Southeast
        Asian Languages and Linguistics, 986
Bibliography of...
        *American Literature, 1142
        *Bioethics, 54
        Black Music, 619
        British Dramatic Periodicals, 1720–1960,
                824n–825
        Contemporary American Poetry, 1945–1985,
                1266
        Discographies, 694
        Early American Architecture, 489n
        English-Language Works on the Babi and
                Baha'i Faiths, 119
        German Literature, 1330n
        Glass, 570n
        Medieval Drama..., 827
                1969–1972, 827n
                1973–1976, 827n
                1977–1980, 827n
        New Religious Movements in Primal Societies,
                126
        Philosophy, Psychology, and Cognate Subjects,
                40
        Published Articles on American Presbyterian-
                ism, 113
        Semiotics, 1975–1985, 987
        Soviet Philosophy, 51n

the Dance Collection of Doris Nyles, 790
the History of Art: BHA, 329, 331n, 333n, (p. 153)
*Bibliotheca Germanica, 1329n
Bibliotheques et musees des arts du spectacle, 600
Bick, Patricia A., 47
Bierley, Paul E., 758
Bigsby, Christopher, 878
Bihallji-Merin, Oto, 404
Bijbelse Encyclopedie, 261n
*Billboard, 680n, 750, 764n, 951n, 959n
Billboard Book of Number One Country Hits, 767n
Billboard Book of Top 40 Albums, 750n
*Billboard Information Network, 750
*Billboard Online, 750n
Billboard Top 1000 Singles, 1955–1992, 764
Billboard's Hottest Hot 100 Hits, 764n
Billman, Larry, 816
Bimson, John J., 285
Bioethics Thesaurus, 54n
*BIOETHICSLINE, 54n
Biographical Dictionaries Master Index, 30n
Biographical Dictionary of...
    Actors, Actresses, Musicians, 1660–1800, 861
    American Cult and Sect Leaders, 208
    Dance, 814
    Film, 961, 968n
    Japanese Art, 386
    Scenographers, 962
    Twentieth-Century Philosophers, 85
Biographical Index to Children's and Young Adult Authors, 1367
*Biography and Genealogy Master Index, 30, 384n, 604n
*Biography Index, 31
*Biography Master Index, 30n
Bishop, Michael, 1307n
Bishop, William W., 1147n
Bjorling, Joel, 127
Black American...
    in Books for Children, 1358
    Women in Literature, 1177
    Writers, 1194n
Black Artist in America: An Index to Reproductions, 335
Black Authors: A Selected Annotated Bibliography, 1143
Black Authors & Illustrators of Children's Books, 1368
Black, David, 584
Black Holiness, 114n
Black Literature...
    *1827–1940, 1143n
    Criticism, 1081, 1090n
Black, Matthew, 281
Black Music...
    Biography, 683
    in the United States, 683n
Black Theology: A Critical Assessment, 114

Black Writers: A Selection of Sketches, 1178
Blackburn, G. Meredith, 1350
Blackburn, Simon, 69n
Blacks in...
    Black and White: A Source Book on Black Films, 924
    the Humanities, 1750–1984, 32
Blackwell Companion to...
    Philosophy (series), 74
    the Enlightenment, 74n
Blackwell Dictionary of Judaica, 181
Blackwell Guide to Recorded Jazz, 768n
Blackwell Philosopher Dictionaries (series), 86
Blaiklock, Edward M., 269
Blain, Virginia, 1190
Blanck, Jacob, 1142
Bleiberg, German, 1313
Bleiler, Everett F., 1117, 1261
Bleiler, Richard J., 1117
Bleznick, Donald W., 1322
Blier, Suzanne P., 405n
Bloom, Allan, (p. 2)
Bloom, Harold, 405n
Blom, Eric, 672n
Bloom, Ken, 774n
Bloomsbury Guide to English Literature, 1171n
*Blues Online, 754n
Blues Who's Who, 754
Blum, Daniel, 857
Blume, Friedrich, 668
Blumhofer, Edith W., 112n
Boase, T. S. R., 416
Boatner, M. T., 1019
Bober, Phyllis P., 500
Bohemian Register, 1179
Bollard, John, 1033n
Bond, Cynthia D., 1146
Bondanella, Julia C., 1309
Bondanella, Peter, 1309
Bonk, Mary R., 1019n
Bontekoe, Ronald, 74n
Book of Mormon, 170n
Book of Saints, 209
Book of World-Famous Music, Classical, Popular and Folk, 637
*Book Review Index, 1348n
Booker, M. Keith, 1240
Booker-Canfield, Suzanne M., 1249
Booklist, 1344n, (p. 151)
Bookpeople: A Multicultural Album, 1368n
Books and Plays in Films 1896–1915, 913n
Books by African-American Authors and Illustrators for Children, 1347
*Books in Print, 644n, 1225n
Bordman, Gerald, 774, 850, 873
Bordon, Carla M., (p. 3)
Borklund, Elmer, 1183
Bort, Barry D., 1341
Bosman, Ellen, (p. 73)

Botterweck, Johannes G., 274
Bottomore, Tom, 77
Boulanger, Norman, 852
Bowden, Henry W., 213
Bowden, John, 160n
Bowers, Faubion, 802
*Bowker International Serials Database Update, 7n
*Bowker Serials Bibliography…, 7n
   Database, 7n
   Supplement, 7n
*Bowker's Complete Video Directory, 911
Bowler, Gail H., 17
Boyce, Charles, 560
Boyd, Margaret A., 549
Boynton, G. R., (p. 6)
Bracken, James K., 1136, (p. 393)
Bradley, Carol, (p. 251)
Bradley, James E., 100
Brady, Anna, 901
Brady, Darlene A., 570
Brandle, Kurt, (p. 152)
Brandon, S. G. F., 142
Brannen, Noah S., 1044n
Braun, Erin E., 9
Braunmuller, A. R., 847n
Bredehoft, Neila, 571
Breed, Paul F., 737
Bremser, Martha, 809
Brett, Vanessa, 567
Brewer, Annie M., 988
Brewer, Ebenezer, 292n
Brewer's Dictionary of…
   Phrase and Fable, 292
   *Phrase and Fable (1894 ed. in hypertext), 292n
   20th-Century Phrase and Fable, 292n
Brewton, John E., 1350
Brewton, Sara W., 1350
Brieger, Peter, 416n, 1134n
Brier, Peter A., 1134n
Briggs, Katharine M., 294, 297
Bright, William, 1003
Brinson, Peter, 808n
Brio, (p. 253)
Bristow, M. S., 660
British and Commonwealth Fiction. *See* Master-
   plots II (series)
British Architects, 1840–1976, 489n
British Catalogue of Music (BCM), 638n
British Dramatists Since World War II, 862
British English for American Readers, 1157
British Film Catalogue, 1895–1985, 912
*British Library Catalogue: Music Library, 638n
British Literary Magazines, 1208
British Writers, 1180
Broadcast Engineering, 900n
Broadside, (p. 257)
Broadway Musicals, 774n
Broadway Song Companion, 775

Brockett, Oscar G., 871
   *Digital Supplement, 871n
Brockman, Norbert C., 138n
Brockman, William S., 613
Broecker, William L., 519
Brogan, T. V. F., 1130n
Bromiley, Geoffrey W., 265, 273n
Bronner, Edwin, 878n
Bronson, Fred, 764n
Brook, Barry S., 661
Brooks, Tim, 927
Brosse, Jacques, 221n
Brown Book: A Directory, 487n
Brown, Catherine S., 1303n
Brown, Gene, 943
Brown, Howard M., 653, 692n
Brown, Jeanne M., (p. 153)
Brown, J. H. U., 440
Brown, Kenneth O., 112n
Brown, Les, 948n
Brown, Lesley, 1017n
Brown, Muriel, 1363
Brown, Patricia F., 408
Brown, Raymond E., 278n–279
Brown, Stuart, 85
Brown, Susan W., 1248
Browne, Steven E., 933
Browne, Turner, 528
Browning, W. R. F., 271n
Brownrigg, Ronald, 220n
Bruccoli, Matthew J., 1087, 1223
Bryan, George B., 869
Bryant, E. T., (p. 251)
Buchthal, Hugo, 408n
Budd, John, (p. 393)
Buddhist Spirituality, 230n
*Buecher Online, 1329n
Bukofzer, Manfred F., 691n
Bulfinch, Thomas, 293
*Bulfinch's Mythology, 293
Bull, Storm, 722
Bulletin analytique: Philosophie, 55n, 132n
Bulletin de la Societe Francaise de Philosophie, 72n
Bulletin of the…
   American Library Association, (p. 152)
   British Theological and Philosophical Libraries, (p. 68)
   Center for Children's Books, 1345n
   John Rylands University Libraries of Man-
     chester, (p. 71, 74)
*Bulletin signaletique…, (p. 36). *See also*
   FRANCIS Bulletin signaletique
Bulletin signaletique: Philosophie. Science
   humaines, 132n, 993n
Bunge, Mario A., 60n
Bunnin, Nicholas, 74n
Bunson, Matthew, 215n
Bunting, Christine, 310

Burden, Ernest, 475n
Burack, Sylvia K., 1106
Burger's Daughter, 1240n
Burgess, Stanley M., 164
Burke, Doreen B., 426n
Burke, Joseph, 416n
Burke, T. E., 28
Burkhardt, Hans, 83
Burnette, Charles, 549n
Burns Mantle Theater Yearbook, 876n
Burr, Charlotte A., 36n
Burr, John R., 36n, 84
Burton, D. M., (p. 70)
Burton, Sarah K., (p. 35, 152)
Buschman, Isabel, 578
Bush, Douglas E., 785n
Bushnell, Brooks, 785n
Business Ethics and Responsibility, 47
Bussagli, Mario, 410
Butler's Lives of the Saints, 210
Butterworth, Neil, 718n
Bynagle, Hans E., 37, (p. 30)
Byrde, Penelope, 593
Bzowski, Frances D., 830

Cabeen, David C., 1300n
Cable, Thomas, 109
Cabrol, Fernand, 167
Cackett, Alan, 759
Cahn, Walter, 501
Calasibetta, Charlotte M., 590
*Caldecott Medal Home Page, 1363n
Calendar of...
    English Renaissance Drama, 1558–1642, 877
    Literary Facts, 1064
Callender, John H., 484
Cambridge Bibliography of English Literature,
    1145n
Cambridge Companion to...
    American Realism and Naturalism, 1258n
    British Romanticism, 1158
    Christian Doctrine, 160
    Early Greek Philosophy, 59n
    English Literature 1650–1740, 1158n
    English Poetry, Donne to Marvell, 1282n
    English Renaissance Drama, 847n
    Greek Tragedy, 848
    Jane Austen, 1256n
    Literature, 1082
    Medieval English Theatre, 847n
    Old English Literature, 1158n
    Oscar Wilde, 1198n
    Renaissance Humanism, 26n
    the Classic Russian Novel, 1334
    the Eighteenth-Century Novel, 1254n
    the French Novel from 1800 to the Present, 1301
    Virgil, 1296n

Cambridge Companions to...
    Literature (series), 26n, 1158n, 1250n, 1334n
    Philosophy (series), 59n
Cambridge Dictionary of Philosophy, 59, 69n
Cambridge Encyclopedia of Language, 997
Cambridge Guide to...
    American Theatre, 846
    English Literature, 1158
    Fiction in English, 1235n
    the Museums of Europe, 14
    World Theatre, 839, 846n
Cambridge Handbook of American Literature,
    1159
Cambridge History of...
    American Literature, 1209
    American Theatre, 878
    English Literature, 1210, 1213–1214n
    Judaism, 222
    Later Greek and Early Medieval Philosophy,
        95n
    Later Medieval Philosophy, 95n
    Medieval English Literature, 1210n
    Renaissance Philosophy, 95n
    Seventeenth-Century Philosophy, 95n
    the Bible, 282
Cambridge Italian Dictionary, 1037
Cameron, Elisabeth, 572
Campbell, Dorothy W., 1194
Campbell, George L., 998
Campbell, James, 1329
Campbell, James E., 569
Canadian Library Journal, (p. 393)
Canadian Writers and Their Works, 1118
Canfield, Christopher J., 1249n
Caplan, H. H., 356
*Card Catalog of the Manuscript Collections of
    the Archives of American Art, 319, 374n
Carey, Patrick W., 212n
Caribbean Women Novelists: An Annotated
    Critical Bibliography, 1118
Carlen, Claudia, 272
Carman, Bliss, 1275n
Carman, John, 46
Carnes, Mark C., 28
Carothers, Diane F., 906
Carpenter, Humphrey, 1364n
Carpenter, Joel A., 112n
Carr, A. R., (p. 69)
Carr, Brian, 80n
Carrigan, Henry J., (p. 69)
Carruth, Gorton, 1170n
Carter, Susanne, 1232
Cary, Tristram, 784n
Case, Donald O., (p. 6)
Cash Box, 766n
Cash Box/Black Contemporary Album Charts...
    1960–1984, 766
    1975–1987, 766n
Cashman, Norine D., 380

Caskey, Jefferson D., 1268
Cassaro, (p. 252)
Cassel's German and English Dictionary, 1038n
Cassidy, Frederic G., 1020
Cassin-Scott, Jack, 592
Castagno, John, 352–353, 446
Catalog of Dictionaries, Word Books, and
    Philological Texts, 1440–1900, 988n
*Catalog of the Avery Memorial Architectural
    Library, 466
Catalog of the Theatre and Drama Collections,
    New York Public Library, 828
Cataloging and Classification Quarterly, (p. 252)
Catalogue and Index, (p. 69)
Catalogue of...
    Music in the Bath Reference Library, 638n
    Printed Music in the British Library...
        to 1980, 638
        *to 1990, 638n
Catch Phrases, Cliches and Idioms, 1021n
Catholic Encyclopedia, 174n
Catholic Fact Book, 174n
Catholic Library World, (p. 68, 73)
*Catholic News Service, 198
*Catholic Periodical...
    and Literature Index, 130, (p. 73)
    Index, 130n
*Catholic Trends, 198n
Catholicism in Early Modern History, 225n
Cats of Any Color, 752n
Cavendish, Richard, 303
Caygill, Howard, 86n
CD Review Digest..., 695
    Annual: Classical, 695n
    Annual: Jazz, Popular, etc., 695n
*CD-Litterature, 1308n
*CD-ROM Bible Database, 231n
CD-ROM Directory, 10n
*CD-ROM Directory with Multimedia CD's, 10
*CD-ROM Finder, 10n
CD-ROM Professional, (p. 8)
*CD-ROMs in Print, 8
*CDWord Interactive Biblical Library, 241n,
    263n, 273n, 276n
Cederholm, Theresa D., 384n
*Celebration of Women Writers, 1057
Census of Antique Works of Art, 500n
Century's English-Japanese Dictionary, 1044n
Century Magazine, 893n
Cerrito, Joann, 387
Chaffers, William, 572n
Chamber Music, 639
Chamberlain, Bobby J., 1042n
Chamberlin, Mary W., 309n
Chambers Concise Encyclopedia of Film and
    Television, 931n
Chamber's Dictionary, 1017n
Chambers, Edmund K., 884
Chambers Film Quotes, 925

Champion, Larry S., 1188
Chan, Wing-tsit, 50
Channeling: A Bibliographic Exploration, 127
Chapman, Robert L., 1022, 1035
Chappel, Vere, 85n
Characters from Young Adult Literature, 1359n
Characters in...
    19th-Century Literature, 1065
    20th-Century Literature, 1065n
    Young Adult Literature, 1359
Charles, Jill, 856, 859
Charleston, Robert J., 574n
Charlton, James, 1115n
Cheap Shots: Video Production for Nonprofits,
    942n
*Checklist of...
    American Copies of Short-Title Catalogue
        Books, 1147n
    the Permanent Collection (National Portrait
        Gallery), 434n
    Writings on American Music, 624n
Chelys, 652n
Chevalier, Tracy, 1289
Chiarmonte, Paula L., 402
Chicano Literature: A Reference Guide, 1310
Chielens, Edward E., 1205
Children's Authors and Illustrators, 1374n
Children's Book Review Index, 1348
Children's Books: Awards and Prizes, 1360n
Children's Catalog, 1344n
Children's Literature...
    Awards and Winners, 1360
    *Review, 1369
Childress, James F., 179
Chilton, John, 762
Chilvers, Ian, 370, 1299n
Chinese Drama: An Annotated Bibliography, 888
Chinese Painting, 457
Chipman, Kathe, 435
Chodorow, Stanley, (p. 27, 39)
Choice, (p. 30, 253)
Choquette, Diane, 126n
Choral Music Reviews Index...
    1983–1985, 647
    II 1986–1988, 647n
Christian Communication, 115
Christian, Nicole, 1337
Christian Social Action, (p. 68)
Christian Spirituality, 230n
Christie's Review of the Season, 350n
Chronicle of...
    American Music, 1700–1995, 687
    Western Fashion, 587
Chronological Outline of...
    American Literature, 1207n, 1211
    British Literature, 1207n, 1211n
Chujoy, Anatole, 795
Church and State in America, 99
Church and Synagogue Libraries, (p. 72)

Church History, 100
Cinema Sequels and Remakes, 1903–1987, 941n
Claassen, Lynda C., 430
Clapp, Jane, 502
Clarke, Mary, 795n, 805n
Classical and Medieval Literature Criticism, 1297
Classical Ballet Technique, 804
Classical Dictionary, 298n
Classical Epic: An Annotated Bibliography, 1298
Classical Mediterranean Spirituality, 230n
Classical Music...
    1925–1975, 694n
    Discography, 1976–1988, 694n
    *Website, 721n
Classical Sculpture, 508n
Classification and Indexing in the Humanities, (p. 69)
Classified Directory of Artists' Signatures..., 356
    American Artists with New U.K. Additions, 356n
Classifying Church or Synagogue Library Materials, (p. 69)
Clayton, Michael, 563
Cleary, R. M., (p. 253)
Clegg, S. M., (p. 254)
Clifford, Mike, 757
Closing of the American Mind, (p. 2)
Clunas, Craig, 409
Clynes, Tom, 679
CNI, (p. 7)
*Coates Art Review: Impressionism, 428
Cobledick, Susie, (p. 152)
Coffin, Tristram P., 299
Coghlan, Ronan, 1164n
Cohen, Aaron I., 685,725
Cohen, Albert, 620n
Cohen, Hennig, 299
Cohen, J. M., 1111
Cohen, M. J., 1111
Cohen, Marshall, 976
Cohen, Selma J., 799, 819
Cohen-Stratyner, Barbara N., 734n, 814
Cohn-Sherbok, Dan, 143, 181
Cohn-Sherbok, Lavinia, 219n
Colby, Michael, (p. 252)
Colby, Vineta, 1101n
Coleman, Arthur, 890n
Coleman, Kathleen, 1304
*Collaborative Bibliography of Women in Philosophy, 48
Collected Editions Historical Series & Sets, 460
Collection Assessment in Music Libraries, (p. 253)
Collection Building, (p. 70)
Collection Management, (p. 69, 253–254, 393)
Collection of Exhibition Catalogs, 351n
Collections of The Nelson-Atkins Museum of Art, 429
Collector's Dictionary of the Silver and Gold, 563
*Collector's Encyclopedia of Heisey Glass, 571

College and Research Libraries..., (p. 6–9, 254, 393–394)
    News, (p. 4, 154)
Collier, Clifford, 811
Collier, Laurie, 1374n
Collinge, N. E., 1000
Collingwood, Donna, 1129n
Collins, Pamela, 719n
Collins Spanish-English/English Spanish Dictionary, 1042n
Collins, William P., 119
Collinson, Diane, 89–90n
Color Compendium, 357
Columbia Dictionary of Modern European Literature, 1066
Columbia Granger's...
    Dictionary of Poetry Quotations, 1133n
    Guide to Poetry Anthologies, 1272
    Index to Poetry, 1133n, 1267, 1272n
    *World of Poetry, 1133, 1273n
Comay, Joan, 220
Comite International Permanent de Liguististes, 992
Commire, Anne, 1374
Commission on...
    Preservation and Access, (p. 5)
    the Humanities, (p. 1, 11)
Communication Among Scientists and Engineers, (p. 70)
Compact Oxford English Dictionary: Complete Text, 1012n
Companion Encyclopedia of Asian Philosophy, 80n
Companion to...
    Aesthetics, 74n
    Contemporary Political Philosophy, 74n
    Epistemology, 74n
    Ethics, 74n
    Metaphysics, 74n
    Scottish Literature, 1160
    the Medieval Theatre, 847
    the Philosophy of Mind, 74n
    the Philosophy of Language, 74n
    the Philosophy of Law and Legal Theory, 74n
    Twentieth-Century German Literature, 1327
    World Philosophies, 74n
Comparative Reader, 1052
Compendium of...
    Modern Instrumental Techniques, 783
    the World's Languages, 998
Complete Actors' Television Credits, 1948–1988, 926
Complete Concordance to the Bible (Douay Version), 249
Complete Dictionary of Furniture, 559
Complete Directory to Prime Time Network TV Shows, 927
Complete Encyclopedia of Television Programs, 1947–1979, 927n
Complete Entertainment Discography, 769n

Complete Film Dictionary, 928
Complete Guide to Modern Dance, 817n
Complete Play Production Handbook, 896n
Complete Stitch Encyclopedia, 580
Complete Stories of the Great Ballets, 805
*Complete Works of Shakespeare, 1189n
Composers and Conductors of Popular Orchestra
    Music, 755
Comprehensive Bibliography of...
    Modern African Religious Movements, 126n
    Music for Film and Television, 771
*Comprehensive Dissertation Index, 22n
Comprehensive Index to Architectural Periodicals,
    470n
Compton, Rae, 583
Computer in Art, (p. 153)
Computer Music Journal, (p. 255)
Computer Readable Databases, 9n
*Computerized Torah Treasure, 239n
Computers and the Humanities, (p. 8–9, 36, 70–71,
    255)
Computers in Libraries, (p. 154, 252)
Computing in Musicology, (p. 255)
Comrie, Bernard, 1008
Concert and Opera...
    Conductors, 717
    Singers, 724n
Concert Music, 1630–1750, 691n
Concise American Heritage Dictionary, 1016n
Concise Baker's Biographical Dictionary, 682n
Concise Chronology of English Literature, 1212
Concise Dictionary of...
    *American Literary Biography, 1182
    *British Literary Biography, 1182n
    Christian Theology, 166n
    Christianity in America, 163n
    Indian Philosophy, 82n
Concise Encyclopedia of...
    Interior Design, 475
    Islam, 184n
    Western Philosophy, 75
Concise Glossary of Contemporary Literary
    Theory, 1073n
Concise History of...
    Modern Painting, 458
    Western Music, 688
Concise Oxford Companion to...
    American Literature, 1159n
    American Theatre, 850n
    Classical Literature, 1299n
    English Literature, 1168n
    the English Language, 1006n
    the Theatre, 845n
*Concise Oxford Dictionary, 1017
Concise Oxford Dictionary of...
    Art and Artists, 370n
    Ballet, 806
    *Current English, 1017
    English Etymology, 1029

French Literature, 1305n
    Opera, 710n
Concise Oxford Russian Dictionary, 1046n
Concordances of Great Books, (p. 36)
Conductors and Composers of Popular Orches-
    tral Music, 755
Conner, Susan, 548
Connor, Billie M., 836
Connors, Martin, 920
Conolly, L. W., 851
Conte, Joseph, 1280
Contemporary African American Novelists, 1243
Contemporary American...
    Architects, 490n
    Composers, 718
    Dramatists, 863
    Poetry: A Checklist, 1266n
    Slang, 1022n
    Women Sculptors, 506
Contemporary Architects, 490
Contemporary Artists, 387
Contemporary Authors...
    A Bio-bibliographical Guide, 552n, 1083,
        1090n, 1100n, 1178n, 1281n, 1315n
    Autobiography Series, 1083n
    Bibliographical Series...
        V.1 American Novelists, 1244
        V.2 American Poets, 1244n, 1281
        V.3 American Dramatists, 1244n
    Cumulative Index, 1083n
    First Revision Series, 1083n
    New Revision Series, 1083n
    Permanent Series, 1083n
Contemporary Black American Playwrights, 867
Contemporary British Dramatists, 864
Contemporary Composers..., 719n
    on Contemporary Music, 719
Contemporary Designers, 551
Contemporary Dramatists, 864n–865
Contemporary Fashion, 594
Contemporary Fiction Writers of the South, 1245
Contemporary Foreign Language Writers, 1289n
Contemporary French Women Poets, 1307n
Contemporary Gay American Novelists, 1246
Contemporary Graphic Artists, 552
Contemporary Jewish-American Novelists, 1247
Contemporary Literary Criticism, 1084–1085n,
    1090
    Annual Cumulative Title Index, 1084n
    Yearbook, 1085
Contemporary Literary Critics, 1183
Contemporary Masterworks, 358
Contemporary Musicians, 756
Contemporary Novel, 1241n
Contemporary Novelists, 1248
Contemporary Photographers, 526
Contemporary Poets..., 1282–1283n
    Dramatists, Essayists, and Novelists of the
        South, 1184

Contemporary Popular Writers, 1185
Contemporary Religions, 140
Contemporary Religious Ideas Bibliographic
     Essays, (p. 67)
Contemporary Southern...
     Men Fiction Writers, 1249
     Women Fiction Writers, 1249n
     Writers, 1186
Contemporary Spanish American Poets: A
     Bibliography, 1311
Contemporary Theatre, Film, and Television, 601
Contemporary Women...
     Dramatists, 866
     Poets, 1283
Contemporary World Writers, 1289
Contento, William G., 1226
Continental Novel, 1292
Conversion Experience in America, 211
Coogan, Michael D., 271
Cook, David A., 973
Cook, Dorothy E., 1231
Cooper, B. Lee, 728, 731, 747
Cooper, David E., 74n
Cooper, Martin, 691n
Cooper, Thomas W., 907
Copeland, Edward, 1256n
Copeland, Sandra K., 577
Copleston, Frederick C., 96
Coptic Encyclopedia, 161
Cordier, Mary H., 1352
CoreFiche, 1231
Corenthal, Michael G., (p. 253)
Cormier, Ramona, 92
Cornish, Graham, 107
Corns, Thomas N., 1282n
Cornwell, Neil, 1337
Corson, Richard, 897
Cortes, Eladio, 1312
Costume and Fashion, 591n
Costume Design on Broadway, 595
Costume Index, 585n
Cotten, Lee, 749n
Cotterell, Arthur, 296
Cottingham, John, 86n
Cottrill, Tim, 1230
Couch, Nena, (p. 2, 7–9, 254, 393–394)
Country Music: The Encyclopedia, 740
Cousins, Ewert, 230n
Covert, Nadine, 323n, 375, 466n
Covey, Preston K., (p. 36)
Cowan, Henry J., 476n
Cowden, Robert H., 715, 723–724n
Cowie, Anthony P., 1026
Cowie, Peter, 949
Cowley, John, 765
Cox, Mary, 376
Coye, Dale F., 1172
Coyle, Martin, 1071
Crabtree, Phillip D., 613n

Craddock, Jim, 920
Crafts Supply Sourcebook, 549
Craggs, Stewart R., (p. 288)
Craig, Doris, 1021n
Craig, Edward, 70
Craigie, William A., 1012n
Crane, Gregory, (p. 9, 71)
Crane, Gwen, 1242n
Craven, Robert R., 716
Craven, Wayne, 505
Crawdaddy, 728n
Crawford, Elizabeth D., 1371n
Crawley, Tony, 925
Creth, Sheila D., (p. 6)
Crim, Keith, 139
Crime Fiction II ... 1749–1990, 1221
Crimes of Perception, 141
Criscoe, Betty L., 1356
Crisp, Clement, 805n, 808n
Critic, 893n
Critical Bibliography of French Literature, 1300
Critical Companions to Popular Contemporary
     Writers (series), 1250
Critical Guide to Catholic Reference Books,
     116, (p. 152, 393)
Critical Index, 921n
Critical Review of Books in Religion, 131
Critical Survey of Drama...
     English Language Series, 889
     Foreign Language Series, 889n
     Supplement, 889n
Critical Survey of Long Fiction...
     English Language Series, 1251
     Foreign Language Series, 1293
Critical Survey of Poetry...
     English Language Series, 1284, 1294n
     Foreign Language Series, 1294
     Supplement, 1294n
Critical Survey of Short Fiction, 1119
Critical Temper, 1187
Critical Terms for Science Fiction and Fantasy,
     1234
Crocker, Richard, 691n
Crofton, Ian, 359
Cronin, Gloria L., 1257
Crosman, Christopher, 323
Cross, F. L., 176
Cross-Cultural Statistical Encyclopedia of the
     World, 157n
Crowell's Handbook of Classical Drama, 848n
Crown's Japanese-English Dictionary, 1044n
Cruden's Complete Concordance, 250
Cruikshank, Dan, 495
Crystal, David, 997, 999
*Cuadra Directory of Online Databases, 9n
Cuddon, J. A., 1069
Cullars, John, (p. 152, 393)
Cultural Atlas of Islam, 223
Cumming, Valerie, 593n

Cummings, David, 672n, 686n, 1091
Cummings, Paul, 388
Cumulative Index to Philosophical Books, 53n
Curley, Dorothy N., 1196
Curran, Stuart, 1158n
Current Biography..., 33, 1101n
    Yearbook, 33n
Current Contents...
    *Arts & Humanities, 21
    *Social & Behavioral Sciences, 21n
Current Issues in Fine Arts Collection Development, (p. 151)
Cuseo, Allen A., 1370
Cutting Edge: New Auction Sources and Computer Projects, (p. 151)
*Cyburbia, 463
Cyclopedia of...
    Literary Characters..., 1067n
        *II, 1067, 1094n
    World Authors, 1086n
        II, 1086, 1094n
Cypess, Sandra M., 1325n

Daedalus, (p. 2)
Damschroder, David, 627
Dance, 818n
Dance as a Theatre Art, 819n
Dance Directory 1990, 810
Dance Encyclopedia, 795
Dance Film and Video Guide, 791n
Dance Handbook, 796
Dance History, 819
Dance in America, 820
*Dance Links, 812n
Dance on Camera, 791
*Dance on Disc, 793n
Dance Resources in Canadian Libraries, 811
Dance Words, 797
Dance World, 813n
Dancemagazine, 812
Dancers and Choreographers, 815
Dancy, Johnathan, 74n
Dandekar, Hemalata, (p. 152)
Dangarembka, Tsitsi, 1240n
Daniel Blum's Theatre World, 857n
Daniel, Howard, 448
Daniel, Lanelle, 887n
Danker, Frederick W., 244
Dante Project, (p. 394)
Database, (p. 8)
David, Jack, 1140
Davies, J. G., 154
Davies, Marion W., 1171
Davies, Martin, 469
Davies, W. D., 222
Davis, Charles H., (p. 6)
Davis, Elizabeth, 636, (p. 252)
Davis, Gwenn, 1269

Davis, Lloyd, 1266
Davis, R. H., (p. 151)
*DDM. See Doctoral Dissertations in Musicology
Dearling, Celia, 665
Dearling, Robert, 665
de Brie, 45n
Debus, Allen G., 769n
Decca Hillbilly Discography: 1927–1945, 767
De Charms, Desiree, 736n–737
De Chiara, Joseph, 484
Decorative Arts and Household Furnishings in America, 533
de Courtivron, Isabelle, 1291
DeCurtis, Anthony, 760n, 770n
Deedy, John, 174n
Definitive Kobbe's Opera Book, 700
De George, Richard T., (p. 30)
De La Haye, Amy, 591n
Delaney, John J., 212
De Lerma, Dominique-Rene, 619
Dell, David J., 121
*Delta Blues Museum, 739n
DeMiller, Anna L., 990
De Montreville, Doris, 1371n
Dent, N. J. H., 86n
Denvir, Bernard, 450
Descartes Dictionary, 86n
Describing Music Materials, (p. 30)
*Design & Applied Arts Index, 534
Design on File, 536
Detective and Mystery Fiction, 1120
Deutch, Yvonne, 303
Deutsch, Eliot, 74n
Deutsches Worterbuch, 1038
Devil on the Cross, 1240n
Development of a System for Treatment of Bible Headings, (p. 69)
Development of the Italian Schools of Painting, 459
Devenney, David P., 645, 775
Dey, Alexander, (p. 29, 37)
Diagram Group, 536, 787
Dialogue, (p. 37)
Diamond, Harold J., 626, (p. 253)
Di Berardino, Angelo, 171
Dickerson, Donya, 1105
Dickinson, Alis, 621
Dickinson, Fidelia, 1297n
Dickinson's American Historical Fiction, 1217
Dictionaries, Encyclopedias, and Other Word-Related Books, 988
Dictionary Catalog...
    Freer Gallery of Art, 321
    New York Public Library.
        *Art and Architecture Division, 320, 328n
        Dance Collection, 792
        Music Collection, 629n, 638n
        Research Libraries, 320n

*Dictionary English-German, German English, 1038n
Dictionary of...
  American Biography, 28n, 1087n, 1173n
  American Catholic Biography, 212
  American Children's Fiction...
    1859–1959, 1361
    1960–1984, 1361n
    1985–1989, 1361n
    1990–1994, 1361n
  American Composers, 718n
  American Idioms, 1019
  American Organist, (p. 256)
  American Proverbs, 1108
  American Regional English, 1020
  American Religious Biography, 213
  American Sculptors, 507
  American Slang, 1022
  Architectural and Building Technology, 476n
  Architecture & Construction, 476
  Art (Grove's), 360
  Art Quotations, 359
  Asian Philosophies, 80n
  Ballet, 809n
  Ballet Terms, 807
  Bible and Religion, 162n
  British Artists, 1880–1940, 452
  British Folktales in the English Language, 294
  Catholic Biography, 212n
  Celtic Mythology, 295
  Christ and the Gospels, 258n
  Christian Ethics, 179n
  Christian Lore and Legend, 162
  Christianity in America, 163
  Cliches, 1021
  Collective Nouns and Group Terms, 1031
  Comparative Religion, 139n, 142
  Concepts in Literary Criticism and Theory, 1068
  Contemporary American Artists, 388
  Costume, 588
  Costume and Fashion, 588n
  Critical Theory, 1068n
  Cults, Sects, Religions and the Occult, 191
  Early Music from the Troubadors to Monteverdi, 721n
  Electronic and Computer Music Technology, 784
  Film Makers, 968n
  Furniture, 560
  Heresy Trials in American Christianity, 163n
  Irish Mythology, 295n
  Islamic Architecture, 477
  Italian Literature, 1309
  Jesus and the Gospels, 258
  Judaism and Christianity, 143
  Landscape Architecture, 478
  Linguistics and Phonetics, 999
  Literary Biography, 1083n, 1087, 1090n, 1182n, 1223n, 1242n, 1280n, 1323n, 1332n, 1366n
  Literary Biography Documentary Series, 1087n
  Literary Biography Yearbook, 1087n
  Literary Terms and Literary Theory, 1069
  Logic As Applied in the Study of Language, 76
  Marxist Thought, 77
  Mexican Literature, 1312
  Modern Critical Terms, 1070
  Modern French Literature, 1301n
  Musical Technology, 784n
  Musical Themes, 658–659n
  Mysticism and the Occult, 195n
  Non-Christian Religions, 182
  Opera and Song Themes, 658n–659
  Pentecostal and Charismatic Movements, 164
  Philosophical Quotations, 71n
  Philosophy
    (Bunge), 60n
    (Flew), 60, (p. 28)
    (Lacey), 61
    (Mautner), 61n
    (Runes), 62
    (Saifulin and Dixon), 63
  Philosophy and Psychology, 40n
  Pianists, 720
  Proper Names and Places in the Bible, 259
  Quranic Terms and Concepts, 260
  Scandinavian Literature, 1328
  Signatures and Monograms of American Artists, 352n
  Slang and Unconventional English, 1022
  Television and Audiovisual Terminology, 929
  Terms in Music: English-German, German-English, 675n
  the Bible (Oxford), 271n
  the Black Theatre, 849
  the Dance, 798
  the Ecumenical Movement, 165
  the History of Ideas, 64
  the Literature of the Iberian Peninsula, 1313
  the Liturgy, 174n
  the Proverbs in England, 1113n
  Theology, 166
  20th-Century Design, 537
  Women Artists, 389
    Born Before 1900, 390
  Word Origins, 1032
  World Mythology, 296
Dictionnaire critique et documentaire des peintres, 391
Dictionnaire d'archeologie chretienne et de liturgie, 167
Dictionnaire des philosophes antiques, 87
Die Musik in Geschichte und Gegenwart, 668
*Digital Supplement to Oscar Brockett's History of the Theatre, 871n

Dillon, Dennis, (p. 11)
Dimmitt, Richard, 930n
Dines, Nicholas T., 484n
Dinner Theatre: A Survey and Directory, 854
Directors and Their Films, 916n
Directory of...
   African-American Religious Bodies, 199
   American Philosophers, 88, 92n, (p. 37–38)
   Blacks in the Performing Arts, 602
   Departments and Programs of Religious
      Studies, 200
   Departments of Religion, (p. 72)
   Electronic Journals, (p. 9)
   Historic American Theatres, 855
   International Periodicals and Newsletters on
      the Built Environment, 464
   Little Magazines...
      1965–1972, 1055n
      1993–1994, 1055n
      1997–1998, 1055n
   Music Faculties in...
      American Colleges, 677n
      Colleges and Universities, 677
   Music Research Libraries (RISM), 678
   *Online Databases, 9n
   Portable Databases, 9n
   Publishers in Religion, 206n
   Record and CD Retailers, 676
   Religious Organizations in the United States,
      201
   the American Theatre 1894–1971, 876n
   Theatre Training Programs, 856
   World Museums, 15n
Directory to Industrial Design, 549n
Dirks, Tim, 776n
*DiscLit: AMERICAN AUTHORS, 1175n
*DISCovering Authors, 1088, 1371
*Dissertation Abstracts...
   *International, 22, 621n
   *Ondisc, 22n
   *Online, 22n
Dixon, Richard R., 63
Dizik, A. Allen, 475
D-Lib Magazine, (p. 9)
Dobree, Bonamy, 1214
Dobson, Richard, 784
Docks, L. R., 770
Doctoral Dissertations in Musicology..., 621
   *Online, 621n
Dodge Collection of Eighteenth Century French
     and English Art, 538
Dogra, R. C., 186n
Dolan, John, 225
Dolbow, Sandra W., 1301
Donahue, Leo O., 581
Doo-Wop: The Forgotten Third of Rock 'n Roll,
   766n
Douay Bible, 232, 249n
Douglas, J. D., 178n

Doumato, Lamia, 421
Dove, Jack, (p. 251)
Down Home Guide to the Blues, 765n
Dox, Thurston J., 646
Drabble, Margaret, 1168
Drake, Greg, 515
Drama Collection: Author Listing, 828n
*Drama Criticism, 890
Drama Criticism: Criticism of the Most Signifi-
   cant, 890
Drama Scholars' Index to Plays and Filmscripts,
   834n
Draper, James P., 1081, 1102
Drew, Bernard A., 941, 1233
Dreyer, M. R., 715n
Dreyer, Sharon S., 1346
Drone, Jeanette M., 698
Drury, Nevill, 195n
Duckles, Vincent H., 612n–614, (p. 252)
Duffy, C., (p. 253)
Duggan, Mary Kay, (p. 254–255)
Duke, Maurice, 1139
Duncan, George S., 570n
Dunkelman, Martha L., 423
Dunlap, Kay, 650
Dunning, John, 944
Durant, Will, (p. 30)
Durham, Weldon B., 874
Durran, Jennifer, (p. 154)
Durusau, Patrick, 109
Dutch Art, 361
Dwady, Doris O., 385
Dworkin, Rita, 1241n
Dyson, Anne J., 1253n

*E-Conflict World Encyclopedia, 660n
Eagle, Dorothy, 1170
Eagleson, Laurie, 652
Earl of Harewood, 700
Early American...
   Cinema, 972
   Choral Music, 645n
   Music: A Research and Information Guide, 611
Early Black American Playwrights and Dramatic
    Writers, 867
Early Christian and Byzantine Architecture, 467
Early Medieval Music up to 1300, 691n
Earth Scale Art, 499
Easterling, P. E., 848
Eastman, Mary H., 289n
Eaton, Jan, 580
Eaton, Quaintance, 712n
Ebersole, Gary, (p. 67)
Ebert, Roger, 949n, 983
Ecumenism, A Bibliographical Overview, (p. 67)
*Eda Kuhn Loeb Music Library, 642
Eddleman, Floyd E., 887
Ede, David, 122

Edgerton, William B., 1066
Editing Group, 1041
Education's Great Amnesia, (p. 2)
Edwardian Fiction, 1235
Edwards, Clive, 559
Edwards, Gary, 520
Edwards, Paul, 66
Eerdmans Analytical Concordance to the Revised
    Standard Version, 251
Eerdman's Bible Dictionary, 261
Eerdman's Handbook to...
    Christianity in America, 224
    the World's Religions, 144
Ehresmann, Donald L., 309, 461, 532
Ehrlich, Eugene, 1033, 1170n
Eight American Authors, 1139n
*Eighteenth Century Short Title Catalogue, 687n
Eighteenth-Century...
    British Novel and its Background, 1254n
    Musical Chronicle, 687
Einstein, Alfred, 691n
Eisler, Rudolf, 68n
Ekdahl, Janis, 496
Electric Chelys, 652n
Electronic and Computer Music, 622
Electronic Bibles and Electronic Texts in Biblical
    Studies, (p. 71)
Electronic Library, (p. 5)
*Electronic Library of Art, 336
Electronic Music Dictionary, 784n
Elenchus Bibliographicus Biblicus, 243n
Elenchus of Biblical Bibliography, 243n
Elert, Nicolet V., 967
ELH, 1061n
Eliade Guide to World Religions, 145
Eliade, Mircea, 145, 151
Elizabethan Stage, 884n
Elkan, Allan, 935
Elkins, A. C., 1061n
Elley, Derek, 984n
Eliot, Julia, 1027n
Ellis, Peter B., 295n
Ellis, Steven, (p. 9)
Ellman, Richard, 1275
Ellwood, Robert, 145n
Emanuel, Muriel, 490
Emblidge, David, 1107
Embree, Lester, 76n
Embroidery and Needlepoint, 576
Emecheta, Buchi, 1240n
Enciclopedia della Musica, 701
Enciclopedia filosofica, 65
Encyclopaedia Britannica..., (p. 2, 20, 393)
    *Online, (p. 65, 149, 250)
Encyclopaedia Judaica, 183
    Decennial Book, 183n
Encyclopaedia of...
    Fashion, 589
    Islam, 184, 190n, 260n

Language, 1000
Occultism, 193n
Oil Painting, 447
Psychic Science, 193n
Religion and Ethics, 146
Sikh Religion and Culture, 186n
the Musical Theatre, 777
Encyclopedia Americana, (p. 393)
Encyclopedia of...
    African American Religions, 147
    Afterlife Beliefs and Phenomena, 196n
    American...
        Architecture, 479
        Religions, 148
        Religious Creeds, 148n
        Religious History, 149
        Silver Manufacturers, 564
    Architecture, 480
    Associations, 606n
    Batik Designs, 581
    Biblical and Christian Ethics, 168
    Biblical Interpretations, 275
    Biblical Theology, 262
    *Bioethics, 78
    British Women Writers, 1290n
    Continental Women Writers, 1290
    Cosmology, 79
    Crafts, 539
    Creation Myths, 296n
    Dance & Ballet, 795n
    Design, 540
    Early Christianity, 169
    Eastern Philosophy and Religion, 80
    Ethics, 81
    Fairies, 297
    Film Festivals, 941n
    Folk, Country, and Western Music, 704n
    Furniture, 560n
    Ghosts and Spirits, 192
    Indian Philosophies..., 49n, 82
        Bibliography, 49, 82n
    Interior Design, 481
    Jazz..., 762n
        in the Sixties, 762n
        in the Seventies, 762n
    Jewish History, 181n
    Jewish Symbols, 181n
    Judaism, 189n
    Keyboard Instruments, 785
    Language and Linguistics, 1001
    Library and Information Science, (p. 149,
        152, 251)
    Literary Terms, 1255n
    Literature and Criticism, 1071
    Modern Architecture, 482n
    Mormonism, 170
    Music in Canada, 662
    Native American Religions, 150
    Novels into Film, 930

Encyclopaedia of... (*continued*)
 Occultism & Parapsychology, 193, (p. 65)
 Painting, 451n
 Percussion Instruments, 785n
 Phenomenology, 76n
 Philosophy, 65n–66, 78n, (p. 30)
 Poetry and Poetics, 1130n
 Pottery and Porcelain, 572
 Recorded Sound in the United States, 663
 Religion...
  *(Eliade), 131n, 151
  (Ferm), 151n
 Religious Controversies in the United States,
   149n, 163n
 Sacred Places, 138n
 Science Fiction and Fantasy, 1222
 Sculpture Techniques, 503
 Southern Literature, 1161
 Textiles, 582
 the American Religious Experience, 149n, 152
 the American Theatre, 1900–1975, 878n
 the Blues, 739
 the Early Church, 171
 the New York Stage...
  1920–1930, 879
  1930–1940, 879n
  1940–1950, 879n
 the Reformed Faith, 172
 Themes and Subjects in Painting, 448
 Theology, 173
 Things That Never Were, 304n
 Visual Art, (p. 149)
 Witches and Witchcraft, 192n
 Women in Religious Art, 362
 World Art, 363, (p. 149)
 World Literature in the 20th Century, 1072,
   1317n
 World Religions, 145n
 World Theatre, 840n
Encyclopedic Dictionary of...
 Language and Linguistics, 999n
 Semiotics, 1002
Encyclopedic Handbook of Cults in America, 194
Encyclopedie des sciences ecclesiastiques, 167n
*Encyclopedie internationale des photographes,
   527
Encyclopedie philosophique universelle, 67
English Fiction...
 1660–1800, 1252n
 1900–1950, 1252
English Language Notes, 1061n
English Novel...
 Explication (and Supps. I–V), 1253n
 1578–1956, 1253
 Twentieth Century Criticism, 1253n
English Poetry...
 *Full Text Database, 1273
 1660–1800, 1264
 1900–1950, 1264n

English Prose, Prose Fiction and Criticism to
   1660, 1252n
English Renaissance Prose Fiction, 1500–1660,
   1254
English Revised Version, 233n
*English-Japanese, Japanese-English Dictionary,
   1044n
English Romantic Poetry, 1264n
Enser, A. G. S., 913n
Enser's Filmed Books and Plays, 913
Ensor, Pat, 313
Ensko, Stephen G. C., 561
*Entertainment Weekly, 951
Entourage: A Tracing File for Architecture, 475n
Ensuring Access to the Accumulated Human
   Record, (p. 5)
Erdman, David V., 1061
Erickson, Millard J., 166n
Erlewine, Michael, 763
Eschbach, Achim, 987
Escritt, Stephen, 537n
Eskind, Andrew H., 515
Espina, Noni, 649n
Esposito, John L., 190
*Essay and General Literature Index, 23
Essays of an Information Scientist, (p. 5, 11)
Essays on Early Modern Philosophers, 85n
Essential Shakespeare, 1188
Essential Terms of Fashion, 590
Esslin, Martin, 840n
Estes, Glenn E., 1366
Esteve-Coll, Elizabeth, (p. 150)
Ethics: An Annotated Bibliography, 46n
Ethnic Music on Records, 696
Ethnoarts Index, 326n
Ethnomusicology, 623n
Ethnomusicology Research, 623
European Artists: Signatures and Monograms,
   352n
European Authors, 1000–1900, 1101n
European Culture: A Contemporary Companion,
   28n
European Writers, 1089
Evans, Hilary, 343n
Evans, Ivor H., 292
Evans, James H., 114
Evans, Joan, 416n
Evans, Martin M., 526
Evans, Mary, 343n
Evans, Patrick, 1215
Ewen, David, 753n
Exegetical Dictionary of the New Testament,
   273n
*Exploring Novels, 1088n, 1255
*Exploring Poetry, 1088n, 1285
*Exploring Shakespeare, 1088n
Exploring Short Stories, 1088n
*Eyeneer Music Archives, 741n

*FABS Electronic Bible System, 242n
*FABS Reference Bible System, 242
Facilities Standards for Art Libraries, (p. 151)
Fackler, Mark P., 108n
Facts Behind the Songs, 741
Facts on File...
    Bibliography of American Fiction, 1919–1988, 1223
    Dictionary of Design and Designers, 553
    Dictionary of Film and Broadcast Terms, 931
    Dictionary of New Words, 1027n
    Dictionary of Religions, 145n
    Dictionary of the Theatre, 840
    Encyclopedia of World Mythology and Legend, 298
Fahey, Michael A., (p. 67)
Fairbanks, Jonathan L., 557
Fairchild's Dictionary of Fashion, 590n
Falk, Peter H., 345, 352n, 399
Falk's Art Price Index, 345n
*Familiar Quotations, 1109
Famous American Playhouses, 885n
Fantasy, 1230n
Fantasy Review, 1230n
Farber, Donald C., 895
Farkas, Andrew, 724
Farmer, David H., 216
Farry, Mike, 206n
Fashion and Costume in American Popular Culture, 585
Fashion in Costume 1200–1980, 591
Fashion Encyclopedia, 589n
Faulhaber, Uwe K., 1331n
Faust, Langdon L., 1174
Feather, Leonard, 760n
Federal Theatre Project, 880
    *Digital Project, 880n
Feiser, James, (p. 31, 36)
Feld, Stuart P., 426n
Feminist Art Criticism, 322
Feminist Companion to Literature in English, 1190
Feminist Writers, 1191
Fenske, Ruth E., (p. 69)
Fenstermaker, John J., 1051
Fenton, R. R., 11
Fenwick, M. J., 1326
Ferguson, Carole, 827n
Ferguson, Everett, 169
Ferguson, F. S., 1147
Ferm, Vergilius T. A., 151n
Ferris, Sharon P., 612
*Festival Finder, 679n
Fhaner, Beth A., 979
Fiction Catalog, 1224
Fiction, 1876–1983, 1225
Fiction, Folklore, Fantasy & Poetry for Children, 1349
Fiction Sequels for Readers 10 to 16, 1355n
Fiction Writers Guidelines, 1128

Fiction Writer's Market, 1128n–1129n
Fidell, Estelle A., 837n
Fidler, Linda M., 615
Fieg, Eugene C., 107n
Fielding, Mantle, 395
Fifteenth Century Central Italian Sculpture, 497
Fifth Book of Junior Authors, 1371n
Fifty Key Contemporary Thinkers, 91n
Fifty Major Philosophers, 89
Fifty Prints of the Year, 441n
Fifty Southern Writers...
    Before 1900, 1245n
    After 1900, 1245
Film and Television Composers: An International Discography, 782
Film as...
    Art, 902n
    Industry, 902n
Film Catalog, 909n
Film Choreographers and Dance Directors, 816
Film Critic, (p. 257)
Film Criticism, 900n
Film Encyclopedia, 932
Film Festival Guide, 952
Film Handbook, 963
Film in Society, 902n
Film Index, 902
*Film Literature Index, 921
Film Music..., 772
    Collections in the United States, (p. 253)
Film Quarterly, 978n
Film Review Index, 975
Film Society Bulletin, (p. 257)
Film Study..., 903
    A Resource Guide, 903n
Film, Television, and...
    Stage Music on Phonograph Records, 782n
    Video Periodicals, 900
Film Theory and Criticism, 976
Filmmaker's Dictionary, 928n
Films and Other Materials for Projection, 918n
Films in Review, 918n
Films of Mack Sennett, 977n
Films on Art, 375n
Film-Video Terms and Concepts, 933
Finder's Guide to Prints and Drawings in the Smithsonian Institution, 430
Fine Art...
    Collections, 431
    Index, 337
    Reproductions, Old and Modern Masters, 431n
Fine Arts...
    A Bibliographic Guide, 309
    Periodicals, 312
Fine Prints of the Year, 441n
Fink, Peter E., 175
Finkelstein, Louis, 222
Finson, Shelley D., 118
Fire Music, 729

Firkins, Ina T. E., 834
Fischel, Jack, 188
Fischer-Schreiber, Ingrid, 80
Fisher, Bob, 203n
Fisher, Kim N., 899
Fitzgerald, Gerald, 705n
Fitzgerald, Louise S., 1292
Fitzgerald, Sheila, 1260
Fitzherbert, Andrew, 127
Fitzmier, John R., 217
Fitzpatrick, Olivia, (p. 150)
Five Hundred Best British and Foreign Films, 977n
5,000 Years of the Art of India, 410
Fleming, John, 418, 482, 544
Fletcher, Banister (Sir), 495
Flew, Anthony, 60, (p. 28)
Fletcher, Banister (Sir), 495
Flexner, Stuart B., 1013, 1034n
Flora, Joseph M., 1184, 1245
Floyd, Samuel A., 683
Fodor, Nandon, 193n
Fogelman, Peggy, 504
Folk and Traditional Music of the Western Continents, 692n
Folk Artists Biographical Index, 554
Folk Music in America, 696n, 726
Folklife Sourcebook, 288n
Folklore and Folklife: A Guide, 288
Folklore of American Holidays, 299
Fontis Artis Musicae, (p. 253–254, 256)
*Footage 91: North American Film and Video Sources, 953n
Foreign Language Annals, (p. 395)
Formal Logic and Philosophic Analysis, (p. 36)
Formation of Islamic Art, 411
Forstner, L. J., 1061n
Fortune, Nigel, 691n
Forum, 893n
Foster, David W., 1314, 1322n
Foster, Donald H., 613n
Foster, Vanda, 593n
Found, Peter, 845n
Foundation Directory, 202n, 955n
Foundation Guide for Religious Grant Seekers, 202n
Fourth Book of Junior Authors, 1371n
Fowler, Roger, 1070
Frame, Pete, 757
France, Peter, 1305
*FRANCIS: Art et Archaelogie 526, 330n
*FRANCIS bulletin signaletique...
    24, Sciences du langage, 993n
    519, Philosophie, 55
    523, Histoire et sciences de la litterature, 1059
    524, Sciences du langage, 993
    526, Art et archeologie (Proche-Orient, Asie, Amerique), 330–331n, 333n
    527, Histoire et sciences des religions, 132
    527, Sciences religieuses, 132n

530, Repertoire d'art et d'archeologie, 331
*FRANCIS
    Philosophie. Science humaines, 132n, 993n
    *Philosophie 21: Sociologie, sciences du language, 993n
    *Sciences du langage, 993n
*Francis Loeb Library/Graduate School of Design, 534
Frankel, Ellen, 181n
Frankovich, Nicholas, 1267
Frazer, James G., 291n, 293n
Freedman, David N., 257
Freedman, Harry, 275
Freeman, Carla C., 381, (p. 151)
Freeman, John W., 705
*Freer Gallery of Art Library, 321n
Freitag, Wolfgang M., 316, (p. 149)
French Romanesque Sculpture, 498
French Sculptors of the 17th and 18th Centuries, 501n
*French Studies Web, 1306n
French Women Writers, 1302
French-Canadian Authors, 1181n
Frick Art Reference Library..., 332, 398
    *Frick Collection, 332n
    Original Index to Art Periodicals, 332
    Sales Catalogue Index, 348
Frick, John W., 855
Fried, Jerome, 300
Friedberg, Joan B., 1353n
Friedrich, Gerhard, 273
Friedrichsen, G. W. S., 1029n
From Headline Hunter to Superman, 915
From Museums, Galleries, and Studios, 323
From Silents to Sound, 964
Frost, Carolyn, (p. 151)
Fry, Stephen M., (p. 253)
Frye, Northrop, 1075n
Fu, Charles W., 50
Fuld, James J., 637
Fuller, Graham, 966
Fuller, Muriel, 1371n
Fund Raiser's Guide to Religious Philanthropy, 202
Funk, Isaac K., 1010
Funk & Wagnall's Guide to Modern World Literature, 1077
Funk & Wagnall's New Standard Dictionary of the English Language, 1010
Funk & Wagnall's Standard Dictionary of Folklore, 300
Funkhouser, Edward, (p. 5)
Furness, Raymond, 1327
Furtado, Ken, 831
Future of the Humanities, (p. 2, 74)

*Gale Directory of...
    Databases, 9
    Publications and Broadcast Media (1999), 6

Gale Discovering Authors Program, 1088n
Galerstein, Carolyn L., 1325
*Gale's Literary Index on CD-ROM, 87n, 1084n,
    1087n, 1090, 1093, 1097n, 1099n–1100n,
    1102n, 1131n, 1216n, 1242n, 1244n,
    1260n, 1280n–1281n, 1297n, 1332n
Gammond, Peter, 746
Gangwere, Blanche, 689
Ganzl, Kurt, 777
Ganzl's Book of the Musical Theatre, 777n
Garber, Daniel, 95n
Gardner, Albert T. E., 426n
Gardner, Helen L., 412, 418n, 1277
Gardner, James L., 125n
Gardner's Art Through the Ages, 412–413n
Garland Encyclopedia of World Music, 664
Garland, Henry, 1332
Garland, Ken, 542
Garland, Mary, 1332
Garon, P., (p. 253)
Garraty, John A., 28
Garrett, L., (p. 68)
*Gateway to Art History, 412n
Gaunt, Marianne, (p. 8, 394)
Gavronsky, Serge, 1307
Gay and Lesbian...
    American Plays, 831
    Literature, 1192
Gaze, Delia, 389
Gealt, Adelheid M., 379, 455
Geduld, Harry M., 943
Gee, Robin, 1129n
Gene Lees Jazzletter, 752n
Genreflecting, 1236
Gentry, Linnell, 740n
Gentz, William H., 162n
George, Leonard, 141
George Mason University. Fenwick Library, 880
Gerber, William, (p. 30)
Gerhardstein, Virginia B., 1217
German Art from Beckmann to Richter, 438
*German Corner, 1329n
*German Fiction Writers...
    1885–1913, 1332n
    1914–1945, 1332n
German Literature, 1331n
*German Literature on the Internet, 1329
*German Studies Web, 1329n
Germer, Mark, (p. 252)
Gerstenberger, Donna L., 1241n
*Getty Research Institute for the History of Art
    and the Humanities, 329n
Getz, Leslie, 815
Gibb, H. A. R., 184
Gibson, Gerald D., 694n
Gifford, Denis, 912n–913n
Gilbert and Sullivan Companion, 778
Gillaspie, Jon A., 638n
Gillen, Eckhart, 438

Gillespie, Cindy S., 1346n
Gillespie, John T., 1344, 1359
Gilmore, Mikal, 745
Ginell, Cary, 767
Gitler, Ira, 762n
Glare, P. G. W., 1045
Glass, Dorothy F., 498n
Glasse, Cyril, 184n
Glatt, Hillary, 288n
Glazier, Loss P., 1149
Glikin, Ronda, 1177n
Gloag, John, 559
*Global Jewish Database, 239n
Glock, Hans-Johann, 86n
Glossary of...
    Art, Architecture, and Design Since 1945, 364
    Contemporary Literary Theory, 1073
    Indian Religious Terms and Concepts, 185n
    Literary Terms, 1074
Goble, Alan, 916
Godden, Malcolm, 1158n
Goddesses in World Mythology, 307n
Godfrey, Donald G., 938
*Gods, Goddesses, and Myths, 295n
Goedeke, Karl, 1330
Goff, Penrith B., 1331n
Golden Bough, 291n, 293n
Goldman, Paul, 449
Goldstein, Franz, 353n
Good Books for Children 1950–1965, 1345n
Goodenberger, Jennifer, 657
Goodfellow, William D., 738
Goodin, Robert E., 74n
Goodrick, Edward W., 253
Gordimer, Nadine, 1240n
Gordon, Steewart W., 653
Gordon, W. Terrence, 987n
*Gordon's Print Price Annual, 439
Gore, Chris, 952n
Gorman, G. E., 105
Gorman, Lyn, 105
Goss, Gordon, 810n
Gottesman, Roberta, 679n
Gould, Constance, (p. 6, 31)
Goulding, Alfred S., 600
Goulet, Richard, 87
Gove, Phillip B., 1015
Grabar, Oleg, 411
Grainger, Brett, (p. 70)
Granger, Edith, 1267
Granger's Index to Poetry, 1267, 1270n, 1350n
Grant, Gail, 807n
Grant, Edmund, 981n
Grant, Michael, 306
Grant, William E., 1242n
Grants and Awards Available to American Writers,
    1103
Graphic Arts Encyclopedia, 541
Graphic Design Materials and Equipment, 549n

Graphics, Design, and Printing Terms, 542
Grattan, Virginia L., 753
Gray, Anne, (p. 253)
Gray, John, 314, 618, 729
Gray, Michael H., 694n
Great American Poetry Bake-Off, 1286
Great Architecture of the World, 474
Great Events from History II, 26
Great Hollywood Musical Pictures, 779
Great Italian Films, 977
Great Masters of the Violin, 720n
Great News Bible, 238n
Great Opera Classics, 702
Great Song Thesaurus, 732
Great Stage Stars, 868
Great Thinkers of the...
    Eastern World, 90
    Western World, 91
Great Writers of the English Language, 1193
Greek and Roman Writers, 1297
Green, Carol H., 1174n
Green, Joann, 896
Green, Joel B., 258
Green, Jonathan, 1022n, 1027n
Green, Kay, 774n
Green, Laura G., (p. 252)
Green, R., (p. 254)
Green, Stanley, 774n, 776
Green, William S., 222n
Greenberg, Martin H., 1226
Greene, David M., 721
Greene's Biographical Encyclopedia, 721
Greenfieldt, John, 1234
Greenstein, D., (p. 9)
Greer, Roger C., 340n
Gregory, Hugh, 761
Gresham, T. L., (p. 69)
Gretes, Frances C., 464
Greutzner, A., 452
Gribin, Anthony J., 766n
Griffel, Margaret R., 709
Griffin, J., (p. 154)
Griffith, Benjamin W., 1007
Griffiths, Trevor R., 898
Grimes, John A., 82n
Grimm, Jakob L. K., 1038
Grimm, Wilhelm, 1038
Griscom, R., (p. 254)
Grosheide, F. W., 261n
Gross, Ernie, 158
Grote, David, 896n, 1157
Grout, Donald J., 688, 713n
Grunder, Karlfried, 68
Grundriss der Geschichte der philosophie, 41
Grundriss zur Geschichte der deutschen
    Dichtung, 1330
Guernsey, Otis L., 876n
Guest, Susan S., (p. 6)

Guide to...
    African Cinema, 934
    American Film Directors, 968n
    American Poetry Explication, 1287
    Art Reference Books, 309n
    Arts and Crafts Workshops, 550
    Basic Information Sources in the Visual Arts,
        (p. 150)
    British Poetry Explication, 1287n
    Buddhist Philosophy, 120
    Buddhist Religion, 50n
    Catholic Literature, 1888–1940, 130n
    Chinese Philosophy, 50
    Chinese Poetry and Drama, 1341n
    Chinese Religion, 120n
    Collecting Fine Prints, 440
    College Courses in Film and Television, (p. 257)
    Critical Reviews...
        Part I: American Drama 1909–1982, 893n
        Part II: The Musical 1909–1989, 773
        Part III: Foreign Drama 1909–1974, 978n
        Part IV: The Screenplay from the Jazz
            Singer to Dr. Strangelove, 978n
        Supp. One: 1963–1980, 978
    Dance Periodicals, 793n
    English and American Literature, 1137n
    English Literature, 1137n
    Exhibited Artists, 392
    French Literature, 1303
    French Poetry Explication, 1304
    Hindu Religion, 121
    Historical Fiction, 1217n
    Indian Philosophy, 49n
    Islam, 122
    Japanese Prose, 1341
    Literary Agents (1999), 1105
    Reference and Bibliography for Theatre
        Research, 823
    Reference Books, 3
    Schools and Departments of Religion, 200n
    Selecting and Using Bible Commentaries, 247n
    *Serial Bibliographies for Modern Literatures,
        1053
    the Gods, 301
    the Oxford English Dictionary, 1012n
    the Performing Arts, 793n
    the Pianist's Repertoire, 651, 656n
    World Cinema, 935
Guiley, Rosemary E., 192, 195
Guilmette, Pierre, 811
Guinness Book of Music, 665
Guinness Encyclopedia of Popular Music, 742
Guinness Guide to Ballet, 808
Guitar and Lute..., 652n
    Music in Periodicals, 652
Guitar Review, 652n
Gunn, Paula, 1138n
Gunton, Colin E., 160
Gunzenhauser, Margot, 801

Guttenplan, Samuel D., 74n
Guthrie, William K. C., 95
Gutteridge, Timothy, 1039n
Gwinup, Thomas, 1297n
Gwynn, R. S., 1280n

Hackett, Jeremiah, 87n
Haftmann, Werner, 460
Hagen, Rainer, 451
Hagen, Rose-Marie, 451
Hahn, H. George, 1254n
Haines, Helen, (p. 392–393)
Halbertal, Moshe, 275n
Hale, Bob, 74n
Hall, Charles J., 687
Hall, Halbert W., 1124, 1229
Hall, Sharon K., 1085
Halliwell, Leslie, 936
Halliwell's Film and Video Guide, 936n
Halliwell's Film Guide, 936n
Halliwell's Filmgoer's Companion, 936
Halpern, Jack, 1044
Hamilton, David, 789, (p. 69)
Hamilton, Linda H., (p. 251)
Hamer, Frank, 576
Hamer, Janet, 576
Hamey, Wayne S., 728
Hamilton, David A., 789
Hammer, Tad B., 940n
Hammond, Anne, 529
Hampton, Benjamin, 972n
Hancock, Ian, 1024
Hand, Raymond Jr., 1033
Handbook of...
    Church History, 225
    Contemporary Fiction for Public Libraries,
        1236n
    Denominations in the United States, 148n
    Latin American Literature, 1314
    Literary Research, 1136n
    Metaphysics and Ontology, 83
    Old Time Radio, 937
    Russian Literature, 1335
    World Philosophy, 84
Handbook to Literature, 1075
Handbuch der...
    Geschichte der Philosophie, 42
    Kirchengeschichte, 225n
Handel's National Directory for the Performing
    Arts, 605n
Handweaving, 578
Hanfmann, George M. A., 508n
Hanna, Archibald, 1227
Hanning, Barbara R., 688n
Hanson, Patricia K., 975
Hanson, Stephen L., 975
Hapka, Christopher, 712n
Hardin, James, 1332n

Harke, Gary L., (p. 68)
Harmon, Justin, 28n
Harmon, William, 1075
*Harmonium Bibliography-Anthologies of
    Music, 635n
Harmony Illustrated Encyclopedia of...
    Country Music, 759
    Rock, 757
Harnes, James L., 1135n, 1254
Haroon, Mohammed, 618n
Harper Atlas of the Bible, 283
Harper Concise Atlas of the Bible, 283n
Harper Dictionary of Contemporary Usage, 1023
Harper Handbook to Literature, 1075n
HarperCollins Bible Dictionary, 263
HarperCollins Dictionary of...
    Art Terms and Techniques, 365
    Philosophy, 62n
HarperCollins Italian Dictionary, 1037n
Harper's Bible...
    *Commentary, 263n, 276
    *Dictionary, 263n, 276n
    Dictionary and Harper's Bible Commentary,
        263n
Harper's Encyclopedia of Mystic & Paranormal
    Experience, 195
Harpole, Charles, 974
Harpsichord and Clavichord Music of the Twen-
    tieth Century, 656
*Harrap's Business Dictionary, 1040n
*Harrap's Concise Dictionary, 1040n
*Harrap's Data Processing Dictionary, 1040n
*Harrap's Science Dictionary, 1040n
*Harrap's Shorter Dictionary..., 1040n
    English-French/French-English, 1039n
Harrap's Standard French and English Dictionary,
    1039
Harris, Cyril M., 476, 482
Harris, Charles W., 484n
Harris, Ian, 140
Harris, Laurie L., 1062, 1065n, 1260
Harris, Sheldon, 754
Harris, Steve, 782
Harris, Wendell V., 1068
Harrison, F. L., 669n
Harrison, R. K., 168, 269
Hart, James D., 1166
Hartdegan, Stephen J., 252
Hartnoll, Phyllis, 845
Hartt, Frederick, 407, 414
Hartzler, Judith, 1236n
Harvard Biographical Dictionary of Music, 684
Harvard Dictionary of Music (New), 672
Harvard Library Bulletin, (p. 252)
*Harvard University Art Museums, 338
Harvey, Paul, 1168n, 1299n, 1305n
Hastings, A. J., 146, 258n
Hathorn, Richmond Y., 848n
Hattaway, Michael, 847n

Haven't I Seen You Somewhere Before?, 941n
Haviland, David S., 479n
Havlice, Patricia P., 432n, 436, 499, 735–737,
 1080n
Hawkins-Dady, Mark, 841, 1193n
Hawthorn, Jeremy, 848n, 1073
Haycraft, Howard, 1101n, 1376
Haynes, Bruce, 654
Hazel, John, 306
Hazen, Edith P., 1133n, 1267
*Hebrew-Greek Transliteration, 241n
Hedblad, Alan, 1374n
Hedstrom, Margaret, (p. 9)
Hegel Dictionary, 86n
Heidegger Dictionary, 86n
Heintze, James R., 611, 634
Heinzkill, Richard, (p. 393)
Helander, Brock, 760
Helbig, Alethea K., 1361n
Heller, Steven, 453
Hellner, Nancy, 831
Henderson, Helene, 1062
Hendler, Herb, 749
Hendrick, George, 1241n
Hendrickson, Robert, 1030n
Heninger, S. K., 1252n
Hennessee, Don, 685n
Henry Holt Encyclopedia of Word and Phrase
 Origins, 1030n
Herald, Diana T., 1236
Herbert, Miranda C., 30, 604
Heritage Encyclopedia of Band Music, 758
Herman, Jeff, 1105n
Herubel, Jean-Pierre V. M., (p. 31, 39)
Herzhaft, Gerard, 739
Herzog, Johann J., 178
Hetherington, Norriss S., 79
Heussman, John W., (p. 70)
Heyer, Anna H., 640n
Hicken, Mandy, 913
Hickey, Morgan, 1179
Hicks, Leta, (p. 253)
High Fidelity, 680n
High Places in Cyberspace, 109
Highfill, Philip H., 861
Hildy, Franklin J., 871n
Hile, Kevin S., 1359
Hiley, David, 691n
Hill, Brad, 617
Hill, Donna, 1371n
Hill, George R., 640
Hill, Holly, 879
Hill, Samuel S., 148n
Hill, Thomas E., 377
Hill, Trevor H., 1144
Hillerbrand, Hans J., 177
Hillier, Bevis, 537n
Hindu Spirituality, 230n
Hinman, Lawrence, (p. 29)

Hinnells, John R., 145n, 153, 221
Hinojosa, Ida N., 1042
Hinson, Maurice, 651, 656
Hirschfelder, Arlene B., 150
Hirschhorn, Clive, 776n
Hischak, Thomas S., 781
*Hispanic Writers, 1315
*Histoire et Sciences des Religions, 132n
Historic America, 485n
*Historic American Sheet Music, 640n
Historical Art Index, A.D. 400–1650, 339, 342n
Historical Atlas of the Religions of the World, 226
Historical Dictionary of...
 American Radio, 938
 Buddhism, 185
 Hinduism, 186
Historical Guide to Children's Theatre in America,
 881
Historical Sets, Collected Editions ... of Music,
 640n
Historisches Worterbuch der Philosophie, 68
History and...
 Encyclopedia of Country, Western, and Gospel,
  740n
 Literature of the Wind Band and Wind Ensem-
  ble, 758n
History of...
 Art, 413, 418n
 Greek Philosophy, 95
 Hispanic Theatre in the United States, 878n
 Ideas, 43
 Italian Renaissance Art, 414
 Keyboard Literature, 653
 Modern Art, 415
 Narrative Film, 973
 Philosophy, 96
 Photography, 510
 the American Cinema, 974
 the Bibliography of Philosophy, 44
 the English Language, 1049
 the Movies, 972n
 the Theatre, 871
  *Digital Supplement, 871n
 Western Music, 688
 Western Philosophy, 97n, (p. 30)
 Western Sculpture, 508
 World Architecture (series), 494
 World Theater, 872
Hit Parade, 739
Hitchcock, H. Wiley, 670, 692n
Hixon, Don L., 685n
Hoad, T. F., 1029
Hobbes Dictionary, 86n
Hochman, Stanley, 844
Hockey, Susan, (p. 8)
Hoffman, Frank W., 1, 731, 766
Hoffman, Herbert, 837n, 1295
Hoffman's Index to Poetry, 837n, 1295
Hoffstetter, Eleanore O., 1333

Hoinkes, Rodney, 463n
Hoke, John R., 484n
Holbrook, Clyde A., (p. 67)
Holley, E. Jens, (p. 67)
Holloway, J. H., (p. 4)
Hollywood Baby Boomers, 965
*HOLLYWOOD HOTLINE, 950n
Hollywood Musical, 776n
Hollywood's Indian, 939
Holm, Kirsten C., 1107
Holman, Hugh C., 1075
Holography Market Place (HMP), 516n
Holte, James C., 211
Holtze, Sally H., 1371n
Holy Bible. *See* Bible for specific versions to
    search
Holy Ground, 112n
Holy Scriptures (Jewish Version), 239
    According to the Masoretic Text, 239n
Home Book of Quotations, Classical and Modern,
    1110
Home Video & Cable Report, 957n
Homosexual Characters in YA Novels, 1370
Honea, Sion M., (p. 252)
Honderich, Ted, 69
Honour, Hugh, 418, 482n, 544
Hood, Phil, 756n
Hook, W. J., (p. 68)
Hooper, Brad, 1123n
Hope, Augustine, 357
Hopkins, Richard, (p. 393)
Horacek, David, (p. 37)
Horn, David, 624n
Horn, Maurice, 552
Hornblower, Simon, 1299n
Houck, Catherine, 589n
Houghton, B., (p. 150)
Houghton, Walter E., 1155
Houston, Helen R., 1219n
Hovland, Michael A., 648
Howard, Eric, 1162
Howatson, M. C., 1299
Howes, Kelly K., 1065
Howlett, Colin, 1046
Hoy, James, 827n
Hubin, Allen J., 1221
Huck, Kathy, 1357
Hudson, Kenneth, 14–15n
Hudson, Winthrop S., (p. 67)
Huffman, Franklin E., 986
Hughes, Andrew, 625
Hughes, Don A., 691n
Hughes, Robert, 406
Hughston, M. R., (p. 151)
Hulet, Clayton H., (p. 68)
Huling, Nancy, 1137
Hultgren, Arland J., 245n
Hultman, Scott, 763n

Human Communication Research, (p. 5)
Humanistic Scholars Project: A Study of Atti-
    tudes, (p. 394)
*Humanities Abstracts, 24n
Humanities and the Library, (p. 2, 30, 67, 73,
    149, 249, 251, 254, 393)
Humanities Computing Yearbook, (p. 395)
Humanities in American Life, (p. 2, 11)
*Humanities Index, 19n, 24
Humble, Malcolm, 1327
Hunt, William D., 479
Hunter, Allan, 931n
Hutchings, Noel, 48
Hutchins, Geraldine L., 1229n
Hutchinson Dictionary of Ideas, 64n
Hutera, Donald, 796

*IAWM, 667n
Iconography of Recorded Sound 1886–1956,
    (p. 253)
Ideas and Styles in the Western Musical Tradi-
    tion, 688n
Identities and Issues in Literature, 1162
Ignashev, Diane M. N., 1338
Illustrated Bible Dictionary, 285n
Illustrated Compendium of Musical Technology,
    784n
Illustrated Dictionary of...
    Bible Life and Times, 264n
    Ceramics, 573
    Glass, 574
    Historic Architecture, 482
    Jewelry, 565
    Knitting, 583
Illustrated Encyclopaedia of...
    Arthurian Legends, 1164n
    Costume and Fashion, 592
Illustrated Encyclopedia of...
    Active New Religions, Sects, and Cults, 191n
    Architects and Architecture, 483
    Movie Character Actors, 966n
Illustrated Guide to Glass, 575
Illustrated Who's Who...
    in Mythology, 302
    of the Cinema, 966
Illustration Index (and supps), 340
Imel, Dorothy M., 307n
Immel, Myra, 1354
Imperial Dance Letter, (p. 256)
IMS Directory of Publications, 6n
IMS/Ayer Directory of Publications, 6n
In the Fog of the Season's End, 1240n
Inada, Kenneth K., 50
*Independent Publishers Group, 1149n
Index by Region, Usage, and Etymology, 1020n
*Index Islamicus..., 133n
    1906–1955 (and supplements), 133

Index of...
  American Periodical Verse, 1268n
  American Print Exhibitions, 1892–1940, 441
Index Thomisticus, (p. 36)
Index to...
  American Photographic Collections, 515
  Art Periodicals (Ryerson Library), 332n
  Biographies of Contemporary Composers, 722
  Black American Writers in Collective Biog-
      raphies, 1194
  *Book Reviews in Religion..., 132
    1949–1974, 132n
  British Literary Bibliography, 1144
  Characters in the Performing Arts, 599
  Children's Poetry, 1350
  Crime and Mystery Anthologies, 1226
  Dance Periodicals, 793
  Fairy Tales...
    1949–1972 (and Supps.), 289
    Myths, and Legends, 289n
  Full Length Plays...
    1895–1925, 832
    1926–1944, 832n
    1944–1964, 832n
  Historic Preservation Periodicals, 472
  Italian Architecture, 473n
  Jewish Periodicals, 134
  Literary Biography, 1080
  Motion Pictures Reviewed by Variety,
    1907–1980, 984n
  One-Act Plays (series), 833
  Opera, Operetta and Musical Comedy Synopses,
    698
  Plays...
    1800–1926, 834
    1927–1934, 834n
    in Periodicals (and supp.), 835
  Poetry for Children and Young People (and
    Supps.), 1350
  Poetry in...
    Periodicals (series), 1271n
    Popular Periodicals, 1268
  Religious Periodical Literature, 135n
  Reproductions of American Paintings, 432, 436n
    Appearing in More than 400 Books, 432n–433
  Reproductions of European Paintings, 432n, 436n
  Social Sciences & Humanities Proceedings, 25
  Song Books, 735n–736
  the London Stage, 1660–1800, 882n
  the Portraits in Odell's Annals, 875n
  the Wilson Authors Series, 1101n
  Two-Dimensional Art Works, 341
Index-Dictionary of Chinese Artists, 366
Indian Literature in English, 1827–1979, 1340n
Indian Music Literature, 618n
Indiana Companion to Traditional Chinese
    Literature, 1340n
Individuals, (p. 28)
Information and Technology: Planning, (p. 36)

Information Needs in the Humanities, (p. 6, 31)
Information on Music, 612–613n
Information Technology in Humanities Scholar-
    ship, (p. 7)
Inge, Thomas, 1194n
Ingman, Heather, 1263
Ingpen, Robert, 304n
Innovators of American Illustration, 453
INSPEL, (p. 151)
Institutum Patriscum Augustinianum, 171
Instrumental Music Printed Before 1600, 653n
Instrumental Virtuosi: A Bibliography, 723
Interior Design Sourcebook, 465
*International Alliance for Women in Music.
    See IAWM
*International Art Catalog, 336n
International Authors and Writers Who's Who, 1091
International Bibliography of...
  the History of Religions, 137n
  Theatre, 829
International Book of Ballet, 808n
International Center of Photography/Encyclopedia
    of Photography, 519
International Cyclopedia of Music and Musicians,
    666
International Dictionary of...
  Architects and Architecture, 491
  Art and Artists, 393
  Ballet, 809n
  Films and Filmmakers, 841n, 967
  Modern Dance, 817
  Opera, 703
  Theatre, 841
  Theatre Language, 842
International Directory of...
  *Art Libraries, 377
  Arts, 378
  Film and TV Documentation Centers, 953
  Little Magazines and Small Presses, 1055
  Philosophy and Philosophers, 88n, 92, (p. 37)
International Discography of Women Composers,
    725
International Encyclopedia of...
  Dance, 799
  Linguistics, 1003
  Women Composers, 685
International English Usage, 1024
International Film...
  Guide, 949n
  Index, 1895–1990, 916
    *on CD-ROM, 916n
  Industry: A Historical Dictionary, 940
  Prizes: An Encyclopedia, 940n
International Guide to Nineteenth-Century
    Photographers, 520
*International Index to...
  Film Periodicals, 922
  Music Periodicals Full Text, (p. 255)
  Television Periodicals, 922n

International Motion Picture Almanac, 954
International Museum of Photography, 511
International Music Journals, 615
International Opera Guide, 715
International Philosophical Bibliography…, 56
International Standard Bible Encyclopedia, 265
International Television & Video Almanac, 954n
International Who's Who in Music and Musicians' Directory, 686n
*Internationale Kunstler Datenbank, 383n
Internationale Zeitschriftenschau fur Bibelwissenschaft, 243
Internet Compendium: Subject Guide to Humanities Resources, (p. 10)
Internet Encyclopedia of Philosophy, (p. 31, 36)
Internet School Library Media Center, 1351n
Interpreter's Bible, 266n, 277
Interpreter's Concise Commentary, 278
Interpreter's Dictionary of the Bible, 257n, 263n, 266
Interpreter's One-Volume Commentary on the Bible, 278n
Interviews and Conversations with 20th-Century Authors, 1153
Introduction to…
    Italian Sculpture, 509
    Library Research in German Studies, 1351
    the New Testament, 278n
Inwood, Michael J., 86
IPG. *See* Independent Publishers Group
Ireland, Norma O., 289, 832n
Irregular Serials and Annuals, 7n
Irvine, Betty Jo, (p. 151)
Irwin, Leonard B., 1217n, 1266n
Irwin, Robert, 1266n
*Islam, 133
Islam and Islamic Groups, 187n
Islam in North America: A Sourcebook, 187
Islamic Desk Reference, 184n
Islamic Literature: Problems in Collection Development, (p. 68)
Islamic Spirituality, 230n
Italian Romanesque Architecture, 498n
Itzchaky, Moshe, (p. 70)
Iwaschkin, Roman, 727
Iz, Fahir, 1043n

Jack, Andrew, (p. 29, 39)
Jackson, Richard, 624n
Jackson, Virginia, 379n
Jackson, W. A., 1147
Jackson, William T. H., 1089n
Jacob, Andre, 67
Jacobs, Arthur, 702
James, Richard S., 615
Jane Austen Encyclopedia, 1256
Janes, Michael, 1039n
Jankowski, Bernard, 202

Janson, Anthony F., 413
Janson, Horst W., 413
Jasenas, Michael, 44
Jazz, 694n
Jazz Discography, 768
Jazz Records 1897–1942, 769n
*Jazz Research, 730n
Jedin, Hubert, 225
Jerde, Judith, 581
Jerusalem Bible, 235, 248n, 259n
Jervis, Simon, 553
Jessop, D., (p. 252)
Jesus and His World, 171n
Jewish American Fiction Writers, 1257
Jewish-American History and Culture, 188
Jewish Daily Forward, 214n
Jewish Encyclopedia, 183n
Jewish Folklore, 290
Jewish Heritage in America, 123n
Jewish Profiles, 214
Jewish Spirituality, 230n
Job Information Lists (MLA), (p. 395)
Jodidio, Philip, 490n
John Willis' Theatre World, 857
Johnson, Jane, 452
Johnson, William, 512
Jones, Charles E., 114n
Jones, Dolores B., 1360
Jones, Lois S., 308, (p. 149, 154–156)
Jones, Malcolm, 1334, (p. 254)
Jones, William G., (p. 6–7, 394)
Jordan, Casper LeRoy, 1177
Journal of…
    Documentation, (p. 5, 31)
    Education for Library and Information Science, (p. 36)
    Indian Philosophy, 49n
    Librarianship, (p. 254)
    Philosophy, (p. 31)
    Religious and Theological Information, (p. 69–70)
    Research in Music Education, (p. 256)
    Scholarly Publishing, (p. 395)
    the American Musicological Society, (p. 256)
    the ASIS (American Society for Information Science), (p. 4, 6–8)
    the Association for Recorded Sound Collections, 694n
    Youth Services in Libraries, (p. 68)
Joyce, Beverly A., 1269
Joyce, Donald F., 31
Joys of Motherhood, 1240n
Judaica Americana…
    A Bibliography, 123
    An Annotated Bibliography, 123n
Judaism and Christianity: A Guide, 101, (p. 67)
Junior Book of Authors, 1371
Junior High School Library Catalog, 1344n

Kaeppler, Adrienne, L., 664n
Kaganov, Nathan M., 123n
Kalfatoric, Martin, (p. 154)
Kallman, Helmut, 662
Kandiuk, Mary, 1181
Kanellos, Nicolas, 878n
Kant Dictionary, 86n
Kaplan, Justin, 1109
Kaplan, Leslie, 1307
Kaplan, Mike, 608, 853
Kardas, Pat, 942n
Karkhanis, Sharad, 123n
Karp, Rashelle S., 838
Karpel, Bernard, 317
Kasher, Menahem M., 275
Kasinec, E., (p. 151)
Kassel, Richard, 675
Katlan, Alexander W., 373
Katz, Bill, 5, 1272
Katz, Ephraim, 932
Katz, Linda S., 5, 1272
Katz, William. *See* Katz, Bill
Kaufmann, Paula T., (p. 6)
Kaufmann, Walter, (p. 2, 11, 74)
Kawachi, Yoshiko, 674
Kearney, Elizabeth J., 1292
Keeping Score...
    Film Music 1972–1979, 772n
    Film and Television Music 1980–1988, 772n
Kehler, Dorothea, 1054
Keller, Dean H., 835
Keller, Michael A., (p. 252)
Kellman, Steven G., 614n
Kelly, Aidan, 158n
Kelly, John N. D., 215
Kelly, Serena, (p. 151)
Kemp, Sandra, 1235
Kendall, Alan, 306n
Kenna, Stephanie, (p. 7)
Kennedy, James R., Jr., 102
Kennedy, Michael, 673n
Kennington, Donald, 730
Kenny, Anthony, 97
Kepple, Robert J., 103
Keranan, Alvin, (p. 2)
Kerensky, Oleg, 808
Kernfield, Barry, 744, 769n
Kersey, Ethel M., 94
Kersley, Leo, 807
Kersten, D. B., (p. 69)
Kerwin, Yala H., 341
Kesler, Jackson, 585n
Kester-Shelton, Pamela, 1191
Keutner, Herbert, 508n
Keveaney, Sidney S., 421n
Key Guide to Electronic Resources: Art, 313
Key Ideas in Human Thought, (p. 28, 30, 39, 73,
    149, 156, 249, 258)
Kiell, Norman, 1058n

Killings, Douglas B., 1297n
Kilvert, Ian S., 1180
Kim, Jaegwon, 74n
Kimbel, Bobby E., 1242
Kimmens, Andrew C., 1101
*King James Version, 231, 234n, 236n, 241n,
    248n, 250n–251n, 254n–256n,
    265n–266n, 270n, 277n
King, Lisabeth A., (p. 9)
Kingsbury, Kenn, 759n
Kingsbury's Who's Who in Country & Western
    Music, 759n
Kinkle, Roger D., 739n
Kinsella, Thomas, 1278
Kipnis, Igor, 758
Kirby, John T., 1052
Kirkpatrick, D. L., 1199–1200
Kister, Kenneth F., 989
Kister's Best Dictionaries for Adults & Young
    People, 989
Kittel, Gerhard, 273
Klein, Leonard S., 1072
Kleinbauer, W. Eugene, (p. 149)
Kleiner, Diane E. E., 509n
Kleiner, Fred S., 412
Kleinbauer, W. Eugene, 311, 467
Kline, Victoria, 1133n
Klingelhofer, William G., 338
Klipsch, P., (p. 69)
Kloessel, Christian J. W., 1253n
Kluepfel, Brian, 516n
Knowing the Score: Preserving Collections of
    Music, (p. 252)
Knowledge: Creation, Diffusion, Innovation, (p. 3)
Knowles, Elizabeth, 1027n, 1114n
Knowles, Mark, 800
Kobbe, Gustav, 700
Koegler, Horst, 806
Kohlenberger, John R., 253
*Kohjien (Japanese) Dictionary CD-ROM, 1044n
Kojien: A Comprehensive Dictionary, 1044n
*Kojien Dictionary, 1044n
Kolar, Carol K., 1079
Komonchak, Joseph A., 175
Kong, Le-Ba, 1041
Konigsberg, Ira, 928
Korab, Balthazar, 479
Koran, 240
Koren, Henry J., (p. 31)
Kornick, Rebecca H., 712
Korwin, Yala H., 341
Kostelanetz, Richard, 682n
Koszegi, Michael A., 104, 187
Koth, Michelle, (p. 252)
Kramers, Johannes H., 184n
Krantz, Les, 372, 525
Kraye, Jill, 26n
Kretzmann, Norman, 95n
Krive, Sarah, 1338

Krommer-Benz, Magdalena, 1050
Krstovic, Jelena O., 1297
Krummel, D. W., 610
Kuhn, Laura, 682n, 703n
Kuhn, Sherman M., 1011n
Kullman, Colby H., 860
Kunitz, Stanley J., 1101n, 1376
Kunst, Jaap, 623n
Kuntz, Joseph M., 1279n, 1287n
Kurath, Hans, 1011
Kuroff, Barbara, 1129
Kusnerz, Peggy A., (p. 152–153)
Kuyper-Rushing, Lois, (p. 254)

Lacey, Alan R., 61, (p. 28)
Lacey, Robin T., 962
Lachs, John, 51
Lacy, Norris J., 1164
La Guma, Alex, 1240n
Lalande, Andre, 72
Lamb, Andrew, 777n
Lambrechts, Eric, 513
Lamolinara, Guy, (p. 73)
Lanasa, Philip J., 1356
Lance, Steven, 947
Landon, Grelun, 740
Landscape Architecture...
    Sourcebook, 462n
    *Virtual Library, 463n
Lang, Bernhard, 229
Lang, Jovian, 174n
Lang, Paul H., 688n
Langenberg, Donald N., (p. 6)
Langer, Adam, 952
Langer, Cassandra, 322
Langman, Larry, 910, 915n, 942, 968n
Langridge, D. W., (p. 69)
Language: An Introduction to the Study of
    Speech, (p. 392)
*Languages of the World, 1040
L'annee philogique critique, 1298n
Lapidge, Michael, 1158n
L'annee philogique critique, 1298n
Larkin, Colin, 742
Larousse Dictionary of Painters, 454
LaRue, C. Steven, 703
Laserlog Reporter, 697n
LASIE, (p. 154)
Last Lines: An Index, 1133n
Latham, Alison, 671n
Latin American...
    Artists' Signatures and Monograms, 446n
    Literary Authors, 1316
    Literary Review, 1316n
    *Literary Review Press, 1316n
    Literature in the 20th Century, 1317
    Short Story: An Annotated Guide, 1318
    Writers, 1319

Laufenberg, Cindy, 751
Laver, James, 591n
Laymon, Charles, 278n
Layson, June, 819
Law, Jonathan, 28n
Lax, Roger, 732
Lazarus, John, 708n
Lazinger, S. S., (p. 7)
LC Authorities Collection, 641n
*LC MARC...
    Hebrew, 134n
    Music, 643n
    Visual Materials, 918n
Le-Ba-Khanh, 1041n
Le-Ba-Kong, 1041n
Leach, Maria, 300
Leach, Marjorie, 301
Leader of the Band, 752n
Leaver, R. A., (p. 253)
Lechte, John, 91n
Lecker, Robert, 1140, 1181
Leclerq, Henri, 167
Ledbesert, D. M., 1039
Lee, John K., 1287n
Leeming, David A., 296n
Leeming, Margaret A., 296n
Lees, Gene, 752n
Leigh, Frederic A., 938
Leigh, Robert, 735n–736n
Leiter, Samuel L., 879
LeMay, Harold, 1027n
Lems-Dworkin, Carol, 618
Leon, Ruth, 812n
Leonard, Bill J., 149n
Leonard Maltin's Movie & Video Guide, 917, 920
Leonardo, (p. 4, 11)
Leonard's Annual Price Index of Art Auctions,
    349
Leonard's Index of Art Auctions, 349n
Lerner, Loren R., 315
Les Brown's Encyclopedia of Television, 948n
Leslie, Serge, 790
Leuchtmann, Horst, 675
Levernier, James A., 1176
Levinson, David, 157
Levi, Anthony, 1303
Lewine, Richard, 775n
Lewis, Anthony, 691n
Lewis, James R., 138, 193n, 196n
Lewis, Robert E., 1011n
Lewis, Susan A., 465
Lexikon der ostlichen Weisheitslehren, 80n
Liberation Theologies: A Research Guide, 117
Library Acquisitions, (p. 68)
Library and Information Science Research,
    (p. 393–394)
Library Catalog of the...
    International Museum of Photography, 511
    *Metropolitan Museum of Art, 324

Library Exorcisms of Stalinism, 1337n
Library Journal, (p. 69, 150–151, 253–254)
Library LANs, (p. 153)
Library Literature, (p. 68)
Library of Congress...
    American Prints, 427
    Audiovisual Materials, 918n
    Catalog: Motion Pictures and Filmstrips, 918n
    Catalog: Music and Phonorecords, 630n, 643n
    Information Bulletin, (p. 73)
    *Prints and Photographs, 427n
    Subject Headings in Philosophy, (p. 35)
Library of Literary Criticism..., 1197
    Through the Beginning of the Twentieth Century, 1197n
Library Quarterly, (p. 5–6, 39, 152, 253, 393)
Library Research Guide to...
    Philosophy, 36
    Religion and Theology, 102
Library Resources and Technical Services, (p. 4, 151)
Library Trends, (p. 6, 8, 71, 254–255)
Licht, Fred, 508n
Liebman, Roy, 964
Life, 978n
Limbacher, James L., 771n–772, 941n
Limelight Book of Opera, 702n
Lincoln, T. D., (p. 68)
Lindenberger, Herbert S., 707
Lindfors, Bernth, 1099
Lindholm-Romantschuk, Yiva, (p. 4, 31)
Lindner, Eileen W., 207
Lineback, Richard H., 57n, 92, (p. 30)
Linguistic Bibliography of the Year, 992n
Linguistics: A Guide to the Reference Literature, 990
Linguistics Abstracts, 999n
*Linguistics and Language Behavior Abstracts: LLBA, 994
Linguistics Encyclopedia, 1003n
Linz, W. M., (p. 69)
Lippy, Charles H., 108, 110, 152, 218n
Lissauer, Robert, 743
Lissauer's Encyclopedia of Popular Music in America, 743
List, Charles J., 36
*Literal English Translation, 241n
Literary Adviser, 596
Literary Exorcisms of Stalinism, 1337n
Literary History of England, 1213
Literary Lifelines, 1092
Literary Market Place (LMP), 1104
Literary Research Guide, 1135n
Literary Text in an Electronic Age, (p. 8, 395)
Literatura Chicana, 1320
Literatura Hispanoamericana, 1314n
Literature and...
    Its Times, 1076
    Western Man, (p. 393)

*Literature Criticism from 1400 to 1800, 1090n, 1093
Literature of...
    American Music III, 1983–1992, 624
    American Music in Books and Folk Music Collections, 624n
    British Domestic Architecture 1715–1842, 468
    Jazz, 730
    Modern Art (LOMA), 327n
    Rock, 1954–1978, 731n
      II, 1979–1983, 731n
      III, 1984–1990, 731
*Literature Online, 1136n
Littell, Franklin H., 227
Litz, A. Walton, 1175n
Lives and Works in the Arts, 34
Lively Arts Information Directory, 606n
*Living Bible, 241n, 248n
Living with Books, (p. 392–393)
Livingston, Alan, 546
Livingston, Isabella, 546
Livingstone, Elizabeth A., 176
LLBA: Linguistics and Language Behavior Abstracts, 994n, (p. 394–395)
Lloyd, Ann, 966
LMP (Literary Market Place), 1104
Local Approach to National Collecting: A UK Feasibility Study, (p. 150)
Locke Dictionary, 86n
Loertscher, David V., 1367
Loflin, Christine, 1240n
Logasa, Hannah, 833
Logos, (p. 69)
LOMA: Literature of Modern Art, 327n
Lombardo, Daniel, (p. 151)
Lomeli, Francisco A., 1310
London Stage...
    1660–1800, 861n, 882
    1890–1899, 883
    1900–1909, 883n
    1910–1919, 883n
    1920–1929, 883n
    1930–1939, 883n
    1940–1949, 883n
    1950–1959, 883n
London Times, 869n
Londre, Felicia H., 872
Lonely Scholar in a Global Information Environment, (p. 6)
Loney, Glenn M., 886
Long, A. A., 59n
Longman Dictionary of Language Teaching, 1004
Longman, Tremper, 247
Longyear, Rey M., 692n
Looking at...
    Art, 379
    European Sculpture, 504
    Photographs, 521
    Prints, Drawings and Watercolors, 449

Looney, J. Anna, 1265
Lopez, Manuel D., 888
Lord, Tom, 768
Los Angeles Public Library, 1354n
Los Angeles Times, 869n
Lossky, Nicholas, 165
Loughney, Katharine, 900
Loughridge, Brendan, 989n
Lounsbury, Warren C., 852
Love, J. W., 664n
Lowenberg, Alfred, 699
Lowry, Anita, (p. 394)
Lucas, Amy, 316n
Lucas, Edna L., 316n
Luce, T. James, 1296
Lucie-Smith, Edward, 419
Ludlow, Daniel H., 170
Ludman, Joan, 425
Ludwig, Richard M., 1206
Luedtke, Tami, (p. 70)
Luhrs, Kathleen, 426
Lundin, Anne H., (p. 67)
Lundin, Edward, (p. 67)
Lute Society of America Journal, 652n
Lute Society of America Newsletter, 652n
Lutheran News, 203n
*Lutheran News Service, 203n
Lutterworth Dictionary of the Bible, 267n
Lyle, Wilson, 720
Lyman, Thomas W., 498
Lynk, William M., 854
Lynn, Richard J., 1341n

MacCann, Donnarae, 1358
Mackillop, James, 295
Mackler, Tasha, 1221n
Macmillan Atlas...
    History of Christianity, 227
    of Rugs and Carpets, 584
Macmillan Bible Atlas, 284–285n
Macmillan Biographical Encyclopedia of Photo-
    graphic Artists, 528
Macmillan Dictionary of Contemporary Slang,
    1022n
Macmillan Encyclopedia of Architects, 492
Macmillan Film Bibliography, 904
MacNeil, Anne, 669
Macquarrie, John, 179
Magazines for Libraries, 5
Magic, Witchcraft, and Paganism in America,
    128
Magill, Frank N., 26, 73, 889, 979–980, 1067,
    1086, 1094–1095, 1119, 1126, 1163,
    1195, 1237–1238, 1251, 1284, 1288,
    1293, 1362n, (p. 30)
Magill's Cinema Annual, 979–980n
Magill's Cyclopedia of Literary Characters,
    1067n

Magill's Literary Annual, 1094n
Magill's Survey of...
    American Literature, 1195
    Cinema, 979n–980, (p. 255)
        English Language Films, 980n
        Foreign Language Films, 980n
        Silent Films, 980n
        Title Index, All Series, 980n
Magnuson, Norris A., 112
Mahalingam, Indira, 80n
Mainiero, Lina, 1174
Major Authors and Illusrators, 1374n
Major Languages of...
    Eastern Europe, 1008
    South Asia, 1008n
Major Modern Dramatists, 891
Major 20th-Century Writers, 1083n
Makkai, Adam, 1019
Malchin, Robert, 638
Malinowski, Sharon, 1192
Mallett, Daniel T., 394
Mallett, Daryl F., 1116
Mallett's Index of Artists, 394
Malm, William P., 692n
Malmkjaer, Kirsten, 1003n
Maltin, Leonard, 917
Man, Myth, and Magic, 303
Management for Visual Arts Resources Collec-
    tion, (p. 150)
Managing Performing Arts Collections ...
    Libraries, (p. 251)
Manchel, Frank, 903
Manchester, Phyllis W., 795
Mandell, Judy, 1128
Manoff, Marlene, (p. 4, 11)
Mansion, Jean E., 1039
Mansukhani, Gobind S., 186n
Mantle, Burns, 876n
Mantle Fielding's Dictionary of American Painters,
    395
Manual of European Languages for Librarians,
    1005
Manuel de bibliographie philosophique, 45
Maple, Amanda, (p. 253)
Mapp, Edward, 602
Marcaccio, Kathleen Y., 9
Marciszewski, Witold, 76
Marco, Guy A., 612–613n, 624, 663, (p. 251)
Marcuse, Michael J., 1135
Marcuse, Sibyl, 786
Marder, Stephen, 1046n
Margolies, Edward, 1216
Mark, Mary, 1057
Markel, Robert, 639
Markey, Karen, (p. 152)
Marks and Monograms on European and Oriental
    Pottery, 572n
Marks, Alfred H., 1341
Marks, Claude, 403

Marley, Judith L., (p. 252)
Marsh, Earle, 927
Martin, Mick, 917n
Martin, Richard, 293, 594
Martindale, Charles, 1296n
Martine, James J., 1244
Martinez, Joseph G. R., 1287n
Martinez, Julio A., 1310
Martinez, Nancy C., 1287n
Marting, Diane E., 1325n
Martinich, Aloysius P., 86n
Marxist Philosophy, 51
Mason, Francis, 805n
Mason, Lauris, 424–425
Mason, Mary G., 1174
Mast, Gerald, 976
Masterpieces of…
    African-American Literature, 1163
    World Literature in Digest Form, 1094n
    World Philosophy, 73n, (p. 30)
        in Summary Form, 73n
Masterplots…, 1067n
    Annual Volume, 1094n
    *Complete CD-ROM, 1094, 1119n, 1163n,
        1237n
    *Cyclopedia of Literary Characters, 1067n
        *II, 1067n
    *Definitive Revised Edition, 1094n
        *Nonfiction, Poetry, & Drama CD-ROM,
        1094n
    1801 Plot Summaries, 1094n
    Revised Category Edition…
        American Fiction, 1237
        British Fiction, 1237n
    2,010 Plot Stories and Essay, 1094n
Masterplots II…, 1067n, 1094n–1095n, 1288n,
    1362n
    *American Fiction, 1067n, 1094n, 1238
    *British and Commonwealth Fiction, 1067n,
        1094n, 1238n
    *CD-ROM, 1067n, 1094n, 1238n
    *Drama Series, 843, 1067, 1094n
    *Juvenile and Young Adult…
        Biography Series, 1362n
        Fiction Series, 1094n, 1362
    *Nonfiction Series, 1094n–1095
    Poetry Series, 1094n, 1288
    *Short Story Series, 1067n, 1094n
    *World Fiction Series, 1067n, 1094n
    Women's Literature Series, 1094n
*Masters Abstracts, 22n
Mather, George A., 191
Mattfeld, Julius, 748
Matthiessen, F. O., 1275n
Matuz, Roger, 397, 1186
Mautner, Thomas, 61n
May, Herbert G., 286
Mayer, N. J., (p. 69)
Mayer, Ralph, 354, 365

Mays, James L., 276
McArthur, Feri, 1006
McArthur, Tom, 1006
McCabe, James P., 116, (p. 67)
McCaffery, Larry, 112
McCaslin, Nellie, 881
McCavitt, William E., 905
McClung, Patricia A., (p. 30)
McColvin, L. R., (p. 251)
McCoy, Garnett, 374
McCoy, Judy, 727n
McCoy, W. U., (p. 251)
McCully, Marilyn, 442
McDonagh, Don, 817n
McElmeel, Sharron L., 1368n
McGinn, Bernard, 230n
McGraw-Hill Encyclopedia of World Drama, 844
McGreal, Ian P., 73, 90–91
McIntire, Dennis K., 686n
McIntosh, L. D., (p. 67)
McKee, Elwood, (p. 252)
McKeown, James M., 524
McKeown, Joan C., 524
McKim, Donald K., 172
McKnight, Scot, 258
McLeish, Kenneth, (p. 2, 30, 39, 73, 149, 156, 258)
McLerran, Jennifer, 355
McManners, John, 228
McMaster, Juliet, 1256n
McNeil, Barbara, 30, 384, 604, 1080
McPheron, William, 1266
McQuaid, James, 515
McRae, Linda, (p. 151)
Mead, Frank S., 148n
Mealand, David L., (p. 71, 74)
Meanor, Patrick, 1242n
Media Access and Organization, (p. 151)
Media in the Movies, 915n
Medieval Music, 625
Medieval Philosophers, 67n
Medieval Sculpture, 508n
Medieval Stage, 884
Mehlman, Felice, 575
Mell, Donald C., 1264
Melton, J. Gordon, 104, 128, 148, 187, 193–194,
    196, 201, 204, 206, 208, 218, 1127, (p. 65)
Mencken, Henry L., 1048
Menendez, Albert J., 1221n
Mercatante, Anthony S., 298
Mercer, Anne, 1203
Mercer Dictionary of the Bible, 267
Mercer, Eric, 416n
Merriam-Webster's Collegiate…
    Dictionary, 1018, 1255n
    Thesaurus, 1018n
Merriam-Webster's Dictionary of English Usage,
    1025
Meserole, Harrison T., 1137
Metford, J. C. J., 162

*Methodists Make News, 203
*Metropolitan Museum of Art, 324, 426n
Metropolitan Opera...
    Encyclopedia, 708
    Guild: The Complete Chronicle of Perform-
        ances, 705n
    Stories of the Great Operas, 705
Metzger, Bruce M., 271
Metzger, Linda, 1178
Mexican Literature: A Bibliography, 1322n
Meyendorff, John, 230n
Meyer, George H., 554
Meyer, Ronald, 1335
MGG, 668
Michael Singer's Film Directors, 968
Michelson, Avra, (p. 7, 394)
*Microsoft Book Shelf, 1009n
Middle-English Dictionary, 1011
Middle Scots Poets, 1265
Mieder, Wolfgang, 1108
Mikotowicz, Thomas J., 870
Miller, Judith, 558
Miller, Leta, 620n
Miller, Martin, 558
Miller, P., (p. 9)
Miller, R. H., 1136n
Miller, Robin F., 1334
Miller, Tamara, (p. 6)
Miller, Terry E., 664n, 726
Miller, Tice L., 846
Miller, William G., (p. 10, 39, 73, 396)
Miller-Lachman, Lyn, 1351
Mills, John, 503
Mills, Watson E., 115n, 267
Miner, Earl, 1342
Mir, Mustansir, 260
Mirror for the Nation, 1227
Mitchell, Robert C., 126n
Mitchell, Theresa, 894
MLA Annual Bibliography, 1060n
MLA Directory of Periodicals..., 1056
    United States and Canada, 1056n
*MLA International Bibliography, 19n, 1060,
    1306n, 1311n, (p. 394–395)
MLA Technical Reports Series, (p. 252)
Mochedlover, Helene G., 836
Modern Age, 1890–1960, 691n
Modern American...
    Literature, 1196
    Novel: An Annotated Bibliography, 1258
    Popular Religion, 110
    Women Writers, 1175n
Modern Arabic Literature, 1339
Modern Arts Criticism, 396
Modern Black Writers, 1095
Modern British Literature, 1196n
Modern Esoteric Spirituality, 230n
Modern Humanities Research Association, 1151
Modern Islamic Art, 411

Modern Language Association...
    *International Bibliography, 1060
    Journal, (p. 395)
    Quarterly, 995n
    Review, 995
Modern Philogy, 1152n
Modern Writers, 1900–1998, 1182n
Molinari, Joseph A., 942
Monaco, James, 970n
Money for...
    Film and Video Artists, 955
    Graduate Students in the Humanities, 18
    Performing Artists, 603
Monogramm-Lexikon, 353n
Monogrammisten und diejenigen, 353n
Monro, Isabel S., 432, 1231
Monro, Kate M., 432
Moravcsik, Michael J., (p. 3, 11)
More Junior Authors, 1371n
More Notes for a Different Drummer, 1353n
Morehead, Philip D., 669
Morganstern, Sam, 658–659
Morley, Sheridan, 868
Moroney, K., (p. 70)
Morris, Mary, 1023
Morris, William, 1023
Morrison, Clinton, 251n
Morrone, John, 1103
Morrow, Baker H., 478
Mortimer, Kristin A., 338
Morton, Brian, 719n
Moshkovitz, Moshe, 929
Moss, Joyce, 1076
Moss, Martha, 517
Mote, Dave, 1185
Motif Index of Folk Literature, 297
Motion Picture...
    Guide, 1927–1984, 981
        Annual, 981n
    Rating Preview Reports, (p. 257)
    Series and Sequels, 941
Moulin, Paulette, 150
Moulton, Charles W., 1096
Moure, Nancy D. W., 433
Movement: From Person to Actor, 894
Movie Guide, 981n
Movie Song Catalog, 772n
Moving Borders, 1274
MPA Press, (p. 257)
Muehsam, Gerd, (p. 150)
Muether, John R., 103
Muldoon, James, 228n
Muller, Richard A., 100
Muller, Sheila D., 361
*Multicultural Resources for Children, 1351n
*Multimedia and CD-ROM Directory, 10
Multimedia Yearbook, 10n
Multi-Purpose Tools for Bible Study, 244
Murder ... by Category, 1221n

Murphy, Bruce, 1063
Murphy, Larry G., 147
Murphy, Maria S., 827n
Murray, James A. H., 1012n
Murray, Les A., 1276
Murray, Linda, 368
Murray, Peter, 368
Murray, Sterling E., 635
*MUSE (MUsic SEarch), 633n
Museum News, (p. 155)
Museum of American Folk Art and Artists
        Encyclopedia, 555
    *Online, 555n
Museum of Modern Art...
    *Art on Film Database, 375n
    Artists Files, 415n
    Artists Scrapbooks, 415n
Museums of the World, 15
Musgrove, John, 495
Music: A Guide to the Reference Literature, 613
Music Analyses, 626
Music and...
    CRC Catalogs, 642n
    Dance Periodicals, 616
    the Mind, (p. 251)
    War, 637n
Music, Books on Music, and Sound Recordings,
    630
Music Catalog (Washington, D.C.), 630n
*Music Cataloging Collection, 641
Music Cultures of the Pacific, the Near East, and
        Asia, 692n
Music Festivals...
    from Bach to Blues, 679
    in America, 679n
Music for Oboe, 1650–1800, 654
Music History...
    During the Renaissance Period, 1425–1520,
        689n
    from the Late Roman ... Gothic Periods, 689
Music in...
    Harvard Libraries, 642
    India, 692n
    Latin America, 692n
    Our Time, 691n
    Western Civilization, 688n
Music in the...
    Baroque Era, 691n
    Classic Period, 692n
    Medieval World, 692n
    Middle Ages, 691n
    Renaissance, 691n–692n
    Romantic Era, 691n
    Royal Society of London, 1660–1806, 620n
    Twentieth Century, 691n
    United States, 692n
Music-in-Print (series), 644
*Music Index..., 631, 750
    *on CD-ROM, 631n

Music Librarianship..., (p. 254)
    A Practical Guide, (p. 251)
    in America, (p. 252)
Music Libraries, (p. 251)
Music Library Association...
    Catalog of Cards, 643
    Notes, 632
    *Sheet Music Collections, 733n
Music Lover's Guide to Europe, 679n
Music Reference and Research Materials, (p. 252)
Music Since 1900, 690
Music Theory...
    from Zarlino to Schenker, 629
    *Online, (p. 255)
*Music Yellow Pages, 676n
Music/AGORCC, (p. 256)
Musical America, 680
Musical and Dance Films, 776n
Musical Heritage Review, 721n
Musical Instruments...
    A Comprehensive Dictionary, 786
    of the World, 787
    *Website, 787n
Musical Settings of American Poetry, 648
Musical Woman, 667
Musik in Geschichte und Gegenwart (MGG), 668
Musiker, Naomi, 755
Musiker, Reuben, 755
Musi*key, 733
Muslim Almanac, 190n
Musto, Ronald G., 117
Myers, Allen C., 261
Myers, Bernard S., 451n
Myerson, Joel, 1087n
Mystery Writer's Marketplace and Sourcebook,
    1129n
Mythical and Fabulous Creatures, 304
Mythological and Classical World Art Index,
    342, 344n
Mythologies, 305

Naden, Corinne, 1359
Nagler, George K., 353n
Nakamura, Joyce, 1374n
Nanji, Azim A., 190n
Nash, Jay R., 981
Nathanail, Paul, 1043
National Anthems of the World, 660
National Directory...
    for the Performing Arts and Civic Centers, 605n
    for the Performing Arts/Educational, 605n
    of Churches, Synagogues, and Other Houses,
        204
    of Corporate Giving, 202n
National Guide to Funding in Religion, 202n
*National Portrait Gallery, Smithsonian Institu-
        tion, 434

*National Register of Historic Places 1966–1994, 486

National Square Dance Directory, 810n

National Trust for Historic Preservation, 487

National Union Catalog…, 643n

*Audiovisual Materials, 918

Native American Authors, 1138n

Natoli, Joseph, 1058

Nault, Clifford A., 1206

Nauman, St. Elmo, Jr., 80n

Navia, Luis E., 52n

Naylor, Colin, 358

Naylor, Lynn, 958

NBC Handbook of Pronunciation, 1033

Neal, James G., (p. 7)

Negro Playwrights in the American Theatre, 1925–1959, 867n

Neilson, William A., 1014

Nelson, C. E., (p. 70)

Nelson, Emmanuel S., 1204, 1243, 1246

Nelson's Bible Encyclopedia for the Family, 268

Nelson's Complete Concordance of the New American Bible, 252

Nelson-Atkins Museum of Art, 429

Nelson-Strauss, Brenda, (p. 252)

Nervous Conditions, 1240n

Ness, Richard R., 915

Nettl, Bruno, 623n, 692n

Neufeldt, Victoria, 1018n

Neuman, Delia, (p. 70)

Neusner, Jacob, 222n

New Age Encyclopedia, 196, (p. 65–66)

New American…
  Bible, 237, 248n, 252n
  Dictionary of Music, 669
  Standard Bible, 231n, 233n, 248n, 270n

New Arthurian Encyclopedia, 1164

New Bible…
  Atlas, 285
  Dictionary, 264

New Blackwell Guide to Recorded Blues, 765

New Cambridge Bibliography of English Literature, 1145, 1273n

New Catholic Encyclopedia, 174

*New City Opera, 705n

New College Encyclopedia of Music, 669n

*New Deal Stage Selections, 880n

New Dictionary of…
  Sacramental Worship, 175n
  Theology, 175

New Directions for Higher Education, (p. 6)

New English…
  Bible, 236, 248n, 265n, 280n
  Dictionary on Historical Principles, 1012n

New English-Chinese Dictionary, 1041

New Everyman Dictionary of Music, 672n

New Grove Dictionary of…
  American Music, 670
  Jazz, 741

Music and Musicians, 612n, 668n, 671, 706n, 788n, (p. 251)
  Musical Instruments, 788
  Opera, 706

New Guide to Modern World Literature, 1077

New Handbook of Living Religions, 153

New Harvard Dictionary of Music, 672, 684n

New International…
  Dictionary of Biblical Archaeology, 269
  Dictionary of Music, 669n
  *Version (Bible), 238, 241n, 248n, 253n, 270n, 277n, 287n

New Interpreter's Bible, 277n

New Jerusalem Bible, 235n

New Jerome…
  Bible Handbook, 279n
  Biblical Commentary, 279

New Jewish Version, 231n, 241n, 248n

New King James Version, 241n

New Moulton's Library of Literary Criticism, 1197

New Oxford Annotated Bible, 234n

New Oxford Book of…
  American Verse, 1275
  Australian Verse, 1276
  English Verse, 1277
  Irish Verse, 1278

New Oxford Companion to…
  Literature in French, 1305
  Music, 673

New Oxford History of Music, 691, 1214n

New Quotable Woman, 1112

New Penguin Dictionary of Quotations, 1111

New Princeton Encyclopedia of Poetry and Poetics, 1130

New Religious Movements in the United States, 126n

New Revised…
  Standard Version, 234n, 254n, 264n, 277n
  Velazquez Spanish and English Dictionary, 1042

New Rolling Stone Encyclopedia of Rock & Roll, 745n

New Schaff-Herzog Encyclopedia of Religious Knowledge, 178

New Shorter Oxford English Dictionary, 1017n

New Standard Jewish Encyclopedia, 189

New Strong's Exhaustive Concordance of the Bible, 255n

New Technologies…
  and New Directions, (p. 6)
  for the Humanities, (p. 7)

New Testament…
  Abstracts, 245–246n
  Christology, 245n

New Twentieth Century Encyclopedia of Religious Knowledge, 178n

New Unger's Bible…
  Dictionary, 270
  Handbook, 270n

New Video Encyclopedia, 942
New Westminster Dictionary of Liturgy and
Worship, 154
New York City Opera, 705n
New York Herald Tribune, 820n
New York Public Library (catalog)...
Theatre and Drama Collections, 828
New York Theatre Critics Reviews, 892n
New York Theatrical Sourcebook, 858
New York Times..., 490n, 773n, 869n, 943n, 982n
Book Review, 453n
Directory of the Film, 982n, 984n
Encyclopedia of Film, 943
Film Reviews, 943n, 982, 984n
*Online Service, 892n
Theatre Reviews, 892
New Yorker, 752n
Newbery and Caldecott...
Awards, 1363n
Medal and Honor Books in Other Media, 1363n
Medalists and Honor Book Winners, 1363
*Newbery Medal Home Page, 1363n
Newby, Gregory B., (p. 7, 11)
Newby, James E., 1143n
Newman, Edwin R., 1033n
Newman, Harold, 565, 573–574
Newsletter of the AIA Document Supplement
Service, 479n
Newsweek, 978n
Ney, Diane, (p. 253)
Nicholls, Ann, 14–15n
Nichols, C. Allen, 1355
Nichols, Larry A., 191
Nielsen, Niels C., 140n
Niemeyer, Suzanne, 603, 1255n
Nienhauser, William H., 1342n
Night Beat, 745
1900–1965 American Premium Record Guide,
770
Nineteenth Century...
Fiction, 1228
French Fiction Writers, 1303n
Literature Criticism, 1090n, 1097
Painters and Painting, 455n
Romanticism in Music, 692n
*Short Title Catalog, 1148n
Nineteenth-Century...
American Choral Music, 645n
American Musical Theater, 781n
*Fiction, 1228n
Musical Chronicle, 687n
Photography, 512
Russian Literature in English, 1335
NIV Exhaustive Concordance, 253
NKJV Exhaustive Concordance: New King
James Version, 255n
No Way: The Nature of the Impossible Practical
Ethics, (p. 29)
*NOEMA, 48n

Noll, Mark, 224
Non-Book Collection (Theatre and Drama), 828n
Nonprint Cataloging for Multimedia Collections,
(p. 151)
Nordquist, Joan, 51n
Norman, Geraldine, 455n
North Carolina Libraries, (p. 73)
Norton, Anne-Lucie, 64n
Norton/Grove Concise Encyclopedia of Music,
671n
Norton History of Music Series, 691n–692n
Nostalgia Entertainment Sourcebook, 956
Notes, (p. 252–254)
Notes for a Different Drummer, 1353n
Novel and Short Story Writer's Market (2000), 1129
Nowlan, Gwendolyn W., 941n
Nowlan, Robert A., 941n
NRSV Concordance Unabridged, 254
NRSV Exhaustive Concordance, 254n
*NTC's American Idioms Dictionary, 1040n
NTC's Classical Dictionary, 298n
NTC's Dictionary of Word Origins, 1029n
NTC's New...
College Greek and English Dictionary, 1043
Japanese-English Character Dictionary, 1044
Nunn, Joan, 591
Nyles, Doris, 790

O'Brien, Jacqueline W., 606
Ochs, Michael, (p. 251)
O'Connor, John E., 939, 972n
Odelaine, O., 259
Odell, George C. D., 875
O'Donnell, Elizabeth, (p. 151)
O'Donnol, Shirley M., 586
*OED2 on CD-ROM, 1012n
Official Catholic Directory, 205
Official Museum Directory, 16
O'Grady, Jane, 71n
O'Hara, Georgina, 589
Old Master Print References, 424–425n
Old Testament...
*Abstracts, 246
Commentary Survey, 247
Olendorf, Donna, 1374n
Olitzky, Kerry M., 214n
Oliver, Evelyn D., 138, 585
Oliver, Mary, 1130n
Oliver, Paul, 765
Olmstead, Elizabeth H., 643
Olsen, Dale A., 664n
Olson, C., (p. 68)
Olszak, Lydia P., (p. 151)
O'Malley, John W., 225n
*On Common Ground, 155
On the...
Air, 944
Screen, 899

101 Stories of the Great Ballets, 805n
Onions, Charles T., 1029n
Online and CD-ROM Review, (p. 9)
*Online Medieval & Classical Library, 1297n
O'Pecko, Michael T., 1333
Opening Night on Broadway, 780
Opera America...
    Annual Field Report, 714n
    Directory of Production Material for Rent, 714n
    Repertoire Survey, 714n
    Season Schedule of Performances, 714
Opera and...
    Church Music, 1630–1750, 691n
    Concert Singers, 724
Opera Companies of the World, 715
*Opera Glass, 700n
Opera Handbook, 708n
Opera in History, 707
*Opera of America, 712n
Opera Plot Index, 708
Opera Production I and II, 712n
Operas in German, 709
Opie, Iona, 1364n–1365
Opie, Peter, 1364n–1365
Opitz, Glenn B., 395, 507
Opus, 697
Organ Literature, 655
Original Index to Art Periodicals, 332
Originals: An A-Z of Fiction's Real Life Characters, 1078
Origins of Judaism, 222n
Orr, Leonard, 1068
Osborne, Harold, 367
Osburn, Charles B., 1306
Oscar Wilde Encyclopedia, 1198
OT Kittel, 274
OTIS Guernsey-Burns Mantle Theatre Yearbook, 876n
Ottemiller, John H., 836
Ottemiller's Index to Plays in Collections, 836
Our Family, Our Friends, Our World, 1351
Our Sister Killjoy, 1240n
Ousby, Ian, 1235n
Outline and an Annotated Bibliography of Chinese Philosophy, 50n
Outline History of Western Music, 690n
Owen, Bobbi, 595
Owens, Irene, (p. 7)
Oxenhorn, Douglas, 955
Oxford Bible Atlas, 286
Oxford Book of English Verse, 1277n
Oxford Classical Dictionary, 1299n
Oxford Companion to...
    African American Literature, 1165
    American Literature, 1166
    American Theatre, 850
    Art, 367, 369n–370n, 543n
    Canadian History and Literature, 1167n
    Canadian Literature, 1167, 1305n

Canadian Theatre, 851
Children's Literature, 1364
Christian Art and Architecture, 368
Classical Literature, 1299
English Literature, 1158n, 1160n, 1168, 1235
French Literature, 1305n
German Literature, 1332
Irish Literature, 1169
Music, 673n
Philosophy, 69
Popular Music, 746
Spanish Literature, 1321
*the Bible, 271
the Decorative Arts, 370n, 543
the English Language, 1006
the Literature of Wales, 1169n
the Theatre, 839n, 845, 850n
Twentieth-Century Art, 369–370n
Oxford Dictionary and Thesaurus, 1034
Oxford Dictionary of...
    Art, 370
    Current Idiomatic English, 1026
    English Etymology, 1029n
    English Proverbs, 1113
    Modern Quotations, 1114n
    Music, 673n, 710n
    New Words, 1027
    Nursery Rhymes, 1364n–1365
    Opera, 710
    Philosophy, 69n
    Popes, 215
    *Quotations, 1111n, 1114
    Saints, 216
    the Bible, 271n
    the Christian Church, 176
    Twentieth Century Quotations, 1114n
*Oxford English Dictionary, 1012, 1017n, 1038n
Oxford English-Greek Learner's Dictionary, 1043n
Oxford English-Russian Dictionary, 1046n
Oxford Encyclopedia of the...
    Modern Islamic World, 190
    Reformation, 177
Oxford Greek-English Learner's Dictionary, 1043n
Oxford Guide to...
    Classical Mythology in the Arts, 27
    the French Language, 1039n
Oxford History of...
    English Art, 416
    English Literature, 1214
    New Zealand Literature in English, 1215
Oxford Illustrated...
    History of Christianity, 228
    History of Western Philosophy, 97
    Literary Guide to Great Britain and Ireland, 1170
    Literary Guide to the United States, 1170n
Oxford Latin Dictionary, 1045
Oxford Russian Dictionary, 1046
Oxford Russian-English Dictionary, 280

Oxford Study Bible, 280
Oxford Thesaurus, 1034n
Oxford Turkish-English Dictionary, 1043n
Ozer, Jerome S., 714

Pacey, Philip, (p. 149, 152)
Packard, Robert T., 479–480
Packard, William, 840
Page, James A., 1098
Page, Michael, 304n
Painting in the Twentieth Century, 460
Painting of the Golden Age, 455
Pakan, William A., 541
*PAL: Perspectives in American Literature, a
        Research, 1134n
Palfrey, Thomas R., 1306n
Palisca, Claude V., 688, 692n
Pallot, James, 981n
Palmer, Frederick, 447
Palmer, Helen H., 1253n
Palmieri, Margaret, 785n
Palmieri, Robert, 785n
Palmist's Companion, 127n
Palmquist, Peter E., 52
Pantzer, Katharine F., 1147
Pao, Miranda Lee, (p. 254)
Papal Encyclicals, 272n
Papal Pronouncements, 272
Parapsychology: A Concise History, 193n
Parapsychology: New Sources of Information, 129
Parapsychology: Sources of Information, 129n
Paravisini-Gebert, Lizabeth, 1118
Paris Opera: An Encyclopedia, 711
Parish, James R., 926
Parker, Harold M., Jr., 113
Parker, Philip M., 157n
Parrinder, Geoffrey, 182
Parrish, Robert, 779, 965
Parry, Pamela J., 435
Partington, Angela, 1114
Partington, David H., (p. 68)
Partnow, Elaine, 1112
Partridge, Elinore Hughes, 1134
Partridge, Eric, 1022
Passmore, John, (p. 30)
Patin, Thomas, 355
Patten, Katherine, (p. 152)
Patterson, Dennis M., 74n
Patterson, Margaret C., 1056n, 1135n
Pauly, Reinhard G., 692n
Pavliscak, Pamela, (p. 7)
Paymer, Marvin E., 741
Payne, Wardell J., 199
Peacock, John, 587
Peake's Commentary on the Bible, 276n, 281
Pearsall, Judy, 1017
Pearson, J. D., 133
Pease, Sandra, (p. 70)

Peck, David R., 1162
Pederson, Jay P., 1259
Peek, Robin P., (p. 7, 11)
Pehnt, Wolfgang, 482n
Pelican History of Art, 417
Pelikan, Jaroslav, (p. 65, 67)
Pen Is Ours: A Listing of Writings, 1146
Pendergast, Sara, 551, 1372
Pendergast, Tom, 1372
Penguin Dictionary of Architecture, 482n
Penguin Dictionary of Decorative Arts, 544
Penguin History of New Zealand Literature, 1215n
Penney, Edmund F., 931
People of the Book, 275
Peoples of the American West, 1352
*Pepper Music Network, 644n
Perennial Dictionary of World Religions, 139
Perez-Stable, Maria A., 1352
Performing and Visual Arts Writing and Reviewing,
        (p. 251)
Performing Arts...
    A Guide to the Reference Literature, (p. 251)
    Biography Master Index, 604
    Directory, 812n
    Guide to the Reference Literature, 597
    Journal, (p. 251)
    *Library Guide, 597n
    *Links, 605n
    Resources, 605
Period Make-Up for the Stage, 897n
Perkins, Agnes R., 1361n
Permanent Bibliographical Series, 1083n
Perna, Michael L., 1323
Perry, Jeb H., 607n
Persky, Robert S., 516
*Perspectives in American Literature. See PAL
Perspectives on the Humanities and Schoolbased
        Curriculum Development, (p. 39)
Peters, Robert, 1286
Petersen, Andrew, 477
Peterson, Bernard L., 867
Petteys, Chris, 390
Pettit, Philip, 74n
Pevsner, Nikolaus, 417, 482n
Phaidon Guide to Glass, 575n
Phillpot, Clive, (p. 151)
Philological Quarterly, 1061n
Philosopher's Guide to Sources, Research Tools,
        (p. 30)
*Philosopher's Index..., 57, (p. 36, 38)
    *A Retrospective Index to Non-U.S. English
            Language Publications, 58n
    *A Retrospective Index to U.S. Publications,
            58n
    Thesaurus, 57n
Philosophical Books, 53n
Philosophical Review, (p. 31)
*Philosophie, 55n
Philosophie, sciences religieuses, 132n

*Philosophische Dokumentation, 55n
Philosophy: A Guide to the Reference Literature, 37, (p. 30)
Philosophy Dissertation Bibliographies and Citations, (p. 31)
*Philosophy in Cyberspace, 39, (p. 29, 37)
Philosophy Journals and Serials, 38
Phonolog Reporter, 697n
Photographers: A Sourcebook, 522
Photographer's Bible, 523
Photographic Art Market, 516
Photography and...
    Literature, 513
    Photographers to 1900, 514
Photography Books Index..., 517
    II, 517n
*Photoletter, 518n
*PhotoMarket, 518n
*PhotoNet, 518
Piano in Chamber Ensemble, 656
Picasso—The Early Years, 1892–1906, 442
Picken, Mary B., 588n
Picture Researcher's Handbook, 343n
Picture Sources 4, 343
Piepkorn, Arthur C., 155n
Pile, John, 537
Pinkard, Bruce, 523
Pinsker, Sanford, 188
Pitou, Spire, 711
Pitts, Michael R., 779, 946
Pizer, Donald, 1258n
Placement Services Bulletin (Theatre), (p. 257)
Placzek, Adolf K., 492
*Planning and Architecture Internet Resource Center, 463n
Play Directing in the School, 896n
Play Index, 837
Plays for Children and Young Adults, 838
Plot Summary Index, 1079
Plum, Stephen H., 36
PMLA, (p. 395)
Pocket Guide to Literature and Language Terms, 1007
Podstolski, Max, (p. 151)
*Poem Finder, 1270n
Poetry by...
    American Women...
        1900–1975, 1269n
        1975–1989, 1269n
    Women to 1900, 1269
Poetry Criticism, 1090n, 1131
Poetry Explication, 1279n, 1287n
Poetry Handbook, 1130n
Poetry Index Annual, 1270–1271n
Poet's Market (1999), 1132
Poggi, Isotta, 128
Poiesis, (p. 36)
Polking, Kirk, 1106n
Pollard, Alfred W., 1147

Pollard, Elizabeth B., 30
Pollock, Bruce, 734
Pollock, D. K., (p. 70)
Polner, Murray, 214
Polyglot Dictionary of Musical Terms, 675
Pope Encyclopedia, 215n
Pope-Hennessy, John, 508–509
Poplawski, Paul, 1256
Popular Entertainment Research, 598
Popular Guide to Classical Music, (p. 253)
Popular Music...
    A Reference Guide, 727
    and Society, (p. 253)
    1900–1919, 734n
    1920–1979, 734
Popular Religious Magazines of the United States, 108n
Popular Song Index, 735, 737n
Popular World Fiction, 1121
Portable Baker's Biographical Dictionary of Musicians, 682n
Porter, James, 664
Portraying Persons with Disabilities...
    An Annotated Bibliography of Fiction, 1353
    An Annotated Bibliography of Nonfiction, 1353n
Post-Biblical Saints Art Index, 344
Poster, 545
Postmodern Fiction, 1122
Potter, Karl H., 49
Potter's Dictionary of Materials and Techniques, 576
Pottery and Ceramics, 569
Poupard, Dennis, 1093, 1100
Powers, John, 125
Practical English-Japanese Dictionary, 1044n
Practical Ethics, (p. 29)
Prebish, Charles S., 185
Preiss, Byron, 1357
Prelinger, Richard, 953n
Preminger, Alex, 1130
Prentice Hall Guide to English Literature, 1171
Prentice Hall History of Music Series, 692
Presbyterians, 217
Present Tense, 214
Preservation Yellow Pages, 487
Presocratic Philosophers, 52n
Pressler, C. A., (p. 253)
Preston-Dunlop, Valerie, 797
Preziosi, Donald, 363n
Price, Derek J. de Solla, (p. 70)
Price Guide to Antique and Classic Cameras, 524
Prichard, Mari, 1364n
Priestly, J. B., (p. 393)
*Primetime Radio Classics, 945n
Princeton Companion to Classical Japanese Literature, 1342
Princeton Encyclopedia of Poetry and Poetics, 1130n

Princeton Studies: Humanistic Scholarship in
     America, (p. 2)
Pringle, David, 1239, 1259
Print Collectors Quarterly, 424n
Print Index, 435
Print Price Index, 443
Print Reference Sources, 425
Printworld Directory, 444
Prior, Barbara Q., (p. 154)
Pritchard, James B., 283
Problems in Literary Research, 1054
Proceedings of the 2nd Conference on Scholarship
     and Technology in the Humanities, (p. 7)
Proctor, Robert E., (p. 2)
Producing Theatre, 895
Professional Goldsmithing, 566
Proffer, Carl R., 1335
ProFile, 488
Profiles in Belief, 155n
Project Muse, (p. 36)
*Projekt Alfred, 1329n
*Projekt Gutenberg, 1329n
Pronouncing Dictionary of Proper Names, 1033n
Pronouncing Shakespeare's Words, 1172
Prophets, 239
Prosyniuk, Joann, 396
Prouty, Howard H., 985
Provine, R. E., (p. 253)
Prown, Sarah, 39n
Prown, Jules D., 456
Pruett, Barbara J., 598
Pruett, James W., 613n
Psychoanalysis, Psychology, and Literature, a
     Bibliography..., 1058n
          Supplement to the Second Edition, 1058n
Psychocriticism, 1058
*Public Broadcasting Report, 957n
Public Library Catalog, 1224
Publishers Weekly, (p. 68)

Quarterly Index Islamicus, 133n
Quartermain, Peter, 1280
Queen, Edward L., 149
Quiller-Couch, Sir Arthur, 1277n
Quinlan, David, 966n
al-Quran: A Contemporary Translation, 240

RAA. See Repertoire d'art et archeologie
Raben, Erik, 768n
Raben, Joseph, (p. 8, 35, 152)
Rabin, Carol P., 679n
Raby, Peter, 1198n
Rachow, Louis, 793n
Radio and Television (and supps.), 905
Radio Broadcasting from 1920 to 1990, 906
Radio Programs, 1924–1984, 945

Radio Soundtracks, 946
Raffe, Walter G., 798
Ragan, David, 798, 970
Rahner, Karl, 166, 173
Rai, Priya M., 124n
Raisch, Martin, 313
Raitt, Jill, 230n
Ramsey, Charles G., 484n
Ramsey, Paul, (p. 67)
Ramsey/Sleeper Architectural Graphic Standards,
     484n
Ramsey, William, 48
Rand, Benjamin, 40
Randel, Don M., 672, 684
Random House...
     College Thesaurus, 1034n
     Portuguese Dictionary, 1042n
     Thesaurus, 1034n
Random House Webster's...
     College Dictionary, 1018n
     College Thesaurus, 1034n
     *Unabridged Dictionary, 1013
*R&TA on CD-ROM, 136n
Rangel-Ribeiro, Victor, 639
Rap Music in the 1980s, 727n
Rasinski, Timothy V., 1346n
Rasmussen, Carl G., 287
Read, Gardner, 783
Read, Herbert E., 458
Reader in Art Librarianship, (p. 149)
Reader's Adviser, 230n, 1354n, (p. 392)
Reader's Digest...
     Bible, 234n
     Family Word Finder, 1034n
     Oxford Complete Wordfinder, 1034n
Reader's Guide to...
     Literature in English, 1193
     Periodical Literature, 1268, (p255)
     the Great Religions, 100n
Realenzyklopadie fur Protestantische Theologie
     und Kirche, 178n
Reardon, Joan, 1269n
Rebman, Elizabeth, (p. 249, 252)
Recent American Opera: A Production Guide, 712
Recent Studies in Myths and Literature, 291
Reclaiming Spirituality, 230n
Recorded Plays, 837n
Redgrave, Gilbert R., 1147
Ree, Jonathan, 75
Reed, Ida, 614, (p. 252)
Reed, W. L., 660
Reelin' and Rockin' 1956–1959, 749n
Reese, Gustav, 691n
*REESWeb, 1336
Reeves, H., (p. 251)
Reference and User Services Quarterly, (p. 69)
Reference Guide...
     for English Studies, 1135
     to American Literature, 1199

to English Literature, 1200
to Russian Literature, 1337
to Short Fiction, 1123
Reference Librarian, (p. 393)
Reference Materials in Ethnomusicology, 623n
Reference Services Review, (p. 54, 253)
Reference Tools for Fine Arts Visual Resources, 310
Reference Works...
    for Theological Research, 103
    in British and American Literature, 1136
Reform Judaism in America, 214n
Rega, Regina, 8
Reginald, Robert, 1116
Reginald's Science Fiction and Fantasy Awards, 1116
Regional Theatre Directory, 859
Rehrauer, George, 904
Rehrig, William H., 758
Reich, Warren T., 78
Reichardt, Jasia, (p. 3)
Reid, Daniel G., 163
Reid, Francis, 898n
Reid, Jane D., 27
Reid, Joyce M. H., 1305n
Reiman, Donald H., 1264n
Reinehr, Robert C., 937
Reisman, Rosemary M. C., 1249
Reisser, Marsha J., 68
Religion, (p. 67)
Religion: A Cross-Cultural Encyclopedia, 157
Religion: A Humanistic Field, (p. 67)
Religion and the American Experience, 1620–1900, (p. 67)
Religion in...
    America, (p. 67)
    Geschichte und Gegenwart (RGG), 156
*Religion Index...
    *One: Periodicals, 131n, 135, (p. 73)
    *on CD-ROM, 135n
    *Two: Multi-Author Works, 135n, (p. 73)
*Religion Indexes: RIO/RIT/IBRR, 131n
Religion Journals and Serials, 107n
Religions of the World, 140n
Religious and Theological Abstracts, 136
Religious Bibliographies in Serial Literature, 106
Religious Bodies in the United States, 206
Religious Cultures of the World, 157n
Religious Holidays and Calendars, 158n
Religious Information Sources, 104
Religious Leaders..., 221n
    of America, 218
Religious Periodicals...
    Directory, 107
    of the United States, 108
Religious Right, 179n
Religious Records, (p. 67)
Renaissance Artists & Antique Sculpture, 500

Repertoire bibliographique de la philosophie, 56n, (p. 38)
*Repertoire d'art et d'archeologie, 329n–331n, 333n, (p. 153)
Repertoire for the Solo Voice, 649n
Repertoire international...
    de la Litterature de l'Art. See RILA
    de la Litterature Musicale. See RILM
    des sources musicales. See RISM
Research and Reference Guide to French Studies, 1306
Research Guide...
    for Undergraduate Students, 1137
    in Philosophy, (p. 30)
Research Guide to...
    Biography and Criticism, 1201
    Musicology, 613n
    Religious Studies, (p. 67, 73)
    the History of Western Art, 311 (p. 149)
Research in Philosophy, (p. 31)
Research Libraries Group. See RLG
Researcher's Guide to Archives and Regional History Sources, (p. 67)
Researching Modern Evangelism, (p. 67)
Resnick, Margery, 1291
Resource Guide to Themes in Contemporary American Song Lyrics, 1950–1985, 747
Resources in...
    Ancient Philosophy, 52
    Sacred Dance, 794
Resources of American Music History, 610n
Reuben, Paul P., 1134n
Reusch, Amy, 812n
Revere, Alan, 566
Revised English Bible, 236n, 280n
Revised Standard Version (Bible), 231n, 234, 236n, 241n, 248n, 251n, 261n, 264n, 265n–266n, 277n, 281n
Revue neo-scholastique de philosophie, 56n
Revue philosophique de Louvain, 56n
Reworlding: The Literature of the Indian Diaspora, 1204n
Reynolds, Barbara, 1037
Reynolds, Frank E., 50n, 120
Reynolds, Judy, (p. 5)
RIBA Bulletin, 470n
Ribeiro, Aileen, 593n
Rice, D. T., 416n
Rice, Timothy, 664
Rice, Thomas J., 1252
Richards, Jack, 1004
Richardson, Alan, 160n
Richardson, Larry L., 1331
Richetti, John, 1254n
Riggs, Thomas, 865, 1123, 1282
*RILA, Repertoire International de la litterature de l'art, 329n, 331n, 333, (p. 153)
Riley, Sam G., 1173

*RILM: Abstracts of Music Literature, 620n, 633, 661n, (p. 255–256)
Ringgren, Helmer, 274
Ripley, Gordon, 1203n
Rise of Music in the Ancient World, 691n
RISM..., 628, (p. 256)
    *Directory of Music Research Libraries, 628n, 678
    *Online Resources, 628n, 678n
Ritter, Joachim, 68
Riverside Shakespeare, 1172
RLG News, (p. 153)
*RLG Research-in-Progress Database, 1060n
Robbins, Ira A., 770n
Robertson, Allen, 796
Robertson, Debra E. J., 1353
Robertson, Jack, 334, (p. 150)
Robinson, Doris, 312, 616
Robinson, Kerry A., 202n
Robl, Ernest H., 343
Roche, Elizabeth, 721n
Roche, Jerome, 721n
Rochelle, Mercedes, 339, 342
Rock and Roll: Dimensions of a Cultural Revolution, (p. 253)
*Rock Net, 750n
Rock Who's Who, 760
Rockabilly: A Bibliographic Resource Guide, 728
Rodriguez, Andres, 1320
Rogal, Samuel J., 1064, 1207n, 1211
Roger Ebert's Book of Film, 949n
*Roger Ebert's Movie Home Companion, 983n
Roger Ebert's Movie Yearbook, 983
Roger Ebert's Video Companion, 983n
Rogers, A. Robert, (p. 36)
Rogers, James, 1021
Roget, Peter, 1035n
Roget's International Thesaurus, 71n, 1035
Roget's II: The New Thesaurus, 1035n
Roginski, Jim, 1363n
Roh, Jae Min, 1098
Rohmann, Chris, 27
Roland, Tom, 767n
Rolling Stone, 728n, 745n, 978n
Rolling Stone...
    Album Guide, 770
    Illustrated History of Rock & Roll, 760n
    Rock Almanac, 749
Rollins, Peter C., 939
Rollock, Barbara, 1368
Roman Catholics, 212n
Roman Sculpture, 509n
Romanesque Architecture, 469
Romanesque Sculpture in American Collections, 501
Romanowski, Patricia, 745n
Romantic Movement...
    A Selective and Critical Bibliography, 1061
    Bibliography, 1061n

Romanticism, 1830–1890, 691n
Rondestvedt, Karen, 1336
Room, Adrian, 292, 298n, 306n, 1029n
Roos, Frank J., 489n
Roosa, Mark S., (p. 252)
Roosens, Laurent, 510
Root, Deane L., 781n
Rose, Barbara, 456
Rosenack, Chuck, 555
Rosenack, Jan, 555
Rosenbach, A. S. W., 123n
Rosenberg, Betty, 1236
Rosenberg, Judith K., 1355
Rosenfeld, Louis, (p. 10)
Rosenblatt, Arthur, 772n
Rosenthal, Harold, 699n, 710n
Ross, Franz, 516n
Ross, Seamus, (p. 7)
Ross, Stanley R., 981
Rossetti, Fabrizia, 459n
Rossetti, Stefania, 459n
Roth, Cecil, 189n
Roth, John K., 46n, 73n
Rothenberg, Jeff, (p. 7, 396)
Roth's American Poetry Annual, 1270n–1271
Rousseau Dictionary, 86n
Rousseau, John J., 171n
*Routledge Encyclopedia of Philosophy, 66n, 70
Routledge History of...
    Philosophy, 98
    World Philosophies, 98n
Rowlands, Eliot W., 429
Rowley, H. H., 281
Rowlinson, William, 1039n
Royal Arts of Africa, 405n
Royle, Trevor, 1160
Ruben, Douglas H., 38
Rubinstein, Ruth, 500
Rudisill, Richard, 522
Rule, Amy, 529
Rumsey, William, 48
Runes, Dagobert D., 62
Ruoff, A. Lavonne B., 1138
Ruppert, James, 1287n
Rusch, Frederik L., 1058
Russell, Bertrand, 97n, (p. 30)
Russell, Sharon A., 934
Rust, Brian, 769n
Ryan, Bryan, 1083n, 1315

Sachar, Brian, 474
Sachs, Curt, 691, 821
Sacramentum Mundi, 173n
Sacred Games, 229
Sadie, Stanley, 670–671, 702, 795, 788, (p. 251)
Sadler, Geoff, 1259n
Sadoul, George, 968n
Saifulin, Murad, 63

St. James Guide to...
Biography, 35
Children's Writers, 1372–1373n
Crime and Mystery Writers, 1259
Fantasy Writers, 1259n
Horror, Ghost and Gothic Writers, 1259n
Native North American Artists, 397
Science Fiction Writers, 1259n
Young Adult Writers, 1372n–1373
St. James Reference Guide to...
American Literature, 1199n
English Literature, 1200n
Salazar, Adolfo, 691n
Salem, James M., 773, 893n, 978n
Saliers, Don E., 230n
Salu, Luc, 510, 513
Salvini, Robert, 508n
Salzman, Eric, 692n
Salzman, Jack, 1159
Samples, Gordon, 834n
Sampson, Henry T., 924
Sander, Reinhard, 1099
Sanders, Andrew, 1214n
Sapir, Edward, (p. 392)
Sartori, Eva M., 1302
Sasse, Howell C., 1038n
Savage, George, 573
Saye, Jerry D., (p. 151)
Scales, P., (p. 151)
Schaff-Herzog Encyclopedia, 178
Schellinger, Paul E., 34
Scheps, Walter, 1265
Schiff, Matthew M., 766n
Schirmer Guide to Schools of Music and
Conservatories, 681
Schlachter, Gail A., 18
Schlessinger, June H., 838
Schlueter, June, 1196n
Schlueter, Paul, 1196n
Schmitt, Charles B., 95n
Schneider, Ben R., 882n
Schneider, Gerhard, 273n
Scholarly Publishing the Electronic Frontier, (p. 7,
11)
Scholes, Percy, 673n
School Library Journal, 1344n
Schonberg, Bent, 813
Schrag, Calvin O., 94
Schuller, Nancy S., (p. 150)
Schuster, R. D., (p. 67)
Schuursma, Ann B., 623
Schwann Long Playing Record Catalog, 697n
Schwann Quarterly, 697n
Schwartz, Elliott, 719
Schwartz, Narda L., 1141
Schwarz, Boris, 720n
Schwarz, Catherine, 1017n
Science, (p. 69)

Science Fiction and Fantasy.... *See also* entry
1124
Book Review Annual, 1230n
Book Review Index 1980–1984, 1230n
Reference Index, 1878–1985, 1124
Research Index, 1124n, 1230n
Series and Sequels, 1229
Science Fiction Book Review Index...
1923–1973, 1230
1974–1979, 1230n
Science Fiction, Fantasy, and Weird Fiction
Magazines, 1218
Science Fiction for Young Readers, 1366n
Science Fiction Index, 1124n,
Science Fiction Source Book, 1125
Science Fiction, the Early Years, 1117
Science Fiction Writers, 1261n
Science of Religion...
Abstracts and Index, 137
Bulletin, 137n
Sciences humaines: Philosophie, 132n
Scientometrics, (p. 5)
*SCIPIO (Sales Catalog Index Project), 345n, 347n
Scott, Frank, 765n
Scott, Mark W., 1093
Screen World, 935n
Screenplay from the Jazz Singer to Dr.
Strangelove, 978n
Scrimgeour, Andrew D., (p. 30)
Scullard, Howard H., 1299n
Sculpture: 19th and 20th Centuries, 508n
Sculpture: Renaissance to Rococo, 508n
Sculpture in America, 505
Sculpture Index, 502
Seaman, D., (p. 151)
Sears, Minnie E., 23, 736
Seaton, Douglass, 688n
Seay, Albert, 692n
Sebeok, Thomas A., 1002
Sefami, Jacobo, 1311
Seguineau, R., 259
Seidel, Linda, 501
Selected Black American, African, and Caribbean
Authors, 1098
Selected Musical Terms of Non-Western Cultures,
674
Selected Theatre Criticism, 893
Selection of Library Materials in the Humanities,
Social Sciences and Sciences, (p. 30)
Semantics: A Bibliography, 987n
Semowich, Charles J., 556
Senior High School Library Catalog, 1344n
Senior, Michael, 302
Sennett, Robert S., 514
Sensitive Issues ... Children's Literature, 1346n
Sentman, Catherine, 679n
Serafin, Steven, 1072, 1076
Serban, William, 570
*Serial Bibliographies, 1053n

Serials Librarian, (p. 31, 39, 54)
Serrano y Sanz, Manuel, 1325n
Seventh Book of Junior Authors, 1371n
Seymour, Nancy N., 366
Seymour-Smith, M., 1077, 1101
SFFBRI, 1124n, 1230n
Shaikh, Farzana, 187n
Shake, Rattle & Roll, 749n
*Shakespeare, 1189
Shakespeare Survey, 1154
Shaland, Irene, 822
Shapiro, Nat, 734
Sharkey, Paulette B., 1363n
Sharp, Avery T., 647
Sharp, Dennis, 483
Sharp, Harold S., 599
Sharp, Marjorie Z., 599
Shatzky, Joel, 1247
Shaw, Deborah, (p. 6, 394)
Shaw, Marian, 23
Sheehan, Steven, 354
Sheehy, Carolyn A., (p. 251)
Sheehy, Daniel E., 664n
Sheehy, Eugene P., 3n
Shelton, James, 10n
Shelton, Pamela L., 1283
Sherk, Warren M., 914
Shoemaker, Kellie, (p. 253)
Short-Fiction Criticism, 1241n
Short History of Opera, 688
Short Oxford History of English Literature, 1214n
Short Story...
    Criticism: Excerpts, 1260
    Index (and supps.), 1231
    Writers and Their Work: A Guide, 1123n
Short-Title Catalogue of Books Printed in
        England...
    1475–1640, 1147–1148n
    1641–1700, 1148
Shorter Encyclopaedia of Islam, 184n, 260n
Shorter New Cambridge Bibliography of English
        Literature, 1145n
Shreeves, Edward, (p. 6)
Shriver, George H., 149n, 163n
Siegfried, Susan, (p. 9)
Sienkewicz, Thomas J., 1298
Sievert, Donald, (p. 36)
Sievert, Maryellen, (p. 36)
Sightlines, (p. 257)
Sikhism and the Sikhs, 124n
Sikhs in...
    Britain, 124n
    Great Britain, 124n
    North America, 124
SIL. *See* Summer Institute of Linguistics
Simon, Alfred, 775n
Simon, R., (p. 73)
Simons, Linda K., 597, (p. 251)
Simple English New Testament, 241n

Simpson, J. A., 1012
Simpson, J. M. Y., 1001
Sims, Norman T., 1343
Sinclair, Janet, 807
Singer, Michael, 968
Singer, Peter, (p. 29)
Singerman, Robert, 123
Singer's Guide to the American Art Song, 649
Singh, A., 1340n
Singleton, Ralph S., 928n
Sir Banister Fletcher's History of Architecture,
        495
Siren, Osvald, 457
*SIRIS, 319n
Sisson, C. H., 1158n
Sivaramamurti, Calembus, 410
Six Contemporary French Women Poets, 1307
Sixth Book of Junior Authors, 1371n
Skinner, R., (p. 153)
Skretvedt, Randy, 956
Slavens, Thomas P., 311, 596, 613n, (p. 65, 67,
        73, 149)
Sleeper, Harold R., 484n
Slide, Anthony, 606, 893, 923, 940, 948, 972
Slide Buyer's Guide, 380
Slingerland, Jean H., 1155n
Sloan, Mary M., 1274
Slonimsky, Nicholas, 675, 682, 690
Sloss, K., (p. 253)
Smailes, Suzanne, (p. 69)
Small Press: An Annotated Guide, 1149
Small Theatre Handbook, 896
Smallwood, Philip J., 1212
Smartt, Daniel, 498
Smiraglia, Richard P., (p. 252)
Smith, Barry, 83
Smith, Colin, 1042n
Smith, Dorman H., 652
Smith, Elizabeth H., 151
Smith, Frederick, 732
Smith, Geoffrey D., 1220n
Smith, Kevin L., (p. 70)
Smith, Lyn W., 433
Smith, Natalia, (p. 8)
Smith, Peter R., 476n
*Smithsonian on Disc: Catalog ... on CD-ROM,
        12
Smitten, Jeffrey R., 1253n
Snodgrass, Mary E., 1161, 1359n
Snow, Joel, 754n
Snow, Maryly, (p. 151)
Social Sciences...
    and Humanities Index, 24n
    *Citation Index, 20n
    *Index, 24n
*Social Scisearch, 24n
Social Theory, 51n
*Society of Children's Book Writers & Illustrators,
        1373n

Sojourners, (p. 70)
Sokol, David M., 530
Sole, Carlos A., 1319
*Something About the Author…, 1374
  *Autobiography Series, 1374n
Song Index, 736
Songs in Collections, 735–737
Songs of the Theater, 775n
Songwriter's Market, 751
Sosa, Ernest, 74n
Sotheby's Art at Auction, 350
Sotheby's Directory of Silver, 1600–1940, 567
Souchal, Francois, 501n
Soukup, Paul A., 115
Soul Music A-Z, 761
Source Readings in Music History, 693
Sourcebook for…
  Hispanic Literature and Language, 1322
  Research in Music, 613n
  the Performing Arts, 606
Sources of Films on Art, (p. 155)
South and Meso-American Native Spirituality,
  230n
South, Malcolm, 304
Southern Weave of Women, 1249n
Spain, Louise, 791
Spanish Artists from the Fourth to the Twentieth
  Century, 398
Spanish, Catalan, and Galician Literary Authors
  of the…
  Eighteenth and Nineteenth Centuries, 1316n
  Twentieth Century, 1316n
Sparkes, A. W., 71
Sparkes, Ivan G., 1031
Spassky, Natalie, 426n
Spawforth, Anthony, 1299n
Speace, Geri, 1080
Speake, Jennifer, 60, (p. 28)
Speaking in Tongues, 115n
Spears, Richard A., 1022n
Spectrum, 697n
Spence, Lewis, 193n
Spink, Amanda, (p. 4)
Spirituality and the Secular Quest, 230n
Spottswood, Richard K., 696
Square Dance and Contra Dance Handbook, 801
Stade, George, 1089
Stage Deaths: A Biographical Guide, 869
Stage It with Music, 781
Stage Lighting Handbook, 898n
Stage Makeup, the Actor's Complete, 897n
Stage Makeup Step-By-Step, 897n
Stagecraft, 898
Stahl, Joan R., (p. 253)
Stained Glass, 570
Staller, Natasha, 442
Stam, Deidre C., (p. 152)
Stambler, Irwin, 740
*Stanford Encyclopedia of Philosophy, 66n

Stangos, Nikos, (p. 150)
Stanke, Don, 965
Stanley, Janet, (p. 151)
Stanley, Janet L., 318
Stapleton, Michael, 1158
Starkey, Edward D., 101, (p. 6)
Stavropoulos, D. N., 1043n
STC, 1147–1148n
Stegemeyer, Anne, 594n
Stein, Eliot, 950n
Stein, Jess, 1034n
Stein, Rita, 891
Steinfirst, Susan, 288
Steinmetz, Sol, 1030
Stephens, Meic, 1169n–1170
Stephens, Michael, 960
Stephens, Norris L., 640
Stern, M., (p. 393)
Sternfield, Frederick W., 691n
Stevenson, Barbara, 381, (p. 151)
Stevenson, Burton E., 1110
Stevenson, George A., 541
Stevenson, Jonathan, 549n
Stewart, Bruce, 1169
Stinson, J., (p. 253)
Stock, Raymond, 249
Stockdale, F. M., 715n
Stone, Ruth M., 664n
Stone, Sue, (p. 5)
Stone, Thomas R., (p. 29)
Storey, John W., 179n
Storia dell'arte italiana, 459n
Storr, Anthony, (p. 251)
Story, Norah, 1167
Story of Philosophy, (p. 30)
Stover, Mark, (p. 71)
Strachan, N. S., (p. 69)
Strang, M. H., 1158n
Stratman, Carl J., 824–825, 827
Strawson, P. F., (p. 28)
Stringer, Jenny, 1168n
Strong, James, 255
Strong's Exhaustive Concordance of the Bible,
  253n, 255
Strunk, W. Oliver, 693
Stuart, Douglas K., 247
Studies in…
  Early Christianity, 169n
  Philology, 996n
  Soviet Thought, 51n
Studwell, William E., 708, 789, (p. 253)
Study of Religion in Colleges and Universities,
  (p. 67)
Sturges, Paul, (p. 5)
Sturm, Terry, 1215
Suber, Peter, (p. 36)
Subject Catalogue of Paintings in Public Collec-
  tions, 426n

Subject Collections: A Guide, 13, (p. 10, 39, 73, 156, 396)
Subject Guide to Classical Instrumental Music, 657
Subject Headings Used ... Library of Congress, (p. 33)
Subject Index to Art Exhibition Catalogues, 348n
Subject Is Murder, 1221n
Suchowski, Amy R., 8
Suggs, M. Jack, 280
Sullivan, Alvin, 1208
Sullivan, Bruce M., 186
Sullivan, C. W., 1366n
Sullivan, Michael, 409n
Summary of Proceedings ... American Theological Library Association...
   50th Annual Conference, (p. 68)
   52nd Annual Conference, (p. 68, 70–71)
   Golden Anniversary Annual Conference, (p. 73)
*Summer Institute of Linguistics, 991
Summer Theatre Directory, 859n
Supernatural Fiction Writers, 1261
Supplementary Russian-English Dictionary, 1046n
Survey of...
   Contemporary Literature, 1094n
   Modern Fantasy Literature, 1126
   Musical Instruments, 786n
   Science Fiction Literature, 1126n
Suskin, Steven, 780
Sutherland, Zena, 1345
Sutton, Brett, (p. 8)
Swartz, Jon D., 937
Sweet, Jeffrey, 876n
Sweetland, James H., (p. 6)
Swift, Gay, 579
Swinfield, Rosemary, 897n
Sykes, Edgerton, 306n
Symphony Orchestras of the United States, 716

Talking Philosophy: A Wordbook, 71
Talmud, 239n
Tanakh: A New Translation, 239n
Tansey, Richard G., 412
Tap Dance Dictionary, 800
Tarbert, Gary C., 1348
Tasman, Dan, 463
Tate, Linda, 1249n
Tatian, Carol, (p. 252)
Tatla, Darshan S., 124
Taub, Michael, 1247
Taylor, Thomas J., 826
Tazawa, Yutaka, 386
TDNT, 273
TDOT, 274
Teaching Philosophy, (p. 36)
Teague, Edward H., 473
Technical Manual and Dictionary of Classical Ballet, 807n

Technology, Scholarship and the Humanities, (p. 7)
Television & Cable...
   Action Update, 957n
   Fact Book, 957
Television & Ethics: A Bibliography, 907
Television Character and Story Facts, 947
*Television Digest, 957n
Television Industry: A Historical Dictionary, 948
Television Writers Guide, 958
Telgin, Diane, 1374n
Templeton, N. G., 863–864, 866
Terminorum musicae index, 675
Terrace, Vincent, 926–927n, 945, 947
Terras, Victor, 1335
Terry, Walter, 803, 820
Teutsch, Betsy P., 181n
*Textes et contextes, 1308
Thames and Hudson Encyclopaedia of...
   Graphic Design and Designers, 546
   Impressionism, 450
Theatre Backstage from A to Z, 852
Theatre Collection: Books on the Theatre, 828n
Theatre Companies of the World, 860
Theatre, Film, and Television Biographies Master Index, 604n
Theatre in the...
   East, 802
   United States, 885
Theatre Notes, (p. 257)
Theatre Research International, (p. 257)
Theatre Survey, (p. 257)
Theatre World, 857n
Theatrical Costume, 585n
Theatrical Designers, 870
Thematic Catalogues in Music, 661
Theological and Religious Reference Materials, 105
*Theological Dictionary of the...
   New Testament, 273–274n
   Old Testament, 274
Theological Libraries at Oxford, (p. 73)
Theologische Realenzyklopaedie, 178
Thesaurus of Book Digests, 1079n
Thieme, Ulrich, 353n, 383
Things Fall Apart, 1240n
Thinkers of the Twentieth Century, 93
Thiongo, Ngugi Wa, 1240n
Third Barnhart Dictionary of New English, 1028
Third Book of Junior Authors & Illustrators, 1371n
1,350 Toughest TV Trivia Questions of All Time, 947n
Thirty-Five Oriental Philosophers, 90n
This Day in Religion, 158
Thomas, Nicholas, 967
Thomas, P. J., (p. 68)
Thomison, Dennis, 335
Thompson, Ellen M., 531
Thompson, E. T., (p. 67)

Thompson, Newton W., 249
Thompson, Oscar, 666
Thompson, Stith, 297n
Thomson, David, 961
Thomson, Ruth G., 832
Thrall, William F., 1075n
Thudium, Laura, 897n
Thurston, Herbert, 210
Thurston, Jarvis A., 1241n
Tibbets, John C., 930
Tibbo, Helen R., (p. 6, 8, 35, 394)
Tijdschrift voor filosofie, 56n
Tilley, Morris P., 1113n
Time-Saver Standards for...
    Building Types, 484
    Housing and Residential Development, 484n
    Interior Design and Space Planning, 484n
    Landscape Architecture, 484n
Title Guide to the Talkies, 930n
Tobey, Jeremy L., 43
Tobin, James E., 212n
Tobin, J. J. M., 1172
Today's English Version, 248n
Todd, Loreto, 1024
Tomasevic, Nebojsa, 404
Tomlinson, Gerald, 159
Tomlyn, Bo, 784n
Topper, D. R., (p. 4)
Torah, 239n
Torbet, Laura, 539
Torres-Seda, Olga, 1118
Totok, Wilhelm, 42
Towers, Deirdre, 791n
Toye, William, 1167
Tracey, Esther M., 340
Traditional Jewelry of India, 568
Trant, Jennifer, (p. 154)
Trapido, Joel, 842
Travis, William G., 112
Treasury of Religious Quotations, 159
Treitler, Leo, 693
Trent, William P., 1209
Tribal Arts Review, 326n
Trouser Press Guide to 90s Rock, 770n
Troxell, Kay, 794
Trudeau, Lawrence J., 890
Truemper, David G., 200
Truitt, Evelyn M., 969
Trujillo, Roberto G., 1320
Trump, Polly, (p. 154)
Tsui-James, E. P., 74n
Tuck, Donald H., 1222
Tucker, Martin, 1187, 1197n
Tufts, Eleanor, 402n
Turner, Harold W., 126
Turner, Jane, 360
Turner, Roland, 93
Tuttle Dictionary of New Words, 1027n
TV Guide, 900n

Twayne's United States Authors Series, 1175n
1,201 Toughest TV Trivia Questions of All
    Time, 947n
12,000 Words: A Supplement to Webster's Third
    New International Dictionary, 1015n
Twentieth Century...
    Artists on Art, 334
    Author Biographies Master Index, 1080
    Authors, 1101n
    Design, 547
    Evangelicalism, 112n
    Ornament, 547n
    Shapers of American Popular Religion, 218n
    Short Story Explication: New Series, 1262n
20th Century Theatre, 886
Twentieth-Century...
    *Caribbean and Black African Writers, 1099
    Children's Writers, 1372n
    Crime and Mystery Writers, 1259n
    German Novel, 1333
    Literary Criticism, 1090n, 1100
    Literary Movements Index, 1062
    Music, 692n
    Musical Chronicle, 687n
    Romance and Historical Writers, 1259n
    Science Fiction Writers, 1259n
    Short Story Explication (and supps and index),
        1262
    Spanish Poets...
        First Series, 1323
        Second Series, 1323n
    Western Writers, 1259n
    Young Adult Writers, 1372n
Twist and Shout, 1960–1963, 749n
2000 Novel and Short Story Writer's Market, 1129
2000 Writer's Market (Writer's Market 2000),
    1107
Tyler, Don, 739
Tyler, Gary R., 890n
Tymn, Marshall B., 1218

Ueberweg, Friedrich, 41
Ulrich's American Periodicals Directory, 7n
*Ulrich's International Periodicals Directory...,
    7, 312n
    Supplement, 7n
*Ulrich's on Disc, 7n
*Ulrich's Plus Computer File, 7n
*Ulrich's Quarterly, 7n
*Ulrich's Update, 7n
Ultimate Film Festival Survival Guide, 952n
Ultimate Guide to Science Fiction, 1239
Underwood, Kent D., (p. 254)
Unger, Leonard, 1175
Unger, Merrill F., 270
Union List of Film Periodicals, 901
United Methodist Information, 203

United Nations Educational, Scientific and
Cultural Organization. *See* UNESCO
*University of Virgina Library Electronic
Center, 1329n
Untracht, Oppi, 568
Unwin, Timothy, 1301
Urdang, Laurence, 1034n
Urmson, James O., 75
U.S. Latino Literature, 1324
Uscher, Nancy, 681
*USF Asian Theatre Site-General, 802n
Utter, Glenn H., 179n

Vampire Book, 1127n
Vampire Gallery, 1127
Vance, Lucile E., 340
Vancill, David E., 988n
van Marle, Raimond, 459
Van Vynckt, Randall, 491
Varet, Gilbert, 45
Varieties of Religious Conversion in the Middle
Ages, 228n
Variety, 607n–608n, 750n, 951n, 959, 985n
Variety and Daily Variety Television Reviews,
945n
Variety Film Reviews, 1907–1980, 607n,
984–985n
Variety International...
Film Guide, 949
Showbusiness Reference, 853n
Variety Movie Guide, 984n
Variety Music Cavalcade, 1620–1969, 748–749n
Variety Obits: An Index, 607n
Variety Obituaries, 607
Variety Presents, 853
Variety Television Reviews 1923–1992, 985
Variety Who's Who in Show Business, 608
Variety's Complete Home Video Directory, 911n
*Variety's Video Directory Plus, 911n
Varley, G., (p. 150)
Vasudevan, Aruma, 1259n
Vaughan, David, 795n
Veinstein, Andre, 600
Velazquez de la Cadena, Mariano, 1042
Vellucci, Sherry, (p. 252)
Vermilye, Jerry, 977
Ver Nooy, Winifred, 833
Victorian Bibliography, 1152n
Victorian Studies, 1152n
Video Movie Guide, 917
Video Source Book, 911n, 919
VideoHound's Golden Movie Retriever, 920
VideoHound's World Cinema, 920n
Vietnamese-English, English-Vietnamese
Dictionary, 1041n
Villamil, Victoria E., 649
Vince, Ronald W., 847
Vinopal, Jennifer, 1306n

Vinson, James, 393
*Virginia, University of, Library Electronic
Center, 1329n
Virtual Musician, 617
Visual Arts...
A History, 418
in the Twentieth Century, 419
Research, 308n
Visual History of Costume...
The Sixteenth Century, 593n
The Seventeenth Century, 593n
The Eighteenth Century, 593n
The Nineteenth Century, 593n
The Twentieth Century, 593
Visual Resources..., (p. 151)
Directory, 381, (p. 151)
Vocabulaire technique et critique de la philosophie,
72
Vocal Chamber Music, 650
Vogelsong, Diana, 462n
Voice of Youth Advocates (VOYA), (p. 253)
Vollmer, Hans, 383n
von Herbert, Jacob, 1330n
Vorgrimler, Herbert, 166
Vorp, Donald M., (p. 70)
Voss, Bonnie L., (p. 68)
Vrana, Stan A., 1153

Wade, Bonnie C., 692n
Waiting for Dizzy, 752n
Wakefield, R. I., 1055n
Wakeman, John, 971
Walch, Margaret, 357
Walford, Albert J., 4
Walford's Guide to Reference Material, 4
Walker, Barbara K., 1262n
Walker, John A., 364, 936
Walker, Thomas D., (p. 8)
Walker, Warren S., 1262
Walkiewicz, Lynn, 57n
Wallace, David, 1210n
Waller, Alfred R., 1210
Waller, Susan, 420
Walsh, Michael J., 106
War and Peace Through Women's Eyes, 1232
Ward, Adolphus W., 1210
Ward, Carlton, 855
Ward, Gerald W. R., 533
Ward, Philip, 1321
Warrack, John, 710
Warren, Gretchen W., 804
Warren, Julian, (p. 31)
Washington Post, 1011n
Wasserman, Stephen R., 606n
Watson, George, 1145n
Watson, Noelle, 1248
Watson-Jones, Virginia, 506
Wayne, Kathryn M., 462

Wearing, J. P., 883
Web Thesaurus Compendium, (p. 36)
Weber, R. David, 18
Webster's New...
    International Dictionary, 1014, 1016n
    World Dictionary of American English, 1018n
    World Dictionary of Music, 675
    World Hebrew Dictionary, 1047
Webster's Third New International Dictionary,
    1013n–1015, 1018n
Weill, Alain, 545
Weiner, E. S. C., 1012
Weintraub, Stanley, 862
Weiss, Anne de la Vergne, 1079n
Weiss, Irving, 1079n
Weixlmann, Joe, 1241
Welch, Robert, 1169
Wellesley Index to Victorian Periodicals,
    1824–1900, 1155
Wellesz, Egon, 691n
Welsh, James M., 930
Wescott, Steven D., 771
*WESS French Studies Web, 1306n
Wessel, Henry, (p. 253)
West, Dorothy H., 837n
West, Ewan, 710
Western European Specialists Section (ACRL),
    1306n
Western Series and Sequels, 1233
Westminster Dictionary of Christian...
    Ethics, 179
    Theology, 160n
Westminster Review, 1155n
Westrup, Sir Jack A., 669n
What Great Paintings Say, 451
What's Happened to the Humanities, (p. 2)
Wheeler, Daniel, 415
Whelan, Keith, 676
Where's that Tune? An Index to Songs in Fake-
    books, 738
Which Dictionary? A Consumer's Guide, 989n
Whitaker, Richard E., 251
Whitburn, Joel, 764
White, Rhea A., 129
White, Lynda S., (p. 151)
Whitwell, David, 758n
Who was Who...
    in American Art, 352n, 399
    in the Theatre, 601n
    on Screen, 969
Who's Who in...
    American Art, 400, (p. 155)
    American Film Now, 970n
    American Music: Classical, 686
    Art, 401
    Canadian Literature, 1203n
    Christianity, 219n
    Classical Mythology, 306
    Fashion, 594n

Hollywood, 970
Interior Design, 493
Non-Classical Mythology, 306n
Religion, 219
the Motion Picture Industry, 970n
the New Testament, 220n
the Old Testament, 220
Writers, Editors, & Poets, 1202
Who's Who of...
    Jazz, 762
    World Religions, 221
Wiberley, Stephen E., Jr., (p. 6–7, 394)
Wick, Robert L., 622
Wicks, Donald A., (p. 70)
Widmann, R. L., (p. 35)
Wiener, Philip P., 64
Wigoder, Geoffrey, 189
Wilcox, R. Turner, 588
Wilde, Deborah N., (p. 9)
Wilderotter, J. A., (p. 71)
Wilhelm, Elliott, 920n
Wilk, Sarah B., 497
Wilkes, Joseph A., 480
Wilkins, David C., 414
Wilkinson, Robert, 90n
Willett, Frank, 405
Willett, Perry, (p. 394)
Williams, David R., 627
Williams, Helen E., 1347
Williams, Hermine W., 713
Williams, Lynn, (p. 154)
Williams, Martha E., (p. 9)
Williams, Peter W., 152
Williams, Sean, 664n
Williams, William A., (p. 36)
Williamson, Mary F., 315
Willis, John, 813n, 945n
Wilmes, Douglas R., 1176
Wilmeth, Don B., 846, 878
Wilson Biographies Plus, 1101n
Wilson, Conrad, 669n
Wilson, Donald S., 154n
Wilson, Frank P., 1113, 1214
Wilson, George B., 809n, 1076
Wilson, John F., 99, (p. 65, 67, 73)
Wilson, Katharina M., 1290
Wilson, Raymond L., 441
Winchester, Barbara, 650
Winfield, Jerry P., 1323
Wing, Donald G., 1148
Wingrove, David, 1125
Winklepleck, Julie, 6
Winokur, Jon, 1115
Witcombe, Chris, 412n
Witham, Barry B., 885
Wittgenstein Dictionary, 86n
Wodehouse, Lawrence, 489
Wold, Milo, 690n
Wolfe, Gary K., 1234

Wolff, Robert L., 1228
Woll, Allen, 849
Women and...
　Religion, 118
　Writing in Russia and the USSR: A Bibliography, 1338
Women Artists in the...
　Modern Era: A Documentary History, 420
　United States, 402
Women Authors of Modern Hispanic South
　　America, 1325n
Women in Music, 685n
Women of Classical Mythology, 307n
Women Philosophers...
　A Bibliography of Books Through 1990, 94n
　A Bio-Critical Source Book, 94
Women Writers...
　in Translation, 1291
　of Spain, 1325
　of Spanish America, 1325n
Women's Fiction Between the Wars, 1263
Wood, David, 642
Wood, D. R. W., 264
Woodard, Gloria, 1358
Woodham, Jonathan M., 547
Woodress, James, 1139n
Woodstock, Clive E., 559
Word of God, 248
World Architecture..., 483n
　Index, 473
World Artists...
　1950–1980, 403
　1980–1990, 403n
World Atlas of Architecture, 474n
World Authors...
　1900–1950, 1101n
　1950–1970, 1101
　1970–1975, 1101n
　1975–1980, 1101n
　1980–1985, 1101n
　1985–1990, 101n
*World Authors Biography Series, 1101n
World Ballet and Dance, 813
World Christian Encyclopedia, 180
World Collectors...
　Annuary, 445
　Index, 445n
　Index, 1946–1972, 445n
　Index, 1946–1982, 445n
*World Council of Churches, 111n
*World Council of Churches Catalogues, 111
World Databases in Humanities, 11
World Encyclopedia of Naïve Art, 404
World Film Directors, 971
World Guide to Terminological Activities, 1050
World History of...
　Art, 418n
　the Dance, 821

*World Literature Criticism 1500 to the Present,
　　1090n, 1102
World Museum Publications, 382
World Painting Index, 432n, 436
World Philosophy...
　A Contemporary Bibliography, 36n
　Essay-Reviews of 225 Major Works, 73, (p. 30)
World Photographers Reference Series, 529
*World Religions Index, 104n
World Spirituality, 230
World Treasury of Modern Religious Thought,
　　(p. 65, 67)
World's Major Languages, 1008
World's Master Paintings from the Early
　　Renaissance, 437
Worldwide Art Catalogue Bulletin, (p. 150)
*Worldwide Art Resources, 313n
Worldwide Bibliography of Art Exhibition Cata-
　　logues, 351
Worterbuch der Philosophischen Begriffe, 68n
Wortman, William A., 1053n
*WPA Federal Theater Project, 880n
Wos, Larry, (p. 36)
Wright, Crispin, 74n
Wright, Christopher, 437
Wright, H. S., (p. 253)
Wright, Lyle H., 1220
Wright, Stephen, (p. 253)
Writer's Digest..., 1105n, 1128n
　Magazine, 1105n
Writer's Directory, 1203
*Writer's Electronic Bulletin Board, 1104n
Writer's Encyclopedia, 1106n
Writers from the South Pacific, 1343
Writer's Guide to Book Editors, 1105n
Writer's Handbook 2000..., 1106–1107n
　International Edition, 1106n
Writer's Market 2000, 1107
Writers of the Caribbean and Central America, 1326
Writers of the Indian Diaspora, 1204
Writers on Writing, 1115
Writer's Quotation Book, 1115n
Writer's Resource, 1107n
Writer's Yearbook, 1128n
Writings, 239n
Wyle, Dorothea E., 561
Wynar, Bohdan S., 2
Wynn, Ron, 763n
Wyngaard, Susan, (p. 150–151)

Yaakov, Juliette, 1224
*Yale University Library Research Guide, 39n
Yancy, Preston M., 1219
Yassif, Eli, 290
Year by Year in the Rock Era, 749
Yearbook of...
　American and Canadian Churches, (p. 72)
　Comparative and General Literature, (p. 396)

Year's Work in...
  English Studies, 1156
  Modern Language Studies, 996
Yellin, Jean F., 1146
Yitzhaki, M., (p. 5)
Yogacara School of Buddhism: A Bibliography, 125
Yolton, John W., 74n, 86n
Young Adult...
  Annual Booklist, 1354n
  Reader's Adviser, 1354
Young, Arthur P., (p. 67)
Young, Jordan R., 956
Young People's Books in Series, 1355
Young, Robert, 256
Young, Robyn V., 1131
Young, William C., 860, 885n
Young's Analytical Concordance to the Bible, 256
Yu, David, 121

Zagars, Julie, 487
Zaimont, Judith L., 667
Zalta, Edward N., 66n, (p. 30)
Zen Buddhism: A Classified Bibliography, 125n
Zheutlin, Barbara, 1107
Zielbauer, Paul, (p. 29)
Zimmerman, Dorothy W., 1302
Zimmerman, Marc, 1324
Ziolkowski, Margaret, 1337n
Zondervan NIV Atlas of the Bible, 287
Zubatsky, David, 1316
Zuck, Virpi, 1328
Zwicker, Stephen N., 1158n

SUBJECT/KEYWORD INDEX

The purpose of this index is to provide access to both broad topics and keywords from titles. Only those organizations associated with more than one discipline are listed here. More specialized organizations will be found in the "Accessing Information" chapter for each discipline, as will bibliographic citations to works about the topics included here. Reference is first to entry numbers; page number entries are in parentheses and preceded by the letter "p".

Abstracting, (p. 6)
Action art, 314
Aesthetics, 74n, (p. 29)
African Americans. *See* Black influence
African art. *See* Art, African
African film. *See* Film, radio, television, and video, African
African literature. *See* Literature, African
African music. *See* Music, African
African religion. *See* Religion, African
Afterlife beliefs, 196n
Aging of literature, (p. 5)
Alternative religions
　bibliographies and catalogs, 126–129
　dictionaries, encyclopedias, and handbooks, 191–196
American Art Association, (p. 153)
American Arts Alliance, (p. 155)
American Association of Language Specialists, (p. 395)
American Association of Museums, (p. 155)
American Catholic Philosophical Association, (p. 38)
American Comparative Literature Association, (p. 396)
American Composers' Alliance, (p. 257)
American Council on the Teaching of Foreign Languages, (p. 395)
American Federation of Arts, (p. 155)
American Federation of Film Societies, (p. 257)
American Film and Video Association, (p. 257)
American Film Institute, (p. 257)
American Guild of Organists, (p. 256)
American language. *See* Language and linguistics; Language, American

American literary magazines, 1205
American literature. *See* Literature, English language
American music. *See* Music, American
American Music Conference, (p. 256)
American Musicological Association, (p. 256)
American Musicological Society, (p. 256)
American Philosophical Association, (p. 37)
American poetry. *See* Poetry, English language
American Society for...
　Information Science, (p. 155)
　Theatre Research, (p. 257)
American Theological Library Association, (p. 73)
Ancient philosophy. *See* Philosophy, ancient
Angels, 138
Anthems, national, 660
Antiques. *See* Applied design, crafts, and decorative arts
Applied arts..., 532. See also Applied design, crafts, and decorative arts
Applied design, crafts, and decorative arts (general). *See also specific crafts and art forms* (Furniture and woodcraft; Jewelry and metalcraft; Ceramics, pottery, and glass; Textiles, weaving and needlecraft; Fashion and costume; Graphic arts)
American, 530–531, 533, 555
annuals, 548
bibliographic guides and bibliographies, 530–534
biographical sources, 546, 551–555n
collections, 538
dictionaries, encyclopedias, and handbooks, 535–547
directories, 548–550

Applied design, crafts, and decorative arts (*continued*)
    English, 538
    French, 538
    history, 545
    indexes, 534
    influences, 530
    modern, 537, 547, 551–552
    supplies, 549
    workshops, 550
    world, 532, 542
Archaeology, 167, 171n, 269, 329n–331
Architecture, (p. 148, 152–154)
Architecture, interior design, and landscape
    architecture
    American, 485, 489–490n, 493
    atlases, 474
    bibliographic guides, 328, 461–465
    bibliographies and catalogs, 466–469
    biographical sources, 489–495
    British, 468
    Byzantine, 467
    Canadian, 315
    Catalogs, 466
    Christian, 368, 467
    dictionaries, encyclopedias, and handbooks,
        474–484
    directories, 485–488
    European, 474
    films and videos, 466n
    firms, 488
    history, 329, 414–415, 467, 482–483, 494–495
    indexes, 470–473
    internet resources, 463
    Italian, 414
    modern, 365, 415, 490
    obituaries, 490n
    periodicals, 464
    Renaissance, 414
    Romanesque, 469
    standards, 484
    Western, 336
    world, 473, 483, 491–492, 494–495
Archives, (p. 7)
Archives of…
    American Art, (p. 155)
    Dance, Music, and Theatre, (p. 258)
ARL, (p. 7)
Art. *See also* Visual Arts, (general) *and specific*
    relevant categories (Painting, drawing,
    and print; Sculpture; etc.)
    American, 317, 319, 352, 371–374, 385,
        388–396, 399–400, 402, 406. *See*
        also specific categories
    African, 318,405
    Asian, 366,386,409–410
    Canadian, 315
    catalogs. *See* Art, libraries
    classical, 342

    criticism, 322, 396
    Dutch, 361
    English, 401
    exhibitions. *See* Visual Arts, sales and
        exhibitions
    films and tapes, 323, 375
    galleries, 372
    German, 438
    history. *See* Visual arts, history and chronology
    Islamic, 411
    Italian, 408, 414. *See also separate categories*
    libraries, 319–321, 324–325, 377
    modern, 325, 327, 334, 358, 365, 387–388,
        415, 419–420
    museums, 379, 382
    naïve. *See* naïve art
    Native American. *See* Native American influ-
        ence, visual arts
    performance. *See* Performance art
    performing. *See* Performing arts
    Renaissance, 408, 414
    sales catalogs. *See* Visual arts, sales and
        exhibitions
    selling, 376
    Spanish, 398
    supplies, 373
    techniques, 354, 365
    theory, 355
    visual. *See* Visual arts
    Western, 311
    women in. *See* Female influence, visual arts
    world, 316, 353, 363, 383–384, 393–394,
        403–404, 407, 412–413. *See also*
        separate divisions
Art catalogs, (p. 150)
Art directors (film), 960
Art Libraries Society…, (p. 155)
    North America, (p. 155)
Art songs, 649
Arthurian legend, 1164
Artist colonies, 18
Artists International Association, (p. 154)
Arts. *See* Art; Visual arts; Performing arts;
    Humanities
Asian art. *See* Art, Asian
Asian dance. *See* Dance, Asian
Asian philosophy. *See* Philosophy, Asian
Association for the…
    Development of Religious Information
        Systems (ADRIS), (p. 72)
    Sociology of Religion, (p. 72)
Association of…
    Architectural Librarians, (p. 155)
    Ethicists, (p. 38)
    Philosophy Journal Editors, (p. 38)
Astrology, 193n
Auction catalog, 346, 350
Audiovisual, 918, 929
Austen, Jane, 1256

Author interviews, 1153
Avery Memorial Architectural Library (collection), 471, 490n, (p. 155)
Ayer, A. J., 71n

Babi, 119
Baha'i religion, 119
Ballet. *See* Dance, ballet
Ballet Theatre Foundation, (p. 256)
Band music, 758. *See also* Music, popular; Music, concert (serious) and opera
Baroque music. *See* Music, baroque
Batik, 581. *See also* Textiles, weaving, and needlecraft
Bertrand Russell papers, (p. 39)
Bible, (p. 120–138). *See also* Religion
    abstracts, 243, 245–246
    atlases, 283–287
    bibliographies and guides, 109, 244, 248
    commentaries, 247, 263n, 275–281
    concordances and quotations, 249–256
    dictionaries, encyclopedias, and handbooks, 257–274
    history, 282
    versions and editions
        Christian, 231–238
        multiple versions, 241–242
        non-Christian, 239–240
Bibliotheque Nationale, (p. 396)
Bioethics, 54, 78
Biographical sources, general, 28–35. *See also specific subject categories*
Black influence
    arts, 32
    film, radio, television, and video, 908, 924
    humanities, 32
    literature, 1081, 1096, 1098–1099, 1143, 1146, 1163, 1165, 1177–1178, 1194, 1216, 1218, 1240, 1243, 1347, 1358, 1368
    music, 618–619, 683, 739, 754, 761, 765–766. *See also* Blues music; Jazz
    performing arts (general), 602
    religion and theology, 114, 147, 199
    theater and drama, 849, 867
    visual arts, 335, 384n
Blues music, 739, 754, 765. *See also* Music, popular
Bohemian, 1179
Book reviews, (p. 4)
British Library, (p. 396)
Broadcast media, 6, 957
Broadcasting. *See* Film, radio, television, and video; Radio; Television
Broadway, 775, 780, 849. *See also* Musical theater and film; Theater and Drama
Buddhism, 120, 125, 185. *See also* Religion, Asian
Buddhist philosophy. *See* Philosophy, Asian
Building arts, (p. 148)

Built environment, 464
Byzantine architecture. *See* Architecture, Byzantine

Cameras, 524
Camp meeting, 112n
Canadian art, 315
Caribbean literature, 1118, 1326
Carpets. *See* Rugs and carpets
Cataloging and classification, (p. 32–35, 69, 252)
Catalogs, types (art). *See* Art catalogs
Catholic Library Association, (p. 73)
Catholicism, 116, 130, 174, 198, 205, 212, 215, 272
CD Reviews (music), 695
CD-ROM (guides and catalogs), 8–11
Center for…
    Applied Research in the Apostolate, (p. 73)
    Hellenic Studies, (p. 396)
Ceramics, pottery, and glass
    bibliographic guides and bibliographies, 569–570
    collecting, 571
    dictionaries, encyclopedias, and handbooks, 571–576
    History, 575
    materials and techniques, 572–573, 575–576
Chamber music. *See* Music, chamber
Channeling, 127. *See also* Alternative religions
Chant, (p. 255)
Charismatic movements, 164
Chicano/chicana literature, 1310, 1320. *See also* Literature, foreign language, Spanish
Children's literature. *See* Literature, Children's and young adult
Chinese art. *See* Art, Asian
Chinese philosophy. *See* Philosophy, Asian
Chinese religion. *See* Religion, Asian
Choreographers. *See* Dance, choreography
Christian architecture. *See* Architecture, Christian
Christian art. *See* Art, Christian
Christian doctrine, 160
Christian lore, 162
Christianity, 101, 112–118, 143, 160–180, 219n, 224, 227–228
Church and Synagogue Library Association, (p. 72)
Church history, 99–100, 171, 180, 225
Church issues, 99–100
Cinema. *See* Film, radio, television, and video
Citation studies, (p. 5, 31, 69, 254, 393)
Classical art. *See* Art, classical
Classical literature. *See* Literature, classical
Classical music. *See* Music, classical
Clavichord music, 655n
Cliches, 1021
Collection development, (p. 6, 10, 31, 68, 150–151, 253)
College Art Association, (p. 155)
Color, 357

Committee on Research in Dance, (p. 257)
Communication, Christian, 115
Comparative literature, 1052
Comparative religion, 139n, 142
Composers, 685, 718–719, 755, 758, 782
Computer art, (p. 149)
Computer music.... *See* Electronic music
    Association, (p. 255)
Computers...
    applications in the humanities, (p. 8–9)
    composition, (p. 394)
    literature and, (p. 394)
    music and, (p. 254)
    performing arts and, (p. 254–255)
    philosophy and, (p. 35–36)
    religion and, (p. 70–71)
    visual arts, (p. 152–153)
Computing. *See* Computers
Concert music. *See* Concert music (serious) and
    opera
Concordances, (p. 36)
Conductors, 249–256
Conference proceedings, 23
Composers, 718–719, 722
Construction, 476, 480, 484n
Contemporary architecture. *See* Architecture,
    modern
Contemporary art. *See* Art, modern
Contemporary film, 601
Contemporary literature. *See* Literature, modern
Contemporary music. *See* Music, contemporary
Contemporary philosophy. *See* Philosophy,
    modern
Contemporary religion, 140, 142n
Contemporary television, 601
Contemporary theater, 601
Coptic religion, 161
Cosmology, (p. 28). *See also* Philosophy, ancient
Costume. *See* Fashion and costume
Council of the Societies for the Study of Religion,
    (p. 72)
Country and western music, 740, 759, 763, 767.
    See also Music, popular
Crafts, 535, 539, 550. *See also* Applied design,
    crafts, and decorative arts
Crime fiction. *See* Mystery and crime fiction
C. S. Pierce Society, (p. 38)
Cults and sects, 191, 194, 208
Culture, 1, 26, 157, 171, 223
Cyberspace, 39

Dance, (p. 250, 256). *See also* Ballet
    American, 820
    annuals, 813
    Asian, 802
    ballet, 803–809
        dictionaries, 807–807, 809
        digests, 803, 805

    techniques of, 804
    bibliographies and catalogs, 790–792, 794
    biographical sources, 814–817
    choreography, 815–816
    collections, 790, 811
    dictionaries, encyclopedias, and handbooks
        ethnic and regional, 801–802
        general, 795–800
    directories, 810–811
    ethnic and regional, 801–802
    film and video, 791, 816
    history, 818–821
    indexes, 789, 793
    information centers, 811–813
    internet resources, 812n
    modern, 817–818
    organizations, 811–813
    periodicals, 616, 812
    resources, 810–811
    sacred, 794
    square, 801
    tap, 800
Dance Educators of America, (p. 256)
Dance Masters of America, (p. 256)
Database guides, 8–11
Decorative arts. *See* Applied design and decora-
    tive arts
Dell Publishing Company, (p. 258)
Descartes, 86n
Design, 531, 534, 536–537, 540, 542, 546–547,
    551, 553. *See also* Applied design,
    crafts, and decorative arts; Architecture,
    interior design and landscape
Detective fiction. *See* Mystery and crime fiction
Detroit Institute of Arts (collection), 538
Dictionaries. *See also* Language and linguistics,
    dictionaries
    Chinese, 1041
    English
        children's, 989
        desk and college, 1016–1018
        etymology, synonyms, pronunciation, etc.,
            1029–1035
        unabridged and scholarly, 1009–1015
        usage, slang, idioms, and new words,
            1019–1028
    French, 1039
    German, 1038
    Greek, 1043
    Hebrew, 1047
    Italian, 1037
    Japanese, 1044
    Latin, 1045
    Middle-English, 1104
    Multilingual and bilingual, 1040
    Russian, 1046
    Spanish, 1036, 1042
Digital libraries, (p. 9–10)
Dinner theater, 854

Disabilities, 1353
Discographies. *See* Music, recordings
Dissertations, 22,621
Dodge Collection, 538
Dominican College Library, (p. 39)
Don C. Allen Collection, (p. 39)
Drama. *See* Theater and drama
Dramatists. *See* Theater and drama, playwrights
Drawing, 421. *See also* Painting, drawing, and
    print
Dumbarton Oaks Library, (p. 155)
Earth scale art, 499
Ecumenical movement, 165
Edwardian fiction, 1235
Electronic information. *See individual titles*
Electronic Bibles, (p. 71)
Electronic music, 622, 784
Electronic publishing, (p. 7–8, 71, 253)
Electronic texts, (p. 8, 71, 253, 394–395)
Embroidery, (p. 577, 579). *See also* Textiles,
    weaving, and needlecraft
Engineering. *See* Design
English language. *See* Language and linguistics;
    Language, English
English literature. *See* Literature, English language
English, regional dialect, 1020
Enlightenment, 74n
English poetry. *See* Poetry, English language
Entertainment, 951, 956. *See also* Performing arts
Epistemology, 74n, (p. 28)
Esperanto Language Society of Chicago, (p. 396)
Ethics, 46–47, 74n, 81, 168, 179, 907, (p. 28)
Ethnomusicology, 623
Etymology, 1029–1030
Evangelicalism, 112
Exhibition catalogs, 351

Fable, 292
Fairies and fairy tales, 289, 297
Fakebooks, 738
Fantasy fiction. *See* Science fiction and fantasy
Fashion and costume
    American, 585–586
    bibliographies and indexes, 585
    biographical sources, 594–595
    dictionaries, encyclopedias, handbooks, etc.,
        586–593
    history, 586–589, 591–593
    modern, 586, 594–595
    theatrical, 585n–586, 595
    Western, 587, 591
Federal Theatre Project, 880
Federation of Motion Picture Councils, (p. 257)
Female influence
    literature, 1057, 1112, 1118, 1139, 1141,
        1146, 1174, 1177, 1190–1191, 1194,
        1232, 1249n, 1256, 1263, 1269,
        1274, 1283, 1290–1291, 1302

    music, 667, 685, 725, 753
    mythology, 307
    philosophy, 48, 94
    quotations, 1112
    religion, 118
    theater and drama, 830
    visual arts, 322, 362, 389–390, 402, 420, 506
Feminism, 1190–1191
Festivals, music. *See* Music festivals
Fiction (English language). *See* Literature, fiction;
    Literature, English language
    bibliographic guides, 1216–1218
    bibliographies and indexes
      of fiction, 1219–1233
      of fiction criticism, 1241, 1243, 1246–1247,
        1250–1251, 1253–1254, 1260,
        1262
    biographical and critical sources, 1240–1263
    dictionaries, encyclopedias, and handbooks,
        1234–1239
Fiction, children's. *See* Literature, children's and
    young adult
Fiction (foreign language), 1290–1293
Fiction, historical. *See* Historical fiction
Fiction, popular. *See also specific genres*
Fiction, postmodern, 1122
Fiction, short, 1119, 1123, 1231, 1241–1242,
    1260, 1262, 1318
Fiction, Renaissance, 1254
Fiction, world, 1121, 1289
Film, (p. 250)
Film catalogs. *See* Film, radio, television, and
    video
Film directors. *See* Filmmakers
Film festivals, 952
Film industry, 940, 959n, 970n. *See also* Film,
    radio, television, and video
Film journalism, 915
Film literature, 904. *See also* Film, radio, televi-
    sion, and video
Film, musical. *See* Musical theater and film
Film directors. *See* Filmmakers
Film performers, 964–966, 969–970
Film quotes, 925
Film, radio, television, and video
    African, 934
    African American, 909
    American, 908–910, 915n, 923, 938, 972, 974
    annuals, 954, 957, 959n, 979, 983
    bibliographic guides, 899–901
    bibliographies and catalogs, 902–907
    biographical sources, 960–971
    British, 912, 977n
    collections, 909, 956
    current awareness services, 950–951, 959
    dictionaries, encyclopedias, and handbooks,
        923–949
    directories, 952–953
    film/video sources (listings), 908–920

Film, radio, television, and video (*continued*)
  funding, 955
  history, 972–974
  indexes, 921–922
  Italian, 977
  nostalgia, 956
  periodicals, 900–901, 921–922, 975
  reviews and criticism, 975–985
  world, 916, 922, 935, 940, 949, 967, 971,
    973, 980
  writing for, 958
Film research, 899, 903, 953, 976
Film sequels, 941
Film theory and study, 903, 976
Filmed books, 913, 930
Filmmakers, 963, 967–968, 971
Filmographies. *See* Film, radio, television, and
    video, film/video listings
Fine art. *See* Visual arts
Folger Shakespeare Library, (p. 396)
Folk art, 554–555. *See also* Naïve art
Folk music, 726. *See also* Music, popular
Folklore. *See* Mythology and Folklore
Funding, (p. 11). *See also* Directories *in each
    major category*
Furniture and wood craft,
  American, 556–557
  Antique, 558
  bibliographies, indexes, and abstracts, 556
  dictionaries, encyclopedias, handbooks, etc.,
    559–560
  history, 557
  world, 558

Gay/lesbian influence, 831, 1192, 1198, 1246, 1270
General reference tools for the humanities
  abstracts, 22
  annuals and current awareness sources, 2, 6,
    17–18
  bibliographic guides
    computerized databases/CD-ROM, 8–11
    library collections (catalogs), 12–13
    periodicals, 5–7
    reference books, 1–4
  biographical sources, 28–35
  dictionaries, encyclopedias, and handbooks,
    26–27
  directories, 5–11, 14–18
  indexes, 19–21, 23–25
Genre fiction, 1236. *See also specific genres*:
    Westerns, Science fiction and fantasy, etc.
Getty Center, (p. 154)
Getty Trust, 329
Ghosts, 192. *See also* Gothic literature
Gilbert and Sullivan, 778. *See also* Musical theater
    and film
G. K. Hall (publisher), (p. 73)
Glass. *See also* Ceramics, pottery, and glass

Heisey, 571
  stained, 570
Gold, 563, 566
Gospel music, 763n
Gospels, 258
Gothic literature, 1127, 1261. *See also* Ghosts
Graphic arts, 541–542, 552, (p. 148)
Graphic design. *See* Design
Greek philosophy. *See* Philosophy, ancient;
    Philosophy, medieval
Guitar music, 652

Handicraft, 535, 539
Handweaving, 578. *See also* Textiles, weaving,
    and needlecraft
Harpsichord music, 655n
Hegel, 86n
Heidegger, 86n
Heisey glass, 571
Heresy and heretics, 141, 163n
Higher education, (p. 2)
Hinduism, 121, 186. *See also* Philosophy, Asian;
    Religion, Asian
Hispanic influence, 1315, 1322
Historic places, 472, 486
Historic preservation, 472, 485–487
Historical fiction, 1217
History, 26, (p. 1–2). *See also under each category*
Hobbes, 86n
Holidays, religious, 158n
Holography, 516n
Hollywood, 779, 965, 970
Horror fiction. *See* Gothic fiction
House Library of Philosophy, (p. 39)
Household furnishings, 533
Humanism, 26n
Humanistic Scholarship, (p. 2–4)
Humanities, general, (p. 1–11)
  definitions of, (p. 1–2)
  disciplines of, (p. 1–2)
  general sources. *See* General reference tools
    for the humanities
  literature of, (p. 2–8)
  relationship to science, (p. 4)
Hymnals and hymnology, (p. 253)

Iconography, (p. 147)
Ideas, 43, 64
Idioms, 1019, 1026
Illustration, 340, 422, 446, 453, 552. *See also*
    Painting, drawing, and print
Imperial Society of Teachers of Dancing, (p. 256)
Impressionism, 428, 450. *See also* Painting,
    drawing, and print
Indian art. *See* Art, Asian; Native American
    influence, visual arts

Indian diaspora, 1204
Indian philosophy. *See* Philosophy, Asian
Indian religion. *See specific religions and also*
    Religion, Asian
Information seeking, (p. 4–8,31)
Interior design, 465, 475, 493. *See also* Archi-
    tecture, interior design, and landscape
    architecture
International Association for the Study of the
    Italian Language and Literature, (p. 396)
International Association of
    Art Critics, (p. 154)
    Music Libraries, (p. 256)
    Teachers of Philosophy, (p. 38)
International Council of Museums, (p. 154)
International Federation
    for Theatre Research, (p. 257)
    of Institutes for Social and Socio-religious
        Research, (p. 72)
International Union of Architects, (p. 154)
Internet, (p. 4, 8–10)
Internet, implications of, (p. 6–7)
Internet resources. *See under specific subject*
    categories
Isham Memorial Library of Harvard, (p. 257)
Islamic architecture, 477
Islamic art. *See* Art, Islamic
Islamic groups, 187n
Islamic religion, 127, 133, 184, 187, 190, 223,
    240, 260
Italian painting, 423, 429
Italian sculpture, 497, 509

J. Paul Getty
    Museum, (p. 154)
    Trust, (p. 154)
Japanese art. *See* Art, Asian
Jazz, 729–730, 744, 752, 762, 768–769. *See also*
    Music, popular
Jesus, 171n, 258
Jewelry and metalcraft
    American, 561, 564
    antique, 562
    Asian, 568
    dictionaries, encyclopedias, and handbooks,
        561–568
    English, 563
    history, 565, 567
    technique, 563, 565–566
Jewish influence, 188, 197, 214, 290, 1247, 1257
Journals. *See* Periodicals *segment for each unit*
Journalists, 1173
Judaism, 101, 123, 134, 143, 181, 183, 189,
    214n, 222
Junior high school readers, 1344

Kant, 86n
Kant Society, (p. 38)
Keyboard instruments, 785
Knitting, 583. *See also* Textiles, weaving, and
    needlecraft

Landscape architecture, 462, 463, 478. *See also*
    Architecture, design and landscape
    architecture
Language and linguistics
    abstracts, 993–994
    annuals, 992
    bibliographies and guides, 986–991
    dictionaries, encyclopedias, and handbooks
        (linguistics), 997–1008. *For general*
        purpose dictionaries, see Dictionaries
    directories, 1050
    history, 1048–1049
    indexes, 992
    internet resources, 991
    periodicals, 995n–996n
    reviews, 995–996
    study and teaching, 991, 996, 1004
Language American, 1048
Language and Literature, (p. 391–397)
    definitions of, (p. 1–2, 391–392)
    disciplines of, (p. 392–393)
    users, (p. 392)
Language, Asian, 986
Language behavior, 994
Language, European, 1005
Language, modern, 995
Language studies, 76
Languages, families of, (p. 391)
Latin American literature. *See* Literature, Spanish
League for Yiddish, Inc., (p. 396)
Liberation theology, 117
Library collections
    art, 310, 319–321, 324–325, 328, 336
    dance, 790, 811
    film, 918, 953
    general, 12–13
    literature, 1147–1148
    music, 620, 629, 638, 642–643
    performing arts (general), 600, 606
    philosophy, 54
    religion, 111
    theater, 828
Library of Congress
    collections, 427
    Music Division, (p. 257)
    Subject Headings, (p. 33–34)
Linguistics. *See* Language and linguistics
Linguistics, applied, 1004
L' institut international de philosphie, (p. 38)
Literary agents, 1105

Literary awards and grants, 1103
Literary characters, 1067, 1078
Literary criticism, 1058, 1070–1071,
    1068–1070, 1084–1085, 1087–1088,
    1093–1095, 1097–1102, 1183, 1197,
    1201. *See also* Literature, English lan-
    guage, biographical and critical
    sources; Poetry, biographical and criti-
    cal sources; Fiction, biographical and
    critical sources
Literary guides, 1062, 1064, 1077, 1083, 1128–1129
Literary manuscripts, 1104
Literary movements, 1061
Literary quotations. *See* Literature, general
    works, quotations
Literary scholarship, 1051, 1054, (p. 393–394)
Literary theory, 1069, 1073
Literature
    African, 1240. *See also* Black influence,
        literature
    African-American. *See* Black influence,
        literature
    aging, (p. 5)
    American. *See* Literature, English language
    Arabic, 1339
    Arthurian, 1164
    Asian, 1340–1342
    Canadian, 1140, 1167
    children's and young adult
        awards, 1356, 1360, 1363
        bibliographies and indexes, 1344–1355
        biographical and critical sources, 1366–1374
        characters in, 1359, 1370
        dictionaries, encyclopedias, and hand-
            books, 1356–1365
        disabilities, 1353
        fiction, 1344–1347, 1355, 1362
        multicultural, 1351
        poetry, 1349–1350
        reviews, 1345, 1348
    Chinese, 1342n
    characters in. *See* Literary characters
    comparative. *See* Comparative literature
    English. *See* Literature, English language
    English language
        abstracts, 1150
        annuals, 1151–1152, 1154
        bibliographic guides, 1134–1137
        bibliographies and catalogs, 1138–1149,
            1151–1152, 1156
        biographical and critical sources, 1173–1204
        criticism, 1134. *See also* Literary criticism
        dictionaries, encyclopedias, and hand-
            books, 1157–1172
        fiction. *See* Fiction, English language
        history and chronology, 1205–1215
        indexes, 1152, 1155, 1194
        periodicals, 1155, 1173, 1205, 1208
        poetry. *See* Poetry, English language

    reference sources, 1265
    study and teaching, 1135–1137, 1150,
        1156, 1199–1201
    European, 1066, 1089, 1290, 1292. *See also*
        specific nationalities
    fiction. *See also* Fiction (English language);
        Fiction (foreign language)
        biographical and critical sources, 1118–1127
        dictionaries, encyclopedias, and handbooks,
            1116–1117
        writers' guides and directories, 1128–1129
    foreign language origin (general), 1289–1293
    French, 1300–1308
    general works
        abstracts, 1059
        bibliographic guides, 1052–1053
        bibliographies, 1058, 1060–1061
        biographical and critical sources, 1080–1102
        dictionaries, encyclopedias, and handbooks,
            1063–1079
        history and chronology, 1076
        indexes, 1062, 1090
        internet resources, 1057
        periodicals, 1055–1056
        plot summaries, 1079
        quotations and proverbs, 1108–1115
        writers' guides and directories, 1103–1107,
            1128–1129
    Germanic/Scandinavian, 1327–1333
        internet resources, 1329
    Greek, 1296–1299
    Indian, 1204, 1340n
    Irish, 1169–1170
    Italian, 1309
    Japanese, 1341–1342
    Latin American, 1314, 1316–1319, 1324. *See*
        also Literature, Spanish
    modern, 1053, 1062, 1065n–1066, 1070,
        1072–1073, 1077, 1083–1085, 1091,
        1096, 1098–1100, 1154, 1183–1186,
        1196
    New Zealand, 1215
    poetry. *See also* Poetry, English language
        biographical and critical sources, 1131,
            1279–1288, 1311
        criticism, 1131, 1294. *See also* Literary
            criticism
        dictionaries, encyclopedias, and handbooks,
            1130
        European, 1294–1295
        explication, 1304
        French, 1304
        popular, 1185
        Quotations, 1133
        Spanish (includes Hispanic/Latin American),
            1311, 1323
        writers' guides and directories, 1132
    romantic period, 1061
    Russian (Slavonic), 1334–1338

internet resources, 1336
Scottish, 1160
South Pacific, 1343
Southern, 1161, 1185, 1245
Spanish (includes Hispanic/Latin American), 1295, 1310–1326
summaries and digests, 1067, 1079, 1094
Victorian, 1152, 1155
Welsh, 1169n
world, 1055, 1060, 1064, 1072, 1076–1077, 1086–1087, 1091, 1101–1102
Little magazines, 1055
Liturgy, 154, 167, 229
Living religions, 139, 153
Locke, 86n
Logic, 76, (p. 28)
Lute music, 652
Lutheranism, 203n

Magazines. *See* Periodical Guides, general; Literature, English language, periodicals
Magic, 128, 293n, 303
Marquand Library of Princeton University, (p. 155)
Masterpieces, 1067, 1094, 1163
Marxist philosophy. *See* Philosophy, Marxist
Medieval art. *See* Art, medieval
Medieval music. *See* Music, medieval
Medieval philosophy. *See* Philosophy, medieval
Metalcraft. *See* Jewelry and metalcraft
Metaphysics, 74n, 84, (p. 28). *See also* Philosophy, ancient
Methodism, 203
Metropolitan Museum of Art, 324
Metropolitan Opera, 705, 708
Minor arts, (p. 148)
Modern art. *See* Art, modern
Modern language…. *See* Language, modern Association, (p. 395)
Modern literature. *See* Literature, modern
Modern music. *See* Music, contemporary
Modern philosophy. *See* Philosophy, modern
Monographs, (p. 4, 31)
Mormonism, 170
Motion Picture Association, (p. 258)
Motion pictures. *See* Film, radio, television, and video
Movies. *See* Film, radio, television, and video
Multiculturalism, 1351, 1368
Museum Libraries, (p. 153–154)
Museums, 14–16. *See also* Art, museums
Music, (p. 249–250)
    abstracts, 633
    African, 618
    African American and black. *See* Black influence, music
    American, 610–611, 624, 634, 645, 649, 663, 670, 686–687, 718, 741–743,

752–754. *See also* Music, concert (serious) and opera
analyses, 626
annuals, 680
anthologies, 635
Asian, 618n
Baroque, 609
bibliographic guides, 609–617
bibliographies and catalogs, 618–628
    instrumental, 651–657
    printed music sources, general, 634–644
    vocal, 645–650
biographical sources, 682–686
Canadian, 662
cantatas, 646
cataloging, 641
chamber, 639, 650. *See also* Music, concert (serious) and opera
choral, 645–647
classical, 686, 697. *See also* Music, concert (serious) and opera
composers. *See* Composers
computers in, 622
concert, (serious) and opera
    American, 712, 716, 739–745, 747
    annuals, 699
    annuals, 614
    bibliographies and indexes, 698
    biographical sources, 717–724
    classical, 702, 705, 711
    contemporary, 686, 690, 712, 714–716, 718–719, 722
    dictionaries, encyclopedias, handbooks, etc., 699–713
    directories, 715
    German language, 709
    history, 707, 711, 713
    plots (opera), 700, 703–706, 708
    recordings, 663, 676, 694–697, 725
    symphony, 716
    world, 715
dictionaries, encyclopedias, and handbooks, 662–675
directories, 676–681
discographies. *See* Music, recordings
education. *See* Music, faculties/schools
ethnic, 696
faculties/schools, 677, 681
festivals, 679
film. *See* Musical theater and film
gothic, 689
history and chronology, 610n–611, 687–693, 748–749
indexes, 631
instruments. *See* Musical instruments
internet resources, 617
librarianship, 632, 636
libraries, 678
medieval, 625

Music (*continued*)
  non-Western, 674
  opera. *See* Music, concert (serious) and opera
  periodicals, 615–616
  popular. *See also* Jazz music; Folk music; Rock
      music, Country and western music; etc.
    bibliographic guides, 726–728
    bibliographies and catalogs, 729–731
    biographical sources, 752–762
    contemporary, 727–731, 734–738, 756
    dictionaries, encyclopedias, handbooks,
      etc., 739–749
    directories, annuals, and current awareness
      sources, 750–751
    printed music sources (songs), 732–738
    recordings, 763–770
  reference sources, 612–614
  research, 611, 613–614, 678
  sets and editions, 640
  settings, 648
  sources, 693
  special collections, 628–630
  stylistic analysis, 626
  symphony. *See* Music, concert (serious) and
      opera
  technology, 784n
  television. *See* Musical theater and film
  thematic catalogs, 658–661
  theory, 627
  Western, 688
  world, 664, 666, 703, 715
Music Educators National Conference, (p. 256)
Music librarianship, (p. 251–254)
Music Library Association, (p. 256)
Musical instruments, 783, 785–788
Musical comedy. *See also* Musical theater and film
Musical theater and film, 771. *See also* Dance
  American, 774
  bibliographies and catalogs, 771–773
  dictionaries, encyclopedias, handbooks, etc.,
    774–781
  recordings, 782
  reviews, 773
Musical themes, 658–659
Musicals. *See* Musical theater and film
Musicians, 666, 671, 682, 720, 723, 752, 756
Musicology, 621
Muslim. *See* Islamic influence
Mystery and crime fiction, 1120, 1221, 1226, 1259
Mystical religions, 195. *See also* Alternative
    religions
Mythology and Folklore
  bibliographies and guides, 288, 290–291
  British, 294
  Celtic, 295
  Classical, 27, 306
  dictionaries, encyclopedias, and handbooks,
    292–307
  indexes, 289
  Jewish, 290
  North American, 288, 299
  themes in art, 27, 342
  women in, 307
  world, 296, 298, 305

Naïve art, 404. *See also* Folk art
National anthems, 660
National Art Education Association, (p. 155)
National Council of...
  Churches, (p. 72)
  Churches of Christ in the USA, (p. 72)
National Federation of Language Teachers
    Associations, (p. 395)
National Music Publishers Association, (p. 257)
National Portrait Gallery (collection), 434
Native American influence
  Film, radio, television, and video, 939
  literature, 1138
  religion, 150
  visual arts, 326n, 397
Native art. *See* Art, African; Art, Asian; Native
    American influence, visual arts
Needlepoint, 577. *See also* Textiles, Weaving,
    and Needlecraft
Nelson-Atkins Museum of Art, 429
Networks. *See* Internet
New age religions, 196. *See also* Alternative
    religions
Non-Christian faiths. *See also* Alternative religions
  bibliographies, 119–125
  dictionaries, encyclopedias, and handbooks,
    181–190
New Testament, 220n, 245–246n, 273–274n
New York Public Library, (p. 155)
Nostalgia, 956
Nouns, 1031
Novel. *See* Fiction; Literature, fiction
Nursery rhymes, 1365

Obituaries, 29
Oboe music, 654
Occult, 191, 193, 195n
Old Testament, 220, 246–247n, 274
Online searching, (p. 9, 36, 70, 153, 252, 255)
Ontology, 84. *See also* Philosophy, ancient
Opera. *See* Music, concert (serious) and opera
Opera companies, 715
Operetta, 698
Oratorios, 646
Orchestra, 716
Organ music, 655
Organizations, (p. 37–38, 72–73, 154–156,
    256–258, 395–396)
Oriental art. *See* Art, Asian
Original works, (p. 10, 250)

Paganism, 128. *See also* Alternative religions
Painting, drawing and print. *See also* Illustration
American, 421–422, 426–427, 432–434, 441, 453, 456
Asian, 457
bibliographies, 421–425
biographical sources, 452–455
British, 452
catalogs and collections, 426–431
collecting, 440
dictionaries, encyclopedias, and handbooks, 446–451
European, 455
German, 438
history, 437, 442, 456–460
indexes, 432–433, 435–436, 441, 443
impressionism, 450
Italian, 414, 423, 429, 459
modern, 415, 458, 460
oils, 447
old masters, 424
Renaissance, 414, 423
reproductions, 432–433, 435. *See also* Visual arts, reproductions
sales and exhibitions, 438–445
themes, 448
watercolors, 449
world, 431, 436–437, 444–446, 451
Palmistry, 127n. *See also* Alternative religions
Papacy. *See* Popes
Parapsychology. *See also* Alternative religions
Paris Opera, 711
Pentecostalism, 164
Percussion music, 785n
Performing arts, (p. 249–258). *See also* Dance; Film, radio, television, and video; Music; Theater
bibliographic guides and bibliographies, 596–598
biographical sources, 601, 604, 608
characters in, 599
definitions of, (p. 249)
disciplines of, (p. 249–251)
directories, 600, 602–603, 605–606, 680
funding, 603
indexes, 599, 607
information centers, 600, 605–610
literature of, (p. 251–254)
obituaries, 607
organizations, 605
psychology of, (p. 251)
reference sources, 596–597
research, 598
resources, 605–606
special collections, 600, 605–606
Periodical guides, general, 5–7. *See also* periodicals *under each major subject category*
Personal religion, (p. 66)
Phenomenology, 76n
Phi Sigma Tau, (p. 38)

Philosophy, (p. 27–29)
American, 88
ancient, 52, 59n, 79, 83, 87, 95
Asian, 49–50, 80, 82, 90
bibliographic guides, 36–39
bibliographies and catalogs
general, 40–45
specialized by topic or country, 46–58
biographical sources. *See* directories and biographical sources
cataloging, (p. 32–33)
classification, (p. 32–33)
definitions of, (p. 27–28)
dictionaries, encyclopedias, and handbooks
general, 59–73
specialized by topic or country, 74–84
directories and biographical sources, 85–94
divisions of, (p. 28–29)
Documentation Center, (p. 37–38)
history, 41–44, 95–98
indexes, abstracts, and serial bibliographies, 53–58
internet resources, 39
Marxist, 51, 77. *See also* Philosophy, Soviet
medieval, 87n, 95n
modern, 74n, 79, 84–86, 88, 91n, 93–94, 95n
of language, 74n
of law, 74n
of mind, 74n
of religion, (p. 66)
periodicals, 38
quotations, 71n
Soviet, 51n, 63. *See also* Philosphy, Marxist
subject headings in, (p. 33–35)
thesaurus, 57n, 71n
Western, 75, 89, 91, 94, 97–98
world, 73, 84, 92–93, 96
Phonetics, 999
Photography, (p. 149)
American, 525
anthologies, 517
bibliographies and catalogs, 510–514
biographical sources, 520, 525–529
collecting, 524
collections, 515
dictionaries, encyclopedias, and handbooks, 519–524
history, 510, 514, 520, 522
indexes, 515
modern, 526–527
sales, 516, 520
techniques, 523
world, 510–511, 527–529
Piano music, 651, 653, 656
Picasso, 442
Picture files, 343
Plastic arts, (p. 148). *See also* Visual arts; Sculpture
Plays. *See* Theater and drama

Playwrights. *See* Theater and drama, playwrights
Poetry, (p. 392) (English language). *See also*
    Literature, poetry
anthologies and collections, 1272–1278
Australian, 1276
bibliographic guides, 1264–1265
bibliographies and indexes, 1266–1271
biographical and critical sources, 1279–1288
children's, 1349–1350. *See also* Literature,
    children's and young adult
databases, 1273
explication, 1287
Irish, 1278
modern, 1266, 1281–1283
musical settings, 648
periodicals, 1268
popular, 1268
romantic, 1264n
Scottish, 1265
Poetry (foreign language), 1294–1295
Political philosophy, 74n
Popes, 215, 272
Popular culture, 1
Popular music. *See* Music, popular
Popularizations, (p. 10)
Popular music. *See* Music, popular
Popular religion, 110, 118n
Porcelain, 572. *See also* Ceramics, pottery, and
    glass
Posters, 545
Pottery. *See* Ceramics, pottery, and glass
Presbyterianism, 113, 217
Preservation, (p. 5)
Primal societies, 126
Print collections, 427, 430
Prints. *See* Painting, drawing, and print; Applied
    design, crafts, and decorative arts
Printmaking, 422, 541–542
Professional literatures, (p. 10)
Progress, (p. 3)
Pronunciation, 1033
Prose, (p. 392–393). *See also* Literature, fiction;
    Fiction
Protestantism. *See specific denominations*;
    Christianity
Proverbs, 1108, 1113
Psychic phenomena. *See also* Channeling; Alter-
    native religions
Psychocriticism, 1058
Psychology, 40
Publishers, 1104

Radio, 905–906, 937–938, 945–946, (p. 250)
Radio broadcasting and credits. *See also* Film,
    radio, television, and video
    old time, 937, 944, 956
Rap music, 727n. *See also* Music, popular

Reference guides, general, 1–4. *See also under*
    specific subjects and categories
Reformation, 177
Reformed faith, 172
Religion, (p. 65–74). *See also* Bible
abstracts, 132, 136–137
African, 126n
American, 148–150, 152, 155, 163, 187–188,
    194, 199–201, 206–208, 224
annuals, 197, 207
Asian, 120–122, 124–125, 133, 184–187, 190
atlases, 223, 226–228
bibliographic guides, 99–109
bibliographies and catalogs
    Christian, 112–118
    general, 110–111
    new alternatives, 126–129
    non-Christian, 119–125
biographical sources, 208–221
controversy, 141
conversions, 211
cross-cultural patterns, 157
current awareness, 198, 203
definitions of, (p. 65)
dictionaries, encyclopedias, and handbooks
    Christian, 160–181
    general, 138–159
    new alternatives, 191–196
    non-Christian, 181–190
directories, 198–202, 204–206
disciplines of, (p. 66)
divisions of, 206
education, 199–200
history, 222, 224–225, 228–230
indexes, 130–131, 133–135
internet resources, 109
leaders, 213, 218, 221n
organizations, 199, 201
periodicals, 106–108
philanthropy, 202
quotations, 159
world, 140, 144–145, 155, 226, 230
Religious Conference Management Association,
    (p. 72)
Religious Education Association, (p. 72)
Religious Public…
    Education Association, (p. 72)
    Relations Council, (p. 72)
Renaissance architecture. *See* Architecture,
    Renaissance
Renaissance art. *See* Art, Renaissance
Renaissance humanism, 26n
Renaissance philosophy, 95n
Renaissance sculpture. *See* Sculpture, Renaissance
Research and researchers. *See* Humanistic
    scholarship
Research Library of the Performing Arts, Lincoln
    Center, (p. 257)
Retrospective guides, (p. 2)

Review writing, (p. 251)
Rock & roll, 745. *See also* Music, popular
Rock music, 731, 749, 757, 761. *See also* Music, popular; Rock & roll
Rockabilly, 728. *See also* Music, popular
Romance fiction, 1259n
Romanesque architecture. *See* Architecture, Romanesque
Romanesque sculpture. *See* Sculpture, Romanesque
Romantic movement. *See* Literary movements
Rousseau, 86n
Rugs and carpets, 584. *See also* Textiles, weaving, and needlecraft

Sacramentum Mundi, 173n
Sacred places, 138n
Saints, 209–210
Scenographers, 962
Science fiction and fantasy
    bibliographic guides, 1218
    bibliographies and indexes, 1222, 1229–1230
    dictionaries, encyclopedias, and handbooks, 1116–1117, 1124–1126, 1234, 1239, 1261
Science of religion, 137, (p. 66)
Scottish Chaucerians, 1265
Scripture. *See* Bible
Sculpture
    American, 496, 505–507
    bibliographic guides and bibliographies, 496–498
    biographical sources, 489–493
    catalogs, 501
    dictionaries, encyclopedias, and handbooks, 503–505
    earth art, 499
    European, 504
    French, 498, 501n
    history, 414–415, 497–498n, 509
    indexes, 499, 502
    Italian, 414, 497–498n, 509
    modern, 415
    Renaissance, 414, 500
    reproductions, 499
    Roman, 509n
    Romanesque, 498, 501
    technique, 503
    Western, 509
Sects. *See* Cults and sects; Alternative religions
Semiotics, 987, 1002
Senior high school readers, 1344
Sennett, Mack, 914
Shakespeare, 1154, 1172, 1189
Sheet music, 644
Short fiction. *See* Fiction, short
Show business, 750, 853, 959
Signatures (artist), 352–353, 356, 446
Sikhism, 124, 186n. *See also* Religion, Asian
Silent film, 910, 964

Silver, 561, 563–564, 567. *See also* Jewelry and metalcraft
Singers, 724, 754
Slang, 1022
Slide collections, 380–381
Slides, (p. 154)
Small press, 1149
Smithsonian Institution, 12, (p. 155)
Social fiction, 1227
Societies, scholarly. *See* Organizations
Society for…
    the Scientific Study of Religion, (p. 72)
    the Study of Southern Literature, (p. 396)
    Women in Philosophy, (p. 38)
Solo voice, 649n
Songs, 732–738, 747–748, 751. *See also* Art songs
Songwriters, 751, 753
Soul music, 761. *See also* Music, popular
Soviet philosophy. *See* Philosophy, Marxist; Philosophy, Soviet
Spanish art, 398
Speaking in tongues, 115n
Special collections, (p. 37–38, 72–73, 155–156, 255–256, 395–396)
Special Libraries Association, (p. 155)
Spirits, 192. *See also* Gothic literature
Spirituality, 230
Square dance. *See* Dance, square
Stagecraft, 898. *See also* Theater and drama, production
Stained glass, 570
Stitchery, 580. *See also* Textiles, weaving, and needlecraft
Student funding, 18
Style, (p. 147)
Supernatural literature. *See* Gothic literature
Swing music. *See* Jazz
Symbols, 162
Synonyms, 1035
Systems. *See* Information systems

Taoism, 80. *See also* Philosophy, Asian
Television. *See* Film, radio, television, and video
Television broadcasting and credits, 907, 926–927, 931, 947
Television industry, 907, 929, 948, 957–958
Textiles, Weaving, and Needlecraft
    bibliographic guides and bibliographies, 577–578
    dictionaries, encyclopedias, handbooks, etc., 579–584
Theater and drama, (p. 250)
    actors, 861, 868–869
    African American. *See* Black influence, theater
    American, 822, 824–826, 830–831, 846, 850, 863, 873, 875–876, 878–881, 885, 887–888

Theater and drama (*continued*)
  annuals and current awareness sources, 857–859
  anthologies, 836
  bibliographic guides, 822–825
  bibliographies and catalogs, 826–829
  biographical sources, 861–870
  British, 825, 877, 882–884n, 862, 864
  Canadian, 851
  catalogs and collections, 828
  children's and young adult, 838, 881
  Chinese, 888
  classical, 848
  contemporary. *See* Theater and drama, modern
  designers, 870. *See also* Theater and drama,
      production; Stagecraft
  dictionaries, encyclopedias, and handbooks
    general, 839–845
    special topics and countries, 846–853
  digests of plays, 843
  direction. *See* Theater and drama, production
  directories, 854–856, 858–860
  education and employment, 856, 894
  full length plays, 832
  history and chronology
    general, 826, 871–872
    special topics and countries, 873–886
  legal considerations, 895
  medieval, 827, 847, 884
  modern, 865–866, 886–887, 891
  one-act plays, 833
  periodicals, 824–825, 835
  play sources (bibliographies and indexes),
      830–838
  playhouses. *See* Theaters
  playwrights, 830, 862–867, 891
  production, 852, 880, 894–898
  recordings, 837n
  regional, 859
  research, 822
  reviews and criticism, 887–893
  special collections. *See* Theater and drama,
      catalogs and collections
  summer, 859n
  training programs. *See* Theater and drama,
      education and employment
  world, 829, 839–842, 844, 871–872, 890
Theater companies, 860, 874
Theater dancing, 802
Theater makeup, 887. *See also* Theater and
    drama, production
Theater research. *See* Theater and drama, research
Theaters, 855, 885n
  small, 896
Theatre Library Association, (p. 257)
Theology, 102–103, 105, 114, 136, 156, 166,
    173, 175, 273, (p. 66)
Top 40 (recordings), 750n

UNESCO, (p. 37)
University Film and Video Association, (p. 257)
U.S. English, (p. 396)
Usage patterns. *See* Use and users of information
Use and users of information, (p. 4–6, 31, 69,
    152, 254, 393)

Value, (p. 3)
Vampires, 1127
Van Pelt Library, (p. 39)
Victorian literature. *See* Literature, Victorian
Video, (p. 250). *See also* Film, radio, television,
    and video
Violin music, 77
Virgil, 1296n
Virtuosi, 720, 723
Visual arts (general), (p. 147–156). *See also*
    Architecture; Applied design, crafts,
    and decorative arts; Painting, drawing,
    and print; Photography; Sculpture
  abstracts, 327, 329–331, 333
  annuals, 325
  artwork, collections. *See* Visual Arts, repro-
      duction and artwork
  bibliographic guides, 308–313
  bibliographies and catalogs, 314–325
  biographical sources, 383–404
  chronologies. *See* Visual arts, history and
      chronology
  definitions of, (p. 147)
  dictionaries, encyclopedias, and handbooks,
      371–382
  directories, 312
  disciplines of, (p. 148–149)
  history and chronology, 311, 407–420
  indexes, 326, 332, 334–335, 337, 339–342, 344
  internet resources/computerized databases, 313
  literature of, (p. 149–151)
  periodicals, 312, 332
  quotations, 359
  reference books, 309–310
  reproductions and artwork, 335–344. *See also*
      Painting, drawing and print,
      reproductions
  research, 308, 311
  sales and exhibitions, 345–351. *See also*
      Painting, drawing and print, sales;
      Photography, sales
  special collections, 12
Vocalists. *See* Singers

War fiction, 1232
Weaving, 634. *See also* Textiles, Weaving, and
    Needlecraft
Websites, (p. 10, 29, 30, 36–38, 71, 73, 154,
    250–251, 255–256, 258, 394–396)

Wesleyan Perfectionist, 114n
Western Literature Association, (p. 396)
Westerns, 1233, 1352
Westminster City Libraries, (p. 155)
Weston College Library, (p. 39)
Wilde, Oscar, 1198
Wisconsin Center for Theater Research, (p. 257)
Witches and witchcraft, 128, 193. *See also*
    Alternative religions
Wittgenstein, 86n
Women. *See* Female influence
Woodcraft. *See* Furniture and woodcraft

World Wide Web. *See* Internet; Websites
Writers' colonies, 18
Writing, 1106–1107, 1115

Yogacara, 125

Zen. *See* Philosophy, Asian